Question 4. The negative aspects of holding false or overgeneralized beliefs about men and women, which we know by the term "stereotypes," led some mid-twentieth century thinkers to attempt to deny the existence of any gender differences. Others emphasized the importance of cultural explanations of such differences and discounted any biological explanations. This latter assertion has proved to be inaccurate.

Your answers are correct!
The negative aspects of holding false or overgeneralized beliefs about men and women, which we know by the term "**stereotypes**," led some mid-twentieth century thinkers to attempt to deny the existence of any gender differences. Others emphasized the importance of **cultural** explanations of such differences and discounted any **biological** explanations. This latter assertion has proved to be **inaccurate**.

Textbook Reference: Gender Research Has Emerged from a History of Sexism, pp. 188–189

Previous Question   Next Question

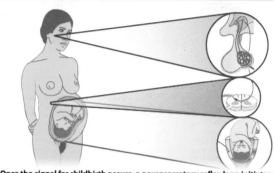

Once the signal for childbirth occurs, a neurosecretory reflex loop initiates uterine contractions. The loop begins when mechanical stimulation of the cervix by the descending fetal head activates sensory nerve endings.

CONTINUE | ◀▶

Textbook Reference: Figure 11.19 The Uterine Contractions of Labor, p. 350

A comprehensive set of study questions
covers the full range of content in every chapter. Each question is referenced to a textbook section for further study.

Animations clearly explain important
concepts and processes in easy-to-follow narratives.

The figure below depicts the female reproductive tract in frontal view. To label the figure, drag each label (bottom) to the appropriate location on the drawing.

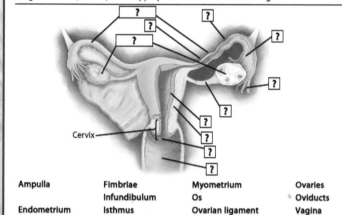

Cervix

Ampulla	Fimbriae	Myometrium	Ovaries
	Infundibulum	Os	Oviducts
Endometrium	Isthmus	Ovarian ligament	Vagina

Correct! The narrow part of the uterus, the cervix, bulges into the deep end of the vagina. A woman can feel her own cervix by inserting two fingers deeply into the vagina while in a squatting position, and she can see her cervix with the help of a mirror, a flashlight, and a speculum.

Textbook Reference: Figure 3.6 The Female Reproductive Tract, p. 62

Drag-and-drop labeling activities
and dynamic step-by-step illustrations simplify complex concepts and reinforce terminology.

Additional features:

Objectives – A set of learning objectives in the form of short-answer questions helps you focus on the important topics in each chapter.

Quizzes – **Multiple choice** quizzes allow you to test your comprehension of each chapter. **Essay questions** help you synthesize and apply the facts and concepts you have learned. (Instructors must register in order for their students to be able to take the quizzes.)

Web Topics – Additional readings on more advanced topics that may be assigned by your instructor.

In addition, the website includes key terms flashcards and a set of Web links for each chapter, as well as a complete glossary.

Web Activities and Topics

The following activities and topics are available on the HUMAN SEXUALITY Companion Website. Page numbers indicate where in the textbook each is referenced.

HUMAN SEXUALITY
THIRD EDITION

HUMAN SEXUALITY

THIRD EDITION

SIMON LeVay • JANICE BALDWIN

Sinauer Associates, Inc. • Publishers
Sunderland, Massachusetts U.S.A.

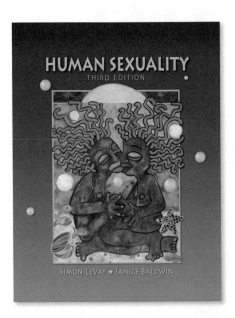

The Cover

The First Kiss, a watercolor by Joanne Delphia (www.jdelphia.com), depicts the sensation of holding one's breath during the first moment of physical contact between new lovers.

Human Sexuality, **Third Edition**
Copyright ©2009 by Sinauer Associates, Inc.
All rights reserved. This book may not be reproduced in whole or in part without permission from the publisher. For information or to order, address:

Sinauer Associates
23 Plumtree Road
Sunderland, MA 01375 U.S.A.
E-mail: publish@sinauer.com
Internet: www.sinauer.com

Library of Congress Cataloging-in-Publication Data
LeVay, Simon.
   Human sexuality / Simon LeVay, Janice Baldwin.
      p. cm.
   Includes bibliographical references.
   ISBN 978-0-87893-424-9
   1. Sex (Psychology) 2. Sex (Biology) 3. Sex—Social aspects. 4. Sexual disorders. I. Baldwin, Janice I. II. Title.
BF692.L48 2009
306.7—dc22   2008046214

About the Authors

Simon LeVay is a British-born neuroscientist turned science writer and teacher. He was educated at Cambridge University and the University of Göttingen, Germany. In 1971, he moved to the United States. He has served on the faculty of Harvard Medical School and the Salk Institute for Biological Studies, and has taught at Harvard, the University of California, and Stanford University. LeVay has authored over 40 scientific studies; the best known of these is a 1991 report in *Science* that described a difference in brain structure between heterosexual and homosexual men. This study helped spark a wealth of new research on the biology of sexual orientation. LeVay is the author or coauthor of nine books, some in the area of human sexuality and others on a broader range of scientific topics. His most recent book is *When Science Goes Wrong: Twelve Tales from the Dark Side of Discovery* (Penguin USA, 2008).

Janice Baldwin is a sociologist at the University of California, Santa Barbara. She is coauthor, with her husband John Baldwin, of numerous studies and articles in the area of sexuality and sex education, as well as the textbook *Behavior Principles in Everyday Life*, now in its fourth edition. The Baldwins co-teach an undergraduate Human Sexuality course that is regularly voted Best Course at UCSB. They also teach an advanced seminar course on the same subject. The Baldwins have been named as Best Professsors on several occasions.

Contents in Brief

Contents

CHAPTER 3 ▪ Women's Bodies 57

CHAPTER 4 ▪ Men's Bodies 85

CHAPTER 5 ■ Sex Hormones and the Menstrual Cycle 115

CHAPTER 6 ■ Sexual Development 149

CHAPTER 7 ■ Gender 187

CHAPTER 8 ■ Attraction, Arousal, and Response 217

CHAPTER 9 ■ Sexual Behavior 251

CHAPTER 10 ■ Sexual Relationships 283

CHAPTER 11 ■ Fertility, Pregnancy, and Childbirth 323

CHAPTER 12 ■ Contraception and Abortion 365

CHAPTER 13 ■ Sexuality across the Life Span 407

CHAPTER 14 ■ Sexual Orientation 453

CHAPTER 15 ■ Atypical Sexuality 491

CHAPTER 16 ■ Sexual Disorders 523

CHAPTER 17 ■ Sexually Transmitted Diseases 551

CHAPTER 18 ■ Sexual Assault, Harassment, and Partner Violence 587

CHAPTER 19 ■ Sex as a Commodity 617

Preface

In 2001, when Simon LeVay and Sharon Valente set out to write a new textbook of human sexuality, they were motivated by the desire to see this vital topic treated in the fashion it deserved—as the subject of enthusiastic but *evidence-based* inquiry. It would seem that this fundamental principle is one that any textbook authors would wish to follow, but in fact it has often taken a back seat to other perceived needs: the need to minimize gender differences, the need to bolster self-esteem, or the need to offer advice, sometimes at the expense of accuracy. For example, one leading textbook in its 2000 edition suggested that men, like women, experience a menstrual cycle—only without the bleeding. The alleged evidence was a 28-year-old magazine article about mood swings in Japanese taxi drivers. LeVay and Valente set out to write a text that "kept it real."

The First and Second Editions of *Human Sexuality* have in fact been recognized as setting new academic standards in the field. According to the *Journal of the American Medical Association,* for example, the book "goes beyond the standard presentation" in that it "normalizes sexuality in the academic curriculum and demonstrates that many aspects of human sexuality are amenable to rational inquiry and critical analysis" (Byne, 2006). We are gratified that the text has been adopted in educational environments ranging from leading universities and medical schools (such as Northwestern University, Vanderbilt University, the University of Lethbridge, Mount Sinai School of Medicine, and Baylor College of Medicine) to community colleges (such as Mt. San Antonio College in Walnut, California).

In addition, *Human Sexuality* has been widely praised for the quality of its writing, graphics, and layout. We hear this not only from professors but also, more significantly, from students. In their anonymous term-end evaluations, for example, students at Stanford University wrote comments such as "really interesting and fun to read," "textbook was great," "thorough and lucid," and "I love the book!" This is the kind of feedback that makes our work worthwhile.

The Third Edition

The Third Edition of Human Sexuality maintains and extends our dedication to the evidence-based approach. For example, our instructions for putting on a male condom no longer state that the man should leave a space at the tip of the condom for his ejaculate. This statement had no basis in research or logic—the man who could burst a condom with his ejaculate has yet to be born—and neither the World Health Organization nor the leading U.S. authorities on condom usage recommend the practice (Warner & Steiner, 2007). Yet it has somehow persisted, like a piece of folklore, in virtually every contemporary sexuality text, including previous editions of this one. By presenting condom use as the simple matter that it truly is, we hope that the instructions in the Third Edition will encourage wider use of condoms.

There are of course many other ways in which the Third Edition differs from its predecessors. Here we lay out the main aspects of the new edition of which users of previous editions should be aware.

Authorship

Sharon Valente has stepped down as coauthor, and we take this opportunity to thank her for her contributions to earlier editions. Joining Simon LeVay for the Third Edition is sociologist Janice Baldwin of the University of California, Santa Barbara. Baldwin was extensively involved in the Second Edition as a reviewer. Both LeVay and Sinauer Associates were impressed by her insightful contributions, so they were delighted when she agreed to coauthor the Third Edition. Their expectations have been fulfilled and exceeded.

Baldwin's background in sociology complements LeVay's biological training. Users who are familiar with earlier editions will notice a significant enrichment of the book in non-biological areas; Baldwin has played a major role in this broadening of the book's perspective. Baldwin co-teaches (with her husband John) one of the largest and most popular human sexuality classes in the United States, and the Baldwins have researched and published in diverse areas of sexology. Thus Baldwin brings to the book a deep understanding of what students need to know, as well as how to communicate it in a fashion that holds their interest and respects their diversity.

Chapter Reorganization

Although the sequence of chapters in the Third Edition remains the same as the Second Edition, we have moved some topics between chapters to better correspond to the sequence that most users prefer. The main changes are as follows:

- Material on the female and male sexual response cycles has been moved from Chapters 2 and 3 to Chapter 8, which is now renamed Attraction, Arousal, and Response. The sexual response cycle is in fact very similar in the two sexes; thus covering them together allows the differences that do exist to be highlighted and discussed.

- Material on the factors responsible for the development of sexual orientation has been moved from Chapter 8 to Chapter 14, and the title of Chapter 14 has been changed from Sexual Minorities to Sexual Orientation.

- Material on transexuality and transgender issues has been moved from Chapter 14 to Chapter 7 (Gender).

- The Afterword has been omitted; some of the material in the Afterword of the Second Edition has been integrated into other chapters.

Updating

Many of the changes in the Third Edition reflect much of what has happened in the area of human sexuality since the Second Edition was published:

- We review numerous new studies documenting progress in research in every area from basic biology to sex therapy. Some of these studies have reopened old controversies, such as one about the nature and prevalence of bisexuality. Other studies may open the door to new fields of inquiry. One example is the surprising discovery that the "stress hormone" CRF plays a key role in the establishment of pair bonds—in prairie voles, at least.

- We update statistics on all relevant topics, including sexual behavior, contraceptive use, marriage, divorce, abortion, public opinion, the world-wide spread of AIDS, and much more. In doing so, we try to emphasize the broad trends, not the year-to-year fluctuations on which the media like to focus.

- We report on new and emerging technologies and drugs for contraception, for infertility, and for the treatment or prevention of sexually transmitted diseases. Examples are the new anti-HPV vaccine Gardasil and the increasing number and popularity of "extended-use" contraceptive pills that reduce or eliminate a woman's menstrual periods.

- We document legal and political events such as the 2008 high court rulings that opened marriage to same-sex couples in California and Connecticut, followed by the November 2008 ballot initiative in California that terminated this short-lived right; the conviction of Mormon polygamist leader Warren Jeffs; and the prostitution-linked resignation of New York governor Eliot Spitzer.

- We observe social trends, such as the threat posed to traditional "gay meccas" by the mainstreaming of lesbians and gay men, the increasing awareness of the sexual needs of old people, and the continuing evolution of college students' relationship styles.

- We refer to some important books that have appeared since the publication of the Second Edition. These range from intimate personal studies such as Laura Carpenter's *Virginity Lost* and Lisa Diamond's *Sexual Fluidity* to the latest edition of Robert Hatcher's monumental reference work, *Contraceptive Technology*.

Ongoing Features

One way that we have strived to maintain both comprehensibility and interest is through the illustrations. One might think that it would be a simple matter to illustrate a book on human sexuality. In reality it is a significant challenge. Illustrating some of the concepts discussed in this book, especially in its more biologically oriented sections, requires a great deal of thought and design skill. Our publisher, Sinauer Associates, is an industry leader in the use of art as a pedagogical medium. Thanks to their efforts, many complex topics such as the regulation of the menstrual cycle and the replication of the AIDS virus have been given a visual representation that gracefully parallels and clarifies the accompanying text.

Boxes are another important feature of the book. There are more than 100 boxes, organized into 7 themes: Biology of Sex, Cultural Diversity, Research Highlights, Sexual Health, Sex in History, Personal Points of View, and Society, Values, and the Law. Within each theme, the subjects range from the serious to the light-hearted, but they all attempt to broaden the reader's horizons with a slightly more in-depth look at a topic than is possible within the main text.

Other aids to learning and revision include key terms (indicated by boldfaced type and defined in a running glossary), FAQS ("frequently asked questions"), discussion questions, chapter summaries, Web resources, and recommended reading materials.

Human Sexuality's Companion Website (www.sinauer.com /levay3e) is an invaluable learning aid. This site parallels the text with a thorough set of study questions, animations, activities, Web topics, quizzes, and other resources. Website activities are linked to the text and are referenced in blue type in the printed text. In addition, a complete set of instructor supplements is available to qualified adopters of the textbook. See the following section for details on the full range of media and supplements that accompany *Human Sexuality*, Third Edition.

Acknowledgments

Producing a modern college textbook such as this one requires the combined efforts of a much larger team of professionals than the two of us who are privileged to have our names on the front cover. The staff members of Sinauer Associates have produced, with great efficiency and good humor, what we consider a textbook of outstanding visual quality and educational value. Those with whom we have had the most enduring contacts are Editor Graig Donini, Production Editor Kathaleen Emerson, and Photo Editor David McIntyre, but many others labored behind the scenes to ensure the book's high quality and timely production. They include Joan Gemme, Janice Holabird, Christopher Small, and Jefferson Johnson. We are very grateful to all of them. We also thank Jean Zimmer for her skillful copyediting, Jason Dirks, Mara Silver, Suzanne Carter, Ann Chiara, Thomas Friedmann, and Nate Nolet for their work on the media and supplements package, Marie Scavotto for her effective work promoting the book, and Susan McGlew for obtaining outside reviews. We take particular pleasure in acknowledging Joanne Delphia's striking composition that graces the front cover. We believe that it conveys the positive, even joyful view of human sexuality that is a central perspective of this book.

Finally, we should mention that John Baldwin's professional and marital ties to Janice have ensured his close though informal involvement in every stage of the project. Whether in their cramped campus office or on some windswept mountain trail, Janice and John have bounced ideas off each other and together have come up with imaginative solutions to the book's challenges. Simon LeVay has also experienced John's enthusiastic involvement during his many visits to Santa Barbara over the last year. We are most grateful for John's contributions to the book.

Third Edition Reviewers

We acknowledge with gratitude the extensive and constructive comments made by people who reviewed chapters or extended portions of the book for the Third Edition. These reviewers are listed below. Helpful comments have also come from the Baldwins' students at the University of California, Santa Barbara.

- Veanne N. Anderson, *Indiana State University*
- J. Michael Bailey, *Northwestern University*
- Phillip G. Batten, *Wake Forest University*
- Stephanie Coday, *Sierra College*
- Lillian Cook Carter, *Towson University*
- James S. Ferraro, *Southern Illinois University*
- Dawn Graff-Haight, *Linfield College*
- Carole Heath, *Sonoma State University*
- Lisa Hoopis, *Planned Parenthood of Rhode Island*
- Fran Jackler, *De Anza College*
- Deborah Kindy, *Sonoma State University*
- Kris Koehne, *University of Tennessee, Knoxville*
- Joseph LoPiccolo, *University of Missouri, Columbia*
- Vance Victor MacLaren, *Thompson Rivers University*
- Jason McCoy, *Cape Fear Community College*
- Laura Miller, *Edinboro University of Pennsylvania*
- Valerie Smith, *Collin College, Central Park Campus*
- Mary Summers, *California State University, Sacramento*
- Soni Verma, *Sierra College*
- Jim Weinrich, *Grossmont College*
- Glenn Weisfeld, *Wayne State University*
- Scott Wersinger, *State University of New York at Buffalo*
- Lester Wright, *Western Michigan University*

Media and Supplements

to accompany *Human Sexuality*, Third Edition

eBOOK

(Available at www.coursesmart.com;
ISBN 978-0-87893-416-4)

New for the Third Edition, *Human Sexuality,* is available as an eBook via CourseSmart. This affordable new electronic version of the textbook is available at a substantial discount off the price of the printed book, as either an online or downloadable ebook. Both versions include features such as highlighting, full-text search, and a notes tool.

FOR THE INSTRUCTOR

(Available to qualified adopters.)

Instructor's Resource Library

(ISBN 978-0-87893-423-2)

The *Human Sexuality* Instructor's Resource Library (IRL) contains a wealth of resources for use in course planning, lecture and presentation development, course website development, student assessment, and more. The IRL includes the following elements:

Instructor's Manual

The *Human Sexuality*, Third Edition Instructor's Manual provides instructors with a variety of resources to aid in planning their course and developing their lectures. For each chapter, the manual includes: a chapter overview, a complete chapter outline, detailed lecture notes, suggested class discussion questions, and other teaching suggestions and resources.

Instructor's Media Guide

New for the Third Edition, the Media Guide offers a wide range of topic-specific video segments that can be used to enhance lectures and inspire discussion. Suggestions for individual segments and full-length programs are included for topics across all chapters of the textbook. Where possible, links are provided to access video segments online. Each segment includes related keywords and concepts. A set of accompanying discussion questions is provided for each chapter.

Test Bank

The *Human Sexuality* test bank consists of a broad range of questions covering all the key facts and concepts in each chapter. The following question types are included for each chapter: essay, multiple choice, fill-in-the-blank, and a complete list of key terms for use in definition questions. The test bank also includes the following additional sets of questions: Companion Website multiple-choice quizzes, textbook end-of-chapter discussion questions, and media guide discussion questions.

Computerized Test Bank

The entire test bank is also provided in Wimba Diploma® format (software included), for easy exam creation and editing. Diploma features drag-and-drop exam creation, export to Blackboard and WebCT, secure Internet testing, and more.

Presentation Resources

BROWSER—A convenient browser interface makes it easy to preview all the content on the IRL.

FIGURES & TABLES—All of the textbook's figures (both line art and photos) and tables are provided as JPEG files in two sizes: high-resolution (excellent for use in Power-Point® or other presentation software), and low-resolution (good for Web pages and other uses). All the artwork has been reformatted and optimized for excellent image quality when projected in class.

PHOTOS—New for the Third Edition, all of the unnumbered photos from the textbook are also included in the Resource Library.

ANIMATED TUTORIALS AND ACTIVITIES—All of the activities from the *Human Sexuality* Companion Website are included for use in the classroom.

POWERPOINT PRESENTATIONS—Two ready-to-use Power-Point presentations are provided for each chapter of the textbook:

- The lecture presentation is a complete lecture outline, covering each chapter and including selected figures—ready to be used as-is or customized as needed.
- The figures presentation includes all the figures, photos, and tables, with titles, making it easy to insert any figure into an existing presentation.

Course Management System Support

New for the Third Edition, *Human Sexuality* now offers a complete e-pack/course cartridge for Blackboard and WebCT. This e-pack includes resources from the Companion Website and the Instructor's Resource Library, as well as the complete test bank, making it easy to quickly include a wide range of book-specific material into your WebCT or Blackboard course.

Video Library

Qualified adopters can select from a wide range of video titles on topics that span the book, all available in either DVD or VHS format. These high-quality videos cover important topics in an in-depth manner, and are a great way to bring an outside perspective into the classroom.

Online Quizzing

The *Human Sexuality*, Third Edition Companion Website features chapter quizzes that report into an online gradebook. Adopting instructors have access to these quizzes and can choose to either assign them or let students use them for review. (Instructors must register in order for their students to be able to take the quizzes.) Instructors also have the ability to add their own questions and create their own quizzes.

FOR THE STUDENT

Companion WebSite

(www.sinauer.com/levay3e)

The *Human Sexuality*, Third Edition Companion Website is comprised of a robust set of study and review aids—all available at no cost to the student. This online companion to the textbook takes the place of a printed study guide

and adds to it a wealth of interactive learning content that helps the student master the full range of material presented in the textbook.

The Companion Website includes the following features:

OUTLINES—Complete outlines of each chapter form the framework for study and review. The outlines include in-context links to all study questions and activities.

OBJECTIVES—Chapter-by-chapter learning objectives help the student focus on the important concepts and topics in each chapter. Each objective is referenced to specific textbook headings and pages.

STUDY QUESTIONS—An extensive set of interactive self-study questions covers the full range of content in every chapter. These are a unique combination of paragraph-style questions that include fill-in-the-blank and multiple-choice elements. Each question is referenced to textbook headings and pages.

ONLINE QUIZZES—Two quizzes are provided for each chapter, as follows (instructors must register in order for their students to be able to take the quizzes):

- *Multiple Choice Quizzes:* These thorough quizzes give the student an opportunity to test their comprehension of the chapter material. Each question includes a reference to the relevant textbook page(s).
- *Essay Question Quizzes:* These short-answer style questions help students synthesize and apply what they have learned in the chapter.

ACTIVITIES (for selected chapters)—Animated tutorials, dynamic (step-through) illustrations, and drag-and-drop labeling exercises all help the student understand complex concepts and learn anatomical and other terms. Relevant activities are referenced throughout the textbook.

FLASHCARDS AND KEY TERMS—Students can quiz themselves on all the important terms introduced in each chapter, or they can browse the list of terms and definitions as a review.

WEB TOPICS—Additional coverage of selected advanced topics is provided via Web Topics, which are referenced in the textbook. Instructors who wish to cover these topics have easy access to them via the companion site.

In addition, the Companion Website includes a complete Glossary, thorough Chapter Summaries, and Web Links for each chapter.

HUMAN SEXUALITY
THIRD EDITION

CHAPTER 1

Human sexuality can be viewed from diverse perspectives.

Perspectives on Sexuality

Sexuality is a central and all-pervasive theme of human existence. At its best, sexuality charges our lives with energy, excitement, and love. It offers a deep sense of connectedness, capable of spanning and healing social divisions. It creates family, the primary unit of society and the cradle of future generations. At its worst, sexuality brings prejudice, anguish, violence, and disease.

To begin our exploration of this powerful and mysterious force, we ask some basic questions: Why study sexuality? What is sexuality "about"? What is the best way to study it? And what should young people be taught about it? We will find that, to do it justice, we must approach human sexuality with open minds, with respect for diversity, and with all the modes of inquiry that have been used to illuminate human nature. Approached in this way, the topic is not just another step in your college career: It is a personal voyage that will help you to enjoy the best that sexuality has to offer, and to avoid the worst.

Why Study Human Sexuality?

There are many possible reasons why you have chosen to take a course in human sexuality. Maybe you're simply curious about a topic that is often treated with embarrassment, evasion, or flippancy. Maybe you are looking for ways to improve your own sex life, or think you have sexual problems that need to be solved. Maybe you are planning a career that requires an understanding of human sexuality.

Regardless of your specific motives, there are many practical benefits to be gained from taking this course and reading this textbook. Here are some examples:

- Improving your understanding of the structure and function of your genital organs, and those of your partners, will help you give and receive more pleasure from sex.

- Learning more about how people communicate on sexual topics will increase your chances of entering into satisfying relationships and avoiding abusive ones.

- Learning about sexual diversity will encourage you to be more accepting of unusual sexual desires and behaviors—whether in others or in yourself.

- Educating yourself about contraception and sexually transmitted diseases will lessen the chance that your sexual behavior may end up harming yourself or your partners.

- Becoming a "sexpert" will be an asset to you in your future career—most especially if you enter the medical field, but also in any career that brings you in contact with other people.
- Educating yourself about sex will enable you to educate others—including your own children.

One of the greatest benefits of a college education is the opportunity to broaden your mental horizons by discussing important topics with people whose backgrounds differ from your own. A human sexuality course provides an especially valuable forum. Whether in formal or informal settings, we encourage you to talk about the many practical and ethical issues raised in this course. And we urge you to do this, not just with your circle of like-minded friends, but with those whose race, nationality, sexual orientation, age, or beliefs differ from your own. In this book we try not to impose our value judgments on you, but we do hope to offer opportunities for you to reconsider your own.

The Meaning of the Word "Sex" Has Broadened

We can get some idea of the broad significance of sex by tracing the meaning of the word **sex** over the centuries. Originally, "sex" meant simply the categories of male or female, based on anatomical characteristics. This meaning persists today, of course. Innumerable bureaucratic forms ask: "Sex: M/F (Circle one)." There are some **intersexed** people (people whose sexual anatomy is ambiguous or intermediate between male and female) for whom this question may pose a real dilemma, but for most of us our sex is an obvious biological given—a reference point on which everything else depends. The anatomical and physiological differences between the sexes, and their development, are primary themes in human sexuality and are discussed in the early chapters of this book.

Starting in the eighteenth century, the meaning of the word "sex" gradually broadened. By the late-nineteenth century it was applied to the whole topic of genital anatomy and function. By the mid-twentieth century "sex" was also used to mean sexual attraction and sexual behavior; in other words, the word referred no longer just to a category but also to a phenomenon and a process. People now "had sex," when earlier they "copulated," "engaged in sexual intercourse," or "made love." As we'll see later, people still don't agree on the precise meaning of "having sex," but they do agree that it means getting together for some sexual purpose. Words and phrases such as "sexiness," "sex-crazed," "sex education," and "sex therapy" have become commonplace, and most of these words relate to sexual attraction and behavior, not to the categories of male or female.

As "sex" came to include sexual behavior, it became a bit of a "dirty word." Toward the end of the twentieth century, therefore, there was a trend toward using another word, **gender**, to substitute for the word "sex" in its original meaning—the categories of male or female. Both academics and lay people began to use phrases such as "persons of either gender" as a genteel alternative to "persons of either sex" (Haig, 2004).

Within the fields of sex research, psychology, and sociology, however, "gender" has a somewhat different meaning. It refers to the collection of cognitive, behavioral, and personality traits that differ (to a greater or lesser degree) between the sexes. In this book, we use the term "gender" only in this sense. The nature of gender differences—and how they arise—is an important and controversial theme in human sexuality.

The word **sexuality** may also be used as a euphemism for "sex" in the same way that "elderly" is used as a euphemism for "old." In this book "sexuality" means more than just "having sex." A more accurate definition of "sexuality" includes sex-

sex 1. The category of male or female. 2. Sexual feelings and behavior.

intersexed Having a biological sex that is ambiguous or intermediate between male and female.

gender The collection of psychological traits that differ between males and females.

sexuality The feelings, behaviors, and identities associated with sex.

ual relationships, gender, and sexual identities; it is a term that embraces all the topics covered in this book. To understand sex fully we must study much more than just "having sex": We must understand sexuality as well.

Sex Is about Relationships

Most sexual behavior takes place in the context of relationships. Not all, of course—for masturbation is a common form of sexual expression that doesn't require a partner. Even with masturbation, however, there may be an *imagined* partner: Men and women who masturbate often fantasize about a desirable partner as an aid to sexual arousal.

Sexual relationships are central to many—perhaps most—people's lives. Even in a sizable textbook such as this one, we can only scratch the surface of this topic, but we will attempt to make several general points. First, sexual relationships are extremely *diverse*:

- They may last a few minutes or several decades.
- They may be motivated by physical attraction, emotional bonding, a sense of duty, a desire to be a parent, a desire to conform or rebel, or economic factors.
- They may be mutually fulfilling, one-sided, unhappy, or abusive.
- They may involve very similar or very dissimilar partners.
- They may involve two individuals or several.
- They may be centered on sex or have sex as a mere incidental feature.
- They may be recognized and approved by society, or they may be hidden, disapproved of, or illegal.
- Sometimes, relationships that the outside world assumes to be sexual are not sexual at all.

Second, real-life sexual relationships are not ideal relationships. We do not get exactly what we want in this world, and we must count ourselves lucky when we come close. Whether we are looking for a partner for a night or for a lifetime, we consciously or unconsciously shop around for the best partner we can get, where "best" refers to all kinds of tangible and intangible qualities that influence our desires. People choose and are chosen. The net result is a matching that confers varying degrees of satisfaction. Almost always, though, there is some degree of mismatch or *conflict* that tests the partners' adaptability and communication skills.

When sexual relationships are challenged by interpersonal difficulties or external events, some endure and some fall apart. Many studies have been conducted, and many volumes written, about what determines the outcome. Our treatment of these issues must necessarily be more superficial than their importance warrants.

Third, sexual behavior and sexual relationships take place in a *moral context*. We all have a sense of what is right or wrong, a sense that is influenced by our upbringing, our life experiences, our religious beliefs (or lack of them), our ability to reason, and perhaps even by our genes. People do not share the same moral values, nor do they necessarily agree on whether a universal code of ethics governs all human behavior and all situations.

Sex Is about Identity

Psychologically speaking, **identity** means the sense of who you are, and it is often defined in terms of the social groups to which you feel you belong. Sexuality strongly influences people's identity. Most obviously, this is true of people's sense of which sex they are—their **gender identity**. The great majority of men and women have a gender identity that corresponds to their anatomical sex, but some

Although most people would not call an interaction between a prostitute and her customer a "relationship," we use the word to refer to any sexual interaction, from a one-time visit with a streetwalker to a lifelong marriage.

identity The sense of self, self-labeling, or group affiliation.

gender identity A person's subjective sense of being male or female.

Transgendered men and women identify with the sex opposite to their anatomical sex. In addition, their transgendered status may itself offer them a unique identity, providing a focus for social life, mutual support, and political action.

individuals have a gender identity that is discordant with their anatomical sex. These **transgendered** or **transexual** individuals may seek to change sex in order to bring their bodies into harmony with their gender identity.

Sexual orientation—the direction of one's sexual attractions—is another important aspect of identity. People who belong to the socially disadvantaged minority orientations—**homosexual** (gay) and **bisexual** men and women—are most conscious of their sexual orientation as an aspect of their identity. Gay people often reach out to one another for sexual fulfillment, social engagement, and political action, and in the process they establish gay communities. Bisexual people do not have to meet other bisexuals for the purpose of sexual fulfillment. Still, they may also develop a strong sense of identity, based in part on their shared experience of prejudice and misunderstanding. **Heterosexuality**, on the other hand, does not usually confer a strong sense of identity—people take it too much for granted.

Other aspects of people's sexuality may also confer a sense of identity:

- People who have group sexual relationships ("polyamorists")
- "Swingers" and others who engage in sex outside of lasting relationships
- People who engage in sadomasochistic practices
- Prostitutes and others whose work involves sex
- People who choose to defer sex until marriage
- People who sacrifice their sexuality in favor of a lifelong religious vocation
- People who have experienced rape or childhood molestation
- People with sexually transmitted diseases (including AIDS)
- People with medical conditions or disabilities that affect sexual expression
- People who do not experience sexual attraction at all (asexuals)

transgender A person who identifies with the other sex.

transexual A person who identifies with the other sex and who seeks to transition to the other sex by means of hormone treatment and sex reassignment surgery. Transexuals can be male-to-female (M-to-F) or female-to-male (F-to-M).

sexual orientation The direction of an individual's sexual feelings: sexual attraction toward persons of the opposite sex (heterosexual), the same sex (homosexual), or both sexes (bisexual).

homosexual Sexually attracted to persons of one's own sex.

bisexual Sexually attracted to persons of both sexes.

heterosexual Sexually attracted to persons of the opposite sex.

People are likely to have some sense of identity and community with others like them. These groups may have Web sites and newsgroups, meeting places, organizations and political goals, and a shared outlook. In other words, our sexual feelings, behaviors, and experiences help establish our place in society, making us sympathetic to others who share our traits and less sympathetic—sometimes downright hostile—to those who do not.

There Are Many Approaches to the Study of Sexuality

Because sexuality affects so many aspects of our lives, it can be studied by many different modes of inquiry. Practitioners of these different disciplines tend to make different assumptions about the purpose, the mechanisms, and the development of sexual feelings and behaviors. They ask different questions and employ different methods to answer them. This section reviews some of the diverse approaches to understanding sexuality that will occupy us later in this book. It also highlights specific examples of the methods that have been developed to study sexuality.

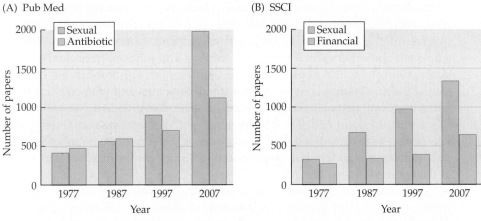

Figure 1.1 **Sex research on the rise** These graphs show the number of research papers that contain the word "sexual" in their titles, retrieved from (A) a biomedical database (PubMed) and (B) a social science database (Social Sciences Citation Index [SSCI]). Titles including the nonsexual terms "antibiotic" and "financial" are shown for comparison.

anatomist Researcher who studies the structure of the body.

endocrinologist Researcher who studies hormones or chemical messengers.

reproductive physiologist Researcher who studies fertility and pregnancy.

neuroscientist Researcher who studies the nervous system.

geneticist Researcher who studies the mechanisms of inheritance.

pathologist Doctor or researcher who studies the diseased body.

microbiologist Researcher who studies microscopic organisms, especially those that cause disease.

Regardless of the specific discipline, however, there has been a marked increase in attention to human sexuality by researchers in recent years (**Figure 1.1**). In part this reflects the increasing acceptability of sex as a topic of discourse by society in general. In addition, it is spurred by increasing awareness of social and economic problems related to sex, such as the AIDS epidemic, teen pregnancy, and divorce.

Biomedical Research Focuses on the Underlying Mechanisms of Sex

Over the years, medical research has gathered vital knowledge about the physical basis of sexuality—in particular, about the structure, function, and development of the male and female genital and reproductive systems. Starting at the time of the Renaissance, **anatomists** made detailed studies of the internal reproductive tracts of men and women (**Figure 1.2**). In the twentieth century, **endocrinologists** and **reproductive physiologists** explored the hormonal systems that make men and women's bodies so different from each other and that give women something that men don't have: a menstrual cycle and the capacity to nurture a fetus. **Neuroscientists** began to lay out the neural control mechanisms that mediate sexual arousal and sexual behavior. **Geneticists** explored how sex is determined and how this process of sex determination can go awry. **Pathologists** and **microbiologists** discovered the causes of sexually transmitted diseases. All these spheres of knowledge, though far from complete, are central to our present-day understanding of human sexuality, and we make no apology for devoting a great deal of space to them in this book.

A valuable medical contribution to sex research has been the physiological observation of sexual responses. The names most closely associated with this approach are those of gynecologist William Masters (1915–2001) and his collaborator (and later his wife) psychologist Virginia Johnson (born 1925) of Washington University School of Medicine (**Figure 1.3**). Starting in the late 1950s, Masters and Johnson recruited volunteers to engage in sexual behavior (solitary or partnered) in their laboratory. They studied their volunteers' sexual responses, not only by visual observation, but also by means of recording

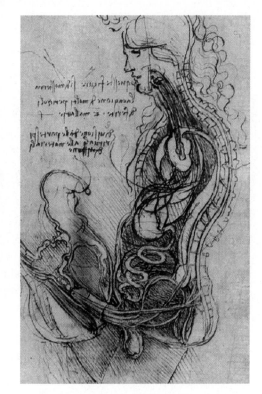

Figure 1.2 **Coitus of a Hemisected Man and Woman (ca. 1492) by Leonardo da Vinci** The copulating couple (with the woman only partially shown on the left) are represented as if they have been sliced down the middle.

Figure 1.3 Sex researchers William Masters and Virginia Johnson, around 1970.

sex therapist A person who treats sexual dysfunctions, usually by recommending behavioral changes and sexual exercises.

endocrinology The study of glands and hormones.

neuropharmacology The study of drugs that affect the brain.

sex hormones Chemical messengers that influence sexual and reproductive processes.

erectile dysfunction A persistent inability to achieve or maintain an erection sufficient to accomplish a desired sexual behavior such as coitus to orgasm. Earlier known as impotence.

neurotransmitter A compound released at a synapse that increases or decreases the excitability of an adjacent neuron.

instruments. These included conventional instruments to record blood pressure, respiration rate, and so on, as well as a set of specially designed devices that recorded penile erection, vaginal engorgement, contractions of the anal sphincter, and other genital processes. Masters and Johnson published their observations in a 1966 book, *Human Sexual Response*. This book, which presented the first comprehensive description of how men and women's bodies perform during sexual behavior, was a best seller. Nevertheless, Masters and Johnson faced vocal criticism from people—both professionals and nonprofessionals—who considered their work prurient (arousing unwholesome sexual interest) or who felt that they focused too much on the mechanics of sex at the expense of love and relationships.

Besides studying the sexual responses of healthy volunteers, Masters and Johnson also studied men and women who suffered from a variety of sexual problems, and they developed techniques for helping such people improve their sex lives. These techniques were described in their 1970 book, *Human Sexual Inadequacy*. Masters and Johnson trained many others in their therapeutic methods; in fact, many of the **sex therapists** practicing today are Masters and Johnson's students or "grandstudents."

The study of the body's chemical messengers (**endocrinology** and **neuropharmacology**) has had a great impact on sexuality:

- Discovery of **sex hormones** in the middle of the twentieth century led to oral contraceptives, in vitro fertilization, drug treatments for breast and prostate cancer, treatments to increase or decrease the sex drive, and treatments to ease sexual dysfunctions associated with menopause.

- Clarification of the chemical mechanisms of penile erection led to the introduction in 1999 of sildenafil (Viagra) for the treatment of **erectile dysfunction** in men, followed more recently by other drugs in the same class. These drugs are improving the sex lives of millions of men and their partners, and (for good or ill) are redefining "normal" sexual performance in men as they age.

- Identification of serotonin and other **neurotransmitters** in the central nervous system led to the introduction of selective serotonin reuptake inhibitors (Prozac-type drugs) for the treatment of compulsive sexual desires and behaviors such as exhibitionism and voyeurism. These drugs may also impair the sexual performance of people who take them for depression.

- Identification of the hormones that regulate the secretions of the pituitary gland led to drugs for the treatment of precocious and delayed puberty.

- Identification of the signaling mechanisms that regulate childbirth led to drugs for the induction of labor and for the prevention of premature labor.

Biomedical researchers often turn to nonhuman animals to deepen their understanding of human nature, including human sexuality. Animal research can mean exploring the physiology of bodily systems: All five advances listed in the previous paragraph were made possible by research in laboratory animals. In addition, researchers study the sexual *behavior* of animals, both in the laboratory and in the wild. They have observed an extraordinary diversity of sexual behavior and sexual relationships: animals that change sex; animals that are both sexes at once, or neither; animals that mate in pairs or in crowds; animals that are heterosexual, homosexual, or bisexual; animals that mate to reproduce, and those that do so for other purposes, including the simple pleasure of it (Judson, 2002; Roughgarden, 2004; Vasey, 2006)). Contrary to what we might conclude from traditional accounts, such as the story of Noah's Ark ("of every living thing, the male and his female, two by two"), there is no standard form of sexuality in the animal

(A)

(B)

Figure 1.4 Myth and reality of sex (A) The biblical story of Noah's ark portrays heterosexual pair-bonding as nature's universal standard. (B) Two female bonobos engage in "genito-genital rubbing."

kingdom to which humans need to conform (**Figure 1.4**). Rather, each species' sexuality is the product of its own evolutionary history.

Psychiatry Is Concerned with Mental "Health" and "Sickness"

Psychiatry, the branch of medicine concerned with mental and behavioral disorders, has naturally had a lot to say about sex. Yet psychiatry's contributions to sex research have been more controversial than those of the other branches of medicine, for several reasons. For one thing, we still have only a very limited understanding of how the brain generates mental states. Thus theories have tended to be highly speculative, and wildly disparate theories have been put forward by different doctors, even at the same time and place (**Box 1.1**).

An even more controversial aspect of the psychiatric approach to sex has been the tendency of doctors to view sexual problems as a health and disease issue. An early example of this approach was the work of the German physician Richard von Krafft-Ebing (1840–1902), who wrote a best-selling treatise entitled *Psychopathia Sexualis* (1886) that dealt with sexual disorders (**Figure 1.5**). This book was a compendium of 237 case histories illustrating all kinds of sexual "deviations," including masturbation, homosexuality, transvestism, fetishism, exhibitionism, pedophilia, bestiality, sadism, masochism, necrophilia (sexual fixation on corpses), coprophilia (sexual fixation on feces), and sexual murder (Jack the Ripper was one of the case histories). A great part of the book's appeal was in the graphic accounts of these "deviations," some of which are shocking even today.

Krafft-Ebing claimed the right to "name" sexual disorders and to "diagnose" people who suffered from them (Davis, 1996). But in doing so, was he responding to a plea for understanding and treatment from deeply disturbed individuals? Or was he seeking to impose his own code of sexual propriety on people who would otherwise have had perfectly harmless and satisfying sex lives, as some modern critics have argued (Szasz, 2000)? Looking at the "deviations" listed

Figure 1.5 Medicalization of sex, Richard von Krafft-Ebing (1840–1902). His 1886 book *Psychopathia Sexualis* is still selling well today, thanks to some lurid descriptions of sexual deviations.

Sex in History

BOX 1.1 Freud and Hirschfeld: Contrasting Theories on Sexual Orientation

About a century ago, two European doctors proposed radically different theories to account for why some people are sexually attracted predominantly to members of the other sex while others are attracted to members of the same sex or to both sexes—a characteristic we now call sexual orientation. In Vienna, Sigmund Freud (Figure A) developed a theory that was based on the concept of an unconscious mind, whose operations could supposedly be probed by psychoanalytic techniques such as free association, the interpretation of dreams, and slips of the tongue. The unconscious mind, though hidden from view and free from moral restraints, nevertheless resembled the conscious mind in many respects–both were capable of rational thought, planning, memory, and emotion.

In Freud's conception, the unconscious mind was more broadly focused in its sexual desires than was the conscious mind. This was particularly true during early childhood, which he believed included autoerotic and homosexual phases as well as incestuous desires directed toward one or the other parent. As we'll see in Chapter 14, Freud thought that the "normal" progression to adult heterosexuality could be derailed in various ways, often involving unconscious emotional processes such as a hostile, too-close, or jealous relationship with a parent or sibling. These phenomena could lead to what Freud called **perversions**; that is, mental states in which adult sexual desires were directed toward atypical targets, such as people of the same sex (homosexuality), inanimate objects (fetishism), and so on. Or they could lead to **neuroses**, in which the sexual element was supposedly repressed from consciousness altogether and reemerged in the form of nonsexual traits and disorders, such as obsessive-compulsive behaviors, depression, or "hysteria."

In Berlin, Magnus Hirschfeld took a radically different view. Hirschfeld proposed the existence of two neural centers in the brain that were responsible for sexual attraction to men and to women. During early fetal life, he suggested, all humans possessed both centers, but later one center grew and dominated, while the other regressed. In men, of course, it was usually the center for attraction to women that persisted, while in women it was the center for attraction to men. Only in the minority of homosexual individuals did development take the opposite course. Hirschfeld believed that sex hormones (then understood in only a very rudimentary way) channeled development in one direction or another, and that people also had a genetic predisposition to same-sex or opposite-sex attraction.

In many ways, the views of Freud and Hirschfeld represented opposite approaches to understanding the mind and sexuality. Freud tried to understand the mind in terms of processes that, though hidden, were inherently *mental*—unconscious thoughts. And he believed interpersonal relationships held the key to sexual orientation and other aspects of adult sexuality. To Freud, getting to your adult sexuality was a long, sometimes chaotic drama in which the unconscious mind took the leading role. Hirschfeld, on the other hand, tried to reduce the mind to relatively simple *nonmental* phenomena such as the growth and activity of nerve cells, hormone secretion, and information encoded in the genes. In Hirschfeld's view, these phenomena controlled sexual development in a manner that was largely independent of family relationships and other aspects of life experience. To Hirschfeld, getting to your adult sexuality was a process that unfolded mechanistically without your active participation—it simply happened to you.

Freud's theories came to dominate most people's ideas about the mind and sexuality through the early and middle part of the twentieth century, while Hirschfeld's theories languished in obscurity. Toward the end of the century, however, there was a noticeable shift of views. To some people, Freud's theories began to seem capricious, poorly substantiated, or inspired by prejudice (against women, especially). Meanwhile, scientific advances tended to bolster a biological view of sexuality. Studies in animals showed that prenatal hormone levels do indeed influence sexual behavior in adulthood, and family studies supported the idea that genes do have some influence on sexual orientation in humans.

Probably the dominant view at present is that both approaches offer potential insights into human sexuality. There must be some biological underpinnings to our thoughts and behaviors, and exploring these underpinnings is likely to tell us a lot about why people differ from one another sexually. On the other hand, it seems likely that there are aspects of human sexuality that need to be studied at the level of thoughts—in other words, by a cognitive approach. Thus, even if neither Freud's nor Hirschfeld's theories turn out to be right, they may both have contributed useful styles of thinking to the discussion.

perversion An obsolete term for atypical sexual desire or behavior, viewed as a mental disorder.

neuroses Mental disorders such as depression that, in Freudian theory, are coping strategies against repressed sexual conflicts.

Sigmund Freud (1856–1939)

Magnus Hirschfeld (1868–1935)

above, there may be some that you practice yourself with no sense of guilt or sickness, some that you have no problem with if other people want to practice them, and some that you think should be prevented at all costs, whether through medical or legal means. But do doctors have the right to decide which is which?

In spite of this controversy, the idea that sexual aberrations can be named and diagnosed has been codified in the American Psychiatric Association's *Diagnostic and Statistical Manual of Mental Disorders* (**DSM**), which is revised periodically (American Psychiatric Association, 2000). The APA underwent a bitter struggle in the early 1970s over the question of whether homosexuality should continue to be listed as a mental disorder (Bayer, 1981). Thanks in part to the efforts of gay activists both inside and outside the psychiatric profession, this diagnostic category was removed in 1973.

Many other questionable sexual "disorders" are still listed in the *DSM*, however; these include "gender identity disorder of childhood" (boys who feel and behave like girls, and vice versa), as well as several disorders straight out of *Psychopathia Sexualis*. There is a difference, though: The *DSM* now emphasizes that (with some exceptions) a sexual condition is not a disorder unless it causes distress to the person who experiences it. In a sense, then, the affected person must participate in the diagnostic process.

The question of what constitutes a sexual disorder in need of treatment comes up in many places in this book, especially in the discussion of homosexuality, transexuality, pedophilia, and other atypical forms of sexual expression. In reviewing this material, we suggest that you look beyond the Greek-sounding terminology (the "philias" and "phobias"). Ask yourself what criteria you would use to distinguish between traits that should be medically treated or legally restrained and traits that can be accepted as part of the diverse tapestry of human sexual expression.

Psychologists Have Taken Diverse Approaches to Sexuality

Psychology, the study of mental processes and behavior, has splintered into all kinds of overlapping subdisciplines, several of which offer unique perspectives on sexuality. Probably the most significant branch in the study of sexuality is **social psychology**—the study of how we think about, influence, and relate to other people. Social psychologists concern themselves with all kinds of sexual matters, such as sexual attraction and sexual relationships, gender differences, homosexuality, sexual assault, intimate-partner violence, and anti-gay prejudice. Social psychology studies may be descriptive or experimental. A *descriptive study* might entail, for example, observing and comparing the flirtatious behavior of men and women in public spaces. In an *experimental study*, the researcher studies the effect of some intervention on the research subjects; such studies commonly have a group of comparison subjects who were not exposed to the intervention ("controls").

The following is an example of an experimental study. Researchers at UCLA are interested in the question of whether portrayals of sexual violence in the media and pornography make men more accepting of such violence, as has been asserted by many feminists. Out of a group of male college students, half were randomly assigned to watch movies that portrayed sexual violence against women—specifically, movies in which a woman was raped but subsequently fell in love with her rapist. The other students (the controls) watched movies that contained no sexual violence. A few days later the students were given a sexual attitudes questionnaire. The results supported the feminist contention: Male students who watched sexually violent movies expressed significantly more accepting attitudes toward sexual violence than the men in the control group. This and other experimental studies have convinced the UCLA researchers that exposure to images of

Diagnostic and Statistical Manual of Mental Disorders (**DSM**) A compilation of diagnostic criteria for mental disorders published by the American Psychiatric Association and updated periodically.

psychology The study of mental processes and behavior.

social psychology The study of our relationship to others.

psychobiologist Psychologist who is interested in the biological bases of mental processes and behavior.

cultural psychologist Researcher who studies the interactions between culture and mental processes or behaviors.

anthropology The study of cultural or biological variations across the human race.

fellatio Sexual contact between the mouth of one person and the penis of another.

sexual violence really does predispose some men to commit sexual assaults against women (Malamuth et al., 2000).

Psychobiologists (or biological psychologists) occupy the interface between psychology and the biological sciences, especially neuroscience and endocrinology. Psychobiologists interested in sexual behaviors often study these behaviors in laboratory animals rather than in humans, because their experiments may involve risk to their subjects or may require killing the animals in order to analyze their brains or other organs. But recent advances in brain-imaging technology have allowed psychobiologists to study the brain basis of sexuality in living humans. For example, Gert Holstege and his colleagues have used positron-emission tomography (PET scanning) to visualize the patterns of brain activity that occur during orgasm.

Cultural (or cross-cultural) **psychologists** concern themselves with the influence of ethnic and cultural diversity on thought, behavior, and interpersonal relationships. Where cultural psychology focuses on differences between entire societies, it overlaps extensively with **anthropology**, especially the branch known as cultural anthropology. The prime research method employed by cultural psychologists is fieldwork: Researchers may spend months or even years embedded in the societies they study, sometimes participating fully in those societies' cultural practices. A pioneer in this field was Margaret Mead (1901–1978), who studied the development of sexual attitudes and gender differences in Pacific Island societies (Mead, 1928, 1935) (**Figure 1.6**).

Cultural psychologists have found that sexual practices and sexual attitudes are far more diverse than you might imagine. A striking example comes from the work of Gilbert Herdt, a cultural anthropologist who now directs the Human Sexuality program at San Francisco State University. Starting in 1974, Herdt spent extended periods of time among the Sambia, a small society indigenous to the highland rainforests of New Guinea. It was known prior to his work that the Sambia engaged in ritualized homosexual practices, but Herdt provided more detail and investigated the symbolic environment in which these practices occurred (Herdt, 2005). The Sambia, he found, believe that boys can become men only by ingesting semen, which is thought to trigger puberty and to instill the qualities of manhood. Before puberty, boys are removed from their families, and for about 10 years they are housed collectively. During this period they must engage in a secret daily ritual that involves male-on-male **fellatio** (oral sex; see Chapter 9). The younger boys take the receptive role, swallowing the ejaculates of the older boys. Later, as they mature physically, they take the insertive role. At the end of the ten-year period the boys, now young men, leave the group and take wives. Contrary to what you might think, this long period of compulsory and exclusive homosexual behavior has no apparent effect on the men's ultimate sexual orientation. It is now known that similar beliefs and practices exist (or existed) widely throughout Melanesia, but sometimes the transfer of semen is accomplished by means of anal rather than oral sex.

Cultural psychologists have also found some striking variations in the criteria used to judge sexual attractiveness (**Box 1.2**) as well as the kinds of sexual relationships that are sanctioned in different societies (for example, monogamous versus polygamous marriages). The topic of sexual diversity will be mentioned frequently throughout this book.

Of course, many diverse ethnic and cultural traditions exist in the United States, so there is ample room for cultural studies of sexuality and gender within our own society. Some Native Americans, for example, preserve

Figure 1.6 Anthropologist Margaret Mead between two Samoan girls, around 1926. Mead depicted Samoa—a group of islands in the South Pacific— as a haven of "primitive" free love, but later studies found that Samoan culture restricted sexual expression in many ways.

Cultural Diversity

BOX 1.2 The Fattening Room

There's an old saying, attributed to the Duchess of Windsor, that "you can never be too rich or too thin." To judge by the rail-thin models and actresses that Americans see on film and TV every day, thinness appears to be the ultimate in female beauty (Figure A). Yet there are societies in which the other end of the size spectrum—obesity—is preferred. Consider for example, the Annang people of southeastern Nigeria.

(A) In the United States, thin is beautiful.

Annang women engage in considerable physical labor, yet calorie-rich food is scarce, so most women are very lean. Before a girl is married off, however, she is secluded in a "fattening room" for several months—sometimes for more than a year. While in the room, the girl is called a *mbobo.* She does no work and has few visitors, but she is fed three large meals every day. The meals consist of high-calorie foods such as yams and rice—expensive luxuries for the Annang,

who generally depend on nutrient-poor cassava. Between meals, the mbobo is instructed in the duties and skills of womanhood. She may also undergo circumcision (see Chapter 3). At the conclusion of the fattening period there is a festival. All the mbobo in the village have their bodies painted, and they dance nude in public to display their fatness. The ceremony includes a great deal of feasting, with food provided by the mbobo's families.

A young man in search of a bride may select one of the mbobo, but he will have to make a substantial bridal payment to her father. The fatter the mbobo, the higher the payment, for all Annang people agree that fat women are the most attractive and desirable as brides.

Why is there such a striking difference between American culture and that of the Annang in the estimation of female attractiveness? According to Pamela Brink of the University of Alberta, who has done fieldwork among the Annang, two related factors make fatness attractive in that culture (Brink, 1989). First, the general scarcity of food and the occurrence of periodic droughts and famines make it difficult for an Annang woman to complete a pregnancy and nurse her baby successfully. A woman who is markedly overweight when she marries is carrying energy reserves that will see her through her first pregnancy—an assurance that is valuable to a potential husband.

The fattening process is also a form of "conspicuous consumption"—a demonstration of wealth on the part of the mbobo's family. To fatten a mbobo, the family not only must provide her with expensive foodstuffs, but must also do without her labor during the time she is secluded. The festival at the conclusion of the fattening process is also very expensive. Thus a fat mbobo and a lavish feast are proof of the family's resources and status. Many families cannot afford to fatten a mbobo, and they must marry their daughters off to less desirable men.

Although the traditional fattening-room practices are on the decline, fatness is still idealized, both among the Annang and more widely in West Africa (Smith, 2001) (Figure B). In some localities, women of limited means put on weight by consuming animal feed or by the use of corticosteroids, even though these drugs produce an unnatural-looking obesity and can be toxic.

In Western countries prior to the Industrial Revolution, full-figured women were greatly admired. In the contemporary United States, however, almost anyone can obtain enough food to gain weight, so obesity does not demonstrate any particular wealth or status. For many women it is more of a challenge to remain thin than to become fat. Perhaps for this reason, and because of awareness of the negative health effects of obesity in our society, being fat is devalued as a measure of attractiveness, and thinness is preferred. Men, too, are now facing increasing pressure to look skinny—on the fashion runway, at least. The *New York Times* recently defined the ideal male model as "an underfed runt" (Trebay, 2008).

The marked difference between the Annang and ourselves in the judgment of female attractiveness suggests that these judgments are not genetically programmed or "hardwired" into our brains. Instead, they seem to depend on cultural traditions and social circumstances. Still, there are some aspects of physical appearance whose attractiveness is judged in a consistent way across cultures, as we will see in Chapter 8.

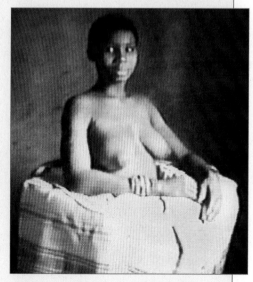

(B) In West Africa, fatness is preferred. This video still, taken from the documentary film *Becoming a Woman in Okrika,* by Judith Gleason and Elisa Mereghetti, shows an *iriabo* (the Okrika equivalent of a *mbobo*) in a fattening room wearing many layers of cloth to accentuate her hips—and her fertility.

evolutionary psychologist Researcher who studies the influence of evolution on mental processes or behavior.

clinical psychologist Clinician (usually not a medical doctor) who assesses or treats mental or behavioral problems.

an ancient tradition that assigns a special, spiritual role to transgendered individuals (Williams, 1986). Some Hispanics, on the other hand, may be influenced by the Latin American culture of *machismo,* which emphasizes stereotypical masculinity. Sexual behavior differs greatly among different groups: Only 27% of Asian-American high school students have ever engaged in penile-vaginal intercourse (coitus), for example, compared with 72% of African-American students (Schuster et al., 1998). Understanding the roots of such cultural differences could aid efforts to reduce unwanted pregnancy and sexually transmitted diseases among teenagers.

Cultural diversity is not a sexual free-for-all. As we shall see, some aspects of human sexuality are remarkably consistent from one society to another. Some examples include:

- The proportion of the population that is homosexual seems to be roughly similar from one society to another (Whitam, 1983).
- Facial beauty is judged fairly consistently across disparate cultures (Perrett et al., 1994).
- Public exposure of the genitals, especially adult women's genitals, is prohibited in almost all cultures (Ford & Beach, 1951).

Evolutionary psychologists seek to explain how evolution has molded our genetic endowment to favor certain patterns of sexual feelings and behaviors. One idea in evolutionary psychology is that, because reproduction is so much more demanding for females than for males, genes have evolved that cause females to be very picky in their choice of sex partners. As a result, other genes have evolved that cause males to engage in competitive and risky sexual displays—displays that are intended to influence females' choices.

It's well established that men are more likely than women to engage in risky behaviors, but it's not clear whether the risks we take in everyday life—such as when we cross a busy street—are actually sexual displays. To help answer this question, an international group of evolutionary psychologists descended on Britain's Liverpool University (Pawlowski et al., 2008). They stationed themselves near the campus's busiest crosswalk and over a period of three months they observed how a thousand men and women crossed the street. Specifically, they noted how much risk the students took in crossing (i.e., whether they crossed when vehicles were approaching) and who else was present when each person crossed. As might have been expected, the researchers found that men took more risks than women. The interesting finding, though, was that the presence of women nearby significantly *increased* the likelihood that a man would attempt a risky crossing, whereas the presence of men nearby did not influence his decision one way or another. Women, on the other hand, paid little or no attention to who was present, regardless of their sex, when they decided whether to cross. The researchers concluded that even a mundane act like crossing a street can be motivated in part by the urge to engage in sexual displays—but only for men. Women do engage in sexual displays—as we'll see later in the book—but these displays don't commonly take the form of risk-taking behavior.

Clinical psychologists deal with emotional, behavioral, and personality problems—problems that often have a sexual element. A related subgroup is sex therapists, who deal specifically with problems that interfere with the enjoyment of sex—problems such as premature ejaculation or lack of sexual desire. In the United States, sex therapists may be certified by the Society for Sex Therapy and Research (SSTAR) or by the American Association of Sex Educators, Counselors, and Therapists (AASECT). Some self-described sex therapists have no formal training or accreditation at all, however: The profession is unregulated in most U.S. states, so it's "buyer beware." **Marriage and family counselors** deal with problems affecting marriage and other intimate relationships—problems that may arise out of sexual difficulties or that, conversely, may arise in nonsexual areas of the relationship but interfere with sexual relations.

Health psychologists focus on the influence that illnesses such as diabetes and arthritis, or symptoms such as fatigue and pain, may have on sexuality. For instance, they will assist survivors of breast cancer, amputation, or heart attacks to cope with how the disease has changed their image of themselves and their relationship with their partner, and will suggest ways to engage in sexual behaviors with less pain or discomfort. Health psychologists also study the psychological aspects of gender inequalities. They may develop programs that empower women to make decisions—to refuse to have sex, for example—in cultures in which such decisions have traditionally been an exclusively male prerogative (Pick, 2003).

Sociologists Focus on the Connection between Sex and Society

Sociology is the scientific study of society. Sociologists make a unique contribution to the study of human sexuality by linking the sexual behaviors and attitudes of individuals to larger social structures.

One way sociologists accomplish this is by taking a demographic approach to sexuality—in other words, by examining how sexual expression varies with age, race, national origin, religious and political beliefs, place of residence, educational level, and so on. Such studies are often carried out by means of *sex surveys*.

The most famous sex survey was conducted by zoologist Alfred Kinsey and his colleagues at Indiana University in the middle years of the twentieth century (**Figure 1.7**). Kinsey's group interviewed about 17,000 Americans about their sex lives; the results were published in two thick, data-rich volumes—*Sexual Behavior in the Human Male* (Kinsey et al., 1948) and *Sexual Behavior in the Human Female* (Kinsey et al., 1953). For example, the reports stated that 37% of men had had at least one sexual contact with another male resulting in orgasm at some time between adolescence and old age. This finding challenged the then-prevailing view of homosexual relationships as some kind of rare aberration. The reports also found marked class differences in sexual behavior and attitudes: Educated, professional people masturbated much more frequently than those with little education or those who worked as laborers, for example.

People are unaccustomed to answering questions about intimate details of their sex lives, or about stigmatized behaviors such as marital infidelity. To encourage honesty, Kinsey took great pains to ensure the confidentiality of his interviewees' identities and of their responses. Such confidentiality is now recognized as an essential ingredient of a valid survey; in fact, surveys are sometimes designed to allow the interviewees to supply answers to sensitive questions in anonymous form, such as through a mail-in questionnaire or by direct entry into a computer.

In spite of the large numbers of interviewees in the Kinsey surveys, their answers were not necessarily representative of the U.S. population as a whole, let alone the entirety of the human race as implied in his

marriage and family counselor Therapist who assesses or treats interpersonal problems arising between spouses or other intimate partners.

health psychologist Person who assesses or treats mental or behavioral difficulties that arise out of physical disease.

sociology The scientific study of society.

Figure 1.7 Sex survey pioneer Alfred Kinsey (1894–1956) (left, seated) and his colleagues (from left to right) Clyde Martin, Paul Gebhard, and Wardell Pomeroy interviewed over 17,000 men and women between 1938 and 1956.

National Health and Social Life Survey (NHSLS) A national survey of sexual behavior, relationships, and attitudes in the United States, conducted in the early 1990s.

General Social Survey (GSS) A long-running periodic survey of the U.S. population run by the National Opinion Research Center.

National Survey of Sexual Attitudes and Lifestyles (NSSAL) A British survey of sexual behavior, relationships, and attitudes conducted in the early 1990s.

script theory The analysis of sexual and other behaviors as the enactment of socially instilled roles.

books' titles. It's possible, for example, that the people who volunteered to participate were relatively free-thinking and sexually adventurous. Also, the great majority of the interviewees were urban whites living in the northeastern United States—many of them in Indiana, where Kinsey was based. Thus statistics reported by Kinsey, such as the 37% mentioned above, are no longer considered reliable.

With the onset of the AIDS epidemic around 1980, the need for detailed information about sexual practices and attitudes spurred a host of new sex surveys. Most notable among them was a 1992 survey conducted by sociologists at the University of Chicago and elsewhere—the **National Health and Social Life Survey (NHSLS)** (Laumann et al., 1994). Besides being more up-to-date than the Kinsey survey, the NHSLS was technically superior in a number of respects, especially in its use of modern random-sampling methods and advanced techniques of statistical analysis, made possible by computers.

On the other hand, the NHSLS was more limited in scope. It included only about 3400 interviewees—too few to draw reliable conclusions about small minorities such as, say, African-American lesbians. It also failed to include people younger than 18 (a group whose sexual activity is of great significance from a public policy perspective) or those older than 59 (the group whose sex lives we know the least about). Finally, some critics have argued that the NHSLS and other recent surveys failed to elicit completely forthright responses from the interviewees, and therefore underestimated the prevalence of stigmatized traits and behaviors such as promiscuity, homosexuality, and abortion (Lewontin, 1995).

The NHSLS is now more than 15 years old. To some extent, its findings are being supplemented by smaller, more focused surveys, as well as by the **General Social Survey (GSS)**, an annual survey administered by the University of Chicago that includes questions on sexuality. The National Center for Health Statistics, a branch of the U.S. Centers for Disease Control, has also entered the sex-survey business (Mosher et al., 2005; Centers for Disease Control, 2007b). These surveys, as well as a British survey called the **National Survey of Sexual Attitudes and Lifestyles (NSSAL)**, (Wellings et al., 1994), will be cited throughout this book. We also occasionally refer to magazine-sponsored surveys, which are more up-to-date and also tend to cover intimate topics that the official surveys ignore. In 2007, for example, *Esquire* and *Marie Claire* magazines commissioned a national random-sample survey that came up with all kinds of interesting information about current U.S. sex practices—such as that men rate their partners' looks as the most powerful turn-on, whereas women give first place to kindness, in each case by wide margins.

Sociologists are interested in the *communities* within which sexual relationships are established and maintained. Most Americans are now city-dwellers. There is a perception that the city is the place where anything goes, where anyone can hook up with anyone, where any fantasy can become fact. Closer inspection shows that this is largely an illusion: Most sexual relationships—even in the city—are tightly constrained by the opportunities and traditions of the community to which the individual belongs. Thus a city has many distinct sexual "markets" within which men and women trade (Laumann et al., 2004).

What is the actual mechanism by which social structures (from the family to the mass media) mold individual feelings and behaviors? One influential idea put forward by sociologists is that they promote a kind of role-playing behavior, in which people are like performers in a play—perhaps a play that is the product of a collective rather than a single playwright. This idea has been referred to as **script theory** (Reiss, 1986; Simon & Gagnon, 1987).

Here's an example of the application of script theory to a sexual topic. Steven Eggermont wanted to know whether television viewing influences teenagers' ideas about how to obtain sexual contacts—specifically, whether they believed that an overtly sexual strategy (such as suggestive touching) or a romantic strategy (the candlelight dinner approach) was more effective (Eggermont, 2006). Television shows, especially those viewed by teens, are filled with examples of both approaches, some successful and some not. Eggermont found that, between the ages of 12 and 15, boys and girls placed increasing faith in the sexual strategy; this change was related to the adolescents' progress through puberty and was little influenced by television exposure. Eggermont also found that television viewing lessened girls' belief in the romantic strategy, while it *strengthened* boys' belief in that strategy. Apparently, television viewing familiarized boys and girls with the sexual scripts thought to be effective with the other sex.

Sociologists May Take an Ethnographic Approach

Sociologists sometimes immerse themselves in their subjects in the same way as cultural anthropologists do. This approach is called **ethnography**, the personal interpretation of a cultural group based on fieldwork. An example is the work of Teela Sanders, of England's Leeds University (Sanders, 2005, 2008). While a graduate student, Sanders spent 11 months closely observing the lives of off-street prostitutes in the city of Birmingham. To do so, she took a position as a health outreach worker, which gave her access to the anonymous, overheated apartments where the women worked. She would bring condoms, lubricant, and information about sexually transmitted diseases, and arrange for the women to get health check-ups. After they came to trust her, many of the women agreed to give Sanders lengthy interviews, which were frequently interrupted by the need to attend to a customer. The women were not above playing jokes on Sanders, such as leading customers to believe that she was one of the sex workers and then watching the resulting embarrassment on the closed-circuit television.

Sanders found a highly structured world inside these illegal brothels. The prostitutes themselves were the financial hubs of networks of complicit coworkers: These ranged from landlords, madams, and maids to photographers, printers, website designers, card boys (who placed the women's cards in telephone booths), drug dealers, peddlers, health workers, and even ethnographers like Sanders herself.

Sanders came to the conclusion that off-street prostitutes are not the passive victims of poverty or drugs—as many streetwalking prostitutes probably are—but women who carefully negotiate the risks and benefits of their trade. And the men seek and obtain more than sex. Money may not buy you love, but—in Sanders' view, at least—it *can* buy you real intimacy, even in the face of social stigma and police harassment. Sanders' findings, which have received a great deal of attention from the British media, suggest that regulation of off-street prostitution might be a sensible alternative to criminalization.

Ethnographers of sex have to be willing to go wherever sex is transacted. Besides brothels, ethnographers have spent months in singles bars, in strip joints, on sordid street-corners, and even—as we'll see in a later chapter—in men's restrooms.

Feminists Emphasize Women's Sexual Rights

Feminism—the belief that women are entitled to the same social, economic, and political rights as men, and the organized pursuit of these goals—has had a profound influence on how Americans think about sexuality.

One feminist pioneer, Margaret Sanger (1879–1966), campaigned tirelessly for women's right to learn about and use contraceptives. In the

ethnography The study of a cultural group, often by means of extended individual fieldwork.

feminism The movement to secure equality for women; the study of social and psychological issues from women's perspectives.

Sex education in the streets. Feminists have encouraged women to learn about their own bodies.

socialization The effect of social influences such as family, education, peer groups, and the media on the development of psychological or behavioral traits.

sexology The scientific study of sex, especially of sexual dysfunctions.

sex research The scientific study of sex.

face of fierce opposition—Sanger spent a month in jail at one point—she and her colleagues opened birth control clinics and helped develop new contraceptive technologies. The Planned Parenthood Federation, a leading provider of contraceptive and abortion services, traces its origins to Sanger's movement.

A second period of feminism began in the 1960s and had its heyday in the 1970s. In the sexual domain, central themes were a woman's entitlement to know her own body, to seek sexual pleasure, to terminate a pregnancy, and to be free from sexual assault and harassment. The bible of this movement was *Our Bodies, Ourselves*, first published by the Boston Women's Health Book Collective in 1970; the book has since been published in innumerable foreign languages from Albanian to Thai.

A dominant idea in 1970s feminism was that differences between the sexes are established by learning and culture—that boys are **socialized** to be sexually aggressive, for example, whereas girls are socialized to be submissive—and could therefore be changed by restructuring society. Influential feminist writers, such as Germaine Greer, downplayed or dismissed the notion that biological factors might contribute to gender differences (Greer, 1971).

In contrast, some feminists such as Carol Gilligan (Gilligan, 1982) emphasized that men and women were fundamentally distinct, or even that women were superior to men in important respects, such as being more caring. These characteristics were thought of either as biological givens or as the consequence of the way women and men interpreted their reproductive functions.

During the 1980s, feminism was shaken up by writers outside of academe, such as self-described pornographer Susie Bright, who reveled in "down-and-dirty" female sexuality and edited a groundbreaking lesbian sex magazine, *On Our Backs*.

Figure 1.8 Chicana lesbian Gloria Anzaldúa (1942–2004) drew feminists' attention to the diversity in women's lives, including their sex lives.

She has since authored innumerable popular books, articles, and online columns that celebrate unorthodox sex. Another voice dissenting from traditional feminism is that of cultural critic Camille Paglia. Paglia sees gender differences as largely innate, and the influence of culture as reining in these differences rather than creating them (Paglia, 1990). Socialization, according to Paglia, is the reason why women can walk the streets with some expectation of safety, not the reason why men commit rape.

Yet another way in which feminism was challenged and transformed in the 1980s was by the voices of diverse minorities, such as those of Chicana lesbians (Anzaldúa & Moraga, 1981) (**Figure 1.8**). These voices were the inspiration for "third-wave feminism," which now concerns itself with everything from sexual freedom in the United States (Baumgardner & Richards, 2000) to the ritual cutting of girls' genitals ("female circumcision") in the Islamic world (Gruenbaum, 2000).

Sex Research Is Becoming a Discipline in Its Own Right

As we have seen, women and men in a variety of academic disciplines and other walks of life have made important contributions to our understanding of human sexuality. Increasingly, however, there is a perception that sex research is an academic discipline in its own right. This discipline is an unusual one in that it demands a training that crosses most of the traditionally established intellectual boundaries.

The study of sex is sometimes referred to as **sexology**, although people who label themselves sexologists tend to be those who focus on sexual dysfunctions. **Sex research** is probably a broader and more widely understood term. However it is named, sex research is now fostered by numerous organizations at local, international, and global levels. In the United States, the Society for the Scientific Study of Sexuality (SSSS or "Quad-S") organizes national and regional meetings and publishes the

Journal of Sex Research and other periodicals. The American Association of Sex Educators, Counselors and Therapists (AASECT) and the Society for Sex Therapy and Research (SSTAR) certify educational programs in sex education and therapy. There are also institutes devoted to research or training in issues of sexuality, such as the Kinsey Institute (which is affiliated with Indiana University), and special-purpose organizations such as the Guttmacher Institute (which focuses on family-planning issues).

At an international level, two organizations stand out. The International Academy of Sex Research (IASR) organizes an annual meeting and publishes the *Archives of Sexual Behavior.* The World Association for Sexual Health (WAS) also holds an annual meeting and has issued a Universal Declaration of Sexual Rights (**Box 1.3**). The abstracts of WAS and IASR meetings are available online and offer an overview of current trends in sex research.

Society, Values, and the Law

BOX 1.3 Declaration of Sexual Rights

The World Association for Sexual Health (WAS) represents 118 national sex-research organizations. At its 1999 World Congress, held in Hong Kong, WAS approved the following Declaration of Sexual Rights. Bear in mind while reading this document that, although it may reflect a consensus among the members of WAS, it touches on topics, such as gay rights and female circumcision (alluded to here as "mutilation"), on which there are differing views in different cultures around the world.

> Sexuality is an integral part of the personality of every human being. Its full development depends upon the satisfaction of basic human needs such as the desire for contact, intimacy, emotional expression, pleasure, tenderness, and love. Sexuality is constructed through the interaction between the individual and social structures. Full development of sexuality is essential for individual, interpersonal, and societal well being. Sexual rights are universal human rights based on the inherent freedom, dignity, and equality of all human beings. Since health is a fundamental human right, so must sexual health be a basic human right. In order to assure that human beings and societies develop healthy sexuality, the following sexual rights must be recognized, promoted, respected, and defended by all societies through all means. Sexual health is the result of an environment that recognizes, respects, and exercises these sexual rights.

1. **The right to sexual freedom.** Sexual freedom encompasses the possibility for individuals to express their full sexual potential. However, this excludes all forms of sexual coercion, exploitation and abuse at any time and situations in life.

2. **The right to sexual autonomy, sexual integrity, and safety of the sexual body.** This right involves the ability to make autonomous decisions about one's sexual life within a context of one's own personal and social ethics. It also encompasses control and enjoyment of our own bodies free from torture, mutilation and violence of any sort.

3. **The right to sexual privacy.** This involves the right for individual decisions and behaviors about intimacy as long as they do not intrude on the sexual rights of others.

4. **The right to sexual equity.** This refers to freedom from all forms of discrimination regardless of sex, gender, sexual orientation, age, race, social class, religion, or physical and emotional disability.

5. **The right to sexual pleasure.** Sexual pleasure, including autoeroticism, is a source of physical, psychological, intellectual and spiritual well-being.

6. **The right to emotional sexual expression.** Sexual expression is more than erotic pleasure or sexual acts. Individuals have a right to express their sexuality through communication, touch, emotional expression and love.

7. **The right to sexually associate freely.** This means the possibility to marry or not, to divorce, and to establish other types of responsible sexual associations.

8. **The right to make free and responsible reproductive choices.** This encompasses the right to decide whether or not to have children, the number and spacing of children, and the right to full access to the means of fertility regulation.

9. **The right to sexual information based upon scientific inquiry.** This right implies that sexual information should be generated through the process of unencumbered and yet scientifically ethical inquiry, and disseminated in appropriate ways at all societal levels.

10. **The right to comprehensive sexuality education.** This is a lifelong process from birth throughout the life cycle and should involve all social institutions.

11. **The right to sexual health care.** Sexual health care should be available for prevention and treatment of all sexual concerns, problems, and disorders.

Sex Education Faces Significant Obstacles

We already mentioned the opposition that Margaret Sanger faced when she attempted to disseminate knowledge about birth control in the early part of the twentieth century. Similar difficulties have plagued education in all aspects of human sexuality and continue to the present day.

Religious conservatives may oppose sex education programs in schools for a number of reasons. They may believe that abstinence until marriage is a moral imperative—even though only five percent of Americans obey it (Finer, 2007). They may see sex education as a private matter that should be the prerogative of parents, not governments. They may believe that, whatever the content of sex education programs, the effect will be to legitimize and promote sexual activity among teenagers, with associated harmful consequences.

Because of pressure from some religious conservative groups, there is a strong emphasis on abstinence in school sex education today. According to a study by the Guttmacher Institute, one in three U.S. teenagers receives no education about birth control. Even among those who do, many do not receive it when they most need it, which is before they start to have sex (Lindberg et al., 2006). Only 14% of U.S. school districts have policies that could be described as comprehensive, meaning that they include both abstinence and contraception as part of a broader program designed to prepare adolescents to become sexually healthy adults (**Box 1.4**).

Some non-profit organizations are dedicated to improving access to comprehensive sex education. Among them are the Sexuality Information and Education Council of the United States (SIECUS) and its Canadian counterpart, SIECCAN.

Health education specialist Clara Haignere has undertaken a detailed review of studies on the effectiveness of school sex-education programs. According to her analysis, abstinence-only programs have little or no effect on teens' sexual behavior. Comprehensive programs, on the other hand, do cause teens to delay sexual activity and make them more likely to use contraception when they do become sexually active (Haignere et al., 1999).

Whatever the deficiencies of sex education in the United States, the teen pregnancy rate has been declining steadily: It is now 36% below its peak in 1990 (National Campaign to Prevent Teen Pregnancy, 2006b), though still above the rates for many other countries. This drop is part of an international trend, and is due largely to improved contraceptive use (Santelli et al., 2007). Thus many U.S. teens seem to be learning about effective contraception from sources other than school sex-education programs. These may include online sources such as Planned Parenthood's Teenwire. Nevertheless, U.S. pregnancy rates remain disturbingly high among Hispanic and African-American teens, two groups that are particularly likely to become sexually active before receiving any education about contraception (Lindberg et al., 2006).

The Political Controversy Reflects Social Divisions

Besides opposing comprehensive sex education in schools, the U.S. government has also opposed international sex-education initiatives. In 1994 the United States had joined 178 other nations in creating the "Cairo consensus," which affirmed the right to comprehensive sex- and family-planning education. But at a follow-up meeting 10 years later, U.S. representatives fought to delete these provisions in favor of abstinence-only education.

Of course, these political attitudes could not exist without considerable public support. In fact, human sexuality classes such as the one you are taking often represent liberal microenvironments. An example: In 2008, one of us (S.L.) polled stu-

Society, Values, and the Law

BOX 1.4 Sex Education: United States and Canada Compared

In the United States, school-based sexuality education varies greatly by location. In recent years, the U.S. government has directed funding for sex education to states that mandate "abstinence-only" programs. Here is a summary of the official policy of one such state, South Carolina (SIECUS, 2004):

Sex education includes instruction in human physiology, conception, prenatal care and development, and postnatal care. Abstinence until marriage is stressed. There is to be no mention of nonreproductive sex practices except to convey the risk of disease transmission. Contraception is [only] taught in the context of marriage. Abortion cannot be discussed, nor can homosexual practices or relationships except to emphasize the risk of disease transmission.

In 2007, the state of Missouri (which receives federal funding) enacted a law banning organizations that perform abortions from providing sex education in public schools. This deprived the state of dozens of highly qualified educators from Planned Parenthood, hospitals, and other agencies.

A few states, including California and Pennsylvania, have rejected federal funding in order to be able to present comprehensive sex-ed programs. California's policy, for example, requires that instruction be age-appropriate, medically accurate, and appropriate for use with pupils of all races, genders, sexual orientations, ethnic and cultural backgrounds, and pupils with disabilities. From grade 7 on, instruction must include information about abstinence while also providing information on other methods of preventing pregnancy and sexually transmitted diseases. This instruction must provide information about the effectiveness and safety of all FDA-approved contraceptive methods in preventing pregnancy, including emergency contraception. Schools that offer comprehensive programs often face protests from parents, some of whom insist on taking their children out of sex-ed classes.

The situation in Canada is very different. The Canadian federal government has established sex-education guidelines that are far more liberal than those of the United States (Public Health Agency of Canada, 2003).

According to the guidelines, "Adolescent sexuality is a central and positive part of the total well-being of young people." Government officials urge comprehensive education including the teaching of contraceptive techniques, discussion of gay, lesbian, and transgender issues, and so on. Sex education is to be provided in an age-appropriate fashion from elementary school through high school. The guidelines urge outreach to homeless and institutionalized youth. Condoms are widely available in schools and, in the province of Quebec, girls can obtain prescriptions for contraceptive pills directly from their school nurses.

According to Canadian sex educator Stephanie Mitelman, parents often demand *more* sex education than schools can provide (Mitelman, 2007). The reason for this is that in spite of the government policy, individual schools vary greatly in the level of funding and training available for sex-ed programs. Least well-served are Canada's native peoples. Partly as a result, their communities have unusually high rates of sexually transmitted diseases, including AIDS.

The teen pregnancy rate is twice as high in the United States as it is in Canada (Guttmacher Institute, 2006).

dents in a human sexuality class at U.C. Santa Barbara about their attitudes to same-sex marriage. All but 1 of the 500-odd students voted for legalization of such marriage, yet over half of the U.S. population at the time was opposed to legalization.

It's important to keep the existence of this conservative climate in mind, and not to dismiss it as ill-intentioned or uninformed. Sexual abstinence, for example, may not be a popular theme in your sexuality class, but the fact is that campaigns promoting sexual abstinence and sexual monogamy, along with condom use by those who are sexually active, have had dramatic effects in reducing HIV infection rates in at least one country in Africa—Uganda—and in doing so have saved countless lives (Singh et al., 2003). Comparable sex-education campaigns have a place in the United States, too, especially in the effort to reduce unwanted teen pregnancy and sexually transmitted diseases.

Ethical Systems Can Be Sex-Negative or Sex-Positive

Social conflicts on issues such as sex education and abstinence result mainly from differences in people's ethical beliefs. Where do these differences arise from? People's sense of right and wrong behavior, in sex as in other spheres of action, derives from many sources: religious teachings, secular humanist ideas, upbringing, past sexual interactions, reasoned thought, and even from ethical "instincts" that we inherit from our evolutionary past. At the risk of oversimplifying the matter, one can say that there are "sex-negative" and "sex-positive" ethical traditions.

Sex-negative traditions label many—perhaps all—sexual behaviors as wrong. Early Christianity was dominated by sex-negative ideas: Abstention from sexual activity was the only truly virtuous state, according to Saint Augustine (see Chapter 10). Among the most sex-positive traditions, on the other hand, are those of some Pacific islands, such as Mangaia in the Cook Islands. Mangaian girls and boys are given instruction in sexual techniques and encouraged to put what they learned into practice, even in the form of casual liaisons (see Chapter 9). Our own contemporary U.S. culture contains a mixture of sex-positive and sex-negative elements—elements that are often at war with each other.

Sexual ethics may be founded on religious or other authority ("homosexuality is against God's law"), on agreed-upon principles such as honesty ("you should tell your partner if you have herpes"), or on an analysis of consequences ("if teens have sex, we'll all have to support the unwanted babies that result"). Because of these varied modes of ethical thought, people (including professional ethicists) have diverging views on what is right and wrong, and sexual ethics may change over time.

At Brandeis University, Bernadette Brooten leads a group that is concerned with the reworking of Jewish and Christian sexual ethics in the light of feminist theory (Brooten, 2008). In the New Testament, Saint Paul roundly condemned sex between women in his Epistle to the Romans. According to Brooten, Paul's condemnation was rooted in his belief in the importance of distinct social roles for men and women, with women in a subordinate position. This distinction was threatened by lesbian relationships (Brooten, 2000). Feminism and other social forces have brought the historical justification for strict gender roles into question, so Paul's denunciation of female homosexuality may have lost some of its moral relevance to contemporary society.

Summary

1. The word "sex" refers to the categories of male or female, or (in more recent usage) the entire phenomenon of sexual attraction and behavior. The word "gender" refers to the constellation of mental and behavioral traits that differ between males and females.

2. Sexual relationships are highly diverse: They may be motivated by a variety of different factors, they may be brief or durable, and they may be socially approved or stigmatized. Most sexual relationships involve some degree of mismatch or conflict that challenges the participants' adaptability and communication skills. Engaging in sexual relationships also requires ethical decisions—decisions that, while influenced by knowledge and reason, are based ultimately on a personal sense of what is right and wrong.

3. Many aspects of sex influence our sense of who we are—our identity. These include characteristics such as male, female, lesbian, gay, bisexual, heterosexual, transgendered, and many others. Sexual identities influence our place in society far beyond the sphere of people with whom we have actual sexual contact.

4. Sexuality can be studied with a wide variety of approaches. The biomedical approach has elucidated many of the anatomical structures and physiological processes that underlie sexual and reproductive life. It has also sought to characterize and treat disorders of sexual desire and behavior, but this effort has involved controversial judgments as to the normality or abnormality of various forms of sexual expression.

5. The psychological approach falls into several subdisciplines. Social psychologists concern themselves with the diverse ways in which sex influences interpersonal relations. Psychobiologists focus on the biological underpinnings of sexual behavior, and often study this behavior in laboratory animals rather than humans. Cultural psychologists study how cultural diversity affects sexual expression. Clinical psychologists and sex therapists deal with problems affecting sexual desire or performance.

6. Sociologists are concerned with the interactions between the sexuality of individuals and larger demographic groupings. Sex surveys are an important tool in this approach. An example of a theoretical social-science approach is sexual script theory: the notion that, as a result of constant interaction with others, people learn to play certain sexual roles. Sociologists also do fieldwork in the environments where sexual transactions take place.

7. Feminists have greatly influenced attitudes about sex. Feminist ideas that have entered mainstream thinking include the belief that women are capable of and entitled to sexual pleasure, have a right to contraception and abortion, are entitled to protection from sexual violence, and are as capable as men in all spheres of life. Feminists have generally favored the idea that sexual attitudes—especially insofar as they differ between the sexes—result from socialization rather than from innate differences.

8. Sexology or sex research is gradually asserting itself as an independent and multidisciplinary field of study. National and international organizations, conferences, and journals are devoted to a rational, evidence-based approach to human sexuality.

9. Educators have faced a difficult struggle to communicate basic information about sex. Even today, there is a widespread fear that instruction in sexual matters, including techniques to avoid sexually transmitted diseases and unwanted pregnancy, may be seen as permitting or even encouraging sexual behavior by teenagers. The amount and nature of sex education provided by public schools varies greatly by location.

10. Ethical traditions can be broadly characterized as sex-negative (such as early Christian views on sex) or sex-positive (such as the attitudes of some Polynesian societies.) The basis for ethical judgments may change over time, leading to a revision of beliefs concerning what is right and wrong in the sphere of sexual behavior.

Discussion Questions

1. After reading the "Declaration of Sexual Rights" (see Box 1.3), do you agree with everything in it? Do you think there are important topics that the Declaration fails to address? Should these rights be incorporated into the laws of all countries, or should local cultural standards (concerning homosexuality and female circumcision, for example) be respected?

2. According to its mission statement, the Sexuality Information and Education Council of the United States (SIECUS) "advocates the right of individuals to make responsible sexual choices." Should people also have the right to make *irresponsible* sexual choices? Where would you draw the line and on what grounds?

Web Resources

American Association of Sex Educators, Counselors, and Therapists www.aasect.org

Archive for Sexology—English language site at the University of Berlin www2.hu-berlin.de/sexology/

Guttmacher Institute www.guttmacher.org

International Academy of Sex Research www.iasr.org

Kinsey Institute for Research in Sex, Gender, and Reproduction www.kinseyinstitute.org

Sexuality Information and Education Council of Canada www.sieccan.org

Sexuality Information and Education Council of the United States www.siecus.org

Society for Sex Therapy and Research www.sstarnet.org

Society for the Scientific Study of Sexuality www.sexscience.org

Statistics Canada www.statcan.ca

World Association for Sexual Health www.worldsexology.org

Recommended Reading

Freud, S. (1905/1975). *Three essays on the theory of sexuality*. Basic Books.

Kinsey, A. C., Pomeroy, W. B., & Martin, C. E. (1948). *Sexual behavior in the human male*. Saunders.

Kinsey, A. C., Pomeroy, W. B., Martin, C. E., & Gebhard, P.H. (1953). *Sexual behavior in the human female*. Saunders.

Krafft-Ebing, R. v. (1886/1999). *Psychopathia sexualis, with special reference to contrary sexual instinct: A clinical-forensic study*. Bloat Books.

Masters, W. H., & Johnson, V. E. (1966). *Human sexual response*. Little, Brown.

Masters, W. H., & Johnson, V. (1970). *Human sexual inadequacy*. Little, Brown.

Mead, M. (1928). *Coming of age in Samoa: A psychological study of primitive youth for Western civilization*. Morrow.

(The books listed above are historically significant works but don't necessarily represent current thinking in sexology.)

Laumann, E. O., Gagnon, J. H., Michael, R. T., & Michaels, S. (1994). *The social organization of sexuality: Sexual practices in the United States*. University of Chicago Press.

Roach, M. (2008). *Bonk: The curious coupling of science and sex*. W.W. Norton.

CHAPTER 2

A male kingfisher offers a fish to a female as a courtship gift.

Sex and Evolution

Our sexuality evolved from the sex lives of nonhuman creatures that preceded us in the long history of life on Earth. By studying this evolutionary process, we can hope to find clues to some very basic "Why?" questions about ourselves: Why are we sexual beings? Why are there two sexes? Why are there approximately equal numbers of men and women? Why do we find some people more attractive than others? Why don't all sex acts lead to pregnancy? Why are men more interested in casual sex than women? Why do some of us cheat on our partners? And why do some of us remain faithful? The study of evolution does not provide complete answers to these questions, but it does remind us that answers are needed. Without the evolutionary perspective, it is too easy to view our own sexuality as the natural order of things, requiring no explanation.

Most of the examples and research studies described in this chapter feature nonhuman animals. This may seem an odd way to begin a textbook on human sexuality. Later in this book, however, we will often have cause to compare ourselves with other animals and to consider human sexuality against the background of the evolutionary principles discussed here.

Diverse Methods of Reproduction Have Evolved

Evolution—the change in the genetic makeup of living populations over time—has led not only to humans, but to over a million other species that currently inhabit our planet, plus millions more that are now extinct. Although we humans like to think of ourselves as the high point of evolution—perhaps even its ultimate goal—scientists have discovered nothing special about our position on the evolutionary tree that would support this notion. Instead, we seem to be just one leaf out of many. And the sex lives of humans, although remarkably diverse, occupy only a fraction of the range of sexual behaviors that exist or have existed on Earth.

The principles of evolution were laid out by Charles Darwin in *The Origin of Species* (1859). Individuals within a single species differ slightly from one another—it may be the length of their nose, the speed of their running, or their preference for one food over another. In part, these differences are **heritable**—they are passed down from parent to offspring. If circumstances favor the survival and reproduction of animals with a certain heritable trait (such as the ability to run fast), that trait will be passed on to more offspring and will become more preva-

evolution The change in the genetic makeup of living populations over time.

heritable Capable of being passed down from parent to offspring.

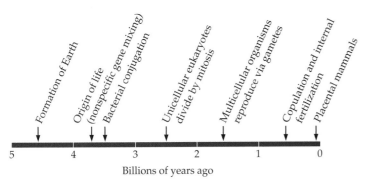

Figure 2.1 **A brief history of sex** Dates are approximate.

lent in succeeding generations. If a trait is disadvantageous, it will be passed on to fewer offspring and will tend to die out. This process is known as **natural selection**: Operating over countless generations, natural selection has produced the complex life forms—including ourselves—that inhabit Earth today.

We now know that heritable traits are encoded by **genes**, and that genes are linear stretches of **DNA (deoxyribonucleic acid)** strung out along **chromosomes** within the nucleus of each cell in an organism. There are an estimated 20,000–25,000 genes in the human **genome** (Human Genome Project, 2005), and any two people will show differences in many of these genes. It is the combined instructions contained in these genes, interacting with the diverse environments in which we develop, that make each of us uniquely human.

The main ingredient in evolution is time—lots of it (**Figure 2.1**). It is now about 4.6 billion years since the formation of Earth, about 3.9 billion years since it became hospitable to life, and at least 3.7 billion years since life actually arose (Rosing, 1999). Thus evolution has had at least 3.7 billion years to create the diversity of species that exists on Earth today.

The nature of the very earliest life forms is a matter of speculation, but the earliest organisms to use DNA as their genetic repository were microscopic, single-celled organisms without nuclei that reproduced by splitting in two. They also readily swapped DNA between individuals. This early form of gene swapping was probably quite disorganized; it may simply have involved the ingestion of fragments of DNA released by dead organisms.

Present-day bacteria also swap DNA, but they do so through a specific mechanism called **conjugation** (**Figure 2.2**). Two bacteria connect by a fine hairlike tube called a *pilus*, and a short piece of DNA called a *plasmid* passes through the pilus from the donor to the recipient bacterium. The plasmid may later become integrated into the recipient bacterium's main genome. One way in which bacterial conjugation affects humans is that it offers a means by which genes conferring resistance to antibiotics can pass from one strain of bacteria to another, thus complicating our efforts to treat infectious diseases.

Organisms composed of nucleated cells—**eukaryotes**—probably appeared between 3 billion and 2 billion years ago. Initially they were all single-celled organisms, like present-day amoebas, followed by multicellular eukaryotes (both animals and plants), which appeared about 1.5 billion years ago. Eukaryotic animals greatly diversified in the so-called Cambrian explosion, 545 million years

natural selection The survival and reproduction of those individuals that are best adapted to their environment.

gene A stretch of DNA that is transcribed as a functional unit; a unit of inheritance.

DNA (deoxyribonucleic acid) The linear molecule that forms the chemical basis of genes in all species except some viruses.

chromosome A rod-shaped nuclear organelle composed of DNA and associated proteins.

genome An organism's entire complement of DNA, including all its genes. In some viruses, such as HIV, the genome is composed of RNA.

conjugation Contact between two bacteria accompanied by the transfer of a short stretch of DNA from one to the other.

eukaryote An organism whose cells contain nuclei.

(A)

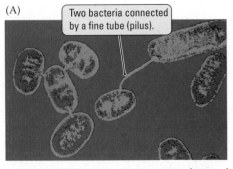

Two bacteria connected by a fine tube (pilus).

1 μm

(B)

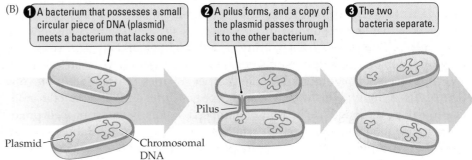

1 A bacterium that possesses a small circular piece of DNA (plasmid) meets a bacterium that lacks one.

2 A pilus forms, and a copy of the plasmid passes through it to the other bacterium.

3 The two bacteria separate.

Plasmid   Chromosomal DNA

Pilus

Figure 2.2 **Bacterial conjugation**

ago, when all the main kinds of body plans that now exist—arthropod, vertebrate, sponge, and so on—first appeared.

Eukaryotic cells usually divide by **mitosis** (**Box 2.1**). When single-celled organisms such as amoebas undergo mitosis, the result is two new daughter organisms. This is a form of **asexual reproduction**, meaning that the offspring carry the genes of only a single parent. Many multicellular animals are also capable of reproducing asexually: A single cell or collection of cells from one organism undergoes repeated mitoses, creating an entire new organism that is genetically identical to its parent. One example that you may be familiar with is the reproduction of hydra and other microscopic animals by a simple budding process; another example is the propagation of plants from cuttings. Although humans don't reproduce by mitosis, mitotic cell divisions are what take us from a single, fertilized egg cell to an organism with billions of body cells.

Nearly all eukaryotic organisms—even single-celled organisms such as amoebas—have the capacity for **sexual reproduction**. The key feature of sexual reproduction is that the offspring carry a mixture of genes from two parents. This mixing occurs through the fusion of two specialized cells known as **gametes** (**Figure 2.3**), each of which contributes chromosomes to the new organism. In order to keep the number of chromosomes constant from one generation to the next, the gametes are usually **haploid**; that is, they contain half the number of chromosomes contained in the regular **diploid** cells of the same species. Haploid gametes are produced by a special sequence of cell divisions known as **meiosis** (see Box 2.1) that takes place within reproductive tissues (**gonads**).

Except for animals that have been produced in the laboratory by artificial cloning techniques, all mammals are the products of sexual reproduction. In fact, most vertebrates reproduce exclusively by sexual means. Among invertebrate animals and plants, many species have the capacity to reproduce either sexually or asexually. The propagation of flowering plants either from seeds or from cuttings is a well-known example. It is rare, however, to find eukaryotic organisms that rely exclusively on asexual reproduction.

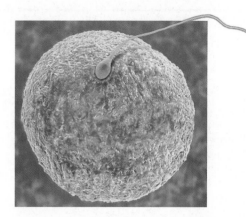

Figure 2.3 Gametes A sperm and an ovum.

Rival Theories Offer Explanations for Sexual Reproduction

The fact that nearly all multicellular organisms are capable of sexual reproduction, and that most vertebrates rely on it exclusively, tells us that the capacity for this form of reproduction must be **adaptive**; that is, it must help the organism to perpetuate its genes in future generations. How does it do so?

Surprisingly, the answer to this very basic question is a bit of a mystery. On the face of it, asexual reproduction is more adaptive than sexual reproduction. This is because an animal that reproduces asexually devotes all its resources to passing on its own genes, and those genes are perpetuated in all of its descendants (**Figure 2.4**). An animal that reproduces sexually, however, dilutes its genes with those of another animal, thus reducing the representation of its own genes in future generations. It seems like a pointless self-sacrifice. This paradox is particularly striking in species in which one sex—usually the female—invests far more in reproduction than the other sex. In such species, it would seem that females would do better to give birth **parthenogenetically** (by asexual "virgin birth") rather than to give some male's genes a free ride into the next generation. If a single parthogenetically reproducing female arose in a population of a million sexually reproducing individuals, then—other things being equal—it would take less than 50 generations for her clonal descendants to replace the entire population. Yet, except for a few unusual species, females engage in sexual reproduction all or some of the time. So other things must not be equal—but in what way, exactly?

mitosis Cell division in which the chromosome number is preserved.

asexual reproduction Reproduction in which all the offspring's genes are inherited from a single parent.

sexual reproduction Reproduction in which the offspring inherit genes from two parents.

gamete A germ cell (ovum or sperm) that fuses with another to form a new organism.

haploid Possessing half the usual complement of chromosomes.

diploid Possessing the full complement of chromosomes.

meiosis A pair of cell divisions that produces haploid gametes.

gonad An organ that produces gametes (a testis in males; an ovary in females).

adaptive Helping the propagation of an organism's genes.

parthenogenesis Asexual reproduction from an unfertilized ovum; "virgin birth."

Biology of Sex

BOX 2.1 The Cellular Basis of Reproduction

Many organisms can reproduce either asexually, by means of mitosis (Figure A), or sexually, by means of meiosis and fertilization (Figure B). Unicellular organisms, and simple multicellular invertebrates such as *Hydra*, reproduce asexually most of the time and sexually less often. Most vertebrates, including humans as well as all other mammals, only reproduce sexually, so their gametes are produced by meiosis (we'll describe an interesting exception in Box 2.2). All other cells in the body are produced by mitosis. (See Web Activity 2.1 Mitosis; 2.2 Mitosis Time-Lapse Video; 2.3 Meiosis; and 2.4 Differences and Similarities between Meiosis and Mitosis.)

(A) Asexual reproduction by mitosis. Only selected phases are shown here.

A diploid cell contains several pairs of homologous chromosomes. One pair is shown here.

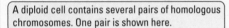

Interphase

Mitosis

G1 Phase
Chromosomes prepare for DNA replication.

S Phase
DNA of each chromosome is replicated to form sister chromatids.

G2 Phase
Each chromosome now consists of two sister chromatids. There is no interaction between homologous chromosomes.

Metaphase
Nuclear membrane breaks down and mitotic spindle forms.

Anaphase
Sister chromatids are pulled apart.

Cell division
Each daughter cell has a copy of every chromosome, so is diploid like its parent.

(B) Sexual reproduction involves meiosis. Only the key phases are shown here.

Mother

Diploid parental cells contain several pairs of homologous chromosomes. One pair is shown here in each cell.

DNA replication. Each chromosome becomes two sister chromatids.

Meiosis I
Homologous chromosomes join to form tetrads.

Genetic exchange takes place between homologous chromosomes…

…which are pulled apart at anaphase.

After cell division, each daughter cell is haploid—it contains half the number of parental chromosomes, each of which consists of two sister chromatids.

Father

Sexual Reproduction May Limit Harmful Mutations

One hypothesis suggests that sexual reproduction is adaptive because it helps organisms deal with the problem of harmful **mutations**. Mutations are random changes in an organism's genome caused by errors in the copying of DNA or by damaging chemicals, sunlight, or radiation. Many mutations are neutral—they have no effect on an organism's ability to survive and reproduce—but of those that are not neutral, far more are harmful than beneficial, just as random changes in computer software are far more likely to degrade its performance than to improve it.

When organisms reproduce asexually, harmful mutations accumulate over the generations. Because all the descendants of a given animal possess exact copies of that animal's genes, there is no way to get rid of a harmful mutation short of eliminating that entire lineage. When organisms reproduce sexually, however, harmful mutations *can* be eliminated. That's because offspring receive a randomly selected half of their mother's genes and half of their father's genes. If one parent carries a particular damaged gene, about half of that parent's offspring will not inherit it—they will inherit the normal version of the gene from the other parent instead.

In reality, most organisms carry numerous harmful mutations. Thus each offspring is likely to inherit some harmful mutations from each parent. But because of the lottery-like nature of sexual reproduction, some offspring will receive a greater total load of harmful mutations, and other offspring will receive

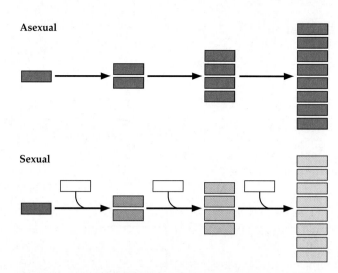

Asexual

Sexual

Figure 2.4 The paradox of sexual reproduction An asexually reproducing female's genes (red) are propagated without loss into future generations, but a sexually reproducing female's genes are mixed with the genes of unrelated males (white), and thus are reduced by half in each ensuing generation.

mutation A change in an organism's genome.

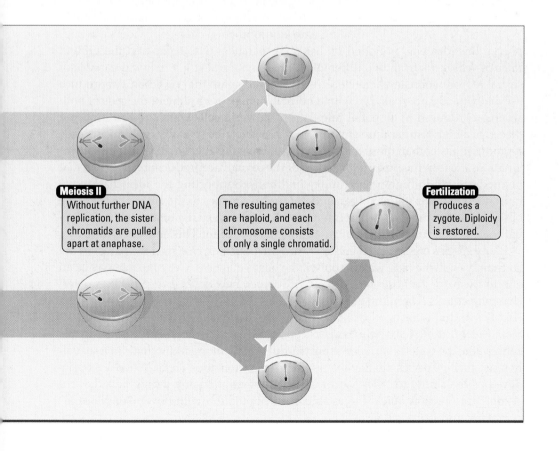

Meiosis II
Without further DNA replication, the sister chromatids are pulled apart at anaphase.

The resulting gametes are haploid, and each chromosome consists of only a single chromatid.

Fertilization
Produces a zygote. Diploidy is restored.

Asexual

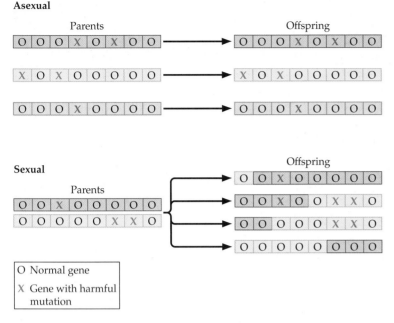

Sexual

O Normal gene
X Gene with harmful mutation

Figure 2.5 Reproduction and harmful mutations In this diagram, each organism is represented as a genome with 8 genes, some of which have harmful mutations (X's). In asexual reproduction (top), each offspring inherits the entire genome of its parent, along with any harmful mutations. In sexual reproduction (bottom), each offspring inherits random chunks of its father's (purple) and mother's (orange) genomes. Thus, some offspring, such as the lowermost one in the diagram, may inherit few or no harmful mutations. If this lucky offspring enjoys great reproductive success and its unlucky siblings die out, the harmful mutations will be eliminated from the population.

Red Queen hypothesis The idea that sexual reproduction is advantageous because it helps defend organisms against parasites.

polymorphism A common genetic variation between individuals in a species.

fewer (**Figure 2.5**). Natural selection will favor the survival and reproduction of the offspring with fewer harmful mutations. Thus sexual reproduction may help maintain an equilibrium state in a population of organisms, in which the appearance of new harmful mutations is balanced by the gradual elimination of old ones.

This advantage of sexual reproduction should outweigh the disadvantage of gene dilution described above, but only under certain conditions (Kondrashov, 1988). There is dispute about whether these conditions generally apply (Lynch et al., 1999; Keightley & Eyre-Walker, 2000; MacCarthy & Bergman, 2007); thus it is not known whether this theory adequately explains why sexual reproduction is so common.

Sexual Reproduction May Generate Beneficial Gene Combinations

Another hypothesis ignores the matter of harmful mutations and attributes the value of sexual reproduction to the novel combinations of genes that it produces. Having offspring with different combinations of genes might be useful because those offspring would have different ways of utilizing the resources available in the environment (eating different foods, for example). In this case, the offspring would compete less with one another for available resources, so that their parents could have more surviving offspring than otherwise possible (Ghiselin, 1974).

Alternatively, the mixing of genes might be useful in dealing with environmental changes. Evidence in support of this idea was provided by British researchers who compared the growth rates of yeast cells from two different strains—a natural strain that was capable of sexual reproduction and a genetically engineered strain that could only reproduce asexually (Goddard et al., 2005). In a normal, benign environment the cells of both strains reproduced at an equal rate. When the yeast cells were stressed by being placed in a high-temperature environment, however, the sexually reproducing cells reproduced faster than those that reproduced asexually. Presumably, new gene combinations arose in the offspring of some of the sexually reproducing yeast cells that favored growth in high-temperature conditions. Supporting the idea that sexual reproduction exists to help organisms cope with changes in the environment is the observation that, in species that can reproduce either sexually or asexually, the sexual route is often adopted when environmental conditions become stressful.

Many species engage in an endless war with parasites, in which the parasites are constantly evolving new ways to outwit the host's defenses. Gene mixing may be an effective way for the host species to rapidly deploy new defenses against these ever-changing attacks (Hamilton et al., 1981; Ridley, 1994). This idea has been called the **Red Queen hypothesis** of sex—named for the Red Queen in Lewis Carroll's *Alice Through the Looking Glass*, who had to keep running to stay in the same place. In this conception, the genetic variations (**polymorphisms**) among individuals in a sexually reproducing species are like the numbers in combination locks: When a parasite develops the ability to "pick" a common combination, many individuals die, but sexual reproduction quickly re-establishes a population with novel, "unpickable" combinations.

Future Research May Solve the Puzzle

We don't know which of these two sexual reproduction hypotheses is correct—perhaps *both* of them are. Several avenues of research may help clarify the issue. One avenue involves the observation of host-parasite interactions in natural, isolated environments such as lakes. These studies have lent some support to the Red Queen hypothesis (Lively & Dybdahl, 2000). Another avenue is "in silico" evolution, in which the evolutionary process is modeled by a computer. This approach can test whether theories—however good they may sound at first—actually have the logical structure required to cause sexual reproduction to persist. Finally, it is worth studying the few species that never engage in sexual reproduction (**Box 2.2**). By analyzing how these species survive without sexual reproduction, we may better understand why sex is so essential for the rest of us.

Why Are There Two Sexes?

The hypotheses previously discussed offer possible explanations for sexual reproduction, but they don't explain the existence of males and females. Across the biological realm, "male" is the name given to individuals with small gametes (sperm, in the case of humans), and "female" is the name given to individuals with large gametes (ova). But why should these two kinds of individuals exist? Why shouldn't a sexually reproducing species consist of individuals that are all alike, any two of which could pair off and fuse their gametes ("sex without sexes," as it were)?

Actually, sex without sexes might well be an ideal arrangement for a species. But because natural selection operates at the individual level, and not at the species level, it does not necessarily produce arrangements that are ideal for the species as a whole. Rather, it produces compromises—states in which the conflicting interests of countless individuals are in dynamic equilibrium. Sex without sexes is not generally an equilibrium state, and here's why. Reproduction requires an **investment**—a commitment of resources. For many organisms, that investment is the time and energy required to produce a gamete. That gamete must be endowed with enough nutrient material so that, once it has fused with the other parent's gamete, it can develop into a new organism. How much nutrient material is required? That depends, in part, on how much nutrient material the *other* parent contributes.

Let's consider a hypothetical sex-without-sexes species, in which the gametes of all individuals are roughly similar in size and nutrient content (**Figure 2.6**). Even so, there will be some natural variation, so that some individuals will produce slightly larger gametes and some will produce slightly smaller ones. Over time, natural selection will favor individuals that produce larger gametes (containing more nutrients) because those gametes stand a better chance of developing into offspring. But individuals that produce smaller gametes will also be favored, because such gametes require a smaller investment. And as long as there are some larger gametes available to fuse with, those smaller gametes can still develop into offspring. The only individuals that are not especially favored are those that produce middle-sized gametes, so those individuals tend to die out. Thus the population gradually diverges into two groups pursuing dif-

investment The commitment or expenditure of resources for a goal, such as reproductive success.

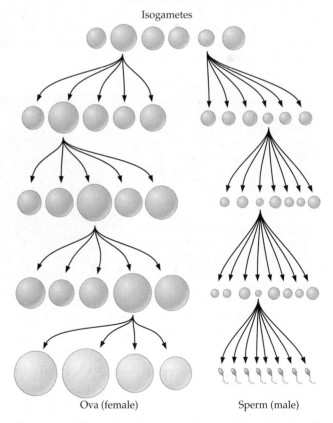

Figure 2.6 Disruptive selection splits a single population of same-sized gametes (isogametes) into large (female) and small (male) types.

Biology of Sex

BOX 2.2 The Paradox of Sexless Species

Cnemidophorus uniparens is a slender whiptail lizard that lives in arid environments in the southwestern United States. Remarkably, this species consists entirely of females, who reproduce parthenogenetically. Although they never reproduce sexually, the lizards do engage in sexual behavior (Figure A). In these encounters, one female takes the "female" role and another takes the "male" role. Any lizard may show either "female" or "male" behavior, depending on where she is in her ovarian cycle. If she is in the preovulatory phase (when eggs are maturing in her ovary), she will exhibit "female" behavior, but if she is in the postovulatory phase (when the eggs are moving down her oviduct and acquiring their shells) she will exhibit "male" behavior. Because neither animal has a testis or penis, however, there is no actual sexual penetration or transfer of sperm. The females' eggs are generated by mitosis rather than meiosis, and they do not require fertilization to develop into offspring.

According to zoologist David Crews, the *C. uniparens* species has arisen recently by hybridization between two other, sexually reproducing *Cnemidophorus* species, and it has inherited their patterns of sexual behavior. The sexual encounters between females, although not involving the transfer of sperm, do facilitate reproduction: The encounters trigger hormonal changes that promote egg development and ovulation (Crews et al., 1986).

If the ability to reproduce sexually is beneficial, how does *C. uniparens* do without it? A key factor may be the recent origin of the species. In the short term, an organism that reproduces asexually may be favored, because its offspring expand clonally and therefore can rapidly fill its ecological niche. Without sexual reproduction, however, *C. uniparens* may accumulate an increasing load of harmful mutations as the generations go by. If so, it may eventually be outcompeted and driven to extinction by sexually reproducing *Cnemidophorus* species.

An even greater puzzle is presented by a group of animals called bdel-loid rotifers (Figure B). These tiny tubelike creatures can be found in almost any freshwater environment, and they move around like leeches (bdelloid means "leechlike"). They are known to have existed for at least 40 million years, because they have been found preserved in amber of that age. And they are not just one species, but an entire class of invertebrates, with at least 352 member species. Yet no one has seen a bdelloid reproduce sexually—in fact, no one has ever come across a male bdelloid. Of course, sex can be hard to spot—an anthropologist from Mars might not discover humans having sex for quite a while. There are many species that normally reproduce parthenogenetically but occasionally engage in sex, and many scientists suspected that the bdelloid rotifers might do the same. According to this idea, even one in a thousand sexual births might be enough to reap the benefits that sexual reproduction is thought to confer.

That hypothesis was tested by Harvard molecular biologist Matthew Meselson and his postdoctoral student David Mark Welch (Mark Welch & Meselson, 2000; Mark Welch et al., 2004). Meselson and Mark Welch analyzed the DNA of several species of bdelloids. They found exactly the patterns that would be expected in organisms that stopped engaging in sexual reproduction tens of millions of years ago.

If the bdelloids have gone without sex for so long, why have they not accumulated lethal levels of harmful mutations? The answer isn't known for sure, but in 2008 Meselson and his colleagues reported a remarkable discovery: Bdelloid rotifers have the ability to take up genes from their surroundings—genes that have leaked out of dying organisms in their environment—and patch them into their own genomes (Gladyshev et al., 2008). Bdelloids are genomic pack rats, so to speak. It is possible that this process, though a random one, leads in time to the selection of organisms in which mutated genes have been replaced by "clean copies." In other words, it may produce the same end-result that is achieved, in the rest of us, by sex.

(A) Pseudocopulation between two whiptail lizards. (Drawing by Patricia J. Wynne.)

(B) A scanning electron micrograph of a bdelloid rotifer, *Rotaria tardigradia*.

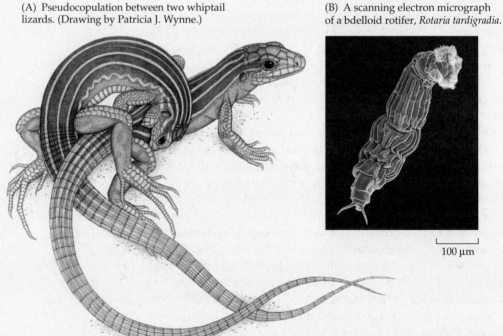

100 µm

ferent strategies. One group follows a "nurturing" strategy and produces large, nutrient-loaded gametes (**ova** or eggs); the other follows an "exploitative" strategy and produces small, nutrient-poor gametes (**sperm**) (see Figure 2.3). The two groups that result are females and males, respectively.

Several other factors come into play. For one, there is the question of mobility. To fuse, gametes need to come together, which usually means that at least one of the gametes has to be motile. It is much easier for small gametes to move than large ones, so gametes produced by males are usually the motile ones. There is also the matter of numbers. Because a small gamete requires so little investment to produce, males can produce many more gametes than females. In fact, some factors that we'll consider below often make it essential for males to produce large numbers of gametes. Thus the total investment in gamete production may end up being similar in the two sexes.

These nudibranchs (marine mollusks related to slugs and snails) are simultaneous hermaphrodites: They produce both sperm and ova at the same time. They do not fertilize themselves, however; instead, they pass sperm from one individual to another.

Hermaphrodites Combine Male and Female Reproductive Functions

Although we usually think of males and females as being two different kinds of individuals within a species, it is not uncommon for individuals to combine male and female reproductive functions within a single body. Such individuals are called **hermaphrodites**. In some species, including most flowering plants and trees as well as some invertebrate animals such as worms and snails, all the individuals are hermaphrodites; there are no pure males or females.

One might imagine that hermaphrodites would fertilize themselves. Such self-fertilization, however, would nullify much of the genetic advantage that sexual reproduction is thought to confer. Thus, in hermaphroditic species there generally exist mechanisms to prevent self-fertilization. Male and female gametes may be generated at different times, or at distant locations on the organism. In the corn plant, for example, the male flower (the *tassel*) is at the top of the plant and develops early, while the female flower (the *ear silk*) is lower on the plant and develops somewhat later. As a result, less than 3% of all corn kernels are the result of self-pollination. In other species of plants, such as the potato, self-fertilization is prevented by molecular tricks that make male and female gametes from the same plant incompatible.

In hermaphroditic animals, there are often behavioral mechanisms that prevent self-fertilization: The animals simply don't inseminate themselves, even though they are physically capable of doing so. Some hermaphroditic mollusks engage in a bizarre behavior called "penis fencing" (for a video clip, see Web Resources at the end of this chapter): Each of the two mating animals acts as if it is trying to inseminate the other while at the same time avoiding being inseminated by the other. They behave in this way because each animal is advantaged if the other takes on the task of producing their offspring.

Can There Be More Than Two Sexes?

There is no known species in which individual organisms have more than two genetic parents. In that sense, two sexes seem to be the limit—on Earth, at least. However, many simple species have multiple "mating types"; each type is defined by unique cell-surface markers, and fertilization is only possible between organisms belonging to different types (Whitfield, 2004). One species of mushroom has over 28,000 mating types. This kind of arrangement promotes the maintenance of genetic diversity.

There are also many species in which individuals of the same sex can have different reproductive roles (Roughgarden, 2004). For example, some individuals of one

ovum A mature female gamete, prior to or immediately after fertilization.

sperm A male gamete, produced in the testis.

hermaphrodite An organism that combines male and female reproductive functions.

There are two main kinds of individuals in a termite nest: fertile "reproductives" (the single queen and king), and sterile workers and soldiers, who may be of either sex. In this photo, workers attend to the queen, the large object in the center. A soldier can be seen at the bottom right.

sex may be temporarily or permanently sterile or reproductively inactive. Well-known examples are found among bees, ants, and termites, in which only a single female in a colony (the queen) is fertile; the rest are sterile workers. In the African fish *Haplochromis burtoni,* only large, brightly colored males mate with females, while small, drab males remain sexually inactive. If the reproductive male in a group dies, one of the inactive males transforms itself physically and behaviorally into a reproductive male (Burmeister et al., 2005).

Why Are There Equal Numbers of Males and Females?

At first, the answer to this question seems obvious. After all, since most humans desire to form sexual partnerships with a member of the other sex, any significant imbalance in the numbers of males and females would leave a lot of people without partners. So it seems only natural that about half of all babies born are boys and half are girls.

It's not really that simple, though. Roughly equal numbers of males and females are also seen in species in which males and females *don't* partner up, or do so in very unequal proportions. Among langur monkeys, for example, a dominant male controls a harem of 12 or so female partners. Among elks, a single bull controls up to 60 females. This leaves most males with no partners; unless they can displace the dominant male, they have little chance of reproducing. In species such as these, wouldn't it be better to have more females than males? In fact, given that males of most species can inseminate large numbers of females, wouldn't it be the best arrangement generally to have an excess of females? That way, resources would be consumed primarily by the sex that needs them to keep the species going.

Again, we have to understand that evolution doesn't necessarily lead to what we might consider the "ideal arrangement" for the species; rather it results in a compromise between the conflicting interests of individuals. Let's imagine that the "ideal arrangement" actually existed, so that among langur monkeys, for example, a female typically gave birth to ten daughters for every son born, and therefore there were ten times as many female langurs as males. For a while, things would be idyllic: Each male would have his harem, every female would have all the offspring she was capable of, and resources would be distributed efficiently.

This situation would not last, however. If a particular female underwent a genetic change such that she produced more sons than daughters, she would gain a tremendous advantage. Each of her sons would be able to mate with numerous females, so she would have far more grandchildren than if she produced mostly daughters. The genes for producing an excess of sons would therefore spread through the population, and the sex ratio would drift toward equality. Conversely, if there were a species in which females produced a dozen sons for

A single dominant bull elk controls a harem of many females, so many subordinate males are left without sex partners.

every daughter born, so that there was a vast excess of males in the population, genes for producing *females* would be advantageous and would spread, and again the sex ratio would drift toward equality. So, in practice, the sex ratio usually remains near equality.

This general principle is liable to be modified by a variety of factors, however, so one doesn't always get a sex ratio of exactly 1:1 (Godfray & Werren, 1996). Among humans, for example, males are more vulnerable than females: At every phase of life, starting with conception, males are more likely to die. This higher death rate among males results both from greater disease susceptibility and from behavioral factors such as greater risk-taking. Thus, if equal numbers of males and females were conceived, there would be an excess of females during the reproductive years. This in turn would increase the value of bearing sons. In reality, the sex ratio at birth does slightly favor males: About 104 to 107 boys are born for every 100 girls (Chahnazarian, 1991).

Evolution Has Led to Diverse Methods of Sex Determination

Seeing that so many species throughout the animal kingdom have settled on the two-sex system, one might expect that the mechanisms of **sex determination**—controlling whether an embryo becomes male or female—would also have become fixed early in evolution, and would now be universal. In fact, however, a variety of sex-determining mechanisms have evolved (Mittwoch, 1996).

Sex May Be Determined by Chromosomes

In humans—and in most mammals—an embryo's sex is determined by the chromosomes it possesses (**Figure 2.7**). Forty-four of our 46 chromosomes are known as **autosomes**; they come in 22 homologous (corresponding) pairs, regardless of a person's sex. With the remaining two chromosomes, the **sex chromosomes**, the situation is more complicated. Females possess a homologous pair of sex chromosomes, termed **X chromosomes**, but males possess one X chromosome and one much smaller chromosome, called a **Y chromosome**.

Now recall that gametes are produced by meiosis, a process of cell division in which the number of chromosomes is halved. Thus ova receive 22 autosomes and one X chromosome. Sperm, however, receive 22 autosomes and either one X or one Y. Thus, when the ovum and sperm fuse at fertilization, the resulting **zygote** receives an X from the ovum and either an X or a Y from the sperm. If an X chromosome is received, the zygote will develop as a female (XX); conversely, if a Y chromosome is received, the zygote will develop as a male (XY). Since there are roughly equal numbers of X-bearing and Y-bearing sperm, the chances of an offspring being female or male are approximately equal.

In humans and nearly all mammals, it is the tiny Y chromosome that determines sex. If one studies humans who possess unusual combinations of sex chromosomes, such as X, XXX, XXY, or XYY, one finds that any individual possessing at least one Y chromosome will be male; all others will be female. This finding indicates that there is a sex-determining gene on the Y chromosome and that the effect of this gene is to confer maleness; in its absence, zygotes develop as females. The sex-deter-

sex determination The biological mechanism that determines whether an organism will develop as a male or a female.

autosome Any chromosome other than a sex chromosome.

sex chromosome Either of a pair of chromosomes (X or Y in mammals) that differ between the sexes.

X chromosome A sex chromosome that is present as two copies in females and one copy in males.

Y chromosomes A sex chromosome that is present only in males.

zygote A cell formed by the fusion of gametes: a fertilized ovum.

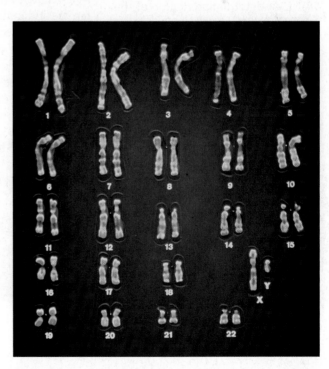

Figure 2.7 Human chromosomes Men and women have the same autosomes (chromosome pairs 1–22), but different sex chromosomes: Women have two X's, men have one X and one Y (as shown here at lower right).

The sex of this crocodile hatchling was determined by its temperature during incubation.

mining gene has been identified: It is named *SRY*. The role of *SRY* in sex development is described in Chapter 6.

Sex May Be Determined by Temperature

Many species of reptiles lack sex chromosomes. In these species, the sex of the offspring is determined by the temperature at which the eggs are incubated. Thus, in a turtle known as the red-eared slider (*Trachemys scripta*), clutches of eggs incubated at 26°C (79°F) develop as all males, clutches incubated at 31°C (88°F) develop as all females, and clutches incubated at intermediate temperatures develop as a mixture of males and females. Among lizards and alligators it's the other way around: Low temperatures produce females, and high temperatures produce males. And in the snapping turtle (*Chelydra serpentina*), both low and high temperatures produce females, whereas intermediate temperatures produce males.

This mechanism of sex determination, though seemingly strange to us, must have some value to the species that employ it. The mechanism does allow the animals to determine the sex of their offspring—by laying eggs under a shady tree or on a sunlit bank, for example, or earlier or later in the season. Whether they make this choice in some advantageous way isn't known. Just the fact of having offspring all of one sex could be beneficial—by eliminating inbreeding among the offspring, for example.

Sexual Selection Produces Anatomical and Behavioral Differences between Males and Females

In many respects, natural selection acts similarly on females and males. It ensures that women and men are both adapted to life on land, for example, and that female and male fish are both adapted to life in water. Yet marked differences can develop between males and females of a single species. Think of peacocks and peahens, for example: The males strut to and fro and shake their gorgeous tail feathers, while the plainer females watch silently, evaluate their prospective mates, and decide which male to mate with. Such differences in the appearance and behavior of males and females result from competition for mates. Charles Darwin called this process **sexual selection**.

Males and Females Follow Different Reproductive Strategies

SRY (*S*ex-determining *R*egion of the *Y* chromosome) A gene located on the Y chromosome that causes the embryo to develop as a male.

sexual selection The evolution of traits under the pressure of competition for mates or of choice by mates.

internal fertilization Fertilization within the body.

gestation Bearing young in the uterus; pregnancy.

lactation The production of milk in the mammary glands.

Two common, though not universal, features of sexual selection among nonhuman animals are competition among males and choice by females. These features

A boar contributed only a single ejaculation to the production of this litter of piglets; the sow must fully provide for them from conception through weaning.

result from the differing strategies adopted by males and females at the origin of the two sexes. Females, as described above, commit themselves to a "nurturing" strategy by virtue of their investment in large, nutrient-rich ova, while males commit themselves to an "exploitative" strategy by virtue of their production of small, nutrient-poor sperm. In some animals, the evolution of these strategies has led to very marked differences in the roles played by the two sexes in reproduction.

Female mammals, for example, carry the burden of **internal fertilization** followed by a prolonged period of **gestation** (pregnancy), which may last from 2 or 3 weeks (in rodents) to 22 months (in elephants). Following delivery of their young, female mammals continue to nourish them through **lactation** (milk production), and usually provide most or all of the care and protection that mammalian infants require. This prolonged investment results in offspring that have a far greater chance of surviving to adulthood than the young of other vertebrates, but it also greatly limits the total number of offspring that female mammals can produce in a lifetime. A female frog can produce hundreds or thousands of tadpoles; a woman can only produce about a dozen children.

Males, however, can often get away with a very small investment in reproduction—a few drops of **semen** containing sperm. In theory, a male mammal could father as many offspring as a female frog produces tadpoles, simply by inseminating female after female and walking away from each. But that is reckoning without two practical constraints: competition from other males, and the ability of females to choose whom they mate with, as we'll see below.

semen The fluid, containing sperm and a variety of chemical compounds, that is discharged from the penis (ejaculated) at the male sexual climax.

Females and Males Are Exposed to Different Reproductive Risks

Females and males typically experience different kinds of risks in their reproductive lives. For a female, the maximum number of potential offspring is rather low, but her chances of having close to this number are quite good, since there will usually be plenty of males willing to mate with her. The variation in the number of offspring that females produce is therefore quite limited. The risk for a female is not so much that she will produce few offspring, but that her offspring will fail to survive and reproduce in their turn. To maximize the likelihood that her offspring will survive, she needs not only to invest her own resources in them, but also to ensure that they are fathered by the best available male. (What "best" means, we'll discuss in a moment.)

Males, as just mentioned, can father numerous offspring, but they can easily end up having none. Earlier, we discussed langur monkeys and elks, species in which dominant males control large harems of females, leaving subordinate males without mates. A dominant male fathers many offspring every year, at least as long as he can maintain his dominant position. Subordinate males will have no offspring unless they can displace a dominant male or evade his surveillance. Although there are wide differences among species, males typically face the real possibility of having few or no offspring. In other words, the variance in reproductive success is usually greater for males than for females, and this encourages the adoption of "risky" sexual strategies by males.

Males Often Compete for Access to Females

Because of this difference in reproductive risks experience by males and females, males often compete with one another for access to females, while females often choose among males. We should emphasize, though, that words such as "compete" and "choose" are really figures of speech. We don't mean to imply that animals consciously try to achieve certain goals—we don't know enough about animals' minds to make such assertions. All we are saying is that animals behave *as if* they have certain goals in mind.

What traits are influenced by sexual selection? Competition among males naturally leads to selection for traits that confer success in that competition. The most obvious traits are large size and physical strength; males are commonly larger and stronger than females, sometimes markedly so, especially among mammals (**Figure 2.8**).

Figure 2.8 Inter-male aggression Male elephant seals compete for access to females, so aggressiveness and large size are assets.

A close-up of a male cecropia moth, showing the feathery antennae that can detect the female moth's sex pheromone at extremely low concentrations.

Along with these physical traits goes the behavioral trait of aggressiveness—the willingness to engage in the interminable bouts of roaring, barking, head-butting, biting, kicking, clawing, and general mayhem that establish a male animal's position in the dominance hierarchy and thus influence his ability to mate with females.

Competition among males also favors traits that assist males in locating receptive females before other males do. Such traits may include well-developed sensory skills that aid them in finding females, such as the ability to detect sexually attractive odors (**pheromones**) and to home in on their source. Another trait that helps males get to females quickly is early sexual maturation—early in life or early in the breeding season.

Yet another trait favored by male–male competition is sexual endurance—the ability to remain reproductively active for a long time. In some species of birds, for example, large numbers of males and females gather at a common mating site. A male bird that can remain sexually active longer than his competitors will have greater mating success, so males are selected for their ability to mate repeatedly over a long period of time. For females, however, the ability to mate repeatedly is less important.

Females Often Choose among Males

What about female choice? One advantageous choice females can make is to mate with healthy, genetically favored males. How can they identify such males? Just the fact that a male has battered other males into submission speaks volumes about his health and fitness, of course. Not all species engage in such male–male contests, however. In these cases, females may choose among males on the basis of their physical appearance or behavior.

CHOICE BASED ON APPEARANCE   One aspect of males' appearance to which females often pay attention is their bodily symmetry. Vertebrates are roughly bilaterally symmetrical, at least in outward appearance. The developmental reason for this symmetry is that, aside from obviously asymmetrical structures such as the heart, a single set of genetic instructions directs the development of both sides of the body. Good genes operating in a good environment will therefore produce a highly symmetrical organism. Poor genes, or a poor environment, will disturb this process, leading to asymmetries. This kind of perturbation, in which the direction of asymmetry is random, is called **fluctuating asymmetry**. A high degree of fluctuating asymmetry has been correlated with a number of disadvantageous characteristics, such as chromosomal defects, infections, exposure to toxins, and environmental stress (Manning & Chamberlain, 1994; Polak & Trivers, 1994). Low fluctuating asymmetry, however, has been correlated with a number of advantageous characteristics, such as high sperm quality in males (Firman et al., 2003).

It turns out that animals are very good at assessing the symmetry of other individuals of the same species, and they prefer to mate with highly symmetrical individuals. For example, manipulating the tail feathers of male barn swallows to make them less symmetrical renders those males less attractive to females (Møller, 1992). Thus there is sexual selection for symmetry, especially in males. In addition, females are selected for the cognitive skills that are required to evaluate symmetry.

Besides symmetry, females often look for other anatomical characteristics in males. Female barn swallows, for example, prefer those males whose outermost tail feathers are not only symmetrical, but are also longer than those of other males. Female deer prefer the males with the largest antlers, female fish often prefer the most brightly colored males, and so on. Generally, the rule is: The bigger and brighter, the better—especially with regard to features that are obviously related to sexual displays.

pheromone A volatile compound that is released by one organism and that triggers a specific behavior in another member of the same species.

fluctuating asymmetry A difference between the left and right sides of the body that results from random perturbations of development.

This preference for "bigger and brighter" seems to be open-ended. If one exaggerates the features that females pay attention to—giving a male barn swallow an artificial tail longer than *any* male normally possesses, for example—such males will be preferred over any "natural" males. Because of this open-ended quality, sexual selection can lead to a runaway process in which the display characteristics of males become highly exaggerated, as has happened with the peacock. Nevertheless, something holds this process in check. The tails of male barn swallows are not getting longer, for example, even though a male with a super-long tail would attract a lot of females. The most plausible reason why the runaway process comes to a halt is that these displays have a *cost* for males. It takes an investment of food to grow long tail feathers. Large antlers hamper a stag's ability to move through the forest. Bright coloration attracts predators. At some point, the cost of these displays balances their reproductive advantage, and an equilibrium situation is reached.

The peacock's ornate tail feather display is used by females to judge his general health and the quality of his genes.

It is precisely the fact that these attractive features have a cost that makes them attractive (Zahavi & Zahavi, 1997). Only a peacock that is genetically well endowed, healthy, and has had ample access to food can sustain the cost of a tail ornate enough to attract peahens. What these displays say is, "I have been able to take on the incredible burden of this tail (or antlers or coloration) and still survive—so I must be a superior animal." And indeed, there is some evidence that these displays are honest advertisements of reproductive superiority. One study, for example, found that male deer with large, complex antlers also had higher-quality sperm than other males (Malo et al., 2005).

CHOICE BASED ON BEHAVIOR   Besides choosing males on the basis of anatomical features, females also choose on the basis of **courtship behavior**. Sometimes this behavior is of practical use to the female in producing young. Female spiders, for example, often demand that their suitors provide some food prior to mating, such as a dead insect (failing which, the female may snack on the male himself). Some female birds demand that the male provide a nesting site or actually construct a nest.

Besides the direct value of such gifts to the female, there's another, more subtle benefit. Demanding that a male provide resources tests his genetic fitness in the same way that demanding anatomical features such as ornate tail feathers does. Thus it may be beneficial to the female to make the male expend resources, even if that expenditure does not benefit her in any direct way.

In fact, there are numerous instances in which courtship by males seems to involve useless make-work. Male bowerbirds, for example, must construct elaborate thatched structures—bowers—and decorate them with hard-to-find items, such as colored shells, berries, and bottle tops, before females will pay attention to their advances. The bowers have no direct value to the females—they are not nests—but they do have the indirect value of testing the male's fitness. Courtship song is another example: Singing for hours at a time offers no direct reproductive benefit, but by doing so, a male bird advertises the fact that he is not foraging—and if he can survive so long without foraging, he must be a well-favored animal. Much courtship behavior has this flavor: Males inflict handicaps on themselves—

courtship behavior Behavior that attracts a mate.

The male satin bowerbird (at right) is not as eye-catching as a peacock, but he makes up for it by building an elaborate bower and decorating its entrances with blue-colored objects, such as shells, berries, or bottle tops. If a female approves of his work, sex will take place within the avenue of the bower.

the behavioral equivalent of peacock's tails—to prove that they are fit enough to withstand them.

So far, we've given the impression that females choose among males simply by assessing their courtship behavior. In fact, however, females often initiate courtship. If you have ever been awakened by the caterwauling from your neighbor's cat, for example, you know that female mammals advertise when they are sexually receptive. At around the time when they ovulate (see Chapter 5), when **copulation** (penile–vaginal sex) can result in fertilization, hormonal changes cause females to undergo **estrus**, or "heat." Besides complex internal processes connected with ovulation, estrus involves the production of auditory, olfactory, or visual signals intended to alert males to the female's receptive state.

Females also may approach individual males and show **proceptive behavior**—behavior designed to elicit reciprocal courtship. Estrous female mice and rats, for example, perform a hopping, darting, and ear-wiggling routine that may induce the male to attempt a mount. During the remainder of their ovarian cycle (when fertilization is not possible), females do not make these displays or approach males, and they forcefully reject male courtship.

Sometimes Males Make Significant Investments in Reproduction

Insofar as females induce males to make an investment in reproduction, they may restore some balance between female and male reproductive strategies. The more resources males invest, the more interest they will have in ensuring their investment is not wasted. If a male has to spend days or weeks wooing a female, or if he has to provide "expensive" nuptial gifts or accomplish burdensome tasks, he may become as committed as the female to seeing that the offspring of their union survive. Otherwise, he will have to start all over again with another female. His life, or the mating season, may simply not be long enough to allow that.

Thus, while there are many species in which males make little or no contribution to the care of their offspring, there are other species in which males make contributions as great as those made by females. This kind of cooperative investment can allow for the evolution of lifestyles that would otherwise be impossible. Pairs of seagulls, for example, take alternating shifts at the nest (incubating eggs or protecting hatchlings) and away from the nest (foraging). A single bird cannot accomplish both tasks, so male investment has been essential to the evolution of seagulls, as well as many other species of birds.

In a few species, males take on the entire responsibility of caring for eggs or young. A male stickleback fish, for example, constructs an underwater nest in which females lay eggs; after fertilizing them, the male spends about 2 weeks guarding the eggs and the newly hatched fry (Kynard, 1978). Some male water birds, such as phalaropes and jacanas, also take on the entire responsibility for incubating eggs and feeding the hatchlings. And in a few species, males take over tasks that seem biologically fated to be handled by females only, such as pregnancy itself. This happens in the curious group of fishes known as sea horses and pipefishes (**Box 2.3**).

copulation Sexual intercourse or coitus.

estrus The restricted period within the ovarian cycle when females of some species are sexually receptive; "heat."

proceptive behavior Behavior by females that may elicit sexual advances by males.

Biology of Sex

BOX 2.3 When Males Get Pregnant

Sea horses comprise about 35 species of fish belonging to the genus *Hippocampus*. (The hippocampus was a horse-headed sea monster in Greek mythology.) Sea horses break all the rules. Their anatomy is peculiar: A horselike head sits atop a strangely ribbed body and a reptilian tail. Their posture is bizarre: They hold themselves vertically in the water, rather than horizontally like most fishes. But oddest of all is their sex life: Like Arnold Schwarzenegger in the movie *Junior*, the *males* get pregnant and give birth to young.

Female and male sea horses form closely bonded, monogamous pairs. The female produces ova in the normal way—that is what defines her as female. But she then deposits the ova in a deep pouchlike cavity in the body of the male, where they are fertilized by the male's sperm. This is the only known example in nature in which fertilization occurs within a male animal's body. After fertilization, the opening of the pouch closes, and the eggs remain sealed off for about 10 days. At the end of that period the pouch reopens, and the young—now tiny sea horses—emerge to face the world (see figure). The female, meanwhile, has prepared another load of ova to deposit in the male's pouch. In the course of a single season, a male may go through a dozen cycles of fertilization,

pregnancy, and parturition, giving birth to a total of several hundred fry.

Because males make the investment of pregnancy, you might think that sexual selection would have effects on sea horses opposite to those it has in most species. That is, one might expect female sea horses to compete for males, and for males to choose among females. But that's not the case, according to Heather Masonjones of Amherst College. Masonjones found that male sea horses fight one another for access to female sea horses, just as happens in so many other species. To understand the reason for this, Masonjones undertook a detailed study of how much energy female and male sea horses expend on reproduction (Masonjones, 2001). Surprisingly, she found that females expend more energy than males. It appears that, even though sea horse embryos develop inside their father, most or all of the nutrients they consume come from the yolk their mother packs into the eggs. In terms of investment, their father does little more than provide a safe haven. And because the females do most of the investing, sexual selection acts primarily on males to make them compete for mates, just as it does in the majority of species.

If Males Invest, Sexual Selection May Work Differently

If males and females invest about equally in reproduction, sexual selection may not lead to any marked anatomical or behavioral differences between the sexes. Male and female seagulls, for example, are nearly the same size, and neither one has any special display feathers or other sexually distinct characteristics. In fact, the only reliable way to tell the sex of a seagull is to examine its internal anatomy.

Among birds, the sex that invests less in parenting tends to be larger and more brightly colored. Usually that sex is the male. Occasionally, however, that sex is the female, as in the red phalarope. Naturalist John James Audubon (1785–1851), who painted these phalaropes, assumed wrongly that the brightly colored bird (right) was the male.

Figure 2.9 Sexual swellings of female baboons appear at the time of ovulation, and thus inform males that they are ready to mate. In addition, the size of each female's swelling is an indicator of her reproductive fitness, so males try to mate with females who have the largest swellings.

If males invest *more* than females in reproduction, and thus are limited in how many offspring they can produce, the effects of sexual selection on the two sexes can actually be reversed. Among phalaropes and jacanas, for example, females compete for the sexual favors of males, and males choose among females. Consistent with this pattern, female phalaropes and jacanas are larger, more brightly colored, and more aggressive than males.

Sometimes, males choose among females because individual females vary in how much they can invest in reproduction. This variation is most obvious in species in which individuals continue to grow after reaching reproductive maturity. Whereas humans stop growing soon after the end of puberty, some animals, such as tortoises, grow throughout their lives. In such species, the oldest and largest females are capable of laying the largest clutches of eggs, so males mate preferentially with the oldest females.

Among some primate species, males invest considerably in reproduction, even if not to the same degree as females. For that reason, there may be competition in and choosing by both sexes. Take baboons, for example. Male baboons are larger than females and compete intensely for mates, as is true in so many other species. In addition, however, female baboons compete for the sexual attention of dominant males. They do this by means of "sexual swellings"—patches of pigmented genital and perianal skin that swell around the time of ovulation (**Figure 2.9**). The females with the largest swellings seem to be genetically favored: They have more offspring than other females, and their offspring are more likely to survive. Thus males try to copulate with the females with the largest swellings (Domb & Pagel, 2001).

It turns out, in fact, that competition among females is much more common than might be imagined on the basis of the traditional "males compete, females choose" concept of sexual selection. Whereas males may compete simply for access to females, females more commonly compete for resources, such as social rank, that enhance their offspring's prospects for survival (Clutton-Brock, 2007).

Diverse Relationship Styles Have Evolved

Evolution has led to a bewildering variety of sexual relationships, from sexual free-for-alls to lifelong, sexually exclusive pairings. Understanding the basis for this diversity can be quite a challenge. Still, we can start with the basic assumption that evolution is always at work. In other words, animals' genes are likely to promote sexual behavior and relationships that offer them the best prospects for leaving copies of those genes in future generations.

Social and Sexual Arrangements Are Not Necessarily the Same

In looking at animal liaisons, we need to distinguish carefully between two phenomena: *social arrangements* and *sexual reality.* In the past, people (including biologists) have tended to take animals' social arrangements at face value—as if these arrangements tell us unambiguously who is having sex with whom. Sometimes they do. It turns out, however, that humans are not the only species in which social and sexual arrangements are imperfectly aligned.

In many species, individuals are essentially solitary or belong to same-sex groups, and they reproduce by mating with strangers (either one or many) whom they never see again. This is the pattern seen in the majority of invertebrates, fishes, amphibians, and reptiles. Among mammals, there is considerable diversity in relationship styles, even between related species. For example, mountain voles (*Microtus montanus*) mate with strangers and immediately go their separate ways, whereas their prairie cousins (*Microtus ochrogaster*) form stable pair bonds (Carter & Getz, 1993).

When reproduction does involve lasting relationships, we see two basic patterns: monogamy and polygamy. In **monogamous** relationships, two animals (usually of the opposite sex) form a **pair bond** for the duration of the breeding season or even for their entire lifetimes. Many birds, such as the seagulls described earlier, pair up for a season. Swans are famous for forming lifelong pair bonds. The belief that bereaved swans die of grief is a myth, however; they actually go searching for a new mate.

In **polygamous** relationships, one animal forms stable bonds with several individuals of the other sex. In most polygamous species, single males form relationships with multiple females. This is the "harem" arrangement described earlier for langur monkeys, and it is technically called **polygyny** ("many females"). The opposite arrangement—a single female with a harem of males—is called **polyandry** ("many males"). It is a rare arrangement, but one animal that does adopt it is the jacana, the water bird we have already described on account of its unusual "females compete, males choose" behavior. In southern Texas one may come across a pond occupied by a single female jacana and several males in a loose social group.

That polygyny is more common than polyandry is consistent with the greater investment in reproduction by females. It simply would not be possible for females of most species to mate with multiple males and have offspring with all of them. Only when the balance of reproduction investment is reversed, as with jacanas, does polyandry crop up.

Some animals, such as lions and chimpanzees, practice a more balanced polygamy in which social groups contain more than one sexually mature adult of each sex, and both males and females mate with multiple partners of the other sex. In such groups, a male's ability to mate is still influenced by his dominance rank. For example, lower-ranking males may have the opportunity to mate with females only at times when the females are unlikely to conceive.

The terms monogamy and polygamy, as just described, refer to bonding relationships, not to sexual behavior as such. Some pair-bonding species mate only within the pair bond, and are therefore called **sexually monogamous**. More commonly, pair-bonded individuals will mate not only with their partners but also, on some occasions, with strangers. Species in which this occurs are called **socially monogamous**. Individuals of polygamous species may also mate with strangers. A male lion will readily mate with a female from outside his pride, for example, if he can get to her before the female members of his pride drive her off. We'll call the willingness to engage in sex outside of an animal's established relationship or relationships **promiscuity**—without, of course, the negative connotation this word sometimes carries when applied to humans.

Male Promiscuity Offers Obvious Evolutionary Benefits

From an evolutionary standpoint, male promiscuity is more or less to be expected: The investment in mating outside the pair bond ("extra-pair sex") is usually so slight that it is "worth it" for the male, even if the chances that the mating will lead to viable offspring are not very great. Thus one has to wonder, not why males of many species are disposed to promiscuity, but why some are not. In some species, sexual monogamy may be imposed on males by females: Females may simply refuse to engage in extra-pair sex. This is true for some species of birds.

monogamy 1. Marriage limited to two persons. 2. A sexual relationship in which neither partner has sexual contact with third parties.

pair bond A durable sexual relationship between two individuals.

polygamy Marriage to or (mostly in animals) mating with more than one partner.

polygyny The marriage or mating of one male with more than one female.

polyandry The marriage or mating of one female with more than one male.

sexual monogamy A sexually exclusive pair bond.

social monogamy A pair bond that is not sexually exclusive.

promiscuity Engaging in numerous casual or short-lived sexual relationships.

Figure 2.10 Deep-sea threesome Two small males have attached themselves permanently to the upper surface of this female anglerfish.

paternity test A test to identify an individual's father by DNA analysis.

Sometimes males mate with only one female simply because they only mate once—period. An extreme example is offered by deep-sea anglerfishes (**Figure 2.10**). In these species, a male homes in on a female and partially fuses with her. His eyes degenerate, and he remains permanently attached to the female, providing her with sperm whenever required. Once attached to his mate in this manner, he is ill-equipped to embark on extramarital affairs!

Why Are Females Promiscuous?

Male promiscuity makes evolutionary sense, but what about female promiscuity? At first glance, it seems there is no reason for it, since females can usually produce all the offspring they are capable of producing with the aid of a single male. But in fact, female promiscuity is fairly common, even in species that have long been considered sexually monogamous.

The best evidence for female promiscuity comes from DNA analysis. Individuals of the same species have numerous differences in their DNA; these differences can be detected with simple enzymatic tests. Offspring inherit their particular DNA sequences from their parents, so by comparing the sequences from the offspring and the individuals who are candidates to be its parents, the true parents can be identified. Since it is usually the identity of the father that is in doubt, the procedure is generally called **paternity testing** (**Figure 2.11**).

Paternity testing has now been done on a wide variety of species, with a wide variety of results. In some socially monogamous birds, up to three-fourths of a female's offspring are fathered by males other than her social mate (Birkhead, 1998). Among chimpanzees, as many as half of all offspring are fathered by males from outside the group to which the mother belongs (Gagneux et al., 1997). In the hamadryas baboon, on the other hand, females seem never to cheat on their male partners, even if their partners are sterile, in which case there would be no offspring (Birkhead, 2000).

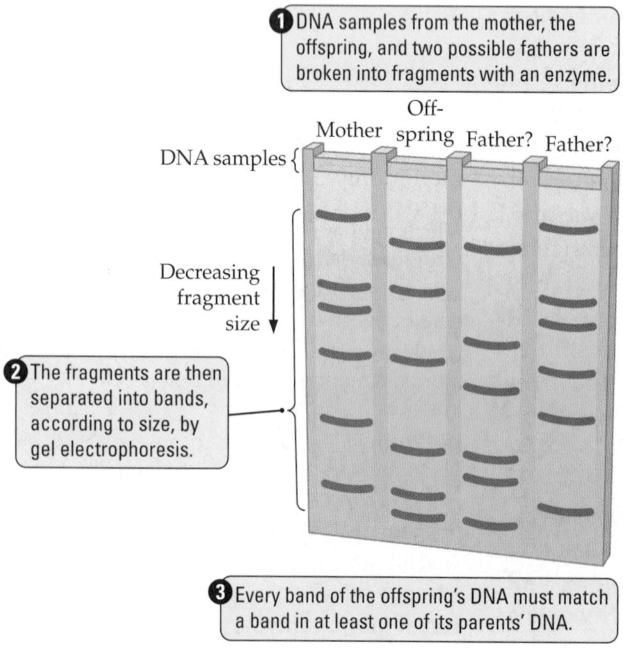

There are a number of possible reasons for female promiscuity, which may differ among species. In species in which males provide resources such as food or protection, obtaining these resources from multiple mates may make promiscuity worthwhile. Another possibility is that socially monogamous females are promiscuous in order to obtain sperm from higher-quality males than their social partners. After all, if males vary in quality, most females will not be partnered with the very best males, so they may seek a higher-quality male. To test this idea, Susan Smith observed the mating behavior of black-capped chickadees (Smith, 1988). She found that when a female chickadee engages in extra-pair sex, she usually does so with a male who was dominant over her social mate during the previous winter. This finding suggests that promiscuous females are indeed shopping for better genes than their regular mates can provide.

Finally, a truly devious reason for female promiscuity may come into play. When the dominant male in a polygynous species is displaced by a new male, the new male may kill the young born to harem females over the following few months. This infanticidal behavior benefits him because the young he eliminates most likely were fathered by the previous dominant male; once the young are removed, the females will quickly become pregnant by the new male. Among langurs (Hrdy, 1977), and probably among other polygynous species, pregnant females will solicit sex with the new dominant male even though, being pregnant already, they cannot conceive young with him. The benefit of doing so is that the new

❶ DNA samples from the mother, the offspring, and two possible fathers are broken into fragments with an enzyme.

DNA samples {

Mother | Off-spring | Father? | Father?

Decreasing fragment size ↓

❷ The fragments are then separated into bands, according to size, by gel electrophoresis.

❸ Every band of the offspring's DNA must match a band in at least one of its parents' DNA.

Figure 2.11 Paternity testing Which male fathered this offspring? (See Web Activity 2.5.)

male protects the offspring of those females that mate with him, rather than killing them. In essence, the females have fooled the male into thinking that the offspring are his. (Again, "fooled" and "thinking" are figures of speech; conscious mental process may or may not be involved.)

Female Promiscuity Leads to Adaptive Responses by Males

While female promiscuity benefits females, it harms the reproductive success of the males who are their social mates. As a result, males of many species have developed behavioral strategies to prevent their mates from engaging in sex with other males. A common behavior of this type is **mate guarding**: A male remains close to a female throughout the period when she is fertile and attempts to keep other males away from her. The importance of this behavior was illustrated in an experiment conducted on red-winged blackbirds. David Westneat prevented male blackbirds from guarding their mates for just one hour, and later used DNA testing to determine who had fathered the females' offspring. That one hour's absence caused the number of offspring fathered by outsiders to skyrocket (Westneat, 1994). Thus, mate-guarding behavior really does limit a female's ability to engage in extra-pair sex. Do you think that human males ever engage in such behavior?

Another way that males may respond to female promiscuity is by producing large numbers of sperm. By sheer force of numbers these sperm compete with the sperm of other males within the females' reproductive tracts. If we compare our close relatives, the chimpanzee and the gorilla, for example, we find that female chimpanzees mate many times with many different males for every time that she becomes pregnant, whereas female gorillas mate with only one or two males per pregnancy. Correspondingly, the testes of chimpanzees are far larger (in relation to overall body size) than those of gorillas, and this allows chimpanzee males to produce ejaculates that contain far more sperm and to ejaculate more frequently. In humans, testis size is intermediate between that of chimpanzees and gorillas, suggesting that female promiscuity and sperm competition have played a role in human evolution, but not an unusually large one.

No primate can compare with the pig, however, in terms of sperm statistics. Pigs mate promiscuously, so sperm competition is probably very strong. Correspondingly, each ejaculate of a male pig (boar) measures a pint or more in volume and contains an average of 750 billion sperm (compared with a mere 350 *million* in men). Furthermore, the boar's penis is long enough to deposit the ejaculate directly into the sow's uterus, rather than into the vagina as in humans—another trait that has been driven by sperm competition.

Males May Copulate with Females by Force

We have seen that the reproductive interests of males and females can be in conflict, and we've already described one grisly consequence of such conflict in primates: infanticide by males who take over harems. Another consequence of conflict is forced copulation. Forced copulation is seen in a wide variety of animals, from insects to primates, and in some of these animals it is clearly an adaptive behavior; that is, it persists because those animals who engage in it have more offspring than they would have otherwise.

Perhaps the most detailed study of forced copulation has been done on scorpionflies by evolutionary psychologist Randy Thornhill of the University of New Mexico (Thornhill, 1980). In these insects, a male is able to mate with a female by one of two strategies. In one strategy, he offers the female a nuptial gift, such as a dead insect; the female approaches the gift-bearing male, and they mate. If a male approaches a female without a gift, the female will attempt to flee. In this case, however, the male may grasp the female and hold her immobile with a spe-

mate guarding A behavior in which a male animal prevents sexual contact between his mate and other males.

(A)

(B)

Figure 2.12 Unforced and coercive sex in the beetle *Tegrodera aloga*. (A) The male (right) courts the female by drawing her antennae into grooves on his head. The female may or may not respond by copulating with him. (B) In an alternative strategy, the male (below) runs up to the female, throws her on her side, and inserts his genitalia as she struggles to free herself from his grasp. (Photographs courtesy of John Alcock.)

cial appendage called a notal organ, which enables him to obtain a forced mating. Because the notal organ has no use other than for forced copulation (it is not required for unforced sex), Thornhill concluded that forced copulation is not a random by-product of scorpionfly evolution, but an adaptive behavior resulting from countless generations of sexual selection.

Only a couple of other species (also insects) have anatomical adaptations that facilitate forced copulation. In fact, quite a few species have the opposite—arrangements of the female anatomy that make copulation impossible without her active collaboration. For example, a female rat's vulva is situated on the underside of her rump and is inaccessible to males unless she exposes it by arching her rump upwards—a behavior called lordosis. It is likely that arrangements of this kind are adaptations to prevent forced copulation.

Most animals do not have anatomical specializations that either facilitate or prevent this behavior, but attempts at forced copulation by males, and resistance by females, have been observed in numerous species (**Figure 2.12**), including species closely related to humans such as chimpanzees (Wrangham & Peterson, 1996). Whether the behavioral proclivity to forced copulation is an adaptation, or merely the by-product of selection for other traits, such as aggressiveness, is not always clear. We revisit this issue in Chapter 18, in which we discuss a controversy about the nature of forced copulation in humans—where it is called rape.

Sometimes, Helping Relatives Reproduce Is a Good Strategy

Genes act within the individual who possesses them. At first thought, therefore, it would seem that a genome should make its owner focus 100% of its efforts on reproducing itself. And there is indeed a lot of selfish sexual behavior in this world: The topic we have just discussed—forced copulation—is an extreme example. But selfless, altruistic behavior is also quite common. In some circumstances altruistic behavior can be adaptive, so that genes promoting it are favored by natural selection. Alternatively, it may be an evolutionary by-product, or—in the case of humans, especially—it may result from cultural processes that have little direct connection with evolution.

One kind of altruistic behavior with an obvious adaptive value is parental care. In evolutionary terms, it's no good having offspring if those offspring don't have offspring in their turn, so it may pay to help one's offspring survive and become sexually mature, even if that limits the number of offspring one can produce. Mammals and birds, in particular, have followed that strategy, but some insects also devote considerable resources to protecting their young. Genes promoting parental care (or at least maternal care) are evidently widespread.

Genes promoting altruistic behavior toward one's offspring survive because the offspring have a good chance of possessing those same genes. (Specifically, any gene in a parent has a 50% chance of being handed down to each offspring.) Therefore, genes for altruism toward one's offspring are helping *themselves* get handed on to the third and future generations. Obviously, genes for *harmfulness* toward one's offspring would not be perpetuated in the same way, nor would genes for altruism toward *strangers*, because those strangers, being unrelated, would have no special likelihood of having inherited the same genes.

Tortoise beetle (*Acromis sparsa*) mother using her body as a shield to guard her young (pupae), Panama.

Parents and offspring are not the only kinds of relatives who inherit the same genes, however. Siblings also co-inherit one half of their genes, on average. First cousins co-inherit about one-eighth of their genes, and so on. Thus, if you happen to possess genes that cause you to help a relative reproduce, those same genes may exist in that relative too. If so, your "altruism" helps propagate those genes into the next generation.

The logic behind this theory was laid out by the British evolutionary theorist W. D. Hamilton in the 1960s (Hamilton, 1964). Hamilton proposed that natural selection causes individuals to devote resources to helping their relatives reproduce, to an extent determined by the degree of relatedness. For example, an individual might be willing to give up having one offspring herself if by doing so she enables her sister to have *two* offspring beyond what she would otherwise produce. In terms of genes, it's a toss-up: either a single 50% copy (a child) or two 25% copies (nephews or nieces). To help a cousin reproduce, however, an individual should sacrifice one offspring's worth of resources only if that sacrifice helps that cousin have *eight* extra offspring—not a likely situation.

Hamilton's theory is known as **kin selection**, and the central concept of kin selection is **inclusive fitness**. You're probably familiar with the use of the phrase "survival (and reproduction) of the fittest" to describe the evolutionary process. What kin selection theory says is that, in considering an individual's "fitness," one has to consider not only how many offspring that individual produces, but all the copies of that individual's genes that persist into future generations, whether in direct descendants or in the descendants of siblings or other relatives.

Kin Selection Explains Some Altruistic Animal Behavior

Kin selection theory does seem to explain quite a lot of social and sexual behavior in the animal kingdom. For example, subordinate males in lion prides and other groups may have few or no offspring of their own, at least as long as they are subordinate. If the dominant male is their brother or other close relative, however, it may still be worth it for them to remain in the group and help him reproduce, for by doing so they are propagating copies of some of their own genes. Kin selection also favors the development of "aunting" behavior in primates—the

kin selection The theory that it can be advantageous, in evolutionary terms, to support the reproductive success of close relatives.

inclusive fitness The likelihood that an individual's genes will be represented in future generations, both in direct descendants and in the descendants of close relatives.

tendency of females to share maternal duties—because the females who share these duties are likely to be sisters or other close relatives.

Probably the most successful application of kin selection theory has been to social insects, such as bees and ants. As described earlier, many individuals in these species are sterile worker females. These individuals work tirelessly to help their fertile sister, the queen, produce enormous numbers of offspring. Why do they do this? It turns out that, due to a peculiarity of inheritance in most social insects, workers are more closely related to the queen than they are to any off-spring they might have themselves. Undoubtedly, this close relatedness fosters the unusual degree of altruistic behavior in these species (Trivers & Hare, 1976).

Kin selection doesn't explain all altruistic behavior, however. Females may adopt orphans who are completely unrelated to them, for example; such behavior is not predicted by kin selection theory. It may still be an adaptation—it might have value as a "rehearsal" for parenting one's own offspring—but it could also be a valueless or even harmful by-product of other adaptations. For example, it could be adaptive for females to nurture infants in their vicinity because those infants are usually their own offspring—so sometimes they nurture the "wrong" infants. While all animals (including ourselves) are products of evolution, it does not follow that *every* behavior has been fine-tuned by natural or sexual selection.

The influence of evolutionary mechanisms on human sexual behavior and attitudes is often difficult to separate from the influence of culture. One attempt to do so is described in **Box 2.4**.

Sex May Acquire Other Functions beyond Reproduction

While reproduction is the primary function of sexual behavior, it is not the only one. We know this because individuals of many species engage in sexual behaviors that cannot generate offspring, such as sex between two males or between two females. Why do they do so?

In part, animals may be motivated to engage in sexual behaviors simply by the physical pleasure that sexual activity brings (Vasey, 2006). Engaging in non-reproductive sex for pleasure alone would not be adaptive in an evolutionary sense. But some species have found functions for nonreproductive sex that are truly adaptive. Notable among these species is our close relative, the bonobo (*Pan paniscus*).

The bonobo is an endangered species of ape that lives along the Congo River in central Africa. Bonobos split off from chimpanzees (*Pan troglodytes*) about 3 million years ago; our own ancestors diverged from the common ancestors of chimpanzees and bonobos about 8 million years ago.

Female and Male Bonobos Engage in Nonreproductive Sex

Like most female mammals, female bonobos advertise when they are willing to copulate (estrus). Bonobos, like baboons, do so by means of their genital swellings. In striking contrast to mammals such as mice, however, the estrus of a bonobo extends over almost two-thirds of her entire ovarian cycle, which lasts about 2 months (**Figure 2.13**). In fact, the bonobo is out of estrus only for a few days around the time of menstruation (the periodic shedding of the lining of the uterus). Although the bonobo ovulates at some point during her estrus, the ovum is only viable for a day or two; sperm do not survive in her reproductive tract for more than a day or two, either. In other words, for most of the time when the female bonobo is willing to have sex, there is no chance that sex will result in pregnancy. From your knowledge of human sexuality, this may not strike you as particularly remarkable, but in evolutionary terms it is a real novelty.

Society, Values, and the Law

BOX 2.4 Does Sexual Morality Have an Evolutionary Basis? —The Case of Incest

Most human cultures have laws, moral teachings, or taboos that prohibit sex or marriage between brothers and sisters. These prohibitions have a rational basis, in that matings between first-degree relatives are far more likely to produce children with inherited diseases and disabilities than are matings between unrelated people (Bittles, 2004). Many people, however, believe that sex between siblings is wrong even if contraception is used or pregnancy is not possible. Thus opposition to incest may involve an intuition-based morality, rather than (or in addition to) a morality based on reason (Greene & Haidt, 2002).

Sexual relationships between adult siblings are in fact very rare, and that's a bit odd, because plenty of other "forbidden" sexual behaviors are quite common. What's more, siblings have ample opportunity to experience sexual attraction to each other and even to fall in love. So why don't they become sex partners more often than they do, particularly in this age of loosened sexual standards?

The answer seems to be that children who are very close in childhood—not just biological siblings, but also foster-siblings and unrelated children who grow up together in communes (Shepher, 1971)—tend not to find each other sexually attractive in adulthood. Consistent with this idea, biological siblings who did *not* spend their childhood together may indeed find each

British poet Lord Byron (1788–1824) had a sexual relationship with his half-sister; the two barely knew each other during childhood.

other attractive, fall in love, and desire to have a sexual relationship. Recently, for example, the marriage of a British couple was annulled when it was discovered that they were twins who had been separated at birth (BBC News, 2008). According to the pioneering Finnish sociologist Edvard Westermarck (1862–1939), this relationship between familiarity during childhood and

sexual nonattraction in adulthood is an evolved mechanism by which the human species reduces the prevalence of incest, with its negative genetic consequences.

Similar mechanisms are seen in animals. Mice, for example, learn the smell of littermates (which carries information about a set of variable genes called MHC markers). After puberty, they avoid sex with animals carrying similar MHC markers—animals who might be close relatives of themselves. Thus, if newborn mice are "adopted" by an unrelated female, they learn to avoid sex with their adoptive relatives rather than with their biological relatives (Penn & Potts, 1998).

Westermarck proposed that, not only our sexual attractions, but also our moral beliefs about sibling incest in general are influenced by being brought up with opposite-sex siblings. To test this idea, psychologists at the University of California, Santa Barbara, surveyed students about their attitudes toward sibling incest (Lieberman et al., 2003). Consistent with Westermarck's proposal, they found that the longer a person had lived with an opposite-sex sibling during childhood, the stronger was that person's moral opposition to sibling incest. The researchers concluded that sexual morality—or this one example, at least—is strongly influenced by evolutionary mechanisms.

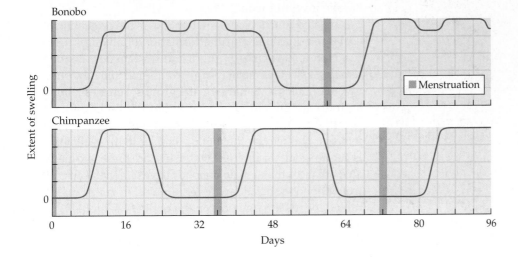

Figure 2.13 Sexual receptivity and the ovarian cycle in a bonobo (above) and a chimpanzee (below). Each graph shows the extent of genital swelling (an indicator of sexual receptivity) on each day of the ovarian cycle, which lasts about 60 days in bonobos and 36 days in chimpanzees. The bonobo is receptive for most of her ovarian cycle, except for a few days around menstruation. The chimpanzee is receptive for a more restricted period in the middle of each cycle, around the time of ovulation. (Data from Jeremy Dahl, Yerkes Primate Center; after de Waal, 1995.)

vulva The female external genitalia.

clitoris The erectile organ in females, whose external portion is located at the junction of the labia minora, just in front of the vestibule.

scrotum The sac behind the penis that contains the testicles.

Not only are female bonobos sexually receptive for most of the ovarian cycle, but they are also receptive when they are not cycling at all. Bonobo mothers nurse their young for several years after they are born, and lactation suppresses ovulation. Thus bonobos cannot become pregnant while they are still nursing previous offspring. Even so, they are sexually receptive throughout this period.

Bonobos have two basic positions for heterosexual copulation. In one, the male mounts the female from the rear, as in nearly all other mammalian species. In the other position, the two animals face each other. This again is an evolutionary novelty. The female bonobo seems well-adapted for this behavior because her **vulva** (external genitalia) faces forward. Although copulation is brief—no more than about 10 to 15 seconds—both the male and the female may experience orgasm, to judge from their grimaces and squeals at climax.

Further accentuating the nonreproductive nature of much bonobo sex, both female and male bonobos engage in frequent homosexual encounters. When two females have sex, they embrace face to face, and each rubs her swollen **clitoris** (the erectile component of the external female genitalia that mediates sexual pleasure) sideways against the other's until both females reach orgasm. This behavior, called genito–genital rubbing (see Figure 1.4), is unique to female–female encounters—it's quite different from the behavior shown by females during sexual encounters with males.

Sexual encounters between males occur in one of two ways. In one kind, the males face away from each other, and one male rubs his **scrotum** (the sac containing the testes) against the other male's buttocks. In the other, the two males rub their penises together while hanging from a tree branch.

Bonobos Use Sex for Conflict Resolution and Alliance Formation

All this nonreproductive sexual activity raises an obvious question—why? Close observation of bonobo colonies in captivity (de Waal, 1995; Parish & de Waal, 2000) and in the wild (Kano, 1992) indicates that bonobos use sex for the prevention and resolution of conflicts. Two bonobos who are faced with a conflict in food allocation, for example, will engage in sex and then divide the food peacefully. This happens regardless of the sex or age of the two animals. Alternatively, one animal may take food from another and "pay" with the currency of sex. When an entire troop of bonobos comes upon a food source—a situation that triggers wild fighting in other species such as chimpanzees—the bonobos engage in extensive bouts of sex with one another before dividing up the food. The bonobos' motto seems to be "Make love, not war."

A related function of sex in bonobos is the cementing of social relationships and the formation of alliances. This function is particularly important for females. Bonobo females leave their natal (birth) groups and join new ones, whereas males stay in their natal groups. Females joining a group are initially unwelcome, but they solidify their position by forming close alliances with high-ranking females. The activity that bonds females in these alliances is genito–genital rubbing. So effective are these sex-mediated alliances that female bonobos have largely taken control of bonobo society away from males. In fact, a male's rank depends in large part on the rank of his mother.

Front-to-front copulation is rare among mammals, but does occur in bonobos and humans.

Because bonobos, like many humans, see more to sex than making babies, we might imagine that the bonobo's sexuality is ancestral to our own. But such an assumption would be risky, for chimpanzees—who are about equally closely related to us—are far more restricted in their use of nonreproductive sex. What is remarkable about the *Hominoidea*—the superfamily that includes gibbons, orangutans, gorillas, chimpanzees, bonobos, and humans—is the diversity of their sexual and social arrangements. Gibbons are monogamous; orangutans are solitary; gorillas are polygynous; chimpanzees are polygamous and male-dominated bonobos are polygamous and female-dominated; and humans—well, that is the topic of the remainder of this book.

Summary

1. The original function of sex—and its only function in many species—is reproduction. The reasons why many species rely on sexual rather than asexual reproduction are disputed. Two general theories have been presented. First, sexual reproduction may promote the elimination of harmful mutations. Second, by mixing genes from different individuals, sexual reproduction may foster the selection of advantageous traits.

2. Natural selection has caused gametes to diverge into female and male forms. Female gametes are large and contain nutrients; male gametes are small and motile. Natural selection also acts to keep the ratio of the sexes near equality in most species, because any imbalance favors animals that have offspring of the minority sex.

3. Sex may be determined by chromosomal mechanisms, as in mammals, or by the temperature at which eggs are incubated, as in many reptiles.

4. Sexual selection, driven by competition for mates, has led to different morphological and behavioral traits in males and females. Because females generally invest more than males in reproduction, males often compete among themselves for access to females. This competition may select for large, aggressive individuals.

5. Females often choose among males. Their choices may be based on morphological features such as symmetry, display feathers, or antlers, or on behavioral traits such as the provision of gifts. Some female choice seems aimed at forcing males to make a greater investment in reproduction than they otherwise would. In species in which males do make significant investments, males become choosier and females become more competitive.

6. A wide variety of relationship styles exist. Animals may engage in sex without establishing any social bond, or they may bond in socially monogamous or polygamous relationships. Polygamy usually involves one male and several females (polygyny); the reverse arrangement (polyandry) is rare.

7. In many socially monogamous or polygynous species, both males and females engage in sex outside these social structures. Promiscuity has obvious benefits for males in terms of increased numbers of offspring. For a female, promiscuity may offer a range of benefits: It may help her gain resources from males, it may give her access to high-quality genes, or it may favorably influence the behavior of males toward her or her offspring.

8. Forced copulation has been observed in many species. In a few species, this behavior is clearly adaptive, increasing the male's likelihood of having offspring.

9. Because close relatives share many genes, evolution has led to altruistic behavior among relatives, including behavior in the reproductive domain. Some altruistic reproductive behavior, such as adoption of orphans, is less easily explained in evolutionary terms.

10. Sexual behavior has developed other functions besides reproduction. Bonobos offer a striking example: In this species, much sex takes place when the female is incapable of becoming pregnant, or between individuals of the same sex. Bonobo sex is directed not only toward reproduction, but also toward the avoidance or resolution of conflicts and the establishment of social bonds.

Discussion Questions

1. Do you think that the sexual behavior of nonhuman animals, as discussed in this chapter, is likely or unlikely to be relevant to an understanding of human sexuality? Why?

2. If the technique of reproductive cloning were perfected and universally adopted by humans, would that affect future human evolution? How would it affect people's moral views about sexual behavior?

Web Resources

Colby, C. Introduction to evolutionary biology www.talkorigins.org/faqs/faq-intro-to-biology.html

Lively, C. M.: Evolution of sex and recombination http://sunflower.bio.indiana.edu/~clively/Research/sex&recomb.html

Newman, L.: Penis fencing in a marine mollusk (video) www.pbs.org/kcet/shape-oflife/video/tv_high.html?ep_hunt_explo2_mov_hi

PBS: Evolution—Show #5: Why Sex? www.pbs.org/wgbh/evolution/sex/index.html

University of California Museum of Paleontology: Evolution 101 http://evolution.berkeley.edu/evosite/evo101/index.shtml

Recommended Reading

Birkhead, T. (2000). *Promiscuity: An evolutionary history of sperm competition.* Harvard University Press.

Buss, D. M. (1994). *The evolution of desire: Strategies of human mating.* Basic Books.

Dawkins, R. (2006). *The selfish gene.* (3rd ed.) Oxford University Press.

Diamond, J. M. (1997). *Why is sex fun? The evolution of human sexuality.* HarperCollins.

Judson, O. (2002). *Dr. Tatiana's sex advice to all creation.* Metropolitan Books.

Ridley, M. (1994). *The Red Queen: Sex and the evolution of human nature.* Macmillan.

Sommer, V., and Vasey, P.L. (2006). *Homosexual behaviour in animals: An evolutionary perspective.* Cambridge University Press.

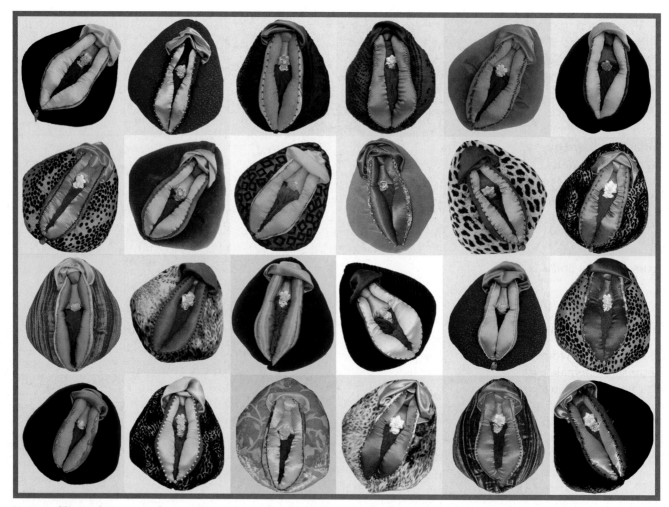

CHAPTER 3

No two alike—vulva puppets by Dorrie Lane (www.houseochicks.com).

Women's Bodies

Women and men are different, both in their bodies—the subject of this and the following chapters—and in their minds. Indeed, bodily differences, especially in the external genitals, are commonly used to decide whether a person is male or female. Yet there are also many similarities between the bodies and minds of men and women—they are only variations on a common theme, after all. And there is considerable diversity *within* the categories of male and female. In fact, some babies are born with bodies that are not easy to categorize as male or female, as we'll discuss in a later chapter.

By presenting women's bodies first, we intentionally distance ourselves from the traditional perspective, which discussed women's sex organs in terms of their equivalence to, or difference from, the sex organs of men. Neither men nor women are the "original" sex from which the other was molded: Women and men coevolved over millions of years from females and males of our ancestral species.

A Woman's Vulva Includes Her Mons, Labia, Vaginal Opening, and Clitoris

Many girls and women have little understanding of their sexual anatomy, in part because the female **external genitalia** are not as prominent as those of men. In addition, girls often learn that it's not nice to inquire or talk about these body parts, or even to take a close look at them. Vague phrases such as "down there" may substitute for specific terms. There are plenty of adult women—and men—who do not know what the word "vagina" means and could not make a reasonable sketch of a woman's genital anatomy. Thus the "naming of parts" and the description of their layout is the crucial first stage of education in sexuality (**Figure 3.1**).

The **vulva** is a scientific term that refers to the entire external genital area in a woman. You rarely see this word used outside books such as this one, which is a pity because there is no common word with exactly the same meaning ("crotch" is close, though it can be used for either sex).

The **mons veneris** (or simply **mons**) is a pad of fatty tissue covered by skin and **pubic hair**. It lies immediately in front of the **pubic symphysis**—the line of fusion between the left and right pubic bones. The mons may serve as a cushion for the woman's pubic area during sex. The hair helps vaporize odors that arise in specialized sweat glands, similar to those in the armpits; these odors may act as pheromones (chemical attractants). The mons with its pubic hair may also be

external genitalia The sexual structures on the outside of the body.

vulva The female external genitalia.

mons veneris (mons) The frontmost component of the vulva: a mound of fatty tissue covering the pubic symphysis.

pubic hair Hair that appears on portions of the external genitalia in both sexes at puberty.

pubic symphysis The junction of the left and right pubic bones, the frontmost elements of the pelvic skeleton.

(A)

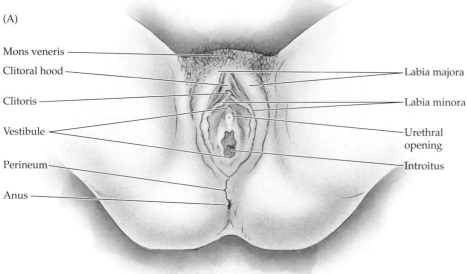

Mons veneris

Clitoral hood

Clitoris

Vestibule

Perineum

Anus

Labia majora

Labia minora

Urethral
opening

Introitus

Figure 3.1 The vulva, or female external genitalia. (A) Vulva with labia drawn
apart to show the vestibule, urethral
opening, and introitus. The perineum
and anus are not part of the vulva. (B)
The labia minora are quite variable in
shape and color from woman to
woman. (See Web Activity 3.1.)

(B)

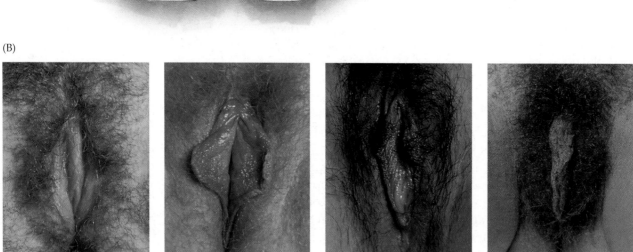

a visual trigger for sexual arousal in a woman's partner, since it is the most easily visible portion of the vulva.

In spite of these possible functions for pubic hair, many women remove some
of the hair or all of it (**Figure 3.2**). Some women leave a pattern they consider aes-
thetically attractive such as a strip, triangle, or heart-shaped patch above the
vulva. A less-hairy vulva may be viewed by some as sexually attractive and may
give better access to the vulva, especially during oral sex. Still, many cultures
(such as that of Japan) have viewed abundant pubic hair as highly erotic.

Hair removal—whether by shaving, plucking, waxing, chemical depilation, or
laser treatment—can cause problems, such as inflammation or infection of the hair
follicles or, in the case of laser treatment, alteration of skin color (Trager, 2006).
Women who choose to shave can lessen the likelihood of problems by using a
triple-bladed razor with shaving gel, shaving with rather than against the hair
direction, shaving less frequently, and applying a mild hydrocortisone lotion after
shaving. Trimming the hair with scissors or clippers is not likely to cause problems.

The **labia majora** (outer lips) are two folds of skin that extend down from the
mons on either side of the vulva. Like the mons, they are padded with fatty tissue, and are hairy on the surfaces nearest to the thighs. The skin of the labia majora is often darker than the skin elsewhere, and it is erotically sensitive, especially
on the inner, hairless sides of the labia.

labia majora The outer lips: fleshy skin
folds, partially covered in pubic hair,
that extend from the mons.

(A)

(B)

(C)

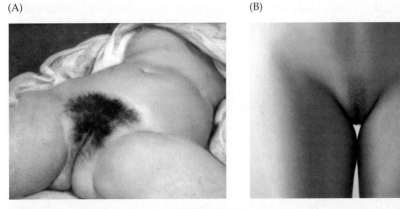
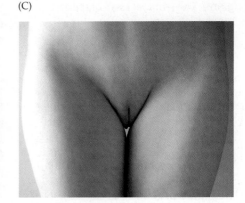

Figure 3.2 Pubic hair—love it or loathe it? (A) Gustave Courbet's 1866 painting *The Origin of the World* put natural pubic hair front and center. (B) A Brazilian wax removes all pubic hair except a narrow strip of trimmed hair. (C) Complete removal of pubic hair.

The **labia minora** (inner lips) are two thin folds of hairless skin that lie between the two labia majora. In some women the labia minora are only visible after parting the labia majora; in other women they protrude to variable degrees (see Figure 3.1B). The labia minora meet at the front, forming the **clitoral hood**, and at the back. The left and right labia minora generally touch each other in the midline, but they enclose a space called the **vestibule**.

The labia minora are amply supplied with glands, blood vessels, and nerve endings, and are very erotically sensitive. The appearance of the labia minora varies greatly from woman to woman. In some women the labia minora are virtually absent, and are represented merely by slight ridges on the inner sides of the labia majora. In other women they extend well beyond the labia majora. In some cultures, the labia minora are not left in their natural state, but are stretched, from childhood onward, with the aim of making the vulva more attractive. A small labia-stretching culture exists in the United States, too. Conversely, some women with naturally prominent or asymmetrical labia consider them unattractive and have them surgically reduced (**Figure 3.3**).

There Is More to the Clitoris than Meets the Eye

Within the vestibule are three important structures: the clitoris, the urethral opening, and the vaginal opening, as well as two glands called Bartholin's glands. The **clitoris** is a complex organ, only a portion of which is visible. The external por-

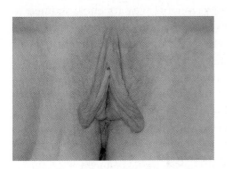
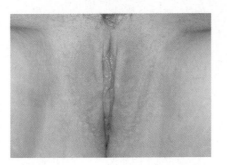

Figure 3.3 A woman's vulva before and after surgical reduction of the labia. (Courtesy of Dr. Robert H. Stubbs.)

labia minora The inner lips: hairless, loose folds of skin located between the labia majora and immediately flanking the vestibule.

clitoral hood A loose fold of skin that covers the clitoris.

vestibule The potential space between the left and right labia minora.

clitoris The erectile organ in females, whose external portion is located at the junction of the labia minora, just in front of the vestibule.

glans The terminal knob of the clitoris or penis.

corpus cavernosum (pl. corpora cavernosa) Either of two elongated erectile structures within the penis or clitoris, which also extend backward into the pelvic floor.

corpus spongiosum A single midline erectile structure. In both sexes, it fills the glans.

smegma A whitish, greasy secretion that builds up under the prepuce of the penis or clitoris.

crus (pl. crura) Internal extension of a corpus cavernosum of the clitoris or penis.

vestibular bulbs Erectile structures deep to the labia minora, on either side of the vestibule.

ischiocavernosus muscle One of the muscles that attaches to the internal portions of the penis and clitoris. It assists with erection and (in men) ejaculation.

bulbospongiosus mucle A muscle that attaches to the base of the penis or clitoris and assists with erection and (in men) ejaculation. In women, the internal portion of the muscle surrounds the introitus.

erection The expansion and stiffening of the penis, clitoris, or nipples in response to sexual stimulation or fantasy.

tion is the clitoral **glans**, a small but highly sensitive knob of tissue positioned at the front of the vestibule. It is about the size of a pearl and like pearls, its size can vary. It is covered, or partly covered, by the clitoral hood, but can be made visible by gently retracting the hood. The shaft of the clitoris, which is about 2 to 3 cm (one inch) long, runs upward from the glans, under the hood. Although the shaft cannot be seen directly, it can be felt, and its outline is visible through the skin of the hood. Both the shaft and the glans are erectile; that is, they are capable of becoming larger and firmer during sexual arousal. The erectile tissue within the clitoral shaft consists of two **corpora cavernosa** (cavernous bodies) that lie side by side. The erectile tissue within the glans consists of a single **corpus spongiosum** (spongy body).

Ointment-like secretions from the underside of the clitoral hood lubricate the motion of the hood over the clitoris, but as these secretions dry and mix with dead cells and bacteria they form a pasty material called **smegma**, which can collect under the hood. Smegma may be removed, or prevented from accumulating, by pulling the clitoral hood back and gently washing the area with soap and warm water.

Two internal extensions of the clitoris, the **crura,** diverge backward and downward from the clitoral shaft, giving the entire clitoris a wishbone structure (**Figure 3.4**). The crura are about 7 cm (3 inches) long and partially enwrap the urethra. Yet another pair of structures, the **vestibular bulbs**, are closely associated with the clitoris (O'Connell et al., 1998). They are curved masses of erectile tissue that surround the vestibule and underlie the labia minora. Like the crura, the vestibular bulbs are considered to be internal portions of the clitoris. Erection of the vestibular bulbs during sexual arousal helps to lengthen and stiffen the vagina.

Two muscles are associated with the clitoris. An **ischiocavernosus muscle** surrounds each crus of the clitoris. Contraction of these muscles during sexual arousal elevates the clitoral shaft and glans, causing the glans to disappear under the clitoral hood. The **bulbospongiosus muscle** forms a sling around the clitoral shaft and then runs downward and backward to surround the vaginal opening. Contraction of this muscle tightens the vaginal opening, increases clitoral erection, and may also help increase the erotic sensations of vaginal penetration by transferring mechanical excitation to the clitoris.

The clitoris, especially the glans, is richly innervated with sensory nerve fibers whose function is to produce sexual arousal. Indeed, the only certain function of the clitoris is sexual pleasure, and its stimulation is the most reliable way for most women to experience orgasm. The clitoris is so sensitive that many women prefer diffuse or indirect stimulation rather than direct touching of the clitoris itself.

Erection of the clitoris is a physiological sign of sexual arousal. During erection, the shaft of the clitoris

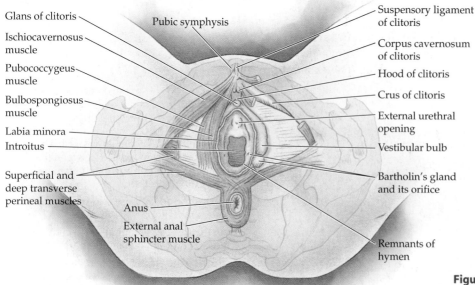

Glans of clitoris
Ischiocavernosus muscle
Pubococcygeus muscle
Bulbospongiosus muscle
Labia minora
Introitus
Superficial and deep transverse perineal muscles
Anus
External anal sphincter muscle
Pubic symphysis
Suspensory ligament of clitoris
Corpus cavernosum of clitoris
Hood of clitoris
Crus of clitoris
External urethral opening
Vestibular bulb
Bartholin's gland and its orifice
Remnants of hymen

Figure 3.4 Dissection of the vulva to show internal portions of the clitoris and the pelvic floor muscles. (See Web Activity 3.2.)

becomes firmer, but the glans remains soft. The reason for this is that the shaft is surrounded by a layer of tough connective tissue that restricts its expansion, whereas the glans is free to expand. The mechanism of erection is described in more detail in connection with the penis (see Chapter 4), where it has been studied in detail.

Typically, the glans of the clitoris is visible in the nonaroused (flaccid) state, but it may disappear under the clitoral hood during erection or with increasing sexual arousal, so sexual stimulation of the clitoris may occur through the hood rather than directly on the clitoral glans (or shaft) itself. Still, there's quite a bit of variation from woman to woman in terms of their clitoral anatomy and what kind of clitoral stimulation they find arousing. The clitoris is more erotically sensitive in the erect than in the flaccid state.

Not all women know that they have a clitoris or understand its function. Discussion of the clitoris can easily get skipped over in sex education classes, and plenty of women have never had a sex-ed class anyway. If they were discouraged, as girls, from exploring their bodies, and their partners have no particular interest in their sexual fulfillment, the structure may remain undiscovered.

Cutting or removal of the clitoris is a central element in female circumcision—a traditional but controversial practice in some cultures (**Box 3.1**). Piercing—usually of the clitoral hood but sometimes of the labia—is becoming an increasingly popular form of self-expression in the United States (Griffin, 2008). It may be done for adornment, to enhance sexual stimulation, or even as a spiritual act. Scrupulous hygiene is required during the procedure and the several-week healing period afterwards to prevent infection.

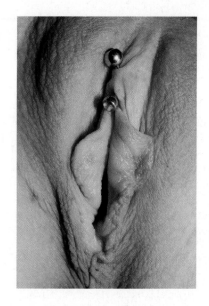

A vertical piercing of the clitoral hood—the most popular genital piercing in women.

The Appearance of the Vaginal Opening Is Variable

The vaginal opening or **introitus** occupies the rear portion of the vestibule. In newborn girls, the introitus is usually covered by an incomplete membranous fold of skin, the **hymen** (also known as the maidenhead or "cherry"). Rarely, the hymen is imperforate; that is, it completely closes the introitus, leaving no opening (Adams Hillard, 2003). This condition is often first diagnosed at puberty, because it causes a blockage of menstrual discharge; it is treated surgically to create a normal opening. More commonly, the hymen has one or several openings that are large enough to allow for menstrual flow after a girl begins to menstruate, and for the insertion of tampons (**Figure 3.5**).

The hymen may tear when a woman first has sexual intercourse, which may lead to some pain and bleeding. This phenomenon has led to the traditional notion that the state of a woman's hymen indicates whether or not she is a virgin. One can certainly debate whether a woman's virginity—or lack of it—should be a matter of concern to anyone besides herself. In any case, the state of her hymen

introitus The entrance to the vagina, usually covered early in life by the hymen.

hymen A membrane, usually perforated or incomplete, that covers the opening of the vagina. It may be ruptured by first coitus or for other reasons.

Figure 3.5 The hymen is highly variable in structure Most commonly it is annular (A); that is, it has a round central opening that is large enough for passage of the menstrual flow and insertion of a tampon, but usually not large enough for coitus. (B) The opening may be crossed by a band of tissue (septate hymen), or (C) by several bands that leave numerous small openings (cribriform hymen). If the openings are very small, or are absent entirely (imperforate hymen), the outflow of vaginal secretions and menstrual fluids may be blocked. First intercourse often tears the hymen but leaves it partially intact. (D) Vaginal childbirth removes all but small remnants of the structure ("parous" refers to a woman who has had at least one child). Familiarity with variations in hymen structure is important for professionals who evaluate female sexual assault victims.

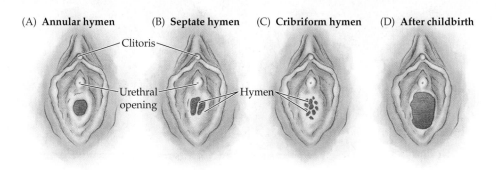

(A) **Annular hymen**   (B) **Septate hymen**   (C) **Cribriform hymen**   (D) **After childbirth**

Clitoris

Urethral opening

Hymen

Society, Values, and the Law

BOX 3.1 Female Circumcision

I was frozen with fear ... I peered between my legs and saw the gypsy woman getting ready ... I expected a big knife, but instead, out of the bag she pulled a tiny cotton sack. She reached inside with her long fingers, and fished out a broken razor blade ... I saw dried blood on the jagged edge of the blade. She spat on it and wiped it against her dress. While she was scrubbing, my world went dark as my mother tied a scarf around my eyes as a blindfold. The next thing I felt was my flesh, my genitals, being cut away.

(Dirie, 1998).

Like Waris Dirie, author of the foregoing account, an estimated 80–120 million women worldwide have been subjected to some form of cutting of their external genitals during childhood or at puberty. The various procedures are referred to collectively as **female circumcision, female genital cutting, or female genital mutilation**. The practice is prevalent in 29 countries, most of them in Africa. Eighty percent or more of the women in Djibouti, Egypt, Eritrea, Ethiopia, Gambia, Sierra Leone, Somalia, and Sudan are believed to have been circumcised. Female circumcision is also practiced in the Middle East, Indonesia, and elsewhere (World Health Organization, 2001). It is particularly associated with Islamic cultures, and although female circumcision is not prescribed in the Qur'an, it is referred to favorably in later Islamic texts and is often perceived to have religious significance.

There are three principal types of female circumcision. In the least invasive version, known as **sunnah**, the clitoral hood is incised or removed. This procedure is roughly analogous to male circumcision as we know it in the United States (see Box 4.1). In practice, however, some part of the clitoris itself is often removed during sunnah circumcision.

In the second procedure, known as **clitoridectomy** or **excision**, the entire clitoral glans and shaft are removed, along with the hood and sometimes nearby portions of the labia minora.

The third procedure, known as **infibulation** or **pharaonic circumcision**, is the most invasive. It is widely practiced in the Sudan and Somalia. (Waris Dirie is Somali.) The procedure

includes clitoridectomy, but goes beyond it to include removal of the entire labia minora and the inner parts of the labia majora. The cut or abraded edges of the two labia majora are then stitched together to cover the vestibule. Only a small opening is left for the passage of urine and menstrual blood. When the woman first has coitus the opening has to be enlarged—by forceful penetration with the penis or other object, or by cutting.

Female circumcision is generally performed by traditional practitioners who lack medical training. It is often done with crude instruments and without anesthesia or attention to sanitary conditions, so there is a risk of potentially fatal complications, including hemorrhage and infection. There has been a recent trend toward the "medicalization" of female circumcision—that is, its performance by trained medical personnel. This trend could reduce the rate of complications. The trend is controversial, however, since it may be seen as legitimizing the practice.

The long-term effects of female circumcision are also controversial. In some cases, especially with infibulation, the procedure can cause serious problems with urination, menstruation, intercourse, childbirth, and fertility. But some

studies have suggested that the harmful effects have been exaggerated (Shell-Duncan & Hernlund, 2000).

Female circumcision may be done simply because it is a tradition in a given culture. A woman who retains her clitoris may be considered ritually unclean or dangerous to the health of a man who has sex with her. However, there may be a second purpose to the procedure: the reduction of female sexual activity, especially outside of or before marriage. This reduction is achieved either by decreasing the pleasure of sexual acts (especially by removal of the clitoris) or by making them physically impossible (as with infibulation). In many cultures in which female circumcision is practiced, a woman who has not undergone the procedure is not marriageable—which often means that she is condemned to a life of poverty.

In the United States, female circumcision has been illegal since 1996. Significant numbers of immigrant women have been subjected to circumcision in their countries of birth, however, so Western medical professionals need to be aware of the phenomenon. Some circumcision of the daughters of immigrants does occur in the United States, but the prevalence of this illegal activity is hard to estimate.

BOX 3.1 (continued)

The practice of female circumcision has been strongly condemned by many Americans on several grounds: that it is harmful and dangerous; that it interferes with women's right to self-expression, especially in the sexual domain; that it subjugates women's interests to the purported interests of men; and that it makes irreversible decisions for children before they are able to make those decisions for themselves.

It's not surprising that many U.S. individuals and organizations have made efforts to have female circumcision banned and eliminated in countries around the world. And, through their membership in the World Health Organization and UNICEF, the United States and other Western nations have helped put pressure on the governments of countries where female circumcision is practiced.

In 2005, the African Union's Protocol on the Rights of Women in Africa was ratified: It requires all 53 member states to prohibit female circumcision. This is a promising step, but its effect is uncertain. In Kenya, for example, female circumcision has been illegal for several years, but in many parts of the country virtually all girls still undergo the procedure.

Although campaigning against female circumcision may seem like an entirely praiseworthy activity, it does potentially conflict with another value, which is respect for cultural diversity and autonomy. While *we* may be tempted to use words such as "mutilation" to describe female circumcision, women in the countries concerned have mostly positive views about the practice, and many girls *want* to have it done as a token of their womanhood and their membership in the culture.

It may be that the greatest progress will come from the work of activist organizations within the cultures concerned. Such organizations now exist in many countries. One possible avenue for change is the institution of "ritual without cutting," in which the traditional rites are preserved but the actual circumcision is omitted. The poster shown here was created by a Gambian organization dedicated to ending female genital mutilation and replacing the rite with one that does not involve cutting.

Waris Dirie, who emigrated to Britain and became a well-known model and author, campaigns against female circumcision on behalf of the United Nations.

female circumcision Any of several forms of ritual cutting or excision of parts of the female genitalia.

sunnah Female circumcision limited to incision or removal of the clitoral hood.

clitoridectomy Removal of the entire external portion of the clitoris.

infibulation The most invasive form of female circumcision, involving clitoridectomy plus the sewing together of the labia majora over the vestibule. Also called pharaonic circumcision.

is not a reliable indicator. The woman may have widened the opening in the hymen during tampon insertion, or she may have deliberately stretched the opening with the intention of facilitating first intercourse.

In many Middle Eastern countries it is traditional for a bride's mother or other relative to display the bloodstained sheets from a window after the bride's wedding night, thereby proving to the community that the marriage was consummated and that the bride was indeed a virgin. Of course there may be no stain, for any number of reasons—the bride was not a virgin; she was a virgin but didn't have an intact hymen; the couple achieved coitus without rupture of the hymen or without sufficient bleeding to stain the sheets; or they didn't engage in coitus because the man ejaculated prematurely or because one or both parties were too anxious or too drunk to perform the act. To guard against any of these possibilities, the mother brings a vial of chicken blood with her.

In some westernized regions of the Middle East this ritual has become a lighthearted tradition. In more conservative communities, however, proof of a bride's virginity is still so important that a woman who lacks an intact hymen may undergo an operation to reconstruct one, before she marries (Bentlage & Eich, 2007).

The opening of the **urethra** is located between the vaginal opening and the clitoris. Given that the main function of the urethra is to convey urine, you might not consider it a sexual structure, but some women do ejaculate from it at sexual climax, as we'll see shortly.

Small glands of unknown function—**Bartholin's glands**—lie on either side of the vaginal opening, just inside the labia minora. They secrete a few drops of fluid prior to orgasm, but they do not play a significant role in lubricating the vagina. It's possible that these secretions help neutralize the normally acidic environment

urethra The canal that conveys urine from the bladder to the urethral opening. It also serves for the discharge of semen or female ejaculatory fluids.

Bartholin's glands Glands at the introitus that discharge a small amount of fluid during sexual arousal.

perineum The region of skin between the anus and the scrotum or vulva.

pelvic floor A muscular sling that underlies and supports the pelvic organs.

pubococcygeus muscle Muscles in the pelvic floor that form a sling around the vagina.

reproductive tract The internal anatomical structures in either sex that form the pathway taken by gametes or the conceptus.

vagina A muscular tube extending 8–10 cm from the vestibule to the uterine cervix.

coitus Penetration of the vagina by the penis.

sexual intercourse Sexual contact, usually understood to involve coitus.

birth canal The canal formed by the uterus, cervix, and vagina, through which the fetus passes during birth.

mucosa A surface layer of cells (epithelium) that is lubricated by the secretions of mucous glands.

of the vagina, thus making it more hospitable to sperm. The main significance of Bartholin's glands, however, is that they sometimes become blocked and form large cysts. These can be drained by a gynecologist.

The **perineum** is the erotically sensitive area between the vaginal opening and the anus (or between the scrotum and the anus in males). Intestinal bacteria can be spread rather easily from the anus across the perineum to the vagina or urethra, possibly causing an infection. For this reason, women are advised to wipe themselves in a backward, not a forward direction after using the toilet.

There are important structures underlying the vulva. We have already described the deep extensions of the clitoris and the two muscles associated with it—the ischiocavernosus and bulbospongiosus muscles. Other muscles of the **pelvic floor**, especially the **pubococcygeus muscle**, have important roles during sex. The steady contraction of these muscles stiffens the walls of the vagina during sex, thus increasing sexual sensations for both participants. These muscles, which contract more strongly at orgasm, increase pleasure, prevent urinary and fecal leakage, and possibly help to keep semen in the vagina. Exercises to increase the tone of pubococcygeus muscle and other muscles of the pelvic floor (Kegel exercises) have been recommended for the treatment of sexual dysfunction as well as to prevent the involuntary leakage of urine or feces (incontinence). Kegel exercises are described in Chapter 16.

The Vagina Is the Outermost Portion of the Female Reproductive Tract

As shown in **Figure 3.6**, the female **reproductive tract** takes the shape of a capital letter T. The stem of the T is formed by the vagina, the cervix, and the body of the uterus. The two horizontal arms of the T are formed by the oviducts or fallopian tubes, whose ends are adjacent to the two ovaries. The reproductive tract serves for transport of the male's sperm and the female's eggs (ova), as well as fertilization, pregnancy, and passage of the fetus during childbirth.

In a woman who is not sexually excited, the **vagina** resembles a collapsed tube that runs about 8 to 10 cm (3 to 4 inches) upward and backward from the vaginal opening (see Figure 3.6). Penetration of the vagina by the penis opens the vagina and constitutes **coitus** or **sexual intercourse**. (Of course, there are plenty of other sexual behaviors that don't involve coitus.) The vagina plays a role in sperm transport and (along with the cervix) forms the **birth canal** through which a fetus is delivered.

The vaginal wall is highly elastic and consists of three layers: a thin cellular lining or **mucosa**, an intermediate muscular layer, and an outermost fibro-elastic layer. The mucosa can be seen by parting the labia minora. When a woman is in a nonaroused state, it is pink in color. The vaginal wall has a series of folds that run around the circumference of the vagina.

The outer third of the vagina, near the vaginal opening, has a different developmental origin than the internal portion (see Chapter 6), and it has a different structure. It is tighter and more muscular, and also more richly innervated, than the deeper portion. Thus most of the sensation during coitus—for both partners—derives from contact between the penis and this outer portion of the vagina.

The vagina is normally inhabited by large numbers of "friendly" bacteria—specifically, lactobacilli—which convert sugars to lactic acid. Because of this bacterial activity, the surface of the vagina is usually mildly acidic (pH 4.0 to 5.0), and this helps to prevent the growth of harmful bacteria. The vagina also normally contains a variety of fungal organisms, especially *Candida albicans*. It sometimes happens that the fungal organisms overgrow, causing inflammation of the

(A) **Midline view**

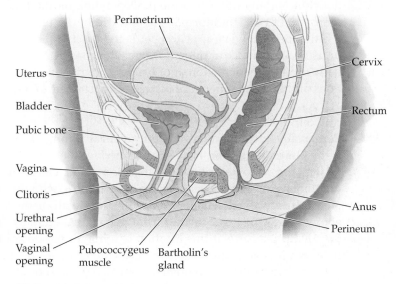

candidiasis A fungal infection, for example, of the vagina. Also called thrush or a yeast infection.

douche To rinse the vagina out with a liquid; the liquid so used.

(B) **Frontal view**

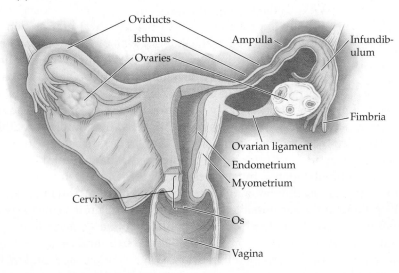

Figure 3.6 The female reproductive tract (See Web Activities 3.3 and 3.4.)

vaginal walls, itching, and possibly a thick white discharge. This condition is called **candidiasis**, vaginal thrush, or (in popular language) a "yeast infection." The condition is diagnosed by microscopic examination of the discharge and is treated with antifungal medications. Some of these medications are available without a prescription. It is better to get a medical diagnosis, however, at least for the first episode, because women sometimes use over-the-counter medications for inappropriate conditions, a practice that can lead to the development of drug-resistant infections (Centers for Disease Control, 2004c). Also, persistent candidiasis can be a sign of an underlying problem with the immune system, such as might be caused by infection with the human immunodeficiency virus (HIV).

One of the factors that can predispose women to candidiasis is frequent **douching**—the rinsing of the vagina with a stream of water or other liquid as a cleansing or deodorizing procedure. Gynecologists discourage douching, because the vagina usually does a good job of looking after its own health and cleanliness. A

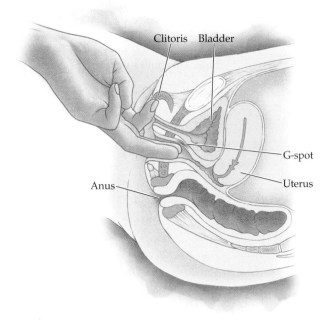

Figure 3.7 Finding the G-spot The G-spot is an area of heightened sensitivity on the front wall of the vagina. Not all women have a G-spot, and some sexologists question its existence altogether.

bacterial vaginosis A condition in which the normal microorganisms of the vagina are replaced by anaerobic species, causing discomfort and a foul-smelling discharge.

Gräfenberg spot (G-spot) A controversial area of increased erotic sensitivity on or deep within the front wall of the vagina.

paraurethral glands Glands situated next to the female urethra, thought to be equivalent to the larger prostate gland in males. Also known as Skene's glands.

anus The exit of the gastrointestinal tract.

sphincter A circular muscle around an orifice whose contraction closes the orifice.

clear, odorless vaginal discharge is normal and does not call for douching or any other treatment. Depending on the time of the menstrual cycle, the normal vaginal discharge may take on a whitish or yellowish appearance. If the discharge develops an unusual appearance or odor, however, this may be a sign of a sexually transmitted infection or of **bacterial vaginosis**. These conditions and their treatment are discussed in Chapter 17.

The G-Spot Is a Controversial Erogenous Zone

Perhaps the most famous and controversial feature of the vagina is the **Gräfenberg spot**, or **G-spot**, named for the sexologist Ernst Gräfenberg, who described it in the early 1950s. Only a minority of women say they have a G-spot, but for those who do, it is an area of heightened sensitivity on the front wall of the vagina, about 3 to 5 cm (1 to 2 inches) from the vaginal entrance (**Figure 3.7**). Deep pressure at this location can trigger the desire to urinate, but it is also said to be sexually arousing and to trigger an orgasm that is different in quality from an orgasm caused by stimulation of the clitoris (Ladas et al., 2004).

What is the structural basis of the G-spot, if it exists? The best candidate is probably a set of **paraurethral glands**, which are located just in front of the anterior wall of the vagina and next to the urethra; their ducts open into the urethra. The paraurethral glands are thought to be developmentally equivalent to the much larger prostate gland in men (Zaviacic & Whipple, 1993). Besides being located in the right place, the paraurethral glands are good candidates for the G-spot because, in some women, orgasms triggered by stimulation of this area are accompanied by ejaculation of fluid from the glands (see below). In 2008, Italian researchers reported that the region containing the paraurethral glands—and therefore possibly the glands themselves—are larger in women who experience orgasm from vaginal stimulation than in those who do not (Gravina et al., 2008). However, there are other possible explanations for the erotic sensitivity in the region of the G-spot: It might be due to stimulation of nerve fibers in the wall of the vagina itself, of the urethra, or of erectile tissue surrounding it.

Some researchers have claimed that every woman has a G-spot and that those who are unaware of its existence can be helped to identify it (Ladas et al., 2004). Some believe that it is a vague term that may be used for any erotically sensitive region within the vagina. Others believe that the G-spot is a complete myth (Hines, 2001). Debate about the G-spot is related to a controversy about vaginal versus clitoral orgasms, which will be considered later in this chapter.

The Anus Can Also Be a Sex Organ

Penetration or manual or oral stimulation of the **anus** (anal sex) is practiced fairly commonly by both heterosexual and homosexual couples (see Chapter 9), so the anus needs to be described along with the more obviously sexual structures. The anal orifice is located at the back of the perineum (see Figure 3.6). It is kept tightly closed most of the time by contraction of the external and internal anal **sphincter muscles**. You can feel these sphincters by inserting your finger a short way into the anus. The external sphincter is under conscious control—you can squeeze down on your finger or release the tension at will. The internal sphincter is under the control of the autonomic nervous system and is therefore less readily controlled by willpower. This is the sphincter that sometimes causes problems during anal penetration, but with experience a person can learn to relax this sphincter too.

Beyond the sphincters lies the **rectum**, the lowermost portion of the gastrointestinal tract. It is usually empty of feces except immediately before a bowel movement. The rectum is a much larger space than the anus, so most of the sensation generated during anal sex (for both partners) derives from penetration of the anus itself (which is both relatively tight and richly innervated), rather than from penetration of the rectum. In women, the structure in front of the rectum is the vagina. Stimulation of this and other nearby structures during anal sex may also contribute to sexual arousal.

The anus and rectum are lined by mucosa, but unlike the vaginal walls, this surface does not provide significant amounts of lubrication. Thus most people who engage in anal sex use some type of lubricant (see Chapter 9). And although we are postponing discussion of sexually transmitted diseases (STDs) to a later chapter, we should stress now that condoms offer significant protection from STDs during anal sex, just as they do during vaginal sex.

The Uterus Serves a Double Duty

The **uterus** or womb—the inward continuation of the female reproductive tract beyond the vagina—is a hollow organ that lies within the pelvic cavity (the portion of the abdominal cavity that is surrounded by the bones of the pelvis). In a nonpregnant woman the uterus is about the shape and size of a small upside-down pear (see Figure 3.6). The narrow part of the pear, the **cervix**, bulges into the deep end of the vagina. A woman can feel her own cervix by inserting one or two fingers deeply into the vagina while in a squatting position, and she can see her cervix with the help of a mirror, a flashlight, and a speculum (an instrument that holds open the walls of the vagina; **Box 3.2**).

A constricted opening—the **os**—connects the vagina to a short canal that runs through the cervix. The cervical canal contains numerous glands that secrete **mucus**. The consistency of this mucus changes with the menstrual cycle, and this is why women experience changes in their vaginal discharge around the cycle. Only around the time of ovulation is its consistency optimal for passage of sperm through the cervix.

The cervical canal opens into the cavity of the uterus proper. The wall of the uterus has three layers: an inner lining (**endometrium**), a muscular wall (**myometrium**), and a thin, outer covering (**perimetrium**) that separates the uterus from the pelvic cavity.

The endometrium must switch between two reproductive functions—the transport of sperm up the reproductive tract toward the site of fertilization, and the implantation and nourishment of an embryo. Because these two functions require a very different organization, the structure of the endometrium changes over the menstrual cycle. A visible sign of this reorganization is **menstruation**—the shedding of part of the endometrial lining and its discharge, along with some blood, through the cervix and vagina.

The myometrium is composed primarily of **smooth muscle**. Unlike the muscles of the pelvic floor, which are composed of **striated muscle**, the uterine musculature is under the control of the autonomic nervous system; muscle contractions cannot be caused by an effort of will. Involuntary contractions of the myometrium during labor play a vital role in delivery of the fetus. Myometrial contractions (often perceived as menstrual cramps) are also thought to aid in the shedding and expulsion of the endometrial lining at menstruation. Menstruation is covered in greater detail in Chapter 5.

rectum The final, straight portion of the large bowel. It connects to the exterior via the anus.

uterus The womb; a pear-shaped region of the female reproductive tract through which sperm are transported and where the conceptus implants and develops.

cervix The lowermost, narrow portion of the uterus that connects with the vagina.

os The opening in the cervix that connects the lumen of the vagina with the cervical canal.

mucus A thick or slippery secretion.

endometrium The internal lining of the uterus.

myometrium The muscular layers of the wall of the uterus.

perimetrium The outer covering of the uterus.

menstruation The breakdown of the endometrium at approximately monthly intervals, with consequent loss of tissue and blood from the vagina.

smooth muscle Muscular tissue that has no microscopic striations. Its contraction is usually involuntary and under the control of the autonomic nervous system.

striated muscle Muscular tissue that has microscopic striations. Its contraction is usually under voluntary control.

Sexual Health

BOX 3.2 Genital Self-Examination

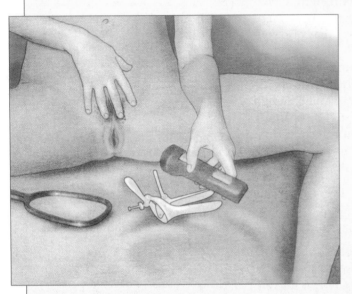

(A) Cervical self-examination

If you're a woman and you've never really taken a close look at your genital area, now may be a good time to do so. Genital self-examination has several potential benefits. If your upbringing has been such that you are reluctant or embarrassed to pay attention to your sexual anatomy, doing so in connection with this course may help you overcome these inhibitions and become more comfortable with your body. Also, it is an opportunity to consider your feelings about your vulva. Are there aspects of the way it looks that seem to you especially attractive, unattractive, or unusual, and if so, why? Vulvas differ greatly from woman to woman, especially in the distribution of pubic hair, the size and visibility of the clitoris, and the shape and color of the labia minora, but your anatomy is no more or less "normal" than any other woman's. Finally, by becoming familiar with your vulva, you can more easily recognize any changes that may call for medical attention.

To get a good look at your vulva you should use a hand mirror and possibly a flashlight (Figure A). Look while in a variety of postures and from a variety of angles. (A full-length wall mirror, used in conjunction with the hand mirror, may be helpful for this.) Make sure you can recognize the parts that are described in the text. Also, explore them with your fingers: What do they feel like to your fingers, and what do your fingers feel like to them? Use your fingers to gently draw back the clitoral hood, and to separate the labia, thus getting a view of the vestibule. If you become sexually aroused in the course of examining yourself, notice how the appearance of your vulva changes.

If you are curious to see the inside of your vagina and your cervix, you will need a flashlight and a vaginal speculum. This is a two-bladed, "duck-billed" device made of plastic that holds the walls of the vagina apart (Figure B). (A speculum can be obtained through women's health organizations. They come in three sizes; a small is probably right unless you have reason to think you need a larger one.) First, wash the speculum and practice opening, locking, and unlocking it. Then lubricate the blades with a water-based lubricant (or just water). With your knees apart, use the fingers of one hand to separate your labia. With the other hand, hold the speculum, with handle up and blades closed, and slide it gently into your vagina. (Sometimes it is easier to hold the speculum sideways for the insertion and turn it handle-up once it is fully in place.) Any discomfort should be a signal to stop and relax, and

if comfortable insertion isn't possible, you should desist. Once the speculum is fully in place, open and lock the blades, so that you now have both hands free to hold the mirror and flashlight. By shining the flashlight onto the mirror, you should be able to illuminate and see your cervix, which looks like a rounded knob with a central hole or slit (the os). The appearance of the cervix varies around the menstrual cycle (due to changes in cervical mucus) and from woman to woman. Some women may see fluid-filled sacs on the cervix protruding through the os; these are usually harmless. To remove the speculum, first unlock and close the blades, then gently withdraw it. The speculum should be carefully washed with soap and water, rinsed, and put away in a clean place. It's not a good idea to share a speculum with others. Self-examination with a speculum helps a woman get to know her own body, but it isn't a practical way to diagnose medical problems or a substitute for regular professional checkups. Another way to see your cervix is during a professional examination: Ask the healthcare provider to let you get the same view the provider does, with the help of a mirror.

(B) A speculum

Cancer Can Affect the Cervix or the Endometrium

Cancer of the cervix (cervical cancer) strikes about 13,000 American women annually and causes about 4400 deaths. The main factor predisposing women to cervical cancer is infection with human papillomavirus (HPV), a virus that is sexually transmitted (see Chapter 17). Less important risk factors include chlamydia

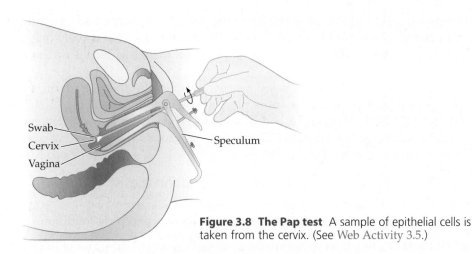

Swab
Cervix
Vagina
Speculum

Figure 3.8 The Pap test A sample of epithelial cells is taken from the cervix. (See Web Activity 3.5.)

Pap test The microscopic examination of a sample of epithelial cells taken from the cervix or (less commonly) the anus.

pelvic examination A visual and digital examination of the vulva and pelvic organs.

colposcopy The examination of the cervix with the aid of an operating microscope.

endometrial cancer Cancer of the endometrium of the uterus.

infection (Koskela et al., 2000), smoking, and immune system dysfunction (cervical cancer is a common complication of AIDS in women).

The death rate from cervical cancer has dropped by about 75% since the 1950s. Much of this reduction can be attributed to the use of regular **Pap tests**—named for the pathologist George Papanicolaou (1883–1962), who developed the test. A Pap test is generally done as part of a **pelvic examination**, which women are encouraged to have annually. In a pelvic exam, the gynecologist or other healthcare provider first inspects the vulva for external problems, and then uses a speculum to hold the walls of the vagina apart so that the vagina and cervix can be visually inspected for lesions, inflammation, or discharges. For the Pap test, a spatula is inserted while the speculum is in place, and a sample of cells and mucus is swabbed from the cervix (**Figure 3.8**). To get a sample from the cervical canal, a swab may be inserted into the cervical os. Pap tests should be done at least once every three years, starting three years after first coitus but no later than age 21.

The sample of vaginal cells and mucus taken from the cervix is spread on a slide and examined under a microscope. If the cells show precancerous changes, the healthcare provider may proceed to a more detailed examination of the cervix using an operating microscope. This procedure is called **colposcopy**. During the colposcopy, the provider may take biopsies or destroy precancerous lesions by freezing or other methods. Follow-up examinations are required to make sure that the lesions do not recur.

If a precancerous lesion escapes detection (most likely because the woman has not had a Pap test for several years, or has never had one), it may progress to true invasive cervical cancer. Symptoms of cervical cancer may include an abnormal, sometimes bloodstained vaginal discharge, pain during intercourse, or bleeding during intercourse. Of course, these symptoms are not specific to cervical cancer, but a woman who experiences them should see a doctor right away to make sure that, if cancer is present, it is detected as soon as possible.

Endometrial cancer (often called uterine cancer) is three times more common than cervical cancer, but only causes 50% more deaths. In other words, the survival rate is better for endometrial cancer: The 5-year relative survival rate (meaning the percentage of women who are still alive 5 years after diagnosis, excluding women who die of other causes) is 84%.

The usual initial symptom of endometrial cancer is abnormal vaginal bleeding or, less commonly, a colorless discharge. A postmenopausal woman who experiences either of these symptoms should seek medical attention, even though the symptoms can also be caused by noncancerous conditions. Less common symp-

hysterectomy Surgical removal of the uterus, sometimes along with the ovaries and oviducts.

fibroid A noncancerous tumor arising from smooth muscle cells of the uterus.

endometriosis The growth of endometrial tissue at abnormal locations.

prolapse The slipping out of place of an organ, such as the uterus.

toms—pelvic pain, a mass that can be felt in the pelvis, and weight loss—are usually associated with more advanced disease. The Pap test does not usually detect endometrial cancer—a diagnosis is usually made on the basis of cells or tissue removed from the uterus.

Except for the earliest-stage cervical cancers, cancers affecting the uterus are usually treated by removal of the entire organ (**hysterectomy**). Sometimes other pelvic organs, such as the oviducts and ovaries, also have to be removed, depending on how advanced the disease is. Chemotherapy, radiation therapy, or a combination of both is commonly added to improve the woman's chances of survival.

Other Uterine Conditions Include Fibroids, Endometriosis, Abnormal Bleeding, and Prolapse

Much more common than uterine cancer are several noncancerous conditions:

■ **Fibroids** are noncancerous tumors of smooth muscle that grow within or outside the uterus (**Figure 3.9**). They are very common: 20% to 25% of women develop them, usually after the age of 30 but before menopause. They can cause pain and abnormal—sometimes heavy—bleeding, but they are often asymptomatic. When fibroids do cause symptoms, they can be removed surgically or destroyed by blockage of the arteries that supply them with blood.

■ **Endometriosis** is the growth of endometrial tissue at abnormal locations within the pelvic cavity, such as on the oviducts, the ovaries, or the outside of the uterus. It is believed that these patches of endometrial tissue are derived from cells in the menstrual discharge that pass backward up the oviducts into the pelvic cavity. The most common symptom of endometriosis is pelvic pain; this pain may be worse before or during the menstrual period, or at the time of ovulation, or it may be ongoing. Endometriosis can cause infertility. There is no simple cure for endometriosis: Pain medications are helpful, as are oral contraceptives. Sometimes the patches of endometrial tissue can be removed surgically.

■ Abnormal endometrial bleeding can be caused by some of the conditions we have already discussed, but it can also occur for a variety of other reasons, or for no apparent reason at all. It can be treated with certain oral contraceptive drugs, by surgery, or (if very persistent) by hysterectomy.

■ **Prolapse** is a downward sagging of the uterus into the vagina. It is caused by weakening of the ligaments that support the uterus and of the muscles of the pelvic floor. The condition is seen most often in elderly women who have had at least one child, because both aging and childbirth weaken the structures that support the uterus. Obesity and smoking are also risk factors. Uterine prolapse may be treated by a variety of surgical techniques or by insertion of a plastic ring that keeps the uterus in place. Kegel exercises help to prevent uterine prolapse.

Problems with the uterus or other pelvic organs can often be detected with a bimanual (two-handed) pelvic examination, which is usually performed as the final step in a pelvic examination. The healthcare provider places two fingers of one hand in the vagina while pressing down on the woman's abdominal wall with the other hand. Using this technique, the provider can feel most of the pelvic organs, including the uterus, oviducts, and ovaries. If the exam

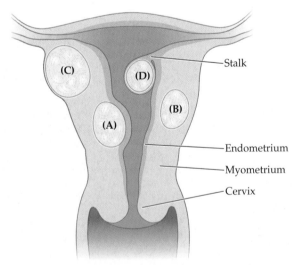

Figure 3.9 Fibroids are noncancerous tumors of the uterus. They may be located on the endometrium (A), within the myometrium (B), or on the outer surface of the uterus (C). Sometimes they are attached to the inner or outer surface of the uterus by a stalk (D).

detects abnormal growths or areas that are unusually tender, they should be investigated further.

Should Hysterectomy Be So Common?

Half a million hysterectomies are performed in the United States annually, and 1 in 3 women have had a hysterectomy by the age of 60. The associated costs exceed $5 billion annually. Are all these operations really necessary, or do they reflect a tradition of medical prejudice against the uterus (**Box 3.3**)?

In a premenopausal woman hysterectomy puts an end to menstruation and renders the woman infertile, but the operation does not have any hormonal effects unless it is accompanied by removal of the ovaries. Hysterectomy should not interfere with a woman's enjoyment of sex or her ability to engage in coitus or experience orgasm. In some cases the cervix can be left intact, making it even less

Sex in History

BOX 3.3 Hysteria

Think "hysteria" and you probably imagine crowds of people running in panic from a nonexistent fire. But the word hysteria derives from the Greek word *hustera,* meaning womb, and it has a long history as a medical term referring to physical and mental problems thought to be caused by that organ. These problems included choking, breathlessness, palpitations, faintness, weight gain, weight loss, too much or too little interest in sex, insomnia or excessive sleep, muscle spasms, depression, irrational fears, and a whole lot more. Up until the early part of the nineteenth century, hysteria was the second commonest medical diagnosis, after fever.

Why was all this blamed on the womb? The fundamental reason was that all doctors were men. Two thousand years of medical tradition held that the male body was the ideal human form; thus female bodies—and in particular women's distinct reproductive organs—were a sign of imperfection, though a necessary imperfection, of course. "The woman is less perfect than the man in respect to the generative parts," wrote the second-century Greek physician Galen. "For the parts were formed inside her when she was still a fetus, but could not emerge and project on the outside, and this, though making the organism that was being formed less perfect, provided no small advantage for the race, for there needs must be a female."

Since the perfect male body had no place for a womb, the belief arose that the womb did not

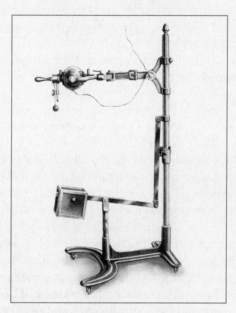

At $200 plus freight charges, the Chattanooga Vibrator was the deluxe solution to hysterical symptoms.

have a fixed abode within a woman's body, but migrated around, causing havoc wherever it went. "It is very much like an independent animal within the body," wrote Galen's contemporary Aretaeus, "for it moves around of its own accord and is quite erratic. Furthermore, it likes fragrant smells and moves toward them, but it dislikes foul odors and moves away from them. When it suddenly moves upward and remains

there for a long time and presses on the intestines, the woman chokes, in the manner of an epileptic, but without any spasms. For the liver, the diaphragm, lungs and heart are suddenly confined in a narrow space. And therefore the woman seems unable to speak or to breathe."

During the nineteenth century many doctors believed that hysteria was due to lack of sexual stimulation. Doctors themselves attempted to relieve the condition by providing the missing stimulation—not by having intercourse with their patients, but by manually stimulating their clitoral area until a "fit of paroxysm"—that is, an orgasm—was reached. This treatment was not considered an improper sexual contact, because it didn't involve penetrating the vagina. The treatment was so time-consuming, however, that doctors devised a variety of mechanical devices to take over the chore: These included shaking tables, water-powered douches, "jolting chairs," and finally the first electrical vibrators (see figure).

In 1896 Sigmund Freud, the founder of psychoanalysis, claimed that hysteria was in the mind, not the womb, but retained the sexual connection. Hysteria, according to Freud, resulted from childhood molestation, and one patient's nervous cough expressed her unconscious wish to perform oral sex on her father. Perhaps in reaction to Freud's wild ideas, hysteria gradually disappeared as a medical or psychiatric diagnosis during the twentieth century.

Sources: Maines, 1999; Ager, 2004.

oviduct Either of two bilateral tubes that lead from the uterus toward the ovaries; the usual site of fertilization. Also called fallopian tube.

cilia Microscopic, hairlike extensions of cells, often capable of a coordinated beating motion.

fimbria A fringe-like set of extensions from the infundibulum of the oviduct.

pelvic inflammatory disease (PID) An infection of the female reproductive tract, often caused by sexually transmitted organisms.

ovary The female gonad; the organ that produces ova and secretes sex steroids.

follicle An oocyte with its supporting cells within the ovary.

oocyte A cell capable of developing into an ovum.

granulosa cells Cells within an ovarian follicle that support the oocyte and secrete sex steroids.

thecal cells Cells located on the periphery of an ovarian follicle that synthesize sex steroids.

antrum A cavity that forms in an ovarian follicle as it matures.

likely that there will be any impairment of the woman's sexual pleasure. In this case, however, she will need to continue having regular Pap tests.

One study found that most women who have a hysterectomy derive more pleasure from sex after the operation (Roovers et al., 2003). Women who undergo hysterectomy also report an improved general quality of life, and these improvements are greater than in women treated for the same conditions by nonsurgical means (Showstack et al., 2006).

Even so, the chances that a woman will undergo a hysterectomy are influenced by factors such as her race, the region of the country where she lives, and even the sex of her physician (having a male physician increases the likelihood of hysterectomy) (Agency for Healthcare Policy and Research, 1998). Some of these factors may be medically relevant; for example, African-American women are much more likely to develop fibroids than white women, and this increases the likelihood that they will have a hysterectomy. Still, women with noncancerous disorders of the uterus should be aware that there is an increasing range of options for treatment. They should not think of hysterectomy as inevitable simply because their mothers had it.

The Oviducts Are the Site of Fertilization

At the upper end of the uterus, the reproductive tract divides into two symmetrical branches, the **oviducts**, also called fallopian tubes or simply "tubes." Each oviduct is about 10 cm (4 inches) long, and forms a pathway between the uterus and the left or right ovary. Fertilization of an ovum by a sperm takes place within an oviduct.

The cells forming the interior surface of the oviducts are lined with **cilia**, microscopic hairlike structures that beat in a coordinated fashion toward the uterus. Sperm moving from the uterus toward the ovary have to swim against the current set up by the beating cilia, rather like salmon swimming upstream, but this current is too slow to offer a serious impediment to healthy, fast-moving sperm.

The portion of each oviduct near the uterus is relatively narrow, but it widens out as it nears the ovary. The oviduct ends in a flared-out opening; the opening has a fringe or **fimbria** that is composed of finger-like extensions. Each fimbria is near, but not actually fused with, the ovary on that side of the body. Thus there is a continuous pathway from the outside of a woman's body via the vagina, up her reproductive tract, and into the pelvic cavity. The body has many mechanisms to prevent the migration of disease-causing organisms up this pathway: For example, the presence of mucus in the cervix acts like a plug, hindering the passage of microorganisms. In some circumstances, however, sexually transmitted organisms can migrate part or all of the way up the pathway, causing inflammation in the reproductive tract or even within the pelvic cavity (**pelvic inflammatory disease**).

The Ovaries Produce Ova and Sex Hormones

The **ovaries**—a woman's gonads—are paired organs located on either side of the uterus. They are egg-shaped structures measuring about 3 cm (1 to 1.5 inches) in length. The ovaries are about the same size and shape as a man's testicles.

Under the microscope, an adult woman's ovary can be seen to contain a large number of **follicles** at various stages of development (**Figure 3.10**). Each follicle consists of a central **oocyte**, or developing egg cell, surrounded by supporting cells known as **granulosa cells**. Outside of these are some more loosely arranged cells called **thecal cells**. The more mature follicles have a central cavity or **antrum**.

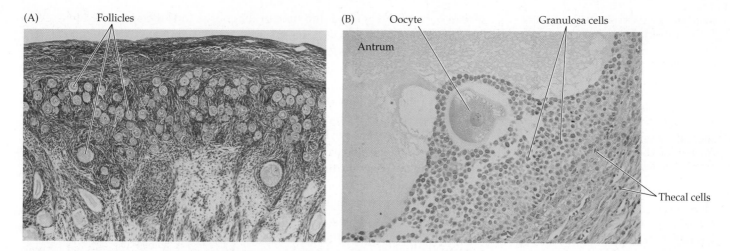

(A) Follicles

(B) Oocyte   Granulosa cells

Antrum

Thecal cells

Figure 3.10 Microscopic structure of the ovary (A) Low-power view of ovary, showing a number of follicles. (B) Higher-power view of part of a single follicle, showing the central antrum and the oocyte surrounded by granulosa cells.

The ovaries have two distinct functions. The first is the release of mature oocytes (**ovulation**). A newborn female has about a million oocytes in each ovary, but their numbers decline throughout life. By puberty a woman has about 200,000 oocytes in each ovary. During her reproductive life she typically releases only one mature ovum from one or the other ovary per menstrual cycle. Thus only a tiny fraction of a woman's oocytes are actually ovulated during her lifetime. Much greater numbers of oocytes die in the process of maturation.

Ovulation occurs when an ovary wall ruptures and releases an oocyte and its surrounding cells (collectively called an **ovum**) into the pelvic cavity. The fimbria of the nearby oviduct catches the ovum, and cilia propel it down into the oviduct, where fertilization may occur if sperm are present. We will have much more to say about all these ovarian processes in later chapters.

The second function of the ovaries is the production and secretion of sex hormones. The granulosa and thecal cells play key roles in the production of these hormones, as we'll see in Chapter 5.

Several medical conditions can affect the ovaries. The most significant is ovarian cancer. This is not a particularly common form of cancer: It strikes about 22,000 American women annually. Risk factors for ovarian cancer include age (the median age at diagnosis is 65), a family history of the disease, possession of cancer-promoting genes, early onset of menstruation (**menarche**), late menopause, not having children, obesity, and prolonged hormone replacement therapy. The use of oral contraceptives for more than 5 years *decreases* the risk of ovarian cancer by about 60%.

Early ovarian cancer is usually asymptomatic, and no screening tests have been shown to reduce mortality in average-risk women. Women with a family history of ovarian cancer can be tested for the possession of cancer-causing genes—these are the same genes that cause breast cancer (see below). Typically, ovarian cancer makes itself known by abdominal swelling, a constant feeling of a need to urinate or defecate, digestive problems, or pain in the pelvis, back, or leg. The accuracy of diagnosis can be improved by measuring blood levels of a marker known as CA-125 (Gordon, 2008), but this marker has not been proven useful as a screening test for asymptomatic women. Treatment typically involves surgery to remove as much of the tumor as possible, as well as chemotherapy. Often the cancer has

ovulation Release of an ovum from the ovary.

ovum (pl. ova) A mature female gamete, prior to or immediately after fertilization.

menarche The onset of menstruation at puberty.

ovarian cysts Cysts within the ovary that can arise from a number of different causes.

polycystic ovary syndrome (PCOS) A condition marked by excessive secretion of androgens by the ovaries.

mammary glands The milk-producing glands within the breasts.

secondary sexual characteristics Anatomical characteristics, such as breasts and facial hair, that generally differ between the sexes but are not used to define an individual's sex.

lobe A subdivision of a gland or other region.

lobules A small subdivision of an organ, such as the breast.

alveolus (pl. alveoli) Microscopic cavity, such as one of those in the breast where milk is produced.

spread beyond the ovary at the time of diagnosis; thus the survival rate is poor: Only about 1 in 2 women survive 5 years.

Another condition affecting the ovaries is the presence of **ovarian cysts** (fluid-filled sacs). These may be discovered when they cause pain, or they may be diagnosed during a pelvic exam. In women of reproductive age, the cysts are usually normal ovarian follicles that have not yet ovulated or that have grown larger than usual. These so-called "functional cysts" usually regress without treatment. Cysts can also be a sign of cancer, however, especially when found in girls before puberty or in postmenopausal women.

Polycystic ovary syndrome (PCOS) is a common but poorly understood condition in which the ovaries secrete high levels of androgens. The condition may cause irregular menstruation, infertility, and a male-like pattern of facial and body hair. Ovarian cysts are often, but not always, present. PCOS is not curable, but most of the symptoms can be controlled with contraceptive pills or other drugs.

The Breasts Have Both Erotic and Reproductive Significance

The breasts (or **mammary glands**) are considered **secondary sexual characteristics**, meaning that they are not components of the genitals, but do differ between the sexes. Although both men and women have nipples, and some men have a certain amount of breast tissue, breasts of significant size are generally a feature unique to women's anatomy. Occasionally, women or men may have extra nipples or breasts (**Box 3.4**).

The breasts lie between the skin and the muscles of the chest wall; some breast tissue extends up into the armpits. Each breast consists of about 15 to 20 **lobes** that are separated from one another by fibrous and fatty tissue (**Figure 3.11**). The lobes are further subdivided into **lobules**, and (in women who are producing milk) each lobule comprises numerous small cavities called **alveoli**. Each alveolus is lined by glandular cells that secrete milk into the central cavity of the alveolus. A layer of muscle cells surrounds each alveolus: When these muscles contract, milk is squeezed out of the alveolus into a system of ducts that connect all the alveoli

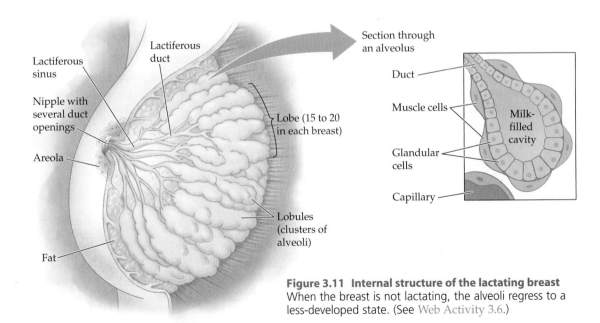

Figure 3.11 Internal structure of the lactating breast When the breast is not lactating, the alveoli regress to a less-developed state. (See Web Activity 3.6.)

Biology of Sex

BOX 3.4 Extra Nipples and Breasts

Some ancient goddesses of fertility were portrayed as possessing numerous breasts where most mortal women have but two. Still, occasional men and women can boast extra nipples (**polythelia**) or breasts (**polymastia**).

Small extra patches of areolar skin—sometimes with miniature nipples at their center—are found in about 6% of people—more commonly in men than in women and more commonly on the left side of the body than on the right (Schmidt, 1998) (see figure). These extra nipples are usually found along the "milk lines"—embryological ridges that run from the armpits to the groin. Mammary glands and nipples originate from characteristic portions of the milk lines in each mammalian species—near the groin in cows, for example—but can also arise in areas outside the milk lines.

Extra breasts in women can become fully functional at puberty. A nineteenth-century Frenchwoman, Therese Ventre, nursed her children from a breast on the side of her left thigh—a highly unusual location off the milk

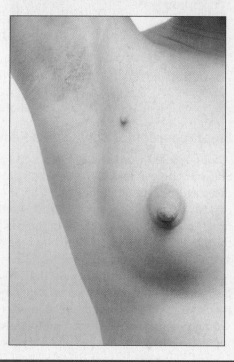

lines—as well as from her two normally located breasts. There has been a traditional (but incorrect) belief that women with extra breasts are unusually fertile. This may be why Anne Boleyn was chosen by King Henry VIII of England as his second wife—unfortunately, the extra breast did not save her from execution after she failed to produce a son (Grossl, 2000). The record number of medically verified breasts in a single person is ten (Deaver & McFarland, 1917).

Extra nipples and breasts may cause discomfort or embarrassment. Extra breasts are also subject to the same diseases as regular breasts. For any of these reasons, surgical removal is an option.

polythelia The condition of possessing more than two nipples; supernumerary nipples.

polymastia The condition of possessing more than two breasts; supernumerary breasts.

---

to the nipple—a process called "milk letdown." The milk then collects in a bundle of **lactiferous sinuses** near and within the nipple. A suckling infant removes milk by compressing the nipple between its tongue and palate, rather than by actually sucking as commonly believed.

The nipples are situated at the tip of the breasts in the center of circular patches of darker skin known as **areolae** (singular: areola). The nipples are capable of erection in response to sexual arousal, tactile stimulation, or cold. Erection is caused by contraction of smooth muscles beneath the nipple, which push the nipple outward.

As with all secondary sexual characteristics, breasts vary considerably among individuals, and there may even be a size difference between a woman's two breasts. Variation in breast size is due largely to differences in the amount of fatty tissue in the breast; women with small breasts usually have adequate glandular tissue to nurse an infant. (Breast-feeding is discussed further in Chapter 11.)

Breasts are of great erotic significance to many people. For women, tactile or oral stimulation of the breasts (especially the nipples) in the appropriate circumstances is sexually arousing. The appearance or feel of the breasts is also an important erotic stimulus to women's sex partners, especially in contemporary Western culture. Probably for this reason, some women are unhappy with their breasts; they may seek to alter their appearance by wearing bras that enhance their breasts or by plastic surgery. The attractiveness of breasts is discussed further in Chapter 8.

lactiferous sinuses One of the storage areas for milk near the nipple.

areola The circular patch of darker skin that surrounds the nipple.

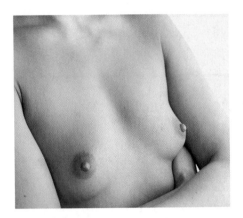
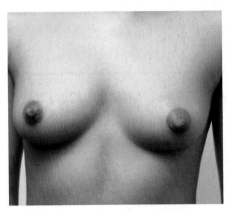
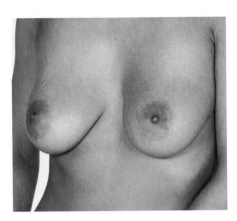

Breasts vary greatly in appearance. There may also be some difference in size between a woman's left and right breasts.

mastectomy Surgical removal of a breast.

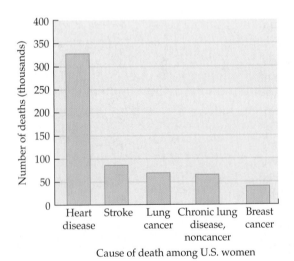

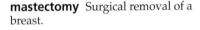

Cause of death among U.S. women

Figure 3.12 Breast cancer is not the leading cause of death among U.S. women. The graph shows the most common causes of death among women in the United States and the number of women who die annually from each of them (Centers for Disease Control, 2008d).

Breast Cancer Mortality Can Be Reduced

About 180,000 women are diagnosed with invasive breast cancer in the United States each year, and about 40,000 women (as well as about 400 men) die of the disease. It is estimated that 13.2% of American women will develop (but not necessarily die of) breast cancer in their lifetime (Mustanski et al., 2005). Women fear breast cancer not just because of the risk of death, but also because one treatment for the disease—surgical removal of the affected breast (**mastectomy**)—may damage a woman's self-image and sex life.

We don't wish to downplay the seriousness of breast cancer, but it is worth pointing out that, contrary to many women's belief, breast cancer is far from being the leading cause of death for women (**Figure 3.12**). Heart disease kills far more women than do all cancers combined. In fact, breast cancer is not even the leading cause of *cancer* deaths among women: Lung cancer kills more women in the United States than does breast cancer. Still, breast cancer is a leading cause of death among middle-aged women.

Many Factors Affect the Risk of Breast Cancer

A number of known factors can increase or decrease the chances that a woman will develop breast cancer:

■ *Genes.* A woman who has one first-degree relative (mother, sister, or daughter) with breast cancer faces twice the risk of getting the disease as a woman who does not. Having two first-degree relatives with breast cancer multiplies her risk fivefold. Certain genes normally protect against breast cancer and other cancers; the most important of these genes are *BRCA1* and *BRCA2*. Women who inherit damaged (mutated) versions of these genes have an 80% risk of developing breast cancer during their lifetime, as well as a heightened risk of developing ovarian cancer (King et al., 2003). Tests for the presence of these genes are available. Mutations in these genes account for only about 10% of all breast cancers, however; in fact, most breast cancers occur in women with no family history of the disease.

■ *Age.* Breast cancer is primarily a disease of older women: About 85% of newly diagnosed cases are in women over 50.

■ *Reproductive history.* Women who had early menarche (before age 12) or late menopause (after age 55), who have had no children, or who had their first child after age 30 have a modestly increased risk of developing breast cancer. Prolonged breast-feeding may offer some reduction in risk.

- *Alcohol.* Women who consume two to five alcoholic drinks per day have about a 1.5-fold increase in risk of developing breast cancer compared with women who consume less than two drinks per day. It is the quantity of alcohol consumed, not the type of drink, that matters (Science Daily, 2007).

- *Obesity.* Women who are obese—especially those who become obese during adulthood and those whose body fat is concentrated at the waist—face an increased risk of developing breast cancer. Some studies suggest that a high-fat diet is a risk factor independent of obesity, but this is uncertain.

- *Exercise.* Women who exercise several hours a week (and who don't have a family history of breast cancer) can cut their risk of developing breast cancer almost in half (Carpenter et al., 2003). This benefit may result from the estrogen-lowering effect of exercise.

- *Medical history.* A history of breast cancer, even when successfully treated, raises the risk of a second, independent cancer in the same or the other breast. A history of high-dose radiation treatment that includes the breast raises the risk of breast cancer. (The X-ray doses associated with mammography are believed to be insignificant in this respect.)

- *Hormones.* The use of oral contraceptives by young women (ages 20 to 34) is associated with a slightly increased risk of breast cancer (Althuis et al., 2003). (Bear in mind, though, that breast cancer is very uncommon in this age bracket whether or not oral contraceptives are used.) The increase in risk disappears by 10 years after cessation of contraceptive use (Collaborative Group on Hormonal Factors in Breast Cancer, 1996). There is little or no risk for older women who use oral contraceptives (Marchbanks et al., 2002). Postmenopausal hormone treatment raises the risk of breast cancer slightly, as discussed in Chapter 13.

Breast cancer offers opportunities for prevention through lifestyle changes (mainly weight control, exercise, and restriction of alcohol intake). These changes are recommended because they have other, additional health benefits besides reducing breast cancer risk. Regular low-dose aspirin was once thought to reduce breast cancer risk, but a large, carefully controlled study showed no such protective effect (Zhang et al., 2008).

Women who are at especially high risk—in particular, those who carry a *BRCA2* mutation—have the option of taking the drug tamoxifen, which provides partial protection against breast cancer (King et al., 2001). Removal of the breasts is an effective but drastic preventive measure that is seldom chosen. In general, because of the limited preventive strategies that are currently available, the emphasis is on early diagnosis and treatment rather than on prevention.

Early Detection Is Important

For many years, the American Cancer Society (ACS) urged women to regularly examine their own breasts for lumps. The ACS withdrew this recommendation in 2003 because of a lack of evidence that these self-exams are useful. According to the results of two very large prospective studies, women who are taught breast self-examination undergo twice as many breast biopsies as other women, but are just as likely to die of breast cancer (Kosters and Goetzsche, 2008). This is probably because the lumps discovered by self-examination, if cancerous, are often too far advanced to be curable.

Breast self-exams remain an option, and instructions on how to perform them are presented in **Box 3.5**. Women who choose not to perform self-exams should remain aware of their breasts and report any changes to their doctor promptly.

Sexual Health

BOX 3.5 Breast Self-Examination

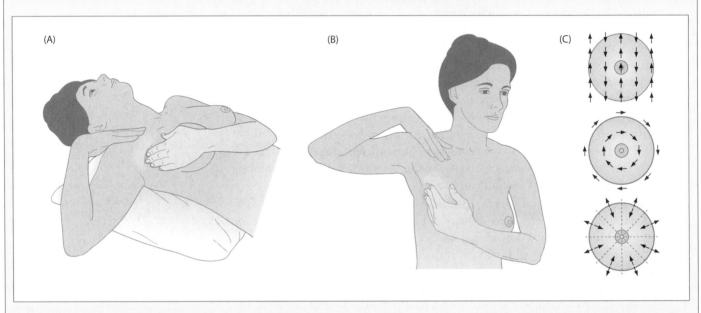

(A) (B) (C)

The best time for breast self-examination (BSE) is about a week after your menstrual period ends, when your breasts are not tender or swollen. If your periods are irregular or you are not menstruating, do BSE on the same day every month.

Lie down with a pillow under your right shoulder and place your right arm behind your head (Figure A).

Use the finger pads of the three middle fingers on your left hand to feel for lumps in the right breast.

Press firmly enough to know how your breast feels. A firm ridge in the lower curve of each breast is normal. (If you're not sure how hard to press, talk with your healthcare provider.)

Move around the breast in a circular, up-and-down, or wedge pattern. Be sure to do it the same way every time, check the entire breast area, and remember how your breast feels from month to month.

Move the pillow to your left shoulder and repeat the exam on your left breast, using the finger pads of the right hand. Repeat the examination of both breasts while standing, with one arm behind your head (Figure B). The upright position makes it easier to check the upper and outer parts of the breasts (toward your armpit), where about half of breast cancers are found.

You may want to do the standing part of the BSE while you are in the shower. Some breast changes can be felt more easily when your skin is wet and soapy.

When examining the breast, follow a regular pattern, such as any one of the patterns shown in Figure C, to ensure that every part of the breast is covered.

Finally, while standing in front of a mirror, check your breasts for any dimpling of the skin, changes in the nipple, abnormal discharge, redness, or swelling.

If you find any changes, see your doctor right away.

Source: American Cancer Society.

Periodic breast exams by a clinician, combined with mammography, are more useful than self-examination.

Mammography is a breast cancer screening technique that uses low-dose X-rays to image the soft tissues of the breast. During a mammogram, each breast is compressed between two plastic plates to spread out the breast tissue and make interpretation of the X-ray image easier (**Figure 3.13**). The procedure can be uncomfortable, but it is very brief. A recent innovation known as cone-beam breast CT allows the breast to be examined without compression; it may become widely available in the next few years (Karellas et al., 2008).

Although there has been some debate about the value of routine mammograms in younger women, the American Cancer Society and other professional organi-

mammography Radiographic inspection of the breasts.

(A)

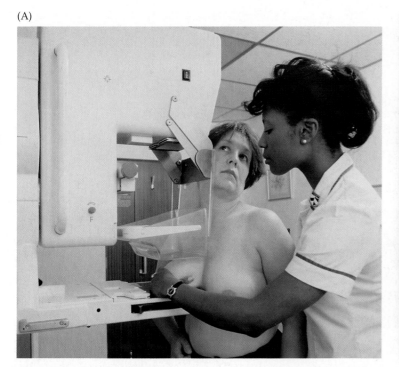

(B)

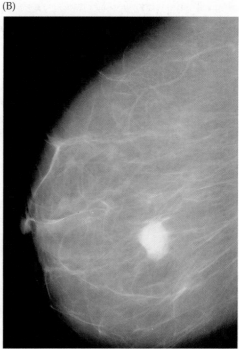

Figure 3.13 Mammography (A) A low-dose X-ray image is taken while the breast is compressed between two plates. (B) This breast lump, visualized as a white patch on the mammogram, is a "ductal carcinoma in situ," the earliest detectable stage and the easiest form of breast cancer to cure.

zations recommend that all women have an annual mammogram from age 40 onward (American College of Obstetricians and Gynecologists, 2002).

If a suspicious lump is seen on the mammogram, further mammography is usually done to establish the lump's position and other characteristics more carefully. An ultrasound examination may be done. Often this more detailed study shows that the lump is not likely to be cancer. If the lump remains suspicious, the next step is a **biopsy**: A sample of the lump is removed with a needle. (Sometimes the entire lump is removed—a more invasive procedure.) Examination of the sample tissue under the microscope allows for a near-definitive determination of whether the lump is cancerous. Only about 1 in 5 biopsied lumps turns out to be cancer.

Treatment Depends on the Diagnostic Findings and the Woman's Choice

If the biopsy shows that the lump *is* cancerous, the woman and her doctors must decide on the best course of treatment, based on the diagnostic findings, the woman's age and other circumstances, and the woman's own wishes. Surgical options range from removal of the lump itself plus some surrounding healthy tissue ("lumpectomy") to removal of the entire breast, chest wall musculature, and regional lymph nodes ("radical mastectomy"), with a number of options in between. Most women with early breast cancer do as well with lumpectomy plus radiation therapy as they do with removal of the entire breast; radical mastectomy has therefore become a much less common operation than it was in the past.

The majority of women diagnosed with invasive breast cancer undergo some kind of surgical treatment. There are several other forms of treatment that they may choose in addition to surgery, either as part of the initial treatment or in the event that the initial treatment fails to eradicate the cancer. These treatments

biopsy A tissue sample from a living person for diagnostic or (less commonly) for therapeutic purposes.

FAQ How big must a breast lump be to be detectable by mammogram or by self-examination?

The typical lump detected by mammogram is 5 mm (0.2 inches) in diameter; by self-exam it is 2 cm (0.8 inches). It is possible to detect smaller lumps with either technique, depending on experience, position and density of the lump, and the general texture of the breast.

Figure 3.14 Coping with mastectomy (A) Anita had a modified radical mastectomy without breast reconstruction. She normally wears a prosthesis. (B) Charlene had her left breast reconstructed immediately after a modified radical mastectomy. These and other breast cancer survivors are featured in the book, *Show Me: A Photo Collection of Breast Cancer Survivors' Lumpectomies, Mastectomies, Breast Reconstructions and Thoughts on Body Image.*

(A)
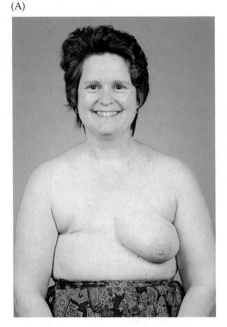

(B)
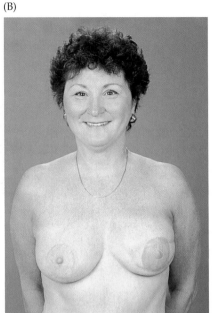

include chemotherapy and radiation therapy, as well as two treatments specific to breast cancer: hormone-blocking therapy with drugs like tamoxifen or letrozole, and immunotherapy with the drug Herceptin. The latter is an antibody that blocks a growth factor receptor present on the cells of some breast cancers. Chemotherapy in women of childbearing age can induce premature menopause, which may be temporary or permanent.

If a woman's breast must be removed, she has several options (**Figure 3.14**). She can simply live with the loss of the breast. She can use an external prosthesis to conceal the absence of the breast. She can also have reconstructive surgery, which can be done either at the time of the mastectomy or at a later date (American Cancer Society, 2007). Reconstructive surgery is not perfect: Even when it is done well, it leaves scars, numbness, and a lack of erogenous sensation in the area of the nipple. Still, many women experience a great deal of psychological benefit from the procedure.

One type of reconstructive surgery involves the insertion of a saline- or silicone gel-filled implant. This is a safe procedure that does not affect the chances that the cancer will recur. Any type of breast implant can cause problems at later times, such as capsular contraction (tightening of the connective tissue capsule that forms around the implant, leading to a distortion in its shape). During the 1980s and early 1990s it was widely believed that silicone gel implants were causing crippling autoimmune diseases. This belief led to successful lawsuits against the implants' manufacturer. A reanalysis of the data, however, found that the implants had no such effect (Tugwell et al., 2001).

Most Women with Breast Cancer Return to an Active Sex Life

Breast cancer and its treatment can affect a woman's sexuality in a number of ways (Kaplan, 1992). First, the grief and fear triggered by a cancer diagnosis are likely to put sexual feelings out of mind, at least for a while. Second, the side effects of cancer treatment may be so debilitating as to make sexual feelings and behaviors impossible. Third, some treatments may have hormonal or other effects

Personal Points of View

BOX 3.6   Is There Sex after Mastectomy?

Here are some postings from a now-defunct online bulletin board for women who have had mastectomies. They illustrate the variety of ways in which mastectomy may affect—or not affect—women's sex lives.

I had surgery for mastectomy 8 years ago. I have to admit at first it affected my sex life. I would not even undress in front of my husband. But now I have come to terms with it. My husband was very patient with me, he understood what I was going through, and I thank him for this. I would not consider having a recon-struction, as I think this could maybe stir up cancer all over again. [There is no evi-dence to support this concern.] I am happy to be able to live a full life—nothing has changed.

Hi, it has been 3 years since my [recon-structive surgery] and I'm still deathly afraid of dating. Always feeling like that moment will come when sex is a 'should I let him see?' I feel like my body looks like such a mess. Being a woman of color I heal differ-ently—I get keloid [a rubbery overgrowth of scar tissue that is more common among dark-skinned people]—so it looks worse on me. I was considering further surgery for correct alignment, but for what? Who looks? I'm a mess. My daughters encour-age me to date but I think it's over for me.

I had breast cancer 10 years ago and did not go for the reconstruction surgery. Since then I think I should have. I am a single woman at the age of 55 and when I meet some man and he is told that I had breast cancer it seems to end the relationship. My self-esteem has suffered due to the rejec-tions, as I still would like to have a mean-ingful relationship with someone some day.

There are men, special men who know what's important, who look past our scars to see who we are. Don't despair, they're out there—don't give up.

I am scheduled for a mastectomy with a reconstruction at the same time. My hus-band and I have been separated for 2 years, but he has been very supportive and loving during this time. I still feel very sexu-al even with all this stress and decision making. I often wonder how I am going to feel with a new breast. He says I am still beautiful without my hair and I will be beautiful with a reconstructed breast.

I had a mastectomy and I could not look in a mirror for years without crying, so I know how you feel. I chose tissue expanders, and now I have new perky breasts. Men turn around to look at me now, a 60-year-old with a body like a teenager! My insurance paid for it, and it has changed my life. Do it, you will never regret it.

---

that decrease physiological arousal or impair libido. Fourth, women who have been through breast cancer treatment, especially if they have had a mastectomy, may fear that they are no longer attractive to their current sex partners, or to potential partners (**Box 3.6**).

Healthcare providers who encourage women with breast cancer to discuss these issues are already helping to resolve them. Even in the days when radical mastectomy was the standard treatment for breast cancer, most women reported no change in key aspects of their sexuality, such as frequency of sex and overall sexual satisfaction (Morris et al., 1977). Women who have breast-conserving sur-geries such as lumpectomy are probably even less likely to report enduring prob-lems with their sex lives (Kiebert et al., 1991). Among women who elect to have breast reconstructive surgery, more than four out of five are very satisfied with the results and report an increase in sexual satisfaction after the reconstruction (Row-land et al., 1993). Of 800 women with breast cancer who were interviewed or quot-ed in one recent book, most spoke positively about their lives, including their sex lives (Peltason, 2008).

Summary

1. A woman's vulva (external genitalia) consists of the mons, clitoris, labia majora and minora (outer and inner lips), and the vaginal opening.

2. A woman's clitoris is a complex erectile organ, only a portion of which (the glans) is visible externally. Stimulation of the clitoris is a major source of sexual arousal in women.

3. The labia majora are two fat-padded folds of skin that form the sides of the vulva. The labia minora are two thinner, erotically sensitive folds of skin that enclose the vestibule—they fuse together at the front to form the hood of the clitoris. The vestibule is the space that encloses the entrance to the vagina and the opening of the urethra.

4. The female reproductive tract includes the vagina, cervix, uterus, and oviducts. At birth, the vagina is partially covered by a membrane (the hymen), which may be ruptured at first intercourse or earlier. The inner surface of the vagina is kept mildly acidic by the action of lactobacilli; frequent douching can disturb the microbial balance, leading to fungal infections (candidiasis) and other problems. The walls of the outer portion of the vagina are more muscular, and more sensitive, than the deeper portion. The G-spot is a controversial site of heightened erotic sensitivity on the front wall of the vagina.

5. The portion of the uterus that connects with the vagina is the cervix, which can be seen by inspection with a vaginal speculum or felt by inserting a finger into the back of the vagina. Cervical cancer is usually caused by sexually transmitted infection with the human papillomavirus; early detection of cancer by means of regular Pap tests has greatly reduced mortality from the disease.

6. The uterus serves as a pathway for sperm transport and also for implantation and development of the embryo; the alternation between these two functions constitutes the menstrual cycle. Medical conditions affecting the body of the uterus include fibroids, endometrial cancer, abnormal bleeding, uterine prolapse, and endometriosis. Hysterectomies (surgical removal of the uterus) may be done more frequently than necessary.

7. The oviducts bring ovum and sperm together for fertilization and transport the resulting embryo to the uterus. The ovaries are the female gonads; they produce ova and sex hormones.

8. A woman's secondary sexual characteristics include her breasts, which combine sexual functions (being a potential source of sexual arousal to herself and her partner) with a reproductive function (lactation). Breast cancer is the second most common cancer affecting women; risk factors include a family history of the disease, age, childlessness, alcohol use, and obesity. It can be detected early by mammography. Most breast lumps are not cancerous. Early-stage cancers can be treated without removing the entire breast. Some breast cancer treatments, especially chemotherapy and mastectomy, present a challenge to women's sexual self-image or sexual function, but most women who undergo them return to sexually active and rewarding relationships.

Discussion Questions

1. Do you think that genital cutting (circumcision) of girls, in countries where it is a traditional practice, should be permitted or banned? What role do you think the United States should take in this matter?

2. Historically, the clitoris has been largely ignored, and even today it may get skipped over in sex-ed classes. What do you think is the reason for this?

3. Women may change the appearance of their vulvas by hair removal, labial surgery, piercing, and so on. Do you see this as a creative form of self-expression, or as the unfortunate consequence of socially imposed ideals of beauty?

4. What was your reaction to reading about all the gynecological disorders described in this chapter? If you're a woman, did you feel hypochondriacal ("I probably have several of them right now"), bored ("I knew everything about them already"), or empowered ("I've learned things that will help me avoid or deal with them.")? If you're a man, did you find it interesting and useful to learn about women's bodies and their disorders, or not? Your instructor and the authors of this book welcome feedback from students.

Web Resources

American Cancer Society www.cancer.org

Endometriosis Association www.endometriosisassn.org

Gray, H. *Anatomy of the Human Body* www.bartleby.com/107

National Breast Cancer Coalition www.natlbcc.org

National Cancer Institute www.nci.nih.gov

National Cervical Cancer Coalition www.nccc-online.org

National Uterine Fibroids Association www.nuff.org

National Vaginitis Association (an industry-sponsored educational panel)
   http://www3.3m.com/pdas-nva/

National Women's Health Information Center www.4woman.gov

National Women's Health Network www.womenshealthnetwork.org

Ovarian Cancer National Alliance www.ovariancancer.org

Tostan (Senegal-based organization opposed to female circumcision) www.tostan.org

University of Delaware histology site (female reproductive system)
   www.udel.edu/Biology/Wags/histopage/colorpage/cfr/cfr.htm

Recommended Reading

American Cancer Society. (2001). *A breast cancer journey: Your personal guidebook.* American Cancer Society.

Angier, N. (1999). *Woman: An intimate geography.* Houghton Mifflin Company.

Boston Women's Health Book Collective. (2005). *Our bodies, ourselves: A new edition for a new era.* Touchstone.

Diree, W. (1998). *Desert flower: The extraordinary journey of a desert nomad.* William Morrow.

Ensler, E. (2007). *The vagina monologues.* Villard.

Gruenbaum, E. (2001). *The female circumcision controversy: An anthropological perspective.* University of Pennsylvania Press.

Komisaruk, B. R., Beyer-Flores, C., and Whipple, B. (2006). *The science of orgasm.* Johns Hopkins University Press.

Lightfoot-Klein, H. (2007). *Children's genitals under the knife: Social imperatives, secrecy, and shame.* BookSurge Publishing.

Love, S. M., and Lindsey, K. (2000). *Dr. Susan Love's breast book* (3rd rev. ed.). Perseus Books.

Northrup, C. (2006). *Women's bodies, women's wisdom: Creating physical and emotional health and healing* (3rd ed.). Bantam.

Peltason, R. (2008). *I am not my breast cancer: Women talk openly about love and sex, hair loss and weight gain, mothers and daughters, and being a woman with breast cancer.* William Morrow.

The male body in action, as captured by stop-motion pioneer Eadweard Muybridge (1830–1904).

Men's Bodies

Men's bodies produce and deliver gametes, called sperm, but men are not designed to carry a pregnancy, so their reproductive anatomy is simpler than that of women. Also, with the exception of some accessory glands and connecting tubing, men's sex organs are visible on the outside of their bodies, so they are relatively familiar. For that very reason, however, they can also be the cause of considerable anxiety: Many men are concerned—often needlessly—about the appearance and performance of their genitals. One of the purposes of this chapter is to normalize the diversity of men's sexual anatomy.

Perhaps because of the social emphasis on male sexuality as performance, there has been more research on male genitals than female genitals, particularly with regard to erection. We therefore take the opportunity of this chapter to discuss the mechanisms and neural control of penile erection, while bearing in mind that erection of the penis and the clitoris probably involve very similar biological processes.

The Male External Genitalia Are the Penis and Scrotum

The parts of the male reproductive system that can been seen from the outside are the penis and the scrotum (**Figure 4.1**). The testicles, or "balls," are indirectly visible as the twin bulges that give the scrotum its shape, but they are part of the internal male reproductive system.

Although men don't usually have the prominent pubic fat pad seen in women, they do have a similar distribution of pubic hair. The hair may extend upward in the midline toward the navel, or merge with the general body hair. Sparse hair usually covers the scrotum.

The Penis Combines Erotic, Reproductive, and Excretory Functions

Developmentally, the **penis** is equivalent to (or homologous with) the clitoris. In a functional sense, however, the penis corresponds to the clitoris, urethra, and vagina all rolled into one, because it is involved in sexual arousal, excretion of urine, and the transfer of gametes from the male to the female. It's no wonder men focus so much attention on the penis and are so gravely concerned when it fails to perform as expected.

The penis in its natural (i.e., uncircumcised) condition has three visible portions: a shaft; a head (or glans); and a foreskin. The **foreskin** is a loose, tubular fold of skin that partially or completely covers the glans. In some males—during

penis The erectile, erotically sensitive genital organ in males.

foreskin The loose skin that partially or completely covers the glans in males who have not been circumcised.

(A)

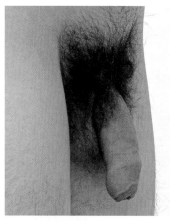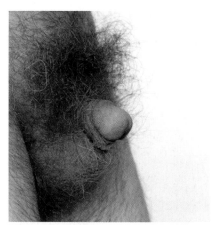

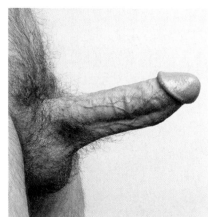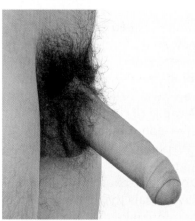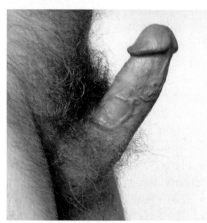

(B)

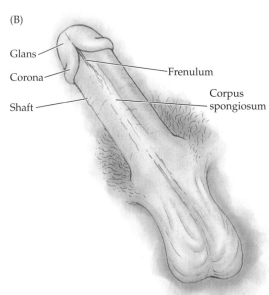

Glans

Corona

Shaft

Frenulum

Corpus
spongiosum

Figure 4.1 The male external genitalia (A) Three penises in the flaccid (above) and erect (below) states. The middle example is an uncircumcised penis; the other two are circumcised. (B) Drawing of an erect circumcised penis seen from below, showing the glans, corona, and frenulum—the most erotically sensitive portions of the penis. (See Web Activity 4.1.)

FAQ Can I get circumcised as an adult?

Absolutely—it's an outpatient procedure done by a urologist. But be sure that you want to be circumcised, because there's no going back. Expect a few days of discomfort and a ban on sex (even masturbation) for about a month.

childhood especially—the foreskin may extend well beyond the tip of the glans, so that urine passes through it as if through an extension of the urethra. In adult males, but not necessarily during childhood (see below), the foreskin can be readily pulled back to expose the glans. Male circumcision is the surgical removal of the foreskin (**Box 4.1**).

Cultural Diversity

BOX 4.1 Male Circumcision

Circumcision in men means the surgical removal of the prepuce or foreskin of the penis. Worldwide, about one-fourth of all men are circumcised. Circumcision is an ancient practice that is religiously prescribed for Muslims and Jews. It has also been practiced as a nonreligious tradition in many cultures (Figure A). Currently, about one-third of all male infants born in the United States are circumcised, but the circumcision rate is declining. It is more common among whites than among African Americans or Hispanics.

Circumcision, which is a fairly simple outpatient procedure (Figure B), offers some medical benefits, but also carries slight risks. Probably the most significant medical benefit is a tenfold or greater reduction in the incidence of urinary tract infections in infancy (McNeil, 2007). Worldwide, circumcision is associated with a lower risk of acquiring ulcerative sexually transmitted diseases and AIDS (Moses et al., 1998). Finally, circumcised men are less likely than uncircumcised men to become infected with a common sexually transmitted virus, human papillomavirus (HPV; see Chapter 17). This makes them less likely to develop penile cancer and it also offers their female partners some protection against cervical cancer (Castellsague et al., 2002).

Besides its medical benefits, circumcision facilitates hygiene. In uncircumcised men, a cheesy substance called **smegma** builds up under the foreskin, and can develop a rancid smell and taste—something that a man's sex partner may find unpleasant, especially when performing oral sex. This problem can easily be avoided, however, if a man washes under his foreskin whenever he takes a bath or shower.

The risks of circumcision include hemorrhage, infection, and—extremely rarely—damage to the penis. Some opponents of circumcision have suggested that the operation reduces the erotic sensitivity of the penis. However, one national study found that circumcision is associated with a lower incidence of sexual dysfunctions, especially erectile dysfunction (Laumann et al., 1997).

(A) Egyptian circumcision, ca. 2300 BCE

Because the procedure offers both benefits and risks, the American Academy of Pediatrics takes no stand on the matter: It suggests that parents make an informed choice in consultation with their doctors (American Academy of Pediatrics, 2007b). The Canadian Paediatric Society takes a somewhat more negative view: It "does not recommend" routine circumcision (Canadian Paediatric Society, 2004).

Some activist groups such as NOCIRC are ardently opposed to circumcision in infancy; they argue that the benefits are too limited to justify imposing the procedure on a child before he is old enough to decide for himself whether he wants to be circumcised or not.

Two other operations on the penis are practiced by certain ethnic groups. In some Polynesian cultures as well as in parts of the Philippines, a slit is made along the top of a boy's foreskin at or before puberty. This operation, called **superincision**, exposes the top surface of the glans and lets the foreskin droop below the glans, but no tissue is removed. Australian aborigines and some other cultures traditionally made a slit along the underside of the penis, exposing the urethra and allowing the glans and part of the shaft to flare outward, giving the penis a flat appearance. This procedure is called **subincision**. For those with strong stomachs, photographs of the procedure (as performed by U.S. body modification enthusiasts) can easily be found on the Internet.

smegma A whitish, greasy secretion that builds up under the prepuce of the penis or clitoris.

superincision An unusual form of male circumcision in which the upper part of the foreskin is incised but not removed.

subincision A form of male circumcision in which a cut is made along the underside of the penis, exposing the urethra.

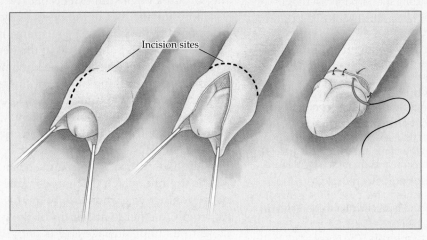

(B) Circumcision surgery

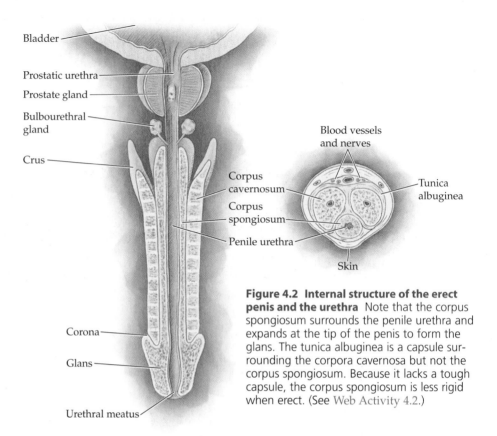

Figure 4.2 Internal structure of the erect penis and the urethra Note that the corpus spongiosum surrounds the penile urethra and expands at the tip of the penis to form the glans. The tunica albuginea is a capsule surrounding the corpora cavernosa but not the corpus spongiosum. Because it lacks a tough capsule, the corpus spongiosum is less rigid when erect. (See Web Activity 4.2.)

corpus cavernosum (pl. corpora cavernosa) Either of two elongated erectile structures within the penis or clitoris, which also extend backward into the pelvic floor.

corpus spongiosum A single midline erectile structure. In both sexes it fills the glans; in males it extends backward along the underside of the penis, surrounding the urethra.

tunica albuginea A fibrous capsule surrounding the corpora cavernosa.

glans The terminal knob of the clitoris or penis.

suspensory ligament A ligament that connects the root of the penis to the pubic symphysis.

penile bulb An expansion of the corpus spongiosum at the root of the penis.

ischiocavernosus muscle One of the muscles that attaches to the internal portions of the penis and clitoris. It assists with erection and (in men) ejaculation.

bulbospongiosus muscle A muscle that attaches to the base of the penis or clitoris and assists with erection and (in men) ejaculation.

urethral meatus The opening at the tip of the penis (in males) or in front of the vagina (in females).

The shaft of the penis contains three erectile structures (**Figure 4.2**): two **corpora cavernosa**, which lie side by side and account for the bulk of the penis's erectile capacity, and a single **corpus spongiosum**, which lies at the midline near the undersurface of the penis. The corpora cavernosa, but not the corpus spongiosum, are surrounded by a tough connective-tissue capsule called the **tunica albuginea**, which limits the expansion of the corpora cavernosa during erection.

The corpus spongiosum extends from the shaft into the **glans**, where it balloons out and fills the entire volume of the glans. Both the corpora cavernosa and the corpus spongiosum extend backward into the body under the pubic symphysis, forming the root of the penis, which is about 5 cm (2 inches) long. The root is attached to the pubis via a **suspensory ligament**.

At the inner end of the root of the penis, the corpus spongiosum expands into a rounded mass of erectile tissue known as the **penile bulb**. The two corpora cavernosa diverge, forming two crura similar to those of a woman's clitoris. As in the clitoris, there are two muscles associated with the root of the penis—the **ischiocavernosus** and **bulbospongiosus** muscles. These muscles are considerably larger in males, and they assist with erection of the penis and with ejaculation. The bulbospongiosus muscle is an integral part of the external anal sphincter muscle; thus the anal sphincter goes into spasm during ejaculation.

The urethra, which discharges urine from the bladder and semen from internal reproductive glands (see below), enters the root of the penis and traverses its length to emerge at the tip of the glans. Within the penis, the urethra runs close to its undersurface and is entirely contained within the corpus spongiosum. The opening of the urethra, which is slit-like in shape, is known as the **urethral meatus**.

The shaft of the penis contains other structures, most notably nerves and blood vessels that play an important role in sexual arousal and erection. The deep structures of the penile shaft are enclosed in a tough, fibrous sheath of connective tissue, or **fascia**. The skin of the penis is hairless and only loosely attached to the underlying fascia.

The glans has a rim, or **corona**, that encircles the penis. On the undersurface of the penis the corona comes closer to the tip of the glans than on its upper surface. In this area lies a loose strip of skin named the **frenulum** that runs between the glans and the shaft (see Figure 4.1). Although stimulation anywhere on the penis can be sexually arousing, the corona and the frenulum are usually the most erotically sensitive regions.

The size of the penis—both in the flaccid and erect states—varies considerably among men. A non-pornographic Web site illustrates some of this diversity and shows the process of erection (see Web Resources at the end of this chapter). Some men are concerned about the size of their penis, but size variations rarely have any practical effect on sexual performance (**Box 4.2**).

Penis piercings are becoming increasingly popular. Men considering such a piercing should carefully review the potential problems, which (depending on the exact site) can include scarring, damage to erectile tissue, nerve damage, interference with urination, and serious infections such as hepatitis and HIV (Grossman, 2008). Selection of an experienced practitioner who uses scrupulous sanitary techniques is paramount.

Considering the demands that may be placed on it, the penis is a remarkably hardy organ. Aside from erectile dysfunction (see Chapter 16) and sexually transmitted infections (see Chapter 17), the penis is subject to only a few medical problems that occur at all frequently:

■ **Balanitis** is inflammation of the glans, caused by poor hygiene and/or infection. It is quite common in uncircumcised men. Treatment involves regular cleaning and antibiotics as appropriate.

■ **Phimosis** is the inability to retract the foreskin far enough to expose the glans. This is the normal condition in male babies, and it persists in many boys into the teen years. There is no need to treat it unless the flow of urine is affected. Phimosis may also develop as a new condition in adults, especially in association with balanitis, in which case surgical treatment may be required.

■ **Paraphimosis** is the entrapment of a retracted foreskin behind the corona of the glans. It can occur as a result of efforts to retract a phimotic foreskin. Paraphimosis is an emergency condition because it can lead to necrosis (tissue death) of the glans. It can usually be reversed without circumcision, but later circumcision is recommended to prevent recurrence.

■ **Peyronie's disease** is an unnatural curvature of the erect penis caused by scar formation in the capsule of the corpora cavernosa—possibly as a late consequence of trauma. (Many men have some natural curvature in their penis.) Peyronie's disease can cause pain or even prevent penetrative sex. Surgical treatments are available.

Penile cancer is rare: It strikes about 1200 men in the United States per year and causes about 300 deaths. Infection with certain types of human papillomavirus (HPV—see Chapter 17) is an important factor predisposing men to penile cancer. Caught early, penile cancer can be treated by fairly minor surgical procedures. If the cancer has invaded the deep structures of the penis, however, part or all of the organ may have to be amputated. It may surprise you to learn that many men

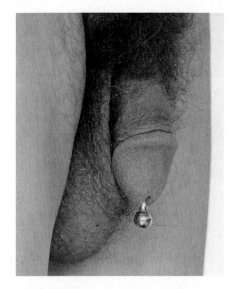

A "Prince Albert" piercing enters the glans through or near the frenulum and exits via the urethra.

fascia A tough sheet or sheath of connective tissue.

corona The rim of the glans of the penis.

frenulum A strip of loose skin on the underside of the penis, running between the glans and the shaft.

balanitis Inflammation of the glans of the penis.

phimosis A tightening of the foreskin, preventing its retraction from the glans.

paraphimosis Entrapment of the retracted foreskin behind the corona.

Peyronie's disease Pathological curvature of the penis.

Research Highlights

BOX 4.2   How Big Should a Penis Be?

Many men fear that they are underendowed—specifically, that their penises are too small to arouse or physically satisfy their partners or that their small size will provoke ridicule from their peers. But because penises—especially erect ones—are rarely seen, it's possible that men develop erroneous ideas about the average or most desirable size of the penis. These ideas could come from watching pornography, for example.

Let's take a look at some objective data. The most reliable study of penis size is probably one published in 1996 by three urologists at San Francisco General Hospital (Wessells et al., 1996b). They measured the flaccid and erect penises of 80 physically normal men. They first measured along the top surface of the flaccid penis, from the skin crease between the penis and the abdominal wall to the tip of the penis. They got a mean length of 8.9 cm (3.5 inches), with a standard deviation of ±2.4 cm (±0.9 inches). Measuring the erect penis the same way, they got a mean length of 12.9 ±2.9 cm (5.1 ±1.1 inches). By pushing the end of the tape measure into the pubic fat pad until it rested against the pubic symphysis, they got a mean "functional erect length" of 15.7 ±2.6 cm (6.2 ±1.0 inches). In two-thirds of the men, the penis's erect length was within 2.6 cm (1 inch) of this mean length. Numerous other studies confirm that 15 cm (6 inches) is about the average length (Templer, 2002).

The San Francisco researchers found that the mean circumference of the shaft of the erect penis was 12.3 ±1.3 cm (4.8 ±0.5 inches). They found no correlation between the length of a man's penis when flaccid and the same penis when erect. However, the length of a man's flaccid penis when stretched out was approximately the length of the same penis when erect.

These data may help male readers judge their own anatomy. It is important, though, to realize that a penis smaller than the range just described is still likely to work just fine in most sexual situations. In vaginal penetration, the dimensions of the penis are pretty much irrelevant, because the elasticity of the vaginal wall makes it a "one-size-fits-all" organ. In anal penetration, a small penis may actually be an advantage. The same is true for oral penetration, since a long penis may cause gagging.

In a large Internet survey, UCLA researchers found that only 55% of straight men were satisfied with the size of their penis, but 84% of straight women were satisfied with the size of their partner's penis, and only 14% wanted it larger (Lever et al., 2006). Thus, unless a lot of men with small penises are lacking partners altogether, many men may be suffering needless anxiety about the adequacy of their penis.

There exists a small industry devoted to the surgical augmentation of the penis. The penis may be lengthened by cutting the suspensory ligament (see figure), followed by many weeks of traction (hanging weights from the penis). This procedure causes the penis to protrude farther from the body. The procedure lengthens only the flaccid penis, however; the erect penis length is not affected. It also drags hairy skin onto the shaft of the penis, which may be considered unattractive.

The girth of the penis can be increased by fat injections, or by transplanting slabs of fatty tissue from the buttocks under the skin of the penis. The procedure leaves visible scars, and the penis often comes to look lumpy or otherwise abnormal over time.

At least one man has died from complications of penis enlargement surgery. Men who undergo the surgery are, on average, dissatisfied with the outcome, and they do not experience improved sex lives afterward (Wessells et al., 1996a; Klein, 1999; Li et al., 2006). Men who are obsessively concerned about the size of their penis can be helped by reassurance or psychotherapy (Wylie & Eardley, 2007).

Some men complain that their flaccid penis retracts inside their bodies. This can be a consequence of obesity: The pubic fat pad may become so thick that the flaccid penis is barely long enough to protrude through it. Weight loss or liposuction may alleviate this problem (Adham et al., 2000). Psychological factors may also be at work, however. In fact, epidemics of delusional penile retraction sweep across some Asian countries (especially southern China) from time to time (Cheng, 1997). This condition is known as **koro**, and its victims attach clamps, strings, and other devices to the penis to prevent its complete disappearance, which they are convinced will be accompanied by their own death.

koro A social panic based on the fear that the penis will retract and disappear, causing death.

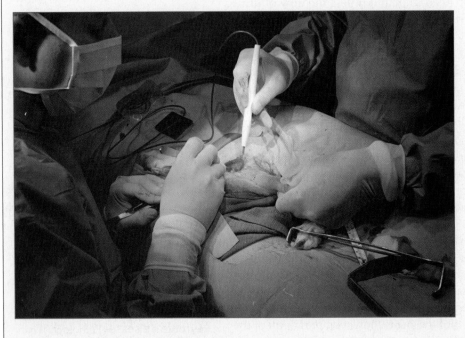

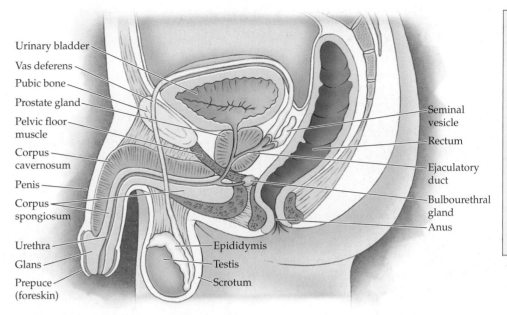

Urinary bladder
Vas deferens
Pubic bone
Prostate gland
Pelvic floor muscle
Corpus cavernosum
Penis
Corpus spongiosum
Urethra
Glans
Prepuce (foreskin)

Seminal vesicle
Rectum
Ejaculatory duct
Bulbourethral gland
Anus
Epididymis
Testis
Scrotum

Figure 4.3 The male reproductive tract Note how the prostate gland surrounds the urethra as it exits the bladder. Enlargement of the prostate can interfere with urination. (See Web Activity 4.3.)

who have had their penis removed develop the ability to experience orgasm through stimulation of nearby areas of skin.

The Scrotum Regulates the Temperature of the Testicles

The **scrotum** or scrotal sac (**Figure 4.3**) is a loose bag of skin that hangs down behind the penis and contains the two testicles. In adult men it is lightly covered with hair, and it possesses numerous sweat glands that help to regulate the temperature of the scrotal contents. Stimulation of the scrotal skin is sexually arousing in most men, though not to the same degree as the most sensitive areas of the penis. Underneath the scrotal skin lies a sheetlike smooth muscle known as the **dartos**. Contraction of the dartos in response to cold (and also during sexual arousal—especially near orgasm) thickens the scrotal skin and causes it to become wrinkled. This makes the skin a more effective insulator and also brings the testicles closer to the body, warming them.

The Testes Produce Sperm and Sex Hormones

The male internal sex organs (see Figure 4.3) have two functions that are similar to those of the corresponding female organs: They produce gametes (**sperm**) and secrete sex hormones. As in women, these two tasks are accomplished by the gonads, which in men are called **testicles** or **testes.** Men do not become pregnant, and correspondingly they lack any structures corresponding to the uterus or oviducts. However, men do need to store large numbers of sperm, mix them with other secretions, and deliver the resulting **semen** to the urethral meatus for ejaculation. These functions require a number of structures, including several specialized glands and assorted pieces of tubing to connect everything together.

The testicles are twin egg-shaped structures that can easily be seen or felt within the scrotal sac (**Figure 4.4**). The testicles are not completely symmetrical: One (usually the left) hangs lower, and one (usually the right) is slightly larger. One

scrotum The sac behind the penis that contains the testicles.

dartos A sheet of smooth muscle underlying the skin of the scrotum, which when contracted causes the skin to become thick and wrinkled.

sperm A male gamete, produced in the testis.

testicle or testis The male gonad: one of the two glands within the scrotum that produce sperm and secrete sex steroids.

semen The fluid, containing sperm and a variety of chemical compounds, that is ejaculated from the penis at male sexual climax.

epididymis (pl. epididymides) A structure attached to each testis through which sperm must pass before entering the vas deferens.

spermatic cord Either of two bilateral bundles of structures, including the vas deferens, blood vessels, and the cremaster muscle, that pass through the inguinal canal to the testis.

inguinal canal A short canal passing through the abdominal wall in the region of the groin in males.

cremaster muscle A striated muscle that wraps around the spermatic cord and the testis.

vas deferens (pl. vasa deferentia) Either of the two bilateral ducts that convey sperm from the epididymis to the ejaculatory duct.

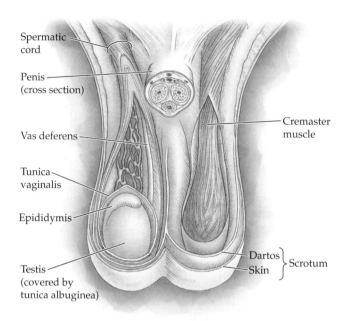

Figure 4.4 The scrotum and its contents (See Web Activity 4.4.)

well-respected psychologist has reported that men with a larger right testicle score well on "masculine" cognitive tests, while men with a larger left testicle score well on "feminine" tests (Kimura, 1994).

Each testicle weighs about 10 to 15 g (0.4 to 0.5 ounces) and lies within a protective capsule. Behind each testis is an **epididymis**, through which sperm pass after leaving the testis. The testis and epididymis can easily be moved around within the scrotum because they lie within a membranous sac, which, developmentally speaking, is an extension of the abdominal cavity, though no longer connected to it after birth.

Before considering the structure of the testis, let's take a look at the **spermatic cord**. This is a bundle of structures that connect the testis with organ systems within the abdominal cavity. It is the testis's "lifeline." The spermatic cord runs through a 4-cm (1.5 inch) long canal—the **inguinal canal**—that passes through the abdominal wall in the region of the groin.

The spermatic cord has a sheetlike covering of connective tissue, and a layer of striated muscle tissue known as the **cremaster muscle**. When it reaches the testicle, the cremaster muscle forms a sling around it. The cremaster contracts automatically in response to cold, pulling the testis toward the body and thus, like the dartos muscle, helping to regulate the temperature of the testis.

Within the spermatic cord runs the **vas deferens**, the tube that carries mature sperm away from the epididymis. In addition, the spermatic cord contains arteries, veins, and nerves that supply the testicle. The arteries and veins run close to each other, an arrangement that facilitates the transfer of heat from the arterial to the venous circulation. This helps keep the temperature of the testicle below the temperature of the remainder of the body.

With all these temperature-regulating elements, it's no surprise to learn that the production of sperm by the human testis requires a specific temperature range, which is 4° to 7°C (7° to 12°F) below core body temperature. This is the reason the testicles migrate out of the abdomen into the scrotum during prenatal development (see Chapter 6). Increasing the temperature of the testes to core body temperature for prolonged periods decreases a man's sperm count. Increased temperature does not affect the other function of the testes—hormone production—to any significant extent.

The internal structure of the testis (**Figure 4.5**) is dominated by the **seminiferous tubules**, a set of about a thousand fine, highly convoluted tubes that occupy the lobes of the testis. The seminiferous tubules are the site of sperm production, or **spermatogenesis**. Unlike oocytes, which are present in the ovaries when a girl is born, sperm are not found in the testes until puberty, when precursor cells begin dividing. The resulting daughter cells continue to divide while embedded within **Sertoli cells** that line the seminiferous tubules.

An important feature of sperm development (as well as ovum development in females) is meiosis. This is the sequence of two specialized cell divisions that halves the number of chromosomes from 46 (the diploid number characteristic of most human cells) to 23 (the haploid number). Meiosis also involves genetic recombination—a shuffling of the DNA that ensures that each gamete is genetically unique (see Chapter 2). Once meiosis is complete, the resulting cells develop the highly specialized structure that characterizes mature sperm.

The developmental sequence that leads from a stem cell to a finished sperm takes 64 days. Of course, huge numbers of sperm are developing simultaneously. The average man produces something like 150 million sperm per day—day after day for several decades. Out of this astronomical total, perhaps two or three sperm will be lucky enough to contribute their genes to the next generation!

seminiferous tubules Convoluted microscopic tubes within the testis; the site of spermatogenesis.

spermatogenesis The production of sperm.

Sertoli cell A type of cell within the seminiferous tubules that nurtures developing sperm and secretes hormones.

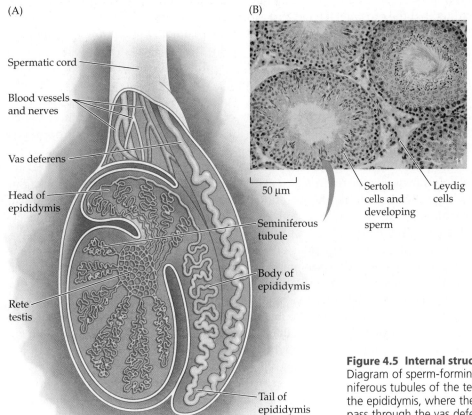

(A)

Spermatic cord

Blood vessels and nerves

Vas deferens

Head of epididymis

Rete testis

Seminiferous tubule

Body of epididymis

Tail of epididymis

(B)

50 μm

Sertoli cells and developing sperm

Leydig cells

Figure 4.5 Internal structure of the testis and epididymis (A) Diagram of sperm-forming pathway. Sperm initially develop in the seminiferous tubules of the testis, and then pass through the rete testis to the epididymis, where they mature further and are stored. They then pass through the vas deferens to the urethra. (B) Cross section of seminiferous tubules. Each tubule measures about 50 micrometers in diameter. The sperm develop while embedded in the cells lining the tubules (Sertoli cells). The cells scattered between the tubules (Leydig cells) secrete sex hormones. (See Web Activity 4.5.)

Besides assisting the process of spermatogenesis, the Sertoli cells produce peptide hormones. (A peptide is a chain of several amino acids—similar to a protein but shorter; see Chapter 5.) One of these hormones plays a role in embryonic sex determination; the other hormones help regulate testicular function in adult men. The spaces between the seminiferous tubules are occupied by **Leydig cells** (also called interstitial cells), which secrete steroid hormones—mainly testosterone. The Leydig cells also secrete peptide hormones that control the process of spermatogenesis. We'll examine the roles of these various testicular hormones in Chapters 5 and 6.

After leaving the seminiferous tubules, the sperm pass through a network of spaces known as the **rete testis** and then enter the epididymis. The epididymis has the shape of the letter C and is attached to the back surface of the testis. It is actually formed by a single, but extremely convoluted, tubule. Sperm spend about a week traversing this tubule, during which time they become about a hundredfold more concentrated. They also mature functionally, gaining the capacity for forward motion. Still, this swimming motion is sluggish and does not contribute to the sperm's movement along the reproductive tract.

A number of medical conditions can affect the testicles, of which the most serious is testicular cancer (**Box 4.3**).

Other Glands Contribute Their Secretions to the Semen

The sperm pass from the epididymis into the adjoining vas deferens. Each vas passes up through the spermatic cord into the abdomen, past the bladder, and down toward the prostate gland (see Figure 4.3). As it enters the prostate, each vas joins with a short duct that adds the secretions of the seminal vesicle (see below) on that side; thereafter, the vas changes its name to the **ejaculatory duct**. While still within the prostate, the left and right ejaculatory ducts join the urethra, which conveys urine from the bladder. From that junction on, the urethra serves for the passage of both urine and semen.

The left and right vasa, as well as the epididymis, are storage reservoirs for mature sperm, which have been concentrated by the epididymis into a pastelike mass. Further progress of the sperm occurs not by fluid flow or by their own motility, but by muscular contractions of the walls of the vas, each of which squeezes a small volume of sperm into the urethra. These contractions occur just before ejaculation.

The **prostate gland** lies in the midline immediately below the bladder. It completely surrounds the urethra as it exits the bladder. The normal prostate is slightly larger than a walnut. The secretion of the prostate is a cloudy alkaline fluid; at ejaculation, this fluid is pumped into the urethra by the contraction of muscle fibers within the gland.

Because the prostate gland is out of sight, and because the role of its secretions (see below) is not widely known, it comes to most people's attention only when it malfunctions, which it does all too commonly, especially in old age (**Box 4.4**).

The **seminal vesicles** are two small glands that lie behind the bladder, close to the vasa deferentia. Their name is misleading: The seminal vesicles are not storage areas for semen, but glands that add their secretions to the semen. As with the prostate gland, the fluid secreted by the seminal vesicles is expelled from the glands at ejaculation.

The last glands in this collection are the **bulbourethral glands**. These two pea-sized glands lie below the prostate gland, and their secretion—a clear mucous fluid—is expelled into the urethra. In many men, secretion from the bulbourethral glands begins early during sexual arousal and can be seen as a drop or two of slippery liquid that appears at the urethral meatus sometime between erection and ejaculation; hence its colloquial name, "pre-cum."

Leydig cells Cells located between the seminiferous tubules in the testis that secrete steroids. Also called interstitial cells.

rete testis A network of spaces between the testis and epididymis, through which sperm must pass.

ejaculatory duct Either of the two bilateral ducts formed by the junction of the vas deferens and the duct of the seminal vesicle. The ejaculatory ducts empty into the urethra within the prostate.

prostate gland A single gland at the base of the bladder, surrounding the urethra; its secretions are a component of semen.

seminal vesicles Two glands situated to either side of the prostate; their secretions are a component of semen.

bulbourethral glands Two small glands near the root of the penis whose secretions ("pre-cum") may appear at the urethral opening during sexual arousal prior to ejaculation. Also known as Cowper's glands.

Sexual Health

BOX 4.3 Disorders of the Testicles

Testicular cancer strikes about 7400 men in the United States annually, but only about 400 of these men die of the disease. In other words, it is usually a curable condition.

Testicular cancer most commonly strikes men in their twenties or thirties. Some very well-known young men, including cyclist Lance Armstrong (Figure A), figure skater Scott Hamilton, and comedian Tom Green have faced

(A) Cyclist Lance Armstrong won the Tour de France seven times, and fathered three children, after being diagnosed with and treated for testicular cancer that had spread to his lungs and brain.

the disease. Testicular cancer can strike at any age, however. Risk factors for testicular cancer include a history of undescended testicles, other developmental abnormalities of the testes, and Klinefelter's syndrome (see Chapter 6). Testicular cancer is usually diagnosed when the individual, or his healthcare provider, notices a lump or an increase in size in one testicle. There may also be a sudden accumulation of fluid in the scrotum, pain in the testicle, or an

ache or heaviness in the lower abdomen, groin, or scrotum. Several diagnostic tests may strengthen the suspicion that a testicular lump is cancer, but the definitive diagnosis is made on the basis of a biopsy, which usually involves removing the entire affected testis (**orchiectomy**) through an incision in the groin.

By itself, the removal of one testis is of no great consequence, since the remaining testis can compensate. Unfortunately, further treatments—lymph node dissection, radiation, or chemotherapy—may be necessary, and these have the potential to interfere with erectile function and sperm production. Men with testicular cancer who may want to father children in the future have the option of depositing semen samples in a sperm bank before treatment. Lance Armstrong used this method and has fathered three children since his diagnosis.

Other noncancerous conditions can affect the testicles and nearby structures:

- **Orchitis** is an inflammation and swelling of a testicle, caused by infection with a variety of organisms, some of which may be sexually transmitted.
- **Epididymitis** is an inflammation of the epididymis, caused by trauma or by infection with *E. coli* or any of a number of sexually transmitted organisms. It is seen most commonly in sexually active young men.
- A **varicocele** is an enlargement of the veins that drain the testicles, causing the spermatic cord to feel like a "bag of worms." This condition may impair fertility, but it can be surgically corrected.
- A **hydrocele** is a collection of fluid in the membrane-lined space surrounding one testicle. It is not dangerous, but can cause discomfort. It can be drained or surgically corrected.
- Testicular torsion is a twisting of a testicle and its spermatic cord, which cuts off the testicle's blood supply. Torsion causes sudden and severe pain; it must be treated within a few hours, or the affected testis may die from the lack of blood.

Regular testicular self-examination (Figure B) is recommended for men at increased risk of

testicular cancer (see above). There are no objective data about its value for men of average risk, but the exam is simple enough and might be lifesaving.

To do the exam, choose a warm location such as the shower, so that the scrotal sac is relaxed. Roll each testicle in turn between thumb and fingers. The surface of the testicle is usually fairly smooth, and the epididymis can be felt as a soft, elongated structure behind and above each testicle. One testicle is normally slightly larger than the other, but it is a matter of concern if one testicle has enlarged from the last time you examined it. Also feel for any lumps, rounded or irregular masses, and changes in the consistency of a testicle, or tender areas. None of these signs are definitive indicators of cancer—in fact, early testicular cancers are often painless—but they merit a visit to your doctor.

While doing a testicular self-examination it is a good idea to examine the remainder of the genital area—especially the penis—for sores, warts, or other lesions that could be caused by a sexually transmitted disease or other condition needing medical attention.

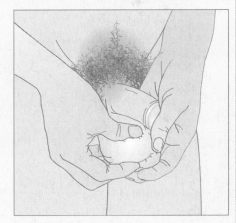

(B) Testicular self-examination

orchiectomy Surgical removal of one or both testicles.

orchitis Inflammation of a testicle.

epididymitis Inflammation of the epididymis.

varicocele Enlargement of the veins that drain the testis.

hydrocele A collection of fluid around a testicle.

Sexual Health

BOX 4.4 Disorders of the Prostate Gland

A healthcare provider can check the condition of the prostate gland by inserting a gloved finger into the anus and feeling the gland through the front surface of the rectum (Figure A). In this way, the provider can assess whether the prostate gland is tender, enlarged, or contains lumps. By massaging the gland, the provider can express a sample of prostatic fluid from the urethra, which can be examined for evidence of prostate disease. A digital rectal exam should be part of an annual health checkup—especially

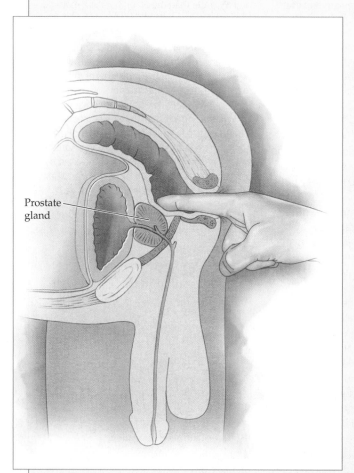

Prostate gland

(A) A digital rectal exam allows the prostate gland to be palpated.

Prostatitis—inflammation of the prostate gland—is a disorder that affects men of all ages. It may be acute or chronic. Acute prostatitis may be caused by infection with *E. coli* or other microorganisms that invade the prostate gland via urine. Since urine is normally sterile, a urinary tract infection must precede or coexist with the prostatitis. The symptoms are pain during ejaculation and urination, ongoing pain in the pelvic region or lower back, and a fever. The condition usually responds to antibiotics.

Chronic prostatitis is a puzzling and difficult-to-treat condition whose symptoms resemble acute prostatitis but which can last for months or years; it may not respond to antibiotics (Schaeffer, 2004). Many men diagnosed with chronic prostatitis actually have no inflammation of their prostate glands, so the term **chronic pelvic pain syndrome** is coming into use as an alternative diagnostic term, especially where there is no demonstrable infection.

Benign prostatic hypertrophy or "enlarged prostate" is a common disorder of older men. The prostate gland grows rapidly at puberty, and then continues to grow slowly throughout adult life. Because the prostate gland lies within a tight capsule, its growth may eventually constrict the urethra where it passes through the gland (Figure B). The term "benign" means that the condition is not cancerous, but it is hardly benign in the popular sense of the word. As the urethra becomes constricted, the bladder has to work harder to expel urine, and the walls of the bladder become thickened and irritable.

More than half of all men in their sixties, and as many as 90% of men in their seventies and beyond, experience chronic urinary problems—weak urine flow, urgency and frequency of urination, and leakage—as a result of this condition. The symptoms may be relieved with a testosterone-blocking drug, finasteride (Proscar), or other drugs, but eventually surgical removal of part of the prostate is often needed. This can be done through the urethra. Unfortunately, the operation can damage the urethral sphincter at the base of the bladder; if so, the man may experience retrograde ejaculation—the ejaculate passes backward into the bladder and is later voided in the urine. This renders the man infertile. Orgasm is still experienced, but its intensity may be reduced.

Prostate cancer is the most common non-skin cancer among American men: Nearly 220,000 cases are diagnosed yearly. One in six men will be diagnosed with prostate cancer in his lifetime, making this condition more common than breast cancer in women. The disease causes about 27,000 deaths annually, which puts it second only to lung cancer in terms of cancer mortality for men. Still, as you can deduce from the numbers, most men who get prostate cancer don't die of it.

The average age at diagnosis is 70 years, and African-American men are much more likely than white men to develop prostate cancer and to die of it. Aside from age and race, a family history of the disease and (possibly) a high-fat diet increase the risk.

The early symptoms of prostate cancer are generally similar to those of benign prostatic hypertrophy—namely, problems with urination. There may also be blood in the urine or semen and pain in the lower back, hips, or upper thighs. Prostate cancer may also be detected by a routine digital rectal exam or by the presence of abnormally high levels of a prostate-derived protein, **prostate-specific antigen (PSA)**, in the blood (National Cancer Institute, 2004). It is not known whether the benefits of routine screening (detecting life-threatening cancers early enough to cure them) outweigh the risks (unnecessary surgery and harmful side effects) (National Cancer Institute, 2008b).

for older men. Men can do a digital examination of their own prostate gland, but it's a bit of a gymnastic feat.

BOX 4.4 (continued)

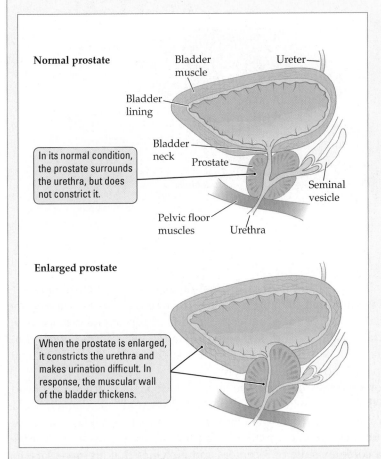

Normal prostate

In its normal condition, the prostate surrounds the urethra, but does not constrict it.

Bladder muscle
Ureter
Bladder lining
Bladder neck
Prostate
Seminal vesicle
Pelvic floor muscles
Urethra

Enlarged prostate

When the prostate is enlarged, it constricts the urethra and makes urination difficult. In response, the muscular wall of the bladder thickens.

(B) Enlarged prostate (See Web Activity 4.6.)

If treatment is undertaken, a common option is **radical prostatectomy**, which means surgical removal of the entire gland plus nearby lymph nodes. Transurethral resection may resolve urinary problems caused by prostate cancer, but it will not generally eliminate the cancer. Radiation therapy can be administered either as an alternative to surgery or as a supplemental treatment. Testosterone-blocking drugs may be also be used. If the cancer is slow-growing, doctors may recommend no treatment but frequent monitoring ("watchful waiting").

The sexual side effects of treatments for prostate cancer may be very significant. Radical prostatectomy puts a permanent end to ejaculation because most of the volume of the normal ejaculate is the secretion of the prostate gland and the adjacent seminal vesicles, whose ducts run through the prostate gland. It is also likely to cause erectile dysfunction because the autonomic nerves that supply the erectile tissue run through the prostate gland. Some surgical procedures are specifically designed to leave the nerves in place, but nerve-sparing surgery is no guarantee that normal erectile function will be preserved. Although there are news stories almost every year about new ways of destroying the prostate gland that don't cause erectile dysfunction, the truth is that this side effect is common (at least as a temporary effect) no matter how the procedure is done. Sildenafil (Viagra) can improve erectile performance after prostatectomy, but only if the nerves and blood vessels supplying the penis are spared (Feng et al., 2000).

If hormonal treatment is used, the man will usually experience a loss of libido and an impairment of erectile function, along with other possible side effects. Since hormonal treatment is often continued for as long as it is effective in keeping the cancer in check, a man who elects this form of treatment must pay a heavy price in terms of his sex life.

prostatitis Inflammation of the prostate gland; may be acute or chronic.

chronic pelvic pain syndrome An alternative, more-inclusive term for chronic prostatitis.

benign prostatic hypertrophy An enlarged but noncancerous prostate gland.

prostate cancer Cancer of the prostate gland.

prostate-specific antigen (PSA) An antigen characteristic of cells of the prostate gland, whose presence at high levels in the blood is suggestive of, but not diagnostic of, prostate cancer.

radical prostatectomy Surgical removal of the entire prostate gland and local lymph nodes.

Bulbourethral secretions do not contain sperm. Nevertheless, they can become mixed with sperm remaining in the urethra from a previous ejaculation. This happens chiefly when a man has sex for a second time without urinating between times. In those circumstances, remnants of the first ejaculate that have remained behind in the urethra get mixed in with the bulbourethral secretions from the second episode. This is of no consequence unless the man is practicing the "withdrawal method" of contraception (withdrawing his penis from his partner's vagina before he ejaculates—see Chapter 12). In that case, he may unwittingly impregnate his partner before he withdraws. "Pre-cum" can also contain disease organisms, and can therefore be responsible for the spread of sexually transmitted diseases.

Figure 4.6 Human sperm Electron micrographic view of a single spermatozoon, showing the acrosome, nucleus, midpiece, and part of the flagellum (tail).

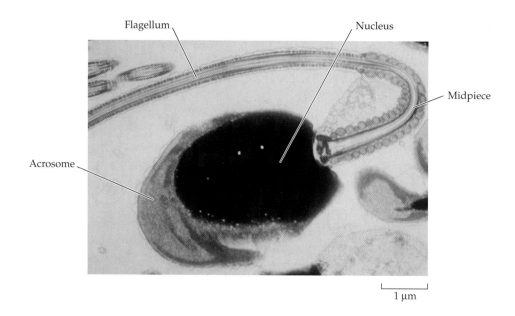

Flagellum

Nucleus

Midpiece

Acrosome

1 μm

What Is Semen?

Semen or seminal fluid (or "cum" in colloquial English) is the thick, cloudy, off-white liquid that is ejaculated from the male urethra at sexual climax. The volume of a single ejaculate usually ranges between 2 and 5 ml (up to one teaspoonful). The most important component of semen is, of course, the sperm (**Figure 4.6**). Each milliliter of semen contains 50 to 150 million sperm, and a normal ejaculate contains between 100 and 700 million sperm.

Each sperm (or spermatozoon) has the familiar tadpole-like structure: a head, containing the cell's nucleus with its all-important DNA, and a motile tail, or **flagellum**, which propels the spermatozoon forward. When we look a little more closely, two other structures become apparent. Capping the nucleus is an **acrosome**, which contains a complex suite of receptors and enzymes that are necessary for successful fertilization of an ovum (see Chapter 11). The part of the tail nearest to the head is slightly thicker than the remainder of the tail and is called the **midpiece**. This section contains mitochondria tightly wound around the tail in a spiral manner. These mitochondria supply chemical energy for propulsion of the sperm.

In spite of the importance of the sperm, they occupy an insignificant proportion (around 1%) of the volume of the semen (**Figure 4.7**). The remainder, called **seminal plasma**, is a mixture of the secretions of the seminal vesicles (about 70% of the total volume) and the prostate gland (about 30%), plus small contributions from the epididymis and the bulbourethral glands. Among the components of seminal plasma are water and salts, plus the following:

- The sugar **fructose**, which the sperm use as an energy source.
- Buffers that keep the pH of the semen alkaline (between about 7.2 and 7.8). These buffers protect the sperm from the acidic environment encountered if they are deposited in the vagina.
- **Fibrinogen**, a protein that can be broken down enzymatically to produce the coagulating agent **fibrin**.
- Calcium binders such as citric acid that prevent premature coagulation of the semen.
- Enzymes derived from the prostate gland. These include an enzyme that converts fibrinogen to fibrin, causing rapid coagulation of the ejaculated

flagellum A whip-like fiber extending from a spermatozoon or other cell that confers motility.

acrosome A structure at the front of a sperm that contains enzymes and receptors required for penetration of the zona pellucida of an ovum.

midpiece The portion of the tail of a sperm that is closest to the head, containing mitochondria.

seminal plasma The noncellular constituents of semen.

fructose A simple sugar (monosaccharide) present in semen.

fibrinogen The precursor to fibrin.

fibrin A protein responsible for the coagulation of body fluids.

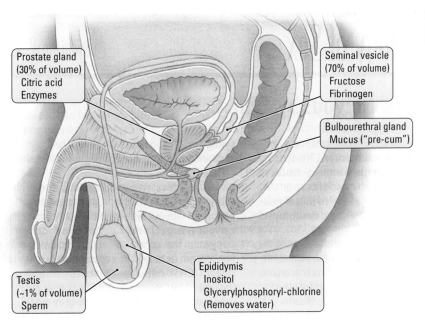

Figure 4.7 Glandular contributions to semen Sperm make up less than 1% of the volume of semen; the rest, known as seminal plasma, comes from various glands.

Prostate gland
(30% of volume)
Citric acid
Enzymes

Seminal vesicle
(70% of volume)
Fructose
Fibrinogen

Bulbourethral gland
Mucus ("pre-cum")

Testis
(~1% of volume)
Sperm

Epididymis
Inositol
Glycerylphosphoryl-chlorine
(Removes water)

semen, as well as another enzyme that slowly breaks down fibrin, relique-fying the coagulated semen. Other prostatic enzymes produce substances required by the sperm.

■ Antioxidants such as ascorbic acid protect the sperm from the damage they might suffer on exposure to air.

■ In men infected with disease-causing viruses such as human immunodeficiency virus (HIV) or hepatitis B virus (see Chapter 17), these viruses may be present at high concentrations in seminal plasma.

The Nervous System Orchestrates Sexual Arousal

Sexual behavior is under the control of two of the body's three major communication networks: the nervous system and the endocrine system. (The third—the immune system—plays little role in sex.) Here we consider the role of the nervous system, focusing on "low-level" functions that are controlled largely by **spinal reflexes**. **Box 4.5** offers a brief refresher course on the organization of the nervous system, emphasizing elements that we'll be referring to in this and later chapters. The role of the endocrine system is discussed in Chapter 5.

Erection Can Be Mediated by a Spinal Reflex

One simple behavior that illustrates the role of the nervous system in sex is the erection of the penis or clitoris in response to tactile stimulation of the genital area. This behavior requires five elements that collectively form a reflex loop running from the genitals to the spinal cord and back:

1. Sensory nerve endings that detect the stimulation;
2. Nerves that convey the sensory information to the spinal cord;
3. A processing center in the spinal cord;
4. Nerves that carry an output signal to the penis or clitoris; and
5. Vascular elements that are responsible for the actual erection.

spinal reflex A reflex mediated by neurons in the spinal cord, requiring no participation by the brain.

BOX 4.5 (continued)

neurotransmitter A compound released at a synapse that increases or decreases the excitability of an adjacent neuron.

synaptic cleft The narrow space between two neurons at a synapse.

central nervous system (CNS) The brain and spinal cord.

gray matter A region of the central nervous system containing the cell bodies of neurons.

cortex The outer portion of an anatomical structure, as of the cerebral hemispheres or the adrenal gland.

nucleus In neuroanatomy, a recognizable cluster of neurons in the central nervous system.

white matter A region of the central nervous system that contains bundles of axons but no neuronal cell bodies.

spinal cord The portion of the central nervous system within the vertebral column.

dorsal horn The rear portion of the gray matter of the spinal cord: It has a sensory function.

ventral horn The portion of the gray matter of the spinal cord nearer to the front of the body, where motor neurons are located.

dorsal root A bundle of sensory axons that enters a dorsal horn of the spinal cord.

ventral root A bundle of motor axons that leaves a ventral horn of the spinal cord.

forebrain The cerebral hemispheres and basal ganglia.

cerebral hemispheres The uppermost and largest portion of the brain, divided into left and right halves.

cerebral cortex Convoluted, layered gray matter that covers most of the brain.

basal ganglia Deep non-cortical structures of the forebrain.

corpus callosum A band of axons interconnecting the left and right cerebral hemispheres.

brainstem The region of the brain between the forebrain and the spinal cord.

medulla The portion of the brainstem closest to the spinal cord.

pons A region of the brain above the medulla.

midbrain The region of the brainstem between the pons and the thalamus.

thalamus The uppermost region of the brainstem.

hypothalamus A small region at the base of the brain on either side of the third ventricle; it contains cell groups involved in sexual responses and other basic functions.

peripheral nervous system The motor and sensory connections between the central nervous system and peripheral structures such as muscles and sense organs.

efferent Carrying signals away from the CNS.

afferent Carrying signals toward the CNS.

ganglia Collections of neurons outside the central nervous system.

autonomic nervous system The portion of the nervous system that controls smooth muscles and glands without our conscious involvement.

sympathetic nervous system A division of the autonomic nervous system; among other functions, its activity inhibits penile erection but helps trigger ejaculation.

parasympathetic nervous system A division of the autonomic nervous system; among other functions, its activity promotes erection of the penis and clitoris.

preganglionic neuron An autonomic motor neuron in the spinal cord.

autonomic ganglion A cluster of autonomic neurons outside the CNS.

postganglionic neuron A neuron with cell body in an autonomic ganglion and an axon that innervates glands or smooth muscles in a peripheral organ such as the genitalia.

Although the brain also plays a significant role in promoting or inhibiting erection, as we'll see later in this chapter, this role is not essential. People who have suffered spinal injuries that prevent communication between the brain and the lower portion of the spinal cord are usually still capable of having erections in response to genital stimulation.

SENSORY INNERVATION OF THE GENITALIA   The penis and clitoris possess a unique class of sensory nerve endings termed **genital end-bulbs** (Halata & Munger, 1986) (**Figure 4.8**). In these structures, the nerve fibers form tangled knots in the dermis (the deeper part of the skin), either immediately under the epidermis (as in the figure) or deeper in the skin. Numerous genital end-bulbs are found in the skin of the glans, but they are also found in the remaining parts of the penis or clitoris and throughout the genital area. In the penis, the highest density of end-bulbs is around the corona of the glans and in the frenulum—the two zones that are generally the most erotically sensitive regions of the penis. It is believed that genital end-bulbs are specialized to sense the kind of tactile stimulation that occurs during sexual behavior.

Of course, the penis and clitoris are not the only erogenous zones: A wide zone of genital skin, as well as the anus and the nipples, are erotically sensitive in both

genital end-bulbs Specialized nerve endings found in erogenous zones, which probably detect the mechanical stimulation associated with sexual activity.

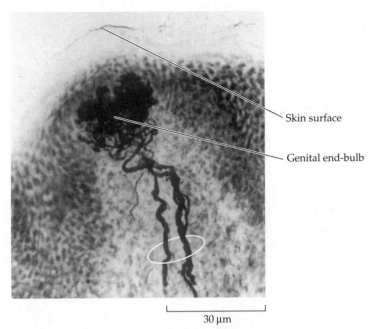

Figure 4.8 Sensory innervation of the penis A bundle of nerve fibers (circled) approaches the skin surface and forms into a dense knot of terminal branches—a genital end-bulb. (From Halata & Munger, 1986; courtesy of Z. Halata and K. Baumann, University of Hamburg.)

Skin surface

Genital end-bulb

30 μm

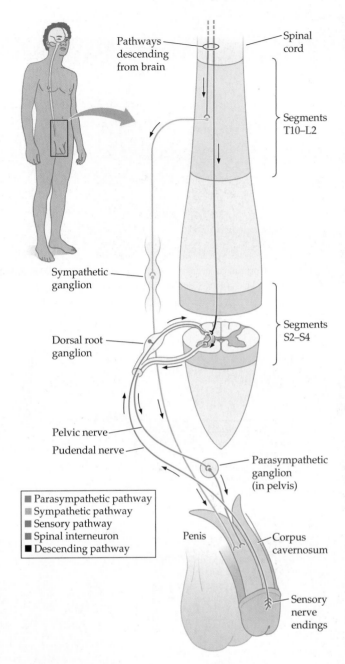

Figure 4.9 Nerve pathways involved in erection Erection depends on the balance of activity in the sympathetic and parasympathetic fibers innervating the erectile tissue. Parasympathetic activity (promoting erection) is triggered by tactile stimulation of the penis (a spinal reflex). Descending inputs from the brain modulate the activity of both the parasympathetic fibers and the countervailing sympathetic fibers, whose activity prevents erection.

sexes, though to a varying degree from person to person. Whether the skin in all these areas contains specialized "genital" receptors is not known.

THE PUDENDAL AND PELVIC NERVES   If we trace the sensory nerve fibers from the penis or clitoris, we find that they travel toward the spinal cord in the left and right **pudendal nerves** (**Figure 4.9**). The sensory fibers enter the sacral segments of the spinal cord by passing through the dorsal roots. The cell bodies of the sensory fibers are located within the dorsal roots, but no synaptic connections occur there—signals go directly into the spinal cord.

The central endings of the sensory nerve fibers form synaptic connections with interneurons (local circuit cells) in the gray matter of the spinal cord. These interneurons in turn form synaptic connections with output neurons, which in this case are preganglionic neurons of the parasympathetic nervous system (see Box 4.5). The cell bodies of these neurons are located in the sacral segments of the spinal cord, and their efferent axons leave the cord in the ventral roots and travel toward the genitalia in the **pelvic nerves**. On reaching ganglia near the bladder, they form synapses with postganglionic parasympathetic neurons, whose axons in turn travel to the erectile tissues in the penis and clitoris.

Before considering how erection occurs, we need to mention another set of nerve fibers that also innervate the erectile tissues. These fibers are components of the sympathetic nervous system. This system also originates in preganglionic neurons in the spinal cord, but its neurons are situated at higher levels of the cord—in

pudendal nerves Peripheral nerves supplying the external genitalia.

pelvic nerves Nerves that convey parasympathetic signals from the lower spinal cord to the genitalia and other organs.

(A)

(B)

Red blood cells

Corpora cavernosa   Corpus spongiosum   Sinusoids

Sinusoids   Trabeculae

80 μm

(C)

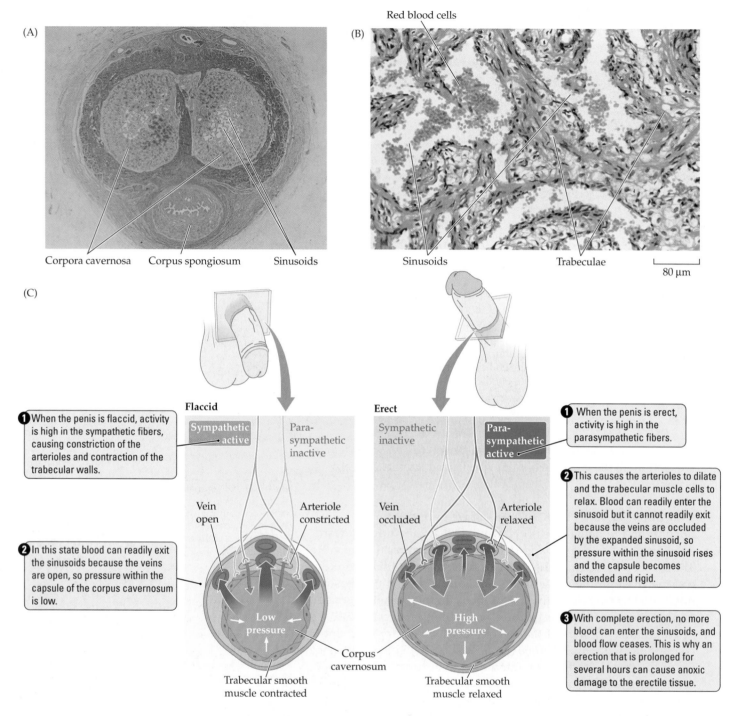

Flaccid

❶ When the penis is flaccid, activity is high in the sympathetic fibers, causing constriction of the arterioles and contraction of the trabecular walls.

Sympathetic active

Para-sympathetic inactive

Vein open

Arteriole constricted

❷ In this state blood can readily exit the sinusoids because the veins are open, so pressure within the capsule of the corpus cavernosum is low.

Low pressure

Trabecular smooth muscle contracted

Erect

Sympathetic inactive

Para-sympathetic active

Vein occluded

Arteriole relaxed

High pressure

Trabecular smooth muscle relaxed

Corpus cavernosum

❶ When the penis is erect, activity is high in the parasympathetic fibers.

❷ This causes the arterioles to dilate and the trabecular muscle cells to relax. Blood can readily enter the sinusoid but it cannot readily exit because the veins are occluded by the expanded sinusoid, so pressure within the sinusoid rises and the capsule becomes distended and rigid.

❸ With complete erection, no more blood can enter the sinusoids, and blood flow ceases. This is why an erection that is prolonged for several hours can cause anoxic damage to the erectile tissue.

Figure 4.10 The mechanism of penile (or clitoral) erection (A) Cross section of the penis, showing the appearance of erectile tissue (in the flaccid state) within the corpora cavernosa. Sinusoids (small white spaces) are separated by trabeculae. (B) Higher magnification of a corpus cavernosum, showing sinusoids (some with red blood cells) and trabeculae (the cellular walls between the sinusoids). (C) Diagram of the erectile mechanism. Note that for simplicity, the illustration shows the penis as if it contains a single, large sinusoid. In reality, thousands of microscopic sinusoids make up the erectile tissue of the corpora cavernosa and the corpus spongiosum. (See Web Activity 4.7.)

the lower thoracic and upper lumbar segments. The axons of these neurons pass out of the cord and travel to sympathetic ganglia, where they form synaptic connections with postganglionic neurons. The postganglionic neurons send their axons to the erectile tissues of the penis and clitoris. The parasympathetic and sympathetic nerve fibers work in opposition to each other in controlling the state of the erectile tissue.

Erectile Tissue Forms a Hydraulic System

Now let's take a look at the erectile tissue itself (**Figure 4.10**). Here we will focus on the two corpora cavernosa, which have been the object of the most study. The tissue within the corpora cavernosa is like a sponge: It consists of irregular, collapsible spaces (**sinusoids**) separated by walls of connective tissue (**trabeculae**). The sinusoids are part of the vascular system; blood enters them via arterioles and exits via veins. The trabeculae contain smooth muscle cells, and contraction of these cells shrinks the spaces, thus diminishing the volume of the erectile tissue as a whole. (It's a "self-squeezing" sponge, as it were.) The other major control element consists of smooth muscle cells in the walls of the arterioles. Contraction of these cells constricts the arterioles, diminishing the flow of blood into the sinusoids.

The flaccid state of the penis and clitoris is not simply an inactive condition in which the erectile tissue receives no input from the nervous system. Rather, it is actively maintained by a continuous flow of impulses in the sympathetic nerve fibers. These impulses, on reaching the nerve terminals in the erectile tissue, cause the release of the sympathetic neurotransmitter norepinephrine. This transmitter, in turn, causes an ongoing contraction of the smooth muscle of the arterioles (thus narrowing the arterioles and restricting the flow of blood into the sinusoids) and of the trabecular walls (thus keeping the volume of the sinusoids low).

Erection results from a *decrease* in this activity of the sympathetic fibers, and a reciprocal *increase* in the activity of the parasympathetic fibers. The parasympathetic fibers release three different neurotransmitters from their nerve terminals in the erectile tissue. The most important of these is **nitric oxide**, which is a dissolved gas (Hedlund et al., 2000). Nitric oxide causes the relaxation of the smooth muscle cells of the arterioles and the trabecular walls. As a result, more blood flows into the sinusoids and the erectile tissue expands. This expansion compresses and closes the veins that receive the outflow from the sinusoids, causing the volume of the erectile tissue to increase further.

With complete erection, no more blood can enter the sinusoids, and blood flow ceases. The pooled blood gradually loses its oxygen, taking on the purplish color of venous blood. (This color change can be observed in the glans, which has only a thin, translucent capsule.) Because of the stasis and deoxygenation of the blood in the sinusoids, an erection that won't go down—a condition called priapism—will cause damage to the erectile tissue if it is prolonged for more than a few hours (**Figure 4.11**).

The ability of the corpora cavernosa to expand is limited by the connective-tissue capsule that surrounds them—the tunica albuginea. It is this resistance to expansion that causes the rigidity of the erect penis. Although both the corpora cavernosa and the corpus spongiosum expand during erection, the corpus spongiosum has a less well-developed capsule, so it does not make much contribution to stiffness. The difference can be appreciated by feeling an erect penis: The corpus spongiosum, which forms the ridge along the underside of the penis and also occupies the entire glans, is much softer to the touch than the rest of the organ. If the

sinusoids A vascular space, such as within erectile tissue, capable of being expanded by filling with blood.

trabeculae Connective tissue partitions separating the sinusoids of erectile tissue.

nitric oxide A dissolved gas that functions as a neurotransmitter in erectile tissue.

Figure 4.11 Priapism is named for the Greco-Roman fertility god Priapus, who was always portrayed with an erection. In this wall painting from Pompeii, Priapus weighs his penis against a bag of gold—an allusion to the wealth of the family that commissioned the painting. (The scale is partially obscured by damage to the painting.) For mere mortals, an erection that won't go down calls for prompt medical attention.

Onuf's nucleus A sexually dimorphic group of motor neurons in the sacral segments of the spinal cord that innervates striated muscles associated with the penis and clitoris.

sexual dimorphism An anatomical difference between the sexes.

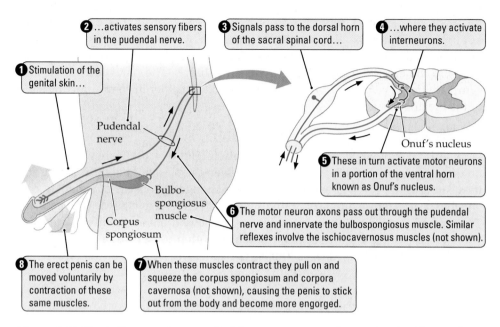

❶ Stimulation of the genital skin…

❷ …activates sensory fibers in the pudendal nerve.

❸ Signals pass to the dorsal horn of the sacral spinal cord…

❹ …where they activate interneurons.

Pudendal nerve

Onuf's nucleus

❺ These in turn activate motor neurons in a portion of the ventral horn known as Onuf's nucleus.

Bulbo-spongiosus muscle

Corpus spongiosum

❻ The motor neuron axons pass out through the pudendal nerve and innervate the bulbospongiosus muscle. Similar reflexes involve the ischiocavernosus muscles (not shown).

❽ The erect penis can be moved voluntarily by contraction of these same muscles.

❼ When these muscles contract they pull on and squeeze the corpus spongiosum and corpora cavernosa (not shown), causing the penis to stick out from the body and become more engorged.

Figure 4.12 The bulbospongiosus and ischiocavernosus muscles are involved in erectile reflexes.

corpus spongiosum were as rigid as the rest of the penis during erection, the urethra would be compressed, and ejaculation might be impossible.

Muscles Are Also Involved in Erection

The two striated (voluntary) muscles, the ischiocavernosus and bulbospongiosus, are also involved in erection of the penis and clitoris (**Figure 4.12**). This reflex action is most obvious in the case of the penis. If a man's penis is already erect but hanging down from the body, a light touch on the sensitive areas of the penis, or even on nearby skin, will cause the penis to jump up and project directly forward or upward. It is also possible to produce the same movement voluntarily, without any stimulation of the genitals. At the same time, the glans of the penis becomes more enlarged. These responses are caused by contraction of the ischiocavernosus and bulbospongiosus muscles, which pull on and squeeze the corpora cavernosa and corpus spongiosum in the root of the penis.

This reflex has the same afferent pathway we described earlier—the sensory fibers running to the spinal cord through the pudendal nerve—but the efferent pathway is different, and does not involve the autonomic nervous system. Instead, the terminals of the sensory fibers in the sacral segments of the spinal cord activate a set of interneurons, which in turn connect with a set of motor neurons in the ventral horn of the cord. These motor neurons form a cell group known as **Onuf's nucleus**. Onuf's nucleus is significantly larger—and contains more motor neurons—in men than in women (Forger & Breedlove, 1986). This difference is one of many **sexual dimorphisms**, or anatomical differences between the sexes, in the human central nervous system (CNS); we will be describing other differences later in this book.

The axons of the motor neurons of Onuf's nucleus run back down the pudendal nerves to the genitalia, where some of them innervate the ischiocavernosus and bulbospongiosus muscles. (Other axons innervate the anal sphincter, the bladder, and other muscles of the pelvic floor.) When impulses reach the endings of the nerves in the muscles (the neuromuscular junctions), they cause the release of the neurotransmitter acetylcholine, which causes the muscles to contract.

The Brain Influences Erection

So far, we have discussed erection as if it were only a spinal reflex triggered by genital stimulation. In fact, however, erection can occur without any tactile stimulation. The stimulus may consist of erotically arousing sights or sounds, or erotic fantasies, as discussed in Chapter 8.

These influences on erection are mediated by higher levels of the CNS (see Box 4.5, Figure C). One brain region that is particularly important for the regulation of sexual excitation (and other drives such as hunger and thirst) is the hypothalamus, which is located at the base of the brain. Descending pathways from the hypothalamus activate lower centers in the brainstem, specifically in the pons and medulla, which in turn send control signals to the sympathetic and parasympathetic neurons in the spinal cord, increasing or decreasing their activity levels. Without going into the details of these pathways—which in any case have not been fully delineated in humans—we can understand that the spinal reflexes mediating genital arousal are not fixed and constant, but are responsive to circumstances: Tactile stimulation of the penis or clitoris may elicit physiological arousal in some circumstances (in the presence of an attractive partner or during sexual fantasies, for example)—but not in others.

Another example of higher-level control of erection concerns erection during sleep. Erections occur during rapid-eye-movement (REM) sleep, the phase of sleep during which vivid dreams are experienced (**Figure 4.13**). The dreams may be erotic in nature, and may sometimes culminate in **nocturnal orgasms** ("wet dreams"), but erections accompany all REM phases, regardless of dream content. The function of nocturnal erections is not certain, but it is suspected that they allow for oxygenation of the genitals and prevent fibrosis and loss of elasticity in the erectile tissue. Nocturnal genital arousal is common in women as well as men, and one study reported that about 1 in 5 young women experience orgasms during sleep (Henton, 1976).

Nocturnal erections are controlled from a center in the pons called the **locus coeruleus**. Here's how it works: Most of the time, the locus coeruleus neurons are active; their activity in turn stimulates activity in the sympathetic neurons of the lumbar region of the spinal cord, thus keeping the penis flaccid. During REM sleep, however, the activity of the neurons in the locus coeruleus drops; this leads to a corresponding drop in sympathetic activity, shifting the balance in favor of the parasympathetic neurons, so an erection occurs.

Ejaculation Requires Coordination of Muscles and Glands

Orgasm, previously discussed in the context of women's sexual arousal (see Chapter 3), is very similar in men. In one study, researchers took men's and women's descriptions of their own orgasms, edited them to remove sex-specific references, and gave them to various experts to sort out by sex. It turned out to be impossible (Vance & Wagner, 1976) (**Box 4.6**).

The main sex difference in orgasm is that nearly all men experience ejaculation as a component of orgasm, whereas only some women do. In men, ejaculation is the forceful ejection of semen from the urethral meatus. It is actually quite a complex process that requires careful coordination of glands and muscles. Luckily, the spinal cord takes care of most of the details.

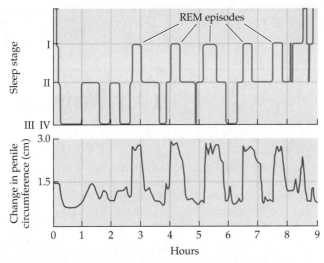

Figure 4.13 Penile erections accompany REM sleep. The graph shows an entire night's sleep (9 hours) for a healthy young man. The upper trace indicates the stages of sleep as determined by electroencephalography (EEG): Stage I is light sleep, stage 2 is an intermediate level, and stages III and IV are both deep, delta-wave sleep. There are 5 REM episodes, shown here as being stage I, although they are actually a distinct kind of sleep characterized by rapid eye movements. The lower trace shows changes in penile circumference (3.0 = maximal erection). Note that the erections occur during the REM episodes. (Data from Brain Information Service, UCLA School of Medicine.)

nocturnal orgasm Orgasm during sleep.

locus coeruleus A nerve center in the pons that helps regulate the state of consciousness.

Personal Points of View

BOX 4.6 Women and Men Describe Their Orgasms

Following are descriptions of orgasms written by students in an introductory psychology course in the 1970s. Some sex-specific words, such as "penis" or "clitoris" have been changed to "genitals." Experts who read these descriptions were unable to tell which descriptions were written by women and which by men.

■ "Feels like tension building up until you think it can't build up any more, then release. The orgasm is both the highest point of tension and the release almost at the same time. Also feeling contractions in the genitals. Tingling all over."

■ "An orgasm . . . located (originating) in the genital area, capable of spreading out further . . . legs, abdomen. A sort of pulsating feeling—very nice if it can extend itself beyond the immediate genital area."

■ "Begins with tensing and tingling in anticipation, rectal contractions starting series of chills up spine. Tingling and buzzing sensations grow suddenly to explosion in genital area, some sensation

of dizzying and weakening—almost loss of conscious sensation, but not really. Explosion sort of flowers out to varying distance from genital area, depending on intensity."

■ "A heightened feeling of excitement with severe, muscular tension especially through the back and legs, rigid straightening of the entire body for about 5 seconds, and a strong and general relaxation and very tired relieved feeling."

■ "Tension builds up to an extremely high level—muscles are tense, etc. There is a sudden expanding feeling in the pelvis and muscle spasms throughout the body followed by release of tension. Muscles relax and consciousness returns."

■ "Intense excitement of entire body. Vibrations in stomach—mind can consider only your own desires at the moment of climax. After, you feel like you're floating—a sense of joyful tiredness."

■ "A building of tension, sometimes, and frustration until the climax. A tightening

inside, palpitating rhythm, explosion, and warmth and peace."

■ "Often loss of contact with reality. All senses acute. Sight becomes patterns of color, but often very difficult to explain because words were made to fit in the real world."

■ "Has a buildup of pressure in genitals with involuntary thrusting of hips and twitching of thigh muscles. Also contracting and releasing of the genital muscles. The pressure becomes quite intense—like there is something underneath the skin of the genitals pushing out. Then there is a sudden release of the tension with contraction of genitals with a feeling of release and relaxation."

■ "Spasm of the abdominal and groin area, tingling sensation in limbs, and throbbing at the temples on each side of my head."

Source: Vance & Wagner, 1976.

As sexual climax approaches, the sympathetic nervous system begins to make itself felt by causing an increase in heart rate, blood pressure, and rate of breathing. Rashes may appear on the front of the body, the neck, or the face, and muscle spasms may also occur. Increased contraction of the ischiocavernosus and bulbospongiosus muscles causes further swelling of the penis, especially the glans, and the pooling of blood within the glans turns it a purplish color. The cremaster muscle draws the testicles upward, sometimes to the point that they disappear from view, and the dartos muscle causes the scrotal skin to become thicker and wrinkled.

Emission Is the Loading of Semen into the Urethra

Immediately prior to ejaculation, the various components of the semen are expelled from their reservoirs into the posterior portion of the urethra (**Figure 4.14A**). This process is called **emission**; it lasts just a second or two and can be felt as a pulsing or flowing sensation at the root of the penis. Emission is triggered by activity in the sympathetic nerve fibers innervating the prostate, the seminal vesicles, and the vasa deferentia, which causes contraction of the smooth muscle in these organs. Once emission occurs, the man has the sense that ejaculation is imminent, although some men are able to halt the process even at this late stage. In that case, the semen simply flows out of the urethral meatus, rather than being forcefully ejaculated.

During emission, the first component to be loaded into the urethra is the fluid secreted by the prostate gland. This is followed by sperm (and a small amount of

emission The loading of the constituents of semen into the posterior urethra immediately before ejaculation.

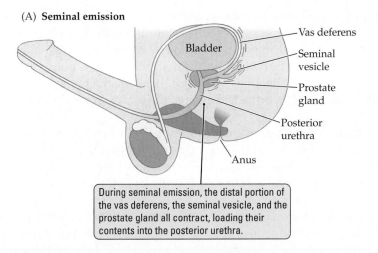

(A) **Seminal emission**

Bladder

Vas deferens

Seminal vesicle

Prostate gland

Posterior urethra

Anus

During seminal emission, the distal portion of the vas deferens, the seminal vesicle, and the prostate gland all contract, loading their contents into the posterior urethra.

(B) **Ejaculation**

Penile urethra

Pelvic floor muscles

During ejaculation, the urethra and the muscles of the pelvic floor contract, ejecting semen out through the urethral meatus.

The urethral sphincter (not shown) at the bladder exit remains closed throughout, which prevents urine from entering the urethra and semen from backing up into the bladder.

Figure 4.14 Seminal emission and ejaculation

fluid) from the vasa deferentia, and finally by the most voluminous component—the secretion of the seminal vesicles. This sequential loading of the urethra is of some functional significance, because the secretions of the prostate gland and the seminal vesicles, when mixed, cause the semen to turn from a liquid to a gel (coagulate) (Finney et al., 1992), a process that normally occurs after ejaculation (e.g., in the vagina). Premature coagulation of the semen within the urethra is prevented by the physical separation of its components.

Ejaculation Is Caused by Contractions of Many Muscles in the Pelvic Floor

Ejaculation (**Figure 4.14B**) is caused by a series of spasmodic contractions of smooth muscle in the walls of the urethra (in response to sympathetic activation) and of the ischiocavernosus and bulbospongiosus muscles, as well as other striated muscles of the pelvic floor. These contractions, which occur in response to a burst of activity in the sacral motor neurons, can be seen in electrical recordings from the muscles involved (**Figure 4.15**). The contractions take place at a rate of about one per second, and the entire sequence lasts no more than about 10 to 15 seconds. The muscles forcefully squeeze the semen-filled urethra, especially in the region between the prostate gland and the root of the penis.

The urethral sphincter at the outflow of the bladder is usually closed, and it constricts even more tightly at ejaculation in order to prevent the pressurized

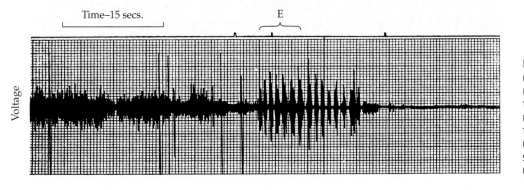

Time–15 secs.

E

Voltage

Figure 4.15 Orgasmic contractions recorded in a male subject This recording was obtained from an electrode placed in the bulbospongiosus muscle. The subject was masturbating to orgasm. Seven spurts of ejaculation (E) occurred in synchrony with the first seven contractions of the muscle. (Courtesy of Roy Levin.)

semen from flowing backward into the bladder (Bohlen et al., 2000). Thus, with nowhere else to go, the semen is expelled from the urethral meatus in a series of spurts of decreasing force. If the man ejaculates into free space, the semen may be propelled some distance from the body, but this projectile ability is quite variable from person to person and declines with age. If he ejaculates within a woman's vagina, the semen may be propelled against the cervix, but not into the cervical canal.

The proper coordination of all these events requires the activity of several centers in the spinal cord. In addition, animal experiments suggest that the brain plays an important role in triggering ejaculation. For example, electrical stimulation of the paraventricular nucleus, a cell group in the hypothalamus, causes penile erection and ejaculation in rats (Chen et al., 1997). The evidence in humans is inconclusive: The majority of quadriplegic men (who have suffered an interruption of the pathways from the brain to the spinal cord) report that they never ejaculate under any circumstances, but a substantial minority (about 40%) do ejaculate (Alexander et al., 1993). This finding suggests that, while spinal circuitry for ejaculation exists, it requires activation from the brain in most men. It is probably an oversimplification to call ejaculation a "spinal reflex."

Nudity Is Culturally Regulated

Women's and men's genitals are often referred to as "private parts." This phrase highlights the fact that cultural factors prohibit or limit public displays of the genitalia. In societies in which women wear clothing of any kind, they are required to cover the vulva while in public. Even in societies in which women traditionally went without clothing, as among the Kwoma people of New Guinea, men were required to look aside when approached by a woman (Ford & Beach, 1951). Men are usually required to cover their genitals, too, but there are exceptions.

The sight of a woman's vulva is sexually arousing to heterosexual men, as has been shown by controlled experiments conducted in strip clubs (Linz et al., 2000).* Thus, social prohibitions against female nudity have the effect of reducing men's arousal, especially in public. Prohibitions against male nudity may have a similar effect on heterosexual women, even if they are not as "visual" as men when it comes to sexual arousal (see Chapter 7). It therefore seems likely that the prohibition of public nudity reduces sexual arousal, sexual coercion, and disputes over potential sex partners—thus facilitating general social cooperation.

Social rules about exposure of the body are indicators of general attitudes toward sexuality. In ancient Greece, male athletes competed without clothing (but out of view of women), and the nude or near-nude body was celebrated in sculpture (**Figure 4.16A**). In early Christian art, however, clothing served to desexualize the body—or indeed, to de-emphasize the body as a whole—as part of an emphasis on humanity's spiritual nature (**Figure 4.16B**).

The nineteenth century was another period when Europeans went to extraordinary lengths to conceal the body. When bathing at the beach, for example, gentlemen wore garments so all-covering as to hamper their ability to swim. These practices were part of a general belief that sexual arousal was dangerous to health, morals, and social order.

---

*In the study, researchers from the University of California, Santa Barbara, arranged for exotic dancers to expose themselves to customers fully naked or with genitals covered. In questionnaires filled out immediately after the show, the customers exposed to the fully naked dancers reported greater erotic arousal. The study was done in response to a Supreme Court ruling which stated that banning nude dancing did not violate the dancers' First Amendment right to free expression because the "messages" received by the customers were the same whether the dancers were clothed or naked.

(A)

(B)

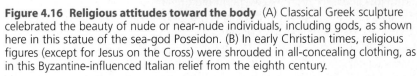

Figure 4.16 Religious attitudes toward the body (A) Classical Greek sculpture celebrated the beauty of nude or near-nude individuals, including gods, as shown here in this statue of the sea-god Poseidon. (B) In early Christian times, religious figures (except for Jesus on the Cross) were shrouded in all-concealing clothing, as in this Byzantine-influenced Italian relief from the eighth century.

Our current society is far freer in its attitudes toward exposure of the body, and far more sex-positive than were our Victorian forebears, but we are certainly not the most liberal contemporary society in these respects. Many consider it unacceptable for women to bare their breasts in public (when breast-feeding a baby for example), and even men may not bare their upper bodies in a wide range of ordinary circumstances, such as at the office or in a classroom. Art depicting nudity may be censored. Correspondingly, anti-sex attitudes are still quite widespread in our society.

Not everyone shares this aversion to nudity. Britain's "naked rambler," Stephen Gough, received widespread public support when he twice walked the length of that country wearing nothing but hiking boots. (His treks, completed in 2006, were interrupted by numerous court appearances and spells in jail.) Less radical advocates for nudity, such as the U.S. Naturist Society, promote opportunities for nudity in private settings. The society believes that anxieties about body image are common and crippling, and that going naked among naked people is the way to resolve them (**Figure 4.17**).

Figure 4.17 Nudism as therapy Nudists (or naturists) believe that going naked helps liberate people from body-image hang-ups.

REFER TO THE

Human Sexuality

WEBSITE AT
www.sinauer.com/levay3e

for activities, study questions,
quizzes, and other study aids.

Summary

1. The male external genitalia comprise the penis and the scrotum. A man's penis contains three erectile structures and encloses the urethra. Its erotic sensitivity is highest on the glans and frenulum. The foreskin, which covers the glans, is removed in the operation of circumcision. Circumcision offers some health advantages, but the prevalence of circumcision in the United States is decreasing. Health problems affecting the penis include inflammation of the glans (balanitis), inability to retract the foreskin (phimosis), entrapment of the foreskin behind the glans (paraphimosis), pathological curvature of the penis (Peyronie's disease), and penile cancer.

2. The scrotum contains the testicles and has muscular and vascular mechanisms for maintaining them below the regular body temperature.

3. A man's internal reproductive structures include six paired structures: the testes, epididymides, vasa deferentia, seminal vesicles, ejaculatory ducts, and bulbourethral glands, as well as two unpaired midline structures, the prostate gland and urethra.

4. The testis contains seminiferous tubules, in which sperm are produced; the tubules are lined by Sertoli cells, which nurture the developing sperm and secrete peptide hormones. Between the seminiferous tubules lie Leydig (interstitial) cells, which secrete steroid and peptide hormones. The most important health problem affecting the testes is testicular cancer. This can affect young men, but is one of the most curable cancers. The epididymis is the location where sperm mature and become more concentrated. The vasa deferentia store sperm and transport them to the urethra. Sperm constitute only about 1% of the volume of the ejaculate.

5. The prostate gland and seminal vesicles add the noncellular portion of semen (seminal plasma), which consists of water, salts, fructose, buffers, fibrinogen, enzymes, and antioxidants. The bulbourethral glands produce a slippery liquid that may be discharged from the urethra in small amounts before ejaculation ("pre-cum").

6. The prostate gland can be affected by inflammation (prostatitis), age-related enlargement (benign prostatic hyperplasia), and prostate cancer. It is possible to screen for prostate cancer by regular digital rectal examination and by a blood test (PSA test). The treatments for prostate cancer (prostatectomy, hormone therapy) often have a serious impact on a man's sex life, and the question of whether and how to treat early-stage prostate cancer is controversial.

7. Sexual functions are regulated by the nervous and endocrine systems. Erection of the penis and clitoris involves a spinal reflex that starts with stimulation of nerve endings in the genital skin. Inputs from the brain powerfully modulate these reflexes. Erection involves the filling of vascular spaces (sinusoids) in the erectile tissue: This process is controlled by the balance of activity in the sympathetic and parasympathetic innervation of the tissue. A key molecule is the neurotransmitter nitric oxide, which is released by parasympathetic nerve terminals and which promotes erection.

8. Emission is the loading of the various glandular components of semen into the urethra. It is followed quickly by ejaculation, in which muscular contractions squeeze the urethra and eject the semen in a sequence of pulses from the urethra. Orgasm is the subjective pleasurable experience that usually accompanies ejaculation, along with the physiological events that underlie it.

9. Most societies prohibit public exposure of the genitals, apparently to regulate sexual arousal and minimize sexual conflicts. There is considerable variation in attitudes toward nudity, however.

Discussion Questions

1. How would you advise a couple who asked you whether they should have their infant son circumcised? Do you think that the baby has a right not to be circumcised until he can make the choice for himself?

2. We downplay the significance of penis size for women's or men's sexual satisfaction, but some writers, such as the author of the Kama Sutra (see Chapter 9), say otherwise. What do you think? (You don't have to discuss your own anatomy or sexual experiences!) If a man who is concerned about his small penis has it enlarged surgically, would you consider that a good idea or not, and why?

3. What's your opinion about the "naked rambler"? Do you sympathize with his actions or not, and why? Do you agree with the Naturist Society that nudism is therapeutic?

Web Resources

Circlist www.circlist.com (a pro-circumcision advocacy group)

Erection Photos www.erectionphotos.com

Guttmacher Institute: In their own right: Addressing the sexual and reproductive health needs of men worldwide. www.guttmacher.org/pubs/itor.html

National Cancer Institute www.cancer.gov (has extensive sections on prostate and testicular cancer)

National Organization of Circumcision Information Resource Centers (NOCIRC) www.nocirc.org (an anti-circumcision advocacy group. Some of the statements on this site, such as that circumcision reduces the length and erotic sensitivity of the penis, are poorly documented.)

Naturist Society www.naturistsociety.com

Prostate Cancer Foundation www.prostatecancerfoundation.org

Prostatitis Foundation www.prostatitis.org

University of Delaware Histology (microscopic anatomy) site: male reproductive system www.udel.edu/Biology/Wags/histopage/colorpage/cmr/cmr.htm

Recommended Reading

Armstrong L., and Jenkins, S. (2000). *It's not about the bike: My journey back to life*. Putnam. (About surviving testicular cancer.)

Bostwick, D. G., MacLennan, G. T., and Larson, T. R. (1999). *Prostate cancer: What every man—and his family—needs to know* (rev. ed.). Villard Books.

Fleiss, P. M., and Hodges, F. M. (2002). *What your doctor may not tell you about circumcision: Untold facts about America's most widely performed and most unnecessary surgery.* Warner Books.

Friedman, D. M. (2001). *A mind of its own: A cultural history of the penis*. Free Press.

Zilbergeld, B. (1999). *The new male sexuality: The truth about men, sex, and pleasure* (rev. ed.). Bantam Books.

CHAPTER 5

Crystals of progesterone, a female sex hormone that maintains pregnancy, viewed in polarized light.

Sex Hormones and the Menstrual Cycle

The endocrine system—the system of glands that secrete hormones into the bloodstream—shares with the nervous system the task of regulating sexual development, sexual functions, and sexual behavior. To produce the full range of sexual functions and behaviors, these two systems must interact in intimate and subtle ways.

Hormones strongly influence activity patterns within the brain and thus have a significant impact on sexual behavior. Conversely, the brain controls the secretion of key hormones that regulate ovarian and testicular functions.

In this chapter we see numerous examples of interactions between the nervous and endocrine systems. None is more striking, however, than the intricate dance of hormonal and neural signals that orchestrate a woman's menstrual cycle—the very core of her sexual physiology.

Sex Steroids Consist of Three Groups

Hormones are signaling molecules secreted into the bloodstream by endocrine glands. Many hormones are active in sexual and reproductive physiology (**Table 5.1**). In this chapter we first consider one class of sex hormones—that of **sex steroids**, which fall into three major subgroups. Later, we discuss other classes of sex hormones that are not steroids, such as proteins, peptides, prostaglandins, and monoamines.

Sex steroids are the hormones that everyone has heard of. In fact, since their original identification early in the last century (**Box 5.1**), they have attained an almost mythical status in popular culture. In part, their reputation derives from the practical uses to which they have been put—contraception, muscle-building, and the restoration of libido, among others. More deeply, though, sex hormones have come to symbolize the "embodiment" of human behavior—the notion that we act the way we do because of internal biological mechanisms as much as or more than because of learning, reason, or morality. Yet this view is a distortion of the truth. Thus one purpose of this chapter is to undo some of the stereotypes that surround sex steroids.

Sex steroids are lipid (fatty) molecules derived from cholesterol (**Figure 5.1**). These hormones fall into three classes with different functional roles in sexual

sex steroid Any of the steroid hormones that are active in sexual and reproductive physiology.

androgen Any of a class of steroids—the most important being testosterone—that promote male sexual development and have a variety of other functions in both sexes.

estrogen Any of a class of steroids—the most important being estradiol—that promote the development of female secondary sexual characteristics at puberty and have many other functions in both sexes.

progestin (or progestagen) Any of a class of steroids, the most important being progesterone, that cause the endometrium to proliferate and help maintain pregnancy. (The term progestin is sometimes reserved for synthetic compounds.)

progesterone A steroid hormone secreted by the ovary and the placenta; it is necessary for the establishment and maintenance of pregnancy.

estradiol The principal estrogen, secreted by granulosa cells in ovarian follicles.

testosterone The principal androgen, synthesized in the testes and, in lesser amounts, in the ovaries and adrenal glands.

5α-dihydrotestosterone (DHT) An androgen that plays an important role in the development of the male external genitalia.

aromatase The enzyme that converts testosterone to estradiol.

5α-reductase The enzyme that converts testosterone to 5α-dihydrotestosterone.

behavior: **androgens**, **estrogens**, and **progestins** (a fourth class of steroids—corticosteroids—is not directly involved in sexual physiology). Within each class are several individual steroids, but we will pay most attention to four key players: the progestin **progesterone**, the estrogen **estradiol**, and two androgens, **testosterone** and **5α-dihydrotestosterone (DHT)**. (The chemical structure of these hormones is shown in Web Activity 5.1 Similarity between Male and Female Steroid Hormones.)

A specific enzyme catalyzes each step in the synthesis of the various sex steroids, but two of these enzymes are of particular importance: **aromatase**, which converts testosterone to estradiol, and **5α-reductase**, which converts testosterone to DHT. The congenital absence of any one of these enzymes can play havoc with a person's sexual development. If a chromosomally male fetus lacks 5α-reductase, for example, it will be born with the outward appearance of a female but will change its apparent sex back to male at puberty. These rare individuals help us understand how hormones regulate the sexual differentiation of the body, as we'll see in Chapter 6. In addition, they cast an intriguing light on an even deeper question—how do we develop an internal sense of ourself as male or female? We will take up the question of gender identity development in Chapter 7.

Testosterone Is a Sex Hormone in Both Men and Women

Perhaps the most widespread misunderstanding about sex steroids is the notion that there is a "male sex hormone" (testosterone) and a "female sex hormone"

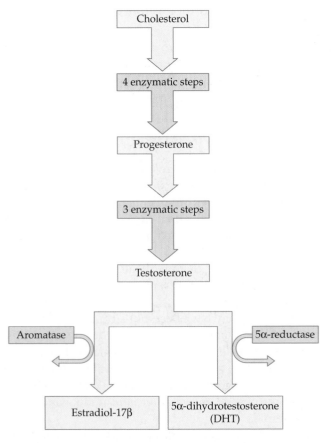

Figure 5.1 The synthesis of the four main sex steroids discussed in this book. Four enzymatic steps convert cholesterol to progesterone. Another three steps convert progesterone to testosterone. Testosterone can be converted either to estradiol (the principal estrogen) or to DHT by the specific enzymes shown. See Web Activity 5.1 for a more detailed version of this diagram.

TABLE 5.1

The Principal Sex Hormones and Their Actions

Class/subclass of hormone	Name	Where produced	Main targets	Main hormonal actions
Sex steroids				
Androgens	Testosterone	Gonads, adrenal cortex	Widespread in body and brain	Masculinizes body and brain during fetal development and at puberty; anabolic effects; maintains libido; feedback inhibition of gonadotropins
	5α-dihydro-testosterone (DHT)	External genitalia, prostate gland, skin (converted from testosterone)	External genitalia, prostate gland, skin	Development and maintenance of male external genitalia and prostate gland; adult male patterns of hair distribution
Estrogens	Estradiol-17β	Gonads	Widespread in body and brain	Feminizes body at puberty; contributes to menstrual cycle; increases density of bone; ends growth of limb bones at puberty; feedback inhibition of gonadotropins; maintains libido (?)
Progestins	Progesterone	Ovary (corpus luteum), placenta	Uterus	Contributes to menstrual cycle; maintains pregnancy
Proteins/peptides				
Releasing hormones	Gonadotropin-releasing hormone (GnRH)	Hypothalamus	Anterior lobe of pituitary gland	Causes release of gonadotropins
Gonadotropins	Follicle-stimulating hormone (FSH)	Anterior lobe of pituitary gland	Gonads	Stimulates spermatogenesis; stimulates maturation of ovarian follicles
	Luteinizing hormone (LH)	Anterior lobe of pituitary gland	Gonads	Stimulates secretion of gonadal steroids; stimulates ovulation
	Human chorionic gonadotropin (hCG)	Conceptus	Ovary	Maintains corpus luteum
Other	Prolactin	Anterior lobe of pituitary gland	Breast	Prepares breast for lactation
	Growth hormone	Anterior lobe of pituitary	Widespread in body	Stimulates growth spurt at puberty
	Inhibin	Gonads	Anterior lobe of pituitary	Feedback inhibition of gonadotropin secretion
	Oxytocin	Hypothalamus (transported to posterior pituitary for secretion)	Breast, uterus	Milk let-down; uterine contractions during labor; role in orgasm(?); (other nonreproductive functions)
	Anti-Müllerian hormone (AMH)	Testis	Müllerian duct	Causes regression of Müllerian duct during male fetal development

(estrogen). This is not a total falsehood—these hormones are present at different levels in the blood of men and women, and (at high levels) they tend to drive the development of the body in different directions—toward a more masculine or a more feminine appearance. However, testosterone (and other androgens) and

Biology of Sex

BOX 5.1 Testicles by the Ton—The Discovery of Sex Steroids

In the 1840s a German zoologist, A. A. Berthold, conducted a set of experiments on roosters that suggested the existence of a male sex hormone. He excised the testes from young roosters and observed that their secondary sexual characteristics (such as their bright red combs) and their sexual behavior were diminished. If he excised the testes and reimplanted them in a bird's abdomen, however, the bird looked and behaved like a normal male. Berthold suggested that the testes manufacture a substance that enters the bloodstream and promotes male development. Analogous experiments done in the 1890s suggested the existence of female hormones.

In the 1880s the elderly French endocrinologist Charles-Édouard Brown-Séquard announced that he had managed to renew his own sexual vigor and general health by injecting himself with extracts of animal testicles. Thus began a craze for rejuvenation remedies involving sex hormones. In the United States, Dr. John "Goat Gland" Brinkley performed innumerable surgical transplants of goat testicles through the 1920s and 1930s. (For women, he offered the "royal jelly" of honeybees.) We now know, of course, that transplanted animal tissues are quickly rejected by the immune system.

In 1929 German chemist Adolf Butenandt isolated and purified the first sex hormone (a form of estrogen) from urine and showed by chemical analysis that it was a steroid. In 1935 a Dutch group purified testosterone from bulls' testicles. American biochemist Edward Doisy purified estradiol from sows' ovaries.

Because these early researchers lacked the analytical techniques that modern biochemists take for granted, their work was extraordinarily laborious. Each step of the purification procedure had to be checked by means of bioassays—testing to see, for example, whether the isolated substances caused a rooster's comb to grow larger. The process was mind-numbingly inefficient. Doisy started with the ovaries of 80,000 sows and ended up with 12 mg of estradiol. The Dutch group started with nearly a ton of bulls' testicles and obtained about 300 mg of testosterone.

After the sex steroids were identified, the next step was to synthesize them. In 1936 the Yugoslav-born chemist Leopold Ruzicka synthesized testosterone. By the early 1940s most of the important sex steroids were being produced by pharmaceutical companies, but their prices were so high as to inhibit their use in research or medicine.

During the 1930s a maverick American chemist, Russell Marker of Pennsylvania State College, became convinced that useful starting materials for manufacturing steroid hormones were to be found in a variety of plants. In 1940 Marker collected 40,000 kg of plant material in the United States and Mexico. Eventually he determined that the best source was a wild yam growing in the mountains near Veracruz, Mexico (see figure). In 1943, with the aid of a mule and a spade and with some assistance from local Indians, he filled many sacks with the plant, brought them back to Mexico City, and turned them into nearly 3 kg of progesterone—which was then worth a steep $8 a

gram. Marker cofounded a Mexican pharmaceutical company, Syntex, to produce the various steroids. Syntex's operations drove down the price of steroids, making them readily available as medicines and research drugs. In

Chemist Russell Marker with a wild yam plant—a rich source of sex steroids.

1951 Carl Djerassi, a chemist working at Syntex, produced a form of progesterone that could be taken orally. This discovery quickly paved the way for the introduction of the oral contraceptive pill.

Sources: Bullough, 1994; Associated Press, 2004c.

estradiol (and other estrogens) are present in both men and women, and they have important hormonal functions in both sexes.

Testosterone is secreted by the gonads (testes and ovaries) and by the **adrenal gland**. In men, by far the larger portion of the testosterone circulating in the bloodstream comes from the testes, where it is produced by the Leydig cells—the cells that occupy the spaces between the seminiferous tubules (see Figure 4.5). In women, the ovaries and the adrenal gland share about equally in the production of testosterone. In the ovary, it is synthesized by the thecal cells that surround the developing ovarian follicle.

adrenal gland A gland near the kidney that secretes a variety of steroids including sex steroids.

TESTOSTERONE LEVELS VARY CYCLICALLY The secretion of testosterone is not constant over time (**Figure 5.2**). In a man's blood, its concentration varies according to two different cycles. The shorter cycle is about 2 to 4 hours in duration. Testosterone levels may fluctuate by three- or fourfold over the course of this cycle. Because of this variation, a single blood sample is a very untrustworthy indicator of average testosterone levels. The longer cycle is a daily one: Mean testosterone levels are higher in the morning (midnight to noon) than in the evening (noon to midnight) (Winters et al., 2001).

In women, blood concentrations of testosterone also vary over time, though more subtly. Testosterone concentrations vary by about twofold over the course of the menstrual cycle, with the highest concentrations occurring around the time of ovulation. Even the peak level in women is far less than the minimum levels seen in men. In spite of these seemingly low levels, testosterone does play an important role in women's sex lives, as we'll see.

Once secreted into the bloodstream, steroid molecules that are free in solution have a half-life of a few minutes, meaning that they have a 50% chance of being removed within that time. The main site of removal is the liver: As blood passes through this organ, nearly 100% of the free steroid molecules are removed and broken down. Some fraction of the secreted steroid molecules are protected from this rapid breakdown by binding to specific carrier proteins in the blood. Nevertheless, the overall half-life of a secreted steroid such as testosterone is only about 45 minutes (Lin et al., 1994). While it might seem wasteful to break down the hormones so quickly, this process allows blood levels of steroids to change fairly quickly and thus to reflect the current rate of hormone secretion. This rapid variation, in turn, allows changes in secretory rates to have an effect on target tissues within less than an hour.

SOME TISSUES CONVERT TESTOSTERONE TO DHT   The Leydig cells (in males) and thecal cells (in females) lack the enzyme 5α-reductase, so they cannot convert testosterone to the more potent androgen DHT. Other cells in the body do possess that enzyme, however. Among them are the Sertoli cells (the cells lining the seminiferous tubules that nurture the developing sperm). The Sertoli cells pick up testosterone that has diffused the short distance from the Leydig cells, convert a portion of it to DHT, and secrete this hormone into the fluid within the seminiferous tubules, where it influences the maturation of sperm.

Many cells in the tissues of the external genitalia, as well as the prostate gland, also produce 5α-reductase. These cells take up testosterone from the blood and convert it to DHT. This local production of the more potent androgen is vital for the normal development of the male genitalia during fetal life, as we'll see in Chapter 6. DHT is also produced in the skin, including the hair follicles, where it helps generate the male-typical pattern of hair distribution.

Estradiol Is Synthesized from Testosterone in Both Sexes

In women, the granulosa cells of the ovaries—the cells within the ovarian follicles that nurture the developing ova—are the main sites for the production and secretion of estradiol. They accomplish this task by picking up testosterone (and other androgens) that have diffused from the nearby thecal cells; the granulosa cells then convert these androgens to estradiol by the action of the enzyme aromatase (**Figure 5.3**). Because the ovarian follicles undergo a process of maturation linked to

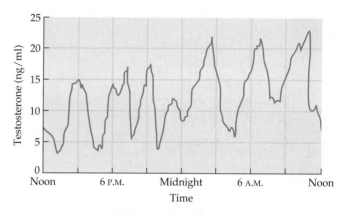

Figure 5.2 Testosterone cycles in a man Testosterone levels in the blood peak every 2 to 4 hours. Mean levels are higher during the night and morning than during the afternoon and evening. (Adapted from Johnson & Everitt, 2000.)

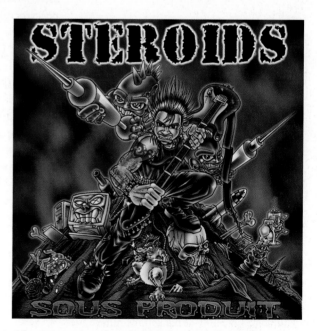

Album cover by a French punk-hardcore band illustrates the popular image of sex steroids.

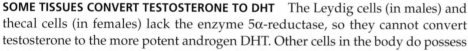

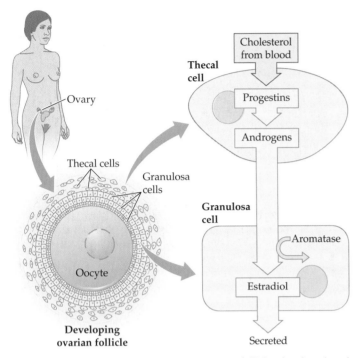

Figure 5.3 Estrogen factory In an ovarian follicle, the thecal and granulosa cells cooperate to produce estradiol.

the menstrual cycle, the concentration of estradiol in the blood varies greatly with that cycle, as we'll describe shortly.

Cells in at least one other tissue—the brain—also possess the enzyme aromatase and are therefore capable of converting testosterone to estradiol.

Progesterone Is a Female Hormone

The progestin progesterone is primarily a female hormone. In women who are undergoing menstrual cycles, progesterone is present in the blood at high levels during the luteal phase of the cycle (see below). It is also present—at even higher levels—during pregnancy. The source of progesterone is the same set of cells that secrete estradiol: the follicular granulosa cells. After ovulation, however, the ruptured follicle transforms itself into a new secretory structure, the **corpus luteum**. The granulosa cells change their appearance and metabolism and are now called **granulosa-lutein cells**. It is in this new guise that they secrete progesterone into the blood. The role of progesterone is to bring the lining of the uterus—the endometrium—into a condition suitable for implantation and pregnancy and to maintain it in that state if pregnancy occurs. Later in pregnancy, progesterone is also secreted by the placenta.

In men, progestin serves mainly as an intermediary metabolite in the synthesis of androgens. However, studies in rodents point to an influence of progesterone on behavior in males—it tends to decrease sexual activity, and it also causes males to act aggressively toward infants (Schneider et al., 2003; Schneider et al., 2005). The relevance of these findings to human behavior remains to be clarified.

Sex Steroids Activate Specific Receptor Molecules

Just as only certain cells synthesize sex steroids, only certain target cells are sensitive to them. What makes a cell sensitive to sex steroids is its possession of specific **receptor** molecules. A hormone fits into its receptor like a key into its lock. There are three different kinds of sex steroid receptor molecules: the androgen receptor, the estrogen receptor, and the progestin receptor. Some cells possess one kind of receptor, some cells possess more than one, and some cells possess none and are therefore insensitive to sex steroids.

In cells that have sex steroid receptors, the level of these receptors is regulated by numerous factors and can therefore vary over time. A cell that is exquisitely sensitive to a steroid at one time may be nearly insensitive to that same steroid a few hours or days afterward. Later in this chapter, we will see how the regulation of receptor levels contributes to sexual functions.

What characterizes individual steroids as androgens, estrogens, or progestins is their ability to bind to and activate androgen, estrogen, or progestin receptors, respectively. But different steroids within a class activate their receptors with different efficacy. Both testosterone and DHT activate androgen receptors, for example, but DHT is twice as potent as testosterone. (In other words, it has the same activating effect at one-half the concentration.)

When steroid hormones bind to their receptors, a sequence of events is triggered within the target cell that affects the activity ("expression") of the cell's genes. These changes in gene expression in turn affect the cell's structure, function, or growth. For example, an endocrine cell might be stimulated to produce and secrete more of its own hormones, or a nerve cell might become more elec-

corpus luteum A secretory structure in the ovary derived from an ovarian follicle after ovulation.

granulosa-lutein cells Cells within the corpus luteum that secrete progesterone.

receptor A molecular structure to which a hormone or neurotransmitter binds. Upon binding, the receptor triggers a specific cellular activity.

trically excitable. The cellular actions of sex steroids are described in greater detail in Web Topic 5.1 Steroid Receptors Control Gene Expression.

Proteins and Peptide Hormones Are Gene Products

Before we discuss the actions of sex steroids, we need to describe the other major class of hormones that regulate sexual functions: **proteins** and **peptides**. Peptides, like proteins, consist of chains of amino acids, but because the chains are shorter the overall size of the molecules is smaller. The distinction between proteins and peptides is somewhat arbitrary.

Oxytocin Is Secreted by Neuroendocrine Cells of the Hypothalamus

Oxytocin, a small peptide, is synthesized in the hypothalamus, principally in the cell bodies of two clusters of large neurons named the supraoptic and paraventricular nuclei (**Figure 5.4**). The hormone is transported down the axons (nerve fibers)

protein A long polymer made up of amino acids.

peptide A polymer of amino acids, usually shorter than a protein.

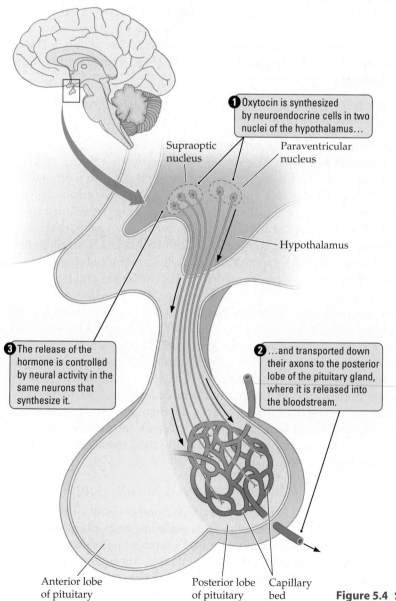

❶ Oxytocin is synthesized by neuroendocrine cells in two nuclei of the hypothalamus…

Supraoptic nucleus

Paraventricular nucleus

Hypothalamus

❸ The release of the hormone is controlled by neural activity in the same neurons that synthesize it.

❷ …and transported down their axons to the posterior lobe of the pituitary gland, where it is released into the bloodstream.

Anterior lobe of pituitary

Posterior lobe of pituitary

Capillary bed

Figure 5.4 Synthesis and release of oxytocin

pituitary gland A gland situated below and under the control of the hypothalamus; its posterior lobe secretes oxytocin and vasopressin, and its anterior lobe secretes gonadotropins and other hormones.

gonadotropin-releasing hormone (GnRH) A hormone secreted by the hypothalamus that stimulates the release of gonadotropins from the anterior lobe of the pituitary gland.

median eminence A region of the hypothalamus where GnRH is secreted, located immediately above the pituitary gland.

follicle-stimulating hormone (FSH) One of the two major gonadotropins secreted by the pituitary gland; it promotes maturation of gametes.

luteinizing hormone (LH) One of the two major gonadotropins secreted by the pituitary gland; it promotes the secretion of androgens and, in females, participates in the regulation of the menstrual cycle.

gonadotropin A hormone that regulates the function of the gonads.

prolactin A protein hormone secreted by the anterior lobe of the pituitary gland that promotes breast development, among other effects.

growth hormone A protein hormone secreted by the pituitary gland that promotes growth.

of these cells to the posterior lobe of the **pituitary gland**. It is stored in the axon terminals there and is released into the bloodstream when a barrage of nerve impulses comes down those same axons.

Oxytocin is present in the blood at low levels most of the time, but it reaches much higher levels under three circumstances: breast-feeding, childbirth, and orgasm. It causes the contraction of smooth muscle in certain tissues that are sensitive to the hormone. One of these is the breast, where oxytocin-induced contractions cause milk letdown. Another is the uterus, where contractions help expel the fetus. Oxytocin may also have effects within the brain. For example, it is thought to contribute to the pleasurable quality of orgasm, and it may also contribute to interpersonal bonding and trust (Zak, 2008).

GnRH Stimulates the Release of Pituitary Sex Hormones

Another peptide with an important sexual function is **gonadotropin-releasing hormone (GnRH)**. GnRH is produced by another set of cells in the hypothalamus (**Figure 5.5**). The axons of these cells end at the base of the brain, just above the pituitary gland, in a structure called the **median eminence**. Here the axon terminals secrete GnRH into a special set of blood vessels ("portal veins") that carry the hormone the short distance to the anterior lobe of the pituitary gland. The function of GnRH is to stimulate the release of two additional hormones, **follicle-stimulating hormone (FSH)** and **luteinizing hormone (LH)**, from glandular cells in the anterior pituitary.

The Pituitary Gonadotropins Are Follicle-Stimulating Hormone (FSH) and Luteinizing Hormone (LH)

The two anterior pituitary hormones whose release is triggered by GnRH are crucially involved in sexual functions. The names for these two hormones, follicle-stimulating hormone (FSH) and luteinizing hormone (LH), refer to their actions in women; nevertheless, they play a vital role in regulating the functions of the gonads in both sexes, as we'll see shortly. The two hormones are therefore known collectively as **gonadotropins**. (The suffix "–tropin" indicates an agent that influences something else—in this case, the gonads.) Both FSH and LH are proteins. The mechanism of action of GnRH on the FSH- and LH-secreting cells is described in greater detail in Web Topic 5.2 Mechanism of Action of GnRH and Other Protein/Peptide Hormones.

The secretion of GnRH into the portal blood vessels is cyclical, with a peak secretion about every 1 to 2 hours. Each pulse of GnRH may trigger a pulse of FSH and LH release, but not all pulses do; thus FSH and LH are secreted in pulses that are somewhat less frequent than the GnRH pulses. A continuous high level of GnRH does *not* cause a sustained release of FSH and LH; rather, the rate of release of the two gonadotropins gradually declines to zero. This fact can be important clinically. If a person's sexual functions are disrupted due to a deficiency in GnRH secretion, synthetic GnRH can be supplied by intravenous infusion, but it has to be infused as a series of pulses mimicking the natural time course of release from the median eminence.

Other Pituitary Hormones Include Prolactin and Growth Hormone

Two other hormones released from the anterior pituitary—both of them proteins—have sex-related functions. **Prolactin**, as its name suggests, plays an important role in preparing the breasts for lactation (see Chapter 11), but it also seems to play a general role in strengthening the effects of other hormones. In addition, prolactin may have behavioral effects. **Growth hormone**, as its name implies, stimulates growth throughout the body. Its main connection with sex is that it

Figure 5.5 Pathway for control of gonadotropin secretion by GnRH

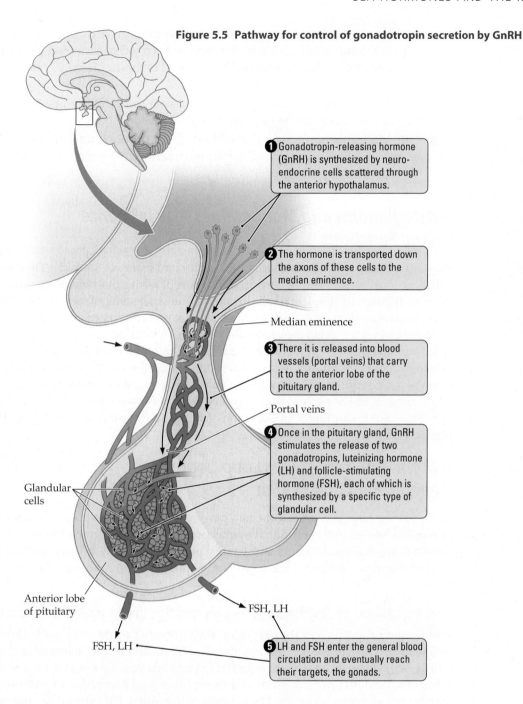

❶ Gonadotropin-releasing hormone (GnRH) is synthesized by neuro-endocrine cells scattered through the anterior hypothalamus.

❷ The hormone is transported down the axons of these cells to the median eminence.

Median eminence

❸ There it is released into blood vessels (portal veins) that carry it to the anterior lobe of the pituitary gland.

Portal veins

❹ Once in the pituitary gland, GnRH stimulates the release of two gonadotropins, luteinizing hormone (LH) and follicle-stimulating hormone (FSH), each of which is synthesized by a specific type of glandular cell.

Glandular cells

Anterior lobe of pituitary

FSH, LH

FSH, LH

❺ LH and FSH enter the general blood circulation and eventually reach their targets, the gonads.

plays an important role at puberty (see Chapter 6). Like prolactin, growth hormone also plays a role in breast development.

Protein Hormones Are Secreted by Other Tissues

We need to describe three protein hormones that are not produced by the brain:

■ **Human chorionic gonadotropin (hCG),** as its name suggests, influences the gonads in the same manner as do FSH and LH; in fact, it is closely related to those hormones in structure. It is synthesized by the **conceptus** (the newly formed organism that precedes a distinct embryo—see Chapter 6) and, later

human chorionic gonadotropin (hCG) A gonadotropin secreted by the conceptus and by the placenta; its presence in a woman's blood is an indicator of pregnancy.

conceptus The developing organism from the 2-cell stage onward, including both embryonic and extraembryonic tissues.

inhibin A peptide hormone involved in the interaction between the pituitary gland and the gonads as well as in other functions.

anti-Müllerian hormone (AMH) A peptide hormone secreted by Sertoli cells that prevents the development of the female internal reproductive tract.

serotonin A monoamine derived from the amino acid tryptophan that functions as a neurotransmitter.

dopamine A catecholamine that serves as a neurotransmitter and also as a hormone, inhibiting the release of prolactin from the anterior lobe of the pituitary gland.

prostaglandins A group of non-steroidal signalling molecules that, among many other functions, help prepare the uterus for childbirth.

monoamines Compounds containing an amine group, including catecholamines and serotonin.

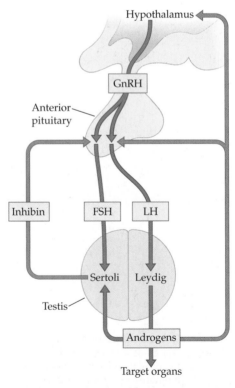

Figure 5.6 Hormonal interactions in the hypothalamic–pituitary–testicular control system Stimulatory influences are shown in blue, inhibitory influences in red.

in pregnancy, by the placenta. Because it is synthesized only during pregnancy, the presence of hCG is a useful indicator that a woman is in fact pregnant; pregnancy tests often depend on the detection of this hormone in a woman's blood or urine (see Chapter 11).

- **Inhibin** is secreted by the gonads and acts on the pituitary gland. It also plays a role locally in the regulation of gonadal function.
- **Anti-Müllerian hormone** is secreted by the testis during fetal life and plays an important role in blocking the development of the female reproductive tract in males (see Chapter 6).

Prostaglandins and Monoamines Also Influence Sexual Functions

Prostaglandins are lipids, but structurally different from sex steroids. They generally act locally, near where they are synthesized, rather than traveling through the bloodstream, so they are not hormones in the strict sense. Among other functions, prostaglandins play a role in preparing the uterus and cervix for childbirth.

Monoamines are small molecules that include dopamine, norepinephrine (also called noradrenaline), epinephrine (adrenaline), and serotonin. **Serotonin** plays a role in sexual function as a neurotransmitter within the central nervous system, but it is not a hormone. **Dopamine**, besides acting as a neurotransmitter, acts as a hormone in the hypothalamic–pituitary control system: It is secreted by the hypothalamus and inhibits the secretion of prolactin from the anterior lobe of the pituitary gland.

A Brain–Pituitary–Testis Loop Controls Gonadal Function in Men

Now that we have introduced the key players, we can look at how they interact to regulate sexual and reproductive functions. First we'll examine the relatively simple hormonal mechanisms that control gonadal function in men. Then we'll turn to the more complex control system responsible for a woman's menstrual cycle.

The Regulation of Testosterone Levels and Spermatogenesis Is Coupled

The hormonal pathways that regulate the functions of the testes are shown schematically in **Figure 5.6**. As already described, the hypothalamus secretes GnRH, which stimulates the secretion of LH and FSH by the anterior lobe of the pituitary gland. LH in turn stimulates the synthesis and secretion of androgens (primarily testosterone) by the Leydig cells of the testes. FSH stimulates the Sertoli cells of the testes to increase the production of sperm (spermatogenesis).

From this, you might imagine that LH and FSH would each be independently responsible for activating one of the two testicular functions—either hormone secretion or spermatogenesis. But that assumption would ignore the purpose of the entire system. From a reproductive standpoint, hormone secretion and spermatogenesis should be *coupled*. There is no biological point in having the testes secrete high levels of testosterone, with all the consequences for a man's physical and psychological state that we'll describe in this and later chapters, unless he is producing sperm—and vice versa. To achieve this coupling, Sertoli cells promote high levels of sperm production only when *both* FSH *and* androgens are present. This coupling is achieved by a process that is described further in Web Topic 5.3 Coupling between Androgen Secretion and Spermatogenesis.

Testosterone and Inhibin Exert Negative Feedback on Gonadotropin Release

The final (and crucial) element in this control system is **negative feedback**. Testosterone circulating in the blood has a damping effect on the secretion of LH: The *higher* the concentration of testosterone in the blood, the *less* LH is secreted by the pituitary (see Figure 5.6). This negative feedback occurs via two routes. The first is a direct effect of testosterone on the LH–secreting cells in the anterior lobe of the pituitary, depressing their response to the GnRH pulses coming from the hypothalamus. The second is an effect of testosterone on the hypothalamus, decreasing the frequency of GnRH pulses.

The entire hypothalamic-pituitary-testicular control circuit—the positive effects of GnRH on LH secretion, the positive effects of LH secretion on testosterone secretion, and the negative effects of testosterone on GnRH and LH secretion—functions to control testosterone levels and to keep them within a normal range. So, for example, if a man loses one testis (perhaps as a result of surgery for testicular cancer), the resulting drop in testosterone levels will allow LH levels to rise, and this rise, in turn, will stimulate the remaining testis to increase its testosterone production, so that the concentration of testosterone in the blood returns to normal or near-normal levels (see Web Activity 5.2 Hypothalamic–Pituitary Endocrine–Axis).

What about the regulation of spermatogenesis? Is there an equivalent signal that feeds back to the pituitary or hypothalamus and regulates the secretion of FSH? In part, such a signal is provided by testosterone: Because testosterone controls the secretion of GnRH and because GnRH stimulates both LH and FSH secretion by the pituitary gland, increasing testosterone levels tend to have a negative feedback effect on FSH as well as LH. However, the Sertoli cells also send a signal back to the pituitary gland that is more directly related to spermatogenesis, in the form of inhibin. In a manner that is not well understood, the level of inhibin secretion by Sertoli cells reflects the rate at which sperm are being produced (Pierik et al., 2003). The secreted inhibin travels in the bloodstream to the pituitary gland, where it directly depresses the secretion of FSH. Thus there is a second, partially independent control circuit that maintains sperm production at normal levels.

Testosterone Has Multiple Functions in Men

Testosterone has an important role in male development, both during fetal life and at puberty. However, we will postpone discussion of these developmental effects of the hormone until Chapter 6. Here, we cover the effects of testosterone in adult men.

We've already described two effects of testosterone in men: the facilitation (in combination with FSH) of spermatogenesis and the negative feedback regulation of LH secretion. Besides these two functions, testosterone has many others—some structural, some metabolic, and some behavioral. What links these effects is that they all contribute—either directly or indirectly—to male sexual function.

TESTOSTERONE SUPPORTS GENITAL TISSUES Most of a man's internal and external genital structures require the presence of testosterone for normal functioning. If an adult man is castrated (that is, both his testes are removed, as may sometimes be necessary to treat testicular cancer or prostate cancer), his prostate gland and seminal vesicles cease to produce their secretions and revert to an anatomically less mature state. However, administration of testosterone causes them to return to a normal functioning state. Not surprisingly, these glands and other genital structures are rich in androgen receptors. These effects of testosterone are height-

negative feedback A control system in which a compound directly or indirectly lowers its own rate of synthesis or secretion.

FAQ **I'm a young guy, but I'm not that interested in sex. Is my testosterone level low?** There are many possible reasons for a low sex drive, ranging from psychological or social factors to hormonal problems. See a sympathetic doctor. A testosterone test can be done, and if your testosterone levels are low, the reason can be investigated and perhaps corrected. In the unlikely case that you need a supplement, your doctor can prescribe testosterone skin patches.

medial preoptic area A region of the hypothalamus involved in the regulation of sexual behaviors typically shown by males.

anabolic Tending to increase tissue mass.

ened by the presence in the target tissues of the enzyme 5α-reductase, which converts testosterone to the more potent androgen DHT.

Testosterone also influences the erectile capacity of the penis. In healthy men, penile erections occur during REM sleep, as described in Chapter 4. These nocturnal erections cease some weeks after castration and return with testosterone treatment. Erections caused by exposure to erotic stimuli (e.g., a sexually explicit video) are only partially impaired after castration, however (Zverina et al., 1990). This residual capacity for erection may be maintained by testosterone from nontesticular sources—most likely the adrenal glands—for men who can still experience an erection after castration have higher circulating levels of testosterone than those who cannot.

TESTOSTERONE INFLUENCES SEXUAL BEHAVIOR   In addition to its influence on genital structures, testosterone influences the central nervous system, facilitating sexual behavior and influencing a variety of other psychological processes. This function has been studied in greatest detail in rats (Meisel & Sachs, 1994). If a male rat is castrated and repeatedly tested with receptive females, he continues to mount them, but he performs intromission (vaginal penetration) and ejaculation less and less often over a period of a few weeks. Eventually, he even stops mounting. Normal behavior can be restored by injection of minute quantities of testosterone into the hypothalamus—quantities that do not raise blood levels significantly. The most sensitive area for restoration of sexual function is a zone toward the front of the hypothalamus known as the **medial preoptic area**. This area is very rich in androgen receptors (**Figure 5.7**), but such receptors are found at lower levels in many brain regions besides the hypothalamus, suggesting that testosterone has more widespread effects.

It should be borne in mind that, as mentioned above, circulating testosterone has a half-life of less than an hour, so testosterone drops to very low levels within a few hours of castration. Yet sexual feelings and sexual behaviors decline over a much longer time span. Evidently, testosterone does not regulate sexuality on a minute-to-minute or hour-to-hour basis. Rather, it influences some fairly durable feature of brain organization, such as synaptic circuitry, that is necessary for sexual behavior—a topic that we'll cover in Chapter 6.

Testosterone also influences sexual behavior in humans. Most men who have been castrated experience a profound decline in or complete cessation of sexual thoughts and sexual behavior. This decline is variable among individuals, however, and can take many months or even years to show itself.

Part of the testosterone that enters the brain is converted to estradiol by the enzyme aromatase. The estradiol formed in this fashion appears to be important for some aspects of sexual function, but there are major differences between species in this respect, and the role of this locally generated estradiol for sexual feelings and behavior in men is uncertain. For more information on this topic, see Web Topic 5.4 Testosterone Conversion to Estradiol.

TESTOSTERONE HAS ANABOLIC EFFECTS   Testosterone and other androgens have a broad influence on body systems, tending to promote tissue growth. These **anabolic** effects are easiest to see in the musculature; in fact, androgens are the main reason why men tend to be more muscular than women after puberty. But androgens also promote the formation of red blood cells, increasing the oxygen-carrying capacity of the blood, and they increase the mass of the liver and kidneys as well. The anabolic effects of androgens is the reason they are abused by athletes (of both sexes), but such use carries significant health risks (**Box 5.2**).

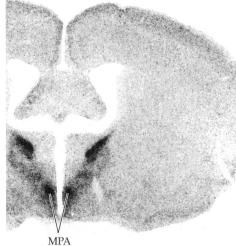

MPA

Figure 5.7 Androgen receptors in the brain This is a cross section of a rat's brain at the level of the hypothalamus. The receptors (present in the dark areas) have been visualized by in situ hybridization, a technique that detects the messenger RNA that codes for the receptor protein. The receptor is present in the medial preoptic area (MPA) of the hypothalamus as well as some other brain regions. (Courtesy of Richard Simerly, Oregon Regional Primate Research Center.)

Biology of Sex

BOX 5.2 Steroids and Sports

In June 2003, officials at the United States Anti-Doping Agency (USADA) received a package mailed by an anonymous track coach (later identified as Trevor Graham, the former coach of track stars Marion Jones and Tim Montgomery). The package contained a used syringe. According to the coach, the syringe had contained an undetectable steroid known as "the clear" that had been used illegally by several athletes to improve their performance.

Athletes have used steroids for decades. Androgens such as testosterone have anabolic effects: They increase muscle bulk and strength—an obvious benefit to athletes. The governing bodies of most sports ban their use, but illicit use (by both men and women) still occurs, and not all androgens are banned in all sports. Baseball slugger Mark McGwire used the androgen androstenedione (the immediate metabolic precursor of testosterone) legally during the 1998 season, when he hit a record-breaking 70 home runs. (In 2004 the FDA banned the sale of androstenedione, and its use in major-league baseball was banned in the same year.) Even some high school athletes use steroids, according to news reports (Associated Press, 2005).

Drug testing has tripped up many steroid users. Cyclist Floyd Landis, for example, had his 2006 Tour de France victory revoked when a urine sample taken during the race was found to contain synthetic testosterone. The widespread use of such tests has motivated a search for substances that have anabolic effects but are not picked up in standard urine or blood tests—the so-called **designer steroids**. When the USADA officials received the syringe from Trevor Graham, they subjected it to lengthy testing, which led to the identification of a synthetic steroid previously unknown to science—tetrahydrogestrinone, or THG (Catlin et al., 2004). The source of the THG was identified as BALCO Labs in Burlingame, California. Eventually BALCO's owner and several other persons associated with the company served prison sentences for their role in the scandal.

According to U.S. prosecutors, illegal use of a designer steroid altered the head and body of Olympic cyclist Tammy Thomas.

UCLA scientists developed a screening test to detect THG, and application of this test to previously taken urine samples identified several prominent U.S. track and field athletes as users of THG. These included Kelli White, the 2003 world champion in the 100- and 200-m competitions. White—who also admitted using two other banned drugs—was stripped of her titles and banned from competition for two years (Associated Press, 2004c), as was the European 100-m champion Dwain Chambers. Four members of the Oakland Raiders football team also tested positive for THG. They were fined but escaped suspension because THG was not specifically listed as a banned drug at the time their urine samples were collected (Gay, 2004).

Sprinter Marion Jones was also identified as a THG user. She pleaded guilty to lying to federal investigators, and her gold medals from the 2000 Olympics (as well as those of her relay teammates) were forfeited (Associated Press, 2007e). She was sentenced to 6 months of imprisonment. Yet another person caught up in the BALCO scandal was baseball slugger Barry Bonds: He was indicted in 2007 for perjury and obstruction of justice regarding his testimony in the case. Bonds and Floyd Landis continue to deny steroid use. More recently, Olympic cyclist Tammy Thomas (see figure) was indicted for lying to a grand jury about drug use: Prosecutors alleged that Thomas experienced abnormal growth of her skull, hands, and feet, deepening of her voice, and growth of a full beard necessitating shaving as a result of taking a designer steroid (Associated Press, 2008b). Thomas has denied drug use, but she has been banned from competition for life.

The use of steroids by athletes is a bad idea not only because it is cheating but also because it can cause significant ill-effects. These include sterility, liver disease, undesirable changes in blood lipids, and pathological aggressiveness ("'roid rage") (Choi & Pope, 1994). In women it can cause excess hair growth, acne, voice changes, and reproductive problems. Perhaps the most systematic abuse of androgens occurred in the former East Germany, where thousands of athletes of both sexes (including minors) were given androgens and other drugs as part of a government-sanctioned program. This program brought numerous world records and Olympic medals to East Germany in the period between 1966 and 1990, but the health effects for the athletes, especially the women, were ruinous (Franke & Berendonk, 1997).

designer steroids Synthetic steroids intended to evade detection in drug tests.

menstruation The breakdown of the endometrium at approximately monthly intervals, with consequent loss of tissue and blood from the vagina.

Estradiol Has Wide-Ranging Effects in Men's Bodies

Besides being produced locally in the brain from testosterone, estradiol is also secreted by the testes, as we described earlier, and it has several important effects (Sharpe, 1997):

- Estradiol facilitates the maturation and concentration of sperm in the epididymis (Hess et al., 1997).
- Estradiol is responsible for terminating the growth of the limb bones at the conclusion of puberty (see Chapter 6). Therefore, those rare individuals who congenitally lack estrogen receptors keep on growing after puberty, reaching a height of 7 feet or more.
- Estradiol maintains the normal density of bone. Low estrogen levels are associated with bone demineralization (osteoporosis). You may know that osteoporosis sometimes occurs as a consequence of estrogen deficiency in postmenopausal women (see Chapter 13), but in fact estradiol is required to maintain normal bone density in both sexes throughout adult life.

Estrogen receptors are found widely throughout the body—in the skin, gut, and heart, for example—so there are probably other actions of estrogens that remain to be discovered.

Menstruation Has Biological and Social Aspects

The menstrual cycle has one obvious external sign: the vaginal discharge of endometrial tissue and blood that women experience at roughly monthly intervals during their fertile years, except when they are pregnant or intensively nursing an infant. This simple outward event—**menstruation**—is brought about by a complex internal mechanism that involves the ovaries, the brain, the pituitary gland, and the uterus.

Before looking at the biological processes underlying the menstrual cycle, let's first acknowledge that menstruation itself has important psychological, cultural, and practical aspects. Most women can remember their first menstrual period—an event that heralds their passage into womanhood more clearly than any other and that is celebrated by special rituals in many cultures. Yet negative attitudes and beliefs about menstruation are also common around the world, especially among men (**Box 5.3**).

Contemporary American women have very divergent attitudes toward menstruation. In 1999, Brazilian gynecologist Elsimar Coutinho published a book, entitled *Is Menstruation Obsolete?*, in which he suggested ways that women could abolish the entire phenomenon. Some women saw his message as a godsend, but others saw it as the ultimate sexist assault—the "perfecting" of women's bodies by making them more like men's. The debate has continued and has intensified with the FDA approval of contraceptive regimes that reduce the frequency of a woman's periods or eliminate them completely (see Chapter 12).

A long-running international debate on the question "Would you stop menstruating if you could?" has enlivened the Web pages of the Museum of Menstruation—nearly a thousand women have voiced their opinions (see Web Resources at the end of this chapter). Here are some contributions:

"I would be the happiest person on earth if I didn't have to menstruate. It's just the worst annoying and unpleasant time that happens too often and for too many years."

"No, I would not stop my periods without good reason. When I menstruate, I feel healthy, alive, and female. In the days leading up to my period, when my body feels full and self-aware, I feel sexy. Good or bad, the experience reconnects me to my body, to my sexuality, and even a conscious awareness of my internal emotional fluctuations."

FAQ **I have heavy periods, and I understand I may be low in iron during those times. What do you recommend?**

Repeated heavy menstrual bleeding can indeed cause iron deficiency. Your healthcare provider can do an examination and blood test to see if that's the case with you—the test can be done at any time in your cycle. You can increase your intake of foods rich in iron (e.g., red meat, liver, fortified breakfast cereals, and some vegetables and legumes), or you can take supplements. In addition, there may be a cause for your heavy periods that is treatable, or they can be made lighter or even abolished by treatment with certain hormonal contraceptives.

Society, Values, and the Law

BOX 5.3 Attitudes toward Menstruation

Across many cultures and historical periods, men have often viewed menstruating woman with distaste, fear, or moral concern. The Roman naturalist Pliny the Elder declared that menstrual blood was a dangerous poison. If a man had sex with a menstruating woman, Pliny wrote, he risked serious harm or even death—especially if the sex act coincided with a total solar eclipse!

According to Judeo-Christian Scripture, a menstruating woman is unclean, as is any person who touches her bedding (Leviticus 15:19–21). In the Orthodox Judaic tradition of *niddut*, a woman must sleep apart from her husband for several days during and after her period and must undergo a ritual cleansing bath (*mikvah*) before returning to him. The Christian theologian St. Augustine taught that sex with a menstruating woman was sinful. The Qur'an likewise prohibits sex with a menstruating woman, and (in some interpretations) prohibits a menstruating woman from praying, fasting, or entering a mosque.

Some cultures have even required women to sleep away from the household altogether during their periods. For example, among the Dogon, a traditional cliff-dwelling people in Mali, Africa, menstruating women have to sleep in a "menstrual hut" for about five nights (see figure). During that time they may work in the fields but may not sleep with or cook for their husbands. A violation of this taboo will, it is believed, bring famine or sickness. The taboo is imposed by the Dogon men, and its ultimate motive is that it gives men precise information about the timing of women's menstruation (Strassmann, 1992, 1996). Why is this information important? In a culture such as that of the Dogon, women experience menstrual cycles (and therefore are able to become pregnant) only for very short stretches of time; the rest of time they are either pregnant or they are intensively breast-feeding their babies, a practice that suppresses the menstrual cycle. Knowledge of the occurrence of menstruation helps men

identify the limited time during which a woman can become pregnant. If she has been adulterous around the time of onset of pregnancy, the father (and all of the people related to him by

A Dogon menstrual hut

the male line of descent) will reject the child as an imposter. Even if the husband wishes to accept paternity, the other members of his lineage, who own land jointly, have the right to overrule his claims. The father and his male relatives have a common interest in guarding against mistaken paternity attributions, so each male line has its own menstrual hut.

In contemporary Western culture, attitudes toward menstruation vary, but the belief that women should avoid vaginal intercourse during their periods is still widespread. A sizable majority (70% to 80%) of men and women do in fact avoid this practice (Barnhart et al., 1995; Tanfer & Aral, 1996). Among some women, this avoid-

ance is bolstered by the idea that sex during menstruation endangers their own health.

Other men and women may avoid sex during menstruation out of a distaste for the prac-

tice, for religious reasons, or because the woman has symptoms associated with menstruation that make her uninterested in sex. A further possible reason may be the low testosterone levels at the menstrual phase of a woman's cycle, which may reduce her interest in sex.

Still, about 20% of women in the United States do engage in vaginal sex during menstruation. These women tend to be white and well educated (Tanfer & Aral, 1996). Some women use a diaphragm (see Chapter 12) or menstrual cup to block the menstrual discharge during sex. Others may simply place a dark-colored towel over their sheets to prevent staining. Alternatively, many couples engage in forms of lovemaking during menstruation that do not involve coitus. (Photo © Beverly I. Strassmann.)

"Damn yes, I would. I have a one-year-old baby and since I got a Norplant [an implanted hormonal contraceptive that is not available in the United States.] inserted, I haven't had my period and have never been happier. I would give anything to feel like this forever. I don't need to bleed for five days to feel like a woman. So bring those tablets on; I am sure women here in Zimbabwe would be happy for that kind of liberation."

menstrual toxic shock syndrome A rare but life-threatening illness caused by a staphylococcal infection and associated with tampon use.

"No. Stopping it via chemicals must surely be harmful—I'll bet they won't find out how harmful for a while. Our bodies do everything for a reason, and shutting things down like that will surely have its effect, though it's not apparent right away."

As far as is known, abolishing menstruation has no harmful effects on the body. It could have negative psychological effects, however, in women who believe that menstruation is important to health. We will discuss menstrual suppression further in the context of contraception (see Chapter 12).

Women Use Pads, Tampons, or Cups during Menstruation

Most American women who menstruate use sanitary napkins ("pads"), panty liners, or tampons in order to absorb their menstrual flow (**Figure 5.8**). Pads and panty liners are worn on the outside of the body—the main difference between them is that panty liners are thinner and only usable for very light flow. Tampons—absorbent plugs, about 3 to 4 cm long (1.5 inches), made of cotton or synthetic fiber—are placed inside the vagina, sometimes with the help of a plastic or cardboard applicator. They have an attached string that hangs outside the body to facilitate removal. About 70% of women in the United States and Canada who are menstruating use tampons (Parsonnet et al., 2005).

Although tampons are very convenient—even allowing such activities as swimming during a woman's period—their use has been linked to a rare but dangerous condition known as **menstrual toxic shock syndrome** (Hanrahan, 1994). This condition, caused by certain strains of the bacterium *Staphylococcus aureus*, is marked by high fever, vomiting, diarrhea, rash, and other symptoms and can be fatal in up to 10% of affected women. The connection between toxic shock syndrome and tampon use was discovered in 1980. Of the 344 women who developed the syndrome in that year (28 of whom died), 70% had used one particular type of extra-absorbent tampon, which has since been withdrawn from the market. Since then, menstrual toxic shock syndrome has become much less common, and deaths are extremely rare.

Tampons range in absorbency from less than 5 g (0.2 ounces—"low absorbency") to 18 g (0.6 ounces) or more ("highest absorbency"). A woman who uses tampons is advised to use the least absorbent tampon compatible with satisfactory function (U.S. Food and Drug Administration, 1999). Tampons should be changed after 4 to 8 hours of use. If the tampon is not saturated after that time (i.e., it still

FAQ I've heard that tampons contain asbestos and dioxins—will they give me cancer?
Tampons don't contain asbestos—that was an old Internet hoax. They may contain minute quantities of dioxins—too little to pose any conceivable health hazard.

(A) (B)

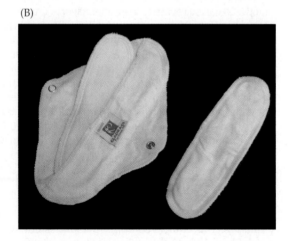

Figure 5.8 Tampons and menstrual pads (A) Tampons come in varying absorbencies and are available with or without applicators. (B) Most menstrual pads are disposable, but these are washable and are made of cotton cloth.

Figure 5.9 Menstrual cups block menstrual flow. The Instead cup (left) is disposable. The Keeper cup (right) lasts for years.

has white cotton showing), the woman should switch to a less absorbent tampon. It's a good idea to have varying grades of tampons available to deal with the varying flow over the course of the period, because the flow usually lessens toward the end of the period. It is also a good idea to use a pad rather than a tampon for some portion of the menstrual period. Any woman who develops a high fever (38.9°C, 102°F) while using a tampon should remove it and seek medical attention immediately. Although toxic shock syndrome is a serious matter, it is hardly a reason for not using tampons. Many millions of women in the United States use them, and only a very few cases of menstrual toxic shock syndrome are reported per year.

As an alternative to pads and tampons, there are also **menstrual cups**: The three most widely available brands are called Instead, Keeper, and DivaCup. These are worn inside the vagina and dam the menstrual flow rather than absorbing it (**Figure 5.9**). They have to be emptied and replaced two or three times a day. The Instead device is made of soft thermoplastic and is for one-time use only. It is placed deep within the vagina against the cervix, so it permits coitus while it is worn. (It does not function as a contraceptive, however.) The Keeper, as its name suggests, is a reusable device—it is made of gum rubber—and it is therefore cheaper over time (and more environmentally friendly) than tampons or pads. It is placed just a little way into the vagina, so coitus is not possible while wearing it. The DivaCup resembles the Keeper and is also reusable, but is made of silicone.

menstrual cup A cup placed within the vagina that collects the menstrual flow.

The Menstrual Cycle Involves the Ovaries, Brain, Pituitary, and Uterus

Now let's return to the biology of the menstrual cycle. What we call the "menstrual cycle" actually consists of two cycles. One is the cycle of hormonal interactions between the ovaries, the hypothalamus, and the pituitary gland. This is sometimes called the "ovarian cycle." The other is the cycle of changes in the endometrium of the uterus, which is responsible for menstrual periods. But the endometrial cycle is driven by the ovarian cycle, so the two cycles cannot get out of synch with each other. Thus it is convenient to speak of a single, overarching "menstrual cycle" that includes all the organs just mentioned.

The uterus is influenced in a dramatic way by the changing levels of ovarian hormones around the menstrual cycle, but it is an entirely passive player, as far as we know. Thus, if the uterus is surgically removed in a premenopausal woman (and the ovaries are left in place), menstruation ceases, but the hormonal fluctu-

ovulation Release of an ovum from the ovary.

mittelschmerz Pain associated with ovulation.

follicular phase The phase of the menstrual cycle when follicles are developing under the influence of gonadotropins.

preovulatory phase An alternative term for follicular phase.

luteal phase The phase of the menstrual cycle between ovulation and the beginning of menstruation.

postovulatory phase An alternative term for luteal phase.

ations of the menstrual cycle continue just as before. If the ovaries are removed and the uterus is left in place, the endometrial cycle ceases and the woman experiences a premature menopause.

The Cycle Is of Variable Length

The length of the menstrual cycle varies greatly among women and can also vary from one cycle to the next in the same woman. Most women have cycles lasting between 24 and 32 days, but cycles as short as 20 days or as long as 36 days are not unusual or unhealthy. Cycle length tends to be irregular for several years after the cycles begin at puberty. Healthcare providers should ask teenage girls about their menstrual cycles, both in order to provide reassurance and to identify problems needing medical attention (American Academy of Pediatrics, 2006). Cycles are also irregular at the approach of menopause.

Even during a woman's reproductive years menstruation can be irregular, infrequent, or absent for a variety of reasons (see below). Menstrual cycles cease during pregnancy and, to a less predictable degree, during the time when a mother is breast-feeding her infant. It has been claimed that the menstrual cycles of women who live together tend to synchronize, but the reality of this phenomenon has been contested (**Box 5.4**).

The Cycle Consists of Menstrual, Follicular, and Luteal Phases

Although menstruation is the obvious outward sign of the menstrual cycle, its most significant internal event is **ovulation**, which involves the release of an ovum from one or the other ovary about midway between one menstrual period and the next. Some women feel abdominal pain (called **mittelschmerz**, a German word meaning "middle pain") at the time of ovulation and may even be able to tell from the location of the pain whether the ovum was released from the left or right ovary.

The portion of the menstrual cycle between menstruation and ovulation is called the **follicular** or **preovulatory phase** because it is marked by the maturation of follicles in the ovaries. The portion of the cycle between ovulation and menstruation is called the **luteal** or **postovulatory phase** because it is marked by the presence of a corpus luteum—a hormone-secreting structure formed from the single follicle that ruptured at ovulation. (Yet another pair of names for these two phases—proliferative phase and secretory phase—refers to processes that take place in the uterus, which we examine later in this chapter.)

A typical 28-day cycle is divided up roughly as follows: The menstrual phase occupies days 1 through 5, the follicular phase occupies days 6 through 14, and the luteal phase occupies days 15 through 28 (**Figure 5.10**). Of these three phases, the luteal phase is the most constant—it usually lasts 14 days—give or take 2 days. Most of the variation in total cycle length is accounted for by variation in the other two phases (see Web Activity 5.3 Ovarian and Uterine Cycles).

The Menstrual Phase Is Triggered by a Drop in Progesterone Levels

During the menstrual phase, much of the inner lining of the uterus—the endometrium—breaks down and is sloughed off. The purpose of this process is to transform the endometrium from a state in which it is capable of sustaining pregnancy to a state in which it facilitates the transport of sperm. The full thickness of the endometrium is not lost during menstruation. The deepest portion remains intact, and this "basal layer" will be the source for regeneration of the endometrium after menstruation ends.

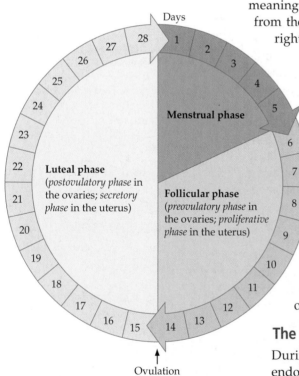

Figure 5.10 A 28-day menstrual cycle When cycles are markedly longer or shorter than 28 days, it is because of differences in the lengths of the menstrual or follicular phases; the luteal phase is nearly always close to 14 days long, as shown here.

Biology of Sex

BOX 5.4 Menstrual Synchrony: Reality or Myth?

Do women who live together get their periods at the same time? Anecdotal accounts have long suggested that they do, but scientific evidence was lacking until 1970. In that year Martha McClintock, then a student at Wellesley College, decided to investigate the matter. Her results ignited a scientific controversy that still rages today.

McClintock kept records of the menstrual periods of the students in her dormitory and found that, over the course of a semester, the periods of women who spent a lot of time together occurred closer and closer in time. Her analysis (McClintock, 1971), appeared to give "menstrual synchrony" scientific grounding.

What's more, her findings resonated with the spirit of 1970s feminism. Here was a biological expression of solidarity among women— a kinship that men knew nothing about and could never join. Before long, menstrual synchrony became common knowledge—something that most people had heard about and probably believed.

Yet the existence of menstrual synchrony remains highly controversial. Although some studies seem to support McClintock's claims, at least in part (Weller et al., 1995; Weller & Weller, 1997), other researchers have failed to detect synchrony, even in circumstances very similar to those of McClintock's original study, or have found methodological problems in the studies that do claim to find synchrony (Arden & Dye, 1998; Yang & Schank, 2006). Two groups of researchers failed to find any menstrual synchrony between cohabiting lesbian couples,

Out of sync Martha McClintock (left) says menstrual synchrony exists; Beverly Strassmann (right) is skeptical.

whom one might imagine would be the *most* likely to synchronize (Trevathan et al., 1993; Weller & Weller, 1998).

One of the most vocal critics of McClintock's work is anthropologist Beverly Strassmann (Strassmann, 1997, 1999). Strassmann studied the Dogon, a traditional West African people who have the custom of sending menstruating women to a "menstrual hut" (see Box 5.3). Because of this practice, it was easy for Strassmann to keep track of the menstrual periods of all the women in the community. She never observed synchronization of cycles, even between women who were sisters or close friends. (She also failed to find any relationship

between menstrual periods and the phases of the moon, a notion that has even wider currency than menstrual synchrony.)

McClintock herself remains adamant that the phenomenon of menstrual synchrony exists, and she claims to have discovered its mechanism— pheromones released by women that supposedly affect the timing of menstruation in other women who smell them (McClintock, 1999). Still, McClintock is willing to admit that the phenomenon may be a lot more complicated than she originally thought. Sometimes women synchronize, she says, sometimes they *de*synchronize, and sometimes they just remain random.

The sloughing-off process is triggered primarily by a drop in the circulating level of the hormone progesterone, which is secreted by the corpus luteum (Johnson, 2007). Blood levels of estrogens also drop at this time. These and other processes are represented diagrammatically in **Figure 5.11**.

There is a negative feedback relationship between estrogen levels and the secretion of the gonadotropins (LH and FSH) by the pituitary gland. This relationship is quite similar to the one we have already described between testosterone and gonadotropin secretion, though with an important extra detail that we'll get to shortly. The negative feedback effect of estrogen is exerted both on the pituitary gland (reducing the sensitivity of the gonadotropin-secreting cells to GnRH) and on the hypothalamus (decreasing the secretion of GnRH). Thus, as estrogen levels fall at the beginning of the menstrual phase, the negative feedback effect diminishes, allowing circulating LH and FSH levels to rise (see Figure 5.11). These

FAQ **Can I get pregnant during my period?**

The chances are low but increase somewhat toward the end of the period, especially if you have long periods or short or irregular cycles. Also, women sometimes experience light bleeding ("spotting") at mid-cycle. If you mistake this for your menstrual period and have unprotected sex, you could very easily become pregnant.

Figure 5.11 Main processes of the menstrual cycle
(A–C) Changes in the circulating levels of the major hormones involved in the cycle. (D) The development of an ovarian follicle, the release of the ovum at ovulation, and the conversion of the follicle to a corpus luteum. (E) The breakdown of the endometrium during the menstrual phase, followed by its regrowth during the follicular and early luteal phases. (See Web Activity 5.4.)

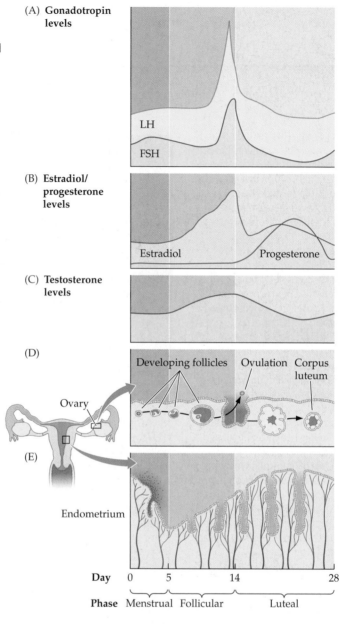

increased gonadotropin levels—in particular, the increase in FSH—promote the development of follicles in the ovaries.

The Follicular Phase Is Marked by the Maturation of Ovarian Follicles

A newborn girl's ovaries contain about 2 million egg cells. These cells, called **primary oocytes**, are arrested in the first of their two meiotic divisions. The traditional belief is that no further oocytes are generated after birth, but recent studies suggest that some new oocytes are generated from a stem-cell population even during adult life (Bukovsky et al., 2005). Even so, the total number of oocytes gradually decreases, so that by the age of puberty a woman is down to about 400,000 oocytes.

Each oocyte is surrounded by a thin layer of granulosa cells, forming a **primordial follicle** (**Figure 5.12**). The ovary consists largely of primordial follicles,

primary oocyte An oocyte arrested in its first meiotic division.

primordial follicle An undeveloped primary oocyte with its surrounding granulosa cells.

(A)

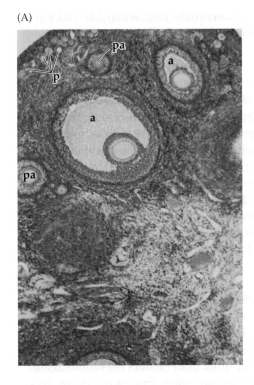

(B)

Figure 5.12 Stages of follicular development (A) Numerous primordial follicles (p) cluster against the outer margin of the ovary. Some have developed into preantral follicles (pa) and a few into antral follicles (a), characterized by their central cavity, or antrum. (B) The single follicle that ovulates transforms subsequently into a corpus luteum, which synthesizes and secretes all three classes of sex steroids; among these, progesterone is vital for the establishment of pregnancy. The corpus luteum is visible here as the oval structure (comprised of dark and light regions) that occupies most of this cross-section of the ovary. It measures about 5 mm across. The light region consists of granulosa-lutein cells, derived from follicular granulosa cells; the darker rim consists of theca-lutein cells, derived from thecal cells. The two pink structures at bottom right are involuted corpora lutea from previous menstrual cycles.

separated by interstitial tissue that includes the thecal cells. As described earlier, thecal cells are the ovarian cells that are capable of synthesizing androgens and thus are equivalent to the Leydig cells of the testis. The granulosa cells are equivalent to the sperm-nourishing Sertoli cells of the testis.

INITIAL STAGES OF FOLLICULAR DEVELOPMENT During a woman's fertile adult life, a constant trickle of primordial follicles—several per day—leave their long-term "frozen" state and enter a process of renewed maturation. In the first stage, which takes about 3 months, the primary oocyte expands in size from about 0.02 mm to about 0.1 mm in diameter—its final size. The layer of granulosa cells also thickens and attracts an outer layer of thecal cells, so that the whole follicle is now about 0.3 mm in diameter and easily visible to the naked eye. At this stage it is called a **preantral follicle**, meaning a follicle that does not yet have a cavity (antrum). At any one time, the two ovaries contain several hundred preantral follicles.

In the next phase (see Figure 5.12), a fluid-filled cavity, or **antrum**, forms within the oocyte. The entire follicle swells as the fluid accumulates. When it reaches a diameter of about 2 mm, a critical event occurs: The follicular cells begin to produce gonadotropin receptors. Specifically, the thecal cells begin to produce receptors for LH, and the granulosa cells begin to produce receptors for FSH. From then on, the follicle is dependent on circulating gonadotropins for its survival and further development.

GONADOTROPIN-DEPENDENT DEVELOPMENT The process of follicular development up to this point has occurred independently of hormones and is therefore oblivious to the menstrual cycles going on at the time. Thus a particular follicle may become gonadotropin-dependent at any point in a cycle, or even while the woman is pregnant. Only those follicles that happen to become gonadotropin-

preantral follicle A follicle that has enlarged but does not yet have an antrum.

antrum The cavity that forms in an ovarian follicle as it matures.

Figure 5.14 Meiosis in the development of human oocytes The process is similar to the generic scheme for meiosis shown in Box 2.1, with two peculiarities. First, there are two halts in the meiotic process: one long halt during meiosis I (from fetal life to adulthood) and a second, shorter halt during meiosis II (from ovulation to fertilization). Second, the cell division at the end of meiosis I is unequal: A single "secondary oocyte" receives most of the cytoplasm, and the other daughter cell is discarded as a bag of chromosomes—the first polar body. (The remainder of meiosis II will be described in the context of fertilization; see Figure 6.3.)

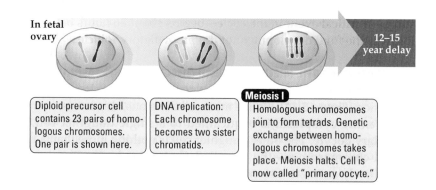

In fetal ovary

12–15 year delay

Diploid precursor cell contains 23 pairs of homologous chromosomes. One pair is shown here.

DNA replication: Each chromosome becomes two sister chromatids.

Meiosis I

Homologous chromosomes join to form tetrads. Genetic exchange between homologous chromosomes takes place. Meiosis halts. Cell is now called "primary oocyte."

granulosa–lutein cells Cells of the corpus luteum, derived from follicular granulosa cells, that secrete progesterone.

theca–lutein cells Cells of the corpus luteum, derived from follicular thecal cells, that synthesize testosterone.

FAQ Can a woman menstruate during pregnancy?

No, but many women experience some light vaginal bleeding early in pregnancy—for example, as the conceptus implants in the uterus. Major bleeding, bleeding accompanied by pain, or any bleeding after the first trimester are reasons to see your doctor promptly.

helpmate is to stretch a small amount of the mucus between thumb and forefinger; during the late follicular phase, the mucus stretches easily, like egg white. This is an indication that the mucus is in a condition to transport sperm. We will come back to this test in the context of methods for avoiding pregnancy (see Chapter 12).

During the Luteal Phase the Uterus Is Prepared for Pregnancy

After ovulation, the ovum may be fertilized by a sperm—a process described in Chapter 6. Alternatively (and more commonly), the ovum simply dies after 12 to 24 hours in the oviduct. The woman's body has no immediate way of "knowing" which of these outcomes has actually taken place, so it must work on the assumption that fertilization has indeed occurred. Therefore, for about 2 weeks after ovulation, both the uterus and the endometrium undergo changes that favor the establishment and continuation of pregnancy, regardless of whether fertilization has occurred or not.

THE CORPUS LUTEUM After the dominant ovarian follicle has released its ovum at ovulation, it undergoes a further transformation and becomes a corpus luteum (see Figure 5.12B). No longer concerned with producing an ovum, the corpus luteum devotes itself entirely to the secretion of sex hormones (see Figure 5.13B). These hormones—primarily progesterone and estrogen—are important for the luteal phase of the cycle or, if fertilization occurs, for sustaining pregnancy.

The two cell types in the follicle—the granulosa and thecal cells—transform themselves into two new cell types named, sensibly enough, the **granulosa-lutein** and **theca–lutein cells**. The granulosa-lutein cells secrete increasing amounts of progesterone, as we saw above, so the blood levels of this hormone increase early in the luteal phase. They also secrete the peptide hormone inhibin.

The theca-lutein cells continue to synthesize testosterone. Some of this testosterone enters the general circulation—its blood levels peak at around the time of ovulation—while another portion of it is taken up by the granulosa-lutein cells and converted into estrogen. Thus, although estrogen levels fall shortly before ovulation, they rise again in the latter part of the luteal phase, reaching a peak that may be as high as the preovulatory peak.

The preovulatory surge of LH and FSH is quickly terminated, in part because of the fall in estrogen levels, which removes the positive feedback effect. Both progesterone and inhibin, secreted by the granulosa-lutein cells, restrain the secretion of the two gonadotropins from the pituitary during the entire luteal phase, thus preventing a second LH surge in response to the estrogen peak late in the phase.

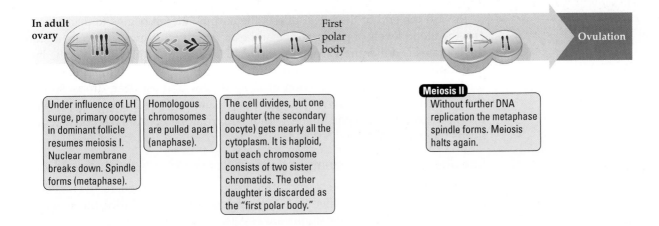

Under influence of LH surge, primary oocyte in dominant follicle resumes meiosis I. Nuclear membrane breaks down. Spindle forms (metaphase).

Homologous chromosomes are pulled apart (anaphase).

The cell divides, but one daughter (the secondary oocyte) gets nearly all the cytoplasm. It is haploid, but each chromosome consists of two sister chromatids. The other daughter is discarded as the "first polar body."

First polar body

Ovulation

Meiosis II
Without further DNA replication the metaphase spindle forms. Meiosis halts again.

In adult ovary

CHANGES IN THE ENDOMETRIUM AND CERVIX During the luteal phase, the endometrium of the uterus thickens further under the influence of progesterone (**Figure 5.15**) and produces a dense, protein-rich secretion. The spiral arteries reach their fullest extent, and the myometrium also thickens. The properties of the cervical mucus change: It takes on a thicker, cloudy appearance, and it can no longer be stretched more than a short distance between thumb and forefinger. Sperm penetrate the mucus poorly at this time. Thus the uterus is least able to transport sperm during the luteal phase, but it is in good shape to nourish the conceptus and to allow for its implantation into the endometrium if fertilization has occurred.

What happens after fertilization (including the completion of the oocyte's meiosis) is the subject of Chapter 6. Here, we are concerned with what happens if fertilization does *not* occur and the menstrual cycle continues.

(A)

(B)

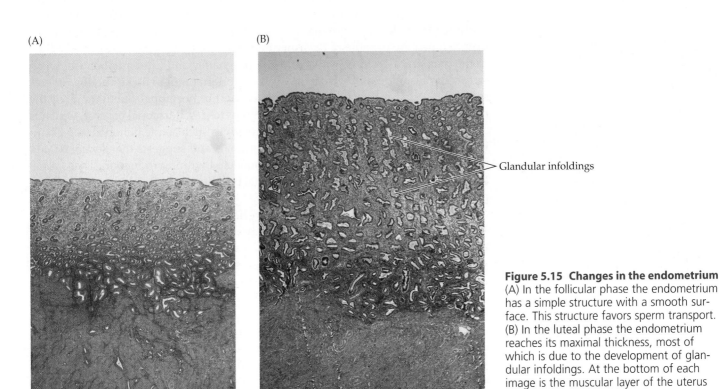

Glandular infoldings

Figure 5.15 Changes in the endometrium (A) In the follicular phase the endometrium has a simple structure with a smooth surface. This structure favors sperm transport. (B) In the luteal phase the endometrium reaches its maximal thickness, most of which is due to the development of glandular infoldings. At the bottom of each image is the muscular layer of the uterus (myometrium).

Toward the end of the luteal phase, the corpus luteum begins to degenerate, and the blood levels of progesterone and estrogen drop. Why the corpus luteum degenerates is not entirely clear. Probably, LH levels are too low during the late luteal phase to sustain its continued functioning. In any event, as the corpus luteum degenerates its production of progesterone and estrogen drops, so that there is no longer any endocrine support for the endometrium. The endometrium therefore breaks down and, along with blood from the disrupted spiral arteries, forms the menstrual flow (See Web Activity 5.5 The Reproductive Years).

Sex Steroids Affect Systems in Women Besides the Reproductive Tract

Although the main function of sex hormones in women is to regulate the functional state of the uterus and other parts of the reproductive tract during the menstrual cycle, they do have other significant effects:

- Estrogens maintain bone density, protecting a woman from osteoporosis. They also protect against pathological blood clotting, including the clots that cause heart attacks.

- Progesterone acts on neural centers in the hypothalamus that control body temperature. Thus a woman's body temperature rises at least 0.22°C (0.4°F) after ovulation, when progesterone levels rise. By keeping track of the timing of this temperature rise, a woman can obtain information about her cycle that is useful in "fertility awareness" methods of contraception. Progesterone also influences mood: It is an anxiety-reducing agent. Thus the fall in progesterone levels toward the end of the luteal phase of the menstrual cycle can cause or contribute to an increase in anxiety and irritability at that time (see below).

The Menstrual Cycle Influences Sexuality

If women's sexual behavior had reproduction as its sole goal, women would engage in coitus only on the six days before and including the day of ovulation, for the great majority of pregnancies result from sex on those days. In fact, however, women are capable of desiring, initiating, and engaging in sex at any time of the menstrual cycle, as well as during pregnancy and after menopause, when fertilization is impossible. Thus the most important point to make about women's sexuality is that it is *not* strictly regulated by the hormonal fluctuations of the menstrual cycle. This emancipation from day-to-day hormonal control, which is also seen among our closest nonhuman relatives such as the bonobos (see Chapter 2), distinguishes us from most other animals and suggests that sexual behavior has acquired functions not directly connected with reproduction. These functions presumably include the interpersonal bonding that sexual pleasure helps to generate (Abramson & Pinkerton, 2002).

Still, women's sexual feelings and behaviors are not completely constant around the menstrual cycle. We've already discussed cultural forces that tend to diminish sexual activity during a woman's menstrual period (see Box 5.3). In addition, however, women are more interested in sex and more sexually active during the six fertile days than they are on any other days of the cycle (Tarín & Gomez-Piquer, 2002; Wilcox et al., 2004). Some studies report a secondary peak in the premenstrual period.

The increased interest in sex at and before ovulation is facilitated by the high levels of circulating estrogens and androgens at that time. The importance of androgens for women's sexual desire is suggested by a set of observations of women who had had their ovaries and uterus removed some years previously (Sherwin & Gelfand, 1987) (**Figure 5.16**). Of these women, one group had been

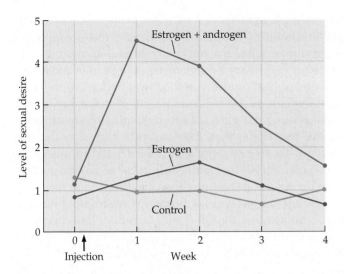

Figure 5.16 Evidence that androgens contribute to female sexual desire Women whose ovaries had been removed were given injections of estrogens alone, estrogens plus androgens, or no injections (control). Only the combined estrogen–androgen injections caused a significant increase in the women's subjectively assessed sexual desire. (After Sherwin and Gelfand, 1987.)

receiving no hormone replacement therapy since their surgeries, one group had been receiving monthly injections of estradiol, and one group had been receiving monthly injections of estradiol plus an androgen. The women who received no treatment or estradiol alone showed low levels of sexual desire, sexual fantasies, and sexual arousal, and these levels changed little over the course of each month. The women who received estradiol plus an androgen, however, experienced greatly increased levels of desire, fantasies, and arousal compared with the other groups, and these levels closely followed the rise and fall of circulating androgens over the course of the month.

Women who have had both their ovaries and their adrenal glands removed, thus eliminating both of their bodies' sources of androgens, experience an even more profound decrease in sexual interest. Again, their sexual interest can be restored by the administration of estrogens plus androgens. (As we will discuss further in Chapter 16, the use of testosterone to restore sex drive in women may incur some undesired side effects.)

Menstrual Problems Are Common But Treatable

Many women experience some kind of health problem associated with their menstrual cycles. These include painful menstruation, physical or psychological problems in the days before the onset of the menstrual period, and irregular or absent menstrual cycles. For most women menstrual problems are quite minor, but for some they are very disruptive or impair fertility. Luckily, a wide range of effective treatments are available for most menstrual conditions.

Menstrual Pain Might or Might Not Reflect Underlying Pelvic Disease

The sloughing off and discharge of endometrial tissue during menstruation is aided by contractions of the outer, muscular layer of the uterus (the myometrium) in a manner somewhat similar to the process of childbirth. These contractions take place under the influence of prostaglandins secreted by the uterus itself, and they are the cause of the **menstrual cramps** experienced by some women during or shortly before their periods. There can also be persistent, aching pain within the pelvis or in the lower back. The pain may be accompanied by nausea or headaches. Menstrual pain is called **dysmenorrhea** when it is severe enough to limit a woman's activities (Mannix, 2008). There are two kinds of dysmenorrhea:

menstrual cramps Sharp pelvic pains that may accompany or precede menstruation.

dysmenorrhea Menstruation accompanied by pain.

premenstrual syndrome (PMS) A collection of physical and/or psychological symptoms that may begin a few days before the menstrual period and continue into the period.

premenstrual dysphoric disorder (PMDD) PMS-associated mood changes that are severe enough to interfere with relationships.

■ *Primary dysmenorrhea* is disabling menstrual pain that is not associated with any diagnosable pelvic condition. It begins at menarche and is especially common among young women who have not had children—as many as 10% of such women experience it. Primary dysmenorrhea can be alleviated with heat (e.g., warm showers, or heating pads on the lower abdomen), calcium supplements, plentiful fluid intake, or nonsteroidal anti-inflammatory drugs such as ibuprofen, which block the action of prostaglandins. Narcotic analgesics may be prescribed for severe cases. Exercise and a high-fiber diet are also thought to be helpful. Another strategy is the use of oral contraceptives: The menstrual period experienced during the "off days" of an oral contraceptive regime is often lighter and less painful than a natural menstrual period. And as described earlier, certain types of hormonal contraception make a woman's periods less frequent or abolish them altogether. Thus hormonal contraceptives are an option for the treatment of dysmenorrhea even in women who do not need them for contraceptive purposes.

■ *Secondary dysmenorrhea* is menstrual pain caused by a pelvic disorder. In affected women, it usually begins not at menarche but at some point during a woman's reproductive life. Among the possible causes are endometriosis, pelvic inflammatory disease, uterine fibroids, and ovarian cysts (see Chapter 3). Intrauterine devices (IUDS; see Chapter 12) and even tampons can sometimes cause menstrual pain. Secondary dysmenorrhea may respond to the same treatments listed above for primary dysmenorrhea. If possible, however, the underlying condition should be corrected. This may require antibiotics or, in some cases, surgery. Menstrual pain associated with IUD use tends to diminish over time.

The main points to know about disabling menstrual pain are that it should be medically investigated to rule out underlying conditions and that effective treatment options are available.

Premenstrual Syndrome Has Physical and Psychological Aspects

It is common for women to experience some form of physical discomfort or negative mood change in the week or two weeks *before* their period. These problems may include any of the following:

■ Breast swelling and tenderness
■ "Bloating"—the sense of being overloaded with fluid
■ Diarrhea or constipation
■ Headache or muscle aches
■ Anxiety or irritability ("premenstrual tension")
■ Depression or crying spells
■ Difficulty in concentrating

If the problems go away soon after the onset of menstruation but recur over several menstrual cycles and are severe enough to interfere with daily living, the condition is called **premenstrual syndrome (PMS)** (Yonkers et al., 2008). In rare cases where the psychological symptoms are severe enough to interfere with relationships—including difficult-to-control anger, for example—they may be diagnosed as a psychiatric condition, **premenstrual dysphoric disorder (PMDD)** (Kaur et al., 2004).

The prevalence of PMS is hard to estimate. About half of all women do not experience PMS at all, 30% to 50% experience mild or moderate symptoms, and no more than about 15% experience severe symptoms (Woods, 1987).

Premenstrual syndrome is often portrayed as something worse than it is.

Some studies indicate that only 3% to 5% of women experience symptoms meeting a strict definition of PMS (Kessel, 2000). The reason that women differ in the extent to which they experience PMS is not so much that their sex hormone levels differ as that their bodies respond to sex hormones in different ways (Schmidt et al., 1998). Progesterone and its metabolites seem to have an anxiety-relieving effect in some women, for example; for these women, the *fall* in progesterone levels during the days before menstruation may have the effect of increasing anxiety.

Treatments for mild or moderate PMS include lifestyle changes such as regular exercise, quitting smoking and excessive drinking, getting sufficient sleep, and managing stress. Women who get a lot of calcium and vitamin A in their diet are much less likely than other women to experience PMS (Bertone-Johnson et al., 2005), and some studies suggest that calcium supplements alleviate PMS symptoms (Thys-Jacobs, 2000).

For severe PMS the physical symptoms may be controlled with diuretics, nonsteroidal anti-inflammatory drugs, or hormonal contraceptives. The psychological symptoms, especially those of PMDD, often respond to treatment with selective serotonin reuptake inhibitors (Prozac-class antidepressants) (Yonkers et al., 2008).

PMS is rarely the monster that it is portrayed to be in popular literature. As described above, the great majority of women experience few or no PMS symptoms, and for those who do experience severe symptoms, effective treatments are available. PMS doesn't disqualify the women who suffer from it from any field of human activity—and dismissing any woman's bad mood or unfriendly behavior with "She's PMSing" is ignorant and sexist.

Menstruation Stops during Pregnancy—and for Many Other Reasons

Most women will notice at some point or another that their menstrual periods have stopped (**amenorrhea**) or have become irregular (**oligomenorrhea**). The most common reasons for amenorrhea are entirely natural and normal ones: The woman is pregnant, is breast-feeding her baby, or has reached menopause. There are also natural reasons for oligomenorrhea: Periods are usually irregular for some time after menarche and during the climacteric—the months or years prior to their final cessation. But many other factors can interfere with menstruation:

- *Some hormonal contraceptives.* It may take months for menstruation to return after the contraceptive is discontinued.
- *Drugs.* Common culprits include steroids, antidepressants, and some cancer drugs.
- *Stress.* This could be caused by physical illness, depression, or social problems.
- *Loss of weight for any reason.* This includes anorexia nervosa, severe dieting, and extreme athletic exercise. A woman is at risk of amenorrhea if her body fat drops below 15% to 17% of total weight.
- *Medical conditions.* These include thyroid dysfunction and pituitary tumors.

A girl may also fail to begin menstruating at puberty (**primary amenorrhea**). This may be due to one of the factors listed above. Alternatively, puberty itself may be delayed for a variety of reasons, or the girl may have a disorder of sex development (see Chapter 6) that makes menstruation impossible.

Unless it is caused by a congenital anomaly, amenorrhea can nearly always be corrected by lifestyle changes or treatment of the underlying condition. Amenorrhea is not harmful in itself—scientists have not identified any health benefit of menstrual bleeding—but the underlying condition may be harmful, and failure to menstruate may cause psychological distress. In addition, a woman is usually unable to become pregnant during the time she is not experiencing menstrual

amenorrhea Absence of menstruation.

oligomenorrhea Infrequent or irregular menstruation.

primary amenorrhea Failure to commence menstruation at puberty.

menorrhagia Excessively heavy menstrual bleeding.

isoflavones Estrogen-like compounds of plant origin.

periods. That is not a sure thing, however; a woman who is breast-feeding, for example, may become pregnant before her menstrual periods return.

The reverse condition, excessively heavy menstrual bleeding, or **menorrhagia**, affects about 10% of all women. Causes are numerous, the most common being hormonal imbalance and fibroids. Treatment is with drugs such as nonsteroidal anti-inflammatory agents or hormonal contraceptives, or surgical treatment of the fibroids. Repeated heavy bleeding predisposes a woman to iron-deficiency anemia, so iron supplements are usually recommended.

Sex Hormone–Related Compounds Exist in the Environment

Compounds with steroid-like or steroid-blocking actions occur naturally in a variety of foods of plant origin. **Isoflavones** are a class of estrogen-like compounds

Biology of Sex

BOX 5.5 Sex Hormones in the Environment

In the 1950s and 1960s, crop dusters spread DDT—an organochlorine pesticide—far and wide across the United States and other countries. Eventually, the crop-duster pilots were found to have abnormally low sperm counts and a variety of other ailments. It turns out that DDT and its breakdown product DDE act like estrogens within the body—both of humans and animals. Although DDT was banned in the United States in 1972, it still lingers in the environment. One hundred tons of DDT, dumped into the sewers of Torrance, California, by the Montrose Chemical Corporation, lie on the seafloor off Los Angeles. This deposit—one of the nation's worst cases of industrial contamination—has had catastrophic effects on wildlife and has necessitated the banning of commercial fishing in the area (see figure).

Besides DDT, numerous other artificial chemicals mimic or block the effects of estrogens or other sex steroids. Because we inadvertently ingest or inhale small quantities of these **endocrine disruptors** in the process of daily living, there is concern about whether they pose a significant hazard to our health. Much depends on the concentrations at which they act. In 1997, for example, a group at the University of Missouri reported that bisphenol A, a common ingredient in plastics, has estrogen-like activity, and that it causes enlargement of the prostate gland in mouse fetuses when fed to pregnant animals at parts-per-billion levels (Nagel et al., 1997). These levels are similar to

the amounts that humans ingest as a result of leaching from plastic food and water containers, especially when the containers are heated (Le et al., 2008). Although the University of Missouri study has had its detractors, a panel convened by the U.S. Environmental Protection Agency has cautiously confirmed its validity (Kaiser, 2000). More broadly, there has been concern that endocrine disruptors might be responsible for the broad decline in sperm counts that has been reported in many industrialized countries. We will review this topic in Chapter 11.

There has also been some concern about hormones that people might ingest by eating meat from hormone-treated livestock. In North America, beef cattle are commonly treated with steroids, especially estrogens and androgens—either the natural hormones or longer-lived synthetic versions. The hormones, which are usually administered via ear patches, promote growth and are therefore of considerable economic significance. The position of the U.S. and Canadian governments is that the amounts of these hormones consumed in meat from treated animals are too small to be of any concern (Balter, 1999). The European Union, on the other hand, has banned the sale or import of hormone-treated beef on health grounds, sparking a trade war with the United States and Canada. In 2008 the World Trade Organization ruled that the E.U. had violated global trade rules by imposing an import ban that was not supported by scientific evidence (EU Business, 2008)

endocrine disruptors Environmental pollutants that have endocrine effects.

present in legumes and beans, especially soybeans, that have mixed estrogenic and anti-estrogenic effects. A soy-rich diet may decrease the risk of breast cancer and alleviate symptoms related to menopause, although the current data are not particularly encouraging (see Chapter 13). The saw palmetto plant contains a variety of bioactive compounds, including antiandrogens. Preparations of saw palmetto, sold as dietary supplements, are widely used for the treatment of benign enlargement of the prostate gland, and they seem to be quite helpful for that purpose (Gordon & Shaughnessy, 2003). Unfortunately, dietary supplements are poorly regulated in the United States, and as a result their content, efficacy, and safety are uncertain. The notion that "natural" products are safer than pharmaceuticals is widespread but mistaken. Synthetic hormones and related compounds also exist as pollutants in the environment. This matter is discussed in **Box 5.5**.

The study of sex hormones and their actions has led to the introduction of many important drugs. These include contraceptives; drugs that increase or lower the sex drive; drugs that treat or prevent cancer of the ovary, breast, and prostate gland; drugs that induce or delay labor; drugs that delay puberty; drugs that treat menstrual symptoms; and drugs that induce abortion. For more on these drugs and their mechanisms of action, see Web Topic 5.6 Drugs Related to Sex Hormones.

Summary

1. Sex hormones may be steroids, proteins and peptides, prostaglandins, or monoamines. The sex steroids are synthesized from cholesterol and fall into three groups: progestins (e.g., progesterone), estrogens (e.g., estradiol), and androgens (e.g., testosterone and 5α-dihydrotestosterone, or DHT). A set of enzymes carries out the synthesis and interconversion of the steroids. The enzyme aromatase converts testosterone to estradiol, and the enzyme 5α-reductase converts testosterone to DHT.

2. Testosterone is secreted by Leydig cells in the testes and by thecal cells in the ovaries as well as by the adrenal glands. Some tissues convert testosterone to the more potent androgen DHT. Other tissues, including the testes, ovaries, and brain, convert testosterone to estradiol. In women, the main source of estradiol is the ovarian follicles, and the blood levels of estradiol fluctuate with the menstrual cycle. Progesterone is a female hormone secreted by the corpus luteum—the reorganized remnants of the follicle that ruptures at ovulation.

3. Peptide and protein hormones are gene products. The peptide sex hormones include two hormones synthesized by neuroendocrine cells in the hypothalamus: oxytocin and gonadotropin-releasing hormone (GnRH). Oxytocin is released into the general circulation from the posterior lobe of the pituitary gland during orgasm, breast-feeding, and childbirth. GnRH is secreted into portal vessels that carry it to the anterior pituitary gland, where it stimulates the release of the gonadotropins into the general circulation.

4. Protein hormones include the two gonad-stimulating hormones (gonadotropins) secreted by the anterior lobe of the pituitary gland: luteinizing hormone (LH) and follicle-stimulating hormone (FSH). Inhibins are protein hormones that are secreted by the gonads and influence the pituitary gland.

5. Prostaglandins are lipid hormones that help prepare the uterus and cervix for childbirth. The monoamine dopamine is a hypothalamic hormone that regulates the release of prolactin from the pituitary gland.

6. In men, testosterone levels and sperm production are regulated by a negative feedback hormonal loop. This involves GnRH secreted by the hypothalamus, the gonadotropins LH and FSH secreted by the pituitary, and testosterone and inhibin secreted by the testes.

7. Testosterone supports the normal structure and function of male genital tissues, has a broad anabolic (tissue-building) effect, guides development in a male direction, and stimulates sexual feelings and behavior. This last effect is seen in both sexes.

REFER TO THE

Human Sexuality

WEBSITE AT

www.sinauer.com/levay3e

for activities, study questions, quizzes, and other study aids.

8. Menstruation—the sloughing off of the uterine lining (endometrium)—is the outward manifestation of the menstrual cycle, which usually lasts between 24 and 32 days. The cycle involves hormonal interactions between the ovaries, the hypothalamus, and the pituitary gland. The resulting cyclical changes in hormone levels regulate the development of ovarian follicles and the state of the endometrium.

9. The menstrual cycle has three phases: the menstrual phase, the follicular phase, and the luteal phase. During the menstrual phase, progesterone and estrogen levels are low, allowing much of the endometrium to be shed as menstrual flow. This change prepares the uterus for its role in sperm transport. LH and FSH levels rise during this phase.

10. During the follicular phase, LH and FSH promote the development of a set of follicles, of which one becomes dominant. The follicles secrete estrogens. Near the end of the follicular phase, rising estrogen levels trigger a surge of LH and FSH secretion, which drives the dominant follicle toward ovulation. In the late follicular phase the uterus is in optimal condition for sperm transport, and the cervical mucus has a highly elastic quality. Nearly all conceptions result from coitus during the 6 days before and during ovulation.

11. Ovulation is the release of an ovum from one ovary. The ovum enters the oviduct, where, if sperm are present, it may be fertilized.

12. During the luteal phase, the remains of the dominant follicle are transformed into a corpus luteum, which secretes progesterone and estrogens. Progesterone causes the endometrium to thicken and prepare itself for implantation of a conceptus. If implantation does not occur by about 14 days after ovulation, the corpus luteum regresses and menstruation begins.

13. Women experience sexual feelings and engage in sexual behavior at all phases of the menstrual cycle, but there is a tendency for their interest in sex to peak in the late follicular phase, when testosterone levels are high.

14. Women may experience painful menstrual periods (dysmenorrhea), a variety of physical and psychological symptoms prior to menstruation (premenstrual syndrome), absence of menstrual periods (amenorrhea), or excessively heavy menstrual bleeding (menorrhagia). There are many causes for these conditions, but effective treatments are usually available.

15. Compounds related to sex hormones are found in some foods and supplements, as well as in the environment. Hormone-related drugs are used as contraceptives, for prevention of menopausal symptoms, for cancer therapy, and for restoration or suppression of sex drive.

Discussion Questions

1. Make a list of anything you have heard about menstruation. Identify the myths and falsehoods. Compare and contrast these misconceptions with the material in the text and, if you wish, with your own experience or observations.

2. If you're a woman, how would you respond to this question: "Would you stop menstruating if you could?" If you're a man, what's your opinion on the matter?

3. Does sexual intercourse during menstruation strike you as appealing or not? Why?

Web Resources

Human ovulation captured on video www.newscientist.com/channel/ being-human/dn14155-human-ovulation-captured-on-video.html

King, M. W. The Medical Biochemistry Page http://themedicalbiochemistrypage.org

McGill Medicine—Menstrual Cycle Home Page sprojects.mmi.mcgill.ca/ menstrualcycle/home.html

Miller, L. (University of Washington) www.noperiod.com (Site devoted to menstrual suppression)

Museum of Menstruation www.mum.org

Recommended Reading

Djerassi, C. (2001). *This man's pill: Reflections on the 50th birthday of the pill.* Oxford University Press.

Johnson, M. A. (2007). *Essential reproduction* (6th ed.). Blackwell.

Nelson, R. J. (2005). *An introduction to behavioral endocrinology* (3rd ed.). Sinauer Associates.

Vliet, E. L. (2001). *Screaming to be heard: Hormone connections women suspect and doctors still ignore* (rev. ed.). M. Evans and Co.

CHAPTER **6**

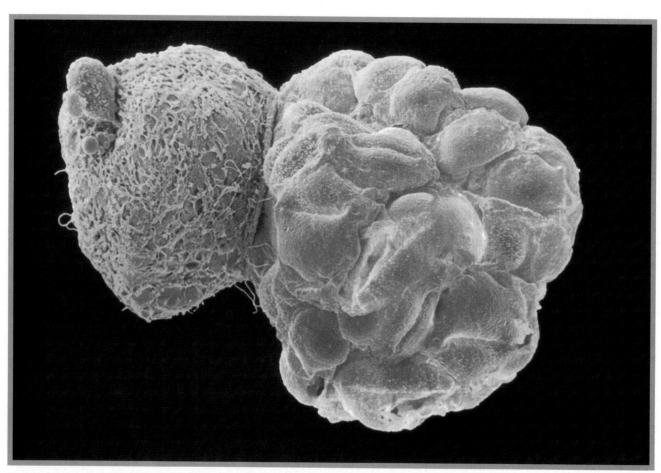

Human blastocyst (at right) hatching from its zona pellucida. The sex of the blastocyst has already been determined by the chromosomes it possesses, but it has not yet begun to differentiate as male or female.

Sexual Development

In Chapter 2 we discussed a number of central questions about sexuality from an evolutionary standpoint —Why are there two sexes? Why do males and females differ in anatomy and behavior? In this chapter we begin a discussion of these same questions from a developmental point of view. What are the actual processes that turn a barely visible blob of protoplasm—a fertilized egg—into an adult human being, complete with her or his unique physical appearance, character, and sexuality? Few questions have so perplexed philosophers and scientists over the centuries, and even today our answers are quite incomplete.

In this chapter we focus primarily on the development of physical differences between the sexes. In the process, we will see that many individuals deviate to some degree from the male and female stereotypes that are described in textbooks. In later chapters we will ask about the origin of sex differences in personality, feelings, and behavior—attributes that are often lumped under the category of "gender." There we will find that these distinctions between the two sexes are even fuzzier than the bodily differences.

Development Passes through Distinct Stages

It's not possible to give an account of human development without drawing a distinction between its usual course and the various ways in which it can deviate from that course. The main text of this chapter describes *typical* sexual development, which progresses through several stages that are controlled by different biological mechanisms; *atypical* sexual development can affect any of these stages and is described in Box 6.1 through Box 6.7. For a discussion of what should be considered "normal" in development, see Web Topic 6.1 The Meaning of "Normal".

Fertilization Is the Fusion of One Sperm with One Ovum

We'll start with a brief general outline of human development before focusing specifically on sex. In the previous chapter, you learned how a secondary oocyte (or unfertilized ovum; **Figure 6.1**) is released from an ovarian follicle at ovulation and transported to the ampulla of the oviduct. Sperm also travel to the oviducts from their site of deposition in the vagina: They find their way primarily by ascending a gradient of increasing temperature (Suarez & Pacey, 2006), but they may be helped along by active contractions of the uterus and oviducts. If sperm are present in the oviduct at

fertilization The entry of a sperm into an ovum, thus transforming the ovum into a genetically unique diploid organism capable of development (conceptus).

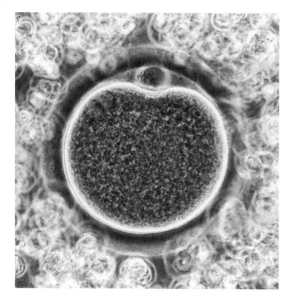

Figure 6.1 An unfertilized ovum The outer wrapping is the zona pellucida. The larger of the two inner structures is the oocyte (shown here halted during meiosis II). The smaller structure, at the 12 o'clock position, is the first polar body—the discarded set of chromosomes from meiosis I. (Micrograph courtesy of R. Yanagimachi.)

the time of ovulation or arrive there within about 24 hours afterward, **fertilization** may occur—that is, a single sperm enters the ovum, producing a **zygote**. If fertilization does not occur within about 24 hours of ovulation the ovum dies, and the luteal phase continues on to menstruation.

Before fertilization can take place, the sperm must undergo two important processes: capacitation and the acrosome reaction (**Figure 6.2**). **Capacitation** involves the removal of masking proteins on the outer surface of the sperm by enzymes present in the uterus and oviducts. Capacitated sperm swim more forcefully and are capable of responding to the presence of the ovum. Once capacitated, a single sperm can live only a few hours, so it must find an ovum or die. The many sperm from a single ejaculation undergo capacitation over a span of several days, however, so a woman can become pregnant from a sexual encounter that took place several days before she ovulates, as discussed in Chapter 11. Once capacitated, sperm are drawn to the ovum by a chemical attractant released by the ovum (Spehr et al., 2003).

The **acrosome reaction** occurs when sperm actually reach the **zona pellucida**— the protective membrane that surrounds the ovum. The sperm's acrosome (see Chapter 4) fuses with its outer membrane, exposing receptors that bind to the zona pellucida as well as releasing protein-digesting enzymes that clear a path through the zona pellucida so that the sperm can reach the ovum's plasma membrane.

The moment a sperm actually fuses with the plasma membrane, an invisible but vital event takes place: The concentration of free calcium ions (Ca^{2+}) within the ovum increases briefly. This increase, in turn, triggers the release of enzymes from the ovum that change the physical properties of the zona pellucida, making it impossible for any other sperm to pass through. If a second sperm did penetrate the ovum, the resulting zygote would possess too many chromosomes and would probably die early in development.

Within the next few minutes, another important event takes place: The ovum completes its second meiotic division (**Figure 6.3**). As with the first division, one daughter cell is just a tiny bag of discarded chromosomes, the

zygote A cell formed by the fusion of gametes: a fertilized ovum.

capacitation A chemical change in the surface of a sperm within the female reproductive tract that allows it to swim more forcefully and respond to the presence of the ovum.

acrosome reaction The opening of a sperm's acrosome, releasing enzymes necessary for penetration of the zona pellucida of the ovum.

zona pellucida The capsule surrounding an ovum that must be penetrated by the fertilizing sperm.

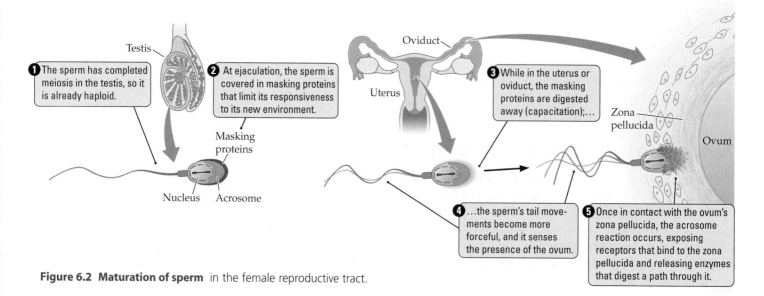

Figure 6.2 Maturation of sperm in the female reproductive tract.

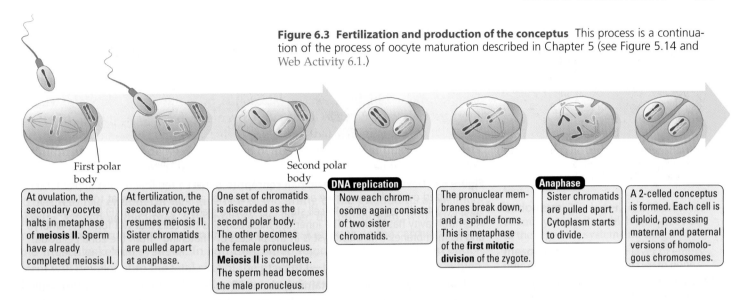

Figure 6.3 Fertilization and production of the conceptus This process is a continuation of the process of oocyte maturation described in Chapter 5 (see Figure 5.14 and Web Activity 6.1.)

At ovulation, the secondary oocyte halts in metaphase of **meiosis II**. Sperm have already completed meiosis II.

At fertilization, the secondary oocyte resumes meiosis II. Sister chromatids are pulled apart at anaphase.

One set of chromatids is discarded as the second polar body. The other becomes the female pronucleus. **Meiosis II** is complete. The sperm head becomes the male pronucleus.

DNA replication
Now each chromosome again consists of two sister chromatids.

The pronuclear membranes break down, and a spindle forms. This is metaphase of the **first mitotic division** of the zygote.

Anaphase
Sister chromatids are pulled apart. Cytoplasm starts to divide.

A 2-celled conceptus is formed. Each cell is diploid, possessing maternal and paternal versions of homologous chromosomes.

First polar body

Second polar body

second polar body; the other daughter cell inherits most of the cytoplasm. The ovum now contains two **pronuclei**: a pronucleus derived from the unfertilized ovum, containing a haploid set (a single set—see Chapter 2) of maternal chromosomes, and a pronucleus derived from the sperm, containing a haploid set of paternal chromosomes.

You might think that the most sensible thing to happen next would be for the two pronuclei to fuse, producing a diploid cell (a cell with the normal double set of chromosomes) with a single nucleus. Such a cell never forms, however. Instead, the two pronuclei undergo a round of DNA replication, so that each chromosome now consists of two identical chromatids. The pronuclear membranes break down, a mitotic spindle forms, the chromatids are pulled apart, and the cell divides. This is the first mitotic cell division of the new organism. Each daughter cell inherits one set of chromosomes from each of the two pronuclei, so these two cells, and all their descendants, are diploid. The polar bodies, containing the discarded chromosomes, eventually break down.

The term **conception** has the same meaning as fertilization. "Conception" is often used when speaking of the age of an embryo or fetus (e.g., "3 weeks after conception"). Less commonly (and never in this book) "conception" is used to mean implantation (see below) or the secure establishment of pregnancy.

The Conceptus Implants in the Uterine Wall

The two-celled organism is called a **conceptus**. This term refers to the entire collection of cells derived from the fertilized ovum, regardless of whether or not they contribute to the tissues of the future fetus. The term "embryo" is not really appropriate at the 2-cell stage or for some time afterward, for reasons we'll see shortly. Nevertheless, the term "embryo" is commonly used to refer to a conceptus from the 2-cell stage onward, especially in the context of in vitro fertilization.

The conceptus remains in the oviduct for about 3 days after ovulation, during which time it undergoes a few more rounds of cell division (**Figure 6.4**). The conceptus does not get any bigger, however; it remains confined within the original zona pellucida. The cytoplasm of the original ovum simply divides into smaller and smaller packets as the cells multiply. At the 4- or 8-cell stage, the conceptus's genes become active for the first time. At about the 16-cell stage, the conceptus becomes a compact mass of cells known as a **morula**. Sometime around the fourth day, the conceptus is swept into the uterus by the action of the cilia lining the oviduct.

second polar body A small body containing the chromosomes discarded during the second meiotic division of an ovum.

pronucleus A nucleus containing a haploid set of chromosomes derived from a sperm or ovum.

conception Fertilization of the ovum.

conceptus The developing organism from the 2-cell stage onward, including both embryonic and extraembryonic tissues.

morula The conceptus when it consists of about 16 to 32 cells arranged in a compact spherical mass.

Biology of Sex

BOX 6.1 Atypical Development: Chromosomal Anomalies

The standard sets of sex chromosomes are XX (female) and XY (male). When nonstandard sets occur, they generally arise during one of the two meiotic cell divisions that give rise to male or female gametes. The anomalies described below are some of the most common.

Turner Syndrome

People with Turner syndrome have either a single X chromosome ("XO") or a single X chromosome plus a truncated portion of a second X chromosome. In either case, they lack a Y chromosome and therefore develop as females. Turner syndrome occurs in approximately 1 in 4000 live births and in an even higher fraction of all conceptions. (Many XO conceptuses die early in development.)

Girls with Turner syndrome usually lack normal ovaries. The germ cells that migrate into the embryonic ovaries require two X chromosomes for their survival and development as oocytes; therefore, in XO embryos the germ cells die. This, in turn, causes the ovaries to regress, leaving nothing but connective tissue ("streak ovaries"). Therefore many girls with Turner syndrome lack gonadal hormones, do not enter puberty, and are infertile. They usually have short stature, and they may have a variety of other physical traits, such as an unusually broad chest and loose skin around the neck ("neck webbing"). Cardiovascular and kidney defects may also occur. Individuals with Turner syndrome are not intellectually disabled, but they tend to have a characteristic array of cognitive deficits, including problems with visuospatial tasks, memory, and attention (Ross et al., 2000). These cognitive deficits are thought to result in part from the brain's lack of exposure to gonadal steroids. Nevertheless plenty of women with Turner syndrome have been very successful in life: These include geneticist Dr. Catherine Ward, current president of the Turner Syndrome Society of the United States (see figure).

Dr. Catherine Ward is a geneticist at Children's Hospital in Akron, Ohio, and president of the Turner Syndrome Society. Her short stature (142 cm, or 4 feet 8 inches) is a feature of Turner syndrome.

Turner syndrome can be treated with growth hormone and androgens to increase childhood growth and with estrogens to induce the development of breasts and other secondary sexual characteristics. Appropriate regimens of estrogens and progesterone can lead to regular menstruation, and women with Turner syndrome can sustain pregnancy with the aid of egg donation and hormonal support.

Klinefelter Syndrome

People with Klinefelter syndrome have a single Y chromosome and two or more X chromosomes (XXY or XXXY). They are male because they possess the *SRY* gene on the Y chromosome. Klinefelter syndrome affects about 1 in 1000 live births.

XXY boys are physically healthy but tend to exhibit some degree of learning disability, especially with respect to language skills (Rovet et al., 1996). On the other hand, some XXY men do well at the college level and beyond. The full Klinefelter syndrome becomes apparent at puberty. It is marked to a variable degree by the following traits: tallness, small testes, gynecomastia (breast development in men), feminine body contours, and sparse facial and body hair. Men with Klinefelter syndrome have low testosterone levels and, in consequence, high levels of luteinizing hormone (LH). Their sperm counts are usually too low for normal fertility. Men with Klinefelter syndrome also tend to have a low sex drive. Nevertheless, these men may be able to become biological fathers by means of special in vitro techniques. Some aspects of Klinefelter syndrome can be alleviated by long-term treatment with testosterone injections or implants.

XYY Syndrome

People with one X and two Y chromosomes develop as males but may have genital anomalies and low fertility and tend to have low intelligence. This syndrome is nearly as common as Klinefelter (about 1 in 1500 live births).

A study of XYY men identified by routine chromosomal analysis at birth found a significantly increased rate of criminal convictions and antisocial behavior compared with XY males in the same birth cohort. Most of this increase was accounted for by the XYY men's lower intelligence, however, rather than being an independent consequence of the chromosomal anomaly (Gotz et al., 1999).

Triple-X Syndrome

Triple-X syndrome is a mild disorder affecting about 1 in 2000 births. The affected individuals have the XXX pattern and develop as females. There are some cognitive deficits, especially in verbal skills (Rovet & Netley, 1983), and fertility is low, but many XXX women are so similar to XX women that they remain undiagnosed.

undifferentiated precursor structures called the **genital ridges**, which are clusters of mesodermal cells on either side of the aorta. To the side of each genital ridge is a transitory, kidney-like structure, the **mesonephros**, that ends up donating tissue to the gonads.

The genital ridges develop at about 4 weeks postconception. A week or so later, cells within the genital ridges of male embryos begin to activate the *SRY* gene. Presumably what happens is that some higher-level gene, present in both sexes, attempts to turn on the *SRY* gene, but this instruction is obeyed only in males because only males have an *SRY* gene to activate.

The product of the *SRY* gene is a **transcription factor**—a protein that binds to and regulates the activity of other genes. It is believed that *SRY* works within the lineage of cells that can become either Sertoli cells or granulosa cells—the gamete-nurturing cells of the testes and ovaries, respectively (see Chapters 3 and 4). When *SRY* is present, these cells develop as Sertoli cells, and the Sertoli cells, in turn, cause the gonads to develop as testes. When *SRY* is absent (i.e., in females), these same cells develop as granulosa cells, and the granulosa cells cause the gonads to develop as ovaries. (Sometimes both ovarian and testicular tissues are present in the same individual; this atypical development is discussed in **Box 6.2**.) These actions involve a sequential cascade of genes, some of which have been identified; the manner in which these genes interact is a topic of current research (Wilson & Davies, 2007).

Although the presence or absence of *SRY* is the initial switch that determines whether a fetus will develop as male or female, many other genes are involved in both male and female development. A key gene in female development, for example, is **DAX-1**, which is located on the X chromosome. *DAX-1* is active in the genital ridges at about the same time that *SRY* is active, but in both sexes rather than just in males (since both sexes have at least one X chromosome). Although the details are not yet completely clear, it appears that *SRY* and *DAX-1* work in opposition to each other (**Figure 6.9**). *DAX-1* promotes the development of ovaries and their key cells, the granulosa cells. In XY embryos, the *SRY* gene overrules the *DAX-1* gene, and therefore the genital ridges develop into testes and the embryo becomes a male.

genital ridge One of two bilateral clusters of cells in the embryo that give rise to the gonads.

mesonephros A transitory embryonic kidney that provides tissue to the gonads.

transcription factor A protein that regulates gene expression.

DAX-1 A gene that promotes development of the ovaries.

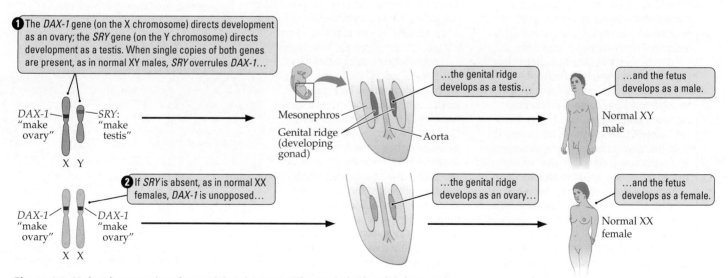

Figure 6.9 Molecular genetics of gonad development The genital ridge develops at the back of the abdomen between the aorta and the mesonephros. It can become either a testis or an ovary.

Biology of Sex

BOX 6.2 Atypical Development: Gonadal Intersexuality

(A) Sleeping hermaphrodite (Roman copy of a Greek original)

How does gonadal intersexuality arise? The majority of affected individuals have two XX chromosomes—the normal female pattern—and the reason they develop testicular tissue is not known. In some of these cases it may be that one X chromosome carries an *SRY* gene that has been translocated from a Y chromosome; testicular tissue could then arise in parts of the embryo in which that X chromosome is active.

A substantial minority of gonadally intersexed people are chromosomal chimeras, possessing some cells or tissue with the XY (male) pattern and some with the XX (female) pattern. Such chimerism can occur if two separate conceptuses of differing chromosomal sex fuse early in development. Alternatively, two sperm (one X, one Y) may penetrate a single ovum, one fertilizing the ovum itself and the other fertilizing one of the polar bodies, which then fails to degenerate and therefore contributes its progeny to the conceptus.

intersexed Having a biological sex that is ambiguous or intermediate between male and female.

disorders of sex development An alternative term for intersexed conditions.

gonadal intersexuality The existence of ovarian and testicular tissue in the same individual. Also called true hermaphroditism.

true hermaphroditism Outdated term for gonadal intersexuality.

Intersexuality is a broad term encompassing a variety of conditions marked by ambiguous or incomplete sexual differentiation. Many pediatricians prefer the term **disorders of sex development** (Lee et al., 2006), but some affected individuals consider that term prejudicial. **Gonadal intersexuality** refers to a rare kind of intersexuality in which a single individual possesses both testicular and ovarian tissue.

Another, more frequently used term for this condition is **true hermaphroditism**. Hermaphrodite, in Greek mythology, was a male–female figure parented by the gods Hermes and Aphrodite (Figure A). As described in Chapter 2, hermaphrodites are common or even the rule in some nonmammalian species. The addition of the modifier "true" distinguishes this condition from pseudohermaphroditism or nongonadal intersexuality (see Boxes 6.3 through 6.5), in which the gonads are entirely of one sex but nongonadal structures are sexually ambiguous.

We dislike the term "true hermaphrodite" for two reasons. First, the word "true" reflects an outdated notion that the gonads are the only "true" arbiters of a person's sex. Second, the term "hermaphrodite" wrongly suggests that gonadal intersexes resemble hermaphroditic animals—that is, that they are capable of taking both the maternal and the paternal roles in reproduction, or even of producing offspring without engaging in sex at all. They cannot do so—in fact, the majority of intersexed individuals are infertile. Thus we prefer—and in this text will use—the term "gonadal intersexuality."

Persons with gonadal intersexuality may possess one ovary and one testis; more commonly, one or both gonads contain both ovarian and testicular tissue (ovotestes; Figure B) (Krob et al., 1994). Generally, the testicular tissue is poorly developed, whereas the ovarian tissue appears normal. The internal reproductive tracts and external genitalia are highly variable, but female structures usually predominate, and individuals affected by gonadal intersexuality tend to look like and identify as women. Several such women have become pregnant and successfully delivered children, but only one instance of a gonadally intersexed person *fathering* a child has been reported.

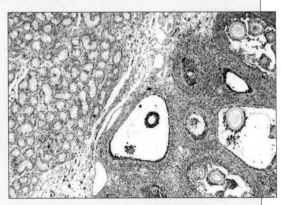

(B) An ovotestis from a dog, showing testicular tissue on the left and ovarian tissue on the right

In XX embryos, on the other hand, *DAX-1* operates unhindered by *SRY*, and therefore the genital ridges develop into ovaries and the embryo becomes a female. Thus, at a molecular level, the process of female differentiation is not simply a "default" process but involves active genetic control from the very beginning.

Sexual Development Involves Growth or Breakdown of Precursor Structures

To produce a male or female human being requires the differentiation of many parts of the body: not just the gonads, but also the reproductive tracts, the genitals, breasts, and many other organs, including the brain. A variety of developmental processes participate in the sexual differentiation of these various organ systems. Some operate within a few weeks of conception; others are delayed until puberty.

Primordial Germ Cells Migrate into the Developing Gonads

Although the gonads develop from the genital ridges under the influence of genes such as *SRY* and *DAX-1*, the gametes themselves—the sperm and the ova—do not originate in the gonads at all. Rather, they are the descendants of a group of cells generated in a transitory extraembryonic region of the conceptus known as the **yolk sac (Figure 6.10)**. About 4 weeks after conception, these **primordial germ cells** migrate into the embryo and home in on the developing genital ridges. It appears that they are attracted by some chemical signal put out by the cells of the genital ridges, for if the ridges are transplanted to some other part of the embryo's body, the primordial germ cells will migrate to the ridges in their unusual location.

Once they have integrated themselves into the gonads, the primordial germ cells (or their descendants) develop into either the stem cells that will give rise to sperm (if they are in a testis) or primary oocytes (if they are in an ovary). Apparently the Sertoli cells (in males) and granulosa cells (in females) play a key role in guiding the developmental pathway of the germ cells.

Male and Female Reproductive Tracts Develop from Different Precursors

At about 6 weeks postconception, when the gonads are beginning to differentiate as ovaries or testes, two separate ducts run from the region of each gonad to the exterior of the embryonic body at the site of the future external genitalia. One of these, the **Wolffian duct**, is the excretory duct for the mesonephros. Because the mesonephros ends up contributing its tissue to the gonads, the Wolffian duct is in direct contact with the gonad. The other duct, the **Müllerian duct**, runs next to the gonad but does not actually contact it. The Wolffian and Müllerian ducts are the precursors of the male and female reproductive tracts, respectively (**Figure 6.11**).

To repeat: Embryos of *both* sexes possess a pair of *both* kinds of ducts. Thus the male embryos need to get rid of their Müllerian ducts and promote the development of their Wolffian ducts, while female embryos need to get rid of their Wolffian ducts and promote the development of their Müllerian ducts.

For females, this process is relatively straightforward, requiring no outside instructions in the form of hormones or other signals. Thus, as originally shown by Jost, the surgical removal of the gonads from an embryo of either sex is followed

yolk sac A transient, early extraembryonic structure; the source of primordial germ cells.

primordial germ cells The cells that give rise to oocytes and to the progenitors of sperm.

Wolffian duct One of two bilateral ducts in the embryo that give rise to the male reproductive tract.

Müllerian duct One of two bilateral ducts in the embryo that give rise to the female reproductive tract.

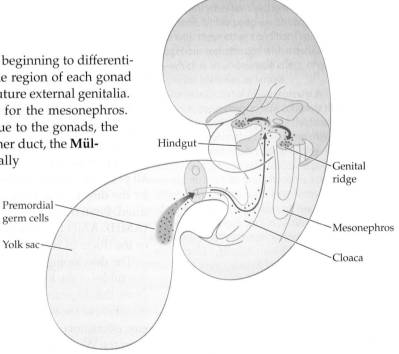

Figure 6.10 Migrating germ cells The cells that will give rise to the embryo's gametes are generated outside the embryo—in the yolk sac—and migrate from there to the genital ridges.

Figure 6.12 Development of the male and female external genitalia from common precursor structures. In males, the urethral folds fuse at the midline to form the penile shaft and enclose the urethra. In females, they remain separate, forming the labia minora.

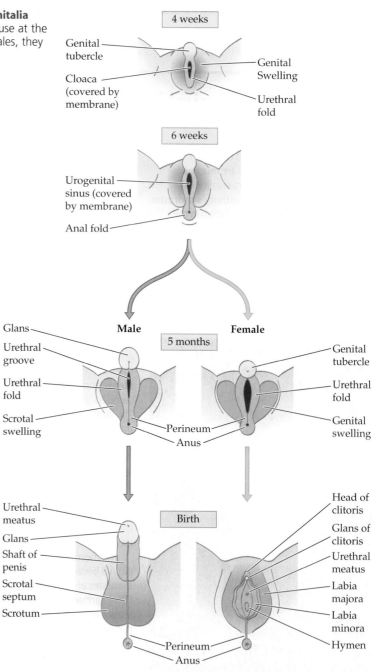

cloaca The common exit of the gastrointestinal and urogenital systems; in humans it is present only in embryonic life.

urethral folds Folds of ectodermal tissue in the embryo that give rise to the labia minora (in females) or the shaft of the penis (in males).

genital swelling Regions of the genitalia in the embryo that give rise to the labia majora (in females) or the scrotum (in males).

A mutation in the gene for the androgen receptor may result in androgen insensitivity syndrome, a condition that produces nongonadal intersexuality (**Box 6.3**).

Male and Female External Genitalia Develop from the Same Precursors

In radical contrast to the development of the internal reproductive tracts, a *single* set of structures gives rise to both the female and the male external genitalia (**Figure 6.12**). Thus the male and female external genitalia are comprised of homologous structures. ("Homologous" means having a common developmental or evolutionary origin.)

At about 4 weeks postconception, the embryo's anogenital region consists of a slit known as the **cloaca**. The cloaca is closed by a membrane. It is flanked by two **urethral folds**, and to the side of each urethral fold is a raised region named the

genital swelling. At the front end of the cloaca is a small midline promontory called the **genital tubercle**. By 2 weeks later, the urethral folds have fused with each other near their posterior (rear) end. The portion behind the fusion point, called the **anal fold**, eventually becomes the anus. The region of the fusion itself becomes the perineum. (Even in adults, the line of fusion is visible as a midline ridge or scar known as the **raphe**, which is seen most easily with the help of a hand mirror.)

During the fetal period, the region in front of the fusion point, which includes the opening of the **urogenital sinus**, gives rise to the external genital structures in both sexes. As with the internal reproductive tracts, the female external genitalia develop by default; that is, in the absence of hormonal or other external instructions. Removal of the ovaries, for example, does not affect the process. (However, the process *can* be affected by a genetic defect in one of the enzymes involved in the synthesis of corticosteroids; this condition is called congenital adrenal hyperplasia [**Box 6.4**]). The genital swellings develop into the labia majora. The urethral folds develop into the labia minora, the outer one-third or so of the vagina, and the crura (deep erectile structures) of the clitoris. The genital tubercle develops into the glans of the clitoris. Remnants of the cloacal membrane persist as the hymen.

The development of the vagina from two different sources is reflected in its anatomical differences in adult women, already alluded to in Chapter 3. The outer portion of the vagina, which develops from the urethral folds, is more muscular and more richly innervated than the inner portion, which develops from the Müllerian ducts.

In male fetuses, the presence of circulating testosterone, secreted by the testes, is required for the normal development of the male genitalia. As with the prostate gland, testosterone has to be converted to the more potent androgen DHT for full genital development. The conversion is performed by the enzyme 5α-reductase. (**Box 6.5** examines the atypical development that occurs as a result of 5α-reductase deficiency.) DHT binds to androgen receptors in the genital tissue and triggers several processes. The urethral folds fuse at the midline, forming the shaft of the penis and enclosing the urethra. (If this midline fusion fails to occur, a condition called hypospadias results, as discussed in **Box 6.6**.) The genital swellings also fuse at the midline, forming the scrotum. The genital tubercle expands to form the glans of the penis. The prostate gland—and probably the homologous paraurethral glands in females—develops from the walls of the urogenital sinus, beneath the urethral folds.

Thus we can define the following homologies: The male scrotum is homologous to the female labia majora, the shaft of the penis is homologous to the labia minora, and the glans of the penis is homologous to the glans of the clitoris. These homologies are approximate; some tissue from the urethral folds probably contributes to the deeper clitoral structures in women, for example.

The Gonads Descend during Development

In fetuses of both sexes, the gonads move downward from their site of origin in the upper lumbar region of the embryo. By about 10 weeks postconception, they are positioned at the rim of the pelvis. In females, the ovaries remain in this position for the remainder of fetal life, but after birth they descend in the pelvis and end up on either side of the uterus.

In males, the movement of the testes is even greater. At 6 to 7 months postconception they descend into the pelvis, and shortly before birth they enter the scrotum. Key to this process are paired structures called **gubernacula**: Each gubernaculum is a fibrous band that attaches at one end to the testis and, at the other

genital tubercle A midline swelling in front of the cloaca, which gives rise to the glans of the clitoris (in females) or penis (in males).

anal fold The posterior portion of the urethral fold, which gives rise to the anus.

raphe The midline ridge of the perineum.

urogenital sinus The common opening of the urinary and genital systems in the embryo.

gubernaculum Either of two bilateral fibrous bands that are involved in the descent of the gonads in the fetus.

Biology of Sex

BOX 6.4 Atypical Development: Congenital Adrenal Hyperplasia

Congenital adrenal hyperplasia (CAH) involves a genetic defect in one of the enzymes that are involved in the synthesis of corticosteroid hormones in the adrenal cortex. (Corticosteroids have functions unrelated to sex, but they are made from the same precursor molecules that give rise to the sex steroid hormones.) Because of this defect, the production of corticosteroids is greatly reduced. The brain and pituitary gland sense this deficit and try to stimulate the adrenal cortex into increased production. The result is excessive growth (hyperplasia) of the adrenal cortex and an overproduction of the precursor steroids, which are then converted into a variety of androgens. The clinical syndrome results both from the lack of corticosteroids—which causes serious metabolic problems in either sex—and from the excess of androgens. The effects of the excess androgens show themselves in XX individuals (chromosomal females) as partial masculinization during fetal and postnatal development. In spite of this partial masculinization, the great majority of XX CAH children are raised as girls.

CAH is a **recessive trait**. If both parents carry a single defective copy of the gene, each of their children (of either sex) has a 1 in 4 chance of inheriting two defective copies and therefore of developing CAH. About 1 in 16,000 live-born children have the classic form of CAH (Carlson et al., 1999), but a larger number have milder forms of the condition. Among Ashkenazic (Central European) Jews, for example, 1 in 27 children have a mild form of the condition (New & Wilson, 1999).

The adrenal cortex begins secreting corticosteroids at about 6 weeks after conception. In CAH-affected fetuses, the excess secretion of androgens begins at some variable time after

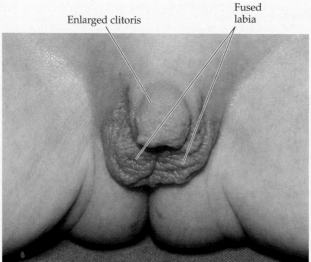

Enlarged clitoris   Fused labia

Partial masculization of genitalia in a CAH girl

that. If the fetus is a chromosomal male (XY), the extra androgens are of little significance because large amounts of androgens are secreted by the testes in any case, and the male differentiation of the genitalia proceeds normally. (After birth, when androgen levels normally drop, the excess androgens in CAH boys may cause too rapid growth and early puberty.)

If the fetus is a chromosomal female (XX), however, problems arise during fetal life. Since AMH is absent, the Müllerian ducts develop in the usual way, so all XX CAH children have a female internal reproductive tract. If the androgen excess occurs early enough in development, it may rescue the Wolffian ducts, which then persist along with the Müllerian duct structures. More commonly, the effects of the excess androgens are seen slightly later in fetal development, during the differentiation of the external genitalia. Although the outcome is variable, the newborn baby's genitalia typically look like female genitalia that have been shift-

ed in the male direction (masculinized). In particular, high levels of prenatal androgens may cause enlargement of the clitoris, and the labia may be partially fused at the midline to form a scrotum-like structure (see figure). If the condition is left untreated, further masculinization may occur at puberty.

Usually, however, the condition is recognized at birth and is treated by lifelong administration of corticosteroids. The treatment supplies the missing hormones and, by doing so, stops the compensatory overproduction of androgens. The masculinized genitalia are often "corrected" surgically by, for example, removing, shortening, or "recessing" the large clitoris early in life. This policy has recently been challenged by some people with CAH and by advocates for the intersexed.

It has recently become possible to treat CAH prenatally. At-risk fetuses can be diagnosed as early as 9 weeks after conception by means of chorionic villus sampling (see Chapter 11). If treatment with a synthetic corticosteroid is started by 10 weeks of pregnancy, masculinization of the external genitalia can be greatly reduced or prevented entirely (Carlson et al., 1999).

An interesting aspect of CAH from a scientific standpoint concerns the possible effects of the prenatal androgen exposure on the fetus's brain and its later psychosexual development. We will postpone our discussion of this issue to Chapter 7.

congenital adrenal hyperplasia (CAH) An intersexed condition caused by a genetic defect in corticosteroid synthesis.

recessive trait An inherited trait that shows itself only when the responsible gene is present on both homologous chromosomes.

end, to the abdominal wall near the developing pubic bone. Because the gubernacula do not lengthen as the fetal body grows, they pull the testes farther and farther downward during fetal life. As the testes enter the scrotum, they draw various structures with them: the vas deferens, blood vessels, and nerves, as well as

Biology of Sex

BOX 6.5 Atypical Development: 5α-Reductase Deficiency

The enzyme 5α-reductase, which is normally present in some androgen target tissues, such as the external genitalia, skin, and prostate gland, converts testosterone to the more potent androgen 5α-dihydrotestosterone, or DHT. Like congenital adrenal hyperplasia, 5α-reductase deficiency is an autosomal recessive trait that causes a form of intersexuality. For the most part it is very rare, but the condition tends to crop up in clusters in genetically isolated communities. The first and most thoroughly studied of these clusters is in the village of Salinas in the Dominican Republic. In 1974, Julianne Imperato-McGinley of Cornell University Medical College, along with several colleagues, reported that 24 XY individuals in the village had an intersexed condition caused by 5α-reductase deficiency (Imperato-McGinley et al., 1974).

Since the affected individuals are chromosomal males (XY), they develop testes. The testicular hormones, AMH and testosterone, as well as the receptors for these hormones, function normally. Therefore, the affected fetuses develop the internal reproductive structures of males, and the female (Müllerian duct) structures regress. But the external genitalia do not fully develop in the male direction without the presence of DHT. Often they consist of labia-like structures instead of a scrotum, a urogenital sinus into which a blind vaginal pouch and the urethra open, and a phallus that resembles a clitoris more than a penis (Figure A). The testicles may be in the

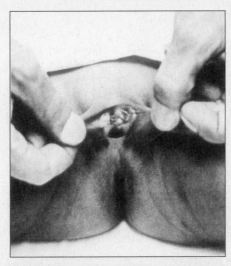

(A) External genitalia of affected child at birth

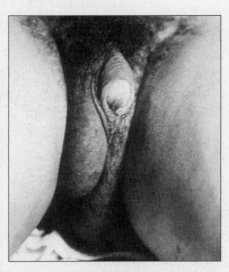

(B) Masculine appearance after puberty

labia or in the inguinal canal. The prostate gland is present but small.

The affected individuals are raised as girls or, in communities that are familiar with the syndrome, as intersexed children. The increase in testosterone levels at puberty, however, is able to accomplish much of what was left undone earlier: the skin of the scrotum becomes pigmented and corrugated, the testes descend if they were in the inguinal canal, and the phallus enlarges to resemble a penis (Figure B). The rest of the body also changes in the male direction: There is a great increase in muscularity, the voice

deepens, and there is no breast development. In effect, girls seem to grow into men. Only a few traits are completely DHT-dependent and therefore do not appear in 5α-reductase-deficient individuals; these traits include acne and a receding hairline. Facial hair is sparse.

One of the most interesting and controversial aspects of the 5α-reductase story is how the affected individuals respond to their apparent change of sex at puberty. We will postpone our discussion of this matter, however, until Chapter 7. (Photographs courtesy of Julianne Imperato-McGinley.)

a portion of the peritoneal lining of the abdominal cavity (**Figure 6.13**). Collectively, these structures contribute to the spermatic cord. Although the testes sit in saclike spaces that are developmentally part of the abdominal cavity, the connection between these spaces and the pelvic cavity is usually sealed off after the testes descend. Thus, even though the cremaster muscle can pull the testes upward in the scrotal sac, the testes cannot move all the way back into the pelvis.

Because the Wolffian ducts are attached to the developing testes before the descent begins, the vasa deferentia (which form from the Wolffian ducts) are drawn out along the course of the descent. That is why the vasa deferentia of adult men take a route that seems unnecessarily circuitous, arching upward over the ureters before they turn downward and medially toward the prostate gland. The kidneys, by moving upward during development, contribute to this circuitous route.

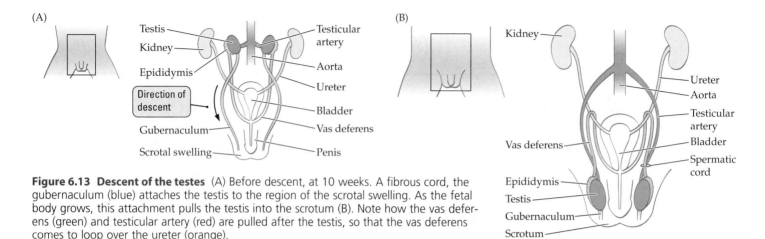

Figure 6.13 Descent of the testes (A) Before descent, at 10 weeks. A fibrous cord, the gubernaculum (blue) attaches the testis to the region of the scrotal swelling. As the fetal body grows, this attachment pulls the testis into the scrotum (B). Note how the vas deferens (green) and testicular artery (red) are pulled after the testis, so that the vas deferens comes to loop over the ureter (orange).

In 2% to 5% of full-term newborn boys, one or both testicles have not yet arrived in the scrotum. In many of these boys, the tardy testicles arrive within a few weeks after birth, but if they are still no-shows at 3 months, the condition is considered pathological and is named **cryptorchidism**. About 1% of boys have this condition (Inan et al., 2008). Usually, the missing testicles have been held up somewhere along the path of their fetal descent—most commonly, in the inguinal canal. Cryptorchidism is associated with lowered fertility and with an increased risk of testicular cancer after puberty. Undescended testicles can often be surgically moved into the scrotum; this procedure is best done before 2 years of age (Lim et al., 2003). If the testicles are near their goal, they may be induced to complete their descent by treatment with gonadotropins or with gonadotropin-releasing hormone (GnRH). Correction of cryptorchidism improves the prospects for fertility but does not eliminate the increased risk of cancer. Once they are in the scrotum, however, the testes can be monitored by regular self-examination, thus increasing the likelihood that any cancer that does develop will be detected at an early stage.

Hormones Influence the Sexual Differentiation of the Central Nervous System

Like male and female bodies, male and female brains differ from each other. These differences contribute to sex differences in cognition, personality, and sexuality. We therefore turn our attention to these brain differences and ask how they arise.

The CNS Contains Sexually Dimorphic Structures

We already described in Chapter 4 how parts of the central nervous system (CNS) differ in structure between the two sexes. The example we cited was Onuf's nucleus in the sacral level of the spinal cord. (Recall from Chapter 4 that "nucleus," in neuroanatomy, means a cluster of nerve cells, not the nucleus *of* a cell.) Onuf's nucleus contains the cell bodies of the motor neurons that innervate some of the striated muscles of the pelvic floor, including those associated with the root of the penis. Onuf's nucleus is larger, and contains more neurons, in men than in women. (See also Web Topic 6.3 Sexual Dimorphism Can Arise as an Indirect Effect of Hormonal Levels.)

The brain also contains sexually dimorphic cell groups. The most extensively studied of these is a cell group in the **medial preoptic area**, the frontmost portion of the hypothalamus. The medial preoptic area is involved (at least in laboratory animals) in the generation of sexual behavior typically shown by males ("male-typ-

Biology of Sex

BOX 6.6 Atypical Development: Hypospadias and Micropenis

Hypospadias is a condition seen in males when the urethral folds fail to fully enclose the urethra (Baskin, 2004). The urethra then opens on the lower surface of the glans, close to the normal position (see figure); on the shaft of the penis; at the base of the penis; on the front of the scrotum; or even on the perineum behind the scrotum. The abnormal opening may be in addition to the regular opening at the tip of the penis or may replace it. Hypospadias is common: As many as 1 in 350 boys have hypospadias severe enough to require surgical repair (Aho et al., 2000), and far greater numbers have milder forms of the condition. In fact, German urologists examined the location of the urethral meatus in 500 "normal" men and found that only 55% of them had a meatus in the supposedly "normal" position at the very tip of the glans. In the other 45% the meatus was located slightly behind the tip on the ventral surface of the glans, or at the level of the corona. Such positioning of the meatus did not impair the men's ability to discharge a single stream of urine, to engage in coitus, or to father children (Fichtner et al., 1995).

The cause of hypospadias in individual cases is not usually known. The condition is thought to result from a variety of endocrinological factors, such as deficits in testosterone synthesis or in the conversion of testosterone to DHT, or from exposure of the mother to steroidal drugs, especially progestins. A variety of techniques, comparable to those used in female-to-male sex reassignment surgery, are employed to repair severe

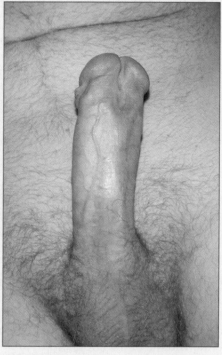

Hypospadias

hypospadias . Noting the benign effect of the mild forms of hypospadias, the German urologists questioned whether surgical repair is warranted when these forms are seen in newborns.

Micropenis means an unusually small penis—less than about 2 cm (0.8 inches) in stretched length—in a newborn male. This

condition, which affects about 2% of boys (depending on exact definitions), can arise from a wide variety of causes, and it is sometimes associated with hypospadias. The treatment of micropenis is controversial. In most cases the penis can be induced to grow larger with a few months' treatment with testosterone, and there are also surgical techniques that can enlarge the penis in early childhood. Sometimes the penis is judged inadequate and the child may be surgically reassigned as a girl. Whichever course is taken, dissatisfaction with the genitalia in adulthood is common (Wisniewski et al., 2001). Nevertheless, children with micropenis who are allowed to grow up as male generally develop into heterosexual men with a strong male identity, enjoy an active sex life, and are indistinguishable from other men in terms of their general mental health (Reilly & Woodhouse, 1989; Lee and Houk, 2004). Thus the justification for sex reassignment in young children with micropenis has been questioned (Calikoglu, 1999).

When older boys are seen by pediatricians on account of a small penis, the real culprit is often obesity, which can cause an average-sized penis to become partially hidden in the pubic fat pad.

hypospadias An abnormal location of the urethral meatus on the underside of the glans, the shaft of the penis, or elsewhere.

micropenis A penis shorter than about 2 cm (0.8 inches) in stretched length at birth.

---

ical" sexual behavior), such as mounting, intromission, and ejaculation, and it may be involved in higher-level traits, such as partner choice, as well. In some species, damage to this area in male animals results in the appearance of behavior patterns typically shown by females (Kindon et al., 1996; Paredes et al., 1998). Thus it may normally play a role in the active suppression of female-typical behavior.

Within the medial preoptic area is a cell group that is larger (on average, at least) in males than in females. In humans it has the name **third interstitial nucleus of the anterior hypothalamus**, or **INAH3** (Allen et al., 1989; Byne, 1998) (**Figure 6.14**). It is the best studied cell group in a chain of nuclei in the base of the brain that are larger in males than in females (Allen & Gorski, 1990). In Chapter 14 we'll review evidence that the size of INAH3 in men is related to their sexual orientation.

The introduction of advanced imaging techniques has led to the discovery that there are numerous structural, functional, and chemical differences throughout

cryptorchidism Failure of one or both testicles to descend into the scrotum by 3 months of postnatal age.

medial preoptic area A region of the hypothalamus involved in the regulation of sexual behaviors typically shown by males.

third interstitial nucleus of the anterior hypothalamus (INAH3) A sexually dimorphic cell group in the medial preoptic area of the human hypothalamus.

(A)

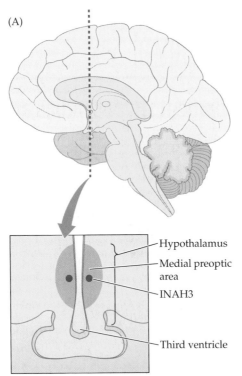

Hypothalamus

Medial preoptic area

INAH3

Third ventricle

Figure 6.14 The third interstitial nucleus of the anterior hypothalamus (INAH3) is larger, on average, in men than in women. (A) INAH3 lies within the medial preoptic area of the hypothalamus, a region concerned with male-typical sexual behavior. The midline slit is the third ventricle of the brain. (B) Micrograph of INAH3 in a man; the nucleus is the oval shaped cluster of darkly stained cell bodies at the center of the micrograph—it measures about 0.5mm across.

(B)

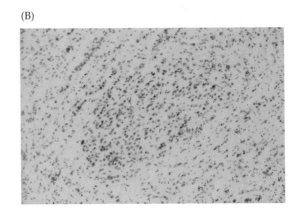

the brains of men and women (Cahill, 2005). In terms of structure, for example, the two cerebral hemispheres are about the same size in women, but in men the right hemisphere is usually slightly larger than the left (Savic & Lindstrom, 2008). In addition, several regions within the cerebral cortex are larger in volume (relative to the volume of the entire brain) in one sex or the other (Goldstein et al., 2001). As an example of a functional difference, a brain structure named the amygdala is involved in the encoding of emotionally laden experiences into memory, but men use the right amygdala for this task, while women use the left amygdala (Canli et al., 2002). And in the realm of chemistry, men's brains produce serotonin—a neurotransmitter involved in the regulation of mood—at a rate 52% higher than women's brains (Nishizawa et al., 1997).

Sexual Dimorphism Arises as a Consequence of Differing Hormonal Levels during a Sensitive Period

How do sex differences in the structure of the CNS arise during development? The best-documented cause is the same as the main cause of sex differences in the rest of the body—the higher levels of circulating androgens in males than in females during development.

Roger Gorski and his colleagues at UCLA studied the development of a sexually dimorphic cell group in the rat's hypothalamus named the **sexually dimorphic nucleus of the preoptic area (SDN-POA)** (Davis et al., 1995). This cell group may be equivalent to the human cell group INAH3 mentioned above. They found that female rats could be induced to develop a large (male-sized) SDN-POA by administration of testosterone and that male rats could be induced to develop a small (female-sized) SDN-POA by castration—that is, by removal of the rat's own supply of testosterone. In either case, however, the manipulation had to be done during a restricted **sensitive period** of development (**Figure 6.15**). In rats, this period begins a few days before birth and ends soon after birth. Comparable treatments in adult rats have little or no effect on the size of the nucleus.

sexually dimorphic nucleus of the preoptic area (SDN-POA) A cell group in the medial preoptic area of the hypothalamus of rodents that is larger in males than females.

sensitive period A period of development during which the survival or growth of a biological system depends on the presence of some factor, such as a hormone.

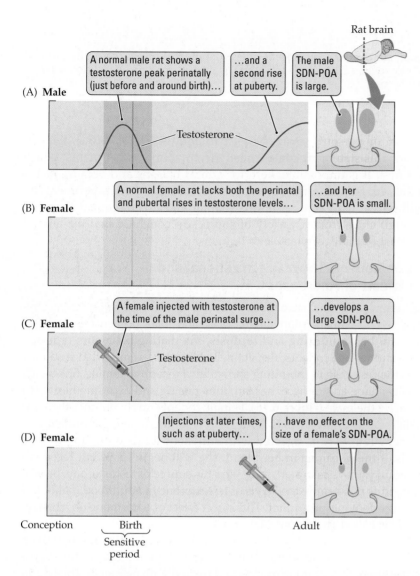

(A) **Male**

A normal male rat shows a testosterone peak perinatally (just before and around birth)...

...and a second rise at puberty.

The male SDN-POA is large.

Rat brain

Testosterone

Figure 6.15 Sexual differentiation in the hypothalamus The presence of testosterone during an early "sensitive period" is necessary for the development of a male-sized SDN-POA in rats.

(B) **Female**

A normal female rat lacks both the perinatal and pubertal rises in testosterone levels...

...and her SDN-POA is small.

(C) **Female**

A female injected with testosterone at the time of the male perinatal surge...

...develops a large SDN-POA.

Testosterone

(D) **Female**

Injections at later times, such as at puberty...

...have no effect on the size of a female's SDN-POA.

Conception   Birth   Adult
                  Sensitive
                  period

Gorski's group found that about the same numbers of SDN-POA neurons are generated in both sexes. Thus testosterone does not influence this initial step in the development of the nucleus. Rather, it influences the *survival* of SDN-POA neurons. Soon after they have started to form the nucleus, SDN-POA neurons produce androgen receptors and in fact become dependent on the presence of testosterone for their survival. Thus in females, whose testosterone levels are low, the majority of SDN-POA neurons die. These cells can be "rescued" not only by systemic administration of testosterone, but also by local injections of miniscule quantities of the same hormone into the hypothalamus itself. This finding supports the notion that androgens act directly on the SDN-POA neurons to promote their survival and development.

We have no direct evidence as to whether similar processes guide the sexual differentiation of INAH3 in humans. If they do, it's likely that the sensitive period is well before birth, rather than around the time of birth, as with rats. That's because humans, with their longer period of development in utero (9 months, versus 3 weeks for rats), are born at a much later stage of brain development.

Early Hormonal Exposure Influences Later Sexual Behavior

Hormone levels during development not only guide the development of anatomical differences between male and female brains; they also have some influence on

Figure 6.16 Copulating rats Mounting and lordosis are the stereotypical sexual behaviors of male and female rodents. The female rat (below) is showing lordosis—an inverse arching of her back that exposes her vulva—in response to being mounted by the male.

mounting A male-typical sexual behavior: climbing onto the female to reach a position in which intromission is possible. (Used mostly for nonhuman animals.)

lordosis In female rodents, an inverse arching of the back that exposes the vulva for intromission by a male.

activational effect The influence of a sex hormone on the function of brain circuitry in adulthood.

organizational effect The influence of a sex hormone on the development of brain circuitry.

an animal or person's sexual *behavior* in adulthood. Of course, the evidence for this statement comes mostly from animal experiments, which we discuss first. It is impossible, both for ethical reasons and because of the prolonged time course of human development, to do equivalent experiments on humans. Still, as we will see later in this chapter and in subsequent chapters, there are enough clues from a variety of sources to conclude that the animal results are at least partially applicable to humans.

Experiments on Rodents Show Organizational and Activational Effects of Androgens

The key observations of animal sexual behavior were made by a group at the University of Texas, led by William Young, in the 1950s and 1960s (Phoenix et al., 1959). Young's group studied **mounting** and **lordosis**, the mating behaviors typically shown by male and female rodents, respectively. Mounting is just what it sounds like; lordosis is the response to mounting shown by a receptive female. She bends her back into a U-shape and deflects her tail, thus raising and exposing her vulva for intromission by the male (**Figure 6.16**). Female rodents rarely mount other animals, and male rodents rarely display lordosis in response to being mounted.

If an adult female rodent is injected with sufficient testosterone to produce male-like levels of the hormone in her blood, she will begin to mount receptive females. If an adult male is castrated, removing his source of testosterone, he will stop mounting. Thus it is simply the levels of testosterone in adulthood that determines whether a rodent mounts or not. This direct effect of a hormone on a behavior in adulthood is called an **activational effect**.

The situation with lordosis is quite different. If an adult male rat is castrated (by removal of his testosterone source) and treated with estrogens, thus mimicking a female hormonal environment, he will *not* show lordosis behavior. But if a male rat is castrated *early in development* and treated with estrogens when he is adult, he *will* display lordosis (**Figure 6.17**). Conversely, if a female rat is treated with testosterone early in development, she will not display lordosis in adulthood, no matter what hormones she is given. In other words, the levels of testosterone during development determines whether a rodent is capable of showing lordosis when exposed to estrogens in adulthood—high levels prevent lordosis, low levels permit it. This is called an **organizational effect** because the levels of testosterone during

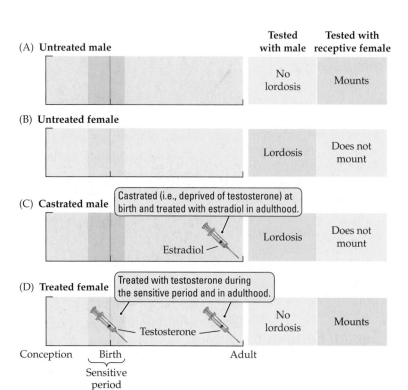

Figure 6.17 Hormones and sexual behavior in rats Sexual behavior depends on the hormonal environment during a sensitive period early in development and in adulthood. (A) Untreated male. (B) Untreated female. (C) Male castrated (i.e., deprived of testosterone) at birth and treated with estradiol in adulthood. (D) Female treated with testosterone during the sensitive period and in adulthood.

development permanently affect the organization of the brain circuitry responsible for a given behavior.

The experiments just described were focused on the motor patterns shown by rodents during sex—mounting or lordosis. In other studies, the animal had to choose between a male and a female partner. This, then, was a test of what we might, in humans, call "sexual orientation." It turns out that organizational effects of testosterone play an important role here: Female rats that were exposed to high levels of testosterone during development are shifted in their partner preference toward females (de Jonge et al., 1988), and males in which the synthesis or action of testosterone was blocked during development are shifted toward preferring male partners (Bakker et al., 1993). Similar effects have been described in a variety of other species.

For more information on the basis of organizational and activational effects, please see Web Topic 6.4 Organizational and Activational Effects of Hormones on the Brain.

Primates Have Multiple Sensitive Periods

How relevant is all this to human sexuality? One way of approaching this question is by extending the rodent research to primates. Researchers led by Robert Goy conducted a multi-year study of female macaque monkeys that had been treated with testosterone during fetal life. Goy's group obtained results comparable to what had already been observed in rats and guinea pigs. Even before puberty, the effects of the prenatal testosterone exposure were obvious. Prepubertal monkeys engage in a lot of "play-sex," in which one monkey mounts but does not penetrate another. Males take the mounting role more commonly than do females. Goy's prenatally treated females also commonly took the mounting role in play-sex. This "masculinization" affected other traits besides play-sex behavior. For example, male prepubertal monkeys typically engage in more "play-fighting" or "rough-and-tumble play" than do females, but prenatal treatment with testosterone increased young female monkeys' engagement in these activities (Goy et al., 1988; Wallen, 1996).

After the treated females reached puberty, Goy's group tested their adult sexual behavior (Pomerantz et al., 1986). They first removed the ovaries from the monkeys and gave them a series of testosterone injections, thus simulating the hormonal environment of a normal adult *male* monkey. The females who had been exposed to testosterone prenatally responded to this endocrinological sex reversal by showing male-typical sexual behavior, especially a style of mounting called the "footclasp mount," in which the mounting animal raises itself on the feet or hind legs of the other animal (**Figure 6.18**). Such behavior was not shown by a comparison group of female monkeys that experienced normal prenatal development, even though they were subjected to the same endocrinological manipulation (ovary removal and testosterone treatment) in adulthood. Thus it was the *prenatal* exposure to testosterone, in combination with the testosterone treatment in adulthood, that caused Goy's females to perform adult-style mounting.

Figure 6.18 When monkeys copulate, the male often grasps the feet or legs of the female with his own feet. Juvenile females who have been exposed to androgens before birth will take the male role in this "footclasp mount" during play-sex, but untreated females will not.

Goy and his colleagues found that monkeys have not just a single "sensitive period," but several. For example, testosterone treatment of females early in fetal life was most effective in promoting mounting behavior, but treatment later in fetal life was most effective in promoting rough-and-tumble play (Goy et al., 1988). It thus appears that the brain circuits mediating different kinds of sex-differentiated behaviors mature at different times and become sensitive to testosterone levels at different times. It is therefore possible, by precise timing of testosterone treatments, not merely to dissociate a monkey's behavior from its anatomy (in other words, producing a monkey with female genitalia but male-like sexual behavior), but it is also possible to dissociate one kind of sex-typical behavior from another (producing a female that participates in rough-and-tumble play but not in male-like play-sex behavior, for example).

We will defer our main discussion of the development of *human* sexual behavior until later chapters. We will make the case, however, that the observations on rodents and primates that we have just described are relevant to human sexual development.

Estrogens seem to play little role in prenatal sexual development, except in the brain, where estradiol (produced by local synthesis from androgens) may help to masculinize brain circuitry, as described earlier. The ovaries do not produce significant quantities of sex steroids before birth. Estrogens are present in embryos and fetuses of both sexes—in particular, they reach the fetus from the mother's circulation, and they are also manufactured by the placenta from androgens secreted by the testes (in males) or the adrenal gland (in both sexes). That these estrogens can influence fetal development to some degree is illustrated by the fact that some newborn infants have visible breast development and may even secrete milk (so-called witch's milk). In general, however, it seems that the fetus, and particularly its brain, is protected from the effects of external estrogens. These protective mechanisms include the chemical alteration of estrogens as they enter the fetal circulation and the existence of binding proteins that lower the levels of the free steroids. Furthermore, laboratory animals and humans that are insensitive to estrogens because of a congenital absence of estrogen receptors experience no obvious abnormalities of prenatal development (Korach et al., 1996). This stands in marked contrast to the situation of genetic males who lack *androgen* receptors: Their fetal development is radically affected (see Box 6.3).

Other Y-Linked Genes Besides SRY Influence Development

So far, we have attributed prenatal sexual differentiation almost entirely to the secretions of the developing testis—AMH and androgens—in males, and to the lack or low levels of comparable hormones in females. Because testis development is controlled by the gene *SRY*, this model places the responsibility for sexual differentiation on the presence (in males) or the absence (in females) of *SRY*, in line with the original hypothesis spelled out by Alfred Jost in the 1940s. But this model is probably incomplete. In particular, other genes on the Y chromosome besides *SRY* influence sexual development. Several Y-linked genes are involved in spermatogenesis (Affara & Mitchell, 2000). Thus, the rare XX individuals who are male by virtue of having a *SRY* gene that has jumped from a Y to an X chromosome during spermatogenesis, as described earlier, have defective spermatogenesis and are sterile because they lack these other Y-linked genes.

There is also at least one gene on the Y chromosome that increases stature, and a part of the reason that men are, on average, taller than women is the fact that they possess this gene (Salo et al., 1995). In fact, it has been reported that male conceptuses grow faster than female conceptuses even before implantation (and therefore long before the testis has begun to secrete hormones). Again, this difference is due to a gene on the Y chromosome that is different from *SRY* (Burgoyne et al., 1995).

Finally, studies on sex-reversed mice indicate that some behavioral differences between male and female mice are influenced by genetic mechanisms that do not involve the *SRY*–testis–hormone cascade (Stavnezer et al., 2000; Arnold et al., 2004). Thus the "classical" mechanism postulated by Jost, while unquestionably of central importance in sexual differentiation, is not the entire story. The non-classical mechanisms remain to be elucidated.

External Factors Influence Prenatal Sexual Development

1957 advertisement for DES in a medical journal. DES caused serious harm to some of the daughters of women who took it.

There is increasing evidence from animal studies that environmental factors operating during pregnancy can affect the sexual development of fetuses. In rats, for example, subjecting a pregnant female to stress (such as forced immobilization or bright lights) or administering alcohol to her affects the later sexual behavior of her male offspring. In general, these males are partially "demasculinized" in their sexual behavior: They are less ready to approach and mount receptive females and ejaculate less often than untreated male rats (Ward et al., 1994). There are also anatomical and chemical changes in the brains of these prenatally stressed rats that are consistent with demasculinization: The volume of the SDN-POA is reduced, and the levels of some neurotransmitters and related compounds are more similar to those typically found in females than in males (Anderson et al., 1986; Reznikov et al., 1999).

Although alcohol and stress can affect fetal development in humans, too, little evidence points to specific effects on sexual development. One external factor that *can* affect human sexual development is the administration of sex hormones or related drugs to pregnant women. Between 1938 and 1971, several million pregnant women in the United States were given the drug **diethylstilbestrol (DES)**, a synthetic estrogen agonist. It was prescribed for women who were at increased risk of miscarriage and even for average-risk women. We now know that DES does not prevent miscarriage and in fact may make miscarriage *more* likely. Administration of the drug to pregnant women was halted when it was found that it caused serious health problems for some of the female children born to those women. About 1 in 1000 of these girls, when they reached young adulthood, developed a cancer of the cervix or vagina that is normally very rare in that age range (Herbst, 1999). Women exposed to DES in utero may also have an increased risk of breast cancer later in life (Palmer et al., 2002). Others have had fertility problems, and some have anatomical abnormalities of the reproductive tract. Males exposed to DES in utero have an increased risk of genito-urinary malformations, but their fertility is not impaired (Wilcox et al., 1995a; Perez et al., 2005). The DES experience highlights the dangers of administering hormone-related drugs to pregnant women.

Biological and Social Factors Interact Postnatally

One of the most common misconceptions about genes and development is that genes run the whole show before birth, and the environment takes over after birth. We've just seen how the environment (meaning, in this case, the mother, as well as factors external to her) can influence prenatal development. Conversely, genes continue to play a major role in postnatal development. Still, it is true that there are far more opportunities for the environment to influence development once a fetus has left the protective cocoon of its mother's uterus.

We will have much more to say about postnatal sexual development in later chapters, but we should mention here a couple of examples of ways in which

diethylstilbestrol (DES) A synthetic estrogen receptor agonist that was once used to prevent miscarriage but that caused cancer and fertility problems in some of the daughters born of these pregnancies.

puberty The biological transition to sexual maturity.

environmental factors influence development during the period between birth and puberty. One such example concerns social isolation. A research group led by psychobiologist Marc Breedlove compared the effects of housing rats one to a cage and in groups from the time of weaning through adulthood (Cooke et al., 2000). They found that male rats raised in isolation were less likely than group-raised rats to respond, with a penile erection, to the presence of an estrous female or to achieve intromission with a female. The isolation also led to anatomical changes in brain organization.

Researchers led by Kim Wallen have conducted a multi-year study of the interaction of hormonal and social factors in the sexual development of rhesus monkeys and other nonhuman primates (Wallen, 1996, 2001). One example of their findings: Monkeys reared in same-sex peer groups show different sexual behavior (during their juvenile life at least) than do monkeys raised in mixed-sex peer groups. In either type of rearing environment, males display more mounting behavior than do females—this difference results from their different prenatal hormonal exposure. But the sex difference in mounting behavior is much less marked among monkeys raised in same-sex groups than among those raised in mixed-sex groups. Apparently, exposure to female peers increases the propensity of male juveniles to mount other animals (of either sex), whereas exposure to male peers diminishes the propensity of female juveniles to mount other animals. Thus prenatal hormone exposure does not rigidly predestine animals' sexual behavior, but generates a predisposition that can be modified by social circumstances.

Puberty Marks Sexual Maturation

During early infancy, the levels of circulating gonadotropins (LH and FSH) are high in both sexes. In girls, the presence of these hormones does not have major or consistent effects on the secretion of hormones by the ovaries, which remains very low throughout childhood. In infant boys, however, the gonadotropins spur the secretion of enough testosterone by the testes to bring circulating testosterone to adultlike levels (Andersson et al., 1998). The function, if any, of this brief postnatal testosterone surge is not known. By about 6 to 9 months of age, testosterone sinks back to very low levels and remains low until **puberty**, the biological transition to sexual maturity.

Although there are no marked differences in sex hormone levels between girls and boys throughout most of childhood, there *are* sex differences in personality and behavior. In part, these differences reflect the different androgen levels to which girls and boys were exposed during fetal life. We will discuss this topic further in Chapter 7.

The Pubertal Growth Spurt Occurs Earlier in Girls than in Boys

The most obvious biological process during childhood is growth (**Figure 6.19**). The rate of growth decreases over time: At the age of 1 year a child is growing in height at a rate of 15 to 20 cm (6 to 8 inches) per year, but by shortly before puberty, growth has slowed to about 5 cm (2 inches) per year. Then comes the pubertal (puberty-associated) growth spurt, in which the growth rate rises briefly to a peak of about 10 cm (4 inches) per year.

The pubertal growth spurt results in a height gain of about 28 cm (11 inches) for boys and 25 cm (10 inches) for girls. About 2 years after the beginning of the growth spurt, however, growth in height finally ceases, as the growth zones in the long bones cease to function and close (that is, they become solid bone).

There is considerable individual variation in the timing of the pubertal growth spurt, but in the contemporary U.S. population it begins at an average age of

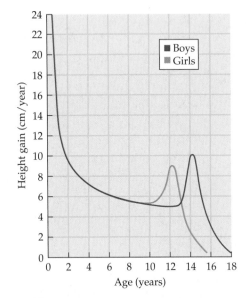

Figure 6.19 Growth velocity curves for boys and girls The pubertal growth spurt begins 1.5 to 2 years later in boys than in girls. It is this extra period of childhood growth in males that largely accounts for the sex difference in adult height.

about 11 (for girls) or 13 (for boys). The age difference allows for about 2 years of additional childhood growth in boys, and this is the principal reason for the 10-cm (4-inch) difference in average height between adult men and women.

The spurt in height is not the only change in growth during puberty. The structure of the skeleton also changes, with girls developing wider hips and boys developing wider shoulders. Body composition also changes: By adulthood, men have 50% more bone and muscle mass than women, and women have twice as much body fat as men. Of course, these are very much statements about averages—there are plenty of muscular women and fat men. Genes influence variations in body composition among individuals of the same sex, and factors such as food availability and athletic training can greatly modify the effects of biological predispositions.

Because of variations in the timing of puberty, these 12-year-old girls vary a great deal in their physical development.

Puberty Is Marked by Visible and Invisible Changes in the Body

More directly relevant to sexuality are pubertal changes in the external genitalia, secondary sexual characteristics, internal reproductive tract, and gonads. In girls, the most noticeable change in the external genitalia is the growth of pubic hair (**Figure 6.20**), but, in addition, the labia majora and labia minora become more prominent, the vagina deepens, and the vaginal wall thickens. Axillary (armpit) hair appears a little later than pubic hair.

The most important secondary female sexual characteristic to appear at puberty are the breasts. Breast development goes through several stages (**Figure 6.21**). The breast first shows itself as a small mound—the **breast bud**—centered on the nipple. As breast development continues, both the nipple and the surrounding areola come to project forward from the breast, and the areola enlarges. With the completion of breast development, the areola lies flush with the breast once more, and only the nipple projects.

Inside a girl's body, puberty is marked by a spurt of growth in the ovaries, uterus, and oviducts. The oviducts, which before puberty have a somewhat contorted course, become straighter. The cervix begins to produce the characteristic secretions of adult life. And in the ovaries, the recruitment of primordial follicles into the process of follicular maturation begins.

The most dramatic event in a girl's puberty is the onset of menstruation, called **menarche** (pronunciations vary—MEN-ar-kee is as good as any). Because menarche is an event rather than a process, and a highly memorable one at that, it is commonly used to date female puberty, even though it occurs long after the beginning of puberty. In the contemporary U.S. population, the average age at menarche is 12 to 13 years, but the range of 11 to 17, or even 10 to 18, is considered normal. There are also ethnic differences

breast bud The first stage of breast development at puberty.

menarche The onset of menstruation at puberty.

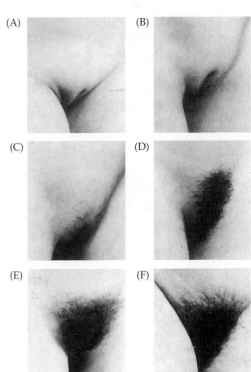

Figure 6.20 Typical development of pubic hair in girls at puberty (A) Prepubertal state: No hair is visible. (B) Sparse, long, downy hair grows along labia. This stage occurs at about 8.8 years in African-Americans and about 10.5 years in white Americans, but with considerable variability. (C) Coarser, curly hair grows along labia. (D) Hair covers labia. (E) Hair spreads over mons veneris but not to the adult extent or density. (F) Hair forms adult-like "inverse triangle" and extends to inner surface of thighs; this final pattern varies considerably among women. (From van Wieringen et al., 1971.)

(A)
(B)
(C)
(D)
(E)

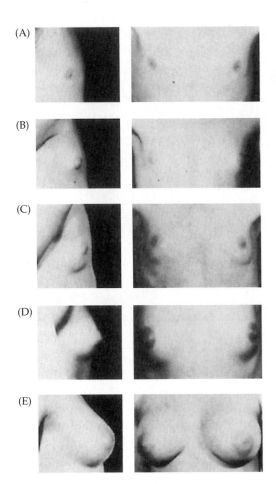

Figure 6.21 Typical development of breasts in girls at puberty seen in side and frontal views. (A) Prepubertal appearance. (B) Breast bud stage: Nipple, areola, and nearby breast tissue form a small mound at about 8.9 years (for African Americans) or about 10 years (for white Americans). (C) Further enlargement of areola and breast. (D) Nipple and areola project out from breast. (E) Adultlike stage: Areola is now flush with the breast; only the nipple projects forward. (From van Wieringen et al., 1971.)

within the U.S. population—the average age at menarche is 12.2 for African-American girls and 12.9 for white girls (Herman-Giddens et al., 1997).

There has been a historical trend toward earlier menarche in a number of Western countries (**Figure 6.22**). In mid-nineteenth-century Europe, the average age at menarche may have been as high as 16 to 17, although there is some uncertainty about the accuracy of these records. According to historian Vern Bullough, 15 is a more likely age (Bullough, 1981). In the United States at the beginning of the twentieth century, it was about 14. Age at menarche decreased at an average rate of more than 1 month per decade during most of the twentieth century (McDowell et al., 2007).

The average timetable for the visible events of female puberty in the U.S. white population is roughly as follows: Breast development begins at 10, pubic hair appears at 10.5, and menarche occurs at 12.9. In the U.S. African-American population, pubic hair appears at an average age of 8.8, breast development begins at 8.9, and menarche is at 12.2 (Herman-Giddens et al., 1997). In both populations, the pubertal growth spurt peaks about 1 year before menarche.

Menstruation may be irregular for the first year or two after menarche. Furthermore, the initial menstrual cycles tend to be anovulatory. For this reason, a young woman may not be capable of becoming pregnant for a year or so after menarche. However, there is much variation in this respect, and the fact that a young woman has only recently begun to menstruate should not lead her to believe that she is incapable of conceiving.

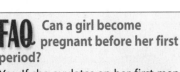 **Can a girl become pregnant before her first period?**

Yes. If she ovulates on her first menstrual cycle (which doesn't always happen), she can become pregnant before her first period, which would normally occur two weeks later. If she does become pregnant her first period won't occur, but since she's not expecting a period she might not discover the pregnancy for many weeks.

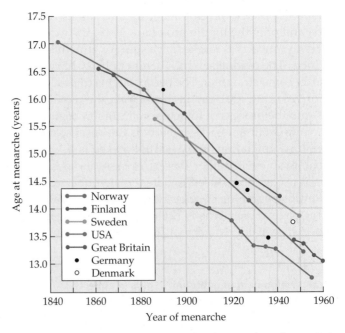

Figure 6.22 Puberty is starting earlier. During the nineteenth and twentieth centuries, girls in Western countries reached menarche at progressively younger ages. The reliability of the nineteenth-century data is uncertain.

Figure 6.23 Typical development of male external genitalia at puberty (A) Prepubertal appearance. (B) Enlargement of scrotum and testes. This stage usually occurs between 11 and 13 years. (C) Increase in length of penis and further enlargement of scrotum. (D) Increase in size of penis, especially the glans. Pubic hair appears. (E) Adult appearance. (From van Wieringen et al., 1971.)

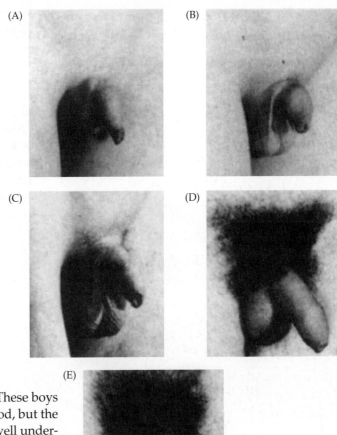

For boys, an early sign of puberty is the enlargement of the testes and scrotum, which begins at the age of 10 to 13 (**Figure 6.23**). Between 11 and 15, the penis grows in length and then in girth, and pubic hair appears. During the same period, the larynx (voice box) grows and the vocal cords thicken, leading to a deepening of the voice. The rate of pubertal growth peaks at about 14.

First ejaculation, which occurs at about age 13, may occur with **masturbation** or during sleep (a **nocturnal emission**). Initially, the semen lacks mature spermatozoa; in fact, a male can be infertile for a year or two after his first ejaculation. As with girls soon after menarche, however, there is no guarantee on this point.

Many boys experience transient development of breasts (adolescent **gynecomastia**) during mid-puberty: about half of all boys do so, according to one longitudinal study (Biro, 1990). These boys tend to have relatively low levels of free testosterone in their blood, but the precise hormonal mechanism of adolescent gynecomastia is not well understood. The enlarged breasts nearly always disappear without treatment.

Facial and axillary hair begins to appear about 2 years after the growth of pubic hair. Body hair may appear soon thereafter, especially on the chest, but its appearance is highly variable among individuals and among ethnic groups. Recession of the scalp hairline at the temples may occur soon after the other events of puberty and does not necessarily presage male-pattern baldness.

One pubertal trait that afflicts many teens, especially boys, is **acne**. The key feature of acne is the blockage of **sebaceous** (oil-producing) **glands** associated with hair follicles—most commonly on the face, neck, or back. The blockage is caused by an excess production and shedding of epidermal skin cells within the glands. The blocked glands become a breeding ground for a common skin bacterium, *Propionibacterium acnes*. The blocked gland is called a whitehead if is below the skin, a blackhead if it reaches the surface, and a pustule or pimple if it becomes inflamed. Severe acne can lead to permanent scarring. The condition can be treated with topical (local) medications containing benzoyl peroxide, salicylic acid, or sulfur. Severe cases may be treated effectively with an oral drug, isotretinoin (Accutane), but this drug can have serious side effects, including fetal defects if taken by pregnant women.

What Drives Puberty?

So far, we have simply described the major phenomena associated with puberty. But what triggers and orchestrates these phenomena? Let's start by looking at the proximate (immediate) causes, then track back to the earlier events that get puberty under way.

The proximate causes of most of the phenomena of puberty are, of course, hormones—in particular, androgens and estrogens, along with growth hormone.

masturbation Sexual self-stimulation. Sometimes also used to refer to manual stimulation of another person's genitalia.

nocturnal emission Ejaculation during sleep.

gynecomastia Enlargement of one or both breasts in a male.

acne A skin disorder caused by blockage and inflammation of sebaceous glands.

sebaceous glands Oil-secreting glands associated with hair follicles.

Although estrogen effects predominate in girls and androgen effects predominate in boys, both androgens and estrogens are needed in both sexes for normal completion of puberty.

Androgen levels rise steadily in both sexes during puberty but reach much higher final levels in men than in women. Androgens are responsible for muscle development, change of voice, and spermatogenesis (in combination with FSH), as well as the appearance of pubic and axillary hair in both sexes. In men, androgens are also responsible for the pubertal development of the external genitalia, prostate, seminal vesicles, sebaceous glands, and facial and body hair (and for male-pattern baldness), but full development of these characteristics requires the conversion of testosterone to the more potent androgen DHT in the target tissues (see Chapter 5). Testosterone also acts on the brain to promote the psychosexual development associated with puberty in both sexes.

Estrogens (in combination with growth hormone and progesterone) promote development of the breasts. Estrogens and progesterone (in combination with FSH and LH) trigger menarche. In males, estrogens are required for the normal functioning of the epididymis in concentrating sperm and are therefore necessary for male fertility. In both sexes, estrogens are responsible for an increase in bone density at puberty, as well as for the closure of the growth zones in the long bones at the end of the pubertal growth spurt. Thus individuals who cannot manufacture estrogens or who lack estrogen receptors fail to stop growing at the end of puberty and may become exceptionally tall (Sharpe, 1997).

What drives the increase in circulating sex steroids during puberty? The initial rise in androgen levels, which triggers the appearance of pubic and axillary hair in both sexes, is due to an increase in androgen secretion by the adrenal glands. The subsequent main increase in sex steroids during puberty, however, is due to their secretion by the gonads. This gonadal secretion is driven by an increase in the release of the gonadotropins LH and FSH.

Gonadotropin secretion is triggered, in turn, by an increase in the secretion of GnRH by the hypothalamus. This increase is a key event during puberty (**Figure 6.24**). The rest of the body seems to be primed from early childhood to heed the call of GnRH (**Box 6.7**); only the lack of GnRH prevents puberty from taking place at 2 or 3 years of age. Thus we would like to know why GnRH secretion increases when it does, rather than earlier or later.

The Body May Signal Its Readiness for Puberty to the Brain

One theoretical possibility is that the hypothalamus possesses an internal clock that counts off the years since birth. That seems not to be the case, however. Instead, it has been suggested that GnRH secretion increases when the body has reached a certain critical weight, weight-to-height ratio, or body fat ratio (the proportion of body weight that is due to fat). The timing of puberty correlates better with body weight than with chronological age. In girls, the pubertal growth spurt begins at an average weight of 30 kg (66 lb). In boys, puberty seems to be triggered at a higher body weight than in girls: about 55 kg (121 lb).

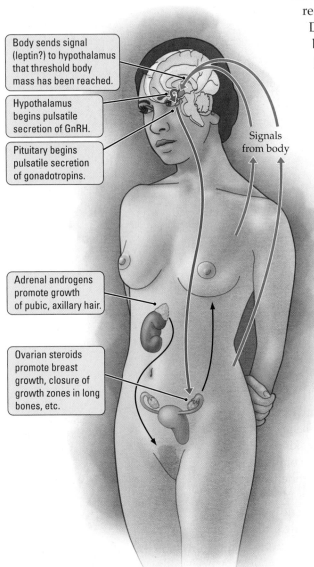

Body sends signal (leptin?) to hypothalamus that threshold body mass has been reached.

Hypothalamus begins pulsatile secretion of GnRH.

Pituitary begins pulsatile secretion of gonadotropins.

Adrenal androgens promote growth of pubic, axillary hair.

Ovarian steroids promote breast growth, closure of growth zones in long bones, etc.

Signals from body

Figure 6.24 Hormonal control of puberty This figure shows the chain of events that drives puberty in girls. The factors that trigger the increase in androgens by the adrenal gland are uncertain but may include a direct signal from body fat stores. The regulation of puberty in boys is similar, except that the principal gonadal steroids are androgens, especially testosterone. (See Web Activity 6.3.)

Biology of Sex

BOX 6.7 Atypical Development: Precocious and Delayed Puberty

Puberty has generally been considered **precocious** if the appearance of pubic hair or breasts, or enlargement of the testicles, begins before age 8 (in girls) or age 9 (in boys) (see figure). These criteria may no longer be realistic, for girls in the United States at least, since 7% of white girls and 27% of African-American girls now have breast development or pubic hair at age 7 (Herman-Giddens et al., 1997). Current guidelines suggest that girls should be evaluated for precocious puberty if they have pubic hair or breast development before age 7 (white girls) or before age 6 (African-American girls) (Kaplowitz & Oberfield, 1999; Muir, 2006). Older girls (e.g., age 8) should be evaluated only if special circumstances apply, such as an unduly rapid progression through the stages of puberty. Criteria for defining precocious puberty in other ethnic groups have yet to be developed.

The cause of most cases of precocious puberty cannot be determined. In medical jargon, such cases are called **idiopathic**. Some cases, however, are caused by tumors at or near the base of the brain. Puberty may also be triggered by disorders affecting the gonads.

Besides potentially causing psychological and social problems, precocious puberty can adversely affect a child's final height. Affected children may initially grow faster than normal, but once the pubertal growth spurt ends, they are likely to be overtaken and left behind by their peers. The earlier puberty begins, the shorter the individual is likely to be in adulthood. Girls who enter puberty at the low end of the normal range (say, at 7 or 8 years of age) suffer little, if any, loss of adult height because their early entry into puberty is partially compensated by an increased duration of the

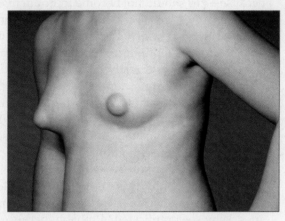

Precocious puberty (breast development, pubic hair, and vaginal bleeding) in a six-year-old girl, caused by a noncancerous, estrogen secreting tumor of the adrenal gland (Kaushal et al., 2007).

pubertal growth spurt (Shangold et al., 1989). This is partly why the recent guidelines for precocious puberty exclude these girls.

Most cases of precocious puberty can be treated with a GnRH analog such as leuprolide (Lupron). You might think that this would be exactly the wrong drug to give, since GnRH normally *triggers* puberty. GnRH's normal action depends on its *pulsatile* secretion, however. If a GnRH analog is administered in the form of monthly depot injections, which maintain constant high levels in the blood, it suppresses the secretion of pituitary gonadotropins and hence the secretion of the gonadal steroids. Growth hormone is sometimes also administered. Although the use of these drugs has been somewhat controversial, they now appear to be quite safe and effective.

Puberty is considered **delayed** if the early signs of puberty do not appear by age 13 (sometimes 14) in girls, or by age 14 in boys.

Delayed puberty is more common in boys than in girls; it is usually idiopathic, in which case puberty eventually starts spontaneously. It is sometimes possible to "kick-start" the process with a short course of testosterone treatment. Brain tumors can also cause delayed puberty.

A rare but fascinating cause of delayed puberty is **Kallmann syndrome** (Gilbert, 2003). In this congenital syndrome, delayed puberty is coupled with the absence of the sense of smell, and sometimes with other developmental anomalies. This coupling is a clue to an odd developmental history. It turns out that the GnRH neurons of the hypothalamus are not generated in the brain at all; instead, they are generated in a region of the ectoderm that gives rise to the olfactory mucosa. These neurons migrate into the brain during embryonic life, following the course of the olfactory nerves. In Kallmann syndrome, the ingrowth of the olfactory nerves is prevented due to a defect in a gene that controls axon growth, and so the GnRH neurons remain stuck in the olfactory mucosa, where they are unable to participate in neuroendocrine regulation. This syndrome, like idiopathic delayed puberty, is usually treated with testosterone replacement, which may need to be continued for life.

precocious puberty Puberty that begins early enough to be considered a medical problem.

idiopathic Lacking an identifiable cause.

delayed puberty Failure of onset of puberty by some criterion age, usually 13 or 14 in girls and 14 in boys.

Kallmann syndrome A developmental syndrome characterized by delayed puberty, inability to smell, and other problems.

Menarche occurs at an average weight of 47 kg (103 lb) in Western countries, but at a significantly lower weight in some developing countries, such as India (Rao et al., 1998). In any given culture, somewhat obese girls tend to experience menarche earlier than thin girls, and very thin girls may not experience menarche at all (**primary amenorrhea**). Furthermore, if women lose most of their body fat after puberty—as can happen during famines, as a consequence of eating disor-

primary amenorrhea Failure to commence menstruation at puberty.

secondary amenorrhea Absence of menstruation in a woman who has previously menstruated normally.

leptin A hormone secreted by fat cells that may play a role in triggering puberty.

kisspeptin A hormone produced in the hypothalamus that is involved in the initiation of puberty.

ders such as anorexia nervosa, or even as a result of extreme athletic activity—their menstrual cycles may cease (**secondary amenorrhea**).

How might the brain know when the body has reached a certain weight or composition? One hypothesis involves the hormone **leptin**, a peptide hormone that is secreted by fat cells (Kiess et al., 2000). In general, leptin levels in the blood provide an indication of how much fat the body has accumulated. It would make sense if a puberty-inducing signal were derived from fat cells, especially in girls, because a girl should not become reproductively mature until she has accumulated the energy stores necessary to sustain pregnancy. Supporting the idea that leptin helps trigger puberty is the finding that children suffering from a mutation in the gene for the leptin receptor do not enter puberty (Clement et al., 1998).

Leptin does not directly activate the GnRH-secreting cells of the hypothalamus, however. Rather, leptin, along with other chemical and neural signals, appears to stimulate a group of hypothalamic neurons that manufacture and secrete a newly-discovered protein named **kisspeptin** (Navarro et al., 2007). Kisspeptin stimulates the GnRH neurons to secrete GnRH, and the rare individuals who lack the receptor for kisspeptin—like those who lack the receptor for leptin—fail to enter puberty.

In summary, puberty is the end result of a long chain of chemical signals: body fat→leptin→kisspeptin→GnRH→gonadotropins→gonadal steroids→target tissues. Why so complicated? Probably because it allows for multiple internal and environmental factors to influence the process, including feedback signals from the target tissues and the gonads.

Dietary Changes May Be the Reason Puberty Is Beginning Earlier

With these insights into the mechanisms that trigger puberty, can we understand why puberty has been occurring at ever-younger ages over the last century or so, as described above? The leading hypothesis is that a progressive *change in diet* over this period has allowed children to reach a body weight that triggers puberty at earlier and earlier ages. In particular, the introduction of cheap, calorie-dense manufactured foods has allowed children not merely to grow faster but also, often, to become moderately or severely obese. These changes could be a large part of the reason for the changing age of puberty, but they may not be the entire reason; for one thing, body weight, though a better indicator than chronological age, is still far from being a precise predictor of the time of puberty. Also, even children of average weight seem to be entering puberty earlier than their predecessors.

Another hypothesis is that endocrine disruptors (hormone-like pollutants in the environment; see Box 5.5) are causing children to enter puberty early. Some studies have reported that children who experience precocious puberty have unusually high levels of such pollutants in their blood (Colon et al., 2000). Still, the idea that endocrine disruptors are contributing to the decreasing age of puberty in the general population is far from proven.

Intersexuality Raises Complex Social and Ethical Issues

We describe a variety of intersex conditions from a biomedical perspective in Boxes 6.1 through 6.7. Certainly, there are medical aspects to intersexuality. Some children with ambiguous genitalia need medical or surgical treatment to save their lives or to correct conditions that greatly interfere with urination, coitus, and the like. Some intersexed people may request surgical treatment to bring their genital anatomy into conformity to the sex with which they identify.

Intersexed people often have nightmarish experiences with the medical profession, however, beginning in early childhood (**Box 6.8**). Often, they become so

Personal Points of View

BOX 6.8 What It's Like to Be Intersexed

Sherri Groveman, a 42-year-old tax lawyer, lives alone in a ranch-style home in one of the sun-baked suburbs of San Diego. She's a pleasant, forthright, freckle-faced, *womanly* woman. So why, within a few minutes of the start of our interview, did I innocently ask: "And did you enjoy playing with other boys—girls, I mean?"

I blushed and apologized, but Groveman wouldn't let me get away with it. It was a Freudian slip *par excellence*—evidence that a part of me considered her a male, regardless of all the evidence to the contrary. And the reason? Because I knew that she had been born with testes and that every cell in her body contained an X and a Y chromosome—the usual biological signature of a male.

Groveman has androgen insensitivity syndrome, which made her developing body unresponsive to the testosterone secreted by her testes. She was born with the outward appearance of a girl, but lacking the internal reproductive tract of either sex.

Groveman's condition was recognized a few weeks after birth when her testes, in the attempt to migrate down into her nonexistent scrotum, became lodged in her groin, where they could be felt as lumps. They were removed surgically, out of concern that they might become cancerous. (This is a legitimate concern in all cases of undescended testicles, but such cancers rarely occur during childhood, so the operation could have been put off for many years.) Groveman was brought up thinking that she had had hernia surgery, but an occasional remark from her mother, to the effect that "not all girls could become mothers," hinted that more might be amiss.

Because Groveman now lacked gonads of any kind, she would need hormone replacement to bring about the bodily changes associated with female puberty. When she was 11, her mother prepared her for this by telling her something slightly closer to the truth: that she had been born with "twisted ovaries" that had been removed to prevent cancer. (The twisted-ovaries story, says Groveman, is a "lie heard round the world"—a standard cover-up recommended by doctors, intended to protect the growing girl's sense of her own femininity.) Groveman learned that she would not menstruate and could never bear children, but she did not learn the real cause, nor was she told of possible difficulties she might later encounter in her

sex life. After this 10-minute conversation, she did not discuss the matter with either of her parents for the next 28 years.

With puberty, her private shame threatened to become a public one. She developed most of the outer features of a woman, but she did not grow pubic hair, which depends on androgens in both men and women. So she had to conceal her lower body in school showers and locker rooms, and from boyfriends. Worse, she found that her vagina was too narrow and short. "Everyone was using tampons," she says, "so I bought some and tried putting one in, but it hurt like hell, because of the narrow entryway." And her vagina was less than 2 inches long—too short for intercourse.

Convinced that she had a dirty secret for which she herself was to blame, Groveman became a "gregarious loner"—outwardly sociable, but shunning intimacy with anyone. The only time her condition was discussed was at her periodic endocrinological checkups. The discussions were not with Groveman herself, though, but among the doctors and medical students who gathered around her crotch. She was told nothing about her condition, and she was asked nothing about her psychological health.

At age 21, Groveman figured out the cause of her condition on her own by rummaging through textbooks in a medical library. She was devastated—not so much at discovering her intersexed status, but at discovering she had been lied to for two decades by parents and doctors. This discovery led to her complete estrangement from the medical profession: She stopped taking estrogens and didn't see a doctor for another 14 years.

"Finding out about myself the way I did really damaged me," she says. "I thought, 'How can I embark on a relationship and not tell my partner? I'd be participating in that same lie that was told to me.' And yet I thought I would *have* to lie. After all, no one told me the information, so I thought it must be so horrible, such a hideous and freakish thing, that if I told anyone else they would bolt."

At the age of 35, however, she did go back to a doctor; she was in a tentative relationship with a man and wanted to know if anything could be done to help her have vaginal intercourse. The doctor confirmed that Groveman had AIS and put her back on estrogens to cor-

rect the severe osteoporosis that had been brought on by the lack of hormones. She also recommended that Groveman use vaginal dilators—plastic tubes that she was to sit on for 15 minutes twice a day. Although these dilators do help some women, Groveman did not like them, and she eventually broke off the relationship with her boyfriend.

In all those years, Groveman had never met anyone resembling herself, and this, she says, was the deepest cause of her loneliness and shame. A few months after the breakup with her boyfriend, however, she came in contact with an AIS support group that was forming in England, and she flew over to attend the inaugural meeting. "There was nothing I would not have given to participate," says Groveman. "I would have cut off my arm—I was that desperate to look into someone else's eyes and have them know what I was experiencing." She has been back for ten subsequent meetings, and she has herself founded a U.S. support group.

The support groups believe that AIS children, like other children, will grow up into sexual adults, but that this development cannot take place properly if the child is sentenced to "solitary confinement," wondering whether they are the only person who suffers from a condition so shaming that no one will talk about it. Thus the groups believe that the best way for parents and affected children to get over their anxieties is to meet and socialize with others who have similar experiences.

Although Groveman identifies as a woman, her identity as intersexed is now just as important to her. Indeed, she is waging a small campaign to have the intersex status more widely recognized: In the "M/F" box on the census form she wrote "I (intersex)," and she is trying (unsuccessfully so far) to have the same designation included on her driver's license. "I want people to acknowledge the reality of intersexuality," she says. "I'm not asking for unusual accommodations."

Groveman doesn't attribute her problems solely to victimization by society. "It's going to be horrible no matter what, there's no way around it," says Groveman. "But I was never sorry that I was born intersexed. I wouldn't trade. This is who I was meant to be in this world."

Source: Interview by Simon LeVay.

3. Puberty is occurring earlier than in the past. Do you think that this creates a social problem? What age of entry into puberty do you think should be considered unacceptably early and a justification for treatment? Do you think it would be a good idea to try to increase the average age of puberty by, for example, restricting children's diets?

Web Resources

Accord Alliance (concerned with disorders of sex development/intersexuality) www.accordalliance.org

Bodies Like Ours (support and information for people with atypical genitals) www.bodieslikeours.org/forums

Hospital for Sick Children: Genital Development www.sickkids.ca/childphysiology/cpwp/Genital/GenitalIntro.htm

National Institute of Child Health and Human Development—Turner Syndrome http://turners.nichd.nih.gov

National Institute of Child Health and Human Development—Klinefelter Syndrome www.nichd.nih.gov/health/topics/klinefelter_syndrome.cfm

Turner Syndrome Society of the United States www.turnersyndrome.org

Recommended Reading

Dreger, A. D. (Ed.) (1999). *Intersex in the age of ethics.* University Publishing Group.

Eugenides, J. (2002). *Middlesex.* Farrar, Straus and Giroux. (Pulitzer Prize–winning novel about a person with 5α-reductase deficiency)

Larsen, W. J. (1998). *Essentials of human embryology.* Churchill Livingstone.

Migeon, C. J., & Wisniewski, A. B. (2003). Human sex differentiation and its abnormalities. *Best Practice & Research Clinical Obstetrics and Gynaecology, 17,* 1–18.

Pinsky, L., Erickson, R. P., & Schimke, R. N. (1999). *Genetic disorders of human sexual development.* Oxford University Press.

CHAPTER 7

Do children's toys reflect real gender differences, create stereotypes, or both?

Gender

In the previous chapters, we discussed sex differences in bodily structure and function and how they develop. We now turn to a topic that is at once more interesting and more controversial: that of sex differences in mental life. Do men and women differ in their cognitive skills, sexual strategies, personalities, behaviors, goals, or values? And if so, how do such differences develop? Are they the products of biological processes, such as the differing hormonal environments that males and females experience before birth? Or do they result from the way our parents treat us in infancy and childhood, from social pressures, or from our own efforts to make sense of the world? Do they perhaps result from a delicate interplay of many factors? And are they fixed or malleable—over the history of the human race, across cultures, or over the course of a single life span? The answers to such questions are not merely of theoretical interest. They are also deeply relevant to social policy, affecting how we educate our children, how we treat wrongdoers, and how we attempt to develop a more just society.

Gender Is a Central Aspect of Personhood

The word **gender**, as used in this book, means the entire collection of mental and behavioral traits that, to a greater or lesser degree, differ between males and females. Thus gender is whatever psychologists can say *about* the two sexes, having defined the sexes by some biological criterion such as (most commonly) the possession of female or male genitals.

Some traits are "highly gendered": That is, the differences between the sexes in those traits are very marked. An example is a person's subjective sense of maleness or femaleness, a trait called **gender identity**. The great majority of males have a secure identity as males, and the great majority of females have a secure identity as females. There are exceptions—transexual and transgendered people—but they form a very small percentage of the population.

An example of a trait that is highly gendered, but less so than gender identity, is that of **sexual orientation**—the direction of an individual's sexual attractions. Most men are predominantly attracted to women, and most women are predominantly attracted to men, but exceptions are common, numbering several percent of the population.

An example of a trait that is much more weakly gendered is verbal fluency. On average, girls outperform boys on tests of this cognitive skill, but it takes the

gender The collection of psychological traits that differ between males and females.

gender identity A person's subjective sense of being male or female.

sexual orientation The direction of a person's sexual feelings: sexual attraction toward persons of the opposite sex, the same sex, or both sexes.

testing of large numbers of children, and the application of statistical tests to the results, to demonstrate the difference.

In our discussion of gender, we first review the aspects of mental life that are known to be gendered to a greater or lesser degree. We then discuss theories about how gender differences arise.

Gender Research Has Emerged from a History of Sexism

In considering differences between the sexes, it would be foolish to ignore certain historical realities: the concentration of economic and political power in the hands of men and the long tradition of prejudice against women. In 1792, when Mary Wollstonecraft published her *Vindication of the Rights of Woman*, it was almost universally accepted that only men had the intellect, personality, and moral qualities required for public life (**Figure 7.1**). Women's qualities, it was agreed, suited them only for nurturing and sustaining roles within the family.

Tremendous changes have overtaken Western countries since Wollstonecraft's time. Considering the opportunities that are open to American women today, we may be tempted to view smugly or judgmentally the way women are still treated in some more traditional regions of the world. But a moment's reflection should show us that there is still unfinished business here at home. A nation that cannot agree on the premise that "equality of rights under the law shall not be denied or abridged . . . on account of sex" (the Equal Rights Amendment to the U.S. Constitution, which was left unratified in 1982), that pays men and women unequally, and that places few women in positions of power or influence is hardly a paragon of gender equity. For these reasons, we should suspect that stereotypes—false or overgeneralized beliefs about classes of people—still influence views of gender, even within the academic community.

In reaction to this history of prejudice, some researchers and feminists have tended to deny the reality of gender differences altogether, or have attributed them entirely to cultural forces rather than to any underlying biological predispositions. For example, the anthropologist Margaret Mead (1901–1978) wrote an influential book entitled *Sex and Temperament in Three Primitive Societies* (Mead, 1935), in which she described three societies in New Guinea. Among the Mundugumor, Mead reported, both men and women were "masculine" by Western standards. Among the Arapesh, both men and women were "feminine." And among the Chambri, gender was actually reversed from what Western societies are familiar with: Women were "masculine" and men were "feminine." Gender, Mead was saying, varies radically from one society to another, and therefore must be determined by culture.

Similarly, during the ferment of feminist thought and culture in the 1970s, many writers emphasized the role of culture or socialization in the molding of gender, to the exclusion of other factors. Germaine Greer, for example, in her 1971 book *The Female Eunuch*, stated categorically that there were no differences between the brains of men and women (Greer, 1971).

Today, most gender researchers consider such views extreme. Mead's research methods, and the interpretations placed on her research by later feminist authors, have been criticized (Freeman, 1983; Goldberg, 1991). Greer's assertion about the identity of male and female brains has been shown to be incorrect. It may be that Mead, Greer, and some other feminist thinkers felt so strongly the need to undermine traditional notions of "biological inevitability" that they were driven to an extreme antibiological position that the evidence did not warrant.

Figure 7.1 Mary Wollstonecraft (1759–1797) was an Anglo-Irish radical thinker who demanded full political and social equality for women, derided marriage as "legalized prostitution," and (in a posthumously published novel, *Maria)* spoke up for women's right to sexual and romantic feelings. She did eventually marry but died a few days after the birth of her daughter Mary (who later married the poet Percy Bysshe Shelley and wrote *Frankenstein*).

The controversy over gender continues today. In a January 2005 speech, Harvard University's President Lawrence Summers speculated that "intrinsic differences" between men and women might be partly responsible for the small number of women in the fields of engineering and physics. His remarks ignited a political and academic firestorm, and the National Organization for Women demanded his resignation, calling his remarks "a public demonstration of sexism and ignorance" (National Organization for Women, 2005). Summers did in fact resign in the following year. We don't discuss the specific issue raised by Summers in this chapter, but we do review the body of evidence suggesting that innate predispositions and life experiences interact in the development of gender-related traits.

Gender Identity May Be Discordant with Anatomical Sex

In its simplest conception, a person's gender identity is his or her response to "Do you feel as if you are a man or a woman?" or some similar question. More than 99.9% of people will give an answer that is consistent with their genital anatomy. Yet there are rare individuals who give a discordant answer to that question: anatomical men who say they feel like women and anatomical women who say they feel like men, as well as others for whom neither "male" nor "female" satisfactorily describes how they think about themselves. The existence of these **transgendered** persons, discussed in greater detail later in the chapter, makes us realize that there must be something more to gender identity than simply reporting on one's genitals. Gender identity is a central and stable aspect of who we are—our personhood. The expression of this identity in gendered behavior—everything from what clothes we wear and how we walk and talk to what sex we claim to be—is called **gender role**.

Although self-identified transgendered persons are quite uncommon, research indicates that gender identity may have a more blurred distribution in the general population than is captured by a simple "male–female" dichotomy. If, for example, people are asked to rate their own "masculinity/femininity" on a scale in comparison with other persons of the same sex, responses are quite spread out: Some women rate themselves as about as feminine as other women, some as more feminine, and some as more masculine, and the same for men (Lippa, 2008). We will revisit this spectrum of subjective masculinity/femininity when we discuss the topic of sexual orientation (see Chapter 14).

Men and Women Differ in a Variety of Cognitive and Personality Traits

Some sex differences are seen in aspects of mental life having to do with perception, motor performance, reasoning, judgments, knowledge, and memory—collectively referred to as **cognitive** traits. For example, men outperform women in some visuospatial skills, such as the ability to mentally rotate 3-dimensional objects (**Figure 7.2**), targeting accuracy, and navigation (Watson & Kimura, 1991; Moffat et al., 1998; Peters et al., 2007). Women outperform men on tasks involving memorization of the location of objects (**Figure 7.3**), fine manipulation, and some verbal skills, such as verbal memory and fluency (Kimura, 1999). These sex differences are moderate to large in size.* Many other cognitive skills show small differences between the sexes.

---

*For statistics buffs, they show effect sizes (*d*) of about 0.5 – 1.0. The measurement and evaluation of sex differences is discussed in detail in Web Topic 7.1 Measuring Sex Differences.

transgendered Having a gender identity that is discordant with one's anatomical sex.

gender role The expression of gender identity in social behavior.

cognitive Related to the aspects of the mind that process knowledge or information.

Wanton violence is predominantly a male activity. Here English and Turkish soccer hooligans do battle in the streets of Copenhagen.

personality The collection of mental and behavioral traits, especially those related to emotions and attitudes, that characterize an individual.

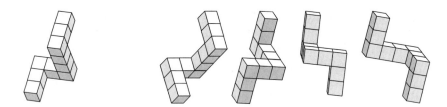

Figure 7.2 Mental rotation task From the four images at right, the subject is asked to select the two objects that could be rotated in space to match the object shown at left. Men generally outperform women in this kind of task.

Other sex differences have to do with feelings, behaviors (including sexual behavior), attitudes, goals, interests, and values—traits that loosely cluster under the term **personality**. Notable among these traits is aggressiveness: Males score higher than women on written tests of aggressiveness, show more verbal and physical aggression in real-life situations, and are more likely to commit violent crimes, both in the United States and across most cultures (Archer, 2004). Women are more likely to express aggression through indirect, nonphysical means, such as malicious gossip (Hess & Hagen, 2006). Another personality difference has to do with interests: Women are more interested in people-related activities and occupations; men have more thing-related interests (Lippa, 2005). This is one of the strongest gender differences, statistically speaking, but it is still only a statement about averages.

One cross-cultural study, based on data from 23,000 men and women in 26 cultures, found robust cross-cultural gender differences in six personality factors: Men scored higher in factors named "assertiveness" and "openness to ideas," while women scored higher in "agreeableness," "warmth," "openness to feelings," and "neuroticism" (Costa et al., 2001).

Figure 7.3A Test of object location memory Study this picture for 1 minute and try to impress upon your memory the position of every item you see. Then look at Figure 7.3B on p. 192. (From Silverman & Eals, 1992.)

There may be differences in the moral sense of men and women. According to Harvard psychologist Carol Gilligan, author of an influential 1982 book, *In a Different Voice* (Gilligan, 1982), women's moral universe is based on caring, whereas men's is based more on justice and rules. Some scientific support for this point of view comes from studies in which women and men's values are surveyed by means of written questionnaires. When women and men are asked to rate the desirability of a variety of traits, the traits rated higher by women include "sensitive," "kind," "understanding," "affectionate," "helpful," and "sincere." When asked to choose the more desirable of two traits, such as "cooperative versus competitive," "patience versus determination," "helping versus being in charge," women tend to choose the more caring alternative. This sex difference has been observed both in the United States and in several Asian countries (Stimpson et al., 1991). A meta-analysis suggests that sex differences in moral reasoning exist, but are small in magnitude—smaller than the differences in moral reasoning that exist among cultures (Jaffee & Hyde, 2000).

Differences in Sexuality Include Attitudes toward Casual Sex, Jealousy, and Frequency of Masturbation

More directly relevant to the overall subject of this book are sex differences related to sexuality. Here we summarize these differences. We will expand on some of them in later chapters.

Men express far more permissive attitudes than women toward casual sex, as well as toward premarital and extramarital sex (Oliver & Hyde, 1993). Men are also more desirous of engaging in casual sex, and make more attempts to do so (Buss & Schmitt, 1993). In one study of college students in 10 major world regions, men consistently expressed a desire for more different sex partners; over half the men, but less than 1 in 5 women, said that they would like to have more than one sex partner in the next month (Schmitt, 2003). Conversely, women are much more likely than men to agree with the statement "I would have sex only if I was in love" and to view sex as a prelude to, or part of, a long-term relationship (Mahay et al., 2000). Asked in a random-sample survey how they would feel after a one-night stand, men were more than three times as likely as women to say they would feel "satisfied," while women were more than twice as likely as men to say they would feel "regret" or "shame" (Esquire, 2007).

Women and men tend to seek different things in their sex partners. Women are attracted to older partners, men to younger ones. Women are more concerned than men with their partners' status or wealth; men are more concerned than women with their partners' physical attractiveness. These differences exist across cultures—in Chinese college students just as much as in American students, for example (Toro-Morn & Sprecher, 2003). Of course, there are any number of exceptions to these generalizations—men who adore powerful older women, for example, and women who are drawn to penniless but handsome youths. But in a statistical sense, the differences hold up very consistently.

Men are more interested in visual sexual stimuli generally, including pornography, and are more sexually aroused by such stimuli, than are women (Murnen & Stockton, 1997; Janssen et al., 2003). Not surprisingly, most pornography is oriented toward consumption by men.

Men and women both experience jealousy, but they tend to experience different *kinds* of jealousy (Buss, 2000). Women are more predisposed to experience *emotional* jealousy—that is, to fear that their male partner may commit himself emotionally to a different woman. Men, however, tend to experience *sexual* jealousy—to fear that their female partner is being physically unfaithful to them.

Concerning actual sexual behavior, far and away the largest difference is that males masturbate more than females, beginning at puberty (Oliver & Hyde, 1993).

Figure 7.3B Test of object location memory Having memorized Figure 7.3A as best you can, look at this picture and identify all the pairs of objects that have swapped places. Women typically do better than men at this task. (From Silverman & Eals, 1992.)

Males also report more frequent sexual intercourse, a younger age at first intercourse, and a larger number of total sex partners than do females, but these differences are in the small to moderate range.

Of course, heterosexual sex partners should balance between the sexes: Men and women should have the same mean number of different partners of the other sex, for example. The apparent sex difference in this measure has a number of potential explanations (Baumeister & Tice, 2000):

- *Dishonest reporting* In line with this hypothesis, one study reported that the sex differences in number of reported partners nearly disappeared when the subjects thought that their truthfulness was being monitored by a polygraph (Alexander & Fisher, 2003).
- *Different definitions of "sex partners"* (i.e., use of a more inclusive definition by men)
- *Different methods of estimation by men and women* (e.g., counting for women versus rough guessing for men)
- *Sampling problems* (e.g., a failure to sample a wide enough age range, or a failure to sample women with many sex partners, such as prostitutes)

It seems likely that women's lesser interest in casual sex and multiple partners limits how many partners heterosexual men have. If so, we would expect that men who desire sexual contact with other men would have more partners than heterosexual men do. And in fact, several studies have reported exactly that: Gay men have more casual sex partners and more total partners than straight men (Laumann et al., 1994). It's not that there's anything psychologically unusual about gay men in this regard—it's just that they're seeking sex partners in a more willing population.

With regard to all these sex differences in cognition, personality, and sexuality, there is still controversy about their magnitude and meaning. Psychologist Janet Hyde has argued that sex differences, if they exist at all, are usually too small to be of any practical significance, but are often exaggerated in the popular imagination—a tendency that she believes has negative consequences both in the workplace and in personal relationships (Hyde, 2005). Others say that Hyde ignores some large and well-replicated differences, which need to be taken into account by those concerned with education and public policy (Lippa, 2006).

Many Gender Differences Arise Early in Life

Children develop some understanding of differences between the sexes at a young age. By 1 year of age, most children distinguish between the faces and voices of males and females (Miller et al., 1982; Leinbach & Fagot, 1993). They generally rely on simple criteria for determining sex, however, such as hair length.

Although they distinguish between the sexes, 1-year-olds probably do not understand that sex is a fixed attribute of individuals. Before about 3 years of age, a child is likely to think that a man who puts on a long-haired wig has become a woman (Kohlberg, 1966). **Gender constancy**—the realization that the sex categories are permanent, and that a man in a wig is still "really a man"—appears by about 3 to 4 years of age (Bem, 1989) (**Figure 7.4**).

What about children's sense of their own sex? It appears that most children can identify their own sex and categorize themselves with other same-sex children by 2 to 3 years of age (Fagot, 1985). This is usually before the age of gender constancy, so children apparently go through a 1- to 2-year period in which they know their own sex but do not know that they are unable to change it.

Boys and girls show quite marked differences in behavior from a young age. Even before birth, male fetuses are more active than females, and this difference in activity level persists throughout childhood (Eaton & Enns, 1986). By 18 months of age, toy preferences begin to diverge: Boys prefer toy vehicles, toy weapons, balls, and construction toys, while girls prefer dolls and toy kitchen implements (Berenbaum & Snyder, 1995; Serbin et al., 2001) (**Figure 7.5**). Boys engage in more rough-and-tumble play and aggression than do girls (Maccoby & Jacklin, 1987; Maccoby, 1998).

By 4 years of age most boys prefer to play with boys, and most girls with girls. This segregation by sex is universal across cultures and is most marked when

gender constancy A child's understanding that sex is a fixed attribute.

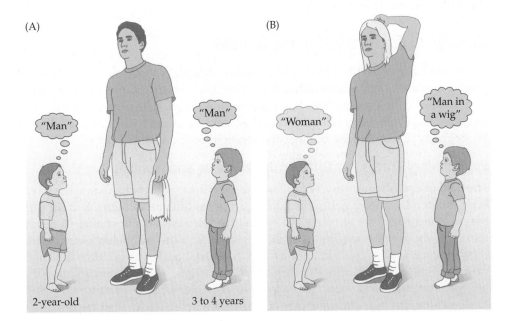

Figure 7.4 Gender constancy (A) A 2-year-old child may think that a man who puts on a long-haired wig has become a woman. (B) By 3 to 4 years of age, the child knows that a person's sex is a fixed attribute.

Figure 7.5 Toy preference test A child is placed within a circle of toys and its play behavior is videotaped. Later, observers measure the amount of time the child spends playing with toys generally preferred by girls and those generally preferred by boys. Examples of data from this kind of study are shown in Figure 7.7.

adults are not present (Fabes et al., 2003). At the same age, girls' and boys' play is governed by different moral rules: Girls appeal to social conventions ("The teacher will be angry if we don't play nicely"), while boys are more likely to refer to principles of justice ("Hands off the car, it's mine!") (Tulviste & Koor, 2005). These different styles of conflict resolution, along with boys' greater physical aggressiveness, may be the main reasons why the sexes segregate in the first place: Girls find themselves disadvantaged in mixed-sex groups because boys ignore their verbal arguments and grab all the marbles, so the girls withdraw (Powlishta & Maccoby, 1990; Maccoby, 1998).

With respect to motor skills, by 2 to 3 years of age boys show greater throwing accuracy and girls show finer control of hand musculature (Kimura, 1999). By elementary school age, differences in cognitive traits begin to emerge; at this age, girls are slightly better at calculating than boys. Boys' superiority in mental visuospatial tasks, such as mental rotation, appears by the age of 9 to 12 (Kerns & Berenbaum, 1991) and in problem-solving tasks by about age 14 (Hyde et al., 1990). This male superiority in visuospatial and problem-solving skills does not translate into better classroom performance, however: Girls tend to get better grades than boys in most subjects and across most age levels.

We mentioned earlier a strong gender difference in interests, with women having more people-oriented interests and men having more object-oriented interests. This difference exists, at least in rudimentary form, on the day of birth: When researchers presented newborn infants with a face and a mechanical mobile, the girls spent more time looking at the face and the boys spent more time looking at the mobile (Connellan et al., 2001).

Biological Factors Influence Gender

So far, we have attempted to describe gender differences without drawing any conclusions about how these differences arise. We now turn to the topic of causes. It turns out that researchers have taken a wide variety of approaches to this topic and have viewed gender through the lenses of several different disciplines. We begin by discussing the biological approach.

Evolutionary Forces Act Differently on Males and Females

The field of evolutionary psychology investigates how gender characteristics have been molded by a long period of human and prehuman evolution. During this period, the struggle to survive and reproduce has favored the spread of genes that predispose their owners to certain sex-specific traits and behavior patterns. Evolutionary psychologists do not usually concern themselves with the question of what these genes are or how they work, but with the ultimate evolutionary rationale for their existence. Here are three examples of how evolutionary psychology attempts to explain aspects of men and women's sexual strategies.

Boys and girls traditionally learned different tasks, but this division of labor during human evolution may have fostered genes for different cognitive skills in the two sexes.

COGNITIVE SKILLS Evolutionary psychologists believe that cognitive differences between the sexes have arisen because of a long-standing division of labor between men and women. Because of their greater physical strength, it is argued, men have always taken a leading role in hunting, warfare, and exploration; while women, because of their biologically mandated role in pregnancy and breast-feeding, have taken a leading role in activities near the home site. Over many generations, such a division of labor might well have favored the spread of genes for different cognitive skills in the two sexes, such as the greater throwing and navigating skills of men and the greater hand and finger dexterity of women.

INTEREST IN CASUAL SEX Men's greater interest in casual sex can be explained in terms of evolutionary processes. The cost of fathering a child—when stripped to its biological essentials—is minimal. In theory, therefore, a man can have hundreds of offspring if he impregnates many different women and walks away from each. Women, however, have to invest so much time and resources into pregnancy and infant care that they are very limited in the total number of offspring they are able to have. Therefore, one can argue, genes evolved that promoted men's interest in casual sex and women's choosiness in who she mated with.

At first glance, casual sex offers women little evolutionary benefit. Nevertheless, it is possible that sex outside of a regular pair bond offers a woman the prospect of conferring better genes on her offspring than those possessed by her regular partner. We will discuss this idea in more detail when we cover the topics of promiscuity and infidelity in Chapter 10.

JEALOUSY Women have always been certain of the identity of their children: Any child to whom a woman gave birth was necessarily her genetic offspring. A man, however, could not be certain which children were his: Even in a supposedly monogamous relationship, there was always the risk that his partner might have sex with someone else and that he might end up helping to rear a child that was not genetically his own. According to David Buss, this difference between the sexes, persisting over countless generations, led to the spread of genes promoting the different styles of jealousy in women and men described above. Men's sexual jealousy served to reduce the likelihood of rearing someone else's child; women's emotional jealousy served to reduce the likelihood that their male partners would abandon them and leave them without resources to rear their children (Buss, 2000; Harris, 2003).

To the extent that these evolutionary theories are correct, one might expect that nonhuman species—especially those closely related to ourselves—would exhibit

Figure 7.6 Monkeys show human-like toy preferences. (A) A female vervet monkey plays with a doll. (B) A male monkey plays with a toy car (Alexander & Hines, 2002).

(A)

(B)

some of the same gender-differentiated traits that humans do, even without the benefit of human culture. As one test of this idea, Gerianne Alexander and Melissa Hines presented male and female vervet monkeys with the same kinds of toys that they had previously used to test children's toy preferences (Alexander & Hines, 2002). The monkeys' preferences were uncannily similar to those of humans: Male monkeys played more with model cars and balls, for example, and female monkeys played more with dolls (**Figure 7.6**). Male and female monkeys played about equally with items that appeal to both boys and girls, such as picture books and stuffed dogs. Similar results have been obtained more recently with rhesus monkeys (Hassett et al., 2008). Since the monkeys had not seen the test items previously, they could hardly have learned to prefer some toys over others. More probably, some internal process of brain differentiation influences toy preferences in both human and nonhuman primates. It's not that there's an innate representation of the concept "car" or of any other toys in the brain, of course. Rather, children and monkeys choose toys that facilitate the behaviors they like to engage in, such as active movement in the case of males.

Experiments Demonstrate a Role for Sex Hormones

In Chapter 6, we mentioned the structural and functional differences between the brains of women and men. These differences result, at least in part, from differences in circulating levels of sex hormones during fetal life, at puberty, and during adult life. So do hormones help generate psychological differences between the sexes?

Experiments in animals certainly suggest so. As described in Chapter 6, biologists have altered the hormonal environment of fetal rats and monkeys—by adding testosterone to a female fetus, for example, or by blocking the action of a male fetus's own testosterone. In postnatal life the treated females behave in many ways like males, and vice versa (Goy et al., 1988).

Although it would obviously be unethical to conduct such experiments in humans, biologists can take advantage of "experiments of nature" in which something similar has occurred spontaneously. One example is the condition of **congenital adrenal hyperplasia (CAH)**. Girls with this genetic condition are exposed to abnormally high levels of testosterone-like hormones (androgens) that are secreted by their adrenal glands during part of their fetal life. Psychologists have found that some, but not all, of the behavioral traits of these girls are shifted in the

congenital adrenal hyperplasia (CAH) A congenital defect of hormonal metabolism in the adrenal gland, causing the gland to secrete excessive levels of androgens.

masculine direction. They engage in more rough-and-tumble play than other girls, for example, and they prefer boys' toys to girls' toys (Berenbaum & Snyder, 1995) (**Figure 7.7**) . The differences persist into adult life, affecting such things as hobby interests and career choices (Berenbaum & Bailey, 2003). Women with CAH are also more proficient than other women at spatial tasks at which males typically excel (Puts et al., 2008). These observations indicate that the high androgen levels experienced by female CAH fetuses influence their gender characteristics after birth. Observations on other "experiments of nature" lend further support to the idea that prenatal hormones influence gender (**Box 7.1**).

But do these results say anything about normal children? To address this question, researchers have estimated testosterone levels in healthy fetuses—by measuring levels of the hormone in the amniotic fluid or in their mother's blood (Hines, 2006; Knickmeyer & Baron-Cohen, 2006). The children born of those pregnancies were studied at various ages after birth. It turned out that fetal testosterone levels predicted a variety of gender characteristics in these children, even within a single sex. The lower a girl's testosterone levels prenatally, for example, the more strongly she would prefer girls' toys over boys' toys when she was 3 years old.

It's difficult to study adults with the same methodology, because of the long time interval involved. To get around this problem, biologists have looked for anatomical markers in adults that may reflect their degree of testosterone exposure prenatally. One marker that has attracted a great deal of attention is the ratio of the length of the index finger to the length of the ring finger—the so-called 2D:4D ratio (**Figure 7.8**). Men typically have a lower 2D:4D ratio than women, and several lines of evidence suggest that this difference comes about as a result of the higher testosterone levels that males typically experience during fetal life (van Anders et al., 2006). Researchers have found that the 2D:4D ratio correlates with many gendered characteristics, even within one sex. A Canadian group, for example, reported that men with lower (more male-typical) ratios are more aggressive than men with higher ratios (Bailey & Hurd, 2005).

These kinds of findings suggest a relationship—presumably a causal one—between the brain's exposure to androgens before birth and a variety of gendered characteristics in childhood and adult life. None of the biological findings allow the conclusion that prenatal hormones *determine* a person's gender characteristics, however. They suggest an *influence*—an influence that may be quite strong for some characteristics and quite weak, or totally absent, for others. Thus there is plenty of room for other factors to play a role. These may include nonhormonal biological processes, such as aspects of brain development that are controlled directly by genes (Davies & Wilkinson, 2006), as well as a variety of entirely nonbiological factors that we discuss next.

Life Experiences Influence Gender

Newborn girls and boys enter a world that imposes gender on them from the very beginning (**Figure 7.9**). Psychologists have discerned a variety of ways in which interactions between individuals, their families, and larger social groups help create or strengthen gendered traits.

Gender Is Molded by Socialization

The primary social influence on gender is the family. Parents and older siblings have myriad opportunities to influence gendered attitudes and behaviors in children. They may do this by the way they dress children, by the way they decorate the child's surroundings, by the toys they provide, by the way they attend to, reward, or punish the child's behavior, and by the activities that they engage the

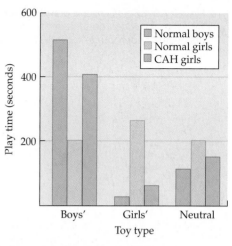

Figure 7.7 Hormones and play
Exposure to androgens during fetal life influences choice of toys during childhood. Normal boys, normal girls, and girls with congenital adrenal hyperplasia (CAH) were observed while playing with toys. The toys available included those generally preferred by boys (e.g., trucks) and those generally preferred by girls (e.g., dolls), as well as gender-neutral toys. The toy preferences of the CAH girls were more like those of boys than of non-CAH girls. (After Berenbaum and Snyder, 1995.)

Figure 7.8 Finger length ratio and gender The 2D:4D ratio is the length of the index finger divided by the length of the ring finger. The ratio is typically lower in men than women, but it also varies with gender characteristics within each sex. (D=digit.)

Figure 7.9 Babies enter a gendered world. Eva and Nicholas have been dressed in the pink and blue outfits deemed appropriate for infant boys and girls.

(A)

(B)

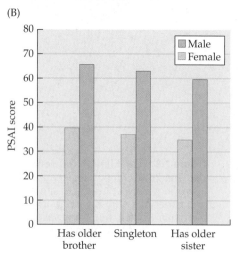

child in. Some parents take great pains to encourage gender-conformity by these various methods, while others take a more lenient stance. Even if they do not set out to influence the child's gender, however, parents and siblings may do so simply by virtue of acting as role models.

OBSERVING SOCIALIZATION Here's just one example of a study in which the influence of family members (older siblings in this case) on children's gender was demonstrated and measured (Rust et al., 2000). A British group of psychologists examined the gender-related behaviors and interests of over 5000 3-year-old children; the researchers reduced the data for each child to a single, unidimensional measure of masculinity-femininity. Some of the children had older siblings of the same or the other sex. As can be readily seen in the data (**Figure 7.10**), those children who had an older sibling of the same sex were more gender-typical than were children who had no siblings (singletons). Conversely, children who had an older sibling of the other sex were less gender-typical than the singletons. These data indicate that the presence of same- or opposite-sex siblings does influence a child's gender characteristics to an appreciable degree. The influence was modest in size: A child's own biological sex was a much stronger predictor of its gender-related traits than was the sex of its older siblings. Girls with older brothers, for example, were far more feminine than any boys, even boys with older sisters. Still, older siblings are

Figure 7.10 Influence of siblings on gender (A) Older siblings act as gender role models. (B) The Pre-School Activities Inventory (PSAI) score is a measure of gender-typical activities and interests in which male-typical traits score higher and female-typical traits score lower. This figure shows the PSAI score for 5542 British 3-year-olds, broken down according to whether they are singletons or have an older brother or sister. The children's gender traits are slightly shifted in the direction of the sex of their older sibling. (After Rust et al., 2000.)

Biology of Sex

BOX 7.1 "Eggs at Twelve"

In the early 1970s Julianne Imperato-McGinley, an endocrinologist at Cornell Medical School, heard stories about a remote village in the Dominican Republic where girls were changing sex at puberty—sprouting a penis and testicles and well-developed muscles just like regular men. Intrigued, she led an expedition to the village. She found that the stories were true. In fact, the phenomenon was so common that the villagers had a name for these children: *guevedoces,* meaning "eggs [testicles] at 12."

Julianne Imperato-McGinley

Imperato-McGinley discovered that the affected children were chromosomally male (XY) but carried a genetic mutation called **5α-reductase deficiency**, which made them unable to convert testosterone to the more potent androgen dihydrotestosterone (DHT) (Imperato-McGinley et al., 1974). DHT is required for the normal prenatal development

of the male genitals. Thus, although the affected children had testicles, the testicles did not descend and their genitals looked—at least to casual inspection—like those of girls. As a result, they were usually raised as girls. At puberty, however, the greatly increased levels of circulating testosterone triggered enlargement of the rudimentary penis and scrotum; the testicles descended, the voice lowered, and the general body build and musculature became that of an adolescent male.

What particularly interested Imperato-McGinley was the affected individuals' gender development. The great majority of these children shifted from a female to a male gender identity at or soon after puberty (Imperato-McGinley et al., 1979). The transition typically took place over a period of several years—subjects felt that they passed through stages of "not feeling like girls," then "feeling like men," and finally being convinced that they were men.

How should this finding be interpreted? Just giving a normal prepubertal girl large doses of testosterone to induce male secondary development would not make her feel like a man. Therefore, it was not just the increased testosterone levels at puberty that induced a male gender identity in the children studied by Imperato-McGinley. Rather, in her interpretation, it was the combination of prenatal testosterone exposure, which had its typical masculinizing effect on the brain, with the rise in testosterone at puberty. Together, these hormonal effects nearly always overrode any effects of being reared as a female.

Imperato-McGinley's conclusions were criticized for a number of reasons. It was suggested, for example, that the children she studied were not really reared as female, but as a kind of intersex. It is true that, as the syndrome

became well known in the area, infants who had the syndrome were recognized by careful inspection of the genitalia at birth, and it was expected that they would change sex. But Imperato-McGinley also reported on 18 children who were raised in the full belief that they were, and would always remain, female. Of these children, 17 developed a male gender identity during puberty (and were sexually attracted to women), and 16 completely changed their public gender role to male. More recently, similar clusters of cases have been found in other isolated communities around the world. Again, most of the affected girls take on a male gender identity at puberty (Imperato-McGinley et al., 1991).

The observations on 5α-reductase deficiency leave many loose ends. What were the gender characteristics of the affected individuals during childhood? What would have happened if the children's brains were flooded with testosterone at puberty, but their bodies for some reason had remained female—would they have accepted their continued female identity, or would they still have transitioned to a male identity, becoming—in essence—transexuals? And what if the whole syndrome were sex-reversed: What if it was a matter of boys developing women's bodies at puberty? Would they be as accepting of membership in the female sex as the 5α-reductase-deficient girls were of membership in the male sex? The remarkable individuals studies by Imperato-McGinley do not provide all the answers to these questions, but they do support the general notion that sex hormones, both before birth and at puberty, powerfully influence a person's gender.

5α-reductase deficiency The congenital absence of the enzyme 5α-reductase, which converts testosterone to dihydrotestosterone.

just one social influence out of many: Parents are probably much more influential, and other influences are exerted by teachers, peer groups, and so on.

REWARDS AND PUNISHMENTS Studies like the one just described demonstrate that social interactions influence gender but don't pinpoint the exact mechanisms. One possible mechanism is simply the administration of rewards when the child shows desired behaviors, and punishments or withdrawal of rewards when the child shows undesired behaviors. In one study focusing on this mechanism, psy-

Personal Points of View

BOX 7.2 The Boy Who Was Raised as a Girl

Bruce and Brian Reimer were monozygotic twins, born in Winnipeg, Canada, in 1965. When the twins were 7 months old they developed phimosis, a common condition in which the foreskin of the penis becomes constricted (see Chapter 4). The parents were advised to have the twins circumcised, but during Bruce's operation, an accident with the electrocautery machine led to the complete destruction of his penis.

The parents were understandably devastated and at a loss as to what to do. Eventually they brought Bruce to sexologist John Money at Johns Hopkins Medical School. Based on his earlier studies of children born with ambiguous genialia, Money believed that children developed a male or female gender identify according to whether they were reared as girls or boys. Since it would not be possible to refashion a normal penis for Bruce, Money recommended that he be surgically transformed into, and reared as, a girl. He told the parents that as long as they treated the child as a girl, she would become a feminine, heterosexual woman.

The parents followed Money's advice. They immediately changed Bruce's name to Brenda and dressed and treated her as a girl. When Brenda was 2 years old, her sex reassignment was completed: Her testicles were removed, and a rudimentary vagina was constructed from the scrotal skin. Her parents dedicated themselves to rearing Brenda and Brian as sister and brother. Money saw the parents and the twins from time to time and advised the parents on the appropriate ways to treat Brenda that would best encourage her femininity.

As the years went by, Money reported in detail on the case in lectures, papers, and books. He claimed that Brenda was developing as a normal girl, apart from a certain tomboyishness. While Brian copied his father, Brenda copied her mother, wrote Money (and colleague Anke Ehrhardt) in a 1972 book (Money & Ehrhardt, 1971): "Regarding domestic activities, such as work in the kitchen and house traditionally seen as part of the female's role, the mother reported that her daughter copies her in trying to help her tidying and cleaning up the kitchen, while the boy could not care less about it." Brenda chose dolls as presents, while Brian chose model cars.

The case became widely cited, both in the popular press and in academic circles, as evi-

David Reimer (1965–2004)

dence for the malleability of gender. "This dramatic case provides strong support for [the idea] that conventional patterns of masculine and feminine behavior can be altered," reported *Time* in 1973. "It also casts doubt on the theory that major sexual differences, psychological as well as anatomical, are immutably set by the genes at conception." "The normality of [Brenda's] development can be viewed as a substantial indication of the plasticity of human gender identity and the relative importance of social learning and conditioning in this process," stated the influential *Textbook of Sexual Medicine* (Kolodny et al., 1979). The case "... illustrated the overriding role of life experiences in molding human sexuality," according to the 1985 edition of the neurobiology textbook *Principles of Neural Science* (Kandel & Schwartz, 1985).

Eventually, Money reported that he had lost contact with the Reimer family. It took detective work by University of Hawaii sexologist Milton Diamond (Diamond & Sigmundson, 1997), and later by journalist John Colapinto (Colapinto, 2000), to discover what had happened to Brenda. It seems that she was never successfully socialized into a feminine gender identity in the way that Money had claimed. Rather, she rebelled against it at every stage. Although a female puberty was induced by means of treatment with estrogen, Brenda loathed her developing breasts. By the age of 15 she had

changed her name to David and was dressing as a boy. David had a double mastectomy, testosterone treatments, and a phalloplasty (reconstruction of a penis). He was always sexually attracted to women, and he eventually married, engaged in coitus with the aid of a prosthesis, and adopted children.

Sadly, David killed himself in 2004 at the age of 38. The exact reason for his suicide is not known, but possible causes include the breakup of his marriage, financial difficulties, the earlier death of his twin brother Brian, and of course his traumatic childhood (Chalmers, 2004).

The case of Bruce, then Brenda, then David Reimer suggests a conclusion different from the one drawn by John Money: Prenatal development seems to strongly influence gender identity and sexual orientation even when rearing conditions, genital anatomy, and pubertal hormones all conspire to produce the opposite result. This conclusion has been reinforced by the study of genetically male children with a condition in which the external genitalia fail to develop. Although surgically reconstructed as girls and reared as such, all are male-shifted in their gender characteristics, and nearly half of them insist they are boys or men (Reiner, 2004). "It's been a monstrous failure, this idea that you can convert a child's sex by making over the genitals in the sex you've chosen," said the author of that study. "If we as physicians or scientists want to know about a person's sexual identity, we have to ask them" (Dreifus, 2005).

dren were shown pictures of boys and girls performing tasks that were either consistent with gender stereotypes (e.g., girls cooking) or inconsistent with those stereotypes (e.g., girls sawing wood). When tested a week later on their recollection of the pictures, children tended to make mistakes that eliminated conflicts with stereotypes—they might recall that they saw boys, rather than girls, sawing wood, for example (Martin & Halverson, 1983). In another study, students were tested on their ability to recall sentences such as "Laura is a good nurse," "Laura is a bad nurse," "Carlos is a good nurse," or "Carlos is a bad nurse." The students recalled the statements that fit gender stereotypes ("Laura is a good nurse," "Carlos is a bad nurse") better than those that conflicted with stereotypes (Cann, 1993). Results such as these suggest that perceptions related to gender do encounter a filter resembling Bem's gender schema.

SEXUAL SCRIPTS Another variation on cognitive developmental models is the **sexual script** theory of John Gagnon and William Simon (Simon & Gagnon, 1986). As the word "script" suggests, this theory asserts that sexual behavior is a form of role-playing, with parts that are learned. We already mentioned one study of sexual scripts in Chapter 1—Steven Eggermont's study of how watching television may teach teenagers to change their strategies for seeking sexual contacts (Eggermont, 2006). People place particular reliance on sexual scripts when interacting with prospective partners that they don't know very well. As we'll describe in more detail in Chapter 10, first dates between heterosexual couples are (or traditionally were) organized according to gendered scripts governing such matters as who pays, what it means to invite someone up for a drink, and how the man and woman negotiate any sexual interactions.

Scripts can change over time under the influence of culture. Early in the twentieth century, for example, oral-genital contact was a form of sex that men largely received from prostitutes and in transient relationships. Now, however, it has become a common and acceptable sexual practice between young adults who are dating, and both males and females take the oral role (Gagnon & Simon, 1987). Thus men and women today read different meanings into oral sex than their grandparents did.

Scripts, according to Gagnon and Simon, influence not only sexual dealings among people, but also the psychosexual development of individuals. They noted that postpubertal boys masturbate a great deal more than do girls, as we mentioned above, while girls' early sexual experiences tend to be with partners. As a consequence, script theory suggests, the meaning of sex for males becomes embedded in the notion of the male's own sexual pleasure, whereas for females it becomes embedded in the notion of relationships.

Some brain scientists are critical of purely cognitive models of mental development. That's because consciousness doesn't necessarily have access to the neural circuitry that underlies our feelings and motivations, or to the processes that modify that circuitry in the face of our life experiences. Joseph LeDoux, for example, stresses the importance of delineating the invisible inner workings of the brain as a basis for understanding mental development and emphasizes that "the self consists of more than what self-aware organisms are consciously aware of" (LeDoux, 2002).

Gender Development Involves Complex Interactions

Gender researchers, like researchers in most other areas, tend to invest themselves in certain approaches to their subject, perhaps due to the training they have received. Some are interested in biological theories, some in socialization, and so on. Yet it is very unlikely that something as complex as human gender could be fully explained by any single approach. Both researchers who have a biological

sexual scripts Socially negotiated roles that govern sexual behavior.

perspective (Wallen, 1996) and those whose focus is on socialization (Maccoby, 1998) agree that nature and nurture interact in the development of most gender-related traits.

Take, for example, a childhood trait such as toy preference. The observations of atypical toy preference in CAH girls strongly suggest that prenatal hormone exposure contributes to the gender difference in this trait. However, many parents give boys and girls gender-specific toys before the age at which gender-specific play emerges—sometimes as early as 9 months (Pomerleau et al., 1990). Furthermore, children whose parents give them gender-specific toys are more likely to prefer and play with such toys than children who are given a mix of toys (Eisenberg et al., 1985; Katz & Boswell, 1986). Thus it seems probable that there is an additive effect of biological predisposition and socialization on the development of toy preference.

The interactions could be more complex than simple addition, however, as illustrated by a study of rape, violence, and other antisocial behavior carried out in New Zealand (Caspi et al., 2002). Males commit many more such acts than females, but not all males are antisocial—why? The researchers established first that boys who had themselves experienced sexual or physical abuse during childhood were more likely than other boys to commit antisocial acts later in life. By itself, this finding merely confirmed a well-known phenomenon, the so-called "victim-perpetrator cycle." But the researchers went on and examined the men's DNA for genes that might also be influencing the behavior. They focused on a gene called *MAOA* that helps regulate the levels of two neurotransmitters, dopamine and serotonin, in the brain. This gene exists in two forms: a fully active form, which was possessed by about 90% of the study population, and a less-active form, which was possessed by the other 10% of the population. Simply possessing one form or the other had no significant effect on a male's likelihood of committing antisocial acts. But when a man *both* possessed the less-active variant *and* had experienced severe childhood abuse, he stood an astonishing 85% chance of committing antisocial acts—a far greater likelihood than if he had suffered the same degree of abuse but possessed the fully active variant of the gene (**Figure 7.13**). In other words, variability in the *MAOA* gene strongly modulates the impact of childhood abuse on sexual and social development, damping the

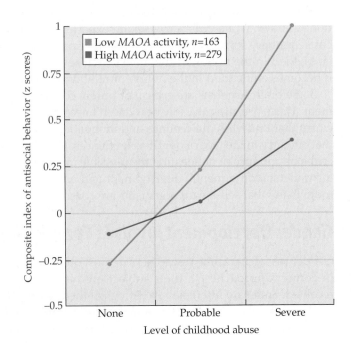

Figure 7.13 Genes and the victim-perpetrator cycle This graph plots the antisocial behavior shown in adulthood by males who experienced differing levels of abuse during childhood (i.e., none, probable, or severe). Men having a less-active *MAOA* gene (orange) showed a much more pronounced effect of childhood abuse than did those with a fully active gene (green). (After Caspi et al., 2002.)

(A)

(B)

Figure 7.14 Social influences work in contradictory ways. (A) Video games may encourage sexual violence. In Grand Theft Auto: Vice City, a man has sex with a prostitute and then beats her to death to get his money back. (B) The criminal justice system may restrain sexual violence: No one wants to join the 90,000 rapists who are serving long prison sentences.

victim-perpetrator cycle when the gene is fully active and amplifying it when the gene is less active. It is a conditional, not an additive interaction. Such complex interactions are probably common.

Another complicating factor is that the influence of socialization is not unidirectional, but can pull people in opposite directions at the same time. Concerning the male disposition to commit sexual violence, for example, there are some social forces that strongly encourage such violence and others that strongly discourage it (**Figure 7.14**). Given all these complexities, it will remain for future generations of researchers to fully tease out the web of causation that establishes gender.

Transgendered People Cross Society's Deepest Divide

The term *transgender* is used in a broad way to encompass all individuals who have the anatomy of one sex but the gender identity of the other. The term **transexual** (also spelled transsexual) is used for the subset of transgendered individuals who seek to change their body into that of the other sex by medical means (i.e., hormone treatment and sex-reassignment surgery). This transition may be in either direction: male to female (M-to-F) or female to male (F-to-M). Transgendered and transexual people have existed in most—perhaps all—human societies (**Box 7.3**). We focus first on transexuals and then take a look at the broader population of transgendered people.

Transexuals Are of More Than One Kind

Imagine yourself waking up one morning in a body of the other sex. Very likely you would be shocked and would move heaven and earth to get back into your "right" body. That is the kind of mental experience transexuals deal with on a daily basis, unless and until they undergo sex-reassignment surgery and transition to the other sex. The unhappiness caused by discordance between anatomical sex and gender identity is given the medical name **gender dysphoria**.

Most F-to-M transexuals (who may call themselves **transmen**) share a similar life history. Even as very young girls they say they are boys or insist that they

transexual A transgendered person who seeks to transition to the other sex.

gender dysphoria The unhappiness caused by discordance between a person's anatomical sex and gender identity.

transman A female-to-male transexual.

Cultural Diversity

BOX 7.3 Transgenders in Cross-Cultural Perspective

Transgendered men and women have probably existed in all human societies. In fact, they have been recognized and given special names in many societies that have no notion of gay people, even though gay people are (by the criteria of our own society, at least) a lot more common. That is probably because being transgendered is a much more visible and striking departure from social norms than is being homosexual.

In many societies, transgendered people have been accorded a special status in society—often, a spiritual or sacred one. Throughout Polynesia, for example, there existed a class of M-to-F transgenders known as **mahus**. There was typically one mahu per village. The mahu dressed in female (or a mixture of female and male) attire, engaged in women's activities, and had sex with conventional men. He was attached to the village headman's household and performed sacred dances. He was traditionally accorded high status, and families encouraged or even trained one of their sons to become a mahu. From time to time, a European explorer or trader took a fancy to a mahu and brought "her" to his ship for sex, only to be shocked by the discovery of his male anatomy.

In several Native American cultures, rituals conducted at or before puberty gave a boy the option to choose between the status of a conventional male and that of a transgendered **two-spirit** (male–female) **person**, or *berdache* (Williams, 1986). Among the Tohono O'odham Indians of the Sonoran Desert, for example, a boy who seemed to prefer female pursuits was tested by being placed within a brushwood enclosure, along with a man's bow and arrows and a woman's basket. The enclosure was then set on fire. If, in escaping the flames, the boy took with him the bow and arrows, he became a conventional man, but if he took the basket, he became a berdache. The berdaches wore special clothes fashioned from male and female attire, practiced mostly female occupations, and engaged in sexual relationships with conventional men. They were often shamans (healers who derived their curative powers from their knowledge of the spirit world), chanters, dancers, or mediators.

The ancient Greek historian Herodotus reported that there were women warriors called **Amazons** among the Scythian tribes north of the Black Sea (Figure A). The Amazons, Herodotus said, cut off one breast in order to use a bow and arrow more effectively. Long thought to be mythical, the existence of Amazons was confirmed by the discovery of female bones,

(A) Amazons battling Greek soldiers

along with weapons, in some Scythian tombs in southern Ukraine (Ascherson, 1996).

A sixteenth-century explorer in northeastern Brazil reported on female warriors among the Tupinamba Indians:

> There are some Indian women who determine to remain chaste: they have no commerce with men in any manner, nor would they consent to it even if refusal meant death. They give up all the duties of women and imitate men, and follow men's pursuits as if they were not women. They wear the hair cut in the same way as the men, and go to war with bows and arrows and pursue game, always in company with men; each has a woman to serve her, to whom she says

she is married, and they treat each other and speak with each other as man and wife.

The explorers were so struck by these women that they named the river that ran through the region the "River of the Amazons."

In India and Pakistan there exists a large group of M-to-F transexuals known as **hijras** (Figure B). Indian hijras are devotees of the Hindu goddess Bahuchara Mata. Hijras remove their entire external genitalia, dress as women, and earn a living by performing dance ceremonies at marriages and the births of male infants. They engage in receptive anal sex with conventional men, often as prostitutes.

In the United States, berdaches were persecuted by white administrators, often by being forced to return to a conventional male role. They lost their respected position in American Indian communities, and words meaning

BOX 7.3 (continued)

berdache, such as the Lakota *winkte*, became terms of abuse analogous to "faggot."

A tragic reminder that these negative attitudes persist occurred in June 2001. Sixteen-year-old Fred Martinez, Jr., a self-described two-spirit Navajo youth, was bludgeoned to death in a desolate area in Cortez, Colorado. The man convicted of his murder, 18-year-old Shaun Murphy, boasted to friends that he had "beat up a fag," according to a police affidavit. No hate crime charge could be added because the state of Colorado did not include sexual orientation or gender identity in its hate crime statute. These categories have since been included.

Sources: Williams, 1986, Nanda, 1990, Quittner, 2001.

mahu A man who took a female gender role in Polynesian society and performed ritual dances.

two-spirit person In Native American cultures, a person with the spirit of both a man and a woman; a transgendered person. Also called berdache.

Amazon A female Scythian warrior; more generally, any tall or powerful woman.

hijra A member of a class of male-to-female transexuals in northern India and Pakistan.

(B) A hijra performs for a marriage.

want to become boys, and they try to express their masculine identity in their clothing, hairstyles, friendships, activities, and career plans. Of course, this usually puts them on a collision course with the gender expectations of family, peers, and the world at large. As they enter puberty they resent the developing signs of womanhood and may seek to hide them by, for example, binding their breasts. In adulthood they seem quite masculine in many respects, and they are usually sexually attracted to women. Thus they are "homosexual" with respect to their birth sex, but they do not identify as homosexual or lesbian. Rather, they identify as heterosexual men. The well-known expression "man trapped in a woman's body" describes them quite aptly.

M-to-F transexuals (or **transwomen**), on the other hand, fall into two contrasting types with different life histories. The first kind, who we may call "classical" M-to-F transexuals, are pretty much the opposite of the F-to-M transexuals just described. As young boys they say that they are girls or insist that they want to become girls, and they try to dress as girls and to play with girls. They dislike the man's body that puberty gives them and may try to pass (be identified by others) as women. Feminine mannerisms, gait, and conversational style seem to come naturally to them—they can often teach women a thing or two about femininity. They are usually sexually attracted to men, but identify as heterosexual women, not as gay men. They are "women trapped in men's bodies." M-to-F transexuals of this type tend to seek sex-reassignment in their teen years or young adulthood—as soon as they are legally allowed to do so or as soon as they can raise the money to pay for it.

transwoman A male-to-female transexual.

transvestism Wearing clothes of the other sex for purposes of sexual arousal. Sometimes applied to cross-dressing for any reason.

autogynephilia A form of male-to-female transexuality characterized by sexual arousal at the thought of becoming a woman.

real-life experience A period of living in the role of the other sex as a prelude to sex reassignment.

There is another kind of M-to-F transexual, however, that is much less well-known to the general public (Freund et al., 1982; Blanchard, 1993). During childhood, these boys are only mildly gender-nonconformist, or not at all. When they grow up they are usually sexually attracted to women, so they are heterosexual with respect to their birth sex. However, their interest in women takes an unusual course, being colored with fetishistic elements. In particular, they are erotically aroused by wearing women's clothes—a trait known as heterosexual **transvestism**. Eventually, this kind of ideation may progress to the point that they are aroused by the idea, not merely of being in women's clothes, but being in a woman's *body* and possessing female genitals. In other words, their desire to become a woman is fueled by the sex drive and by the desire to incorporate the object of their attractions into themselves, rather than by a female gender identity as such. Feminine mannerisms, gait, and conversational style do not necessarily come naturally to these transexuals, and so they may take lessons on how to act like a woman. They tend to seek sex reassignment later in life, often after they have been heterosexually married and fathered children.

A Canadian sexologist, Ray Blanchard, gave this second developmental pathway the name **autogynephilia**, meaning "being attracted to oneself as a woman." Some sex researchers believe that most or all M-to-F transexuals who are sexually attracted to women are autogynephilic, which would make them at least as numerous as classical M-to-F transexuals (Bailey, 2003). Others don't find a close correlation between a M-to-F transexual's sexual orientation and whether or not that person displays characteristics of autogynephilia (Veale et al., 2008). Among M-to-F transexuals themselves, some have strongly opposed the concept of autogynephilia, seeing it as equivalent to calling transexuals mentally ill (James, 2004). Others have embraced the concept and added important details to its theoretical underpinnings (Lawrence, 2004).

Sex Reassignment Is a Multistage Process

No form of psychiatric treatment can bring a transexual person's gender identity into concordance with their biological sex. In fact, any attempt to do so would be experienced as a violation of personhood. Therefore, doctors and therapists have followed a different strategy, helping transexual people to achieve their dream of changing their anatomical sex and their social gender role (**Figure 7.15**). Transexuals call this process transitioning.

One way in which a transexual person can transition is with the help of a gender identity clinic. These clinics usually follow the standards of care laid out by the World Professional Association for Transgender Health (World Professional Association for Transgender Health, 2008).

At a gender identity clinic, the sex-change process has several distinct stages. First, the client is evaluated psychologically and physically. This stage may include psychotherapy, with the goal of probing the client's history, mental health, and motivation, and education about the sex-reassignment process and the inevitable limitations of the results.

In the second stage, known as the **real-life experience**, the client lives in the community for a period of time—usually 1 to 2 years, but sometimes less—as a member of the other sex. The idea is to ensure that the client can function in the desired gender role. This can be a very difficult time for the client because many transexuals cannot pass easily as a person of the other sex without medical treat-

Figure 7.15 Transexual pioneer In 1952, George Jorgensen created a sensation by having sex-reassignment surgery in Denmark and returning to the United States as Christine.

ment (and, often, not even after such treatment). Furthermore, the clinic generally encourages the client to dress in a fashion that is very stereotypical for the other sex, which may produce a caricature-like result.

In the third stage, the client is given hormones to begin the process of bodily change: estrogens for a M-to-F transexual or androgens for an F-to-M transexual. The hormones' effects are not permanent, so this treatment usually continues for life. Sometimes the treatment accompanies or even precedes the real-life experience.

When an intact man is given estrogens, their effects include changes in body fat distribution to a more female pattern, a decrease in the frequency of erections, and, possibly, a cessation of ejaculations. The breasts may enlarge, sometimes to a degree that makes later breast augmentation surgery unnecessary. Estrogens do not abolish facial hair or reverse baldness, however. The M-to-F client often has to undergo a lengthy process of beard removal by electrolysis or laser treatment.

When an intact woman is given androgens, a beard appears, though sometimes only a very thin one. The voice deepens, and the body fat distribution changes in a male direction. Because hormones do not remodel the skeleton, however, the general body shape may remain similar to that of the client's original sex, so that passing as the new sex may be difficult.

The fourth stage of transitioning is **sex-reassignment surgery**. For an M-to-F transexual, the key procedures are removal of the penis and testicles, construction of a vagina, labia, and clitoris (**Figure 7.16**), and breast augmentation. Other procedures that may be done include surgery to the vocal cords (to raise the pitch of the voice), reduction of the laryngeal cartilage (Adam's apple), reduction of the nose and some other facial structures, and liposuction to the waist.

For an F-to-M transexual, surgery can include removal of the breasts, ovaries, oviducts, uterus, and vagina. (The breasts may be removed before the real-life experience if they are large enough to make passing as a man impossible.) In addition, a scrotum and penis may be constructed (i.e., scrotoplasty and phalloplasty). Removal of the ovaries may have particular significance because, in some U.S. states, it is a requirement for a legal change of sex.

Construction of a penis that looks natural, contains a functioning urethra, and can be made to have an erection (with the aid of a pump/reservoir system or some kind of stiffening device: see Chapter 16) is a very costly multistage process, and the results are far from ideal. Frequently, the new urethra develops narrowings (strictures) or unwanted openings to the outside (fistulas), which necessitate further surgery. Urinary tract infections can occur. Furthermore, there is major scarring in the body region that is used as the source of graft tissue. Because of the expense and the imperfect results, many F-to-M transexuals forgo a phalloplasty. In some clients, the clitoris can be enlarged by hormonal treatment and surgery to produce a small penis (**Figure 7.17**) (Hage, 1996). This is not generally usable for coitus, but it may be capable of erection and orgasm, and the procedure may also be psychologically and socially beneficial in confirming a male identity. Even with this simpler procedure, however, complications requiring further surgery are common.

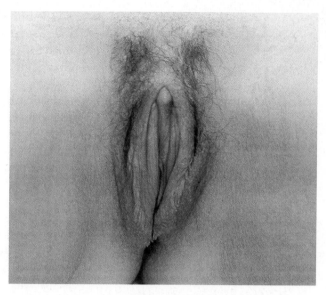

Figure 7.16 The vulva after sex-reassignment surgery The clitoris is constructed from the top surface of the penis with its nerve supply intact, and may therefore be capable of triggering orgasm. The clitoris and adjacent labial tissue are covered with mucosa derived from the penile urethra, giving them a pink color. The remainder of the penile skin, including the glans, is inverted to form the vagina. Often, additional skin must be grafted from other areas to make the vagina deep enough for coitus. (Courtesy of Eugene A. Schrang, M.D.)

sex-reassignment surgery Surgery to change a person's genitals or other sexual characteristics.

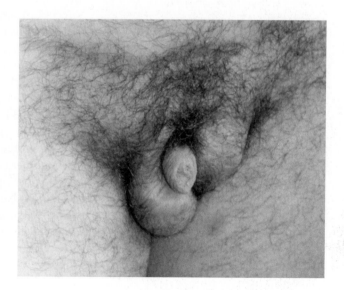

Figure 7.17 Transformation of the clitoris into a small penis by hormone treatment and surgery. This procedure is a simpler, less invasive, and less expensive alternative to the construction of a large penis usable for penetrative sex (phalloplasty). This F-to-M transexual also had a scrotum constructed from labial skin, with testicular implants.

The fifth stage of transitioning is surgical, endocrinological, and psychological follow-up, which may last for several years. Postoperative transexuals have to make many practical decisions (for example, whether to be open about the sex change or to conceal their past), and they face all kinds of personal and social challenges. Even getting an amended birth certificate may be a struggle.

Establishing sexual and affectional relationships is often difficult. Postoperative transexuals who can pass as members of their new sex have to deal with the problem of whether and when to let their prospective partners know about their history. When a heterosexual man finds out that his female partner was born a man, he may refuse to accept the reality of the sex change and may therefore reject the woman and possibly even assault her. Luckily, there are also people who are willing to accept transexuals as truly belonging to their new sex, or who are even specifically attracted to transexuals. Some transexuals remain in a relationship that existed prior to their transition.

Not all transexuals who wish to change sex do so via the "official" route just described. Some pursue another strategy (Denny & Bolin, 1997): They learn about sex reassignment through peer networks, obtain hormones on the black market, and, when they feel they are ready for surgery, go straight to a private surgeon. Of course, such self-medication carries significant risks (Moore et al., 2003).

The long-term outcome of sex-reassignment surgery is mostly good. In a recent survey of 232 postoperative M-to-F transexuals operated on by a particular surgeon, the overwhelming majority were well satisfied and felt that the surgery had greatly improved the quality of their lives (Lawrence, 2003). Some studies have reported that a significant proportion of postoperative transexuals are dissatisfied or depressed (Eldh et al., 1997). Better preoperative counseling and postoperative support would no doubt improve these outcomes.

Among the factors that correlate with long-term satisfaction are young age at reassignment, good general psychological health, a body build that permits passing as the other sex, good family and social support, and the success of the surgical procedure itself. Most experts now believe that a transexual's sexual orientation, and whether they are autogynephilic or not, are not useful predictors of the success of sex reassignment, and should not therefore be used as criteria for accepting or rejecting a person for medical assistance with the process.

Because age at treatment seems to be so important, some centers (especially in Europe) are now treating children at or before puberty. Their strategy is to postpone puberty with hormone-blocking drugs, thus preventing the appearance of difficult-to-reverse traits such as a beard or breasts. A few years later, when the child is considered old enough to give informed consent, the definitive hormonal and surgical treatment is undertaken.

One problem that affects most transexuals is the expense of transitioning: Sex reassignment can easily cost $30,000 and may run up to $150,000 or more if a multistage phalloplasty is involved. Governments and insurance companies provide little or no assistance in most cases. (Medicaid does sometimes pay for sex-reassignment surgery, however.) How is a teenager or young adult to raise this kind of money? For a few, the answer is through prostitution; transgendered prostitutes are much in evidence in some large cities (see Chapter 19). For the majority, the expense of sex reassignment imposes a frustrating waiting period that may drag on for many years.

Some Transgenders Do Not Want Surgery

The whole philosophy behind transexuality and sex-reassignment surgery is *medical:* The idea is that transexuals have a "problem" that needs to be "treated" in order to make them "well." Not all transgendered people accept this medical model. To some, it is *society* that has a "problem" with gender-variant people, and it is society that needs to be "treated."

Certainly it is true that contemporary U.S. society has what seems like a pathological aversion to transgendered people, who are victimized by abuse and hate crimes at a much higher rate than are lesbians and gay men. Could it be that the desire to change one's genital anatomy represents the internalization of these hostile attitudes? Kate Bornstein (**Figure 7.18**), a gender theorist who is herself a postoperative M-to-F transexual, put it this way:

> People think that they have to hate their genitals in order to be transsexual. Well, some transsexuals do hate their genitals, and they act to change them. But I think that transsexuals do not 'naturally' hate their birth-given genitals—I've not seen any evidence of that. We don't hate any part of our bodies that we weren't taught to hate. We're taught to hate parts of our bodies that aren't 'natural'—like a penis on a woman or a vagina on a man (Bornstein, 1994).

Figure 7.18 Kate Bornstein, a M-to-F transexual, believes that social pressures force people into impossible-to-live-up-to gender categories.

To some extent Bornstein's point of view is supported by anthropological research. In the native culture of Samoa, for example, transgendered persons (called *fa'afafine*) rarely desire sex reassignment, because it is socially acceptable to possess a penis and yet live in a gender role that is not male (Vasey & Bartlett, 2007).

Many transgendered Americans do not seek sex reassignment either, for a wide variety of reasons. They may not see any contradiction between living as a woman while possessing the genitals of a man, or vice versa. They may not have the money, they may be put off by the less than ideal results, or they may be perfectly satisfied with cross-dressing and "passing" as a person of the other sex. This choice also gives them the option of switching between male and female roles. They may even get satisfaction from *not* passing—from being recognizable as a "gender outlaw" or "genderqueer" rather than trying to deceive everyone.

This is how one 18-year-old "transman," who has had a mastectomy but no genital surgery, put it: "Some transmen want to be seen as men—they want to be accepted as born men. I want to be accepted as a transman—my brain is not gendered. There's this crazy gender binary that's built into all of life, that there are just two genders that are acceptable. I don't want to have to fit into that" (Quart, 2008).

Transgenders and Transexuals Struggle for Awareness and Acceptance

Some controversy surrounds the treatment of strongly gender-nonconformist children. According to prospective studies, only a minority of children who express a wish to be of the other sex continue to feel the same way after puberty (Green, 1987; Drummond et al., 2008). This has led some therapists to favor a strategy in which the child is encouraged to revert to a sex-typical gender role (Zucker, 2005). Their thinking is that this will help the children avoid social stigmatization and bullying. Others believe that this strategy is traumatizing, and these children stand a better chance at happiness if they are allowed to express and develop their transgendered identity (see Web Resources at the end of this chapter). Occasionally, a transgendered child's school will support this policy (Santiago, 2006).

Transgendered adults have had a difficult struggle to gain recognition as a group distinct from lesbians and gay men. Of course, the introduction of sex-reas-

(A)

(B)

Figure 7.19 Transgendered teen Gwen Araujo (left) and three of the men who beat her to death.

signment surgery in the 1960s, with all the attendant publicity, did educate the public about the phenomenon of transexuality, but it also prompted most people to accept the medical model of transexuality, which, as just mentioned, is rejected by some transgenders.

One factor that has hampered the advancement of transgendered people is that they are relatively few in number. Thus their political activism has generally taken place under the umbrella of the much larger gay rights movement. In fact, transgendered persons participated in the "Stonewall Rebellion"—the 1969 riot in New York that was a key event in the modern gay rights movement (see Chapter 14). Still, like bisexuals, transgenders have fought to clarify their separate identity. In gay rights and gay pride marches and parades, transgendered people form their own contingents, and these events now usually carry names such as "March for Lesbian, Gay, Bisexual, and Transgender Equality."

Legal protections for transgendered people lag behind those for gays and lesbians, even though the transgendered population is at greater risk of violence and discrimination. An attempt to introduce a federal Employment Non-Discrimination Act, with protections for transgendered people, failed in 2007. On the positive side, the first-ever Congressional hearings devoted to transgender issues were held in the following year.

Only 12 states have statutes that provide transgendered people with protection from discrimination, and only seven states and the District of Columbia currently include gender identity in their hate crime statutes (National Center for Transgender Equality, 2007). One notorious case that was prosecuted as a hate crime was the murder of 17-year-old Gwen (born Edward) Araujo of Newark, California, in 2002 (**Figure 7.19**). According to trial testimony, Araujo was beaten to death by four men: The men allegedly had sex with Araujo and then killed her after they discovered she was anatomically a male. Two of the men pleaded guilty to manslaughter and two were convicted of murder, but the jury rejected the hate-crime enhancement.

Summary

1. Gender is the entire collection of mental traits that differ between men and women. Gender identity is a person's core sense of being a man or a woman. Gender role is the social expression of gender identity.

2. Men outperform women in some cognitive traits, such as visuospatial skills. Women outperform men in fine movements, verbal fluency, and some aspects of memory. Personality differences include greater aggressiveness in men. In the area of sexuality, men and women differ in frequency of masturbation (men masturbate more frequently), attitudes toward casual sex (men are more approving), and styles of jealousy (women are more likely to experience emotional jealousy; men are more likely to experience sexual jealousy). All these gender differences show considerable overlap between the sexes, and their significance is debated.

3. Many gender differences arise early in life. Most children distinguish perceptually between males and females by 1 year of age, can identify their own sex by 2 to 3 years, and understand the immutability of sex by 3 to 4 years. Males are more active than females beginning in fetal life. Boys are more aggressive than girls. Boys and girls prefer different toys, and both prefer to associate with children of their same sex. Sex-specific interaction styles develop within these same-sex groups. Differences in other cognitive traits emerge gradually during childhood.

4. Biological factors influence gender. These include genes that have evolved to help men and women improve their reproductive success. A role for sex hormones, especially during prenatal life, is illustrated by experiments on animals, by observation of humans affected by endrocrinological disorders, and by the study of anatomical markers (such as finger-length ratios) that are correlated with gender traits.

5. Socialization influences gender. This can happen through the innumerable rewards and punishments that children receive from parents and others. Imitation is also an important mediator of gender learning. The feminist movement has discouraged gender stereotyping and may have had the effect of lessening gender differences.

6. A variety of cognitive developmental models stress the importance of children's thought processes in the development of gender. The understanding of gender develops sequentially in young children. Gender schemas are frameworks of beliefs that influence perception and that tend to encourage categorical notions about gender. In sexual script theory, gender learning involves the social negotiation of roles, such as those to be played by the man and woman in heterosexual relationships.

7. Transgendered people are those whose gender identity does not match their biological sex. Transsexuals are transgendered people who seek to change their anatomical sex: They may transition from male to female (M-to-F) or from female to male (F-to-M).

8. All F-to-M transexuals and some M-to-F transexuals have a childhood history of strong gender-nonconformity. They dislike the bodily changes induced by puberty and may attempt to conceal them. They are usually homosexual in the sense that they are sexually attracted to persons of the same birth sex as themselves. They usually identify not as gay, however, but as heterosexual individuals of the other sex. Some heterosexual M-to-F transexuals have a different developmental history, in which the desire to change sex develops out of a wish to incorporate their sexual targets (women) into their own bodies (autogynephilia).

9. Sex reassignment is a multistage process involving living for some period in the identity of the other sex, followed by hormonal treatments and sex-reassignment surgery. Genitals can be transformed into those of the other sex, but the procedure is expensive and, particularly in the case of F-to-M reassignment, yields imperfect results. Nevertheless, many transexuals are satisfied with the results of sex reassignment and are able to surmount the social and sexual challenges of post-transition life.

10. Other transgendered people do not seek sex reassignment for a variety of reasons. Some believe that sex reassignment would be unnecessary if society could be persuaded to loosen its rigid ideas about gender. All transgendered people face discrimination and the risk of violence, and most states and the federal government fail to offer them specific protections.

REFER TO THE
Human Sexuality
WEBSITE AT
www.sinauer.com/levay3e
for activities, study questions, quizzes, and other study aids.

Discussion Questions

1. Do you think that this chapter presents a balanced account of psychological differences between the sexes, and of research into the origins of these differences? If not, why? Did anything you read surprise you or cause you to reconsider your beliefs in this area?

2. After reading this chapter, what do you think of former Harvard University President Lawrence Summers' comments about why there are so few women in engineering and physics? If you were a college president would you consider it important to change this gender imbalance, and how would you go about it?

3. How would you react if your young daughter insisted she was a boy and asked to go to school in boys' clothes? Would you mention the possibility of sex-reassignment surgery?

Web Resources

Gender Inn (a bibliographic source for books, articles, and Web sites concerning gender) www.uni-koeln.de/phil-fak/englisch/datenbank/e_index.htm

National Public Radio: Two families grapple with sons' gender preferences (This radio program describes two opposing therapeutic strategies for helping transgendered children.) www.npr.org/templates/story/story.php?storyId=90247842&sc=emaf

World Professional Association for Transgender Health www.wpath.org

Recommended Reading

Bailey, J. M. (2003). *The man who would be queen: The science of gender-bending and transsexualism.* Joseph Henry Press.

Baron-Cohen, S. (2004). *The essential difference: Male and female brains and the truth about autism.* Basic Books.

Berenbaum, S. A., Moffat, S., Wisniewski, A. B., and Resnick. S. (2003). Neuroendocrinology: Cognitive effects of sex hormones. In M. de Haan and M. H. Johnson (Eds.), *The cognitive neuroscience of development.* Psychology Press.

Colapinto, J. (2000). *As nature made him: The boy who was raised as a girl.* HarperCollins.

Fausto-Sterling, A. (2000). *Sexing the body: Gender politics and the construction of sexuality.* Basic Books.

Geary, D. C. (1998). *Male, female: The evolution of human sex differences.* American Psychological Association.

Hines, M. (2004). *Brain gender.* Oxford University Press.

Lippa, R.A. (2005). *Gender, nature, and nurture* (2nd ed.). Erlbaum.

Maccoby, E. (1998). *The two sexes: Growing up apart, coming together.* Harvard University Press.

Mealey, L. (2000). *Sex differences: Developmental and evolutionary strategies.* Academic Press.

Nanda, S. (1999). *Gender diversity: Crosscultural variations.* Waveland Press.

Rhoads, S. E. (2004). *Taking sex differences seriously.* Encounter Books.

Sax, L. (2005). *Why gender matters: What parents and teachers need to know about the emerging science of sex differences.* Doubleday.

CHAPTER **8**

In parts of Burma women traditionally enhanced their beauty by stretching their necks with metal rings—a practice now aimed mostly at promoting tourism.

Attraction, Arousal, and Response

I n sex, one thing leads to another. To be more specific, a predictable sequence of mental and bodily processes characterizes sexual interactions. In this chapter we present these stages as follows: sexual attraction to a potential sex partner; psychological sexual arousal; and the physiological changes in the genitals—the sexual response cycle—that precede and accompany sexual behavior. This sequence is not universal. There are times when people engage in sex without prior attraction or arousal, for example, and only become aroused as a *consequence* of their behavior. But it is a useful storyline or framework for discussing the key processes underlying sexuality.

To describe the basic structure of this sexual storyline, we must postpone consideration of many issues that relate to it in important ways: how we negotiate sexual interactions, how we enter into sexual relationships, what specific forms of sexual contact we engage in, and how the aging process influences our sexual psychology and performance. What is left, however, is the central core of sex: wanting it, and getting it.

Sexual Attraction: It Takes Two

Sexual attraction is an erotically charged orientation toward a specific other person. The attraction may be calm and controlled ("He is a really charming guy"), or it may be madly impetuous ("If I don't have sex with her in the next 5 minutes, there is no God"). It may be felt at first meeting, or it may build over time. The attraction may be mutual, or it may be one-way. It may be accompanied by feelings of love and commitment, or not.

Sexual attraction is different from simple *liking*. In fact, we may be sexually attracted to people we dislike or to people we don't know well enough to like or dislike. Sexual attraction is also different from the judgment that a person is attractive. A heterosexual woman might judge that another woman is attractive, for example, but not be sexually attracted to her. Sexual attraction is also different from mate choice: We may choose to marry someone, cohabit with someone, or even have sex with someone for entirely nonsexual reasons. And sexual attraction is different, at least in part, from romantic love.

Because sexual attraction involves two people, we may approach it in two ways. First, we may ask, What causes a person to be attractive? Second, we may

fluctuating asymmetry A difference between the left and right sides of the body that results from random perturbations of development.

ask, What causes a person to experience attraction? Both questions are important, but we begin with the former. We are asking, essentially, What is beauty?

Beauty Is Not Entirely in the Eye of the Beholder

If we define beauty as the attributes that combine to make a person sexually attractive, then beauty can include many things, ranging from physical traits such as appearance, voice quality, and odor to less tangible attributes such as personality, behavior, and social circumstances. But our looks are the first cues to attractiveness that are available to others. So we consider physical appearance before other aspects of beauty (**Figure 8.1**).

The saying "Beauty lies in the eye of the beholder" suggests that everything is subjective or idiosyncratic—that there are no objective characteristics that make a person more or less attractive to people in general. In fact, however, psychologists have found a considerable degree of consensus on the topic of beauty. And they have identified certain characteristics that influence the attractiveness of faces and other physical features, no matter who is doing the judging.

SYMMETRY We mentioned in Chapter 2 that animals look for symmetry in their mates. So do humans, both in industrialized countries and in hunter-gatherer societies (Little et al., 2007). The more symmetrical a person's face, the more attractive, sexy, and healthy that person seems to others (Fink et al., 2006) (**Box 8.1**). Symmetry raises the attractiveness of the remainder of the body, too.

In Chapter 2, we discussed a possible evolutionary explanation for why asymmetry is unattractive (Thornhill & Gangestad, 1999a). (We are referring here to random, or **fluctuating asymmetry**—not the planned asymmetry of, say, the heart within the thorax.) Because a single genetic program guides the development of the

Figure 8.1 Human faces offer astonishing diversity, and no two people would place them in the same order of attractiveness. Yet there do seem to be some universals that affect people's judgment.

Research Highlights

BOX 8.1 Twins, Symmetry, and Attractiveness

(A) **Symmetry and attractiveness** Unmanipulated photographs of monozygotic twins 1 and 2. Which do you find more attractive?

(B) **"Double-left" and "double-right"** composite images of twin 1 (above) and twin 2 (below). Which of the pairs are more similar to each other?

Psychologist Linda Mealey (1956–2002) and her colleagues studied the relative attractiveness and facial symmetry of monozygotic ("identical") twins (Mealey et al., 1999). If you want to "play along," first answer the questions under the photographs, and then read further.

Monozygotic ("identical") twins share the same genes, but the vicissitudes of development ensure that they do not end up looking perfectly identical. Mealey gathered photographs of 34 pairs of monozygotic twins and had a large number of college students choose the more attractive member of each pair. In the example shown in Figure A, most students rated twin 2 as more attractive than twin 1.

To compare the visible symmetry of the two faces, Mealey used a computer to make two composites of each face. In each composite, one half of the image—say, the left—was the real image of the left side of the person's face, while the other half was a mirror-reversed version of

that same left half—we'll call this the "double-left" image. The other composite was the "double-right" image. Obviously, the more symmetrical the original face, the more similar the double-left and double-right composites of that face would look.

Mealey asked another set of students to look at these composites and judge whether the composites for twin A or for twin B were more alike. This was a judgment as to which twin's face was more symmetrical. Consistently, the twin who was judged more symmetrical by this test was also judged more attractive, even though the two kinds of judgments were made by different raters. In the examples shown here (Figure B), the lower pair of images, made from the more attractive twin 2, was judged more similar to each other than the upper pair of

images, made from the less attractive twin 1. Because twins 1 and 2 started out with the same genes, it appears that environmental factors or random processes triggered asymmetrical development in twin 1, with a corresponding reduction in attractiveness.

left and right sides of the body, a high degree of fluctuating asymmetry can arise only if the genetic program has been derailed in some way. Either the person's genes were of poor quality, or they ran into some kind of interference (such as an infection) during development. Indeed, people with asymmetrical features are more likely to suffer from a variety of disorders—including extremely premature birth, certain forms of intellectual disability, schizophrenia, and psychological and physiological distress—than are more symmetrical persons (Shackelford & Larsen, 1997). Thus it is plausible that evolution would favor the spread of genes that give us the ability to assess symmetry as well as the motivation to prefer it.

Figure 8.2 The face that changes sex Seven frames from a movie of a face that gradually morphs from hypermasculine (left) through androgynous (center) to hyperfeminine (right). The faces at the two extremes are generally rated the most attractive. (The complete movie can be seen at http://www.psych.nmsu.edu.) (From Johnston et al., 2001.)

Of course, there are other cues to a person's health besides symmetry. These include clear skin, glossy hair, freedom from visible defects and diseases, and so on. All such cues to health are also criteria for physical beauty.

MASCULINITY–FEMININITY It is possible to computer-generate a face that morphs continuously from a hypermasculine face through an androgynous face to a hyperfeminine face (**Figure 8.2**). Most people judge faces near the extremes of this range to be the most attractive (Johnston et al., 2001). This finding suggests that masculinity–femininity is an important dimension of attractiveness.

The actual cues to the masculinity–femininity of faces are things such as jaw width (wider in males), mouth and nose width (wider in males), chin size (larger in males), lip fullness (fuller in females), eyebrow bushiness (bushier in males), and eye size (larger in females). Such differences are largely generated under the influence of androgens (male traits) and estrogens (female traits) at puberty. Thus faces seem to become more attractive the more sexually differentiated they are.

Why are these sexually differentiated traits attractive, in an evolutionary sense? In part, they simply announce that the person has undergone a sex-typical puberty and is therefore likely to be fertile. In addition, the traits may be advantageous in themselves. Victor Johnston, for example, has suggested that the extreme masculine face represents the "healthy hunter," who would be well adapted for survival in early human evolution: The wide mouth and nose facilitate a high respiration rate during strenuous exercise, for example, while the prominent brow ridges may keep sunlight and sweat out of the eyes (Johnston et al., 2001) or protect the eyes from wounds during fights (Weisfeld, 1999).

BABYFACEDNESS We just mentioned that traits indicative of passage through puberty (and therefore of fertility) are considered attractive. Thus you wouldn't expect that making an adult face more like a young child's would increase its attractiveness, but that is exactly what a research group at the University of Regensburg, Germany, has reported (Braun et al., 2001). The researchers first quantified the facial proportions of children by computer-averaging the faces of a number of actual 4- to 6-year-old children and measuring the layout of facial features on this averaged image. Then they generated an adult woman's face by averaging the faces of 64 actual women (**Figure 8.3A**). This adult face was judged as quite attractive, but its attractiveness increased as it was progressively morphed toward the standard childlike face (**Figure 8.3B–F**). In the example shown in the figure, viewers found that a 30% admixture of "babyfacedness" produced the most attractive face.

What is the explanation of this paradoxical finding? It seems that the main features of children's faces that enhance the attractiveness of adult women's faces are

(A)　　　　(B)　　　　(C)　　　　(D)　　　　(E)　　　　(F)

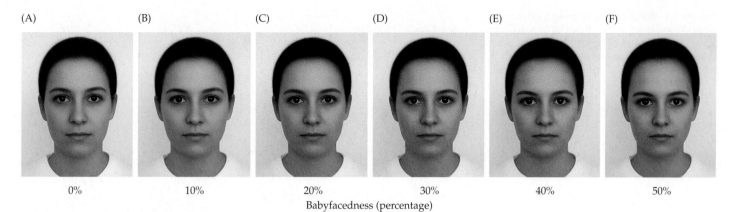

0%　　　10%　　　20%　　　30%　　　40%　　　50%

Babyfacedness (percentage)

Figure 8.3 Babyfacedness increases attractiveness. A face generated by computer-averaging the faces of 64 adult women (A) and the same face morphed with increasing percentages of babyfacedness, as indicated below each image (B to F). (G) The bar graph shows the percentage of viewers who rated each image as the most attractive of the six. (Photos courtesy of Martin Gruendl.)

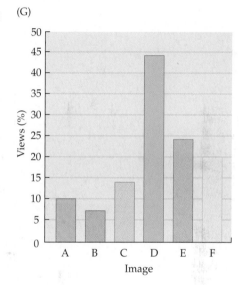

the low position of the facial features on the head, a prominent forehead, large eyes, and a small nose. These features help to elicit the positive, protective feelings that adults commonly experience when they view young children. Thus adult women who happen to have somewhat "babyfaced" features—supermodel Kate Moss is an example, according to the German researchers—may co-opt those positive feelings, in addition to whatever attractiveness they may have by virtue of "adult" characteristics (Zebrowitz, 1997).

The Attractiveness of Bodies May Be Related to Reproductive Success

Men's and women's bodies are more distinct than are men's and women's faces. Like facial attractiveness, bodily attractiveness is often a matter of being near one or the other extreme of the masculine–feminine continuum. Thus body parts that differ relatively little between the sexes, such as the hands and feet, also contribute relatively little to judgments of attractiveness. In general, then, it is likely that the attractiveness of a body signals information about its sexual differentiation under the influence of sex hormones, and hence about its fertility, strength, health, and other traits important for reproduction.

One simple variable, the **waist-to-hip ratio**, has an important influence on attractiveness (Singh, 1994a,b, 1995). After puberty, women store much of their fat in the area of the hips, buttocks, and thighs. Men tend to accumulate their fat higher in the body, at the waist and above. For this reason, and also on account of skeletal differences between the sexes, the ratio of the body circumference at the waist to the body circumference at the hip is lower for women than for men, and this holds across a wide range of body sizes, from leanness to obesity (**Figure 8.4**).

Women judge men to be most attractive if they have a waist-to-hip ratio of 0.9, while men judge women to be most attractive if they have a waist-to-hip ratio of 0.7–0.8. These preferences hold up across diverse cultures. Both men and women perceive variations in waist-to-hip ratio as providing information about a person's health. There is some evidence that this perception is well grounded: Men and women with ratios far from the "optimum" for their sex are at increased risk for a variety of diseases.

Although the waist-to-hip ratio may be a universal indicator of attractiveness, absolute body fatness is not. In contemporary U.S. culture, thin women are generally considered more attractive than those who are of average weight or obese, at least to judge by the appearance of successful female models and film stars. In

waist-to-hip ratio The ratio of the width of the body at the waist to the width at the hip.

Figure 8.4 Waist-to-hip ratio and attractiveness Women are most attracted to men with a waist-to-hip ratio of 0.9 (shaded row); this is true whether men are underweight (row I), normal weight (row II), or overweight (row III). Men are most attracted to women with a waist-to-hip ratio of 0.7–0.8.

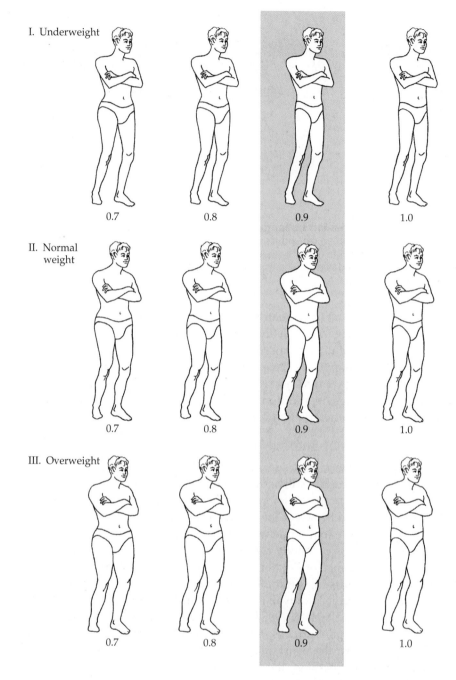

I. Underweight

0.7   0.8   0.9   1.0

II. Normal weight

0.7   0.8   0.9   1.0

III. Overweight

0.7   0.8   0.9   1.0

some non-Western cultures where food is scarce, obese women may be strongly preferred, as we discussed in Chapter 1 (see Box 1.2). The same was true in some periods of Western history (**Figure 8.5**). In fact, simply causing a man to feel hungry makes him rate heavier women more attractive (Nelson & Morrison, 2005; Swami & Tovee, 2006). This is an example of how situational factors can influence judgments of attractiveness.

Female breasts are obviously sexually attractive to many men, but the issue of breast *size* is less clear. Psychological research has produced equivocal findings. One study found that increasing breast size had *no* effect on the perceived attractiveness of women to men (Horvath, 1981). A more recent study found that men did prefer breasts of larger-than-average size, but not nearly as large as women *thought* men liked (Thompson & Tantleff, 1992).

In terms of men's bodies, the two studies mentioned above found that the width of the shoulders and the size of the pectoral muscles ("pecs") influenced women's ratings of male attractiveness, presumably by increasing their perceived strength (**Figure 8.6A**). Men have used clothing and adornment to increase their apparent shoulder width since time immemorial. Interestingly, women with a need to assert strength (such as historical female monarchs and contemporary women in the male-dominated business world) have followed the same strategy (**Figure 8.6B**).

As with women's breasts, there is a disconnect between reality and perceptions when it comes to male muscularity (Frederick et al., 2005; Frederick & Haselton, 2007). Women do like muscularity in men, but the optimal degree of muscularity is only moderate. Men tend to think that extreme muscularity is the most attractive to women, but it isn't. For that reason men's magazines tend to show images of body-builder types, whereas women's magazines are more likely to show men with "swimmers' bodies."

Are these various cues to attractiveness genetically hardwired into our brains, or are they a matter of learning and culture? One way this question has been addressed is by making comparisons across cultures (Bernstein et al., 1982). In the case of female breasts, some human cultures place little emphasis on them as sexually attractive features and do not require women to cover them. This is the case in the traditional culture of Mali (West Africa), for example (Dettwyler, 1994). In non-Western cultures that do consider the breasts sexually attractive, the preferred appearance may range from small and upright to long and pendulous (Ford & Beach, 1951). These variations suggest that cultural factors are important influences on at least this one aspect of beauty.

People generally find faces of individuals from their own ethnic group more attractive than faces from other groups—a finding that almost certainly reflects an influence of culture. However, individuals in different cultures rely on similar cues to attractiveness. Furthermore, people make consistent judgments of faces from other cultures. The way that Caucasians rank the attractiveness of Japanese faces, for example, is similar to the way that Japanese rank those same faces (Perrett et al., 1994). In other words, the judgment of beauty

Figure 8.5 Ample-bodied women were admired in seventeenth-century Europe, as illustrated in this painting, *The Judgement of Paris*, by Peter Paul Rubens.

(A) (B)

Figure 8.6 Shouldering the male role (A) Broad, muscular shoulders are generally considered attractive in men. (B) Women who wish to project authority in a male-dominated field may use shoulder pads to give a similar appearance.

depends on a blend of cultural and universal factors. Mass communications are globalizing the cultural standards of beauty, sometimes making them seem universal (**Box 8.2**).

If there is any universality to attractiveness, we may wonder whether very young children are sensitive to it. It seems that they are. When newborn infants are presented with pairs of images of faces, one of which has been rated by adults as more attractive than the other, the infants spend more time looking at the more attractive face (Slater et al., 1998).

From the general appearance of a person's face and body, we can assess their age, which is an important criterion for attractiveness in women, at least according to men. When judging women solely by physical appearance, men find women decreasingly attractive as women progress from the late teen years onward (Mathes et al., 1985). A preference for women of youthful appearance is found in men of all ages, but is most marked for younger men. Women's judgments of men's physical attractiveness do not vary nearly so much with the men's age, but women generally prefer men who are somewhat older than themselves.

The cosmetic enhancements that people use to increase their own attractiveness often involve the exaggeration of sexually differentiated traits. Breast augmentation is a well-known example in Western society. Lips, which are typically fuller in women than in men, are also augmented by women in some non-Western societies, sometimes to a remarkable degree (**Figure 8.7**).

It's worth stressing that the process of judging visual attractiveness is a largely *unconscious* process. When men are asked to choose the more attractive of two women's faces, for example, and then asked why they found that face more attractive, they will give detailed, persuasive reasons for their choice, as if they had carefully thought the matter through before choosing. But if they are deceived into thinking that the face they *rejected* was the one they chose, they usually fail to notice the deception and give equally detailed and persuasive reasons why *that* face was the more attractive one (Johansson, 2005). This phenomenon has been called "choice-blindness." It's as if consciousness simply provides a plausible explanation for choices that are really made at a much deeper level of the mind.

Attractiveness Involves Senses Besides Vision

Although we tend to rely on our eyes in assessing the physical attractiveness of potential partners, other senses also play a role. If that were not true, blind people could not experience sexual attraction, but they do. Here's how one blind person expressed it on an online bulletin board: "If anything I think being blind has made me kinkier and more intense as you touch a lot more. Being blind, I would have to say sex is better and deeper, feeling your way around a body you get to know everywhere."

Besides touch, hearing and olfaction may also be important. Men's voices are generally deeper-pitched than those of women, reflecting the sexual differentiation of the larynx at puberty. Women find men with deep voices more attractive than those with higher-pitched voices, and in hunter-gatherer societies fertile women bestow their favors more readily on deep-voiced men (Apicella et al., 2007). Men, on the other hand, prefer women's voices that are higher-pitched than average (Feinberg et al., 2008). These are further examples of sexually differentiated traits being particularly important criteria for physical attractiveness.

Everyone knows that body odor can have a strong influence on a person's attractiveness. Some researchers, however, have gone further,

Figure 8.7 Improving on nature A stretched lower lip, produced by insertion of progressively larger plugs or plates, is considered attractive in parts of Chad and Ethiopia. This woman is Ethiopian.

Cultural Diversity

BOX 8.2 Beauty and Culture

Among *People* magazine's 100 Most Beautiful People of 2008 were actors Angelina Jolie (appearing on the list for the sixth time) and Brad Pitt (making his eighth appearance) (Figure A). The fact that certain individuals, such as Jolie and Pitt, have such a lock on the most-beautiful lists supports the idea that there is something universal about standards of beauty. Scientists have made some progress in discovering what these standards are, as discussed in the text of this chapter.

At the same time, the worldwide idolization of certain Hollywood stars also illustrates a very different idea, which is that notions of beauty diffuse around the world, changing people's "local" ideals of beauty as they spread. This phenomenon would have been impossible before the Industrial Revolution, when most people lived in villages, rarely traveled, and had no access to images of people they hadn't met. Now, it seems, it is unavoidable.

Within the United States, there has been much discussion of how the dominant white culture has caused some nonwhites to change their appearance in a "white" direction—as exemplified by the popularity of hair-relaxation among many African-American women. But beyond our borders, the diffusion of Western standards of beauty has had more dramatic effects. Throughout much of Asia, many or most of the advertising models featured in women's

magazines are Western (Frith et al., 2004). This kind of sustained attention to Western culture has made Caucasian traits more beautiful than Asian ones in the minds of many Asians. In South Korea, for example, there are more plastic

(A) Angelina Jolie and Brad Pitt   (B) Rihanna   (C) Jason Castro

surgeons per capita than anywhere else on Earth (Donohoe, 2006), and many of these surgeons are kept busy giving Koreans more Western-looking eyes (Yoo, 2008). In Fiji, fat used to be beautiful, but the introduction of television in the early 1990s, with an emphasis on American programs such as *Melrose Place* and *Beverly Hills 90210*, led to obsessive dieting and an epidemic of eating disorders among young people (Becker, 2004). In India, a country

that has been exposed to a dominant white culture for centuries, skin-lightening products are a $200 million annual market (Rashid, 2006).

Yet today's ideals of beauty will eventually be discarded on the trash heap of cultural history. Even now, Brangelina's throne is threatened by younger, sometimes nonwhite icons such as 20-year old Barbadian singer Rihanna (Figure B), who made *People's* list for the first time in 2007. And the dreadlocks sported by 2008 *American Idol* finalist Jason Castro (Figure C) illustrate the phenomenon whereby the beauty standards of overseas cultures (Black Jamaican in this case) infiltrate Hollywood's own domain.

claiming that specific sex pheromones in men and women influence sexual arousal through unconscious olfactory mechanisms. This topic is highly controversial and is not well understood at this time, but we'll mention just one intriguing experiment. Randy Thornhill and Steven Gangestad had women sniff T-shirts previously worn by men they hadn't seen. Those women who were in the fertile phase of their menstrual cycles rated as most attractive the shirts worn by men with physically symmetrical bodies—even though the women were unable to assess the men's bodily symmetry directly (Thornhill & Gangestad, 1999b). As mentioned earlier, symmetry is considered attractive and is thought to be a cue to good genes. Thus it appears that some aspect of men's body odor is correlated with physical symmetry and likewise offers a cue to their reproductive fitness.

Besides the issue of pheromones, there have been claims that people use olfaction to avoid inbreeding: more specifically, that they prefer the body odor of persons who are genetically different from themselves in a class of genes called the major histocompatibility complex, or MHC (Wedekind & Furi, 1997). Rodents are known to use this kind of olfactory mechanism to avoid inbreeding, but the situation in humans is less clear. For one thing, women who are asked to rate the visual attractiveness of male faces tend to prefer men who are *similar* to themselves in their MHC genes, rather than different (Roberts et al., 2005). More research is needed to clarify this issue.

Behavior Influences Sexual Attractiveness

All this talk of physical beauty can have a downside because it can provoke anxiety among people who think that their faces or bodies fall short of the standards necessary to attract a desirable partner. Yet this kind of anxiety is seldom justified. For one thing, people tend to underestimate their own physical attractiveness. For another, they can improve their attractiveness by means of all the technologies—from cosmetics to plastic surgery—that human ingenuity has devised. And most important, they can influence their attractiveness through their behavior.

In fact, we may speak of a "behavioral beauty" that can be at least partially independent of physical beauty. Behavior and personality tend to influence attractiveness more slowly than appearance does, because they are not so immediately apparent. But even in a still photograph, behavior matters: Smiling faces are judged to be more attractive than those with neutral expressions, at least when the faces are looking directly at the observer (Jones et al., 2006).

Presumably, sexual attractiveness influences the desirability of partners for casual encounters or dating relationships more than it does for longer-term, live-in relationships such as marriage, because long-term relationships involve so much more than sex. To get some insight into the spectrum of traits that influence sexual attractiveness, therefore, we do best to look at studies that have questioned men and women about the traits they would value in a casual or short-term sex partner. Most such studies report that physical appearance is the most important criterion used by both men and women in choosing casual sex partners (Regan & Berscheid, 1997), but many personality traits are also highly rated, including trustworthiness, warmth, and a sense of humor (Regan et al., 2000). These are traits that are likely to be important in any relationship. It may be that, even when people are "hooking up," they are still unconsciously evaluating the person they are hooking up with as a potential long-term partner (Sprecher & Regan, 2002). In any event, general "likability" traits seem to intensify sexual attraction.

To fully understand behavioral beauty it is necessary to go beyond surveys and use tests that are closer to real-life situations. Both men and women say that they value a sense of humor in their sex partners, for example, but what do they actually mean by that? To find out, one group of psychologists presented subjects with photos of people along with humorous or nonhumorous statements that they had supposedly written. For women subjects, the humorous statements increased the attractiveness of the people in the photos, as expected. For men, however, the humor had no such effect (Bressler & Balshine, 2006).

Why then do men say that they value a sense of humor in their partners? A follow-up study revealed the reason (Bressler et al., 2006). Male subjects find their partners sexually attractive when they respond with laughter to the *subjects'* jokes, not when they make their own jokes. Subjects label their partners' appreciation of

---

FAQ **I'm stepping out to snare a man. Any tips from psychology?**

Wear red. This boosts a woman's attractiveness by 1.25 points on a 7-point scale, compared with any other color of clothing (Elliott and Niesta, 2008.)

their wit a "sense of humor." In a potentially sexual situation, laughter often signals sexual receptivity; thus, when men say they find a "sense of humor" attractive they might simply mean that they are glad when a sexual situation shows signs of moving toward actual sex.

In one study, men and women were asked to list desirable characteristics in romantic partners and then were invited to a "speed-dating" event (an event in which people meet a large number of potential partners in a sequence of brief one-on-one conversations). The people whom the subjects chose for future dating were not those whose characteristics matched the subjects' previously stated preferences (Eastwick & Finkel, 2008). For example, a woman who rated high earnings as the most important criterion for selecting a romantic partner actually chose the lowest-earning of the men she talked with at the event. Thus people might not have a clear idea of what they are looking for in a sex partner until they actually meet someone who appeals to them—another example of the limited role of conscious processes in sexual attraction.

It's been reported over and over again that men are more interested than women in the physical attractiveness of their prospective sex partners, whereas women are more interested than men in their partners' wealth or social status (Buss, 1989; Regan et al., 2000). But what happens when women themselves acquire wealth or power? According to several studies, such women have a preference for even wealthier or higher-status partners, as if the important criterion is that their partners be wealthier or of higher status than themselves (Buss, 1995). To the extent that this is the case, affluent women risk pricing themselves out of the market. Some studies report different results, however: namely, that women who have many resources tend to focus more on their partners' physical attractiveness and less on their pocketbooks (Moore et al., 2006). If this latter idea is correct, it could explain why, in this age of financial independence for women, young men make more effort to look good than their fathers did.

The importance of behavioral factors in sexual attraction comes to the fore when people are actually negotiating sexual interactions—when they are flirting, in other words. We will take up this topic in the context of sexual relationships (see Chapter 10).

At speed dating events, such as this church-sponsored event in England, people's choices may not be based on conscious criteria.

Familiarity Both Increases and Decreases Attraction

How attractive we find people (and things in general) is strongly influenced by our prior experience, but this influence can work in either direction, making people and things more attractive or less attractive. In general, mere exposure to any stimulus—whether it be the music of a particular composer or a particular kind of food—makes us like that stimulus better when we encounter it again, even if we don't remember having experienced it before. The same is true of faces: The mere fact of having seen a face before makes us judge it as more attractive than if we are seeing it for the first time (Peskin & Newell, 2004).

One face we see a lot of is our own, so are we especially attracted to our own face or to faces like our own? That's a tricky question to answer. For one thing, most of us are heterosexual, so our faces are the wrong sex—for *sexual* attraction, at least. Also, recognizing one's own face carries a lot of cognitive baggage—thoughts that could interfere with judgments of attractiveness. A Scottish research group got around these problems in an ingenious way: They took photographs of their subjects, then changed their apparent sex by computer-morphing techniques (Penton-Voak & Perrett, 2000a). The subjects did not recognize themselves in their morphed "twins"; nevertheless, they found their "twins" more attractive than the "twins" of other subjects. This could be taken as support for the idea that self-similarity contributes to attractiveness.

Figure 8.8 Familiarity increases liking. The subject likes a mirror-reversed image of herself better than a real image—because she is more familiar with herself as seen in a mirror. The subject's friend prefers the real image—because she is more familiar with a direct view of the subject.

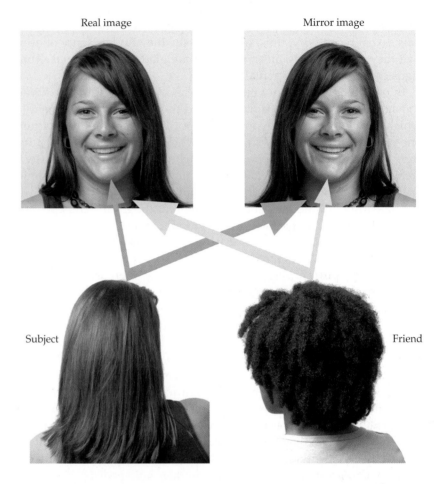

Real image   Mirror image

Subject   Friend

A related study was conducted by psychologists at the University of Wisconsin (Mita et al., 1977) (**Figure 8.8**). The researchers showed subjects photographs of themselves as well as the same photographs after left-right reversal. The subjects liked the mirror-reversed photos better than the unaltered ones. Friends of the subjects, however, liked the unaltered photos of the subjects better. The researchers reasoned that subjects were used to seeing themselves in mirrors, whereas their friends were used to seeing them directly; in both cases, long exposure to the image had increased its attractiveness.

We are in fact attracted to people who resemble ourselves in a variety of traits—attitudes, age, race, educational level, social status, and so on (McPherson et al., 2001). This tendency is called **homophily**. However, most studies of homophily have been done on nonsexual forms of attraction, such as childhood friendship or social networks. With regard to sexual attraction, homophily is usually assessed by comparing the characteristics of couples who are already in sexual partnerships, such as married couples. Such couples certainly do resemble each other in many traits (Price & Vandenberg, 1980).

Again, however, this doesn't really show that people are sexually *attracted* to people like themselves. For one thing, people are not usually able to partner with the person they find most attractive (Berscheid et al., 1971). They have to be satisfied with a relationship they feel is "fair" (Hatfield, 1978; Lawrence & Byers, 1995), and this usually means a relationship between rather similar people. In addition, sexual partnerships are usually established within a socially circumscribed environment (Laumann et al., 2004). People commonly meet their partner in their neighborhood, at school, or at work. In some cultures, the choice of partner may be strongly constrained by social customs. (For example, marriages may be

homophily The tendency to be attracted to people who resemble oneself.

"arranged," or interracial dating may be stigmatized.) All of these factors are likely to cause sexual partners to resemble each other more than would be expected on a chance basis, even if people have little intrinsic preference for similar sex partners.

There are some circumstances in which familiarity can *reduce* attractiveness. For example, being close to another child (such as a sibling) during early childhood makes it unlikely that one will find that person sexually attractive in adult life. This seems to be an evolved mechanism whose adaptive value is that it reduces the likelihood of incestuous matings (Bevc & Silverman, 2000). Olfaction may be involved in this process, because opposite-sex siblings develop an aversion to the scent of each other's bodies (Weisfeld et al., 2003).

Sexual familiarity may also reduce attractiveness. In animals, it's well known that males who have just mated will mate again more promptly if presented with a novel female. This is called the **Coolidge effect.***

There has never been a full-scale test of the Coolidge effect in humans, but here's something close: Researchers at the University of North Dakota (Plaud et al., 1997) recruited male psychology students for a study that involved listening to erotic tapes narrated by a female student. (As if further incentive were needed, the students received $20 and research credit.) The students' sexual arousal—monitored by strain gauges placed around their penises—declined if the same tapes were repeated (**habituation**) but remained high if new tapes were played. The habituation effect lasted for several weeks at least.

Habituation also affects real sexual relationships: Both men and women derive less and less sexual satisfaction from their steady relationships as the duration of the relationship increases, and this effect is relationship-specific; that is, it is not accounted for simply by the aging process (Klusmann, 2002). It's likely, however, that couples can counteract this habituation to some extent by introducing forms of novelty other than novel partners. These could include novel sex positions, novel practices such as bondage and dominance, sex in novel locations, and so on. In addition, other forms of satisfaction, such as emotional satisfaction, may counterbalance sexual habituation.

Although we don't discuss falling in love until Chapter 10, we should mention the obvious, which is that falling in love vastly increases the physical and behavioral attractiveness of the beloved. Physical flaws and distracting tics may suddenly seem like so many facets of perfection—for as long as love lasts, at least. In this situation, beauty may truly lie in the eye of the beholder.

Perceived Attractiveness Varies around the Menstrual Cycle

Another way in which attractiveness is affected by factors intrinsic to the viewer has to do with the menstrual cycle. Two research groups have found that women prefer men with more masculine faces near the time of ovulation, when they are most likely to conceive, and prefer less masculine faces at other times (Penton-Voak & Perrett, 2000b; Johnston et al., 2001). Some popular accounts have presented this as a wild swing in women's preferences, from macho hunks to nurturing sweeties and back, but the real shift is quite subtle—much less than a single step in the 7-step series of images shown in Figure 8.2.

Coolidge effect The revival of sexual arousal caused by the presence of a novel partner.

habituation A psychological or physiological process that reduces a person's response to a stimulus or drug after repeated or prolonged exposure.

---

*This calls for a brief digression to explain how the phenomenon of arousal by a novel sex partner came to be associated with the name of Calvin Coolidge—yes, the 29th president of the United States. According to legend, the President and Mrs. Coolidge were once touring a farm. Soon after their arrival they were taken off on separate tours. When Mrs. Coolidge passed the chicken pens she paused to ask the man in charge if the rooster copulated more than once each day. "Dozens of times," was the response. "Please tell that to the President," Mrs. Coolidge requested. When the President passed the pens and was told about the roosters, he asked, "Same hen each time?" "Oh no, a different hen each time." "Please tell that to Mrs. Coolidge," said the President.

These changes in women's perception of male attractiveness around the menstrual cycle have a tempting explanation in terms of evolutionary psychology: Women may be primed to look for "good genes" when good genes are most useful—during their fertile period. During the rest of their cycle they may be drawn to other males, such as their regular partner (who, by the law of supply and demand, is not likely to be the most genetically favored male out there).

Does this mean that partnered women are more likely to engage in sex outside the partnership during the fertile days of their cycle? It seems that they are (Gangestad & Thornhill, 1998). We are not suggesting that partnered women consciously set out to have babies by that "tall, dark stranger." Indeed, a tall, dark baby might be hard to explain to the rest of the family. To the extent that women engage in extra-pair sex, they often take care *not* to get pregnant. But their evolutionary history, mediated by the ebb and flow of sex hormones around the menstrual cycle, does seem to influence their sexual desires.

Women's sexual attractiveness to men also varies around the menstrual cycle. University of New Mexico psychologists demonstrated this by recording the tips received by female lap-dancers in "gentlemen's clubs" (Miller et al., 2007) (**Figure 8.9**). Tips were much higher near the time of ovulation than at any other time in the women's cycles. The researchers did not identify what exactly was more attractive about the women near the time of ovulation, but other studies have reported a variety of subtle changes in women's appearance, including an increased facial attractiveness at that time (Roberts et al., 2004). Near ovulation, women's behavior also subtly changes to make them more attractive: They pay more attention to grooming, make-up, ornamentation, and clothes (Haselton et al., 2007).

Some People Do Not Experience Sexual Attraction

All this talk of sexual attraction probably resonates with experiences you have had in your own life. But what do you make of these comments?

> I've never in my life had a dream or a sexual fantasy about being with another woman. So I can pretty much say that I have no lesbian sort of tendencies whatsoever. But I've never had a dream or a sexual fantasy about being with a man either—that I can ever, ever remember.

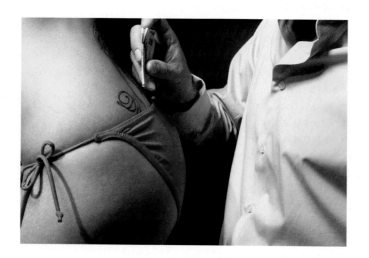

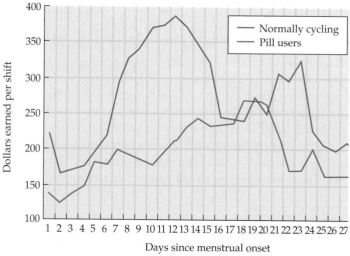

Figure 8.9 Lap dancers' earnings around the menstrual cycle. In normally cycling women, there is a broad peak in earnings between about days 9 to 14 after the onset of menstruation. This peak corresponds approximately to the fertile window leading up to ovulation. In women on contraceptive pills, which often prevent ovulation, this peak is absent (Miller et al., 2007).

I didn't find the act something I enjoyed. I guess I thought, "What's the big whoop? Why are they so interested in this thing?" I don't get anything out of it.

(Prause & Graham, 2007).

asexual Describes a person who never experiences sexual attraction.

fantasy An imagined experience, sexual or otherwise.

For reasons unknown, a small number of people experience no (or very little) sexual attraction over their entire lifetime. These **asexual** people may still experience romantic attraction in the sense of desiring psychological intimacy with a specific partner, but they do not desire to express that intimacy in physical sex. Sometimes they derive no pleasure from masturbation either.

Asexuality is different from a conscious decision not to engage in sexual relationships (sexual abstinence). Nor does it stem from problems in sexual performance such as erectile dysfunction, from conditions that impair general social interactions such as autism, from a morbid fear of sex, or from repressed homosexuality. Because cultural forces (including this book) emphasize the central place of sexuality in human life, asexual individuals may be made to feel impaired, but in reality they function well in society.

According to one study—the source for the two quotations above—self-identified asexual men and women say that their lack of sexual motivation has both positive and negative effects on their lives. On the plus side, they have more free time and are spared the complications of negotiating sexual relationships, the health hazards of sex, and unwanted pregnancies. On the negative side, they may worry about what is wrong with them, and they may have difficulty maintaining close relationships while rebuffing sexual advances. In fact, asexual people often do enter into sexual relationships, simply for the purpose of maintaining the relationship.

Another study found that about 1% of the population is asexual (Bogaert, 2004). According to this study, asexual people are more likely than others to be female, short, unhealthy, uneducated, and of low socioeconomic status. But they can also be male, tall, well-educated, healthy, and good-looking. An example is David Jay, the 25-year-old St. Louis resident who founded the Asexual Visibility and Education Network (see Web Resources at the end of this chapter). "Asexuality is not an illness," says Jay. "People are using it as their sexual orientation." His Web site sells T-shirts proclaiming "Asexuality—It's not just for amoebas any more" (Westphal, 2004).

This mention of "sexual orientation" reminds us that a person's sexual orientation—defined as their predisposition to experience sexual attraction to one sex or the other, or to both—is the most dramatic example of an internal trait influencing sexual attraction. Because of its personal and social significance, however, we dedicate an entire chapter to it (see Chapter 14).

Sexual Arousal Has Multiple Roots

Sexual arousal is an acute psychological state of excitement marked by sexual feelings, attractions, or desires. In addition, it is a physiological state marked by changes in the genitalia. Psychological and physiological arousal usually go together, but not always. Sexual arousal may be triggered by external events, such as the appearance of a sexually attractive person or by some particular aspect of that person, such as their sexually suggestive behavior or their nudity. However, arousal may come entirely from within, apparently triggered by nothing (spontaneous sexual arousal).

Fantasy Is a Common Mode of Sexual Arousal

Sexual **fantasy**—imagined sexual experiences during waking hours—is a route by which internal mental processes promote sexual arousal. The great majority of men and women engage in sexual fantasy. It might occur when no actual sexual behavior is possible—mentally undressing classmates during a boring lecture would fall into this category. Or it might accompany masturbation or sex with a partner. In either of these cases, it might add a great deal of arousal and might even be necessary to reach orgasm.

Men engage in sexual fantasy quite a bit more than women, both in the regular course of the day and during masturbation or sex with a partner (Leitenberg & Henning, 1995). In one study, heterosexual male and female college students were asked to keep written records of all their sexual fantasies as they had them. The men averaged 7.2 fantasies per day, as compared with 4.5 for the women (Jones & Barlow, 1990). In another study, over 4000 men and women were asked whether they had thought about sex within the previous 5 minutes. Among 14- to 25-year-olds, the sex difference was not great: 52% of the men and 39% of the women said "yes." Among 26- to 55-year-olds, the total amount of sexual thought decreased, but men continued to fantasize more than women: 26% of the men and only 14% of the women said "yes" (Cameron & Biber, 1973).

The content of sexual fantasies varies a great deal, but the common items are fairly similar to the kinds of behaviors people actually engage in. According to one study of heterosexual college students (Hsu et al., 1994), over half of both males and females reported that they had recently fantasized the following activities: touching and being touched sensually, oral–genital sex, naked caressing, watching a partner undress, seducing a partner, having intercourse in unusual positions, walking hand in hand, being seduced, and having sex in an unusual location.

There are some gender differences in the content of fantasies (**Figure 8.10**). In the study just described, men were much more likely than women to fantasize manually stimulating their partner's genitals, having more than one partner simultaneously, having sex with a virgin, watching a partner undress, making love with the possibility of being discovered by a third party, having sex with a famous person, engaging in anal sex, and forcing a partner to submit. The only behavior that women fantasized significantly more often than men was getting married. In general, the men were more adventurous in their fantasies: Women nearly always fantasized about sexual behaviors that they had at some time actually engaged in, while men frequently fantasized about sexual behaviors that they had never engaged in, such as whipping a partner or being whipped.

The fantasies of lesbians and gay men are similar to those of straight men and women, aside from the sex of their imagined partners (Price et al., 1985). Questions about fantasies are often used to assess sexual orientation, under the assumption that the sex of a person's fantasy partners should give a more truthful indication of what they find arousing than asking them directly about their attraction to men and to women. This assumption, however, is debatable. In the Hsu et al. (1994) study, for example, 19% of the men and 33% of the women (all of whom identified as heterosexual) reported having had at least one recent fantasy of engaging in sex with a same-sex partner. Does that mean all these people were actually sexually attracted to same-sex partners in real life? Not if we are to go by their self-identification

In your fantasies you can have sexual experiences that might not be advisable in real life.

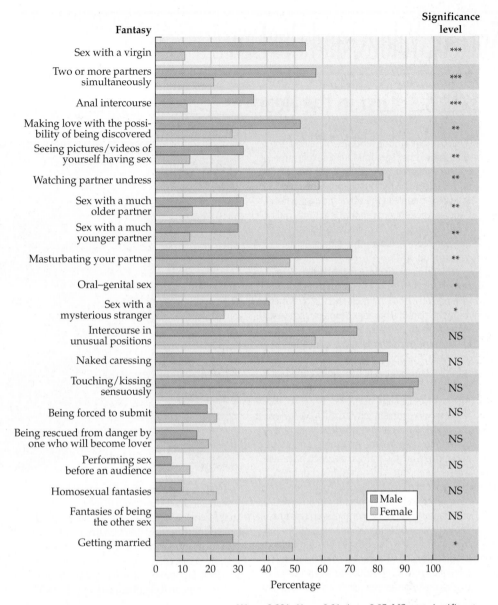

Figure 8.10 Selected recent sexual fantasies reported by 160 heterosexual college students, arranged in approximate order from the most male-biased to the most female-biased. (Data from Hsu et al., 1994.)

*** $p < 0.001$; ** $p < 0.01$; * $p < 0.05$; NS: not significant.

as heterosexual, which by definition means they are attracted only to the other sex. The Hsu finding illustrates the limitations of a simple unidimensional scale of sexual orientation.

To some extent, the sexual fantasies of men and women differ in a way that is consistent with stereotypes about male and female sexuality: Men are more likely to focus almost exclusively on the visualization of explicit sexual behavior, and their fantasies often involve taking a dominant role in sex acts. Women's fantasies, however, tend to include more romance, affection, and indications of committed relationships (such as the marriage fantasy mentioned above) and may involve taking a more passive role in sex acts (Ellis & Symons, 1990; Leitenberg & Henning, 1995).

People sometimes feel guilty about their sexual fantasies, especially if the fantasies involve behaviors in which they wouldn't want to engage in real life. Yet people who can enjoy a range of sexual fantasies without experiencing guilt seem to have a generally more satisfying sex life (**Box 8.3**).

Society, Values, and the Law

BOX 8.3 Lust in the Heart

During the 1976 presidential election campaign, Jimmy Carter held an 18–20-point lead in the polls over incumbent Gerald Ford until he gave an ill-advised interview to *Playboy* magazine. During a portion of the interview that Carter thought was not being recorded, the conversation turned to the moral status of adultery. Carter, a Baptist minister, admitted that he had "lusted in his heart" for many women. (Later, he explained that he was referring to the period before his marriage.) When it appeared in *Playboy,* Carter's admission triggered a major drop in his popularity, and he briefly trailed Ford before recovering to win the election.

Considering that most people have experienced similar fantasies, Carter's admission hardly seems like a cause for deep moral concern. Yet the Christian religion—which condemns adultery—has traditionally held that imagining a sinful deed such as adultery is itself sinful. As Jimmy Carter reminded *Playboy*, "Christ said, 'I tell you that anyone who looks on a woman with lust has in his heart already committed adultery.'" Partly because of this teaching, many people feel guilty about having sexual fantasies that would violate their own moral code if acted out in real life.

Scientific research cannot by itself decide moral questions, but it can sometimes provide information that is useful in making moral judgments. Suzana Cado and Harold Leitenberg (Cado & Leitenberg, 1990) studied two groups of people who experienced sexual fantasies

(which might include fantasies of having sex with some other person) during sexual intercourse. One group of subjects consisted of men and women who felt guilty about their fantasies; the people in the other group did not. Cado and Leitenberg reported that the "guilty" men and women had more sexual dissatisfaction and more sexual dysfunction than the other group.

This finding could mean that guilt about sexual fantasies causes sexual dysfunction. Alternatively, both the guilt and the dysfunction might be part of a broader problem with sexual expression, caused perhaps by attitudes learned in the home or during religious education. In any event, therapists generally attempt to reassure clients about the harmlessness, and possible benefits, of sexual fantasies—even those that involve "deviant" acts.

More of a problem may arise if a person has a strong desire to actually engage in potentially harmful sexual behavior. An example might be a pedophile who has a strong desire to have sex with children, but is trying not to act on that desire out of moral concern or fear of punishment. Very likely, such a person would experience fantasies of sexual contact with children. Should a therapist encourage him to suppress these fantasies or change their content (thus keeping the potential crimes as far from his mind as possible), or should he be encouraged to give his fantasies free rein (thus allowing him

to vent his desires in a harmless way)? Most researchers have concluded that it is beneficial to steer the pedophile's fantasies away from children (Johnston et al., 1992), on the assumption that such fantasies are a link in the chain that leads to actual child molestation (McKibben et al., 1994). Still, more research is needed to test this assumption (Leitenberg & Henning, 1995).

Many women have fantasies in which they are sexually coerced, raped, or otherwise subjected to force by a partner (Knafo & Jaffe, 1984). Is it healthy or unhealthy for women to have such fantasies? In one study (Strassberg & Lockerd, 1998), women who reported engaging in force fantasies (more than half the total number of women in the sample) were, if anything, better adjusted sexually than those who did not—they suffered from less guilt about sex, for example. They also engaged in more sexual fantasies generally than other women. They did not differ from other women in terms of their actual experience of sexual coercion or molestation. Does a woman who fantasizes about rape want to be raped in real life? Of course not: The woman having the fantasy is "running the show" and can call it off whenever she wishes, unlike the situation of an actual sexual assault.

Arousal Occurs in Response to a Partner

Being with an actual or potential sex partner in real life is a potent trigger to arousal, especially if that person is judged sexually attractive. In such a situation, both

Men

Women

Figure 8.11 Men look at crotches; women don't. These images were obtained by tracking the gaze of a large number of men and women while they viewed a photograph of baseball Hall of Famer George Brett. (Image courtesy of Kara Pernice, from Nielsen & Pernice, 2008.)

men and women are aroused by looking at the partner's face, but men also find looking at their partner's genital area arousing, as we mentioned in our discussion of nudity in Chapter 4. Men are more likely than women to report that they are highly aroused by watching their partner undress (Laumann et al., 1994). Even in totally nonsexual situations, in fact, men tend to look at people's crotches, but women don't (**Figure 8.11**).

Arousal increases as flirting or other forms of sexual negotiation proceed (see Chapter 10). It increases even further as actual sexual contact is initiated, because sensory signals from the genitals and other body regions feed into the brain circuits that mediate arousal.

In order to identify the brain regions that are involved in sexual arousal, researchers have shown erotic film clips to subjects who are undergoing functional brain imaging (**Figure 8.12**). Among the brain regions that light up under these conditions is a region of the cerebral cortex named the anterior cingulate cortex. This region also lights up when people who are in love simply view a photo of their beloved (Bartels & Zeki, 2004) and when people are given euphoria-inducing drugs such as cocaine. Thus it seems to be involved in the processing of "happy" states.

For reasons that are not well understood, sexual arousal appears to operate in a more specific manner in men than in women. Men are aroused (psychologically and genitally) by erotic images that are appropriate to their sexual orientation; that is, straight men are aroused by images of women, and gay men are aroused by images of men. Women, on the other hand, are aroused by erotic images of both women and men, regardless of whether they identify as straight, lesbian, or bisexual (Chivers et al., 2004; Suschinsky et al., 2008). And when men and women watch erotic heterosexual videos, men look mostly at the women, whereas women look about equally at the men and the women (Lykins et al, 2008). It may be that these differences reflect a greater fluidity of sexual orientation in women than in men—a topic we will discuss in Chapter 14. Alternatively, it may be that women are more interested in the totality of the sexual interaction and perhaps wish to know whether both partners are sexually aroused.

(A)

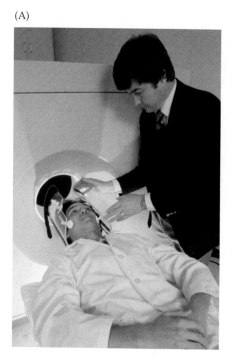

(B)

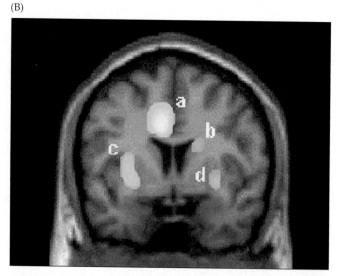

Figure 8.12 The brain and sexual arousal (A) Person undergoing a PET scan. The standing man is Michael Phelps, coinventor of the PET technology. (B) Brain activity specific to sexual arousal in men. This image shows the difference between scans during sexual arousal and scans in nonsexually aroused states. The anterior cingulate area of the left hemisphere (a) is one of the regions that is most active during sexual arousal. The other active regions visible in this slice are components of the basal ganglia. (B courtesy of Jérôme Redouté.)

Sexual Arousal Is Influenced by Other Forms of Arousal

misattribution of arousal The tendency of nonsexual arousal, such as fear, to facilitate sexual arousal.

A number of scientific studies suggest that emotional arousal of any kind—whether it consists of fear, anger, hilarity, or some other emotion—can promote sexual arousal. This phenomenon is called **misattribution of arousal**. In one well-known study by Donald Dutton and Arthur Aron (Dutton & Aron, 1974), a female interviewer approached men who were crossing one of two footbridges in British Columbia, Canada. One bridge was fear-inspiring: It was a rickety, narrow, 230-foot (70-m) -high footbridge that spanned a rock-strewn gorge. The other was a solid, wide bridge that crossed a small rivulet at a height of only 10 feet (3 m). The interviewer asked the men to write a story based on a picture they were shown. They were also offered the interviewer's phone number. The men who crossed the fear-inducing bridge included significantly more sexual content in their stories than did the men who crossed the safe bridge, and more of the former called the woman's phone number (50% versus 12.5%).

By itself, this experiment is inconclusive: It could simply be that the men who crossed the high bridge had more risk-taking or novelty-seeking personalities than those that crossed the low bridge, and these personality differences could have influenced the men's responses to the interviewer. But more recent studies have reported similar findings in better-controlled situations. In one study, for example, men and women entering or

Nonsexual arousal, such as that caused by riding a roller coaster, can facilitate subsequent sexual arousal.

exiting a roller-coaster ride were shown photos of a person of the other sex: They rated the photos more attractive on leaving the ride, when they had been brought into a heightened state of excitement by the just-completed ride (Meston & Frohlich, 2003).

This kind of misattribution of arousal occurs most readily when the original exciting event (the ride, in this case) has already terminated, rather than when it is still happening. That's probably because the cause of the arousal is less apparent to the person, so they are more likely to attribute it to some new stimulus, such as the photograph. On the other hand, arousal declines fairly quickly after most exciting events—say, in 10 minutes or so. Because of this rather brief interval, it's not clear to what extent misattribution of arousal affects people's decision-making in real-world sexual situations.

Hormones Influence Sexual Arousability

Do biological factors influence sexual arousal? The first thing one thinks of in this context is testosterone. A popular misconception is that this hormone influences sexual arousal—particularly in men—on a minute-by-minute or hour-by-hour basis. A man who is feeling "horny" (that is, who is experiencing an unfocused sense of sexual arousal and is motivated to find some way of satisfying it) might comment that he "can feel the testosterone flowing," or the like.

In reality, testosterone does not seem to have any short-term influence on the sexual feelings of either men or women. For example, a research group at Georgia State University (Dabbs & Mohammed, 1992) wondered whether heterosexual couples would be more likely to have sex on evenings when the testosterone level of one or both partners was high. They recruited a number of couples and had them take saliva samples early and late in the evening over many nights. Salivary testosterone levels (which correlate well with the level of free testosterone in the blood) were no higher early on the "sex" evenings than on the "no sex" evenings, in either the men or the women. Testosterone levels *were* higher *late* on the "sex" evenings—after sex had occurred—than late on the "no sex" evenings. This finding suggests that sexual activity triggers a rise in testosterone but that high testosterone does not trigger a desire for sexual activity.

There is evidence, however, that testosterone has a longer-term influence on our capacity to experience sexual arousal. The clearest connection between testosterone levels and sexual arousability is found in boys around the time of puberty. In one study of boys in grades 8, 9, and 10 of a public school system, those boys who were experiencing the rise in testosterone levels associated with puberty were much more likely to experience sexual feelings and engage in sexual behavior than boys of the same age whose testosterone levels had not yet risen (Udry et al., 1985). This finding is consistent with research in nonhuman animals, which suggests that testosterone activates brain circuits involved in male-typical sexual behavior. One might imagine an alternative interpretation: that the rise in testosterone at puberty stimulates only physical maturation, and that psychosexual development occurs as an indirect effect involving learning or social forces. The researchers noted, however, that the boys' sexual motivation was less closely related to their degree of physical maturation than it was to their testosterone levels. More recent longitudinal studies by the same research group have supported a role for testosterone in the onset of sexual feelings and behavior—in both boys and girls (Halpern et al., 1997, 1998).

An ideal experiment would be to vary testosterone levels in children artificially and then study the effects on their sexuality. Normally, conducting such an experiment would be unethical, but some boys with delayed puberty receive testosterone as part of their treatment (Finkelstein et al., 1998). A group of such

hypogonadal Producing insufficient levels of sex hormones.

classical (Pavlovian) conditioning A form of behavioral learning in which a novel stimulus is tied to a pre-existing reflex.

boys agreed to participate in a study in which their testosterone treatments were alternated with placebo treatments in a double-blind design (that is, neither the patients nor their doctors knew who was receiving the real hormone). The researchers then studied the boys' sexual ideation and behavior over a period of 21 months. The treated boys did think more about sex, and they engaged in more sexual touching and "necking." Still, the effects were not particularly strong, and the researchers concluded that social effects must also play an important role in determining when adolescent boys begin to engage in sexual behavior.

Testosterone levels do influence sexual arousability in adult men; in fact, men who have a profound reduction in testosterone levels for any reason (**hypogonadal** men) suffer a gradual decline in sexual desire and activity, and this decline can be reversed by testosterone replacement therapy (Wang et al., 2000). Most men seem to have levels of testosterone that are well above the "ceiling" for its effect on arousability, however. In other words, variation in the testosterone levels of healthy men does not account for variation in their sexual feelings and behavior—or it does so to only a small degree. Testosterone is one of many substances used as aphrodisiacs (**Box 8.4**), but it's doubtful that testosterone enhances sexual desire or performance in healthy men.

The situation in women is more complex because at least two groups of hormones are involved—androgens (including testosterone) and estrogens—and their levels vary around the menstrual cycle. Testosterone levels in women are quite low compared with those in men—roughly 10 to 20 times lower—so it is less likely that these levels are at a "ceiling." In other words, there is more potential for changes in testosterone levels to modulate sexual arousability in women than in men.

The Pennsylvania State University study of children with delayed puberty, described above, included girls as well as boys. The girls were treated with oral estrogens, which had almost no effect on the girls' sexual thoughts or behaviors. In general, it appears that testosterone is more important than estrogens in influencing female sexual arousability, both in adolescent girls and in adult women, and may contribute to changes in women's sex drive around the menstrual cycle (Morris et al., 1987; Udry & Talbert, 1988; Van Goozen et al., 1997; Davis, 2000). Estrogens may have important indirect effects on sex, however: A reduction in estrogen levels, such as the decline that occurs at menopause, may lead to vaginal dryness and hence to painful intercourse, which in turn may cause a decline of interest in sex.

Conditioning May Influence Arousal

Classical or **Pavlovian conditioning** is the name given to a form of associative learning first studied by Ivan Pavlov in the early twentieth century. Pavlov observed that dogs salivate automatically when they smell food (an "unconditioned reflex"). Pavlov rang a bell every time a dog was given food. Over time, the dog began to salivate at the sound of the bell alone, as if it were food (a "conditioned reflex").

It's a plausible idea that classical conditioning influences sexual arousal. In one Canadian study (Lalumiere & Quinsey, 1998), researchers repeatedly showed male subjects a photograph of a moderately attractive, partially nude woman. Some of the subjects viewed the photo by itself; the others viewed it in conjunction with a highly arousing video of heterosexual sex. Over time, the men who viewed the photo alone were less and less strongly aroused by it—this is an example of the *habituation* that we described earlier in the chapter. But the men who repeatedly viewed the photo in conjunction with the arousing video were *more* strongly aroused by the photo alone at the end of the study than they were at the start. This, the researchers concluded, demonstrated the effect of classical conditioning, which they believe tends to counteract the habituation process.

Biology of Sex

BOX 8.4 Aphrodisiacs

Fetch me that flow'r; the herb I showed thee once.

The juice of it, on sleeping eyelids laid,

Will make or man or woman madly dote

Upon the next live creature that it sees.

—(Oberon, in Shakespeare's *Midsummer Night's Dream*)

Aphrodisiacs—named for the Greek goddess of love, Aphrodite—are substances intended to improve one's own sexual desire, sexual performance, or sexual pleasure or to cause someone else to respond to one's advances or to fall in love with oneself. In the latter case, they may be called "love potions."

Traditionally, the belief that certain substances are aphrodisiacs has been based on magical thinking, especially the "law of similarity," which holds that "like produces like" (Frazer, 1922). Thus aphrodisiacs have been derived from things that resemble penises (e.g., rhinoceros horns) or vulvas (e.g., oysters) or from sex organs or secondary sexual structures of animals, such as bull's testicles, the bacula (penis bones) of harp seals, and deer velvet (the skin covering the growing antlers of male deer). The flower used by Oberon as a love potion, the love-in-idleness, or wild pansy, is purple in color and thus resembles blood, the supposed seat of passionate feelings.

It's not likely that any of these substances work, at least by objective criteria. A New Zealand research group recently went to the trouble of conducting a double-blind, placebo-controlled trial of deer velvet and found absolutely no effect on men's sexual function or that of their partners (Conaglen et al., 2003). Still, these natural aphrodisiacs may have a beneficial effect through the power of suggestion.

Ginseng root has long been used in Eastern medicine as a treatment for sexual dysfunctions. Controlled scientific studies support ginseng's usefulness: It facilitates sexual behavior in male rats (Murphy et al., 1998) and helps alleviate erectile dysfunction in men (de Andrade et al., 2007). Botanicals such as ginseng are poorly regulated, however, and are not necessarily safe simply because they are natural products. Treatments for erectile dysfunction are discussed in detail in Chapter 16.

Another class of substances that are sometimes used as aphrodisiacs is that of recreational drugs. Here the issue is not so much whether they work—they often do—but their safety. Here are some examples:

- Amyl nitrite ("poppers") and related drugs such as butyl nitrite, which are administered by inhalation, produce a brief "rush," during which time sexual feelings are enhanced and the pleasurable sensations of orgasm are intensified. It is very dangerous to use these drugs in combination with Viagra or related drugs, since a life-threatening drop in blood pressure can result. Even used alone, they can have serious harmful effects in people with cardiovascular or breathing problems.

- Marijuana, the most widely used illicit drug in the United States, tends to exaggerate preexisting personality traits and thus has very different effects in different people. In some, it induces relaxation or heightened sensitivity that makes sex more enjoyable. In others it increases anxiety or impairs the physical skills required for a satisfying sexual experience.

- Methamphetamine ("speed") is a highly addictive drug that has a reputation as a powerful aphrodisiac. Many people use it primarily to enhance their sexual experiences. With repeated use, however, it damages the brain's dopamine system and makes sexual pleasure unattainable even with the help of the drug.

- Cocaine in moderate doses can enhance sexual sensations but in high doses or with chronic use can cause erectile difficulties as well as the inability to achieve orgasm (in both men and women). Overdoses are potentially fatal. Cocaine use has declined in recent years.

- MDMA ("Ecstasy") is a serotonin-related drug that can increase sexual arousal as well as general energy and euphoria. It can have serious adverse effects in people with cardiovascular problems. It can also cause psychological problems such as depression and anxiety that persist after drug use ceases. In addition, Ecstasy tablets are often contaminated with other drugs.

- Alcohol is a central nervous system depressant that can facilitate sexual expression by removing inhibitions. In high doses it can impair performance.

A safety issue that applies to the use of all recreational drugs in a sexual context is that they may impair judgment, thus promoting unsafe sex, sexual victimization, or sexual encounters that are later regretted. For the use of Viagra as a performance-enhancer by men who do not have erectile dysfunction, see Box 16.2.

aphrodisiac A substance believed to improve sexual performance, enhance sexual pleasure, or stimulate desire or love.

Male deer grow new antlers with astonishing speed before every breeding season. No wonder that the covering of the antlers—deer velvet—is prized as an aphrodisiac.

Classical conditioning could influence how sexual arousal changes over time in real-life situations such as steady relationships. Thus, we may be more strongly aroused by our partner over time, simply because of the arousing effect of sexual interactions with that partner. This process could help counteract the potentially negative aspects of long-term relationships, such as boredom and the decreasing physical attractiveness that accompanies aging.

It has also been suggested that conditioning could explain the development of unusual sexual desires such as fetishisms. We discuss this idea in Chapter 15.

Sexual Arousal Follows a Response Cycle

In Chapters 3 and 4 we described some of the genital phenomena that accompany sexual arousal in women and men. We now attempt to tie these phenomena together into a coherent sequence or process—the **sexual response cycle**. This cycle goes forward in a fairly similar way regardless of how arousal occurs (e.g., through partnered sex or by solitary masturbation).

The best-known description of the overall response cycle is the one developed by Masters and Johnson, in which they divided the process into four phases: excitement, plateau, orgasm, and resolution.

In the Excitement Phase, Genital Responses Begin

The **excitement phase** is just what it sounds like: the period during which sexual arousal begins. In women it is marked by swelling and opening up of the labia minora, vaginal lubrication, a deepening in the color of the labia minora and the vaginal walls (caused by vasocongestion), erection of the clitoris and nipples, swelling of the breasts, and an increase in heart rate and blood pressure (**Figure 8.13**). According to Masters and Johnson, the uterus swells and elevates within the pelvis. The use of modern imaging techniques has provided partial confirmation for the elevation, but not for the swelling (Schultz et al., 1999).

In men the excitement phase is marked mainly by erection of the penis (**Figure 8.14**). In healthy and highly aroused young men the process of erection takes only a few seconds. Usually, the corpora cavernosa become erect first, followed more slowly by the corpus spongiosum. In older men, men who have health problems affecting erection, or men who are not highly aroused, the process of penile erection may take many minutes.

Also during the excitement phase, contraction of the cremaster muscle begins to elevate the testicles. The skin of the scrotum becomes thicker and more wrinkled, due to contraction of an underlying muscle layer. The nipples may also become erect.

Of course, various components of the excitement phase don't always occur together or to the same degree. The duration of the excitement phase also varies, from less than a minute to an hour or more.

In the Plateau Phase, Arousal Is Maintained

The **plateau phase** is a state of high arousal that may be maintained for some time, from several minutes to several hours (in the case of extended lovemaking). In women, physiological events that occur during the plateau phase include the thickening and tightening of the outer third of the vagina and the surrounding muscles of the pelvic floor. This causes the outer part of the vaginal canal to narrow, so that (if coitus is occurring) it grips the penis more tightly. This tense outer region of the vagina and surrounding tissues is called the **orgasmic platform**. The inner part of the vagina, in contrast, tends to balloon out and lengthen, so that it does not grip the penis at all tightly during coitus.

sexual response cycle The sequence of physiological processes that accompany sexual behavior.

excitement phase The beginning phase of the sexual response cycle.

plateau phase The phase of the sexual response cycle during which arousal is maintained at a high level.

orgasmic platform The outer portion of the vagina and surrounding tissues, which thicken and tense during sexual arousal.

Figure 8.13 Genital changes in women during the sexual response cycle.

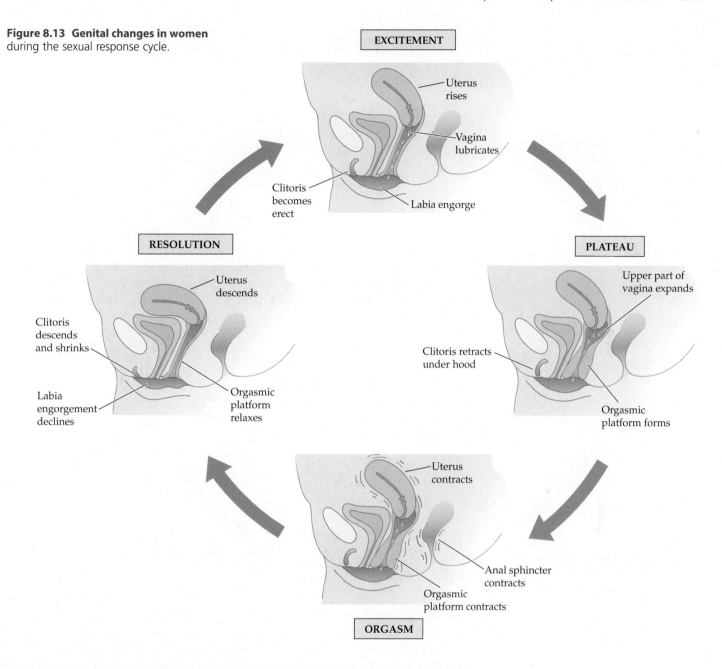

During the plateau phase, the glans of the clitoris usually disappears under its hood. The breasts may swell further, and the areolae may become engorged and swollen, making the nipples appear less prominent than before. In some women, the breasts or other parts of the body may take on a flushed appearance. Heart rate and blood pressure increase further, and there is a general increase in muscle tension (**myotonia**) throughout the body.

In men, secretions from the bulbourethral glands ("pre-cum") may appear at the urethral opening during the plateau phase. The erection of the penis becomes stronger, and the testicles are elevated farther and swell due to vasocongestion. Heart rate and respiration rate increase, and there is a general increase in muscle tension.

The term "plateau," which means a flat region in a graph, suggests a steady state in which not much is changing, physiologically speaking. This may be misleading, however. Sometimes a person will pass rapidly from excitement through plateau to orgasm: In this case the plateau phase may be a brief period of rapid-

myotonia A general increase in muscle tension.

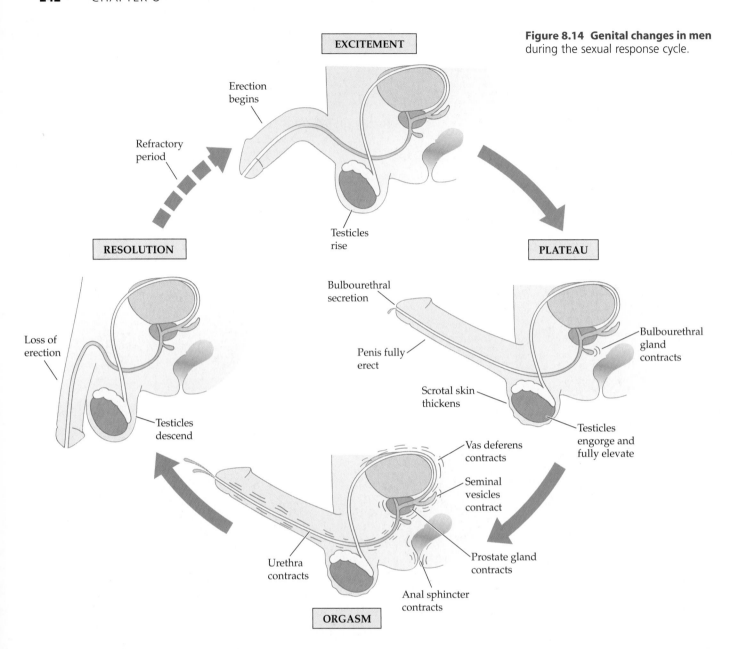

Figure 8.14 Genital changes in men during the sexual response cycle.

EXCITEMENT

Erection begins

Refractory period

Testicles rise

RESOLUTION

PLATEAU

Loss of erection

Testicles descend

Bulbourethral secretion

Penis fully erect

Scrotal skin thickens

Bulbourethral gland contracts

Testicles engorge and fully elevate

Vas deferens contracts

Seminal vesicles contract

Prostate gland contracts

Urethra contracts

Anal sphincter contracts

ORGASM

ly increasing arousal that is difficult to distinguish from the excitement phase. If the plateau phase is maintained for an extended time, however, there are likely to be periodic increases and decreases in arousal depending on the stimulation the person is experiencing, distraction, fatigue, and other factors. Thus the plateau phase is more of a general concept than a definable episode within each and every sexual experience.

Orgasm Is the Climax of Sexual Arousal

Orgasm is the subjective experience of intense pleasure and release at sexual climax, as well as the accompanying physiological processes. As previously discussed in Chapter 4, it is very similar in men and women. Orgasm is usually felt as a brief sequence of muscle contractions in the genital area, but the sensation often radiates out to involve other parts of the body. Respiration rate, heart rate, and blood pressure all reach peak levels during orgasm. Muscle contractions may occur anywhere in the body. In men orgasm is accompanied by two genital events described in

orgasm The intense, pleasurable sensations at sexual climax and the physiological processes that accompany them.

Biology of Sex

BOX 8.5 Female Ejaculation

You might think that ejaculation would be a purely male experience, but according to one survey 40% of women say that they experience a discharge of fluid at sexual climax (Darling et al., 1990). Although first described in Western scientific literature in the mid-twentieth century (Grafenberg, 1950), female ejaculation was described in Indian manuscripts dealing with sex as early as the eleventh century (Syed, 1999).

As with male ejaculation, the fluid is discharged from the urethra. The discharge seems to be of two kinds. In one kind of ejaculation, a small amount (a few drops to a teaspoonful or so) of an opalescent (pearly) fluid is discharged, usually without great force. In another kind, a larger quantity of clear fluid is discharged, sometimes with sufficient force to project the fluid away from the woman's body. For the most part, different women report experiencing the two different kinds of ejaculation.

The low-volume, opalescent ejaculate appears to be a secretion from the paraurethral glands. As described earlier, these small glands, which are probably equivalent to the much larger prostate gland in men, lie just in front of the front wall of the vagina, in close proximity to the urethra. The ducts of these glands open into the urethra about 2 cm (1 inch) back from the ure-

thral opening. Consistent with this interpretation, the low-volume ejaculate contains an enzyme characteristic of secretions from the male prostate gland: prostatic acid phosphatase

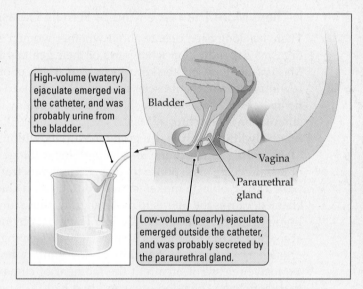

High-volume (watery) ejaculate emerged via the catheter, and was probably urine from the bladder.

Bladder

Vagina

Paraurethral gland

Low-volume (pearly) ejaculate emerged outside the catheter, and was probably secreted by the paraurethral gland.

Gary Schubach conducted his experiment to determine the origin of fluids ejaculated by women. A catheter was inserted into the bladder, and the women masturbated to orgasm.

(Belzer et al., 1984). The functional role of this kind of ejaculation in women, if any, is unknown. Because the male ejaculate consists in part of prostatic secretions, the paraurethral ejaculation in women is a partial parallel to male ejaculation—minus the sperm, of course.

The high-volume, clear ejaculate has been much more controversial, with some sexologists doubting the reality of the phenomenon or dismissing it as urine. To solve the riddle, sexologist Gary Schubach recruited volunteers who stated that they experienced large-volume ejaculations (Schubach, 1996). Schubach observed that these women did indeed expel large volumes—100 ml (3 ounces) or more—of watery fluid from the urethra at orgasm.

To investigate the origin of this fluid, Schubach passed a fine rubber tube (catheter) through the urethras of some of the women, past the ducts of the paraurethral glands and into the bladder (see the figure). The women then masturbated (or were stimulated by their partners) to orgasm. The idea was that if the fluid was urine, it should exit the urethra via the inside of the catheter, but if it was a secretion from the paraurethral glands or other nearby glands, it should exit the urethra *outside* the catheter. In all cases, all the high-volume fluid expelled at orgasm exited via the inside of the catheter. Schubach's conclusion: High-volume female ejaculation involves the expulsion of urine from the bladder. Some of the women also released the low-volume, opalescent ejaculate, and this fluid emerged outside the catheter, consistent with an origin in the paraurethral glands.

Chapter 4: emission, in which the various components that make up semen are loaded into the urethra, and ejaculation, in which the semen is forcefully expelled from the urethral opening. Some women also ejaculate during orgasm (**Box 8.5**).

Masters and Johnson, as well as more recent sex researchers, have investigated the physiological basis of the spasms experienced during orgasm. We described some of the research on men in Chapter 4). In women, the spasms derive from intense contractions of the bulbospongiosus muscle and nearby pelvic-floor muscles, which cause tightening of the outer portion of the vagina. The anal sphincters, the uterus, and even the oviducts may also undergo contractions. The contractions occur about once per second, and a total of about 8 or 10 occur in a typical orgasm.

In both men and women, orgasm is accompanied by the surgelike release of a hormone named **oxytocin** from the pituitary gland (Carmichael et al., 1994). Oxy-

oxytocin A hormone secreted by the pituitary gland that stimulates uterine contractions and the secretion of milk.

tocin contributes to the contraction of smooth (involuntary) muscles such as those in the wall of the uterus and in breast tissue. (It plays an important role in childbirth and breastfeeding, and possibly also in the formation of durable sexual relationships, as we'll see in Chapter 10. Thus its release during orgasm may contribute to the contractions that accompany orgasm. In addition, however, oxytocin released during orgasm acts directly on the brain, helping generate the pleasurable sensations of orgasm. The evidence for this is that, if the release of oxytocin is blocked, the physiological events of orgasm occur more or less normally, but the pleasurable quality of the orgasm is greatly reduced (Murphy et al., 1990). Administration of oxytocin may help some individuals experience orgasm who otherwise have difficulty doing so (Ishak et al., 2008).

Is There More Than One Kind of Female Orgasm?

There has long been debate about whether women experience different kinds of orgasms depending on what parts of their genitals are stimulated. According to Masters and Johnson, the key physiological sign of orgasm in women—spasmodic contractions of the muscles around the outer part of the vagina—are the same no matter how orgasm is reached, and are probably the result of direct or indirect stimulation of the clitoris (Masters & Johnson, 1966). Masters and Johnson placed relatively little emphasis on erotic sensitivity within the vagina itself.

According to Josephine and Irving Singer (Singer & Singer, 1972), a "uterine orgasm" occurs in response to deep vaginal penetration when the penis (or other penetrating object) makes direct contact with the cervix. This contact, they claimed, causes the uterus to move slightly, thus stimulating nerve endings in the lining of nearby abdominal organs. The most obvious sign of a uterine orgasm, according to the Singers, is a characteristic gasping pattern of breathing as the orgasm approaches, followed by an involuntary holding of breath and then an explosive release of breath at the moment of climax. The Singers also reported that there were "blended orgasms" that had features of both the uterine orgasm and the regular, "vulval" orgasm described by Masters and Johnson.

Researchers who study the G-spot also claim that stimulation of that spot triggers an orgasm different from the kind that results from clitoral stimulation. Although both types of orgasms involve contraction of the pelvic floor muscles, only a G-spot orgasm involves major contractions of the uterine musculature, it is claimed (Ladas et al., 2004). Whether the G-spot orgasm is the same as the Singers' uterine orgasm is unclear.

There is definitely room for more research in this area. While it is possible that women experience more than one kind of orgasm, it is also possible that stimulation of different sites leads to the same kind of orgasm, varying perhaps in intensity but not in its physiological basis.

Brain Imaging Suggests Where Orgasm May Be Experienced

The subjective experience of orgasm must result from some kind of activity in the brain, but where in the brain does that activity occur? To study this question, a Dutch group (Holstege et al., 2003) used a functional brain imaging technique (PET scanning). The researchers took scans in two conditions: when the subject was being manually stimulated by his female partner but was not experiencing orgasm, and in the same situation when he *was* experiencing orgasm (**Figure 8.15**). One scan was then digitally subtracted from the other to show the pattern of activity that was specifically associated with orgasm. The researchers found that the most active region was a zone in the midline of the brain including part of the thalamus and nearby structures. Interestingly, this same region has been shown to be active during a heroin rush. It contains many neurons that use dopamine as a neuro-

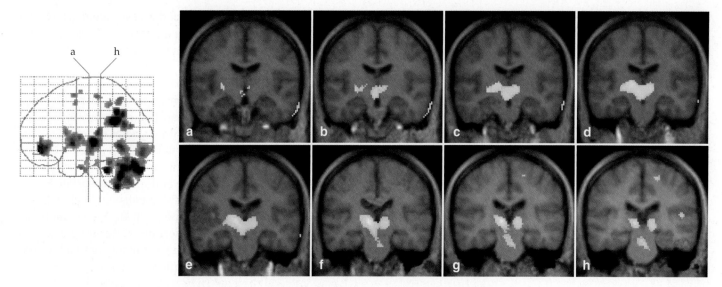

Figure 8.15 Brain activity during orgasm in a man, as revealed in a PET scan. The most active areas (yellow) involve subcortical structures such as the thalamus. (Courtesy of Gert Holstege.)

transmitter; dopamine is believed to be involved in brain processes that have to do with pleasure and reward. Activity in the cerebral cortex—seat of our intellectual lives—decreases greatly during orgasm. More recently, the Dutch group extended their observations to women: Again, there was activation of dopamine-related systems and a general drop in activity in the cerebral cortex (Georgiadis et al., 2006). The researchers speculate that this drop represents a switching-off of cognitive or behavioral processes that would otherwise inhibit orgasm.

In the Resolution Phase, Arousal Subsides

The **resolution phase** is the period during which the physiological signs of arousal reverse themselves—clitoral erection, vasocongestion, and lubrication subside, the vaginal and pelvic-floor muscles relax, the breasts lose their swollen appearance, and heart rate and blood pressure return to normal levels. Psychological arousal usually subsides too, and there is often a sense of relaxed contentment. Full resolution typically takes about 15 minutes, but resolution is slower if an orgasm has not occurred.

The Phases May be Linked in Different Ways

Although the excitement, plateau, orgasm, and resolution phases are the building blocks of the sexual response cycle, individual cycles may be assembled in a variety of ways (**Figure 8.16**). In one type of cycle (shown in orange in the figure), the person passes sequentially through the four phases in the sequence just described—excitement, plateau, orgasm, and resolution. This might be called the "standard version" of the response cycle.

A second type of cycle (shown in red in the figure) skips the orgasm phase: The person passes from excitement to the plateau phase, and then directly to the res-

resolution phase The phase of the sexual response cycle during which physiological arousal subsides.

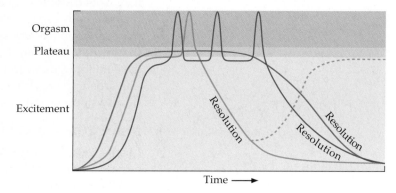

Figure 8.16 Patterns of sexual response In the pattern shown in orange, a single orgasm is experienced before loss of arousal (resolution), but a new cycle of arousal may begin after resolution (dashed line). In the pattern shown in blue, the person passes through excitement to the plateau phase and then experiences more than one orgasm, returning to the plateau phase between orgasms. In the pattern shown in red, the person experiences the plateau phase but no orgasm.

status orgasmus An orgasm or uninterrupted sequence of orgasms that last from 20 seconds up to a minute or more.

refractory period A period of reduced or absent sexual arousability after orgasm.

olution phase. We have become acculturated to think of this as a sign of something wrong or missing: We might say that the person "failed to achieve" orgasm. Still, the fact is that it is a common type of cycle. Women may describe it as a fully satisfying sexual experience—in fact some women never experience orgasm but nevertheless express satisfaction with their sex lives. Alternatively, they may feel frustrated, and they may even be left with an aching sensation in their pelvic area, perhaps due to prolonged vasocongestion and the resulting tissue anoxia.

Men are less likely than women to be satisfied with a sexual experience that doesn't include orgasm—only 34% of men, compared with 50% of women, believe that sex without orgasm can be satisfying, according to a large British survey (Wellings et al., 1994). Besides the loss of the pleasure and release associated with orgasm, men sometimes experience testicular pain ("blue balls"), which is likely due to vasocongestion and anoxia (Chalett & Nerenberg, 2000). Men sometimes plead "blue balls" by way of pressuring their partner into continuing a sexual encounter. That's hardly a compelling argument, because in that situation the condition—if real—could easily be relieved by masturbation.

Some People Experience Multiple Orgasms

A third type of cycle involves multiple orgasms (the blue line in Figure 8.15). A multiple orgasm means a sequence of at least two orgasms, between which the person descends only to the plateau phase of genital arousal (Amberson & Hoon, 1985). It does not refer to having an orgasm, losing one's arousal completely, and then quickly entering another arousal cycle that culminates in a second orgasm.

Multiple orgasms are far more common in women that in men. One survey of college-educated U.S. nurses found that about 43% of them usually experienced multiple orgasms (Darling et al., 1991). No doubt many more women could experience multiple orgasms if they wanted to or if they had the cooperation of their partners. However, women are not necessarily more satisfied with multiple orgasms than with a single orgasm, as many men would imagine. Reports of large numbers of sequential orgasms—up to 50 or so—concern women who are masturbating, rather than engaging in coitus.

Masters and Johnson reported that women can sometimes experience a sequence of orgasms that follow directly one upon the other, so that the woman doesn't even descend into the plateau phase between them. The orgasms may be considered to form one single, unusually prolonged orgasm. This condition, which they named **status orgasmus**, can last from 20 seconds up to a minute or so.

A few men also experience multiple orgasms (Dunn & Trost, 1989). Often, only one orgasm in the series—usually the last—is accompanied by ejaculation, while the previous ones are "dry." Some sexologists believe that all men can learn to have multiple orgasms. For those who wish to try, instructions are available online (Silverberg, 2008). The key, it is said, is learning to separate orgasm from ejaculation by stopping stimulation just short of ejaculation.

Men Experience a Refractory Period

In men, there is a period of time after orgasm during which further sexual stimulation does not lead to renewed erection or a second orgasm. According to Masters and Johnson, this **refractory period** lasts between 30 and 90 minutes. The length of the period varies greatly with age, however, being negligible in some boys around the age of puberty but extending over a day or more in some older men. While the early part of the refractory period may be *absolute*—that is, the man cannot be physiologically aroused by any means—it may be followed by a *relative* refractory period during which the man can be aroused by stronger than usual stimuli, such as a novel sex partner. This is probably related to the Coolidge effect, described earlier.

The Masters and Johnson Cycle May Be Incomplete

Masters and Johnson's four-stage model of sexual response is primarily a description of physiological processes—things that one can observe or measure during sexual behavior such as erection or changes in blood pressure. Since Masters and Johnson's time there have been efforts to place the physiological response cycle in a larger psychological context.

One important issue is this: Do the physiological markers of sexual arousal—erection, vasocongestion, lubrication, and so forth—correspond to *psychological* or *subjective* arousal, meaning the person's sense of being sexually excited? There appears to be a difference between men and women in this respect. A man's psychological arousal is usually closely tied to his genital arousal—his mind and his penis are one, so to speak. Women, however, do *not* always feel sexually excited when their genitals are showing every sign of arousal (Suschinsky et al., 2008). It may be that a woman's genital arousal is less obvious to her than is penile erection to a man, or women may be acculturated to ignore the messages from their genitals. But the reason for this potential disconnect between physiological and psychological arousal in women remains mysterious and deserves further study. For one thing, it may affect whether drugs that increase genital arousal offer any psychological benefit for women with sexual dysfunctions.

Another issue is this: Where does sexual *desire* fit into the overall response cycle? According to Helen Singer Kaplan, sexual desire is the psychological state that precedes and leads to physiological arousal (Kaplan, 1979). This makes intuitive sense: We want to engage in sex, so our genitals become aroused. But here again, there may be a difference between men and women. For men, Kaplan's model is generally accepted. In the case of women, however, several researchers have moved away from Kaplan's model (Basson, 2000, 2001). Psychiatrist Rosemary Basson proposes that many women, especially those in established relationships, are not motivated to engage in sexual behavior by what we would usually think of as sexual *desire*—horniness, sex hunger, the urge to merge, or whatever you want to call it. Rather, they have an *interest* in sex that flows from a wish for intimacy with the partner or from an expectation of benefits that may flow from a sexual interaction. This interest is responsive, cognitive, or even intellectual in quality, rather than being the expression of a biological drive. Once physical interactions begin, however, and the physiological processes of sexual arousal are triggered, genital sensations provide a "feedback" stimulus that reinforces sexual interest and gives it more the quality of true sexual desire, so a self-reinforcing cycle is set up. Again, this model has implications for the treatment of sexual dysfunctions in women (see Chapter 16).

Cognitive psychologists have developed quite complex models of the thought processes that underlie sexual behavior. Susan Walen and David Roth, for example, developed a cognitive model of the sexual response cycle that explicitly incorporates mental processes and causal connections (Walen & Roth, 1987) (**Figure 8.17**). This model begins with perception of a sexual stimulus, which triggers the

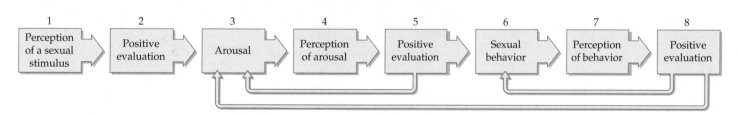

Figure 8.17 Walen–Roth cognitive model of a positive sexual experience The arrows represent causal links between one cognitive state and another. (After Walen & Roth, 1987.)

evaluation of that perception, which in turn (if positive) triggers sexual arousal. The arousal itself is then perceived and evaluated, and a positive evaluation reinforces arousal (a positive feedback loop) and also triggers sexual behavior. That behavior, in turn, is perceived and evaluated, with further feedback effects.

This model has definite merits in terms of its focus on mental events and how they are connected. It might also help explain some sexual dysfunctions. For example, a young woman may be distracted from monitoring her own arousal by other concerns. (Is her partner going to withdraw in time? Is her partner being satisfied?) According to the model, this lack of attention to her own arousal breaks the feedback loop and therefore interferes with arousal itself and with resulting positive evaluations.

The Walen-Roth model does not include any explicit inhibitory processes, but in reality cognitive mechanisms can exert a strong inhibitory influence on sexual arousal (Janssen & Bancroft, 2006; Sanders et al., 2008). Such inhibition can save people from becoming aroused under socially inappropriate circumstances, such as when a doctor is examining a patient. But it can also lead to chronic sexual difficulties—in people who have had a very repressive upbringing, for example, or in those who are excessively anxious about their sexual performance. We will return to this issue when we discuss sexual disorders (see Chapter 16).

Summary

1. Sexual attraction is a response to another person that is influenced by objective attributes of that person, as well as by both durable and varying characteristics of the person experiencing the attraction.

2. One objective attribute that increases a person's attractiveness is facial and bodily symmetry. One reason we may find symmetry attractive is because it indicates that a person had a healthy development.

3. The "masculinity" and "femininity" of faces is an important part of their attractiveness. The majority of people find very masculine or very feminine faces most attractive.

4. The attractiveness of bodies is also often a matter of their masculinity or femininity. The waist-to-hip ratio differs between the sexes and is an important determinant of attractiveness across many cultures.

5. Youthful appearance—another cue to fertility—is an important criterion of physical attractiveness in women, but less so in men.

6. Attractiveness is strongly enhanced by general "likability" traits such as trustworthiness, warmth, and a sense of humor. When people are given the opportunity to select partners from a large group, however, they don't generally choose the partners who correspond most closely to their stated preferences. This suggests that some aspects of attraction operate below the level of conscious thought.

7. Other factors modulating sexual attraction include familiarity and, in women, the phase of the menstrual cycle.

8. Some asexual individuals never experience sexual attraction. They might not engage in sexual relationships, or they might do so simply to satisfy their partners.

9. Sexual arousal may be triggered internally or by external factors. Internal processes include erotic dreams and sexual fantasies. Fantasies are a healthy part of most people's sex lives.

10. External events that cause emotional arousal of any kind—even fear—can enhance sexual arousal.

11. Testosterone plays an important role in conferring the capacity for sexual arousal in males, especially at puberty. Testosterone does not play a minute-by-minute role in sexual arousal, however. Both testosterone and estrogens may contribute to sexual arousability in women; testosterone is probably the more important of the two.

12. Classical conditioning may increase arousal to a specific sexual partner over time.

13. The sexual response cycle has four phases: excitement, plateau, orgasm, and resolution.

14. The subjective experience of orgasm is similar in women and men. Many women but few men experience multiple orgasms in a single cycle. Sometimes a response cycle does not include orgasm. A cycle without orgasm may be perceived as sexually satisfying, or it may leave the person dissatisfied and in discomfort from vasocongestion that is slow to resolve.

15. Men but not women experience a refractory period after orgasm during which they cannot enter a new cycle. The length of the refractory period increases with age but can be shortened by situational factors such as exposure to a novel partner.

16. Cognitive models of the sexual response cycle emphasize the role played by a person's thoughts and feelings during the cycle.

Discussion Questions

1. Cultural influences shape sexual arousal and attractiveness. Identify the culture of your ancestors, and identify the attributes that your culture finds sexually attractive (e.g., are skinny women or those with "curves" and "meat on their bones" more attractive?).

2. Consider your reaction as you walk around campus or other areas and see people holding hands, kissing, lying on the grass in a passionate embrace, or almost having intercourse. What are your reactions to seeing such behavior? How does your reaction differ depending on whether the couple is homosexual or heterosexual? Do you think we should have rules or limits on the extent of public displays of affection or arousal?

3. Should sexual partners discuss what is arousing for each person? What are the costs and benefits of this type of communication? What are your attitudes toward talking with an intimate partner about what is arousing and what is not? Imagine for a moment that your partner had a fascination with your feet and wanted to kiss and touch them. How would your attitudes encourage or discourage this discussion?

4. As a class, make a list of words or phrases (e.g., common expressions, slang, words in other languages) that are used for (a) a woman who has sex with numerous partners; (b) a woman who doesn't engage in partnered sex at all; (c) a man who has sex with numerous partners; and (d) a man who doesn't engage in partnered sex. After the list is complete, discuss the attitudes and values it illustrates about men's and women's sexuality. Do you think that a double standard exists?

Web Resources

Asexuality Visibility and Education Network www.asexuality.org

Gruendl, M. Beautycheck (study of attractiveness, using digitally manipulated faces) www.uni-regensburg.de/Fakultaeten/phil_Fak_II/Psychologie/Psy_II/beautycheck/english/index.htm

Recommended Reading

Buss, D. (1994). *The evolution of desire: Strategies of human mating.* Basic Books.

Langlois, J. H., Kalakanis, L., et al. (2000). Maxims or myths of beauty? A meta-analytic and theoretical review. *Psychological Bulletin* 126: 390–423.

Thornhill, R., and Gangestad, S. W. (2004). The evolution of human attractiveness and attraction. In A. Moya and E. Font (Eds.), *Evolution: From molecules to ecosystems.* Oxford University Press.

CHAPTER 9

Erotic temple sculptures at Khajuharo in Northern India

Sexual Behavior

Which human behaviors do you consider sexual? Which of these, if any, do you engage in or find enjoyable? Which do you consider morally acceptable, and which strike you as repugnant? Probably no two people would give precisely the same answers to these questions. In this chapter, we survey common forms of sexual behavior, with a central emphasis on sexual practices in the contemporary United States and other Westernized countries. We will defer a discussion of atypical sexual practices to Chapter 15.

Everyone has to make important decisions about their sex life. Questions arise, such as: Do I want to have sex at all, and if so, under what circumstances, and in what kind of a relationship? Do I want to have children, and if not, how should I prevent pregnancy? How can I best reduce the likelihood of acquiring or transmitting diseases in the course of sexual encounters? These important topics will be discussed in later chapters. For the moment, we deal with sexual behavior itself.

People Have Differing Ideas about What Constitutes Sexual Behavior

"I did not have sexual relations with that woman, Miss Lewinsky." History will probably record these words as the most famous utterance of the 41st president of the United States, William Jefferson Clinton. It turned out that Clinton and White House intern Monica Lewinsky had engaged in oral sex (specifically, mouth–penis contact, or **fellatio**) to the point of ejaculation. Was that "having sex"? Not according to Clinton—and there are plenty of people who agree with him: Over half of young people surveyed in the 1990s stated that oral–genital contact did not constitute "having sex," even if it included orgasm (Richter & Song, 1999; Sanders & Reinisch, 1999). There is a wide perception, especially among men, that "real" sex is one thing and one thing only: a man inserting his penis into a woman's vagina and keeping it there until he ejaculates.

For the purposes of this book, we take a more inclusive view: We consider any behavior sexual if it is accompanied or followed by physiological signs of sexual arousal, such as penile erection or vaginal lubrication—whether or not ejaculation or orgasm occurs. Even behaviors that are not accompanied by physiological arousal should probably be considered sexual if they are perceived to be such by the participants. And "sex," by our definition, can involve a single person, two or more people of any sex, or even a human and an animal. Of course, the bound-

fellatio Sexual contact between the mouth of one person and the penis of another.

When President Bill Clinton denied having sex with White House intern Monica Lewinsky, it focused national attention on what "having sex" means.

masturbation Sexual self-stimulation. Sometimes also used to refer to manual stimulation of another person's genitalia.

autoerotic Providing sexual stimulation to oneself or being aroused sexually by oneself.

Unsweetened corn flakes were introduced at the Battle Creek Sanitarium in Michigan by anti-masturbation crusader John Harvey Kellogg. His brother Will added sugar to the flakes and successfully marketed them as a breakfast cereal.

aries of sexual behavior are difficult to define precisely: Hugging or kissing, for example, may be sexual in some contexts and not in others. But it's probably better to be overinclusive here than to omit behaviors that are significant modes of sexual expression for some people.

Masturbation Is a Very Common Form of Sexual Expression

We have already discussed one way in which people can arouse themselves sexually: through sexual fantasy (see Chapter 8). Fantasy is not a behavior because it doesn't involve *doing* anything in the external world. But people also have the capacity to arouse themselves sexually through physical stimulation of their own bodies—**masturbation**.

The term "masturbation" is sometimes used to indicate any kind of manual stimulation of the genitals, including those of a partner. Most commonly, though, the term is reserved for **autoerotic** (self-arousing) behavior, whether by use of the hand or by other means such as vibrators or pillows, and we use it in that sense here.

Negative Attitudes toward Masturbation Are Still Prevalent

Masturbation is a normal, common, and healthy sexual behavior. It's not always perceived that way, however. If you felt a certain anxiety when you realized the topic of this section, be assured that you are not alone. In this age of relative openness about sexuality, masturbation is the one common form of sexual expression that still triggers a great deal of embarrassment, guilt, or denial—not just for people who practice it, but also for people who talk about it. During the planning of the National Health and Social Life Survey (NHSLS—see Chapter 1) federal administrators demanded that questions about masturbation be removed from the interview protocols. Then, after the project became privately funded, the interviewers themselves balked at the idea of asking about the topic. In the end, questions about masturbation had to be placed on a special form that subjects could fill out by themselves. In the NSSAL (the equivalent British survey), masturbation fared even worse: Reactions to the topic were so negative that it had to be dropped from the survey.

It's not just sex surveys that have problems with masturbation. Although "masturbation" is not one of the "seven forbidden words" that have been banned from the airwaves by the Federal Communications Commission, it might just as well be on the list, considering the rarity with which it is spoken. What's more, it's not just the word, but the entire concept, that is largely excluded from public discourse (**Box 9.1**).

Part of the reason for the difficulty people have in discussing masturbation is historical. In Victorian times, masturbation was considered disgusting, sinful, and unhealthy and was referred to with morally loaded terms such as "self-pollution." According to many authorities of the time, masturbation led to "degeneracy," a condition of physical, mental, and moral decay that affected not just the masturbator, but also any offspring that he or she might have (Hare, 1962). In that period, it was believed that the consumption of rich or highly flavored foods provoked masturbation and that bland foods discouraged it. Two bland foods that are still popular today—the graham cracker and Kellogg's Corn Flakes—were specifically introduced with the hope of reducing the prevalence of masturbation and sexual arousal. (Sylvester Graham was a minister and moral campaigner; John Harvey Kellogg was a doctor.) Health manuals recommended a variety of methods for discouraging masturbation, and one could even purchase mechanical

Society, Values, and the Law

BOX 9.1 The Dreaded *M* Word

Joycelyn Elders, pediatrician and director of the Arkansas Department of Health, was appointed U.S. Surgeon General by President Bill Clinton in 1993. Elders had (and still has) a passionate interest in reducing sexually transmitted diseases and unwanted pregnancies, and she felt that simply preaching abstinence was not an effective strategy for accomplishing these goals. Her support for programs that encouraged contraception led conservatives to call her the "Condom Queen."

In December 1994, Elders gave a speech at a United Nations–sponsored conference on AIDS. Afterward, she was asked about masturbation as a form of safe sex. Masturbation, she replied, "is a part of human sexuality, and it's a part of something that perhaps should be taught." Specifically, she recommended that information

about masturbation be included in a comprehensive program of sex education in schools.

When Clinton learned of her statement and learned that it was going to be published in *U.S. News and World Report*, he fired her. Dr. Elders was unrepentant. "Masturbation," she later wrote in an online column, "is not a four-letter word, but the President fired me for saying it. In this so-called 'communications age,' it remains a sexual taboo of monumental proportions to discuss the safe and universal practice of self-pleasure. No doubt, future generations will be amused at our peculiar taboo, laughing in sociology classes at our backwardness, yet also puzzled by it given our high rates of [sexually transmitted] disease and premature pregnancy. We will look foolish in the light of history" (Elders, 1997).

Joycelyn Elders

devices that made masturbation impossible. (Actually, such devices are still for sale, though they now seem to be used as bondage toys more than as aids to abstinence.)

Few people are campaigning against the evils of masturbation in the United States today, but few people speak out in favor of the practice, and children may still absorb negative attitudes about it from their parents. Furthermore, the Roman Catholic Church (as well as some other denominations and religions), still holds that masturbation is sinful.

Another reason for masturbation's bad reputation is the belief that it is an activity practiced only by people who cannot get access to "real" sex. The derogatory terms "jerk" (whose meaning has been influenced by the phrase "jerking off," slang for male masturbation) and its British equivalent "wanker" mean a person who is so unattractive or socially inept that they are driven to have sex with the one person who cannot turn them down: themselves.

Thus several factors combine to make people feel bad about masturbation. In the NHSLS study, about half of all the respondents who stated that they masturbated also stated that they felt guilty after they did so. The youngest age group interviewed (18 to 24 years) reported the highest levels of guilt.

Several Demographic Factors Influence Masturbation

What is the reality of masturbation? In the NHSLS study (**Figure 9.1**), about half of the interviewees stated that they had masturbated at least once during the previous 12 months. The frequency with which these people masturbated, however, was strongly influenced by their sex (men masturbated more than women), age (older people masturbated less often than younger people), ethnicity (African-Americans masturbated less than other groups), religion (nonreligious and non-

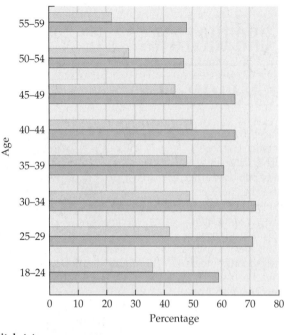

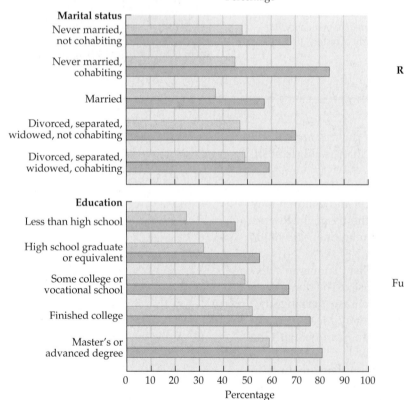

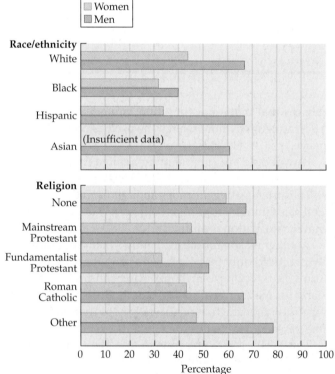

Figure 9.1 Biological and cultural factors influence whether people masturbate. These histograms show the percentages of various groups who acknowledge having masturbated at least once in the previous 12 months, as categorized by (counterclockwise from top left): age, marital status, education, religion, and race/ethnicity. (Data from NHSLS.)

Christian people masturbated more than Christians), educational level (higher educational attainment was associated with more frequent masturbation), and marital status (unmarried people masturbated more than married people).

While the data in Figure 9.1 illustrate two apparent biological influences on the frequency of masturbation (sex and age), they also show how strongly cultural factors influence the practice. The strong association between educational level and frequency of masturbation is particularly interesting. Highly educated people are less religious than other groups, and they also tend to believe that pleasure is one of the main reasons for engaging in sex. Both these factors might make highly educated people less inhibited about engaging in masturbation (or reporting that they masturbate).

Men experience orgasm during masturbation more frequently than women do. In the NHSLS study, 82% of the men but only 61% of the women stated that they always or usually had an orgasm when masturbating. This sex difference is not unique to masturbation: Women are less likely than men to have an orgasm during sex with a partner, too. In fact, the average woman is more likely to experience orgasm when masturbating than when engaged in sex with a partner (Hite, 2003).

Asked *why* they masturbated, the men and women in the NHSLS survey gave similar answers: They did it to relieve sexual tension, for the physical pleasure, and/or because a partner was not available.

The NHSLS data lend only limited support to the notion that partner unavailability is the major reason for masturbation. Married people did masturbate less than unmarried people, but that could have been in large part because the married interviewees were older than the unmarried ones, and the frequency of masturbation declines with age. More telling is the comparison between unmarried people who were and were not cohabiting with a partner. Those who had a partner masturbated as often as or more often than those who did not have a partner. Thus it doesn't seem that people have a certain fixed endowment of sexual need that they can allot either to partnered or to unpartnered sex. Many people who masturbate simply add it to their other sexual activities.

Women Use More Diverse Techniques of Masturbation than Men

Most of what is known about how people masturbate comes from the work of Masters and Johnson, who observed several hundred men and women masturbating as part of their overall studies of sexual behavior (Masters & Johnson, 1966). Women use quite diverse methods of masturbation (**Figure 9.2**). One common technique involves manually stimulating the area of the clitoris with a circular or to-and-fro motion of the fingers. Alternatively, pulling on the labia minora causes the clitoral hood to move to and fro on the clitoral glans, thus stimulating the clitoris indirectly. Another way of stimulating the clitoris is for a woman to cross her legs and squeeze them together rhythmically. Yet another technique is to rub or press the genital area against some object, such as a bed or pillow. Women sometimes use electric vibrators, either to stimulate the genitalia directly, or attached to the back of the hand so as to give the fingers an extra vibratory motion.

Many men imagine that women masturbate by thrusting their fingers or an object deeply into the vagina, thus simulating coitus. Some women do this, but it is quite a bit less common than clitoral stimulation. Some women can give themselves a different kind of orgasm by deep pressure in the region of the G-spot.

While manually stimulating the genitals, many women stimulate the nipples or breasts with their free hand. In fact, some women can bring themselves to orgasm by breast stimulation alone. A small number of women can experience orgasm by fantasy alone, without any kind of physical stimulation of the body (Whipple et al., 1992).

Men's techniques of masturbation tend to be less varied than women's (**Figure 9.3**). The usual method is to grasp the shaft of the erect penis with one hand and move the hand rhythmically up and down, thus stimulating the most sensitive areas of the penis: the glans, corona, and frenulum.

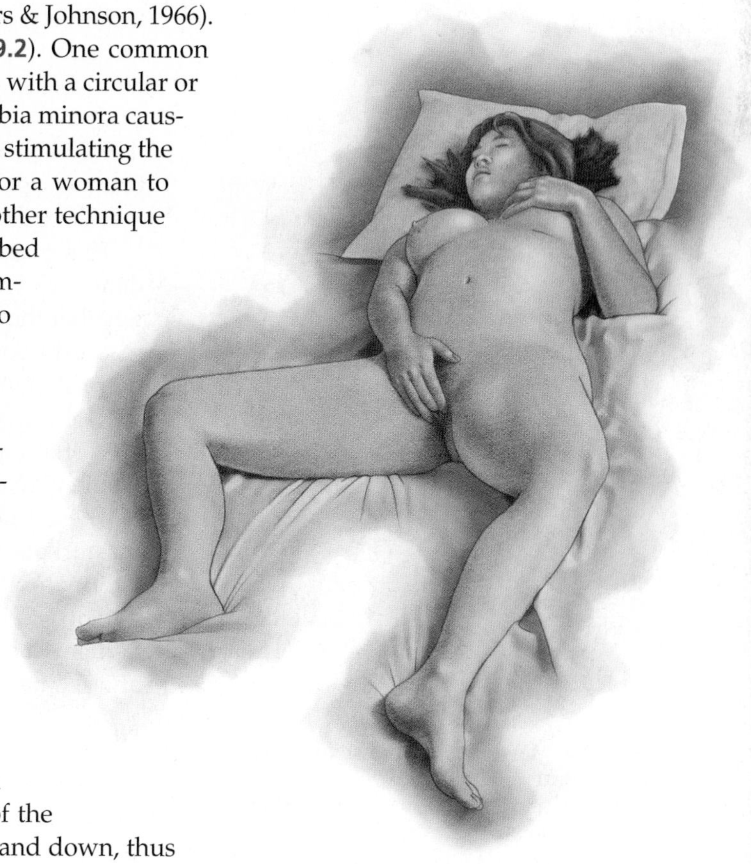

Figure 9.2 Female masturbation

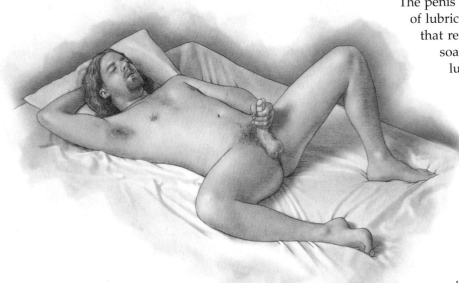

Figure 9.3 Male masturbation

The penis does not produce a significant amount of lubrication (and neither does the hand!). For that reason, some men like to use saliva, oil, soapsuds, or a water- or oil-based sexual lubricant—whatever feels good and does not irritate the penis. Alternative methods of masturbation include lying in contact with an object such as a pillow or the edge of a bed and thrusting against it. Some men like to stimulate the nipples or anus with their free hand while masturbating with the other, but few can reach orgasm without direct stimulation of the penis.

Most men take about 2 to 3 minutes from the beginning of masturbation to the point of orgasm, compared with about 4 minutes for women, though these data are old and need to be replicated (Kinsey et al., 1948; Kinsey et al., 1953). Some men and women like to draw out the experience over a period of many minutes, perhaps approaching orgasm several times and then easing off before finally climaxing; others like to reach orgasm as quickly as possible.

Gay People Masturbate More Than Heterosexuals

Intuitively, one might imagine that gay men and lesbians would enjoy masturbation more than heterosexual men and women, and might masturbate more frequently. Gay people's own bodies, after all, are of the sex that they find sexually attractive, so autoerotic behavior might be more arousing for them than for straight people. According to the NHSLS data, gays and lesbians (or people with recent homosexual experience) do masturbate far more frequently than do heterosexual men and women (**Figure 9.4**).

This difference was confirmed in a survey of male German college students: Gay students not only masturbated more frequently (regardless of whether they were partnered or not), but also derived greater pleasure from masturbation (Schmidt, 2000). Furthermore, gay male students were far more likely than straight male students to masturbate in front of a mirror—48% of gay students had done so in the previous 12 months, versus only 18% of straight students (G. Schmidt, pers. comm.). Comparable data for women are not available.

These findings suggest that gay people's relatively greater interest in masturbation may result from a greater erotic response to their own bodies, although other explanations are possible. This is not meant to imply that gay people are, in general, erotically focused on themselves. Both lesbians and gay men are as "other-directed" in their sex lives as heterosexual men and women (see Chapter 14).

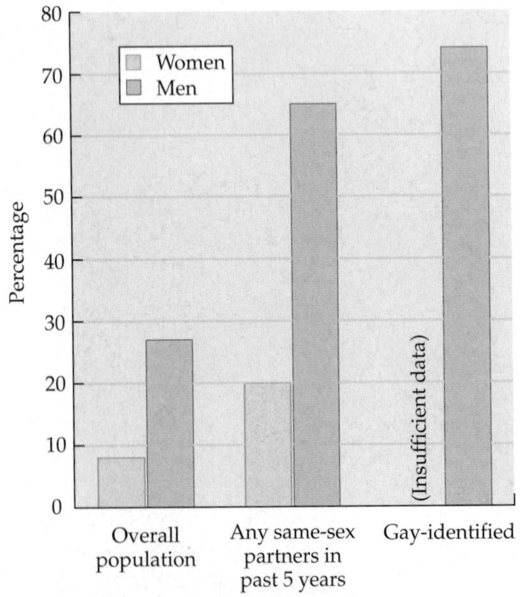

Different Cultures Have Different Attitudes toward Masturbation

In the *International Encyclopedia of Sexuality*, which is a compilation of reports by sex researchers from about 50 countries (Francoeur, 2001), masturbation is most commonly presented as something practiced by children or adolescents; adults seldom masturbate, it is said, and they often consider the prac-

Figure 9.4 Masturbation and sexual orientation Homosexual behavior or identity is associated with a high frequency of masturbation. These histograms show the percentages of men and women who masturbate at least once per week. (Data from NHSLS.)

tice shameful, ridiculous, or unhealthful. Nevertheless, many of the researchers stress the difficulty of finding out the true prevalence of masturbation. In addition, most of the countries represented in the Encyclopedia are either Western or have been strongly influenced by Western ideas about sex.

What about truly non-Western cultures? Some cultures have taboos against male masturbation on account of beliefs about semen: that it is contaminating or, conversely, that it is so valuable that its loss will cause ill health or even death. Nevertheless, there are examples of more positive attitudes. Hortense Powdermaker, an American anthropologist who spent a decade living in a Melanesian village in New Ireland (part of Papua New Guinea) during the 1920s, wrote as follows:

> A woman will masturbate if she is sexually excited and there is no man to satisfy her. A couple may be having intercourse in the same house, or near enough for her to see them, and she may thus become aroused. She then sits down and bends her right leg so that her heel presses against her genitalia. Even young girls of about six years may do this quite casually as they sit on the ground. The women and men talk about it freely, and there is no shame attached to it. It is a customary position for women to take, and they learn it in childhood. They never use their hands for manipulation [of their genitals]. (Powdermaker, 1933, cited in Ford & Beach, 1951.)

In Chapter 4 we mentioned Gagnon and Simon's idea that the high rate of masturbation by pubertal boys plays a role in focusing male sexuality on the physical pleasure of sex. Conversely, it has been suggested that the relatively low frequency of masturbation by girls might hinder their development of the ability to experience sexual pleasure and orgasm in partnered sex. Some therapies aimed at overcoming sexual problems in women, especially the inability to experience orgasm, therefore involve instruction in masturbation (see Chapter 16).

deep kissing Kissing with entry of the tongue into the partner's mouth.

The Kiss Represents True Love—Sometimes

To anyone familiar with the poetry and music that depicts the kisses of dying lovers—Shakespeare's Romeo and Juliet, and Wagner's Tristan and Isolde, among many others—or who remembers the great screen kisses of Clark Gable and Vivien Leigh (in *Gone with the Wind*) or of Heath Ledger and Jake Gyllenhaal (in *Brokeback Mountain*), to name just a few, the kiss signifies one thing and one thing only: a passionate love that transcends life itself.

In reality, of course, kisses come in many different degrees and flavors, from the no-contact "air kiss" and the perfunctory cheek peck to the wildest oral adventures that tongue, lips, and teeth are capable of. A kiss may mean nothing, it may be a way of saying that "real sex" is on the way, or it may solemnify the union of two souls "till death do us part."

Surprisingly, kissing is not as ubiquitous a custom as we Westerners might imagine. Anthropologists Clellan Ford and Frank Beach listed eight non-Western societies in which kissing of any kind was unknown (Ford & Beach, 1951). One of these societies was that of the Thonga, who live in the southern lowlands of Mozambique. "When the Thonga first saw Europeans kissing," wrote Ford and Beach, "they laughed, expressing this sentiment: 'Look at them—they eat each other's saliva and dirt.'"

Even in the United States, attitudes toward kissing vary. In the Kinsey studies of the 1940s, well-educated men and women were much more likely than less-educated people to report engaging in **deep** ("French") **kissing**—another example of the association between education and more liberal attitudes toward sexual practices. It is likely that deep kissing has become more broadly accepted today than it was in Kinsey's time,

The Kiss, completed in 1898 by Auguste Rodin, was originally intended to represent Paolo and Francesca, the doomed lovers in Dante's *Inferno*.

foreplay Sexual behavior engaged in during the early part of a sexual encounter, with the aim of increasing sexual arousal.

afterplay Sexual behavior engaged in after coitus or orgasm, or at the end of a sexual encounter.

necking Kissing or caressing of the head and neck.

petting Sexually touching the partner's body (often taken to exclude the breasts or genitalia).

heavy petting Sexually touching the partner's genitalia or breasts.

fondling Any kind of sexual touching of the partner's body.

tribadism Sexual behavior between two women, who lie front-to-front and stimulate each other's vulvas with thrusting motions.

although rising concern about HIV-AIDS and other sexually transmitted diseases may discourage deep kissing in a casual context—even though it is very rare for HIV to be transmitted by any kind of kissing.

Of course, mouths can roam farther than a partner's mouth. Almost every body part is licked, sucked, bitten, or chewed on in the heat of somebody's passion. Breasts are a perennial favorite. Oral–genital contacts are discussed below. Even the sucking of toes ("shrimping") can be highly arousing to both partners.

"Petting" and "Fondling" Refer to a Variety of Noncoital Behaviors

Simple touching of another person's body can be a powerfully intimate and sexual act (Davis, 1999). People engage in all kinds of hand-to-body and body-to-body contacts, sometimes as **foreplay** (behavior designed to increase pleasure and arousal prior to some "main event," such as coitus), but also often as the "main event" in itself, or as **afterplay**. "Necking," "petting," and "heavy petting" are words traditionally used to describe some of this behavior: **Necking** means kissing and touching confined to the head and neck; **petting** means touching naked skin below the neck—usually excluding the breasts or genitalia; **heavy petting** means touching the breasts or genitalia. **Fondling** is a broader term that could include any of these behaviors. Sometimes "petting" is used to describe anything short of coitus or anal penetration, in which case it would include oral–genital contact. "Outercourse" is another term to describe noncoital or nonpenetrative sexual contact, especially when it is practiced as a way to avoid pregnancy. Some kinds of petting may be accompanied by orgasm, but the participants are not "having sex" by many young people's way of thinking (see above).

General body-to-body contact, accompanied by rubbing or thrusting motions of the pelvis that stimulate the clitoris or penis, is a common part of sexual activity for many people, and may readily lead to orgasm. When two women engage in this activity, rubbing their vulvas against each other's bodies with pelvic thrusting motions, it is called **tribadism** (**Figure 9.5**).

Oral Sex Is Increasingly Popular

Oral sex has become an increasingly prevalent activity among younger people over the last few decades, both in the United States and Britain. Thus, paradoxically, younger people are more likely than older people to have engaged in oral sex at some point during their lifetime. In the NSSAL (British) study, for example, only 50% of women in the 45–59 age bracket said that they had ever participated in any kind of oral sex, but 83% of women in the 25–34 age bracket had done so.

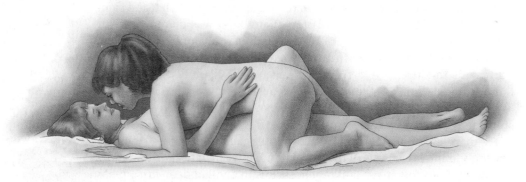

Figure 9.5 Tribadism

The corresponding figures for men were 62% and 88%. Of course, there are always alternative explanations of such data, such as that older people forget some of the things they did in their wilder years. The Kinsey surveys of the 1940s reported much lower rates of oral sex than the recent NSSAL and NHSLS studies, however, suggesting that the increase over time is real.

Oral–genital contacts are of three main kinds: mouth–penis contact (fellatio, also known as a "blow job," "sucking off," "going down on," or "giving head"), mouth–vulva contact (cunnilingus, "eating," or "going down on"), and mouth–anus contact (anilingus or analingus, "rimming").

Fellatio Is Oral Stimulation of the Penis

Fellatio, like most sex, is a pretty simple matter (**Figure 9.6A**). One person (the "insertee") takes the insertor's penis into her or his mouth, and usually runs the lips rhythmically up and down the shaft of the penis, keeping them fairly tight so as to provide optimal stimulation. The insertee may also use the tongue to stimulate the most sensitive portions of the penis, the corona and frenulum. As a variation, the insertee may lick the scrotum or take one or both testicles into the mouth.

The insertor often wants his penis to go deeper and deeper into his partner's mouth as he becomes increasingly aroused, but this may cause gagging, depending on the length of the man's penis and his partner's experience. As with every aspect of two-person sex, good communication is key.

Fellatio can be continued to the point that the insertor ejaculates. Here again, however, communication is important. Some people don't like the experience of receiving the ejaculate in the mouth, or have concerns about disease transmission. The taste and odor of semen varies from man to man, and is also affected by diet—strongly odorous foods such as garlic are particular offenders. As to swallowing the ejaculate, the perennial question is: How many calories does it contain? The answer: an insignificant amount—less than 5 calories.

In heterosexual contexts, men typically enjoy fellatio more than women do (**Figure 9.7**). Thus it seems that women engage in fellatio to give their male partners pleasure more than as a directly pleasurable experience for themselves. The NHSLS study also found cultural differences: For example, more-educated people tended to enjoy it more than less-educated people.

Not a great deal is known about fellatio in non-Western cultures. One well-studied exception is the Sambia of New Guinea. As we described in Chapter 1, rit-

(A)

(B)

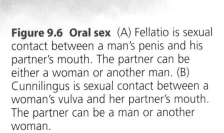

Figure 9.6 Oral sex (A) Fellatio is sexual contact between a man's penis and his partner's mouth. The partner can be either a woman or another man. (B) Cunnilingus is sexual contact between a woman's vulva and her partner's mouth. The partner can be a man or another woman.

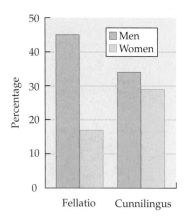

Figure 9.7 Popularity of oral sex The graph shows the percentages of men and women who find fellatio and cunnilingus "very appealing." (Data from NHSLS.)

FAQ I've heard that blowing into a woman's vagina is dangerous. Is it?
Blowing into a pregnant woman's vagina as if trying to inflate a balloon may indeed cause an air embolism (blockage of arteries with air) that can be fatal. Whether this can happen in a nonpregnant woman is unclear—we suggest you avoid vigorous blowing.

cunnilingus Sexual contact between the tongue or mouth of one person and the vulva of another.

anilingus Sexual contact between the mouth or tongue and the partner's anus.

ualized fellatio is practiced between older and younger Sambia youths and is believed to confer the qualities of manhood on the younger boys (the insertees). Besides its ritual significance, this activity provides a sexual outlet for the older youths, who have no access to women because they are sequestered in all-male groups.

Cunnilingus Is Oral Stimulation of the Vulva

In **cunnilingus** (see Figure 9.6B), a woman's partner explores her vulva with lips and tongue. The tongue provides very effective sexual stimulation for many women because it is soft, wet, warm, and highly mobile. Thus it is much easier to stimulate the clitoris and labia minora in an uninhibited way with the tongue than with, say, the fingers, which may provide too-harsh stimulation to the most sensitive areas, such as the glans of the clitoris. For some women, cunnilingus is the only way by which they regularly achieve orgasm (Hite, 2003).

Considering that men enjoy fellatio more than women, you might expect that women would enjoy cunnilingus more than men. In the NHSLS study, however, slightly more men than women said that they found cunnilingus "very appealing" (see Figure 9.7). Again, there were cultural differences: Cunnilingus was more popular among more-educated men and women than among the less educated.

If a couple arrange themselves in a mutual head-to-genital position, they can perform oral sex on each other simultaneously (**Figure 9.8**). This practice is often called "69" or "soixante-neuf" (French for 69). While sixty-nining can be very exciting, it has two possible drawbacks. The first is that each partner may be distracted from enjoying what is going on at one location by the need to attend to the other location. Also, when fellatio is performed in the 69 position, the tongue of the insertee is located on the upper, less sensitive surface of the penis and cannot easily reach the area of the frenulum.

There is little information about the prevalence of **anilingus** (mouth–anal contact). This practice can be very arousing because the skin around the anus is erotically sensitive. Sometimes anilingus is performed as a prelude to anal penetration. Many people avoid anilingus, however, because of negative associations

Figure 9.8 Mutual oral sex may be called "69" or "soixante-neuf." Though shown here between a man and a woman, any sex combination can perform this activity.

with defecation or because of health concerns, which are to some extent justified (see Chapter 17).

Most Sexual Encounters Include Coitus

Penetration of the vagina by the penis is called **coitus**, or "fucking," in blunt English. (The phrase "sexual intercourse" is usually taken to mean coitus, but it is a less well-defined term that could include other behaviors.) Coitus is central to many people's sex lives. Ninety-five percent of sexual encounters between opposite-sex adults include coitus, according to the NHSLS study, and it is usually the final behavior in an encounter. Still, same-sex couples have equally satisfying sex lives without the option of coitus. A focus on coitus as the be-all and end-all of sex may unduly limit people's sexual satisfaction, most especially where there are performance problems such as erectile dysfunction (see Chapter 16).

Coitus Can Be Performed in Many Different Positions

Perhaps the most striking thing about human coitus, compared with coitus in animals, is the wide variety of positions that a couple may adopt to perform it. Among animals, only our closest primate relatives exhibit any significant degree of flexibility in this regard: Bonobos, for example, engage in both front-to-front and rear-entry coitus. But humans can and do attempt an almost unlimited number of different positions, a few of which are sketched in **Figure 9.9**.

If you actually tried a large range of positions such as those shown in Figure 9.9, you would probably find that each provided a somewhat different physical and emotional experience, and thus might be preferable in some particular situation. Some positions, for example, allow the man to make thrusting motions of his pelvis but restrict the woman's mobility. Some allow the reverse, while others allow both partners some degree of freedom. Thus there may be positions that are appropriate when one or the other partner is in an aggressive, take-control mood or, conversely, desires to play a passive role. In some positions, the hands of one or both partners are free to explore and stimulate erogenous zones; in others, the arms and hands may be occupied in supporting the weight of the body. Some positions require strenuous exertion and cannot be maintained for long periods of time, while others are more relaxed and may be suitable for couples who want to

FAQ Recently, I've noticed some minor bleeding from my vagina after sex—is that something to worry about? Post-coital bleeding can have many causes, including yeast infections, sexually transmitted diseases, fibroids, uterine polyps (growths from the endometrium), and precancerous changes in the cervix. It is definitely a reason to see your doctor.

coitus Penetration of the vagina by the penis.

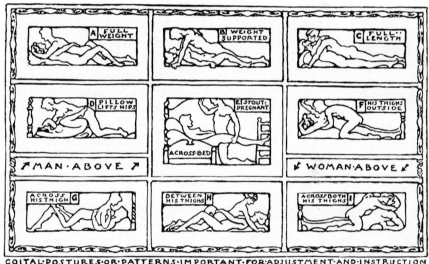

Figure 9.9 Coitus (penile–vaginal penetration) can be performed in numerous positions. These illustrations are from a 1940s manual used by physicians in marriage counseling.

engage in prolonged, leisurely sex, or for obese or frail people. Yet others may be suitable if the woman is advanced in pregnancy. Some positions allow for eye contact between the man and the woman; this may be crucial for a head-over-heels-in-love couple, but less so for other couples. Some positions provide more erotic stimulation to the man, and others provide more stimulation to the woman; such considerations may be relevant if the couple is trying to reach orgasm simultaneously. Some positions provide the woman with more clitoral stimulation, and some stimulate the area of the G-spot, which may affect the quality of the woman's orgasm or whether she experiences one at all. In short, there seems to be every reason for couples to experiment and to communicate, not just for variety's sake, but so as to suit their sexual behavior to their needs.

The Man-Above Position Is the Traditional Favorite

In spite of the possible advantages of experimentation, Americans tend to stick to one tried-and-true position for coitus, in which the woman lies on her back with her legs parted and the man places himself above her, supporting his upper body with his hands or elbows (**Figure 9.10**). This man-above position is also referred to derisively as the "missionary position," a phrase apparently invented by Alfred Kinsey (Priest, 2001). At the time of his surveys in the 1940s, Kinsey estimated that 75% of Americans had never tried any other position for coitus.

With coitus in the man-above position, one partner guides the man's penis into the woman's vagina. If the woman does this, it may give her a sense of control that otherwise is lacking in the man-above position. Because the man is above, he has to do most of the "work" of coitus (i.e., the pelvic thrusting); the woman's freedom of movement is restricted by the man's body, especially if he is much larger than she is. This position has the advantage of allowing eye contact during sex but the disadvantage that the man's hands are not free to roam over the woman's body.

Simple variations on the man-above position include the woman's achieving more hip flexion by curling her legs around the man's back or even draping them over his shoulders. Such positions allow the man's penis to extend more deeply into the vagina than when the woman's legs are straight or only slightly bent at the knees.

The man-above position generally provides good erotic stimulation for the man—sometimes too good, if he tends to ejaculate more rapidly than he or his partner would like. For the woman, it is more variable. Some women are well stimulated by coitus in this position; for others, there is insufficient stimulation, especially of the G-spot, since the penis is directed toward the rear wall of the vagina (**Box 9.2**).

The Women's Movement Encouraged Alternative Positions

Since Kinsey's time, the sexual revolution and the women's movement have spurred Americans to try other positions besides the man-above position. The connection between the women's movement and changes in coital position was well illustrated in 1975, when stu-

Figure 9.10 The man-above position for coitus is also called the "missionary position."

Research Highlights

BOX 9.2 Progress in Coitus Research

In Chapter 1 (see Figure 1.2) we showed Leonardo da Vinci's anatomical drawing of a couple engaged in coitus. Of course, Leonardo didn't really cut people in half in the way that he depicted it—he just imagined it—and as a result, the anatomical details are highly suspect. Leonardo showed the man's penis sticking straight out from his body like a flagstaff. He also had some odd ideas about internal anatomy. If you look back to the drawing, you'll see that there's a tube running from the woman's uterus to her breast, which has no basis in reality. The scientific value of Leonardo's study, however, lay not so much in its veracity, or lack thereof, as in its implied message: that sex was a suitable subject for study.

Half a millennium later, gynecologist Willibrord Schultz and his colleagues at the University Hospital in Groningen, Holland, decided to check on Leonardo's conception of coitus by means of magnetic resonance imaging (MRI) (Schultz et al., 1999). It wasn't easy. First, there was the question of space. If you have ever been inside an MRI machine, you'll know that it's a tight fit: The tube you lie in is only 20 inches in diameter. Imagine having someone else in there with you, and then going through the contortions required even for missionary-position sex. The researchers had to select smallish volunteers, and in fact, the first couple that succeeded in achieving penetration in the MRI machine was a pair of amateur acrobats.

The researchers had an even more serious problem, however: The male volunteers' penises did not stand up well to the study's high-stress conditions. It took nearly a minute to acquire a single MRI image, and the men just couldn't

keep their penises stationary and erect inside the women's vaginas for that length of time.

Five years after the start of the study, however, two unexpected breakthroughs occurred. The researchers obtained a new MRI machine that could generate an image in a mere 12 seconds, and sildenafil (Viagra) came onto the market (see Chapter 16). By swallowing a pill an hour before entering the machine, the men were able to maintain an erection as long as necessary. At last the researchers obtained sharp pictures of the man's fully erect penis deep within the woman's vagina (see figure).

In these pictures, the penis is not straight, as depicted by Leonardo, but bent upward, with the hinge point near the abdomen. Thus the entire penis (including the root of the penis within the man's body) has the shape of a boomerang.

In the images, the sensitive lower surface of the penis presses against the back wall of the woman's vagina, an arrangement that may be highly stimulating to the man. Yet the penis makes little contact with the front wall of the vagina, which is the location of the controversial G-spot. (The particular women who participated in the study said they did not have G-spots.) These findings support the notion that positions other than the missionary position would provide better stimulation to the female partner, especially if she desires stimulation of the G-spot.

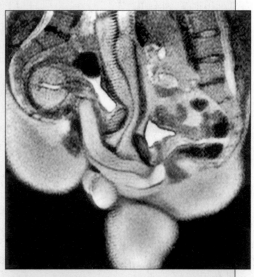

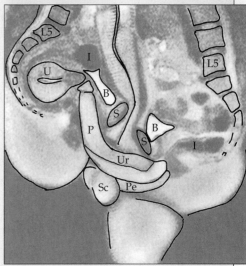

MRI image of coitus (top) with explanatory drawing (bottom). P = penis; Ur = urethra; Pe = perineum; U = uterus; B = bladder; I = intestine; L5 = fifth lumbar vertebra; Sc = scrotum; S = pubic symphysis. (From Schultz et al., 1999).

dents at Smith College celebrated their school's centennial with T-shirts proclaiming "A Century of Women on Top."

One alternative is the woman-above position (**Figure 9.11**). In this position the man lies on his back, and the woman either lies on top of him in a face-to-face arrangement (which allows full body contact) or sits upright. The woman-above position gives the woman greater control, since she generates much of the thrusting motion. In general, the woman-above position may give the man somewhat less erotic stimulation than the man-above position, and the woman may receive somewhat more stimulation. (This may be helpful if the man tends to reach orgasm more rapidly than the woman does, which is common.) Furthermore,

Figure 9.11 The woman-above position for coitus In this position, the woman is more in control and does most of the thrusting. The man may receive less stimulation, which can be a good thing if he tends to reach orgasm prematurely.

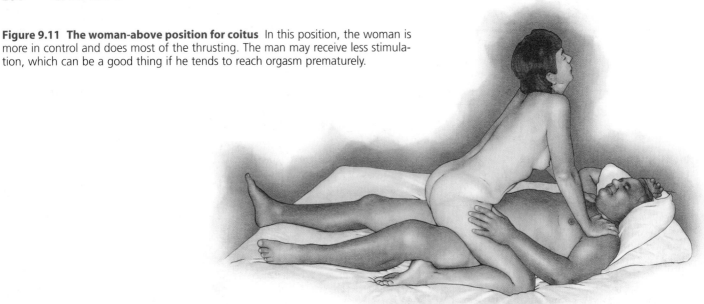

especially when the woman adopts a sitting position, it is relatively easy for her or the man to manually caress her breasts or her clitoris, thus increasing her erotic stimulation further. In a variation of the woman-above position, the woman sits upright but faces away from the man. This "reverse cowgirl" position allows for deep penetration, but it doesn't allow for eye contact. Perhaps for that reason, it is not popular: Only about 1 in 50 Americans chose it as a favorite in the *Esquire/Marie Claire* survey (*Esquire*, 2007).

Another alternative is the side-by-side position (**Figure 9.12**), in which the woman and the man face each other, but each lies with one side directly on the bed (or floor, or grass!). Coitus in this position tends to be relatively relaxed, since neither partner's thrusting is aided by gravity, and penetration tends to be shallow. This may be desirable if the intention is to prolong the sexual encounter or if health concerns restrict one or both partners' ability to expend energy. One problem with side-by-side coitus, however, is that limbs tend to get trapped under bodies and may go numb in the middle of the action. In addition, the penis rather easily becomes dislodged from the vagina, and reinsertion can be awkward in the side-to-side position.

In rear-entry coitus (**Figure 9.13**), the man faces the woman's back. There are a number of ways of accomplishing rear-entry coitus: The couple may lie side by

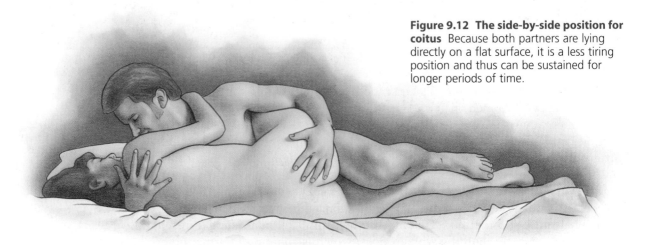

Figure 9.12 The side-by-side position for coitus Because both partners are lying directly on a flat surface, it is a less tiring position and thus can be sustained for longer periods of time.

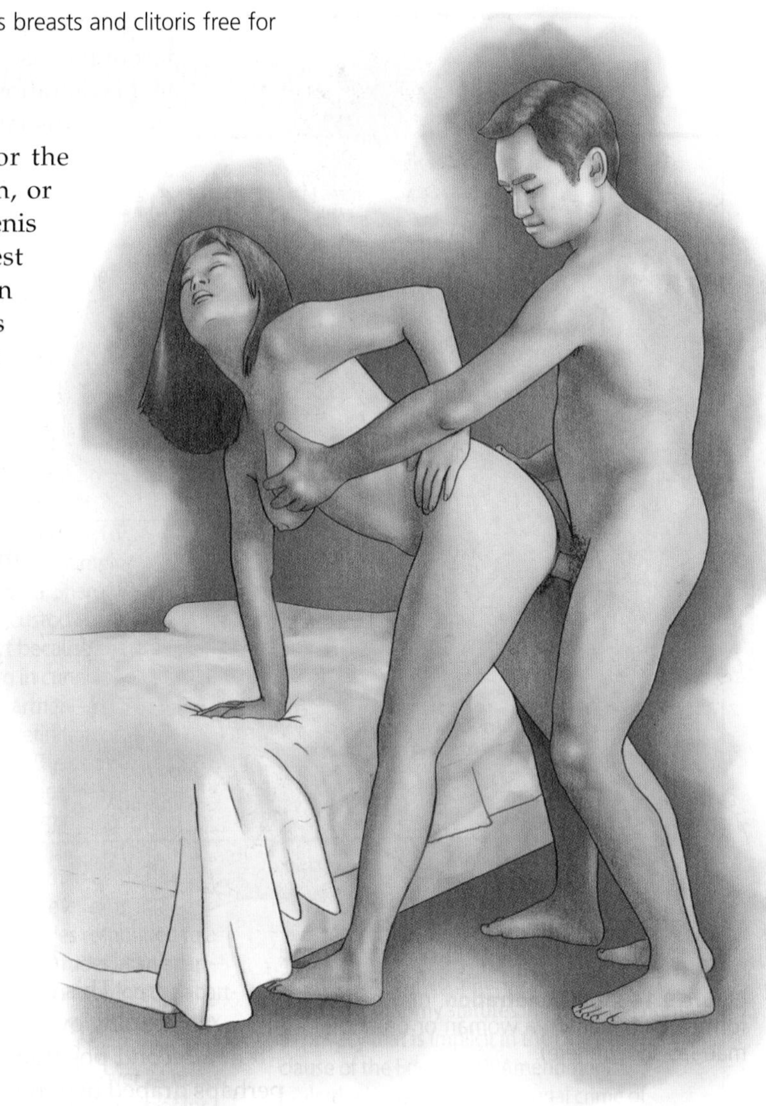

Figure 9.13 Rear-entry coitus This position leaves the woman's breasts and clitoris free for manual stimulation by either partner.

side with the woman turned away from the man, or the woman may be lying prone or in a crouched position, or standing and leaning over some object. Because the penis enters the vagina from the rear, it comes into strongest contact with the vagina's front wall, and penetration tends to be fairly shallow. There are rear-entry positions that give deep penetration, however, such as when the woman is crouching on her knees with her chest down on the surface.

As indicated by its slang name, "doggy-style," rear-entry coitus is a reminder of our kinship with the animal world. It has a number of potential advantages and disadvantages. The man may find contact with the woman's back and buttocks arousing, and the fact that the woman's front is free makes it easy for either partner to stimulate her breasts and clitoris during coitus. Rear-entry coitus in the side-by-side position may be the most comfortable position for a woman in the later stages of pregnancy. In rear-entry coitus, the angle of penetration of the vagina is ideal for women who like stimulation of the G-spot, but there is no direct stimulation of the clitoris. Another possible disadvantage is that eye contact is limited.

Anal Sex May Be a Part of Either Heterosexual or Male Homosexual Behavior

By **anal sex** (**Figure 9.14**), we mean penetration of the anus by the penis ("butt-fucking"). Anal sex should be distinguished from rear-entry coitus, in which the penis penetrates the vagina from behind. Until recently, anal sex was illegal in some states (**Box 9.3**).

Although anal sex is often thought of in connection with sex between men, it is not rare in heterosexual sex. Heterosexual couples may engage in anal sex in order to avoid pregnancy, to avoid "having sex" in the narrow sense of the phrase, because the greater tightness of the anus (compared with the vagina) may be stimulating to the man, because anal stimulation is arousing to the woman, or simply for the sake of variety. In the 2005 National Center for Health Statistics study, 35% of women and 40% of men (age 25 to 44) said that they had engaged in anal sex with an opposite-sex partner (Mosher et al., 2005). In one survey of female and male college students, 18% of the respondents stated that they had engaged in anal sex (Baldwin & Baldwin, 2000). Apparently, most of the students who engaged in anal sex were risk-takers: They were unlikely to have used condoms during either anal or vaginal sex.

The mechanics of anal sex deserve some discussion. The anus is normally kept closed by the tonic contraction of two **sphincter** muscles, the external and internal sphincters (see Chapter 3), and the internal sphincter may go into an even

anal sex Penetration of the anus by the penis, or any sexual behavior involving the anus.

sphincter A circular muscle around an orifice whose contraction closes the orifice.

Personal Points of View

BOX 9.6 On Seeing a Sex Surrogate

Mark O'Brien was a Berkeley-based writer who, as a consequence of childhood polio, had to spend most of his life inside an iron lung. In a 1990 article for *The Sun,* O'Brien described his efforts to achieve sexual fulfillment. The following is a condensed version of the article, which is available in full on the Web (O'Brien, 1990).

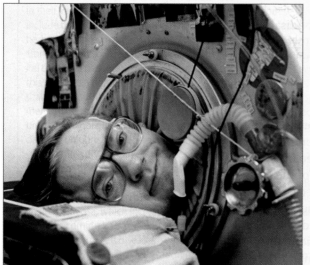

Mark O'Brien (1949–1999)

On the phone, Cheryl had explained that she would interview me for the first hour of the session; then, if I agreed, we would do 'body awareness exercises.' I was too scared to ask what this meant, but said I would give it a go.

When March 17 arrived, I felt unbearably nervous. Vera, one of my morning attendants, dressed me, put me in my wheelchair, and pushed me to Marie's cottage. Once inside, Vera put a sheet I had brought with me on the double bed. Then she lowered me onto it. The bed was close to the floor, unlike my iron lung. Since it's difficult for me to turn my head to the left, Vera pushed me over to the left side of the bed, so that Cheryl could lay next to me and I could still see her. Then Vera put the hose of my portable respirator near my mouth, in case I needed air. I thought it likely because I'd never been outside the

iron lung for an hour without using the portable respirator. I was all set.

Oh God, would she ever come? Perhaps she had found out what an ugly, deformed creep I am and was breaking the appointment.

A knock on the door. Cheryl had arrived. I turned my head as far to my left as I could. She greeted me, smiling, and walked to where I could see her better. She doesn't hate me yet, I thought. Marie went out the door with Vera, saying that she would return at 1. Cheryl and I were alone. 'Your fee's on top of the dresser,' I said, unable to think of anything else to say. She put the cash into her wallet, and thanked me.

She wore a black pantsuit, and her dark brown hair was tied behind her head. She had clear skin and large brown eyes and she seemed tall and strong, but then I'm 4' 7" and weigh sixty pounds. As we talked, I decided that she was definitely attractive. Was she checking out my looks? I was too scared to want to know.

Talking helped me to relax. I began to tell her about my life, my family, my fear of sexuality. I could see that she was accepting me and treating me with respect. I liked her, so when she asked me if I would feel comfortable letting her undress me, I said, 'Sure.' I was bluffing, attempting to hide my fear.

My heart pounded—not with lust, but with pure terror—as she kneeled on the bed and started to unbutton my red shirt. She had trouble undressing me; I felt awkward and wondered if she would change her mind and leave once she saw me naked. She didn't. After she took my clothes off, she got out of bed and undressed quickly. I looked at her full, pale breasts, but was too shy to gaze between her legs.

Whenever I had been naked before—always in front of nurses, doctors, and

attendants—I'd pretend I wasn't naked. Now that I was in bed with another naked person, I didn't need to pretend: I was undressed, she was undressed, and it seemed normal. How startling!

She stroked my hair and told me how good it felt. This surprised me; I had never thought of my hair, or any other part of me, as feeling or looking good. Having at least one attractive feature helped me to feel more confident. She explained about the body awareness exercises: first, she would run her hand over me, and I could kiss her wherever I wished. I told her I wished that I could caress her, too, but she assured me I could excite her with my mouth and tongue. She rubbed scented oil on her hands, then slowly moved her palms in circles over my chest and arms. She was complimenting me in a soft, steady voice, while I chattered nervously about everything that came to mind. I asked her if I could kiss one of her breasts. She sidled up to me so that I could kiss her left breast. *So soft.*

'Now if you kiss one, you have to kiss the other,' she said. 'That's the rule.'

Amused by her mock seriousness, I moved to her right breast. She told me to lick around the edge of the nipple. She said she liked that. I knew she was helping me to feel more relaxed, but that didn't make her encouragements seem less true.

I was getting aroused. Her hand moved in its slow circles lower and lower as she continued to talk in her reassuring way and I continued my chattering. She lightly touched my cock—as though she liked it, as though it was fine that I was aroused. No one had ever touched me that way, or praised me for my sexuality. Too soon, I came.

After that, we talked a while. I asked Cheryl whether she thought I deserved to be loved sexually. She said she was sure of it. I nearly cried. She didn't hate me. She didn't consider me repulsive.

She got out of bed, went into the bathroom, and dressed. By then it was nearly 1. The door opened. It was Marie and Dixie. They asked me about the experience. I told them it had changed my life. I felt victorious, cleansed, and relieved.

sports accidents, or falls. A complete injury at the cervical (neck) level results in almost total loss of movement and sensation below the neck (**quadriplegia**), while injuries at lower levels usually affect the legs and the lower portion of the trunk, including the genitalia (**paraplegia**).

One option adopted by many men and women with spinal cord injuries is to make increased use of parts of the body whose movement and sensation is unimpaired. In quadriplegics that may mean primarily the mouth, while for paraplegics it may include the hands and breasts. Many people with spinal cord injuries report that the erotic sensitivity of their unaffected body regions increases over time, so much so that the person may experience orgasm, or highly pleasant sensations comparable to orgasm, from sexual use of those regions. In some cases the sensations may be experienced as if they were coming from the genitalia ("phantom orgasm").

A man with a spinal cord injury may or may not be able to have an erection. If the injury is to the lowest (sacral) portion of the spinal cord, the man is unlikely to be able to have an erection under any circumstances, because the parasympathetic neurons that provide the major drive for erection are located there. If the injury is high in the spinal cord, he probably will be able to have erections in response to sensory stimulation of the genitalia because the entire reflex loop from the genitalia to the spinal cord and back is intact. However, if the spinal injury is complete, the man will not feel any sensations from his penis, erect or not. Nor will he have erections in response to erotic sights or fantasies ("psychogenic erections") because the long pathways between the brain and the lower spinal cord have been interrupted. Some men with injuries at lumbar (lower-back) levels can have psychogenic erections, apparently mediated by sympathetic pathways that leave the cord at thoracic (chest) levels, but these erections are weak and short-lived and therefore are not generally usable for coitus (Rehman & Melman, 2001). Viagra and similar drugs have proved helpful for men with spinal cord injuries who have difficulty obtaining or maintaining an erection, but only if at least a partial erection can be obtained without the drug (Schmid et al., 2000).

Figure 9.16 Paraplegia typically strikes young men. Sexual expression is still possible but requires adaptability.

Ejaculation may be possible for men with lower-level injuries, especially if they are incomplete, but a complete upper-level injury generally makes ejaculation impossible because it cuts off signals from the brain centers that are involved in triggering this process. Even if ejaculation is possible, it is not likely to be accompanied by the normal subjective sensations of orgasm. Ejaculation may occur retrogradely (into the bladder) due to the failure of the sphincter at the upper end of the urethra to close.

Men with spinal cord injuries who wish to engage in coitus are usually capable of doing so. If the man is paraplegic, he can take the man-on-top position. He may have to push his flaccid penis into the woman's vagina by hand (the "stuffing" technique); the woman can help this process by actively contracting the muscles of the vaginal walls. The man's penis may then become erect as a result of reflex action as the woman performs thrusting motions. If the man is quadriplegic, the woman does best to kneel astride him and place his penis in her vagina; again, the penis may become erect in response to this stimulation. An additional complication is urinary incontinence. If a urinary catheter is in place, it can be

quadriplegia Paralysis affecting almost the entire body below the neck.
paraplegia Paralysis affecting the lower half of the body.

kept in place with the aid of a condom or tape; this, then, will necessitate the use of a lubricant.

Women with spinal cord injuries have deficits roughly comparable to men: Besides the loss of movement and sensation (depending on the level and severity of the injury), women may lose vaginal lubrication (necessitating use of a lubricant). With lower-level injuries, engorgement of the vulvar tissues may be lost as well. Coitus is possible in several positions, however, including the man-on-top position, or side by side with either front or rear entry.

In one laboratory-based study (Sipski et al., 2001), somewhat fewer than half of the women with spinal cord injuries were able to reach orgasm, compared with 100% of a control group of women. Ability to reach orgasm was lowest with complete injuries affecting the lowest (sacral) region of the spinal cord. Among women who did reach orgasm, the time required to do so was longer than among the control women, but the orgasms themselves were similar in quality.

Paraplegic and quadriplegic women can sustain a pregnancy and deliver a baby vaginally, although there is a somewhat increased risk of complications and of premature birth. Contraception presents some special problems for women with spinal cord injuries.

If you are an able-bodied and sexually active young person, you might be wondering whether sexual interactions are really worth it for spinal-cord–injured men and women or their partners. The answer, however, is often a resounding yes—whether in terms of physical pleasure, intimacy between partners, or the psychological reward of accomplishing such a basic human activity in the face of a major challenge.

Many Intellectually Disabled People Are Competent to Make Sexual Choices

Traditionally, intellectually disabled children and adults (who used to be described as "mentally retarded") were sequestered in institutions. The motive was protection, and they were rarely given the opportunity to make any active decisions for themselves, least of all in the area of sexuality. Often they did not receive any sex education, out of concern that this might encourage sexual behavior. Intellectually disabled women (and, to a lesser extent, men) were sometimes sterilized involuntarily, either out of concern that they would not be able to fulfill their parental roles or because of fear that any children they had would themselves be retarded.

Nowadays, people with mild or moderate intellectual disabilities often participate in community life and may live in independent or semi-independent settings. There has been an increasing acknowledgment that most intellectually disabled people have sexual feelings—only some profoundly disabled people seem to lack them. Intellectually disabled people have the same constitutional right as other people (under the right to privacy) to make informed choices about sexual activity, if they are capable of doing so. They also have a right to protection from sexual exploitation, however. Balancing these rights can be difficult.

In general, it is illegal, as well as reprehensible, for anyone to have sexual contact with an intellectually disabled person if that person lacks the mental capacity to give informed consent. Mental capacity means knowledge about sex, the intelligence to understand the risks and benefits of sexual activity (including an awareness of the social and moral nature of sexual relations), and the ability to make a decision free of coercion. No one can give consent on behalf of the disabled person (Stavis, 1991). Thus, if a person is judged by psychiatrists or others not to be capable of giving consent, caregivers have a responsibility to protect that person from all sexual contact with others because such contact would be sexual assault or statutory rape. Institutional staff may realize that an intellectually disabled person of borderline capacity has the wish to engage in sex and may therefore be motivated to judge that person competent. The downside of doing this is that if the judgment of competence holds up, the disabled person may be sexually exploited by others with little recourse.

Luckily, many intellectually disabled people are well within the bounds of competence and chiefly need education in such matters as potential sexual behaviors, appropriate partners, privacy, sexual exploitation, STDs, pregnancy prevention, and the like (Lumley & Scotti, 2001). The Arc, a national organization of and for the intellectually disabled, asserts the right of these people not only to engage in sexual relationships, but also to marry and have children and, if they do have children, to receive assistance in raising them (The Arc, 2007).

Summary

1. Sexual behavior is difficult to define precisely, but it includes much more than coitus (penile-vaginal sexual intercourse). Any behavior that is accompanied by physiological signs of sexual arousal, or that is perceived as sexual by the participants, may be included.

2. Historically, attitudes toward masturbation or autoerotic behavior have been quite negative. These attitudes derive from moral teachings, from the notion that masturbation is unhealthy, and from a sense that people who masturbate are those who can't find a sex partner. Even today, many people feel guilty about masturbating.

3. According to the NHSLS, about half of U.S. adults masturbate at least once per year. Factors associated with higher rates of masturbation include male sex, a younger age, and a higher educational level. Factors associated with lower rates of masturbation include being married, having religious beliefs, and being African-American. Gay people masturbate more than heterosexuals and derive more enjoyment from it. Masturbation does not seem to be simply a substitute for sex with partners.

4. Men tend to use a single technique for masturbation—direct manual stroking of the penis—whereas women use a greater variety of techniques, such as manual stimulation of the clitoris, labia, or vagina, or rubbing of the vulva against objects. Men experience orgasm during masturbation more frequently than do women.

5. Kissing is an important form of sexual expression in the United States, where it often has strong romantic significance, but it is not practiced in all human cultures.

6. Petting or fondling includes a variety of behaviors short of penetrative sex, including sensuous touching and kissing of the body. It may be a prelude to penetrative sexual interaction (foreplay), or it may form the entire sexual encounter, especially among adolescents.

7. Oral sex means contact between the mouth and the penis (fellatio), the vulva (cunnilingus), or the anus (anilingus). Oral sex has become increasingly popular among younger people in the United States and Britain, where 80% to 90% of young people have engaged in it. Like many noncoital sexual behaviors, it is more common among well-educated people.

8. About half of U.S. men, but fewer women, find fellatio very appealing. Cunnilingus is enjoyed about equally by men and women; about a third of the U.S. population finds it very appealing. Oral sex may be performed mutually in a head-to-genital arrangement; this behavior is called sixty-nining, or *soixante-neuf*.

9. Most adult heterosexual couples engage in coitus as the culmination of a sexual encounter. The most popular and traditional position for coitus in the United States is with the man above ("missionary position"), which requires the man to do most of the pelvic thrusting. The women's movement of the 1970s encouraged the exploration of other positions, such as the woman-above position and rear-entry coitus. Each position may have particular advantages and disadvantages for certain couples or in certain situations.

10. Anal sex (penetration of the anus by the penis) is practiced in both male–male and female–male encounters. About 10% of Americans engage in heterosexual anal sex at least once a year. Anal sex can be performed in a variety of positions and does not damage the anus or rectum.

11. Some couples like to make coitus almost the entirety of a sexual encounter, while others include much foreplay and afterplay, or even dispense with coitus altogether. In general, women prefer more protracted lovemaking and do not place as much emphasis on coitus as do men. Thus sexual encounters between women tend to be considerably longer than heterosexual encounters. Women generally take longer to reach orgasm than do men, so men might have to learn to postpone their own orgasms in heterosexual encounters if the man and woman wish to experience orgasm at close to the same time.

12. Vibrators are electrically powered devices that deliver erotically arousing vibratory stimulation. They may be used by men or women, but they are particularly associated with use for masturbation by women and to help women reach orgasm in partnered sex. Dildos are unpowered, sometimes penis-shaped objects used for vaginal or anal penetration, in either partnered or solo sex.

13. Different cultures vary greatly in the openness with which they discuss sexual behavior. The classic how-to manual on sexual behavior is the *Kama Sutra* (India, fifth century or earlier). This book demonstrates that explicit discussion of sex is not the sole prerogative of modern Western society. Contemporary India, however, has less positive attitudes toward sex than those described in the *Kama Sutra*.

14. Some cultures are more sex-positive than others. In many Pacific Island cultures, such as that of Mangaia, children receive instruction and initiation into sexual practices at puberty. An important aim of this instruction is to encourage sexual pleasure and to ensure that men help their partners experience multiple orgasms.

15. Some disabilities interfere with sexual behavior by limiting movement or making movement painful. Arthritis is the leading culprit in this respect, with 15% of the U.S. population affected. Nevertheless, people with arthritis can usually engage in pleasurable and rewarding sex by advance preparation and by choosing positions for sex that put the least stress on affected joints.

16. Spinal cord injuries can cause a near-complete loss of movement and sensation in the body below the neck (quadriplegia) or in the lower half of the body (paraplegia). Although conscious sensations from the genitalia are often lost, reflex penile erection and vaginal lubrication and engorgement may be preserved, depending on the level and completeness of the injury. Most people with spinal cord injuries can engage in coitus if they desire it, and women with spinal cord injuries can sustain pregnancy and deliver a baby vaginally.

17. Most intellectually disabled people experience the same sexual feelings and desires as everyone else. They have a right to make informed choices about sexual behavior if they are capable of doing so. Facilitating the exercise of this right must be balanced against the need to protect intellectually disabled people from sexual exploitation. With appropriate education, many intellectually disabled people can enjoy active sex lives, and some become parents and raise children.

Discussion Questions

1. Why do you think college graduates engage in a greater variety of sexual behaviors than do people who did not go to college?

2. Do you agree with Joycelyn Elders, U.S. surgeon general under President Clinton (see Box 9.1) that teaching about masturbation would help reduce unwanted pregnancies and sexually transmitted diseases?

3. Are there any sexual behaviors described in this chapter that you think people in general should not engage in? Is your view based on your moral beliefs, on practical (e.g., health) considerations, or some other reason?

4. Would it be a good or a bad thing if Mangaian attitudes toward sex became the rule in the United States today? How would it change our society?

5. Masturbation is often a stigmatized topic. Make a list, on a piece of paper, of all the things you have ever heard about masturbation; don't record your name. After a list of all these items from each member of your class is recorded on a chart or board, compare and contrast your views of these ideas, particularly the myths and misconceptions. Discuss how misconceptions about masturbation arose throughout history and have influenced our behavior.

6. Consider your attitudes and beliefs about whether the government should regulate the kinds of sex acts that American adults engage in (see Box 9.3). Should oral or anal sex be prohibited? Imagine that you are testifying before a Senate committee, and argue what should or should not be permitted or prohibited. How might the Supreme Court rule on the decision you make?

7. You have a friend whose arthritis makes sexual intercourse very uncomfortable. He fears he may have to give up sex because he can't find a comfortable position. What changes might you suggest to help him find a more comfortable approach?

Web Resources

Nerve.com, an online magazine devoted to sex and culture www.nerve.com

Sexual Health InfoCenter, Better Sex www.sexhealth.org/bettersex/

Society for Human Sexuality www.sexuality.org

The Lover's Guide www.loversguide.com

Recommended Reading

Comfort, A., and Park, C. (1998). *The new joy of sex and more joy of sex.* Pocket Books.

Cosmopolitan (2007). *Cosmo's steamy sex games: All sorts of naughty ways to have fun with your lover.* Hearst.

Dodson, B. (1987). *Sex for one: The joy of self-loving.* Harmony Books.

Gregersen, E. (1983). *Sexual practices: The story of human sexuality.* Franklin Watts.

Joannides, P. (2000). *Guide to getting it on!* Goofy Foot Press.

Kaufman, M., Silverberg, C., and Odette, F. (2007). *The ultimate guide to sex and disability: For all of us who live with disabilities, chronic pain, and illness* (2nd ed.). Cleis Press.

Stengers, J., and Van Neck, A. (2001). *Masturbation: The history of a great terror.* (K. A. Hoffmann, Trans.) Palgrave.

Schell, J. (2008). *Lesbian sex: 101 lovemaking positions.* Celestial Arts.

Silverstein, C., and Picano, F. (1992). *The new joy of gay sex.* HarperCollins.

Sipski, M. L., and Alexander, C. J. (Eds.) (1997). *Sexual function in people with disability and chronic illness: A health professional's guide.* Aspen Publications.

Vatsyayana (1991). *The Kama Sutra of Vatsyayana.* (R. F. Burton, Trans.) Arkana.

CHAPTER 10

Sexual relationships lie at the core of human society.

Sexual Relationships

In previous chapters we discussed sexual attraction, sexual arousal, and sexual behavior. Now we step back and take a look at the interpersonal frameworks within which partnered sex may occur—in other words, sexual relationships.

Of course, we have to interpret the word "relationship" broadly if we are to encompass the full expression of human sexuality. In common discourse, a "one-night stand"—or an even briefer sexual encounter between strangers—may not constitute a relationship, but for our purposes it does. So does a partnership that lasts a lifetime. So do sexual encounters that involve coercion or payment, although we defer discussion of these two topics to later chapters. What interests us here is the dynamic that brings people together as potential sex partners and keeps them together for minutes, days, or decades.

Sexual Relationships Are Motivated by Many Factors

What propels people into sexual relationships? According to the contemporary Western ideal, there are two leading factors: physical attraction and romantic love.

Certainly, these powerful forces inspire many sexual encounters and lasting relationships. But they may be mingled with, or entirely replaced by, a wide variety of other motives. These include the desire for status, security, or profit; the desire to conform or to follow moral beliefs—or, conversely, to rebel; the desire to arouse jealousy; and finally, of course, the desire to have children. Most sexual relationships are probably fueled by some combination of these forces.

Because of this complex web of motives, sexual relationships involve more than just two people. They are played out in a larger social, economic, and moral context. Let's begin with the last of these and consider how ethical traditions—the moral structures handed down from countless past generations—have viewed and molded sexual expression.

Religion and the Law Influence Sexual Morality

A major thread in Western thought is the idea that sexuality is morally suspect, an inferior state of being, or a threat to the integrity of society. Of course, successful societies have had to permit enough sex to allow for reproduction, but some have hedged sexuality with numerous restrictions. This has often been done through religious teachings.

double standard The application of different moral standards to males and females.

celibate Living under a vow not to marry or (by implication) to engage in sexual relations.

procreation Production of offspring.

fornication Obsolete term for sex between unmarried persons; viewed as a sin.

Ancient Jewish Doctrines Forbade Many Sexual Behaviors

The restrictions laid down by the religious leaders of ancient Israel and incorporated into the Book of Leviticus (part of the Jewish Torah and the Christian Old Testament) have been fundamental to Western moral tradition. According to Leviticus, God gave Moses a list of prohibited sexual behaviors, along with appropriate punishments for transgression—sometimes death. The forbidden behaviors included adultery, incest (including sex with relatives by blood and by marriage), sex during menstruation, sex between men, and sex with animals.

Leviticus did not prohibit marital sex, and numerous passages in the Old Testament attest to the positive moral status of the marriage bond and of sex within that bond. Nor did Leviticus prohibit sex between an unmarried man and an unmarried woman. Other biblical passages, however, made clear that a woman who was not a virgin when she married could be stoned to death (Deuteronomy 22). No equivalent punishment was laid down for men, showing that the **double standard** was already well in place in early Jewish society.

Christianity Began with Negative Views of Sexual Expression

Early Christian thinkers thought poorly of *any* kind of sexual behavior or sexual desire. This attitude was influenced by several factors: the belief that Jesus himself had been **celibate** (unmarried and sexually inactive), a reaction to the sexual excesses of the Roman Empire, an ascetic trend in Greek philosophy, and the personalities of two particular men who helped mold the ethical structure of early Christianity—St. Paul (who died ca. 64 CE) and St. Augustine (354–430 CE). Both of these men had conversion experiences that led them to condemn sexual desires (**Box 10.1**).

Virginity, or at least celibacy, thus became the most virtuous of states for Christian men and women. Certainly, most Christians did get married and have sex, but in doing so they yielded the high moral ground to the faith's ascetic monks, nuns, friars, and hermits. Since the twelfth century, all Roman Catholic clergy (but not the clergy of the Eastern Catholic and Orthodox churches) have been required to be celibate.

In the thirteenth century St. Thomas Aquinas (1225–1274) restored a measure of moral legitimacy to sex within marriage. He based his argument on "natural law," holding that the natural purpose of sex, intended by God, was to produce children (**procreation**). Aquinas used that same argument to condemn any kind of nonmarital, extramarital, or nonprocreative sex, including some kinds that were not specifically mentioned in Leviticus. These included sex between unmarried people (called **fornication** in Christian tradition), masturbation, and even nocturnal emissions. Though marital sex was permitted, the Church applied all kinds of restrictions, analogous to the traditional Hindu restrictions described in Chapter 9. These rules forbade sex during and after menstruation and pregnancy as well as on Fridays and holy days, during Lent, and so forth.

Aquinas's teachings remain at the core of modern Roman Catholic teachings about sex (Pope John Paul II, 1981). The Vatican has slightly liberalized its doctrines in recent years, however. It has acknowledged that sex, besides its direct procreative function, supports procreation indirectly by helping to cement the marital bond. Concordant with that view, it has sanctioned the timing of marital sex so as to avoid pregnancy—the "fertility awareness" methods of contraception. Such a practice would have shocked Aquinas.

Other conservative churches, such as the Eastern Orthodox churches, the Southern Baptist Church, and the Church of Jesus Christ of Latter-Day Saints (Mormons), agree fully with the Roman Catholic position in condemning all sex-

Sex in History

BOX 10.1 Sex and *The City of God*

(A) A fourteenth-century depiction of St. Augustine.

After the Bible, no book has influenced Western ideas of morality more than *The City of God*, written by St. Augustine (Figure A), who served as Bishop of Hippo in Roman North Africa between 412 CE and 427 CE. Augustine was brought up as a Christian but left the faith and spent his teen years in Carthage, where he had two mistresses and fathered a son. As he recounts in his *Confessions*, he was torn by guilt and prayed to God: "Give me chastity and continence, but not yet." ("Continence," in this context, means sexual self-restraint.) After some years in Italy, at the age of 33 he reconverted to Christianity, becoming a celibate hermit and ultimately a bishop.

Augustine began work on *The City of God* soon after Rome was sacked by the Visigoths.

During that event, many pious virgins were raped. Some people held that these women had sinned and that they should have committed suicide rather than yield to the conquerors. Augustine, in contrast, held that they retained their virtue because chastity is lost by intention, not by the mere act of intercourse.

This idea of sinfulness being in the individual mind is an important theme in *The City of God*. To Augustine, the doctrine of the Fall of Man meant that all humans are born in a state of sin (Figure B). As told in Genesis, Adam and Eve's sexual awareness arose directly from their sin of eating the forbidden fruit. As a result, they covered their genitals with fig leaves. Sexual desire, Augustine wrote, is part of our punishment for Adam and Eve's sin. It is a sin in itself, even when not expressed in sexual behavior. The fact that couples desire privacy during sex shows that they are aware that sex is wrong.

The sinfulness of sex, according to Augustine, lies in the fact that it is driven by passion (lust) rather than by the will. Thus, if Adam had not sinned, a man's penis would have been like other parts of his body—under voluntary control—and a couple could have had sex with no more passion than during any other activity of life. As it is, he wrote, sexual arousal is a physiological necessity if intercourse is to take place, and this means that sex is not consistent with virtue. Nevertheless, a husband and wife can lessen the sinfulness of sex by concentrating on the intention to procreate and minimizing their sexual arousal.

Augustine's views on sex were shared by some of his contemporaries, such as St. Jerome. Although there was also a sex-positive tradition within the early Church, the sinfulness of sexual arousal became a major theme of Christianity through the Middle Ages. The most popular medieval manual of moral doctrine, written by the French friar Vincent of Beauvais (ca. 1190–ca. 1264), stated that "a man who loves his wife very much is an adulterer ... An upright man should love his wife with his judgment, not his affections" (Boswell, 1980).

Some Christian sects have gone so far as to require universal celibacy, even though this requirement imperiled the sects' continued existence. One example was the Harmonist sect, a group of German immigrants who established themselves in Pennsylvania in 1804. Like many members of the early Church, they renounced sex in expectation of the imminent Second Coming of Christ. Although they adopted some children and also gained some adult converts, by 1876 they were mostly elderly, and the last

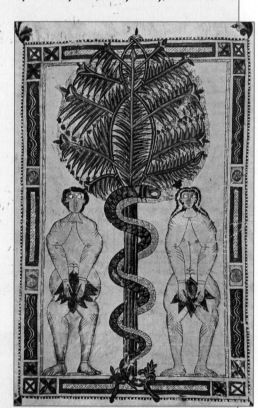

(B) Adam and Eve as depicted in a tenth-century Spanish manuscript.

member of the sect died around 1920. The Roman Catholic Church, in contrast, abandoned St. Augustine's doctrine of the sinfulness of sex in marriage, forbade contraception and abortion, and now has about a billion adherents worldwide.

ual relationships outside marriage. Because these churches incline to moral absolutism, they often attempt to influence government policies in ways that would impose their moral views on the entirety of society—by opposing legislation that extends protections to unmarried or same-sex couples, for example.

Many mainstream Protestant denominations in America are divided on issues of sexual ethics. For this reason, and also because of the emphasis these denominations place on the role of individual conscience, they tend to come out with nondogmatic or ambiguous position statements on these issues. Here are two examples:

> Although all persons are sexual beings whether or not they are married, sexual relations are only clearly affirmed in the marriage bond (United Methodist Church, 2000).

> We believe it is best to postpone intercourse until marriage. If a teenage couple decides to have a sexual relationship, they have the responsibility to use effective contraception (Presbyterian Church [U.S.A.], 1998).

The most liberal denominations, such as the Religious Society of Friends (Quakers) and the Unitarian Universalist Association (which incorporates traditions from other religions besides Christianity), do not attempt to lay down specific rules of sexual conduct. In general, the Quaker and Unitarian Universalist congregations look favorably on all loving relationships, including sexual relationships between two men or two women, and they are more concerned with issues of social justice than with what people do in their bedrooms.

Some Religions Are More Permissive than Christianity

Contemporary Judaism has two main branches, Orthodox and Reform Judaism. Orthodox Jews follow scriptural teachings (the Torah) as literally as possible and tend to be quite restrictive in sexual matters. Reform Judaism, the numerically preponderant branch in North America, is much more liberal in sexual matters, as may be exemplified by its actions relating to homosexuality and gay people. As early as 1977 the Central Conference of American Rabbis (CCAR), the main voice of Reform Judaism, called for the decriminalization of homosexual behavior and for an end to discrimination against gay people. During the 1980s rabbinical schools began accepting openly gay or lesbian students. In 1996 the CCAR called for the legalization of same-sex civil marriage, and in 2000 it resolved to permit rabbis to officiate at same-sex weddings (Central Conference of American Rabbis, 2000).

Reform Jewish rabbis are permitted to officiate at same-sex weddings, such as this wedding between two men.

Islam's founder, Muhammad (who died in 632 CE), was very different from Jesus: He was a civil ruler, a successful general, and a sexually active man with many wives. He condemned homosexuality but encouraged most other forms of sexual expression, especially within the context of marriage. As Islam spread, some ascetic movements developed within it, such as the monastic Sufis of Persia, but by and large Islam remained a sex-positive religion. Nevertheless, Islamic cultures have a long tradition of restricting women's freedoms, especially in the sexual domain. Islamic fundamentalism has led to severe restrictions on sexual expression in some countries, and there have been reports of severe punishments, including flogging and death by stoning, for people accused of engaging in nonmarital or extramarital sex. These punishments are suffered more frequently by women and gay people than by heterosexual men.

The founder of Buddhism, Siddhartha Gautama, or Buddha (who died ca. 483 BCE), renounced earthly pleasures at the age of 29, and his religion emphasizes self-denial as the way to escape suffering. Many Buddhist men lead ascetic, celibate lives as monks, but some branches of Buddhism, as in pre-Western Japan, permitted and even praised homosexual relationships within the monasteries. The general Buddhist populations, however, have always been expected to participate fully in life, including sexual relationships.

One particular branch of Buddhism known as Tantric Buddhism emphasizes the control of physical and mental functions, including sexual activity, as a means to enlightenment. Rather than simply condemning erotic desire, Tantric Buddhism seeks to rechannel it. Tantric sex—which is part of a larger framework of yoga practices—may involve prolonged sexual encounters combined with meditation, concentration, and breath control. During Tantric sex, little thrusting or other movement occurs. The man may postpone his orgasm or avoid it altogether, or he may learn to ejaculate retrogradely (into the bladder)—a mode of release that is accompanied by a less exciting orgasm (Yogani, 2004). (Whether this practice has long-term consequences on health or fertility is not known.) Much of what is taught and written about Tantric sex in the United States today is of dubious historical authenticity.

Humanism Has Influenced American Attitudes and Laws

Humanism is a tradition that derives moral principles from a basic premise of human worth. These principles include such ideas as equality; the right to freedom of thought, expression, action, and worship; and the obligation to respect the rights of others. If this sounds like a summary of the Declaration of Independence and the U.S. Constitution, that's no coincidence: The framers of those documents were strongly influenced by humanists such as Thomas Paine (1737–1808), and more broadly by the rationalist, anti-clerical movement in eighteenth-century Europe known as the Enlightenment.

Humanistic principles underlie the right to privacy—the idea that governments should not intrude unnecessarily in people's private lives. Although the Constitution does not spell out such a right, the U.S. Supreme Court has held that it is implied by that document—especially by the due process clause of the Fourteenth Amendment. The constitutional right to privacy has had an enormous impact in the area of sexuality: It has been invoked by the Supreme Court to strike down state laws banning contraceptives, abortion, interracial marriage, and gay sex (**Box 10.2**). Many of the controversies about sexual matters that plague contemporary U.S. society reflect the tension between the openness of humanism and the more restrictive ethics of Christian tradition (Klein, 2006).

People's Moral Judgments about Sex Depend on Its Context

In a series of studies begun in the 1960s, sociologist Ira Reiss showed that people judge the morality of heterosexual behavior by the relationship within which it occurs: The more affectionate, intimate, or committed the relationship, the more likely people are to consider sexual acts morally acceptable (Reiss & Miller, 1979). Some nonheterosexual behaviors, however, may be judged without regard to the relationship within which they occur.

As to how committed a heterosexual relationship need be for sex to be morally acceptable, people's views on this question are influenced by their beliefs about the purpose of sex (DeLamater, 1987). People who believe that the main purpose of sex is procreation tend to be the most restrictive, disapproving of nonmarital sex or of sex acts that cannot lead to pregnancy. People who believe that sex has a major purpose in cementing relationships tend to approve of sex between

Society, Values, and the Law

BOX 10.2 Who May Marry?

Early in the morning of July 11, 1958, Richard Loving and his wife Mildred were asleep at their home in Central Point, Virginia, when three policemen burst into their bedroom. "Who is this woman you're sleeping with?" they demanded of Richard. Mildred replied: "I'm his wife," and Richard pointed to the marriage certificate hanging on their bedroom wall. "That's no good here," responded the sheriff, and he arrested both of them.

Mildred Jeter and Richard Loving

The Lovings were an interracial couple (Richard was white, Mildred was African American). They had married out of state and returned to Virginia to live. They were convicted of violating Virginia's 1924 Racial Integrity Act, which made marriage between a white and nonwhite person a felony.

In his sentencing opinion, the judge in the *Loving* case wrote as follows: "Almighty God created the races white, black, yellow, malay, and red, and he placed them on separate continents. The fact that he separated the races shows he did not intend for the races to mix." Although this makes the statute appear to be based on (misguided) moral grounds, historians and jurists believe that it was motivated by white supremacist thinking, because it did not ban marriage between nonwhite persons of different races.

The Lovings were sentenced to a year in prison, but the sentence was suspended provided that they left the state and did not return for 25 years. They moved to Washington, D.C., where they appealed the case. In its 1967 *Loving v. Virginia* decision, the U.S. Supreme Court struck down the Virginia statute and affirmed the right to marry across racial lines. The justices based their ruling on the due process and equal protection clauses of the Constitution. These have been interpreted to grant a fundamental right to marry that cannot be denied to certain couples on account of a mere perception of immorality. Some state Supreme Courts (beginning with California, in a 1948 case titled *Perez v. Sharp*) had reached the same conclusion before the *Loving* decision.

Among the many beneficiaries of *Loving* are the current U.S. Supreme Court justice Clarence Thomas and his wife, an interracial couple who live in the same state where Mildred Jeter and Richard Loving were convicted a half-century ago.

Although the constitutional battle over interracial marriage has been resolved, the legal principles that were debated then have been brought back into focus by the current debate over same-sex marriage (see Chapter 14). The laws banning such marriage are rooted in a traditional moral condemnation of sex between men or between women. But in 2003 the U.S. Supreme Court struck down all laws banning gay sex, thus undercutting some of the justification for laws banning gay marriage.

In 2008, when the California Supreme Court heard arguments on the gay marriage issue, proponents of such marriage argued that the Court's 1948 *Perez* ruling set a precedent that was equally applicable to same-sex couples. Opponents countered that, if an open-ended right to marriage were recognized, there would be no way to prevent polygamous marriage or marriage between siblings. The California Supreme Court struck down the state laws banning gay marriage, however, citing the *Perez* precedent.

Richard Loving died in 1975, Mildred in 2008. In her last public statement before her death, Mildred Loving spoke out in favor of gay couples' right to marry (Martin, 2008).

unmarried people if the relationship is a committed one, but disapprove of extramarital or casual sex. People who believe that the purpose of sex is primarily recreational, or to give pleasure, tend to consider any type of consensual heterosexual sex morally acceptable. We may call these three views of sex the traditional, relational, and recreational perspectives (**Figure 10.1**).

Demographic Factors Affect Sexual Attitudes

Surveys such as the National Health and Social Life Survey (NHSLS) (Laumann et al., 1994) have found that basic demographic facts about a person, such as sex, age, educational level, region of residence, race/ethnicity, and religion, predict that individual's moral beliefs on sexual issues:

■ *Sex*. Women are more likely than men to have a traditional perspective, disapproving of casual, nonmarital, and extramarital sex. This observation goes along with a wide body of research indicating that women take a more relationship-oriented view of sex than do men (see Chapter 4). Women are not more conservative on abortion issues, however (Gallup News Service, 2004).

■ *Age*. Older people are more likely to have a traditional perspective than younger people. This reflects the fact that older people grew up when social attitudes were more conservative than they are now, and that older people are more likely to be married and to have children, both of which tend to make people's views more conservative.

■ *Education*. Increasing educational level is associated with relatively permissive attitudes. Highly educated people, whatever their religious affiliation, are likely to be tolerant or accepting of homosexual relationships, for example.

■ *Region*. People living in the northeastern United States or on the West Coast are less likely to have a traditional perspective on sex, and more likely to have a recreational perspective, than are people in other regions. For residents of the southern states, it's the reverse (NHSLS data). Although these differences are largely explained by differences among these regions in educational level and religious affiliation, there also seem to be local cultures that influence people's sexual morality.

■ *Race/ethnicity*. Race or ethnicity is not strongly predictive of sexual attitudes, but African Americans and Hispanics tend to be less approving of homosexuality and abortion than whites.

■ *Religion*. Conservative Protestants, such as Baptists, tend to have a traditional perspective, while people with no religious affiliation tend to have a recreational perspective. Catholics and mainstream Protestants have a wide range of attitudes, but most have a relational perspective. The NHSLS, like other surveys, found that many American Catholics disagree with the official Vatican line on sexual issues.

The combined influence of just two demographic traits—sex and age—on sexual attitudes is very strong. **Figure 10.2**, which is based on data from the British National Survey of Sexual Attitudes and Lifestyles (NSSAL) (see Chapter 1), shows the percentage of interviewees who disapproved of "one-night stands." Fewer than half of young men disapproved of this behavior, but over 90% of women in the oldest age bracket did so.

Although survey data imply that people's sexual attitudes can be predicted to a considerable extent from their demographic characteristics, we don't mean to downplay the individual aspects of moral reasoning. People may be influenced by all kinds of life experiences to rethink their beliefs—by facing the reality of an unwanted pregnancy, by having a daughter or son "come out" as gay, and so on. You might feel that your own attitudes are permanent and the only correct ones, but if you write them down and check again in 20 years, you may be surprised by how much they have changed.

Americans' Attitudes Have Changed over Time

While on the topic of changing attitudes, let's take a look at how the moral stances of Americans on sexual topics have changed over the last few decades. The General Social Survey (GSS)—a project of the National Opinion Research Center at the University of Chicago—has asked Americans a standard set of questions on a variety of topics since the early 1970s (**Figure 10.3**). The GSS has found a decline in the percentage of the population who consider sex before marriage "always

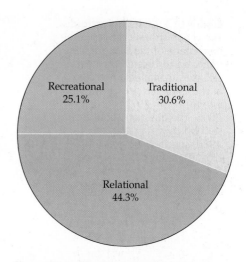

Figure 10.1 Moral perspectives on sexuality Americans can be grouped into three perspectives reflecting different ideas about the purpose of sex. (Data from NHSLS.)

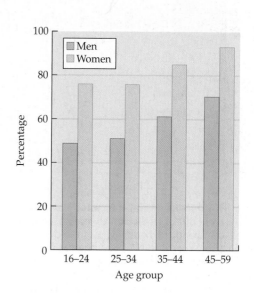

Figure 10.2 Sex and age strongly influence sexual attitudes. The percentages of NSSAL interviewees who stated that "one-night stands" are always or mostly wrong varied with their sex and age.

Figure 10.3 Changing attitudes
This graph shows changes in the percentage of the U.S. population who considered premarital sex, extramarital sex, homosexual sex, and teen sex "always wrong," from 1972 through 2006. The question about teen sex (which was first asked in 1986) specified 14- to-16-year-olds. (Data from General Social Survey.)

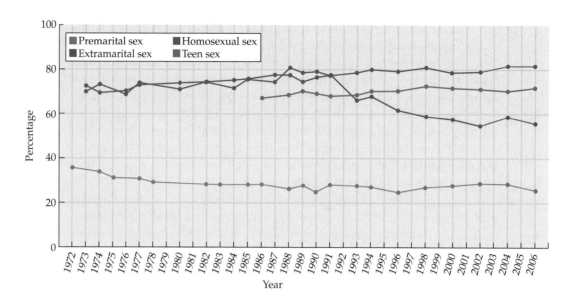

wrong" and a corresponding rise in the percentage who consider it "not wrong at all." When interviewees are asked specifically about sex between 14- to-16-year olds, however—a question that was first asked in 1986—opinions are far more negative and have not changed significantly over the period during which the question has been asked.

With regard to extramarital sex, public opinion has actually become more negative. Between 1973 and 2006, the percentage of people who believe that extramarital sex is "always wrong" increased from 70% to 82%.

With regard to sex between two adults of the same sex, opinion has changed in a more complicated way. During the 1980s, when public concern about AIDS was at its height and the disease was largely blamed on gay men, disapproval of homosexual behavior increased. Since the early 1990s, however, there has been a very marked liberalizing trend. By 2006 only a slight majority of the population (56%) believed that gay sex was "always wrong."

Attitudes in Other Countries Differ from Those in the United States

How does American opinion on sexual morality compare with opinion in other countries? In 1997 the Gallup Organization conducted a survey of moral issues in 16 countries (Gallup Organization, 1997) (**Figure 10.4**). One of the questions asked whether it was wrong for a couple to have a child out of wedlock. Nearly half of Americans thought that this was wrong, placing the United States pretty much in the middle of the spectrum of world opinion. The residents of some countries, such as India and Singapore, were much less permissive on this question, whereas those in other countries, especially in Europe, were much more permissive. (European permissiveness on this score may in part reflect the prevalence of long-term cohabitations, which offer children a stable, two-parent environment without the formality of marriage.) That the United States should fall somewhere in the middle of world opinion is perhaps to be expected, given the wide mix of ancestries and cultures its people represent.

In spite of the diversity of attitudes toward the morality of sex, it's worth emphasizing a belief that represents a common moral ground for many people— the idea that it's not the sex act itself, but its context, that has moral significance. In particular, sexual behavior that may endanger established relationships is very broadly disapproved of. Whereas only about 1 in 5 Americans thinks that nonmar-

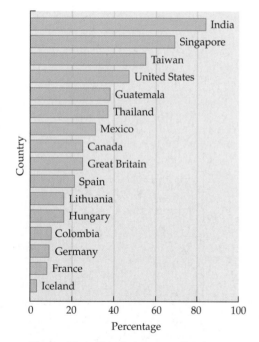

Figure 10.4 Moral stances on having a child out of wedlock vary greatly around the world. This graph shows the percentage of persons in 16 countries who believe that it is morally wrong for a couple to have a baby if they are not married. The true figures for India, Mexico, and Colombia are probably higher than given here because rural areas, which are usually more conservative, were not sampled in these countries. (Data from Gallup Organization, 1997.)

ital sex is always wrong, 4 in 5 think that *extra*marital sex is always wrong. The British NSSAL study came up with very similar findings but, in addition, found that cohabitational and even *non*cohabitational sexual relationships were viewed as morally protected, albeit not to the same degree that marriages are: Most of the interviewees felt that people in such relationships should not engage in sex outside the relationship. Evidently, most people place a high moral value on lasting sexual relationships—even when they are not formalized by marriage—and see sexual monogamy as an important factor in preserving them.

casual sex Sexual encounters that do not take place within a durable sexual relationship.

Casual Sex Has More Appeal to Men than to Women

By **casual sex**, we mean sexual encounters that the participants do not view as part of a durable sexual relationship. It includes sex between people who have known each other only very briefly, as well as sex between those who have known each other for some time but do not intend the encounter to be the beginning of a longer sexual relationship.

We mentioned above that men and women differ in their attitudes toward casual sex, with men far more likely than women to consider "one-night stands" morally acceptable. Does this difference in moral stance translate into differences in behavior? Psychologists Russell Clark and Elaine Hatfield performed a rather sneaky "real-life test" of this question (Clark & Hatfield, 1989, 2003). They recruited attractive male and female college students as confederates and had them approach unwitting students of the other sex somewhere on a U.S. college campus (**Figure 10.5**). They were told to say "I have been noticing you around campus and I find you to be very attractive." Then they asked one of three questions: "Would you go out with me tonight?" "Would you come over to my apartment tonight?" or "Would you go to bed with me tonight?"

The male and female "targets" were about equally willing to go out with the confederate—about half assented to this request. When the request was phrased in ways that referred more explicitly to the desire for casual sex, however, women's responses rapidly fell off—in fact, not a single woman agreed to go to bed with the male confederate, and the women often lent emphasis to the rejection with comments such as "What's wrong with you, creep, leave me alone!" Men's responses, however, became more positive as the proposal became more explicit: 69% of the men agreed to go to the female confederate's apartment, and 75% agreed to go to bed with her, sometimes adding comments such as "Why do we have to wait until tonight?" In other words, reducing a casual date to its sexual essentials robbed the date of all its appeal to women, but actually *enhanced* its appeal to men! When you consider that some of the men must have been in ongoing relationships, some must have been gay, and some must have been otherwise engaged that evening, a 75% acceptance rate to having sex is fairly astonishing. Of course, we don't know whether men and women in other age ranges, or who are not college students, would respond in the same way, but it seems likely that the sex difference would be the same.

A replication of Clark and Hatfield's experiment was performed more recently on a college campus in London, England, with virtually the same results as in the original study (British Broadcasting Corporation, 2002). A third study, conducted in Austria, did manage to find a few women who assented to sex with an attractive male stranger, but these women made up only 6% of the total (Voracek et al., 2005).

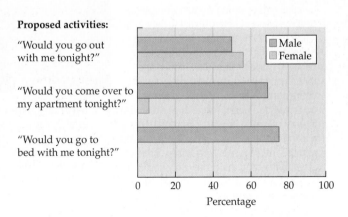

Proposed activities:

"Would you go out with me tonight?"

"Would you come over to my apartment tonight?"

"Would you go to bed with me tonight?"

Figure 10.5 Sex differences in willingness to engage in casual sex The figure shows the percentage of male and female college students who agreed to three activities proposed by an attractive but unfamiliar student of the other sex. (After Clark & Hatfield, 1989.)

On the basis of these data, you might think that a straight man's quest for casual sex would be fruitless, and that his only recourse would be to go to a prostitute. This may be the case in some cultures, and may have been the case historically in our own culture, but the current reality is different. Some women *do* agree to casual sex, and may even initiate it. And those sexual encounters may be with men or with other women (**Box 10.3**).

There are several possible reasons why women are more willing to engage in casual sex or brief relationships today than they were in earlier generations. The availability of reliable contraception—and, if necessary, legal abortion—are probably the most important reasons. In addition, a woman who is known to have engaged in premarital sex, even casual sex, suffers much less damage to her reputation than her mother or grandmother would have—let alone a woman from the time of Leviticus. By and large, men no longer expect their brides or cohabiting partners to be virgins. Still, the fear of disease, the fear of being labeled a "slut," and the fear of vio-

Society, Values, and the Law

BOX 10.3 Getting the BUG

When Britney Spears and Madonna performed a passionate, spit-swapping kiss at the 2003 MTV Video Music Awards, they put their seal of approval on a form of behavior that has been rapidly gaining popularity, or at least public attention: sexual intimacy between young women who are not lesbians. The practitioners may describe themselves as "heteroflexible," "gayish," or (in the case of college students) "four-year queer" or "BUG" ("bisexual until graduation").

There is a long tradition of romantic, physically intimate friendships between teenage girls or young women who later become pillars of heterosexual society (Faderman, 1981; Vicinus, 1989). What distinguishes the current trend is that the behavior is overt rather than hidden and that much of it is quite casual. In fact, part of the purpose of these "lesbian" interactions may be a heterosexual one—to arouse the interest of males. "It's very common to see girls making out at parties," a male Rutgers student told the *Star-Ledger* of New Jersey. "I think it's an attention-getting thing; they only do it in front of guys." A 22-year-old woman said, "The waitresses where I work are doing it right in front of the cooks. They're doing it for attention" (O'Crowley, 2004).

Other young women engage in sexual interactions with other women for reasons that

have nothing to do with attracting men or with establishing a lesbian identity. It may be a matter of experimentation, the desire to give physical expression to a close friendship, the pressure to follow a trend, or a preference for the safety and mutual understanding of a same-sex relationship. Here's one student's (abbreviated) account:

I had small crushes on women before, but nothing beyond the realm of my imagination had happened—until I met Amy. Our

attraction was, at first, that of two best friends destined to keep in touch for life. But by the end of one listless summer an undeniable sexual heat had developed between us. One night, we got drunk on cheap swill and did the deed. Embarrassed, we giggled over our small feat for weeks. It was the first and last time we'd make love. But, hot damn, it was amazing!

I had other encounters with women, but none quite matched the heady rush that followed the first. I quickly became disenchanted with the notion of, well, going down. How could men manage this for minutes on end? And the soft, sweet feminine touch was no match for the firm, male thrust. There was no getting around it: I was straight.
(Anonymous, 1999)

According to one longitudinal study by Lisa Diamond of the University of Utah, more than a quarter of all young women who identify as bisexual or lesbian give up that identity within 5 years (Diamond, 2003). It's not that their sexual attractions change, according to Diamond. Rather, it had to do with changes in the way they interpret or act on those attractions. These findings mesh with studies described in Chapter 14, which find that women are generally more fluid in their sexual orientation than are men.

lence are three very real concerns that limit women's willingness to embark on casual sexual relationships.

The average college student thinks that his or her peers are much more sexually active, and with more partners, than is actually the case, according to a study of four campuses (Scholly et al., 2005). Thus one factor promoting casual sex at the college level could be a desire to conform to perceived—but inaccurate—social norms.

Hooking Up—The New Norm?

Although young women may be as averse to sex with total strangers as they ever were, many are becoming much more open to engaging in casual, uncommitted sex with acquaintances—sometimes including people they have met that same evening. This practice is often called **hooking up**. Hookups may involve anything from kissing to coitus, are typically unplanned, and arise out of social get-togethers, group outings and the like.

Hookups often arise out of small social gatherings.

The colloquial terms "friends with benefits" and "booty calls" have much the same meaning as hooking up. The term "friends with benefits," however, incorporates the notion that the relationship, though devoid of romantic commitment, is facilitated or legitimized by the trust and comfort of a previously established nonsexual friendship (Bisson & Levine, 2007).

hooking up Uncommitted sex with an acquaintance.

To social critics who have a "traditional" or "relational" perspective on sex, hooking up is a sign of moral decay or presents a practical danger to young women. In a 2007 book, *Washington Post* journalist Laura Sessions Stepp argued that hooking up is emotionally damaging to women, leaves them ill-prepared to embark on more meaningful relationships, and lowers their perceived worth. "In a smorgasbord of booty," Stepp writes, "all the hot dishes start looking like they've been on the warming table too long" (Stepp, 2007). Those who take a recreational perspective on sex tend to dismiss this view as old-fashioned sexual conservatism. "[Stepp] resurrects the ugly, old notion of sex as something a female gives in return for a male's good behavior," wrote one reviewer in Stepp's own newspaper, "and she imagines the female body as a thing that can be tarnished by too much use" (Dobie, 2007). Yet some college psychiatrists, such as Miriam Grossman of the University of California, Los Angeles, have taken viewpoints quite similar to Stepp's (Grossman, 2007). Grossman complains that young women are not warned that engaging in sexual behavior will create strong but unreciprocated feelings of attachment. "No condom will protect her from the heartache and confusion that may result," Grossman asserts. Her solution: "I'd like to see war declared on our campus hookup culture." What do you think?

Casual Sex Is More Accepted in the Gay Male Community

Casual sex is more prevalent among gay men—especially among gay men without steady partners—than in the heterosexual population. Explanations for this phenomenon may include the following:

- Gay men are not restrained by women's reluctance to engage in casual sex.
- Pregnancy is not an issue.
- Gay men, who may already be stigmatized by society for their sexual orientation, are less likely to pay attention to public opinion on the topic of casual sex.

In addition to gay bars, which are an important feature of gay male life in many U.S. cities, other institutions offer the opportunity for sexual encounters on an even more casual or totally anonymous basis (Leap, 1999). These include encounters in bathhouses, public toilets, and outdoor cruising locations such as parks and freeway rest areas, as well as encounters arranged via personal ads or the Internet.

Although engaging in casual sex carries little stigma in gay male communities, that does not mean that all gay men engage in it or approve of the practice. Some limit their sexual activity because of the risk of acquiring AIDS or other diseases. Some live in rural areas where potential partners are scarce. Some believe that casual sex gives the gay community a bad name (Signorile, 1997). And, most importantly, many gay men are involved in monogamous relationships and have no desire to engage in casual sex—or feel that doing so would endanger their relationship.

In the NHSLS study, men who identified as homosexual or bisexual reported an average of 3.1 sex partners in the previous 12 months. That is well above the 1.8 partners reported by men who identified as heterosexual, but far fewer than was the norm in some urban gay communities in the pre-AIDS era (Bell & Weinberg, 1978).

There do exist bars and other locations where lesbians can meet, but little is known about casual sex between women. The NHSLS survey interviewed too few lesbians for the data to be meaningful. The much larger NSSAL survey identified 175 women who had had at least one sexual encounter with another woman. Of these women, only one had had more than 10 female partners, and none had had more than 20. Although the nature of the encounters was not investigated, the low numbers suggest that casual sex between women is uncommon. This is not just a matter of lack of opportunity: Lesbians express the same low interest in casual sex and multiple sex partners as do heterosexual women (Bailey et al., 1994).

Negotiating Sex Involves Flirting

Back in the 1980s, when singles bars were the uncontested focus of the singles scene, independent sex researcher Timothy Perper used them to study how men and women negotiate a casual sexual encounter (Perper, 1985). Perper found that men and women engage in rather stereotyped behaviors. Contrary to what one might imagine, women often take the first step in the interaction. This behavior includes looking at, approaching, and talking to the man. A process of escalation then occurs, which involves the progressive turning of the man and woman toward each other, and the synchronization of body movements. Synchronization begins with apparently coincidental synchronization of hand or head movements, such as reaching for a drink, and may progress to complete synchronization of body movements, such as swaying in time to music. At each step, one partner may validate the other's escalation or may break the process by failing to synchronize, thus allowing the process to cool off or terminate. At some point, the man typically takes a more controlling role, in which he makes the sexual nature of the interaction more explicit.

Psychologist Monica Moore has studied women's flirting behavior (Moore, 1998). Like Perper, she finds that women's body language is crucial in the early stages of sexual interactions. Behaviors that serve as solicitations include smiling, short darting glances, prolonged eye contact, lip licking, nodding, tossing the hair back, playing with the hair, touching the neck, raising the skirt slightly, and walking by a man with hips swinging and breasts pushed forward. In a social situation such as a singles bar, Moore found that the likelihood of a man approaching a woman was very strongly correlated with the number of such solicitations that she performed. In other words, flirting works.

Austrian ethologist Irenäus Eibl-Eibesfeldt spent years observing flirting behavior on several continents as well as on Pacific islands (Eibl-Eibesfeldt, 2007). He found a remarkable consistency in these behaviors across cultures: Almost everywhere, for example, a woman who is interested in a man will exhibit a sequence of behaviors that include smiling, arching the brows, looking down and to the side, and then putting her hands near her mouth and laughing. These behavioral patterns are almost as consistent and unconscious as the "proceptive" and "receptive" behaviors of nonhuman animals. Thus nature may have equipped us with a standard set of flirting behaviors as well as the ability to interpret and respond to them.

Dating Relationships Are Often Short-Lived

One step up the relationship hierarchy from hookups are sexual relationships between people who are not married or cohabiting but nevertheless feel some degree of commitment to each other. We may call these **dating relationships**. Sometimes a relationship of this kind leads to cohabitation or marriage. Sometimes it is a brief romance that breaks up when the pair find themselves incompatible, find better partners, or get separated by external circumstances such as the end of a school year. Sometimes it is a durable relationship between two people who for some reason don't want to or are unable to live together. Although we think of dating relationships as being the hallmark of the teenage years or young adulthood, plenty of older people—unmarried, divorced, or widowed—also engage in them.

Because of the informality of these relationships, no clear terminology describes them, though phrases such as "partners," "girlfriend/boyfriend," "seeing each other," "going together," "they're an item," or "they're dating" are clear enough. Except among the most traditionally minded couples, relationships of this kind usually include some degree of physical intimacy, but not necessarily coitus or other genital contact. Some men and women engage in sex outside the dating relationship, but more commonly dating relationships are expected to be sexually exclusive. Thus a person who dates a succession of partners over a period of time is usually engaging in **serial monogamy**—a very common lifestyle, especially among adolescents and young adults.

First Dates May Follow a Script

A dating relationship begins, of course, with a first date. On a first date, both partners often feel considerable uncertainty about what is going to happen, even if they have known each other for some time in a nonsexual way. On a first date between heterosexual college students, the man typically has a greater desire for sex, and a greater expectation of sex, than does the woman, and this expectation of sex increases if alcohol is consumed (Mongeau et al., 2004; Morr & Mongeau, 2004).

Because of the uncertainty associated with a first date, the participants often follow socially established rituals, which researchers call scripts (see Chapter 1). The ritualization of the first date is particularly marked when the date is "blind," that is, when the two people are complete strangers to each other. With a date between heterosexual college students, the traditional script demands that the man take the leading, active role: He picks up the woman, plans and pays for the activities, initiates any sexual intimacy, and takes her home. The woman takes the reactive role, accepting or rejecting the date, the activities, and the sex (Rose & Frieze, 1993). This pattern conforms to the traditional expectation that men will be the ones who initiate sexual interactions and women the ones who say "yes" or "no," thus setting limits (Metts & Cupach, 1989). The gender-based scripts for

Flirting is the same the world over. It includes behaviors such as smiling and playing with the hair, as shown by this young woman in India.

dating relationship A nonmarital sexual relationship between two persons who do not live together but who see each other on a more-or-less regular basis.

serial monogamy Engagement in a series of monogamous relationships.

First dates may be heavily scripted.

first dates between college students have been quite durable over time, in spite of the more equal roles now played by young women and men in most social interactions (Laner & Ventrone, 2000)

Violations of dating scripts do occur, of course. It's not uncommon for the woman to initiate the date, for example. If she does so, however, the subsequent script changes. Most significantly, the man usually has a greatly increased expectation that sexual intimacy will occur (Mongeau & Carey, 1996). In reality, heterosexual first dates that are initiated by women tend to include relatively little sexual intimacy, so men's expectations in this regard are often disappointed (Mongeau & Johnson, 1995). This is a potential source of conflict and may be a factor in predisposing some men to commit date rape. Many women are aware that allowing the man to do the paying may be read as entitling him to sex, and therefore insist on paying their share.

Most of the research on dating has been carried out on college students, who offer a convenient, captive population for study by university-based social scientists. But when Paul Mongeau compared the dating goals of heterosexual college students with those of older, single adults, he found striking differences (Mongeau et al., 2007). Whereas the college students showed the traditional gender-based differences (males more interested in sex, females in developing a friendship or having fun), many of the older adults were seeking to initiate a lifelong relationship, and this was as true for the men as it was for the women. What's more, the older adults of both sexes placed more emphasis on nonphysical aspects of attractiveness, such as caring and good conversational skills, than did the college students. How would you explain these differences between the two groups?

As a dating relationship continues, the social scripts that organized the first date are gradually replaced by **interpersonal scripts**—sets of rules and expectations that are generated by the dating couple themselves (Metts & Cupach, 1989). These scripts allow for increasing self-disclosure, intimacy, and nonverbal communication. Also, the gender difference in the expectation of sexual intimacy diminishes. That's because women become more willing to engage in sex as the relationship becomes more committed (Buss, 1995).

Same-Sex Dates Have Their Own Scripts

Same-sex dating has not been the subject of a great deal of study, but it's worth raising a few points. First, in many environments (such as high school, college, or work) there is a presumption of heterosexuality. Thus, for a same-sex date to occur, there has to be an initial recognition or mutual disclosure that the two people are open to a same-sex relationship. This disclosure, once achieved, may promote a more rapid development of the relationship than would be typical for an opposite-sex couple. Conversely, some same-sex couples may have difficulty achieving intimacy because of inculcated negative feelings about homosexuality (internalized homophobia: see Chapter 14).

For women especially, sexual exploration and the development of a homosexual or bisexual identity may occur in the context of a preexisting and intense same-sex friendship (Peplau et al., 1999). In such cases, the two people may essentially be in love before the question of sexual attraction and sexual behavior comes

interpersonal scripts Patterns of behavior that develop between couples.

into play at all. Dating under these circumstances has a very different meaning than it does in dates between most heterosexual or male–male couples, in which the two people are typically not very emotionally intimate on their first date but may be very conscious of sexual attraction and the possibility of sexual behavior.

The cultural scripts that regulate heterosexual dating —especially those related to gender roles—may be less relevant in the gay and lesbian communities. Still, certain expectations apply, such as the idea that a person who provides resources (e.g., drink and transportation) is accruing a degree of entitlement. Within some gay subcultures, such as the gay leather or BDSM communities (see Chapter 15), an explicit negotiation of the kind of sexual role-playing that the two men will engage in is likely (Townsend, 2007).

Dating Relationships May Evolve Rapidly

Noncohabitational relationships are often very dynamic—they are processes, rather than states of being. The process may be one of growing love, leading to cohabitation or marriage, or of gradual realization by one or both partners that "this was not meant to be," with a resulting breakup.

Often this dynamic process is viewed as being entirely intrinsic to the relationship—in other words, as an exploration of mutual attraction and compatibility. But a concurrent, external process involves a sexual "marketplace." In this process, each person consciously or unconsciously assesses whether they have the best possible partner, given their own sense of self-worth and the range of other options available (Lawrence & Byers, 1995). If either partner believes that they are not getting what they deserve in the relationship, that partner will feel less commitment to the relationship, and the chances of a break-up are increased (Sprecher, 2001).

Given that there are so many alternative partners out there, it may seem odd that dating couples become committed to each other at all. There appears, however, to be a tendency to idealize the partner that helps stabilize the relationship (Murray & Holmes, 1999). This idealization does not mean blindness to a partner's shortcomings, but a minimization of their importance as well as a tendency to construct mental representations in which the partner's perceived faults are tied to virtues and thus balanced by them. ("Yes, he drinks too much, but only socially, and that's part of his outgoing personality that I like so much.")

We will postpone our discussion of more durable sexual relationships (cohabitations and marriages) to Chapter 13, where we will also discuss sexual relationships that involve more than two people (polyamory and polygamy). Instead, we now turn our attention to the emotional underpinnings of sexual relationships.

Love Cements Many Sexual Relationships

Love, in some form or another, is the glue that holds couples in sexual relationships. Long celebrated in poetry and art (**Box 10.4**), love has recently come under the scrutiny of psychologists and even brain scientists, though no consensus has been reached on what exactly love is, or what causes it.

There Are Different Kinds of Love

One thing that is clear is that there are several aspects to love, or several kinds of love. Some types of love, such as the nurturing care that a mother gives her child, the liking that forms the basis of friendships, or the charitable feelings that Jesus instructed his followers to direct toward all fellow humans, are not sexual. Even within the context of sexual relationships, different aspects of love are apparent. Most strikingly, the quality of love tends to change over the duration of a relation-

Sex in History

BOX 10.4 Love in Literature

We've mentioned that men tend to be more oriented toward physical attraction and women toward commitment. The following two poems about love contradict that association. First, a surviving fragment of a 2500-year-old love poem by the Greek lyric poet Sappho (in prose translation by H. T. Wharton) expresses the overwhelming physical immediacy of her love:

> That man seems to me peer of gods, who sits in thy presence, and hears close to him thy sweet speech and lovely laughter; that indeed makes my heart flutter in my bosom. For when I see thee but a little, I have no utterance left, my tongue is broken down, and straightway a subtle fire has run under my skin, with my eyes I have no sight, my ears ring, sweat pours down, and a trembling seizes all my body; I am paler than grass, and seem in my madness little better than one dead. But I must dare all . . .

In contrast, this sonnet by William Shakespeare (1564–1616) focuses on love as an enduring commitment:

> Let me not to the marriage of true minds
> Admit impediments; love is not love
> Which alters when it alteration finds,
> Or bends with the remover to remove.
> O, no, it is an ever-fixèd mark

> That looks on tempests and is never shaken;
> It is the star to every wand'ring bark,
> Whose worth's unknown, although his
> height be taken.
> Love's not Time's fool, though rosy lips and
> cheeks
> Within his bending sickle's compass come;
> Love alters not with his brief hours and
> weeks,
> But bears it out even to the edge of doom.
> If this be error and upon me proved,
> I never writ, nor no man ever loved.

And here are two literary observations on falling *out* of love:

> To think that I've wasted years of my life, that I've longed to die, that I've experienced my greatest love, for a woman who didn't appeal to me, who wasn't even my type!

(*Swann's Way*, by Marcel Proust, translated by Scott Moncrieff and Terence Kilmartin)

> Methought I was enamored of an ass . . .
> O, how mine eyes do loathe his visage now!

(Titania in Shakespeare's *Midsummer Night's Dream*)

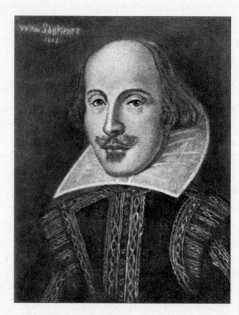

William Shakespeare (1564–1616)

ship, starting with passion and developing over time into a calmer but deeper bond (Hatfield & Rapson, 1993). The early kind of love is called romantic love, passionate love, or limerence (Tennov, 1979) and, popularly, "falling in love" or "being head-over-heels in love." The later kind of love is called companionate, realistic, or mature love.

Here's how one teenager explained the difference (Montgomery & Sorell, 1998): "Being in love with someone and loving someone are two different things; when you're *in love* with someone, you think they're just wonderful and everything they do is perfect and they have no faults. When you *love* someone you know about their faults and you realize that they may not be exactly as you want them to be, but you love them in spite of it."

Romantic Love May Be a Human Universal

Romantic love—being *in love*—is an intense and erotic attraction that involves the idealization of the loved person. It does not require familiarity with the loved person, nor need it be reciprocated. In fact, familiarity and reciprocation may hasten the end of romantic love by helping to transform it into companionate love.

Some anthropologists and historians have maintained that romantic love is a product of Western industrial society, or that in preindustrial societies it was experienced by only the leisured elite classes (Aries, 1965; Stone, 1988). To test this notion, William Jankowiak and Edward Fischer combed through anthropological sources that described courtship, marriage, and family relations in 166 cultures (Jankowiak & Fischer, 1992). They found clear evidence for the existence of romantic love in 147, or 86%, of these cultures. For most of the remaining cultures there was no clear evidence one way or the other. Jankowiak and Fischer concluded that the capacity for romantic love is a human universal or near-universal.

Jankowiak and Fischer cite examples that document the existence of romantic love in cultures very different from our own. In one interview with an anthropologist, Nisa, a woman of the hunter-gatherer !Kung people of the Kalahari Desert of southern Africa, drew a distinction between a husband and a lover. A relationship with a husband is "rich, warm and secure," she said, while that with a lover is "passionate and exciting, although often fleeting and undependable." She added that "when two people come together their hearts are on fire and their passion is very great. After a while, the fire cools and that's how it stays" (Shostak, 2000).

In *The Jade Goddess,* a tale from the Chinese Sung Dynasty (928–1233 CE), a man by the name of Chang Po falls in love with a woman who is already engaged to someone else. He sinks into prolonged despair, but when he finally expresses his feelings to her, she reveals that she feels the same way about him, and they elope. They suffer from poverty and isolation and eventually decide to return home. On the eve of their return Chang Po draws his beloved into his arms and says, "Since heaven and earth were created you were made for me and I will not let you go. It cannot be wrong to love you" (Lin, 1961). The story is strikingly similar to the romances that were celebrated during the same period by the wandering minstrels of Europe, although there was little contact between the European and Chinese cultures.

Even if the capacity for romantic love is universal, modern Western culture is probably unusual in the emphasis it places on romantic love as a prerequisite for marriage. In many cultures, including our own until a century or so ago, choices of marriage partners were generally made by parents or decided by a variety of economic or other practical considerations in which love played little role. If a young man and woman were in love and wanted to marry, elopement was often a necessity.

Being in Love May Be the Justification for Marriage or Sex

"Love and marriage," crooned Frank Sinatra in 1955, "go together like a horse and carriage." Yet as recently as the 1960s, only 30% of women said that being in love was a necessary condition for marriage. The corresponding figure for men was over 60%. By 1984, these figures had risen to over 80% for both sexes (Simpson, 1986). Presumably, women's increasing economic independence has diminished their need to marry for nonromantic reasons such as economic security or social status. By the 1990s, less than 4% of Americans said they would marry someone they didn't love, compared with 50% of Indians and Pakistanis—in whose countries arranged marriages are still common (Hatfield, 1994).

Falling in love also seems to give people permission—women especially—to engage in sexual intercourse for the first time. In the NSSAL study, 58% of women mentioned "being in love" as a reason they first had intercourse. Only 30% of men mentioned this factor, however; a much more frequently cited reason for men was "I was curious about what it would be like."

People Fall in Love with Attractive Persons Who Show Some Interest in Them

What actually causes person A to fall in love with person B? We can point to several factors likely to be involved. First, person A is likely to be lonely or "looking for love." In fact, the best protection against falling in love is to be in love already. Second, person B should be *attractive* to person A. Third, B should display some interest in A. The degree of interest may be very small and may have no sexual content in B's mind, but it may still be enough to trigger A's passion. In other words, falling in love is often a reciprocation of the expression of positive feelings by the beloved (Curtis & Miller, 1997).

Is it possible to fall in love "at first sight"? About half of the U.S. population thinks it is; in fact, 44% of men and 36% of women say that it has happened to them (Gallup Organization, 2001). Since there is no objective test for "being in love," it is hard to confirm or refute their claims. But the fact that many people say they have experienced love at first sight highlights the fact that familiarity is not a necessary ingredient for romantic love.

Researchers Are Probing the Biological Basis of Love

Speaking of objective tests, there has been some research aimed at finding a biological basis for love. One interesting line of animal research focuses on voles (Nair & Young, 2006). As we mentioned in Chapter 2, closely related species of these small mammals differ in their sexual and social behavior. Prairie voles form lifelong pair bonds that are established at first mating (**Figure 10.6**), whereas mountain voles and meadow voles are sexually promiscuous and do not form pair bonds (Carter & Getz, 1993). Detailed examination of the brain and endocrine system suggest that pair bonding in prairie voles is mediated by several hormones or neurotransmitters, including two peptides released by the posterior lobe of the pituitary gland: oxytocin (see Chapter 5) and a closely related peptide, vasopressin (Carter, 1998). A research group at Emory University facilitated pair-bond formation in the promiscuous species of voles by injecting these hormones directly into their brains or by injecting a gene that caused their brains to produce more receptors for the hormones (Lim et al., 2004). When the researchers created a strain of genetically modified mice that possessed the gene for the prairie vole's vasopressin receptor, these mice showed greater affection for each other than do ordinary mice (Young et al., 1999).

Genes also contribute to variability in attachment formation within a single species. Among male prairie voles, for example, some individuals bond strongly to their partners and contribute to the care of their young, whereas others do nei-

(A)

(B)

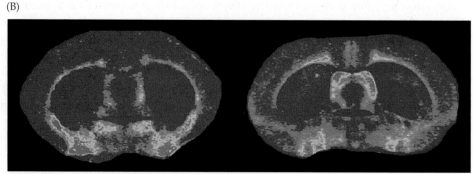

Figure 10.6 Prairie home companions (A) After mating, male and female prairie voles tend to stay together in a monogamous partnership until one of them dies. The male and female voles share parental duties. This behavior contrasts with that of the closely related mountain vole, which does not form pair bonds. (B) Receptors for the hormone vasopressin (indicated here by red, orange, and yellow) are distributed differently in the brains of the monogamous prairie vole (left) and the nonmonogamous mountain vole (right). This difference probably contributes to the behavioral differences between the two species. (Courtesy of Zuoxin Wang and Thomas Curtis.)

ther. The Emory researchers found that this behavioral difference is caused in part by slight differences in the DNA control sequences that regulate the production of the vasopressin receptor (Hammock & Young, 2005).

Another intriguing observation concerns a peptide hormone known as corticotropin releasing factor (CRF). This is a "stress hormone" that is secreted during states of fear or anxiety. Thus it was surprising to find that tiny injections of CRF into a brain region concerned with emotion and social bonding (the nucleus accumbens, part of the forebrain) greatly facilitated pair bond formation in prairie voles (Lim et al., 2007). This cross talk between the stress and social-bonding systems offers a possible biological explanation for "misattribution of arousal"—the phenomenon, described in Chapter 8, whereby putting someone in a state of high anxiety or fear causes them to find a potential sex partner more attractive than they otherwise would.

None of these observations on rodents prove that oxytocin and vasopressin play a role in triggering romantic attachments between humans, of course, but such attachments do probably have *some* kind of neurochemical basis. There has been speculation that neurotransmitters of the catecholamine family, such as dopamine, norepinephrine, and a related compound called phenylethylamine, might be important for sexual attraction and love in humans (Fisher et al., 2006). Researchers have also begun to delineate the brain circuitry involved in romantic love, using functional imaging techniques (**Box 10.5**).

One Theory Proposes that Love Has Three Components

Psychologist Robert Sternberg of Yale University has proposed that love is comprised of three elements: **passion**, **intimacy**, and **commitment**. These elements can be represented as the three vertices of a triangle (Sternberg, 1986) (**Figure 10.7**). When each of the three elements is present in the same amount, they form an equal-sided triangle whose size is proportionate to the degree of love. When the three elements are present to an unequal degree, they form an unequal-sided triangle.

The passion element in Sternberg's triangular model is the motivational component. It is strongest in the initial heat of romantic love. It is the "urge to merge," in both the physical and psychological senses. Intimacy is the emotional component: It refers to the feelings of closeness and connectedness in a relationship. It is expressed in the desire to promote the well-being of the beloved, in self-disclosure to the beloved, and in valuing the beloved in one's life. Commitment is the cognitive component. It refers, in the short term, to the decision that one loves the beloved. In the longer term, it refers to the commitment to maintain the loving relationship—as expressed in the marriage vows, for example. It is the element over which one has the greatest conscious control.

Just as the three primary colors can be combined in different proportions to create a variety of hues, the three elements of Sternberg's love triangle can be combined in different ways, producing different kinds of love, which can be represented by triangles of differing shapes (**Figure 10.8**). Sternberg names these kinds of love as follows:

- *Liking* is the kind of love in which intimacy is high but passion and commitment are low. It corresponds to what we usually call friendship.
- *Infatuation* is the kind of love in which passion is high but intimacy and commitment are low. It corresponds to "love at first sight," when one loves a person without knowing them well or thinking much about the matter.
- *Empty love* is the kind of love in which commitment is high, but passion and intimacy are low. It could be the final, stagnant stage of a romantic relationship in which passion and emotional involvement have waned, but there is still a

passion The overwhelming feeling of attraction typical of the early stage of a loving relationship.

intimacy The sense of connectedness in an established relationship.

commitment The cognitive component of love: the decision to maintain a relationship.

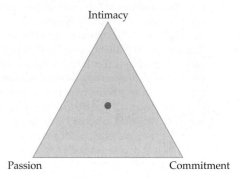

Figure 10.7 Sternberg's love triangle Robert Sternberg proposed that love consists of three elements—passion, intimacy, and commitment—that can be represented as a triangle.

Research Highlights

BOX 10.5 This Is Your Brain in Love

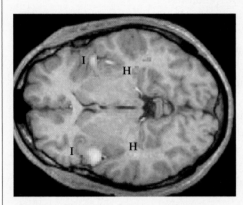

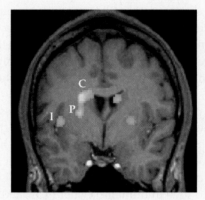

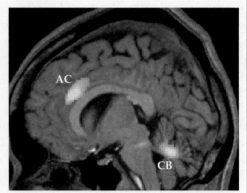

(A) A horizontal slice (front to the left, left side at top), showing activity in an infolded region of the cerebral cortex called the insula (I), and in the hippocampus (H).

(B) A frontal slice, showing activity in the insula and in two regions of the basal ganglia: the caudate nucleus (C) and the putamen (P).

(C) A near-sagittal (midline) slice, showing activity in the anterior cingulate cortex (AC) and the cerebellum (CB).

Neuroscientist Semir Zeki, of University College, London, along with his Swiss graduate student Andreas Bartels, wanted to find out what brain regions might underlie the experience of romantic love (Bartels & Zeki, 2000, 2004). They put up posters around London that advertised for men and women who were "truly, deeply and madly in love." Seventy women and men responded. The subjects had had a relationship with their beloveds for an average of about 2 years—thus they were not in the first flush of falling in love.

The subjects filled out a "passionate love questionnaire" (Hatfield & Sprecher, 1986), which asked them to rate their agreement with statements such as "For me, X is the perfect romantic partner," "I will love X forever," and "I eagerly look for signs indicating X's desire for me." Seventeen subjects (11 women and six men—all heterosexual) who scored highly on the questionnaire were rolled into a **functional magnetic resonance imaging (fMRI)** scanner. This high-tech mind reader constructs an image of the brain in which changes in blood flow (induced by brain activity) are represented as color-coded pixels. It produces images comparable to those produced by positron emission tomography, discussed in Chapter 4, but with better spatial resolution.

To allow the subjects to experience the emotion of romantic love while lying in the unromantic bowels of the fMRI scanner, Bartels and Zeki gave each subject a photograph of their beloved to gaze at. Of course, a whole lot goes on in the brain when you look at a picture, most of which has nothing to do with the emotion of love. To get rid of the irrelevant informa-

tion, the researchers alternated the picture of each subject's beloved with pictures of several other friends with whom the subject was not in love. They then digitally subtracted the scans taken while the subjects viewed the "friend" pictures from those taken while they viewed the "beloved" pictures, creating images that represent the brain regions that became more or less active when a subject viewed their beloved's picture. These images, the researchers argue, show the brain regions involved when a person experiences the emotion of romantic love.

One of the regions that becomes more active is the insula, a deeply infolded zone of the cerebral cortex (Figures A and B). The insular cortex has been known to play a role in emotions—both negative and positive ones—for some time. The insula in the left hemisphere was far more active than the corresponding region in the right hemisphere, casting doubt on the validity of the popular notion that the left and right hemispheres are the homes of reason and emotion, respectively.

Another region that became more active was the anterior cingulate cortex—a region that also becomes active when people view sexually arousing material without being in love (Figure C) (see Chapter 8). This observation makes sense, since we expect erotic arousal to be a component of romantic love.

Among the regions whose activity *decreased* during the experience of love were zones previously implicated in the experience of painful emotions such as sadness, anger, and fear. These regions include the prefrontal cortex of the right

hemisphere and a deep (subcortical) structure known as the amygdala. It appears that the brain regions serving positive and negative emotions have a reciprocal, seesaw relationship, such that love diminishes anger, and vice versa.

Most of the regions that were activated during the experience of romantic love have previously been shown to be active while a subject is under the influence of euphoria-inducing drugs such as opiates or cocaine. Apparently, both romantic love and those drugs activate a "blissed-out" circuit in the brain.

Still, this finding raises the usual question one must ask when attempting to measure tough-to-define emotional experiences: Are Bartels and Zeki studying what they think they're studying? All their subjects were in relationships with their beloveds, suggesting that they were *happily* in love. But romantic love is often unrequited, and that is far from a happy experience—it can lead to depression, even suicide. If Bartels and Zeki had tested a bunch of *unhappy*—but definitely "in love"—lovers, they might have found a pattern of activity very different from the one they reported. In other words, it is uncertain whether all the brain centers that lit up in their experiments are truly involved in the experience of love itself, rather than the euphoria that accompanies love when it is reciprocated (fMRI images from Bartels & Zeki, 2000).

functional magnetic resonance imaging (fMRI) A form of magnetic resonance imaging that maps brain activity by detecting the associated changes in blood flow.

conscious commitment to keeping the relationship going. But it could also be the first stage of an arranged marriage, leading to more complete love. Thus "empty love" may be a poor choice of terms that undermines Sternberg's assertion that commitment is a valid constituent of love.

- *Romantic love* is the kind of love in which both intimacy and passion are high, but commitment is low. Sternberg mentions the love of Romeo and Juliet, and of Tristan and Isolde, as examples of romantic love in this sense.

- *Companionate love* is the kind of love in which intimacy and commitment are high, but passion is low. It frequently occurs in marriage and cohabitations after physical attraction has abated.

- *Fatuous love* is the kind of love in which passion and commitment are high, but intimacy is low. According to Sternberg, it is seen in whirlwind romances in which two lovers rush off to get married and set up a home together without ever getting to know each other very well. These are high-risk relationships, although there is always the possibility that intimacy will develop.

- *Consummate love* is the kind of love in which all three elements are present in full. It represents the kind of love that most of us strive for and, having achieved, try to maintain—with variable success.

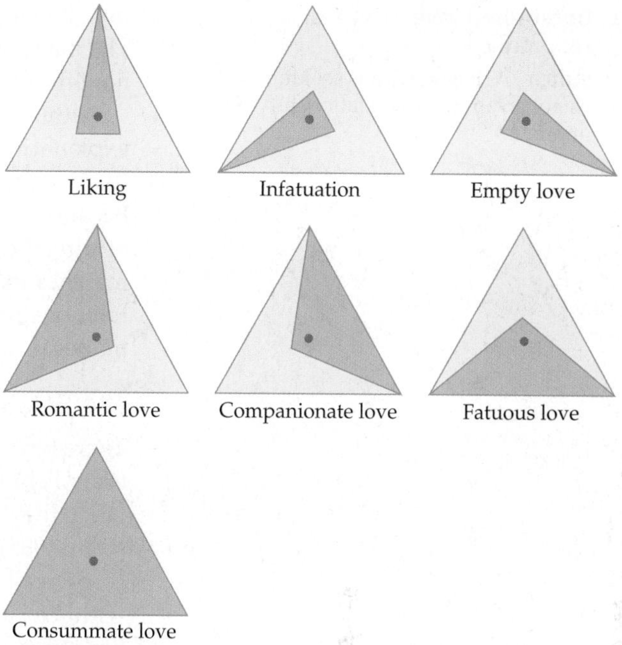

Figure 10.8 Sternberg's seven types of love combine passion, intimacy, and commitment in different proportions. (See Web Activity 10.1.)

Besides asserting that love is made up of these three elements in various combinations, Sternberg claims that people are most likely to be satisfied with their love relationships when their own and their lovers' triangles match or nearly match (Sternberg & Barnes, 1985) (**Figure 10.9**). When a couple's triangles are mismatched, as when one partner is high on commitment but low on passion, while the other is the reverse, both partners are likely to be dissatisfied.

Sternberg's theory has attracted a great deal of attention. One obvious prediction of the theory is that it should be possible to detect the existence of the three distinct components of love—passion, intimacy, and commitment—by giving people questionnaires about their loving relationships. Studies of this kind have produced mixed results, but one study, by Robert Lemieux, did produce a result favoring Sternberg's model (Lemieux & Hale, 1999). The researchers gave 233 unmarried male and female college students a 20-item questionnaire, in which the subjects were asked to rate their degree of agreement or disagreement with statements such as "My partner is sexually exciting." Analysis of the responses revealed three factors corresponding to the three elements of Sternberg's love triangle. Seven of the questions (including the one just cited) contributed primarily to the "passion" factor. Another seven (including "There are things I can tell my partner that I can't tell anyone else") contributed primarily to the "intimacy" factor. The remaining six questions (including "I think of our relationship as a permanent one") contributed mainly to the "commitment" factor.

Lemieux and Hale's study bolstered Sternberg's triangular theory of love. It also found sex differences in two of the three factors: Women scored higher on both "intimacy" and "commitment" than did men, whereas both women and men scored about equally on "passion." Thus the "average" loving relationship between a man and a woman is likely to be somewhat unbalanced, with the woman experiencing more intimacy and commitment than her partner. For both men and women, the strength of all three factors contributed to their degree of satisfaction with the relationship, but the strength of the "intimacy" factor was the best predictor of satisfac-

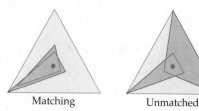

Figure 10.9 Couples may have matching or unmatched love triangles. Each member of the couple on the left (represented by blue and purple) has triangles approximating Sternberg's "infatuation." In the couple on the right, one member's triangle corresponds to "infatuation" and the other member's to "companionate love." According to Sternberg, the couple on the left is more likely to be satisfied with their relationship, because there is more overlap between their triangles.

unrequited love Love that is not reciprocated.

suitor A person who is seeking to establish a romantic relationship with another.

tion. Lemieux and Hale later replicated their study using married men and women. The main difference was that, as one might imagine, the "commitment" factor was now the best predictor of satisfaction (Lemieux & Hale, 2000).

Although Sternberg's theory is more a description of what love *is* than an explanation of how love comes about, it is potentially useful in studying how relationships run into trouble and how broken relationships might be healed. Because each partner's love triangle will change its shape and size over the course of a relationship, mismatches are very likely to develop. Identifying such mismatches may allow a counselor to focus a couple's attention on aspects of their relationship that need work. The simple, graphical nature of Sternberg's theory makes it suitable for use in a therapeutic setting.

The Relationship of Commitment to Love Is Debated

There have been quite a few other efforts to dissect love. To mention just one, Beverley Fehr of the University of Winnipeg has studied the terms that people use when they are asked to freely describe concepts such as "love" and "commitment" (Fehr, 1988). If commitment is one component of love, as Sternberg's model proposes, then all the terms that people use to describe commitment should be contained within a larger list of terms used to describe love. In fact, however, Fehr found that her subjects used two different, though partially overlapping, lists of terms to describe the two concepts (**Figure 10.10**). Furthermore, some of the terms used to describe commitment were quite negative, such as "feeling trapped." Thus, to rescue Sternberg's model, one would have to say that it uses special meanings of "love" or "commitment" that are somewhat different from the way most people think of these terms: specifically, a broader meaning of "love" or a narrower meaning of "commitment." Indeed, it is likely that most people are not comfortable with the intellectual aspect of love contained within Sternberg's notion of "commitment."

Here's the heart of the debate: Can you *decide* to love someone, or is love simply something that *happens* to you? Most Americans think of it as something that happens to you. Yet, as psychoanalyst Erich Fromm (1900–1980) pointed out, the cognitive aspects of love help us understand how arranged marriages not uncommonly grow into successful, loving relationships. "One neglects to see an important factor in erotic love, that of *will*," Fromm wrote. "To love somebody is not just a strong feeling—it is a decision, it is a judgment, it is a promise. If love were only a feeling, there would be no basis for the promise to love each other forever" (Fromm, 1956).

All in all, we can say that each individual's experience of love is unique and personal. We create our own narratives of love that reflect not only our individual personalities and experiences but also our exposure to popular culture (**Box 10.6**).

Unrequited Love Is Painful for Both Parties

The ultimate in mismatched love triangles is unreciprocated or **unrequited love**, in which one person's affection for another is not returned. These ill-starred relationships are very common: By college age, most men and women have experienced episodes of unrequited love, both as the **suitor** and as the rejector (Baumeister et al., 1993). Because romantic love is characterized by a longing for union with the beloved, unrequited love can be viewed as the most extreme or purest form of romantic love—one in which the desire for union is not diluted by its actual attainment.

Unrequited love can also be thought of as part of the matching process by which people find long-term mates. If, as we have sug-

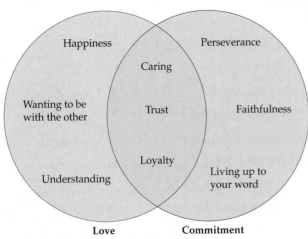

Figure 10.10 Love and commitment Beverley Fehr found that people use partially overlapping lists of terms to describe "love" and "commitment." Some of the terms are shown here.

Personal Points of View

BOX 10.6 Love Stories

Wes and Gina have been going out for six months, and there are times when Wes thinks that Gina sees the two of them as being involved in a competition rather than a relationship. She is determined to be the best at everything—not just at racquetball and other naturally competitive ventures, but at things as seemingly uncompetitive as taking down phone messages. Wes sees Gina as someone who could turn this seemingly mindless task into a challenge of who can take down the better, more comprehensive messages. Gina also turns the romantic aspects of their relationship into a competition. One of her favorite things to do is to play a kissing game with Wes; the two of them sit so that there are just a few inches between their lips, and the winner is the one who resists the temptation to kiss the other the longest. Gina has never lost this game, as Wes always succumbs to his desire to kiss her; after all, he knows that if he does not kiss her, they will sit there all day, because Gina would never give Wes the satisfaction of winning (Sternberg, 1998).

To Yale psychologist Robert Sternberg—he of Sternberg's love triangle—intimate relationships tend to follow certain well-worn story lines. Gina, for example, is following the "game story," in which the relationship is seen as a zero-sum game—one in which there is a winner and a loser.

Sternberg describes 26 different kinds of stories. Here are some more examples:

- *The fantasy story:* Alexis thinks that Cory, an office co-worker, may be the knight in shining armor who will romance and care for her for the rest of their days.
- *The addiction story:* Kevin has a neurotic need for Amanda and is preoccupied with the fear of losing her.

The fantasy story

- *The religion story:* Brenda believes that God brought Timothy to her so that they can imitate God's love in their mutual relationship.
- *The teacher-student story:* David expects Jessica to be the dutiful recipient of his lectures about life and what really makes people tick.

- *The business story:* Although well off, Kathy focuses more on the economic security of her marriage to Warren than on fostering passion or romance.
- *The war story:* Bob sees his relationship with Dierdre as a series of disputes to be fought over.

These love stories are not factual descriptions of relationships but subjective interpretations of them. A story is not necessarily good or bad: It depends in part on whether the other person's story fits in with it. If Jessica is comfortable playing the "student" role to David's "teacher," for example, the relationship may thrive. If Dierdre, like Bob, subscribes to a war story, the battles may go on for years without harm. Thus, relationships that seem (to outsiders) to be doomed to failure may last, while others that seem ideal may quickly end.

Where do these love stories come from? In part, they reflect an interaction between individuals and society, especially popular culture. Books and movies tell the same love stories over and over again. Wes and Gina's "game story," for example, is the theme of the movie *Who's Afraid of Virginia Woolf?,* in which Richard Burton and Elizabeth Taylor engage in an elaborate and increasingly bitter game of make-believe.

People may go through several relationships while enacting the same stories, and each relationship may fail in the same way. "Will he never learn?" think his friends. On the other hand, people are capable of changing their love stories over time—perhaps with the help of insights developed in the course of therapy. "That love is a story closes off no options to us," concludes Sternberg. "Instead, it makes us aware of the infinite options we can create as we write the stories of our lives and loves."

gested earlier, there is a sexual marketplace in which people find partners of roughly their own "worth," there has to be a trial-and-error process by which people find out what their own worth is. In the old days of arranged marriages, this kind of market negotiation was done by parents or match-makers. Now, a chain of unrequited or short-lived relationships may achieve the same thing. An

This late nineteenth-century Japanese woodblock print, *Reflected Moonlight*, depicts Lady Ariko, a poet of the medieval Heian court, with her lute, preparing to drown herself because of her unrequited love for a lord. Lady Ariko's poem, which appears at the top right of the print, expresses the anguish of the rejected lover: *"How hopeless it is/it would be better for me to sink beneath the waves/perhaps there I could see my man from Moon Capital."*

obsessive relational intrusion
Obsessive pursuit of a person by a rejected lover.

stalking Obsessive pursuit of a previous, current, or desired sex partner in such a way as to put that person in a state of fear.

adolescent may start by having a crush on the captain of the team, the class president, or some other figure whose abilities, looks, or social standing places them far above what the adolescent has to offer. Rejection may be followed by pursuit of a somewhat more appropriate partner, and so on, until a good match is found.

This is not to say that in unrequited love affairs the rejector is always more attractive (in some objective sense) than the unhappy suitor. There is, of course, a hefty dose of idiosyncrasy and quirkiness in love. Sometimes a person will see nothing in a suitor whom everyone else is salivating over. Sometimes a difference in sexual orientation will prevent love from being reciprocated, whatever the suitor's attractiveness. Sometimes the rejector, though idealized to virtual sainthood by the suitor, is really a ne'er-do-well who would ruin the suitor's life if they ever did connect. But commonly, rejectors fail to respond positively to suitors' advances because they rate the suitors as offering less than they "deserve."

Rejection in Love Damages Self-Worth

The experience of unrequited love is painful for the suitor, of course. There is not merely the failure to obtain what, for a few desperate weeks at least, seems like the only thing worth having on Earth. There is also the humiliation of rejection—being told, in some way or another, that one is not "good enough." Rejection in love is a crushing, if short-lived, blow to one's self-esteem. Yet the suitor does at least have a "script" to follow. The role of the unrequited lover is familiar to everyone; it is celebrated in one popular song after another. It is a dramatic role with its prescribed times for grief, anger, acceptance, and moving on.

Most people can follow this script and emerge unscathed and perhaps stronger for the experience. For a minority, however, especially those with controlling or manipulative personalities or poor communication skills, it may be difficult to take "no" for a final answer, and a single-minded pursuit of the desired person may ensue (Sinclair & Frieze, 2001). This pattern, termed **obsessive relational intrusion**, can lead eventually to criminal **stalking** (see Chapter 18).

The Rejector May Experience Guilt

As psychologist Roy Baumeister and his colleagues point out, the experience for the *rejector* is very different but often equally painful (Baumeister & Dhavale, 2001). At the beginning, certainly, the rejector may get a psychological boost from the realization that they are the object of someone's affection, even if not the particular someone they would have liked. Later, however, the rejector is likely to experience considerable guilt. This guilt has three sources: guilt at having led the suitor on, even if unintentionally or to a small degree; guilt at not returning the suitor's affection—a violation of the social norm of reciprocity; and guilt at inflicting humiliation on the suitor by telling that person that they are not loved in return.

Furthermore, the rejector's role is largely "unscripted": There are few social models for how a rejector is supposed to behave or feel. Thus the rejector may end up failing to communicate the rejection clearly to the suitor, perhaps representing it as a matter of unfortunate circumstances that might conceivably be overcome in the future. The rejector might even weasel out of making any explicit rejection at all—by avoiding the suitor, for example. When one considers that the suitor is likely to read the most optimistic interpretation into anything the rejector says or does, the potential for misunderstanding is great.

In fact, by analyzing numerous accounts of unrequited love told from the perspective of both suitors and rejectors, Baumeister's group found systematic biases in the way the episodes were recalled (**Figure 10.11**). Suitors were much more likely than rejectors to recall that the rejector initially reciprocated the suitor's advances and that the rejector led the suitor on. Rejectors, however, were more likely than suitors to recall that the rejector gave the suitor an explicit rejection and that the suitor persisted unreasonably in spite of the rejection. The researchers interpreted these biases as representing efforts by suitors to rebuild their self-esteem and by rejectors to justify themselves and reduce their feelings of guilt.

Rejection in love is bound to be a painful experience, but exactly *how* painful depends both on the style of rejection and the nature of the relationship between the two people (Young et al., 2008). Face-saving rejections ("I'm not ready for a relationship," or "You used to date my friend, so it would not be right") are somewhat less traumatic than baldly direct rejections ("I'm not interested," or "I don't feel the same way about you"). But much more important is the nature of the relationship. If the two people are friends, their friendship may well survive the romantic rejection and could even blossom into a romance later, so the rejection is not too traumatizing. (This is the storyline of countless movies, after all.). If they have already entered into a romantic relationship, however, no amount of tact is likely to cushion the blow of rejection, for, whatever the exact words the rejector uses, they are interpreted as meaning: "Getting into a relationship with you has been a disappointment." Real tact is not getting into an unworkable relationship in the first place.

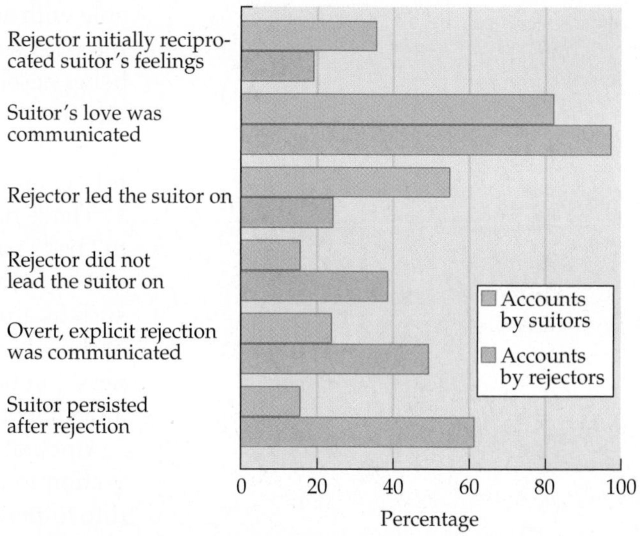

Figure 10.11 Unhappy memories When college students were asked to recall their experiences of unrequited love—both experiences in which they were rejected and experiences in which they did the rejecting—the two kinds of narratives differed markedly. The figure shows the percentage of "suitor" and "rejector" narratives that included the six listed assertions. (Data from Baumeister et al., 1993.)

Life Experiences Mold Our Sexual Relationships

Although we usually think of ourselves as entirely free agents in our romantic lives, the fact is that life experiences for which we are not directly responsible have an impact on our relationship styles. Here we briefly consider two such factors: our early relationship with our parents, and the social group in which we live.

Relationship Styles Are Influenced by Childhood Attachments

According to a school of thought known as **attachment theory**, parenting styles profoundly affect the child's developing personality (Bowlby, 1973; Ainsworth et al., 1978). If parents—the mother, especially—respond sensitively to the young child's needs, the child becomes securely attached; that is, it will become confident in the parent's love, will respond positively to the parent, and will seek contact with her or him, but will not be unduly disturbed by separation. If the parent is rejecting or emotionally distant, however, the child may avoid intimate interactions with the parent. If the parent is inconsistent or unresponsive, the child may become anxious or ambivalent and may become extremely upset when separated from the parent. These last two parent-child relationships are described as insecure attachments.

According to attachment theory, these styles of relating to parents—secure, avoidant, and anxious-ambivalent attachment—can persist into later childhood and adulthood, influencing how people relate to peers and also to romantic partners (Hazan & Shaver, 1987). People who were securely attached as children have a basic self-confidence and trust that allows them to enter into intimate relationships with relative ease. People who were avoidant as children may be uncomfort-

attachment theory The idea that relationship styles are influenced by the quality of the early parent–child bond.

able with adult intimacy and may strike potential romantic partners as cold. People who were anxious or ambivalent as children may have an unrealistic fear of being deserted, and this may cause them to seek an emotional "merger" that actually has the opposite effect of driving the partner away. To some extent, these different developmental trajectories have been verified in longitudinal studies that follow individuals from infancy through to adulthood (Simpson et al., 2007).

That's not to say that the young child is an entirely passive recipient of "good" or "bad" parenting. There may be traits in children themselves that tend to provoke certain styles of parental treatment (Sroufe, 1985). These could be physical traits, such as attractiveness or unattractiveness, or psychological traits. As an example of the latter, a Canadian group has presented evidence that unmasculinity ("sissiness") in boys may provoke rejection by their fathers, which may in turn lead to attachment anxiety in their adult romantic relationships (Landolt et al., 2004).

Understanding how attachment difficulties can be "transmitted" from one generation to another can lead to strategies for helping adults who have persistent difficulties in establishing or maintaining intimate relationships (Holmes, 2001). In addition, it is relevant to the issue of violence between intimate partners (Chapter 18); there is evidence that men who assault their partners have a childhood history of insecure attachment (McClellan & Killeen, 2000). In theory at least, promoting secure attachments between parents and their young children could have highly beneficial effects on sexual relationships in adulthood (Bowlby, 1988).

Relationship Styles Are Influenced by Communities

At various points in this book, we've touched on cross-national differences in how sexual relationships are constructed: arranged marriages in India, freewheeling sexual expression in Mangaia, and so on. What is perhaps less obvious is that there are enormous differences even within U.S. urban populations. Cities comprise numerous subcommunities that differ in cultural traditions, wealth, and opportunities, and these differences shape how individuals seek and enter into sexual relationships (Laumann et al., 2004). You might think that anyone in, say, Chicago would be free to connect with anyone else in Chicago, but in practice they're not. Communities are mostly organized by locality (i.e., they form a geographic patchwork). A young woman living in a Mexican-American community might not travel frequently outside that community, so most of her social contacts will be within it. If she or her parents are Catholic churchgoers, there may an expectation of conformity to Catholic teachings concerning sexual relationships as well as a resistance to any prospective non-Catholic mates, and she may be given few opportunities to meet young men on her own. Thus her prospective mates are likely to be family friends—perhaps distant relatives or immigrants from the same country.

Traditional institutions such as churches and families have lost a lot of their influence over mate choice and relationship style for many Americans, but that doesn't mean that we make sexual decisions in a social vacuum—far from it. Think about your own situation. As a college student, you probably enjoy independence in the sexual realm and are exposed to a greater variety of potential partners than is available to many Americans. But your friendship network—perhaps the group you live with—powerfully influences your judgments of the attractiveness of potential partners. Your friends may actually set up dates for you, or at least express opinions about the suitability of people you date or are thinking about dating. Their opinions, to a considerable degree, become yours. You absorb community standards of attractiveness, sexual behavior, and relationship styles. If your social network were a group of factory workers, a street gang, or a religious community, the sexual standards you absorbed would differ accordingly.

Couples in Relationships Resemble Each Other

One striking fact about couples is how similar their two members commonly are to each other. In Chapter 8 we described the concept of homophily; that is, the fact that people tend to be attracted to others who resemble themselves. It's not surprising, then, that couples should resemble each other to some degree, but the actual extent of that resemblance *is* surprising. According to the NHSLS, couples resemble each other far more than would be expected by chance in race or ethnicity, religion, age, educational level, and socioeconomic status. This is true not just for married and cohabiting couples, but for couples in short-term partnerships as well (Black & Lichter, 2004). This resemblance also extends to height, eye color, physical attractiveness, intelligence, and personality variables (Feingold, 1988). The tendency of sexually partnered couples to resemble each other is called **homogamy**. (Sometimes this term is reserved for married couples.)

To some degree, homogamy is an accident—a consequence of the fact that, as we just mentioned, people tend to find mates among the people they commonly encounter, who are likely to be of the same race, age, religion, and so on. This observation shows that sexual relationships are embedded in larger social structures, but it doesn't say whether homogamy has any *effect* on relationships, either for good or for bad.

There is some evidence, however, that homogamy does contribute to the success and stability of sexual relationships. Longitudinal studies have found that couples who resemble each other in a variety of respects are more likely to stay together, and express greater satisfaction with their relationships at later times in the relationship, than couples who are less alike (Hill et al., 1976; Meyer & Pepper, 1977; Caspi & Herbener, 1990; Caspi et al., 1992). Similarity between couples may strengthen relationships because companionate love—the hallmark of long-term relationships—is exactly that: a companionship. Like friends, couples who are similar to each other tend to have shared interests and attitudes. Thus they communicate approval to each other, bolster each other's self-esteem, and help stabilize each other's personalities.

In addition, outside forces tend to stabilize relationships between couples whose members are similar. For example, a couple's two birth families are more likely to interact socially and to actively support the couple's relationship if the couple is of the same race than if they are of different races. Similarly, people in general tend to be less supportive of couples who differ greatly in age than of age-matched couples, as if there is something not quite legitimate about a relationship between two people who are distinctly different in age.

In spite of these stabilizing influences, homogamy also presents hazards. In particular, similarity tends to undermine the mystery and tension associated with romantic love and sexual attraction. One can speculate that similarity between couples contributes to the reduction in sexual activity that often occurs over the duration of a long relationship. With heterosexual couples, of course, there is always the difference of sex: Gender-based differences offer an enduring mystery that might help to sustain erotic interest. With same-sex couples, however, gender-based differences are likely to be less marked, though they are not necessarily entirely absent. The similarity of same-sex partners may present a challenge to the maintenance of erotic interest over time. In particular, it may contribute to "lesbian bed death"—the low frequency of sex that has been reported for established lesbian couples (Blumstein & Schwartz, 1983). A similar phenomenon has been described for many long-term gay male relationships, although it has not been given a special name (McWhirter & Mattison, 1984).

Couples may resemble each other.

homogamy The tendency of sexually partnered couples, or married couples, to resemble each other in a variety of respects.

Communication Is a Key Factor in the Success of Relationships

Another important factor thought to influence the success of relationships is communication. In fact, many therapists name communication problems as the number one reason for dissatisfaction in marriages and other long-term relationships. According to several longitudinal studies, couples who communicate well before or at the time of marriage are likely to be satisfied with their relationships when interviewed several years later. Couples who communicate poorly early on (even though they may be just as happy at that stage) are likely to be dissatisfied with their marriage later. And couples who communicate via aggression are likely to be separated or divorced a few years later. These correlations are so strong that researchers can predict with 65% to 90% accuracy the state of a marriage 5 years down the road, simply on the basis of communication styles at the outset (Markman, 1981; Rogge & Bradbury, 1999).

Further bolstering the importance of communication in relationships are studies that demonstrate the benefit of interventions to improve communication skills. A research group at the University of Denver's Center for Marital and Family Studies, led by Howard Markman and Scott Stanley, focused on couples who were planning to marry (Markman et al., 1993). Some of the couples participated in a five-session Prevention and Relationship Enhancement Program (PREP), aimed at improving communication and conflict resolution skills. Five years later, the couples who took the PREP course had significantly better communication skills and lower levels of marital violence than the control couples. Furthermore, the couples who took the course were more likely to be together after 5 years: Only 8% of them had divorced or separated, compared with 19% of the control couples. In general, marital preparation courses have quite a good track record: Participants do about 30% better than nonparticipants on most measures of success, at least over the first few years of marriage (Carroll & Doherty, 2003).

The good results reported by PREP and other comparable programs have prompted some states to consider making premarital counseling programs mandatory for all marrying couples, with the hope of improving the statistics on marriage duration and divorce (see Chapter 13). It is far from certain that a mandatory program would have the same benefits as a voluntary one, however, since motivation tends to be a key factor in self-improvement programs. The idea of governments telling people how to run their marriages is also offensive to some.

Communication May Be Inhibited by Upbringing or by the Gender Barrier

Communication is a skill that permeates every aspect of a relationship. We focus here first on communication in the area of sexuality itself—which is after all the topic of this book—and then take a look at more general aspects of communication between intimate partners.

Many couples are reluctant to communicate at all about sexual issues. This reluctance results in part from a tradition of silence about sexual matters that is instilled in young children. Parents tend not to discuss sexual function or genital anatomy with their children, nor do they typically disclose much about their own sex lives or sexual problems. Children quickly learn that sex is a taboo subject. The result is a sense of shame that may profoundly inhibit communication in adulthood.

In heterosexual relationships, the gender barrier may compound communication problems. Boys and young men tend to talk about sexual matters among themselves; so do girls and young women. This leads almost to separate lan-

What went wrong? Many couples find it difficult to discuss sexual problems because they have been socialized to discuss sex only in same-sex groups.

guages: Young men, for example, may be perfectly comfortable using words such as "dick" and "pussy" among themselves, but the same words may seem vulgar when used with a female partner. So men are obligated to use words such as "penis" and "vagina," which may put them in an uncomfortable, almost clinical mindset. When this language difficulty is combined with limited knowledge about the other sex's anatomy and physiology, communication may be severely inhibited. Similarly, girls and young women may discuss sexual and relationship issues at great length among themselves but be quite unprepared to bring up these same issues with men.

Couples may also be reluctant to discuss sexual matters for a more subtle reason: They may fear that bringing sexual matters out into the open will destroy the "mystery" of sex, thus reducing it to just another uncomfortable topic of conversation. There may be some validity to this point of view. If a couple has a satisfying sex life without explicit verbal communication, there is certainly no reason to force it on them. There are many ways to communicate "This is fun" or "I'd rather do it this way" other than in words. Still, not even the most intimate of partners are mind readers, so problems not clearly communicated tend to remain unresolved and to multiply.

Additionally, cultural factors inhibit communication in certain groups. Asian Americans, especially Asian-American women, may find it a very foreign concept to discuss sex or relationship problems, either with a partner or with a therapist (Del Carmen, 1990). Hispanic Americans, too, have a custom of marital silence on sexual issues. This custom derives in part from the traditional expectation that men will exhibit tough, independent masculinity, or **machismo** (Guerrero Pavich, 1986). In addition, some immigrants from impoverished or socially conservative countries may lack the most basic knowledge about sexual anatomy and physiology, which makes communication even more difficult. Counterbalancing these problems, however, is a sense of teamwork or mutual obligation that many minority and immigrant couples possess, as well as the strong involvement of extended families in the maintenance of marital relationships. These factors contrast with the more individualistic approach to relationships that typifies European-American culture.

With all these obstacles, quite ordinary acts of communication can seem all but impossible in the domain of sex and intimate relationships. "I wish you'd help me reach orgasm," "Sorry, but I don't feel like sex tonight," "I'd like to have sex more often," "I'm missing the hug you used to give me when I came home," "I feel jealous when you spend so much time with Chris," and any number of other statements and requests may be invested with all kinds of negative overtones. Yet if they do not get said, it only gets harder and harder to say them. Finally, just making such a statement seems so out of line that it carries the unspoken subtext: "And, by the way, our relationship is going down the tubes."

Premarital Programs Teach Communication Skills

Programs such as PREP teach basic communication skills that are often as relevant to work and general social life as they are to sexual relationships. At the core of all communication, for example, is one person saying something and the other person listening and responding. In premarital counseling programs, couples may practice this interaction in a formalized manner. The couple may be seated facing and looking directly at each other, perhaps touching each other. One partner ("Pat") holds a speaker's token such as a square of linoleum (representing "the floor"), and makes a statement such as, "Kim, I find myself feeling hurt when you just breeze in and start chatting with the kids as if I'm not there." Pat then yields the "floor" to Kim, who replies in a fashion that paraphrases what Pat has just said, such as,

machismo The traditional Latino culture of manliness, which delineates sharp gender roles and gives men certain obligations and privileges.

"You mean, I seem to just take you for granted?" Pat may clarify the initial statement: "Not all the time, just when the kids are around." Then Kim gives a response representing a proposed resolution: "You may be right, Pat—sorry! I can understand how you must feel. However much I love the kids, you're the number-one person in my life, and I want to make sure you know it." And so on.

Contrived though such "active listening" exercises may seem, they teach two important points: the right of one partner to make a clear statement of a potential problem without interruption, and the obligation of the other to provide some feedback—to acknowledge understanding the statement and to process it in a way that will bring the interaction to a satisfactory close. In other words, "uh-huh" might not be a fruitful response to each and every one of your partner's utterances. It's not expected that couples will continue to pass floor tiles to and fro for the rest of their natural lives, but the hope is that the notion of ordered, reciprocal communication will persist.

Active listening exercises do run the risk of turning sexual relationships into therapy sessions. Partners are not therapists—that is, they are not outsiders whose role is simply to empathize, but players *within* the drama. Thus it doesn't necessarily help to tell your partner how much you understand their point of view unless that understanding is accompanied by action and resolution. Here's how one marriage-counseling researcher, John Gottman of the University of Washington, presents the issue:

> Let's say my wife is really angry with me because I repeatedly haven't balanced the checkbook and the checks bounce. . . . What would it accomplish if I say 'I hear what you're saying, you're really angry with me, and I can understand why you're angry with me because I'm not balancing the checkbook'? That's not going to make her feel any better—I still haven't balanced the damned checkbook! ...Real empathy comes from feeling your partner's pain in a real way, and then doing something about it (Wyatt, 2001).

Although writers such as Gottman often frame their discussion in terms of heterosexual marriage, the principles they put forward are applicable to any relationship that a couple values and wishes to sustain. In fact, even the less durable relationships that are common in the college years can be viewed as opportunities for exploration and learning in the field of communication, just as much as in the field of sexuality.

Self-Disclosure Facilitates Trust

An important role of communication is to allow for self-disclosure. It's not possible to form an intimate relationship with the mask that a person presents to the workaday world, but only with the inner person. That requires a voluntary disclosure of the rational and irrational thoughts, happy and painful memories, and hopes and fears for the future that lie hidden within each of us.

According to Susan and Clyde Hendrick of Texas Tech University (Hendrick, 1981; Hendrick et al., 1988; Hendrick & Hendrick, 1992), self-disclosure proceeds in a stepwise fashion: A disclosure by one partner tends to provoke an equivalent disclosure by the other, so that trust gradually builds between the two. In the Hendricks' studies, self-disclosure between partners predicted satisfaction in the relationship and a likelihood that the relationship would endure.

Self-disclosure—in particular, the disclosure of emotions—is often more difficult for men than for women, in our culture at least. Except for the emotion of anger, boys and young men are typically permitted little freedom to reveal their feelings, and by adulthood they may be quite deficient in "emotional expressiveness." Therapy aimed at reawakening men's ability to communicate their feelings may have a major beneficial influence on their relationships (Levant, 1997).

How Couples Deal with Conflict Affects the Stability of Their Relationship

Conflicts are inevitable in all but the briefest relationships, but how conflicts are handled is a good indicator of the likelihood that a relationship will last. John Gottman and his colleagues have carried out numerous longitudinal studies of conflict styles in marriage; typically, the researchers videotape conflict-laden interactions between partners early in their relationship, analyze and quantify the communications within the interaction, and then follow the relationship for a period of years.

One of the key findings is that the expression of anger is not necessarily a bad thing (Gottman & Krokoff, 1989). Disagreement and anger cause unhappiness at the time they are expressed, but couples who express conflicts through disagreement and anger are actually *more* likely to be satisfied with their relationships a few years down the road than couples who use other conflict styles, such as stone-

Getting angry does not necessarily threaten the stability of a relationship, but negative interactions must be balanced by more numerous positive ones.

walling, withdrawal, or contempt. What's more, expressing one's anger is associated with better general health: In one large-scale longitudinal study, women who clammed up during marital conflicts had a fourfold greater chance of dying within 10 years than did women who actively expressed their anger (Eaker et al., 2007).

That doesn't mean that couples should just lay into each other—far from it. For one thing, negative communications such as the expression of anger have to be balanced with positive ones. The University of Washington researchers have found that a certain *ratio* of positive to negative interactions in discussing problems—about five times as many positive interactions as negative ones—characterizes stable marriages (Gottman & Levenson, 1999). When negative communications are too frequent, they may come to taint the entire relationship, but when they are too rare, it may be a sign that marital problems are not being processed at all.

A common interactive style involves an initial, conflict-laden conversation that breaks off without a resolution, followed by a later, more positive conversation on the same topic. This "repair" conversation seems to be one of the most crucial processes in marriage. Gottman's group was able to predict, with 92.7% accuracy, whether a couple would divorce or not in the following 4 years, simply on the strength of their positive interactions during the repair conversation (Gottman & Levenson, 1999). This degree of predictability is remarkable when one considers that the likelihood of divorce is also influenced by completely unrelated factors, such as the loss of a job (Lester, 1996). Thus the old advice to "kiss and make up"—and to find a resolution to the problem that triggered the conflict—seems to be right on the mark. There are few if any differences between same-sex and opposite-sex relationships in this respect (Gottman et al., 2003).

Therapy based on insights of this kind is known as **behavioral couples therapy (BCT)**. This form of therapy is particularly successful in helping rescue troubled relationships where alcohol or substance abuse by one partner is a factor (Addiction and Family Research Group, 2004). This may be because poor communication is one of the factors that predisposes people to alcohol and substance abuse, as well as making it hard to deal with once established. The BCT therapist

behavioral couples therapy (BCT)
Therapy focused on improving styles of communication between partners in relationships.

emotionally focused couples therapy
Therapy focused on uncovering emotional problems that harm relationships.

jealousy Fear that a partner may be sexually or emotionally unfaithful.

sexual jealousy Fear that one's partner is engaging in sexual contacts with another person.

emotional jealousy Fear that one's partner is becoming emotionally committed to another person.

will introduce the couple to simple behavioral exercises, such as participating in a daily "abstinence trust discussion" or filling out a weekly "Catch Your Partner Doing Something Nice Worksheet," that bring social-learning and cognitive principles to bear on the problems faced by the couple.

In contrast to this "behavior-first" approach to couples therapy, **emotionally focused couples therapy** aims to uncover emotions, such as fear or sadness, that lie behind behavioral traits such as withdrawal or aggression (Johnson, 2004). Once identified, it is believed these emotions can be worked through in increasingly positive cycles of interaction between the two partners. The proponents of emotionally focused therapy report that most couples see a lasting improvement in their relationship after only 8 to 12 sessions of therapy (Johnson, 2003).

Love, Jealousy, and Infidelity Are Intertwined

Jealousy is the unpleasant feeling caused by the fear or realization of one's partner's infidelity.[*] Infidelity, in this context, could mean anything from an actual sexual contact or relationship with a third party to a mere indication of interest in someone else—as evidenced by looking at, flirting with, or spending time with that person. At any one time, about 1 in 10 college students is experiencing jealousy, according to an Italian study (Marazziti et al., 2003).

Jealousy can be an acute sensation—the instant stab of jealousy that we may feel when our beloved shows attention to a potential rival. This feeling probably involves a physiological stress response. Alternatively, it can be a gnawing, suspicious frame of mind that takes over a jealous person and colors all their interactions with their partner—the "green-eyed monster" that settled on Shakespeare's Othello.

We can break down jealousy into two kinds. The first, **sexual jealousy**, is a fear that one's partner is engaging or seeking to engage in sex with another person. The second, **emotional jealousy**, is a fear that one's partner is committing himself or herself to another person and might therefore abandon the relationship. Men and women can experience both kinds of jealousy, but men typically experience sexual jealousy more strongly than women, and women typically experience emotional jealousy more strongly than men. This sex difference exists across many or all cultures (Buss, 1989).

Jealousy Can Have a Positive Function

Although some sociologists have discussed jealousy as a purely cultural phenomenon (Reiss, 1986), evolutionary psychologists see the capacity for jealousy as a hardwired adaptation to certain inescapable facts about reproduction. First, female mammals make a much greater biological contribution to reproduction than do males, but in some species, such as ours, this imbalance may be countered by the extra resources (e.g., food and protection) that males contribute. Second, females can be certain that any offspring they bear are their own; males, however, cannot be certain that they fathered their mate's offspring. Thus, during human evolution, the major risk for a woman was that a man would take up with another mate, leaving her with insufficient resources to rear her children alone. The major risk for a man, however, was that he would unwittingly devote a great deal of time and effort to helping rear children who were actually fathered by another man. According to David Buss of the University of Texas, these differences in risks explain why men and women tend to experience different kinds of jealousy: Men are more anxious

---

[*]Jealousy is different from *envy*—the distress caused by another person's possession of something that one lacks.

not to be cheated on sexually, whereas women are more anxious not to be deserted (Buss, 2000).

Because our capacity for jealousy has evolved, it is "built in;" thus it is not always a rational process. A husband doesn't say to himself, "Oh, my wife's on the pill, so I'm not worried if she sleeps around." A childless lesbian couple isn't impervious to jealousy simply because there are no children for whom resources are needed. Evolution knows nothing about pills or sexual orientation: It simply provides everyone with an emotional mechanism that has been effective in the past for protecting people's reproductive interests.

Jealousy is neither a good thing nor a bad thing, but rather a psychological function that can have both positive and negative consequences. The negative consequences can be truly horrendous: About 13% of all homicides are spousal murders, most of them triggered by jealousy. Battered women who seek refuge in shelters are commonly there because of spousal jealousy. And many more relationships are poisoned by less extreme expressions of the same emotion. When people learn to respond appropriately to problematic situations, however, they can overcome the problems that jealousy creates.

Jealousy can help maintain relationships that are threatened by third parties.

Jealousy often arises when people in relationships receive sexual advances from outsiders. These "mate-poaching" efforts are not uncommon and seem to be universal across human cultures (Schmitt, 2004). In addition, people in relationships may be tempted to cheat on their partners—not all men and women, and not all the time, but often enough to demonstrate that love—the main glue of relationships—is not always strong enough by itself to preserve monogamy. That's where jealousy attempts to take over the job. And that's where jealousy can have a positive value for the person who experiences it, painful though it is.

Jealousy is part of the mechanism that detects and gives salience to cheating by a partner and that motivates action to prevent or end it. As Buss points out, there must have been an evolutionary spiral in which skill at cheating and skill at detecting cheating spurred each other's development. In any event, humans today are extremely good at both. And although jealousy is often dismissed as irrational or pathological, it's surprising how often "irrational" jealousy turns out to be well founded, even when the signs of infidelity are subtle.

Jealousy Can Become a High-Stakes Game

The spiral gets even more convoluted, however. Women, in particular, may *intentionally* attempt to provoke their partner's jealousy by mentioning their attraction to another man or by openly flirting with another man. If a woman's flirtation is successful in attracting a response, this raises her attractiveness in the eyes of her partner. This is because people rarely rely entirely on their own estimation of a partner's attractiveness—they also take other people's opinions into account. What's more, the woman closely monitors her partner's response to the flirtation. If he isn't jealous or stoically hides his jealousy, she may perceive this nonresponse as a lack of commitment to their relationship. Thus a demonstration of jealousy can be an important confirmation that the relationship is strong (Buss, 2000).

We mentioned earlier that couples tend to be roughly matched in attractiveness (in the broad meaning of the word). Nevertheless, there are couples who are

delusional jealousy Persistent false belief that one's partner is involved with another person.

extra-pair relationship A sexual relationship in which at least one of the partners is already married to or partnered with someone else.

unmatched in this respect or who become so in the course of a relationship. In such cases, the more attractive partner is more likely to be unfaithful. That's partly because the more attractive partners feel that they are not getting their "fair market value" in the relationship (Hatfield et al., 1979) and partly because they are approached more often by third parties. Correspondingly, the less attractive partners in unmatched relationships are more committed to those relationships, and they experience more intense jealousy when confronted with the possibility of infidelity (Hansen, 1985). In other words, the more difficult people think it would be to replace their partner with another of equal value, the more susceptible they are to jealousy.

Several therapists have laid out useful techniques for distinguishing healthy jealousy, which can help strengthen and maintain loving relationships, from jealousy that is merely destructive, as well as techniques for overcoming the latter kind (Barker, 1987; Dryden, 1999). Self-destructive jealousy, aggressive jealousy, or jealousy that is based on persistent false beliefs about the partner (**delusional jealousy**) obviously merit therapeutic intervention. Still, one way to deal with jealousy is to act on it, specifically by making oneself more physically attractive to one's partner or by going out of one's way to demonstrate love and commitment. "Men who are successful at keeping their partners often step up their displays of love when threatened with a possible partner defection," writes Buss. "Men who fail in these displays tend to be losers in love" (Buss, 2000).

Extra-Pair Relationships Have Many Styles and Motivations

As we've just discussed, the capacity for jealousy exists because people who are in coupled relationships, whether dating, cohabiting, or married, may also engage in sexual relationships outside their ongoing partnership. We now turn our attention to the forms and motivations of such **extra-pair relationships**. ("Extramarital relationships" is a better-known phrase, but it is not inclusive enough for our purposes.)

About the only thing that all extra-pair relationships have in common is that, as mentioned earlier in this chapter, they tend to incur social disapproval. Monogamy and serial monogamy are considered the ideal forms of sexual relationship, and anything that violates these norms is stigmatized, though to varying degrees depending on circumstances. Even fantasies about sex with a person outside the partnership are widely considered a form of infidelity, in spite of the fact that most men and about half of all women experience such fantasies (Yarab et al., 1998).

If we discount fantasies, we are still left with a broad range of behaviors that fall into the category of extra-pair relationships. These behaviors include casual flirting, fondling, genital contact and coitus, and falling in love. Extra-pair relationships may be single encounters, brief "flings," longer "affairs," or a succession of such relationships with a variety of different partners. They may take place with or without the knowledge or acquiescence of the person's regular partner, who may be a spouse, cohabitational partner, or girlfriend or boyfriend. They may take place in "real life" or on the Internet (**Box 10.7**).

Personal and Evolutionary Factors Influence Infidelity

Why do some men and women in our society engage in extra-pair relationships while others do not? Many factors come into play here. Moral beliefs, concern for their partners' feelings, or fear of the consequences restrain many people from engaging in extra-pair sex even though they would like to. Conversely, lack of physical satisfaction, communication, or love in the primary relationship, or prolonged absence of the primary partner, can drive some people into affairs. So can

Society, Values, and the Law

BOX 10.7 We Just Clicked

When John Goydan of Bridgewater, New Jersey, filed for divorce from his wife Diane and sought custody of their two young children, his legal papers contained dozens of emails, some of them sexually explicit, that Diane had exchanged with a man who called himself "The Weasel." Diane and the Weasel never met, but to John their online romance amounted to adultery. Similarly, "Nadja" considered that her attorney husband "Steve" had cheated on her when their children found erotic correspondence between him and a woman named "Galaxy Queen" on the family computer—even though Steve and Galaxy Queen had confined their romance to the Internet (Associated Press, 1996).

What drives people to commit Internet infidelity? For the most part, it's the same reasons that have driven people to cheat on their partners since time immemorial. But the Internet offers special incentives—what has been called the "triple-A engine" of accessibility, affordability, and anonymity (Cooper, 2002). Anonymity, in this context, includes selective disclosure and deception: in other words, a level of control over how the other person perceives you that would never be achievable in the "real" world. And of course it means safety—no hard-to-explain hickeys, no mysterious phone hang-ups, and no STDs. A secure password covers everything.

Diane and Steve's escapades took place in the 1990s, when text emails were about the only option for cyberlovers. Now the profusion of microphones, webcams, and videochat-oriented websites allow for the exchange of everything but pheromones (Ruberg, 2007). But the closer an electronic romance comes to resemble the real thing, the more likely that it will be perceived as cheating. When Monica Whitty had 234 subjects complete a story that dealt with Internet infidelity, most did so in ways that revealed their belief that such actions constituted cheating and were harmful to established relationships (Whitty, 2005). Often, this belief was based on the sense that, while online physical intimacy is simulated, the emotional intimacy that may go along with it amounts to real betrayal.

John and Diane divorced—after a countersuit by Diane claiming invasion of privacy and wiretapping. As for Nadja and Steve, extended marriage therapy and a major change in lifestyle saved them from a breakup.

the sense that one is not getting what one deserves in the primary relationship because one's partner is perceived as less attractive or desirable than oneself. So can the sheer excitement of having a new partner or of falling in love all over again. People may also cultivate secondary relationships to provoke a jealous response on the part of the primary partner, to "get even" with the primary partner if that partner is already having an affair with someone else, or to precipitate an end to the primary relationship. Finally, gay people who are heterosexually married may find their only sexual satisfaction in secondary relationships.

People who are in the early stages of a relationship may cultivate a "back burner" relationship with another partner, perhaps an "ex." This strategy could be either a form of insurance in case the main relationship doesn't work out or simply a means to increase sexual enjoyment or attention. "Back burner" affairs are less common when primary relationships have lasted for some time and have turned into cohabitations or marriages. These more mature relationships are exposed to another danger, however, related to the transition from romantic to companionate love. This transition reopens the possibility of romantic love—but with a different person. It's the stuff of soap operas, but it's often the stuff of real

Figure 10.12 Marriage is an interlude of monogamy, according to NHSLS data. The graph shows the percentage of men and women born between 1943 and 1952 who said they had more than one sex partner before, during, or after their first marriage.

life, too: a man or woman may be deeply attached to his or her regular mate but may also be head over heels in love with someone else.

That infidelity has evolutionary roots is suggested by the fact that promiscuity is common among nonhuman animals, including many species that form pair bonds ("socially monogamous" species). As we discussed in Chapter 2, male animals probably engage in extra-pair sex because it is a relatively inexpensive way to have more offspring, whereas females are more likely to do so to acquire the resources provided by the extra-pair male or to give her offspring better genes than those provided by her regular mate.

Evolutionary psychologists argue that similar forces influence human behavior. Steve Gangestad and Randy Thornhill, for example, believe that when women have sex outside of their marriages or regular partnerships, they are unconsciously shopping for better genes. They are said to do this by choosing men who are physically symmetrical—a sign of good genes (see Chapter 8)—and by engaging in extra-pair sex during the phase of their menstrual cycles during which they are most likely to conceive (Gangestad & Thornhill, 1997).

In addition to these apparent evolutionary forces, we should bear in mind the obvious social factors that influence women and men in different ways when it comes to extra-pair relationships. Men's infidelities tend to be viewed more leniently than those of women, and men often have greater ability to devote time and resources to an outside relationship than women do, especially if the woman is pregnant or the couple already has children. The most convincing evidence for evolved gender differences, in the area of infidelity as in all other aspects of sexuality, would come if they were to show themselves even on a perfectly level social playing field—something that does not yet exist.

Extra-Pair Relationships Are Uncommon

Given all these possible reasons for extra-pair relationships, it's actually somewhat surprising how uncommon these relationships are (**Figure 10.12**). In the NHSLS, more than 90% of the women and more than 75% of the men reported that they had been completely monogamous over the entire duration of a marriage or cohabitation, whereas many of these same people had multiple partners *before* and *after* those long-term relationships.

It's possible, of course, that the interviewees were less than honest about their extramarital relationships. One study found that married women were six times more likely to admit to a recent extramarital relationship when entering their responses into a computer than when they were questioned in a face-to-face interview, as was done in the NHSLS study (Whisman and Snyder, 2007). David Buss has concluded from a review of numerous studies that 30% to 50% of American men and 20% to 40% of American women have at least one extramarital affair over the course of a marriage (Buss, 2000). Still, even that conclusion is compatible with the idea that most Americans are monogamous for the greater part of their married lives.

Summary

1. People enter into sexual relationships for a variety of reasons: sexual attraction and love; nonspecific sexual arousal; the desire for status, security, or profit; the desire to conform or to rebel; and the desire to have children.

2. Sexual relationships are influenced by individual and societal attitudes concerning the morality of sex. The Christian religion was very anti-sex in its early days, but current teachings are more diverse. Some other religions have embraced sexuality more warmly. To some degree, U.S. law and public opinion acknowledge that people have a right to freedom of sexual expression.

3. People tend to judge the morality of sexual behavior by its context, being more approving of sex in committed relationships than of casual or extramarital sex. Beliefs about the morality of sex are tied to beliefs about its purpose. Americans can be grouped into several clusters with characteristic attitudes on sexual matters; to a considerable degree, a particular person's beliefs can be predicted by demographic characteristics such as age, sex, religion, and educational level. Americans have become far more accepting of sex between unmarried individuals over the past several decades.

4. Casual sex is more appealing to men than to women. In the college environment, "hooking up" (uncommitted sex between acquaintances) is an increasingly common practice. But the prevalence of casual sex in the college environment is lower than most students believe. Casual sex is more accepted and prevalent in the gay male community than among heterosexuals or among lesbians.

5. In environments in which casual sex is negotiated, such as singles bars, women tend to initiate sexual encounters. Flirting behaviors by both sexes are quite stereotyped across cultures.

6. Noncohabitational ("dating") relationships tend to be fluid and short-lived, leading either to a live-in relationship or to separation. First dates in the college environment follow gendered scripts. On these dates, men tend to focus on the prospects for sexual contact more than women do. Among older singles, both men and women focus more on seeking a life-long partner.

7. Romantic love exists in most or all cultures. Certain hormones and neurotransmitters and particular regions of the brain may play a specific role in romantic love.

8. One theory of love proposes that it consists of three elements—passion, intimacy, and commitment—whose relative contributions may be represented by a triangle. The shape of a person's "love triangle" changes over the course of a relationship. A couple is most likely to be satisfied with their relationship when their triangles match.

9. Unrequited love is painful to both suitors and rejectors: to suitors because it denies them their love object and diminishes their self-esteem, and to rejectors, because it causes them guilt.

10. According to attachment theory, young children's relationships with their parents establish patterns that are echoed in romantic relationships during adulthood.

11. Partners in relationships tend to resemble each other in a variety of respects. Homogamy contributes to satisfaction in relationships but may contribute to a decline in erotic interest between long-term partners.

12. Couples' communication styles predict their satisfaction with and the durability of their relationship. Couples commonly have difficulty communicating about sexual matters for many reasons, such as a culture of sexual shame as well as the gender divide. Some premarital counseling programs teach communication skills.

13. Self-disclosure is an incremental and reciprocal process in relationships that builds intimacy and trust.

14. The way couples deal with conflict is strongly predictive of how long the relationship will last. Optimal strategies involve not the avoidance of anger but a balancing of angry interactions with numerous positive interactions, and the follow-up of hostile interactions with positive "repair" conversations. Couples therapy may focus on altering behavior or on unearthing hidden emotional problems.

15. Jealousy, though a painful experience, has a positive function in protecting relationships against infidelity and in testing the strength of love bonds. Sex differences in jealousy—sexual jealousy in men and emotional jealousy in women—may reflect the different reproductive interests that men and women have had over the course of human evolution. Some forms of jealousy are damaging and merit treatment, but well-grounded jealousy can spur constructive efforts to improve the relationship, if those involved have learned to respond effectively to problematic situations.

16. Many circumstantial factors influence whether people in long-term partnerships engage in sexual relationships outside those partnerships. In addition, infidelity may have evolutionary roots because it offers the possibility of more offspring for men and

of better-quality offspring for women. National surveys suggest that most married Americans are in fact monogamous for most or the entirety of their marriage.

Discussion Questions

1. Compare and contrast your beliefs about what is right or wrong in the sexual domain with your peers' and your parents' beliefs (e.g., consider extramarital sex, premarital sex, casual sex, promiscuity, age of consent, homosexual behavior, contraception, abortion, and divorce). Identify the moral perspective (see Figure 10.1) that best describes your beliefs. Discuss how your attitudes have or have not changed over time.

2. If you have had an experience with a relationship breakup, describe your reactions to that breakup, how it felt, and what you learned. If you have not had a breakup, imagine the circumstances that would distress you enough to lead to a breakup.

3. Discuss what is important to you in a relationship about communication and conflict negotiation. Are you reluctant to discuss sexual issues? Why? Consider your ability to communicate in light of those factors discussed in the text that hinder communication.

4. Discuss your experiences with jealousy and compare them with those of your peers.

5. Which method do you think is more effective for selecting a marriage partner—arranged marriage, or falling in love? Why?

Web Resources

American College Health Association www.acha.org/

Beliefnet (interfaith site with considerable discussion of sexual and relationship issues) www.beliefnet.com

Go Ask Alice: Relationships (from Columbia University's Health Services) www.goaskalice.columbia.edu/Cat8.html

Gottman Institute: Relationship Quiz www.gottman.com/marriage/relationship_quiz/

SexInfo: Love and Relationships (from the University of California, Santa Barbara) www.soc.ucsb.edu/sexinfo/?article=A2J8

Recommended Reading

Buss, D. M. (2000). *The dangerous passion: Why jealousy is as necessary as love and sex.* The Free Press.

Easton, D., & Liszt, C. A. (1998). *The ethical slut: A guide to infinite sexual possibilities.* Greenery Press.

Fisher, H. (2004). *Why we love: The nature and chemistry of romantic love.* Henry Holt.

Gottman, J. M., Gottman, J. S., Declaire, J. (2006). *Ten lessons to transform your marriage: America's love lab experts share their strategies for strengthening your relationship.* Crown.

Hatfield, E., and Rapson, R. L. (1996). *Love and sex: Cross-cultural perspectives.* Allyn and Bacon.

Klein, M. (2006). *America's war on sex: The attack on law, lust, and liberty.* Praeger Publishers.

Markman, H., & Stanley, S. (2001). *Fighting for your marriage: Positive steps for preventing divorce and preserving a lasting love* (rev. ed.). Jossey-Bass.

McNaught, B. (2008). *Are you guys brothers?* AuthorHouse.

Parrinder, G. (1996) *Sexual morality in the world's religions.* Oneworld Publications.

Pierce, C., & Morgan, E. T. (2008). *Finding the doorbell: Sexual satisfaction for the long haul.* Nomad Press.

Sternberg, R. J., & Weis, K. (2008). *The new psychology of love.* Yale University Press.

CHAPTER 11

From conception through delivery, pregnancy brings about many changes in a woman's body.

Fertility, Pregnancy, and Childbirth

n earlier chapters we described the processes of conception and implantation, as well as the sexual differentiation of the embryo and fetus. We now take a broader look at pregnancy and childbirth from the perspectives of both the fetus and its parents. In this chapter we assume that couples want to become parents—and parents of a healthy child. We will see how a couple can optimize their chances of achieving this goal, and how medical science has improved their odds of doing so. In Chapter 12 we will take the opposite tack, looking at strategies to prevent pregnancy and childbirth.

Pregnancy and Childbirth Raise Major Health Concerns

In the past, pregnancy and childbirth were events to which women looked forward with a mixture of joy and terror. Joy, because producing and rearing children defined much of a woman's existence. And terror, not just because of the pain of childbirth, but because of the grave risk that pregnancy would end in the death of mother, baby, or both.

Before the advent of modern medicine, no amount of wealth or power could avert the human cost of reproduction. Remember England's King Henry VIII (1491–1547) and his six wives? Yes, he had a couple of them beheaded, but two of the remaining four—Jane Seymour and Kathryn Parr—died in or soon after childbirth. Of these six women's 11 children, most died in infancy, and only three reached adulthood. Memorials to the millions of women who have died in childbirth are everywhere, from India's fabled Taj Mahal to a humble stone in the pioneers' graveyard at Coloma, California, that records the death of 32-year-old Hannah Seater and her newborn son in 1852.

Today the prospects for pregnant women and their fetuses are far brighter than in the past. If we exclude pregnancies that are terminated by induced abortion, 80% of all established pregnancies in the United States culminate in the delivery of a live child. Once a child is born, it has a better than 99% chance of surviving infancy. And only about 1 in 10,000 pregnancies now leads to the death of the mother (Centers for Disease Control, 2004b, 2007e).

Still, there is always room for improvement, especially because the statistics for some U.S. minorities are much worse than those for the general population. And parents want not just a live child, but one who is in the best possible shape to face the rigors of life "on the outside." To achieve this goal, it helps for parents to learn as much as possible about pregnancy and childbirth and about the factors that promote or compromise the health of the mother and her fetus.

Pregnancy Is Confirmed by Hormonal Tests

We say that pregnancy is "established" not at fertilization, but several days later, when the embryo (more accurately called a conceptus—see Chapter 6) implants in the uterine wall and starts to secrete the hormone human chorionic gonadotropin (hCG). This hormone blocks the regression of the corpus luteum that normally takes place at the end of the luteal phase of the menstrual cycle. Menstruation therefore does not occur, and a missed menstrual period is the usual way that a woman learns that she is pregnant.

Unfortunately, the absence of a menstrual period at the expected time is not a totally reliable indicator of pregnancy. Many women have irregular periods anyway, and even in a woman who is normally very regular, a period can be missed or delayed as a result of illness, stress, or some other reason. Conversely, some "spotting" (light bleeding) can occur even when a woman is pregnant.

Other signs may help to confirm the pregnancy, including breast tenderness, fatigue, and nausea (the beginning of the "morning sickness" that can plague some women during the first 3 months of pregnancy; see below). In addition, a woman who has been monitoring her basal body temperature as a means to determine her "fertile window" (see below) may notice that her temperature stays high, rather than falling as it usually does at the end of the luteal phase. None of these signs is foolproof, however, and this is why pregnancy tests are important.

Pregnancy tests detect the presence of hCG in the mother's blood or urine. The most sensitive (and expensive) laboratory tests can detect hCG in the mother's blood almost immediately after implantation—several days *before* a woman would notice a missed period. The more usual, less sensitive laboratory tests detect pregnancy with about 98% accuracy at the time of the missed period. To get a laboratory test, a woman must see a healthcare provider.

Another option is to purchase a home pregnancy test kit. These kits are convenient and popular—about 20 million are sold in the U.S. every year. They work by means of specific antibodies that bind to hCG in the woman's urine and then trigger a color reaction on a test strip (**Figure 11.1**). Various brands are available, ranging in price from about $7 to $17. Most of these tests can detect pregnancy by the first day after a missed period, and some can do so 3 days *before* a missed period.

Unfortunately, home pregnancy tests are not nearly as reliable as laboratory tests. Although most of the products claim "99% accuracy," that figure refers to their use by professionals in unrealistic laboratory conditions. In real-world use, many home test results are incorrect (Cole et al., 2004). The main problem is a high rate of false negatives: test results indicating that the woman is not pregnant when in fact she is. False negatives can occur because of too-early testing, too-dilute urine, or failure to follow the instructions correctly. A false negative result can cause a woman to postpone getting prenatal care and may lead her to continue the consumption of alcohol or drugs that are capable of harming the embryo (see below). Thus it is a good idea to follow up a negative test with a second test a few days later. To facilitate retesting, some test kits are available as two-packs.

There is a great need for a more reliable home pregnancy test. A small step in that direction took place in 2003 with the introduction of the Clearblue Easy test. This test shows the words "pregnant" or "not pregnant" in place of the traditional indicator stripes and thus reduces the likelihood of misinterpretation.

The secretion of hCG is presumptive evidence of pregnancy. Definitive clinical evidence of pregnancy can be obtained at 5 to 6 weeks by means of an **ultrasound scan**. This technique generates an image using high-frequency sound waves that are reflected off structures within the mother's body. It can determine whether one or more embryos are present, and by 2 to 3 weeks later it can detect the fetal heartbeat.

ultrasound scan An imaging procedure that depends on the reflection of ultrasonic waves from density boundaries within the body. Also called ultrasonographic scan.

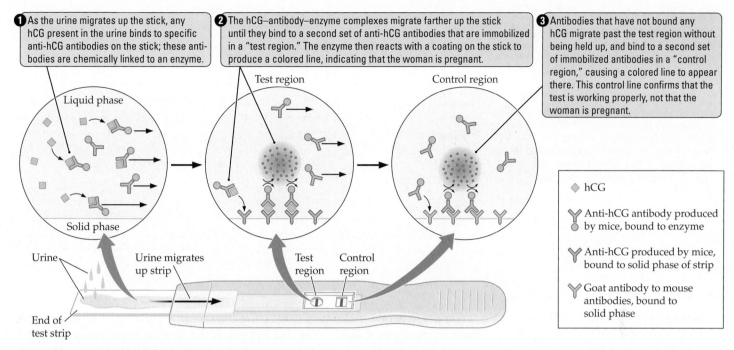

1 As the urine migrates up the stick, any hCG present in the urine binds to specific anti-hCG antibodies on the stick; these antibodies are chemically linked to an enzyme.

2 The hCG–antibody–enzyme complexes migrate farther up the stick until they bind to a second set of anti-hCG antibodies that are immobilized in a "test region." The enzyme then reacts with a coating on the stick to produce a colored line, indicating that the woman is pregnant.

3 Antibodies that have not bound any hCG migrate past the test region without being held up, and bind to a second set of immobilized antibodies in a "control region," causing a colored line to appear there. This control line confirms that the test is working properly, not that the woman is pregnant.

Test region

Control region

Liquid phase

Solid phase

Urine

Urine migrates up strip

Test region

Control region

End of test strip

◆ hCG

Ⓨ Anti-hCG antibody produced by mice, bound to enzyme

Ⓨ Anti-hCG produced by mice, bound to solid phase of strip

Ⓨ Goat antibody to mouse antibodies, bound to solid phase

Figure 11.1 How a home pregnancy test works The user holds one end of the test stick in her urine stream for a few seconds (or dips it in a collected specimen). (See Web Activity 11.1.)

The Likelihood of Pregnancy Can Be Maximized by Tracking Ovulation

For a fertile young couple that is having sex several times a week without any form of contraception, there is about a 20% chance of pregnancy per month. This translates into a 93% chance within the first year. If a woman does not become pregnant after a year of unprotected sex, the couple is described as **subfertile**. This doesn't mean that there is no further chance of pregnancy, but rather that an investigation to find out why pregnancy has not occurred is warranted.

There are many steps a couple can take to increase the chances of pregnancy. The most important concerns the *timing of coitus* with respect to the woman's menstrual cycle. An ovum remains viable for no more than 24 hours after ovulation, so coitus after that time in the cycle has very little chance of resulting in pregnancy. Coitus is most likely to result in pregnancy when it takes place on the same day as ovulation: There is about a 33% chance of success on that day (Wilcox et al., 1995b) (**Figure 11.2**). Because sperm survive in the female reproductive tract for several days, pregnancy can also result from coitus up to 5 days prior to ovulation, but there is a lower likelihood of success. At 5 days prior to ovulation, the chance of success drops to 10%. It is unlikely, though not impossible, that pregnancy will result from coitus on any other day of the cycle.

To take advantage of this information, a couple needs to know the day of ovulation. If a woman has a very regular cycle that is near 28 days in length, it may be sufficient simply to count the days from the beginning of the previous menstrual period. Assuming that the luteal phase lasts approximately 14 days, the total cycle length minus 14 days gives the approximate interval from the beginning of menstruation to the next ovulation.

subfertility Difficulty in establishing a pregnancy; arbitrarily defined as the absence of pregnancy after a couple has had frequent unprotected sex for 12 months.

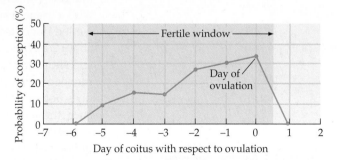

Figure 11.2 The likelihood of conception depends on when coitus occurs with respect to the day of ovulation. (After Wilcox et al., 1995b.)

Figure 11.3 A typical basal body temperature chart for one menstrual cycle and the first day of the next cycle. Day 1 is the first day of menstruation. Ovulation (on day 14 in this example) is marked by a slight dip in temperature, followed by a rise of at least 0.2°C (0.4°F) over the following 48 hours. The higher temperature is sustained for the duration of the luteal phase. Random spikes, such as the one here on day 10, are common and should be ignored. If the cycle is longer than 28 days, ovulation is likely to occur later than day 14.

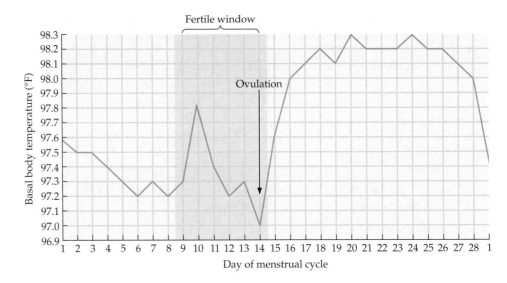

basal body temperature (BBT) Body temperature measured in the morning before getting out of bed.

cervical mucus Mucus, the consistency of which varies around the menstrual cycle, secreted by glands in the cervix.

A more accurate method of estimating the day of ovulation is to track **basal body temperature (BBT)**. To use this technique, the woman measures her temperature with a digital thermometer or a special-purpose BBT thermometer every morning before getting up. Typically, a woman's basal body temperature is relatively low during the follicular phase (say, about 36.3°C or 97.4°F), dips slightly on the day of ovulation, and rises sharply to a level above the follicular phase level (say, to 36.8°C or 98.2°F) on the day after ovulation, staying high for the remainder of the luteal phase (**Figure 11.3**). What matters is the *change* in temperature, not the absolute temperature, which may vary from woman to woman and with the measurement technique being used.

Since the main indicator is the rise on the day *after* ovulation, when coitus no longer stands a good chance of leading to conception, it is not helpful for getting pregnant on that particular cycle. Rather, the woman has to follow her temperature over several cycles to determine the usual interval between the onset of menstruation and ovulation. This information can then be used to time coitus during future cycles.

If the basal body temperature does not show the midcycle rise, it is possible that ovulation is not occurring. If the rise is not sustained for at least 10 to 12 days, the luteal phase may not be long enough for pregnancy to be established (see below). These potential problems can be investigated and treated by fertility specialists.

Another way to estimate the time of ovulation is by examining the consistency of the **cervical mucus** present in the vagina. The woman takes a sample of the mucus by inserting a finger into her vagina or even simply by wiping her vulva with a tissue. Then she tests the stretchability of the mucus by touching her mucus-wetted finger to her thumb and gently separating her finger and thumb again. For about 2 days, ending on the day of ovulation or the day before, the mucus is clear and slippery, and it stretches out into a thin thread between finger and thumb, like raw egg white (**Figure 11.4**). During the rest of the cycle it is white and thick and does not stretch out into a thread, or there is no mucus present at all. With experience, these changes in the property of the mucus can be felt as changes in vaginal sensations, from dry or sticky to slippery, and then back, even without doing a digital test. The 2 days marked by the most stretchable mucus, and possibly the following day, are the most favorable times for coitus if pregnancy is desired.

Yet a third way to estimate the day of ovulation is to detect the surge in luteinizing hormone (LH) that begins about 36 hours before ovulation (see Chap-

Figure 11.4 Cervical mucus test For about 2 days prior to ovulation, the cervical mucus can be drawn out into a thread between finger and thumb.

ter 5). Home test kits designed to detect the LH surge are available; they are usually called "ovulation tests," which is slightly misleading. They work in a fashion similar to home pregnancy tests. In over 90% of cycles, ovulation occurs within 2 days of the LH surge as detected by the kit, according to one study (Behre et al., 2000), so sex during those 2 days has a high likelihood of leading to conception. To save on test kits, it makes sense to get an idea of when to expect ovulation, by means of one of the methods described above, before starting to test.

Besides timing sex to coincide with ovulation, couples can take other steps to improve their chances of pregnancy. The man's ejaculations should not be too frequent, otherwise the total number of sperm deposited during a single ejaculation may be too low; spacing ejaculations at 24-hour or 48-hour intervals may be optimal. Coitus should be in the man-above position; gravity helps the ejaculate pool near the cervix rather than flowing out of the vagina, as can happen in the woman-above position. The woman should remain lying on her back, preferably with knees raised, for half an hour after coitus. Also, douching should be avoided.

Infertility Can Result from a Problem in the Woman or in the Man

Subfertility and **infertility** (total inability to achieve pregnancy) are surprisingly common. About 15% of couples have enough difficulty establishing a pregnancy that they seek medical attention. Fertility problems are about equally likely to be caused by a disorder on the man's side as on the woman's side, but it's usually the woman that gets investigated first, simply because couples are likely to seek help from gynecologists when they have fertility problems. Occasionally there is a problem on both sides. In about 25% of cases the cause cannot be identified.

A Variety of Factors Can Reduce Sperm Counts

The most common group of conditions affecting fertility is characterized by insufficient or poor-quality sperm in the man's semen. Sperm-related problems are the cause of about 25% of all couples' difficulties in achieving pregnancy. The usual rule of thumb is that a man is likely to be subfertile (i.e., have difficulty becoming a father) if there are fewer than 20 million sperm per milliliter of semen or if the fraction of the sperm that move normally is less than 50%. Abnormal sperm morphology (**Figure 11.5**) can also impair fertility, but only if the percentage of abnormal sperm is very high—above about 90% (Guzick et al., 2001).

What causes insufficient or defective sperm? There are many possible causes. Undescended testicles, sex chromosome anomalies, infections that cause blockage of the reproductive tract, and intensive chemotherapy can all cause irreversible reduction or failure of spermatogenesis. Heating of the testes, as can occur with too-tight clothing or with strenuous exercise, causes a lowered sperm count that is usually reversible. Environmental toxins can also cause lowered sperm counts, and they are suspected of having contributed to a general reduction in sperm counts in the population of the United States and other countries over the last several decades (**Box 11.1**).

In cases of problems with sperm quality, a couple can take various steps to achieve pregnancy. If sperm numbers are too low, semen can be collected over a period of time and frozen. Then the entire collected amount can be placed in the woman's vagina or directly into her uterus at a time coinciding with ovulation. This procedure is called **artificial insemination**. If the sperm comes from the woman's partner, the tech-

infertility Inability (of a man, woman, or couple) to achieve pregnancy.

artificial insemination An assisted reproduction technique that involves the placement of semen in the vagina or uterus with the aid of a syringe or small tube.

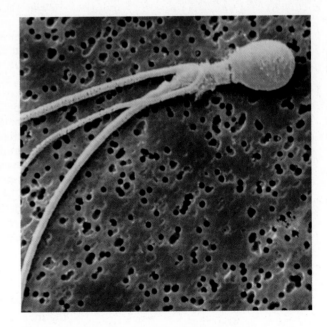

Figure 11.5 Abnormal (multi-tailed) sperm

Research Highlights

BOX 11.1 Are Sperm Counts Declining?

In 1992 a Danish research group published some disturbing news about male fertility (Carlsen et al., 1992). According to their meta-analysis of about 60 prior studies that employed standardized sperm-counting techniques (Figure A), average sperm counts in several Western countries dropped by nearly one-half between 1940 and 1990—from 113 million to 66 million sperm per ml of semen. This drop was accompanied by a drop in ejaculate volume

(A) Sperm are counted in a precisely calibrated chamber, but slight variations in counting procedures could result in a false impression of changing sperm counts over time.

(from 3.4 ml to 2.75 ml) and by an increase in the prevalence of certain male reproductive disorders, such as undescended testicles (cryptorchidism) and testicular cancer.

The Danish findings have been contested. In 1999, for example, a group at Columbia University in New York argued that the apparent fall in sperm counts in the United States was an illusion caused by variations in where the sampling was done (Saidi et al., 1999). Specifically, many of the early U.S. studies were done in New York, where (according to the New York researchers, at least) sperm counts are higher than in the rest of the country. The later studies were done in other cities, such as Los Angeles, where sperm counts are said to be lower.

Another, even more extensive meta-analysis was published in 2000 by a group led by Shanna Swan of the University of Missouri (Swan et al., 2000). This study basically confirmed the original Danish claim (Figure B) and presented new evidence that the decline continued at least through 1996. Another Danish study reported that the median sperm count in unselected young Danish men had fallen to 41 million sperm per ml (Andersen et al., 2000). This level is already in a "gray zone" within which fertility may be affected. Furthermore, a French group found that sperm counts measured at a single sperm bank in Paris declined markedly between 1973 and 1992, belying the Columbia group's geographic explanation (Auger et al., 1995). Thus the decline in sperm counts appears to be real, although some experts remain skeptical (Fisch, 2008).

If the decline in sperm counts is real, what is causing it? One trivial explanation—more frequent ejaculation—has been ruled out by studies that control for the length of abstinence prior to specimen donation. Lifestyle changes such as the increased popularity of tight-fitting pants and underwear, which keep the testes too warm, are a possible cause. Most attention, however, has been focused on the possibility that the decline is caused by environmental pollutants, especially by "endocrine disruptors"—agricultural pesticides and other industrial chemicals that mimic or antagonize sex hormones (see Box 5.5). Agricultural workers do suffer a decline in sperm counts that is related to their degree of pesticide exposure (Abell et al., 2000). Whether endocrine disruptors are responsible for the decline in

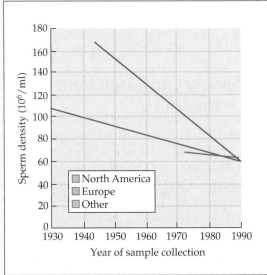

(B) Sperm counts have declined fastest in Europe, more moderately in North America, and barely at all in other parts of the world, according to a review of 101 studies (Swan et al., 2000). The reliability of this conclusion depends on a variety of assumptions, such as that the measurement techniques have remained constant over time. Some researchers have contested these findings.

sperm counts in the general population is less certain (Juberg, 2000). However, the steep sperm count declines in agricultural countries such as Denmark, where pesticide use is intense, suggest this possibility. Shanna Swan's group has reported that sperm counts are lower in a rural area of Missouri, where pesticide use is high, than in cities such as New York or Los Angeles and that individual men in Missouri with high levels of pesticide metabolites in their urine have lower sperm counts than men with lower urinary pesticide levels (Swan, 2006).

nique is usually called "artificial insemination by the husband," or AIH (although the man could equally be the woman's cohabitational partner). Men with normal sperm counts may also store their own sperm for future AIH use. They may do this in advance of medical procedures that could affect their fertility, such as chemotherapy, radiation treatments, or surgery on the testes or reproductive tract (including sterilization).

In Vitro Fertilization Can Circumvent Many Sperm Problems

Some sperm quality problems may require the use of **in vitro fertilization (IVF)**, a technology introduced by British researchers in 1978. "In vitro" means "in glass"—in a petri dish, in fact. In the standard IVF procedure (**Figure 11.6**), the

in vitro fertilization (IVF) Any of a variety of assisted reproduction techniques in which fertilization takes place outside the body.

(A)

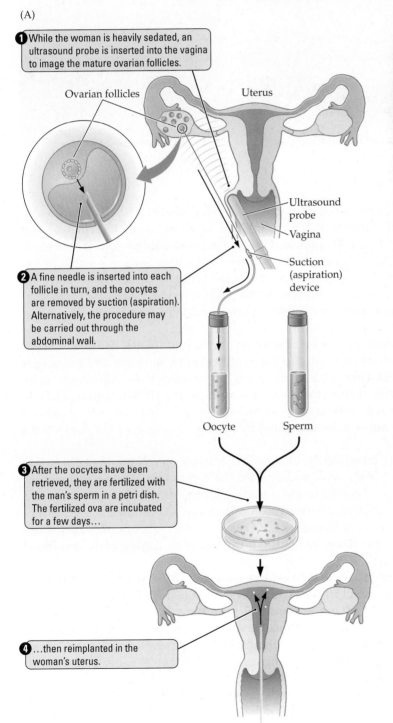

❶ While the woman is heavily sedated, an ultrasound probe is inserted into the vagina to image the mature ovarian follicles.

Ovarian follicles

Uterus

Ultrasound probe

Vagina

Suction (aspiration) device

❷ A fine needle is inserted into each follicle in turn, and the oocytes are removed by suction (aspiration). Alternatively, the procedure may be carried out through the abdominal wall.

Oocyte   Sperm

❸ After the oocytes have been retrieved, they are fertilized with the man's sperm in a petri dish. The fertilized ova are incubated for a few days...

❹ ...then reimplanted in the woman's uterus.

(B)

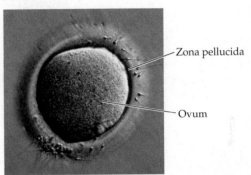

Zona pellucida

Ovum

Figure 11.6 Standard in vitro fertilization (A) The steps in the procedure. (B) An ovum being fertilized by sperm in vitro. Many sperm attach to the zona pellucida—the coat around the ovum—but only one enters the cytoplasm of the ovum and fertilizes it. In a natural fertilization within a woman's oviduct, fewer sperm would be present. (See Web Activity 11.2.)

Figure 11.7 Intracytoplasmic sperm injection The technician uses a stereomicroscope and micromanipulators to perform the procedure. As can be seen on the video monitor, the ovum (in the center of the screen) is immobilized by gentle suction from a flat-tipped pipette (at left). A sharp, fine-tipped pipette (at right) is then inserted through the zona pellucida, and a single sperm (not visible) is injected into the cytoplasm of the ovum.

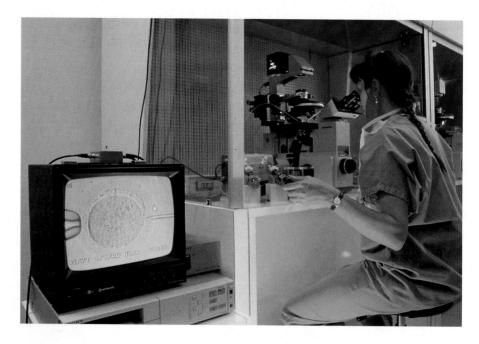

zonal drilling An assisted reproduction technique in which a hole is drilled through the zona pellucida of an ovum to facilitate fertilization.

subzonal insemination An assisted reproduction technique in which sperm are injected into the space between the zona pellucida and the plasma membrane of an ovum to facilitate fertilization.

intracytoplasmic sperm injection (ICSI) An assisted reproduction technique in which a single sperm is injected into the cytoplasm of an ovum.

preimplantation genetic screening Testing of in vitro fertilization embryos for genetic defects prior to implantation.

woman is given hormones to promote the development of a batch of follicles on a precisely timed schedule. When the follicles are nearly ready to ovulate, a fine needle is passed into each follicle under ultrasound control, and its oocyte is flushed out. As many as two dozen oocytes can be harvested in a single procedure. The collected oocytes are placed in a petri dish, and the man's sperm are then added. This procedure costs about $12,000 for a single cycle.

If the man's sperm are not capable of performing even this simplified fertilization task, further variations on IVF are available. A hole can be drilled through the zona pellucida to allow direct access to the oocyte itself (**zonal drilling**). One or several sperm can be injected into the space between the zona and the oocyte (**subzonal insemination**). Or a single sperm can be injected directly into the cytoplasm of the oocyte (**intracytoplasmic sperm injection [ICSI]**) (**Figure 11.7**). In fact, even a man who produces no mature sperm at all may be able to father a child: Precursor cells can be harvested by needle aspiration of the man's testis and used instead.

ICSI has greatly increased the likelihood of infertile men becoming fathers, and it has become one of the most widely used IVF techniques. There remains some concern that the oocyte could be damaged by the procedure. A carefully controlled study found few differences between naturally conceived children and those conceived by ICSI, but the ICSI children did have a higher rate of undescended testicles and were more likely to require hospitalization during early childhood (Ludwig et al., 2008).

Regardless of the exact IVF procedure used, the artificially fertilized ova are usually kept in tissue culture for several days, during which time they divide several times (**Figure 11.8**). It is possible at this stage to remove a cell or two from the embryos without harming them; the sex and genetic makeup of the removed cells can then be determined. This **preimplantation genetic screening** is useful if one of the parents carries a disease-causing gene and the couple wants to ensure that their child does not inherit it (Sermon et al., 2004; Kuliev & Verlinsky, 2008).

A number of embryos—often about four—are then placed in the woman's uterus simultaneously, in order to maximize the chance that at least one of them will implant. If several implant, the woman is offered the opportunity to have the number reduced by abortion (often euphemized as "fetal reduction"), but this practice can present risks to the remaining fetuses, and it also presents ethical problems for some women. Most of the high-number multiple births that have attracted headlines over the past few years involve mothers who have undergone IVF or other assisted reproduction procedures (see below) and have declined abortion. High-number multiple pregnancies are associated with all kinds of serious risks to the fetuses and the mother; only a few have the happy outcomes that the media like to focus on. Thus, in one study of 11 high-number multiple pregnancies (mostly quadruplets), 9 of the 48 fetuses were stillborn, and at least 9 of the remainder suffered disabilities that were still evident at the age of 2 years (Lipitz et al., 1990). According to professional guidelines, healthy young women should receive no more than 2 embryos on their first IVF attempt (American Society for Reproductive Medicine, 2004).

A more common problem, however, is not multiple fetuses, but zero fetuses. Nearly two-thirds of all IVF attempts do not lead to a successful pregnancy, so couples may have to repeat the procedure several times, at mounting expense and with no guarantee of ultimate success. (Some clinics offer partial or full refunds if the woman does not become pregnant.) The prospects are particularly poor for women over 40 who use their own oocytes (Centers for Disease Control, 2004a). Still, half a million babies have been born in the United States by IVF and related technologies (collectively known as **assisted reproductive technology [ART]**) (American Society for Reproductive Medicine, 2008).

In an alternative procedure, oocytes are harvested from the woman as before, but they are placed directly in the woman's oviducts, along with sperm from the man. Fertilization then takes place in the oviduct. This procedure is called **gamete intrafallopian transfer (GIFT)**.

There remain some questions about the safety of assisted reproductive technology (Schieve et al., 2004). According to a meta-analysis of 169 studies on the topic (Holden, 2004), babies conceived through ART have two to three times the risk of prematurity, low birth weight, and infant mortality, compared with non-ART babies—even if they are singletons rather than multiple births. These findings suggest that ART doesn't yet imitate nature closely enough.

Sperm Can Be Donated

Sometimes the male partner is completely sterile or the couple does not want to use his sperm, as, for example, when he carries a gene for a serious disorder. Some single women also want to become pregnant, as do some women who are partnered with other women. In all such cases, women can use **artificial insemination by donor (AID)**. In this procedure, sperm from a third party are placed in the woman's vagina or uterus. **Sperm banks** provide suitable semen at fairly low cost. Sperm donors are usually college students who are paid a small fee to donate semen (by masturbation). The donors are screened for heritable medical problems (in themselves or their families) and for infections such as human immunodeficiency virus (HIV) that might be transmitted to the recipient woman. Information about potential donors' physical appearance, field of work or study, and other interests is usually available to potential recipients.

Some women, especially lesbians, may arrange the whole matter themselves with the help of a male friend and a turkey baster or a needleless syringe. Although

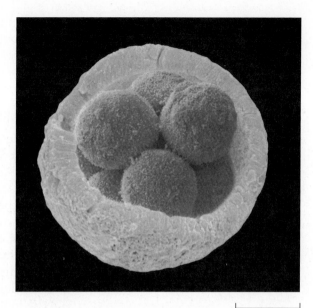

Figure 11.8 A human embryo (more accurately called a conceptus), 3 days after in vitro fertilization. In this scanning electron micrograph, part of the zona pellucida has been removed to reveal the embryo within. At this stage, the embryo consists of about 8 cells, and it can be reimplanted, allowed to mature further in vitro, or frozen for future use.

50 μm

assisted reproductive technology (ART) In vitro fertilization and related technologies.

gamete intrafallopian transfer (GIFT) An assisted reproduction technique in which ova and sperm are placed together in a woman's oviducts without prior in vitro fertilization.

artificial insemination by donor (AID) Artificial insemination using sperm from a man who is not the woman's partner.

sperm bank A facility that collects, stores, and provides semen for artificial insemination.

secondary amenorrhea Absence of menstruation in a woman who has previously menstruated normally.

oligomenorrhea Infrequent or irregular menstruation.

surrogate A person who stands in for another; for example, as a sex partner or as the bearer of a child.

this option is simple and inexpensive ($0.99 for the baster), it is probably a bad idea for both medical and legal reasons. The donor may not be adequately screened for genetic problems or communicable diseases, and there may be future disagreements about the donor's rights or obligations with respect to any child who is produced.

Abnormalities of the Female Reproductive Tract May Reduce Fertility

The second most common group of conditions affecting fertility is characterized by abnormalities of the woman's reproductive tract. Such conditions are responsible for about 20% of infertility cases. The commonest site of abnormalities is the oviducts. They can become scarred, obstructed, or denuded of cilia as a consequence of pelvic inflammatory disease (PID)—a general term for infections of the uterus or oviducts, usually caused by sexually transmitted organisms such as chlamydia or gonorrhea (see Chapter 17). Another condition that can interfere with fertility is endometriosis. Although surgery can sometimes restore fertility in such conditions, it often fails to do so. In such cases it is possible to take the oviducts out of the equation by performing IVF and placing the resulting embryos directly in the uterus.

Failure to Ovulate Can Be Dealt with by Drugs or by Oocyte Donation

Another 20% or so of infertility cases are caused by problems with ovulation. We mentioned the failure to begin menstrual cycles at puberty—primary amenorrhea—in Chapter 6. A postpubertal (but premenopausal) woman may also stop cycling (**secondary amenorrhea**) or cycle irregularly (**oligomenorrhea**). These conditions can be caused by weight loss, athletic training, stress, certain drugs, a pituitary tumor, or reduced ovarian sensitivity to gonadotropins. Sometimes, failure to ovulate can occur in a woman who is experiencing normal menstrual periods. Most ovulatory problems can be reversed by lifestyle changes, psychotherapy (if the cause is an eating disorder, for example), or drug treatment.

If the woman's oocytes cannot be used, oocytes can be obtained from donors (Klein & Sauer, 2002). Obtaining oocytes from female donors is more complex and expensive than sperm donation, however, because the donor must undergo hormone treatment followed by surgical aspiration of the oocytes from the ovaries, as described above for IVF. The donors—who are often college students—are typically paid a few thousand dollars. For both sperm and oocyte donations, there is a market for donors who are perceived to have desirable traits, and higher fees may be paid in such cases, especially for oocytes (**Box 11.2**).

Surrogate Mothers Bear a Child for Someone Else

If the woman cannot sustain a pregnancy at all—say, because her uterus is malformed or has been removed or because her general medical condition makes pregnancy inadvisable—an option is to use a **surrogate** mother. Gay male couples who wish to have children may also resort to this option. In traditional surrogacy the surrogate agrees to be artificially inseminated with semen from the man, and she then carries any resulting fetus or fetuses to term. If the woman who cannot sustain a pregnancy can nevertheless produce oocytes, those oocytes can be fertilized with the man's sperm by IVF and then implanted in the surrogate.

Either way, when the child (or children) is born, the surrogate gives it up for adoption by the couple. The surrogate is usually paid about $20,000 to $25,000 plus expenses—and the total cost to the couple is $60,000 or more. Although detailed contracts spell out the various parties' obligations, surrogacy can be a psychological and legal minefield, and some critics question the propriety of a couple's use of another woman's body to carry their child, especially where the

Society, Values, and the Law

BOX 11.2 Designer Gametes

Most women who donate oocytes for IVF are motivated principally by the desire to help infertile couples have a baby and are paid about $2000 to $4000 per procedure. But some wealthy couples are willing to lay out much larger sums for donors who they think will produce oocytes of exceptional genetic quality. Their hope, of course, is to have unusually gifted or attractive children. This desire has led to the development of a cutthroat market for "über-eggs." Ads in college newspapers now mention payments of $50,000, $80,000, or even $100,000 for suitable donors (Figure A). Few, if any, women have actually received payments at these levels, which are largely advertising hype, but payments of $20,000 or so are not uncommon. At this level, a young woman can pay her way through college with a few donations.

We are looking for a special egg donor.

COMPENSATION
$100,000

This ad is being provided for a particular client and is not soliciting eggs for a donor bank or registry. We provide a unique program that only undertakes one match at a time and we do not maintain a donor database.

Please visit
▬▬▬▬▬.com
for full program details

(A) This advertisement was placed in the student newspaper of Brown University in 2007.

What does it take to be a high-end donor? Beauty, brains, athletic achievement, and social skills—probably in that order. The ads demand SAT scores at the 1300 level or even higher, and

it helps if the woman is an accomplished cellist and track star, won the Intel Science Talent Search, and is fluent in Norwegian and Japanese. The "beauty" part is fuzzier, but probably more important; there may be an advertised height and race requirement, but everything depends on the reactions of the couple when they meet the potential donor. "You look even more gorgeous than the pictures," was one couple's reaction to meeting Rachel, a tall, strawberry blonde graduate student with a creamy complexion and blue-green eyes. Rachel earned about $18,000 for that "donation" and later made others at a higher price (Weiss, 2001).

The American Society for Reproductive Medicine has serious reservations about the commercialization of oocyte donation (American Society for Reproductive Medicine, 2007). High payments may be essentially coercive, causing women to ignore their own psychological reservations or the possible risks of the procedure. This may be particularly true for women of limited means or with high expenses, such as students at the Ivy League colleges where much of the recruitment is done. Women facing such large inducements may conceal negative aspects of their medical or family history. Furthermore, paying high prices for "genetically favored" gametes may imply that all humans do not have equal intrinsic worth, contrary to the values that many Americans hold dear. And last, high prices may ultimately restrict oocyte transfers to the very rich.

For all these reasons, the American Society for Reproductive Medicine recommends that compensation be limited to $5000 unless special circumstances justify a higher amount and that no payment should be above $10,000. Furthermore, payments should not vary according to the race or other personal characteristics of the donor. It is clear, however, that some

agencies are ignoring these guidelines. And while greed no doubt plays a role in this, one can make the countervailing ethical argument that high payments increase the total number of donors, to everyone's benefit.

(B) Nobel prizewinner and eugenics enthusiast William Shockley (1910–1989) was a tireless sperm donor.

Because it is so much less demanding for men to donate sperm, they rarely receive more that $100 per donation, whatever their desirability as fathers. But sperm donations can be repeated frequently, so with a sufficient work ethic a sperm donor can earn as much as an egg donor, if not more.

A few men have donated sperm for ideological reasons, believing that they were benefiting the human race by spreading their own "superior" genes (Figure B).

surrogacy involves "reproductive tourism" to third-world countries (Chu, 2006). Twelve U.S. states refuse to recognize the legality of surrogacy contracts. Yet there is also an altruistic aspect to surrogacy for some women: "Being a surrogate is like giving an organ transplant to someone, only before you die," one woman told *Newsweek*, "and you actually get to see their joy" (Ali & Kelley, 2008).

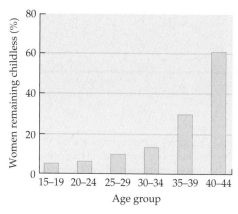

Figure 11.9 Age and infertility The graph shows the percentage of women who remain childless after a first marriage in spite of continued efforts to produce a child, grouped by age at marriage. Note that the likelihood of infertility rises rapidly in the mid-thirties. (After Johnson & Everitt, 2000.)

Down syndrome A collection of birth defects caused by the presence of an extra copy of chromosome 21.

Adoption Is Limited by the Supply of Healthy Infants

Adoption is a low-tech but often very successful way for infertile couples to have children. The main problem with adoption from the perspective of would-be parents is a severe shortage of the preferred adoptees—that is, healthy infants of the same race or ethnicity as themselves. Excluding adoptions between relatives, the number of adoptions in the United States has decreased greatly over the last 30 years and is now only about 50,000 per year (U.S. Department of Health and Human Services, 2004). The main reason for the decline is the greater willingness of unmarried mothers to keep their babies, but legalized abortion and better access to contraception may also play a role. Older or "special-needs" children (i.e., children with disabilities or other medical or psychological problems) are much more readily available; so are sets of siblings who want to be adopted together. Sixty percent of children awaiting adoption in the United States are from racial or ethnic minorities. Adopting from overseas is an alternative, though usually an expensive one (Adoptive Families, 2008).

Fertility Declines with Age

A major factor affecting fertility is age—both of the woman and the man. You might imagine that couples stay completely fertile until the woman's menopause, whereupon fertility drops to zero. In reality, fertility drops off steadily beginning in young adulthood, as shown in **Figure 11.9**. Already by their mid-thirties about 1 in 4 couples is infertile. This decline in fertility has several causes, including more frequent failure of ovulation, decreasing sperm counts and sperm quality, and an increased likelihood of spontaneous abortion early in pregnancy.

Children who are born to older parents, especially older mothers, also stand a greater risk of having chromosomal abnormalities. One of these is **Down syndrome**, caused by an extra copy of chromosome 21 (i.e., three copies instead of two). Down syndrome usually includes mild or moderate intellectual disability and a characteristic facial appearance (**Figure 11.10**). It affects 1 in 885 births at a maternal age of

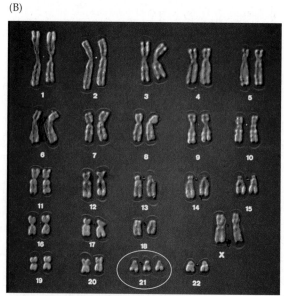

Figure 11.10 Down syndrome (A) A child with Down syndrome; the syndrome is marked by a characteristic facial appearance and sometimes by other physical anomalies. (B) Chromosome set of a person with Down syndrome, showing the three copies (circled) of chromosome 21.

30, but the rate gradually increases to 1 in 25 births at a maternal age of 45 and older. Because the great majority of babies are born to younger women, however, 4 out of 5 children with Down syndrome are born to women *under* 35. For that reason, the American College of Obstetricians and Gynecologists now recommends that all pregnant women be offered screening, regardless of their age (American College of Obstetricians and Gynecologists, 2007).

Increasing paternal age also raises the chances that a child will suffer from physical malformations, as well as mental conditions such as Down syndrome, autism, and schizophrenia (Reichenberg et al., 2006; Yang et al., 2007). This is because the sperm precursor cells are constantly dividing to produce new sperm. Thus an older man's sperm are the product of a greater total number of cell divisions, and each round of DNA replication carries some small risk of introducing a harmful mutation. In addition, chronic exposure to toxins such as solvents or tobacco smoke increase the likelihood that a man's children will have developmental problems (Cordier, 2008). Nevertheless, most children of older fathers are healthy.

A postmenopausal woman can become pregnant with the aid of reproductive technology: Donated oocytes can be fertilized in vitro (usually with her husband's sperm) and the embryos placed in her uterus. The pregnancy must be supported with hormone treatments. The oldest woman known to have become a mother by this procedure is Carmen Bousada, who gave birth to twin sons—her first children—in Barcelona, Spain, a week before her 67th birthday. According to news reports, Bousada deceived the California clinic that provided the donor eggs for her pregnancy, saying that she was only 55 years old at the time (ABC News, 2007). Less than a year after giving birth, Bousada was reported to have been diagnosed with cancer (Mills, 2007).

Adriana Iliescu, who gave birth to a daughter at age 66 with the help of artificial reproductive technology, was the oldest known woman to give birth before Carmen Bousada broke her record by a few months.

Many Embryos Do Not Survive

Nature has not completely mastered the difficult task of creating a normal embryo. Some large fraction—perhaps more than 50%—of all human embryos are genetically abnormal and have little or no chance of giving rise to a viable child. Most of these defects occur at the very earliest stages of development. If the ovum is fertilized by two sperm rather than one, for example, the resulting embryo will have three sets of chromosomes rather than the normal two. In some cases, environmental factors such as alcohol consumption, general anesthesia, or X-ray exposure around the time of ovulation may trigger chromosomal abnormalities.

The great majority of abnormal conceptuses are lost at some point in their development. Many fail to implant, and the mother is never aware of their existence. Others implant briefly, causing a transient release of hCG and a slight prolongation of the luteal phase, but then die, so that menstruation ensues. Of pregnancies that proceed far enough to be detected clinically, about 20% are subsequently lost by spontaneous abortion, usually during the first 3 months. At least half of all spontaneously aborted embryos and fetuses have chromosomal abnormalities, whereas only 0.5% of live-born babies have them.

Rh Factor Incompatibility Can Threaten Second Pregnancies

One major cause of fetal loss is blood group incompatibility, especially when the fetus possesses the blood group antigen known as **Rh factor** and the mother does not. (Rh is short for rhesus, the species of monkey used in early studies of the disorder.) Rh factor, like other blood group antigens, is a molecular label on the surface of red blood cells. In cases of Rh incompatibility the fetus will have inherited the factor from its father. The combination of Rh-negative mother and Rh-pos-

FAQ **I have a birth defect. Will I pass it on to my children?** Children of mothers with birth defects are at increased risk of being born with that same defect, especially for cleft palate/lip and limb defects (Skjaerven et al., 1999). Still, 96% of the children of mothers with birth defects are free of all defects. The effects of paternal defects have not been well studied but are likely to be similar.

Rh factor An antigen on the surface of red blood cells that, when present in a fetus but not in its mother, may trigger an immune response by the mother, resulting in life-threatening anemia of the fetus or newborn.

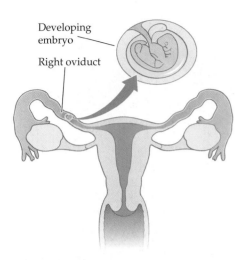

Developing
embryo

Right oviduct

Figure 11.11 Ectopic pregnancy can occur in the oviduct (as shown here), on the ovary or cervix, or elsewhere.

itive father is common—it is the case for about 10% of all couples in the United States—but only a minority of their pregnancies are marked by problems. These problems arise when the mother develops antibodies against Rh and those antibodies cross the placenta and attack the fetus. This does not happen routinely, because the fetus is immunologically isolated from the mother. Nevertheless, the mother may develop anti-Rh antibodies at childbirth if the fetus bleeds into the maternal circulation during delivery. These antibodies develop too late to affect that child, but they may attack a subsequent fetus, destroying its red blood cells and rendering it severely anemic. Such an attack can kill the fetus or newborn child, or it can leave the child intellectually disabled.

Luckily, the initial immune response to a mother's first Rh-positive fetus can be blocked by the administration of an Rh-specific immunoglobulin, either soon after delivery or during the pregnancy itself. By binding to Rh, the immunoglobulin hides it from the maternal immune system. If severe anemia does occur in a subsequent pregnancy, the fetus or the newborn child may have to undergo a blood transfusion.

Ectopic Pregnancy Can Endanger the Mother's Life

Another serious condition that causes fetal loss is **ectopic pregnancy**, which is implantation of the fetus at a location other than the uterus (Mukul & Teal, 2007) (**Figure 11.11**). This happens in about 1% of all pregnancies. The most common site of ectopic pregnancy is the oviduct ("tubal pregnancy"), but other possible sites include the cervix, the ovary, and elsewhere within the abdominal cavity.

Ectopic pregnancies can be caused by congenital malformations of the oviducts or uterus, by damage to the oviducts resulting from PID or appendicitis, or by treatment with certain sex steroids and contraceptives that interfere with the normal movement of the embryo into the uterus. Ectopic pregnancies may occur without any of these predisposing factors, however. The rate of ectopic pregnancy is increasing, and the main culprit is the increasing prevalence of PID due to chlamydia infections (see Chapter 17).

Ectopic pregnancy commonly leads to early spontaneous abortion. Alternatively, as the embryo grows, it may cause internal hemorrhage or rupture of an oviduct, both of which are emergencies that threaten the mother's life. Recognition of the condition is hampered by the fact that the woman may not know she is pregnant—the symptoms can appear within 3 weeks of the beginning of pregnancy. Therefore, if a woman of childbearing age has engaged in coitus recently and experiences abdominal pain, shoulder pain, pain on defecation or urination, abnormal vaginal bleeding, or signs of shock, she should see a doctor right away.

Ectopic pregnancy can usually be diagnosed by an ultrasound scan or by monitoring the levels of pregnancy hormones in the blood. If these hormones rise more slowly than in a normal pregnancy, an ectopic pregnancy is suspected. The condition is treated surgically or with a drug (methotrexate) to induce abortion. Whatever the woman's views on abortion, she should bear in mind that an ectopically implanted embryo cannot survive under any circumstances, so her only choice is whether or not to safeguard her own health. Even if one oviduct has to be removed, which is often the case, the woman can still become pregnant via the remaining oviduct. She has an elevated risk of experiencing another ectopic pregnancy and therefore needs to be monitored closely, but 90% of subsequent pregnancies are located normally in the uterus.

Pregnancy Is Conventionally Divided into Three Trimesters

Let's return to the happier topic of normal pregnancy. First of all, how long does a normal pregnancy last? Logically, we would time pregnancy from fertilization,

ectopic pregnancy Implantation and resulting pregnancy at any site other than the uterus.

or perhaps from implantation, but neither of these events can be used for timing because they don't usually make themselves known to the mother. The only relevant date that the mother is likely to remember is the onset of her last menstrual period, which occurs about 2 weeks before fertilization. Thus pregnancy is conventionally timed from that date, and a fetus is said to have a **gestational age**, which is calculated based on the number of weeks that have elapsed since the onset of her last menstrual period—even though the embryo didn't actually exist for the first 2 weeks of that time.*

According to the oft-cited **Naegele's rule**, a pregnant woman's due date is 9 months plus 1 week (about 281 days) after the onset of her last menstrual period. The true average is probably 3 to 8 days longer than this and is longer for a woman's first pregnancy than for later pregnancies (Mittendorf et al., 1990). Eighty percent of natural births occur within 2 weeks before or after the due date.

In the context of prenatal care, pregnancy is usually divided into three **trimesters**, each three months long. These time periods do not correspond to any particular biologically significant milestones but are simply convenient ways to refer to early, middle, and late pregnancy. The growth and appearance of the fetus over the first half of pregnancy is shown in **Figure 11.12**.

The Fetus Secretes Sex Hormones to Sustain Pregnancy

The fetus takes control of its mother's body in many respects. It is true that the mother's ovarian hormones—especially progesterone and estrogens—are initially required to bring the endometrium into a state that can sustain implantation. However, the implanted embryo usurps this system, first by secreting hCG, which

---

*Some authorities, as well as previous editions of this textbook, have used "gestational age" to mean age timed from the date of fertilization. The usage we adopt in this edition is the one most widely recommended (American Academy of Pediatrics, 2004).

gestational age A fetus's age timed from the onset of the mother's last menstrual period.

Naegele's rule A traditional rule for the calculation of a pregnant woman's due date: 9 calendar months plus 1 week after the onset of the last menstrual period.

trimester One of three 3-month divisions of pregnancy.

FAQ I'm pregnant, but I'm still having my periods. What's up?

If you're pregnant, the bleeding is not your normal menstrual period. Minor bleeding commonly occurs around the time of implantation. If you're bleeding at later times, consult your doctor promptly; it could be something harmless, but it could also signal a serious problem with your pregnancy, such as an ectopic pregnancy or a miscarriage.

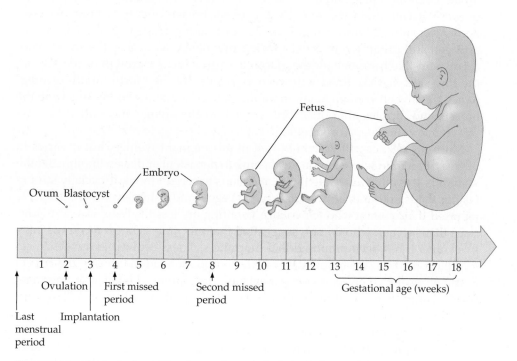

Figure 11.12 Embryonic and fetal growth and changes in appearance through the 18th week of pregnancy.

prevents the corpus luteum from regressing and therefore keeps progesterone levels high, and later by secreting its own supply of estrogens and progesterone. These hormones enter the mother's circulation, eventually rising to levels not experienced at any other time of her life. Their main role is to sustain the endometrium, but they also prepare the uterine musculature for childbirth and the breasts for lactation. Estrogens are secreted by the fetus's adrenal glands, and progesterone is secreted by the placenta. Thus, by less than 2 months into a pregnancy, the pregnancy will continue normally even if the mother's ovaries have to be removed for some reason.

Women May Experience Troublesome Symptoms during Early Pregnancy

The first trimester is in many ways the most significant period of pregnancy. During this time, the embryo implants in the uterine wall and sets up a system of hormonal and metabolic communication with the mother. By 8 weeks of gestational age (which is just 6 weeks from fertilization) it has developed from a tiny, featureless disk of cells into a miniature human being with all its organ systems present. It is now referred to as a fetus. By the end of the first trimester the fetus is about 10 cm (4 inches) in its longest dimension (crown–rump length) and weighs about 50 g (2 ounces). The external genitalia have differentiated as male or female, and most of the fetus's organ systems are functioning at some primitive level.

The first trimester is an important period for the mother as well. She typically learns that she is pregnant, a piece of news that may bring delight or anxiety. She has to decide, perhaps in discussions with her partner, whether to continue the pregnancy or not. Assuming that she goes ahead with it, she is likely to experience some of the early symptoms of pregnancy, especially breast tenderness and morning sickness.

Breast tenderness is a sign that the breasts are preparing for nursing the infant, even though it will be months before they can actually be used for that purpose. Recall from Chapter 6 that the female breasts undergo a burst of development at puberty under the influence of rising estrogen levels. The rise of estrogen and progesterone levels during pregnancy, as well as the secretion of a prolactin-like hormone by the placenta, causes further growth of the alveoli, the tiny sacs that are lined with secretory cells. By the fourth month of pregnancy the alveoli contain small amounts of secreted material. By this time the breasts and nipples are noticeably larger, and the areolae have often become wider and more deeply pigmented.

Morning sickness affects about half of all pregnant women, but it varies in degree, from mild nausea upon awakening to persistent and even life-threatening vomiting. It is often associated with aversions to certain foods, especially strong-tasting foods and animal products (meats, eggs, and fish). Several studies have reported that women who experience vomiting are less likely to have a miscarriage than women who do not, suggesting that morning sickness has some positive value. It has been proposed that morning sickness evolved as a mechanism to protect the fetus from potentially toxic compounds in food during the critical first few weeks when its organ systems are developing (Flaxman & Sherman, 2000). Eating bland food tends to alleviate the condition, which usually disappears by the end of the first trimester.

Other symptoms experienced by many women during the first trimester include frequent urination, tiredness, sleeping difficulties, backaches, mood swings, and, sometimes, depression. The woman's male partner may develop analogous symptoms and may even gain weight faster than the pregnant woman.

The phenomenon of pregnancy-like symptoms in men is known as **couvade**. The average woman gains only about 1 to 2 kg (2 to 4 lb) during the first trimester.

Prenatal Care Provides Health Screening, Education, and Support

When a woman finds out that she is pregnant (if not before), she can take many practical steps to safeguard her own and her embryo's health. These steps include seeking out prenatal care, ensuring good nutrition, avoiding harmful substances, and learning about exercise and sex during pregnancy.

Numerous studies have shown that prenatal care benefits almost every aspect of pregnancy: It decreases the likelihood of maternal, fetal, or neonatal death; fetal prematurity; and low birth weight. Unfortunately, prenatal care is not as widely utilized in the United States as it is in European countries. In 2002, 16% of pregnant American women received no prenatal care during the critical first trimester (Centers for Disease Control, 2004b). African-American, Hispanic, poor, unmarried, uneducated, and teenage women are particularly likely to miss out on first-trimester care and to receive inadequate care at later times in their pregnancies. The reasons women receive inadequate care have to do with psychosocial factors, such as ambivalence about the pregnancy or not believing that prenatal care will be helpful, more than a lack of access to care (Johnson et al., 2007).

What does prenatal care accomplish? Even before she becomes pregnant, a woman can be tested for her immunity to German measles (**rubella**). If a woman is not immune to this disease and contracts it during pregnancy, the fetus can suffer serious developmental defects, such as deafness and intellectual disability. Therefore it is a good idea for a nonimmune woman to be vaccinated before pregnancy begins. She can also be tested for HIV; this is important because an HIV-positive woman may pass the virus on to the fetus during pregnancy or at birth, and antiretroviral therapy reduces the risk that this will happen from about 25% to 2% (Centers for Disease Control, 2007f).

The first post-conception healthcare visit typically takes place soon after the first missed period. At this point the healthcare provider takes a history and does a general examination, a Pap smear, a cervical culture (to test for gonorrhea and other conditions), a rubella test (if not done previously), and a test for blood type and Rh factor. A clinical pregnancy test may be done, even if the woman has already done a home pregnancy test. The provider advises the woman on nutrition and related matters, answer her questions, and help her make informed decisions about how to manage her pregnancy and childbirth.

On one or more occasions during the first trimester, the provider conducts a pelvic exam (see Chapter 3). In addition to the pelvic exam, many providers perform an ultrasound exam at some point during the first trimester, especially if there is some indication of a problem. This exam permits determination of fetal age, the number of fetuses, and the presence of any abnormalities such as ectopic pregnancy. It is not usually possible to discern the fetus's sex by ultrasound during the first trimester.

Adequate Nutrition Is Vital to a Successful Pregnancy

An expectant mother needs an additional 250 to 300 calories per day in addition to what she needs to support herself. At term (just before childbirth), a woman typically weighs 9 to 15 kg (20 to 35 lb) more than her prepregnancy weight; this

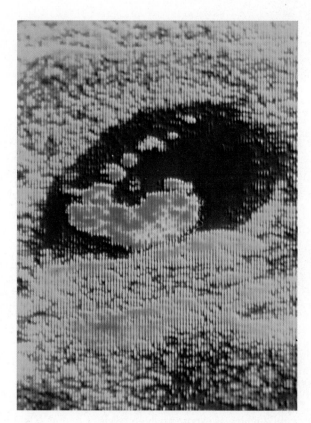

False-color ultrasound image of a fetus after 8 weeks.

couvade Pregnancy-like symptoms in the male partner of a pregnant women.

rubella German measles, a viral infection that can cause developmental defects in fetuses whose mothers contract the disease during pregnancy.

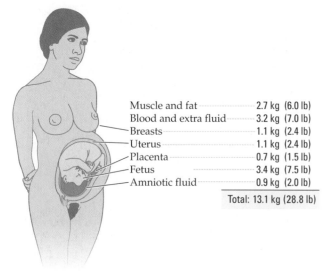

Muscle and fat .... 2.7 kg (6.0 lb)
Blood and extra fluid .... 3.2 kg (7.0 lb)
Breasts .... 1.1 kg (2.4 lb)
Uterus .... 1.1 kg (2.4 lb)
Placenta .... 0.7 kg (1.5 lb)
Fetus .... 3.4 kg (7.5 lb)
Amniotic fluid .... 0.9 kg (2.0 lb)

Total: 13.1 kg (28.8 lb)

Figure 11.13 Where do those extra pounds go? The distribution of extra weight for a woman who gains 13.1 kg (28.8 lb) during pregnancy.

fetal alcohol syndrome A collection of physical and behavioral symptoms in a child who was exposed to high levels of alcohol as a fetus.

Figure 11.14 A boy with fetal alcohol syndrome and his adoptive parents Typical facial features include short eye slits, a flat mid-face, a short nose, an indistinct groove between nose and lip, and a thin upper lip.

includes the weight of the fetus, placenta, and amniotic fluid, as well as her own increased fat deposits, enlarged breasts, and increased volume of blood and tissue fluids (**Figure 11.13**). Besides sheer calories, a pregnant woman needs to consume adequate amounts of other nutrients, especially protein, calcium, iron, vitamin A (but see below), and folic acid (or folate).

Women who begin pregnancy with a normal weight are most likely to produce a healthy child (Cnattingius et al., 1998). Underweight women risk producing an underweight child, who is more likely to suffer a variety of medical problems. Women who are overweight face an increased risk of certain serious disorders during pregnancy, including diabetes and hypertension. Being either underweight or overweight is associated with an increased likelihood of premature birth, which also may have adverse consequences for the child (see below).

Tobacco, Alcohol, Drugs, and Radiation Can Harm the Fetus

As well as consuming the right foods, a pregnant woman needs to avoid a number of agents that can harm the fetus (**Table 11.1**). Alcohol and tobacco head this list. Heavy alcohol consumption increases the likelihood of birth defects and infant mortality, and it is associated with a specific cluster of symptoms known as **fetal alcohol syndrome** (Merrick et al., 2006). Children with this syndrome are small, have a characteristic facial appearance, and may be intellectually disabled or have behavioral problems (**Figure 11.14**). There is some uncertainty as to whether consuming one or two drinks a day is harmful, but most experts recommend complete abstention from alcohol during pregnancy. Caffeine can also be harmful: A daily intake of 200 mg or more (the amount in a 12-ounce serving of coffee) doubles the risk of miscarriage (Weng et al., 2008).

Smoking is one of the most harmful practices a woman can engage in during pregnancy (Shea & Steiner, 2008). It increases the likelihood of spontaneous abortion, premature birth, low birth weight, and congenital malformations. Its ill effects continue after a child is born: One-third of all cases of sudden infant death syndrome can be attributed to the mother's smoking during pregnancy (Mitchell & Milerad, 2006). Unfortunately, at least 1 in 9 American women smokes during pregnancy (Centers for Disease Control, 2004b).

Many drugs—including prescription, over-the-counter, and recreational drugs—can harm the fetus. A particularly dangerous drug is isotretinoin (Accutane and its generic equivalents), which is used for the treatment of severe acne. Accutane causes fetal malformations. Because teenage girls have high rates of both acne and unintended pregnancy, the possibility of disaster is real, despite educational programs and stringent prescribing requirements (iPledge, 2005).

Addictive drugs such as cocaine, heroin, and nicotine cause the baby to be born in an addicted state, as well as having other harmful effects. A pregnant woman, or one who may become pregnant, should discuss all drugs she is taking with her doctor; often, drugs that are harmful to the fetus or whose safety has not been established can be replaced with safer ones.

TABLE 11.1

Examples of Substances, Organisms, and Physical Agents that Can Harm the Developing Fetus

Agent	Possible consequences
Drugs	
Alcohol	Fetal alcohol syndrome
Tobacco	Spontaneous abortion, prematurity, low birth weight, addiction of neonate, sudden infant death
Isotretinoin (Accutane)	Heart, brain malformations; intellectual disability
Thalidomide	Limb defects, deafness, blindness
Vitamins A and D (in excessive amounts)	Fetal malformations
Androgens, estrogens	Abnormalities of external genitalia and reproductive tract, especially in females
Diethylstilbestrol (DES)	Reproductive cancers (females); reduced fertility (males)
Aspirin (late in pregnancy)	Interferes with blood clotting, potentially causing hemorrhage in mother, fetus, or neonate
Heroin	Spontaneous abortion, low birth weight, respiratory depression of neonate, addiction of neonate
Cocaine	Neonatal intoxication and addiction
Infections	
Rubella	Damage to ears, eyes, heart
Genital herpes	Spontaneous abortion, premature birth, birth defects
HIV	AIDS in infancy/childhood
Chlamydia	Premature birth, neonatal eye infection
Physical agents	
X-rays	Increased risk of childhood cancer
Nuclear radiation	Increased risk of childhood cancer
Cosmic radiation (high-altitude flight)	Possible increased risk of childhood cancer, for very frequent flyers
High body temperature (over 38°C or 100.4°F) in early pregnancy (from fever, excessive exercise, saunas)	Variety of birth defects

Vitamin A, though essential for normal fetal development, can cause malformations in excessive doses. Of particular concern is "preformed vitamin A," which is present in liver and eggs and is often added to breakfast cereals, nonfat milk, and other foodstuffs (check the ingredient list for "retinyl palmitate," "vitamin A palmitate," or similar compounds). Pregnant women should limit their intake of these substances to no more than 100% of the recommended daily allowance.

Another agent that can harm the fetus is radiation. X-rays during pregnancy should be avoided if possible, but the chances of ill effects are low, so the medical benefits of the X-ray may outweigh the risks in some cases.

The Second Trimester Is the Easiest

The second trimester begins at 13 weeks of gestational age. Most women experience the second trimester as a period of calm and well-being. Morning sickness and most of the other unpleasant symptoms of early pregnancy usually disap-

quickening The onset of movements by the fetus that can be felt by the mother.

nuchal translucency test The ultrasonographic measurement of the skin fold at the neck of a fetus, useful in the prenatal diagnosis of Down syndrome and other congenital anomalies. Also called nuchal fold test.

amniocentesis The sampling of the amniotic fluid for purposes of prenatal diagnosis.

alpha-fetoprotein A protein whose presence at elevated levels in the blood of a pregnant woman is suggestive of neural tube defects in the fetus.

spina bifida A congenital malformation caused by incomplete closure of the neural tube.

chorionic villus sampling The sampling of tissue from the placenta for purposes of prenatal diagnosis.

pear. Only the need for frequent urination persists, and in fact may become worse as the enlarging uterus presses on the bladder. Signs of pregnancy become obvious: The abdomen swells, stretch marks may begin to appear, and the breasts may expel small amounts of colostrum, the special milk that nourishes newborn infants.

Around the middle of the second trimester the mother will begin to feel the fetus's movements. This event, known as **quickening**, has always had great psychological significance—it is a major step in the bonding of the mother with her child. In early Christian doctrine, quickening marked the entry of the soul into the fetus, so that abortion before quickening was not necessarily a sin. The beginning of fetal movement does not mean that the fetus is now a conscious being, however: The cerebral cortex, which is probably the main locus of consciousness, is still at an extremely rudimentary stage of development at the time of quickening.

Tests Can Detect Fetal Abnormalities

At prenatal care visits during the second trimester, the healthcare provider monitors the fetus's growth and well-being. In addition, tests may be done to check for congenital disorders. These tests may include ultrasound scans, amniocentesis, and chorionic villus sampling. These procedures can also be used to determine the fetus's sex (**Box 11.3**).

An ultrasound scan done at the beginning of the second trimester or slightly earlier can come up with evidence suggestive of congenital abnormalities, including Down syndrome. One particular feature of the fetus—the thickness of the skin fold at the neck—is particularly correlated with the likelihood of Down syndrome and other anomalies. When the measurement of this skin fold (called a **nuchal translucency test** or nuchal fold test) is combined with biochemical tests, about 90% of fetuses with Down syndrome can be identified.

If the nuchal translucency test is positive, or if there are other reasons to be concerned about fetal abnormalities, more invasive tests may have to be done. In **amniocentesis** (**Figure 11.15A**), the doctor first determines the precise position of the uterus and the fetus with an ultrasound scan and then passes a thin needle through the front wall of the abdomen into the amniotic sac in which the fetus is floating, avoiding the fetus itself. A sample of the amniotic fluid, containing some free-floating cells derived from the fetus or its membranes, is withdrawn. These cells are then grown in tissue culture and examined for chromosomal abnormalities. The fluid itself is tested for a protein called **alpha-fetoprotein**, whose levels are raised if the fetus has a neural tube defect such as **spina bifida** (incomplete development of the spine and spinal cord). Amniocentesis is usually done at about 15 to 18 weeks of pregnancy, but it is sometimes done as early as 11 weeks. The procedure carries a slight risk (less than 1 in 1000) of causing a miscarriage (Eddleman et al., 2006).

An alternative to amniocentesis is **chorionic villus sampling** (**Figure 11.15B**). In this procedure, a catheter is passed through the cervix and a sample of tissue is taken from the placenta. (Chorionic villi are the tissue projections from the placenta that serve to increase the area of contact with the mother's blood.) The procedure may also be done with a needle passed through the abdominal wall. Chorionic villus sampling is usually done at 10 to 12 weeks of pregnancy. Although it has the advantage of producing results earlier than amniocentesis, chorionic villus sampling identifies only chromosomal and genetic abnormalities, not spina bifida, and the risk of harm to the fetus, though still low, is slightly higher than with amniocentesis.

In the great majority of cases, the outcome of these tests is reassurance that the baby is probably healthy. Unfortunately, a few women do receive the devastating

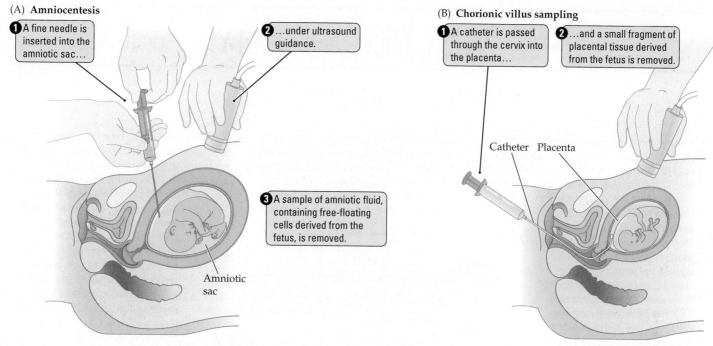

(A) **Amniocentesis**

1 A fine needle is inserted into the amniotic sac...

2 ...under ultrasound guidance.

3 A sample of amniotic fluid, containing free-floating cells derived from the fetus, is removed.

Amniotic sac

(B) **Chorionic villus sampling**

1 A catheter is passed through the cervix into the placenta...

2 ...and a small fragment of placental tissue derived from the fetus is removed.

Catheter   Placenta

Figure 11.15 Screening for congenital disorders

news that their fetus has a serious genetic abnormality. In some cases, such as congenital adrenal hyperplasia, it may be possible to prevent harm to the fetus by drug treatment during pregnancy. If not, the majority of women choose to abort the fetus. (Women who are opposed to abortion under any circumstances tend not to seek prenatal testing in the first place.) The earlier diagnosis offered by chorionic villus sampling (as compared with amniocentesis) makes the decision to have an abortion psychologically easier and medically safer.

Sex during Pregnancy Is Healthy

As the second trimester rolls on, the mother will have switched to looser clothing to accommodate her expanding belly, but otherwise the progress of her pregnancy at this time is fairly uneventful. One topic that couples often think about as the mother grows larger is sex: Is it a good idea in the latter half of pregnancy? In particular, can it harm the fetus? The answer is that, in a normal pregnancy, the fetus is well protected from almost anything the couple might do during sex. The only sex practice known to be dangerous during pregnancy is blowing air into the vagina.

About the only other way that sex can harm the fetus is if the mother acquires a sexually transmitted disease (STD) from her partner. Such diseases can be transmitted to the fetus during pregnancy or as the fetus passes through the birth canal. Organisms that cause only mild or moderate problems for adults can be catastrophic for fetuses or newborns. Thus pregnant women who are sexually active should be extra vigilant concerning the possibility of acquiring an STD.

It has been widely thought that sex late in pregnancy may increase the likelihood of premature childbirth, but research indicates it does not (Sayle et al., 2001). Even engaging in coitus right up until the woman's due date has no effect on the timing of labor (Schaffir, 2006).

The foregoing applies to *normal* pregnancies. Some medical conditions may make coitus unwise, especially toward the end of pregnancy. These can include threatened miscarriage or premature birth, vaginal bleeding, leakage of amniotic

Society, Values, and the Law

BOX 11.3 Choosing Children's Sex

As they plan for pregnancy, some couples would prefer their child to be of a particular sex, male or female. At times their preference has a specific medical reason. In particular, if the child is at risk of inheriting a genetic disorder that crops up predominantly in one sex, the couple may want a child of the other sex. This usually means a girl, because most sex-linked disorders affect boys. More commonly, couples want a child of a particular sex for some social reason. For example, they may have one or more children of one sex and now want to "balance" the family with a child of the other sex.

In many cultures boys are commonly preferred over girls. Boys are wanted because they will help with farm work, because they will bring money into the family, or because their children will carry on the family name. Girls are less desired in some cultures because marrying them off requires hefty bridal payments or because they may be essentially lost to their birth family after marriage and therefore will not support the parents in their old age. Some people do prefer girls—often because they are seen as easier to raise—and many have no preference, but boys are preferred over girls in nearly all countries. The figure shows people's preference for a boy or a girl in 16 countries. Interviewees were asked "Suppose you could only have one child. Would you prefer that it be a boy or a girl?" Interviewees who expressed no preference are omitted (Gallup Organization, 1997).

In the past, there have been many superstitions about how to have a child of a particular sex, but only one technique actually worked: killing or abandoning newborn children of the unwanted sex. Female infanticide still persists to some extent in India and China. One 28-year-old Indian woman, who had poisoned her second daughter by feeding her oleander sap, justified her action as follows: "A daughter is always liabilities. How can I bring up a second? Instead of her suffering the way I do, I thought it was better to get rid of her" (Dahlburg, 1994).

The introduction of obstetric ultrasound provided a simple and inexpensive means to

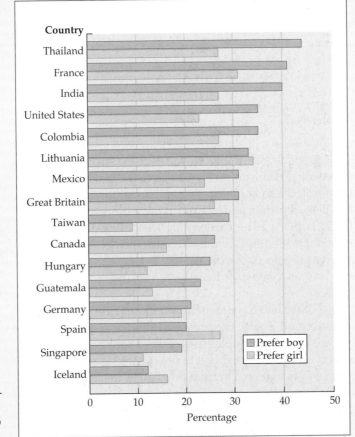

visualize a fetus's genitals and hence to determine its sex. This can be done as early as 12 to 14 weeks of pregnancy. As a consequence, the practice of aborting female fetuses has become prevalent in some countries, especially India and China, and the sex ratio of newborn children is becoming markedly skewed toward males. In China's Hainan province, for example, 135 boys are now born for every 100 girls (Shanghai Star, 2002). In India, an estimated 10 million female fetuses had been aborted on account of their sex by 2006 (Jha et al., 2006).

Considerable efforts have been devoted to developing techniques for selecting a child's sex before pregnancy is established. Because X chromosomes are larger than Y chromosomes, X-bearing sperm contain slightly more total DNA than Y-bearing sperm. A technique called flow cytometry can sense this difference and thus sort out the two kinds of sperm, but not with 100% accuracy. The developers of this technology claim a 90% success rate in producing girls and a 75% success rate in producing boys. The technology is not currently available pending FDA approval.

The most reliable method of selecting a child's sex is by preimplantation genetic screening. Several embryos are produced by in vitro fertilization, and only embryos of the preferred sex are implanted in the woman's uterus. Although this is mostly done to avoid sex-linked diseases, some fertility clinics offer the service for the purpose of "family balancing."

As with so many issues in the area of reproductive technology, the possibility of selecting children's sex triggers strong reactions. Some say that the practice is morally offensive or will have bad social consequences, such as a skewed sex ratio (Fletcher, 1983). Others say that it is a good idea because children will be more like what their parents want and therefore more loved. Some say the practice should be banned; others believe it should be left up to the mother, or to both parents, to decide (Cowan, 1992). Fearing a critical shortage of marriageable women, Chinese authorities are introducing severe penalties for sex-selective abortion as well as financial incentives for having daughters, such as free education for girls (Yardley, 2005). The government of India criminalized sex-selective abortion in 1995, and it recently announced a financial incentive plan similar to China's (Ramesh, 2008).

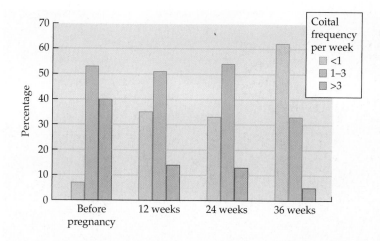

fluid, certain abnormalities of the placenta, and, possibly, the presence of more than one fetus. The woman's healthcare provider can advise her on this score.

Regardless of whether sex in late pregnancy is safe for the fetus, it may be less than satisfactory for the couple. Sexual activity generally drops off markedly during pregnancy. In one prospective study of first pregnancies (Robson et al., 1981), sexual activity dropped off in the first trimester, remained level over the second, and then dropped off again in the third, when only 38% of women engaged in one or more acts of coitus per week (**Figure 11.16**). Marital conflict, depression affecting the mother, a history of previous miscarriages, and the couple's belief that sex could harm the fetus were all linked to a decrease in sexual activity during pregnancy.

Couples who do continue to have sex late in pregnancy can make it more enjoyable by exploring new positions (**Figure 11.17**). The man-above position generally becomes awkward; the side-by-side position may be preferred (see Chapter 9). If coitus is uncomfortable in any position, manual or oral contacts may be excellent alternative ways to make love.

Moderate Exercise during Pregnancy Is Beneficial

Another issue that concerns some women is exercise. Traditionally, pregnant women were thought of as fragile creatures that needed to be spared any kind of exertion. It's now clear that, except in the case of certain problem pregnancies, exercise has a positive value in maintaining the woman's health and sense of well-being. It is especially useful in counteracting backache, constipation, mood swings, and sleeplessness.

The American College of Obstetricians and Gynecologists (ACOG) recommends that pregnant women engage in moderate, low-impact forms of exercise such as brisk walking and swimming. ACOG adds two caveats: First, a woman should avoid doing exercises that involve lying on her back after 20 weeks of pregnancy, and second, she should avoid exercises that significantly raise her body temperature, especially during the first trimester or when she has a fever already. Paula Radcliffe, world record holder in the marathon, delivered a healthy daughter after training up until the day before she went into labor (Kolata, 2007).

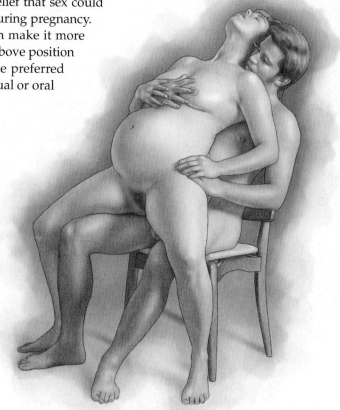

Figure 11.17 Sex during the later stages of pregnancy may be facilitated by a willingness to try new positions or sexual activities other than coitus.

Moderate exercise is beneficial for pregnant women. Swimming and brisk walking are recommended.

The Third Trimester Is a Time of Preparation

The third trimester begins at 27 weeks of gestational age. At this time, the fetus already weighs about 900 g (2 lb) and has a decent chance of surviving if born prematurely, although its survival would entail weeks of intensive neonatal care and a six-figure hospital bill. During the third trimester, the fetus increases rapidly in weight; at the time of fastest growth, which is around 33 weeks, the fetus is gaining about 50 g (2 ounces) every day. By the time of birth it has reached a weight of about 3.4 kg (7.5 lb).

During the third trimester, the fetus performs many of the behaviors that it will need to survive outside its mother, including breathing motions. The mother, and possibly her partner, may be awakened frequently at night by its vigorous movements. The mother's uterus also undergoes occasional, irregularly spaced contractions. These **Braxton-Hicks contractions** (or "false labor") are normal and do not endanger the fetus. Only if the contractions come at regular intervals and become gradually more frequent, stronger, and longer-lasting need a woman be concerned that true labor is beginning.

Women's experience of the third trimester varies greatly. Some women sail through it serenely, while others are overwhelmed by physical problems (backache, urinary frequency, fatigue, or sleeplessness) or by anxiety about childbirth and motherhood. Couples may find themselves bonding more closely than at any previous time in their relationship, or there may be increasing tension. Depression is not uncommon at this time: About 1 in 8 middle-class women experiences clinical depression during the weeks before she gives birth, as does 1 in 4 impoverished inner-city women (Hobfoll et al., 1995). Understandably, depression is particularly common among women who do not have a partner.

A Hospital Is the Best Location for Childbirth if Complications Are Foreseen

On a more positive note, the third trimester is a time of preparation for birth. By this time, the mother will probably have decided where to have her baby. If it is her first baby, she and her partner should be taking classes in preparation for the birth.

Concerning where to have the baby, there are three choices: at home, in a hospital, or (in some areas) in a stand-alone facility known as a **birthing center**. Most

Braxton-Hicks contractions Irregular uterine contractions that occur during the third trimester of pregnancy. Also called false labor.

birthing center A facility specializing in childbirth care.

births in the United States take place in hospitals. The great advantage of this location is the immediate availability of medical expertise and equipment in case anything goes wrong. The disadvantage is that a hospital can be a relatively impersonal and sometimes intimidating environment, and the mother may feel that less attention is paid to her wishes for the birth process than if she were in her own home.

Many hospitals have taken steps to make their childbirth facilities more welcoming and to involve the woman and her partner in decision-making. Some hospitals have "birthing rooms"—rooms that are more homelike and less clinical than traditional delivery rooms. Hospitals now encourage the presence of the woman's partner at the birth—sometimes even if the baby has to be delivered by cesarean section (see below). Most hospitals also encourage immediate mother–child contact after the birth, so long as there are no serious medical problems that make that impracticable.

A birthing center (if one is available) offers a compromise between hospital and home. However, it may be staffed by midwives rather than by obstetricians, and it will not have the same equipment as a hospital. Thus it may still be necessary to move the mother to a hospital if complications arise. For that reason, a birthing center that is part of a hospital complex may be preferable to one that is some distance away.

An important consideration influencing the choice of location for a birth is the estimated likelihood of complications. The healthcare provider will advise the mother to have her child in a hospital if labor begins prematurely, if the fetus is not optimally positioned for birth, if there is more than one fetus, if the mother's pelvis is unusually narrow, or if there exist any other medical conditions that increase the risk of complications. For low-risk pregnancies, there are no good studies comparing the outcomes of home and hospital births; research in this area is needed (Vedam, 2003). Thus, especially for low-risk pregnancies, there is no reason why the mother's wishes concerning the birth location should not be respected.

Childbirth Classes Prepare Parents for Birth

Many different kinds of childbirth classes are available to parents. Nearly all provide general education about pregnancy, childbirth, and infant care and encourage breast-feeding. Some of the classes incorporate the ideas of the French "prepared childbirth" pioneer Fernand Lamaze. Reacting against the use of general anesthetics during labor, which was widespread in the 1950s and 1960s, Lamaze asserted that women could experience a pain-free childbirth without anesthetics. His followers today do not make such an extreme claim (Lamaze International, 2002). The **Lamaze method** teaches breathing exercises and techniques for relaxing abdominal and perineal muscles. His method also teaches women how to reduce the perception of pain. For example, light stroking of the abdomen or thighs (**effleurage**) reduces the perceived intensity of painful signals from the uterus or birth canal during labor. Similarly, the woman can cause painful sensations to recede by focusing visual attention on something in the environment, such as a picture on the wall; by listening to words spoken by her partner; or by imagining pleasant scenery or experiences.

Lamaze teachers do not oppose anesthesia during labor if it seems necessary, and a fair proportion of women who take Lamaze classes do receive some kind of anesthesia. Another type of childbirth preparation, the **Bradley method**, stresses "natural" childbirth and places a lot of

Lamaze method A method of childbirth instruction that focuses on techniques of relaxation and other natural means of pain reduction.

effleurage Light rhythmic stroking—a part of the Lamaze childbirth method.

Bradley method A method of childbirth instruction that stresses the partner's role as birth coach and that seeks to avoid medical interventions.

Childbirth classes help expectant mothers and their partners prepare for the physical and psychological demands of labor.

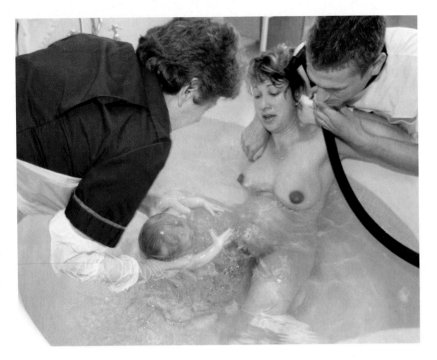

A water birth

weight on the role of the woman's partner as "birth coach." Although developed by a physician, it is more anti-medical in flavor than the Lamaze method, and women who take classes based on the Bradley method are less likely to accept anesthesia or other medical interventions during labor than women who take Lamaze classes (Monto, 1996).

Most hospital-based childbirth classes do not closely follow either the Lamaze or the Bradley model, but are based on the experience of the people teaching them. They tend to be eclectic, practically oriented, and responsive to the parents' needs, rather than being based on some overarching theory of childbirth management. As with prenatal care in general, there are significant social disparities in usage of childbirth classes: For instance, African-American mothers are only half as likely to have ever attended a class as white mothers (Lu et al., 2003).

One form of childbirth that has gained some popularity recently is water birth. The mother (often with her partner and midwife) sits in a pool or tub of warm water during delivery, and the baby is born underwater. (The baby does not take its first breath until it is brought above the water surface.) The advantage of this style of childbirth is said to be its gentleness. Some hospitals and birthing centers have birthing tubs available, or they can be rented.

The Fetus Also Makes Preparations for Birth

While the parents are preparing themselves for childbirth, so is the fetus. Although the fetus's growth rate slows dramatically after 33 weeks, its organ systems undergo rapid maturation. Much of this preparation for birth is orchestrated by corticosteroids secreted by the fetus's adrenal glands. In response to hormonal instructions from the fetus's hypothalamus and pituitary glands, the adrenal glands pump out increasing amounts of corticosteroids during the third trimester, and there is a particularly significant surge of these hormones about a month before birth. Among their effects are important changes in the lungs that facilitate the inflation of the lungs when the newborn takes its first breath of air. Corticosteroids also instruct the fetus's liver to manufacture **glycogen** that will be used to supply the brain's critical glucose needs before, during, and just after birth. Rising corticosteroid levels before birth also affect blood production, switching the hemoglobin in red blood cells to a different form that is better suited to an air-breathing lifestyle.

Labor Has Three Stages

The process of childbirth is referred to scientifically as **parturition**, and more commonly as **labor**. During most of pregnancy, parturition is prevented by the inability of the uterine musculature (myometrium) to contract in an organized manner, as well as by the cervix, whose thick wall contains a dense network of connective tissue that resists expansion. Thus the Braxton-Hicks contractions, described earlier, put some downward pressure on the fetus, but this pressure is easily resisted by the cervix, so the fetus does not move into the birth canal.

Before labor begins, the fetus changes its position in the uterus, as its head sinks deep into the pelvis against the cervix (**Figure 11.18**). This event, called

glycogen A polymer of glucose used for energy storage.

parturition Delivery of young; childbirth.

labor The process of childbirth.

engagement (or "lightening"), is often noticed by the mother when a bit of extra space opens up between her breasts and her swollen belly. In first pregnancies, engagement may occur a week or more before birth; in later pregnancies, it occurs shortly before or during labor.

Labor itself takes place in three stages. The first stage consists of the uterine contractions that open the cervix. The second stage is the actual delivery of the baby. The third stage is the period from the delivery of the baby to the delivery of the placenta.

Animal Studies Suggest that the Fetus Issues the Signal for Parturition

What causes these processes to commence? The immediate causes of parturition are fairly well understood. Cervical softening is triggered by prostaglandins and nitric oxide. Both of these substances are produced locally in the uterus and cervix. Uterine contractions are triggered by prostaglandins and by the hormone oxytocin (**Figure 11.19**). Secretion of oxytocin by the mother's pituitary gland is a reflex: Stimulation of the cervix as the fetus passes through it causes neuronal signals to be sent to the spinal cord and from there to the hypothalamus, where the cell bodies of the oxytocin-secreting neurons are located (see Chapter 5). These neurons then release a surge of oxytocin from their terminals in the posterior lobe of the pituitary, and the oxytocin triggers a contraction of the myometrium.

Of course, there must be higher-order controls that decide *when* these processes should begin. In large animals that have been studied in the laboratory, such as sheep and goats, the ultimate signal derives from the fetus—specifically, from

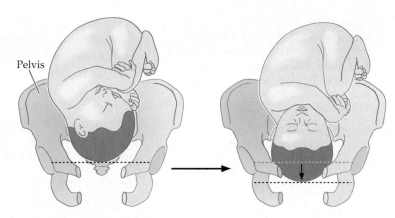

Pelvis

Figure 11.18 Engagement is the sinking of the fetus's head deep into the mother's pelvis.

engagement The sinking of a fetus's head into a lower position in the pelvis in preparation for birth. Also called lightening.

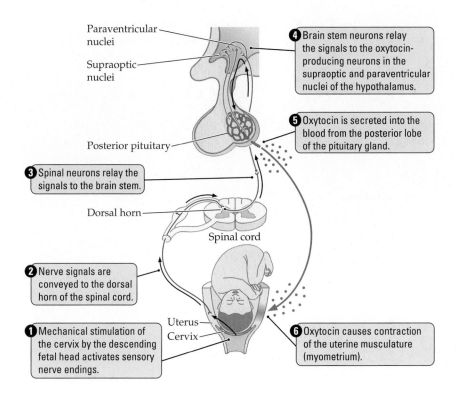

Paraventricular nuclei

Supraoptic nuclei

Posterior pituitary

3 Spinal neurons relay the signals to the brain stem.

Dorsal horn

Spinal cord

2 Nerve signals are conveyed to the dorsal horn of the spinal cord.

1 Mechanical stimulation of the cervix by the descending fetal head activates sensory nerve endings.

Uterus
Cervix

4 Brain stem neurons relay the signals to the oxytocin-producing neurons in the supraoptic and paraventricular nuclei of the hypothalamus.

5 Oxytocin is secreted into the blood from the posterior lobe of the pituitary gland.

6 Oxytocin causes contraction of the uterine musculature (myometrium).

Figure 11.19 The uterine contractions of labor result from a neurosecretory reflex involving oxytocin. (See Web Activity 11.3)

contraction In childbirth, a periodic coordinated tightening of the uterine musculature, felt as a cramp.

softening The elimination of connective tissue from the cervix, allowing it to thin out and dilate during labor. Also called ripening.

its hypothalamus, which somehow "knows" when it is time to be born. The hypothalamus orders the fetus's adrenal glands to increase their secretion of corticosteroids over and above the already high levels existing in late pregnancy, and these hormones induce an increase in estrogen secretion by the fetal side of the placenta. The estrogens enter the maternal circulation, promote prostaglandin secretion in the uterus, and facilitate the oxytocin reflex.

In women, the signals that initiate parturition are poorly understood. It is possible that the human fetus's brain also sends out a triggering signal, because malformed fetuses that lack brains are often born late (Mannino, 1988).

The First Stage of Labor Is Marked by Uterine Contractions and Cervical Dilation

Labor may be heralded by the discharge of the mucus plug that seals off the cervix during pregnancy. The plug may be tinged red with blood, and this event is therefore traditionally called the "bloody show." The amniotic sac may also rupture early in labor, or it may be ruptured by a healthcare provider. The rupture produces a gush or leakage of amniotic fluid from the vagina ("water breaking"). In other cases the sac does not rupture until later in labor, and occasionally a baby may be born "in the caul"—that is, in an unruptured, fluid-filled amniotic sac.*

The first stage of labor can last anywhere from a couple of hours to 24 hours or more. The two main processes that permit parturition are the strong, coordinated **contractions** of the uterus and the elimination of much of the connective tissue in the cervix (**softening** or ripening) (**Figure 11.20**). The contractions are medi-

---

*A baby that comes "gift wrapped" in this fashion is considered lucky in some cultures: Specifically, it will not die by drowning.

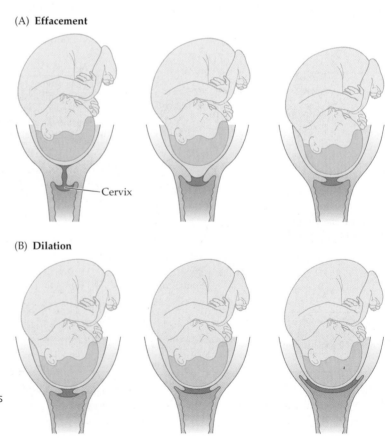

(A) **Effacement**

Cervix

(B) **Dilation**

Figure 11.20 Cervical changes during labor (A) Effacement is the thinning of the cervix. (B) Dilation is the opening of the cervix, from fully closed to a width of 10 cm (4 inches).

ated by the pituitary hormone oxytocin. The effect of the contractions is not yet to move the fetus downward, but to pull the cervix upward, so that the vagina and cervix together form a single, continuous **birth canal**. Early in labor, the contractions are fairly mild and spaced 15 to 20 minutes apart. Later, they become more intense and closely spaced—about every 3 minutes.

The softening of the cervix, which is mediated by prostaglandin hormones secreted by the uterus itself, allows the cervix to thin out (**effacement**) and the cervical canal to gradually open up enough for passage of the fetal head (**dilation** or dilatation). When this opening process is complete, the canal measures 10 cm (4 inches) in diameter.

The last part of the first phase of labor, when the cervix dilates from 8 to 10 cm (3 to 4 inches), is sometimes called the **transition**; it is a short period of very intense and frequent contractions. The transition is the part of labor that is most likely to be painful and exhausting, and it is here that the woman can most usefully apply what she has learned in her prenatal classes: relaxing rather than fighting the contractions, and directing her attention to other sensory inputs.

Many forms of anesthesia are available for women who are experiencing a great deal of pain during labor. These include intravenous general anesthetics such as barbiturates, opiate analgesics, tranquilizers, spinal anesthetics (that numb much of the lower part of the body), and nerve blocks that numb the area of the vulva. Anesthetics that act systemically (i.e., those administered orally or intravenously) will reach the fetus and have the potential to depress its responsiveness during labor and after birth.

Another disadvantage of anesthetics is that they may impair the mother's ability to assist the birth process. One technique that reduces these problems is the injection or continuous infusion of a morphine-like drug or local anesthetic into the back, just outside the membrane that wraps the spinal cord (**epidural anesthesia**). Recent modifications of this technique minimize the impairment of the mother's ability to move. Still, no single method is appropriate for all situations (American Society of Anesthesiologists, 2007). Pregnant women do well to discuss the issue of anesthesia and develop a birth plan ahead of time with their healthcare provider.

Forms of natural pain relief may be useful to many women. These include such seemingly simple activities as walking, pelvic rocking, showering, using a hot tub, sitting on a "birth ball," breathing exercises, and guided imagery.

Delivery Is Accomplished by Uterine Contractions Aided by "Bearing Down"

The second stage of labor is the actual passage of the fetus through the birth canal. This movement happens because the cervix is anchored by ligaments and connective tissue sheets to the pelvic floor. Thus, once the first-stage contractions have pulled the cervix up to its maximum extent, further contractions must pull the fundus of the uterus down, toward the birth canal, and this movement inevitably pushes the fetus through the canal.

Although the delivery of the fetus can be accomplished purely by uterine contractions, women usually feel an urge to push, or "bear down": that is, to assist the birth process by voluntary contraction of the muscles of the abdominal wall and the diaphragm. This assists the process by adding intra-abdominal pressure to the intrauterine pressure produced by the uterine contractions.

The second stage of labor is quite variable in duration: It may last just a few minutes, or it may take several hours. It is usually lengthier and more stressful for a woman's first delivery than for subsequent deliveries. The second stage is usually perceived as less painful than the transition phase of the first stage.

birth canal The canal formed by the uterus, cervix, and vagina, through which the fetus passes during parturition.

effacement Thinning of the cervix in preparation for childbirth.

dilation In childbirth, the expansion of the cervical canal. Also called dilatation.

transition The final phase of dilation of the cervix during labor.

epidural anesthesia Anesthesia administered just outside the membrane that surrounds the spinal cord.

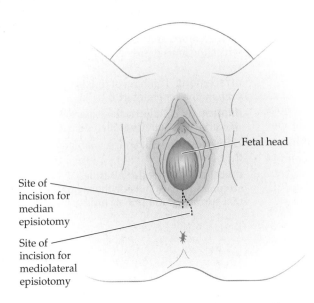

Figure 11.21 Episiotomy is a surgical cut made to expand the vaginal opening, facilitating passage of the fetus's head. The cut may be made in the midline or diagonally to one side.

crowning The appearance of the fetal scalp at the vaginal opening.

episiotomy A cut extending the opening of the vagina backward into the perineum, performed by an obstetrician with the intention of facilitating childbirth or reducing the risk of a perineal tear.

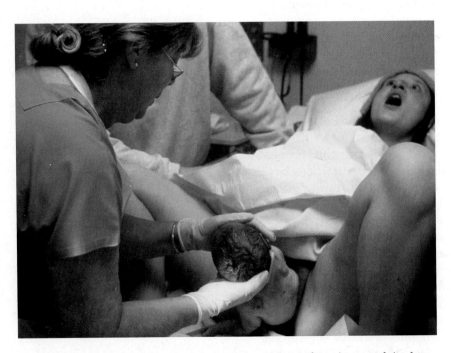

The hard part is over: Once the head and shoulders are free, the rest of the fetus emerges easily.

Toward the end of the second stage, the baby's head appears at the vaginal opening (**crowning**). At this point, if it seems likely that the delivery of the head will tear the vaginal wall, the provider may make an incision in the perineum to extend the vaginal opening a short distance backward, toward the anus (**Figure 11.21**). This procedure, called an **episiotomy**, is done under local anesthesia.

The thinking behind doing an episiotomy is that, if the vaginal wall is likely to rupture anyway, it is better to make a clean incision that can be neatly sewn up afterward. Still, many people feel that episiotomies are done too often, mostly to hurry delivery along, even though speedy delivery does not convey any particular medical benefit (Eason & Feldman, 2000). Episiotomy may increase the chances that the woman will subsequently experience pain during coitus (Hartmann et al., 2005; Ejegard et al., 2008). Medical students are now taught not to perform episiotomies routinely; still, the procedure may have to be done if there is fetal distress (Cleary-Goldman & Robinson, 2003). Some authorities recommend perineal stretching exercises during late pregnancy as a way to make tears or episiotomy less likely (Mayo Clinic, 2008).

The Newborn Child Adapts Quickly

Once the fetus's head and shoulders have exited the birth canal, the rest of the body follows fairly readily. The compression of the fetus's chest as it passes through the canal effectively "squeegees" the fluid out of its lungs, thus preparing them for their first breath. With the passage of the entire body through the canal, the second stage of labor is complete.

At this point, the newborn infant is still attached to the placenta by the umbilical cord, so it is still getting its oxygen from its mother's lungs. Very shortly after birth, however, it takes its first breath, probably in response to cold and tactile stimulation. Then, in a beautifully orchestrated feat of physiology, the infant's circulatory system reorganizes itself: The fetal system, which largely bypasses the lungs, is replaced by the definitive circulatory pattern, in which the lungs receive all the blood from the right side of the heart.

The cessation of pulsation in the umbilical blood vessels can be readily seen. At this point, the cord is clamped and cut (sometimes by the mother's partner), and the baby is finally a free-living organism. The mother is often given the chance to hold and perhaps breast-feed her baby, at least for a short while. In many hospitals the mother has the option of keeping the baby with her, unless the baby has some health problem that necessitates moving it to the nursery.

The Third Stage Is the Expulsion of the Placenta

The third stage of labor consists of further uterine contractions that separate the placenta from the uterine wall and expel it (along with the other fetal membranes) through the birth canal. This usually takes about 30 minutes, but it can range from a few minutes to an hour or more. The expelled placenta is called the **afterbirth**.

The fetal blood in the afterbirth and the umbilical cord can be donated to a cord-blood bank; it is of potential use in the treatment of leukemia and related diseases. Banking the blood for the baby's own future use is a growing trend—fostered by a for-profit industry—but it doesn't make a whole lot of sense, given the low chance that the baby will ever need it (American Academy of Pediatrics, 2007a).

The process of labor can be shortened, or eliminated entirely, by delivering the baby through **cesarean section (C-section)**, but the increasing popularity of this practice raises serious concerns (**Box 11.4**).

Premature and Delayed Births Are Hazardous

Labor is considered premature if it occurs more than 3 weeks before the mother's due date. In most cases of premature labor the cause is not known, but predisposing factors include multiple fetuses, teen pregnancy, the mother's use of tobacco or drugs, malnutrition, and a variety of illnesses during pregnancy. Premature labor can sometimes be halted with the use of drugs; if not, it leads to **premature birth** or **pre-term birth**. This happens in about 10% of all pregnancies in the United States.

Premature birth is dangerous to the baby's health: About 75% of all neonatal deaths (aside from those associated with congenital defects) strike the 10% of babies who are born prematurely. Pre-term babies, especially those who are small for their gestational age or who are born very prematurely, also have a much higher likelihood of suffering long-lasting physical and behavioral disabilities than do babies delivered at term (Schothorst & van Engeland, 1996; Lopez Bernal & TambyRaja, 2000). Even so, the majority of "preemies" do fine and, though small at birth, eventually catch up with their peers.

Labor is considered **delayed** if it occurs more than 3 weeks post-term: About 10% of babies are born at least this late. Like premature labor, delayed labor has risks. The fetus may grow too large to pass through the birth canal, and in a minority of cases the placenta may cease to adequately nourish the fetus, so that it is born too small for its gestational age. Post-term babies are about three times more likely to die neonatally than are babies born at term. To avoid these ill effects, labor may be **induced** with drugs such as oxytocin and prostaglandins. This practice itself carries some risk, but it does at least allow for the date of delivery to be planned ahead of time (**Box 11.5**).

The Period after Birth Places Many Demands on Parents

The weeks after birth are called the **postpartum**. Although there can be medical problems for the mother during this period, including serious ones such as infections acquired during the birth process, its main feature is physical recovery from the stresses of pregnancy and childbirth. A vaginal discharge continues for a few days after parturition and is then replaced by small volumes of a dark, bloody discharge known as **lochia**; this ceases after a few weeks, but spotty bleeding may continue for 6 to 8 weeks. The uterus gradually shrinks back to its original dimensions, episiotomy or C-section incisions heal, and the mother's levels of estrogen and progesterone, which drop precipitously at delivery, eventually return to more normal levels.

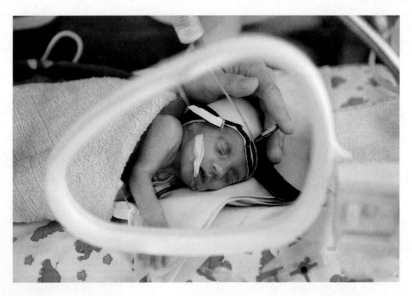

Premature infants have a good chance of surviving, but they require intensive medical care and may end up with some kind of disability. This preemie was photographed through an access hole in its incubator.

afterbirth The placenta, whose delivery constitutes the final stage of labor.

cesarean section (C-section) The delivery of a baby through an incision in the abdominal wall and the uterus.

premature birth Birth that occurs more than 3 weeks before a woman's due date. Also called pre-term birth.

delayed labor Labor that occurs more than 3 weeks after a woman's due date.

induced labor Labor induced artificially by drugs.

postpartum The period after birth.

lochia A bloody vaginal discharge that may continue for a few weeks after childbirth.

Sexual Health

BOX 11.4 Cesarean Section

A cesarean section, or C-section, involves the delivery of a baby through a surgical incision in the front of the abdomen and the uterus (see figure). The procedure is so named because Julius Caesar was supposedly born by this method. (We know that he wasn't because his mother was alive during his childhood; no mothers survived C-section section before the Renaissance.)

In the United States today, almost 1 in 3 hospital births is by C-section (Agency for Healthcare Research and Quality, 2008). The comparable figure in Canada is 1 in 4 births (Canada.com, 2007). Both these figures represent huge increases over the last decade—and this has happened in the face of government policies to *reduce* the number of C-sections.

Cesarean sections are done when vaginal delivery is deemed inadvisable for a variety of medical reasons: if the mother's pelvis is too narrow for the size of the fetus, when labor does not progress after a prolonged period and the mother or fetus are becoming exhausted, or when certain complications occur during labor. A C-section may also be performed if the fetus's position is unfavorable for birth—that is, it is in some orientation other than head down and cannot be manipulated into the head-down position—or the placenta is blocking the baby's passage into the birth canal. Another medical reason for a C-section may be to avoid exposing the baby to an infection present in the birth canal, such as herpes.

Still, as many as 18% of C-sections are performed simply because the mother requests the procedure. Usually she does so out of fear of a painful childbirth (Wax et al., 2004), but some-

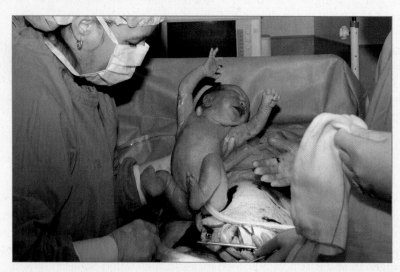

A baby being delivered by cesarean section

times because she believes that a vaginal delivery will impair her sex life afterward or even because she doesn't want to devote time to attending childbirth classes. What's more, there are nonmedical reasons that make some doctors also favor C-sections: These procedures are much less likely than vaginal deliveries to lead to malpractice suits, and preplanned C-sections are easier to fit into a doctor's schedule than unpredictable natural births (Kotz, 2008).

Emergency C-section may well save the life of mother or child, but any C-section, even an elective one, causes the mother weeks of debility right at the time when she needs to be recovering from pregnancy and supporting her baby. Both immediate and long-term complications can occur (Declercq et al., 2007). A review of 79

studies, including randomized trials, indicated that elective C-sections present significantly more risks to mother and child than natural childbirth (Belizan et al., 2007). What's more, returning to natural childbirth after an earlier C-section, though usually safe, does raise the likelihood of one serious complication—a rupture of the uterus during labor.

The World Health Organization believes that governments should try to keep national C-section rates no higher than 5% to 10% of all births, but the United States and Canada are moving in the other direction. If the present rate of increase were to continue—which is not terribly likely—natural birth would become a minority practice in the United States around the year 2015.

Psychologically, the postpartum is a highly variable experience. On the plus side, the mother has the relief of putting pregnancy behind her and the joy of a new baby. Over the first few days after parturition these positive feelings tend to dominate. After that, however, the mother faces a great deal of stress. She finds herself back home and devoting a great deal of time and effort to looking after her infant, yet she still needs quite a bit of "mothering" herself. In this situation, the degree of support she receives from her partner or others makes an enormous difference to her psychological well-being.

Postpartum Depression May Be Accompanied by Disordered Thinking

Many women experience variable moods after childbirth, including periods of sadness and crying ("baby blues"). In some women this sadness is sufficiently

Sex in History

BOX 11.5 The Blackout Babies

The New York skyline during the 1965 blackout

On November 9, 1965, electrical power went out over most of the northeastern United States, putting a stop to all business activities for over 24 hours. Television sets flickered and failed, and darkness covered the land. So how did people fill this unexpected void in their lives?

The answer seemed to be forthcoming 9 months later. On Wednesday, August 10, 1966, the *New York Times* ran a front-page story under the headline "Births Up 9 Months After Blackout." The *Times*'s reporters had learned of unusually high numbers of births in several New York City hospitals on Monday, August 8. Later articles reported that the birth rate declined over the following days and was back to normal by the end of the week. New Yorkers, it seemed, had found a "creative" way to deal with their time off during the power outage.

The only problem with this story was—it didn't happen! Mondays are always busy days in maternity wards. That's because many deliveries are induced and can therefore be planned ahead of time. These induced deliveries tend to pile up on Mondays because obstetricians don't like to work on weekends any more than the rest of us do. As shown by statisticians Alan Izenman and Sandy Zabell, the August 8 birth peak was actually no higher than any other Monday peak in New York City (Izenman & Zabell, 1981). Furthermore, the variability in the length of pregnancy means that, even if there was a city-wide orgy of unprotected sex on November 9, one would not expect a surge in births to occur on a precise day in August of the following year.

The *New York Times* later backpedaled on its report, but to no avail: The "blackout babies" became an unshakable urban legend. Similar stories have appeared in the media on many occasions since then, for example in early October of 2000, 9 months after all those drunken millennium celebrations.

intense and sustained to be diagnosed as **postpartum depression** (Georgiopoulos et al., 2001). This susceptibility to depression peaks in the period between 10 and 20 days after the birth, when mothers are 7 times more likely to experience depression or other mental disorders requiring hospitalization, as compared with mothers of older children (Munk-Olsen et al., 2006). Depression can linger for several months after the birth, however.

In a small minority of women, postpartum depression is accompanied by a serious disruption of thinking: This is called **depressive psychosis**. On rare occasions, this disorder can lead to infanticide or suicide. In a uniquely tragic case in June 2001, a Houston woman with a prior history of severe postpartum depressive psychosis drowned her 6-month-old daughter as well as her four older children. At her 2002 trial the woman, Andrea Yates, pleaded not guilty of murder by reason of insanity, but she was found guilty and sentenced to life in prison. An appellate court reversed her conviction and ordered a new trial. In the 2006 retrial the jury accepted her insanity defense, and Yates is now confined in a state mental hospital.

postpartum depression Depression in a mother during the postpartum phase.

depressive psychosis Depression accompanied by seriously disordered thinking.

TABLE 11.2

Main Constituents of Mature Human Milk

Water	Approximately 90%
Sugar (lactose)	Approximately 7%
Fat	3–6%
Proteins	0.8-0.9%
Amino acids	Includes all essential amino acids
Vitamins	Includes A, B_1, B_2, B_{12}, C, D, E, K
Energy content	Approximately 650 calories per liter (19 calories per fluid ounce)

wet nurse A woman who breast-feeds someone else's infant.

infant formula Manufactured breast milk substitute.

In many non-Western cultures, the contraceptive effect of prolonged breast-feeding plays an important role in spacing out a woman's children.

provides it with about 700 calories of energy. Most of that energy comes from the fat content of the milk. Of the proteins in milk, some are digested to provide amino acids for protein synthesis, while others resist digestion and serve as enzymes, antibodies, growth factors, and the like (Lönnerdal, 2003).

Infant Formula Is an Alternative to Breast Milk

Over most of human history, mothers had little choice but to breast-feed their babies. If they could not do so or did not wish to, their only option was to have the baby breast-fed by another woman who had milk to spare—perhaps because she had lost her own infant. Such women were called **wet nurses**. In the twentieth century, however, breast-feeding largely gave way to bottle-feeding in western countries, and the industrial production of **infant formula** began. Most formula is based on cows' milk; soy-based formula is recommended only for infants who cannot digest cows' milk.

By the 1950s only about 1 in 5 American women breast-fed their infants, but starting in the 1970s the numbers began to rise again. This shift was propelled by medical research, which demonstrated that breast-feeding has specific health benefits, and by the women's movement, which rejected the image of breast-feeding as demeaning. Breast-feeding became a cause, spearheaded by La Leche League International. Currently, about 77% of American mothers breast-feed their babies initially, but only about 1 in 3 women still does so at 6 months (Centers for Disease Control, 2008a).

Breast-Feeding Has Many Advantages and Some Drawbacks

Breast-feeding, as compared with bottle-feeding, has many advantages:

- *Health benefits for the baby* Breast-fed babies are less likely to develop infectious illnesses such as pneumonia, botulism, bronchitis, bacterial meningitis, staphylococcal infections, influenza, ear infections, rubella, and diarrhea, and are also less prone to asthma. These benefits are experienced mainly during the period of breast-feeding; the long-term physical health of breast-fed and bottle-fed infants is about the same. But there do seem to be long-lasting cognitive benefits: In one randomized trial, prolonged, exclusive breast-feeding was associated with a higher IQ and better academic performance at the age of 6 (Kramer et al., 2008).

- *Health benefits for the mother* By stimulating the release of oxytocin, breast-feeding helps shrink the uterus to its prepregnancy size and reduces postpartum bleeding. It also helps the mother shed the excess weight she gained during pregnancy. (Breast-feeding is nature's own liposuction.) It may also reduce her risk of ovarian cancer and early (premenopausal) breast cancer.

- *Psychological benefits to the mother and infant* Breast-feeding helps establish a close bond between mother and child. Breast-feeding is usually pleasurable and relaxing for the mother.

- *Convenience and expense* Breast-feeding is much less expensive than bottle-feeding, even considering the extra food the mother must consume to support it. Breast-feeding is more convenient than bottle-feeding in the sense that no preparations are required: The breast milk is always there, perfectly prepared, at the right temperature, and sterile.

- *Contraceptive effect* Breast-feeding suppresses ovarian function by interfering with the pulsatile secretion of GnRH from the hypothalamus (McNeilly, 2001). Normal menstrual cycles do not usually begin until 6 weeks after parturition at the earliest. In some non-Western cultures women nurse their children for several years after birth, and the associated reduction in fertility is a major factor creating substantial intervals between births. It takes intensive nursing to achieve a marked contraceptive effect, however, and most American women stand a good chance of becoming pregnant even if they continue to nurse. The first ovulation after parturition may not be preceded by a menstrual period, so nursing women receive no foolproof signal that fertility has returned.

Breast-feeding also has several potential disadvantages:

- *Health problems for the mother* Women who breast-feed sometimes develop inflamed nipples, which makes nursing painful, or their breasts become uncomfortably engorged with milk. About 20% of women develop an inflammation or infection of the breast (**mastitis**), often as a consequence of cracked nipples or a blocked milk duct (Kinlay et al., 2001). These conditions can be easily treated, however.

- *Health problems for the baby* The infant can acquire some infections, including HIV and hepatitis, from the mother via her milk. Many drugs (including contraceptives) can pass from the mother to the child via milk and may harm the child. A mother who is taking medication and plans to breast-feed should discuss all drugs with her physician.

- *Inconvenience* Although breast milk comes already prepared and warmed, the process of feeding it to the baby takes considerable time—several hours each day. It is a real challenge for working women. One option is for the woman to remove milk with a breast pump and refrigerate it so that a caretaker—or perhaps the mother's partner—can feed it to the baby later by bottle.

Numerous organizations would like to see more women breast-feed their babies. Still, if a woman cannot do so for one reason or another, she should not feel that she has failed her child. Formula-fed infants can thrive as well as breast-fed ones.

If a mother does breast-feed her infant, when should she stop? The American Academy of Pediatrics has recommended that babies be exclusively breast-fed for 6 months, with continued partial breast-feeding for 1 year or more (American Academy of Pediatrics, 2005). The World Health Organization has recommended 2 years of breast-feeding. The average for nonindustrial societies is 3 to 5 years. Very few American mothers continue to breast-feed beyond 1 year, and those that continue to 2 years might face strong societal disapproval. Many Americans view the breasts primarily as sex organs and consider the breast-feeding of a 2-year-old to be something akin to sexual child abuse. There have been cases in which children have been legally removed from their mothers on account of too-lengthy breast-feeding (Healy, 2001).

Biological Mechanisms May Contribute to Maternal Behavior

We mentioned that breast-feeding helps to cement the mother–child bond. This observation brings up the question of whether there is a "chemistry" to mother love—some hormone or neurotransmitter that causes a mother to devote herself

mastitis Inflammation of the breast.

so selflessly to her helpless infant. Some people think that there is, and point to the two hormones primarily involved in lactation, prolactin and oxytocin. Both of these hormones are known to play a role in the generation of maternal behavior in animals, including rodents and larger animals such as sheep. During pregnancy, prolactin "primes" certain centers in the brain, especially in the hypothalamus and nearby, changing their synaptic wiring in such a way as to prepare the animal to show maternal behavior (Mann & Bridges, 2001). After parturition, prolactin and oxytocin released by suckling, combined with visual and olfactory cues, trigger the actual display of maternal behavior. Thus, by suckling, the offspring not only obtain milk, but also "push their mother's buttons," causing her to groom them, protect them, fetch them if they stray, and so on.

Similar mechanisms may well operate in humans and other primates, too, but the situation is more complex. For one thing, many female primates show "aunting" behavior—that is, they will temporarily mother another female's infant, even if they have never been pregnant themselves. They may even permanently adopt a strange infant—as, of course, humans sometimes do. Indeed, even rodents will often show maternal behavior to strange pups, given enough exposure to them. Thus the hormonal changes induced by pregnancy, parturition, and lactation may play a role in human maternal behavior, but they can hardly be the whole story.

Summary

1. The onset of pregnancy is marked by a missed menstrual period and other symptoms. It can be confirmed by urine or blood tests that detect the human chorionic gonadotropin hormone (hCG) secreted by the implanted embryo.

2. To enhance the chances of pregnancy, coitus should be timed to occur at or just before ovulation. The time of ovulation can be estimated by tracking basal body temperature or changes in cervical mucus or by the use of test kits that detect the surge of luteinizing hormone prior to ovulation.

3. Infertility or subfertility can be caused by problems in the man or in the woman. If this condition results from a low sperm count or sperm quality, in vitro fertilization may still make pregnancy possible. An alternative is artificial insemination with donated sperm.

4. Abnormalities of the female reproductive tract, resulting from sexually transmitted infections or other causes, can reduce fertility. The oviducts are the commonest site of such problems. These abnormalities can sometimes be corrected surgically. Alternatively, embryos produced by in vitro fertilization (IVF) can be placed directly in the uterus.

5. Problems with ovulation can often be treated with drugs. An alternative is the use of donated eggs.

6. If a woman cannot sustain pregnancy at all, surrogate motherhood and adoption are possible options.

7. Fertility declines steadily with age in both sexes. Age also raises the likelihood of fetal abnormalities such as Down syndrome.

8. Many embryos do not survive. Many of those that fail to implant or die early in pregnancy are abnormal. Other conditions, such as ectopic pregnancy or Rh factor incompatibility, can cause fetal loss or harm the fetus or the mother.

9. Pregnancy lasts about 9 months and is conventionally divided into 3 trimesters. The first trimester may be marked by symptoms such as morning sickness. It is a critical period of fetal development during which the main body plan is laid out and organ systems develop. This process can be impaired by maternal infection or poor nutrition

REFER TO THE

Human Sexuality

WEBSITE AT

www.sinauer.com/levay3e

for activities, study questions, quizzes, and other study aids.

or by use of alcohol, tobacco, or a variety of drugs. Prenatal care offers important benefits, but many women do not receive such care in early pregnancy.

10. The second trimester is usually easier for the mother. The fetus can be screened for congenital abnormalities and its sex determined at this time. Moderate exercise benefits the mother. The frequency of sexual activity tends to decline during pregnancy, but for most women there is no health reason for abstaining from coitus.

11. In the third trimester both the parents and the fetus make preparations for birth. Childbirth classes teach strategies to facilitate delivery and to minimize pain.

12. Labor has three stages. In the first stage, uterine contractions and cervical softening prepare the birth canal for the passage of the fetus. In the second stage, the fetus passes through the canal and is "delivered". Rapid physiological changes adapt it to an air-breathing existence. In the third stage, the placenta (afterbirth) and fetal membranes are expelled.

13. Difficult births may necessitate surgical widening of the vaginal opening (episiotomy) or delivery via an abdominal incision (cesarean section). In the United States, both of these procedures are done more commonly than is necessary. Various forms of anesthesia are available if labor is excessively painful. There are also forms of pain relief that do not rely on medications.

14. Premature or delayed labor is associated with increased risks of harm to the fetus.

15. The period after birth (postpartum) is a time of recovery for the mother but is marked by depression with disordered thinking in a few women.

16. The birth of a child, especially a first one, can bring great happiness, but it also causes major stresses. Marital satisfaction tends to decline after the transition to parenthood, and the frequency of sexual activity decreases.

17. Hormones prepare the mother's breasts for lactation and mediate the release of milk during nursing. The content of milk changes during the weeks after childbirth. Breast-feeding has significant advantages over formula feeding, but formula-fed infants can thrive too.

Discussion Questions

1. Imagine that for some reason you or your partner were not able to become pregnant by sexual intercourse. Discuss your preference for some alternative method of becoming parents (e.g., adoption, assisted reproductive technology, or surrogate motherhood). Discuss what the pros and cons of each solution would be for you.

2. Do you think that IVF clinics should help postmenopausal women who want to become pregnant, regardless of their age?

3. Imagine that you or your partner were pregnant and learned that the embryo had a genetic defect such as Down syndrome. Discuss the costs and benefits of the options available to you (e.g., abortion, delivering the child and putting it up for adoption, or keeping and raising the child) and the rationale behind each one.

4. Do you think that the capability to select a child's sex prenatally is a good thing or a bad thing, and why? Do you think the practice should be permitted, discouraged, restricted, or banned?

5. Imagine that you or your partner are happily pregnant and expect a normal delivery. Would you elect to deliver the child at home, in a hospital, or in a birthing center? Would you prefer a medical doctor or a certified nurse-midwife to deliver your baby? Why?

6. Your baby is born and is healthy. Discuss the pros and cons of breast-feeding versus bottle-feeding. Which would you select? How long would you breast-feed? Give your reasons.

7. What reasons can you list for *not* having children?

Web Resources

American College of Obstetricians and Gynecologists www.acog.org

American Society for Reproductive Medicine www.asrm.org

IFCONLINE—Independent Fertility Counseling Online www.infertility-info.com/

National Down Syndrome Society www.ndss.org

Society for Assisted Reproductive Technology www.sart.org

Recommended Reading

American College of Obstetricians and Gynecologists (2000). *Planning your pregnancy and birth* (3rd ed.). ACOG.

Carson, S. A., Casson, P. R., & Shuman, D. J. (1999). *The American Society of Reproductive Medicine complete guide to fertility.* Contemporary Books.

Cunningham, F. G., et al., (2005). *Williams obstetrics* (22nd ed.). McGraw-Hill.

La Leche International (2004). *The womanly art of breastfeeding* (7th ed.). Plume.

Mayo Clinic (2004). *Guide to a healthy pregnancy.* Collins.

Varney, H., Kriebs, J. M., and Gegor, C. L. (2004). *Varney's midwifery* (4th ed.). Jones and Bartlett.

CHAPTER 12

Condoms are reliable contraceptives when used properly.

Contraception and Abortion

The previous chapter treated pregnancy as a natural and desired consequence of vaginal intercourse. For most men and women, however, there are substantial periods of life during which they want to engage in sexual relationships but do not want to produce children. Human ingenuity has come up with a wide variety of methods for preventing pregnancies and—if necessary—terminating them. These methods, often referred to collectively as family planning, are the topic of this chapter.

Birth Control Has a Long History

In the ancient Mediterranean world, "birth control" was accomplished largely through the neglect, abandonment, or outright killing of unwanted babies. Various forms of contraception were also used, though probably with limited success. These methods involved placing some substance, such as olive oil or a vinegar-soaked sponge, in the vagina before sex or douching with wine or vinegar afterward. The withdrawal method of contraception is mentioned in the biblical story of Onan, who "spilled his seed upon the ground" to avoid impregnating his deceased brother's wife (Genesis 38).

Male condoms—sheaths placed over the penis—also have a long history. The eighteenth-century Italian adventurer and ladies' man Giacomo Casanova (**Figure 12.1**) popularized their use, both as contraceptives and to prevent the transmission of disease. At that time, most condoms were made from animal intestines, and they were so expensive that they had to be used repeatedly. Mass-produced rubber condoms (hence "rubbers") became available at the end of the nineteenth century, followed by latex condoms in the 1930s.

Diaphragms—barriers that cover the cervix—were originally natural objects, such as squeezed half-lemons. (Besides acting as a barrier, the lemon's acidity had some spermicidal action.) A reasonably effective artificial diaphragm was invented in the 1880s. Diaphragms were the main form of contraception used by women until the 1960s. In the 1920s Ernst Gräfenberg (of "G-spot" fame) developed an effective intrauterine device (IUD); this probably worked by interfering with sperm transport.

Scientific discoveries about the endocrinological basis of the menstrual cycle led to the introduction of oral contraceptives ("the pill") for women in the 1960s. Oral contraceptives, which contain sex steroids, were so effective that they almost eliminated the fear of unwanted pregnancy for many women and thus helped spur the "sexual revolution" of that time. Most recent developments in contraceptive technology employ sex steroids or related compounds.

Figure 12.1 Giacomo Casanova (1725–1798) made the testing of condoms into a social activity.

Feminists Led the Campaign to Legalize Contraception

The history of contraception in the United States is not merely a story of technological advances, however, but also one of profound social conflict. At least until the end of the nineteenth century, contraception was viewed by many as morally offensive because it subverted what was thought to be the natural or divinely intended function of sex: procreation. Indeed, that is still the official position of the Roman Catholic Church today. Early proponents of contraception were harassed, fined, or jailed.

Margaret Sanger (1879–1966) and other early feminists led the struggle to legalize contraception in the twentieth century (**Box 12.1**). The birth control movement did not achieve definitive success until the 1960s and 1970s, when two decisions of the U.S. Supreme Court (*Griswold v. Connecticut*, 1965, and *Eisenstadt v. Baird*, 1972) overthrew laws that banned the use or distribution of contraceptives. These rulings were based on a constitutional right of privacy and in fact helped establish that right.

Following these decisions, federal and state governments began supporting family planning initiatives—for example, through the Medicaid program. The AIDS epidemic, which began around 1980, spurred the social approval of one form of contraception—condoms—because it offered protection against the transmission of HIV. But contraception remains controversial in some quarters even today, especially with regard to its use by teens. Much of this debate centers on whether schools should provide information about contraception and access to contraceptives. Because of this controversy, the U.S. government has been much less active in the field of contraception services, education, and research than governments in many other industrialized countries. Thus, much of the burden of education and service provision has fallen on nongovernmental organizations.

Contraception Has Not Yet Solved the Problem of Unwanted Births

Currently, 90% of American women aged 15 to 45 who are sexually active and fertile but do not want to become pregnant are using some contraceptive technique. On the basis of this high rate of contraceptive usage, you might imagine that the great majority of pregnancies would be planned and would lead to the birth of wanted babies. Unfortunately, as you can see from **Figure 12.2**, fewer than half of all pregnancies have that outcome; the remainder end in induced abortion, spontaneous abortion (miscarriage), or unwanted or mistimed births. More than 3 million unwanted pregnancies occur in the United States each year. Half of these result from not using any method of contraception, but the other half result from failure of a method that *was* used, though perhaps not properly (Finer & Henshaw, 2006).

Another practical problem is financial: Many medical insurance plans do not cover contraceptive drugs or devices that require a prescription, or do so less generously than for other kinds of drugs and devices. Federal legislation to mandate equal coverage of contraceptive and noncontraceptive prescription drugs and services has been introduced in Congress on more than one occasion but has not yet been enacted. Providing full contraceptive coverage in employment-based medical plans is estimated to cost no more than about $21 per employee per year (Guttmacher Institute, 2002).

Different Users Have Different Contraceptive Needs

A wide variety of contraceptive methods are available, each of which has certain features that make it more or less attractive for particular users. Contraceptive

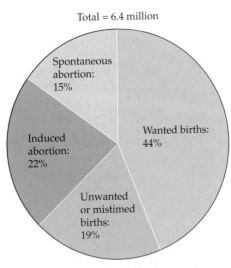

Total = 6.4 million

Spontaneous abortion: 15%

Induced abortion: 22%

Wanted births: 44%

Unwanted or mistimed births: 19%

Figure 12.2 Fewer than half of all U.S. pregnancies lead to the birth of a wanted child. This chart shows the outcome of the 6.4 million pregnancies that are established in the United States per year. (Data from Guttmacher Institute, 2008b.)

Sex in History

BOX 12.1 Margaret Sanger and the Birth Control Movement

Margaret Sanger was born in Corning, New York, in 1879. Her mother, Anne Higgins, died at age 50 after bearing 11 children, and Sanger attributed her early death to the burden of too-frequent pregnancies. Sanger trained as a nurse and in 1902 married an architect. The couple had three children and then moved to New York City and became involved in socialist causes. One of the people who influenced Sanger was the anarchist Emma Goldman.

Working as a visiting nurse in New York's Lower East Side, Sanger came to realize that unrestricted births were putting a crushing economic and health burden on working-class women. In 1914 Sanger began publishing a radical feminist monthly called *The Woman Rebel,* which included appeals for the right to practice birth control. Sanger was indicted under the Comstock Laws, which forbade the dissemination of information about contraception. She jumped bail and spent a year in Europe. While there, she visited a birth control clinic in Holland, where women were being fitted with a new type of diaphragm, and she later imported this diaphragm into the United States.

Sanger returned to the United States in 1915 to face the charges against her, hoping to make her trial into a showcase for the birth control cause. The charges were dropped, however, because of widespread public sympathy for Sanger—especially because her only daughter had died that same year. She therefore went on a national lecture tour to promote birth control and was arrested in several cities.

In October of 1916 Sanger opened the country's first birth control clinic, the Brownsville Clinic in Brooklyn, New York. The police closed it down after just nine days of operation. Sanger was arrested and, because she refused to pay a fine, spent 30 days in prison. While in prison she taught contraceptive methods to other inmates.

The Brownsville affair drew widespread sympathy and financial support to her cause. Although she lost the appeal of her conviction, the appellate court did rule that physicians could provide contraceptive information for medical reasons. This ruling allowed Sanger's group to open a doctor-staffed birth control clinic, and others followed. In 1917 Sanger began publication of a monthly, the *Birth Control Review,* and in 1921 she founded the

American Birth Control League, forerunner of the Planned Parenthood Federation.

During the 1920s Sanger broadened her arguments for birth control, including some ideas that were espoused by eugenicists. She advocated the involuntary sterilization of the intellectually disabled as well as measures to decrease the reproduction rate of various social

Food and Drug Administration approved the first contraceptive pill.

Sanger died in 1965, just a few months after the U.S. Supreme Court, in *Griswold v. Connecticut,* declared that married couples had the right to use birth control. Despite her misguided eugenicist views, Sanger's life and work were important, not just for her achievements

Margaret Sanger (1879–1966) (seated, center) and staff of the American Birth Control League, circa 1921

groups that she considered "unfit." Eventually, Sanger was perceived as too radical for the movement she had started. She resigned the presidency of the American Birth Control League in 1928 and thereafter gradually gave up her role as leader of the birth control movement in the United States. After the Second World War, however, she came out of retirement to help found the International Planned Parenthood Federation, and she served as its president from 1952 to 1959.

Sanger was always trying to find improved birth control techniques. After sex steroids were synthesized, she arranged for funding to support research into hormone-based contraceptives—research that paid off in 1960 when the

in the area of birth control, but because she set an example of nonviolent direct action in the service of social progress—an example that was followed by many other movements later in the twentieth century.

In Britain, Marie Stopes (1880–1958) had a career quite comparable to that of Sanger. Her sex manual, *Married Love,* caused enormous controversy on its publication in 1918. She opened Britain's first birth control clinic in 1921. The organization named for her, Marie Stopes International, now provides reproductive health services in 38 countries.

Sources: Margaret Sanger Papers Project, 2000; Planned Parenthood Federation, 2000.

Ideally, couples who engage in sex will cooperate to ensure that pregnancy doesn't occur, but a self-reliant method, or one that is evident in use, may allay concerns about a partner's reliability.

options in Canada are quite similar to those in the United States (Fisher & Black, 2007). Here are the main issues that people who are choosing a contraceptive technique should consider.

- *How reliable is the method?* With some methods, such as oral contraceptives, fewer than 1% of users will become pregnant in a single year, provided they practice the method properly. This percentage is called the **perfect-use failure rate** of the method. All humans are fallible, however; for example, a woman may forget to take the pill for a day or two, or a man's fingernail might tear a condom while he is putting it on. Thus the **typical-use failure rates** of contraceptive methods tend to be higher—about 6% for the pill. Only a few methods have typical-use failure rates below 1%; these are methods that you can basically forget about once you have taken the initial steps. We summarize information about usage and reliability of the most common methods of contraception in **Table 12.1**.

- *How safe is it for me?* We describe any risks associated with the various methods listed below. Individual users may have risk factors that make specific methods inadvisable for them.

- *Do I need the method to be reversible?* For most young people the answer is yes, but for older adults who are certain they don't want more children, irreversible methods (sterilization) may be preferable.

- *Do I need STD protection?* The STD protection offered by condoms is an important added advantage, especially for women and men who are not in long-term monogamous relationships. Of course, condoms can be used in combination with methods that don't offer STD protection, such as pills.

- *How easy is the method for me to use?* Some methods, such as condoms, require some time and attention before or during every sexual encounter. Some methods require taking pills on a rather precise schedule. Some require regular visits to a healthcare provider. How burdensome these requirements are depends on your individual circumstances and personality.

- *How much will it cost?* Some methods require substantial upfront expenditure, some require continual purchases over time, and some are free or nearly so.

- *Will I be in control?* For some users, it may be important to be in charge of the contraception method, rather than leaving the responsibility to potentially unreliable partners.

Physical Methods Block Sperm Transport

We begin with reversible physical methods, some of which have a long history of safe and successful use.

Male Condoms Are Reliable When Properly Used

The **male condom (Figure 12.3)** is a disposable sheath that is placed over the penis before coitus. It works simply by preventing semen from entering the vagina; thus it is described as a **barrier method** of contraception. Some condoms come precoated with the spermicide nonoxynol-9, which kills sperm chemically. The amount of spermicide on coated condoms is probably not enough to be effective

perfect-use failure rate The percentage of women using a contraceptive technique correctly who will become pregnant in a year.

typical-use failure rate The percentage of women using a contraceptive technique with a typical degree of care who will become pregnant in a year.

male condom A sheath placed over the penis as a contraceptive and/or to prevent disease transmission.

barrier method Any contraceptive technique in which a physical barrier, such as condom or diaphragm, prevents sperm from reaching the ovum.

TABLE 12.1

Usage and Failure Rates of the Most Common Contraceptive Techniques

Method	Usage (percentage of all contraceptive users who use this method)[a]	Failure rate (percentage of women using this method who become pregnant in 1 year)	
		With perfect use	With typical use
No method	10.7	85.0	85.0
Physical methods			
Male condom	17.9	2.0	15.0
Female condom	—	5.0	21.0
Diaphragm	0.3	6.0	16.0
Cervical cap[b]	—	18.0	24.0
IUD	2.0		
Paragard (Copper-T)		0.6	0.8
Mirena		0.2	0.2
Spermicides			
Sponge[b]	—	9.0	16.0
Other	—	18.0	29.0
Hormone-based methods			
Pill	30.5	0.3	8.0
Injection (Depo-Provera)	5.3	0.3	3.0
Implant	1.3	0.05	0.05
Patch[c]	—	0.3	8.0
NuvaRing[c]	—	0.3	8.0
Behavioral methods[d]			
Periodic abstinence	1.2	1.0 – 9.0	25.0
Withdrawal	4.0	4.0	27.0
Sterilization			
Male	9.2	0.1	0.1
Female	27.0	0.5	0.5

Source: Guttmacher Institute, 2005; Trussel, 2007.

[a]Where not listed, usage is small or unknown.

[b]For these methods, failure rates are higher for women who have already had a child.

[c]Typical-use failure rates for the patch and the NuvaRing are estimates.

[d]Failure rates for behavioral methods are estimates.

in the event that the condom breaks, however, and the presence of the spermicide shortens the shelf life of the condom and increases its cost. In addition, as discussed later in this chapter, the frequent use of spermicides can cause health problems for the woman. For all these reasons, spermicide-coated condoms are not recommended.

Most condoms are made of latex. Some are made of polyurethane plastic, and some of animal intestinal tissue. Latex condoms are the cheapest: They cost less than $0.50 apiece when bought in multipacks, and several programs distribute them free. When used properly (**Figure 12.4**), they are an effective contraceptive, and they also provide substantial protection against transmission of STDs, including HIV. Condoms should be used in conjunction with water-based or silicone lubricants only. Oils, fats, lotions, petroleum jellies, and

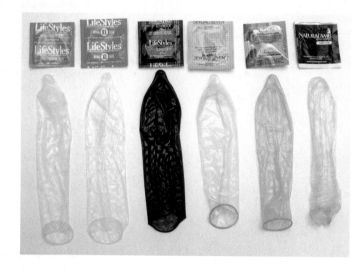

Figure 12.3 Male condoms come in a variety of types, sizes, and even flavors.

Figure 12.4 How to use a condom
These are the instructions recommended by an expert committee of the World Health Organization. (Warner and Steiner, 2007.)

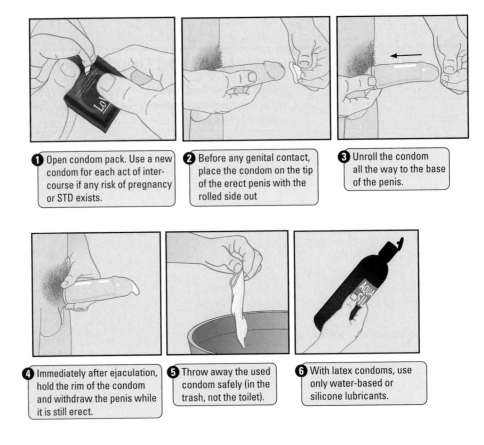

❶ Open condom pack. Use a new condom for each act of intercourse if any risk of pregnancy or STD exists.

❷ Before any genital contact, place the condom on the tip of the erect penis with the rolled side out

❸ Unroll the condom all the way to the base of the penis.

❹ Immediately after ejaculation, hold the rim of the condom and withdraw the penis while it is still erect.

❺ Throw away the used condom safely (in the trash, not the toilet).

❻ With latex condoms, use only water-based or silicone lubricants.

any lubricants containing those substances will weaken the latex and may cause the condom to break.

Some men and women are allergic to latex. Another potential disadvantage of latex condoms is that they may lessen the sensations of coitus, especially for the man. In fact, as many as 33% of young men experience erection difficulties when using a condom, either because of the lessened sensation or because of the tightness of the condom, and this is a common reason why men don't use condoms consistently (Graham et al., 2006). For men who tend to ejaculate earlier than they want to, on the other hand, the decreased sensation can be an advantage.

If any of these factors discourage the use of latex condoms, polyurethane or natural-tissue condoms can be tried. Both of these are more than twice as expensive as latex condoms. The polyurethane condom is thinner and slicker than latex, so it allows more sensation. It lacks the odor and taste of latex, and it is not damaged by oil-based lubricants. It is also less stretchy than latex, which means that it doesn't feel as tight, but it is important to get a well-fitting condom, otherwise it may slip off. It is an effective contraceptive, and its disease-preventing abilities are probably as good as latex condoms.

Natural-tissue condoms are also effective contraceptives, but they are known to be *ineffective* in preventing the transmission of HIV and other viral STDs. That's because they have pores large enough to permit the passage of viruses. Thus, they should be used only if STDs are not a concern.

Condoms come in quite a variety of sizes, styles, colors, and even flavors. A standard-size condom, which measures about 180 mm (7 inches) long by 51 mm (2 inches) across when flat, will fit most men after a fashion, but there are smaller ("snugger fit") and larger ("large," "magnum," "magnum XL") condoms available. There are also condoms whose width is greater near the tip, condoms with various kinds of ribbed or bumpy surfaces, condoms with a skin desensitizer (to delay the man's orgasm), and condoms that glow in the dark. If condoms are going to be a part of your life for the foreseeable future, it may be worth ordering one of the sampler kits that are available on the Internet. These kits contain many different types of condoms from a variety of different manufacturers. (Testing them all could provide material for an interesting term paper.) Just be wary of natural-membrane or novelty condoms that may not provide adequate contraception or disease protection.

Most or all latex condoms meet or exceed international standards for failure-resistance, according to a 2005 study by Consumers Union (Reuters News Service, 2005). The best-performing condom in that study was Durex Extra Sensitive Lubricated Latex, and the worst-performing (but still adequate) condom was one distributed by Planned Parenthood. (Planned Parenthood has since introduced an improved line of condoms.)

Condoms do sometimes break. The reasons include use of old, defective, or inappropriately sized condoms, insufficient lubrication, use of oil-based lubricants, and unusually vigorous sex. Strategies to prevent breakage include inspection of the condom before and during sex, use of plenty of water-soluble lubricant, changing condoms during prolonged coitus, or using thicker condoms.

To get some idea of condom breakage rates under conditions of expert but real-world usage, a group headed by longtime contraceptive expert Robert Hatcher of Emory University interviewed prostitutes in legal brothels in Nevada, where condom usage is legally mandated (Albert et al., 1995). The prostitutes reported breakage rates of about 1 per 1000 usages. They often used doubled-up condoms, with lubricant between to reduce friction—this practice did not lead to condom failure as some guidelines have suggested. When the researchers undertook the noble task of examining the used condoms from 372 sexual encounters at the brothels, they found not a single broken condom. Over a 5-year period, over 20,000 HIV tests were performed on legal Nevada prostitutes, and every single test came back negative. The message is clear: Used correctly, condoms are very reliable.

Advantages of the male condom:

- It is cheap and readily accessible.
- It is reliable when properly used.
- It offers significant protection against STDs and thus helps protect fertility.
- It lacks the possible side effects of hormone-based contraceptives.
- It is fully and immediately reversible.

Disadvantages of the male condom:

- Putting on a male condom can be intrusive during sex because it cannot be put on until the man already has an erection. However, the man and woman can cooperate in putting on the condom, thus incorporating the procedure into the lovemaking process.
- The man must maintain his erection for as long as the condom is in use, so he must withdraw promptly after ejaculating.
- Erotic sensation may be reduced, especially for the man. (An innovative design called the Inspiral has a loose-fitting spiral rib near the tip that improves sensation by generating friction against the penis.)
- Reliability is less than ideal in typical use, mostly because of failure to use condoms consistently. Reliability is highest when both partners are involved in condom use decisions (Crosby et al., 2008).

Figure 12.5 The Reality female condom is made of polyurethane. It is an effective contraceptive but it is not widely used.

Female Condoms Are Relatively Intrusive

The **female condom** (Reality condom, Femidom) is made of polyurethane. It resembles a large, nonelastic male condom, but it is stiffened by rings at each end (**Figure 12.5**). The ring at the closed end lies inside (but is not attached to) the condom; it fits around the cervix rather like a diaphragm (see below). The attached ring at the open end is larger and stays outside the body. Thus the condom covers the entirety of the vagina and adjacent parts of the vulva. The condom comes with lubricant on the inside, and additional lubricant for the outside is supplied with the condom.

To insert the condom, the inner ring is first squeezed between the fingers and then pushed into the vagina with a finger until it can't be felt. This draws most of the condom into the vagina, but the larger end should remain outside. During coitus, the man's penis should be guided into the inside of the condom. After use, the outside end should be twisted to enclose the contents and the condom gently pulled out. This should be done before the woman stands up. As with male condoms, the female condom should be disposed of in the trash, not the toilet.

Reality condoms cost about $3 to $4 each, making them much more expensive than male condoms. They are also harder to find.

Advantages of the female condom:

■ The female condom is the only contraceptive controlled by the woman that probably offers substantial protection from STDs, including HIV. (This statement is based on permeability tests, not real-life clinical trials [Centers for Disease Control, 2002b].) Its disease-preventing action may be even better than that of the male condom because it covers parts of the vulva adjacent to the vagina that may be susceptible to genital warts and other infections.

■ It can be inserted ahead of time, thus avoiding any interruption of lovemaking.

■ It does not require the man to maintain an erection during use.

■ It is easily and immediately reversible.

■ It can be used for anal sex if the inner ring is removed.

Disadvantages of the female condom:

■ Some couples find that the female condom reduces erotic sensation and, in fact, generates nonerotic noises. The female condom tends to be less appealing to men than to women; part of the reason for this is that the protruding free end (which covers part of the vulva) is considered by some unaesthetic.

■ There is the possibility that the man will unwittingly insert his penis into the vagina outside of the condom, thus nullifying its barrier function.

■ Sometimes the entire condom may be drawn into the vagina during coitus. If this happens the condom should be replaced with another. To prevent this occurrence, it is sometimes necessary to hold the outer portion of the condom.

■ Male and female condoms should not be used simultaneously because the friction between them may pull one of them out of place.

Most couples prefer the male condom to the female condom (Macaluso et al., 2000), and the female condom is not widely used in the United States or overseas. Still, its obvious advantages make it well worth a try. Some couples may find that it is quite acceptable, and they may be able to deal with the noise problem by adding extra lubricant. New versions of the female condom, with different designs and made from different materials, are on the horizon and may become available

female condom A plastic pouch inserted into the vagina as a contraceptive and/or to prevent disease transmission.

during the lifetime of this textbook edition (McNeil, 2007b). An acceptable, affordable female condom would be of great help in the battle against AIDS in developing countries, where men sometimes resist using condoms.

Diaphragms and Cervical Caps Are Inconvenient but Have Few Side Effects

The **diaphragm** (**Figure 12.6**) used to be a very popular form of contraception prior to the development of oral contraceptives, but it is now used by fewer than 1 in 50 women. It is a dome-shaped piece of latex or rubber that is stiffened by a rubber-covered metal spring or strip around its perimeter. It fits against the walls of the vagina, covering the cervix. It works by preventing sperm from entering the cervix. However, sperm can migrate around the edges of the diaphragm, and it must therefore be used in conjunction with a spermicidal cream or jelly. Diaphragms, like latex condoms, are damaged by oil-based lubricants (**Box 12.2**).

Figure 12.6 Diaphragms have lost popularity in the United States but are still widely used elsewhere.

Advantages of the diaphragm:

■ It is somewhat less intrusive than condoms because it can be inserted ahead of time and does not usually affect sensation during sex.

■ It is relatively cheap. Although it requires a medical visit for initial fitting, the diaphragm itself costs between $25 and $50 and lasts for a year or two, so the only ongoing expense is for the contraceptive cream.

■ Long-term use of the diaphragm is associated with a lowered risk of cervical cancer, probably because the diaphragm offers some protection against infection of the cervix with human papillomavirus, the virus that causes cervical cancer.

diaphragm A barrier placed over the cervix as a contraceptive.

Lea's shield A type of diaphragm with a one-way valve.

Disadvantages of the diaphragm:

■ It is inconvenient, both because of the necessity for professional fitting and because of the need for insertion, removal, and cleaning.

■ It can occasionally get dislodged during coitus.

■ The diaphragm's failure rate is significantly greater than that of hormone-based methods and even slightly greater than that of condoms. The failure rate is even higher for women who have previously given birth.

■ It provides much less disease protection than condoms.

■ The spermicide may cause irritation, which may increase the risk of STD transmission.

■ Some women find that they develop urinary tract infections with diaphragm use.

A new diaphragm, the **Lea's Shield**, was approved by the FDA in 2002 (**Figure 12.7**). This silicone rubber device incorporates a one-way valve. This valve lets trapped air escape from behind it, thus helping the device form a close seal against the cervix, and it also allows for passage of cervical mucus. An important feature of Lea's

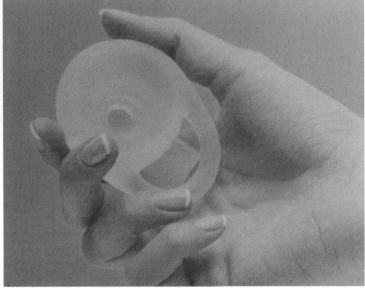

Figure 12.7 Lea's Shield is a silicone diaphragm with a central valve and a loop-like handle.

Sexual Health

BOX 12.2 How to Use a Diaphragm

The keys to successful use of a diaphragm are selection of the appropriately sized diaphragm (done by a experienced professional), proper timing of insertion and removal, correct use of spermicide, correct placement, and care and regular inspection of the diaphragm.

The diaphragm can be inserted immediately before coitus or up to 6 hours earlier. If inserted more than 2 hours prior to sex, however, the contraceptive cream may dissipate, reducing its effectiveness.

Before insertion, empty your bladder. Place about a teaspoonful of contraceptive cream or jelly in the center of the hollow side of the diaphragm, and spread it around so that it covers that side and also the rim. Do not use Vaseline or any oil-based lubricant: These are ineffective and can damage the diaphragm.

Find a comfortable position for inserting the diaphragm. Fold the diaphragm between thumb and fingers, but not so tightly as to squeeze out the spermicide. Push it far up into the vagina so that the upper part of the rim lodges in the hollow beyond the cervix. With your index finger, push the front part of the rim until it sits snugly behind the pubic bone. Use your finger to check that the diaphragm is lying snugly against the cervix.

Between inserting the diaphragm and having sex you can pursue regular activities, go to the toilet, etc., and the diaphragm will stay in place. If you have a bowel movement, wash your hands thoroughly and then recheck that the diaphragm remains properly located.

Repeated coitus can occur without removing or replacing the diaphragm, but more spermicide should first be inserted outside the diaphragm with the aid of an applicator. The diaphragm must be left in place for at least 6 hours after coitus, but no more than 24 hours, since doing so may raise the risk of toxic shock syndrome.

Male condoms can be used in conjunction with a diaphragm. This helps reduce the failure rate, and it is a particularly good idea while you are learning how to use the diaphragm. The use of a condom also greatly increases protection from sexually transmitted diseases.

To remove the diaphragm, lift the front rim away from the cervix with your index finger and pull it away, following the direction of the floor of the vagina. It helps to bear down gently while doing so.

Wash the diaphragm with mild soap, rinse it thoroughly, dry it completely, and, by holding the diaphragm up to the light, check it visually for holes or other damage. Dust the diaphragm with cornstarch, and store it in its container in a place that is protected from heat.

Have the fitting rechecked by a professional within a few weeks if you have only recently begun having sex. Otherwise, have it rechecked if you have gained or lost 4.5 kg (10 pounds) or have been pregnant, or in conjunction with an annual health examination.

1 Put spermicidal cream or jelly around the rim of the diaphragm and in the center of the hollow side.

2 Fold the diaphragm.

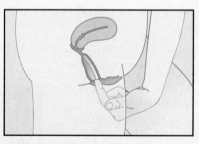

3 Insert the diaphragm, hollow side up, and push it into the vagina.

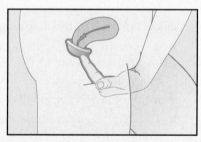

4 Feel with a finger to make sure that the diaphragm is properly covering the cervix.

shield is that one size fits all. For that reason it is sold over the counter in some countries, though not yet in the United States. The prescribing clinician will usually check that the woman has learned to place the shield correctly. Testing so far suggests that Lea's Shield is about as reliable as a regular diaphragm, or possibly more effective in women who have not had a prior pregnancy. It has a rather short usable life, however—about 6 months.

The **cervical cap** (**Figure 12.8**) is smaller and more steeply domed than the diaphragm. It is held in place not by fitting against the walls of the vagina, but by holding like a suction cup onto the cervix itself. Like the diaphragm, it must be prescribed and individually fitted. Spermicide is placed inside the cap; it is then

cervical cap A small rubber or plastic cap that adheres by suction to the cervix, used as a contraceptive.

folded and inserted like a diaphragm. After insertion, the woman feels with a finger to ensure that it is sitting right on the cervix. Like the diaphragm, the cap can be inserted an hour or two before intercourse and must be left in place for at least 6 hours afterward, but it can be left in place for as long as 48 hours in total. More spermicide should be inserted, without removing the cap, before each repeated act of intercourse. The advantages and disadvantages of the cervical cap are similar to those of the diaphragm, but there are some differences:

Advantage of the cervical cap (compared with the diaphragm):

■ The cervical cap is an alternative to the diaphragm for women whose vaginal anatomy makes a diaphragm difficult to fit.

Disadvantages of the cervical cap (compared with the diaphragm):

■ Its failure rate is somewhat higher than that of the diaphragm, especially in women who have had children.

■ It is somewhat more difficult to insert properly.

■ Even if properly inserted, it can be dislodged from the cervix during coitus.

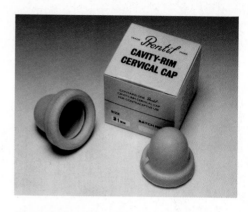

Figure 12.8 The cervical cap holds onto the cervix by suction. Like the diaphragm, it must be used in conjunction with spermicide. (Photo courtesy of Cervical Cap Ltd.)

A variant of the traditional cervical cap, the **FemCap**, was approved by the FDA in 2003 (**Figure 12.9**). It is a silicone rubber device shaped like a sailor's cap, with a dome and a raised brim. It also has a strap to aid in removal. The raised brim is designed to lie snugly against the walls of the vagina, thus deflecting sperm toward the groove between the brim and the dome, where they encounter spermicide. To assist the snug fit, the FemCap comes in three sizes. Even so, typical-use failure rates range from 14% to 29%—the higher numbers applying to women who have previously delivered a baby. A number of women experience problems with insertion or removal of the cap or find that its presence causes discomfort (Mauck et al., 2006).

In general, diaphragms and cervical caps may be good options for women who need to be in charge of their own contraception but cannot or do not want to use hormone-based methods.

FemCap A type of cervical cap that has a raised brim.

spermicide A chemical that kills sperm, available as a contraceptive in a variety of forms, such as foams, creams, and suppositories.

Spermicides Are Not Very Reliable When Used Alone

Some women use **spermicides** as their sole method of contraception. Spermicides are sperm-killing chemicals, most commonly nonoxynol-9, that destroy sperm with a detergent-like action that disrupts their cell membranes. Spermicides come in the form of contraceptive foams, jellies, creams, suppositories ("inserts"), sponges, or dissolvable films (**Figure 12.10**). They are placed deep in the vagina no more than 2 hours ahead of time (and preferably much closer to the time of coitus). Suppositories need time to dissolve, so they should be inserted at least 10 minutes before coitus. All spermicides must be left in place for at least 6 hours afterward in order to complete the killing of sperm; therefore, the woman should not rinse out her vagina during this time. If a woman has coitus again during this 6-hour period, she must insert more spermicide before each act.

One spermicide contraceptive, the Today sponge, sits against the cervix like a diaphragm and thus presents a partial physical barrier in addition to releasing spermicide. It is said to be effective for multiple acts of intercourse over 24 hours.

Advantages of spermicides:

■ They are readily available without a prescription.

■ They are inexpensive.

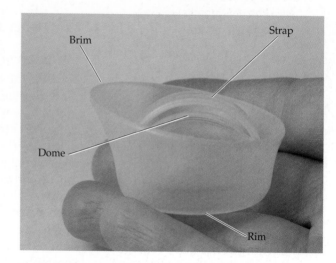

Figure 12.9 The FemCap has a dome that fits over the cervix and a raised brim that lies against the walls of the vagina.

(A)

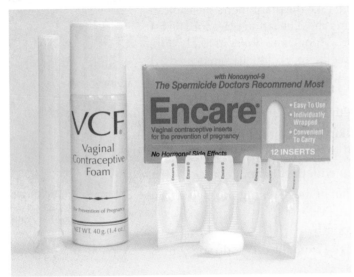

(B)

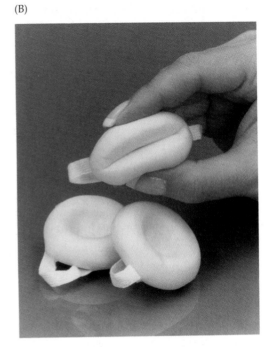

Figure 12.10 Spermicides come in a variety of forms. Vaginal contraceptive foam and Encare inserts (A) and the Today sponge (B) contain the spermicide nonoxynol-9. (B photo courtesy of Allendale Pharmaceuticals, Inc.)

■ They have few side effects, except in the case of allergic reactions and irritation, which is mostly associated with frequent use.

Disadvantages of spermicides:

■ Spermicides can hardly be recommended as the sole means of contraception because their failure rate is quite high—about 25% for the foams and possibly higher for the suppositories. They are better suited for use in combination with barrier methods. The Today sponge may be a little better, with a reported 15% to 19% failure rate in typical use.

■ Spermicides, used alone, offer no significant protection against several sexually transmitted diseases, including gonorrhea, chlamydia, and HIV. In fact, frequent use of spermicides (more than twice a day) can cause genital irritation or lesions, thus increasing the likelihood of acquiring or transmitting HIV and other infections (Centers for Disease Control, 2002).

Intrauterine Devices Require Little Attention

Intrauterine devices (IUDs) are plastic objects, often in the shape of a T, that are placed in the uterus. Their mechanism of action is not fully understood. They probably work by causing a low-grade inflammation of the uterus that interferes with sperm transport (Grimes, 2007). Some IUDs also release progestins; we will discuss the contraceptive action of progestins in the section on hormone-based contraceptives below.

Currently, only two models of IUDs are available in the United States: the **Para-Gard** (also called the "Copper-T") and the **Mirena**. Fewer than 1% of American women use IUDs, but they are much more popular elsewhere: An estimated 85 million women use them worldwide, and nearly all users are very satisfied with them. IUDs have a unique combination of features that makes them well worth considering.

An IUD must be inserted by a trained health care professional. It is passed through the cervix while folded up inside an inserter; once it is in the uterus, the

intrauterine device (IUD) A device placed in the uterus as a contraceptive.

Paragard A copper-containing IUD.

Mirena A hormone-releasing IUD.

(A) (B)

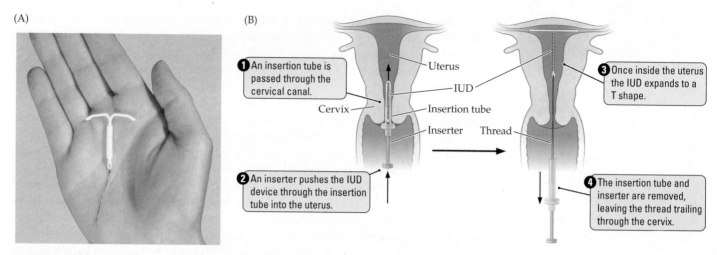

Figure 12.11 IUD insertion (A) The Mirena IUD. (B) Insertion of the ParaGard IUD. The Mirena is inserted in a similar way.

inserter is removed, and the IUD unfolds (**Figure 12.11**). A plastic thread, attached to the bottom of the T, is left trailing through the cervix. Every month after her period the woman or her partner must ensure the thread is in place and that no part of the IUD itself has moved down into the vagina. The thread also helps in the removal of the IUD, which is done by a professional. (Women should never attempt to remove their own IUDs.) The ParaGard can be left in place for up to 12 years. The Mirena, which releases a progestin, lasts for 5 years.

Advantages of the IUD:

■ Both the ParaGard and the Mirena IUDs are highly effective; in fact, they are nearly as effective as female sterilization.

■ There are few side effects and no systemic hormonal side effects, even with the hormone-releasing Mirena.

■ Once inserted, IUDs are convenient and nonintrusive, requiring only the monthly thread check.

■ With the Mirena, menstrual cramping and bleeding may be reduced and sometimes abolished altogether.

■ IUD contraception is reversible immediately on removal of the device (but see below).

■ For reasons that are not well understood, IUDs offer significant protection against endometrial cancer (Hubacher & Grimes, 2002).

Disadvantages of the IUD:

■ The one-time costs are fairly high—$200 to $600. But there are no ongoing costs, unless condoms are added for disease prevention. A user would save money, compared with even the cheapest contraceptive pills, after only about 2 years of use.

■ Some cramping and irregular bleeding may occur, but these symptoms usually go away after a short period of use. With the ParaGard, menstrual flows may be increased.

■ IUDs offer no protection against STDs.

■ IUDs increase the risk of ectopic pregnancy (see Chapter 11). Women who are at increased risk of ectopic pregnancy for any reason should not use an IUD.

For women who have an STD while an IUD is in place, the IUD may increase the likelihood of pelvic inflammatory disease (PID) or worsen a preexisting disease. PID can damage the oviducts and lead to infertility. For this reason, some experts are reluctant to recommend IUDs for young women who have not had children. Still, the likelihood of IUD use leading to infertility is very small. In fact, a large-scale study conducted in Mexico found no association between the use of copper IUDs and damage to the oviducts (Hubacher et al., 2001). Women who currently have an STD or pelvic inflammatory disease should not receive an IUD, and women who are at increased risk of acquiring STDs because they have multiple sex partners are also advised against using this form of contraception.

Couples who have had children and are thinking about sterilization may want to consider an IUD: It is reversible, less invasive, less expensive, and nearly as effective. IUDs may also be a suitable way to extend the intervals between pregnancies. Even young women who have not had children may want to consider trying an IUD. The slightly increased risk of PID may be balanced by the health and psychological benefits of greater contraceptive efficacy compared with barrier methods or oral contraceptives. In short, the IUD is a form of contraception that deserves to be more popular in the United States than it currently is—especially for women whose STD risk is low because they are in a monogamous relationship.

Hormone-Based Methods Are Easy to Use

A variety of hormonal contraceptive methods are available. They differ in the kinds and amounts of hormones they contain as well as in their form of delivery. Because oral contraceptives (pills) are so popular—they are the choice of more than 1 in 4 women who use any kind of contraception—and because they come in a number of significantly different formulations, we will devote most of our attention to them.

constant-dose combination pill An oral contraceptive regimen in which all pills (except any dummy pills) contain the same drug dosage.

Contraceptive pills (**Figure 12.12**) contain either a combination of two hormones—an estrogen and a progestin—or just one hormone, a progestin. Both hormones are synthetic. Synthetic steroids are used because they are broken down in the body much more slowly than the natural hormones, so that the pills need be taken only once a day. Nearly 4 in 10 of all undergraduate college women use contraceptive pills. They typically pay $20 to $30 for a month's supply through student health centers (Associated Press, 2007a), but discount pharmacies such as Wal-Mart and Target offer them for as little as $9 per month in many states.

Combination Pills Offer Health Benefits

The most commonly used type of contraceptive pill is the **constant-dose** (or "monophasic") **combination pill** (Nelson, 2007). Such pills, of which there are many different brands as well as generic versions, usually contain between 20 and 50 mcg of estrogen and between 0.1 and 1.0 mg of progestin. (Part of the reason for the varying progestin doses is that progestins vary in potency: 0.1 mg of one may be the equivalent of 1.0 mg of another.) Typically, a woman takes one pill a day for 21 days, followed by no pills or inactive

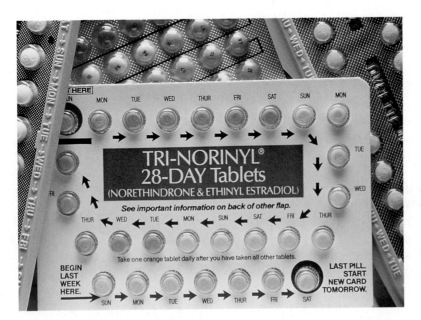

Figure 12.12 A variety of combination contraceptive pills in 28-day dispensers. Note the orange dummy pills for the 7 no-drug days, seen at the bottom of the photograph.

"dummy" pills for 7 days. Some formulations that contain very low doses of hormones shorten the drug-free interval to 4 or even 2 days. It is expected that additional brands of constant-dose pills will switch to a shorter drug-free interval in the future.

A second, more recent kind of combination pill is the **triphasic** (or "multiphasic") **combination pill** (examples are Ortho-Novum 7/7/7, and Tri-Norinyl). In these pills, the amounts and ratios of estrogen and progestin vary around the cycle, the idea being to minimize the total doses of hormones and decrease side effects. As with most constant-dose pills, triphasic regimens involve a 7-day drug-free interval. Triphasic pills are more expensive than constant-dose pills.

One site of action of combination pills is the brain—specifically, the hypothalamic–pituitary control system (see Chapter 5). The progestin component of the pill exerts a negative feedback on the hypothalamus and pituitary gland, decreasing the secretion of follicle stimulating hormone (FSH). The estrogen component augments this effect by increasing the levels of progestin receptors. It also has an FSH-suppressing effect of its own. Because FSH is suppressed, the FSH-dependent maturation of ovarian follicles does not occur; therefore, there is no ovulation. This suppression of ovulation is the main route by which the combination pill prevents pregnancy. A second site of action is the uterus: The hormones in combination pills cause the cervix to secrete thick mucus that prevents sperm from entering the uterus.

Combination pills also cause development of the endometrium as would happen naturally during the postovulatory phase of the menstrual cycle. During the drug-free portion of the cycle, therefore, the endometrium breaks down and bleeding occurs. This bleeding simulates a natural menstrual period, although the menstrual flow may be less than a woman normally experiences.

Ovarian follicles develop during the drug-free interval, just as they do during the early days of a normal menstrual cycle. A woman is just as well protected from pregnancy during the drug-free days as during the rest of the cycle, because the further development of these follicles is suppressed as soon as the next cycle of pills begins. If a woman forgets to begin the next cycle of pills, however, the developing follicles can proceed to ovulation within a couple of days or so, potentially leading to pregnancy. Thus, if she is in doubt about the number of drug-free days that have elapsed, a woman does better to restart the cycle too early rather than too late.

Many physicians prefer to prescribe pills containing as little estrogen as possible (i.e., 20 mcg or thereabouts) because it is primarily the estrogen in combination pills that is responsible for the health risks associated with these products (see below). Low-estrogen combination pills are as effective in preventing pregnancy as are higher-estrogen products. They do not always regulate the woman's menstrual cycle as effectively, however, and this can be a reason why some women discontinue low-estrogen combination pills (Thorneycroft & Cariati, 2001).

Advantages of combination pills:

■ With perfect use, combination pills are extremely reliable: Less than 1% of women correctly using combination pills will become pregnant per year. Unfortunately, it is easy to forget a pill or two. In fact, one group of researchers who installed electronic sensors in women's pill boxes found that about half the women forgot to take three or more pills per cycle (Potter et al., 1996). Thus, the typical-use failure rate is about 8%—significantly better than condoms or behavioral methods, but significantly worse than sterilization or the IUD. Remember, though, that a woman doesn't have to be "typical": She can come close to "perfection" by planning her pill-taking schedule carefully or by adding condoms to the mix.

triphasic combination pill An oral contraceptive regimen that varies the doses of estrogens and progestins around the menstrual cycle.

FAQ Is it safe to take St. John's wort while on the contraceptive pill?
No. St. John's wort, an unregulated botanical, accelerates the breakdown of the pill's ingredients in the body and may therefore raise the likelihood of pregnancy.

- They are convenient and neither interfere with the spontaneity of sex nor diminish the sensations of coitus.

- They are easily reversible. Fertility should return to normal levels by 3 months after stopping the combination pill. (If the woman doesn't wish to become pregnant, she should use an alternative contraceptive technique immediately after stopping the pill.)

- They have very significant health benefits quite aside from the avoidance of pregnancy (which is a health benefit in itself). Use of combination pills for 10 years is associated with an 80% reduction in the risk of both ovarian and endometrial cancer, and this reduced risk persists for at least 20 years after stopping pill usage. Many women experience lighter menstrual flows and diminished or absent menstrual cramps, premenstrual symptoms*, and mid-cycle pain when on the pill. Pill usage also reduces the prevalence or severity of iron-deficiency anemia, endometriosis, ovarian cysts, noncancerous conditions of the breast, acne, and hirsutism (excessive facial and body hair). The health benefits of contraceptive pills can be so great, for many women, that some experts recommend their use even by women who don't need contraception.

Disadvantages of combination pills:

- They offer no protection against STDs, including HIV. (However, condoms can be added for disease protection.)

- The woman needs to remember to take the pills regularly each day.

- The method is not evident to the woman's partner unless he is present every day when she takes the pill. Thus he has no objective assurance that effective contraception is being practiced.

- The combination pill can have several side effects, some of them serious or, in rare instances, fatal. Frequently reported side effects include nausea, breast pain, increased breast size, irregular bleeding, abdominal pain, back pain, decreased vaginal lubrication, weight gain, blotchy discoloration of the skin, emotional lability (for example, crying for little reason) or depression, and decreased or increased interest in sex. In a placebo trial of one triphasic combination pill, however, only breast pain and emotional lability were substantially more frequent in the patients who received the real pill, and even with these two side effects, the differences did not quite reach statistical significance (Redmond et al., 1999). Among the less common but more serious side effects are hypertension (increased blood pressure) and disorders of blood clotting, including coronary thromboses (heart attacks), venous thromboses (clots in large veins), pulmonary embolisms (clots that get carried to the lungs), and strokes (clots or hemorrhages in cerebral arteries). Although these complications are not common, the reality of the increased risk has been well established. The risk for women over 35 who smoke is particularly high, and such women are usually advised not to use combination pills. The warning signs for complications are summarized in the acronym ACHES, which stands for Abdominal pain, Chest pain, Headaches, Eye problems, and Severe Leg Pain. Any of these conditions are reason for a pill user to contact her healthcare provider, as are severe mood swings or depression, yellowing of the skin or eyes, or two missed periods or other signs of pregnancy.

---

*One combination pill, Yaz, is specifically FDA-approved for treatment of premenstrual symptoms, especially psychological ones. Yaz was tested against a placebo, however, not against other combination pills, so it may not in fact be superior to other pills when used for this purpose.

- Method failure (that is, pregnancy) is somewhat more likely in women weighing over 70.5 kg (155 pounds) than in lighter women, especially if they use low-dose pills (Holt et al., 2002).

- Early formulations of the pill, which included high doses of estrogens, moderately increased the risk of breast cancer. Current formulations either have no effect on breast cancer risk or have only a slight effect that is restricted to women under 35. This latter risk, if it exists, is very small because the base rate of breast cancer in young women is so low. Even women who are at high risk of breast cancer because of a family history of the disease do not appear to incur any increased risk if they use combination contraceptive pills (Silvera et al., 2005). Preliminary evidence suggests, however, that women who carry the breast cancer gene BRCA2 (but not BRCA1) may face an increased risk of breast cancer if they use the pill for prolonged periods of time (Haile et al., 2006).

- Combination pills should not be used by nursing mothers because the hormones can reach the baby via the milk.

Continuous Use of Combination Pills Eliminates Menstrual Periods

The standard combination-pill regimen calls for a 7-day drug-free interval every month, which allows for withdrawal bleeding akin to a menstrual period. The only function of a menstrual period, however, is to prepare the woman's uterus to receive and transport sperm. If pregnancy is not desired, menstrual periods offer no known health benefit and in fact present health concerns such as menstrual pain, premenstrual symptoms, and iron-deficiency anemia in some women.

For many years, therefore, some physicians have prescribed combination pills in such a way as to provide a drug-free interval only once every 2 months, once every 3 months, or never (Nelson, 2000). Such "off-label" prescribing is done to increase the pill's efficacy and to eliminate the menstrual period and the symptoms associated with it.

A new preparation, **Seasonale**, was approved in 2003. A woman takes this pill continuously for 12 weeks, followed by a 7-day drug-free interval, and so on. Thus she experiences four menstrual periods per year instead of thirteen. A slightly different version, **Seasonique**, contains the same drugs except that the pills taken during the 7-day interval contain a low dose of estrogen rather than being completely inert. Yet another recently introduced pill, **Lybrel** (Anya in Canada and Britain), contains the same drug combination as Seasonale or Seasonique, but at lower doses. Lybrel is packaged for continuous year-round use with no drug-free intervals at all. The FDA's approval of these drugs signals the agency's blessing of planned menstrual suppression in healthy women.

The main advantage of these **extended-use regimens** is the reduction in the number of menstrual periods, which should be a major benefit to women who have menstrual problems. On the other hand, there are potential disadvantages. For one thing, Seasonale, Seasonique, and Lybrel are expensive. With the advice of her doctor, a woman might be able to get the same benefit from an appropriate regimen of much cheaper, generic contraceptive pills.

More significantly, irregular spotting or breakthrough bleeding is common, especially in the early months of use, and can sometimes be quite severe. Also, a woman's total number of days of exposure to estrogen is greater than with conventional combination pills because of the reduced number (or total lack of) drug-free days. However, there is no clear evidence for differences in health risks, health benefits, or contraceptive reliability between extended-use and conventional combination pills.

As a 37-year-old smoker, this woman faces a relatively high risk of experiencing serious side effects if she uses combination contraceptive pills.

Seasonale An extended-use contraceptive pill.

Seasonique An extended-use contraceptive pill.

Lybrel A contraceptive pill designed for complete elimination of menstrual periods.

extended-use regimen A regimen of contraceptive pills that allows for fewer or no menstrual periods.

progestin-only pill An oral contraceptive that contains progestin but no estrogen. Also called the "mini-pill."

Progestin-Only Pills Have Fewer Side Effects

The **progestin-only pill** contains a very low dose of a progestin and no estrogen. A brand called Ortho Micronor, for example, contains just 0.35 mg of the progestin norethindrone. Compare that with the 1.0 mg of norethindrone, plus an estrogen, in the combination pill Ortho-Novum 1/35 and its generic equivalents. How can a pill that contains so much less of an active ingredient have a reliable contraceptive effect? And if it does, why don't the combination pills go out of business? The answer is that the progestin-only pill works differently from the combination pill, requires greater care in use, and has some unique side effects.

The progestin-only pill does not reliably shut down ovulation, although it does do so in some women. It works mainly through its effect on the cervical mucus, making it viscous (thick) and hostile to sperm transport. It may also make the endometrium hostile to implantation. These actions of progestin require lower doses than its actions on the hypothalamus and do not require the presence of estrogens.

The effects of each progestin-only pill last a very short time—barely 24 hours. Therefore, a woman who uses this method of contraception must be very careful not to miss a dose, or even to delay a dose by more than a few hours. There is no 7-day drug holiday every month, as with the combination pill: The progestin-only pill must be taken every single day for as long as contraception is required.

With perfect use, the progestin-only pill is just as reliable as the combination pill. There is a widespread assumption that it is less reliable in typical use because of the requirement for accurately timed dosing. This has not been documented in clinical trials, however (Raymond, 2007).

Many of the advantages and disadvantages of progestin-only pills are similar to those of combination pills. Here we compare the two kinds of pills.

Advantages of progestin-only pills:

- Progestin-only pills lack the estrogenic side effects of combination pills (although weight gain can still be a problem). They are a good alternative for women who experience serious side effects with the combination pill or who fall in risk groups for which the combination pill is contraindicated.
- Progestin-only pills can be used by mothers who are breast-feeding their infants, beginning 6 weeks after birth.

Disadvantages of progestin-only pills:

- Unlike the combination pill, the progestin-only pill tends to disrupt the menstrual cycles of women who were previously quite regular. In fact, irregular bleeding and spotting are reasons some women discontinue this form of contraception. This effect is highly variable from woman to woman, however, and does not have major health consequences so long as total blood loss is not increased. Plenty of women continue to have regular menstrual cycles while using progestin-only pills—presumably, these are women in whom the pill does not suppress ovulation.

Given the wide variety of contraceptive pills available—with more coming on the market all the time—a woman who is considering this form of contraception should consult with a knowledgeable professional who can recommend a pill suited to her needs and who can suggest appropriate changes if side effects crop up. Because a woman may be taking birth control pills for years, it is important that she keeps herself well-informed to ensure that she is taking the one best suited to her.

FAQ I missed taking a pill—what should I do?
Take the missed pill right away even if it means taking two on one day. If you're on progestin-only pills, abstain from coitus or use an alternative contraceptive method for 48 hours. Planned Parenthood's Web site has more information.

Hormones Can Be Administered by Non-Oral Routes

We now shift our attention to hormone-based contraceptives that are administered by some route other than by mouth. The methods we consider depend entirely on the slow release of hormones from some kind of "depot"—a reservoir or store that is inside or outside of the woman's body. The general advantage of non-oral over oral contraceptives is that they don't require taking a pill every day. Most women on the pill forget to take it from time to time, and this fact makes non-oral hormonal contraceptives more reliable in typical use.

A general disadvantage of the non-oral methods is that they have been in use for a much shorter time than the pill, so their reliability and possible long-term effects (whether beneficial or harmful) have not been as thoroughly researched. It's reassuring that the hormones used are generally similar to those in contraceptive pills, but non-oral administration does introduce some functional differences. For example, the rate of drug delivery is usually more constant than with a once-a-day pill, and the drug does not pass through the liver before reaching the rest of the body as happens with pills. These differences could affect the cumulative drug load experienced by hormone-sensitive tissues.

Depo-Provera Lasts Three Months

The contraceptive **Depo-Provera** is administered by intramuscular injection or (in a different formulation called **Depo-SubQ Provera**) by subcutaneous injection (Goldberg & Grimes, 2007). Depo-Provera is a slow-release (depot) form of a progestin, medroyxprogesterone acetate (**Figure 12.13**). A single Depo-Provera injection provides contraception for 3 months. Costs vary by provider, but a year's contraception can cost somewhere between $200 and $300, which is roughly comparable to the annual cost of an oral contraceptive. The subcutaneous formulation can be self-injected, which may save on medical costs.

Depo-Provera is usually administered within a few days of the onset of menstruation to ensure that the woman is not pregnant. Repeat injections should not be delayed more than 2 weeks beyond the 3-month approved period, or pregnancy may occur.

Initially, a woman who uses Depo-Provera may experience irregular bleeding. After a year of use, however, at least 50% of women experience complete cessation of menstruation. Some women consider this a worrisome side effect, while others consider it a convenience.

Advantages of Depo-Provera:

- With a typical-use failure rate of 3%, Depo-Provera is more reliable than contraceptive pills. Failures are almost always caused by neglecting to get injections on time—something that a conscientious woman should be able to avoid.

- It doesn't require the user to do anything aside from getting the injections. Teenagers can easily conceal their use of Depo-Provera from their parents, if that should be necessary.

- As with progestin-only pills, the lack of an estrogen component may make it safer for some women.

- The eventual cessation of menstrual periods may appeal to women with menstrual problems.

Disadvantages of Depo-Provera:

- The repeated medical visits may be burdensome to some women.

- Depo-Provera offers no protection against STDs.

Depo-Provera An injectable form of medroxyprogesterone acetate, used as a contraceptive in women or to decrease the sex drive in male sex offenders.

Depo-SubQ Provera A form of Depo-Provera designed for subcutaneous injection.

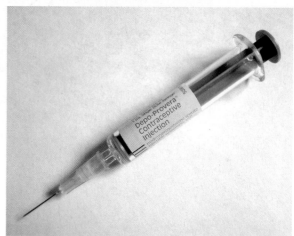

Figure 12.13 Depo-Provera is an injectable progestin that provides three months' contraceptive protection.

Ortho Evra   A contraceptive patch.

- Irregular, sometimes prolonged bleeding is a common problem, especially in the early months of use. Approximately 20% to 25% of women discontinue Depo-Provera during the first year for this reason. Less common side effects can include loss of sex drive, depression, liver damage, weight gain, acne, and hair loss.

- Once injected, Depo-Provera cannot be removed, so if side effects occur it may take 3 months for them to go away.

- Although Depo-Provera is a fully reversible contraceptive, it may take as long as a year for a woman to return to full fertility after discontinuing the injections.

- Some women experience a loss of bone density while on Depo-Provera. Bone density increases again after a woman stops use of Depo-Provera; it's uncertain whether this recovery is complete, however, especially for adolescents. Women who are on Depo-Provera should make sure they are getting adequate calcium in their diet or via supplements. Because of this risk, the FDA discourages the use of Depo-Provera for more than about 2 years unless other birth control methods are unsatisfactory (Pfizer, 2004).

Transdermal Patches Last a Week

Transdermal patches look like large square Band-Aids, but they contain a hormonal contraceptive that diffuses slowly into the body through the skin. The only transdermal contraceptive patch currently available in the United States is **Ortho Evra (Figure 12.14)**. Ortho Evra contains an estrogen and a progestin, so it's equivalent to a combination-pill oral contraceptive. The woman has many choices as to where to place the patch, but she should not place it on a breast, and she should select a new location each time (to reduce the likelihood of skin reactions).

Each patch is left on for 1 week. The woman uses three in a row and then goes for a week without a patch, so there is a 4-week cycle, just as with the combination pill. She will probably have (or begin) a period during the patch-free week. She should apply a new patch after the 1-week gap, even if her period hasn't yet stopped.

Generally, the advantages and disadvantages of Ortho-Evra are similar to those of combination contraceptive pills, but there are a few differences:

Advantages of Ortho Evra (compared with combination pills):

- It requires fewer actions on the part of the user, and compliance is better (Burkman, 2004). As a result, the reliability in typical use may be higher, but data are lacking.

- It is more evident in use and thus offers more assurance to the woman's partner that effective contraception is being used.

Disadvantages of Ortho Evra:

- There may be local skin reactions, which, if severe, could necessitate discontinuance.

- Sometimes the patch may become loose or fall off, but this is uncommon.

- As with the combination pill, Ortho Evra is not advised for women over 35 who smoke.

- Ortho Evra is nearly twice as expensive as generic combination pills.

- For women who weigh more than 90 kg (about 200 lb), the patch might not deliver enough hormones for reliable contraception. (This may be a particular concern when using

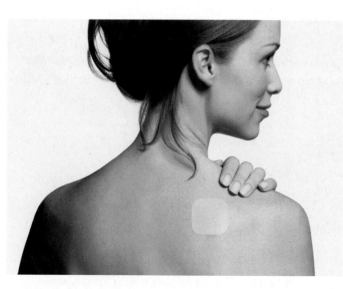

Figure 12.14 The Ortho Evra patch releases an estrogen–progestin combination that is absorbed through the skin.

the Canadian version of the Evra patch, which contains 20% less estrogen than the U.S. version.)

■ The risk of serious side effects, such as heart attacks, may be higher with the patch than with the pill. At least a few deaths—and perhaps as many as 50—have been attributed to use of the patch, and sales fell by 80% after the FDA warned the public of the potential risk (Harris & Berenson, 2008).

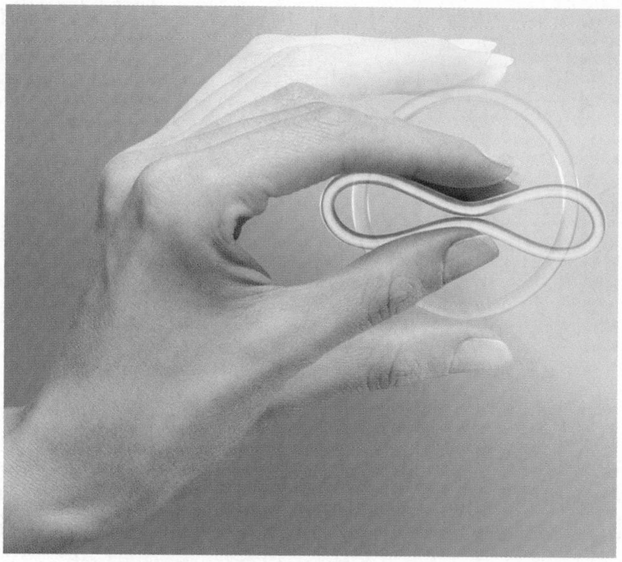

Vaginal Rings Last Three Weeks

Contraceptive hormones can be absorbed from the vagina, and the **NuvaRing (Figure 12.15)** takes advantage of this phenomenon. It is a flexible ring, about 54 mm (2.1 inches) in diameter, and is placed deep within the vagina. (Its exact placement doesn't matter.) Like the combination pill and the Ortho Evra patch, it releases a combination of an estrogen and a progestin. The ring is kept in place for three weeks, then there is a week's break to allow for a menstrual period, and then a new ring is inserted.

The advantages and disadvantages (and the cost) of the NuvaRing are similar to those of the Ortho Evra patch, with some differences.

Figure 12.15 The NuvaRing is a flexible hormone-releasing ring that is placed in the vagina.

Advantages of the NuvaRing (compared with Ortho Evra):

■ The woman has to take fewer actions per month (two versus four), which may improve compliance.

■ There are no skin reactions.

■ Estrogen exposure is lower.

■ The ring is not visible.

Disadvantages of the NuvaRing:

■ The ring may occasionally slip out. (It should be washed in cool water and replaced.)

■ It can cause vaginal irritation or a discharge.

■ Approximately 15% of women and 30% of their partners report feeling the NuvaRing during coitus on at least some occasions (Szarewski, 2002). However, the ring can be taken out before coitus; if so, it should be replaced within 3 hours.

■ The NuvaRing must be protected from heat prior to use.

A new vaginal ring, developed by the Population Council, is in final clinical trials. If approved, a single ring will be usable for 12 months on a 3-weeks-on, 1-week-off basis.

Implants Are Extremely Reliable

Contraceptive implants are rods containing contraceptive hormones that are implanted under the skin. They are as reliable as sterilization, even in typical use, but are fully reversible. The only implant currently available in the United States is the **Implanon**. This is a flexible, matchstick-sized rod, which releases a progestin. A healthcare provider inserts the rod under the skin of the woman's upper arm—the procedure takes about 1 minute. The implant provides protection against pregnancy for 3 years.

Advantages of Implanon (compared with Ortho-Evra or NuvaRing):

■ It requires no action on the part of the user beyond the insertion and removal.

NuvaRing A contraceptive ring placed in the vagina.

contraceptive implants A device implanted in the body that slowly releases a hormonal contraceptive.

Implanon An implanted hormonal contraceptive.

- Because the user does not have to do anything, it is probably more reliable. It may be the most reliable of any hormonal contraceptive technique in typical use, although experience is limited.

Disadvantages of Implanon:

- Beginning and ending the use of Implanon are more complex than with the other techniques.
- Initial expenses are higher—$400 to $800 for the exam, the Implanon, and the insertion. Removal costs about $100.
- Because it contain a progestin only, irregular bleeding is common. Up to 30% of women have the implant removed by 2 years after implantation, often because of bleeding.
- The reliability of Implanon in women weighing over 100 kg (220 lb) is uncertain.

Behavioral Methods Can Be Demanding

For couples who do not want to use "artificial" contraception of any kind for moral or other reasons, there are contraceptive options that depend simply on the manner or timing of sexual encounters. Although these options are considered by some to be more "natural" than other forms of contraception, and although they are inexpensive and free of the side effects of other methods, they make such demands on their users that their reliability in typical use is well below that of the best artificial methods.

In Fertility Awareness Methods, Couples Avoid the Fertile Window

Nearly all pregnancies result from coitus during the fertile window, which is the 6-day period leading up to and including the day of ovulation. Therefore, couples who avoid coitus during the fertile window will greatly decrease the likelihood of pregnancy (Jennings & Arevalo, 2007). We discussed methods for identifying the fertile window in Chapter 11 in the context of overcoming fertility problems. **Fertility awareness methods** of contraception put these techniques into reverse. They are sometimes called "rhythm methods" or "periodic abstinence methods" (**Figure 12.16**).

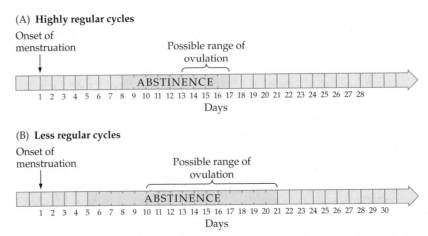

fertility awareness methods
Contraceptive techniques that rely on avoiding coitus during the woman's fertile window. Also called rhythm methods or periodic abstinence methods.

Figure 12.16 Timing methods make different demands on women with regular and irregular cycles. (A) A woman who cycles quite regularly needs to abstain from unprotected sex for only about 9 days per month. (B) A woman who cycles irregularly may have to abstain for 16 days or more because of greater uncertainty as to when ovulation will occur.

Unfortunately, very different requirements exist when information about the fertile window is used for contraception compared to when it is used to achieve pregnancy. When the aim is to achieve pregnancy, it is quite sufficient to identify just the day of ovulation, since this is the day when coitus is most likely to result in pregnancy. When the aim is to *avoid* pregnancy, however, the earlier fertile days are of great consequence: The couple must abstain from coitus beginning at least 5 days *before* ovulation.

STANDARD DAYS METHOD This is the simplest fertility awareness method: It is usable by women who have rather regular menstrual cycles lasting between 26 and 32 days. (About 3 out of 4 women meet this criterion.) Counting the first day of menstruation as day 1, the couple simply abstains from coitus on days 8 to 19 or uses condoms on those days. The reason why the period of abstinence is so much longer than the 6-day fertile window is that the timing of the fertile window is not precisely known.

Figure 12.17 CycleBeads may help women apply the standard days method of contraception. (Photo courtesy of Cycle Technologies, Inc.)

Some women use CycleBeads, a set of color-coded beads (**Figure 12.17**) to help them keep track of the days on which they may and may not have unprotected sex: The woman pushes a rubber ring from bead to bead each day, and the color of the current bead tells her whether coitus is safe or not. Unfortunately, if a woman forgets to move the ring or moves it more than once in a day she has no way of telling that she has made a mistake. Marking days on a wall calendar is better in that respect.

CALENDAR RHYTHM METHOD In this method, the woman first keeps track of the length of her menstrual cycles over 6 to 12 cycles and notes the length of the shortest and longest cycles. She subtracts 18 from the number of days in her shortest cycle to identify the first no-sex day in her cycle, and she subtracts 11 from the number of days in her longest cycle to identify the last no-sex day in her cycle. So, for example, if her shortest cycle is 24 days and her longest cycle is 34 days, then she must abstain from unprotected sex from day 6 (24 minus 18) to day 23 (34 minus 11) of her cycle. This method is usable by women with cycles that are too irregular for the standard days method, but it is very demanding and also rules out a large number of days. For these reasons it is not widely used or recommended.

CERVICAL MUCUS METHOD In this method, the woman monitors changes in her cervical mucus around the menstrual cycle. In the simplest version of the method, called the TwoDay method, the woman does not concern herself with what the mucus is like but simply notes each day whether she has *any* secretions. She asks herself two questions: "Do I have any secretions today?" and "Did I have any secretions yesterday?" If the answer to *both* questions is no, the chances of becoming pregnant are low. If the answer to *either* question is yes, the chances of becoming pregnant are high. The TwoDay method has been validated in large-scale studies; used correctly, fewer than 4 out of 100 women will become pregnant per year (Arevalo et al., 2004; Institute for Reproductive Health, 2008), but typical-use failure rates are higher. Other methods, which involve checking the consistency of the mucus, are also available (Planned Parenthood Federation, 2008). These methods may be slightly more reliable than the TwoDay method, but a direct comparison has not been done.

SYMPTO-THERMAL METHOD This method combines awareness of cervical secretions with the monitoring of body temperature: The woman measures her basal

standard days method A simplified calendar method of contraception usable by women with regular cycles.

calendar rhythm method A fertility awareness method of contraception that takes account of variability in the length of a woman's menstrual cycles.

cervical mucus method A fertility awareness method of contraception that depends on observing changes in the cervical mucus.

sympto-thermal method A rhythm method of contraception that uses the measurement of basal body temperature and the testing of cervical mucus to determine the time of ovulation and the fertile window.

body temperature every day with a digital thermometer before getting up. She stops having unprotected sex on the first day of cervical secretions. Her temperature drops slightly on the day of ovulation and then rises abruptly by at least 0.22°C (0.4°F) on the day after ovulation, as described in Chapter 11. Unprotected sex can resume 2 days (or, to be extra safe, 3 days) after the rise in temperature.* For both the cervical mucus and the sympto-thermal methods, the woman needs to have at least one detailed consultation with a family-planning provider; otherwise she is likely to make mistakes while she is familiarizing herself with the techniques.

Advantages of fertility awareness methods:

■ They are inexpensive or free.

■ They are usable by people who consider other forms of contraception morally wrong.

■ They avoid the side effects and health risks of other forms of contraception.

■ They are completely and immediately reversible.

Disadvantages of fertility awareness methods:

■ They are considerably less reliable than some other methods (see Table 12.1). This is a particular problem because users of these methods are often opposed to the use of abortion as a backup measure in the event pregnancy occurs. However, a couple who is using a fertility awareness method to have children less frequently rather than to avoid pregnancy altogether might find the method perfectly adequate.

■ They require a great deal of abstention from coitus. Of course, the couple could use an alternative form of contraception such as condoms during the fertile period, but fertility awareness methods appeal most to people who don't want to use any kind of artificial contraceptive technology.

■ The more accurate fertility awareness methods (i.e., cervical mucus, sympto-thermal) are quite demanding of time and attention. Only highly motivated users will do well with them.

■ With the calendar rhythm method, a woman needs to keep track of her cycles for at least 6 months before even beginning to use the method.

■ There is no protection from STDs, including HIV, if condoms are not used.

The Withdrawal Method Is Simple but Challenging

In the **withdrawal method** of contraception (also called "coitus interruptus"), the man simply removes his penis from the woman's vagina before he ejaculates. It sounds simple, so why does the method have a 27% failure rate with typical use?

Part of the reason for this is that some sperm may be present in the pre-ejaculatory fluid, or "pre-cum." Normally, this fluid contains no sperm, but it could contain some if the man ejaculated earlier, did not urinate afterwards, and is now having sex for a second time. If this were the only way in which the method could fail, however, it would probably be one of the most reliable forms of contraception. The real reason why the method is so unreliable is that the man doesn't always pull out in time. He simply gets carried away, or he ejaculates without sufficient warning. Also, he may spill semen on the labia, from where some hardy sperm may make it all the way into the woman's reproductive tract.

withdrawal method A method of contraception in which the man withdraws his penis from the vagina prior to ejaculation.

*An ovum survives for no more than 24 hours after ovulation. The 2–3 day wait is necessary because of uncertainty in the temperature determination and also because of the slight chance that a second ovulation might occur up to 24 hours after the first.

Advantages of the withdrawal method:

- It requires no advance preparation. Thus, it is frequently used during unplanned sexual encounters when no other contraceptive method is available.
- It is free.
- It enables the man to take responsibility for contraception.
- It can be combined with condom use for extra protection.
- There are no medical side effects or health risks.

Disadvantages of the withdrawal method:

- Reliability is poor. It is not recommended for men who ejaculate prematurely or have difficulty telling when they are going to ejaculate, or for teenagers.
- It provides little or no disease protection.
- In some men it can cause anxiety and diminish sexual pleasure.

Although we are not enthusiastic about the withdrawal method given the availability of better contraceptive options, the method has been of great importance in global terms. It has played a key role in the "demographic transition"—the dramatic decline in family size that accompanies modernization. Thanks to the withdrawal method, countries such as Turkey have undergone the demographic transition without the widespread adoption of medical contraceptive techniques (Cebeci Save et al., 2004). And it is of course a valuable last resort if a couple has engaged in coitus without any advance planning and ejaculation is now approaching.

Noncoital Sex Can Be Used as a Means of Avoiding Pregnancy

Knowing that only penile–vaginal intercourse can lead to pregnancy, many couples engage in other forms of sexual activity, including everything from kissing and fondling to body-on-body contact, hand stimulation of the genitals, and oral and anal sex. Sometimes these alternative forms of sex are promoted as a way to avoid pregnancy; in that context, they may be referred to as **outercourse**—the opposite of intercourse. (Some people exclude any form of penetrative sex from the definition of outercourse.)

outercourse Sexual activities other than coitus, promoted as a means to prevent unwanted pregnancy and avoid sexually transmitted diseases.

Advantages of noncoital sex:

- It is completely reliable if adhered to. (Semen must not be deposited near the vaginal opening, however, or transferred to the vagina after ejaculation by manual or body contact.)
- It is free and requires no preparation.
- There are none of the side effects that may be associated with other forms of contraception.
- For teens who have not yet engaged in coitus, it may be valued as a way to preserve "vaginal virginity."
- There is some STD protection, depending on what kinds of noncoital activities are engaged in. (Anal sex is at least as risky as coitus, and more so in the case of HIV.)

Disadvantages of noncoital sex:

- It misses out on what many heterosexual men and women consider the most pleasurable and intimate kind of sex.

Noncoital sex is an excellent form of contraception for responsible couples who communicate well.

emergency contraception Use of high-dose contraceptives after unprotected sex to prevent pregnancy.

Plan B A progestin used for emergency contraception.

■ It may be difficult to refrain from coitus once noncoital sex is under way, and if coitus does happen, contraception may not be available.

The main keys to successful outercourse are to decide what kinds of sex you will and will not engage in, discuss this with your partner *before* any sexual behavior begins, and have condoms ready in case plans change.

There Are Contraceptive Options after Unprotected Coitus

You got carried away. He said he was going to pull out. She said she was on the pill. The condom broke. The diaphragm slipped. Who cares how it happened—it's 11:00 P.M., ovulation is tomorrow, and a few million sperm are going gangbusters for the cervix. Your whole life—as a parent—is passing before your eyes. What next?

A woman's first impulse is to rinse out the contents of her vagina—preferably with something that will kill sperm. Coca-Cola is said to be the traditional favorite of teens.* Some women use water, a commercial douche, or spermicidal foam.

None of these methods is recommended as a regular form of postcoital contraception. Even the spermicidal foam, which is probably the best of the options just mentioned, is a highly unreliable way to prevent pregnancy when applied after coitus, because some sperm are likely to have gotten beyond the reach of the spermicide before it is ever placed in the vagina. Any of these methods may prevent pregnancy on a one-shot basis—if you're lucky. But the point is, you really can't afford to leave it to luck.

For that reason, it would be best for a woman in this situation to assume that sperm have made it to the safety of her cervix. She now has two effective options to prevent pregnancy: taking a high dose of contraceptive pills, or having an IUD inserted.

The pill method is called **emergency contraception**. The main way by which emergency contraception works is by preventing ovulation—and therefore conception. Conflicting data exist on whether it also works after ovulation—by interfering with transport of sperm, ovum, or embryo, or by disrupting fertilization or implantation. What is known is that emergency contraception does not interrupt an established pregnancy.

Emergency contraception is thought to work better, the sooner it is employed after coitus. Although often called the "morning-after pill," the method retains some efficacy for up to 5 days. Emergency contraception is not nearly as reliable as conventional hormone-based contraception, but it is well worth using given a woman's limited options. If emergency contraception fails and a pregnancy is established, the fetus will not have been harmed by the pills.

The recommended emergency contraception method is to take 1.5 mg (1500 mcg) of the progestin levonorgestrel. This dosage is contained in **Plan B**, a formulation packaged specifically for emergency contraceptive use (**Figure 12.18**). Plan B may be purchased without a prescription by women (or men) aged 18 or older. Those under age 18 require a prescription. In some parts of the United States many pharmacists refuse to sell it, citing moral scruples. In Canada, Plan B can be purchased over the counter without proof of age.

The two pills in a Plan B package can be taken together or (as stated on the package insert) 12 hours apart. The same dosage can be

Figure 12.18 Plan B is a progestin, levonorgestrel, specifically packaged for use as an emergency contraceptive.

*The 2008 Ig Nobel Prize—an award honoring comical science—was bestowed on two groups who studied whether Coca-Cola is an effective spermicide. One group found that it is, the other found that it isn't.

taken by using conventional progestin-only contraceptive pills. For example, one can take 40 Ovrette pills (either together or as two 20-pill doses 12 hours apart). A single one-month pack of Ovrette does not contain sufficient pills. Regardless of whether the source is Plan B or another brand, emergency contraception based on levonorgestrel reduces the likelihood of pregnancy by 60% to 90%.

Although less optimal, it is also acceptable to use estrogen–progestin combination pills. For example, a woman can take 10 Alesse pills—so a single 1-month pack contains more than enough pills. Planned Parenthood maintains a Web page that lists dosages for many brands. Don't use brands that are not listed on Planned Parenthood's site or another trustworthy site, unless you are certain that you are getting the identical dosage of the identical drugs as are in a listed pill. And forgive us if we're insulting your intelligence, but it's important not to use the dummy pills that may be provided for the drug-free week of the cycle!

When using combination pills, the pills should not be taken all at once but should be divided into two equal dosages taken 12 hours apart. Because of the high doses used, the estrogen-containing combination pills can cause vomiting. It is a good idea to take an anti-nausea pill, such as Dramamine, 30 minutes before the first dose of contraceptives, because if vomiting does occur an unknown fraction of the contraceptive dose may be lost. A woman who vomits after the first dose should take an anti-nausea pill before the second dose, or she can insert the pills in her vagina, pushing them as far in as possible with her fingers.

In trials that directly compared the two approaches, pregnancy rates observed in women who used Plan B or its equivalents were about half the rates using combination pills (Stewart et al., 2007). In other words, the high-dose levonorgestrel regimen is significantly more reliable.

The other strategy to prevent implantation is to have an IUD inserted. The ParaGard IUD is used for this purpose. Of course, this is a much more expensive and inconvenient option than taking pills. However, it is nearly 100% reliable—only 10 failures have ever been reported—and it can be done up to 10 days after coitus, rather than 5 days with the pills. (With a 10-day wait, it may work by inducing an early abortion.) Furthermore, the IUD can be left in place, in which case it will provide very reliable contraception for up to 12 years. Alternatively, it can be removed as soon as the woman has had her next menstrual period.

Sterilization Is Highly Reliable

Sterilization is a surgical procedure that puts an end to fertility. Various procedures have this effect. We focus on surgical procedures that are used to terminate fertility *electively* in otherwise healthy men and women: **vasectomy** in men and **tubal sterilization** in women. Both methods work by preventing sperm from reaching ova.

Sterilization is a serious issue for any individual or couple to face. Although, as we'll see below, sterilization procedures can be successfully reversed in some cases, there is no guarantee of success, so people who choose sterilization should be clear in their minds that they want to lose their fertility for good. They may want this under a number of circumstances:

- They simply don't want children and are certain they will never change their minds. (However, healthcare providers may be reluctant to sterilize healthy young men or women who don't have children.)

- They have had enough children and are confident that they will want no more, even if they remarry or their children die.

- A medical condition makes pregnancy a serious health hazard.

FAQ I don't have sex very often. Could I just rely on emergency contraception?
It is not recommended. Emergency contraceptive pills are less reliable than other methods of contraception and can be more expensive.

---

sterilization A surgical procedure to eliminate fertility in either sex.

vasectomy A male sterilization techniques that involves cutting or tying off the vasa deferentia.

tubal sterilization A female sterilization technique that involves cutting, cauterizing, or tying off the oviducts. Also called tubal ligation.

■ They have a significant likelihood of passing on a serious congenital disorder.

About 40% of all users of contraception rely on sterilization of the male or female partner as their contraceptive technique. The majority of people who choose sterilization are married couples with children. One in six American men over 35 has had a vasectomy.

Although the sterilization procedure is simpler, cheaper, and safer in men than in women, 72% of all sterilizations in the United States are done on women.

Vasectomy Is a Brief Outpatient Procedure

Vasectomy is a very simple and safe procedure that is usually done under local anesthesia (**Figure 12.19**). The physician locates the vas deferens inside the scrotal sac, makes a small incision, and cuts out a short segment of it. The free ends are tied, cauterized, or sealed with clips to prevent them from rejoining. The incision is then closed with a couple of stitches and the procedure is repeated on the other side. In an alternative "no scalpel" procedure, the scrotal skin is pierced with sharp-tipped forceps. Because the incision is so small, it needs no stitches and heals faster. With either method, however, the man can go home directly after the procedure.

The man should refrain from strenuous exercise for a couple of days after surgery. He can usually resume sexual activity in about a week. He is not yet sterile, however, because sperm remain in the portion of each vas deferens above the cut. It takes about 15 to 20 ejaculations to get rid of these sperm. The man's semen must be checked microscopically for absence of sperm before he can engage in unprotected coitus.

Complications of the procedure can include bleeding, infection, and—in about 18% of cases—the appearance of lumps formed by leaked sperm. These usually clear up by themselves, but they can be treated surgically if necessary. About 1 in 50 men experience chronic testicular pain after vasectomy. The pain can be treated by a variety of methods including surgical modification or reversal of the vasectomy if necessary (Christiansen, 2003).

Vasectomy costs between $250 and $1000 for the complete treatment—that is, the medical exam, the procedure, the follow-up, and the semen exam. It is extremely reliable; early failure can result if the man resumes unprotected sex too soon, and late failure can result from surgical errors, spontaneous reconnection of a vas deferens, or other unusual causes.

About the only way that vasectomy can harm a man's sex life is if he feels psychologically damaged by the procedure. For most men, it's quite the reverse: They and their partners are able to enjoy sex more because they no longer have to worry

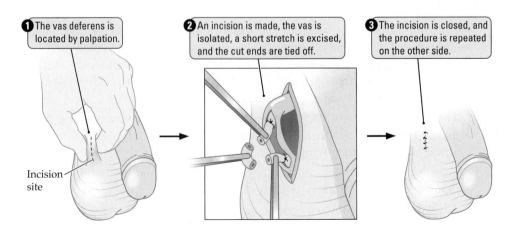

Figure 12.19 Vasectomy is a relatively simple procedure that can be performed under local anesthesia. (See Web Activity 12.1.)

❶ The vas deferens is located by palpation.

❷ An incision is made, the vas is isolated, a short stretch is excised, and the cut ends are tied off.

❸ The incision is closed, and the procedure is repeated on the other side.

Incision site

about contraception or pregnancy. The procedure has no effect on sexual desire, the ability to perform, testosterone levels, or secondary sexual characteristics. Although some early studies reported an increased rate of prostate cancer in vasectomized men, the current consensus is that there is no causal connection between vasectomy, prostate cancer, or any other serious medical condition (Goldacre et al., 2005; Pollack et al., 2007). Because sperm form such a small component of semen, there is no noticeable reduction in the volume of the ejaculate.

Of course, there are men who for one reason or another end up wanting the procedure reversed. There is an operation called **vasovasostomy** in which the surgeon, using an operating microscope, locates the two cut ends of each vas and sews them together. The procedure is expensive, however, and has no more than about a 50% chance of success. Quite aside from the difficulty of getting a functional reconnection, the man may have formed antibodies against his own sperm, which interfere with sperm production.

Some men deposit a sperm sample in a sperm bank prior to the vasectomy procedure, with the hope that they can become fathers via artificial insemination in case they change their minds. However, there is no assurance that this will be possible, as frozen sperm can deteriorate over time, and there will be only a limited amount available.

Advantages of vasectomy:

■ It is almost 100% reliable.

■ Once accomplished, it is totally convenient, and free.

■ Vasectomy is cheaper and safer than tubal sterilization.

Disadvantages of vasectomy:

■ Vasectomy is not reliably reversible. Attempts at reversal are very expensive.

■ The up-front expenses are considerable.

■ There is no STD protection.

Tubal Sterilization Is More Invasive and Expensive

Female sterilization is quite analogous to male sterilization: The oviducts are tied and cut (**tubal ligation**), cauterized, or closed off with clips or other devices (**Figure 12.20**). The result is that ova and sperm cannot meet. Tubal sterilization is a

vasovasostomy Surgery to reverse a vasectomy.

tubal ligation Female sterilization by tying off the oviducts.

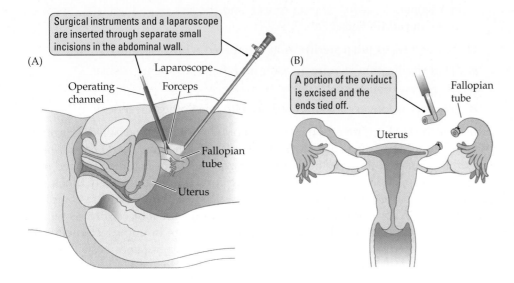

Figure 12.20 Tubal sterilization (A) Laparoscopic procedure for tubal ligation. (B) A portion of the oviduct may be excised and the ends tied off, as shown here, or the oviduct may be closed off by cauterization or the application of clips. (See Web Activity 12.2.)

laparoscopy Abdominal surgery, such as tubal sterilization, perfomed through a small incision with the aid of a laparoscope (a fiber-optic viewing instrument).

mini-laparotomy Abdominal surgery, such as tubal sterilization, performed through a short incision.

Essure A method of tubal sterilization that blocks the oviducts by use of implants.

more invasive procedure than vasectomy, however, since it involves entering the abdominal cavity. Many sterilizations are done after childbirth or after an abortion. Female sterilization costs $1000 to $2500, or up to $6000 if the procedure requires hospitalization.

There are two main kinds of female sterilization procedures, called laparoscopy and mini-laparotomy ("mini-lap"). These procedures differ not so much in what is done to the oviducts, but in the surgical approach. In a **laparoscopy**, no extended incision is made in the abdominal wall. Instead, a viewing instrument (laparoscope) is inserted through one tiny incision, and an instrument to clamp or cut the oviducts is inserted through another. Sometimes the two instruments are combined into one and only a single incision is made. The laparoscopic procedure is the least stressful, requires no stitches afterward, and can be done under either local or general anesthesia. Often, the woman can go home the same day.

In a **mini-laparotomy** or "mini-lap," a small scalpel incision about 2.5 cm (1 inch) long is made somewhere between the navel and the mons pubis. The oviducts are located and pulled to the incision, where they are tied and cut, or closed with clips, and then allowed to slip back into their normal position. The incision is then sewn up. Recovery takes a few days.

Tubal sterilization, like any internal surgery, can occasionally cause hemorrhage or infection. General anesthesia, if used, also carries some risk. These or other complications occur in 1% to 4% of cases, but they can usually be dealt with effectively. In the United States there are 1 to 4 deaths for every 100,000 tubal sterilizations. In general, one can say that tubal sterilization is a very safe procedure, but not quite as safe as vasectomy.

Like vasectomy, tubal sterilization has no effect on other aspects of sexual functioning. Menstrual cycles usually continue as before, and a woman's interest in sex and her physiological reactions during sex are undiminished. She may enjoy sex more because she is no longer concerned about pregnancy.

In some cases, tubal sterilization can be reversed by microsurgical techniques, but the operation is very expensive and success is quite unpredictable. The advantages and disadvantages of tubal sterilization are very similar to those of vasectomy, but there are a few important differences between the two.

Advantages of tubal sterilization (compared with vasectomy):

- A woman may find it easier to undergo sterilization herself than to persuade her partner to do so.
- For unknown reasons, tubal sterilization is associated with a 39% decrease in a woman's risk of ovarian cancer, and the risk of endometrial cancer is also reduced (Pollack et al., 2007).

Disadvantages of tubal sterilization (compared with vasectomy):

- Tubal sterilization is more invasive and therefore slightly riskier.
- It is more expensive.
- Recovery is longer (but shorter than with most other surgeries).

In 2002 the FDA approved a new method of tubal sterilization called **Essure**. In this method, the oviducts are blocked internally with small metal coils. These implants are passed through the vagina, cervix, and uterus and then pushed into the proximal portions of both oviducts. The coils do not effectively block the oviducts by themselves, but they provoke a tissue reaction that causes complete blockage within about 3 months. (Successful blockage must be confirmed with a special X-ray procedure before the woman can engage in unprotected coitus.) Essure can be performed in a doctor's office without general anesthesia. As with any novel procedure, data on long-term efficacy and safety are lacking.

Disabled Persons Have Special Contraceptive Needs

Many men and women with physical and mental disabilities are sexually active, but they may face special problems related to contraception (Best, 1999). If they have a movement disorder, arthritis, multiple sclerosis, or a spinal cord injury, they may not be able to put on a condom, insert a diaphragm, or check an IUD. Oral contraceptives are not advisable for women with reduced mobility because they may raise the risk of blood clots. IUDs are not advisable if the woman does not have normal sensation in the pelvic area. If the disabled person has a nondisabled partner, the couple may agree to leave contraception to that partner. That may not be an option if the disabled person is not in a steady relationship, however.

Contraception is a particularly important issue for intellectually disabled female adolescents and young women, who face a heightened risk of sexual abuse and who may not be able to comply with the usual contraceptive regimes. Careful counseling, repeated over time and tailored to the particular young woman's needs, is often required. Progestin hormone injection methods may be particularly useful for these women; the reduction in menstrual periods associated with these contraceptives may be an advantage in itself. Still, the ethical requirement for informed consent applies to intellectually disabled persons just as it does to other people.

There Is Active Research into New Contraceptive Methods

We have already mentioned some variants on current contraceptive technologies that are in various stages of testing and that might become available during the lifetime of this edition. But researchers are also working on radically new contraceptive technologies (Gabelnick et al., 2007). The following are a few lines of research that have the potential to change the practice of contraception in the more distant future.

One novel strategy is to interfere with the chemical signals involved in fertilization or implantation. It's known, for example, that human sperm carry an olfactory receptor that is sensitive to the chemical compound bourgeonal (a component of many perfumes). Apparently ova secrete bourgeonal, or something like it, to attract sperm. Thus a drug that blocked the bourgeonal receptor might well prevent fertilization.

Another strategy focuses on blocking sperm production itself. This can be done by treating men with a combination of a long-acting androgen and a progestin, delivered by injection, which together block the secretion of the two gonadotrophic hormones, LH and FSH, by the pituitary gland. With these hormones eliminated, sperm production stops. The secretion of testosterone by the testes also ceases, but the missing testosterone is replaced by the androgen in the drug cocktail. Developing the right synthetic hormones for this application and avoiding undesirable side effects has proved challenging, but the World Health Organization is beginning to test possible drug combinations in human trials. Success in this quest could have a major impact on contraceptive practices worldwide.

British and Japanese researchers are working on a "dry orgasm pill." This uses a variety of drugs that partially paralyze the smooth muscle of the vas deferens and urethra (Kobayashi et al., 2007). The drugs reduce or eliminate the ejaculate or prevent the sperm component from being added to the ejaculate. If this approach proves successful, it would render a man infertile for just a few hours, so he could take the pill in anticipation of a particular sexual encounter rather than as a months-long strategy.

Several Safe Abortion Procedures Are Available

induced abortion An abortion performed intentionally by medical or surgical means.

therapeutic abortion An abortion performed to safeguard a woman's life or health.

elective abortion An abortion performed in circumstances when the woman's health is not at risk.

An **induced abortion** is the intentional termination of a pregnancy. In this chapter we use "abortion" to refer exclusively to induced abortions (**Box 12.3**).

An abortion may be induced in order to safeguard the mother's health (**therapeutic abortion**) or because the woman chooses not to carry the fetus to term (**elective abortion**). An elective abortion may be performed because the pregnancy was not wanted (contraception failed or was not used, or the pregnancy resulted from rape), or because the fetus is known or suspected to suffer from some defect or disease. In some countries, but not in the United States, abortions are commonly performed because the child is of the nonpreferred sex—usually female. India and China are most frequently mentioned in this regard.

The moral status of abortion, and the degree to which governments should restrict or regulate the practice, are highly contentious issues in contemporary society. In this chapter, we first describe the technology of abortion and then discuss the social conflicts that surround it.

Society, Values, and the Law

BOX 12.3 Abortion in the United States: Some Key Statistics

■ Twenty-two percent of all established pregnancies in the United States (aside from those that end in miscarriage) are terminated by abortion. There are 1.2 million abortions annually. Assuming the continuation of current trends, about one-third of American women will have an abortion by the age of 45.

■ Most abortions are done for social, not medical, reasons (see Table).

■ Young, single women are the major recipients of abortion. Seventeen percent of all abortions are performed on teenagers.

■ Minority women are disproportionately represented among abortion recipients.

■ Fifty-four percent of women who have abortions were using some kind of contraceptive technique when they became pregnant.

■ Eighty-nine percent of all abortions are performed within the first 12 weeks of pregnancy.

■ Fewer than 3 in 1000 abortions result in a complication requiring hospitalization. Legal abortion performed by 8 weeks of pregnancy has a 1 in 1,000,000 chance of causing the mother's death. Abortion performed at or after 21 weeks has a 1 in 11,000 chance of causing the mother's death.

■ Abortion is legal in all U.S. states. Thirty-five states require minors to notify or obtain consent from their parents (or, failing that, from a court). About 13% of abortions in the United States are paid for with public funds.

■ The clinics of the nonprofit Planned Parenthood Federation perform 20% of all abortions in the United States. One of the largest for-profit abortion providers is Family Planning Associates, with 20 clinics in California and Illinois.

Source: Guttmacher Institute, 2008a.

Most Important Reason Given for Abortion	
Not ready for a(nother) child/timing is wrong	25
Can't afford a baby now	23
Have completed my childbearing/have other people depending on me/children are grown	19
Don't want to be a single mother/am having relationship problems	8
Don't feel mature enough to raise a(nother) child/feel too young	7
Would interfere with education or career plans	4
Physical problem with my health	4
Possible problems affecting the health of the fetus	3
Was a victim of rape	<0.5
Husband or partner wants me to have an abortion	<0.5
Parents want me to have an abortion	<0.5
Don't want people to know I had sex or got pregnant	<0.5
Other	6
Total	100

Source: Finer et al., 2005.

Abortions can be performed either by physically removing the fetus and its membranes from the uterus (**surgical abortion**) or by administering drugs that cause the death and expulsion of the fetus in a manner that resembles a miscarriage (**medical abortion**). Currently, surgical abortions are much more common than medical abortions.

Vacuum Aspiration Is the Standard First-Trimester Surgical Method

Surgical abortions are carried out in different ways depending on the age of the fetus. During the first trimester, most surgical abortions are performed by **vacuum aspiration (Figure 12.21)**. This procedure—which accounts for the great majority of all abortions in the United States—is done on an outpatient basis with local anesthesia or sedation. The healthcare provider first dilates the cervix by passing a series of metal rods of increasing diameter through the cervical canal.

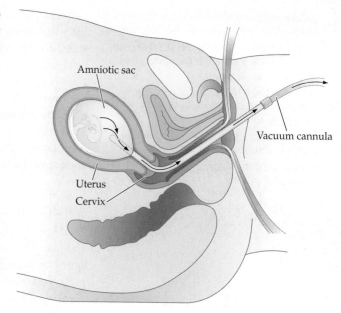

Figure 12.21 Vacuum aspiration is the abortion procedure most commonly used in the first trimester.

Once the cervix has been dilated, the provider passes a cannula (tube) into the uterus. The other end of the cannula is connected to a pump that applies suction. (With very early abortions, suction may be applied by hand, using a syringe.) The suction breaks up the embryo or fetus and its membranes and removes them from the uterus. This process takes less than 5 minutes. The extracted tissue is examined to ensure that the abortion is complete. The provider may insert a curette (a metal loop) to clean the walls of the uterus of any remaining tissue.

The woman remains in the clinic or doctor's office for an hour or so before being allowed to go home. She may experience some bleeding and cramping over the following week or two. The woman should refrain from coitus for 2 weeks to allow the cervix to close fully. Complications are rare but can include heavy bleeding, infection, or perforation of the uterus.

Dilation and Evacuation Is Used Early in the Second Trimester

Vacuum aspiration abortions can be performed up to about 14 week of pregnancy, but the majority of second-trimester abortions are performed using a different procedure, called **dilation and evacuation (D and E)**. Most D and Es are done in the period from 13 to 16 weeks, but they are sometimes done at up to 20 weeks or even later.

D and Es are usually performed under general anesthesia in a hospital but may be performed with sedation in an outpatient setting. The procedure is fairly similar to vacuum aspiration, but the cervix has to be dilated more widely. Therefore, a two-day procedure is commonly employed. On the first day, a stick made from the seaweed *Laminaria* is inserted into the cervical canal. The laminaria absorbs fluid and expands, gently opening the cervix. On the following day, a suction cannula is used to remove fluid and some tissue, and then the remainder is removed with forceps or other instruments. Finally, the lining of the uterus is cleaned with a curette.

The D and E is a very safe procedure, but it has a somewhat greater likelihood of complications, such as excessive bleeding, than vacuum aspiration abortion.

Induced Labor and Hysterotomy Are Performed Late in the Second Trimester

Late in the second trimester, the D and E procedure becomes more risky, and alternative surgical techniques may be used. In one method, the provider simply

surgical abortion An abortion induced by a surgical procedure.

medical abortion An abortion induced with drugs.

vacuum aspiration An abortion procedure in which the conceptus is destroyed and removed by suction.

dilation and evacuation (D and E) A procedure involving the opening of the cervix and the scraping out of the contents of the uterus with a curette (spoon-like instrument). D and E may be done as an abortion procedure or for other purposes. The term is sometimes used to refer to vacuum aspiration.

saline-induced abortion An abortion induced by use of a strong salt solution.

hysterotomy An abortion performed via a surgical incision in the abdominal wall and the uterus.

mifepristone A progestin receptor antagonist used to induce abortion. Also known as RU-486.

misoprostol A prostaglandin used in medical abortions.

methotrexate A drug used in some medical abortions.

induces premature labor. This may be accomplished by injecting a salt solution into the amniotic sac (**saline-induced abortion**). Alternatively, and more commonly, labor is induced by administration of a prostaglandin. The drug is either injected into the amniotic sac or administered by means of a vaginal suppository. Contractions usually begin within an hour or so, and the fetus is expelled within 48 hours.

If the woman's health is such that labor seems risky, the fetus may be removed by means of a surgical incision in the abdomen and the uterus (**hysterotomy**). Neither induced labor nor hysterotomy is performed very frequently—each of them accounts for fewer than 1% of all abortions in the United States, and there are legal restrictions on these procedures in some states.

Medical Abortions Are Two-Step Procedures

Medical abortions can be performed anytime up to 7 to 9 weeks after the start of the last menstrual period. The drug most commonly used is **mifepristone** (trade name Mifeprex; also known as RU-486). Mifepristone is an antagonist of progestin receptors—the cellular molecules that recognize and respond to progesterone and similar hormones. Recall that progesterone, secreted by the corpus luteum and later by the placenta, is required to keep the uterus in a state capable of sustaining pregnancy (**Figure 12.22**). In the presence of mifepristone, the progestin receptors do not "see" progesterone, so it is as if progesterone is absent. The endometrium begins to break down and ceases to support the fetus, which detaches from the endometrium and dies.

In about 5% of women the remains of the fetus and its membranes are expelled by spontaneous uterine contractions. In most cases, however, it is necessary to give a second drug, the prostaglandin **misoprostol**, to induce contractions. Misoprostol should be taken orally and not, as was earlier recommended by some clinics, by being inserted in the vagina. (Use of this latter route has been tentatively linked with fatal infections in a few women.) The misoprostol is usually taken 2 or more days after the mifepristone. Bleeding begins within 24 hours of taking misoprostol, and the entire abortion process takes no more than a few days. A follow-up visit to the clinic is necessary to make sure that the abortion is complete.

There are a number of circumstances in which women should not use mifepristone or in which special steps need to be taken to allow it to be used safely. For that reason, a woman should not bypass medical assessment by buying the drug via the Internet. If she cannot take mifepristone, she may still be able to have a medical abortion by use of a different drug, **methotrexate**. This drug, which is

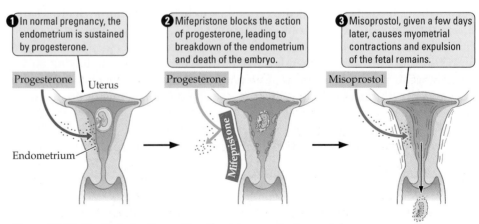

Figure 12.22 Medical abortion with mifepristone and misoprostol

usually given by injection, kills rapidly dividing cells, and thus it has a direct toxic effect on the fetus. It must be followed by misoprostol to induce contractions. The abortion process takes longer with methotrexate than with mifepristone (Creinin & Pymar, 2000).

There is a small difference in reliability between the two methods: Mifepristone works in about 96% of cases, and methotrexate works in 90% of cases. If either procedure should fail, the woman should have a surgical abortion because the fetus may well have been seriously damaged.

Mifepristone was developed in France and had been widely used in Europe for several years before it was approved by the FDA in 2000. It has been used safely by millions of women around the world. American pro-choice activists (see below) hoped that the introduction of the abortion pill would encourage general-care providers, such as family doctors, to offer abortion—thus making it difficult for abortion foes to monitor or interfere with the process. This has not happened to any great degree, however, in part because special training is required before a doctor can prescribe mifepristone. In fact, the great majority of all abortions in the United States are still surgical.

Here are the advantages and disadvantages of medical abortion compared with surgical abortion:

Advantages of medical abortion (compared with a surgical abortion):

■ It requires no invasive surgical procedure.

■ It can be performed earlier than surgical abortion—as soon as pregnancy is confirmed.

■ The abortion may seem more like a natural miscarriage.

Disadvantages of medical abortion (compared with a surgical abortion):

■ Medical abortions take longer. A surgical abortion is over within minutes, whereas a medical abortion typically takes a few days and requires a total of two or three visits to the provider.

■ Medical abortions cannot be performed after 7 to 9 weeks from the beginning of the last menstrual period.

■ Medical abortions generally cost $100 to $300 more than surgical abortions.

■ For anyone who is trying to conceal the abortion, having the abortion at home may be a disadvantage.

■ Another disadvantage of having the abortion at home is the possibility of seeing the fetal remains, which may disturb some women.

■ For some women it may be psychologically harder to cause the abortion themselves (by taking pills) than to let a professional provider take care of the matter (as with a surgical abortion).

Abortions Do Not Cause Long-Lasting Ill-Effects

Neither medical nor early surgical abortion impairs a woman's fertility (Paul & Stewart, 2007) or causes any problems during subsequent pregnancies (Virk et al., 2007). There may be some increased risk of spontaneous abortion during pregnancies subsequent to a second-trimester D and E abortion.

Although a woman may feel stress or sadness immediately after an abortion, the procedure does not cause any long-lasting psychological harm to the great majority of women. In fact, there may be psychological benefits such as enhanced self-esteem (Major et al., 2000). A very small number of women—about 1% of all women who obtain abortions—do seem to experience lasting depression or stress. These are largely women who were depressed before their abortion. The idea that

The abortion debate is often portrayed as a face-off between extreme pro-life and pro-choice activists, but many Americans hold intermediate positions.

pro-life Opposed to abortion; believing that abortion should be illegal under most or all circumstances.

pro-choice Believing that abortion should be legal under some or all circumstances.

millions of previously healthy women are psychologically crippled by a "post-abortion syndrome," analogous to the post-traumatic stress disorder suffered by battle-scarred soldiers, is a myth propagated by abortion opponents (Bazelon, 2007).

Americans Are Divided on Abortion, but Most Favor Restricted Availability

In its landmark 1973 decision in *Roe v. Wade*, the U.S. Supreme Court ruled that states could not enact outright bans on abortions performed before the age of fetal viability, which was taken to mean before the end of the second trimester of pregnancy. Since that time, Americans have remained divided on the issue of abortion.

The abortion debate is often portrayed as if there are simply two opposing camps: **pro-life**, meaning people who believe that elective abortion is always wrong and that it should be a criminal offense, and **pro-choice**, meaning people who believe that women should be allowed to make all abortion decisions for themselves. When Americans are asked "Do you consider yourself pro-life or pro-choice?" most will identify themselves as one or the other, with roughly equal numbers of people taking each point of view (Gallup Organization, 2005).

When polls ask Americans about abortion in more detail, however, it becomes apparent that their views are not strictly polarized. For example, many people believe that abortion should be permissible in the first trimester, but far fewer believe that it should be permissible in the second or third trimester (Goldberg & Elder, 1998) (**Figure 12.23A**). In this respect, Americans tend toward a more conservative position than was spelled out in *Roe v. Wade*, which made abortion legal in both the first and second trimesters.

Furthermore, while 60% of Americans think that the *Roe v. Wade* decision was a good thing, this does not mean that they agree with the core of the decision,

(A)

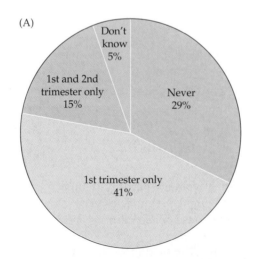

(B)

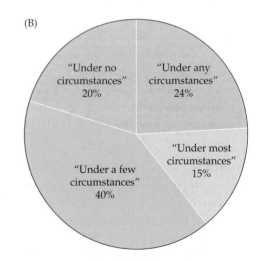

Figure 12.23 Americans' views on abortion are not as simple as "pro-life vs. pro-choice." (A) Abortion is considered more acceptable when it is done early: The graph shows the percentage of U.S. adults who believe abortion should be permitted during different time intervals within pregnancy. (B) Only minorities of Americans have extreme opinions in response to the question "Under what circumstances should abortion be legal?" posed in a 2005 Gallup poll. (A data from Gallup Organization, 2006a; B data from Religious Tolerance.org, 2006.)

which was that a woman has a right to an early abortion for any reason. Americans generally are in favor of the notion that a woman should be able to have an abortion if her life is at risk, if the fetus is likely to have a congenital disorder, or if the pregnancy resulted from rape. In contrast, they are *not* in favor of the idea that a woman should be allowed to have an abortion for a reason of mere convenience—such as the fact that having the baby would interfere with her career. Seventy percent of Americans believe that abortion under these circumstances should be illegal, contrary to the *Roe v. Wade* ruling. Only a minority of Americans believe that abortion should be illegal under all circumstances or legal under all circumstances (**Figure 12.23B**). The most common opinion is that abortion should be legal under a limited set of circumstances.

How do views on abortion vary with major demographic variables? First, women and men do not differ significantly in their representation in the pro-choice and pro-life camps, but women hold their opinions more strongly than men (Gallup News Service, 2004). This is hardly surprising, given that the abortion issue affects women more directly than it affects men.

The four main variables that correlate with abortion views are religious beliefs, political affiliation, educational level, and age. People with strong religious beliefs or who are Republicans are more likely to have restrictive views on abortion, while Democrats, people who have high levels of educational attainment, and younger people are more likely to have permissive views (Religious Tolerance.org, 2005).

The Abortion Debate Focuses on Specific Issues

Because the majority of Americans do not hold extreme views on abortion, pro-life and pro-choice activists generally wage their battles over positions in the center, not over the absolute banning or legalization of abortion. Several questions have been the focus of intense debate:

■ *Should abortion be restricted by imposing conditions on it, such as mandatory 24-hour waiting periods or mandatory counseling about alternatives to abortion?* Abortion foes have been quite successful in these areas. The U.S. Supreme Court has ruled that such restrictions are constitutional (*Planned Parenthood v. Casey,* 1992), and many states have enacted some or all of them. In 2006 the Supreme Court let stand a New Hampshire law that requires a minor to obtain consent from her parents (or a judge) for an abortion.

■ *Should abortions be banned after a certain duration of pregnancy?* Abortion foes have been less successful here. *Roe v. Wade* permitted the banning of abortion after the age of fetal viability and implied that this age was at the end of the second trimester. Later Supreme Court rulings, however, stated that only an individual doctor could decide whether a particular fetus was viable or not and that viability was not linked to a fixed fetal age.

■ *Should certain late abortion procedures, such as partial-birth abortion (known medically as "intact D and X"), be banned?** In 2003, President Bush signed a ban on these procedures, with no exceptions for medical necessity. In 2007 the Supreme Court upheld this law. Intact D and X was a rarely performed procedure, but the 2007 decision signaled an increasing willingness on the part of the Supreme Court to approve restrictions on abortion.

■ *Should indigent women's abortions be paid for by public funds?* Currently, states are required to fund such abortions only when pregnancy results from incest

> **FAQ Will the government pay for my abortion if I can't afford it?**
> Medicaid pays for some abortions in all states, but many states restrict these payments to cases of medical necessity, rape, or incest.

---

*In this procedure, which was never common, the provider manipulated the fetus into a breech position and then delivered its lower body. Before the head was delivered, the provider punctured it and suctioned out the brain, thus easing delivery and ensuring that the fetus was not born alive.

or rape or when the mother's life is in danger. Some states voluntarily fund abortions in other circumstances.

- *Should anti-abortion protesters be kept away from people entering or leaving abortion clinics?* This contentious issue has been the subject of several Supreme Court rulings. Currently, fixed "buffer zones" around a clinic entrance are legal, but "floating" buffer zones (meaning that a person entering or leaving a clinic may not be approached, wherever they are physically located) are not.

- *Should embryonic stem cells derived from aborted fetuses be used for medical purposes?* Under current policy, federal funding may be used to support medical research involving stem cell lines in existence before August 2001, but not research using the much larger number of stem cell lines that have been obtained since that time. Partly in reaction to the federal restrictions, California voters in 2004 approved a $3 billion bond measure to support stem cell research in that state, and other states have followed suit.

The Availability of Abortion Varies by Location

Partly because of the fierce controversy over abortion, the availability of abortion varies greatly within the United States. In many large metropolitan areas there are plenty of abortion providers. In fact, because of the falling numbers of abortions, there is considerable competition among clinics, and a woman may therefore be able to obtain a reasonably priced procedure.

In nonmetropolitan areas and in the South, it may be difficult to locate an abortion provider. In the entire state of Mississippi, where anti-abortion forces have come to dominate political life, only a single abortion clinic remains in operation. This clinic, which is located in the city of Jackson, has faced severe restrictions and harassment for many years (Associated Press, 2004b). Yet Mississippi is a state with a heightened need for abortion providers because public schools are restricted to abstinence-only sex education and emergency contraception is hard to obtain. Mississippi abortion law is the most restrictive permitted under *Roe v. Wade*: Abortion is not legal after 12 weeks.

One-third of all American women live in counties where there is not a single abortion provider (Guttmacher Institute, 2008b). Although some doctors may refuse to perform abortions as a matter of personal conscience, another motivating factor is fear of harassment or even violence. During the 1990s at least 11 abortion providers or other persons associated with abortion clinics were murdered by anti-abortion activists (**Figure 12.24**), and in 2001 the operations of hundreds of abortion clinics were disrupted by hoax anthrax letters sent to them through the postal service.

One thing that most pro-life and pro-choice activists agree on is that contraception is preferable to abortion. Improved access to contraceptive services, better education in contraceptive methods, development of new methods, and changes in religious attitudes toward contraception all have the potential to greatly

Figure 12.24 Anti-abortion extremism In 1994 Paul Hill shot and killed an abortion provider and a clinic security guard. Hill was sentenced to death and was executed in 2003. These pro-life activists were expressing their support for Hill at the time of his execution.

reduce the number of abortions performed in the United States. In fact, abortion rates have been falling steadily for years. In 2005 (the most recent year for which data are available) the abortion rate was 19.4 abortions per 1000 women aged 15 to 44. This represents a 34% drop from the peak rate of 29.3 recorded in 1981 (Jayson, 2008).

Some Countries Use Birth Control to Regulate Population Growth

Although we have examined contraception and abortion largely from the point of view of the individual, society as a whole also has an interest in regulating births. Many developing countries see population control as the key to economic development and protection from famine. China, for example, has imposed strict limits on reproduction via its "one-child policy." This policy limits most urban couples to one child; couples in rural areas may have a second child if the first was a daughter. The one-child policy is realized to a considerable extent through abortion: Considerable pressure is put on women who have a child to terminate any later pregnancies.

Until recently, India has been less successful in reining in its population growth, but it is now beginning to do so, thanks largely to a state-run sterilization program. The program is voluntary but is backed by strong incentives and peer pressure.

Some developed countries, on the other hand, are economically threatened by declining birth rates and aging populations. This is particularly true of Japan, whose population will decline by at least 14% by 2050 (Efron, 2001), but 38 other countries also face declining birth rates. The governments of many of these countries are initiating programs to increase the number of births; for example, by making child support payments, providing child care so that mothers can work, and so on.

The population of the United States is expected to grow only moderately over the next few decades. Thus the U.S. government feels no need to actively curb or encourage population growth and generally leaves family-planning decisions to individuals.

"One couple should give birth to only one child" reads this billboard in Beijing China. In 2007, residents clashed with police in protest over an official birth control program that, according to residents, included forced abortions.

Summary

1. Although various forms of contraception have been known since ancient times, moral repugnance, restrictive laws, and lack of knowledge prevented effective contraception in the United States until the twentieth century. Margaret Sanger led the struggle to legalize contraception, to educate the public about contraceptive methods, and to introduce improved methods. Contraception was not fully legalized in the United States until 1972. Even today, about three million unwanted pregnancies occur in the United States every year, on account of non-use of or failure of contraceptive methods.

2. All currently available contraceptive methods have advantages and disadvantages. Different people have different contraceptive needs in terms of reversibility, reliability, cost, and so on, so no one method is best for all users.

3. Male condoms (sheaths that cover the penis) require careful use to prevent failure and are somewhat intrusive, but they are cheap, readily accessible, and offer significant protection against STDs. They are the only male method (aside from withdrawal) that is reversible. Female condoms offer similar benefits but are far less popular than male condoms.

4. Diaphragms and cervical caps are other barrier methods of contraception. They are used in conjunction with spermicides to prevent the entry of sperm into the cervix. They are less intrusive than condoms, but they provide less pregnancy and disease protection and are fairly inconvenient to use. Spermicides used by themselves are not very reliable, and overuse of spermicides can cause irritation and raise the risk of STD transmission.

5. Intrauterine devices render the uterus hostile to sperm transport. They are very reliable and quite convenient once inserted. They offer no STD protection.

6. Contraceptive pills contain either a combination of estrogen and progestin or progestin only. They work by blocking ovulation and by rendering the uterus hostile to sperm transport. They are fairly convenient once prescribed, nonintrusive, and very reliable if taken regularly. They offer no STD protection. Estrogen-containing pills may have a number of side effects as well as some long-term health risks and benefits. Progestin-only pills often cause irregular bleeding.

7. Some contraceptive pills may be taken in an extended fashion that reduces the frequency of menstrual periods or eliminates them entirely.

8. Hormone-based contraceptives may also be administered by long-term injections (Depo-Provera), by contraceptive patches (Ortho Evra), by vaginal rings (NuvaRing), or by implants placed under the skin (Implanon). These non-pill methods have the advantage of greater reliability in typical use than birth control pills.

9. In fertility awareness methods, couples avoid sex near the time of ovulation, which they can determine by a variety of techniques, including simple calendar calculations, temperature measurements, or examination of cervical mucus.

10. In the withdrawal method, the man withdraws his penis prior to ejaculation. Globally, this method has made a major contribution to population control, but many couples find it difficult to practice, especially if the man tends to ejaculate early or without warning.

11. Noncoital sex (outercourse) is a reliable form of contraception if adhered to strictly.

12. Emergency contraception involves taking a high dose of oral contraceptives within 5 days after unprotected sex or failure of a barrier contraceptive. This method prevents ovulation. It is less effective than regular contraception and has side effects. Another possible postcoital contraceptive technique is the insertion of an IUD.

13. Sterilization is the cutting and/or tying off of both vasa (in men) or oviducts (in women). The procedure blocks gamete transport and is nearly completely reliable in preventing pregnancy. The majority of sterilizations are done in women, but the procedure is simpler, safer, and less expensive in men. Although intended to be permanent, sterilization can be reversed in some cases. Sterilization is generally chosen by couples who have all the children they desire.

14. In the United States, 1.2 million abortions are performed every year. Most abortions are done in the first trimester of pregnancy and are performed by the vacuum aspiration method, in which the cervix is dilated and the contents of the uterus suctioned out under local anesthesia. A slightly more complex procedure, dilation and evacuation, is used early in the second trimester.

15. Early abortions may also be induced with drugs. Medical abortion is a two-step procedure involving the administration of a drug that terminates the pregnancy (usually mifepristone), followed about 2 days later by a second drug (misoprostol) that induces contractions and the expulsion of the fetal remains. Neither medical nor surgical abortions cause long-lasting physical or psychological harm to the mother.

16. The moral and legal status of abortion is contentious. The extreme anti-abortion (pro-life) position is that abortion is always wrong and should be illegal, except perhaps when done to save the mother's life. The extreme opposing (pro-choice) view is that a woman should have the right to choose abortion under any circumstances. Most Americans describe themselves as pro-life or pro-choice but actually hold to an intermediate position, believing that abortion should be permitted under certain limited conditions, such as early in pregnancy or when the fetus has a congenital defect.

Discussion Questions

1. Your sister or best friend asks you to help her decide which contraceptive method is best for her. She says she could not take pills, use a diaphragm, or use the rhythm method because she is too forgetful. She does not want to have to contemplate an abortion because it is against her values. Recommend two forms of contraception that would be suitable. Compare their actions and side effects. Compare their reliability.

2. A teenager tells you that she has no risk of getting pregnant because she can tell when her boyfriend is about to ejaculate by the look on his face, and she makes him pull out. Explain to her the facts of this method of contraception, suggest an alternative method, and describe how it works and its advantages and disadvantages.

3. What are your own views about abortion? What changes, if any, would you like to see in current laws relating to abortion in your state?

Web Resources

Guttmacher Institute www.guttmacher.org

Male Contraception Coalition (covers research on male contraception) www.malecontraceptives.org

Marie Stopes International www.mariestopes.org.uk

National Abortion and Reproductive Rights Action League www.naral.org

National Abortion Federation www.prochoice.org

National Right to Life Committee www.nrlc.org

Planned Parenthood Federation of America www.plannedparenthood.org

Recommended Reading

Chesler, E. (1992). *Woman of valor: Margaret Sanger and the birth control movement in America.* Simon and Schuster.

George, R. P. and Tollefsen, C. (2008). *Embryo: A defense of human life.* Doubleday. (Makes the case that an embryo is a full human being entitled to legal protection.)

Hatcher, R. A., Trussell, J., Nelson, A. L., et al. (2007). *Contraceptive technology.* (19th ed.) Ardent Media.

Solinger, R. (2005). *Pregnancy and power: A short history of reproductive politics in America.* NYU Press.

Wicklund, S. (2007). *This common secret: My journey as an abortion doctor.* Public Affairs.

CHAPTER 13

The role of sexuality in human lives varies across the life span.

Sexuality across the Life Span

No two lives are alike, yet sexuality does unfold in a somewhat predictable manner across the life span. In fact, a person's age is one of the best predictors of their sexual behavior and relationships. Sex researchers tend to focus on a narrow age range within the total life span—from adolescence to midlife—when sexuality has its greatest social relevance. Here we develop a view of sexuality as a work that is already in progress at birth and that remains so until death.

Some Forms of Childhood Sexual Expression Are Common

There are several possible ways one might study childhood sexuality. One method is retrospective: This involves asking adolescents or young adults to recall their sexual feelings and sexual behavior during their childhood. Another is to ask children themselves about their sex lives. Yet another is to observe children's sexual behavior directly or to obtain such observations secondhand from parents or other caregivers.

None of these approaches is completely satisfactory. Adults have very limited memories of their childhood and no recollection at all of their infancy. Infants cannot be interviewed about their sex lives. Older children can be interviewed, but their understanding may be limited, and their replies might be too easily influenced by suggestion. In addition, parents might be reluctant to permit questioning of their children on sexual matters. Direct observation of children's sexual behavior might be difficult if the behavior is infrequent. Ethical or legal considerations might also limit the use of this approach. Thus observational studies have generally involved asking parents or teachers about sexual behavior they happened to have witnessed among children under their care, rather than direct observation of such behavior by researchers.

Because of these problems, the total number of studies of childhood sexuality has been very limited: One recent review identified just 12 retrospective studies and 11 observational studies, most of them conducted outside the United States (de Graaf & Rademakers, 2006).

For all these reasons, we cannot expect to reach definitive conclusions about childhood sexuality. Nevertheless, it is a topic that is well worth studying for two important reasons. First, childhood sexuality is the precursor of adolescent and adult sexuality and may therefore help us understand how the diversity of adult sexual behavior arises. Second, a knowledge of normal childhood sexuality seems like a precondition for understanding how children are affected by sexual abuse

Do young children have a sex life? There are wildly diverging opinions on this question.

and for developing strategies to help them mend the damage caused by that abuse (Bancroft, 2003).

In Contemporary Western Culture, Children Are Insulated from Sex

Before the nineteenth century, families generally slept together, so young children sometimes observed adult sexual behavior. Also, because farming was the commonest occupation, children saw animals mating, becoming pregnant, and giving birth. Climate permitting, young children frequently went naked, so it was easy for them to explore their own anatomy and that of their siblings.

During the nineteenth century, however, there developed a belief that children needed to be kept in a state of sexual innocence. Although there have been changes since then, especially in terms of formalized sex education, children today often experience a "conspiracy of silence" on sexual matters. Many parents, for example, do not permit their children to see them naked or to witness their sexual encounters, in part because clinicians and therapists have suggested that these experiences are harmful to children and may even represent a form of sexual abuse (Kritsberg, 1993). Research on this topic has led to reassuring findings, however. In one 18-year longitudinal study (the UCLA Family Lifestyles Project) young children who saw their parents naked or engaging in sex were no more likely to experience psychological problems in later childhood or adolescence than children who did not (Okami et al., 1998). In fact, there was a tendency for them to have *fewer* problems—a finding that is in line with another, retrospective study (Lewis & Janda, 1988).

Children, especially younger ones, express a lot of curiosity about "where babies come from" and other sexual matters. Some parents are very forthcoming, using these questions as an opportunity to teach their children the basic facts of sexuality in an age-appropriate fashion (**Box 13.1**). But other parents are evasive: They may give fairy-tale explanations, tell the child that they are too young to know such things, or express disapproval of the questions. Thus many children remain remarkably ignorant of sexual matters.

Parents also communicate diverse values to their children—values that may be broadly sex-positive, broadly sex-negative, or a mixture of the two. As an example of the last, some parents communicate respect for heterosexual relationships but express disgust for "faggots" and "dykes," thus communicating homophobic attitudes to their children before the children even have a clear grasp of what homosexuality is.

Some Children Engage in Solitary Sexual Activity

What about children's actual sexual behavior? Newborn babies may already exhibit penile erections or vaginal lubrication (Martinson, 1976; Masters et al., 1982). In fact, erections have been detected in male fetuses several weeks before birth by means of ultrasound imaging. These physiological processes continue to occur through infancy and childhood. They are not necessarily brought about by what we would normally consider *sexual* stimuli, however. According to Kinsey's group (Kinsey et al., 1948), penile erections in young boys are triggered by a

Nudity allows children to familiarize themselves with anatomical sex differences.

Sexual Health

BOX 13.1 Talking with Children about Sex

Talk early and often. Toddlers should learn the names for their genitals along with other body parts ("These are your toes, and this is your penis"—or "vulva" or "vagina"). Progress from there in an age-appropriate manner through high school. Each stage facilitates later stages: It's a lot easier to talk about a man putting his penis into a woman's vagina if you and the child have already become comfortable with talking about those body parts.

Use teachable moments. Rather than postpone everything to a "big talk about sex"—which may never happen—take advantage of opportunities that arise, such as when the child is undressing, sees a sibling or parent's genitals or nude art, witnesses sexual intimacy on television or in real life, or sees animals mating or giving birth. Take advantage of a subsequent pregnancy and childbirth, or the puberty of a sibling, to talk about these processes. Above all, respond accurately and simply to the child's questions. If a child asks about the meaning of a word he hears from peers, respond candidly and in a relaxed, nonjudgmental manner. The question "Where do babies come from?" needs to be answered several times over in increasing detail, beginning with something like "Babies grow in a special place inside the mother" and later explaining about eggs and sperm and how they come together. Respond to things the child has heard or witnessed at school or from friends: If the child announces that "Andy has two mommies," for example, that would be a good opportunity to talk about gay relationships and alternative parenting styles.

Balance negatives with positives. If you see your child masturbating, for example, then (depending on your own beliefs on the topic) you may want to say something like "That feels good, doesn't it? It's fine to do that, but it's best to do it in your bedroom. People like to do that when they're by themselves." When talking about sexual behavior, talk in an age-appropriate way about the physical and emotional pleasure of sexual contact and intimate relation-

ships—including the specific body parts, such as the clitoris, that are involved—as well as the responsibilities and risks that sexual intimacy involves.

Anticipate events. That's especially important for the bodily and psychological changes that accompany puberty. A mother can teach her daughter (or her son, for that matter) about menstruation either in words or with aids such as pictures or her own unused and used tampons. Puberty comes earlier than parents expect, and by the time schools get around to the subject, half the class may have pubic hair. There are dozens of books suitable for kids—check out the Web booksellers' sites under the search term "puberty."

Acknowledge diversity. Help your child or teen understand that there is no single "normal" size or shape for genitals or breasts; no single "normal" time for the growth spurt, menarche, a sexual relationship, falling in love, or marriage; and no single "normal" sexual orientation.

Communicate your values. Let your child know your views on when sex is acceptable—whether it should be restricted to marriage or to emotionally committed relationships, or whether it has a place outside of those relationships. If you believe that your teen is ready for some forms of sexual contact, but not for others, say so. Ask for your child's views on these questions, and if you disagree, present the reasons for your point of view rather than simply laying down the law. Explain the core values, such as respect for others or your religious beliefs that underlie your opinion.

Give practical advice. Bear in mind that most teens become sexually active well before leaving home. Adults can help teens

avoid the serious pitfalls of adolescent sexuality without encouraging them to engage in sex. Explain the specific steps they can

There are many opportunities to teach one's child about sex and reproduction.

take to reduce the likelihood of pregnancy and STDs. Remember that, depending on your school's sex-ed policy, there may be little or no instruction in contraceptive methods, especially in such practical matters as where to obtain contraceptives. It's unlikely that you'll be able to answer all the spoken or unspoken questions your teen will have about sex, so tell them about teen-oriented sex-education Web sites such as www.teen-wire.com and www.sexetc.org.

Very young children's tactile exploration may lead to autoerotic behavior.

wide variety of physical stimuli (e.g., the motion of a car or sitting in warm sand) or exciting or fearful events (e.g., playing exciting games, being asked to go to the front of the class, punishment, or looking over the edge of a building). Thus it seems that erections in young boys are part of a generalized arousal response.

Infants and young children of both sexes commonly touch their genitals. The great majority of mothers in European countries report having witnessed such behavior, whereas only about half of American mothers say that they have seen genital touching (Friedrich et al., 2000; Larsson et al., 2000). This cross-national difference could be real, but it could also reflect a greater openness of European mothers to the concept of childhood sexuality.

Of course, simply touching one's genitals may or may not be sexual in motivation. By 15 to 19 months of age, however, some girls and boys rhythmically stimulate their genitals by hand or by rubbing their genitals against an object (Galenson, 1990). Roughly 1 in 5 parents has witnessed such masturbatory behavior in their child before the age of 6; again, the numbers are higher in some European countries than in the United States (Friedrich et al., 1998; Larsson & Svedin, 2002b).

Interpersonal Sexual Activity Can Occur during Childhood

Besides solitary sexual activity, children's sexual behavior may involve others (**Table 13.1**). It is common for young children to show their genitals to adults or to other children and to attempt to view the genitals of others. Such behavior begins in the second year of life, and about half of all parents have witnessed them by the time a child reaches the age of 5 or 6. Not only parents but also preschool staff report seeing this kind of behavior (Davies et al., 2000; Larsson & Svedin, 2002b).

In addition, there may be sexual or quasi-sexual contacts between children. Children often kiss and hug each other. They may also attempt to touch each other's genitals. Sometimes these behaviors are incorporated into games such as "show," "doctor," "house," and the like. In "doctor"—just in case your childhood memories are hazy—one child complains of some pain and another investigates its cause. The genitals are often examined—even if the "pain" is an earache. In one study, about half the mothers reported that their children had engaged in this type of sexual play before the age of 6. Children who did so were no more likely to be maladjusted as teenagers than children who did not (Okami et al., 1997). In later childhood children may graduate from fantasy-based games such as "doctor" to more adultlike sexual games such as "7 minutes in heaven," in which two children go into a closet and are given that much time to kiss or fondle, while the others giggle outside.

Only very small numbers of children engage in more adultlike sexual behavior, such as coitus (or pretended coitus), oral or anal sex, or insertion of a finger or an object into the vagina or anus (see **Table 13.1**). At first glance, this might seem surprising, given that coitus-related behaviors (presenting and mounting) are almost universal among the young of nonhuman primates. Bear in mind, however, that children (at least in contemporary American culture) have little opportunity to observe adults engaged in sexual behavior beyond kissing and hugging.

TABLE 13.1

Children's Sexual Behavior[a]

Behavior	Girls	Boys
Talking about sex	28	30
Looking at pornographic pictures	13	22
Kissing and hugging	44	34
Showing genitals	23	28
Other child touching your genitals	19	17
Touching, exploring genitals of other child	19	17
Inserting objects into other child's vagina or rectum	4	10
Other child inserting objects into your vagina or rectum	2	2
Putting penis in other child's mouth	—	5
Other child putting penis in your mouth	1	2
Vaginal intercourse	1	4
Anal intercourse	0	3

Source: Larsson & Svedin, 2002a.

[a]The table shows the percentage of young adults who recalled having engaged in various voluntary sexual activities with other children when they were 6–10 years of age.

Because imitation may play a large role in the learning of interpersonal sexual behavior in childhood, one would not expect to see many children attempting coitus or other forms of penetrative sex.

The data in Table 13.1 refer only to voluntary sexual behavior between children. Sometimes a child will coerce another child into some kind of sexual activity. In one study, 13% of adolescents recalled childhood experiences of being coerced into a sexual contact by another child—the method of coercion being trickery, bribes, threats, or physical force. Eight percent recalled being the perpetrator in such coercive acts (Larsson & Svedin, 2002a).

For the most part, solitary and interpersonal sexual behaviors by children seem to be harmless. Children who engage in sexual play with other children are just as likely to be well-adjusted in the teenage years as children who did not, according to one longitudinal study carried out at UCLA (Okami et al., 1997). When adolescents or young adults are asked to describe how childhood sexual experiences made them feel, most reply with positive descriptors such as "curious," "excited," or "happy," and most say that these experiences were "normal." But a minority report that the experiences made them feel "shamed," "guilty," or "embarrassed." Girls experience more negative feelings than boys; children who are coerced experience more negative feelings than those who participate willingly; and Americans experience more negative feelings than Europeans (Larsson & Svedin, 2002a; Reynolds et al., 2003).

Cultures Vary in Their Attitudes toward Childhood Sexuality

Cross-cultural studies indicate that children in many societies engage in sexual behavior, but societies vary in whether they encourage, tolerate, or suppress it (Frayser, 1994). In Chapter 1 we mentioned the tolerance shown by the people of Mangaia toward sexual expression by children. The Chewan people of Malawi encourage their children to play at being husband and wife in little huts situated away from the village. The Lepcha people of northern India believe that coitus is necessary for girls to mature into women. Similarly, as we discussed in Chapter 1, several tribes in New Guinea believe that male-on-male fellatio is necessary for boys to develop into men (Herdt, 2005).

More commonly, however, adults exert some degree of restraint on children's sexual expression. There are usually mild restraints on heterosexual play or masturbation during early childhood, but they may become stronger during later childhood. These restraints are stronger in societies in which sexual restraint is expected of adults; thus, children are essentially being trained to develop the sexual attitudes they will show in adulthood.

Some Children Have Sexual Contacts with Adults

In the United States and other Western countries, sexual contacts between adults and children are crimes. Nevertheless, these contacts are not rare. There have been no random-sample surveys of children inquiring about their sexual experiences with adults, but a number of surveys have asked adults to recollect such experiences from their childhood. In these surveys, about 15% of women and 7% of men report that they had at least one childhood sexual experience involving physical contact with an adult (Gorey & Leslie, 1997). If one includes noncontact experiences, such as exposure of a man's genitals to a child, the percentages are higher.

Sexual assaults against children have become much less frequent in recent years: The incidence of substantiated cases fell by 39% between 1993 and 2003 (Koch, 2005). Although changes in methodology may be partly responsible, the decline is at least in part a real one.

Most Adult–Child Contacts Involve Older Children and Are Single Encounters

According to the National Health and Social Life Survey (NHSLS), most children who have sexual experiences with adults or adolescents have only one such experience, or if they have multiple experiences, they are all with the same partner. For girls, that partner is most often an adult male and less often an adolescent male. For boys, it is most commonly an adolescent female, less often an adolescent male, and even less often an adult male. The data also showed that 80% to 90% of adult–child contacts involve the adult touching the genitals of the child. Oral contacts and vaginal or anal penetration are much less common.

How old are children when they have sexual contact with adults or adolescents? The most likely age bracket for a child to have sexual contact with a male is 7 to 10 years, but about one-third of such contacts occur in the under-7 age bracket. The most likely age bracket for a boy to have contact with a female is 11 to 13 years. The females involved are usually adolescents who are a few years older than the boys.

What about the adults who have sexual contacts with children? As shown in **Table 13.2**, only a very small percentage of these adults are strangers to the children with whom they have contact. Most are relatives or family friends. Boys are most likely to have contacts with family friends, while girls are most likely to have contacts with relatives. As the table shows, girls as a group are equally likely to have contacts with fathers and stepfathers. Many more girls live with their fathers than live with stepfathers, however; thus a girl who lives with a stepfather has a relatively higher likelihood of experiencing a sexual contact with him than girls who live with their fathers.

TABLE 13.2

Percentage of Adult–Child Sexual Contacts Identified by Relationship and Child's Sex

Relationship of adult to child	Child's sex	
	Girl	Boy
Father	7	1
Stepfather	7	1
Older brother	9	4
Other relative	29	13
Teacher	3	4
Family friend	29	40
Mother's boyfriend	2	1
Older friend of child	1	4
Other person known to child	19	17
Stranger	7	4

Source: NHSLS.

Note: The percentages add up to more than 100 because some children had contacts with more than one adult.

Some Kinds of Adult–Child Sex Are More Harmful than Others

The effects of adult–child sex on children are controversial. In the minds of most members of the public, politicians, and jurists, as well as some therapists, such contacts are always extremely harmful to the child. Adult–child sex is widely referred to as "sexual abuse of children." It is a criminal offense on the part of the adult everywhere in the United States, and people convicted of it ("child molesters") are punished more severely than almost any other criminals. Sentences of 60 or more years of imprisonment may be imposed, even in cases in which the adult does not use force (Tran, 2001). Just writing down a fictitious description of (highly abusive) adult–child sex in his private journal cost one Columbus, Ohio man a 7-year prison sentence (Doulin, 2001). (After he had served 18 months, the American Civil Liberties Union [ACLU] helped secure a retrial, and the case appears to have been dropped since then.)

However, cross-cultural studies suggest that adult–child sex may not always have serious harmful consequences. We have mentioned several examples of cultures in which such contacts are or were common, accepted, and without obvious damaging effects. These are often cultures, such as that of ancient Greece, in which young unmarried men have little sexual access to women and have sexual contacts with pubertal or prepubertal boys instead. (Of course, we lack detailed information about the mental health of the affected children in this particular case, so we cannot be sure that they were unharmed.)

Many studies have focused on the effects of adult–child sexual contacts in the United States and other contemporary Western cultures. These include studies of children known to have had such contacts as well as surveys of adults who recollect such contacts from their childhood. When children who have had sexual contacts with adults are viewed as a single group, they do experience more negative consequences than control groups of children who have not had such contacts. The harmful consequences include both short-term effects (e.g., fearfulness, depression, inhibition of emotions, hostility, and antisocial behavior) and long-term effects (e.g., mood disorders, phobias, panic disorders, antisocial personality, suicidality, substance abuse, poor academic performance, premature sexual activity, sexual promiscuity, exposure to sexually transmitted diseases, and sexual victimization of others) (Green, 1992; Kendall-Tackett et al., 1993; Paolucci et al., 2001).

A somewhat different picture emerges, however, when the details of the adult–child contacts are taken into account. The children who are most likely to experience adverse effects are, not surprisingly, those who were coerced into a sexual contact (Molnar et al., 2001). Sexual contacts that are repeated over a long period of time, that are with a family member (incest), or that involve a very large age difference may also be more likely to cause harm than isolated or nonincestuous contacts or those with a small age difference between the child and the older person. Contacts that involve sexual penetration are more harmful than those that do not (Najman et al., 2007). Girls are also more likely to suffer harm than boys. According to meta-analyses and original studies by psychologist Bruce Rind of Temple University and his colleagues, most children who experience sexual contacts with adults suffer no long-term adverse consequences, or only mild ones (Rind et al., 1998; Rind, 2001).

The issue of adult–child sex and its consequences is greatly complicated by problems of recall. Ideally, children would give reliable testimony about sexual contacts they had recently experienced, and adults would have accurate memories of childhood sexual experiences. Unfortunately, neither is necessarily the case. Children can be induced to believe and report events that didn't happen, and adults can be induced to "recover" supposedly repressed memories of childhood sexual abuse, even when such memories are demonstrably false (**Box 13.2**).

Society, Values, and the Law

BOX 13.2 Sex and Suggestibility

In 1984, Peggy McMartin Buckey, along with her son Raymond and four others, faced over 200 counts of child molestation—crimes that were alleged to have taken place at the McMartin Preschool in Manhattan Beach, California (Figure A). During their trial—the longest in U.S. history—extraordinary allegations surfaced. These allegations involved not merely sexual abuse of young children, but also underground satanic rituals involving animal sacrifice. After 7 years (including a retrial for Raymond Buckley), all the defendants were acquitted.

(A) Peggy McMartin Buckley and Raymond Buckley

The core issue in the trial was the believability of the 349 children who told social workers and investigators that they had experienced, witnessed, or been told about sexual abuse at the school. It became apparent during the trial that many of these children were inculcated by their interviewers with false memories of events that never happened. We may never know whether there was any kernel of truth to the McMartin allegations, but what is certain is that unscrupulous investigators, overzealous prosecutors, and sensation-seeking media blew the case up into a hysterical witch hunt.

Sadly, the McMartin case was not the last of its kind. In 1989, Robert Kelly, the owner of the Little Rascals day-care center in North Carolina, was charged, along with six others, with molesting 29 children at the center. Young children described not merely being sexually abused but also witnessing the ritual killings of babies and the disposal of their bodies in a lake. (No babies were ever reported missing.) Some of the alleged

abuse occurred in ships on the ocean, or even in outer space. The defense argued that the children's stories were inculcated, but Kelly was convicted and sentenced to 12 life sentences. Dawn Wilson, the center's cook, was also sentenced to life imprisonment. In 1995 their convictions were overturned because of legal errors by the prosecution, and all the charges were later dropped.

In the same year that the North Carolina appeals court reversed Kelly and Wilson's convictions, 43 men and women were arrested in the picturesque apple-growing town of Wenatchee, Washington, and charged with raping and molesting 60 children. Among the defendants were the pastor of the local Pentecostal Church and his wife. The whole case was driven forward by a police detective whose 9-year-old foster daughter accused 90 people of satanic ritual abuse. Again, children were pressured by therapists to "remember" episodes of molestation and assault. The pastor and his wife spent 135 days in jail before being acquitted, but 26 defendants were convicted. Nearly all had their convictions overturned, but some spent several years in prison. The City of Wenatchee, as well as the state of Washington, ended up paying large settlements to the defendants.

There is a close connection between these cases and the epidemic of "recovered memories" that swept the United States in the late 1980s and early 1990s. In 1992, for example, a Missouri woman who was in therapy with a church counselor "remembered" that she had been repeatedly raped by her father—a minister—between the ages of 7 and 14, that she became pregnant as a result, and that she was forced to perform an abortion on herself with a coat hanger. When her story was publicized, her father had to resign his post as a minister. Before he could be tried, however, a medical examination revealed that the daughter had never been pregnant and, in fact, was still a virgin. The therapist paid $1 million in settlement of the case.

Numerous studies document that memories can be inculcated. The leading figure in this field of research is Elizabeth Loftus (now at the University of California, Irvine), who testified at the McMartin trial and in many similar cases (Loftus & Davis, 2006) (Figure B). In her best-

(B) Elizabeth Loftus

known experiment, Loftus instilled her subjects with a false memory of having been lost in a shopping mall as a child, along with various things that happened to the child while lost. Others have instilled "childhood memories" of hospitalization for an ear infection, of the sprinklers going off in a store, of an accident at a wedding reception, and the like. Nothing distinguishes these false memories from real ones—except that they are false.

Several circumstances promote the inculcation of false memories. One is that the initial account comes from a trusted or authoritative person. Another is that the subject is interviewed repeatedly. Oftentimes, details that the subject denies in initial interviews are gradually incorporated into the false memory of the event. Both these factors operate in many sexual abuse cases, Loftus says. Another dangerous but common practice is for interviewers to encourage their subjects to exercise their unfettered imagination. Loftus quotes one therapist as recommending that interviewers tell the client: "Spend time imagining that you were sexually abused, without worrying about accuracy…Who would have been likely perpetrators?" But, as Loftus's research has shown, the mere act of imagining a fictional past event facilitates the process of "remembering" it.

The sexual abuse of children does happen, and when it does it's a tragedy. But there's something about these crimes, or the rumor of them, that has often triggered "moral panics" in which common sense and elementary principles of justice fall by the wayside (Jenkins, 1998).

Sources: Lyon, 1998; Schneider & Barber, 1998; Associated Press, 1999; Landsberg, 2000; Rohrlich, 2000; Lyman, 2005.

Strategies to Prevent Adult–Child Sex Are Quite Effective

None of this should be taken as an attempt to minimize the fact that some children are indeed traumatized by sexual abuse. These children are at risk of developing **post-traumatic stress disorder**, just as are adult rape victims (see Chapter 18). One aspect of this disorder is **dissociation**—the tendency to "stand outside" the traumatic experience and to fail to experience the normal emotional responses to it. Another common trait shown by sexually abused children is self-blame. Therapy may be focused on helping the child to experience the missing emotions and to realize that the adult perpetrator was the sole guilty party.

Many schools have programs intended to teach young children how to avoid sexual encounters with adults by learning to distinguish between "good touch" (e.g., patting and hugging) and "bad touch" (e.g., genital fondling). One simple instruction that children often receive is never to allow anyone to touch them on parts of their body that are covered by a bathing suit. There has been some concern that such programs might inculcate sex-phobic attitudes, especially considering that U.S. schools do not provide general sex education for young children. A study of college-age women, however, concluded that women who underwent these prevention programs in childhood were as well adjusted sexually as other women and were much less likely to have experienced adult–child sexual contact subsequent to the instruction (Gibson & Leitenberg, 2000). Thus these programs seem to be quite effective.

Preadolescence May Be Marked by an Increase in Sexual Interest

The period between about 8 and 12 to 13 years of age is often called **preadolescence**. During this period the biological processes of puberty begin. Preadolescence may be marked by some degree of increased sexual feelings and behavior, but this varies greatly from one individual to another.

In the United States, where many young children receive little or no sex education, the early preadolescent years (say, around age 8 or 9) are the time when most children learn about coitus and other "facts of life." Much information is spread through peer networks, so comical misunderstandings are the rule. For example, children may fail to understand the difference between the anus and the vagina or may think that babies grow in the mother's stomach and emerge via the belly button. Late in elementary school, students usually have one gender-segregated lesson on the basics of puberty. Middle-school students may be exposed to school-based sex-education classes for the first time, but the content and message of these classes varies greatly from school to school (see Box 1.4).

Preadolescent Children Segregate by Sex

Preadolescent children spend much of their free time in all-male or all-female groups. Obviously, this pattern of socialization minimizes their opportunities for heterosexual interactions. Nevertheless, some older preadolescents do engage in sexual behavior with the other sex. In one study of students in an urban public school system, 30% of students entering the sixth grade (approximately 11 years old) stated that they had already engaged in sexual intercourse (Kinsman et al., 1998). The students who had done so differed in a number of respects from those who had not: They were more likely to be male, African-American, from poorer neighborhoods, from single-parent families, and to have engaged in nonsexual risky behavior. Nationwide, the proportion of children who experience coitus before the age of 13 is only 7%, but it varies greatly with ethnicity (**Figure 13.1**).

post-traumatic stress disorder A cluster of physical and psychological symptoms that can affect persons who have experienced severe trauma.

dissociation The distancing of oneself from the emotions evoked by some traumatic experience or memory.

preadolescence The age range including the beginning of puberty, from approximately 8 to 12 or 8 to 13.

likely that such communities offer adolescents few constructive goals and therefore give them little motivation to avoid sexual behavior, especially risky sexual behavior such as unprotected coitus (Billy et al., 1994).

Another factor associated with the early initiation of sexual activity is having a significantly older boyfriend or girlfriend (VanOss Marin et al., 2000; Halpern et al., 2007). This is hardly surprising, given that older partners are likely to be more sexually experienced.

Television probably promotes early entry into sex by familiarizing adolescents with sexual relationships and behaviors among young people, often in a highly glamorized and unrealistic fashion. According to the American Psychiatric Association, girls are being prematurely sexualized by exposure to inappropriate images and role models in the media and advertising (American Psychiatric Association, 2008).

Some cultural forces work against early sexual initiation. Among them are virginity pledge programs (for example: True Love Waits and Silver Ring Thing) that are run by religious organizations. The efficacy of these pledge programs is very limited, however (Brückner & Bearman, 2005; Rosenbaum, 2006). School-based abstinence programs fare even worse. In one study mandated by the U.S. Congress, students were randomly assigned to attend or not attend such programs and then followed up on for several years. Attending a program had no effect on any measure of the teens' subsequent sexual behavior (Trenholm et al., 2007). After publication of the report, Congress *increased* spending on abstinence programs (Beil, 2007).

Males Masturbate More than Females

One of the commonest sexual behaviors among adolescents is masturbation. But adolescents often feel guilty about masturbating, believe that the practice is harmful, and use allegations of masturbation as schoolyard insults (Savin-Williams & Diamond, 2004). Thus adolescents are often reluctant to admit that they masturbate, making the topic a difficult one to do research on. In one longitudinal study, for example, only about one-third of 13-year-old boys said that they masturbated, but when these same subjects were reinterviewed in adulthood more than twice as many said that they had masturbated at that age (Halpern et al., 2000a). In general, it seems clear that the frequency of masturbation increases during early and mid-teen years and that boys masturbate more frequently than girls. But girls have been catching up: In the mid-twentieth century only 39% of young women said that they had ever masturbated during childhood or adolescence; by the early twenty-first century, 84% reported having done so (Bancroft et al., 2003a). Although substantial numbers of both boys and girls begin masturbating before puberty, the onset of masturbation is much more closely synchronized with the onset of puberty in boys than it is in girls (**Figure 13.3**). This suggests a more powerful hormonal influence on masturbation in boys.

The Sexual Behavior of American Teens Has Increased and Diversified

Adolescent sexuality in the United States has changed greatly over the last half century or so. In the period immediately after the Second World War, most adolescents' goals were focused on completing schooling, entering the labor force, marrying, and starting a family. Adolescents dated, and this behavior was important for adolescents' social standing and the development of gender-appropriate roles, but dating generally involved sexual behavior short of coitus. Engaging in coitus endangered the social status of adolescent and unmarried young adult females. The status of males was not endangered in the same way (exemplifying the "double standard"). Males generally found it difficult to persuade females to have intercourse with them, and some turned to prostitutes.

(A) Males

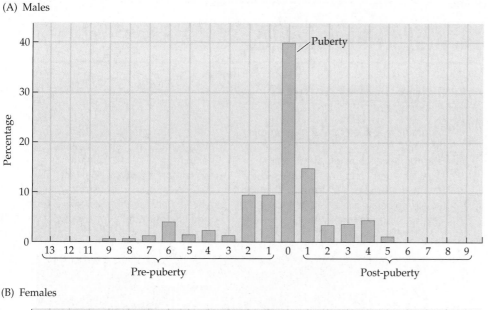

Pre-puberty   Post-puberty

Figure 13.3 Masturbation and puberty Male and female college students were asked about the age at which they first masturbated and their age at puberty, defined as menarche (girls) or first ejaculation (boys). The graphs show that the onset of masturbation is closely tied to puberty in boys (A), but not in girls (B). (Data from Bancroft et al., 2003a.)

(B) Females

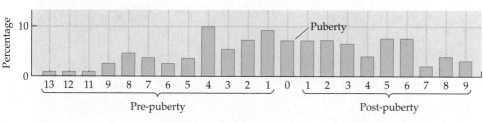

Pre-puberty   Post-puberty

Many social changes since the 1940s have caused teenage sexual activity to increase, especially among girls (**Figure 13.4**). One was the introduction of oral contraceptives in the 1960s. Another was the legalization of abortion in the United States in 1973. Yet another was the introduction of effective treatments for some sexually transmitted diseases. These factors reduced the risks of coitus to women, including adolescent women. Another factor was feminism, which encouraged women to attend college, enter the labor market, and postpone or avoid marriage. These changes reduced the importance of marriage to women's social and economic status, so that preserving their "marriageability" by refusing to engage in coitus lost much of its value. But "losing one's virginity" is still a significant event in many women's and men's lives (**Box 13.3**).

All in all, these changes have led to a considerable increase in the proportion of adolescents who engage in heterosexual intercourse, as well as in the total number of their sex partners, as compared with 50 or 60 years ago. Nevertheless, there has been a leveling off of—or slight decrease in—adolescent sexual activity in the United States in recent years: Between 1991 and 2007, the proportion of sexually active 9th- through 12th-graders dropped from 37.5% to 35%, according to the Youth Risk Behavior Survey (Centers for Disease Control, 2008j).

Noncoital Sex Is Popular among Teens

Oral sex is common among teens; by age 17, over half of all teens have engaged in it, according to the National Health Statistics survey (Mosher et al., 2005). In part, oral sex is popular because it is a way to have sex to the point of orgasm without loss of "virginity" or risk of pregnancy. In addition, teens may believe that oral sex avoids the disease risks that are associated with coitus. (This is only true in a limited way, as we'll discuss in Chapter 17.) In the late 1990s social commen-

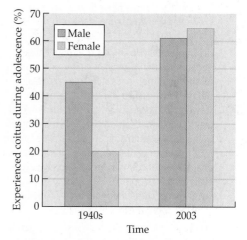

Figure 13.4 Coitus has become more common among teens. The graph shows the percentages of females and of males who experienced coitus during adolescence in the 1940s and in 2003. The 1940s data refer to coitus by age 19; the 2003 data refer to coitus by grade 12. (Data from Kinsey et al., 1948; Kinsey et al., 1953; Centers for Disease Control, 2004d.)

Research Highlights

BOX 13.3 Losing It

What does losing one's virginity mean? Does it mean *anything* anymore? Vanderbilt University sociologist Laura Carpenter set out to find the answers to these questions by conducting in-depth interviews with 61 young women and men from diverse social backgrounds and sexual identities, most of whom had already lost their virginity (Carpenter, 2005). Comments from four of them appear below.

Kelly: "Virginity is supposed to be something special and cherished and wonderful and something to keep and you give to someone who is … I don't know if *lose* is the right word … I'll say you give to someone, whenever you find the right person."

Emma: "I just did not want to be a virgin … And looking back, that wasn't particularly intelligent or mature … But at the same time, that was how I viewed it when I was a virgin."

Jason: "[Losing one's virginity is] sort of the year zero in between the part of life before sexual activity and then, the one after … the moment between having never had sex and having had it."

Carrie: "I think it's a really great way to honor God, in the sense of knowing that, whatever He has for me is going to be better than the things I can pursue on my own."

Traditionally, losing one's virginity meant engaging in penile-vaginal intercourse (coitus) for the first time. That's still a common belief, but not universal. To some of Carpenter's interviewees, losing virginity was more of a mental event than a mechanical one. So, for example, being raped would not cause one to lose virginity. Also, other sexual behaviors such as oral or anal sex might count as loss of virginity, especially for gay people.

Carpenter discerned four basic modes of thinking about the loss of virginity:

■ *Virginity loss as a gift* "Gifters" (such as Kelly) believe that virginity is something valuable to be given to a partner in a loving relationship—though not necessarily in a marriage. To gifters, virginity is not really "lost," because it becomes part of the extended self that includes the intimate partner. To gifters, the emotional aspect of losing one's virginity is more

important than the physical pleasure of the event. Before they lose their virginity, many gifters engage in a great deal of "heavy petting" and oral sex as a substitute for coitus. Although most gifters are female, some are male. Gifters want to lose their virginity to another gifter, but it

Donna (Tori Spelling) preserved her virginity through seven seasons of *Beverly Hills 90210*, finally gifting it to her future husband David (Brian Austin Green).

often doesn't work out that way, due to the shortage of male gifters. Gifters may be disappointed if they find that their partners do not reciprocate their feelings with lasting love and affection.

■ *Virginity loss as erasing a stigma* To some young people (such as Emma) virginity is a sign of "irredeemable dorkiness"—a stigma that only becomes more oppressive as the teen years roll by. Often the stigma is dealt with by claiming not to be a virgin. Losing one's virginity is seen as an end in itself and does not have to happen in the context of a loving relationship. Besides physical pleasure, it brings social status. Many of the "stigmatized" do not engage in petting and oral sex before proceeding to

coitus. They often prefer to lose their virginity with a sexually experienced partner, who may be a casual friend or acquaintance, even though such partners may mock virgins' sexual "incompetence." Because the stigmatized seize the first opportunity for coitus, they often do not use contraception or safer sex. Most of the "stigmatized" are male, but some are female.

■ *Virginity loss as a part of a process* Some young people see the loss of virginity as not something intrinsically good or bad, but as part of the process of growing up into male or female adulthood. This point of view has been influenced by the work of anthropologists who have described coming-of-age rites in non-Western cultures. "Processors" (such as Jason) see first coitus as one developmental "stepping-stone" out of many. They typically have sex with partners they are dating but don't wait for the perfect partner, as gifters do. Lesbians and gay men were disproportion-

BOX 13.3 (continued)

ately likely to take this perspective, since they experienced virginity loss as intertwined with the process of coming out.

■ *Virginity loss as a sacrament* Some religious young people such as Carrie—mostly evangelical Christians—see abstinence as a form of worship and losing one's virginity (with one's eventual spouse) as a mutual gift to God. These young people typically avoid almost all sexual intimacy before marriage. If they

do yield to temptation, they may rededicate themselves to abstinence, thinking of themselves as "born-again virgins."

Looking back on the encounters that marked their loss of virginity, some of Carpenter's subjects recalled emotional or physical pleasure, or satisfaction at having accomplished one of life's watershed tasks. But many recalled the event as disappointing, physically painful (women especially), or downright embarrassing. Here's how one young man saw it:

Bill: "I was so nervous, it was my first time, and … I didn't want to look foolish. … I tried to do what I saw the people do in the porno movies, move my body in a certain way, and do it really fast. … She was saying to me 'There's another person here, you know.' I ejaculated very quickly. I was, like, just interested in getting myself off and didn't even think about her. … I felt like I had really fucked this thing up."

tators suggested that these beliefs were driving the emergence of a new culture of oral sex among adolescents (Lewin, 1997; Stepp, 1999).

If these were the main reasons why adolescents engage in oral sex, however, we would expect there to be a period of time when they have engaged in oral sex but haven't yet experienced coitus. In reality, this is the case for only about 1 in 10 teens (Mosher et al., 2005). Much more commonly, adolescents have their first experience of oral sex shortly after they first experience vaginal sex (Lindberg et al., 2008). This suggests that, for most teens, oral sex is something they add to their sexual repertoire because of the pleasure it brings, not as a substitute for coitus. Anal sex is much less common than oral sex—only about 1 in 10 adolescents has engaged in it—but again, it is practiced mainly by teens who have already begun to experience coitus.

There are some ethnic differences in these activities. African-American adolescents are more likely to have experienced coitus than similar-age adolescents of other races (**Figure 13.5**), but they are less likely to have engaged in noncoital behaviors, especially cunnilingus. In this, they reflect the attitudes of their elders, because oral sex is much less popular among African Americans generally than it is among whites (Laumann & Michael, 2000). Hispanics are more like white Americans in this respect.

Asian Americans and Pacific Islanders (AAPI) are a small but very diverse group who often get overlooked in surveys. Far fewer AAPI high-school students have ever engaged in coitus than have students of other origins. This could be read as consistent with the stereotype of Asian Americans as the "model minority." When AAPI teens do finally engage in coitus, however, they are just as likely to do so without protection or while under the influence of alcohol or drugs (Grunbaum et al., 2000), so their "modelness" doesn't necessarily carry over into the details of their sexual activities. Part of the reason for this may be a traditional reluctance of Asian Americans to discuss sexual matters within their families or with healthcare providers: 4 out of 10 Asian-American females never discussed sexual matters with their parents, and most of the remainder were "very uncomfortable" having such discussions, according to one survey (National Asian Women's Health Organization, 1997).

Teenagers can easily run into legal problems when they engage in sexual activities, especially if one partner is older than the other. A remarkable example concerned a Georgia youth, Genarlow Wilson, who had oral sex with a willing 15-

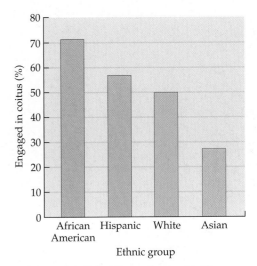

Figure 13.5 Ethnicity and sexual initiation This graph shows the percentage of U.S. high school students in various ethnic groups who have engaged in coitus. (Data from Schuster et al., 1998.)

Teen sexual relationships often have a playful quality.

year-old girl when he was 17. In 2005 Wilson was convicted of aggravated child molestation and sentenced to 10 years of imprisonment. Two years later the Georgia Supreme Court ruled that the sentence was cruel and unusual punishment and ordered him released. Age-of-consent laws are complex and highly variable from state to state. Detailed information for particular U.S. states and other countries is available online (see Web Resources at the end of this chapter).

Teen Sexuality Is Central to Identity Development

Although public attention focuses mainly on the possible negative consequences of adolescent sexuality and on ways to prevent its expression, we shouldn't ignore the positive role that sexuality plays in the process of growing up. Adolescence involves the development of a sense of self and a social identity independent of one's parents (Erikson, 1968; Steinberg, 2004). Answering questions about one's sexuality figures centrally in this process. Teens must answer many such questions: What is my sexual orientation? What am I looking for in sexual relationships? How attractive am I? Who can I attract as a sexual partner, and what is my best strategy for entering into a partnership? How does my sexuality relate to other aspects of my identity, such as my career goals, my ethnic origins, or my religion?

The development of a sense of self is vital to practical sexual concerns. For example, both young women and young men need to be able to refuse unwanted sex, especially sex without a condom. In one study of African-American teenage girls in Birmingham, Alabama, girls with a high evaluation of themselves—including a positive ethnic identity, high self-esteem, and a positive body image—communicated better with their partners concerning condom use and were more likely to refuse unprotected sex than other girls (Salazar et al., 2004). Some studies have failed to identify a beneficial effect of self-esteem, however (Boden & Horwood, 2006).

Development of a sense of self is not a purely intellectual process—it is not achieved simply by reason or introspection. Rather, it requires social exploration. This exploration takes place chiefly in the milieu in which sexual interactions are likely to arise; namely, in one's peer group—hence the transfer of energy and allegiance from parents to peers that characterizes adolescence (Brown, 1999). This is not to say that parent-teen interactions are unimportant, however. In the Birmingham study, for example, girls who spoke frequently with their parents about sexual matters were nearly twice as likely to refuse unwanted sex as those who did not (Sionean et al., 2002).

With the loosening of traditional attitudes over the last few decades has come an increasing interest among adolescents in issues of gender and sexual orientation. Most teens, regardless of their sexual orientation or gender identity, are likely to know of the existence of sexual minorities and the cultures that they have established—if only that there is a gay bar somewhere in town. Many teens are personally acquainted with one or more gay or (less likely) transgendered people. They therefore see a greater range of options open to themselves. This doesn't mean that all is now well for gay, bisexual, or transgendered youth. Far from it—increasing openness has created problems for some of them. Still, adventuresome teenagers may explore gender and sexual orientation issues in ways that were completely off limits to earlier generations.

Is Dating Outdated?

For many adolescents, sexual exploration involves **serial monogamy**, in which the youth has a series of exclusive relationships with girlfriends or boyfriends (or both). Within such serial relationships adolescents can discover what gives them pleasure and how to interact intimately with another person. Typically, the sexual content of these relationships progresses during the adolescent years from kissing and fondling to noncoital orgasmic contacts, and possibly to coitus.

Nevertheless, steady relationships may be losing their overriding importance among sexually active teens today, according to investigations by the *New York Times* and some other newspapers (Denizet-Lewis, 2004; Gootman, 2004). Casual sex seems to be becoming more common. Dating may be replaced by group outings from which sexual interactions sometimes evolve. Even that most time-hallowed of dating rituals, the high-school prom, is changing—more and more teens are attending proms in groups without specific partners, and group dances such as the Cha Cha Slide are gaining in popularity. Terms such as "hooking up" (sexual intimacy between acquaintances) "friends with benefits" (acquaintances who hook up on a somewhat regular basis) or "fuckbuddies" (a similar but more explicit term), are replacing "date," "girlfriend," or "boyfriend." "The couple thing is overrated," one 17-year-old girl told the *Times*, "It gets too clingy."

Somewhat contradicting this apparent trend are the dry statistics collected by the Centers for Disease Control. According to their National Youth Risk Behavior Survey, the percentage of high-school students who have had four or more sex partners actually fell—from 18.7% to 14.9%—between 1991 and 2007 (Centers for Disease Control, 2008j). Why the discrepancy? The trend noted by journalists may be regionally limited, students may be more open about their sexual behavior rather than actually engaging in more behavior, or it may be that much of the increase in sexual behavior doesn't involve coitus and therefore isn't counted as "sex."

Teen Pregnancy Is Declining but Is Still Too Common

Teenage pregnancy is not an inherently bad thing, of course. Nature designed females to start having children soon after puberty, and in many developing countries females are expected to marry in their mid-teens and bear children shortly thereafter. There are some advantages to becoming a mother early. These include a decreased risk of breast cancer later in life, a lesser likelihood of fertility problems, and the ability to look after and enjoy one's children while still in the full vigor of young adulthood. Some teenagers—with help from their partners, their parents, or social services—are able to successfully incorporate pregnancy and motherhood into their lives, and those who have difficulty may eventually recover from the disadvantages of early, unassisted motherhood. In fact, the very experience of being a mother helps some previously aimless teenagers focus on their life goals and strive for success (SmithBattle, 2007).

In spite of these positive points, the outcome of pregnancy is not a happy one for most American teenagers (National Campaign to Prevent Teen and Unplanned Pregnancy, 2008). The majority of these pregnancies (about 4 out of 5) are unintended, and one-third of all teen pregnancies end in abortion (Jones et al., 2002). When these unintended pregnancies are allowed to go to term, the children born of them are less likely to be breastfed and more likely to suffer health problems than other children. If the pregnancy is intended, it may be for less than satisfactory reasons, such as a desire for the self-esteem or social status that is imagined to go with motherhood. The father

This teenage mother and her child are likely to face economic hardship.

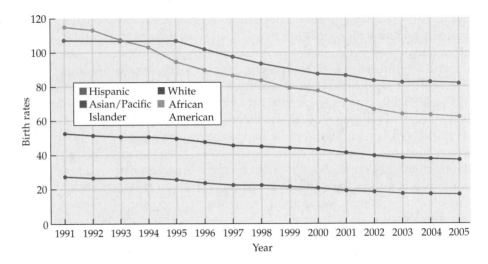

Figure 13.6 Teen birth rates have dropped. This graph shows birth rates (births per 1000 females per year) for U.S. females aged 15–19, by race/ethnicity. (Data from Centers for Disease Control, 2007a.)

may be out of the picture before the child's birth or soon thereafter—oftentimes his name does not even appear on the birth certificate. When the father can be identified, he is typically several years older than the mother. Most teen fathers do want to be involved in their child's life, but circumstances often make a positive supporting role difficult. If the mother and father marry, the likelihood of marital breakdown is high. Pregnancy and motherhood impair teenagers' opportunities for education and employment, so children of teenage mothers typically grow up in poverty and are more likely to drop out of school than other children.

Happily, teen birth rates have been declining steadily in all ethnic groups in the United States over the last 15 years—most markedly among African-American teens (**Figure 13.6**). The decline is due to a decrease in pregnancy rates, not to an increase in abortion. The decline in the pregnancy rate is due mostly (86%) to improved contraceptive use and only to a small degree (14%) to an increase in abstinence among teens (Santelli et al., 2007). In spite of the decline, there is much still to be done: Teen birth rates are far higher in the United States than in many other developed countries (**Figure 13.7**).

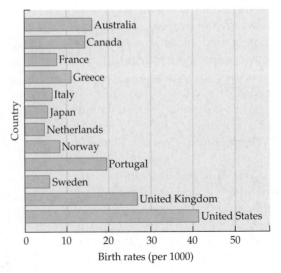

Figure 13.7 The United States still leads in teen births. This bar graph shows the 2004 birth rates per 1000 females aged 15–19, for selected countries (Data from National Campaign to Prevent Teen Pregnancy, 2006a.)

In Young Adulthood, Conflicting Demands Moderate Sexual Expression

In Chapter 10 we discussed the kinds of sexual relationships that adults may engage in. We now attempt to describe how those relationships structure individual life courses. We begin with collective data—data that describe generic Americans, with their off-white skin color, predominantly heterosexual orientation, and 2.1 children.

Most Young Men and Women Have Only a Few Sex Partners

The median age at first marriage in the United States is now about 28 for men and 26 for women, up from 23 and 21 in 1970 (U.S. Census Bureau, 2008). Assuming an age of 13 for puberty, Joe Median can therefore expect a period of 15 years between puberty and marriage, and Jane Median can expect a period of 13 years. By many measures, this period includes Joe and Jane's peak sexual years. It includes the years of most frequent sexual behavior (including mas-turbation) (Kinsey et al., 1948; Kinsey et al., 1953; Now, 2004), of greatest fertility, and of greatest physical attractiveness (for females as judged by males, at least—see Chapter 8). Typically, Joe and Jane spend a portion of this period without a sexual relationship, a portion dating (with varying degrees of sexual intimacy), and a por-tion (usually about a year) cohabiting with the partner they ultimately marry.

Given all one reads and hears about sex among young adults, the actual statis-tics from the National Health and Social Life Survey (NHSLS) may be surprising (**Figure 13.8**). Between age 18 and the time of first marriage or cohabitation—what we might call the young adult dating years—men and women have fairly low numbers of sex partners. In all demographic groups, significant numbers of indi-viduals have *no* new sex partners during the dating years (they may have no part-ners at all, or a continuation of a relationship they began before age 18). In no group does the majority have more than four new partners.

In one random survey of college undergraduates (University of Arizona Cam-pus Health Service, 2005), 42% said they did not have sexual intercourse with anyone in the previous year, 40% had one partner, and only 1% had more than five

Young adults typically spend several years dating and relating before they move in with a partner.

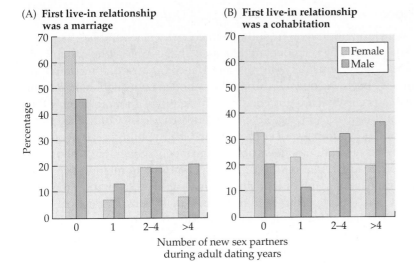

(A) First live-in relationship was a marriage

(B) First live-in relationship was a cohabitation

Number of new sex partners during adult dating years

Figure 13.8 Two routes to a live-in relationship Women and men whose first live-in relationship is a marriage (A) have relatively few sex partners during the dating years compared with people who enter cohabitations (B). The graphs show the percentage of women and men born between 1963 and 1974 who had the stated numbers of new sex partners between the age of 18 and the time of their first live-in sexual relationship. (Data from NHSLS.)

Married or cohabitating? These days, it can be hard to tell the difference.

partners. Some students who are not sexually active—often the more religiously minded ones—describe themselves as practicing "secondary abstinence." This means that they have made a conscious decision not to have sex after having been sexually active at some earlier age.

Cohabitation Is an Increasingly Prevalent Lifestyle

Most men and women hope to enter into a durable, live-in sexual relationship—a cohabitation or marriage—eventually. Often, a desire for children comes into play here, but even people who don't want children commonly want to be part of a long-term, loving relationship.

Cohabitation is the word we use to describe the relationship of a couple—heterosexual or homosexual—that lives together in a sexual relationship without being legally married. Cohabitation has become an increasingly prevalent form of relationship over the past few decades, both in the United States and in other Western countries. For nearly all men and women born before 1940, the first live-in sexual relationship was marriage. Among men and women born after 1953, however, about half made cohabitation their first live-in relationship, and today the majority of young people will enter into a cohabitation at least once in their lives.

What factors influence the choice of cohabitation or marriage as a first live-in relationship? According to the NHSLS, younger people, as well as people whose parents separated while they were children, are more likely to cohabit; members of conservative Protestant denominations, as well as people who put off their first sexual experience until after the age of 18, are more likely to marry. City dwellers are more likely to cohabit, country folk to marry.

Although so many people now make their first live-in relationship a cohabitation, only a small fraction of the U.S. population (about 7% of men and women aged 18 to 59) is cohabiting at any given time. That's because cohabitations are typically short-lived: According to the NHSLS data, about half of all cohabiting couples either married or split up within a year of moving in together. Roughly equal numbers of cohabitations ended in marriage and in separation. (A smaller number ended in the death of one partner.)

Cohabitation is becoming even more popular in Canada than in the United States. Among the Canadian provinces, Quebec leads the trend: 29% of Quebecois couples are cohabiting (Wu, 2007). This is the same percentage as in Sweden, long considered the world capital of liberal sexual attitudes.

Marriages Preceded by Cohabitation Are Less Durable

Cohabitation signals a withdrawal from the sexual marketplace and has the flavor of a "trial marriage." In that vein, one might expect that couples who cohabit and then marry would have unusually durable marriages because the incompatible couples would have been weeded out during the period of cohabitation. In fact, the reverse is true: Marriages that are preceded by cohabitation end more quickly than those that are not (Bumpass & Sweet, 1989; Centers for Disease Control, 2002a).

The reason for this paradox is not entirely clear. One hypothesis is that couples who cohabit have less traditional views about marriage in general and show this by divorcing more readily. A second hypothesis is that live-in relationships tend to last a certain time, so if some of that time is used up in cohabitation the marriage will be that much shorter. A third hypothesis is that the experience of cohabitation somehow reduces subsequent marital stability. According to one detailed study (De Vaus et al., 2003), the first hypothesis was the correct one in the past, when cohabitation was rare and only unconventional people cohabited, but the

cohabitation A live-in sexual relationship between two persons who are not married to each other.

second explanation appears to be the main or even the entire explanation today, when cohabitation is commonplace. The researchers could find no evidence for the third hypothesis; in fact, they speculated that the net effect of the cohabitation experience (for the most recent cohabitors) is to stabilize subsequent marriage. In other words, encouraging couples to marry directly rather than to cohabit first would not increase the length of their entire live-in relationships, but might actually shorten them.

Cohabitation Has Diverse Meanings

Some cohabitations differ from trial marriages in significant ways. About 40% of cohabiting couples have children, for example (including children of the couple and children from prior relationships). Some cohabitations are lengthy—about 20% last more than 5 years. Some are between elderly people—widowed or divorced—who see no particular need to marry because they will not have children or who prefer not to marry in order not to disturb pension or inheritance arrangements. Some are same-sex couples, for whom legal marriage is not an option in most states.

What is cohabitation like for the participants, as compared with marriage? The answer seems to depend on whether the participants view their cohabitation as a prelude to marriage or not (Smock, 2000). For those who do, the cohabitation is experienced very much like a marriage. For those who do not, there is (on average) poorer management of conflicts and less overall satisfaction with the relationship than would typically be seen in a marriage. Part of the reason may be that these cohabitations are less well connected to social support networks such as extended families and friends.

Many cohabiting couples appreciate the informality of their relationship. They may be less burdened by social expectations and less constrained by traditional roles than if they were married. It may be easier to preserve financial independence, if that is desired. And breaking up, if it comes to that, is less of a public embarrassment. On the down side, cohabiting couples are often denied many rights provided automatically to married couples. Therefore, cohabitation can bring bureaucratic hassles, especially if there are children. People who cohabit have to draw up wills, durable powers of attorney, and other documents if they want their wishes to be respected in case of incapacity or death.

For many couples, cohabitation is not perceived as an alternative to marriage but as an alternative to *dating* (Manning & Smock, 2007). In other words, the decision to cohabit may be driven more by economic considerations or convenience than by a deep sense of commitment. "We were paying rent in two places and living in one," a 23-year-old told *USA Today*. "It seemed financially reasonable [to cohabit], and we're pretty compatible" (Jayson, 2005). Given that dating relationships tend to be short-lived, we wouldn't necessarily expect couples who cohabit as an alternative to dating to stay in specific cohabitations for long periods of time. And indeed, "serial cohabitation" is an increasingly prevalent lifestyle.

Because increasing numbers of college students live in coed dorms, where sexual relationships arise and dissolve fairly easily, serial cohabitation may simply be seen as the continuation of a culture initiated in college. Given all that we have said about gender differences in the desire for commitment, however, serial cohabitation may be a less satisfactory arrangement for women than it is for men. In fact, serial cohabitation is something that many women drift into on account of poverty or other disadvantageous circumstances rather than because of any actual preference for such a lifestyle (Lichter et al., 2006).

We tend to think of cohabitation as a product of liberal Western attitudes toward sexuality. Yet even some conservative cultures around the world have sanctioned impermanent sexual relationships. The Shi'ite branch of Islam, for example, has a

mut'a A contract to marry for a fixed period of time.

bigamy In law, the crime of marrying someone while already married to another spouse.

polygamy Marriage to more than one spouse at a time.

polygyny Marriage of one man to more than one woman.

concubine A woman who cohabits with a man but is not his wife, usually in polygamous cultures.

temporary marriage known as **mut'a** (Arabic). The terms of this marriage, including its duration, are specified by the partners in advance. Mut'a may last for as little as 30 minutes if the man and woman want to have just a one-time sexual encounter, or it might last for a year if a man is living away from home for that period of time and wants a temporary wife for the duration. It is a real marriage in the sense that any offspring of the relationship are legitimate. It is open to unmarried women and to married or unmarried men. In some parts of the Islamic world, however, short-term mut'a has become a legal cover for prostitution.

Marriage Takes Diverse Forms

Most, if not all, human cultures have formalized heterosexual unions in some way, but the manner in which this has been done has varied greatly. In ancient Israel, one way for a couple to marry was simply to let it be known that they had had intercourse (Biale, 1984). In India, a wedding is an elaborate ceremony that takes up the best part of a week and involves lengthy rituals and enormous expense, particularly on the part of the bride's parents. In the United States, getting married can mean anything from a quick visit to a government office to a multimillion-dollar union of dynasties.

The Formalization of Sexual Unions Has Social and Personal Functions

Formalizing sexual unions by marriage has a variety of purposes. In many cultures, women have been viewed as men's property; in such cultures, marriage was a transaction marking the transfer of a woman from her father to her husband. More positively, marriage has functioned in several ways to create an environment favorable for child-rearing. First, marriage was traditionally a means to identify the man responsible for the support of a woman and her children. Even today, husbands are usually required to contribute to the support of all children their wives bear during their marriage, no matter who fathered them. Second, by publicly identifying two people as a couple, marriage places an obligation on others to respect the sexual exclusivity of their relationship, thus reducing social friction. Third, marriage may bring the couple's extended families together; this was an important function of marriage in traditional societies, in which marriages were often used to end vendettas or to create social alliances. Finally, by making it difficult for a man and woman to separate, marriage is intended to stabilize their union and ensure that they stay together long enough to rear their children.

Many Societies Have Permitted Polygamy

Nearly all Americans think of a marriage as involving just two people, and the law reinforces this attitude: Anyone who marries someone while still married to someone else is committing the crime of **bigamy**. Thus you might be tempted to think that monogamy is the only normative form of sexual relationship around the world.

Anthropological studies suggest the reverse: **Polygamy** is, or has been, commonplace. Out of 853 preindustrial societies analyzed in one survey, 84% permitted men to have more than one female mate (**polygyny**), and in most of these cultures polygynous unions were legally recognized (Fisher, 1989). Today, most Islamic countries permit polygyny, as does India, though only for its Muslim citizens.

The exact arrangements in polygynous societies vary. Often, the first mate has some kind of official status as "principal wife." In some societies polygynous relationships are permitted but not legally formalized. In such cases, the later mates may be **concubines** whose attachment to the household is impermanent and whose children have no inheritance rights.

Given that there are roughly equal numbers of men and women in most societies, not every man in a polygynous society can have multiple wives. In fact, most men in such societies have just one wife at best; it is the wealthy and powerful men who have many. The extreme cases were the **harems** associated with Oriental rulers. According to Jewish legend, King Solomon had a harem of a thousand wives, each of whom prepared a banquet every evening in the faint hope that he would dine with her. Harems were traditionally watched over by **eunuchs** (castrated men).

A marked excess of women can occur in societies whose menfolk have been decimated by warfare. In fact, a close reading of the passage in the Koran that authorizes Muslims to engage in polygamy suggests that the institution was intended to help the numerous war widows of early Islamic society as well as their fatherless children (Hasan, 1996).

Polygamy is connected to the idea that women are men's property—if a rich man has many cattle, why shouldn't he have many wives? Thus the Christian prohibition of polygamy, which distinguishes it from many other religions, such as Islam, can be viewed as an attempt to assure some equity in marriage. Still, shades of polygamy persist in Western culture: Some wealthy men support mistresses, and a polygamous culture persists among some fundamentalist Mormons (**Box 13.4**).

Societies in which one woman takes more than one husband or mate (**polyandry**) have been very uncommon. They have tended to be societies in which resources are so limited that a man cannot maintain a wife and children on his own. That has been true for high-altitude communities in Tibet and other parts of the Himalayas (Samal et al., 1997). In these communities, a woman may marry two or more brothers, an arrangement that prevents the subdivision of scarce arable land. Less formal arrangements of the same kind tend to crop up in other parts of the world, such as southern Africa, where low-income male migrant workers live together in communal groups. These groups often share a common girlfriend—an arrangement that has been disastrous in terms of HIV transmission. Female prostitution can also be viewed as a kind of polyandry.

harem 1. The quarters for wives and children in a polygamous Muslim household. 2. In some species, the group of females who live and mate with a single male.

eunuch A man who has been castrated.

polyandry Marriage of one woman to more than one man.

polyamory The formation of nontransient sexual relationships in groups of three or more.

swingers Couples who agree to engage in casual sexual contacts with others.

group marriage Three or more people living together in a marriage-like relationship.

Polyamory Includes a Variety of Nonmonogamous Relationships

Somewhat related to polygamy is **polyamory**. This is a catch-all term for people who openly and intentionally participate in nonmonogamous relationships. Some polyamorists are **swingers** or "mate swappers": These are usually couples (married or otherwise) who engage in casual sex with likeminded others. To swingers, this behavior may be seen as a way of avoiding the desire or necessity for secret extramarital affairs (Gould, 1999).

Other polyamorists, however, form stable, sexually linked groups of three or more people who usually live together as a family. This phenomenon is called **group marriage**, or polyfidelity. Group marriage has surprisingly deep roots in America. One group of about 250 people, the Oneida Community in upstate New York, flourished from 1848 to 1881. Every man in the community was considered to be married to every woman, and exclusive sexual relationships were forbidden. Excessive preg-

Tibetan polyandrous family. Cai Zhuo with her two husbands, who are brothers, and their son.

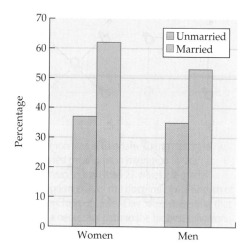

Figure 13.10 Happily married The graph shows the percentage of married women and men and unmarried women and men who call themselves "very happy" (when given the choices of "very happy," "fairly happy," and "not too happy"). (Data from Gallup Organization, 2000.)

prenuptial agreement A contract signed before marriage, spelling out the disposition of wealth in the event of divorce.

postnuptial agreement A financial agreement between spouses.

covenant marriage A form of marriage that requires a stronger vow of commitment than a regular marriage and that makes divorce harder to obtain.

tual nature of marriage is the appearance of custom-designed legal agreements. These include **prenuptial agreements**, which are used primarily to specify the distribution of wealth in the eventuality of divorce, **postnuptial agreements**, which are similar agreements made after marriage, and **covenant marriages** (available only in Louisiana, Arkansas, and Arizona), which are less easily dissolved than conventional marriages.

Second, a companionate marriage implies some kind of equivalence between husband and wife. Indeed, past generations would be amazed at the similarity of the roles of men and women in present-day marriages—especially in terms of the distribution of breadwinning, household, and decision-making responsibilities. That's not to say that women earn as much as men (they don't) or that men do their fair share of housework (they don't), but the fact that these activities are shared at all is a major break from the past.

This increasing equivalence has been brought about not only by the education of women and their entry into the labor market, but also by the decline in the number of children produced by women during marriage. If we visit the home of Joe and Jane Median—who have married each other since we last met them—we will find that *they do not have a single child in their home with them.* In other words, the number of married-couple households with no children under 18 is greater than the number of such households with one or more children, so the median number of children living in a household is zero (U.S. Census Bureau, 2001). This lack or small number of children minimizes the biologically distinct roles of men and women.

Husbands and wives have become all-purpose companions: They are expected to be romantic partners, friends, economic collaborators, fellow workers in the home, and colleagues in parenting. And they are expected to sustain all these relationships with far less support from relatives or neighbors than was customary a generation or two ago. It is no small challenge, but for many it works: Married people are significantly happier than the unmarried (**Figure 13.10**).

Marriage Is Becoming a Minority Status

So is marriage on the way out? That depends on how you look at the numbers. Currently, over 90% of Americans marry at least once. This suggests that marriage is still an attractive institution to most people. However, this percentage disregards the length of time for which people are married, which is shrinking (see below). In addition, there is no guarantee that the younger, not-yet-married generation will mimic the behavior of their elders with regard to marriage. (That's why we don't use the term "premarital sex" in this book.)

The percentage of the population that is not married at any given time is steadily rising, and the percentage that is currently married is steadily falling. The United States passed a notable landmark in 2005, when for the first time less than half of all households (49.7%) consisted of married couples (Roberts, 2006).

There are many regional and ethnic differences in marriage rates, however. African-American women, for example, are far less likely to be married or cohabiting than other groups. (U.S. Census Bureau, 2001) (**Figure 13.11**). A large part of the reason is the shortage of available young black men (Eckholm, 2006). Because black men have a much higher death rate than black women, and are much more likely than black women to be incarcerated or partnered with non-blacks, the effective sex ratio in the black community is skewed strongly toward women. This imbalance is worsened by the relatively high unemployment rate among young black men, which makes them less desirable as live-in partners. Thus black women are often single, even though they generally prefer to be partnered (Oropesa & Gorman, 2000). All of these statements apply largely to African-

(A)

(B)

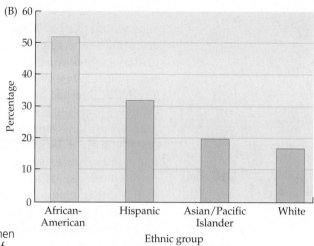

Figure 13.11 Single parenthood (A) African-American women are much more likely to be single mothers than are women of other racial or ethnic groups. (B) The graph shows the percentage of family households that are not headed by a married couple; the great majority of these are single-mother families. (Data from U.S. Census Bureau, 2001.)

Americans living in the inner city, however; among those who live in the suburbs, living arrangements are much more like those of other middle-class Americans. Furthermore, black single-mother families are often strengthened by the presence of other relatives in the household or by strong kinship links outside of it (Barnes, 2001).

Most Married Couples Are Satisfied with Their Sex Lives

Marriage has many functions, but this book is about sexuality, so our main concern is with marital sex. Here the picture is somewhat paradoxical: Married (and cohabiting) couples generally seem happier with their sex lives than the frequency of their sexual activities would suggest.

NHSLS data illustrating this point are shown in **Figure 13.12**. The figures show that married women, as a group, are less likely than dating women to have sex more than twice a week. They are also less adventurous sexually, at least in terms of a lesser likelihood of engaging in oral sex (either fellatio or cunnilingus). In addition, women in any long-term relationship, including marriage, are less likely to experience orgasm reliably than are women in short-term dating relationships. Paradoxically, women's physical satisfaction with sex is much greater in long-term relationships than in short-term relationships, and their emotional satisfaction is higher in marriage than in any other class of relationship. Data for men (not shown) are roughly comparable, except that men have a high likelihood of experiencing orgasm regardless of the kind of relationship they are in.

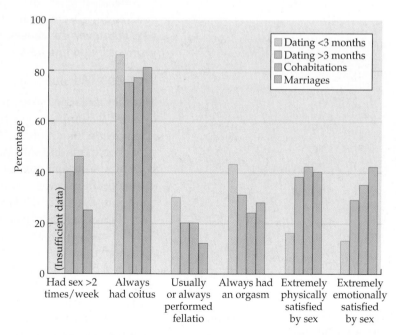

Figure 13.12 Married women have sex less frequently, engage in less oral sex, and are less likely to experience orgasm, but are more likely to derive physical and emotional satisfaction from sex, compared with women in dating relationships. (Data from NHSLS.)

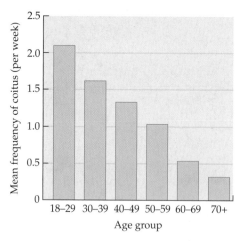

Figure 13.13 Marital sex becomes less frequent with increasing age. (Data from National Opinion Research Center, 1998.)

habituation The psychological process that reduces a person's response to a stimulus or drug after repeated exposure.

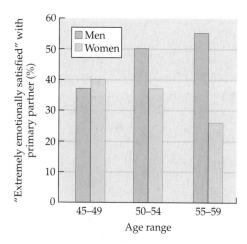

Figure 13.14 Emotional satisfaction changes with age. Between the ages of 45 to 59, men become more emotionally satisfied with their partners (usually their spouses), but women become less satisfied. (Data from NHSLS.)

Marriage Makes Sex More Satisfying for Women

Why would this be? There could be two different reasons. These results could be an artifact reflecting different demographic characteristics among the various groups studied. Alternatively, it could be that marriage somehow confers satisfaction—especially emotional satisfaction—on the sexual aspects of relationships. The NHSLS researchers carried out a statistical analysis to resolve this question (Waite & Joyner, 2001) and came up with the following answer. For men, demographics are key—when men are matched for other characteristics, they are about equally likely to be satisfied by sex within marital and nonmarital relationships. For women, however, the finding is *not* an artifact. In other words, women derive extra emotional satisfaction from sex within a married relationship simply by virtue of that relationship being a marriage. We may speculate that the reason for the extra satisfaction is the high level of commitment and exclusivity represented by the institution of marriage—qualities that are more important to women than to men.

The Frequency of Sex Declines during Marriage

Sexual interactions between married partners tend to fall off over time (Christopher & Sprecher, 2000; Bozon, 2001). Several factors are at work here. First, there is a loss of sexual interest associated with increasing familiarity between the partners (**habituation**) and the dimming of passionate love. This factor seems to be responsible for a decline in the frequency of coitus over the first year or two of marriage. Partners may become less physically attractive with aging, and even if they don't, there may be a *perception* of diminished attractiveness, prompted by exposure to beautiful people outside the relationship (**Box 13.5**). There is also a long-lasting decline in sexual interest and frequency of coitus following the birth of children. Finally, there is a decline in sexual behavior associated with the process of aging itself. This age-related decline may have a number of components, including a lessening of the physiological processes associated with arousal, a decreasing sex drive due to falling blood levels of gonadal steroids, and a general decrease in health and fitness, including an increased likelihood of obesity. Whatever the causes, the frequency of marital sex declines steadily as the years go by (**Figure 13.13**).

Women's Marital Satisfaction Declines during Middle Age

Marital satisfaction also falls off over time, although to a highly variable degree (Musick & Bumpass, 2006); some couples remain highly satisfied with their marriage over a long lifetime. The birth of the first child is associated with a significant drop in marital satisfaction (Tomlinson, 1987; Crohan, 1996), in part because both husbands and wives tend to see themselves as having to shoulder an unfair share of family responsibilities. Other landmarks, such as the entry of the oldest child into adolescence (Gottman & Notarius, 2000) and retirement (Lee & Shehan, 1989), may also be associated with decreased marital satisfaction.

On the whole, wives are less satisfied with their marriages than are husbands (Schumm et al., 1998). A particularly striking change happens between the ages of 45 and 59. At the commencement of this period, men and women's emotional satisfaction with their primary sex partner (usually their spouse) is about the same, but during this period men's satisfaction increases substantially, while women's satisfaction falls (**Figure 13.14**). Thus, by their late fifties, men are more than twice as likely as women to describe themselves as "extremely emotionally satisfied" with their partners. Physical satisfaction follows a very similar trend. In considering possible reasons for this sex difference, bear in mind that by their late fifties many men and women are in a second or later marriage and

Research Highlights

BOX 13.5 Contrast Effects and Marital Woes

Thanks to the media, we are now being bombarded with nonstop images of extremely attractive people—something that our great-grandparents were rarely exposed to. Is this

why we don't stay married as long as our great-grandparents did? Some researchers think so and have come up with evidence to back up their belief.

Back in 1980, psychologists Douglas Kenrick and Sara Gutierres of Arizona State University had a bunch of male college students perform a fairly untaxing task: They had to watch *Charlie's Angels*—a TV show that featured Farrah Fawcett (see figure) and other beauties of the 1970s. Another bunch of "control" students didn't watch the show. Then all the students were asked to judge the suitability of an average-looking woman as a blind date. The men who had seen *Charlie's Angels* rated the woman significantly less attractive than did the controls. Evidently, seeing extremely beautiful women had made the average-looking woman less attractive by a contrast effect (Kenrick & Gutierres, 1980).

Can such a contrast effect influence the attractiveness of one's own partner? Apparently so. In 1989, Kenrick's group published a study in which they showed men nude magazine centerfolds. After seeing the pictures, the men rated their own partners less attractive than did men who had seen nonattractive images, and they even rated their love for their partners as less intense (Kenrick et al., 1989).

The researchers did an equivalent study on women. Women's ratings of the attractiveness of their partners were unaffected by viewing photos of naked men. When women viewed photos of men that were accompanied by descriptions of the men's leadership qualities and achievements, however, there *was* an

effect: They rated their satisfaction with their current partners lower than did women who viewed pictures of men described as unambitious or ineffectual. Of course, this finding fits with other evidence that women's judgments of attractiveness are strongly influenced by non-physical attributes, such as social position.

Do these contrast effects actually influence the durability of marriages? To find out, sociologists Satoshi Kanazawa (of Indiana University of Pennsylvania) and Mary Still (of Cornell University) tried to think of a profession that involved frequent contact with attractive young people. They chose teaching. They identified 646 male and female teachers (junior high, high school, and college) from data in the General Social Survey and compared them with non-teachers matched for a variety of demographic factors that are known to influence divorce rates. The male teachers—but not the female teachers—were significantly more likely to be divorced or never married than the nonteacher controls. That, Kanazawa and Still surmise, is because male teachers are constantly seeing attractive young women—and the contrast effect makes their own wives seem unattractive (Kanazawa & Still, 2000).

You may well be able to think of alternative explanations for Kanazawa and Still's finding. But just to be safe, you might want to dump that teacher boyfriend before he dumps you.

that older men typically have more choice in the marriage market than do older women.

Some researchers have argued that women's declining marital satisfaction over time is a cohort effect: That is, today's younger women may simply be more successful than their elders in getting what they want from marriage, sexually and otherwise (Carpenter et al., 2007). If so, their satisfaction with their marriages may not decline in the future—or not as much as would be expected.

Many Factors Bring Relationships to an End

A large fraction of all marriages end in separation or divorce. (We refer to these events as "breakups" or "marital disruption.") In the preceding section (and in Chapter 10), we discussed some of the family circumstances and psychological factors that seem to promote or prevent the breakup of marriages. In a broader, demographic sense, the likelihood of marital disruption is linked to four major

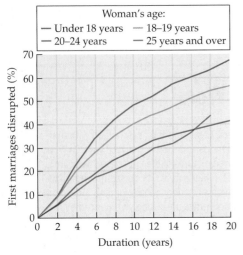

Figure 13.15 Teen marriages are less durable. The percentage of first marriages that have broken up rises faster over time for marriages in which the woman is either younger than 18 or aged 18–19 than for marriages at older ages. (Data from U.S. Census Bureau, 2001.)

factors: the passage of time, age at marriage, ethnicity, and educational level (Centers for Disease Control, 2001; Hurley, 2005).

The likelihood of marital disruption is highest during the first few years of marriage, but breakups continue at significant rates thereafter. About 1 in 5 of all first marriages ends within 5 years, and 1 in 3 ends within 10 years. The overall divorce rate—the fraction of all marriages that end in divorce or separation—is about 45% (Hurley, 2005).

Marriage during the teen years increases the risk of disruption (**Figure 13.15**). If the woman is under 18 at the time of marriage, the chances of breakup within 10 years are double what they are for the marriages of women who are over 25 (1 in 2 versus 1 in 4). The reasons for the vulnerability of teen marriages probably include the immaturity of the partners, the economic stresses of early marriage, and the fact that some teen marriages are "shotgun" (forced by pregnancy).

African-American couples are more likely to break up than whites or Hispanics, and Asian Americans are less likely to break up (**Figure 13.16**). This ethnic effect is quite strong: By 10 years after marriage, about 1 in 2 black couples, 1 in 3 white and Hispanic couples, and only 1 in 5 Asian-American couples has broken up.

A college education does wonders for marital stability: The divorce rate for people with a 4-year college degree is less than half what it is for those without such a degree, and this difference persists even after factoring out the higher age at which college-educated people marry. What do you think might be responsible for this difference?

Dissimilarity between Husbands and Wives Shortens Marriages

Other factors are associated with an increased likelihood of marital disruption. In Chapter 8 we described the concept of homophily—the idea that people are attracted to others who resemble themselves. Homophily seems to influence marital stability, according to NHSLS data. Thus married couples that have different religions are more than twice as likely to break up as couples that share the same religion. Couples that differ in ethnicity are 69% more likely to break up than couples that do not. Large age differences also increase the chances of a breakup. The reason for these trends is not entirely clear. Besides possible direct effects, such as marital tensions arising from the partners' differences or a lack of shared interests, there are likely to be indirect effects: Couples that differ in religion or ethnicity may be exposed to social prejudice and may be more isolated from their extended families than couples who share the same religion or ethnicity. Thus their marriages may receive less external support.

When individual divorced people are asked about why their marriages ended, they do not refer to demographic variables, but rather to specific problems in their own marriages. These problems include extramarital relationships, sexual or psychological incompatibility, money problems, drinking and drug use, and so on (White, 1991). In non-Western societies, infertility is also a major reason for divorce (Betzig, 1989; Inhorn, 1996). The discovery that the bride was not a virgin may trigger a divorce in some Muslim countries. In 2008 a French court sparked a national outcry when it granted a Muslim man's request for divorce on those grounds (Associated Press, 2008c).

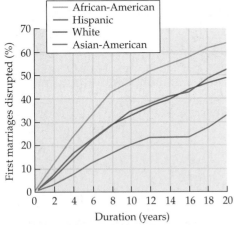

Figure 13.16 Ethnicity influences the durability of marriage. The percentage of first marriages that have broken up rises fastest for marriages in which the wife is African American and slowest for marriages in which the wife is Asian American. (Data from U.S. Census Bureau, 2001.)

Marital Disruption Can Have Negative and Positive Consequences

In the immediate aftermath of a divorce, negative emotions such as anger, guilt, sadness, or fear for the future often predominate. Yet divorce is a mixed bag in terms of its effects on the man and woman and any children they may have.

Divorced Men and Women Can Suffer Physical, Psychological, and Economic Damage

When marriages end, there are all kinds of negative consequences that go far beyond the bitter feelings of the breakup itself (Smock, 1993; Amato, 2000). Divorced people suffer higher rates of psychological and physical ill health (including higher mortality) than do married people. They are less happy, less sexually active (Stack & Gundlach, 1992), more socially isolated, and more prone to substance abuse. Divorced women—who usually retain custody of children—generally suffer a severe drop in per capita household income. (Divorced men, on the other hand, may see a rise in per capita household income.) The children of divorced parents experience a heightened risk of depression, behavior problems, low academic performance, substance abuse, criminality, and early sexual activity (Amato, 2000). Couples who separate without divorcing may suffer similar problems: This is particularly relevant to separated African-American couples, who tend to remain in that state without divorcing for much longer than do white or Hispanic couples (Centers for Disease Control, 2002a).

Statistically, this interracial couple stands a much higher chance of breaking up than do couples of the same ethnicity. Interracial couples may lack the social supports that help sustain marriage.

Of course, not all these ill effects can be blamed on divorce or separation per se: They may well be the ongoing consequences of the kind of marriage that preceded the break-up. People who divorce are generally unhappy in their marriages, and if divorce were not possible, they might become even less happy and might eventually experience impairments in their mental and physical health at least as severe as those that affect divorced men and women. What is really desirable is to increase people's marital satisfaction so that they won't want to split up in the first place; we discussed some strategies to accomplish this in Chapter 10.

Divorce May Be the Start of a New Life

To some extent, the concept of divorce as an unmitigated evil has arisen from a religious conservative tradition that uses terminology such as "failed marriages" and "broken homes," that refers to the children of divorced parents as "victims," and that sees rising divorce rates as a symptom of society's "moral decay" (Coltrane & Adams, 2003). In reality, marital disruption can also have positive consequences (Hetherington & Kelly, 2002). In fact, if it didn't, it would be hard to explain why divorce is so popular—there are about 1.2 million divorces in the United States annually, compared with about 2.4 million marriages (**Figure 13.17**). The benefits of divorce include escape from an unhappy, possibly abusive relationship and the potential for forming a better one. Divorce is always a challenge, but for some people, women especially, it can be the key that reveals previously untapped sources of talent, energy, and resolve. For married men and women who are homosexual or bisexual, divorce may be an opportunity to "come out of the closet" and develop same-sex relationships.

For divorced or separated people who are parents, the existence of children adds complexity to the search for sex partners and new relationships. Children may not be too comfortable with the idea of their parent bringing dates home and sleeping with them. Parents sometimes opt to deal with this issue by confining their dating activities to times when the children are with the other parent. Making children's feelings paramount may not be a recipe for self-fulfillment, however. In an alternative and perhaps more positive strategy, the children can be drawn

Figure 13.17 Divorce, Vegas-style Former Miss USA Shanna Moakler celebrated her 2006 split from drummer Travis Barker with a party at the Bellagio Hotel, complete with divorce cake.

into the parent's quest for new social and romantic contacts. The organization Parents Without Partners (see Web Resources) is geared toward this approach: Its chapters organize functions at which single parents, along with their children, can meet others who are similarly situated.

Most Divorced People Remarry

Most divorced men and women marry again. Men remarry more quickly than women, but even among women, 54% remarry within 5 years (Centers for Disease Control, 2002a). The chances of remarrying are influenced by age at divorce (younger women are more likely to remarry) and ethnicity (African-American women are less likely to remarry). Remarriage brings economic and other benefits, especially to women. It is also associated, not surprisingly, with an increase in sexual activity—clear evidence that the general decline in sexual behavior during marriage is not solely a biological effect of aging.

Unfortunately, children of divorce tend to remain disadvantaged when their mothers remarry: The adverse effects that strike children of divorced parents (see above) also strike stepchildren at about the same frequency (Coleman et al., 2000). Stepchildren are twice as likely to suffer from behavioral problems as are children who live with their biological parents (Bray, 1999; Evenhouse & Reilly, 2004). Nevertheless, the majority of stepchildren do well in school and don't have emotional or behavioral problems (Ganong & Coleman, 2003).

Another downside of remarriage is that later marriages are somewhat less durable than first marriages. For example, a woman 25 years old or older who marries for the first time has a 1 in 4 chance of breaking up within 10 years, but if she has been married previously, she has a 1 in 3 chance of breaking up within the same period. In other words, experience gained from the first marriage doesn't seem to stabilize later marriages. Bear in mind, though, that it's a special subset of people who remarry: namely, those who have already divorced at least once. These people may see less moral or practical value in lasting marriages, or they may have personality traits or economic circumstances that undermine marital stability.

Menopause Marks Women's Transition to Infertility

Starting in the early or mid-forties, women may find that their menstrual periods become less regular. This change marks the onset of a gradual transition to infertility—a phase called the **climacteric** or "change of life." The first portion of the climacteric, when a woman misses some menstrual periods but has not stopped menstruating completely, is called the **perimenopause**. The cessation of menstrual cycles—the **menopause**—occurs at an average age of 51 in U.S. women. Because of the irregularity that commonly precedes the menopause, a woman can't *know* that her last period was in fact her last until some time afterwards. Conventionally, menopause is said to be "confirmed" after 12 months without a period—in the absence of health factors that might be responsible for the amenorrhea. There is considerable variation in the age at menopause: Some women reach menopause in their early forties; others continue to menstruate into their late fifties or even early sixties. However, the oldest women known to have become pregnant by natural means have been in their mid-fifties.

Although people often focus on the negative aspect of menopause, namely the loss of fertility, evolutionary biologists look at it in a different way, asking why women have evolved the capacity for many years of active life *after* cessation of reproduction—something that is unusual in the animal realm. They suspect that the reason has to do with the resources, such as food and knowledge, that postmenopausal women have been able to provide to their adult children, thus enabling their children to be more prolific and successful parents. This is the so-called "grandmother hypothesis" of menopause (Hawkes et al., 1998). It is supported by data showing that, in premodern times, women who lived for many years after menopause had more surviving grandchildren than those who did not (Lahdenpera et al., 2004).

Menopause is an aspect of aging, but it comes at what we now consider midlife.

Menopause May Be Caused by Depletion of Oocytes

It's not known exactly what triggers menopause or why women reach menopause at such variable ages. However, women who have fewer pregnancies, who have short cycle lengths, who have had one ovary removed, or who don't use oral contraceptives are all likely to experience earlier menopause than other women (Cramer & Xu, 1996). In women who smoke, these effects are accentuated. Heredity also influences the timing of menopause (Cramer et al., 1995).

These findings suggest that women are born with the capacity for a certain number of ovarian cycles and that the main reason for the transition to infertility may be the depletion of oocytes—the ovarian cells that develop into ova—and the diminishing ability of any remaining oocytes to respond to pituitary hormones (Santoro, 2005). By the time of menopause, the ovaries contain very few oocytes. Consistent with this view, the secretion of pituitary gonadotropins (FSH and LH) does not decrease at menopause, but rather *increases*—in response to the decline in blood levels of ovarian steroids (Johnson & Everitt, 2000). Thus, although the brain tells the ovaries when to *start* cycling (at menarche), it apparently doesn't tell them when to *stop* cycling.

Surgical removal of the uterus (hysterectomy) in a premenopausal woman puts a stop to menstruation but not to the hormonal processes that underlie the menstrual cycle. If the ovaries are removed, however, menopause occurs immediately.

Decreased Hormone Levels Affect Some Women's Sexual Responses

Menopause influences women's sexuality in a number of ways. First, the reduction in circulating ovarian hormones, especially estrogens, has direct effects on

climacteric The transition to infertility at the end of a woman's reproductive life, lasting for several years and culminating in menopause.

perimenopause The phase prior to menopause that is marked by irregular menstrual cycles.

menopause The final cessation of menstruation at the end of a woman's reproductive years.

vasomotor control The physiological regulation of peripheral blood flow.

hot flashes (hot flushes) Episodes of reddening and warmth of the skin associated with menopause.

osteoporosis Reduction in the mineral content of bone, predisposing to fractures.

the body. These effects can include a reduction in vaginal lubrication in response to sexual arousal, a rise in the pH (decrease in acidity) of vaginal fluids, and sometimes a thinning of the walls of the vagina. In some women these changes may lead to painful coitus and vaginal inflammation. However, two-thirds of perimenopausal and postmenopausal women do not experience these vaginal symptoms (Agency for Healthcare Research and Quality, 2005).

Menopause (and perimenopause) may be accompanied by a variety of other symptoms that can influence sexual expression indirectly. The reduction in estrogen levels often leads to instability in the control of blood vessels (**vasomotor control**), so that many menopausal women experience **hot flashes** or **hot flushes** (dilation of blood vessels in the skin, causing reddening, a sensation of warmth, and sometimes perspiration, followed by a cold chill), night sweats, headaches, tiredness, and heart palpitations (bouts of accelerated or irregular heartbeats). Sleep problems are also common. The extent to which these menopausal symptoms occur and how bothersome women find them is highly variable, and there are even differences among ethnic groups; for example, African-American women seem to experience more extreme vasomotor symptoms than other groups (Avis et al., 2001). Many of these menopause-related symptoms disappear within a few years after menopause, even without medical treatment.

Lowered estrogen levels may also have long-term heath effects. The most significant of these are a loss of bone density (**osteoporosis**), which carries a risk of fractures and vertebral compression (**Figure 13.18**), and changes in blood lipid chemistry, which increase the risk of atherosclerosis and heart attacks. In addition, there are noticeable effects on the skin (loss of thickness, elasticity, hydration, and lipid content).

(A)

(B)

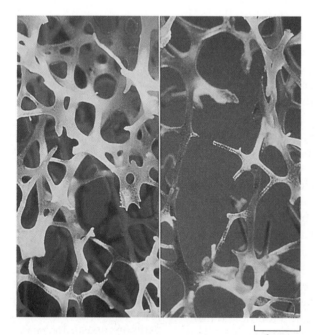

1 mm

Figure 13.18 Osteoporosis (A) Low estrogen levels after menopause can lead to thinning of the mineral structure of bone. These are scanning electron micrographs of normal bone (left) and osteoporotic bone (right). (B) Osteoporosis can cause spinal fractures resulting in increasingly stooped posture, but exercise, diet, and drugs can help prevent this process.

Women Typically Experience Some Decline in Sexual Desire at Menopause

Menopausal women often experience a decrease in sexual desire and sexual arousal. This decline probably results mainly from the combined effects of menopause we have just listed. Other factors, such as direct effects of declining gonadal steroid levels on the brain systems that mediate sexual arousal, could also play a role.

Still, the decline in sexual desire associated with menopause is fairly modest in degree. Other factors, such as relationship issues, attitudes toward sex and aging, general health, and cultural background have larger effects on sexual desire and sexual function than does menopausal status (Avis et al., 2005; Hayes et al., 2008). Bear in mind that androgens play a significant role in female sexual desire, and although some androgens come from the ovaries, they are also secreted by the adrenal glands. This latter supply continues after menopause and is often sufficient to maintain a high level of sexual interest.

The psychological effects of menopause on sexuality are diverse. For women who believe that the main or only purpose of sex is reproduction, the loss of fertility at menopause may lead to a loss of interest in sex. For the larger number of women who see a recreational or emotional significance in sex, menopause may actually be welcome because it removes the fear of unwanted pregnancy and makes contraception unnecessary. Such women may get increased pleasure from sex for that reason. (The risk of sexually transmitted infections may still make the use of condoms advisable, of course.)

Hormone Therapy Can Reduce Menopausal Symptoms

Menopausal women have the option of taking sex steroids or other drugs to compensate for the loss of their own ovarian hormones and thus to alleviate the symptoms of menopause. This practice, once referred to as "hormone replacement therapy," is now called **menopausal hormone therapy (MHT)** (Simon & Snabes, 2007). The most common regimen is a combination of estrogens and progestins. It is the estrogens that alleviate symptoms such as hot flushes and vaginal dryness. Progestins are added to protect the woman from one unfortunate side effect of the estrogen treatment, which is an increased risk of endometrial cancer. For women who have had a hysterectomy, progestins have little benefit, and the therapy may consist of estrogens alone. For women in whom vaginal symptoms are the main problem, estrogen can be administered directly to the vagina by means of a ring, tablets, or cream (American Academy of Family Physicians, 2004). About 1 in 4 menopausal women in the 50 to 55 age bracket uses MHT. Lower-income women are much less likely to use MHT than are middle- or upper-income women (Finley et al., 2001).

Postmenopausal Hormone Therapy Is Controversial

Until recently, large numbers of women took hormones for many years or decades *after* menopause. The rationale behind this **postmenopausal hormone therapy** was that it would not merely continue the benefits of menopausal therapy but would also offer long-term protection against some of the major health risks for postmenopausal women, including osteoporosis (which predisposes women to fractures of the hip and other bones), cardiovascular disease, and perhaps dementia. In 2002, however, a large-scale placebo-controlled trial, the Women's Health Initiative (WHI) study, came up with disturbing findings: Postmenopausal women using combined estrogen/progestin therapy did enjoy some protection from osteoporosis (and also from colon cancer), but these benefits were outweighed by an *increased* risk of cardiovascular disease, breast cancer, and even dementia (Women's Health Initiative, 2002; Shumaker et al., 2003) (**Figure 13.19**).

menopausal hormone therapy (MHT) Use of hormones to treat symptoms occurring during or soon after menopause.

postmenopausal hormone therapy Hormone treatment extending for a long time after menopause.

Figure 13.19 Risks may outweigh benefits for postmenopausal hormone therapy. The bar graph shows the predicted number of extra cases (red bars) or fewer cases (green bars) of the listed conditions experienced by 10,000 women on long-term combined estrogen-progestin therapy per year. (Data from U.S. Food and Drug Administration, 2004c.)

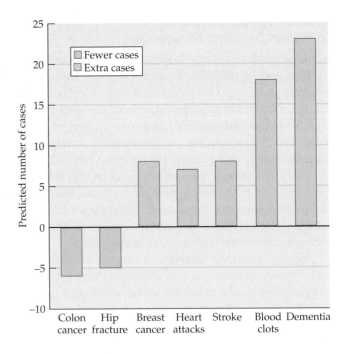

Estrogen-alone therapy decreased the risk of osteoporosis, and possibly also breast cancer, but slightly increased the risk of stroke and dementia (Anderson et al., 2004; Shumaker et al., 2004).

During the year after the WHI results were published, millions of American women stopped using hormone therapy. Over this 12-month period, the U.S. breast cancer rate dropped by 7%—the largest one-year drop in the incidence of any cancer. The decrease was even greater—12%—among women in the 50 to 69 age range, who were the ones most likely to be using hormone therapy (Ravdin et al., 2007). Although the causal link remains to be proven, it is very likely that thousands of estrogen-dependent cancers were "stopped in their tracks" as women discontinued hormone treatment.

Most of the women in the WHI study began hormone treatment about 10 years *after* menopause. This led some experts to suggest that the ill-effects might be caused by exposing the body to hormones after a long hormone-free gap. This explanation no longer appears to be valid, however, at least with regard to breast cancer risk: Women who initiate hormone therapy at or very soon after menopause increase their risk of developing this disease by 60% after 5 years of therapy and more than double their risk after 10 years (Prentice et al., 2008).

On the basis of these and other findings, the FDA and NIH have recommended that hormone therapy be generally restricted to the short-term relief of menopausal symptoms and that hormones should be taken in the lowest doses that provide adequate relief of symptoms. Even in this application, however, there is some question about the usefulness of hormone therapy because (in some women at least) the therapy seems merely to *postpone* menopausal symptoms, rather than *prevent* them (Ockene et al., 2005).

Long-term use of hormone therapy, according to the FDA, should be considered primarily by women with severe osteoporosis. There do exist, however, several kinds of drugs that combat osteoporosis without raising breast cancer risk, or that actually lower it.

There has been a search for alternative, more "natural" therapies for menopausal symptoms and for long-term postmenopausal use. In particular, there has been interest in **isoflavones**, which are plant-derived molecules with an estrogen-like structure. One meta-analysis of isoflavone trials found a "marginally significant" benefit in prevention of hot flushes (Coon et al., 2007). The long-term safety of isoflavones is unknown. In a more general way, lifestyle choices such as exercise (especially weight-bearing exercise such as walking), keeping slim, not smoking, and eating a healthful, calcium-rich diet are probably more valuable than any medication in reducing postmenopausal health risks.

Women using hormone therapy are sometimes given testosterone. The rationale for adding testosterone is to improve sexual function, and it appears to be quite effective for this purpose (Somboonporn et al., 2005; Kingsberg et al., 2007). But there are significant safety concerns with the use of this drug in women, especially for long-term treatment. For this reason, a testosterone patch for use by women has not yet been approved by the FDA, although it is available in some other countries. We will discuss this issue in more detail in the context of sexual dysfunctions (see Chapter 16).

There Are Ethnic Differences in the Psychological Experience of Menopause

The Study of Women's Health Across the Nation (SWAN) is a multicenter, federally funded study that has followed a large and diverse group of American women across the climacteric (see Web Resources). Among the interesting findings from this study is the observation of differences in the way American women of differing ethnicities experience the menopause (Sommer et al., 1999; Sampselle et al., 2002). White women tend to medicalize menopause, to suffer more psychosomatic symptoms, and to be relatively concerned about a perceived loss of youthfulness and attractiveness. African-American and Latina women report more physical symptoms associated with menopause, and yet they tend to adopt a more positive, even welcoming view of the event—as a normal life stage that allows them to restructure their priorities, with a greater emphasis on self-fulfillment. Regardless of ethnicity, a fear of menopause before the event commonly gives way to a sense of emancipation after it arrives.

Men's Fertility Declines Gradually with Age

Men do not experience a sudden or complete cessation of fertility comparable to menopause. Instead, they experience a gradual reduction in fertility and sexual function with aging, evidenced by declining sperm counts and ejaculate volume, an increased likelihood of erectile dysfunction (see Chapter 16), and decreased sexual desire and frequency of sex. More general changes associated with aging include loss of muscle bulk and bone density, changes in the skin and hair, and possible cognitive changes such as memory impairment. Although there is a decline in blood levels of testosterone and other hormones (such as growth hormone) with aging, there doesn't seem to be any good correlation between testosterone levels and sexual activity among normal older men, any more than there is among younger men (Sadowsky et al., 1993).

Some people refer to this collection of changes as the "male menopause" or **andropause** (Mooradian & Korenman, 2006), but these terms are misleading if they suggest that the changes are sudden or that there is a total cessation of reproductive function. Although sperm counts decline, some men in their eighties have fathered children.

There has been considerable recent interest in the use of testosterone replacement therapy to treat aging men with low testosterone levels and sexual or other problems (Brawer, 2004). At this point, there is little information about the long-term conse-

isoflavones Estrogen-like compounds of plant origin.

andropause In men, the gradual decline of fertility with age; a hypothetical male equivalent of menopause.

quences of such treatment. One concern is that it might increase the risk of developing prostate cancer or accelerate the growth of preexisting, undiagnosed cancers.

The Sex Lives of Older People Have Traditionally Been Ignored

Our knowledge of sexuality in old age is quite limited. There has been a traditional assumption that older people are asexual, and any indications to the contrary (such as sexual behavior by the residents of nursing homes) have generally been viewed with embarrassment and disapproval. It didn't help that the two big national surveys we have referred to in this book, the American NHSLS and the British NSSAL, restricted their samples to men and women under 60, as if the sex lives of older people were nonexistent or unimportant. Indeed, the very word "old" has been largely excluded from social discourse and has been replaced by euphemistic terms such as "senior," "elderly," and the like. Still, since the time of those large national surveys there have been attempts to make up for their inattention to older men's and women's sex lives (Schiavi, 1999; Hayes & Dennerstein, 2005; Lindau et al., 2007).

We may speculate that younger people's discomfort with the notion of sexuality in old age originates in a failure of empathy. In other words, when faced with the fact that older people engage in sex, they imagine themselves having sex with an older person—that is to say, with someone they might well find sexually unattractive, and so they are repelled. What they *fail* to imagine is being *in the mind* of an older person, whose ideas of attractiveness may be quite different from their own. In particular, judgments of attractiveness are influenced by familiarity and intimacy, so an older person may find their spouse of many years sexually attractive even though few younger people would concur. In a survey commissioned by the American Association of Retired Persons (AARP), 53% of women over age 75 and 63% of men over age 75 reported strong physical attraction to their partners. These percentages were actually *higher* than for women and men in younger age brackets (American Association of Retired Persons, 1999).

The fact is that nearly everyone continues to have sexual feelings into old age, and many people express these feelings behaviorally in one way or another. In considering sexual expression in old age, it's important not to fall into either of two traps (Meston, 1997). On the one hand, there is the danger of subscribing to folklore about the inevitable decline of sexual intimacy with aging. On the other hand, there is the temptation to expect or demand patterns of sexual expression similar to those of younger people. Certainly, old age brings physical changes and illnesses that may affect sexual expression. These problems may necessitate some changes in sexual behavior, but they rarely make sexual behavior impossible or unrewarding to the older person or their partner.

Aging Is Accompanied by Physiological Changes in the Sexual Response

Let's look first at some of the physical changes associated with aging (Thienhaus, 1988; Gelfand, 2000). Older people—and we are being deliberately vague about precise ages, because these changes occur slowly and vary from one person to the next—experience changes in the physiological processes underlying sexuality. For men, these changes include the following:

The sexuality of this older couple is important to the well-being of their relationship.

- The penis becomes erect more slowly in response to either tactile or mental stimulation. The erect penis is less hard. Some degree of erectile dysfunction is reported by two-thirds of normal older men (Litwin, 1999).
- Ejaculatory volume is smaller, and the ejaculate is discharged less forcefully. (It may flow out slowly or even be discharged retrogradely into the bladder.)
- The erection is lost more rapidly.
- The refractory period (time before another erection and ejaculation are possible) is longer.

Women may experience the following changes:

- There are atrophic changes in the vagina, vulva, and urethra. The walls of the vagina become thinner, and the entire vagina may become shorter and narrower. (This condition can be alleviated with local application of estrogens as described above.)
- There is decreased vaginal lubrication.
- There are fewer contractions during orgasm.
- There is a more rapid decrease in arousal after orgasm.

Medical Conditions, Drugs, and Social Factors Can Impair the Sexuality of Older People

Sexual performance can also be impaired by medical conditions that become commoner with advancing age. These conditions include arthritis, heart disease, osteoporosis, incontinence, diabetes, chronic obstructive pulmonary disease (emphysema and chronic bronchitis), and obesity. Surgeries such as prostatectomy, colostomy, mastectomy, hysterectomy, or heart surgery can affect sexual performance, either directly, or indirectly by causing pain, embarrassment, or poor self-image.

Older people take more prescription drugs than younger people, and many of these drugs can interfere with sexual performance (Mooradian, 1991). Examples include anti-hypertension drugs, diuretics, tranquilizers and antidepressants, cancer chemotherapy, ulcer medicines, and anticoagulants. (Individual drugs vary, as do patients' responses to them; alternative drugs can often be prescribed that do not impair sexual desire or performance.) Excessive alcohol use impairs sexual performance in older people just as it does in younger people.

Psychological and social factors that can impair sexual expression in older people include depression, poor self-image, performance anxiety, bereavement, lack of an available partner, and the internalization of the negative expectations of others, especially the older person's children and medical professionals.

When older people are asked to express their current concerns about sexual matters, gender differences emerge that are quite in line with what we have learned about younger people. In particular, men mention problems of performance, especially erectile dysfunction, whereas women mention relationship problems, including the lack of a partner (Wiley & Bortz, 1996; Avis, 2000). Both sexes report that their level of sexual activity has declined in the past 10 years and say that they wish they were more active. The two factors that seem to influence older people's sex lives the most are their health status and their sense of how sexually responsive their partners are (Bortz et al., 1999).

With all these potential problems, you might imagine that older people would be mired in misery. In fact, however, people generally become happier as they age (Yang, 2008), perhaps because of a diminishing gap between what they want and what they have. In the area of sexuality, this could mean an increasing realism about sexual goals and satisfaction with what is attainable, as the AARP study mentioned above suggested.

Coping Strategies May Require Flexibility

Concerning the availability of a partner, recall that women not only live longer than men, but also tend to marry men who are older than themselves. This age difference may be even more marked in second or later marriages. The combination of these two factors makes for long widowhoods: A 50-year-old woman whose husband is 5 years older than herself can expect (on average) to become a widow at age 75 and to live for 10 years thereafter.

Single men aged 75 and over are in short supply (**Figure 13.20**). Two-thirds of men in that age bracket are married and living with their wives, whereas only 29% of women over 75 are married and living with their husbands (U.S. Census Bureau, 2001). Thus the odds are stacked against a widowed woman in that age bracket being able to remarry.

Of course, there are other possibilities: Some widowed or divorced older women form sexual relationships with younger or married men, for example. But such choices will strike many older women as inappropriate or immoral. People's attitudes tend to be conditioned by the environment in which they grew up, so today's older people—who came of age before the sexual revolution of the 1960s—are likely to be less open to unconventional sexual relationships. In the AARP survey mentioned above, two-thirds of women over age 75 said it was wrong to engage in sex with anyone but a legally married spouse—a far higher percentage than for women in younger age brackets (American Association of Retired Persons, 1999). (Thus the legalization of same-sex marriage has the potential to expand older women's partnering choices.)

The same attitudes apply to actual sexual behavior. For older couples that have difficulty with coitus (because of physiological changes in one or both partners),

(A)

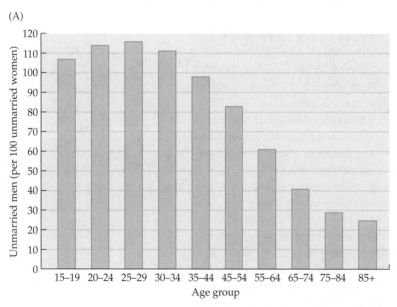

(B)

Figure 13.20 The tilting playing field (A) This graph shows the number of unmarried men per 100 unmarried women in the U.S., by age bracket. At younger ages there is an excess of unmarried men, but in later years they are in increasingly short supply. (B) Because of the imbalance between the sexes, a single, older man may be a hot property. (A, data from U.S. Census Bureau, 2007.)

it might make good sense to practice oral sex instead. However, people born before about 1942 came of age at a time when oral sex was relatively uncommon and was practiced mainly by the better-educated levels of society. This age cohort did not necessarily join the rush to oral sex in the 1960s; in fact, nearly half of them have never had a single experience of fellatio or cunnilingus, according to NHSLS data, and many of them probably consider these behaviors immoral. Obviously, it may be hard for such people to accept or enjoy oral sex now that they are well into their retirement years, even if it is suggested to them by healthcare providers or others.

Some Older People Remain Sexually Active

In 2007 University of Chicago sociologists published a large, random-sample study of the sex lives of older Americans (Lindau et al., 2007). Most men and women are sexually active in their late fifties and early sixties, but activity declines quite markedly over the following two decades, especially for women (**Figure 13.21**). The researchers set the bar very low to qualify for "sexually active" status (at least one episode of partnered sex within the previous 12 months). However, even in the oldest age group, over half of those who were sexually active by that criterion did in fact have sex at least two to three times per month. In addition to partnered sex, plenty of older men and women masturbated: About half of the men and one-fourth of the women reported having done so at least once in the previous 12 months.

The main reasons for the lack of sexual activity in the older age groups included the lack of a partner (especially among women), health problems in the interviewee or the interviewee's partner, and sexual dysfunctions including erectile difficulties and a loss of interest in sex. (As we'll discuss in Chapter 16, lack of interest in sex is not really a "dysfunction" unless it is perceived as causing a problem.)

Age 85—the upper age limit in the 2007 study—is not necessarily the end of life, of course. In one study carried in the 1980s, psychologists interviewed 200 healthy men and women aged 80 to 102 who lived in retirement communities (Bretschneider & McCoy, 1988). Most were unmarried. The researchers found that the most common sexual activity among these people was touching and fondling without coitus, followed by masturbation and then coitus. As has been consistently reported in other studies, the frequency with which these older people engaged in most sexual behaviors was predicted by the frequency with which they engaged in the same behavior earlier in life. In other words, people are creatures of habit, and they don't change their sexual behavior as they age unless they have to. The one activity whose frequency was not predicted by earlier frequency was coitus. That was probably because of age-associated physical problems described above as well as social factors, such as loss of a spouse.

Although some people believe that sex in middle or old age carries health risks (especially for people with heart disease), a number of studies suggest the opposite; namely, that older people who engage in frequent sex live longer (**Box 13.6**). Of course, there may be medical circumstances in which exertion of any kind is to be avoided, but the exertion of intercourse is no greater than that of other activities that people regularly engage in, such as climbing stairs.

It seems likely that, as baby boomers (people born shortly after the Second World War and who lived through the sexual revolution of the 1960s) enter their retirement years, there will be an increasing focus on sexual activity and sexual satisfaction among older people. Not only are baby boomers more interested in sexual variety and less tied to the notion that sex is only for reproduction, but they also have a greater sense of entitlement with regard to

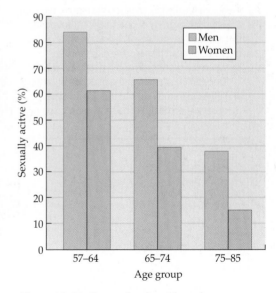

Figure 13.21 Sex and aging These bar graphs show the percentage of men and of women who are sexually active (at least one episode of partnered sex in the previous 12 months) at increasing ages. (Data from Lindau et al., 2007.)

Research Highlights

BOX 13.6 Sex and Death among Welsh Cheesemakers

The idea that sexual activity is debilitating to health—especially for men, who have to expend precious semen in the sexual act—is widespread in human cultures. To test the truth of this idea, epidemiologist George Davey Smith of the University of Bristol, England, along with two colleagues, descended on the quiet town of Caerphilly, Wales, renowned for its cheese (Davey Smith et al., 1997) (see figure).

Most of the men in this town are participating in a longitudinal study of factors that affect long-term health. Nine hundred and eighteen of them (aged 45 to 59, mostly married) answered a question about how often they experienced orgasm. (Before the researchers could survey the entire adult population of the town, local doctors persuaded them to delete this particular question.)

By 10 years later, 150 of the 918 men had died. The men who had told the researchers that they had a high frequency of orgasm (at least two orgasms per week) were the least likely to have died. Those who had an orgasm between once a week and once a month were 60% more likely to have died (after adjustment of the data to allow for age differences). Those who had an orgasm less than once a month were *twice* as likely to have died. Even when the researchers adjusted for a variety of potentially confounding factors, such as social class, blood pressure, and presence of heart disease, the differences between the groups remained nearly as great.

One can't be certain of the direction of cause and effect in a study such as this. It's possible that preexisting health conditions caused some

men to be relatively inactive sexually and also shortened their lives. Alternatively, the men who had frequent sex might have had a lower death rate because they were in more loving marriages, rather than more sexually active ones.

Caerphilly's annual cheese race offers healthy exercise, but frequent sex may be even more beneficial.

Still, the findings are consistent with a number of other studies that have reported lower mortality or a lower incidence of myocardial infarction in men and women who were more sexually active

or who derived more enjoyment from sex (Abramov, 1976; Persson, 1981; Palmore, 1982).

Given the apparent protective effect of orgasms, the researchers commented that a public health campaign, modeled on the "at least five a day" campaign to get people to eat fruits and vegetables, might be in order—with some adjustment of the recommended frequency, of course.

---

personal fulfillment generally. Thus they will be far less ready to give up sex if physiological or social problems get in their way. The huge demand for Viagra when it came on the market in 1998 was a harbinger of things to come: Both men and women are likely to demand effective medical treatments for age-associated sexual dysfunction. They will also make sure that sexual expression by older people is recognized and respected, rather than being pushed into the closet.

Summary

1. Physiological responses suggestive of sexual arousal are seen in infants and young children, but they seem to be triggered by a wide range of stimuli, such as strong emotion of any kind. Masturbation is common in young children, and other sexual behaviors, such as the display of genitals or the inspection of other children's genitals, are

also seen. These behaviors may be incorporated into sexual games such as "doctor." Young children rarely engage in adultlike sexual behavior, however.

2. Some non-Western societies tolerate or encourage childhood sexual behavior, while others attempt to restrain it. In the contemporary United States, children are often prevented from engaging in or learning about sexuality.

3. Some children, usually older ones, have sexual contacts with adults. These contacts are usually one-time events rather than ongoing relationships. Most adults who have sexual contacts with children are relatives or acquaintances of the child, rather than strangers. Coercive or repeated adult–child sexual contacts can cause long-lasting psychological trauma. Noncoercive, sporadic contacts may cause little or no harm.

4. In late childhood (preadolescence), children tend to socialize in same-sex groups and to impose strict gender codes. This practice can be traumatic for gender-nonconformist children. Although segregation by sex limits opportunities for heterosexual encounters, a few children do engage in coitus before the age of 13.

5. Puberty is marked by special celebrations or rites in many cultures. Examples practiced in the United States are the Jewish bar/bat mitzvah and the Hispanic quinceañera.

6. Adolescence is usually defined as the teen years. In early adolescence, rising sex hormone levels trigger an increasing interest in sex. Most adolescent males masturbate frequently, but females do so less often. Adolescent heterosexual behavior gradually progresses from kissing and fondling to coitus, oral sex, and, sometimes, anal sex. Some characteristics of teen sexual behavior reflect personal and demographic factors such as intelligence, education, and ethnicity. Women's changing expectations as well as the availability of reliable contraception have modified teen sexual behavior over the last several decades.

7. Teen pregnancy has declined over the last two decades thanks to improved use of contraceptives, but it is still much higher in the U.S. than in Canada or other developed countries. It is also higher among Hispanics and African Americans than among whites or Asian Americans. Teen pregnancies are often terminated by abortion. Teenage mothers and their children face numerous problems, but some thrive.

8. Young adults typically spend a few years "hooking up" and/or dating before they enter their first live-in relationship, but the average number of sex partners during this period is quite low. During the dating years, sexual desires have to compete with other interests, such as pursuit of education or career advancement.

9. For many adults, their first live-in relationship is a nonmarital cohabitation. Cohabitation may serve simply as a convenient alternative to dating, or it may represent a committed relationship without the legal trappings of marriage.

10. Many past and present human societies have allowed polygamy. In the United States group marriage and Mormon polygamy (which is no longer permitted by the Mormon church) exemplify nonstandard marital arrangements.

11. Western society is moving from a traditional, one-size-fits-all institution of marriage to a greater variety of live-in sexual relationships. Because women have fewer pregnancies than in the past and are more likely to be in the labor market, distinct gender roles in marriage have diminished. People are marrying later and divorcing more readily; marriage may soon become a minority status for American adults. Nevertheless, most people desire to be in some kind of monogamous, long-term relationship.

12. Married men and women tend to have less sex than those who are dating or cohabiting, and they are less adventurous sexually, but their physical and emotional satisfaction with their sex lives is high. For women, simply being married makes sex more satisfying. However, sexual interactions and marital satisfaction tend to fall off over time.

13. One in three marriages breaks up within 10 years. The likelihood of breakup is increased by a number of factors, such as early (teen) marriage, dissimilarity between husband and wife, and cohabitation before marriage.

14. Divorced people suffer a variety of physical and psychological ill effects, but most divorced men and women remarry within 10 years.

15. Menopause—the cessation of menstrual cycles—is the culmination of a gradual transition to infertility in women. The hormonal changes of menopause can impair the physiological processes of sexual arousal and may be accompanied by a decline in sexual interest and activity.

16. Hormone therapy can alleviate menopausal symptoms but may have unpleasant side effects that cause many women to discontinue treatment, as well as long-term health risks including an elevated risk of breast cancer. Postmenopausal women are advised to used hormones only at dosages and for lengths of time that are sufficient to control symptoms.

17. Men experience a gradual decline in fertility, physiological arousal, and sexual interest, rather than a rapid transition to infertility. A few men father children in old age.

18. Many people continue to experience sexual desire into old age. The physical expression of this desire may be compromised by declining physiological responsiveness (for example, erectile dysfunction or loss of vaginal lubrication) or by a variety of medical conditions, drugs, or social circumstances. Nevertheless, many older women and men continue to engage in sexual behavior, including masturbation, coitus, and noncoital contacts.

Discussion Questions

1. What are your attitudes and values about what is normal sexuality during childhood? If you were a parent and found your child "playing doctor" (engaging in sexual exploration) with the child next door, how would you respond?

2. What kind of sex education would you want your child to receive in elementary school, middle school, and high school?

3. Describe your ideal marriage partner or cohabitational partner and their characteristics (e.g., appearance, personality, and occupation). What circumstances or conflicts (if any) do you think would lead you to consider a separation or divorce (e.g., infidelity, refusal to have children, disease, or cross-dressing)?

4. Identify the myths and "what you have heard" about menopause. Contrast these descriptions with the facts. What behaviors are characteristic of menopause? Do men have a "change of life"?

5. Describe the advice you would give to your mother or an older female friend who asks you to explain the pros and cons of hormone replacement therapy. Do you think that the fact that menopause is a natural part of the aging process should discourage women from attempting to counteract its effects with hormone treatment?

6. Think about your grandparents and people who are older than 60. What are your beliefs and thoughts about sex among these people? What do you think are the barriers to enjoying a happy sex life after 60?

Web Resources

Ages of consent in North America
   http://en.wikipedia.org/wiki/Ages_of_consent_in_North_America (This article appears to be accurate and up-to-date, but Wikipedia articles can change unpredictably.)

Alternatives to Marriage Project www.unmarried.org

American Psychological Association—Aging and human sexuality resource guide
www.apa.org/pi/aging/sexuality.html

Divorcenet www.divorcenet.com

Gay Teens Resources www.gayteens.org

Janssen, D. F. Growing Up Sexually: A World Atlas www2.rz.huberlin.de/
sexology/gesund/archiv/gus/indexatlas.htm

National Campaign to Prevent Teen and Unplanned Pregnancy
www.thenationalcampaign.org

National Healthy Marriage Resource Center www.healthymarriageinfo.org

North American Menopause Society www.menopause.org

Parents Without Partners www.parentswithoutpartners.org

Sex, Etc.—A Web site for teens by teens www.sexetc.org

Sexinfo (University of California, Santa Barbara) www.soc.ucsb.edu/sexinfo/

Silver Ring Thing (virginity pledge program) www.silverringthing.com

Study of Women's Health Across the Nation
www.edc.gsph.pitt.edu/swan/public/index.html

Teenwire (Planned Parenthood site) www.teenwire.com

Worldwide ages of consent www.avert.org/aofconsent.htm

Recommended Reading

Bancroft, J. (Ed.). (2003). *Sexual development in childhood.* Indiana University Press.

Bogle, K.A. (2008). *Hooking up: Sex, dating, and relationships on campus.* New York University Press.

Bray, J. H., & Kelly, J. (1998). *Stepfamilies: Love, marriage, and parenting in the first decade.* Broadway Books.

Butler, R. N., & Lewis, M. I. (2002). *The new love and sex after 60.* Ballantine Books.

Carpenter, L. M. (2005). *Virginity lost: An intimate portrait of first sexual experiences.* New York University Press.

Crowley, C., & Lodge, H.S. (2005). *Younger next year.* Workman Publishing.

Crowley, C., & Lodge, H.S. (2005). *Younger next year for women.* Workman Publishing.

Furman, W., Brown, B. B., and Feiring, C. (Eds.). (1999) *The development of romantic relationships in adolescence.* Cambridge University Press.

Hetherington, E.M. & Kelly, J. (2002). *For better or for worse: Divorce reconsidered.* W.W. Norton and Co.

Levine, J. (2002). *Harmful to minors: The perils of protecting children from sex.* University of Minnesota Press.

North American Menopause Society (2003). *Menopause guidebook.* Can be ordered at www.menopause.org.

Regnerus, M. (2007). *Forbidden fruit: Sex and religion in the lives of American teenagers.* Oxford University Press.

Steinberg, L. (2004). *Adolescence* (7th ed.). McGraw-Hill.

CHAPTER 14

Gay relationships are an increasingly visible aspect of human diversity.

Sexual Orientation

The direction of our sexual attractions—to the other sex, to our own sex, or to both sexes—has a profound influence on our personal and public lives and how we are viewed and treated by others. In this chapter we first ask what sexual orientation is and how it develops. We then turn to the social aspects of sexual orientation. Here we largely ignore heterosexuality, because that is to some degree the leading theme of most other chapters of this book. Instead, we focus on gay people—lesbians and gay men. What is causing their rapid emergence from a history of discrimination and exclusion? How do their life courses differ from those of heterosexual men and women, beginning in childhood? What subcultures exist within the larger gay community? What causes some people to fear or dislike lesbians and gay men, and how can these negative attitudes be changed?

Finally, we take a look at what might be the least well understood sexual orientation: bisexuality. Bisexuals are the subject of considerable scientific and social controversy. Does bisexuality even exist—or are we *all* bisexual? And by being attracted to both women and men, do bisexuals enjoy the best of all possible worlds—or the worst?

There Is a Spectrum of Sexual Orientations

Sexual orientation is the dimension of personality that describes the balance of our sexual attraction to the two sexes. At either end of this dimension are **heterosexuality** (attraction only to persons of the other sex) and **homosexuality** (attraction only to persons of one's own sex). Between these two endpoints lie degrees of **bisexuality**—sexual attraction to both sexes. The colloquial terms "straight" and "gay" have come to replace the more clinical-sounding "heterosexual" and "homosexual" in most contexts, and bisexual people may simply call themselves "bi." The term "gay" can apply to either homosexual men or homosexual women. An alternative term that applies only to homosexual women is "lesbian." This term comes from the Greek island of Lesbos, home of the ancient poetess Sappho, who wrote passionate love-poems to other women.

In his pioneering studies, Alfred Kinsey developed a 7-point scale of sexual orientation that ranged from group 0 (exclusively attracted to the opposite sex) to group 6 (exclusively attracted to the same sex), with the intervening groups defining various degrees of bisexuality. Although well-known to the public, the "Kinsey scale" is less widely used by researchers than it was in the past, chiefly because

sexual orientation The direction of a person's sexual feelings toward persons of the same sex, the other sex, or both sexes.

heterosexuality Sexual attraction only (or predominantly) to persons of the other sex.

homosexuality Sexual attraction only (or predominantly) to persons of one's own sex.

bisexuality Sexual attraction to persons of both sexes.

Figure 14.1 Spectrum of sexual orientation
This bar graph shows the direction of sexual attraction for U.S. men and women aged 18 to 44 (Mosher et al., 2005).

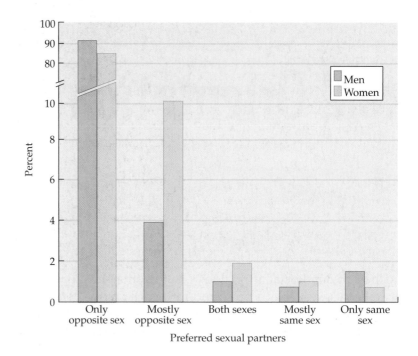

it suggests finer gradations of sexual orientation than are usually supported by the underlying data. Instead, researchers often use a five-point scale (**Figure 14.1**).

In terms of numbers, the distribution of sexual orientations is strongly biased toward the heterosexual end of the spectrum. In most random-sample surveys, at least 85% to 90% of men and women say that they are attracted sexually only to persons of the other sex, and another several percent say that they are attracted "mostly" to the other sex. At the other end of the spectrum, less than 2% of men and less than 1% of women say that they are attracted only to persons of the same sex as themselves. Similar results have been obtained when people have been asked how they think about themselves: In a 2003 Canadian national survey, for example, 1.3% of men and 0.7% of women said that they considered themselves homosexual (Statistics Canada, 2004). If one includes in the definition of gay people those who say they are attracted "mostly" to the same sex, their numbers rise to about 2% to 3% of the population (Laumann et al., 1994; Wellings et al., 1994). The true figures could well be somewhat higher, given that some respondents may be reluctant to admit to a homosexual orientation, but even surveys that have paid a great deal of attention to assuring the respondents' privacy and confidentiality have not come up with significantly higher numbers.

Sexual Orientation Is Not an Isolated Trait

Lesbians and gay men have traditionally been thought of as having many characteristics of the other sex. Words such as "effeminate" or "queeny" have been applied to gay men, and "mannish" or "butch" to lesbians, usually with derogatory implications. These are stereotypes—false or overgeneralized beliefs about classes of people.

Some gay people themselves, however, have promoted the idea that they are **gender-variant** (**Figure 14.2**). Others have rejected this notion, asserting that they differ from straight people only in "who we love."

You probably know at least one or two gay people. If you happen to be gay yourself, you may have scores of gay friends and acquaintances. Either way, you

gender-variant Atypical in gender characteristics.

can hardly have avoided noticing that lesbians and gay men are a very mixed bunch. Some are entirely conventional in their gender characteristics, some are a trifle nonconformist, and some are flagrant gender rebels. Straight people are not always so "straight-acting," either. But are there gender-related differences between gay and straight people considered as entire groups?

Psychologists have studied this issue by examining gender-related traits in large numbers of gay and straight people. They find that gay people—*on average*—do differ in a number of gender-related traits from straight people of the same sex:

- During childhood, boys who later become gay men tend to engage less in rough-and-tumble play, aggressive behavior, and athletics, to be less focused on typical boys' toys and boys' activities, to enjoy interacting with girls, to have a social reputation as a "sissy," and to have less stereotypically male career plans. For girls who later become lesbian, the opposite is true: Such girls tend to be very active physically, to be considered a tomboy, to have male-typical career plans, and so on (Bailey & Zucker, 1995). Although these findings are based largely on the recollections of gay and straight adults, which could be distorted, they have been confirmed by the study of home videos: Raters who watched childhood video clips provided by gay and straight adults (without knowing which was which) rated the "pre-gay" children as far more gender-nonconformist than the "pre-straight children" (Rieger et al., 2008). It is not possible to predict with certainty the future sexual orientation of even extremely gender-nonconformist children, but many or most of them do become gay adults, according to prospective studies (Green, 1987; Drummond et al., 2008) (**Box 14.1**).

Figure 14.2 Novelist Radclyffe Hall (1880–1943) (standing, with her partner Una Troubridge), portrayed lesbians, including herself, as resembling men.

- In adulthood, gay men are (on average) gender-atypical in some of the sex-differentiated cognitive traits that were discussed in Chapter 7 (Wilson & Rahman, 2005). They are less aggressive than straight men, perform less well on male-favoring tests such as mental rotation and targeting accuracy, and perform *better* on some female-favoring tests such as verbal fluency (**Figure 14.3**) and object-location memory. Lesbians also score in gender-atypical fashion in some tests—doing better than heterosexual women in mental rotation and worse in object-location memory, for example.

- On average, gay men describe themselves as less masculine than do straight men, and lesbians describe themselves as less feminine than do straight women (Lippa, 2000). Gays and lesbians also tend to be less gender-conformist than their straight counterparts in their choice of occupations and recreational interests, and this difference holds up across several different regions of the world (Lippa, 2002, 2008).

- To some extent, it is possible to identify a person's sexual orientation on the basis of unconscious behaviors such as

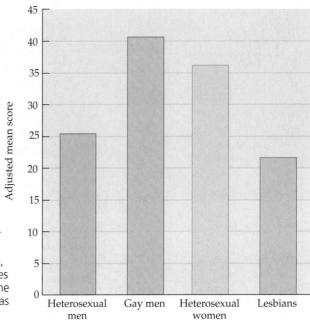

Figure 14.3 Gay men and lesbians are sex-atypical in verbal fluency. The bar graph charts the mean scores of heterosexual men, heterosexual women, gay men, and lesbians (60 individuals per group) in tests of the type "In one minute, list as many words as you can that have the same meaning as 'dark'." The scores have been adjusted for age and IQ. The results for gay men were about the same as for heterosexual women, while the results for lesbians were about the same as for heterosexual men. (After Rahman et al., 2003a.)

Research Highlights

BOX 14.1 Boys Will Be Girls

There has long been "folk wisdom" to the effect that feminine boys have a high chance of becoming gay when they grow up. In the late 1960s, psychiatrist Richard Green of UCLA initiated an ambitious prospective study to test the truth of this notion (Green, 1987). He recruited 66 families in which there was a son (aged 4 to 10) who was markedly feminine. These were not just slightly unmasculine boys. Here's an excerpt from one interview Green had with a 5-year-old boy, "Richard," whose parents brought him to Green because of his persistent cross-dressing, role-playing as a girl, and avoidance of male playmates:

> *Green*: Have you ever wished you'd been born a girl?
> *Richard*: Yes.
> *Green*: Why did you wish that?
> *Richard*: Girls, they don't have to have a penis.
> *Green*: They don't have to have a penis?
> *Richard*: They can have babies. And— because they—it doesn't tickle when you tickle them here.
> *Green*: It doesn't tickle when you tickle them here? Where your penis is?
> *Richard*: Yeah. 'Cause they don't have a penis. I wish I was a girl.

> *Green*: You wish you were a girl?
> *Richard*: You know what? I might be a girl.

Green also recruited 56 boys as matched controls; these boys were chosen without regard to their gender characteristics. He interviewed the boys and their parents repeatedly during the boys' childhood, adolescence, and (in many cases) young adulthood.

The central finding of the study could hardly be more striking. The control boys became, with one slight exception, totally heterosexual (see figure). Of the feminine boys, the majority became bisexual or homosexual. Since some of these boys were only in their mid-teens at their last interview, it is quite possible that some of them moved further toward exclusive homosexuality as they entered adulthood. Although many of the feminine boys wished they were girls, most of them actually became fairly conventional gay men without markedly feminine traits, and only one expressed an interest in sex-reassignment surgery.

In spite of the marked difference in outcomes for the two groups, we should make a couple of cautionary points. First, some of the feminine boys were entirely heterosexual at

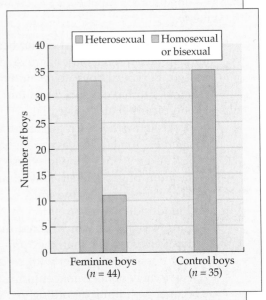

their last interview (in fact, "Richard" was one of these). Thus childhood characteristics are not entirely predictive of adult orientation, even for these extreme gender-nonconformist kids. Second, most gay men do not have a history of such radical gender nonconformity during their childhood; in fact, some recall a very conventionally masculine childhood.

body motions and voice quality (Pierrehumbert et al., 2004; Johnson et al., 2007b). This ability is referred to colloquially as **gaydar.** Some of the behaviors detected by gaydar are gender-atypical in gay people.

In short, there is a partial correlation between sexual orientation and other aspects of gender, and any theory of sexual orientation needs to explain the existence of this correlation. Gays and lesbians are certainly not transgendered, but they are distinctly atypical, on average, in some gender-related traits. These differences between gay and straight people are generally more consistent for men than for women.

Diverse Theories Attempt to Explain Sexual Orientation

What causes a person to become heterosexual, bisexual, or homosexual? This is a question that has aroused a great deal of interest and controversy over the years. In popular discourse, the question has often been phrased in such forms as "What makes people gay?"—as if heterosexuality didn't require any explanation. In reality, of course, heterosexuality, homosexuality, and bisexuality all need some kind of explanation.

gaydar The ability to recognize gay people on the basis of unconscious behaviors, voice quality, gait, and so on.

Most theories of sexual orientation could be described as either psychodynamic or biological. Psychodynamic theories attempt to explain the development of a person's sexual orientation in terms of internal mental processes, especially as they are affected by interaction with others, rewards and punishments, and so on. Examples include psychoanalytic theory and socialization theory. Biological theories, in contrast, attempt to explain sexual orientation in terms of phenomena such as brain circuitry, hormones, genes, and evolution. It is unlikely that either class of theory, by itself, can provide a complete understanding of sexual orientation.

Freud Put Forward Elaborate Developmental Theories to Explain Both Heterosexuality and Homosexuality

Throughout most of the twentieth century, thinking about sexual orientation centered on the psychoanalytic theories of Sigmund Freud. Freud saw heterosexuality as the "normal" end stage of a complex, multistage process of psychosexual development (Freud, 1905/1975). This process, he believed, included a homosexual phase in early childhood that is later forgotten. The "normal" developmental process could be disrupted by abnormal relationships within the family: These could include a mother who was too "close-binding" or "seductive" toward a child, a father who was too distant or hostile, intense sibling rivalry, or penis envy—the trauma supposedly suffered by a girl when she discovers that she lacks a body part possessed by her father or brother. If these phenomena blocked "normal" development, the child might remain stuck in the early homosexual phase. Freud suggested a variety of other mechanisms by which a person might become homosexual. None of them have been substantiated by scientific research.

Freud himself spoke positively about homosexual people and did not think that they could readily be "converted" to heterosexuality. Many of Freud's followers in the United States, however, thought otherwise. Until recent times, when homosexuality became more socially accepted, many gay men who wished to become straight underwent long and expensive courses of psychoanalysis. The hope was that by uncovering and working through the childhood events and relationships that were thought to be responsible for their "condition," these men could attain the "normal" end point of psychosexual development: heterosexuality. However, successful transformations occurred rarely, if ever, and many gay men were severely traumatized by this kind of therapy (Duberman, 1991). Freudian theory also traumatized the parents of gays and lesbians by making them feel responsible for their children's homosexuality. Still, some contemporary psychoanalysts have reworked Freudian theory in a more gay-positive vein (Isay, 1989; Drescher et al., 2003).

Sexual Orientation Has Been Attributed to Socialization

One potentially very powerful form of socialization consists of sexual interactions. In this vein, it has often been suggested that both male and female homosexuality result from molestation during childhood, from rape during young adulthood, from consensual same-sex experiences in boarding schools, or from other early sexual experiences. Again, though, the evidence does not support such ideas. People who attend single-sex boarding schools do have more homosexual experiences during that time than people who don't attend such schools, but they are no more likely to be gay in adulthood (Wellings et al., 1994). And lesbians are no more likely to have been molested during childhood than are straight women (Dominguez et al., 2002).

Socialization effects could, of course, be much subtler than those just described and could include important cognitive aspects. Women, in particular, whose sexual feelings are more strongly modulated by considerations of love and intimacy

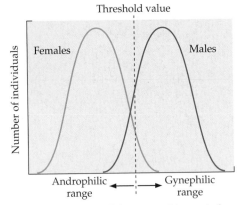

Threshold value

Females | Males

Number of individuals

Androphilic range ←——→ Gynephilic range

Androgen level during sensitive period

Figure 14.4 The prenatal hormonal theory of sexual orientation In its simplest form, this theory proposes that adult sexual orientation depends on the level of androgens to which the brain is exposed during a sensitive period of fetal development. Most males and a few females exceed some threshold of androgen exposure and therefore become attracted to females. Most females and a few males fall below that threshold level and therefore become attracted to males. In the figure, the threshold has been arbitrarily set at a value that would produce more homosexual males than females, corresponding to what has been observed in most studies.

gynephilic Sexually attracted to women.

androphilic Sexually attracted to men.

than are those of men, may for that reason be more responsive to the vagaries of individual life history and to culturally based identities and sexual scripts (see Chapter 1), which might give their sexual orientation greater fluidity than that of men (Peplau & Garnets, 2000; Diamond, 2008b). At the height of the feminist movement in the 1970s, for example, a number of women expressed their sense of solidarity with the community of women by entering into lesbian relationships, and some later returned to relationships with men (Whisman, 1996).

In Chapter 7 we described the work of John Money, who proposed that parents guide their children's developing gender and sexual orientation by innumerable rewards and punishments—by operant conditioning, in other words. We described how Bruce Reimer, the boy who was reared as a girl, became Money's poster child for this theory but later became Money's nemesis when he changed his sex back to male and developed a clear heterosexual orientation (see Box 7.2). Although it seems likely that parental influence does mold some aspects of children's gender characteristics, there is no positive evidence for an influence on sexual orientation. In particular, there is no evidence that children who later become gay adults are exposed to any parental "training" in that direction.

Biological Theories Focus on Prenatal Hormones and Genes

The leading biological theory of sexual orientation proposes that sexual orientation, like other aspects of gender, reflects the sexual differentiation of the brain under the influence of prenatal sex hormones. In the simplest version of this theory (**Figure 14.4**), everything depends on androgen levels during a sensitive period of prenatal development. Fetuses whose brains are exposed to high levels of androgens during this period (mostly males, but a few females) will be sexually attracted to women (**gynephilic**) in adult life; conversely, fetuses whose brains are exposed to low levels of androgens (mostly females, but some males) will be sexually attracted to men (**androphilic**) in adult life. Alternatively, it might be not the hormone levels themselves but the brain's sensitivity to hormones that differs between "pre-gay" and "pre-straight" fetuses.

The prenatal hormonal hypothesis could explain why gay people are, on average, gender-atypical in a variety of traits besides their sexual orientation, as described above. We would just need to suppose that differences in androgen levels during development affect the differentiation not just of brain circuits that are responsible for sexual orientation, but also some brain circuits that mediate some other gendered traits—specifically, those whose brain circuitry happens to differentiate in the same fetal time-period.

The prenatal hormonal theory has a solid basis in animal research: The preference of animals such as rats for male or female sex partners can be modified by manipulation of their androgen levels during development (de Jonge et al., 1988, Bakker et al., 1993). Of course, it is not ethically possible to do comparable experiments in humans. As we mentioned in Chapter 7, however, the condition of congenital adrenal hyperplasia (CAH), in which human fetuses are exposed to high levels of androgens regardless of their sex, offers an equivalent "experiment of nature." Women with CAH are more likely to experience same-sex attraction and engage in same-sex relationships than are control groups of women such as their unaffected sisters (Dittmann et al., 1992). This suggests that the findings of the animal studies are relevant to humans too.

Of course, CAH is a rare medical condition. Do the findings in CAH-affected persons say anything about healthy people? To study this question, researchers have looked for biological markers related to sexual orientation in the general population. Neuroscientist Simon LeVay focused on the hypothalamus. In Chapter 5 we mentioned animal experiments indicating that a region at the front of the hypothalamus known as the **medial preoptic area** is involved in the regulation of sexual behaviors typically shown by males, including the preference for female partners (**Figure 14.5**). Within the medial preoptic area is a cell group that is sexually dimorphic: It is typically larger in males than in females. In humans it has the name **INAH3**. Again, based on animal experiments, it appears that this sex difference results from differences in circulating sex hormone levels during the prenatal period when this region of the brain is developing. LeVay measured the volume of INAH3 in autopsy tissue from gay and straight men. He reported that the volume was significantly smaller in the gay men than in the straight men and not significantly different from the volume found in women (LeVay, 1991). A replication study found a difference of the same kind, though smaller in degree (Byne et al., 2001). And more recently, a research group at Oregon Health Sciences University made similar findings in the brains of sheep—a species in which about 8% of males are naturally homosexual (Roselli et al., 2004).

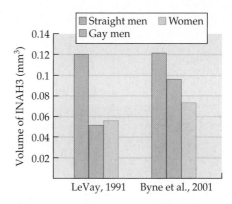

Figure 14.5 Hypothalamic structure and male sexual orientation Two autopsy studies found that the sexually dimorphic cell group known as INAH3 is smaller in gay men than in straight men, but they did not agree on the magnitude of the difference (LeVay, 1991; Byne et al., 2001).

Functional differences between the hypothalamus of gay and straight people have also been described. A Swedish research group used a PET scanner to study brain activity patterns in subjects who were sniffing odorous compounds derived from human sweat or urine—substances that may act as pheromones. For example, one compound, called androstadienone (AND), is derived from male armpit sweat, and it has a positive effect on women's mood even when delivered at concentrations too low for conscious detection (Lundstrom & Olsson, 2005). In the Swedish study, the front part of the hypothalamus, which includes the medial preoptic area, was active in heterosexual women and gay men while they were sniffing AND but inactive in heterosexual men (**Figure 14.6**). A follow-up study reported that this brain region was also inactive in lesbians when sniffing AND. The researchers obtained the opposite results when using a substance released by women: The front region of the hypothalamus was active in heterosexual men and lesbians, but not in heterosexual women or gay men (Savic et al., 2005; Berglund et al., 2006). These findings, which remain to be replicated by other researchers, suggest that functional connections between the olfactory system and the hypothalamus differ between homosexual and heterosexual individuals of the same sex. Whether these differences result from early biological processes of brain development, or from the sexual or social experiences of gay and straight people in adult life, is not known.

A variety of other biological differences between gay and straight people have been reported. These include differences in the relative size of the left and right cerebral hemispheres (Savic & Lindstrom, 2008), in the function of the inner ear (McFadden & Pasanen, 1999), in eye-blink reflexes (Rahman et al., 2003b), and even in body features such as the relative lengths of the fingers (Williams et al., 2000; Manning et al., 2007) and the rotation direction of scalp hair whorls (Klar, 2005). None of these traits are "diagnostic" of an individual's sexual orientation, but differences emerge when large numbers of gay and straight subjects are compared. In most of these

medial preoptic area A region of the hypothalamus involved in the regulation of sexual behaviors typically shown by males.

INAH3 (third interstitial nucleus of the anterior hypothalamus) A cell group in the hypothalamus that differs in size between men and women and between gay and straight men.

(A) Heterosexual women   (B) Homosexual men   (C) Heterosexual men

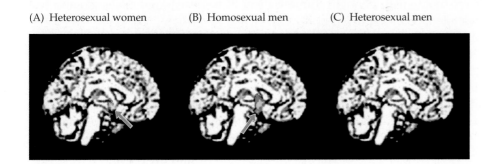

Figure 14.6 Brain function and sexual orientation The PET scans show the averaged brain activity of (A) heterosexual women, (B) homosexual men, and (C) heterosexual men, elicited by breathing air containing androstadienone, a volatile compound that is present in men's sweat. There is an active response to the odor in the hypothalamus of heterosexual women and gay men (see arrows) but not in the hypothalamus of heterosexual men. (From Savic et al., 2005.)

studies, the traits under study are reported to be sex-atypical, (or intermediate between the sexes) in gay men or lesbians, and such findings have been interpreted as further evidence in support of the prenatal hormonal hypothesis. Still, the exact processes by which these traits come to differ between the sexes, let alone how they come to differ between gay and straight people, remain to be nailed down.

Even if correct, the prenatal hormone theory is not an ultimate explanation of sexual orientation because it does not explain why androgen levels (or sensitivity to androgens) should differ between "pre-gay" and "pre-straight" fetuses. It is possible that a variety of different ultimate causes, including both endogenous and environmental processes, could modulate fetal hormone levels or hormone responsiveness, and hence ultimately influence sexual orientation.

One possibility is that a fetus's *genes* affect prenatal hormone levels or sensitivity to hormones. Family and twin studies have shown that genes do indeed have a significant influence on sexual orientation (Wilson & Rahman, 2005). Monozygotic or "identical" twins—who share the same genes—are much more likely to share the same sexual orientation than are nonidentical twins, who do not (Kendler et al., 2000). Genetic factors account for as much as half of the overall diversity in men's sexual orientation, according to some studies. Genes have a weaker but still measurable influence on women's sexual orientation. Whether this genetic influence works through the prenatal hormonal pathway, however, or through some quite different mechanism, remains to be determined. Attempts to locate the specific genes that influence sexual orientation have so far yielded only suggestive findings (Hamer et al., 1993; Mustanski et al., 2005). If future studies do identify specific genes, this will open the door to a more detailed study of the biological pathways that are involved.

Further discussion of the mechanisms underlying sexual orientation is available in Web Topic 14.1 The Categorical Perception of Sex May Influence Sexual Orientation.

The Basis for Defining Homosexual People Has Changed over Time

Currently, we think of homosexual or gay people (lesbians and gay men) as people whose sexual feelings are directed predominantly toward people of the same sex as themselves. Whatever the actual determinants of sexual orientation, we think of gay people's sexual desire as a durable attribute that helps define who they are.

It hasn't always been that way. Certainly, there is occasional mention in ancient literature of the notion that particular individuals are attracted to the same or to the other sex (**Figure 14.7**). The more usual concept over the past 2000 years, however, has been that everyone shares roughly the same sexual feelings—a predominant desire for the opposite sex, with some capacity for same-sex attraction. In societies in which women were secluded and therefore inaccessible to unmarried men, as in ancient Greece, many men had sex with male youths, but this behavior was not usually thought to mark them as a special kind of person and was often tolerated or approved of.

Some early Christians, such as St. Paul, strongly disapproved of homosexual behavior by either men or women. They represented such behavior as a willful violation of a person's true nature as heterosexual, however, and not as a sign of some deep difference between heterosexual and homosexual persons. This attitude persisted through most of western European history. Sexual behavior between men was called sodomy and was thought of as a wicked behavior that anyone might be inclined to engage in if not restrained by morality or the law. Sexual behavior between women was largely ignored.

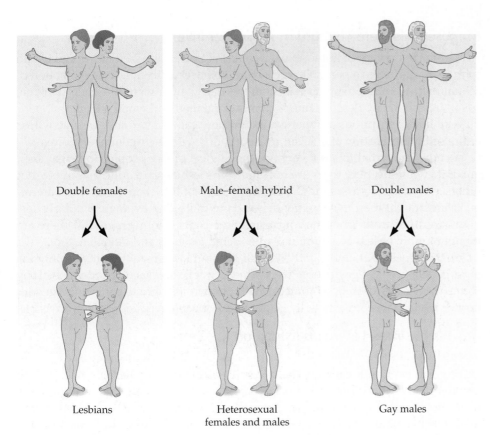

Figure 14.7 Theory of origins In Plato's *Symposium* (drinking party), written in Athens during the fourth century BCE, a participant presents an extemporized creation myth to account for the existence of persons of different sexual orientation. All humans, he said, originally consisted of double creatures, each with four arms, four legs, and two sets of genitals. Some were double females (left), some were male-female hybrids (center), and some were double males (right). These creatures were cut in two by an angry god, forming the humans we know today. Sexual desire is the desire to be reunited with one's other ancestral half. Thus humans descended from the double females are lesbians, humans descended from the hybrids are heterosexual women and men, and humans descended from the double males are homosexual men. This is one of the few instances in classical literature in which a writer makes a clear distinction between gay and straight people and considers how such differences might have arisen.

Double females

Male–female hybrid

Double males

Lesbians

Heterosexual
females and males

Gay males

Several factors facilitated the development of the concept of a homosexual *identity*. One was the growth of cities, which allowed homosexual men to find each other and form social groups. By the mid-nineteenth century, most large cities in Europe and the United States had some kind of homosexual male subculture. There was no equivalent homosexual culture for women, but many educated American women formed **Boston marriages**—same-sex cohabitations that were quite likely sexual but were not viewed as such by society at large (Faderman, 1981). (The phrase "Boston marriage" has recently developed a somewhat different meaning, referring to lesbian couples who do not have sex with each other.)

Another factor promoting the recognition of a homosexual identity was the development of "companionate" marriage that emphasized intimacy between husband and wife (see Chapter 13). Fulfilling this expectation of heterosexual intimacy was difficult for many homosexual people, and it made same-sex affairs more dangerous. Thus there was an increase in the numbers of homosexual men and women who remained unmarried and who were therefore available to populate a homosexual subculture. The "confirmed bachelor"—a man who rejected marriage and who might well be homosexual—became a familiar social type in the nineteenth century.

A third factor was the attention paid to same-sex desire by nineteenth-century doctors. Most prominent among these was the German sexologist Richard von Krafft-Ebing, whose 1886 book *Psychopathia Sexualis* was mentioned in Chapter 1. Krafft-Ebing and other early sexologists portrayed homosexuality as a mental disorder. This might not seem particularly advantageous to gay people—in fact, it led to traumatic attempts to "cure" them. However, it did strengthen the notion that homosexuals were a distinct kind of people and thus contributed to the development of gay and lesbian self-awareness.

Boston marriage In nineteenth-century New England, the cohabitation of two women.

A "Boston marriage" was the cohabitation of two women—often academics—in nineteenth-century New England. In most cases we do not know whether these relationships were sexual or not, though it is likely that some were. This photograph shows social reformer and Nobel Peace Prize winner Jane Addams (right) (1860–1935) with her benefactor and life companion Mary Rozet Smith (1868–1933).

(A)

(B)

A woman's privilege is to change her mind, and actress Anne Heche (who starred in *Psycho* and *Wag the Dog*) has certainly done so. For 2 years in the mid-1990s she dated actor Steve Martin. Then she lived for 3 years with lesbian comedian Ellen DeGeneres (A). They planned to have a baby and get married, but in August 2000 they broke up. (B) A year later Heche married Coleman Laffoon, a cameraman she met while working on a documentary about DeGeneres. They split up in 2007. How do you label someone like Heche? Is she straight, lesbian, bisexual, or just a trendsetter?

butch Masculine-acting, often used to describe certain lesbians.

femme Feminine-acting, often used to describe certain lesbians or bisexual women.

Homosexuals Were Thought of as Gender Inverts

Although the concept of homosexual people became established in the nineteenth century, it was tied to a particular idea about homosexuality, which was that homosexual men were like women and homosexual women were like men (Hekma, 1994). Indeed, many descriptions of homosexual men and women from that period read like descriptions of what we would now call transexuals—people whose entire self-identification and social role is at odds with their genital anatomy.

We now know that this is a very one-sided view of gay people: Some gay men are quite feminine, but others are not, and some lesbians are quite masculine, but others are not. As discussed in the earlier sections of this chapter, gay men do differ from straight men in some gender-specific traits—on average. Similarly, lesbians do differ from straight women in some traits—on average. But there are plenty of more or less conventionally gendered lesbians and gay men, too.

We may guess that, in the early days of gay and lesbian culture, it was only the most gender-atypical gay people who came to public and medical attention. They were, in essence, exposed, or "outed," by their own inability to conform to gender norms, while more conventionally gendered gay people remained largely invisible.

Gay People Were Later Subdivided on the Basis of Gender Characteristics

During the twentieth century, the diversity of gay people became much more apparent (Faderman, 1991; Chauncey, 1994). To accommodate this recognition, a new idea took hold—that there are two kinds of lesbians and two kinds of gay men. The two kinds of lesbians were called **butch** and **femme**: The butch lesbians looked, dressed, and acted like men and took a dominant role in sex, while the femme lesbians were like heterosexual women and took a submissive role in sex. A lesbian couple would consist of a butch–femme pair. Similarly, gay men were thought to be of two kinds, sometimes referred to as tops and bottoms: Tops were defined by a preference for the insertive role in anal intercourse and were relatively masculine and dominant generally, while bottoms preferred the receptive role and were more feminine. With this thinking, lesbian and gay male relationships were "regularized." Although they were same-sex relationships, they mimicked heterosexual relationships in the sense that they were formed by the union of a more masculine-gendered and a more feminine-gendered partner.

This general conception of gay sexuality persisted through the 1950s and was very much part of gay and lesbian culture. According to an oral history of mid-twentieth-century lesbian life in Buffalo, New York, young, working-class women who entered the lesbian culture had to first figure out whether they were butch or femme. After this fateful decision was made, all their relationships, social roles, and sexual behaviors were governed by their identity as one or the other (Kennedy & Davis, 1983).

To some degree this culture of complementary gender types still exists today. The 10-year-old son of a lesbian couple living in Decatur, Georgia, put it this way: "One of my moms is kind of like my dad, and my other mom is the girly mom" (Bagby, 2008). But in general, today's gay and lesbian communities are characterized by a kaleidoscopic variety of "types" and a generally more playful attitude toward gender. Self-identified butch and femme lesbians still exist, but the rules have loosened. No one would be surprised to see two butch or two femme lesbians forming a couple, for example.

In addition, the lesbian/straight and gay/straight dichotomies are themselves under siege, especially among women. While some women remain out-and-out lesbians, others move fluidly between relationships with both men and women. Of course, one might call these women bisexuals (see below), rather than lesbians.

However, they may reject any such labels themselves, preferring to define their sexual desires in terms of the specific people they are attracted to, rather than by overall classes of partners. Thus they challenge the centrality of sexual orientation as we currently define it.

The Gay Community Has Struggled for Equal Rights

As with some other minorities, gay people's identity has been powerfully molded by a history of oppression and by the struggle to overcome that oppression. Thus to understand the gay community today it is necessary to have some knowledge of its political history, a history that begins in Europe rather than in the United States.

The Gay Rights Movement Began in Germany

The world's first gay rights organization, the Scientific-Humanitarian Committee, was founded in Berlin in 1897. The main figure behind this group was Magnus Hirschfeld (see Box 1.1), a gay Jewish doctor and sexologist who developed a biological theory of sexual orientation and gender (Wolff, 1986). For 30 years Hirschfeld led the struggle to have the German sodomy statutes overthrown. His organization drew considerable public interest and sympathy and seemed close to success on several occasions, but it was ultimately broken up by the Nazis. Several thousand German homosexuals—nearly all men—were sent to concentration camps, where most of them died. The identifying symbol that homosexual men were forced to wear in the camps—a pink triangle—was later adopted as an icon for the gay rights movement worldwide.

After the Second World War, gay activism moved to the United States (Marcus, 2002). The first enduring American gay rights organization, the Mattachine Society, was founded in Los Angeles in 1950, and the first lesbian organization was founded in San Francisco 5 years later. These organizations functioned largely as support groups for gays and lesbians, who were generally reviled at that time. In the mid-1960s, more politically active gay organizations sprang up on the East Coast and began a series of actions, such as picketing the White House to protest the firing of gay federal employees (**Figure 14.8**).

Figure 14.8 Early gay activists
Members of the Washington offshoot of the Mattachine Society and other East Coast groups picketing the White House in 1965.

Early on the morning of June 28, 1969, a riot broke out outside the Stonewall Inn, a bar in New York's Greenwich Village that catered to gay men, transvestites, and transexuals (Duberman, 1993). The riot was in response to a police raid—something that gay bars endured frequently in those days. The rioting evolved into street demonstrations that continued for several nights. These demonstrations were followed by the formation of more confrontational gay rights organizations. The "Stonewall Rebellion" is often viewed as the starting point of the modern gay rights movement.

At the time of the Stonewall Rebellion, the status of gay people in the United States was still quite dismal. Homosexuality was officially listed by the American Psychiatric Association as a mental disorder, and many gay people were attempting to be "cured" of it (Duberman, 1991). Most Americans thought that sex between two men or two women was morally wrong, most states had sodomy statutes, and gay relationships had no status under the law. Gay people had no legal protection from discrimination and were often dismissed from public or private employment on the basis of their sexual orientation. Not a single openly gay person had ever been elected to public office, and there were virtually no gay role models in any occupation. Bars represented almost the entirety of gay social life.

The 1970s were a period of rapid change. The first gay rights marches took place in 1970. In 1971, the National Organization for Women officially acknowledged the role of lesbians in that organization. In 1973, homosexuality was deleted from the *DSM,* the American Psychiatric Association's handbook of mental disorders. In 1974, the first openly gay person won elected office, and others followed (**Box 14.2**).

During the 1970s, urban gay districts such as San Francisco's Castro Street drew thousands of young gay men from around the country and became the center of their sexual, social, and political lives (D'Emilio, 1990). Homosexuality became a topic of considerable public interest, and while many people continued to despise gays and lesbians, others became sympathetic. By 1977, about 40 cities had enacted some kind of antidiscrimination ordinance.

The AIDS epidemic, which began around 1980 and continues today, caused the deaths of 266,000 gay men* by 2006 (Centers for Disease Control, 2008b) and deeply traumatized the survivors. The initial public and political response to AIDS was to ignore it or dismiss it as a "gay disease" (Shilts, 1987). In reaction, countless thousands of gay men were motivated to involve themselves in AIDS activism and gay activism. Lesbians, who during the 1970s had been involved in feminist causes more than in specifically lesbian or gay ones, joined forces with gay men and founded co-gender organizations. Gays and lesbians **came out of the closet** in droves. Americans came to *know* gay people—not just the distant, famous ones, but also family members, neighbors, and coworkers. The percentage of Americans who said that they personally knew someone who was openly gay rose from 30% in 1983 to 73% in 2000 (Rubin, 2000).

The collective effect of these disclosures was immense, bringing the most unlikely allies to the gay cause. When archconservative Republican Senator Barry Goldwater of Arizona discovered that his grandson Ty Ross was gay, he began to support gay causes, including nondiscrimination statutes and the right of gay people to serve in the military. "I'm an honorary gay by now," the 85-year-old Goldwater said on one occasion (Grove, 1994). In 2004, Vice President Dick Cheney—a conservative by any standard—refused to support President Bush's call for a federal ban on gay marriage. "We have a gay daughter," Cheney said, "so it's an issue we're very familiar with. Freedom means freedom for everyone" (BBC News, 2004).

come out of the closet (or "come out") Reveal a previously concealed identity, such as being gay.

---

*More accurately, these were men who acquired HIV infection from sex with men—not all were gay.

Sex in History

BOX 14.2 Harvey Milk

If the American gay rights movement has a martyr, it is City Supervisor Harvey Milk of San Francisco. Born to a New York Jewish family, Milk was always conscious of Jewish history and thus of the need to struggle actively against oppression. He moved to San Francisco in 1972 and, after two failed attempts, won election to the Board of Supervisors in 1977. He was the first openly gay man to be elected to city government in the United States.

During his short tenure as supervisor, Milk helped lead the successful campaign to reject California Proposition 6, the "Briggs Initiative," which would have forced the state to fire openly gay teachers. He was instrumental in passing San Francisco's first gay rights ordinance. And he encouraged gay activism with a series of public speeches, which often acknowledged the example set by the black civil rights struggle. "The blacks did not win their rights by sitting quietly in the back of the bus," he declared at the 1978 San Francisco Gay Pride parade. "They got off! Gay people, we will not win our rights by staying quietly in our closets. We are coming out! We are coming out to fight the lies, the myths, the distortions! We are coming out to tell the truth about gays!" Milk was also inspired by the black civil rights movement to call for a gay and lesbian March on Washington.

On November 27, 1978, shortly after Proposition 6 was rejected, Milk and San Francisco Mayor George Moscone were shot dead in their City Hall offices by Dan White, an anti-gay city supervisor and former police officer who represented a conservative blue-collar district of the city. At his trial, a psychiatrist testified that White's addiction to junk food was a sign of mental disorder; this became the infamous "Twinkie defense." White received an extraordinarily light sentence—fewer than 8 years in prison. When the sentence was announced, gay men rioted, torched police cars, and broke down the doors of City Hall. In retaliation, anti-gay police officers attacked a gay bar and clubbed most of the customers.

White was released after just 5 years but committed suicide 2 years later. The March on Washington that Milk had called for took place in October of 1979; it was the first of several increasingly effective national demonstrations for gay rights. Milk's life has been commemorated in a biography (Shilts, 1982), plays, music, and a 2008 feature film starring Sean Penn.

Harvey Milk (1930–1978) (center) with San Francisco Mayor George Moscone (left)

As a result of this pro-gay trend, there have been important judicial and legislative decisions affecting gay people in recent years. In 2002, the U.S. Supreme Court ruled that state laws banning gay sex were unconstitutional (see Box 9.3). In 2003, the Massachusetts Supreme Court paved the way for gay marriage in that state, and the Supreme Courts of California and Connecticut followed suit in 2008 (**Box 14.3**). By 2008, 20 states and many cities had enacted laws banning some forms of discrimination on the basis of sexual orientation, and 13 of these states also include gender identity as a protected category (National Gay and Lesbian Task Force, 2008b).

Society, Values, and the Law

BOX 14.3 Gay Marriage

On May 17, 2004, Julie and Hillary Goodridge were married by a Unitarian Universalist minister on Boston's Beacon Hill, in the presence of their 8-year-old daughter Annie (see figure). The Goodridges and hundreds of other lesbian and gay male couples who married in Massachusetts on that day were making history—they were the first gay couples to enter into fully legal civil marriage in the United States, thanks to a successful lawsuit in which the Goodridges were the lead plaintiffs.

In 2008 California's Supreme Court likewise ruled that a state law banning same-sex marriage violated gay people's rights under the equal-protection clause of the California constitution, thus making California the second U.S. state to legalize same-sex marriage. In the November 2008 election, however, California voters amended the state's constitution to eliminate the right to same-sex marriage. The voters' action consigned thousands of already-married gay couples to a legal limbo that the courts will have to deal with.

In October 2008, Connecticut's Supreme Court issued a similar ruling to California's. Also, the governor of New York announced a policy to recognize out-of-state same-sex marriages. Thus same-sex marriage is effectively available to New Yorkers, who can simply cross the border to Connecticut or Massachusetts to get married.

Eight other states have introduced legal unions or partnerships that confer some or all of the benefits and responsibilities of marriage, though without the name. Gay marriage is legal in Canada, the Netherlands, Belgium, and Spain; nine other countries authorize same-sex civil unions.

Most Americans are opposed to gay marriage, however. In 1996 Congress passed the Defense of Marriage Act (DOMA), which prohibits federal recognition of same-sex marriages, and most states have enacted laws or constitutional amendments banning same-sex marriages. The constitutionality of these laws and the question of whether States have to recognize same-sex marriages performed in other states will eventually be decided by the U.S. Supreme Court.

Former President George W. Bush criticized Massachusetts' "activist judges" for "forcing" gay marriage on an unwilling society and bypassing the legislative process. Yet there is a striking parallel with the history of interracial marriage (see Box 10.2): In the face of popular and political opposition, state and then U.S. Supreme Court justices ruled that such couples had a constitutional right, under due process, to marry. It's doubtful that Bush would claim that those judicial decisions were wrong, but it's difficult to see a legal distinction between one case and the other.

In spite of the current popular opposition to gay marriage, it seems likely that it will eventually become commonplace. Between 1996 to 2006 the proportion of the U.S. population opposed to same-sex marriage fell from 67% to 56%, according to Gallup Polls (Religious Tolerance.org, 2007; Gallup, 2008). And young people are much more favorably inclined toward gay relationships than are their elders; in 2007, 61% of college freshmen believed that gay marriage should be legal (Vara-Orta, 2007), and a 2004 national poll by the *Los Angeles Times* found that 59% of the U.S. population believes that gay marriage is "inevitable." The examples of Massachusetts and California, though they initially provoked a hostile backlash, may eventually help to "normalize" the concept of gay marriage. As one of the May 17 Massachusetts brides commented, "When everyone wakes up tomorrow and sees that nothing bad happened—it's the same world it was the day before, there are only more people who are equal to them—they're going to see there was nothing to fear" (Associated Press, 2004a).

Unfortunately, same-sex marriages are no more immune from problems than heterosexual ones. The Goodridges separated two years after their pioneering Massachusetts marriage, and gay divorces are now commonplace. Because the federal government does not recognize same-sex marriages, it does not grant a tax-deduction for same-sex alimony payments, thus imposing an extra financial burden on divorcing gay couples (Linzer, 2008).

Gay People Are in Transition

Because of this rapid, ongoing change of attitudes, the current status of gays and lesbians in American society is full of paradoxes:

- A slight majority of Americans continue to believe that sex between men or between women is morally wrong (see Figure 10.3), but on many questions of practical significance a majority of Americans now take a pro-gay view (**Figure 14.9**).

"Should gays be protected under civil rights laws in the way that racial minorities and women have been protected, or not?"

Figure 14.9 Changing views on gay people, based on national polls by the Los Angeles Times. (Data from Mehren, 2004.)

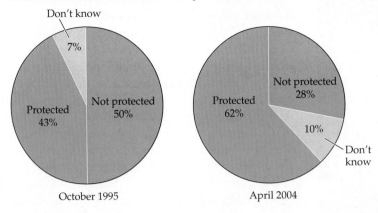

October 1995   April 2004

"If you had a child of elementary school age, would you object to having a gay person as your child's teacher, or would that not bother you?"

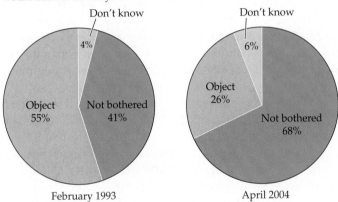

February 1993   April 2004

- Gays and lesbians are being discharged from the armed services in considerable numbers (612 men and women in 2006), but most Americans now think that gays should be able to serve openly in the military (Pew Research Center, 2006; Tyson, 2007).

- Over 1400 hate crimes based on sexual orientation were reported to the FBI in 2006 (Federal Bureau of Investigation, 2007), yet many gay people say they feel safer and more accepted than ever before.

- Civil same-sex marriage is not available anywhere except in Massachusetts and Connecticut, yet more and more gay couples consider themselves married, and many raise children.

- Gays claim that they are campaigning for "equal rights" (Human Rights Campaign, 2008), but their opponents say gays want "special rights" (Focus on the Family, 2007).

Gay Rights Are a Global Issue

The status of lesbians and gay men varies greatly around the world. The United States has been a leader in gay people's political struggle over the last several decades—in fact, some other countries, such as Britain, use the word "Stonewall" in the names of their own gay rights organizations, as if to acknowledge the worldwide significance of that 1969 riot.

This Israeli soldier can be open about his homosexuality without risking discharge.

Some countries, especially in western Europe, have a tradition of social tolerance that has allowed their gay citizens to sidestep some of the inequities that their American counterparts have experienced. In France, for example, sex between men has been legal since 1791. Also, the "religious right" is a much less significant political force in most European countries than it is in the United States. Thus, with relatively little effort, gay couples have acquired the full legal rights of marriage in three European countries and domestic partnership rights nearly equivalent to marriage in several others. In many European countries anti-gay discrimination and gay-bashing are less common than in the United States, and gay culture flourishes. The 1950 European Convention on Human Rights has been interpreted to protect the rights of sexual minorities, the Council of Europe has required its member nations to rescind their sodomy statutes, and the European Court of Human Rights has ruled that lesbians and gay men must be allowed to serve openly in member nations' armed forces. Canada is also more accepting of gay people than the United States, as exemplified by the fact that same-sex marriage is legal throughout the country.

In contrast, there are other parts of the world where lesbians and gay men are still subject to extreme persecution (International Gay and Lesbian Association, 1999). In fact, most countries ban homosexual behavior completely, ban it for one sex, or have a higher age of consent for gay sex than for heterosexual sex. Only five countries in Africa, six in Asia, one in the Middle East (Israel), and seven in the Americas allow the same rights of sexual expression for gay and straight people. Homosexual acts are a capital offense in Iran and a few other Islamic countries. Police harassment of gay people is common in many countries, especially in the Balkan nations, Central and South America, and China. Killings of gay people on account of their sexual orientation happen frequently in Central and South America. Brazil is one of the worst offenders: An estimated 1600 Brazilians are believed to have been killed on account of their sexual orientation or gender identity between 1980 and 1997 (International Gay and Lesbian Association, 1999).

Growing Up Gay Presents Challenges

It's possible that, at some future time, a person's sexual orientation will be of as little significance as, say, their handedness. For now, however, many gay people still have to grow up in a hostile environment, and the experience of this hostility may strongly color their worldview as adults.

We mentioned above that many gays and lesbians are somewhat gender-nonconformist as children. Of course, there's a lot of variation among individuals. Some pre-gay children act like miniature transexuals and cannot be cajoled or forced by any means to behave like conventional kids of their own sex. Others fit easily into the conventional mold. The majority are probably somewhere in the middle—not quite conventional boys and girls but not outrageously unconventional either.

A pre-gay child's position on this gender continuum strongly affects their growing-up process. Markedly gender-nonconformist children "out" themselves before they even enter kindergarten. Parents may already suspect—with good reason—that the child is likely to become gay, and they may do everything in their power to prevent it, including punishment and various kinds of "therapy." A "sissy" boy may quickly become the least favorite child in the family—especially in the eyes of his father. For tomboyish girls, it's less predictable—some such girls thrive. In any case, tomboyishness is much less reliable a predictor of future homosexuality in girls than is femininity in boys (Bailey & Zucker, 1995).

Initially, a gay child's experiences in school may be unremarkable, but trouble often crops up in the preadolescent years (age 8 through 13). Because children form same-sex social networks at this age and rigorously enforce gender norms, a child who is gender-nonconformist to any extent may be excluded from friendship groups and even verbally abused. This can happen even before the child becomes aware of same-sex attraction—in fact, some of these children don't become gay at all. But it's all the same to their peers. Terms of abuse such as "faggot" and "dyke" are used commonly in preadolescent and adolescent school society, and teachers do not always make serious efforts to stop this abuse. As the child gets older, things may go from bad to worse as abusive words are supplemented by abusive deeds. Many gay and lesbian adolescents are now announcing their homosexuality, either to close friends or to the whole world (Floyd & Bakeman, 2006), but this openness can bring severe retribution in some communities (**Box 14.4**).

Gay adolescents who are more conventional in their gender characteristics have the option of passing as straight, and many do. Quite commonly, such teens go into an "overachiever" mode, in which excellence in academics or other fields serves to mask their problematic sexuality. Although this course of action may prevent the kind of harassment that more obviously gay teens experience, it may inflict its own wounds: specifically, a hemming in of normal self-expression that interferes with psychological development and with sexual and social relationships in later life.

It's not possible to provide a single image of what it's like to grow up gay. For some youths, like those described in Box 14.4, it can be an unrelenting torment. Some are rejected by their parents or run away from home, perhaps becoming prostitutes in the nearest big city. Some contemplate or attempt suicide (Richardson, 1995), although whether the rate of attempted or completed suicide is higher among gay than straight youth is uncertain (Savin-Williams, 2001). Not surprisingly, those gay adolescents and adults who experienced harassment for gender-nonconformity during their childhood have an increased likelihood of psychological distress as compared with gay adults who never experienced such harassment (Skidmore, 2006; Plöderl, 2008).

Yet, for increasing numbers of today's adolescents, growing up gay can be relatively painless or, indeed, a very positive experience (Savin-Williams, 2005). What has made such a difference for today's gay youth is the existence of role models, the frequent discussion of gay issues on youth-oriented television shows and online sites, the presence of support organizations such as Gay-Straight Alliances in some schools, the efforts of some teachers to confront anti-gay attitudes and bullying, and the greater willingness of some parents to accept and love their gay children. Much depends on the kind of environment in which gay adolescents find themselves. But given the continuing trend toward tolerance and even positive acceptance of gay people, we may expect that the experience of adolescence will improve even further for the next generation of gay youth. In fact, public-health experts have already noted a marked reduction in the prevalence of mental health problems among young gay people, as compared with their gay elders—presumably as a consequence of the more benign environment in which they are coming of age (Meyer et al., 2008).

Personal Points of View

BOX 14.4 Hatred in the Hallways

Human Rights Watch is an international organization that investigates human rights abuses, usually far from our shores. In 2001, however, it published an investigative report on human rights abuses suffered by gay children in public schools right here in the United States (Human Rights Watch, 2001a). Here are two fairly typical stories from the Human Rights Watch report.

"Nikki L.," California

Everyone thinks I have a problem. They blame me, they blame my mom. They want me to be quiet. But I'm a lesbian. I feel like I've always known it. But I didn't get into trouble 'til seventh grade. I told a friend. Next thing I know, everyone seems to know. I got yelled at—on the playground, in gym, in the hall, in classes.

Only one teacher ever did anything. Miss Johnson, my English teacher—I love her—she made them stop it. I felt safe with her. I would go to her room for lunch and recess. She made me feel safe. She liked my poetry—encouraged me to write.

But everywhere else was bad. I tried to defend myself. I'm little but I'm tough. When kids hit me, I hit back. I got suspended twice. Three days each. A group of boys tried to beat me up, but I kicked them. I was just defending myself, but the vice-principal thinks I have a reputation. He calls me a "hard ass." I'm tough. I'm not gonna let anyone just push me around and hit me.

But I got really sick of going to school. I would tell my mom I was feeling sick so I didn't have to go to school. Finally she called the school. The principal said I needed to document three incidents before they would do anything. There were about 20 to 30 kids, mostly boys, who harassed me. My grades dropped.

Then one day I was walking home and some kids threw a brick at me. It hit me in the head. They were calling me a "fucking dyke." I sorta lost consciousness and my head was bleeding. That did it. I decided to never go back to school. I'm too scared.

Now I do independent study. My grades are back up. It's good. I don't have many friends. They are all a lot older than me. But that's okay—I like older people. They don't care if I am a dyke.

"Dylan N.," Nevada

Dylan N. told his family that he was gay when he was 12, but that fact came as no surprise to them. "From a young age, I was set aside as different," he explained when Human Rights Watch interviewed him in December, 1999 in Atlanta, Georgia.

During the first semester of his sophomore year, Dylan appeared on a local public-access television program as a participant in a discussion about the experiences of lesbian, gay, bisexual, and transgender students in high school. When word spread among his classmates that he was gay, they subjected him to constant harassment because of his sexual orientation. Some of his peers began to taunt him routinely by calling him a "fag," "butt pirate," "fairy," "homo," "queer," "sissy," "ass licker," "AIDS whore," and other derogatory terms. "It was all part of the normal daily routine," said Dylan.

The verbal harassment escalated almost immediately into physical violence. Other students began spitting on him and throwing food at him. One day in the parking lot outside his school, six students surrounded him and threw a lasso around his neck, saying, "Let's tie the faggot to the back of the truck." He escaped from his tormentors and ran inside the school. Finding one of the vice principals, he tried to tell her what had just happened to him. "I was still hysterical," he said. "I was trying to explain, but I was stumbling over my words. She laughed."

The school took no action to discipline Dylan's harassers. Instead, school officials told him not to discuss his sexual orientation with other students. "Looking back on it, I was so out," he said. "I tried to start GSAs [gay–straight alliances]. Like, I tried to do so much."

After the lasso incident, the harassment and violence intensified. "I was living in the disciplinary office because other harassment was going on. Everyone knew," he said. "It gave permission for a whole new level of physical stuff to occur." To escape the relentless harassment, Dylan asked for a transfer to another school in the district. When the semester ended, the district placed him in an alternative school for students with poor academic records or behavioral problems.

"The principal [at the alternative school] had a real issue with me," Dylan said. "The principal told me he wouldn't have me acting like a faggot at

Derek Henkle ("Dylan N.")

school. After a semester there, I realized that it was not a place where I could get an education."

Dylan was successful in securing a transfer to a traditional school the following year, when he was 15, but school officials again directed him not to discuss his sexual orientation with other students.

The gag rule imposed on him by the school did not protect him from his peers, who learned that he was gay from his former classmates at his first school. "It was the same thing all over again," he said. "They'd push me up against the lockers and call me a fag. They'd chase me around campus in their cars, screaming and yelling `fag' out the windows." Once, he told us, a teacher walked out of the room while some of his classmates were throwing things at him.

On another occasion, a group of students surrounded him outside the school, punching him, shouting that he was a "bitch," and jeering while security officers stood nearby. When the fight ended, he related, "I was completely bloody. I was bleeding from both lips, my nose, behind my ear."

Dylan tried to return to his second school, the alternative school, but school officials turned down his request to be placed there again. "What they did was they put me in the adult education program. Their justification was, I would be around people who were much more accepting. What they didn't tell me was I would have no chance of getting a high school diploma," he said.

"Dylan," whose real name is Derek Henkle, sued his school district for violation of his constitutional rights to free speech and equal protection (Lambda Legal Defense and Education Fund, 2000). In an August, 2000 settlement the district agreed to pay Henkle $451,000 and to institute a strict antiharassment policy (Reich, 2002). Henkle became a gay activist and journalist.

Coming Out Is a Lifelong Process

Although there are some analogies between gay people and ethnic minorities, there is one major difference: Ethnic minority children are usually brought up by parents of that same minority, whereas most pre-gay children are brought up by straight parents. Thus, whether or not gay people are "born gay" in a *biological* sense, they are usually "born straight" in a *social* sense: They are born into a predominantly straight culture, and everyone (including probably themselves) expects them to become heterosexual adults. Coming out of the closet, though it may involve a dramatic moment or two, is really a lifelong voyage away from the social expectation of heterosexuality and toward a fully integrated gay identity. That individual voyage repeats, to some extent, the social and political history of gay people as a whole.

The process of coming out has several elements. The first is coming out to oneself; that is, realizing and consciously accepting that one is gay. Although it is only the first step in the process of coming out, it is the hardest step for many gay people, especially those who grow up in a social setting that strongly disapproves of gays and lesbians or whose religion labels homosexual behavior as immoral. Many gay people live in denial for many years, perhaps even for their entire lives. Particularly if they are fairly conventional in their gender traits, they may stereotype gay people as "swishy" or "dykey" and fail to recognize themselves within those stereotypes. They may actually engage in homosexual behavior for many years without considering same-sex desire to be part of their identity. "I was convinced that I wasn't a homosexual," said former Republican Congressman Robert Bauman, who, though married, led a secret gay life for 20 years. He was exposed by the FBI in 1980, at the age of 43, and was voted out of office a few weeks later. "It took me almost 3 years of religious and psychiatric counseling for me to acknowledge that I was gay," he said later (Marcus, 1992).

The second element is coming out to others. Of course, that's usually a gradual process: A gay adolescent may come out first to another gay youth, a best friend, a sibling, or a counselor. Parents tend to find out late; gay adolescents fear parental rejection, sometimes with good reason. If parents have anti-gay views, they may react very negatively to their child's disclosure, and this can cost a gay teen a home, a college education, and much more. However, many parents whose initial reaction is negative go through a rapid change of heart after their child comes out, and may even take an activist role and join a pro-gay organization such as Parents, Families and Friends of Lesbians and Gays (PFLAG). Among minority and immigrant families especially, there is a strong instinct to close ranks around a family member who is perceived to be victimized or stigmatized by society.

The third element of coming out is joining a gay or lesbian community. For some gay men, that means moving to a big city that has a well-developed gay community. An example is West Hollywood, California, an independent city within Los Angeles whose population is about one-third gay men. Lesbians tend to be more scattered, but some smaller cities, such as Northampton, Massachusetts, have become centers of lesbian life. In locations such as West Hollywood and Northampton, gay people can find communities that offer sex partners, acceptance, and a wide range of gay or lesbian cultural institutions (**Box 14.5**).

Moving to a "gay mecca" has lost quite a bit of the significance it once had for young gay people, however. That's because many young lesbians and gay men can now find other gay people, be openly gay, and experience some degree of organized gay life in the communities in which they grow up. In addition, the Internet, with its gay "megasites" such as PlanetOut.com and its endless opportunities for gay networking, chat, and cybersex, has delivered the gay community to

The National Coming Out Day logo, created by Keith Haring. National Coming Out Day is an opportunity for closeted gays and lesbians to reveal their sexual orientation.

> **FAQ** I'm a woman who's had several boyfriends, but they all turned out to be gay. Is something wrong with me?
> Women who associate predominantly with gay men ("fag hags" in gay slang) may do so because they appreciate the gay male sensibility, because they feel safe in such relationships, or because they want intimacy without sex. There's nothing wrong with you, but if you want a lasting sexual relationship you need to look elsewhere.

Society, Values, and the Law

BOX 14.5 Gay Meccas: West Hollywood and Northampton

Los Angeles has been an important center of gay life and gay activism since the first gay rights organization, the Mattachine Society, was founded there in 1950. During the subsequent decades, gay culture focused on an unincorporated area east of Beverly Hills, where gay bars could not be raided by the Los Angeles Police Department. In 1984, this area incorporated as the City of West Hollywood; it currently has a majority of gay men on the City Council, and about one-third of its residents are gay men.

West Hollywood's gay culture centers on Santa Monica Boulevard, which is lined with gay bars, clubs, coffeehouses, a gay bookstore, gymnasiums, theaters, design showrooms, clothing stores, hair salons, and galleries, as well as the offices of a gay church (the Metropolitan Community Church, a national gay-focused organization). On weekend evenings, the western end of the boulevard, known as Boystown, is thronged by young gay men of every race and gender who pack into the bars and clubs there or cruise one another (check out one another sexually) in the street. The boulevard also hosts Los Angeles' annual Gay Pride parade as well as gay-oriented Halloween and Mardi Gras festivities.

The streets behind the boulevard are lined with apartment blocks housing thousands of gay men, many of whom work (or are seeking work) in the entertainment industry. Most of these apartment blocks are arranged around a central courtyard with a pool and are little gay worlds in their own right.

The eastern end of the Boulevard is seedier. The main signs of gay life here are male prostitutes—both hustlers and male-to-female transgenders. There is also a gay sex club on the boulevard just beyond the city limits, in which men can engage in group sex in a nearly pitch-dark labyrinth.

The collision of Hollywood, homosexuality, and a warm climate has fostered an obsession with looks, physique, and sexual performance in West Hollywood that is rivaled in the United States only by Miami's South Beach. Alcohol, drug use, and sexually transmitted diseases are significant problems in West Hollywood, and it

has one of the highest rates of HIV infection in the nation.

Lesbians are fairly well represented in West Hollywood, too, but their real strength is in small woman-oriented cities such as Northampton, Massachusetts. Northampton is home to a leading women's college, Smith College. The area can boast a long history of woman-loving women, most notably the poet Emily Dickinson (1830–1886), who lived in nearby Amherst.

Northampton's current mayor, Clare Higgins, is lesbian, but the city is not lesbian-dominated, and there is no lesbian street scene analogous to West Hollywood on a Saturday night. Rather, lesbians blend in seamlessly with heterosexual and bisexual women, collaborating with them in business and in academic work. There are an annual Gay Pride march and festival at which lesbians predominate (see fig-

ure), a lesbian softball league, and other lesbian-oriented sports and cultural events, as well as lesbian-owned bookstores, cafes, and restaurants. To a casual visitor, however, it might not be obvious who the lesbians are. In fact, there are said to be at least three categories of homosexual women in Northampton: "lesbians," who tend to be politically active lesbian feminists; "gay women," who are often professional women who dress and act fairly conservatively; and "dykes," who revel in the masculine stereotype that the word "dyke" suggests and are likely to be political radicals.

Smith College is, of course, lesbian-friendly. It offers several lesbian-oriented courses and has an active lesbian, bisexual, and transgender alliance. The majority of the students are straight, however, and Smith has to combat its image as a "lesbian school" in order not to scare away nonlesbian applicants (Greene, 2004).

gay youth in their own homes. Meanwhile, cities such as West Hollywood that are known for their nightlife are being invaded by gay-friendly straight people (Abcarian, 2006). Gay meccas now face something of an identity crisis (Brown, 2007).

One problem with moving to a gay mecca is that it may also represent a flight from other aspects of a gay person's cultural identity. In becoming openly gay and moving to gay meccas, many young gay people isolate themselves from their ethnic roots, their religion, and their extended families. Here is how one San Francisco Bay Area lesbian leader, Abby Abinanti, expressed the matter:

> When I went to Eureka, to my Yurok tribe, I felt as though I was somewhat accepted but they were not always ready for me as a queer, so I had to keep that part hidden a little. It felt easier for me to live in San Francisco than at home. But when I was in San Francisco, in a lesbian group, I felt they couldn't understand the Indian part of me. They're different from what I'm used to: different values, different approaches, a different sense of humor. They didn't know about those families back home I grew up with, the disputes, the importance of questions like 'How's the fishing?' There was no place where all of me was validated (Faderman, 1991).

Thus, an important fourth element of coming out for gay people is integrating the gay side of their identity with other aspects of who they are. This may involve returning to their roots or participating in organizations that straddle the boundary that they have crossed—e.g., gay Catholic groups or gay Asian groups or gay Deaf groups. They can also become active politically in their own communities to raise awareness of the fact that gay people are among them. In these ways, they break down the psychological compartments within their own lives. Close friendships between gay and straight young people are increasingly noticeable and offer an important avenue toward the full integration of gay people into contemporary society (Tillman-Healy, 2001).

Lesbians and Gay Men Are Well Represented in Certain Occupations

Lesbians and gay men are found in all walks of life. Yet, as we mentioned above, gay people are more likely to violate gender norms in their occupational choices than are heterosexual men and women (Lippa, 2008). Concerning the specific occupations that may attract lesbians and gay men, there is relatively little hard information, but a lot of speculation. Lesbians do seem to be overrepresented, and particularly successful, in professional sports such as golf and tennis, but, of course, only a tiny fraction of all lesbians are in this field.

Gay men seem to be overrepresented and especially successful in the creative arts, and this is true across many cultures (Whitam & Dizon, 1979). In fact, a survey of one group of male creative artists—professional dancers—concluded that one-half or more of the men in this field are gay (Bailey & Oberschneider, 1997). Another set of occupations in which gay men seem to be disproportionately represented are those involving personal service or caring; many are nurses, teachers, flight attendants, or waiters. Occupations that combine artistic creativity and personal service, such as hairstyling, floristry, and interior design, are the most stereotypical of all gay male occupations—these are the occupations in which practitioners are gay until proven otherwise.

One point of mentioning these apparent occupational preferences is to highlight the fact that gay people are not simply people who get together to have sex, nor are they simply a community united in political resistance to oppression. They also, to a degree, share common interests and a common sensibility (the "camp" humor of gay men, for example). If and when gay people are fully accepted by mainstream society, it is not likely that they will

Gay ballet dancer Rudolf Nureyev (1938–1993) and lesbian tennis star Martina Navratilova illustrate stereotypical occupations for gay men and lesbians, respectively. These occupations probably do have far more than their share of gay or lesbian practitioners, but most gay people are not in these or other stereotypically gay fields of work.

be completely assimilated and disappear from view as a distinct group, as has happened to left-handers, for example. More probably, homosexuality will retain a special salience, and gay people will be valued for their unique gifts.

Gay People Who Belong to Minorities Have Special Concerns

As far as is known, roughly the same proportions of different racial or ethnic groups in the United States (whites, African Americans, Hispanics, Asian-Pacific Islanders, and Native Americans) are gay or lesbian. Nevertheless, the experience of being gay can be different for members of minorities. For one thing, there were until recently few or no role models for gay people within their own minority communities. Certainly, there have long been prominent minority leaders who have been homosexual—among African Americans, for example, there was Pauli Murray (1910–1985), a leading civil rights lawyer and cofounder of the National Organization for Women, and Bayard Rustin (1912–1987), a close aide to Martin Luther King Jr.—but those individuals' sexuality was not a matter of public knowledge.

The situation is now changing; a number of minority public figures are openly gay. Among Hispanics, for example, we could mention skater/AIDS activist Rudy Galindo, author/playwright Cherríe Moraga, and actor Wilson Cruz. There are also hundreds of organizations of gay people who belong to minorities, some of them catering to very specific groups such as Vietnamese-Americans in Southern California (see Web Resources at the end of this chapter).

Nevertheless, many minority gay people have to deal with cultural traditions that make heterosexual marriage into a near-sacred obligation (for oldest sons in many Asian-American cultures, for example) or that place taboos on the discussion of sexual topics in general, especially for women. Thus, acknowledging their own gay identity might, for some minority gay people, come at a cost of distancing themselves from their communities or their cultural roots, as we indicated earlier in the quotation by Abby Abinanti, a lesbian Native American.

Immigrant families in particular may see their children's homosexuality as a sign that they are losing them to an alien culture, but this reaction can be overcome. Here's how one first-generation Chinese-American woman, who belonged to a support group for Asian-American lesbians and bisexual women, put it:

> "[My parents] always had this perception of 'Who are these people you always hang out with?'—shadowy people that they didn't know, a bad influence, or whatever. But as soon as they met other Asian [lesbian] women, who spoke the same language as we do at home, it made a really big difference, and now they're meeting other parents, and it's just made a world of difference, because before they felt very isolated" (LeVay & Nonas, 1995).

Racism exists within the gay community, as is made clear by the informal writings of gay people who belong to minorities (Chaudhary, 2000; ColorQ World, 2000; Tat, 2005). For example, plenty of white gay men may seek out nonwhites for casual sex but reject them for durable relationships. These attitudes, when combined with other stressors, such as homophobia and poverty, that gay minority people may experience significantly contribute to mental-health difficulties among these minorities as well as to unsafe sex practices (Derby et al., 2001; Wilson, 2004).

Interracial relationships among gays and lesbians are actually quite common, however, and are fostered by specific organizations such as the National Association of Black and White Men Together (see Web Resources). Still, they are beset by stereotypes. White gay men who date Asians, for example, may be caricatured as "rice queens" who seek Asians because of their smooth bodies or their perceived exoticism, submissiveness, or femininity rather than for their individual qualities, while Asian gay men who date whites may be construed as self-loathing or as seeking a white partner for reasons of mere economics or status (Gay Asian Pacific Support Network, 2001). Also, interracial gay relationships are even less likely to have the support of the partners' birth families than are same-race gay relationships.

How is it that so many interracial gay relationships thrive in the face of these difficulties? We may speculate that the difference in race supplies some of the vital "otherness" that, in heterosexual relationships, is automatically provided by the difference in gender. An analogous mechanism causes most deaf gay people to partner with hearing people (LeVay & Nonas, 1995). Deaf gay communities within a given city are so close-knit as to make everyone seem like members of the same family and thus inappropriate as sex partners.

Members of sexual minorities who are nonwhite may develop their own cultural institutions. A striking historical example is that of the "vogueing balls"—elaborate contests in dance, drag and "realness" that sprang up among gay and transgendered men in New York's Hispanic and black communities in the 1980s. The lifestyle surrounding these balls constituted a parallel universe that was largely unknown to most Americans until it was made the topic of a notable documentary film, *Paris is Burning* (1991).

Gay Sex Has Its Own Style

With the exception of coitus, most sexual behaviors that male–female couples engage in are also practiced by same-sex couples. It's worth pointing out some differences, however. Most obviously, no one has gay sex in order to procreate, so physical pleasure and emotional intimacy are the main reasons for engaging in sex.

Among the sexual behaviors practiced by female couples are kissing, fondling, oral or manual breast stimulation, body-to-body rubbing involving the vulva (tribadism), cunnilingus, rimming (anilingus), manual stimulation of the clitoris, penetration of the vagina or anus with a finger or sex toy, and sex play involving elements of bondage/dominance/sadomasochism (BDSM play; see Chapter 15). Among behaviors practiced by male couples are kissing, fondling, nipple stimulation, body-to-body rubbing involving the penis, fellatio, anal penetration with a finger or the penis, intercrural (between-the-thighs) intercourse, and BDSM play. Many of these behaviors can be either unidirectional or reciprocal (for example, reciprocal fellatio, or "69").

Same-sex couples take their time over sex (Masters & Johnson, 1979). Lesbians may spend a great deal of time on breast and nipple stimulation, for example, before focusing on the genitals and may extend the entire sexual interaction for well over an hour. Gay men also enjoy nipple stimulation. (In BDSM play, nipple clamps may be used to provide more intense and long-lasting stimulation.) Gay men often bring each other close to orgasm and then back off, thus prolonging sexual pleasure and causing a more intense orgasm when it finally arrives.

Although nearly all lesbians and many gay men confine their sexual behavior to paired encounters in the privacy of their own bedrooms, some gay men have sex in other places, including outdoor locations such as public toilets (**Box 14.6**), parks, and freeway rest areas and indoor semi-public locations such as sex clubs and "back rooms" attached to gay bars. Some of this sexual activity occurs in groups rather than pairs.

One reason gay men have sex in places such as parks and toilets is simply the lack of other options. Gay men who live with their parents, who are heterosexually married, or who live some distance from where they meet their sex partners may not be able to bring their sex partners home. Cohabiting gay men who are

Research Highlights

BOX 14.6 The Tearoom Trade

On June 11, 2007, Larry Craig, the senior U.S. senator for the state of Idaho, was arrested in a men's bathroom at the Minneapolis-St. Paul International Airport and charged with lewd conduct. According to a report by a plain-clothes police officer, Craig solicited the officer for sex by making foot-to-foot contact and hand signals while the two men were sitting in adjacent stalls of the bathroom. Craig pleaded guilty to a lesser charge of disorderly conduct and was given a suspended 10-day jail sentence. After the matter became public knowledge Craig, who is married to a woman, denied that he had engaged in any improper conduct or that he is gay (Murphy & Stout, 2007). However, eight gay men told the *Idaho Statesman* that they had had sex with Craig or had been "hit on" by him at various times during his political career (Associated Press, 2007d). Craig attempted, unsuccessfully, to withdraw his

guilty plea. After initially saying that he would resign from the U.S. Senate, he later decided to stay in office but not to seek reelection.

Whatever Craig's sexual orientation, this incident drew public attention to the topic of gay men engaging in sex in public restrooms—something that has been going on for as long as public restrooms have existed. In his 1970 book *Tearoom Trade*, ethnographer Laud Humphreys documented—in unblushing detail—the goings-on in a restroom located in a city park somewhere in the Midwest during the mid-1960s. (Restrooms used for gay sex were commonly called "tearooms.")

Humphreys was able to study this illegal behavior because he pretended to be one of the participants. He posed as a person who was aroused by watching others engage in sex—a voyeur (see Chapter 15). He also served as a

lookout who warned the participants of the approach of strangers or police officers.

Humphreys found that the commonest kind of sex practiced in the tearoom was fellatio. He collected all kinds of numerical data about the length of time spent in the toilet, the men's movements and signals, and even such minor details as what proportion of fellators swallowed the ejaculate (four-fifths).

Humphreys could not obtain personal information about the participants in the restroom because the sex was anonymous. But he traced over 100 participants by their car license plates, and he later called at their homes in disguise, posing as a social health researcher. By this subterfuge he obtained detailed information about them. He found that about half of the men were married and living with their wives. Although married, many of these men had "role-segregated" marriages that involved relatively little day-to-day interaction between the spouses.

Humphreys' book won the annual prize of the Society for the Study of Social Problems, but it evoked both positive and negative reactions. The positive reviews noted Humphreys' skill and courage in exploring a little-known corner of society's sexual underworld. Critics focused on the fact that Humphreys' subjects did not participate voluntarily, or even wittingly, in the study—a violation of the norms of sociological research.

Since the 1970s, the explosion of gay culture has made "tearooms" less necessary than in the past, as Humphreys predicted. But that hasn't dimmed some gay men's interest in them. Apparently, many present-day gay men seek out partners in public toilets more for thrill-seeking purposes than from necessity. This was presumably the case with British pop icon George Michael, who was arrested for soliciting sex from an undercover police officer in a public restroom in Beverly Hills, California, in 1998 (see photo). Michael was convicted of lewd conduct and fined $810, but he more than recouped his losses with his music video *Outside*, which reenacted the event, with Michael in the role of the policeman.

seeking extra-pair sex may be in the same situation. But another reason is probably the thrill-seeking aspect of sex in public places—the sense of hunting for a partner and being hunted, combined with the possibility of public disclosure. Yet another reason is the opportunity to have sex with a number of different partners in a short time.

These motivations are probably relevant to the culture of sex in **bathhouses**. Gay bathhouses are facilities in which large numbers of men engage in sex in a semi-public environment. A bathhouse may have a pool, but the real action is in a warren of dimly lit corridors, cubicles, and steam rooms, in which men engage

bathhouse A facility, usually in the form of a private club, used for casual sex between men.

in brief sexual encounters, most of which do not culminate in orgasm. There are also community rooms (e.g., TV rooms, weight rooms) in which there may be conversation and social life. Because bathhouses usually operate as private membership facilities, they are often exempt from police action. Early in the AIDS epidemic, bathhouses were closed down in many cities, though this action stirred conflicts within the gay community between sexual libertarians and AIDS activists (Shilts, 1987). Many still operate or have reopened, however, usually under city regulations that attempt to discourage sex or enforce safe sex practices.

Although gay male culture includes and is fairly accepting of outdoor sex, bathhouses, and the like, it's worth reemphasizing that large numbers of gay men live in very ordinary monogamous relationships that, aside from their same-sex aspect, are indistinguishable from the relationships of most heterosexual Americans. These different lifestyles reflect something of a political dichotomy within the gay male community. More conservative gay men are anxious to emphasize the normality and conventionality of gay culture, hoping that this will speed the acceptance of gay people by mainstream society (Bawer, 1993; Sullivan, 1995). The legalization of same-sex marriage may be viewed as a step in that direction. More radical gay men see their role as breaking down society's traditional taboos concerning sex and restoring its status as a primitive, creative, and even spiritual life force (Thompson, 1995; Warner, 2000). Something of the same dichotomy exists among lesbians, too, but the sexual revolutionaries are in a smaller minority (Atkins, 1999).

There are other subtypes among gay people that form the basis of sexual subcultures. Among gay men there exists an extensive BDSM culture, which overlaps with the "leather community." BDSM practitioners are not necessarily gay, of course, but they are a far more visible and accepted subculture within the gay community than in the heterosexual world (**Figure 14.10A**). Leather bars are common in gay communities. Gay leather art is widespread. Some lesbians are also into leather or BDSM practices (Samois, 1987). Most gay people think of leather and other BDSM practices as a normal but minority sexual interest.

Another gay subculture is that of **bears** (Wright, 1996). A stereotypical "bear" is a big, bearded man with plenty of body hair and a noticeable beer gut (**Figure**

Gay men's personal ads often include references to "top" and "bottom," but in reality many gay men are versatile in their sexual behavior.

bear In gay slang, a burly gay man with plenty of body hair; more generally, a member of a gay male subculture that rejects many of the prevailing standards of gay male attractiveness and behavior.

(A)

(B)

Figure 14.10 There are sexual subcultures among homosexual men. Shown here are the covers of two magazines serving different sexual interests. *Bound and Gagged* ceased publication in 2005.

Changing One's Sexual Orientation Is Difficult or Impossible

gay bashing Hate crimes against gay people. Sometimes includes verbal abuse as well as physical violence.

implicit association test A psychological test that is intended to reveal unconscious or unstated preferences.

As we mentioned earlier, during the 1950s and 1960s many gay men (and a few lesbians) tried to become straight by psychoanalysis or other treatments. The market for this kind of treatment has dwindled in recent years, but there is still enough demand to keep a small number of therapists in business (NARTH, 2008). In addition, various ministries offer prayer-based conversion (Love in Action, 2008), and organizations of "Ex-Gays" attest to the efficacy of conversion (Exodus International, 2008).

The general opinion in the psychological community is that conversion treatments are ineffective and potentially harmful (Haldeman, 1994). It therefore came as a surprise to many when, in 2001, Columbia University psychiatrist Robert Spitzer reported the results of a survey of 200 one-time gays and lesbians who claimed to have changed their sexual orientation through conversion therapies or ministries. On the basis of detailed telephone interviews, Spitzer concluded that 66% of the men and 44% of the women had indeed achieved "good heterosexual functioning" (Spitzer, 2003).

It shouldn't really be surprising that highly motivated gays and lesbians can enter into heterosexual relationships and function sexually in those relationships because we know that many gays and lesbians were heterosexually married and had children before they "came out." A more cogent question would be: Does conversion therapy cause a person to develop a pattern of sexual attraction and arousal that is fundamentally different from what they experienced prior to treatment?

Answering this question would require a clinical study of people before and after treatment—for example, by physiological assessment of their genital responses to erotic videos. Such a study hasn't yet been done. In the meantime, it seems fair to say that changing sexual orientation through therapy or ministry is at best extremely difficult. At worst, it is a traumatic, expensive, and futile exercise that can only delay a gay person's progress toward self-acceptance.

Homophobia Has Multiple Roots

Anti-gay activist Fred Phelps demonstrates outside the courthouse during the trial of two men accused in the 1998 murder of gay University of Wyoming student Matthew Shepard.

Antagonistic feelings and behaviors directed toward gay people are very common. They range all the way from the simple belief that all homosexual behavior is morally wrong—an attitude held by about half of all Americans—to the killing of lesbians and gay men by a few hate-filled **gay-bashers**. The use of **implicit association tests** reveals that most people have an automatic preference for straight people over gay people (**Figure 14.11**). In an experimental study, researchers led heterosexual men to believe that a coworker was gay; this caused them to psychologically distance themselves from the coworker, regardless of whether they were overtly prejudiced against gay people or not (Talley & Bettencourt, 2008).

The word homophobia literally means the *fear* of homosexuality, but it has come to be used for the entire spectrum of anti-gay attitudes and behaviors, and that is how we use it here. A variety of different factors probably contribute to homophobia, so it may be difficult to unravel the causes of a particular person's anti-gay attitude or to figure out what sparked a particular hate crime.

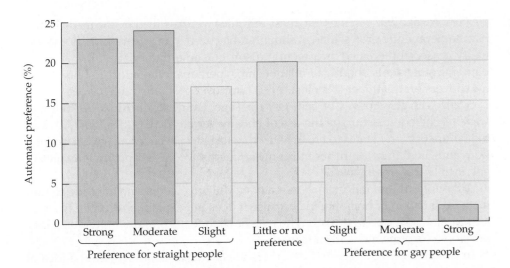

Figure 14.11 Most men and women have an automatic preference for straight people. The bar graph shows data from a Web-based implicit association test taken by about 150,000 subjects. The test uses reaction times to assess the strength of unconscious mental linkages between values (good/bad) and a variable of interest (gay/straight in this case). (Data from Nosek et al., 2004.)

Cultural Indoctrination Transmits Homophobia across Generations

Some children and adults learn to dislike homosexuality and gay people by receiving anti-gay messages from parents, teachers, religious authorities, political figures, and so on. The fact that the children of gay parents are more tolerant of homosexuality than are other children (see above) is a simple illustration of the importance of that learning process. The messages can be quite vocal and explicit: The Roman Catholic church, for example, labels homosexuality a moral disorder, calls gay sex sinful, and has actively opposed numerous gay rights initiatives in the United States and worldwide. In 2003, the Vatican asserted that it is "gravely immoral" for a Catholic legislator to vote for the legalization of gay marriage (Congregation for the Doctrine of the Faith, 2003). Regular participation in organized worship is the strongest demographic predictor that a person disapproves of gay sex (**Figure 14.12**). (Nevertheless, plenty of religious denominations or individual congregations are gay-affirmative.)

Many heterosexual people hold negative beliefs about same-sex relationships—that they are less loving and less stable than opposite-sex relationships, for exam-

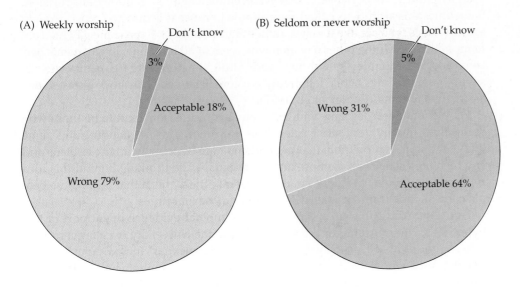

Figure 14.12 Organized religion and anti-gay attitudes These charts show the percentages of Americans who believe that gay sex is morally acceptable or morally wrong, for (A) those who worship weekly and (B) those who seldom or never worship (Gallup, 2006b).

ple (Testa et al., 1987). In the past, these attitudes were instilled by the medical and psychotherapeutic professions. Although it has been many years since homosexuality ceased to be listed as a mental disorder, some therapists still make disparaging statements about gay relationships, perhaps in an effort to find clients for conversion treatment (Nicolosi, 1991; Nicolosi & Nicolosi, 2002).

Silence can also convey an anti-gay message. Examples include the failure of some teachers to discourage the use of abusive terms such as "fag" and "dyke," the failure of many states to enact hate crime legislation covering sexual orientation, and the failure (until recently) of the media to present positive images of gay men and women.

Although cultural indoctrination is a powerful force, it does not provide an ultimate explanation of homophobia because it does not explain how anti-gay social attitudes arose in the first place. Thus we have to focus on how individuals may develop or express these attitudes.

In Chapter 13 we suggested that the widespread discomfort with the idea of old people having sex arises from a failure of empathy. The same process may well occur with gay sex (LeVay, 1996). A heterosexual man, when he thinks about homosexuality, imagines himself engaging in sex with another man. Because he is heterosexual, this idea is a turn-off, and he transfers this aversion to men who actually engage in such behavior. What he fails to do is put himself in the *mind* of a man who is sexually attracted to men.

This model readily explains why homophobic attitudes among men are directed against gay men much more than against lesbians. Heterosexual men are not turned off by imagining themselves doing what lesbians do, which is to say having sex with a woman. In fact, most heterosexual men are aroused by the idea of two women engaging in sex. Laws have traditionally ignored sex between women rather than punishing it, and hate crimes against lesbians are far less common than those against gay men (Federal Bureau of Investigation, 2003).

Homosexuality Is Seen As Transgressive

Another motivation for anti-gay prejudice is the sense that gay people break rules—not just society's rules, but what seems to some heterosexual people to be the natural order of things. Gay people break these rules by engaging in gay sex, but, in addition, they may do so to the extent that they are recognizably gender-nonconformist. In fact, the earliest experience of anti-gay prejudice that many pre-gay children experience is really a prejudice against gender transgression. Sometimes this attitude is called **femiphobia** because it is directed most strongly against males who act like females, rather than vice versa. Even some gay men are femiphobic, devaluing other gay men who seem at all feminine. In gay men's personal ads, for example, "masculine" and "straight-acting" are frequently cited as sought-after qualities, while femininity is often dismissed with stock phrases such as "no fats or fems" (Bailey et al., 1997).

People who view lesbians and gay men as transgressors tend to be those who themselves live by very strict rules (Young-Bruehl, 1996). Extending this same line of thought, is it possible that people who hate or actually attack lesbians and gay men are themselves homosexual or bisexual? The thinking behind this idea is that a homophobic attitude is part of a defense mechanism that helps these people control, hide from, or mask their own homosexual urges.

One study did come up with some experimental evidence in support of this hypothesis. Henry Adams and his colleagues at the University of Georgia recruited two groups of self-described "exclusively heterosexual" men: One group consisted of men who scored very high on an index of homophobic attitudes, while the other group scored low (Adams et al., 1996). (The questionnaire used in the

femiphobia Prejudice against femininity in males.

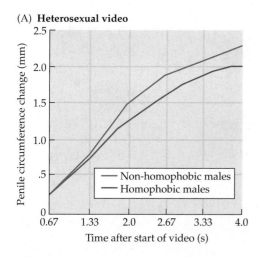

(A) Heterosexual video

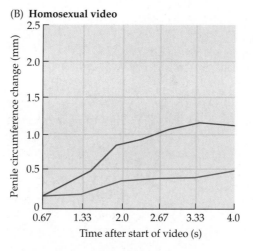

(B) Homosexual video

Figure 14.13 Do homophobic men have homosexual urges? These graphs show the penile responses of homophobic and nonhomophobic men, all of whom identified themselves as heterosexual, to videotapes containing heterosexual or homosexual images. Both groups responded to the heterosexual videos, but only the homophobic men responded to the homosexual videos. (After Adams et al., 1996.)

study is available online—see Web Resources). The researchers then showed the men videotapes of male–female, female–female, and male–male sex. During the viewing, the men's sexual arousal was monitored by penile plethysmography (measurement of penile erection). When asked, all the men said that they were aroused only by the heterosexual and "lesbian" tapes. According to the plethysmographic data, however, the homophobic men (but not the nonhomophobic men) were also aroused by the "gay male" tapes, though not to the same extent as by the heterosexual tapes (**Figure 14.13**). The researchers concluded that strongly homophobic attitudes are associated with homosexual feelings that the person denies or is unaware of. More research is needed to reach any definitive conclusion on this matter, however.

From time to time, politicians, preachers, and others who promote an anti-gay agenda are themselves outed as homosexual. A striking example occurred recently in Spokane, Washington. Republican mayor James West had been a state senator for many years, during which time he had proposed or supported numerous anti-gay initiatives, including a bill to bar gays and lesbians from teaching or other positions at public schools. In 2005, a local newspaper published allegations that West was meeting young men on a gay Internet site for sex and had offered some of these men positions at City Hall (Morlin, 2005). West admitted he was gay and lost his job in a recall election. Another much-publicized example was that of evangelical preacher Ted Haggard, founder of the New Life Church in Colorado Springs. Haggard, who is married to a woman and has five children, condemned homosexuality on scriptural grounds and opposed gay marriage. In 2006 a male prostitute alleged that Haggard had paid him for sex on many occasions. Haggard resigned his ministry. "There is a part of my life that is so repulsive and dark that I've been warring against it all of my adult life," he wrote in his resignation letter (Haggard, 2006).

Overcoming Homophobia Is a Grassroots Enterprise

Considerable research has been done on methods to overcome anti-gay attitudes. Because these attitudes have such diverse roots, it is unlikely that any one strategy will be successful by itself.

To some extent, the reduction of homophobia can be engineered through legislation and other public policy measures—by the passage of nondiscrimination and hate crime statutes, for example. Thirty-two states and the District of Columbia now have hate crime statutes that include sexual orientation, and 12 of these also include gender identity as a protected category (**Figure 14.14**). Also, the gay-

Figure 14.14 Hate crime laws This map shows the states (pink) that have hate crime laws covering sexual orientation and those (red) whose laws cover both sexual orientation and gender identity (National Gay and Lesbian Task Force, 2008a).

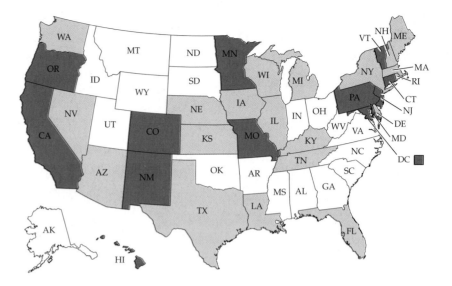

positive attitudes of leaders such as former President Bill Clinton doubtless have had a significant effect on public attitudes generally.

Nevertheless, social science research suggests that people's attitudes toward gays and lesbians, as in other matters, are most readily influenced by interactions with relatives, friends, coworkers, and other people with whom they have ongoing associations (Sears & Williams, 1997). Recent history supports that view; for example, as mentioned earlier in the chapter, there has been a large increase over the last two decades in the number of Americans who know a gay person and a dramatic easing of anti-gay attitudes over the same period. This, in turn, suggests that further progress will be achieved most readily by a continuation and extension of these interactions, particularly in those parts of America and in those walks of life in which they have been sparse up to now.

Bisexuals Are Caught between Two Worlds

Bisexual ("bi") men and women are people who experience a significant degree of sexual attraction to both sexes. That might seem like an unalloyed benefit—doesn't it just increase the possibilities for pleasure, intimacy, and sexual variety? That may in fact be the case, but in addition bisexual people face some unique problems and challenges.

The Prevalence of Bisexuality Depends on Definitions

Population-based surveys suggest that bisexuality—when defined as *any* degree of sexual attraction to both men and women—is more prevalent than exclusive homosexuality in both sexes. The majority of bisexuals defined in this manner, however, are much more attracted to the other sex than to the same sex (the "mostly opposite sex" column in the bar graphs of Figure 14.1 describes such a bisexual orientation). If bisexuality is defined as a roughly *equal* attraction to the two sexes, however, it is far less common, especially in men.

Indeed, some sexologists have contested the notion that true bisexuality exists in men at all—at least at the level of genital arousal. Kurt Freund, for example, studied sexual orientation by measuring men's penile tumescence while they viewed erotic photographs of men and women; he claimed never to have encountered a man who was aroused both by adult men and adult women (Freund, 1974). In a more recent study, researchers at Northwestern University specifically advertised for men who identified as "bisexual," but when they showed these men erotic images of men and women, they all showed much greater genital arousal to one sex (usually men) than the other (Rieger et al., 2005).

It is also the case that "bisexual" is commonly used as a self-identifier by young men who are on their way to coming out of the closet; as many as 40% of self-identified gay men say that they described themselves as "bisexual" at some point during early adulthood, according to one magazine survey conducted in the 1990s (Lever, 1994). Thus many self-identified "bisexual" young men can be expected to come out as gay within a few years (Stokes et al., 1997), and it is possible that many of the men in the genital arousal studies just described fall into that category. Alternatively, they may be men whose subjective feelings of arousal, or their romantic attractions, are not congruent with their patterns of genital arousal.

Still, there is little reason to doubt the validity of these men's self-identification, whatever their patterns of genital arousal may be. Some bisexuals have protested what they consider the attempted "erasure" of bisexuality in the Northwestern study and in media reports of it (Hutchins, 2007).

No one doubts the reality of bisexuality in women. In fact, at the level of genital arousal, most or all women seem to be bisexual: They show genital arousal to erotic videos of either men or women, regardless of their stated attraction to one sex or the other or their self-identification as heterosexual, lesbian, or bisexual (Chivers et al., 2004). These findings, which are consistent with a body of other evidence, do not disprove the existence of exclusive heterosexuality and exclusive homosexuality in women. Rather, they show that, in women, there is no straightforward connection between patterns of physiological arousal and those of verbally stated sexual attraction. Most men can figure out their sexual orientation by monitoring their genitals; few women can do so.

Psychologist Lisa Diamond followed about 80 young women over a period of 10 years (Diamond, 2008a, b). At the onset of her study, all the women described themselves as "lesbian," "bisexual," or "unlabeled." Over the course of the study many of the women changed their self-descriptions, but there was no overall trend in one direction or another. Rather, the women adopted identities that matched their current relationship patterns. Diamond's work suggested not only that women's sexual orientation is more fluid than men's, but also that there is little distinction between different kinds of nonheterosexual women, such as "lesbian" and "bisexual," when women's lives are viewed over a longer term.

Another complicating issue is that many self-identified bisexuals are not attracted to men and to women in the same way. For example, a bisexual man may be more emotionally attracted to women but more physically drawn to men (Matteson, 1991). Alternatively, the strength of a person's attraction to one or the other sex might change over the life span. Unidimensional measures of sexual orientation do little justice to these complexities.

Bisexuals Face Prejudice

For bisexuals, the crucial part of the coming out process is letting go of the notion that they must be either gay or straight (Fox, 1991; Weinberg et al., 1995). Even after they have accomplished this realization themselves, they must constantly deal with other people who have not (**Box 14.7**). In fact, negative attitudes toward bisexual people (**biphobia**) are more widespread than are anti-gay attitudes (Herek, 2002) (**Figure 14.15**).

Part of the reason for this prejudice is a widespread belief that people who claim to be bisexual are deceiving themselves or lying—that they are actually either heterosexual or homosexual (Dworkin, 2001). Another potentially harmful stereotype about bisexual people is that they need to express their sexual attrac-

biphobia Prejudice against bisexuals.

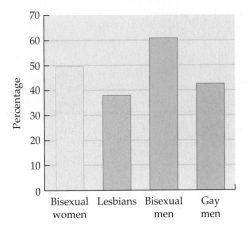

Figure 14.15 Bisexuals are more disliked than homosexuals. The graph shows the percentage of heterosexual college students who rated bisexual women, lesbians, bisexual men, gay men, and as either "very" or "somewhat" unacceptable. (Data from Eliason, 1997.)

Personal Points of View

BOX 14.7 Scenes from Bisexual Life

The following is excerpted from an autobio-graphical essay by bisexual activist and writer Elizabeth Reba Weise (Weise, 1991):

I came of age in that odd non-time, the 1970s, the decade that felt like a long afternoon nap after the rush and activity of the sixties. So let me begin by explaining how I *didn't* become a bisexual. It wasn't because I have an overactive libido, and it wasn't because it was a hip thing to do in the glitter rock seventies. It did have to do with everything else in the universe, or per-haps nothing.

When I was thirteen I made a list of all the things I wanted to do in my life. Two of the top items were someday having a girl-friend and someday having a boyfriend. I wrote romantic stories about meeting amorous young women over the recorder music files at the library and then falling in love on rainy walks after folk dances. And even in those stories, when the other woman would declare herself to be a les-bian, I'd say, 'And I'm bisexual.' . . .

So I went home to Seattle, bound and determined to finally *be a lesbian*. . . . And before my big chance came again, I fell in love—with a man. We met at a party where the lines of sexual preference were tenuous at best....In that atmosphere your interest and not your persuasion mattered. I remember thinking, 'But he was supposed to be a woman.' However, he *was* clear-thinking and deep-minded and appreciated good science fiction. . . .

That went on for many years. At times we lived together, at times we lived apart.

During one of those times I went to the lesbian support group at the university the night they talked about bisexuality, and kept going back. One evening a born-again baby dyke, all het up [excited] about her newly won status as Oppressed Person, shouted at me, 'You oppress us by sleeping with men! You steal our woman energy!' I stopped going to the support group....

Then, finally, I found a girlfriend.... It was a wonderful thing to be young, in love, and a dyke. It was vindication. Walking down the street hand-in-hand just daring anyone to say anything, I suddenly felt as if every-thing in my life had fallen into place. I was attracted to a woman. I was in love with a woman. I was a lesbian.

But reality broke through soon enough. There was the fact that I wasn't a 'real' dyke, defined by [lesbian comedian] Kate Clinton as 'penis-pure and proud.' Again, after the honeymoon of acceptance, everyone was waiting for me to renounce my feelings for men. I wasn't part of the family.

My girlfriend and I broke up. I got back together with my boyfriend. I began an exis-tence as a closeted bisexual in the lesbian community. My hair got shorter and shorter. One day I realized that I felt uncomfortable walking down the street hand-in-hand with my lover for fear someone would see us and my cover would be blown.

I moved out again. A friend and I rented a huge old blue farmhouse in the middle of Seattle and by default started a bisexual women's household.... We were a femi-

Elizabeth Reba Weise

nist bisexual nexus. We held support groups, potlucks, slumber parties, dance parties, and political screaming argu-ments. It was everything I'd always want-ed from the lesbian community, without the fear of being thrown out. Being a part of the Seattle Area Bisexual Women's Network gave me the support to stop worrying about what other people thought about my sexuality and get on with life. We helped each other relearn that it's what you do and not who you sleep with that matters.

tion to both men and women and therefore are incapable of being in a durable monogamous relationship (Spalding & Peplau, 1997). "Bisexual by definition means promiscuous," said former U.S. Senator Don Nickles, in opposing legal protection for bisexuals (ReligiousTolerance.org, 2008). Bisexuality refers to a per-son's sexual feelings and not their sexual behavior, however. Some individual bisexuals may be promiscuous—plenty of straight and gay people are too—but there are also bisexuals who are in lasting monogamous relationships with a part-ner of either the same or the other sex (Yoshizaki, 1991).

Other negative views that bisexuals may have to contend with are that they are "oversexed" or that they are responsible for the spread of AIDS. In general, these false beliefs may reflect people's unfamiliarity with bisexual men and women.

Two-thirds of college students say that they have no bisexual friends or acquaintances, and those two-thirds have more negative attitudes toward bisexuals than do other students (Eliason, 1997).

These negative views about bisexual people are changing, especially among the young and well educated. College students in particular are more open to sexual experimentation and, perhaps for that reason, are leading a trend toward greater acceptance of bisexuality (see Box 10.3).

Bisexuals have lagged behind gays and lesbians in developing a community identity (Highleyman, 2000). A Bisexual Center was founded in San Francisco in 1976, and various regional bisexual organizations sprang up. Bisexuals formed their own contingents in gay rights marches beginning in the late 1980s, and the 1993 March on Washington for Lesbian, Gay and Bi Equal Rights was the first national event to include "bi" in its name. BiNet, a national-level bisexual organization, was formed in 1990. Several important books by or about bisexuals appeared in the early 1990s (Hutchins & Kaahumanu, 1991; Weise, 1992; Weinberg et al., 1995), and others have followed more recently (Fox, 2004).

Bisexuals debate whether they should ally closely with lesbians and gay men, forge an independent social identity, or act as some kind of bridge between heterosexual and homosexual people. The bisexual community is very much in a state of evolution.

Summary

1. Sexual orientation defines how a person's disposition to experience sexual attraction varies with the sex of their potential partners. It can be represented on a 5- or 7-point scale from heterosexual (attracted to people of the opposite sex only), through varying degrees of bisexuality, to homosexual (attracted to people of one's own sex only.) A small percentage (2% to 3%) of the population is homosexual. Exclusively homosexual men are more common than exclusively homosexual women. The percentage that is bisexual depends greatly on the definition used but is always higher in women than in men.

2. Lesbians and gay men, although very diverse, tend to be sex-atypical in their self-described masculinity–femininity, in cognitive and personality traits, and in occupational interests. This gender nonconformity is evident in children who later become gay adults.

3. A variety of theories have been put forward to explain how sexual orientation develops. According to Freudian psychoanalytic theory, heterosexuality emerges from a complex sequence of stages of psychosexual development; the disruption of several of these stages may lead to homosexuality. According to socialization theories, a child's ultimate sexual orientation is molded by innumerable rewards and punishments given by parents and others.

4. According to biological theories, sexual orientation is affected by factors such as prenatal hormone levels, which are thought to influence the organization of brain systems responsible for sexual attraction. Genes also influence sexual orientation, especially in men, but the specific genes that are involved have not yet been identified.

5. The idea that same-sex desire defined a specific class of "homosexual" people first became prevalent in the late nineteenth century as a result of urbanization, the rise of companionate marriage, and the writings of sexologists. Initially, homosexual men and women were thought of as "gender inverts"—people born with many physical and psychological traits of the other sex.

6. In the twentieth century it became apparent that homosexual people were not all alike. This led initially to the concept of a "butch/femme" or "top/bottom" duality, but more recently it has become apparent that gay people include a wide variety of "types" that cannot easily be shoehorned into gender categories. Sexual orientation is a more fluid concept than originally conceived, especially for women.

REFER TO THE

Human Sexuality

WEBSITE AT
www.sinauer.com/levay3e
for activities, study questions,
quizzes, and other study aids.

7. The modern gay rights movement began in nineteenth-century Germany and spread to the United States after the Second World War. A key event was the Stonewall Rebellion, a riot in New York City in 1969 that led to the politicization of the gay community. The AIDS epidemic, which began around 1980, devastated gay male communities. It was also the spur to more effective political action and to greater openness on the part of gay people.

8. The rapid advances made by lesbians and gay men have made them the focus of a cultural conflict between conservative and progressive forces in American society. The same conflict is playing itself out worldwide; in some countries, gay people have gained greater acceptance than in the United States, while in others they are more severely stigmatized.

9. Pre-gay children who are markedly gender-nonconformist typically experience taunting, abuse, or efforts to normalize them. For gay people, psychological development is a process of "coming out." This process involves several stages: self-realization and self-acceptance, disclosure to others, joining the gay community, and integrating one's homosexuality with other aspects of one's cultural identity.

10. Gay sex and gay relationships are quite similar to their heterosexual counterparts. Gay men tend to more sexually adventurous and to have more partners than lesbians or heterosexual people, but monogamous gay relationships are also common.

11. Many lesbians and some gay men are parents, either from earlier heterosexual relationships or as a result of a variety of reproductive strategies that are open to gay couples. The children of gay parents generally thrive: They may experience some taunting in school, but they are as well adjusted as the children of straight parents, and they tend to be more tolerant and empathetic.

12. Anti-gay attitudes and behaviors (homophobia) have multiple roots. These roots include cultural indoctrination, an aversion to the idea of engaging in sex with a same-sex partner, an image of homosexuality as a transgression of social rules, or a defense mechanism against one's own real or feared homosexual tendencies. Overcoming homophobia depends primarily on personal interactions at a grassroots level.

13. Bisexual men and women have the advantage of a wider potential range of sexual experience, but they also face social stigma ("biphobia"). They may be mischaracterized as closeted gay people, as oversexed, as spreaders of AIDS, or as inconstant partners. Bisexuals have attempted to forge a social and political identity that is at least partially separate from that of gay people.

Discussion Questions

1. How do your views on homosexuality compare with those of your grandparents, your parents, and your college peers?

2. Take the "gay-straight" Implicit Association Test at https://implicit.harvard.edu/implicit/demo/selectatest.html or the Homophobia Questionnaire at www.pbs.org/wgbh/pages/frontline/shows/assault/etc/quiz.html. Do you think that the test reveals anything about your attitude toward gay people?

3. Your friend tells you, "I can tell if a person is gay without even asking them." Do you agree or disagree with this statement? If you agree, what cues you in to a person's sexual orientation?

4. You are a board member of a local school district. This school district proposes to start a program in which openly gay faculty would provide support, information, and role models for students. Would you support or discourage this program? Give a rationale for your answer. What would the effect of the program be on the students?

5. Imagine that you have always been attracted emotionally and sexually to your own sex and that your family has rather traditional religious and conservative views. Would you tell your family about your attraction? If you were to disclose your sexu-

al orientation to your family, how would you do it? What do you think their response would be?

6. Researchers find more evidence of bisexuality and sexual fluidity among women than among men. Do you think this says something profound about men and women's sexuality, or does it have more to do with how boys and girls are acculturated to think about sexual attraction and sexual relationships?

7. In 2008, the Ad Council ran a public service announcement featuring actress Hilary Duff, who urged young people not to use the put-down, "That's so gay." Do you agree with Duff, or was this an example of unnecessary "political correctness"?

Web Resources

American Civil Liberties Union—Lesbian and gay rights page
   www.aclu.org/lgbt/index.html

American Institute of Bisexuality www.bisexual.org

Asian Pacific Islander Queer Women and Transgender Coalition www.apiqwtc.org

BiNet USA www.binetusa.org

Gay Asian Pacific Support Network www.gapsn.org

Homophobia questionnaire
   www.pbs.org/wgbh/pages/frontline/shows/assault/etc/quiz.html

Human Rights Campaign (political and educational organization for the gay, lesbian, bisexual, and transgender communities) www.hrc.org

Lambda Legal (main gay and lesbian legal organization) www.lambdalegal.org

National Center for Lesbian Rights www.nclrights.org

National Gay and Lesbian Task Force (serves the same communities as the Human Rights Campaign, but with an emphasis on grassroots activism)
   www.thetaskforce.org

OutProud—The National Coalition for Gay, Lesbian, Bisexual, and Transgender Youth
   www.outproud.org

Parents, Families and Friends of Lesbians and Gays (PFLAG) www.pflag.org

Unid@s-National Latina/o Lesbian, Gay, Bisexual, and Transgender Human Rights Organization www.unidoslgbt.org

United Lesbians of African Heritage www.uloah.com

Recommended Reading

Diamond, L.M. (2008). *Sexual fluidity: Understanding women's love and desire.* Harvard University Press.

Faderman, L. (1991). *Odd girls and twilight lovers: A history of lesbian life in twentieth-century America.* Columbia University Press.

Herek, G. M. (Ed.) (1998). *Stigma and sexual orientation: Understanding prejudice against lesbians, gay men, and bisexuals.* Sage Publications.

Rust, P. C. R. (Ed.) (2000). *Bisexuality in the United States: A social science reader.* Columbia University Press.

Savin-Williams, R. C. (2001). *Mom, Dad, I'm gay: How families negotiate coming out.* American Psychological Association.

Siegel, L. and Olson, N. L. (Eds.) (2001). *Out of the closet, into our hearts: Celebrating our gay family members.* Leyland.

Townsend, L. (1997). *The leatherman's handbook* (Silver jubilee ed.). Masquerade Books.

Wright, L. (Ed.) (1997). *The bear book: Readings in the history and evolution of a gay male subculture.* Harrington Park Press.

CHAPTER 15

For some, sexuality is inextricably tied to fetish objects or to behaviors outside the sexual norm.

Atypical Sexuality

Most of us, at one time or another, have experienced a bizarre sexual fantasy or have tried out some "kinky" sexual practice. Such thoughts and behaviors may add spice to our sex lives and help maintain our interest in sexual relationships. However, have you ever been sexually aroused by a horse? Have you ever masturbated while holding an item of lingerie? Have you ever enjoyed having your sex partner inflict pain on you during sex? For some people—most of whom are men—such unusual sexual desires come to dominate their lives. These desires only become problematic if they cause distress to the people who experience them or if they are acted out in behaviors that harm others or run afoul of the law. In this chapter we describe a variety of atypical sexual desires and behaviors, discuss theories about what causes them, and present treatment options if treatment is called for.

Sexual Variety Is the Spice of Life

The blows fell rapidly and powerfully on my back and arms. Each one cut into my flesh and burned there, but the pains enraptured me. They came from her whom I adored, and for whom I was ready at any hour to lay down my life.

She stopped. "I am beginning to enjoy it," she said, "but enough for today. I am beginning to feel a demonic curiosity to see how far your strength goes. I take a cruel joy in seeing you tremble and writhe beneath my whip, and in hearing your groans and wails; I want to go on whipping without pity until you beg for mercy, until you lose your senses. You have awakened dangerous elements in my being. But now get up."

I seized her hand to press it to my lips.

"What impudence." She shoved me away with her foot. "Out of my sight, slave!"—
Venus in Furs (Sacher-Masoch, 1870/2000).

Does this passage strike you as an example of healthy sexuality? Or was one or both of the participants mentally deranged? Richard von Krafft-Ebing, the encyclopedist of sexual aberrations who was mentioned in Chapter 1, was so impressed by Leopold von Sacher-Masoch's (autobiographical) account of sexual humiliation that he actually borrowed the author's name to define a psychiatric disorder—masochism.

Today, however, most sex researchers believe that only a small province within the realm of atypical sexuality needs to be cordoned off as "diseased" (**Figure 15.1**). That province will be covered later in this chapter. For now, we discuss

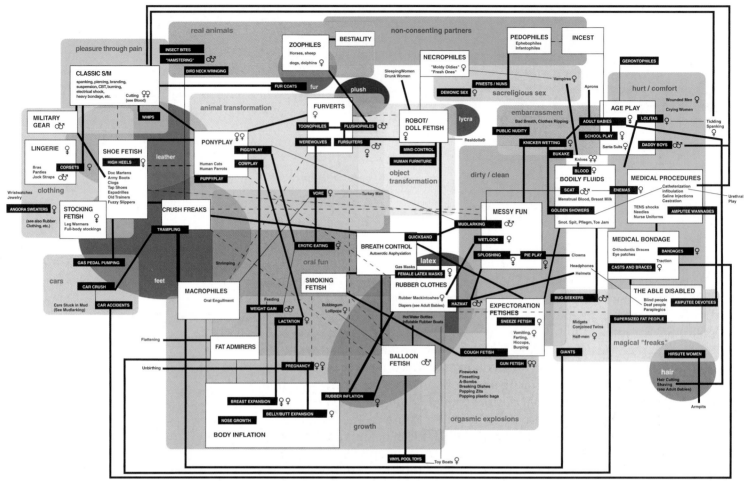

Figure 15.1 A map of "deviant" sexuality by Katharine Gates (see Recommended Reading at the end of this chapter), showing the clustering of traits into conceptual categories, with their links. Only small regions of this map cover forms of sexual expression that are definitely abnormal or illegal (especially the blue section labeled "non-consenting partners"), but other regions may be considered pathological if they cause distress to the people who experience them. This diagram should be viewed as one writer's attempt to organize the diversity of atypical sexual expression, rather than as a definitive or consensus-based analysis. (© Katherine Gates/deviantdesires.com.)

variant sexual interests and practices as, at worst, harmless oddities and, at best, creative strategies to enrich sexual experience and to strengthen relationships.

Fetishism Is Sexual Arousal by Inanimate Objects, Substances, or Body Parts

Most of us find that certain items of clothing or certain perfumes are especially effective in enhancing a partner's sexual attractiveness—whole industries depend on that fact. For many of us, particular body parts—e.g., breasts, penises, buttocks, legs, or feet—carry a special erotic charge. "I'm a legs man," someone might say, or, "Guys' buns really turn me on." When these kinds of specific attraction come to play an important role in a person's sexual life they are known as **fetishisms**.

Sometimes, the objects of fetishistic desire are *things*: shoes, lingerie, jockstraps, or other items of clothing, for example (**object fetishism**). Alternatively, the fetishism may focus on *materials*—such as leather, rubber, silk, or fur—that are arousing regardless of the specific object into which they are fashioned (**media fetishism**). (Sacher-Masoch was a fur fetishist as well as a masochist.) Fetishistic

fetishism Sexual arousal by inanimate objects, materials, or parts of the body.

object fetishism Sexual arousal by inanimate objects. Also called form fetishism.

media fetishism Sexual attraction to materials such as rubber or silk. Also called material fetishism.

attraction to *body parts*, such as feet, is known as **partialism**. Besides normal body parts, a few people have a fetishistic attraction to abnormal body parts such as deformed feet or amputation stumps. In fact, there seem to be few restrictions on the possible targets of fetishistic desire, but the most common ones are closely associated with people or with sexual activities.

Some people—mostly men*—invest a lot of energy in pursuing fetishistic interests. A foot-fetishist might incorporate foot worship into sexual foreplay with his partner. He might spend a lot of time watching foot-fetish videos or visiting foot-fetish Web sites. He might belong to groups of people who share the same interest. A lingerie fetishist might spend a lot of time purchasing (or stealing) items of women's underwear and viewing and touching them during masturbation.

That fetishistic interests are common is made obvious by a visit to any sex shop or sex-toy Web site, where a wide variety of fetish-related objects are available. Fetish-related videos comprise 25% or more of the output of some large adult-video companies, and some smaller companies, such as Kink Video and Redboard Video of San Francisco, specialize entirely in fetish videos. (The term "fetish" is used broadly in the sex industry, however, and may include bondage/dominance and almost any other sexual behavior aside from conventional intercourse.)

At what point does someone with fetishistic interests deserve to be called "a fetishist"? Usage varies: Some authorities would reserve the term "fetishist" for a person whose interest clearly crosses the line to a mental disorder (see below), but others hold that someone can be called a fetishist if they are strongly invested in fetishism even if they are not diagnosable as having a mental disorder. We take the latter view—*we use the term "fetishist" without any necessary implication that the person has a mental disorder.*

The Internet has had a major impact on the lives of fetishists, as it has for all people with minority sexual interests (**Box 15.1**). It has facilitated communication among fetishists, thus bolstering self-acceptance and satisfaction and reducing the likelihood that fetishists will feel the need to seek psychological help. It has also promoted awareness about fetishism in the general population. Thus the Internet has played a key role in "normalizing" fetishism and other variant forms of sexual expression.

People Cross-Dress for a Variety of Reasons

Some people repeatedly or continually wear the clothes of the other sex. Both men and women may **cross-dress**, and they do so with a wide variety of motives:

PRACTICAL REASONS   There may be entirely nonsexual reasons for cross-dressing. Women have often cross-dressed in order to pass as men and thus obtain male employment or other privileges of masculinity. Male attire may be more practical for many activities. In fact, as women have gained increasing parity with men, traditionally masculine attire, such as blue jeans, has become unisex.

DOING DRAG   Men or women may dress as the other sex for entertainment purposes or to mock stereotypical gender expectations or fashion norms. In

Fetishism is erotic fixation on inanimate objects or, as here, on certain body parts.

partialism   Fetishistic attraction to specific parts of the body.

cross-dress   To wear the clothing of the other sex, for any of a variety of reasons.

Drag artist at Rio de Janeiro's Carnaval

---

*Because of the strong predominance of men in many forms of atypical sexual expression, we will sometimes use male pronouns in this chapter. As we describe, however, women are represented to a variable extent.

Personal Points of View

BOX 15.1　Rubber Fetishism and the Internet

The following is an interview with "Ataraxia," a 59-year-old Pittsburgh man who is a rubber fetishist (or "rubberist") and founder of the International Association of Rubberists and its Web site, Rubberist.net:

Is rubber fetishism a mental illness?

That's what I thought for the first half of my life. I got out of the Navy because of it. And on the way out their psychiatrists told me, "There's not a whole lot we can do to cure this, so why don't you learn to enjoy it?" That's where I came up with "Ataraxia," which means "peace of mind."

What kinds of problems do fetishists have?

One problem is spousal: With many of them, their wives are either not into it at all, or they barely tolerate it. And then there's the social aspect, where people think that we're kinky and therefore dangerous. We're not: We don't hurt anybody.

What's the purpose of Rubberist.net?

The aim is to help others go through that process I went through. Before the Internet, fetishists might think they were the only one in the world.

What can they find on the site?

Personal stories, as well as practical information, like how to make rubber clothing or where to get it. News, culture, surveys. And a way to meet other rubberists. They can post on a bulletin board or jump into a conversation. About 1000 rubberists visit the site every day.

What kinds of people visit the site?

Ninety percent or more are male. There's some confusion because some are transgendered. True female rubberists are rare. As for sexual orientation, my site tends to be heterosexually oriented, but it includes a lot of material that is not specifically straight or gay. There are plenty of gay rubber sites. Life is easier for gay fetishists—they can find partners without too much trouble.

Heterosexual rubber fetishists may have a hard time finding sympathetic partners.

What are the options for straight ones?

They can grin and bear it, or they can reach some sort of compromise, as I did with my wife. Some of the younger women are more open to it.

Is there a connection between rubber and BDSM, like there is between leather and BDSM?

Yes, a large proportion of rubberists are into that—mostly the bondage side of it.

What's the psychology of rubber fetishism?

Mostly it's the sense of encasement. The term is "total enclosure," which means covering every inch of your body with rubber—making two or three layers if you can. It's a combination of the sense of tightness and being shielded from the rest of the world. I think it's a "return to the womb" kind of thing—the warm, moist, enclosing environment, it seems like a womb. It seems to be a phenomenon of the industrialized world. About a third of our members are from England.

---

this case their clothing, makeup, and hairstyle is likely to be an over-the-top caricature, not a real attempt to replicate the typical dress of the other sex. Many, but not all, **drag** artists are gay men, in which case they may be called "drag queens."

TRANSGENDERED CROSS-DRESSING　For transexual and transgendered people, wearing the clothes of the other sex may be a vital expression of their gender identity. In that sense, one could debate whether the practice should be called

drag　The wearing of exaggeratedly feminine clothing by a man, often for entertainment purposes.

"cross-dressing" at all, given that it conforms to the sex the person identifies with. (Certainly it should not be called cross-dressing *after* a transexual has transitioned to the other sex.) Typically, transexuals attempt to *pass* as the other sex, not to *parody* it, although some transgendered people do adopt styles of dress and hairstyle that defy gender norms for either sex. It's important to note that erotic arousal is not the primary motivation for transgendered cross-dressing, although a transgendered person may well feel "sexier" and more interested in attracting a sex partner when cross-dressed.

TRANSVESTIC FETISHISM   Another class of cross-dressers comprises heterosexual men who wear women's clothes because they find the practice itself sexually arousing. This is therefore a form of fetishism, and its technical name is transvestic fetishism, or simply **transvestism**. (Again, the use of the term "fetishism" here is not intended to brand this form of sexual expression as a mental disorder.) Transvestic fetishism is not rare: One random-sample study of the general population of Sweden found that 2.8% of men and 0.4% of women had engaged in at least one episode of transvestic fetishism (Langstrom & Zucker, 2005).

Many heterosexual transvestites keep their cross-dressing secret for fear of public ridicule or rejection by their partners. Others venture out in public while cross-dressed, and they may be sexually excited by doing so. Many heterosexual transvestites are married (Docter & Prince, 1997); some conceal their cross-dressing from their wives, but others tell their wives or are found out. The wife is commonly disturbed by the initial discovery and may worry that her husband is gay. Some wives come to accept their husband's cross-dressing, and the couple may even incorporate it into their sexual activities (Talimini, 1982).

It seems that there is a continuum of traits in which heterosexual men's sexual desires move from their usual target—women—to *representations* of women that can be progressively stripped away, co-opted, and internalized (Blanchard, 1993; Bailey, 2003). The first stage in this continuum is regular fetishism, in which a woman's identity is represented by an object, such as a piece of feminine attire that is separable from the woman and can be completely owned and controlled by the man. In the second stage (transvestic fetishism), the clothing that represents the woman is put on, rather than simply viewed or handled. This practice may progress to fantasies of *being* an alluring woman, including the possession of breasts and female genitalia. In the extreme stage, the man may seek sexual satisfaction in actually transitioning to the female sex (**autogynephilia**—see Chapter 7). Most fetishists do not progress through this series of traits, of course, but autogynephiles often have regular fetishism and transvestic fetishism in their history. A fairly typical life history, which illustrates the blurring of fetishism, transvestism, and borderline autogynephilia, is presented in **Box 15.2**.

Certainly, not all heterosexual cross-dressers go this route. For others, cross-dressing may lose some of its erotic significance over time and become a matter of gender expression more than sexual expression. Such men may join The Society for the Second Self (more commonly known as Tri-Ess), a support organization that publishes a magazine and organizes events at which heterosexual cross-dressers can socialize in a safe and accepting atmosphere. Support of this kind is important because heterosexual cross-dressers may encounter a lot of misunderstanding, ridicule, or abuse.

Sadomasochism Involves the Infliction or Receipt of Pain or Degradation

In regular discourse, the word **sadist** may be applied to any cruel person, and the word **masochist** to anyone who is a "glutton for punishment." More properly,

transvestism Wearing clothes of the other sex for purposes of sexual arousal. Sometimes applied to cross-dressing for any reason.

autogynephilia A form of male-to-female transexuality characterized by a man's sexual arousal at the thought of becoming a woman.

sadism Sexual arousal by the infliction of pain, bondage, or humiliation on others, or by witnessing the recipient's suffering.

masochism Sexual arousal from being subjected to pain, bondage, or humiliation.

The *Femme Mirror* is the magazine of Tri-Ess, an organization for heterosexual cross-dressers.

Figure 15.3 BDSM sex scenes require careful negotiation of consent.

adult baby An adult who obtains sexual satisfaction from acting as a baby or toddler.

should be avoided. These kinds of communications are of particular importance in male–male BDSM scenes, which tend to involve heavier interactions with greater risk of injury than what typically takes place in male–female or female–female BDSM scenes. BDSM scenes that challenge the bottom's tolerance or that approach the boundaries of safety or consent are known as "edge play."

Prior consent, even in written form, is not necessarily a legal defense if unwanted pain or actual injury does occur during a BDSM scene. In general, a person cannot legally consent to being assaulted or injured, but the application of this principle to BDSM cases is unclear.

On the surface, BDSM activities involve entirely negative feelings such as pain, fear, and anger. Dedicated BDSM practitioners, however, assert the very opposite: that the relationship of power, trust, and dependency that exists between top and bottom represents a condition of heightened intimacy and that a participant in a BDSM scene may enter an altered state of consciousness that amounts to a spiritual experience (Mains, 1984).

"Adult Babies" Reenact Infancy

As may be appreciated from a perusal of Figure 15.1, there is almost no limit to the range of atypical sexual interests. One "fringe" example is that of men who derive sexual satisfaction from acting as infants or toddlers. Psychiatrists occasionally see men of this kind (Pate & Gabbard, 2003), and there are psychiatric terms such as "infantilism" to describe the trait, but most men who have it don't consider it an illness or seek professional help, and they simply call themselves **adult babies**.

Adult babies may wear diapers or toddler clothes, sit in baby chairs, drink from baby bottles, sleep in cribs, and talk and act in a babylike fashion. Sometimes there are BDSM elements: The man may play a role in which returning to babyhood is a punishment to which he is forced to submit. Adult babies are not interested in sexual contacts with actual babies.

If a man's sexual interest is largely focused on the wearing of diapers, he may call himself a "diaper lover." Diaper lovers may masturbate while wearing diapers, or they may act in more authentically babylike fashion by wetting or soiling the diaper. Some diaper lovers wear diapers under their regular clothes during daily activities, like an adult with incontinence.

As with so many other minority sexual interests, adult babies have been "normalized" by the Internet. In the past they may have thought they were the only person in the world to have an erotic interest in babyhood, but now there are many Web sites and Internet-based groups that serve them. There are sites, for example, on which adult babies can hire "baby-sitters" who will play that role for an hourly fee, doing such things as pampering, feeding, or disciplining the adult baby, or changing his diapers.

"Paraphilia" Is the Psychiatric Term for Problematic Sexual Desire or Behavior

There is no precise or objective boundary between normal and abnormal sexual feelings and behaviors. Social norms, moral teachings, legal proscriptions, and medical theories all have something to say on the matter, but they do not necessarily agree, nor does what they say remain constant over time. In the United States of a century ago, homosexuality lay well outside the bounds of "normal" sexuality: Psychiatrists called it a disease, nearly everyone considered it immoral, and the law prohibited it. Little has changed about homosexuality itself over the intervening years, but it is now no longer labeled a disease or a crime, and it is increasingly accepted as a normal aspect of sexual diversity. Clearly, then, social attitudes strongly color what is considered sexually normal and what is considered abnormal, sick, or wrong.

The term **paraphilia** is used by psychiatrists to cover any unusual and problematic form of sexual expression. According to the 2000 edition of the American Psychiatric Association's *Diagnostic and Statistical Manual of Mental Disorders* (*DSM-IV-TR*), paraphilias are "recurrent, intense sexually arousing fantasies, sexual urges, or behaviors involving (1) nonhuman objects, (2) the suffering or humiliation of oneself or one's partner, or (3) children or other nonconsenting persons. . . . The behavior, sexual urges or fantasies cause clinically significant distress in social, occupational, or other important areas of functioning" (American Psychiatric Association, 2000). Paraphilias can sometimes be diagnosed even if the person who has them does not experience any subjective distress or impaired functioning. This is mostly relevant in the context of paraphilias that involve criminal activity.

The *DSM* lists seven specific paraphilias—fetishism, transvestism, masochism, sadism, exhibitionism, voyeurism, and pedophilia—as well as unspecified "other conditions." The prevalence of paraphilias is unclear because people are generally unwilling to admit to them. The paraphilias that come to medical or legal attention most often are those that involve victims (**Figure 15.4**).

Three main issues need consideration in the context of diagnosing paraphilias:

■ *Is there distress?* As with medical problems in general, it is the fact that the person experiences suffering and seeks relief from that suffering that is the prime criterion for a diagnosis of a paraphilia. The suffering might be caused by guilt, damage to the man's marriage, a failure to establish intimate relationships, or interference with his daily life. Still, as just mentioned, a diagnosis of a paraphilia may be appropriate even if there is *no* subjective distress, especially if they motivate a person to victimize others.

■ *Is the ideation or behavior required for arousal?* If the person is *incapable* of sexual arousal or orgasm without a specific behavior or fantasy, it is especially

paraphilia An unusual form of sexual arousal or behavior that is considered to be a psychological problem.

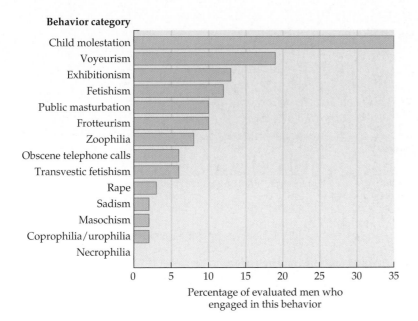

Behavior category

Percentage of evaluated men who engaged in this behavior

Figure 15.4 The prevalence of paraphilias among men being evaluated clinically for suspected inappropriate sexual interests. Of course, these behaviors are biased toward those that bring men to medical or legal attention; namely, those that involve victims. No men in this sample had necrophilic interests. (Data from Abel & Osborn, 2000.)

likely that a diagnosis of a paraphilia is appropriate. Still, this criterion has to be flexible. Some behaviors that are clearly paraphilic occur in binges separated by periods of perfectly ordinary sexual expression, or in a secret "shadow-life" that parallels a conventional, sexually active marriage.

■ *Is there a victim?* If the person's sexual behavior engages others without their consent or actually harms them, a diagnosis of paraphilia is made more likely. Again, this cannot be an absolute criterion, however. Rape, for example, is clearly a sexual behavior that has a victim, but it is considered simply as a crime rather than a paraphilia, unless there are other aspects indicating mental illness.

We can make some generalizations about paraphilias. They are often extensions or exaggerations of common sexual desires and behaviors (**Figure 15.5**). Far more men than women develop them. Paraphilias begin at an early age—usually around the time of puberty or early adolescence—and tend to become more pronounced over time. People who start out with one kind of paraphilia may eventually exhibit multiple forms; by the time they come to professional attention, 54% of paraphiliacs report experiencing more than one paraphilia, and 18% report four or more paraphilias (Abel & Osborn, 2000). Certain personality traits are common among paraphiliacs: These include a lack of social skills (especially in dealing with women), a sense of inadequacy, depression, and sometimes a sense of rage against women. Paraphiliacs commonly have cognitive distortions, believing, for example, that their behaviors are sexually exciting or beneficial to the people whom they target.

In this section we focus on those paraphilias that, when acted out, involve victims. These include three of the paraphilias listed in the *DSM*—exhibitionism, voyeurism, and pedophilia—as well as four "other conditions"—frotteurism, zoophilia, necrophilia, and paraphilic rape. By omitting discussion of fetishism, transvestism, masochism, and sadism in this section, we do not mean to imply

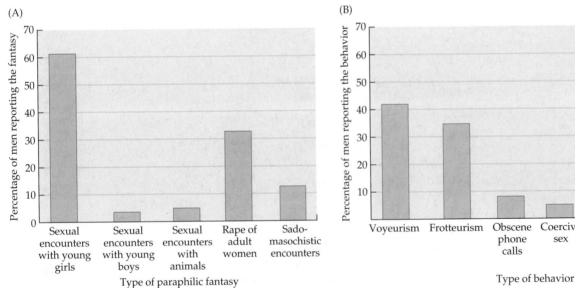

Figure 15.5 Atypical fantasies and behaviors in the general male population. (A) Percentage of men who experience paraphilic sexual fantasies during masturbation or intercourse. (B) Percentage of male college students who admit having engaged in paraphilic or criminal sexual behaviors. (A after Crepault & Couture, 1980; B after Templeman & Stinnett, 1991.)

that they are never paraphilic—they do deserve that diagnosis when they cause severe distress or harm, as discussed above.

Exhibitionists Expose Themselves to Nonconsenting Persons

The paraphilia called **exhibitionism** refers to people (nearly always men) who expose their genitals to nonconsenting persons, usually women or children, for purposes of sexual arousal. Typically, an exhibitionist (or "flasher") will station himself in some location where women are present, but which offers little danger of his being identified or arrested. As a woman approaches, the man will step into her line of sight and open his coat to expose his genitals. Alternatively, he may remove a book or newspaper that conceals them. During this action, the man may fantasize having a sexual interaction with the woman. He may masturbate and ejaculate while doing so; alternatively, he may flee and masturbate later, using his recollection of the event as an arousing stimulus. In legal terms, this behavior is the crime of **indecent exposure**.

Exhibitionism is defined *behaviorally*—by what people do—rather than as a sexual preference. Exhibitionists are no more strongly aroused sexually by exposing themselves than by other forms of sexual expression, to judge from penile plethysmographic studies (Marshall & Fernandez, 2003). Rather, exhibitionists often exhibit high rates of many different kinds of sexual behaviors—a trait called hypersexuality (see below) (Murphy & Page, 2008).

An exhibitionist often misinterprets his victim's reactions—whether of shock, fear, or amusement—as a reciprocation of his sexual interest. Because of this cognitive distortion on the exhibitionist's part, the woman's emotional reactions tend to reward him and promote a continuation of his behavior. Women who encounter an exhibitionist do best to stay calm and simply walk away, although there is the option of attempting to have the man arrested if circumstances permit.

Exhibitionism is very common. It accounts for over one-third of all sex crimes reported to the police, even though most victims do not file police reports (Riordan, 1999). Exhibitionists seen at one clinic admitted to having committed an average of over 500 exhibitionist acts each (Abel & Rouleau, 1990). About half of all adult women have been the victim of an exhibitionist at least once in their lives, and of the women who have had such experiences, over half were first victimized before the age of 16 (Riordan, 1999).

Related to exhibitionism is obscene telephone calling, in which the perpetrator (almost always a man) calls a known or unknown victim (usually a woman) and makes sexual suggestions or utters obscenities. As with exhibitionism, the obscene telephone caller is sexually aroused by the reaction (real or perceived) of the woman he is exposing himself to, the only difference being that the exposure is auditory rather than visual.

Most exhibitionists and obscene telephone callers are shy men who lack social skills—especially in their interactions with women—and they tend to experience general feelings of inadequacy (Dwyer, 1988; Matek, 1988). Exhibitionist behavior usually begins in adolescence and persists for many years. As with most paraphilic behaviors, however, it becomes less common in later life, probably because of the drop in testosterone levels that accompanies aging (Barbaree, 2008).

Because exhibitionism is a "hands-off" behavior, with no physical contact between the exhibitionist and his victim, there is a tendency to take it lightly, or even humorously. (Legally, indecent exposure is generally a misdemeanor, not a felony.) Doubtless some women who are the victims of exhibitionists are able to make light of the experience and suffer no significant harm. But exhibitionism is a serious matter for three reasons. First, many victims of indecent exposure are in fact traumatized—they may develop an incapacitating fear of sexual crime, for

exhibitionism A paraphilia involving exposure of the genitalia to strangers, sometimes with masturbation; also called "flashing."

indecent exposure The crime of exposing the genitals or female breasts in public—exact legal definitions vary.

FAQ I've been getting obscene telephone calls—what should I do?
Hang up immediately. Use an Anonymous Call Rejection or Privacy Manager option to block the calls, or change your telephone number. In some places you can have the calls traced by dialing *57 after the call (there is a charge); in other places you must file a police complaint before having calls traced—check with your local phone company or college operator.

example (Cox & Maletzky, 1980; Riordan, 1999). Second, some of the victims are children. And third, exhibitionists are more likely to reoffend than are other sex offenders, and more than one-third of these repeat offenses are more serious, "hands-on" sexual crimes (Firestone et al., 2006).

Voyeurs Are Aroused By Watching Others

Voyeurs, or "peepers," are men who are erotically focused on watching people (usually women) while they are undressing, naked, engaged in sexual behavior, or urinating or defecating (Mann et al., 2008). Typically, voyeurs carry out their activities in a discreet fashion, such as by peering through a bedroom window from a dark location. Thus, even though they may masturbate while watching, they are usually safe from arrest and may never come to the attention of the women who are being observed. Some voyeurs may use mirrors or camera phones to peer under women's clothing, or look through peepholes into dressing rooms or toilets. Occasionally, voyeurs may be emboldened to enter people's homes in order to watch them while they sleep. As with some other paraphilias, the risk of discovery may add to the sexual excitement of voyeuristic practices. A recent twist on voyeurism is offered by Internet sites that allow people, for a membership fee, to spy on the homes of young women.

Voyeurism is very common (Abel & Osborn, 2000). It could be considered an extension of normal male sexuality, which includes a strong visual component. The biblical story of David and Bathsheba, for example, begins with King David spying on the naked Bathsheba from the roof of his palace. Many adolescent or adult males might take advantage of an opportunity to watch women who are undressed or engaged in sexual activity, especially if they can do so "guilt-free" because the woman's bedroom is in plain sight from their own window or from the street. About half of all adolescent males report having engaged in such behaviors (McConaghy, 2005). The popularity of pornographic movies and pornographic images on the Internet reflects a similarly widespread voyeuristic interest. Voyeuristic acts were not crimes in either Canada or the United Kingdom until 2004; they are now misdemeanors. In some U.S. jurisdictions voyeuristic acts remain legal so long as no trespassing, photography, or video-recording is involved.

Frotteurism Involves Surreptitious Physical Contact

A **frotteur** is a man who has physical contact with others—usually women—in public places without their consent and often without their knowledge (**Box 15.3**). He seeks out women in places that are sufficiently crowded that physical contact goes unnoticed—subway cars, elevators, crowded bars, sporting events, and the like. He rubs his erect penis, hand, leg, or an object such as a newspaper against the woman's thighs, buttocks, vulva, or breasts. According to the *DSM*, the man fantasizes about having an intimate relationship with his victim, but this idea does not appear to be supported by any evidence (Lussier & Piché, 2008). Because he may ejaculate under his clothes during the behavior, the frotteur may wear a plastic bag or plastic wrap around his penis to prevent any visible staining of his clothes. If he is arrested, evidence of such precautions may be used to prove his criminal intent. Other frotteurs may expose themselves and ejaculate directly onto their victim's clothing, however.

Again, frotteurism could be viewed as an extension of normal sexuality; most heterosexual men would like to "cop a feel" of an attractive female stranger with whom they find themselves in close proximity, and all too many men actually indulge this wish. In surveys, one-third of young men say that they had committed at least one act that would meet the definition of frotteurism (Templeman & Stinnett, 1991; Freund et al., 1997). Still, a great deal of the "groping" that is done

voyeurism A paraphilia involving spying on persons while they are undressing, naked, or engaged in sex.

frotteurism A paraphilia involving touching or rubbing the clothed genitals against a stranger without their consent or without their knowledge, as in a crowded public place.

Society, Values, and the Law

BOX 15.3 Frotteurism on Public Transit

Once, when I felt a surreptitious hand on my nether parts, and fed up with just silently standing there, I turned and shouted to the man behind me, "Take your hands off me!" The response was: "I don't know what you are talking about. You are making improper accusations." The men around stood silently by, and it was I who was embarrassed (Katz, 2006).

This description, by a New York City subway commuter, typifies the experience of many women who have to travel on crowded trains and buses. In surveys, at least one-third of college women say that they have been "groped" (Fisher et al., 2000), and very often they feel unable to respond effectively.

When the Los Angeles County Metropolitan Transportation Authority dispatched six undercover officers to deter theft on buses and trains, the officers quickly discovered that frotteurism was a much more common criminal activity. Often the victims were unaware of what was going on, or they were aware and distressed but did nothing (Liu, 2002).

Occasionally, transit officials conduct stings to catch offenders. One sting in New York City netted 13 suspected gropers and flashers (exhibitionists) (Hartocollis, 2006). The associated publicity may have served as a short-term deterrent to potential offenders. Still, sexual offenses in transit systems are a worldwide problem that shows no signs of going away. Some cities, such as Tokyo and Mexico City, have tackled the prob-

lem by banning all men from at least one car in every train (see figure).

Women can take certain steps to protect themselves, such as remaining alert, moving to less crowded areas within the train or bus, and using bags or other items as barriers between them and potential offenders. Camera phones are useful tools to deter offenders or to identify them to law enforcement. Still, when crowding becomes extreme it is difficult to distinguish innocent contacts from criminal ones. Sometimes women only discover after leaving the vehicle that their clothes have been soiled by a man's ejaculate.

Here are two accounts from New Yorkers who were able to exact some measure of retribution against frotteurs:

A hand went up my skirt and down my panties. I gasped. The nearest woman asked what was wrong. I said, "That guy's got his hand inside me." Just then, the train pulled into 161st Street. The crowd threw the guy out the door, like a watermelon seed (Randall, 2006).

A man sat down next to me in the aisle seat, then began worming his fingers under my hip as we sat side by side. I got up immediately, making sure to step on his foot and grind my heel as hard as I could as I passed him. It certainly made me feel good; I can't say the same for the perp (Andrews, 2002).

The Tokyo subway provides women-only cars as a measure against frotteurism.

in public places represents the persistent activity of dedicated frotteurs, rather than the occasional acts of otherwise conventional men.

Zoophiles Are Sexually Fixated on Animal Contacts

Sexual contact between humans and nonhuman animals—a behavior traditionally called **bestiality**—is depicted in European cave paintings that were created 15,000 to 20,000 years ago (Peretti & Rowan, 1983). In modern societies, this behavior is not particularly rare. In the Kinsey studies, about 8% of men stated that they had had at least one sexual contact with an animal (Kinsey et al., 1948). Of men raised on farms, nearly half reported at least one sexual contact with an animal, and about 17% reported a contact leading to orgasm. In such contacts, the man may penetrate the animal vaginally or anally or may induce the animal to fellate him.

For women, the numbers are considerably lower: 3.6% of the women in the Kinsey studies reported having some kind of sexual contact with an animal—

bestiality Obsolete term for sexual contact between a person and an animal.

zoophilia A persistent preference for sexual contacts with animals, considered as a paraphilia.

necrophilia A paraphilia involving sexual arousal from viewing or having contact with dead bodies.

Would-be necrophiliacs (from top to bottom) Nick Grunke, Alex Grunke, and Dustin Radke.

usually a household pet—after adolescence (Kinsey et al., 1953). These contacts usually involved generalized body contact. Only very occasionally was the woman brought to orgasm by the contact; those cases generally involved dogs that were induced to lick the woman's vulva. Anyone who visits bestiality-related pornographic Web sites might conclude that sexual interest in animals is an all-female trait; in reality, of course, these sites present images of women because they are intended for heterosexual male consumption.

Most human–animal contacts occur during the preadolescent or adolescent years and constitute only a tiny fraction of the person's total sexual activity. They can hardly be considered signs of a paraphilia. A few people—mostly men—do persist in having sexual contacts with animals throughout their lives, however, largely to the exclusion of human sexual contacts. This condition is called **zoophilia**. In one study, two-thirds of zoophiles stated that they would rather have sex with an animal than with a human (Williams & Weinberg, 2003). In a case study, a man was found (by penile plethysmography) to be sexually aroused more strongly by horses than by any other species, including humans (Earls & Lalumiere, 2002). A first-person account (also written by a horse-lover) asserted that zoophilia is a matter of romantic intimacy and not merely physical gratification (Matthews, 1994).

People who engage in persistent sexual contacts with animals often display other kinds of paraphilic behavior. There seems to be a connection between human–animal sex and generalized psychiatric disturbance: In one study, 55% of psychiatric inpatients had a history of human–animal sexual contacts or fantasies, compared with 10% to 15% of controls (Alvarez & Freinhar, 1991).

In Necrophilia, Nonresistance of the Partner May Be Arousing

Necrophilia is a sexual fixation on corpses. It is a rare paraphilia, with probably fewer than 200 cases having been reported in the medical literature. Still, there is enough interest in necrophilia to keep some Internet bulletin boards busy. Necrophiliacs may take positions as mortuary workers or other jobs that give them access to dead bodies. (Of course, the overwhelming majority of mortuary workers are not necrophiliacs.)

Necrophiliacs may view or touch a dead body while masturbating or may actually have penetrative sex with it. Apparently, it is the lack of resistance or rejection by the dead person that is a key motivator for necrophilic behavior (Rosman & Resnick, 1989). In fact, some men are turned on when their (living) sex partners feign unconsciousness, "play dead," or join them in necrophilic fantasies. Such activities may not be entirely harmless, because some men have committed murder to satisfy their necrophilic interests.

Not all states criminalize sex with corpses, and in those that do the interpretation of the law is often murky, as was highlighted by a recent bizarre case in Wisconsin. In September 2006, 20-year-old Nick Grunke saw an obituary of a young woman who had died a few days earlier in a motorcycle accident. Grunke was so smitten with the young woman's photograph that he conceived a plan to disinter her body from the local cemetery and have sex with it. Grunke, his twin brother Alex, and another friend drove to the cemetery late at night, after stopping off at WalMart to purchase some condoms. Once at the cemetery, the three men dug down to the woman's vault, but could not pry it open. Shortly thereafter they were apprehended by the police and charged with attempted third-degree rape. Wisconsin had a statute banning sex with corpses, but the defendants argued that it only applied to cases where the sex act took place in conjunction with a murder. The trial court, and an appeals court, agreed with them. But the prosecutors appealed the case all the way to the Wisconsin Supreme Court, and those justices took a different view. They ruled in 2008 that the statute did cover sex with a dead person who had not been murdered, and they sent the case back to the lower court for further proceedings, which have yet to take place (Supreme Court of Wisconsin, 2008).

Sexual Violence Can Be Paraphilic

Not all violent forms of sexual expression warrant diagnosis as paraphilias. Consensual S/M scenes are not usually an indication of a paraphilia, nor are most cases of rape (though rape is a crime, of course). If a person has a persistent and distressing fixation on sexual violence, however, or commits acts of nonconsensual sexual violence *because the violence itself is sexually arousing,* the person is probably diagnosable as having a paraphilia. Terminology varies: The condition may be called paraphilic rape syndrome, paraphilic sadism, or something similar; it is not specifically listed in the *DSM*.

Some of the most notorious serial killers, such as Jack the Ripper, or Jeffrey Dahmer—who killed and dismembered 17 boys or youths in the Milwaukee area for sexual gratification—would fit the description of paraphilic sadists (Jentzen et al., 1994). (Dahmer was also a necrophiliac.) Paraphilic sexual killers often have a complex mental disorder, including brain damage, psychosis, and a history of severe childhood abuse (Pincus, 2001). Nevertheless, these crimes are not impulsive. Typically, they are carefully planned and involve hours or days of torture before the victim is finally killed. The perpetrator often records his crimes on videotape or in diaries.

One sexual serial killer who generated enormous publicity was Gary Ridgway (the "Green River killer"). In 2003, Ridgway pleaded guilty to murdering 48 young women and girls—mostly prostitutes—in the Seattle area over a period of 16 years (*Seattle Times*, 2004). He killed most of the women by strangling them during sexual encounters. In his confession Ridgway expressed contempt for prostitutes, but this seems to have been merely what permitted him to direct his murderous sexual impulses at them, rather than being the actual motive, which—while obviously pathological—remains obscure. Ridgway escaped the death penalty by agreeing to provide information about his victims and the location of their bodies.

Eating the remains of sex-murder victims, as Jeffrey Dahmer did, is a recurrent theme in such cases—it seems to represent the ultimate in the internalization of the desired love object. A truly macabre case from Germany drew worldwide attention in 2003. (Skip the rest of this paragraph if you have a weak stomach!) Forty-two-year-old Armin Meiwes, who had fantasized about cannibalism since childhood, advertised on an Internet chat room for a man who was willing to be slaughtered and eaten. A computer analyst named Bernd Brandes volunteered, wrote his will, and bought a one-way ticket to the town where Meiwes lived. After hours of sadomasochistic sex, which included the cooking and eating of Brandes' penis by both men, Meiwes stabbed Brandes to death, butchered and froze his body, and ate much of it over the following months. On account of Brandes' documented consent, Meiwes was only convicted of manslaughter and was sentenced to 8 years of imprisonment, but in 2005 a higher court ordered a retrial, and in 2006 Meiwes was convicted of murder and sentenced to life imprisonment. Meiwes was described by court-appointed psychiatrists as having a "schizoid personality," a condition marked by emotional coldness, a lack of intimate relationships, and an excessive preoccupation with fantasy. What about Brandes? He evidently had a "vore fantasy"—an erotic fixation on being eaten alive that is usually acted out in some innocuous fashion such as pretending to be a Thanksgiving turkey (Gates, 2000).

Some masochists inflict pain or suffering on themselves without the aid of a partner. A particularly dangerous form of this behavior is **autoerotic asphyxia**, in which the practitioner partially asphyxiates himself while masturbating. Although

Gary Ridgway—the Green River serial killer—said that he killed prostitutes because he hated them and because "I thought I could kill as many of them as I wanted without getting caught."

autoerotic asphyxia Self-strangulation for purposes of sexual arousal.

Research Highlights

BOX 15.4 Autoerotic Asphyxia

"When you find my body hanging . . . with a tight noose around my neck, do not look for a murderer. I have executed myself. I say execute rather than suicide because I didn't really intend to hang unto death." This cryptic note was found next to the strung-up, half-naked body of a young Canadian man. Indeed, the cause of his death was not murder, nor was it suicide. It was autoerotic asphyxia—a sexually charged near-death experience that went a step too far (Blanchard & Hucker, 1991).

People who practice autoerotic asphyxia do so in order to increase the intensity of orgasm by constricting the flow of blood to the brain during masturbation. The practitioners of this behavior—nearly all male—may tighten a belt around their necks or suspend themselves by a noose, often using a closet rail, rafter, or tree. The cerebral cortex is partially knocked out by the resulting lack of oxygen, and its normal inhibitory influence on lower centers of the brain is removed. This probably results in the same kind of heightened, woozy orgasm that some people experience with the use of nitrite inhalers or "poppers." But autoerotic asphyxia carries a dire risk of accidental death if the practitioner passes out before he has time to release the constricting ligature.

One of the most famous cases of suspected autoerotic asphyxia was that of Australian rock star Michael Hutchence (lead singer for INXS), who died in 1997 at the age of 37. Hutchence hanged himself from a closet rail, using a belt. His death was officially ruled a suicide (Hand, 1998), but numerous details pointed toward autoerotic asphyxia as the cause of death, according to Hutchence's fiancée, Paula Yates (Barrie, 1999).

For many practitioners, autoerotic asphyxia is about more than experiencing a supernormal orgasm. To judge by the death scenes of victims, it is often linked with a complex of paraphilic elements, including bondage, punish-

ment, and execution by hanging. The victim's body may be tied up around the ankles and genitals as well as the neck, and sadomasochistic literature or images are often found in the vicinity. Transvestism can also play a role: One victim was found dressed in women's clothes and surrounded by documents containing passages such as "the law of the land for any man dressed as a woman and found guilty is that he be hanged." Another victim was found hanging in front of a computer that had been playing a "snuff video" (a movie depicting a real or staged murder, perhaps in a pornographic context (Vennemann & Pollak, 2006).

As with Hutchence, many possible cases of autoerotic asphyxia come to light only when the person has died. But on the basis of a few studies of living practitioners, it seems that the behavior typically begins experimentally, in adolescence. In some men the behavior develops such intensity that it becomes their only possible sexual outlet. A few studies suggest that experience of sexual abuse in childhood may provoke the behavior, but this is far from certain.

Autoerotic asphyxia is not extremely rare as a cause of death among young men. Over 400 such deaths have been reported in the forensic literature (Sauvageau & Racette, 2006). What's more, many cases of autoerotic asphyxia are misidentified as suicides, either because the family covers up the evidence that the deceased was masturbating or because the authorities make a default assumption that a hanging is a suicide. But even if there are no

obvious clues at the scene, such as magazines or bondage gear, an alert pathologist may spot other indications of the true cause of death: The victim may place a thick cloth between the ligature and his neck in order to prevent rope burns, for example, or the closet rail may show wear from repeated use.

Rock star Michael Hutchence may have been a victim of autoerotic asphyxia.

Men in whom autoerotic asphyxia has developed into a compulsive behavior should seek psychotherapeutic treatment in an attempt to rechannel their sexual energy. Unlike many paraphilias, this one is simply too dangerous to be a reasonable risk. Unfortunately, the secrecy with which most men practice autoerotic asphyxia usually ensures that medical examiners, not psychiatrists, are the first to find out about it.

this behavior can have the aim simply of enhancing sexual arousal, it is often connected with BDSM ideation and practices (**Box 15.4**).

Some Adults Desire Sexual Contact with Children

Few topics in the area of human sexuality arouse such strong feelings, or are the focus of so many news stories, as that of sexual contact between adults and children. We discussed this issue from the point of view of the children who experience such contacts in Chapter 13, where we described the harm that many such children suffer. Here we revisit the issue from the point of view of the adults: people (usually men) who are sexually attracted to children or youths below the legal age of consent, or who actually engage in sexual contact with them.

Pedophilia and Child Molestation Are Not Synonymous

The terms **pedophile** and **child molester** denote different but overlapping populations (Camilleri & Quinsey, 2008) (**Figure 15.6**). A pedophile is a person—usually a man—who has a persistent sexual attraction to prepubescent children. Usually he is less strongly attracted, or not attracted at all, to physically mature adults, but this is not part of the official definition of pedophilia. Some pedophiles molest children, but some do not—perhaps because they believe it is wrong, are afraid of the consequences, or can obtain sufficient sexual gratification from older partners or from fantasies.

A child molester (or sexual offender against children) is any adult who has had sexual contact with a prepubescent child—the actual age limit varies between jurisdictions. It is primarily a legal definition. Some child molesters are pedophiles; others molest children for a variety of other reasons, such as the lack of available older partners, the desire to hurt one of the child's parents (perhaps an ex-girlfriend of the perpetrator), alcohol or drug intoxication, or neurological damage. The majority of child molestation convictions are for nonpenetrative acts, such as touching a child's genitals or buttocks.

Some adults are primarily attracted to postpubertal teenagers—say, in the 13-to-17-year range. These adults do not fit the definition of pedophiles given above. The term **ephebophile** is sometimes used to designate this group. Since many people experience sexual attraction to some youths in this age bracket, the defining feature of ephebophiles is really their low sexual interest in adults. In lay discourse and in the media the distinction between pedophiles and ephebophiles is often blurred—any men who are attracted to, or have sex with, adolescents below the age of legal consent are commonly referred to as pedophiles or child molesters.

Pedophiles generally become aware of sexual attraction to children in early adolescence—at the same time that non-pedophilic men become aware of sexual attraction to women or to men. Thereafter, pedophilic attraction remains unchanged over the life span. In other words, pedophilia is experienced as an orientation, similar to the heterosexual or homosexual orientations of non-pedophiles (Seto, 2008).

Some child molesters have sexual interactions with their own children or stepchildren (**intrafamilial child molesters,** or **incest offenders**). Others have interactions with children outside their immediate families (**extrafamilial child molesters**). There are differences between these two types of molesters. Extrafamilial molesters are more likely to engage in penetrative sex with their victims, to injure their victims, to molest boys, to repeat their offenses, and to be exclusive pedophiles (as assessed by penile plethysmography), as compared with men who molest their own children (Rice & Harris, 2002; Blanchard et al., 2006). Nevertheless, even men who molest their own children usually show more sexual arousal to images of children than do men who have no history of such offenses.

Female pedophiles and child molesters are uncommon, but they do exist. Incarcerated female child molesters generally have severe psychiatric disturbances (Green & Kaplan, 1994), but the majority of women who have sexual contacts with prepubescent boys are probably never apprehended, because the affected boys tend not to view the contacts as abusive (McConaghy, 1998).

Cases in which female teachers enter into sexual relationships with male teenage students grab the headlines from time to time. In one much-publicized

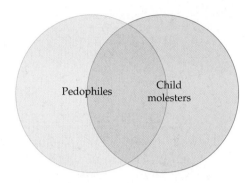

Figure 15.6 Pedophiles and child molesters are distinct but partially overlapping populations.

pedophile A person whose sexual feelings are directed mainly toward prepubescent children.

child molester An adult who has had sexual contact with a prepubescent child.

ephebophile A person whose sexual feelings are directed mainly toward postpubertal teenagers.

intrafamilial child molester A person who has had sexual contact with his own children or stepchildren. Also called incest offender.

extrafamilial child molester A person who has had sexual contact with children outside his immediate family.

case, a 34-year-old Seattle teacher, Mary Kay LeTourneau, who was married and the mother of four children, started an affair with a 13-year-old student, Vili Fualaau, and had two children by him. After LeTourneau served a seven-year prison sentence, she and Fualaau reunited, and in May 2005 they married. The Fualaaus earned a reported $750,000 from the sale of their wedding video to "Entertainment Tonight" (Kiyomura, 2005).

Attraction May Be to Girls, Boys, or Both

Most pedophiles have a preference for children of one sex. Heterosexual pedophiles predominate; they outnumber homosexual pedophiles by about 2:1 or 3:1 (Blanchard et al., 1999; Blanchard et al., 2000). (Because gay men are sometimes accused of being pedophiles, it's worth emphasizing the obvious: Homosexual pedophiles are not the same thing as regular gay men, any more than heterosexual pedophiles are the same thing as regular straight men.) Men who are attracted to younger children do not distinguish between males and females as sharply as do most adult men, to judge from their physiological responses to images of nude boys and girls (Freund et al., 1991). This finding makes some kind of sense, because prepubescent boys and girls resemble each other much more closely than adult men and women resemble each other.

There are differences between homosexual and heterosexual pedophiles (Langevin et al., 1978; Freund et al., 1987). Homosexual pedophiles who come to the attention of the law are more likely than heterosexual pedophiles to have had sexual contacts with multiple children. They are more likely to have had contacts with children who were strangers to them or only slightly acquainted with them. They are more likely to reoffend after conviction. Finally, homosexual pedophiles tend to be more emotionally disturbed and to have lower levels of intellectual function.

It Is Uncertain Whether Pedophiles Have Distinctive Personalities

Pedophilia generally begins early—at adolescence—and persists over the lifetime. As a pedophile becomes an adult, it becomes increasingly difficult for him to associate with children without arousing suspicion. He may engage in youth work, child care, or similar activities in order to do so. Of course, most people in these lines of work are not pedophiles.

What are pedophiles like as people? Early studies suggested that they are deficient in social skills, lack empathy, lack self-esteem or self-assertion, are lonely and psychologically distressed, experience cognitive distortions (such as the belief that children benefit from having sex with them), are emotionally disturbed, and have disordered thought processes akin to schizophrenia (Langevin et al., 1978). It has also been reported that pedophiles suffer from a variety of other paraphilias such as exhibitionism and voyeurism. Still, more recent research finds that pedophiles are rather unremarkable people, with few distinguishing characteristics except for a relatively low level of intellectual function (Quinsey & Lalumière, 2001; Cantor et al., 2004). Because studies of pedophiles are based almost entirely on men who have been arrested for child molestation, the characteristics of noncriminal pedophiles are unknown (Seto, 2008). In other words, the question of whether there is a typical "pedophile personality" remains unanswered.

Like other paraphilias, pedophilia is an exaggeration of a sexual interest that exists quite widely in the male population. You may be reluctant to believe that many "normal" men are sexually aroused by children, but this has been demonstrated by penile plethysmography. Arousal is generally greatest in response to older children and to children of the same sex as the adults whom the subject finds arousing (that is, to girls in heterosexual men and to boys in homosexual men) (Freund et al., 1989).

In a survey of 193 male college students, about 1 in 5 respondents stated that they were sexually attracted to some "small children" (Briere & Runtz, 1989) (**Table 15.1**). Interestingly, the students who acknowledged these interests differed from the other students in a number of respects. They reported more traumatic early sexual experiences, had more sex partners, used pornography more frequently, acknowledged a greater likelihood of raping a woman, and had attitudes supportive of sexual dominance over women. Of course, few, if any, of these students were likely to go on to molest children (or rape women) in real life. There was no suggestion that any of these men were more sexually interested in children than in adults. But the findings illustrate that the capacity for sexual arousal by children is not rare.

TABLE 15.1

Male Students' Sexual Interest in Children[a]

Type of interest	Percentage of students
Experienced sexual attraction to some small children	21
Had sexual fantasies involving children	9
Masturbated to fantasies involving children	5
Might have sex with a child if they could avoid detection	7

Source: Briere & Runtz, 1989.
[a]Surveyed anonymously.

NAMBLA Opposes Age-of-Consent Laws

Men who engage in sexual behavior with children or underage youths risk arrest and lengthy prison sentences. So do men who produce, sell, or buy pornographic or other representations of such behavior or pictures of minors that are deemed obscene. Thus the activities of pedophiles and ephebophiles are greatly restricted. However, they are at least theoretically entitled to freedom of thought and political expression. One organization that exercises these rights is the North American Man–Boy Love Association (NAMBLA), which was founded in Boston in 1978.

NAMBLA advocates the abolition of all age of consent laws. It argues that at least some boys are capable of giving meaningful consent to sex, that noncoercive man–boy sexual relationships are harmless and in fact potentially beneficial to the boy, and that other laws offer protection against genuinely abusive adult–child sexual relationships. It also points out that some other cultures have tolerated or even encouraged man–boy relationships and that some widely admired figures have been sexually attracted to boys or have been accused of engaging in sexual contact with them. NAMBLA paints age-of-consent laws as violating not just the rights of boy-loving men, but also those of man-loving boys. Its Web site carries numerous testimonials that are stated to have been written by such boys. NAMBLA does not advocate the legalization of coercive sex, nor does it recommend breaking the law. It does provide outreach to incarcerated sex offenders, however.

One can of course offer rebuttals to NAMBLA's arguments. It is questionable whether younger children at least could give consent in the full sense of the word. The issue of the effects on children of sexual contacts with adults is discussed in Chapter 13; while it does appear that older boys may be psychologically unharmed by willing relationships with adults (Green, 1992), such relationships may cause them to become prematurely sexually active, which introduces a variety of health and social risks. The positive testimonials presented by NAMBLA could be countered by negative ones, such as the allegations of long-lasting harm by some men who had childhood sexual contacts with Catholic priests (**Box 15.5**). There is also the question of parents' rights if a man engages in sex with their child without their consent. And the fact that other cultures have condoned man–boy sex does not in itself show that such behavior is morally acceptable for our own culture.

The age of legal consent varies significantly from jurisdiction to jurisdiction. In the United States it ranges from 16 to 18, depending on the state. Internationally, the age of legal consent is commonly 14, 15, or 16—Canada's age of consent

Society, Values, and the Law

BOX 15.5 Priests Who Molest Minors

In January 2002, a defrocked Roman Catholic priest, John Geoghan, was convicted by a Massachusetts court of sexually fondling a 10-year-old boy in a swimming pool and was sentenced to a 9-to-10-year prison term. In addition to that boy, more than 130 people accused Geoghan of molesting them while they were minors. The Archdiocese of Boston has paid several multimillion-dollar settlements to groups of Geoghan's victims.

The Geoghan case was nothing new. Another Massachusetts priest, James Porter, had been convicted in 1992 of abusing 28 children and was sentenced to 18-to-20 years of imprisonment, and similar cases have occurred around the country. What prompted a particular outcry in the Geoghan case, however, was the role of Geoghan's superiors. Reporters for the *Boston Globe* discovered that Cardinal Bernard Law (the Archbishop of Boston), as well as other church officials, had known that Geoghan was an incorrigible sex offender. Instead of dismissing him or turning him over to prosecutors, they shuffled him from parish to parish over a period of 30 years, thus giving him the opportunity to molest new and unsuspecting victims. Furthermore, another 80 priests in Boston alone had been accused of similar offenses and had also been protected by church officials. (Their names have since been given to prosecutors.) Besides moving abusive priests around, church officials used another strategy to keep the abuse quiet: In many cases, they paid large sums of money to victims on condition that the victims remain silent about their experiences.

The 2002 scandal spread like wildfire. In 2004, a committee of U.S. bishops reported that 4393 priests—4% of all clerics—had allegedly abused as many as 10,000 minors since 1950 (Lobdell & Stammer, 2004). Large legal settle-ments were reached between the Catholic Church and victims in many states. Just one diocese—that of Los Angeles, California—settled with about 500 victims for $600 million, and at least five dioceses have filed for bankruptcy protection on account of the financial burden imposed by their abuse cases (Flaccus, 2007).

To put these events in perspective, it's worth stressing three points:

1. The recent spate of allegations concerns events that happened over several decades; there is no evidence of a sudden recent increase in the prevalence of abuse of minors by priests.

2. Some allegations are likely to be false. Also, some people whose accusations are true may exaggerate the harm caused by the abuse in the hope of maximizing their monetary compensation. Others have suffered real and long-lasting harm, however, including loss of their religious faith.

3. Catholic priests are not the only people who may take advantage of positions of influence to sexually abuse minors. High school teachers, social workers, youth services providers, and non-Catholic clerics and rabbis are charged with sexual offenses against minors from time to time.

The victims of priestly abuse are of both sexes and range in age from prepubescent to adult, but there seems to be a preponderance of teenage males. As we discussed in Chapter 8, teens are sexually attractive to many adults, so many of the abusive priests could be gay men who preferentially target teens for practical reasons, such as accessibility and ease of control, not because they have an unusual proclivity for young partners. Some, however, may be ephebophiles. Only a

John Geoghan

minority of the abusive priests appear to have a preference for prepubescent children, so most do not fit the clinical definition of pedophiles, even though this term is commonly used in media accounts of the scandals.

Some observers connect the problem of abusive priests with the Roman Catholic Church's long-standing requirement for priests to be celibate. In an editorial in March 2002, for example, the *Pilot* (the newspaper of the Boston archdiocese) raised the question of whether there would be fewer incidents of abuse if celibacy were optional and women could become priests (Paulson, 2002).

John Geoghan was sentenced to a 9-to-10-year prison term, but in 2003 he was murdered in prison by a fellow inmate.

was raised from 14 to 16 in 2008.* Thus there does seem to be room for debate, even among those opposed to adult–child sex in general, about whether older minors are capable of giving meaningful consent to sexual activity with adults.

---

*The age of consent in a given jurisdiction may vary according to the relative ages of the partners, whether they are married, whether the older person is in a position of authority, what sexual acts are engaged in, and (in some countries) whether the sexual contact is heterosexual or homosexual. Wikipedia has up-to-date and detailed articles on the ages of consent in North America and elsewhere.

Sex Offenders Do Not Necessarily Repeat Their Offenses

Sex offenders, especially offenders against children, are widely perceived as incorrigible monsters who will inevitably repeat their offenses if given the chance. This perception has led to draconian measures against convicted sex offenders: very long prison sentences, denial of parole, detainment after the completion of sentences, and compulsory drug treatments (see below). Registration of sex offenders' addresses, and access by the public to this information, are mandated in all states. In some states the police are required to notify the public when a registered sex offender moves into a neighborhood. These requirements are known as "Megan's laws," named for Megan Kanka, a 7-year-old New Jersey girl who was raped and murdered by a known child molester in 1995. The molester had moved onto the Kankas' street without their knowledge.

Some sex offenders do indeed repeat their offenses—sometimes to an extraordinary degree. One 63-year-old man, arrested in San Jose, California, in 2005, had prior arrests or arrest warrants for child molestation in five other states as well as in Brazil. He was in possession of handwritten lists that allegedly contained the names of 36,000 children along with codes that, police suggested, indicated the manner in which he had molested them (Reed et al., 2005). In 2007 he was sentenced to life in prison.

On the other hand, sex offenders as a group are *less* likely to repeat their offenses than are people convicted of many other kinds of crimes. Overall, 68% of released prisoners are rearrested for a serious offense within 3 years, but only 43% of released sex offenders are rearrested for a serious offense, and only 5.3% for a sex crime (U.S. Department of Justice, 2004b). (Some offenders may repeat their offenses at a later date, of course, or reoffend without being apprehended.) The perception that sex offenders are unusually prone to reoffend (**recidivism**) is fostered by distorted media coverage, which focuses preferentially on sex-offense recidivists and often provides inaccurate information about them (Berlin & Malin, 1991).

Several factors can predict an increased likelihood of recidivism in these offenders (Hanson & Bussière, 1998). The best predictors are measures of antisocial tendencies (such as antisocial personality disorder or a general criminal history) as well as measures of atypical sexual interests (for example, child molesters who are pedophiles are more likely to reoffend than those who are not). Not surprisingly, a person who has already committed more than one offense or whose prior offense involved violence has an increased likelihood of offending again (Prentky et al., 1997; Firestone et al., 2000).

Given our knowledge of these factors, it may be possible to direct prevention strategies toward the subset of sex offenders who are particularly likely to reoffend and to allow the remainder to rejoin the community. The current practice of forcing sex offenders to move from city to city for years after they have completed their sentences (**Box 15.6**) neither prevents recidivism nor protects the public.

There Are Numerous Theories of Paraphilia

Understanding the cause or causes of paraphilias might help prevent them or lead to effective treatments. Yet theories to explain why people develop paraphilias are very diverse (Laws & O'Donohue, 2008). This may in part reflect the diversity of paraphilias themselves, ranging as they do from minority sexual interests such as fetishism—that only become paraphilic by virtue of the distress they may cause—to highly abnormal desires that may trigger grave sex crimes. What follows is a brief summary of the ideas that have been put forward regarding the development of paraphilias.

FAQ **What crimes result in registration as a sex offender?** Occasionally, people have ended up as registered sex offenders as a result of trivial offenses such as public urination, but the great majority of registered offenders have been convicted of serious crimes such as rape, sexual assault, and sexual offenses against children. National and state registries can be searched online: They list each offender's convictions.

recidivism The tendency of convicted offenders to reoffend.

Society, Values, and the Law

BOX 15.6 The "Geographic Cure"

Got a sex offender on your doorstep? How about forcing him out of your community and letting someone else deal with the problem? That's a common strategy for dealing with sex offenders in the United States.

In 2000, twice-convicted child molester Aramis Linares moved in with his sister's family in Monrovia, California. In accordance with state law, Linares notified the Monrovia Police Department of his address. The police, in turn, petitioned the state's Department of Justice to have Linares declared a "high-risk" sex offender. The state did so, and this designation allowed the police to notify the public. They handed out fliers and gave the local media details of Linares' crimes, his address, and his description. Public protests erupted immediately, and Linares eventually had to move out of Monrovia. But the Monrovia police went further: They gave him a one-way ticket to Reno, Nevada, and escorted him to the plane.

A more disturbing case was that of 43-year-old Nathaniel Bar-Jonah. After kidnapping two boys in his home state of Massachusetts, Bar-Jonah spent 12 years in a treatment center for sexually dangerous offenders. While in detention, he confessed to many bizarre sexual fantasies, including cannibalistic urges. In 1991, however, two psychologists testified that he was no longer a threat to society, and he was released. Within a month, he was arrested in the attempted kidnapping of another boy. Bar-Jonah avoided jail by agreeing to move to Montana—which he did. Montana authorities were not fully informed about Bar-Jonah's criminal history.

Within months of arriving in Great Falls, Bar-Jonah was charged with molesting an 8-year-old boy whom he was babysitting. Prosecutors dropped the charges after the boy's mother refused to let him testify. But in December 2000, Bar-Jonah was arrested and charged with the 1996 kidnapping and murder of 10-year-old Zachary Ramsay. Authorities claimed that Bar-Jonah had butchered the boy's remains and fed some of them to unsuspecting neighbors. This trial was postponed for years, but in

2003 Bar-Jonah was convicted of unrelated child-molestation charges and given a 130-year prison sentence. He died in prison (of natural causes) in 2008.

According to Connie Isaac, executive director of the Association for the Treatment of

Juan Carlos Martin was one of about 20 Miami-area sex offenders who were told to live under the Julia Tuttle Causeway after zoning restrictions barred them from residential areas.

Sexual Abusers, moving a convicted sex offender from state to state "has absolutely nothing to do with the treatment of the offender and has nothing to do with public safety. It's a good way for one jurisdiction to wash their hands of the problem and say 'It won't be my kid and I don't know anyone in Montana.'"

Another tactic used by many states and cities is to enact zoning restrictions that have the effect of excluding sex offenders from entire communities (see figure). A 2006 Georgia law, for example, banned the state's 15,000 registered sex offenders from living within 1000 feet of a school, school bus stop, church, child-care

facility, park, or skating rink. The collective effect of these restrictions was to effectively bar sex offenders from any habitable area. The Atlanta-based Southern Center for Human Rights (SCHR) described the 2006 law as an "election year stunt" and contested it in court. In 2007 the

Georgia Supreme Court overturned the law on the grounds that it amounted to unconstitutional seizure of property (Associated Press, 2007a). The legislature responded by passing a modified but equally restrictive law in 2008. Within minutes of the governor's signature it was challenged in federal court by SCHR and other advocacy groups (Southern Center for Human Rights, 2008). These groups claim that the law will drive offenders underground, disconnect them from social supports, and thus increase the likelihood of recidivism.

Sources: Dear & Sibley, 2000; Goldberg, 2001; Skornogoski, 2003; Associated Press, 2008a.

Biological Factors May Predispose to Paraphilia

To some extent, paraphilias run in families. In one study, 18.5% of paraphiliacs had first-degree relatives (parents, siblings, or children) who were also paraphiliacs, whereas only 3% of people with other psychiatric conditions had paraphiliacs in their families—a sixfold difference (Gaffney et al., 1984). This finding suggests that a tendency to develop a paraphilia could be inherited, though other explanations for the family clustering are possible.

A variety of biological abnormalities have been reported in paraphiliacs (Langevin & Watson, 1996). In one recent study, researchers performed MRI scans of the brains of 65 pedophilic sex offenders and 62 people guilty of offenses that were not sexual. They found deficiencies in the cerebral white matter (fiber connections) in the pedophiles—deficiencies that were not seen in the other offenders (Cantor et al., 2008). The researchers suggested that pedophilia results from a disconnection between brain regions that regulate sexual expression.

Previously normal men and women can develop abnormal sexual desires and behaviors after damage to certain specific brain regions, especially the temporal lobes of the cerebral cortex (Mendez et al., 2000). Diffuse damage to the cerebral cortex, such as occurs in Alzheimer's disease, can also lead to paraphilic behaviors, perhaps by removing the inhibitions that normally restrain such behavior.

Paraphilias May Result from Learning Processes

It has been suggested that paraphilias and other atypical forms of sexual expression develop by classical (Pavlovian) **conditioning** or some other learning process. According to this idea, an adolescent might, for example, happen to have a sexually gratifying experience while focusing on his girlfriend's shoes. The sexual pleasure experienced—especially that of orgasm—confers attractiveness on the previously neutral stimulus (the shoes). The person may continue to fantasize about shoes or use real shoes during subsequent bouts of masturbation. This practice may continually reinforce the erotic significance of shoes until they become an indispensable focus of sexual activity. (We re-emphasize that shoe fetishism is not a paraphilia if it does not cause distress.)

This idea could conceivably account for why most paraphiliacs are male. Male teenagers masturbate much more than females, so there is more opportunity for reinforcement of paraphilic ideation.

To test the conditioning theory, several research groups have attempted to generate paraphilia-like arousal patterns in a laboratory setting. In one study, for example, normal male volunteers were repeatedly shown images of a piggy bank in conjunction with erotically arousing images. After three weeks of exposure to these pairings the men developed penile arousal responses to the piggy bank alone (Plaud & Martini, 1999) (**Figure 15.7**). Conditioning experiments of this kind have generally yielded rather weak or inconsistent results, however. This could be because the subjects were adults, whose sexuality may be less malleable than that of young adolescents.

Some Paraphilias May Represent Disorders of Courtship

We have mentioned that several kinds of paraphilias seem like extensions of normal male sexuality. By that, we do not mean to imply that normal men stand on the brink of mental illness—they do not. Nor are we suggesting that paraphilias are actually healthful. Rather, paraphilias are abnormal and unhealthful in part because they represent elements of male sexuality that have been torn out of their normal psychological environment, isolated, and allowed free expression without the inhibitions that usually restrain them.

conditioning The modification of behavior by learning through association and/or reinforcement.

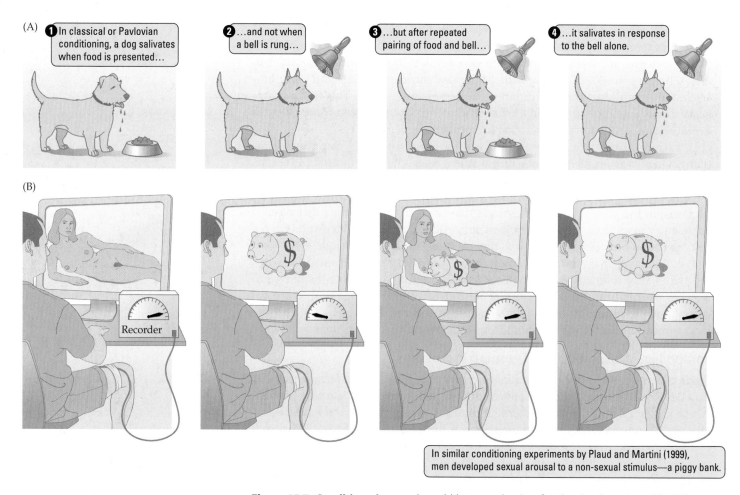

Figure 15.7 Conditioned arousal could be a mechanism for the development of fetishisms.

Kurt Freund and his colleagues developed this idea in terms of what they referred to as **courtship disorder** (Freund & Blanchard, 1986). The normal process by which a man acquires a sex partner consists of four stages: (1) location and evaluation of a potential sex partner, (2) initial nontactile interactions, such as smiling, displaying attractive features, and talking with the partner, (3) tactile interactions such as embracing and fondling, and (4) genital sex. Each of these stages has a paraphilic counterpart: (1) voyeurism, (2) exhibitionism and obscene telephone calling, (3) frotteurism, and (4) paraphilic rape.

Freund's perspective on paraphilias as courtship disorders may help explain why men with one paraphilia commonly have others. It is as if some higher organizing principle that normally ties the elements of male courtship together into a coherent, purposeful, and interactive sequence has been lost, leaving the individual elements in a state of psychic anarchy that allows them to be expressed in isolation. Because the elements of courtship are normally tied together into highly regulated sequences in all animals, it is possible that studying the cognitive and neural systems that organize courtship in nonhuman animals might offer insights into the causes and treatment of paraphilias (Freund & Seto, 1998).

Paraphilias May Represent a Sexual Escape Route

courtship disorder A paraphilia or cluster of paraphilias seen as a disorder of normal courtship behavior.

Another idea is that paraphilias are caused by the blockage of normal avenues of sexual expression. If a person can't explore typical sexual relations, he might turn to alternative, atypical ones.

What could cause such a blockage? As mentioned above, some (but not all) studies have reported that paraphiliacs are deficient in social skills and relate poorly to women. Such personality traits might hamper adolescents' attempts to establish normal sexual relationships and might therefore drive them into paraphilic behaviors. After all, most paraphilic behaviors require only rudimentary social skills (e.g., pedophilia, exhibitionism) or no social skills at all (e.g., paraphilic object fetishism, voyeurism, zoophilia, necrophilia).

It is doubtful that this idea could provide a complete explanation for the development of paraphilias, however, because plenty of socially inept men are not paraphiliacs, and some paraphiliacs have normal social skills. One must also keep in mind the possibility that the social ineptness and other negative psychological traits *result* from the paraphilia, rather than cause it. After all, it is difficult to relate gracefully to a woman if one is interested only in her underwear. Still, this kind of theory has some plausibility, and some treatment strategies are based on it (see below).

The Cycle of Abuse May Contribute to Paraphilias

There is a widespread belief that the experience of emotional, physical, or sexual abuse during childhood makes people more likely to engage in abusive behaviors themselves during their adult lives. This idea is called the **cycle of abuse** (Garland & Dougher, 1990).

Most victims of childhood abuse do not become abusers. In fact, their traumatic experiences may make them especially careful not to inflict similar harms on others. Nevertheless, abusers do often have a history of childhood victimization. It has been reported, for example, that child molesters are more likely to have been sexually molested during childhood than either people who committed offenses that were not sexual or sexual offenders whose offenses were against adults (Lee et al., 2002).

It is not known why abused children should become abusers. Perhaps taking on the role of abuser allows the affected individual to mask his childhood trauma (Stoller, 1975; Bentovim, 1993). Alternatively, the initial abuse might have had pleasurable features for the victim, such as sexual arousal or the receipt of gifts and attention from the abuser; these pleasurable features might foster a desire to engage in that same behavior (as abuser) in the future. Finally, the initial experience might simply "normalize" the behavior, eliminating the sense that it is something alien or taboo and therefore making it psychologically easier to practice that same behavior in later life. It is even possible that there is no causal connection between being abused and becoming an abuser: The correlation might result from some other unknown factor that raises the likelihood both of being abused during childhood and perpetrating abuse as an adult.

Paraphilias May Be Facilitated by Other Psychological Traits

It is possible that certain personality traits or disorders, though not paraphilic in themselves, make the development of paraphilias more likely. One such trait is **hypersexuality**—an excess of sexual desire that shows itself in compulsive masturbation and the devotion of a great deal of time to sexual fantasy, pornography use, and the pursuit of sex partners, to the detriment of other life goals. The cause of hypersexuality is not known, but many paraphilic men are hypersexual (Kafka, 2003, 2008), and their hypersexuality seems to be a powerful driving force behind their engagement in paraphilic behaviors.

Other conditions or traits that may promote the expression of paraphilic behaviors include **obsessive–compulsive disorder (OCD)**, attention deficit/hyperactivity disorder (ADHD), impulsivity, alcohol and drug dependency, mood disorders, and personality disorders (Laws & O'Donohue, 2008). We will have more to say about OCD and a related concept, sexual addiction, in the following chapter.

cycle of abuse The cycle in which some abused children grow up to repeat similar forms of abuse on others. Also called victim–perpetrator cycle.

hypersexuality Excessive sexual desire or behavior.

obsessive–compulsive disorder (OCD) A mental disorder marked by anxiety, repetitive thoughts or urges, and behaviors that temporarily relieve those urges.

Multiple Causal Factors May Interact

The proposed causes of paraphilia that we have just discussed are inadequate explanations when considered separately, because none of them has a very high likelihood of leading to the development of a paraphilia. Thus some researchers have put forward models that involve the interaction of multiple causal factors. In Chapter 7 we described one study that showed how childhood abuse, when combined with the possession of a certain gene, greatly increased the likelihood that a male would commit antisocial acts in adolescence or adulthood (Caspi et al., 2002). Do analogous interactions lie behind the development of paraphilias?

In one integrative model (Ward & Beech, 2008), three sets of factors converge to cause criminal paraphilic behavior. These are (1) biological factors (i.e., genetic predisposition and brain developmental factors), (2) ecological niche factors (i.e., the person's social, cultural, and personal circumstances), and (3) neuropsychological factors (i.e., motivation, memory, action selection, and so on). In the model, these factors maintain positive feedback loops, such that the offender's behavior has consequences in the outside world or in his own mind that reinforce the paraphilia. For example, an exhibitionist who exposes himself to a woman may experience a lessening of anxiety, which reinforces the behavior.

Of course, when presented with multiple competing theories of causation, it is easy to say "It's all of the above." Integrative models need to be tested as rigorously as single-factor models, but they are rarely specific enough to allow for such testing. A comprehensive and persuasive picture of how people come to develop and act on paraphilic desires remains a goal for the future.

Theories of Causation Have Suggested a Variety of Treatments

Most paraphiliacs do not seek treatment of their own accord. They may be pressured into doing so by spouses, or they may be referred to mental health professionals by the courts. For convicted sex offenders, attending some kind of risk-reduction program may be a condition of their sentencing or parole.

The fact that the paraphiliacs themselves are not usually the initiators of their treatment makes that treatment difficult, both practically and ethically. In a practical sense, the paraphiliac may lack the motivation that is a precondition for success in most forms of psychotherapy. Ethically, a therapist working with such a person must walk a fine line between serving the client (responding to his need for help) and serving the state (protecting society from harm) (Laws, 1999). Ideally, those two goals will be brought into alignment—that is, the therapist will help the client accept that treatment to reduce his paraphilic desires or behaviors is in his best interests. Even if he is not convinced that there is anything wrong with his paraphilic desires, the client may come to agree that progress in treatment will save his marriage, help him get out of prison, or save him from future legal problems. Of course, a client who is incarcerated may be highly motivated to feign a disappearance of his paraphilic interests. A child molester may learn to control his penile responses during plethysmographic testing, for example, so as to make it seem that he is no longer aroused by images of children. Some reports of treatment successes probably result from uncritical acceptance of such "cures."

When a sex offender is initially seen by a clinician, he will first undergo a process of assessment. The clinician will attempt to establish a trusting relationship and will seek to obtain a detailed history that provides information not only about the offenses that brought the person to the attention of the law, but about his whole range of sexual desires and behaviors, his childhood and adolescence, and the presence or absence of other psychological problems such as OCD. The offender's sexual interests will be tested by penile plethysmography or some other technique, and various questionnaire-type tests will probe for personality disorders or intellectual disabilities.

Treatment plans often involve the simultaneous application of several treatment modalities. Some of these modalities are based in the individual theories of causation discussed above.

Conditioning Is Intended to Change Sexual Desires

If paraphilias result from conditioning or other forms of learning, then it might be possible to treat them by driving the learning process in reverse or by fostering new learning processes that lead to more normal sexual desires or behaviors. The best-known of these techniques is **aversion therapy**. This technique employs appropriately timed aversive (unpleasant) experiences to turn something that was previously experienced as attractive into something unattractive or even repulsive. If a man is attracted to prepubescent boys, he is shown pictures of boys, or told to masturbate to fantasies of boys, but these pleasant experiences are accompanied or quickly followed by something unpleasant such as the smell of ammonia or disgusting images. Alternatively, the man is required to generate his own aversive stimuli by imagining some unpleasant sight such as vomit or feces (**covert sensitization**). The idea is that, after many repetitions of this procedure over weeks or months, the man will gradually lose his sexual interest in young boys as they become more and more strongly associated with the unpleasant experience. These various forms of treatment are sometimes referred to collectively as **behavior therapy**.

Psychotherapy Is Aimed at Preventing Repeat Offenses

Other forms of treatment are aimed not so much at actually changing a man's underlying sexual interests as at lessening the chances that he will reoffend. In **cognitive therapy** (which is often combined with the conditioning treatments just described) the aim is to correct the disordered thinking that the man uses to justify or rationalize his behaviors. For example, the man may believe that his behavior is sexually arousing to his victims or benefits them in some way. In that case,

therapy will be aimed at helping him realize that his behavior is harmful, rather than helpful, and will attempt to awaken some empathy toward his victims. In fact, empathy training is one of the most commonly used techniques in the treatment of sex offenders (Morin & Levenson, 2008).

Another approach seeks to remove blockages to normal sexual expression. The therapist will attempt to strengthen the man's social skills, self-esteem, assertiveness, and intimacy. The man may be encouraged to practice interactions with women, including such basic matters as how to behave on a date as well as how to deal with conflicts and jealousy.

In yet another approach, called **relapse prevention therapy**, the offender is trained in how to identify the situations that may trigger a repeat offense and how to avoid or cope with those situations. This may include mental tricks such as "thought stopping" that interrupt obsessive ideation, as well as very practical issues such as avoiding locations that offer temptations to offend. These programs also

Relapse prevention. Social worker Karen Swearingen leads a discussion in an education group for sex offenders at the Circleville Juvenile Detention Center in Ohio.

aversion therapy A form of behavior therapy that attempts to eliminate unwanted desires or behaviors by associating them with some unpleasant experience, such as a noxious smell.

covert sensitization A variation of aversion therapy in which the unpleasant experience is provided by the subject's own imagination.

behavior therapy Treatment of paraphilias or other disorders based on conditioning or other theories of behavioral psychology. Also called behavior modification.

cognitive therapy Therapy based on changing a person's beliefs and thought processes.

relapse prevention therapy Therapy aimed at training a person to avoid or cope with situations that trigger criminal behavior.

encourage the development of peer relationships that can give the offender a sense of purpose and acceptance.

These various forms of therapy are often conducted in small groups. Group therapy doesn't just save money: Peer interaction is an important therapeutic tool in itself (Levenson & Macgowan, 2004).

The Efficacy of Psychological Treatments Is Doubtful

Although some of these therapeutic strategies have been employed, alone or in combination, for many decades, there is surprisingly little evidence that they work, whether "working" is taken to mean curing paraphilias or merely stopping criminal recidivism. Certainly there are any number of case studies that report on the apparent benefits of the various approaches. But the more rigorous the investigation, the less benefit they demonstrate. Probably the most thorough study was the Sexual Offender Treatment and Evaluation Project (SOTEP), funded by the state of California (Marques et al., 2005). The study began in 1985. Sex offenders were randomly assigned to be treated with a state-of-the-art intervention program that focused on relapse prevention or to receive no treatment. Individual offenders were treated for many years, both during and after incarceration. Follow-ups continued until 2005. The outcome: Whether an offender participated in the program, dropped out of the program, or never took the program made no difference to the likelihood that he would reoffend! Other studies have failed to detect any improvement in treatment outcomes in studies conducted recently compared with those published decades ago, in spite of the many new treatment modalities that have been introduced in the intervening years (Camilleri & Quinsey, 2008). "We now have a 50-year history of such treatments," wrote two leading experts recently, "and it is entirely reasonable to ask: What have we got to show for it? The answer, sadly, is very little" (Laws & O'Donohue, 2008).

Drug Treatments Interact with Neurotransmitters or Hormones

Given the questionable success of psychological interventions, many researchers and clinicians have turned to drug treatments, either alone or, more commonly, in conjunction with psychological treatments (Bradford, 2001). One class of drugs that has been widely used is that of **selective serotonin reuptake inhibitors (SSRIs)** (Prozac-class antidepressants). These drugs affect the activity of two neurotransmitters, serotonin and dopamine, in the brain. For reasons that are not well understood, they tend to lower a person's interest in sex. Although this is a bothersome side effect when these drugs are given to treat depression, it is helpful in lowering the sex drive of paraphiliacs. In addition, these drugs tend to relieve obsessive-compulsive conditions, which, as mentioned above, often contribute to paraphilias. SSRIs are used in the treatment of the less-severe paraphilic offenders, such as exhibitionists. Although they are widely believed to be helpful, their efficacy has not yet been documented in controlled trials.

A more radical pharmaceutical approach is to interfere with testosterone, the principal hormonal driver of male sexuality (**Figure 15.8**). One drug use for this purpose is medroxyprogesterone acetate, or Depo-Provera. As described in Chapter 12, Depo-Provera is a synthetic, injectable progestin that is used as a long-term contraceptive in women. In men Depo-Provera depresses the secretion of GnRH by the hypothalamus, which results in a steep decline in testosterone secretion by the testes (see Chapter 5). The end result is a profound drop in plasma testosterone levels and a concomitant reduction in sexual desires and behaviors. Similar results can be obtained with leuprolide (Lupron), a drug we mentioned in

selective serotonin reuptake inhibitors (SSRIs) A class of drugs, including antidepressants such as Prozac, that depress sexual function.

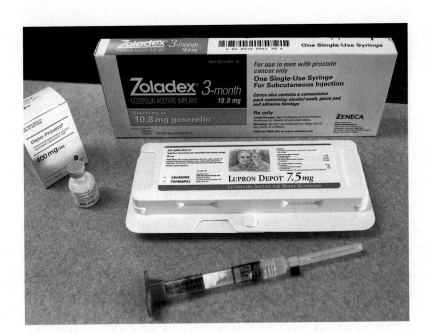

Figure 15.8 Drugs used to treat sex offenders include the injectable progestin Depo-Provera and the GnRH blockers Lupron and Zoladex.

Chapter 6 in connection with the treatment of precocious puberty. Yet another drug, cyproterone acetate, blocks testosterone receptors, thus making the body and brain insensitive to the hormone.

These drugs are far from ideal. They do not "cure" paraphilias in the sense of redirecting the person's sexual desire into normal channels; they simply decrease desire and arousal generally. That effect has been well documented in controlled trials conducted in paraphilic men (Bradford & Pawlak, 1993). There have not been any such trials to test the effects of these drugs on recidivism, however.

Some states have mandated Depo-Provera treatment for convicted or recidivist sex offenders. These laws raise ethical and practical problems and are sometimes counterproductive because they restrict treatment options (Stone et al., 2000).

Castration Is a Treatment of Last Resort

Surgical castration (removal of the testicles) removes a man's main source of androgens. The surgery is followed by a rapid drop in circulating androgen levels and a slower, somewhat variable decline in sexual desires and behaviors, including physiological responses such as erection and ejaculation (Zverina et al., 1990). Castration may be more effective than other treatments for the prevention of sexual recidivism (Meyer & Cole, 1997) . According to one review of studies of castrated sex offenders—most of whom had committed multiple and/or violent offenses prior to surgery and were therefore at a very high risk for reoffending—only 1% to 7% did in fact reoffend (Prentky et al., 1997).

The Association for the Treatment of Sexual Abusers (ATSA), which represents the therapists who treat sex offenders, is opposed to castration. The ATSA argues that castration is not necessarily effective because some castrated men retain sexual desires and behaviors. They also point out that castrated men can obtain testosterone illegally, thus reawakening their sexual desires (Association for the Treatment of Sexual Offenders, 1997). Even so, some states, such as Texas and California, have begun to reintroduce the operation on a voluntary basis, and this has led to the release of a few offenders who otherwise would likely have spent the rest of their lives behind bars.

Summary

1. Most variations in sexual desire and behavior are not mental disorders but represent minority interests or a means of adding excitement to sexual relationships.

2. Fetishism is sexual arousal by objects, materials, or body parts. Transvestic fetishists are sexually aroused by cross-dressing, but not all cross-dressers are fetishists—others may cross-dress for practical reasons, for entertainment purposes, or as an expression of a transgendered identity.

3. Bondage/dominance and sadomasochism (collectively known as BDSM) involves sexual arousal by the infliction or receipt of humiliation, degradation, or physical pain. BDSM practices generally take place in safe, consensual settings.

4. The boundary between normal and abnormal sexuality is imprecise and subjective and is defined socially as well as medically. According to the American Psychological Association (APA), paraphilias are sexual feelings or behaviors that are targeted at nonhuman objects or nonconsenting people, or that involve suffering or humiliation, and that cause significant distress or social dysfunction. Paraphilic behaviors directed at nonconsenting people are illegal.

5. In general, paraphilias are extensions or exaggerations of normal sexual feelings or behaviors. Far more men than women have paraphilias. It is common for a person to develop multiple paraphilias over time. Paraphiliacs who commit sex offenses often have deficient social skills, psychological problems, and some have suffered child abuse.

6. Exhibitionists are sexually aroused by exposing their genitals to others (usually women) in public places. Making obscene phone calls is a variation on exhibitionism. Voyeurs spy on women who are undressed or engaged in sex. Frotteurs make body contact with women in crowds. Autoerotic asphyxia is often combined with BDSM elements; it is a highly dangerous practice.

7. Although rape is not generally considered a paraphilia, the commission of violent sexual acts because the perpetrator experiences the violence itself as sexually arousing is paraphilic. Paraphilic sadism has motivated many notorious serial killers.

8. Pedophiles are sexually attracted to prepubescent children more than to adults. Pedophiles and child molesters are overlapping but nonidentical groups. Most pedophiles are attracted to children of one sex more than the other. Ephebophiles are attracted to postpubertal teenagers.

9. Sex offenders repeat their offenses (recidivism) less often than many other kinds of offenders. Certain factors, such as mental retardation, alcohol use, and a history of violence or sexual contact with unrelated children are associated with an increased likelihood of recidivism.

10. A variety of theories attempt to explain paraphilias. Some see them as the result of distorted learning processes or as the result of a blockage of normal sexual expression. Some categorize paraphilias as forms of obsessive–compulsive disorder. Other theories point to the victim–perpetrator cycle as a possible cause of sexual offenses, especially against children. Some biological theories attribute paraphilias to neurological, endocrinological, or genetic disturbance.

11. The various theories of paraphilia have led to diverse forms of treatment. Behavioral approaches, such as aversion therapy, attempt to help paraphiliacs unlearn their paraphilias and relearn normal sexual desires.

12. Psychotherapeutic approaches include cognitive therapy, which attempts to correct the paraphiliac's thinking; social skills training programs, which encourage normal communication with women; and relapse prevention programs, which help sex offenders identify and avoid situations in which they are likely to reoffend. In controlled trials, the behavioral and psychotherapeutic approaches have not been shown to reduce the likelihood that a paraphilic sex offender will reoffend.

13. Biological approaches include the use of drugs that reduce testosterone levels or block testosterone's effects, as well as selective serotonin reuptake inhibitors. The drugs appear to be quite effective but can have serious side effects. Castration is an effective but highly controversial method of preventing recidivism by men who commit repeated, serious sex crimes.

Discussion Questions

1. Do you think society should place any legal restrictions on the expression of noncoercive sex practices (e.g., those undertaken as a solo activity or with a consenting partner)? Give a rationale for your point of view.

2. People with paraphilias often find it very difficult to give them up. Compare the advantages and disadvantages of various treatments (e.g., psychotherapy, behavior therapy, drug therapy).

3. Entertainers who are strippers, burlesque dancers, or peep show dancers certainly exhibit themselves. Are they exhibitionists?

4. If you were confronted by an exhibitionist who exposed himself, what would you do? Why?

5. A pedophile who has been arrested for molesting a child argues that he has a sexual compulsion that he cannot resist. Do you think treatment should be legally mandated? Which treatments do you think would be best for him, and why?

6. Recently the Catholic Church has faced a major controversy over reports that priests have had sexual contacts with minors. In several cases, the priests received counseling and were moved to another parish, where they repeated their behavior. Take a position about what an institution (e.g., religious or educational) should do about reports of child molestation. Should the institution handle the accusation itself, or should it turn the matter over to the police? If the reports of molestation are accurate, how should the perpetrators be treated? What should be done to prevent further incidents?

7. Imagine that you're a therapist who is counseling a couple. The woman has caught the man cross-dressing. What questions would you ask him to find out what's really going on and whether he has a paraphilia? How would you advise the couple?

8. How would you respond if you learned that a sex offender had moved into your neighborhood? How can public safety be balanced against the right of someone who has "served his time" to get on with his life? Are there better strategies than the "geographic cure"?

Web Resources

American Professional Society on the Abuse of Children www.apsac.org

Association for the Treatment of Sexual Abusers www.atsa.com

Tri-Ess (organization for heterosexual cross-dressers) www.tri-ess.org

United States Department of Justice: Dru Sjodin National Sex Offender Public Web site www.nsopr.gov/

Recommended Reading

De Sade, Marquis (republished 1966). *The 120 days of Sodom, and other writings.* (Translated by Richard Seaver and Austryn Wainhouse). Grove Press.

Dekkers, M. (1994). *Dearest pet: On bestiality.* W.W. Norton.

Gates, Katharine (2000). *Deviant desires: Incredibly strange sex.* Juno Books.

Henkin, W. A., and Holiday, S. (1996). *Consensual sadomasochism: How to talk about it and how to do it safely.* Daedalus.

Laws, D. R., and O'Donohue, W. T. (Eds.) (2008). *Sexual deviance: Theory, assessment, and treatment* (2nd. ed.). Guilford Press.

Sacher-Masoch, L. v. (republished 2000). *Venus in Furs.* Viking Penguin. Full text available online at http://www.gutenberg.net/etext04/vnsfr10.txt.

Weinberg, T. S. (Ed.) (1995). *S and M: Studies in dominance and submission.* Prometheus Books.

CHAPTER 16

Smoking greatly increases the risk of erectile dysfunction in men, as shown pointedly in this antismoking poster.

Sexual Disorders

We turn now from unusual forms of sexual expression to more common problems that can interfere with even the most conventional of sex lives. A number of physiological and psychological conditions can impair sexual interest or arousal or make sexual interactions painful or unrewarding. Most of these conditions are deficiencies, such as a lack of interest in sex or a difficulty with erection, lubrication, or orgasm. Some, however, represent overexcitable states, such as premature ejaculation and excessive sexual behavior. Either way, these disorders are common. For the most part, they are more readily treatable than the paraphilias discussed in the previous chapter. The major factor impeding their successful treatment is people's reluctance to discuss sexual problems openly with their partners or to seek appropriate professional advice and therapy.

The Prevalence of Sexual Disorders Is Controversial

Large numbers of women and men have problems with some aspect of sexual function. The most widely cited survey data on this topic come from the National Health and Social Life Survey (NHSLS), although unfortunately, that survey covers only women and men aged 18 to 59 (Laumann et al., 1994; Laumann et al., 2000). The survey asked about seven kinds of sexual disorders or dysfunctions (these two terms have similar meanings): lack of interest in sex, lack of pleasure in sex, pain during sex, problems with erection or lubrication, inability to reach orgasm, climaxing too early, and anxiety about sexual performance. The percentages of the participants who acknowledged suffering from these problems (for a period of at least several months during the previous 12 months) ranged from a low of 3% (men who experienced pain during sex) to a high of 33% (women who lacked interest in sex). Forty-three percent of the women and 31% of the men reported having experienced at least one of these problems during the previous 12 months.

Some experts believe that the NHSLS conveyed an exaggerated impression of the prevalence of sexual disorders because the survey did not ask whether the interviewees experienced *distress* or whether their lives or relationships were *impaired* as a result of their condition. As with the atypical modes of sexual expression discussed in the previous chapter, it is questionable whether a condition should be labeled a sexual disorder if it is not experienced as such by the person who has it. Surveys that have taken the personal impact of a condition into

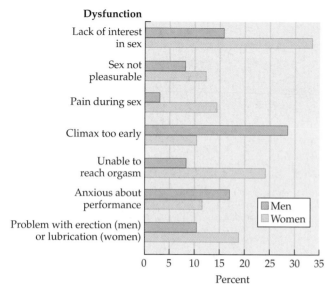

Figure 16.1 Sex differences in the prevalence of sexual dysfunctions These bar graphs refer only to ages 18–59, the ages that were surveyed. (Data from NHSLS.)

sex therapist A person who treats sexual disorders, usually by means of psychotherapy and sexual exercises.

account have come up with lower estimates of the prevalence of sexual disorders—perhaps about half the rates reported by NHSLS (Simons & Carey, 2001; Bancroft et al., 2003b).

Men and Women's Sexual Problems Differ

One aspect of the NHSLS findings that is widely accepted is that men and women tend to experience different kinds of sexual problems. In the NHSLS data (**Figure 16.1**) the leading problems for women were a lack of interest in sex, an inability to experience orgasm, problems with physiological arousal (especially vaginal lubrication), and pain during sex. For men, climaxing too early (premature ejaculation) was the leading problem, followed by anxiety about performance and a lack of interest in sex. Studies of people who seek professional help for sexual problems echo this kind of distinction (**Figure 16.2**). This is how Sandra Leiblum, a leading authority on sex therapy, has summarized the distinction: "Men are typically motivated to seek treatment for *problems with sexual performance.…* In contrast, women often enter treatment expressing *concerns about sexual feelings…*" (Leiblum, 2007b).

We should emphasize right away, though, that these stereotypical differences mask a lot of overlap and commonality between the problems encountered by the two sexes. There are performance issues that are quite common among women, such as difficulty experiencing orgasm, and some men are troubled by a lack of interest in sex, especially as they age.

In this chapter we first describe problems related to sexual performance. We deal with men's and women's performance problems separately because symptoms and treatments for such problems usually differ between the sexes. Later we cover issues of excessive or diminished interest in sex; in this section we cover both sexes together because the problems and their treatments are fairly similar between the sexes.

Whether we are talking about performance or feelings, however, sexual problems affect *relationships*. Although just one person may seek professional advice, that person's partner often needs to be drawn into the effort to understand the roots of the problem and to develop and execute a successful treatment plan.

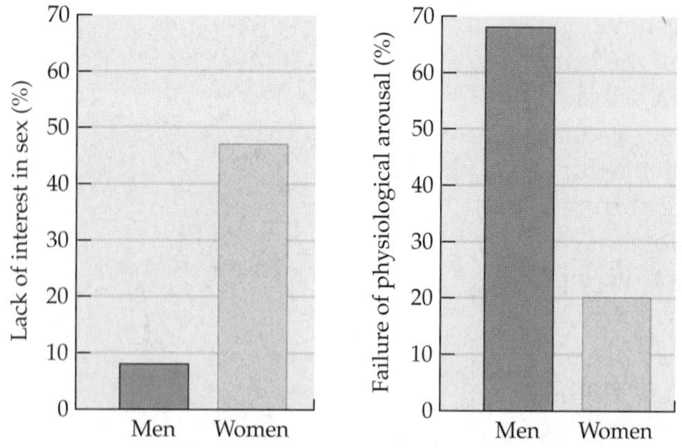

A Multidisciplinary Approach to Treatment Is Preferred

A person suffering from a sexual disorder may visit a family doctor, a psychotherapist, or some other nonspecialist provider. Sometimes these professionals resolve the problem satisfactorily: For example, a family doctor might write a prescription for Viagra that successfully treats a man's erectile dysfunction, or a therapist might help a person work through relationship difficulties that are interfering with sexual pleasure.

Commonly, though, sexual problems are complex and multifactorial. In this case the person or couple who has the problem may benefit from the combined insights of a group of experts—experts who focus on sexual disorders from different perspectives. Among these experts might be a clinical psychologist or psychotherapist who specializes in sexual problems (often called a **sex therapist**), a physician who treats genital or hormonal disorders, and a physiotherapist who can give instruction on Kegel exercises and other methods of improving genital function. When several such experts work together in a sexual-disorders clinic (which may be

Figure 16.2 Sex differences in a clinical population The bar graphs show the percentages of 533 men and 577 women attending a sexual problems clinic who complained of lack of interest/enjoyment in sex and failure of physiological arousal. (Data from Warner & Bancroft, 1987.)

a freestanding private practice or a department in a hospital or medical school) they are in the best position to identify useful lines of therapy and to avoid costly and time-consuming mistakes.

While many different kinds of treatments may be offered to persons with sexual disorders, as described in various sections of this chapter, sex therapists commonly use a core of therapeutic techniques to treat a variety of disorders. Examples of these are given in **Box 16.1**.

Sexual disorders can be primary, secondary, or situational. A **primary disorder** is lifelong. A **secondary disorder** is one that appears after some period of normal function. A **situational disorder** is one that appears in some circumstances but not in others.

Sex therapists may recommend a combination of psychotherapy, sexual exercises, and drugs to alleviate sexual problems. Success is most likely when both partners participate in therapy.

Erectile Dysfunction Has Many Causes and Treatments

Erectile dysfunction (once called impotence) is a recurrent inability to achieve an adequate penile erection or to maintain it through the course of the desired sexual behavior—if such inability causes distress to the man or difficulty between the man and his partner. The condition may be partial or complete, and it may be a primary, secondary, or situational disorder. Although erectile dysfunction can certainly occur in young men, it becomes much commoner as men age. In fact, it affects about one half of all men over the age of 60 and the majority of men who are 70 or older. Nevertheless, younger men are more likely to be severely distressed by erectile dysfunction and are more likely to seek treatment.

primary disorder A disorder that is not preceded by any period of healthy function.

secondary disorder A disorder that follows some period of healthy function.

situational disorder A disorder that appears only in certain circumstances.

erectile dysfunction A persistent inability to achieve or maintain an erection sufficient to accomplish a desired sexual behavior such as coitus to orgasm.

Erectile Dysfunction Can Have Physical or Psychological Causes

A great variety of factors can cause or contribute to erectile dysfunction, ranging from entirely physical factors to entirely psychological ones. Here are some of the chief villains:

- *Behavioral/lifestyle factors* include smoking (which doubles the risk of erectile dysfunction), chronic alcohol abuse, obesity, and lack of exercise.
- *Medical conditions* include diabetes, hypertension, atherosclerosis ("hardening of the arteries"), and prostate surgery.
- *Drugs* include certain tranquilizers, diuretics, and antidepressants, among others.
- *Injuries* include spinal cord injury, injury to the nerves and blood vessels that supply the penis, and injury to the penis itself.
- *Psychological factors* include performance anxiety, distraction, inadequate stimulation, relationship difficulties, stress, and depression. (See Web Topic 16.1.)
- *Developmental issues* include childhood trauma, sexual orientation issues, and religious taboos.

Smoking, alcohol use, and obesity all increase the risk of erectile dysfunction.

Sexual Health

BOX 16.1 Techniques of Sex Therapy

Sex therapists are psychotherapists who have special training in the treatment of sexual disorders. They may have certification from the American Association of Sex Educators, Counselors, and Therapists or the American Board of Sexology (see Web Resources at the end of this chapter), but the profession is largely unregulated. They may work alone or in collaboration with other specialists.

As with psychotherapists in general, sex therapists take a client's (or couple's) history, assess the problem, and offer treatment. The treatment may involve drugs (which will have to be prescribed by a physician) and talk (such as efforts to help the client correct false beliefs, reduce anxiety, or resolve relationship difficulties). In addition, however, the therapist may recommend that their clients practice certain exercises intended to relieve a variety of sexual problems. Here we describe two kinds of exercises that have rather general application. Other exercises that are designed to treat specific disorders are described in the text.

Sensate focus (also called non-demand pleasuring) is a set of touching exercises that is intended to be practiced by couples who want to build closer intimacy (see figure). The partners, who are usually nude, take turns (perhaps 10 to 15 minutes before switching) at touching (the "giver") or being touched (the "receiver"). Initially, touching is restricted to general body surfaces, with no touching of genitals or breasts. There may be a progression to include erogenous zones in later sessions, but there is no coitus. Anxiety is reduced because the experience is less of a "performance" than regular sex. The receiver is encouraged to concentrate simply on the pleasure of the sensation and to let go of any obligation to reciprocate (see figure). The only communication that the receiver should provide is to let their partner know if the touching becomes uncomfortable. This can be a valuable exercise for people who have difficulty deriving pleasure from sex because they are too wrapped up in making sure that their partner is being satisfied. The giver is also learning to enjoy sex in a novel way—namely, through the tactile experience of giving pleasure to a partner, without any direct stimulation of their own

erogenous zones. In fact, the giver's fingers may become erogenous zones in themselves. The tactile stimulation received in this way may not

In sensate-focus exercises, one partner is pleasured by the other but lets go of any responsibility to reciprocate.

lead to physiological arousal, but the very fact that it doesn't may be a good thing. It may allow the giver, like the receiver, to experience sexual pleasure entirely free from the need to perform physiologically.

Unlike sensate focus, **Kegel exercises** are designed to be performed alone, and their goal is to make sex more pleasurable by improving genital and orgasmic function. Kegel exercises were originally developed for the treatment of urinary incontinence (leakage). Because incontinence is more common in women than in men, Kegels are often thought of as being "for women," but actually they can benefit both sexes. The aim is to strengthen the muscles of the pelvic floor. The first step is to identify the muscles that need to be exercised. The usual recommendation is for the person to sit on the toilet with knees apart, to begin to urinate, and then to voluntarily interrupt the flow of urine. The muscles that accomplish this are the ones

that need to be contracted during the exercises. An alternative technique, if the client is female, is for her to insert a finger, a dildo, or a special purpose Kegel exerciser into the vagina and squeeze down on it. Once the person has learned how to contract the pelvic floor muscles, they should begin a regular program of exercises. At the beginning it may be difficult to hold a contraction for more than a second or so. But with practice it will be possible to hold the contractions for longer periods of time. One recommended regimen to aim for is a set of ten 3-second contractions, three times a day. Kegel exercises are said to improve sexual arousal and provide stronger, more pleasurable orgasms. They may be combined with self-generated sexual fantasy. One controlled study found that Kegel exercises enhanced sexual arousal after 1 week (Messe & Geer, 1985).

sensate focus A form of sex therapy that involves graduated touching exercises.

Kegel exercises Exercises to strengthen pelvic floor muscles, with the aim of improving sexual function or alleviating urinary leakage.

Older men are less likely than younger men to achieve erections by purely psychogenic means, such as by anticipation of a sexual encounter or viewing a naked partner; they are more likely to require direct physical stimulation of the penis.

Often, erectile dysfunction results from an interplay of physical and psychological factors, which reinforce each other and need to be disentangled (Goldstein, 2000; Rosen, 2007).

Ideally, erectile dysfunction should be evaluated by both a urologist and a mental-health specialist (psychiatrist, psychotherapist, or sex therapist) to identify the cause of the dysfunction and to initiate a course of treatment. The urologist will focus on possible biological problems and will ask questions such as: Does the patient ever have erections on waking in the morning? (Most men have such erections, at least on occasion; if the patient never does, there may be a biological cause for the dysfunction.) The urologist can also conduct tests that directly evaluate the erectile capacity of the penis and can evaluate the patient for the variety of medical conditions and drug treatments that can cause erectile dysfunction. The mental health specialist will ask detailed questions about the patient's sexual functioning and how long the problem has lasted and will try to discover whether relationship difficulties or stressful events are contributing to the problem.

Simple Measures May Alleviate the Problem

Sometimes the cause of the problem can be removed rather simply. If the problem is caused by a prescription drug, for example, it may be possible to substitute another drug that does not have the same effect. Lifestyle changes such as quitting smoking, reducing alcohol consumption, losing weight (if the patient is obese), and beginning an exercise program may alleviate erectile difficulties. If the man can develop an erection but loses it during sex, he may be able to maintain the erection for a longer period simply by placing a constricting elastic band ("cock-ring") around the penis after the erection has developed. (Such a device should be taken off as soon as it has served its purpose, to avoid damaging the erectile tissue.)

Viagra and Similar Drugs Have Become the Leading Treatments

If these simple measures fail or are not applicable, further intervention is required. Ideally, perhaps, the man would undergo careful study to tease out the web of causes that lie behind his condition. In the real world, it is more likely that he will receive a prescription for one of the three Viagra-class drugs that have been approved for treatment of erectile dysfunction: sildenafil (Viagra), vardenafil (Levitra), or tadalafil (Cialis). It is simpler and quicker for a primary-care physician to give the patient a drug prescription and see whether it works rather than to send him off for lengthy medical and psychological investigations that might yield inconclusive results. Whether this is the right or wrong philosophy, the fact is that 25 to 30 million men take these drugs worldwide (Rosen, 2007). Their efficacy in improving the quality of life of men with erectile dysfunction has been well documented in placebo-controlled trials (Ralph et al., 2007), and the men's partners also experience much more satisfying sex lives as a result (Fisher et al., 2005).

Viagra-class drugs work by increasing the responsiveness of the erectile tissue to nitric oxide, the neurotransmitter that is chiefly responsible for penile erection. At the usual doses, these drugs do not cause erection unless some nitric oxide is being released by nerve terminals in the penis. What this means is that simply swallowing a sildenafil tablet does not produce an erection—there has to be sexual excitation as well. And if the nerves are not active—if they have been destroyed in the course of prostate surgery, for example—then sildenafil is unlikely to work, no matter how sexually excited the man may feel.

Regular exercise is one of the best ways to lower the risk of male erectile dysfunction.

Advertising for Viagra, Levitra, and Cialis links the drugs with relatively young, healthy men.

Sildenafil and the other drugs must not be taken in conjunction with certain other substances, most especially nitrite-containing recreational drugs (inhaled recreational drugs with names such as "amyl," "rush," or "poppers"). The reason for this is that combining these drugs can cause a life-threatening drop in blood pressure. Nor should they be taken by people who have the eye disease retinitis pigmentosa. The drugs can cause a variety of undesirable side effects, such as headache, facial flushing, or visual disturbances. Tadalafil is longer-acting than the other two drugs—it works for up to 36 hours. This appeals to many men because it allows for greater spontaneity in sexual activities (Dean et al., 2006). The long course of action may also prolong the side effects or adverse drug interactions, however.

Do these drugs do anything for men who *don't* have erectile dysfunction? Most medical authorities say that they do not improve the sexual performance of healthy men, but the porn industry says otherwise (**Box 16.2**). In the view of some critics, Viagra and its look-alikes are being deliberately marketed to healthy men. "The advertising and promotion have become disengaged from any notion of a medical condition or a disease," says feminist psychologist Leonore Tiefer. "Now you take these drugs because you're less perfect than you want to be. It's like teeth whitener" (Tuller, 2004). Whether you have erectile difficulties or not, we advise against taking these drugs without an appropriate medical consultation and prescription.

Locally Applied Drugs Require Only That the Erectile Tissue Be Functional

Some men are not helped by Viagra-class drugs, even if their erectile dysfunction has a clear biological cause. This includes men whose penile nerves have been destroyed by prostate surgery, as mentioned above. Achieving an erection is not impossible in such situations, however. The drug **prostaglandin E₁ (alprostadil)** produces a very reliable erection in any circumstances, so long as the erectile tissue itself is still intact. The man does not even have to be sexually aroused. Unfortunately, this drug has to be delivered by self-injection into the corpora cavernosa (**Figure 16.3**). For that reason, and also because it is a very expensive form of treat-

prostaglandin E₁ (alprostadil) A hormone that is injected into the penis to produce an erection.

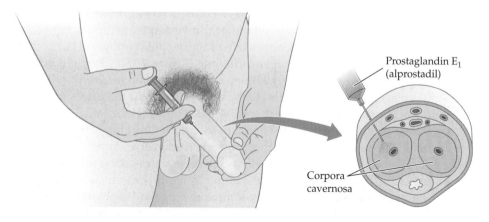

Figure 16.3 Prostaglandin E₁ (alprostadil) produces an erection when injected directly into the corpora cavernosa.

Society, Values, and the Law

BOX 16.2 Better Porn through Chemistry

Pudgy, hairy, and none too good-looking, Ron Jeremy starred in 1900 pornographic movies over a 25-year career. His secret: being able to get an erection on command and to perform in front of the cameras once, twice, maybe even three times per day. Thanks to some mysterious physiological endowment that differentiated him from regular mortals, Jeremy was Mr. Reliable Provider in the world of heterosexual pornographic movies, an industry that is based in Los Angeles's San Fernando Valley. And that's important, because unlike the feature films that are produced a few miles away in Hollywood, porno movies are made on a tight budget ($10,000 to $20,000) and an even tighter schedule (usually 3 days' shooting). A single failure to perform may cost a day's delay and spell the difference between profit and loss.

Beginning around the year 2000, though, Jeremy began seeing more competition, thanks to a little blue pill called Viagra. The competition came from "pretty boys"—actors who may have been easier on the eye than Jeremy but who, until 1999, couldn't hold a candle to him in the performance department. Now they could.

Cheyne Collins, 34, is one of the new breed. "Back then, you could only do one, maybe two scenes a day," he told the *Los Angeles Times* in 2001. "Now we're doing five." Collins admits to using Viagra at least some of the time, especially if he's not in the mood "or I'm tired or sick that day." And the production staff love it. "I put Viagra right up there with the polio vaccine, as far as making my job easier," said director

Michael McCormick of Metro Productions. Typically, directors give their male actors a 30-minutes warning before their curtain call so that they can take their pill and be ready for action when the cameras start rolling.

Viagra is widely used as a recreational drug. Porno actors, like anyone else, can readily obtain the pill by answering a few questions on the Internet. The manufacturer, Pfizer, emphasizes that Viagra is for men with erectile dysfunction only and that the maximum dosage is one pill per day. Still, Pfizer's advertising suggests otherwise. Initially, the commercials featured old men with bona fide erectile dysfunc-

tion, such as prostate cancer survivor and former U.S. Senator Bob Dole. More recently, the ads have featured much younger and more virile-looking men—the kind of men who are less likely to have erectile dysfunction.

Within the porno industry, Viagra has so opened up the field to competition that the established actors are having a difficult time holding onto their turf. Hundreds of men now compete for jobs that previously were assigned to a few trusty stalwarts, and that's causing hard feelings. "No *real* star uses Viagra," claims Ron Jeremy.

Source: Huffstutter & Frammolino, 2001.

---

ment, about half the men who try the technique give it up (Sexton et al., 1998). Another form of the drug is administered by means of a soft pellet that is pushed into the urethra, but this has its own drawbacks: It can cause an aching pain in the penis, as well as low blood pressure, and it could trigger a miscarriage if the man has unprotected sex with a pregnant woman.

Erectile Dysfunction Can Be Treated with Devices and Implants

There are also nondrug methods to help men with erectile dysfunction. One such method is a **vacuum constriction system** (**Figure 16.4**), versions of which are made by several manufacturers. The man lubricates his penis, places a clear plastic cylinder over it, and then draws a partial vacuum inside the tube with the aid of a pump powered by hand or by a battery. The vacuum draws blood into the erectile

vacuum constriction system A device for treating erectile dysfunction that creates a partial vacuum around the penis, thus drawing blood into the erectile tissue.

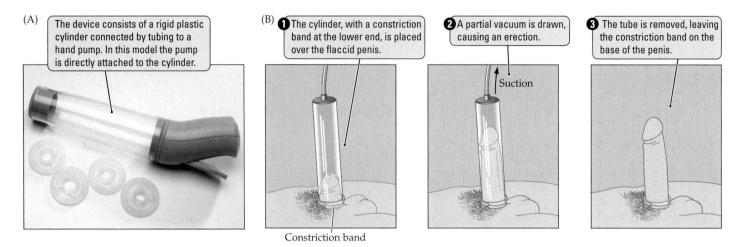

(A) The device consists of a rigid plastic cylinder connected by tubing to a hand pump. In this model the pump is directly attached to the cylinder.

(B) ❶ The cylinder, with a constriction band at the lower end, is placed over the flaccid penis.

❷ A partial vacuum is drawn, causing an erection.

Suction

❸ The tube is removed, leaving the constriction band on the base of the penis.

Constriction band

Figure 16.4 Vacuum constriction systems produce an erection by drawing blood into the penis.

tissue. Once an erection has been attained, the man slips a constriction band around the base of the penis to maintain the erection after the cylinder is removed.

The major disadvantage of vacuum systems is that using them interrupts lovemaking in a major way. This almost precludes their use by a man who is engaged in casual dating, but an established couple that takes a lighthearted approach to sex may be able to work the vacuum system into their lovemaking routine. The constriction band often interferes with ejaculation. Another disadvantage is that overenthusiastic pumping can pull blood right out of the vessels into the tissue spaces. The resulting bruises can take a week or more to heal. (FDA-approved systems have pop-off valves that limit the depth of vacuum that can be attained.)

The advantages of vacuum systems are that they are safe (if properly used), effective, and among the least expensive forms of treatment. Also, they do not require that the innervation of the penis be intact. Only about one-third of men who try vacuum systems continue to use them for long periods, however (Dutta & Eid, 1999).

A more invasive and expensive treatment involves the surgical insertion of **penile implants** (Mulcahy, 1999) (**Figure 16.5**). One kind of implant is a semi-rigid or malleable plastic rod that keeps the penis permanently stiff enough for coitus. It is relatively easy to have inserted surgically, but the permanent erection may be difficult to conceal and therefore embarrassing in some circumstances. Another kind of implant is inflatable; it is filled from a reservoir that is implanted under the groin muscles. The pump and valves that control the filling and emptying are placed in the scrotum, where they can be accessed manually through the skin. This kind of implant is costlier and more prone to malfunction, and the erect penis is not usually as long as it was originally. On the plus side, the inflatable implant is more discreet and produces a more natural-seeming erection than the semi-rigid implant.

Placing implants in the penis is likely to damage the erectile tissue and reduce or eliminate any natural erectile capacity that the man still has. Therefore, implants should be considered a therapy of last resort, after drugs and other methods have failed.

With the advent of effective drug treatments for erectile dysfunction, implants have lost most of their popularity, but they are still useful for men whose erectile tissue has been damaged by scarring or other processes. Having an implant does not usually interfere with the capacity for orgasm or ejaculation. About 80% of men who have penile implants, as well as their partners, are satisfied with them.

penile implant An implanted device for treatment of erectile dysfunction.

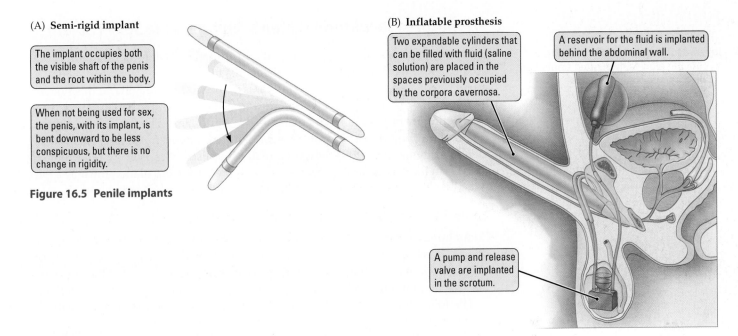

(A) **Semi-rigid implant**

The implant occupies both the visible shaft of the penis and the root within the body.

When not being used for sex, the penis, with its implant, is bent downward to be less conspicuous, but there is no change in rigidity.

Figure 16.5 Penile implants

(B) **Inflatable prosthesis**

Two expandable cylinders that can be filled with fluid (saline solution) are placed in the spaces previously occupied by the corpora cavernosa.

A reservoir for the fluid is implanted behind the abdominal wall.

A pump and release valve are implanted in the scrotum.

Psychological Treatments May Be Useful

If a man's erectile dysfunction does not respond to medical treatments, or if there are factors suggesting that his problem results from psychological or relationship issues, he may be referred to a sex therapist. One common objective in sex therapy is to reduce anxiety. This may be accomplished by means of sensate-focus exercises, as described in Box 16.1. The particular aim will be to help the man enjoy sensual contacts without worrying about whether he has an erection or not. Another approach is cognitive: Here the aim is to overcome misperceptions, such as the idea that a first-class erection and coitus are the be-all and end-all of sex. When the man realizes that he can fully satisfy his partner by means other than coitus, his anxiety may be reduced to the point that his erectile difficulties also decrease (LoPiccolo, 1992). Simply reassuring men that it is normal for the process of erection to take longer as they age can be very helpful.

Even more important may be efforts to resolve relationship problems. These problems may be of various kinds (Rosen, 2007). The man's self-esteem in the relationship may be traumatized by a loss of status, such as may follow loss of a job or development of an illness. His experience of intimacy may be damaged by an extramarital (or extrapair) relationship or by the birth of a child. His partner's or his own perceived attractiveness may be diminished by aging, obesity, or alcoholism. The impact of these issues on erectile function may be lessened by bringing them out into the open and trying to resolve them, either in one-on-one psychotherapy, in couples therapy, or even in group therapy.

Sex therapy can be combined with drug treatment. For example, a man who suddenly regains the capacity for coitus, thanks to sildenafil or another drug, might need help in restarting a sexual relationship that has been "frozen" by avoidance or apathy over a period of years. What's more, his erectile difficulties may have been masking, or standing in for, some other sexual problem such as a lack of interest in sex. Alternatively, the man's interest in sex may reemerge all too strongly. If, as sometimes happens, the man's partner had been quietly relieved that his erectile dysfunction put an end to their lovemaking, the new demands put on her (or him, if it's a same-sex relationship) may spark resentment and conflicts. Sex therapists may be able to help couples work through such problems.

Premature Ejaculation Is Men's Number One Sex Problem

premature ejaculation Ejaculation before the man wishes, often immediately on commencement of coitus. Also called rapid ejaculation.

Premature ejaculation (sometimes called rapid ejaculation) is ejaculation that occurs before the man wants it to. If the man's intention is to engage in coitus, he might ejaculate before he can place his penis in the woman's vagina, at the moment he does so, or quickly thereafter. Some authorities give a particular cut-off time for a definition of premature ejaculation—the World Health Organization says that ejaculation must occur within 15 seconds of commencement of coitus (World Health Organization, 1993)—but it's really the distress caused by the problem, more than the precise timing, that is relevant. Premature ejaculation must be a persistent problem, not just an occasional phenomenon, to merit a diagnosis.

There Are Different Kinds of Premature Ejaculation

Premature ejaculation is the leading form of sexual dysfunction among young and middle-aged men (see Figure 16.1). As with erectile dysfunction, it can be a primary, secondary, or situational disorder. As an example of the last of these, premature ejaculation might occur during partnered sex but not during masturbation.

The following two vignettes (Althof, 2007) illustrate some of this diversity:

Jim, a 58-year-old businessman in his second marriage, typifies men with lifelong rapid ejaculation. He described never being able to last more than 15 seconds with any sexual partner. He had tried masturbating prior to lovemaking and tried to distract himself with nonsexual thoughts. He had read books about premature ejaculation and diligently practiced the exercises, to no avail. This "disability" was a great source of shame for him, and he felt that it had greatly interfered in his relationships prior to marriage and in both of his marriages. His wife, Claire, was supportive and praised Jim for going "all out to please her after his orgasm." They appeared to have a good relationship, and neither partner had significant psychological problems.

John, a 6-foot-2-inch, well-muscled, 30-year-old, never-married police officer sought consultation because he had developed rapid ejaculation with his new partner of 6 weeks. John prided himself on his masculinity and said that he could not understand why this was happening to him now. There was a bragging quality to John as he detailed his sexual history…. The essential question in my mind was what was different now. With some embarrassment John revealed that he was intimidated by Kim. She was a beautiful, successful woman, the CEO for a small corporation, and he felt "dominated" by her. I asked whether he had ever been in a relationship with any other woman where he felt dominated. At first he said no, and then he laughed and recalled that many years ago there was such a woman and yes, he also suffered from rapid ejaculation with her.

The causes of premature ejaculation are not well understood. The traditional view, espoused by Masters and Johnson, was that it results from learning. They suggested that a man whose early sexual experiences are conducted in haste and anxiety (with a prostitute, perhaps, or in the back seat of a car) might become conditioned to reaching orgasm very quickly (Masters & Johnson, 1970). Another hypothesis, based on animal research as well as pharmaceutical studies in humans, is that lifelong premature ejaculation is caused by a dysfunction in certain receptors for the neurotransmitter serotonin (Waldinger, 2004). Psychological theories seem most plausible in cases where premature ejaculation is situational (as with John, above), while biological theories may account better for lifelong premature ejaculation that affects a man in all circumstances (as with Jim in the first vignette).

Drug Treatment May Be Effective

Premature ejaculation is treated with drugs or sex therapy. The combination of both is often the most effective approach (Althof, 2007).

The drugs used to treat premature ejaculation are mostly selective serotonin reuptake inhibitors (Prozac-class antidepressants). One of them, paroxetine (Paxil), may be the most effective (Waldinger & Olivier, 2004). In one randomized, double-blind study of men with severe premature ejaculation, a 6-week course of Paxil increased the time between commencement of coitus and ejaculation from about 20 seconds to two and a half minutes (**Figure 16.6**), whereas the placebo had no effect at all. In uncontrolled studies, individual men using antidepressants for premature ejaculation may last as long as 10 minutes before ejaculating (Althof, 2007).

While the usual form of treatment involves the man taking the drug daily and continuously, some men take it only on days when they plan to have sex. This "as needed" treatment mode is probably not as effective as continuous dosage, but it is cheaper and more convenient, especially for men who don't have sex very often.

Sex Therapy May Help Men to Regulate Excitation

One aspect of sex therapy is simply talking through the history of the man's condition and the factors that may exacerbate it. In the second vignette above, for example, it quickly became clear that interpersonal dynamics lay behind John's premature ejaculation—specifically, the power relationship between John and his partners—and this became the focus of discussion. In other cases, it may be useful to concentrate on cognitive distortions. These distortions can range from discounting the positive ("My partner says our lovemaking is satisfying because she doesn't want to hurt my feelings") to all-or-nothing thinking ("I am a complete failure because I come quickly") or catastrophizing ("If I fail tonight my girlfriend will dump me") (Althof, 2007).

Sex therapy exercises may be very useful. These can include the same sensate-focus exercises already described. There are exercises specifically designed for premature ejaculation, however. One example is the **stop-start method**:

- Initially, the man masturbates alone, bringing himself to a medium level of excitement. (He may be taught to think about sexual arousal on a 10-point scale, 10 being orgasm, and to focus on staying in the 5-to-7 range.) He learns to recognize what this level feels like and then stops masturbating to allow his state of arousal to decrease. This is repeated a few times, until he is finally allowed to masturbate to orgasm. He does this several times a week for several weeks, with the goal of being able to stimulate his penis for 15 minutes without ejaculating.

- In the next stage, the man and his partner are together, in a position such as that shown in **Figure 16.7A**. She (assuming it's a woman) stimulates his penis by hand or orally, but he asks her to stop before he climaxes. Masters and Johnson recommended that the partner firmly pinch or squeeze the man's penis, just below the glans, at the time that stimulation ceases, as a means of reducing his arousal (**Figure 16.7B**). Again, the goal is to be able to experience this stimulation for 15 minutes without ejaculation.

- The third stage progresses to coitus. The woman simply places the man's penis in her vagina, and the couple lie still for a prolonged period. The idea is that the man gets accustomed to the sensations of coitus without being too excited. Then the woman begins to move somewhat, but the man tells her to stop whenever he approaches orgasm. The woman can apply the squeeze technique in this situation too, as necessary: She can squeeze the base of his penis when it is still partially inserted in her vagina. After several repetitions, the man is allowed to ejaculate. As the exercises proceed, the man should be able to defer his ejaculation for a longer and longer time.

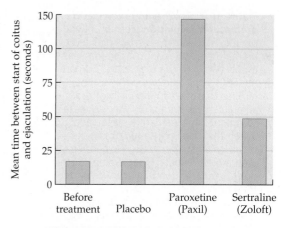

Figure 16.6 Drug treatment for premature ejaculation Effect of 6 weeks of treatment with a placebo or one of two SSRIs. (Data from Waldinger et al., 2001.)

stop-start method A sex therapy technique for the treatment of premature ejaculation that involves alternating between stimulating and not stimulating the penis.

Figure 16.7 Sex therapy exercises for premature ejaculation Position of couple for "stop-start" exercises directed at premature ejaculation. (A) The man lies on his back with his legs apart. His partner lies to one side and partly astride him, so that she can manually or orally stimulate his genitals. (B) The "squeeze technique" for premature ejaculation. When the man is close to orgasm, he communicates this fact to his partner with a prearranged signal. (Some couples do this with random timing.) The partner then grasps the man's penis with a thumb on the frenulum and squeezes firmly for a few seconds. This diminishes the man's urge to ejaculate and possibly causes a partial loss of his erection.

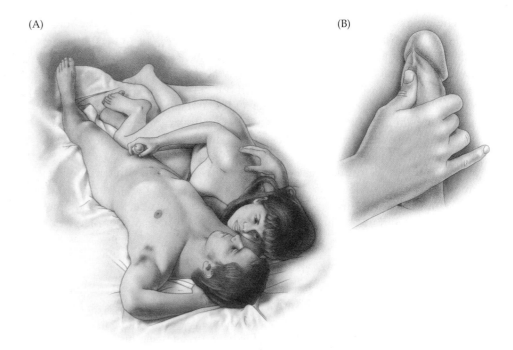

(A)　(B)

According to some experts, Kegel exercises are also useful: They help men get to know and control the muscles that participate in ejaculation.

How helpful are these sex therapy exercises to men with premature ejaculation? Masters and Johnson claimed success rates of over 90%, even at 5 years after treatment, but more recent studies have come up with less positive findings: Many couples report some continuing or recurring difficulties after the termination of treatment (Hawton et al., 1992). Various methods to prevent relapses, such as repeating the initial exercises periodically and having periodic follow-up visits with the therapist, have been recommended.

Treatment failure and relapses can occur with any form of treatment, whether drug therapy, psychotherapy, or the combined approach. "While these cases are discouraging," writes an expert in the field, "in general the majority of men and couples achieve modest gains sexually, psychologically, and relationally in treatment" (Althof, 2007).

Delayed Ejaculation Can Be a Side Effect of Several Drugs

Delayed (or absent) **ejaculation** is the opposite of premature ejaculation: The man can reach the point of ejaculation with difficulty or not at all. Sometimes delayed ejaculation is specific to a certain kind of sexual behavior, such as coitus or partnered sex generally; in other cases, the man may not be able to reach orgasm under any circumstances. Either way, it is a fairly uncommon problem.

Delayed ejaculation can have specific causes, such as neurological damage. It can also result from the use of certain drugs, including anti-hypertensive drugs, major tranquilizers, and antidepressants. In many cases, psychological causes are suspected; this is particularly likely with delayed ejaculation that follows some life event, such as a relationship crisis. In some cases, the man merely needs to receive more effective stimulation.

When delayed ejaculation is a side effect of drugs such as antidepressants, it can usually be treated by switching to a different drug or by adding a second drug that counteracts this side effect. Sildenafil is an example of a drug that can be used for this purpose (Rothschild, 2000). If the man has never experienced ejac-

delayed ejaculation Difficulty achieving or inability to achieve orgasm or ejaculation. Also called male orgasmic disorder.

ulation or orgasm, a consultation with a urologist is warranted, to see whether there is some congenital abnormality of the internal reproductive tract.

Concerning psychological causes, therapists hold quite diverse views. According to one school of thought, the condition represents an inhibition that results from hostility toward women or some other deep-seated conflict; this inhibition may be overcome by the use of prolonged and intense sexual stimulation (Kaplan, 1974). In another model, delayed ejaculation represents a lack of desire or arousal (Apfelbaum, 2000). In this model, intense stimulation should be avoided; instead, the man needs to acknowledge his lack of desire as a first step in treatment. Given these conflicting ideas, it is understandable that no psychological treatment for delayed ejaculation has been proven effective by objective research (Hartmann & Waldinger, 2007). It may be that a better understanding of the neural regulation of ejaculation and orgasm will lead to improved treatments, both for delayed and for premature ejaculation.

Sexual Pain Is Uncommon in Men

It is quite unusual for men to complain of pain during sexual activity, but it does happen: About 3% of men reported such pain in the NHSLS study (see Figure 16.1). Pain may be associated with infections, especially acute prostatitis, which can cause severe spasms of pain during ejaculation. The somewhat mysterious condition called chronic pelvic pain syndrome (also called chronic prostatitis—see Chapter 4) can also cause pain during sex or at ejaculation (Luzzi & Law, 2006). Uncircumcised men can have problems with retracting their foreskins (phimosis): If the foreskin is insufficiently mobile, coitus may be painful. A man in that situation may be able to avoid pain by using a condom, but a urologist can often resolve the problem with minor surgery or by performing a circumcision. There are other uncommon sources of pain, such as allergic reactions to latex or soap. A few men experience pain in the penis after ejaculation for no obvious reason.

Female Sexual Arousal Disorder Involves Insufficient Genital Response

In women, the three early processes of physiological arousal are vaginal lubrication, engorgement of the vaginal walls, and clitoral erection. The absence or insufficiency of any of these processes makes coitus unpleasurable and often downright painful. **Female sexual arousal disorder** is a term used to refer collectively to these problems. As we mentioned in Chapter 8, psychological or subjective arousal may or may not accompany physiological arousal.

Insufficient lubrication during sex is a common complaint, especially after menopause. In postmenopausal women, the condition may well respond to hormone treatment (see Chapter 13). Estrogens may also be administered orally or directly to the vagina in the form of creams, tablets, or slow-release rings (Mayo Clinic, 2005). If poor lubrication is the woman's only problem, hormone treatment may be an "overkill" remedy; over-the-counter water-based lubricants do a good job, are inexpensive, and have few, if any, side effects. The lubricant may be applied to the woman's vagina or to her partner's penis.

Erectile dysfunction is usually thought of as an exclusively male problem, but women can experience a lack of clitoral erection. Clitoral erectile dysfunction can coexist with absence of vaginal engorgement; both can be caused by diseases that compromise the blood vessels supplying the genitalia (Goldstein & Berman, 1998).

The FDA has approved one device for the treatment of problems with female physiological arousal (**Figure 16.8**). Called the Eros Clitoral Therapy Device, it is

female sexual arousal disorder
Insufficient physiological arousal in women, such as to make sex unpleasurable or painful.

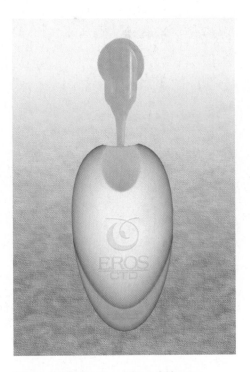

Figure 16.8 The Eros Clitoral Therapy Device increases blood flow to the clitoris and the surrounding area by drawing a partial vacuum. No constriction band is used.

persistent genital arousal disorder
Long-lasting physiological arousal in women, unaccompanied by subjective arousal or pleasure.

dyspareunia Pain during coitus.

vulvar vestibulitis syndrome A form of dyspareunia marked by inflammation of the vestibule and increased tension in pelvic floor muscles.

a miniature version of the vacuum systems used to treat male erectile dysfunction. A soft plastic cup is placed over the clitoris, and a partial vacuum is drawn. The vacuum increases blood flow into the clitoris and into the vaginal walls. In small-scale, uncontrolled studies, women who used the device reported moderate benefits in terms of increased sensation, lubrication, and satisfaction with sex. Some women also reported more orgasms (Wilson et al., 2001; Munarriz et al., 2003).

Because sildenafil has proved so successful in the treatment of erectile dysfunction in men, it was hoped that it might prove equally useful in women with sexual arousal disorder. Results so far have been disappointing, however. One large U.S. study found no benefit at all from use of the drug—it merely caused unpleasant side effects such as headaches (Basson et al., 2002). One subgroup of women *are* helped by sildenafil, however: These are women who experience arousal difficulties as a side effect of antidepressant medications (Nurnberg et al., 2008).

Psychotherapy and sex therapy can play an important role in the treatment of female arousal disorder. We will postpone discussion of this topic until after we have covered other aspects of sexual dysfunction in women.

Rarely, women experience the very opposite of female arousal disorder: They are troubled by frequent, unwanted, or near-continuous physiological arousal, including vasocongestion, tingling, and sensitivity of the genital area and sometimes the breasts too. Even orgasms may occur without any obvious trigger. This condition is called **persistent genital arousal disorder** (Leiblum, 2007a). Because the physiological arousal is completely disconnected from any subjective sexual arousal or desire, it is extremely distressing. One woman described it as feeling like "hormonal rape." The symptoms do not disappear with a single orgasm but may require many orgasms over hours or days to resolve. No simple treatment has been discovered for this condition, though some women have been helped by locally applied anesthetizing agents, by physical therapy, or by cognitive therapy.

There Are Many Reasons for Sexual Pain in Women

Pain during coitus (**dyspareunia**) is far more common among women than among men (see Figure 16.1), and it is especially common among young women. Dyspareunia can severely impact women's sex lives and relationships.

The following are the common causes of dyspareunia:

- Developmental malformations, intersexed conditions, or a persistent unruptured hymen
- Scars from vaginal tearing during childbirth or from episiotomy, hysterectomy, sexual assault, or female circumcision
- Vaginal atrophy (a thinning of the vaginal walls that occurs with aging)
- Acute or chronic infections or inflammation of the vagina, internal reproductive tract, or urinary tract, including several STDs and pelvic inflammatory disease
- **Vulvar vestibulitis syndrome** (a common form of vulvar pain associated with low-grade inflammation of the vestibule and increased tension in the pelvic-floor musculature)
- Endometriosis
- Allergic reactions to foreign substances, such as latex, spermicides, or soap
- Insufficiency of physiological arousal, especially of vaginal lubrication
- Vaginismus (see below)

The treatment of dyspareunia depends on the diagnosis. Infections may be treatable with antibiotic, antiviral, or antifungal drugs. If the problem is vaginal dryness, a lubricant can be used, or the woman's natural lubrication may be improved by prolonging foreplay or by clitoral stimulation before coitus. (Her partner may need some education in this matter.) If the dryness is associated with vaginal atrophy, treatment with estrogens (by mouth or by local administration) is an option. If there is a suspected latex allergy, polyurethane condoms can be substituted. Endometriosis can be treated with drugs or with surgery. Psychological problems and relationships difficulties are often associated with dyspareunia, as either a cause or a result of the condition, and it often takes a combination of physical treatments and psychotherapy to work through these issues (**Box 16.3**).

vaginismus Inability to experience coitus due to spasm of the muscles surrounding the outer vagina, pain, or fear of pain.

Vaginismus May Make Intercourse Impossible

Some women have no obvious vaginal pathology, and yet they cannot experience coitus: Penetration of the vagina by the penis is impossible on account of some

Sexual Health

BOX 16.3 Dyspareunia: A Case History

This is an abridged account of a case history described by Yitzchak Binik, Sophie Bergeron, and Samir Khalifé of McGill University Health Center and reproduced by permission (Binik et al., 2007).

Heather and Steven, ages 31 and 35, were referred by their gynecologist with a diagnosis of vulvar vestibulitis syndrome. The gynecologist had also referred them to a physical therapist, and pelvic floor rehabilitation had already begun when the couple came to see us.

Heather and Steven had been married for 5 years and reported a good relationship. Heather was an accountant and Steven was a pharmacist. They planned to have children but wanted to wait until the genital pain problem was resolved. The couple had begun to limit all forms of sexual contact and both experienced self-doubt, each wondering how they were contributing to the problem.

Their family histories were similar; each had one parent who had been depressive and who was absent for long periods of time from the daily routine of family life. The two had always done well in school, excelled in sports, and had had significant past romantic relationships before meeting one another. They currently lead busy and active lives, with many nights taken up by work or sports.

The genital pain had begun a few years ago but had been bearable until a year previous,

when it had worsened following a particularly stressful time in Heather's career. The problem had affected Heather's sexual desire, which fluctuated but had generally decreased. They both believed that intercourse was an important part of sex and felt inadequate for not engaging in it more often.

Initial goals were to explore factors related to Heather's desire fluctuations and to decrease the intensity of her genital pain. Among the first issues that we worked on was lifting some of the obstacles to having uninterrupted time together and to find ways to connect other than sex. Heather often leaned on Steven for support, and in return Steven tended to overprotect Heather to the point of neglecting his own needs. We also did some cognitive restructuring to separate sex from intercourse and to reduce catastrophizing about pain. Information was provided about vulvar vestibulitis, and sex education focused on broadening their definition of sex and on decreasing the emphasis they placed on intercourse. Both were very receptive to these interventions and made significant attempts to integrate new knowledge and behaviors between sessions.

Heather and Steven were seen for a total of 18 sessions. The couple learned to create high-quality moments for intimacy and sex and felt more connected than at the start of therapy.

They developed coping strategies, for example, opening up more to each other about their respective difficulties. In doing so, they learned that they could cope with intermittent episodes of pain.

During therapy we learned that both felt unlovable at times and that this drove many of their reactions to each other. Heather improved her management of emotions, and Steven began to concentrate more on his own needs. At the end of therapy, both reported that sexual desire was no longer a major issue and that the pain was negligible.

Both Heather and Steven dealt with their difficult childhoods by placing a high value on creating a healthy marriage; in addition, they were obviously committed to doing whatever work was necessary to ensure this outcome. The fact that they had previously enjoyed pain-free sex may have contributed to Heather's recovery from pain and restoration of her sexual desire. The relationship work that was accomplished during the course of therapy helped Steven become less passive both inside and outside of the bedroom. Finally, the increased emotional intimacy of the couple along with the decreased focus on intercourse may have helped the couple to reinject passion into their sex life.

(A) **Vaginismus**

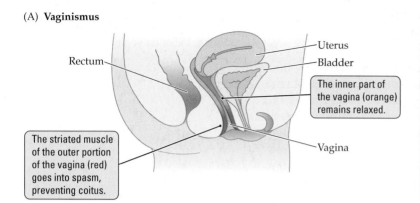

Rectum

Uterus

Bladder

The inner part of the vagina (orange) remains relaxed.

Vagina

The striated muscle of the outer portion of the vagina (red) goes into spasm, preventing coitus.

(B) **Vaginal dilators**

Figure 16.9 Vaginismus (A) The usual explanation of vaginismus is that the striated muscle of the outer portion of the vagina (red) goes into spasm, preventing coitus. The inner part of the vagina (orange) remains relaxed. (B) In one treatment for vaginismus, the woman uses progressively larger dilators in combination with relaxation exercises.

combination of muscle spasm and either pain or fear of pain. This condition is known as **vaginismus**. Penetration of the vagina by a finger, a tampon, or a gynecologist's speculum may likewise be impossible.

The usual explanation for why penetration is impossible in vaginismus is that the nearby muscles—either those of the vaginal walls (**Figure 16.9A**) or the entire musculature of the pelvic floor—go into spasm, so that the outer third of the vagina is tightly closed. Some experts question whether muscle spasm is a useful criterion to define vaginismus, however. They speculate that muscle spasm might not be the cause of the condition so much as a reaction that develops as a defense against anticipated pain (Reissing et al., 2004). In fact, it is not fully agreed that vaginismus is a distinct condition separate from vulvar vestibulitis syndrome and other forms of dyspareunia (Binik et al., 2007).

Some researchers consider vaginismus to be an aversion to coitus stemming from early traumatic experiences (such as experiencing or witnessing sexual assault), from the inculcation of very strict religious attitudes toward sex, or even from simple ignorance about sex. In one study, women with a diagnosis of vaginismus were more likely to report a history of childhood sexual abuse than were a control group of women (Reissing et al., 2003), but it is certainly not the case that all women with vaginismus were sexually abused, or vice versa.

A mix of psychotherapy and sex therapy are the currently favored options for treatment of vaginismus. The psychotherapy may be aimed at identifying and overcoming the root cause of the woman's aversion to coitus. The sex therapy may include general exercises such as sensate focus. A behavioral technique specific to vaginismus, however, is the use of **vaginal dilators** (**Figure 16.9B**): The woman inserts progressively larger-diameter probes into her vagina while doing relaxation exercises. The hope is that the woman will gradually cease feeling anxious during vaginal penetration. In one study, nearly all the women treated with this form of therapy were able to engage in intercourse after about six sessions (Schnyder et al., 1998). Physical therapy to help women monitor and regulate their pelvic floor muscles is also useful (Rosenbaum, 2007).

Vaginismus doesn't necessarily interfere with a woman's capacity for sexual arousal or orgasm. Even when vaginismus makes coitus impossible, a couple may still have an active sex life using other means of stimulation. Sometimes it is only when a couple want to have children that they seek professional help for the condition.

vaginal dilator A plastic cylinder used to enlarge the vagina or to counteract vaginismus.

Difficulty in Reaching Orgasm Is Very Common among Women

Some women experience considerable distress in their sex lives on account of a persistent and recurring difficulty in reaching orgasm (**anorgasmia**, or female orgasmic disorder). Ten to 15 percent of U.S. women have never experienced orgasm under any circumstances (Althof & Schreiner-Engel, 2000). An estimated two-thirds of all women do not experience orgasm regularly during coitus without other stimulation (Kaplan, 1979). In the NHSLS study, 71% of women (compared with only 25% of men) said that they did not always experience orgasm during sex with their regular partner. But plenty of women are satisfied with their sexual relationships in spite of infrequent or absent orgasms, so the percentage who could be said to have anorgasmia as a clinical disorder is lower than these high numbers might suggest (Bancroft et al., 2003b).

Psychotherapy and Directed Masturbation May Be Helpful

Anorgasmia can be caused by drugs, especially by antidepressants and antihypertensive drugs. Such cases can usually be treated by adjusting dosage, switching drugs, or adding another drug to counteract the effect. A variety of medical conditions, especially those that cause neurological damage, such as diabetes or multiple sclerosis, can interfere with orgasmic function. So can pelvic surgery, including hysterectomy in some women.

More commonly, anorgasmia does not have any obvious biological cause. In such cases, the clinician or therapist will suggest different strategies depending on the details of the problem. If the woman can experience orgasm with masturbation but not with partnered sex, it may be possible to suggest modifications of partnered sex that will allow orgasm to occur. First, the therapist will reassure the couple that it is normal for a woman not to experience orgasm with coitus alone. They should be encouraged to add clitoral stimulation—by hand or mouth, or with a vibrator (**Figure 16.10**). This stimulation can be provided by either partner and can take place before, during, after, or instead of coitus. Increasing the duration of sexual activity (for example, by helping a male partner delay his orgasm) or trying different coital positions may also resolve the problem.

One variant on the man-above position, known as the **coital alignment technique**, is said to be particularly effective (Pierce, 2000). In this technique, the man positions himself a few inches farther forward than usual and lies in direct contact with the woman's body, though without placing his entire weight on her. Instead of deep thrusting, a reciprocal rocking motion by both partners provides rhythmic contact between the base of the man's penis and the woman's clitoris.

Encouraging couples to communicate better about their sexual feelings and the sexual activities that are most arousing can be very helpful as well. Men do not automatically know what their female partner finds sexually arousing. A man may rush from foreplay to coitus before his partner is sufficiently aroused, in which case coitus may be a turn-off for her, rather than a turn-on. The man may stimulate the

anorgasmia Difficulty experiencing or inability to experience orgasm. In women, also called female orgasmic disorder.

coital alignment technique A variation of the man-above position for coitus that increases clitoral stimulation.

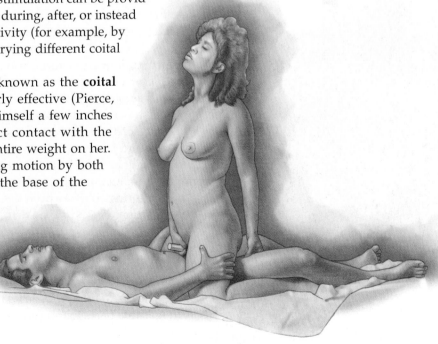

Figure 16.10 Helping a woman experience orgasm during partnered sex If a woman has difficulty experiencing orgasm during coitus, it may be helpful to adopt a position, as here, that allows either partner to provide clitoral stimulation by hand or with a vibrator.

discrepant sexual desire The situation in which one partner in a relationship has much more interest in sex than the other.

hypersexuality Excessive sexual desire or behavior.

woman's nipples or clitoris too strongly—these are tender areas, after all. A post-menopausal woman may take longer to become aroused than she did earlier in her life. All these things can make it difficult for the woman to experience orgasm. In an environment in which the woman feels free to let her partner know whether what he is doing is working or not, these difficulties can often be resolved.

If the woman does not experience orgasm under any circumstances, a somewhat different strategy is called for. Bear in mind that over half of all women say that they never masturbate (NHSLS data). Thus, if they are open to trying masturbation, they may be easily helped to experience orgasm for the first time. Sex therapy for anorgasmia often includes a directed program of self-stimulation, which may begin with general exploration of the naked body and later extend to genital stimulation. Vibrators are particularly useful in these kinds of exercises. Sometimes this directed masturbation program is accompanied by exercises in the use of fantasy or erotic materials. In addition, the woman may be encouraged to perform Kegel exercises, although these are more helpful in improving the quality of orgasm than in helping women experience orgasm. Sensate-focus exercises with a partner are often added.

As might be expected, directed masturbation programs are most successful at helping women reach orgasm during masturbation. The great majority of women are able to do so by the end of a sex therapy program, but fewer are able to transfer this new-found capacity to partnered sex (Heiman, 2007).

Directed masturbation programs work better for women with primary (lifelong) orgasmic disorder than for women who develop the problem after some years of satisfactory orgasmic functioning (Althof & Schreiner-Engel, 2000). In the latter group of women, the problem more usually reflects relationship difficulties, other psychological issues, or medical conditions that are not addressed by masturbation training.

Too Much Interest in Sex Can Cause Problems

We now shift from disorders of sexual performance to disorders characterized by too much or too little sexual desire or sexual behavior. Of course, it is difficult to define what constitutes "too much" or "too little" in the area of sexuality. Still, these conditions can cause serious problems for individuals and relationships, especially when the levels of sexual activity desired by two partners are very different (**discrepant sexual desire**).

Excessive sexual desire or behavior is called **hypersexuality**. A variety of medical conditions can trigger hypersexual behavior, including dementias, psychoses, epilepsy, and injury to certain parts of the brain. Some drugs (both prescription and recreational) or alcohol can have similar effects. In most of these conditions, the abnormal nature of the person's sexual behavior is obvious because it represents a radical departure from their sexual behavior prior to the onset of the medical condition.

Is Excessive Sexual Behavior an Addiction or a Compulsion?

More difficult to evaluate is excessive sexual behavior by adults who do not have medical conditions such as those listed above. Some people—men, for the most part—spend several hours each day engaged in masturbation, reading or viewing pornography, participating in sex-related online chat rooms, using commercial phone sex services, seeking casual sex partners in bars, cruising the streets for prostitutes, or having anonymous sex with multiple partners in bathhouses or sex clubs. They may feel that they have lost control of their own behavior. In fact,

Sex addict? Two-time Golden Globe winner David Duchovny (seen here with Michele Nordin) plays a sex-obsessed character on the cable TV show *Californication*, but in 2008 he entered a rehabilitation facility, stating that he was suffering from real-life sexual addiction.

these activities may so take over people's lives as to destroy their careers and marriages and expose them and their partners to HIV and other STDs. Hypersexuality is often associated with paraphilic behaviors such as exhibitionism, and in fact hypersexuality itself is sometimes viewed as a paraphilia (see Chapter 15).

According to Patrick Carnes, a well-known writer on addiction issues, hypersexual behavior is often symptomatic of **sexual addiction** (Carnes, 2001). Sex addicts, Carnes says, go through a four-stage cycle resembling the cycle experienced by drug addicts (**Figure 16.11**). The stages are:

1. An increasing craving for sex
2. The ritualized search for sex, such as spending time in online chat rooms
3. Sexual behavior itself, which might be masturbation or sex with partners
4. A period of guilt or despair after the bout of sexual behavior

Carnes has suggested that programs like those that treat addictions to substances, such as Alcoholics Anonymous, could be an effective treatment for sexual addiction. A number of such programs (such as Sexaholics Anonymous) have in fact been initiated, but the efficacy of these programs is uncertain.

The use of the term "addiction" in a sexual context, while it may seem reasonable to laypeople, is controversial among scientists. Addiction, as traditionally defined, is to a *substance* (heroin, for example), and it is characterized by a specific cluster of neurochemical features that have not been well documented in hypersexuality. For example, substance addiction responds to opiate-blocking drugs, but hypersexuality usually does not. For that reason, many experts prefer to use the phrase **compulsive sexual behavior** or obsessive–compulsive sexual disorder to refer to the condition that Carnes calls sexual addiction (Coleman, 1996). This designation acknowledges a key attribute of the behavior—namely, that it is experienced as being carried out against a person's will and often in a self-destructive manner. However, this designation links excessive sexual behavior with other compulsive behaviors, such as compulsive hand-washing, rather than with substance addiction.

Compulsive Sexual Behavior Can Often Be Treated with SSRIs

If there is a medical cause for hypersexuality, treating that cause will likely alleviate the problem. Otherwise, psychotherapy to explore the origins of the behavior may be helpful. If it seems that the behavior is a mechanism to escape some internal conflict or difficult life situation, helping the person find a resolution to that problem may lessen the need for the behavior. In addition, however, drug therapy can be very effective (Bradford, 2001). Selective serotonin reuptake inhibitors (SSRIs) are the drugs most commonly used for this purpose. Indeed, the effectiveness of these antidepressants in the treatment of many cases of hypersexuality could be taken as supportive evidence that these behaviors belong to the family of obsessive–compulsive disorders, since SSRIs are known to be helpful in the treatment of those conditions. In more serious cases of hypersexuality, especially those in which there is underlying brain pathology that cannot be corrected, it may be necessary to use drugs that lower testosterone levels or that block testosterone's effects.

Lack of Desire for Sex Is Not Necessarily a Problem

About 1 in 3 women and 1 in 6 men within the 18-to-59 age range say that they lack interest in sex (see Figure 16.1). The proportion of people who are uninterest-

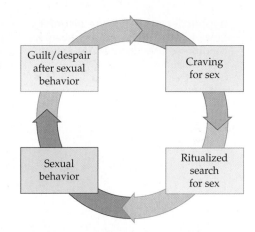

Figure 16.11 Compulsive sexual behavior often takes the form of a four-stage cycle. (After Carnes, 2001.)

sexual addiction The idea that a person may be addicted to certain forms of sexual behavior by a mechanism similar to that of substance addiction.

compulsive sexual behavior Sexual behavior perceived subjectively as involuntary and diagnosed as a symptom of a compulsive disorder. Also called obsessive–compulsive sexual disorder.

hypoactive sexual desire disorder
Low or absent interest in sex, when this condition causes distress. Also called low sexual desire.

ed in sex probably increases among older people. If a person lacks interest in sex and this lack of interest causes distress or interferes with the person's marriage or relationship, it is considered a clinical condition and is called **hypoactive sexual desire disorder**, or simply low sexual desire. The number of people who have a clinically defined hypoactive sexual desire disorder is much lower than the number of people who say they lack interest in sex; for example, no more than 3% of men in the general population are estimated to have the disorder (Simons & Carey, 2001). Many people who lack interest in sex, especially those who are elderly, are not troubled or harmed by this lack of interest and should not be considered as having a problem of any kind. Lesbians in long-term relationships are said to be especially likely to lose interest in sex (**Box 16.4**).

Sexual Health

BOX 16.4 Sexual Minorities and Sexual Dysfunction

Men and women who belong to sexual minorities face the same kinds of sexual problems and dysfunctions as do heterosexual men and women and benefit from the same kinds of treatments. Yet there are certain ways in which sexual orientation or gender identity is especially relevant in the context of sexual dysfunctions:

■ Some homosexual men and women are in heterosexual marriages or relationships. The homosexual partner may have performance difficulties or avoid sex as a result of a lack of sexual attraction, and this in turn is likely to create problems for the heterosexual partner and for the relationship as a whole. Surprisingly, though, many homosexual people perform quite well in heterosexual relationships. It's not uncommon to hear their partners say, after they come out of the closet, "I had no idea—we had great sex!" Even when the sex isn't great, there may be great intimacy.

■ Gay men and lesbians may have a sense of shame or self-hatred about their homosexuality ("internalized homophobia") or a difficulty accepting their sexual orientation. This may affect their performance within homosexual relationships or their ability to communicate effectively about their sexual needs. With the increasing social acceptance of homosexuality, however, identity and shame issues have become much less prevalent than in the past.

■ Some gay men have developed an unreasonable fear of sex because of the AIDS

epidemic, anxiety about sexual practices in a relationship in which one of the partners is HIV-positive, or feelings of guilt as AIDS "survivors."

■ Anal penetration, practiced by some gay men, can present performance difficulties for either the receptive or the insertive partner. Fear of pain may make relaxation of the anal sphincter difficult, and a man with erectile dysfunction will have more difficulty with anal penetration than with vaginal penetration. Advice on how to deal with these problems is not always easy to come by (see Chapter 9).

■ Transgendered and transexual people may have special concerns about sexual practices; they may be dissatisfied with their genitals and not wish to use them in sex, or, if they have undergone sex-reassignment surgery, they and their partners will have to deal with the functional limitations of their new genitals—which may include difficulty experiencing orgasm (see Chapter 7).

■ Although all couples can lose interest in sex with each other over time, this seems to occur particularly commonly for lesbians, who report lower frequency of sex than women in heterosexual relationships. Still, the sex that lesbian couples do have may be of high "quality": It tends to last longer and to be more varied, it is more likely to include orgasm, and it is less likely to be undertaken in response to a partner's request, as compared with the sexual experiences of heterosexual women

(Nichols & Shernoff, 2007). Lesbian couples who wish to reinject some passion into their relationship can follow the same recommendations that apply to all established couples: Make time for each other, introduce novelty (dates and trips, new sexual positions or sex toys, sex in new locations), express romantic feelings, and resolve conflicts.

Men and women who belong to sexual minorities may fear that they will not receive understanding treatment from heterosexual doctors and therapists and therefore fail to seek help with their sexual problems. This fear is often groundless, but some healthcare professionals do still fail to recognize either the commonalities between the problems of gay and straight people (performance problems, desire problems, relationship problems) or the special concerns of sexual minorities, as listed above. The American Psychological Association's Division 44 consists of over 1500 gay or gay-affirmative members and has published guidelines for psychotherapy with lesbian, gay, and bisexual clients (American Psychological Association, 2000). The Association of Gay and Lesbian Psychiatrists provides referrals (Association of Gay and Lesbian Psychiatrists, 2008). Regional lists of gay healthcare providers and therapists are available on the Web, but word-of-mouth is often a more effective way to locate a suitable provider. There are also some transgendered sexologists and therapists, such as Dr. Anne Lawrence of Seattle (Lawrence, 2008).

Hormone Treatment May Restore Sexual Desire

Gonadal hormones play a significant role in influencing sexual desire. In men, testosterone is the key player. The role of testosterone was well illustrated in one double-blind, placebo-controlled study (Bagatell et al., 1994). Healthy male volunteers were given a drug that lowered their blood testosterone levels to well below normal. By the end of the 6-week treatment period the men had a greatly reduced interest in sex, experienced fewer sexual fantasies, and engaged less often in masturbation and sexual intercourse. By contrast, men who received the testosterone-lowering drug but also received enough testosterone to keep their blood testosterone levels normal did not differ in their sexual responses from the men who received only a placebo.

Unlike erectile dysfunction, for which testosterone treatment is not very helpful (see above), hypoactive sexual desire disorder in men often does respond to such treatment, especially in men whose testes are secreting lower than normal levels of testosterone (**hypogonadal** men). With the availability of transdermal delivery methods (patches), treatment with testosterone and related androgens has increased in popularity. Testosterone treatment carries significant risks, however: It has the potential to cause or worsen prostate disease, liver disease, and heart disease, and it may lower fertility, accelerate balding, and cause mood problems. It is not the "fountain of youth" for normally aging men.

Psychological factors probably play a significant role in hypoactive sexual desire disorder in men. These factors can include inculcated sex-negative attitudes, relationship difficulties, stress, depression, and a feedback effect from erectile dysfunction. Alleviating these difficulties through psychotherapy, relationship counseling, or behavioral sex therapy may be more effective than drug treatment for some men, but studies in this area are few and have generally yielded disappointing results, according to one recent review of the literature (Maurice, 2007).

Estrogen or Androgen Treatment May Improve Sexual Desire in Women

The diagnosis and treatment of hypoactive sexual desire in women is more complex than in men. Traditionally, clinicians assessed women's sexual health by asking how often they engaged in intercourse. The answer to this question can give an erroneous notion of the state of a woman's sexual desire, however. She may be engaging in intercourse in response to sexual advances by her partner but have little or no interest in sex herself. Conversely, she may have a great interest in sex but not be able to gratify that interest because of a lack of partner availability or because of her partner's disinterest. To determine whether a particular woman really has a troubling lack of sexual desire requires a sympathetic ear and thoughtful questioning.

Women's sexual desire is supported by two classes of hormones, estrogens and androgens, although there is still considerable uncertainty about their relative roles (Meston & Bradford, 2007). The levels of these hormones drop when levels of body fat are very low (as a result of starvation, anorexia nervosa, or some athletic training regimens) as well as after menopause. In these circumstances, sexual desire often declines or disappears. Some women continue to initiate sexual activity long after menopause, however. Their behavior may reflect the importance of cultural factors in sexual desire, or it may be due to the continuing presence of steroids secreted by the adrenal glands.

In premenopausal women who are not menstruating and have low sexual desire (because of low body weight, for example), an interest in sex usually reappears when body weight returns to normal and menstruation resumes. In post-

As a means of restoring interest in sex, using testosterone patches has benefits, limitations, and risks—for both sexes.

hypogonadal Suffering from low function of the testes or ovaries, usually taken to indicate a deficiency of sex steroids.

Sexual Problems, 2001). The group proposed categorizing these problems under four major headings:

- *Sexual problems due to socio-cultural, political, or economic factors* These include lack of information about sex or access to relevant services, culturally imposed anxiety about one's attractiveness or shame about one's sexual orientation, conflicts between one's own cultural norms and those of the dominant culture, and lack of interest in sex due to family and work obligations.

- *Sexual problems relating to the partner and the relationship* These include sexual inhibition resulting from relationship conflicts or unequal power, different desires, poor communication, or the partner's health or sexual problems.

- *Sexual problems due to psychological factors* These include sexual aversion due to past trauma, problems to do with attachment or rejection, depression, anxiety, or fear of the consequences of sex or of refusing sex.

- *Sexual problems due to medical factors* These include painful intercourse or lack of physiological arousal caused by physical issues listed earlier in this chapter.

Women in the real world, such as the woman in the case history above, might well have problems in several of these categories. Viewed in this way, women's sexual problems demand a "biopsychosocial approach" to treatment (Leiblum, 2007c), but turning this idea from a catchphrase into an objectively assessable treatment program will require a great deal of clinical and laboratory research. In fact, there are political aspects to the issue too, for society as a whole may need to be reeducated to take greater account of women's concerns and their sexual rights. If this is true for the United States and other Western countries, how much more might it apply to societies in which women's voices are not yet heard?

Summary

1. Sexual disorders are common. Among women, the most frequent problems are a lack of interest in sex, difficulty experiencing orgasm, and a lack of vaginal lubrication. Among men, the commonest problems are premature ejaculation, anxiety about performance, and a lack of interest in sex. Sexual dysfunctions are clinical problems requiring treatment only if they cause distress. Treatment may involve some combination of drugs, psychotherapy, and sex therapy exercises.

2. Many conditions can lead to problems with penile erection, including smoking, use of alcohol and certain prescription or recreational drugs, diabetes, cardiovascular disease, spinal cord injury, and prostate surgery. Among psychological factors that may impair erectile function, performance anxiety is probably the most important. Treatment of erectile dysfunction can include alleviation of the underlying disorder, psychotherapy, or the use of a drug such as Viagra. Among the nondrug treatments available are vacuum devices and penile implants.

3. The causes of premature ejaculation, a very common sexual dysfunction, are poorly understood. A man who ejaculates prematurely may be helped by sex therapy exercises in which he learns to maintain himself at a medium level of arousal for extended periods of time. Premature ejaculation can also be treated with selective serotonin reuptake inhibitors (SSRIs).

4. Difficulty in reaching ejaculation or orgasm is fairly uncommon in men but may be caused by certain drugs, such as SSRIs. It may be treated by changing or adding drugs or by sensate-focus exercises in which the man and his partner progressively explore each other's bodies while avoiding performance demands.

5. Female sexual arousal disorder refers to difficulties with vaginal lubrication or engorgement or with clitoral erection. Insufficient lubrication is common, especially after menopause; it can be dealt with by the use of lubricants. Hormone replacement

often restores physiological arousal in postmenopausal women. Sex therapy exercises may be helpful.

6. In women, painful coitus (dyspareunia) can result from a wide variety of biological causes, including developmental malformations, scars, vaginal atrophy, infections, allergies, and insufficient lubrication. It can often be treated by correction of the underlying condition. In vaginismus, coitus is not possible, due to some combination of pelvic muscle spasm and pain or fear of pain. It is treated by psychotherapy and sex therapy exercises, including the use of vaginal dilators.

7. Many women have problems with orgasm. Some have never experienced it, and some do not experience it during partnered sex or during coitus. A biological cause for orgasmic dysfunction cannot usually be identified. Sex therapy for anorgasmia may include a program of directed masturbation or sensate-focus exercises. A woman may be helped to experience orgasm during partnered sex or coitus by adding effective clitoral stimulation, trying different positions, or extending the duration of the sexual interaction. It may also be helpful to address relationship problems.

8. Excessive sexual desire or behavior (hypersexuality) in either sex can be caused by neurological damage, various mental illnesses, or certain drugs. Hypersexuality may include frequently repeated and seemingly involuntary involvement in masturbation, partnered sex, pornography use, telephone sex, and the like. Such behaviors may be classed as compulsive disorders, and like other such disorders, they often respond well to SSRIs. The use of the term "sexual addiction" to describe these conditions is controversial.

9. Lack of interest in sex (hypoactive sexual desire disorder) is more common among women than among men. Sex hormone levels strongly influence sexual desire. In men, lack of interest in sex often responds to treatment with androgens. In women, it may respond to estrogens, androgens, or a combination of the two. Androgen treatment can cause unwanted or harmful side effects in both sexes, however, and the benefits may be limited, especially in women. Sex therapy may help people with low desire "let go" of thought patterns that interfere with sexual pleasure, such as a perceived obligation to ensure their partner's satisfaction. The efficacy of sex therapy in the treatment of hypoactive sexual desire disorder needs to be objectively tested. Lack of sexual desire needs to be evaluated in a broad context, which includes not just medical problems but also psychological, relationship, and socioeconomic issues.

Discussion Questions

1. "Many people have sexual disorders but are prevented by embarrassment or ignorance from seeking treatment that could help them." "Many people have unrealistic expectations about sex and therefore demand treatments, such as drugs or psychotherapy, when there's really not much wrong with them." Which of these two statements describes contemporary U.S. society more accurately, in your opinion, and why?

2. A married woman friend complains to you that she cannot reach orgasm during intercourse with her husband. If you were a therapist, what questions would you ask her and what recommendations would you give her?

3. An older male friend complains that he has been unhappy with his sexual performance and unable to sustain an erection over the past 2 years. How would you advise him about the various treatment options available?

4. Do you think that anxiety about performance, or excessive attention to one's partner's sexual satisfaction, can interfere with one's own sexual pleasure or performance? If so, what steps could be taken to alleviate the problem?

5. Some old people have lost interest in sex but are not bothered by that fact. If they were to take a pill that somehow restored their sex drive, do you think that would improve their lives, or would it simply create extra problems for them?

Web Resources

American Association of Sex Educators, Counselors, and Therapists www.aasect.org

American Board of Sexology www.americanboardofsexology.com

Sexual Health InfoCenter www.sexhealth.org

Society for Sex Therapy and Research www.sstarnet.org

Recommended Reading

Berman, J., Berman, L., and Bumiller, E. (2001). *For women only: A revolutionary guide to overcoming sexual dysfunction and reclaiming your sex life.* Henry Holt.

Heiman, J. R., and LoPiccolo, J. (1988). *Becoming orgasmic: A sexual and personal growth program for women* (2nd ed.). Simon and Schuster.

Kaplan, H. S. (1995). *The sexual desire disorders: Dysfunctional regulation of sexual motivation.* Brunner/Mazel.

Kaschak, E., and Tiefer, E. (2002). *A new view of women's sexual problems.* Haworth Press.

Leiblum, S. R. (Ed.). (2007). *Principles and practice of sex therapy* (4th ed.). Guilford Press.

Weeks, G. R., and Gambescia, N. (2002). *Hypoactive sexual desire: Integrating sex and couple therapy.* W. W. Norton.

Zilbergeld, B. (1999). *The new male sexuality* (rev. ed.). Bantam.

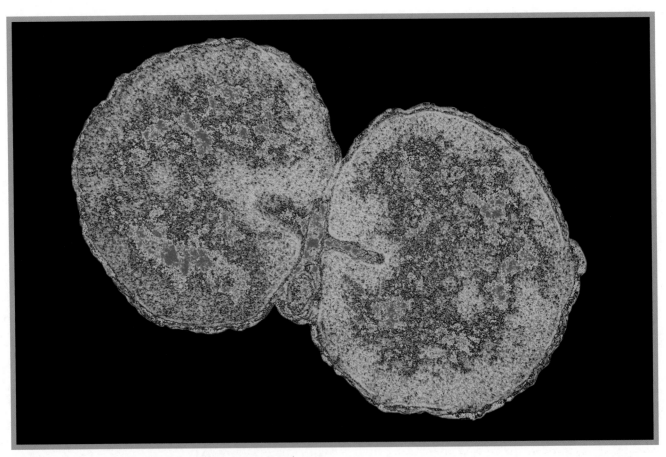

CHAPTER 17

Neisseria gonorrhoeae, the bacterium that causes gonorrhea.

Sexually Transmitted Diseases

The sustained intimacy of sexual contact offers an ideal opportunity for many disease-causing organisms to spread from one person to another. Some of these organisms are highly specialized for transmission by the sexual route, while others can spread either sexually or by alternative means. The existence of sexually transmitted diseases (STDs) has always added an element of risk to sex, and it has strongly influenced people's sexual behavior and attitudes. The AIDS epidemic, which struck the United States in the late 1970s and continues to cause immense human suffering worldwide, is just the most recent example. Medical research has brought spectacular advances in our knowledge of the causes of STDs and in many cases has given us the power to prevent or treat them. Yet there are deep social conflicts about how the battle against STDs should be conducted. These conflicts, rooted in moral differences about the nature and purpose of sexuality, have undercut the effectiveness of public health campaigns aimed at eliminating STDs.

Women and men who educate themselves about STDs can greatly reduce their risk of acquiring one. If they do contract one, they are in a better position to participate in effective treatment and can minimize the risk of passing the disease on to others.

Venereal Diseases Were Seen as Punishment for Sexual License

Until about a generation ago, sexually transmitted diseases* were called **venereal diseases**, after Venus, the Roman goddess of love. The archetypal venereal disease was **syphilis**, the first European cases of which were described in the mid-1490s, a year or two after Christopher Columbus discovered the New World. It is likely that Columbus or his sailors brought the disease from the Americas, where it had been endemic (Rothschild et al., 2000). For centuries, syphilis was essentially untreatable; it spread inexorably and returned to America with the colonists. By 1918, an estimated 1 in 22 Americans was infected (Amstey, 1994).

During the nineteenth century, there was very little sympathy for people with syphilis. They were thought to have brought the disease on themselves by engag-

---

*The term "sexually transmitted infections" is also commonly used. This term emphasizes the fact some people have been infected with STD-causing organisms but have not (yet) experienced any symptoms.

venereal disease Obsolete term for a sexually transmitted disease.

syphilis A sexually transmitted disease caused by a spirochete, *Treponema pallidum*.

Anti-VD (venereal disease) posters in the mid-twentieth century often blamed prostitutes and promiscuous women for the spread of syphilis and gonorrhea.

ing in a sinful behavior. Except for innocent wives infected by their husbands, people with syphilis were denied admission to hospitals for the poor. The facial disfiguration that commonly accompanied late-stage syphilis was taken as proof that the disease was a divine retribution for wrongdoing.

Until the mid-twentieth century, young men commonly used prostitutes as a sexual outlet prior to marriage—a practice that was highly conducive to the spread of syphilis and other venereal diseases. Men preferred to have sex either with very young prostitutes, who might still be free of infection, or with much older prostitutes, who were thought to have reached a noninfectious stage of the disease. Men also used primitive condoms to protect themselves from syphilis and other diseases. Many other men refrained from sex altogether for fear of infection. Thus syphilis and other venereal diseases helped make sex into something frightening and evil.

Syphilis still exists in America, but in recent years it has come tantalizingly close to being eliminated. This has resulted from medical advances, beginning with the discovery of the causative bacterium in 1905 and the introduction of the first effective antibiotic 4 years later. Grassroots activism and public health campaigns have also played an important role, as well as the decline of prostitution as a social institution. Unfortunately, as we'll see, the disease is proving harder to wipe out than was expected just a few years ago.

The history of AIDS has mimicked that of syphilis in many respects: the importation of the disease from another continent (Africa), its rapid spread, the initial lack of any effective treatment, the stigmatization of those who were affected, and the gradually increasing success in combating the epidemic, thanks to medical advances, social activism, and public health campaigns. The main difference is that the process has been compressed into a couple of decades rather than half a millennium. Also, syphilis can now be cured; AIDS, so far, can only be held at bay.

STDs Are Still a Major Problem in the United States

Here are some basic statistics that give some idea of the magnitude of the STD problem in this country (American Social Health Association, 2006):

- Nineteen million new infections with STD-causing organisms occur in the United States every year.
- One in two sexually active Americans acquires an STD by the age of 25.
- The United States has the highest incidence rates for curable STDs of any developed country—higher than many developing countries. The rate for gonorrhea, for example, is 8 times higher than in Canada and 50 times higher than in Sweden, even though sexual activity patterns are roughly comparable.

Some STDs occur much more commonly than others. Furthermore, because some STDs are readily treatable while others persist for a lifetime, there are enormous differences in the numbers of Americans who are carrying the various STDs at any one time (**Table 17.1**).

Some STDs are reportable, meaning that medical professionals who encounter cases are required to notify state or federal authorities. The main federally reportable STDs are syphilis, gonorrhea, chlamydia, and HIV/AIDS. Of course, many cases of these diseases go undiagnosed or unreported. The prevalence of STDs that are not reportable, such as herpes, is usually estimated on the basis of surveys.

There are very marked differences in the incidence of STDs in different racial/ethnic groups in the United States. African Americans in particular experience very high STD rates. The chlamydia rate is about 9 times higher among

TABLE 17.1

Estimated Incidence and Prevalence of Some Important STDs

STD	Incidence (estimated number of new cases per year)	Prevalence (estimated number of people currently infected)
Trichomoniasis	5 million	Not available
Syphilis	32,000	Not available
Gonorrhea	700,000	Not available
Chlamydia	4 million	Not available
Genital herpes	1 million	45 million
Human papillomavirus (HPV)	6.2 million	20 million
Hepatitis B	60,000	417,000
HIV/AIDS[a]	56,000 (reported AIDS diagnoses)	1,040,000

Source: National Prevention Information Network, 2008.

[a]HIV infections are not all by sexual contact.

blacks than among whites, the gonorrhea rate is 18 times higher, and the syphilis rate is about 10 times higher (Centers for Disease Control, 2006b). The HIV/AIDS rate is 8 times higher among black men and 23 times higher among black women, compared with the rates for white men and women (Centers for Disease Control, 2008f). The rates for Hispanics and Native Americans are also elevated, though less markedly. A variety of geographic, socioeconomic, and cultural factors combine to produce these disparities (Kraut-Becher et al., 2008).

In this chapter we discuss those STDs that are most commonly encountered in the United States and Canada (**Table 17.2**). We describe them in a sequence based on the type of organism that causes them, beginning with insects and progressing down the size scale to viruses. To an approximation, this also represents a sequence of increasing seriousness: Insects are an annoyance, but viruses can be killers.

We intend this chapter to be an educational overview of STDs rather than a specific source of medical advice for STD sufferers. That's because, for one thing, we are not medical doctors. For another, the information we provide may not be up to date at the time you read it. Therefore, if you have (or someone you know has) an STD, we urge you (or them) to get medical attention. There are also Web sites that carry up-to-date information on STDs and their treatment, such as the site of the Centers for Disease Control (see Web Resources at the end of this chapter).

Insects Are More of an Annoyance than a Danger

Three species of insects—head lice, pubic lice, and scabies mites—commonly infest human skin. Of these, pubic lice and scabies mites are frequently spread by sexual contact and are therefore discussed here. Louse and mite infestations hardly warrant being called "diseases" since they do not generally lead to serious systemic effects, but they are very bothersome conditions that, luckily, can be quickly and effectively treated.

Pubic Lice Itch, and That's All They Do

Pubic lice (*Phthirus pubis*) are popularly known as "crabs," but they are insects (**Figure 17.1**). They are small but visible—a large adult louse may measure about

pubic lice Insects (*Phthirus pubis*) that preferentially infest the pubic region.

TABLE 17.2

Basic STD Facts[a]

STD (Causative organism)	Symptoms	Diagnostic tests	Treatment
Insects			
Pubic lice	Itching at site of infestation	Visual recognition	Topical insecticidal lotion
Scabies (Scabies mite)	Itching, rash	Microscopic examination of skin scrapings	Topical insecticidal lotion
Protozoa			
Trichomoniasis (*Trichomonas vaginalis*)	Foul-smelling vaginal discharge, vaginal itching	Microscopic examination of discharge	Oral metranidazole (Flagyl)
Bacteria			
Syphilis (*Treponema pallidum*)	Primary: chancre at site of infection Secondary: rash, fever Latent period: none Tertiary: widespread organ damage	Primary: Microscopic examination of discharge Secondary: blood test (antibodies to *T. pallidum*)	Penicillin by injection
Gonorrhea (*Neisseria gonorrhoeae*)	Thick, cloudy discharge from urethra, vagina, or anus; may be asymptomatic or cause PID	DNA test on discharge or urine	Oral antibiotics (cephalosporins)
Chlamydia (*Chlamydia trachomatis*)	Thin discharge from urethra, vagina, or anus; local pain or irritation; often asymptomatic	DNA test on urine or swabs from penis, cervix, etc.	Oral azithromycin
Viruses			
Herpes (Herpes simplex virus 1, Herpes simplex virus 2)	Recurrent outbreaks of blisters or fissures localized to site of infection; may be painful	DNA tests on swabs from sores, or on blood	Oral acyclovir (Zovirax), valacyclovir (Valtrex), or famciclovir (Famvir); not curable
Genital warts (Human papillomavirus type 6 or 11)	Painless genital or anal warts	Visual recognition	Destruction of warts by freezing or podophyllin application
Precancerous changes in cervix or anus (Human papillomavirus type 16, 18, or others)	None at early stages	Microscopic examination of sample from cervix (Pap test)	Prophylactic vaccine against HPV types 16 and 18 available (Gardasil)
Hepatitis B	Jaundice, fever; most people recover, a few progress to chronic hepatitis and liver failure	Blood test (antibodies to virus)	No specific treatment for acute infection; several oral antivirals available for chronic hepatitis
Hepatitis A	Jaundice, nausea, flu-like illness; does not progress to chronic hepatitis	Blood test (antibodies to virus)	No specific treatment
HIV/AIDS (Human immunodeficiency virus)	Acute flu-like illness; after latent period, opportunistic infections, cervical cancer, lymphoma, wasting	Blood test (for antibodies to virus; alternatively, DNA test)	Combination of several oral antiviral drugs (HAART); not curable

[a]This table lists only the major STDs and their typical symptoms, most commonly used diagnostic tests, and usual forms of treatment.

a millimeter across and is dark or tan-colored, while newly hatched lice are considerably smaller and colorless. Pubic lice are flat, so they can lie very close to the skin; this makes them hard to dislodge. In addition, they grasp two nearby hairs with their clawlike legs, anchoring themselves in place. Once anchored, they burrow their mouthparts into the skin between the hairs and gorge themselves on their host's blood.

Pubic lice are happiest living among pubic hairs because the spacing between hair shafts in that region is optimal for them. They can also spread to other hairy areas of the skin, however, such as the armpits, eyebrows, and the general body surface of hairy people. They can even spread to the scalp, especially around the edges. Still, the scalp is the preferred hunting ground of another louse—the head louse.

Pubic lice lay eggs ("nits"), which they glue onto hairs near their base. Each nit can be seen as a tiny dark lump near the base of a hair. It takes about a week for the nits to hatch and begin the cycle anew. Both the lice and their nits may fall off the body and end up on bedding, underwear, or towels. The lice can survive in these locations for 2 days at the most, but the nits can survive for a week. It is therefore possible to acquire a louse infestation either by direct contact with an infested person or by using that person's bedding, clothing, or towels. Most infestations are probably passed on by direct contact, however. Sleeping with someone is the most favorable situation for transmission.

The "disease" part of a pubic louse infestation is simply the itching that the lice cause—plus any damage done by scratching. The amount of blood lost is trivial and, fortunately, pubic lice don't seem to transmit more dangerous disease agents.

Diagnosing pubic lice is a simple matter of looking for the insects in the region of irritated skin, digging one out, and watching it wave its legs. Pubic lice are probably the one STD that you don't need a medical degree to diagnose.

Pubic lice are treated with insecticidal lotions or shampoos. Medications containing permethrin or pyrethrins (for example, Rid) are available over the counter. The lotion should be applied to all hairy areas, left on for the exact period of time specified in the instructions, and then washed off. All clothes, sheets, and towels that might harbor pubic lice must be washed and dried at a high heat setting. (Items that cannot be washed can simply be left in a sealed plastic bag for 2 weeks or dry-cleaned.)

The over-the-counter medications to treat lice infestations do not always work well; if they don't, it may be necessary to see a doctor and get a prescription for a more effective insecticide, Lindane. Because Lindane is potentially toxic if misused, it is important to follow instructions carefully. It should not be used by pregnant or nursing women. Pubic lice and nits may also be removed by close shaving of affected areas. As with any STD, all recent sex partners should be notified.

Figure 17.1 Scanning electron micrograph of pubic lice The claws at the ends of the insects' legs are structured to clamp onto oval-shaped hair shafts.

1 mm

Scabies May Be Transmitted Sexually or Nonsexually

Scabies is an infestation with a parasitic mite, *Sarcoptes scabiei* (**Figure 17.2**). The mites themselves are not usually seen, because they spend most of their time in tunnels that they dig within the superficial layers of the skin. The tunnels themselves are visible as reddish tracks, spots, or pustules. If the infested person is sensitive to the scabies mite, there may also be a generalized rash even in places where no mites are located. Unlike lice, the scabies mite does not require hairy skin. In fact, it is commonly found in hairless areas such as the wrists, elbows, between the fingers, and the knees, penis, breasts, or back.

The female mite lives for about 2 months below the skin in its tunnels, laying eggs every few days. The eggs hatch after 3 to 8 days. The young go through a couple of juvenile stages and then return to the skin surface as adults to mate. Impregnated females burrow into the skin again, completing the cycle.

scabies Infestation with a mite (*Sarcoptes scabiei*) that burrows within the skin.

Figure 17.2 A scabies mite (left) and a severe case of scabies rash (right)

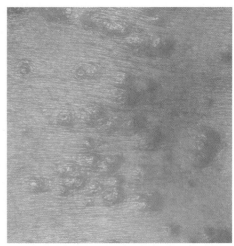

200 µm

trichomoniasis (or "trich") Infection with the protozoan *Trichomonas vaginalis*.

asymptomatic carrier Someone who is infected with a disease organism but is not experiencing symptoms.

The itching caused by scabies infestations can be severe and may interfere with sleep. Infested people may scratch themselves to the point of causing sores, which can become infected. Scabies spreads from person to person quite easily, so it is common wherever people live in crowded conditions. Sexual contact is just one of many modes of transmission.

Scabies is best diagnosed by a physician, who may examine skin scrapings under a microscope. The recommended treatment is a topical application of permethrin lotion, which is left on for several hours or overnight before being washed off. Because the eggs may not all be killed, a repeat treatment 7 to 10 days later may be necessary. As with pubic lice, possibly infested items must be washed and dried on a hot cycle or left unused for 2 weeks.

Trichomoniasis Is Caused by a Protozoan

Trichomoniasis ("trich") is an infection of the vagina or the male urethra and prostate gland with *Trichomonas vaginalis*. This organism is not a bacterium, but rather a single-celled nucleated (protozoan) organism with a bundle of whiplike flagella (**Figure 17.3**). In women, trichomoniasis is marked by a foul-smelling, greenish, or frothy discharge from the vagina. There may be vaginal itching and redness, as well as abdominal discomfort or the urge to urinate frequently. Some women, however, have no symptoms. (People who are infected with a disease organism but show no symptoms are referred to as **asymptomatic carriers**.) Women who do have symptoms develop them within 6 months of infection, which usually happens through coitus. *T. vaginalis* survives poorly outside a human host or even on the outside of the body, so nonsexual transmission is thought to be rare. An estimated 2 million women in the United States develop trichomoniasis every year, so it is a very common condition. About one-fourth of all cases of vaginitis (inflammation of the vagina) are caused by *T. vaginalis*.

In men, *T. vaginalis* infection is usually asymptomatic. Sometimes it is marked by a slight discharge from the urethra, the urge to urinate frequently, and pain during urination.

Trichomoniasis is usually diagnosed by microscopic examination of specimens from the vagina or the urethra. A more sensitive diagnostic method is to culture (grow) the organism from specimens; this process takes a few days and is more expensive. Trichomoniasis can usually be cured with a single oral dose of metronidazole (Flagyl or its generic equivalents). Some strains of *T. vaginalis* are resist-

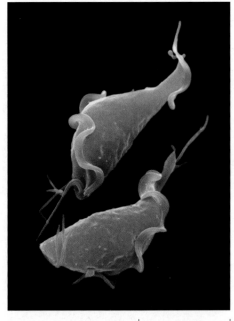

20 µm

Figure 17.3 *Trichomonas vaginalis*, the single-celled organism that causes trichomoniasis, as seen in a colorized scanning electron micrograph. The bundle of whiplike processes carry receptors that specifically recognize and bind to the cells of the vaginal lining.

ant to metronidazole, however, and the drug should not be used during pregnancy. The infected person's partner should be treated at the same time, whether symptomatic or not; otherwise partners may continue to swap the infection back and forth between them.

Bacterial STDs Can Usually Be Treated with Antibiotics

The main sexually transmitted bacterial infections in the United States are syphilis, gonorrhea, and chlamydia. These are serious diseases that can be fatal in themselves (syphilis), impair fertility (gonorrhea and chlamydia), or facilitate HIV infection (all three). Treated promptly, however, they can be readily cured, and complications can be avoided.

Syphilis Is Down but Not Out

Syphilis is caused by infection with a corkscrew-shaped bacterium, or **spirochete**, with the name *Treponema pallidum* (**Figure 17.4**). Syphilis is spread by direct contact, nearly always sexually. (It can also spread from mother to fetus.) If not treated, syphilis can last a lifetime and eventually cause death.

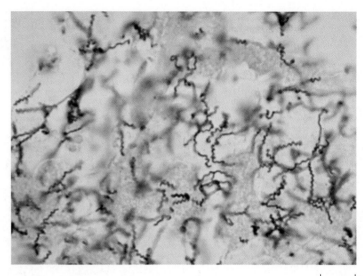

|_____|
10 μm

Figure 17.4 *Treponema pallidum,* the bacterium that causes syphilis. The bacteria are the dark, corkscrew-shaped threads. The yellow objects are cells of the host.

Untreated Syphilis Progresses through Three Stages

A man or woman acquires syphilis by sexual contact with a person who is in the primary or secondary stage of the disease. Most commonly, infection comes from a syphilitic sore, or **chancre** (**Figure 17.5**), which exudes a fluid containing huge numbers of spirochetes. The chancre is often painless. It may be visible on the penis or labia, or it may be hidden inside the vagina, on the cervix, inside the anus or rectum, or even inside the mouth. Thus it may or may not be possible to tell whether a partner has a chancre.

The spirochetes penetrate the skin and multiply at the site of infection. Between 10 and 90 days (usually about 21 days) after infection, a chancre appears at that same site. This condition is known as **primary syphilis**. The chancre starts as a red bump that then breaks down, becoming a sore or ulcer. The chancre has a hard, rubbery rim and a wet or scabbed-over interior. If left untreated, it will heal by itself within 3 to 6 weeks. Because a chancre is a break in the skin, it greatly facilitates the transmission of an even more serious pathogen, HIV.

Secondary syphilis may begin while the primary chancre is still visible, or it may be delayed for several weeks. The main sign of secondary syphilis is a painless rash, which classically affects the palms of the hands and the soles of the feet but may also occur elsewhere (**Figure 17.6**). The rash takes the form of red or reddish-brown blotches. It is often accompanied by a fever, swollen lymph nodes, sore throat, and muscle pain. If left untreated, these symptoms generally disappear within a few weeks.

In many individuals, the *T. pallidum* spirochetes are not eliminated at the end of the second stage but continue to multiply in the body, even though the symptoms are gone. After about a year of this **latent phase**, the person is no longer infectious to sex partners. A pregnant woman can pass the organism to her fetus, however. The fetus may be stillborn, die neonatally, or suffer severe neurological impairment.

spirochete Any of a class of corkscrew-shaped bacteria, including the agent that causes syphilis.

chancre A primary sore on the skin or a mucous membrane in a person infected with syphilis. (Pronounced SHANK-er.)

primary syphilis The first phase of syphilis, marked by the occurrence of a chancre.

secondary syphilis The second phase of syphilis, marked by a rash and fever.

latent phase An asymptomatic phase of syphilis or other infectious disease.

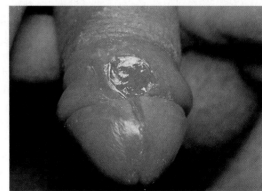

Figure 17.5 Primary syphilitic sore (chancre) on the penis

Figure 17.6 Secondary syphilitic rash may appear on the hands, as here, on the soles of the feet, or elsewhere on the body.

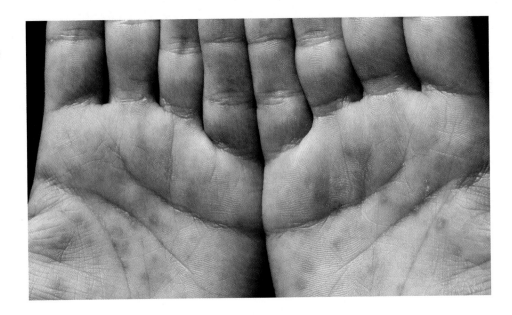

tertiary syphilis The third phase of syphilis, marked by multiple organ damage.

During the latent phase, the organism continues to multiply at a slow rate. It may gradually invade the cardiovascular system, the bones, the liver, and the nervous system without initially causing any symptoms.

Eventually—sometimes decades after infection—syphilis may begin to do serious damage. This phase is called **tertiary syphilis**; it occurs in about 15% of untreated individuals. Large ulcers may appear on the skin or internal organs. The disease may attack the heart, the central nervous system, or the skeleton. Tertiary syphilis is now thankfully rare, but its very rarity, combined with the variety of sites that may be attacked, can make it difficult to diagnose.

Syphilis Has Resisted Elimination

Syphilis is diagnosed by recognition of the clinical signs and symptoms, by finding *T. pallidum* in the fluid discharge from the primary chancre, or by detecting antibodies to *T. pallidum* in the blood. During the first year after infection, a single large injection of penicillin is curative; at later times a more prolonged course of the drug may be required. Having had syphilis in the past does not protect a person from reinfection.

The introduction of effective antibiotic treatment, along with other public health measures, greatly reduced the prevalence of syphilis in the United States from the 1 in 22 rate in 1918, mentioned earlier. In 2000 the rate of new cases was so low (about 2.5 new infections per 100,000 people) that public health officials spoke hopefully of eliminating the disease. Since then, however, the syphilis rate has rebounded to 3.5 new infections per 100,000 people (Centers for Disease Control, 2007h).

There are really two interconnected syphilis epidemics in the United States. One is a heterosexual epidemic among African American men and women in the South. This epidemic has persisted for well over a century (**Box 17.1**). The other is a more recent series of outbreaks among gay and bisexual men in large cities such as Los Angeles, New York, and Atlanta. The interconnection comes about because some heterosexually identified black men also engage in sex with men, either on account of a broader sexual interest than their self-identification suggests or because they are in prison, where about 13% of all new cases of syphilis are reported (Kahn et al., 2004).

Society, Values, and the Law

BOX 17.1 The Tuskegee Syphilis Study

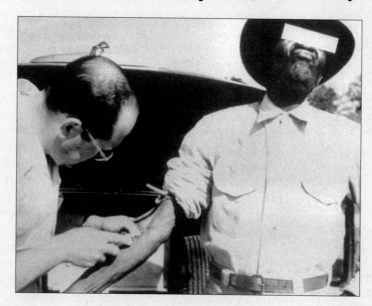

One of the most shameful episodes in the history of American medicine began in 1932, when Public Health Service researchers initiated a study of the effects of untreated syphilis on several hundred African-American men living near Tuskegee, Alabama (Reverby, 2000) (see figure). The aim of the project was to follow the natural history of the disease, to study whether there were differences between the disease in black and in white people, and to compare symptoms during life with autopsy findings after death. (The study initially had a treatment element, but this was soon abandoned.)

The researchers, some of whom were based at the Tuskegee Institute (now Tuskegee University, a historically black college), recruited black farmers, renters, and laborers who had latent syphilis. That is, they had progressed beyond the first two stages of the disease but had not yet shown systemic symptoms. Most were poor and poorly educated. Among the incentives that attracted men to the study or kept them in it over the years were medical examinations and blood tests, free trips to Tuskegee, and the promise that burial expenses would be covered. Most of the subjects thought that they were being treated for their condition, but in reality they only received dubious medications such as "tonics."

At the time the study began, a treatment for syphilis existed—the organic arsenical compound Salvarsan—but effective treatment required weekly injections over many months, and serious side effects were common. Some doctors thought that the treatment was worse than the disease for people in the latent stage. Because of this uncertainty, as well as the expense of treatment and the belief that poor rural blacks were unlikely to cooperate with the treatment regimen, this population was often not given drugs for syphilis. In other words, the Tuskegee subjects were not initially treated in any unusual way.

The study continued for decades, and 13 research papers described the findings. In 1947, a far more effective antibiotic, penicillin, was recognized as the standard of care for syphilis. In the same year, the Nuremberg Code was promulgated in response to the atrocities committed by doctors in Nazi Germany. The code declared that informed consent must be a condition for participation in medical experiments. Nevertheless, the Tuskegee experiment continued, and the subjects were not told that a simple and effective treatment was now available. In fact, the researchers went to considerable lengths to prevent the subjects from receiving treatment at the hands of other doctors. Thus the moral status of the study changed radically.

The study did not end until 1972, when a CDC researcher who was opposed to the continuation of the study gave an account of it to an Associated Press reporter. The ensuing publicity led to the rapid termination of the project. By that time, however, dozens of the subjects had died of the disease, and 22 wives, 17 children, and 2 grandchildren had contracted it, probably as a result of the nontreatment of the subjects.

In 1974 a lawsuit brought on behalf of the survivors was settled for $10 million. In May 1997, President Clinton, responding to pressure from civil rights activists and the Black Congressional Caucus, formally apologized to the survivors in a White House ceremony. In response, one of the survivors, Herman Shaw, declared that "it is time to put this horrible nightmare behind us as a nation. . . . We must never allow a tragedy like the Tuskegee study to happen again."

The Tuskegee study exemplified a long tradition of abusive medical research on black Americans (Washington, 2007). As if the facts of the Tuskegee study were not ethically troubling enough, fictional allegations about it are in wide circulation, such as the notion that the Tuskegee doctors actually infected their subjects with syphilis. Not surprisingly, many African Americans have developed a deep suspicion of mainstream medicine. Conspiracy theories that may seem outlandish to others, such as the idea that the AIDS virus was manufactured and spread by the federal government with the intent of wiping out black people, find a certain resonance among less-educated African Americans.

Research practices have changed greatly since the time the Tuskegee study was begun, and it is unthinkable that such a project could be carried out in the United States today. Even so, much needs to be done to ensure that minority interests are properly addressed in medical research. Furthermore, ethical concerns somewhat similar to those arising from the Tuskegee study have been raised by the practice of testing drugs and vaccines in developing countries, usually on relatively poor, nonwhite populations. Researchers and ethicists debate whether these research subjects must be given world-class medical care or whether they may be treated according to lower standards that are more comparable to those currently existing in their communities (Wendler et al., 2004).

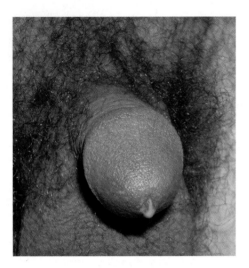

Figure 17.7 Gonorrheal urethritis in men is usually marked by painful urination and a discharge of pus from the urethra.

gonorrhea A sexually transmitted disease caused by infection with the bacterium *Neisseria gonorrhoeae.*

pelvic inflammatory disease (PID) An infection of the female reproductive tract, often caused by sexually transmitted organisms.

epididymitis Inflammation of the epididymis.

Gonorrhea Can Lead to Infertility

Gonorrhea ("the clap," "the drip") is a very common STD. The disease is caused by infection with the bacterium *Neisseria gonorrhoeae.* The symptoms of gonorrhea develop quickly—within 2 to 10 days after infection in most people. In women, the initial site of infection is usually the cervix. Symptoms include a yellow or bloody vaginal discharge, bleeding during coitus, and a burning sensation when urinating. Sometimes—perhaps in the majority of cases—the initial infection is asymptomatic. In men, the usual site of infection is the urethra, and the symptoms are a discharge of pus from the urethral meatus (**Figure 17.7**) and pain on urination. Like women, men can be infected with gonorrhea without experiencing symptoms (Mimiaga et al., 2008).

Both men and women can be infected rectally through receptive anal sex. The symptoms of rectal infection include a rectal discharge, anal itching, and sometimes painful bowel movements with fresh, bright red blood on the surface of the feces. In women, a vaginal infection can spread to the rectum. Infections of the mouth or pharynx can occur as a result of oral sex, especially fellatio, with an infected person.

In women, a gonorrheal infection can spread into the uterus and oviducts, causing **pelvic inflammatory disease (PID)**. In some women, PID symptoms are the first symptoms of gonorrhea to be noticed. These symptoms can include abdominal cramps and continuous pain, vaginal bleeding between menstrual periods, vomiting, and fever. PID may cause scarring of the oviducts, resulting in infertility or subfertility and a heightened risk of ectopic pregnancy. In men, the infection can spread to the epididymis (causing pain in the scrotum) or to the prostate gland. **Epididymitis**, like PID, can affect fertility. Other organ systems can be affected in both sexes, and babies can become infected—usually in the eyes—during the birth process. To prevent this, all newborns in the United States are given antibiotic eyedrops.

Gonorrhea is usually diagnosed by the detection of *N. gonorrhoeae* DNA in the discharge or in urine. The organism can also be identified by being cultured (grown in the lab).

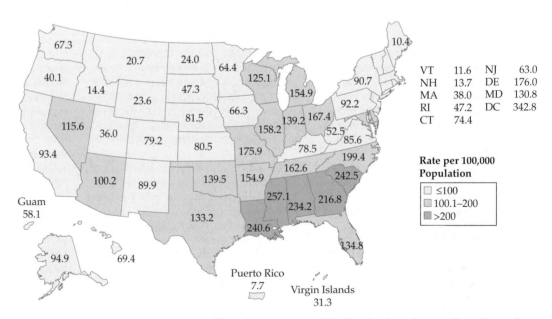

Figure 17.8 Geographic distribution of gonorrhea Gonorrhea is most prevalent in the southeastern United States. The map shows the new cases per 100,000 people in 2006. (Data from Centers for Disease Control, 2007g.)

About 700,000 new cases of gonorrhea are reported in the U.S. annually, with by far the highest incidence rates in the South (**Figure 17.8**) and among African Americans. Nevertheless, the pattern has been changing in recent years: Rates in the South and among African Americans have been falling, and rates in the West and among whites have been rising (Centers for Disease Control, 2006b).

At one time, gonorrhea was readily treatable with standard antibiotics such as penicillin and tetracycline. Unfortunately, the *N. gonorrhoeae* organism has shown a remarkable ability to develop drug resistance. The DNA test that is commonly used to diagnose gonorrhea provides no information about which antibiotics the infection will respond to. The CDC therefore recommends that all cases be treated with a class of antibiotics (cephalosporins) to which all strains of gonorrhea are known to be sensitive. This policy could backfire if it encourages the emergence of cephalosporin-resistant gonorrhea, because after that no new drugs are close to approval.

It's important for infected people to notify their partners so that the partners, too, may be treated before serious complications develop. Women in particular may have few or no symptoms, at least initially, so they may not seek medical treatment unless they know that their sex partner is infected.

Chlamydia Causes a Common Infection with Serious Complications

Chlamydia is a relatively newly recognized STD. Reported cases in the United States rose from 3 to 207 per 100,000 people between 1984 and 1997, and chlamydia is now the most common of all reportable infectious diseases; 1,030,000 cases were reported in 2006, and many more probably went unreported (Centers for Disease Control, 2007b). This increase did not represent the explosive spread of a new disease, as with AIDS, however. Rather, the increase was due in part to increased recognition of a condition that had previously been diagnosed as a nonspecific genital infection.

The causative agent, *Chlamydia trachomatis* is a bacterium, but an unusual one: Like viruses, it lives inside cells and exists outside of cells only in the form of inert infective particles. Besides its role in causing an STD, *C. trachomatis* is a leading cause of blindness in tropical countries, where it is transmitted by eye-seeking insects.

In the United States and Canada, chlamydia is usually spread by genital contact. Symptoms appear a few days to 3 weeks after infection. In men, the organism infects the urethra, causing a thin discharge (different from the thick discharge of gonorrhea) and burning pain during urination. Like gonorrhea, the organism can migrate farther up the male reproductive tract and cause epididymitis or prostatitis.

In women, the organism infects the cervix (**Figure 17.9**) or urethra, causing irritation, a thin vaginal discharge, and painful urination. But 75% of infected women (as well as 50% of infected men) experience no symptoms. In both men and women, chlamydia infections can also occur in the rectum and in the mouth or throat if those parts have been involved in sexual contact with an infected partner.

Like gonorrhea, chlamydia can migrate up the female reproductive tract and cause PID (whether the initial infection was symptomatic or not). Up to 40% of women with untreated chlamydia infections develop PID; 20% of these women with PID will become infertile, and 9% of them will have an ectopic pregnancy. About half of all cases of PID are probably caused by chlamydia infections.

As with gonorrhea, chlamydia can spread from an infected woman to her infant during childbirth, causing a serious but treatable eye or respiratory infection. Testing (and, if necessary, treatment) of all pregnant women is recommended.

chlamydia A sexually transmitted disease caused by infection with the bacterium *Chlamydia trachomatis*.

Figure 17.9 (A) Normal cervix and (B) cervical inflammation caused by chlamydia, as seen on visual examination through the vagina. (Not all healthy cervixes look exactly like the one on the left.)

(A)   (B)

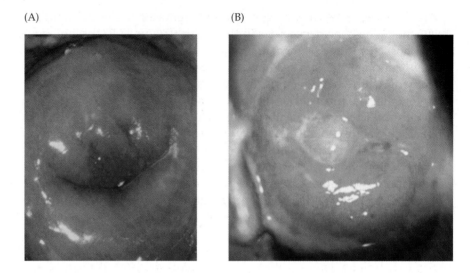

Chlamydia is diagnosed from cell samples obtained from the penis or cervix. (The cervical sampling procedure is different from the Pap test described below.) It can also be diagnosed from urine samples. Chlamydia can be cured with a single dose of an antibiotic, usually azithromycin. Reinfection from an infected partner can easily occur, so it's important that partners be tested and successfully treated before they resume sexual contact.

The demographics of chlamydia are poorly understood because of underreporting and other factors. Reported cases among women outnumber those among men by about 5 to 1, but this is probably due to the fact that there have been extensive campaigns to screen for chlamydia among women. Chlamydia is common among young, sexually active men and women across the United States. As many as 1 in 10 of all adolescent girls are infected, and the figures for older adolescents in urban areas may be even higher. By age 30, about half of all sexually active women show evidence of current or prior chlamydia infection.

The CDC recommends that all sexually active women under 25 be tested for chlamydia once per year, as well as older women who have had a new sex partner and all pregnant women (Centers for Disease Control, 2007b). Since the test merely involves giving a urine sample—and taking a single dose of an antibiotic if it is positive for chlamydia—it is a small price to pay for peace of mind.

The Status of Bacterial Vaginosis as an STD Is Uncertain

Bacterial vaginosis is a condition in which the normal vaginal microorganisms are replaced by a variety of other bacterial species (Schwebke, 2000). The pH of the vaginal secretions rises (becomes less acidic), the vagina develops a characteristic fishy odor, and there may be itching, pain, and a thin, off-white discharge. Many women who have bacterial vaginosis have no symptoms.

Bacterial vaginosis is uncommon in women who have not had sexual intercourse, but it is very common among sexually active women, especially those who have multiple partners. Vaginal douching, which disturbs the bacterial ecosystem within the vagina, increases the likelihood of developing vaginosis (Brotman et al., 2008).

While it is clear that engaging in sex increases the likelihood of developing bacterial vaginosis, it is not clear whether sexually transmitted organisms are

bacterial vaginosis A condition in which the normal microorganisms of the vagina are replaced by other species, causing discomfort and a foul-smelling discharge.

responsible for the condition. That does seem to be the case for female–female sexual contact, however: Lesbians whose partners have bacterial vaginosis are about 20 times more likely to have the condition themselves, compared with lesbians whose partners do not have it (Berger et al., 1995; Marrazzo et al., 2002). As to the question of heterosexual transmission, at least one of the organisms that characterize bacterial vaginosis, *Gardnerella vaginalis*, can also infect men; such infections may be asymptomatic or they may be accompanied by urethritis. Nevertheless, the CDC does not recommend routine treatment of male partners of women with bacterial vaginosis.

In a minority of women, bacterial vaginosis may lead to serious complications, such as pelvic inflammatory disease and (in pregnant women) premature delivery. Having bacterial vaginosis makes it easier for a woman to acquire or transmit HIV (Atashili et al., 2008).

The condition can be treated effectively with antibiotics. Relapses can occur; treating the male partners of affected women does not reduce the likelihood of recurrence. This observation argues somewhat against the idea that heterosexual transmission of causative organisms is an important route for acquisition of bacterial vaginosis.

Urethritis Can Be Caused by a Variety of Organisms

Infections of the urethra (**urethritis**) are very common. They are not necessarily caused by sexually transmitted bacteria, but they often are. We already mentioned gonorrhea as a cause of urethritis in men. Urethritis caused by other organisms, especially when it occurs in men, is referred to as **nongonococcal urethritis (NGU)**. The main agents are *Chlamydia trachomatis*, discussed above, and a group of organisms called **mycoplasmas**, the smallest cellular organisms known. (Sometimes "NGU" is taken to exclude chlamydia as well as gonorrhea.) Another potential agent is *Gardnerella vaginalis,* also mentioned above.

Urethritis causes pain during urination and, often, a urethral discharge. The infection can spread to the bladder (cystitis) and reproductive tract. If gonorrhea has been ruled out, the doctor may treat the urethritis with antibiotics without attempting to identify the specific organism responsible. As with any STD, partner notification is important.

Viral STDs Can Be Dangerous and Hard to Treat

Viruses are extremely small infectious particles (10 to 100 nanometers in diameter). When not inside a host cell, viruses are metabolically inert but infectious. A viral particle consists of a core of genetic material (either DNA or RNA) and proteins, surrounded by a **capsid**—a crystal-like array of proteins with associated sugar molecules. In some viruses the capsid is contained within a lipid **envelope** resembling a cell membrane.

A virus's genome is extremely limited in size: It may possess as few as 10 genes, compared with about 1000 genes for a bacterium. Once inside a host cell, the viral genes take over the cell's metabolic machinery in order to replicate themselves. This replication may occur right away and be followed by the release of new viral particles. Alternatively, the viral genes may persist in the cell in an inactive form for months or years before coming out of hiding and generating new viral particles.

Many viral diseases are self-limiting because they trigger an effective immune response in the infected person. Some viruses have found ways to protect them-

urethritis Inflammation of the urethra, usually caused by an infection.

nongonococcal urethritis (NGU) Urethritis not caused by gonorrhea.

mycoplasmas A group of very small cellular organisms that may cause urethritis.

virus An extremely small infectious agent. When not inside a host cell, viruses are metabolically inert but infectious.

capsid An array of protein molecules surrounding the core of a virus.

envelope A lipid outer membrane possessed by some viruses.

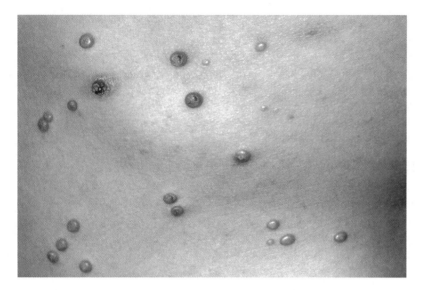

Figure 17.10 Molluscum contagiosum takes the form of small growths on the skin.

molluscum contagiosum A skin condition marked by small raised growths; it is caused by a pox virus.

oral herpes Herpes infection of the mouth, caused by HSV-1 or (less commonly) HSV-2.

genital herpes An infection of the genital area caused by HSV-2 or (less commonly) HSV-1.

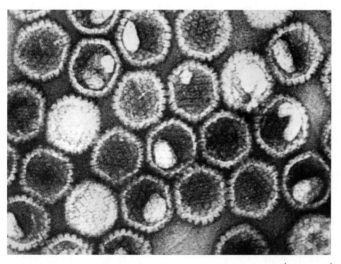

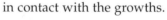

150 nm

Figure 17.11 Particles of herpes simplex virus 2 (HSV-2), the usual causative agent of genital herpes, are shown in an electron micrograph, using negative contrast. The shell-like structures are viral capsids—arrays of proteins that form cages around the viral DNA. Each capsid measures about 200 nanometers in diameter. The DNA cores are visible as dense, light-colored clumps within some of the capsids.

selves from their host's immune system, however. Viral infections are not treatable with antibiotics. A variety of effective antiviral drugs have been introduced over the last two decades, but these drugs are rarely curative and they often have serious side effects. Some are also very costly—users pay as much as $20,000 for a year's supply for the most advanced drugs.

In this section we discuss six viruses or classes of viruses: a pox virus, herpes simplex viruses, cytomegalovirus, human papillomaviruses, hepatitis viruses, and the human immunodeficiency virus. This sequence corresponds approximately to the increasing seriousness of the diseases they cause.

Molluscum Contagiosum Is a Self-Limiting Condition

Molluscum contagiosum is a skin condition caused by a pox virus. It is characterized by small, bump-like growths on the skin up to about the size of a pencil eraser (**Figure 17.10**). Each bump has a central pit or dimple. The virus is transmitted by direct skin-to-skin contact or by contact with infected clothing or towels. Nonsexual transmission is common, especially among children. Molluscum in the genital area is most likely the result of sexual transmission, however. The condition does not cause any serious health problems, and it usually disappears within a year of its first appearance, but a variety of treatments is available. Because it is so contagious, people with molluscum should take care to prevent others from coming in contact with the growths.

Genital Herpes Is a Lifelong but not Life-Threatening Infection

The genetic material of herpesviruses is DNA (**Figure 17.11**). Two herpesviruses, herpes simplex 1 and 2 (HSV-1 and HSV-2), may be transmitted sexually. HSV-1 commonly causes **oral herpes**, often in the form of "fever blisters" or "cold sores" on the lips. Oral herpes may be spread by sexual or nonsexual contact. If a person with oral herpes performs oral sex on another person, however, that other person may acquire a genital HSV-1 infection. The proportion of genital herpes infections that are caused by HSV-1 has been increasing in recent years and is estimated to reach 30% to 50% among college students, probably because of the increasing popularity of oral sex. The more common cause of **genital herpes**, however, is HSV-2, which is usually transmitted directly from the anogenital area of one person to that of another.

The initial symptoms of HSV-2 infection usually occur within 2 weeks after exposure, taking the form of an outbreak of sores at the site of infection. This site is most commonly somewhere in the genital or anorectal area or on the

(A)

(B)

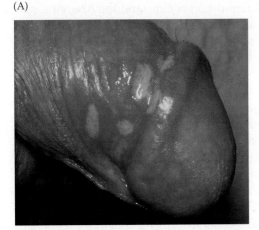

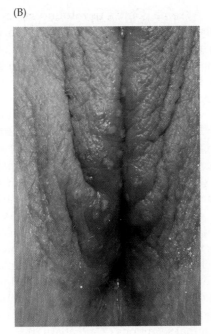

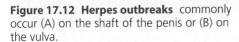
Figure 17.12 Herpes outbreaks commonly occur (A) on the shaft of the penis or (B) on the vulva.

surrounding skin, but may be elsewhere on the body or around the mouth. The most frequently affected sites are the penis in men and the labia, clitoral hood, or vaginal walls in women.

The outbreak may be preceded by tingling or itching at the site where the outbreak is about to occur. Such anticipatory signs are useful, especially in later outbreaks, because they can warn the person to abstain from sex or use protection (to decrease the likelihood of giving herpes to a sex partner) and to start taking medication (see below). Shortly after any anticipatory signs, a reddish, slightly elevated spot or cluster of spots appears. A day or so later, the spots turn into blisters (**Figure 17.12**). The blisters then break, leaving sores or ulcers that give rise to a clear discharge. Alternatively, there may be fissures (cracks) in the skin or mucosa, rather than blisters. The discharge from the blisters or fissures contains immense numbers of viral particles and is highly infectious. After a few more days, the sores crust over, dry up, and gradually heal and disappear.

Herpes outbreaks may be painless or mildly itchy—especially if they occur on a less sensitive patch of skin. In that case, they may not come to the person's attention at all. Alternatively, the outbreaks may be quite painful. If they are in a site that is contacted by urine, the act of urination may be extremely painful.

The first outbreak may be accompanied by fever and swollen lymph nodes or, rarely, by more serious symptoms. Also, the virus can be spread to other parts of the body, including the eyes, by the person's fingers.

Recurrent Outbreaks Are the Rule

Unless the immune system is compromised, the primary infection is quickly resolved, and the sores disappear within a couple of weeks. The herpesvirus has a trick up its sleeve, however. Some viral particles enter the terminals of sensory nerve fibers in the vicinity of the infection site. They then travel up the nerve fibers to the nerve cell bodies, close to the spinal cord. Once the viral particles have reached a cell body, they may remain inert for weeks or months. In this location, they are protected from the host's immune system.

At some point, a new round of viral replication occurs, and the new viral particles travel in the opposite direction, back to the original infection site or nearby, where they cause another outbreak of sores. Because the host's immune system has already been exposed to the virus, the second and later outbreaks are usually less severe than the first, and during these later outbreaks the virus cannot be spread to other parts of the body.

A few people infected with genital herpes caused by HSV-2 may experience only the initial outbreak, but the great majority continue to experience outbreaks indefinitely. Typically, the frequency of outbreaks decreases over time, from a median of 6 outbreaks in the first year to 3 outbreaks in the fifth year (Benedetti et al., 1994). When genital herpes is caused by HSV-1, recurrent outbreaks are much less frequent and less severe than with HSV-2.

It is widely believed that most HSV-2 infections are asymptomatic, because the majority of people who have been infected (as documented by the presence of antibodies to HSV-2 in their blood) deny any history of herpes outbreaks. This belief may be erroneous, however. In one study, researchers recruited HSV-2-positive women who said that they had never had a herpes outbreak and gave them careful instructions on how to examine themselves. Within a few months, most of the women reported at least one outbreak, and the virus was detected in their vaginal secretions (Wald et al., 2000). Presumably, many of the remaining women would have reported outbreaks if they had monitored for longer periods. Thus, truly asymptomatic HSV-2 infection may not be common among women—it may just be that the outbreaks are painless and in an inconspicuous location. It is thought that "asymptomatic" men also suffer periodic outbreaks that are not recognized (Leone & Corey, 2005).

During outbreaks, herpes sufferers can very easily transmit the disease to their sex partners. People with herpes are generally most infectious from the time they experience the first symptoms to the time that all their sores are dry and crusted over. HSV-2 can sometimes be detected on the affected area of skin during times when no outbreak is present, and some evidence suggests that transmission between outbreaks is a possibility (Mertz et al., 1992). Nevertheless, the great majority of transmissions probably occur during outbreaks. People with herpes who carefully watch for outbreaks and who abstain from sex while they are present are going a long way toward protecting their partners from infection.

Is There a Stress Connection?

Many people believe that stress triggers their herpes outbreaks or increases their frequency, and some scientific studies support this idea (Sainz et al., 2001). However, these studies have usually failed to account for observer bias—that is, for the fact that stressful events occurring right before outbreaks are remembered better, simply because they are followed by an outbreak.

To get around this problem, two prospective studies required herpes sufferers to keep logs of stressful events and to seal the logs or deposit them in the mail at regular intervals, even daily (Rand et al., 1990; Herpetic Eye Disease Study Group, 2000). In neither of these studies did statistical analysis reveal any tendency for sufferers to record an increased frequency of stressful events before they knew they had an outbreak. In one of these studies, the sufferers had the opportunity to retrospectively add mention of earlier stressful events. These people did indeed add many reports of such events for the days before each outbreak, apparently because of observer bias. Thus there is a real possibility that the link between stressful events and herpes outbreaks is fictitious or exaggerated. There is some evidence, however, that persistent stress and anxiety can increase the likelihood of herpes outbreaks (Cohen et al., 1999).

Herpes Can Have Serious Effects

Although recurrent herpes outbreaks, even over a lifetime, do not present a serious threat to health, a herpes infection can have more serious effects. First and foremost, a herpes-infected pregnant woman can transmit the infection to her child during the birth process, and the infection can be fatal to the infant or leave it severely disabled. Mother-to-infant transmission can be prevented by delivering the baby via cesarean section.

There is also some evidence that herpes infection increases the risk of cervical cancer, possibly by assisting the main causative agent, human papillomavirus (see below). Studies on this topic have yielded contradictory results, however (Lehtinen et al., 2002; Smith et al., 2002).

Drug Treatment Can Shorten or Prevent Outbreaks

Genital herpes is sometimes diagnosed simply from the patient's history and from clinical observation of the sores. Herpes is often difficult to recognize, however, and other, more serious diseases can closely mimic herpes. Also, simple inspection cannot distinguish between herpes caused by HSV-1 and HSV-2, but the distinction is important because of the difference in the long-term course of the two diseases. For all these reasons, both the CDC and independent experts recommend that the diagnosis be confirmed by laboratory tests on either samples swabbed from the sores or on blood samples (Leone & Corey, 2005; Centers for Disease Control, 2006a).

The mainstay of treatment is **acyclovir** (Zovirax, and generic equivalents). Some related drugs, such as valacyclovir (Valtrex) and famciclovir (Famvir), are also used. There is no difference in efficacy between acyclovir and the much more expensive valacyclovir (Tyring et al., 1998).

Acyclovir is available as a topical ointment (which is of dubious value) and as oral tablets (which are highly effective). If a course of oral acyclovir is started at the first sign of an outbreak, the outbreak is shortened and may never get to the point of producing a discharge. People who are bothered by frequent or painful outbreaks can take acyclovir or valacyclovir on a continuous basis as a preventive measure (Gupta & Wald, 2006). Doing so reduces the frequency of outbreaks or eliminates them entirely, and it also lowers (but doesn't eliminate) the chance that partners will be infected. After taking acyclovir continuously for a long period of time (say, 2 years), some herpes sufferers find that they can stop taking the drug and yet experience few or no further outbreaks. In general, however, herpes is considered incurable with current therapy.

Herpes Is Extremely Common

The fact that herpes is a lifelong infection makes it the most common STD in the United States in terms of the number of people currently infected (see Table 17.1). According to the most recent national data, which were gathered in 1999-2004, 17% of Americans aged 14 to 49 have been infected with HSV-2 (Xu et al., 2006). This is a substantial decline from 10 years earlier, when 21% were infected. Much of the decline was among teenagers, and it may be due to behavioral changes as well as to greater use of drugs to suppress outbreaks and thus reduce transmission. Doctor visits for herpes more than doubled between 2001 and 2006 (Centers for Disease Control, 2007d), but this increase may not result from any recent increase in infection rates. Rather, it may be a response to the heavy promotion of Valtrex (valacyclovir), a drug that requires a doctor's prescription.

Given the 17% figure, it's clear that a sexually active person has a high likelihood of encountering an HSV-2-positive partner at some point. About 90% of persons infected with HSV-2 are unaware that they are infected (Leone & Corey,

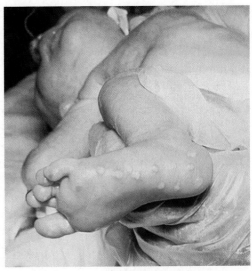

This baby acquired a potentially fatal herpes infection from its mother during the birth process.

acyclovir A drug used in the treatment of genital herpes.

cytomegalovirus (CMV) A virus that can be transmitted sexually or nonsexually. It can be hazardous to fetuses and persons with weakened immune systems.

human papillomavirus (HPV) Any of a group of viruses that can be sexually transmitted and which cause genital warts or other lesions; some types predispose infected persons to cancer of the cervix or anus.

genital warts Wartlike growths on or near the genitalia or anus, caused by infection with human papillomavirus.

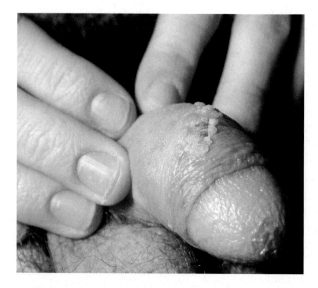

Figure 17.13 Genital warts on the penis

2005), so a partner's statement that he or she does not have herpes should be viewed in that light.

Cytomegalovirus Is a Common Infection that Can Harm Fetuses

Cytomegalovirus (CMV) is a DNA virus related to the herpes simplex viruses, but it doesn't cause skin lesions such as those seen in herpes infections. In fact, most people don't show any symptoms, which is a good thing because an estimated 50% to 80% of the world's population are infected with CMV at some point in their lives, and once an infection has occurred the virus cannot be completely eliminated from the body. Some people develop a prolonged fever accompanied by mild hepatitis, and people with compromised immune systems can develop serious CMV infections of the retina, esophagus, and other organs.

CMV is very easily transmitted in body fluids, including by oral ingestion. Thus young children commonly become infected from their playmates. Young adults who did not become infected as children may well acquire infection sexually or they may do so by contact with young children. People who work in day care facilities and nursery schools are at particular risk.

A major concern with CMV is mother-to-fetus transfer. A woman who becomes infected for the first time during pregnancy, or within 6 months before becoming pregnant, has an approximately 30% chance of passing the virus on to her fetus. A fetus infected in this way has about a 10% chance of dying or developing serious problems such as intellectual disability or deafness. A woman who became infected well before becoming pregnant has very little chance of passing CMV on to her fetus. If she so chooses, a woman can be tested for CMV before she plans to become pregnant. (The test detects antibodies to CMV in the blood.) If she is CMV-negative, or if she is not tested, she can reduce the risk of becoming infected during pregnancy by ordinary hygienic measures such as frequent hand-washing—especially after diaper-changing or other contacts with young children. Pregnant women who experience a prolonged fever should be evaluated for possible CMV infection and (if it is confirmed) they should be counseled about possible harm to the fetus.

Human Papillomaviruses Can Cause Genital Warts—and Cancer

Human papillomaviruses (HPV) are DNA viruses that fall into about 100 different types, out of which about 30 are sexually transmitted. These viruses infect the cells lining the urogenital tract or the skin near the genitalia. Once inside a host cell, the virus can remain in an inactive form, or it can spur cell division, leading to the appearance of **genital warts (Figure 17.13)** or other skin lesions. The types of papillomaviruses that cause common skin warts do not generally infect the genitals.

Genital warts usually appear a few months after infection, but many infected people have no warts or other symptoms. The warts are benign (noncancerous) tumors that are typically located at the vaginal opening, within the vagina, on the cervix, on the penis, at or within the anus, or even in the mouth. They can be single soft, pink bumps or more elaborate, cauliflower-like growths. They can be unattractive and they are highly infectious, but they are usually painless and do not often cause serious health problems.

Visible genital warts are most frequently caused by HPV types 6 and 11. Rarely, these types may later cause cancers of the external genitalia (for example, of the penis, labia, or anus), but this does not happen frequently enough to be a matter of real concern.

HPV types 16 and 18 are not a common cause of raised genital warts. They can cause other kinds of lesions in the genital region, including flat lesions that may be precancerous, but most commonly there are no symptoms. The problem with these HPV types is that, in women, they can eventually promote the development of cervical cancer (**Figure 17.14**). In fact, HPV infection is the principal cause of this disease. A key strategy in preventing the progression from HPV infection to cervical cancer is the Pap test. Most genital warts do *not* contain the types of HPV that predispose women to cervical cancer.

These same two types of HPVs (16 and 18) can cause anal cancer; in fact, they are as much the cause of anal cancer as they are of cervical cancer (Daling et al., 2004; Uronis & Bendell, 2007). Men and women who engage in unprotected receptive anal sex are therefore at increased risk for this disease. HPV promotes anal cancer more efficiently when the immune system is damaged (as in people with AIDS) and when the person is a smoker. The incidence of anal cancer has approximately doubled over the past 30 years (Johnson et al., 2004). The main reason for the recent increase is the improved survival of people with AIDS, which has allowed time for HPV-infected anal tissue to develop into cancer (D'Souza et al., 2008). Still, anal cancer remains a rare disease, with an annual incidence of 1.5 per 100,000 in the United States and a death rate only about one-tenth of that (National Cancer Institute, 2008a). Some specialists recommend regular anal Pap tests for at-risk groups (Goldie et al., 2000), but there is no positive evidence of benefit from such screening, and the CDC does not recommend it.

In addition, HPV infection is an increasingly common cause of cancers of the mouth and throat (Chaturvedi et al., 2008) and of the vulva. Although none of these HPV-caused cancers are common, they illustrate the fact that HPV's carcinogenic potential is rather nonselective: What matters most is which part of the body is initially infected by the virus.

Unlike the situation with HSV or CMV, the fact that a pregnant woman has been infected with any type of HPV is unlikely to have any adverse effect on her fetus or newborn child. Very rarely, the infant can develop warts in the mouth or respiratory tract; these are treatable, but recurrences can occur.

An estimated 50% to 75% of sexually active men and women acquire an HPV infection at some point in their lives, and HPV is the commonest STD in the United States in terms of the number of new infections per year (see Table 17.1). In one study that followed a large group of HPV-negative female college students, over 60% had acquired an HPV infection by 5 years later (Baseman & Koutsky, 2005). Most infected people eventually clear the virus from their bodies and become noninfectious to others within a couple of years from the initial infection, but an estimated 20 million Americans are currently infected and potentially infectious to others. Over 5 million new HPV infections occur annually.

A clinician can remove genital warts by a variety of means, such as by cutting them off, by freezing them with liquid nitrogen, or by the application of podophyllin or other agents. HPV may not be eliminated from the body by these treatments, however, and the warts sometimes recur.

An HPV Vaccine Is Available for Females

In 2006 the FDA approved Gardasil, the first vaccine against HPV. The vaccine provides complete protection against the two types of HPV (16 and 18) that cause

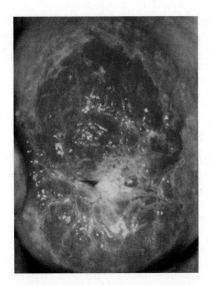

Figure 17.14 Cervical cancer as seen on visual examination through the vagina. Compare with the normal cervix shown in Figure 17.9A. Most cases of cervical cancer are caused by HPV infection.

FAQ I'm a guy whose girlfriend has HPV. Should I get my own HPV status checked? There is no approved lab test to check for HPV in men. Many men have been infected with HPV. The great majority suffer no ill effects, recover from the infection, and become non-infectious to others.

hepatitis viruses Viruses that cause liver disease.

hepatitis B Liver disease caused by the hepatitis B virus, a virus that is often transmitted sexually.

jaundice Yellowing of the skin and mucous membranes, caused by liver disease.

70% of all cervical cancers, as well as the two types (6 and 11) that cause 90% of genital warts. Gardasil is approved for use in females aged 9 through 26—the CDC-recommended age for vaccination is 11 or 12. The vaccine is given as three injections over 6 months and costs $375 for the complete series, but there are various programs to help defray the cost. It is not yet known how long the protection lasts, but if booster shots are required they will not be necessary until many years after the initial vaccination.

To be effective against a given HPV type, the vaccine must be administered *before* a person becomes infected by that type. Ideally, therefore, girls should be vaccinated before they become sexually active. However, even if a girl or young woman has become sexually active and has acquired an HPV infection, the vaccine will still protect against the HPV types to which she was not exposed.

HPV vaccination is not a substitute for regular Pap tests, even if the vaccine was administered before the onset of sexual activity. That's because 30% of all cervical cancers are caused by HPV types that are not included in the vaccine.

The efficacy of the vaccine in older women and in men is currently being studied. The potential value of the vaccine in men is to reduce the risk of genital warts and penile, anal, and oral cancers due to HPV. In addition, it could help reduce the incidence of cervical cancer by reducing the transmission of HPV from men to women.

The introduction of HPV vaccines is potentially a major advance in the battle against STDs as well as cancer. The vaccine will not have a dramatic effect on cervical cancer mortality in the U.S. or Canada, however, because Pap testing has already greatly reduced the number of deaths caused by the disease. In fact, some experts believe that Gardasil was approved too rapidly and is being overpromoted in the U.S., given the uncertainties that surround its long-term efficacy and safety (Rosenthal, 2008). The most dramatic benefits could be in the developing world, where few women undergo regular Pap testing. It will take a significant reduction in cost, however, before widespread use of an HPV vaccine in third world countries is likely (Kaiser, 2008).

Hepatitis Viruses Can Be Sexually Transmitted

Viruses that attack the liver, called **hepatitis viruses**, belong to a number of unrelated types, of which the best known are hepatitis A, B, C, D, and E. The most important of these viruses in terms of sexual transmission is hepatitis B, followed by hepatitis A.

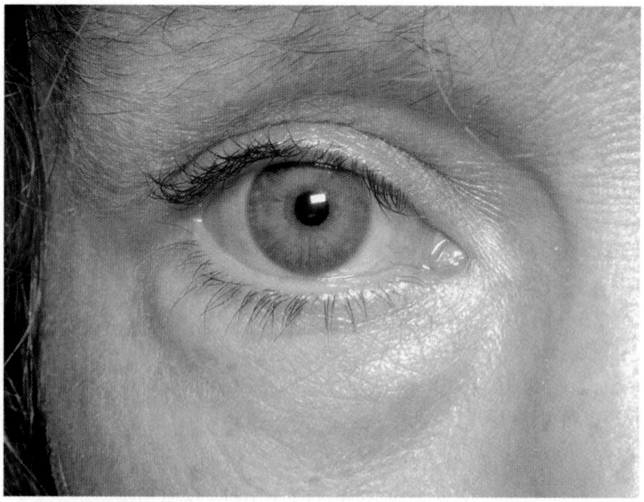

The **hepatitis B** virus is a small DNA virus. It can be picked up by coitus or by anal or oral sex with an infected partner, as well as by contact with contaminated blood (by sharing needles, for example). The signs and symptoms of hepatitis B include **jaundice** (yellowing of the skin and mucous membranes—**Figure 17.15**), fever, general malaise, and tenderness and swelling of the liver (located in the upper right quadrant of the abdomen). The majority of people with hepatitis B recover uneventfully and become noninfectious to others, but in about 6% of infected people the infection progresses to a chronic state, which can lead to scarring (cirrhosis) of the liver, liver cancer, and fatal liver failure. Chronically infected people remain infectious to others. Five drugs are available for treatment of hepatitis B, but they need to be taken for many months and are more likely to suppress symptoms than to actually eliminate the virus from the body. Liver transplantation may be necessary, but not enough livers are available to cover demand.

Figure 17.15 Jaundice is a yellowing of the skin and mucous membranes, seen most easily in the whites of the eyes. It is caused by liver disease, including sexually transmitted hepatitis infections.

Currently, about 46,000 people acquire a hepatitis B infection in the United States each year. This represents an 80% drop in infection rates since 1991, when routine vaccination of children was implemented. Nevertheless, about 1 million Americans are living with a chronic hepatitis B infection (Centers for Disease Control, 2008e).

The genetic material of **hepatitis A** is not DNA, but RNA. This virus is transmitted by the fecal–oral route; that is, viral particles in the feces of an infected person get into the mouth of another. It is often spread by food handlers, but it can also be spread sexually, especially by the practice of mouth-to-anus contact (called anilingus, or rimming) or by anal penetration. The symptoms are similar to those of hepatitis B but are usually milder. The disease does not progress to a chronic state, and no one remains infectious after recovery. There is no specific treatment.

Individual vaccines are available against hepatitis A and against hepatitis B, as well as a combined vaccine against both A and B (Twinrix). The combined vaccine is administered as three injections over 6 months; it costs $120, but there are no-cost programs for those at high risk.

The hepatitis C virus is another important cause of chronic liver disease. It is not commonly transmitted via sexual contact, however.

AIDS Is Caused by the Human Immunodeficiency Virus

Acquired immune deficiency syndrome (AIDS) is a relatively new disease. It was first described in 1981. Nearly uniformly fatal if untreated, the disease has spread as a devastating epidemic in the United States and worldwide (**Table 17.3**). It is caused by the **human immunodeficiency virus (HIV)** (**Figure 17.16**).

HIV evolved from a very similar virus that infects chimpanzees in west-central Africa (Keele et al., 2006). The virus spread to humans quite recently—probably in the 1950s. The first people to be infected may have been involved in the killing and butchering of chimpanzees for "bush meat." Although the first human cases must have been in Africa, the first outbreak to be recognized as a new disease struck gay men in San Francisco, Los Angeles, and New York in the mid-to-late 1970s. HIV has since spread by other routes, including heterosexual sex, contaminated needles, blood transfusions, and perinatal transmission from mother to child, but more than half of all new infections in the United States still result from sex between men (**Figure 17.17A**). Young gay and bisexual men, and African Americans of both sexes (**Figure 17.17B**), are particularly at risk of acquiring and passing on the virus. AIDS has spread around the world, but it has caused the worst humanitarian disaster on the continent where it originated—Africa (**Box 17.2**). (See Web Activity 17.1 Milestones in the Global HIV/AIDS Pandemic.)

hepatitis A Liver disease caused by the hepatitis A virus. It is sometimes transmitted sexually.

acquired immune deficiency syndrome (AIDS) The disease caused by the human immunodeficiency virus (HIV); its onset is defined by the occurrence of any of a number of opportunistic infections, or on the basis of blood tests.

human immunodeficiency virus (HIV) The retrovirus that causes AIDS.

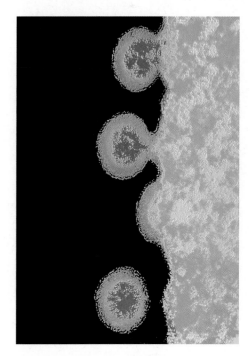

Figure 17.16 HIV particles This false-color electron micrograph shows HIV particles budding off an infected cell. Each viral particle is about 0.0001 mm across.

TABLE 17.3

HIV/AIDS Statistics for the United States and Worldwide, 2006–2007

	United States	Global
Cumulative AIDS deaths	560,000	25 million
AIDS deaths per year	15,000	2.0 million
Persons currently infected with HIV	1,040,000	33 million
New HIV infections per year	56,000	2.7 million

Sources: Centers for Disease Control, 2008g, h; UNAIDS, 2008.

(A)

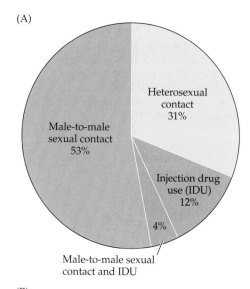

(B)

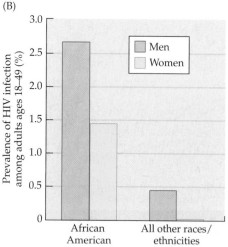

Figure 17.17 The demographics of HIV infections in the United States. (A) Mode of infection. (B) Comparison of prevalence of HIV infection in African Americans and all other races/ethnicities. (A data from Centers for Disease Control, 2008f; B data from Centers for Disease Control, 2008i.)

retrovirus An RNA virus whose genome is translated into DNA within the host cell.

HIV is an RNA virus, but once inside the host cell, the viral RNA is transcribed into DNA and inserted into the cell's own genome. This makes HIV a **retrovirus**—"retro" because the direction of transcription is opposite from the usual DNA-to-RNA direction. **Box 17.3** explains how HIV enters a host cell and uses the host's metabolic machinery to replicate itself.

Sexual Transmission Is Chiefly By Coitus and Anal Sex

In this discussion, we are mainly interested in the sexual modes of HIV transmission; this is a sexuality textbook, after all. To evaluate the risks of transmission, it's important to understand that HIV exists in several body fluids of infected people—blood, semen, vaginal fluid, breast milk, tears, and saliva—but in very different concentrations. The levels of HIV in tears and saliva are very low. Kissing—even deep kissing—an HIV-infected person carries a very low risk of transmission. Because of the possibility that there might be blood or open sores in the infected person's mouth, however, the risk is not completely zero. For that reason, the CDC recommends against open-mouth kissing with an HIV-infected person.

HIV is present at high concentrations in semen and vaginal fluid. Thus there is at least a theoretical risk of transmission by oral sex; that is, a person who takes the oral role in fellatio or cunnilingus with an HIV-infected partner has a chance of acquiring an infection. Transmission by fellatio has been documented by actual case studies (Public Health Agency of Canada, 2004), but the risk is lower than with vaginal or anal sex. The risk of transmission by cunnilingus is extremely low, but there have been a few cases where the virus was apparently transmitted by this route (Centers for Disease Control, 2000). Presumably, the likelihood of transmission in the reverse direction, from the mouth of an HIV-infected person to the penis or vagina of their partner, is also very low. There is one reported case of oral–anal transmission.

The sexual behaviors that carry a high risk of HIV transmission are unprotected (condomless) coitus and anal penetration. The risk of transmission to the receptive partner is about fivefold higher for anal sex than for coitus (Varghese et al., 2002). This is probably because the rectal mucosa possesses immune-system cells that pick up the virus (Owen, 1998). Nevertheless, vaginal transmission is common. It has been estimated that a single act of coitus between an HIV-positive man and an HIV-negative woman has an approximately 1 in 1000 chance of infecting the woman (Varghese et al., 2002). This may not seem like a high risk, but bear in mind that a young couple may easily engage in coitus more than 100 times per year. The transmission risk probably varies greatly depending on the stage of the infected partner's disease. According to one study conducted in Africa, the risk of transmission per sex act is more than 10 times higher soon after infection than during the latent phase of the disease (see below) but rises again after AIDS itself sets in (Wawer et al., 2005). Treatments that reduce viral loads presumably reduce the risk of transmission, though not to zero.

Transmission occurs more readily in the penis-to-vagina and penis-to-anus directions than in the reverse directions, but reverse transmission does occur. Transmission in either direction is facilitated by the presence of preexisting STDs such as syphilis, gonorrhea, herpes, and chlamydia. In fact, any condition that causes ulcers or other damage to the skin or mucosa increases the risk of transmission. Coitus during a woman's menstrual period increases the risk of woman-to-man transmission.

The risk of acquiring HIV by any kind of sexual contact between women is low (Bevier et al., 1995), but occasional instances have been reported. Of course, bisexual and lesbian women can contract HIV infection from sex with men or from injection drug use.

Society, Values, and the Law

BOX 17.2 AIDS in Africa

The AIDS pandemic is not just mind-numbing statistics but also countless individual tragedies. Here is how one Ugandan girl testified at an African AIDS meeting in 1997:

My names are Kevina Lubowa. I am 14 years old. I have four brothers and two sisters younger than me. I have come here to say something about AIDS and its problems. AIDS means acquired immune-deficiency syndrome. It's a terrible disease. It killed both my mother and father in 1992. It killed all brothers and sisters of my father. It has killed many men and women in Uganda.

Some houses have been closed. But our house was not closed because my father and mother left me with four brothers and two sisters. I look after them. I also look after my grandfather who lives near us, because his wife died and nobody was there to look after him. He is 84 years old. He lost his wife in 1992. The grandfather does not see. He has eye problems. It is me who looks after the family. Our food is not enough. Some days we don't get food. We eat cassava with boiled water as sauce. We don't have money to buy sugar or tea leaves.

Because I am a girl people think I am weak. So they come home and steal our cassava and firewood. Because I am a girl, even when I see them I can do nothing. Some people in the village are not friends. They shout at us. They don't give us advice; we don't have any one to call father or mother; we feel sad when we see other children laughing with their father and mother. In short, this is how I find life. (Abridged from United Nations Development Program, 1997).

Kevina is one of nearly 12 million children orphaned by AIDS in sub-Saharan Africa (AVERT, 2008). And because 25 million people in that region are currently infected with HIV, the number of orphans is likely to rise dramatically. AIDS is the leading cause of death in Africa, and in several African countries life expectancy has fallen by 20 to 30 years on account of the epidemic.

Why has AIDS taken a worse toll in Africa than elsewhere? We can point to several factors:

■ The prevalence of untreated STDs, which facilitate the transmission of HIV, and of tuberculosis, which is deadly in people with AIDS. Malaria, which is endemic in many African countries, facilitates transmission of HIV from mother to fetus (Brahmbhatt et al., 2003).

■ The low prevalence of male circumcision in some regions of Africa; these regions have the highest HIV rates (Bailey et al., 2001). Male circumcision, even in adulthood, reduces the risk of female-to-male transmission by more than half in African populations (McNeil, 2007a).

■ A traditional double standard in sexual matters: a culture which permits married men to have sex with "girlfriends" or prostitutes but which rarely allows wives to refuse sex or to demand the use of condoms (Isiramen, 2003).

■ Widespread labor migration, which increases the likelihood that workers will have multiple sex partners.

■ A generally low level of education, which has permitted the spread of harmful myths about AIDS, such as the idea that a man can be cured by having sex with a virgin, or even with a child or baby (Flanagan, 2001).

■ Lack of resources, at either the individual or governmental level, or of sufficient foreign aid. Until recently, this has made medical treatment inaccessible to all but a privileged minority.

Poverty is the common thread linking most of these factors. Yet there are some hopeful signs:

■ Risk reduction campaigns have reduced HIV infection rates in some countries, such as Uganda (see text).

■ International aid to combat AIDS in Africa has increased. In 2003, President Bush pledged $15 billion over 5 years to combat

A local drama group performs a play to raise awareness of HIV in Moshi, Tanzania.

AIDS—most of it earmarked for Africa—but the implementation of this pledge remains uncertain and controversial.

■ Antiretroviral treatments have become simpler (two pills a day rather than ten), cheaper (as little as $250 for a year's supply under the special contracts negotiated for the African market), and more widely available. By 2007, 1.3 million Africans were receiving such treatment, but this represented only 30% of the people who need it (Nduru, 2007). Treatment success rates are as high in Africa as in developed countries (LaFraniere, 2005).

HIV Infection Progresses in a Characteristic Way

Now let's look in more detail at the course of the disease following HIV infection. During the weeks after the initial infection, the virus multiplies inside cells in the person's blood and lymph nodes. Its main target is the **CD4 lymphocytes**, a type

CD4 lymphocytes A type of lymphocyte that carries the CD4 receptor; one of the major targets of HIV.

Biology of Sex

BOX 17.3 HIV's Replication Cycle

If you know little and care less about molecular biology, you might want to skip this page. But learning how HIV replicates itself within the cells of an infected person's immune system is central to understanding how the virus causes disease, as well as how anti-HIV drugs work and how better drugs might be designed in the future. So, if you have any interest in these topics, we urge you to read through this explanation.

The most important target of HIV is a type of immune system cell called the CD4 lymphocyte, which is a "T cell," so called because it matures in the thymus gland. The designation CD4 refers to a characteristic receptor molecule on its cell membrane called the **CD4 receptor**. HIV also targets some other immune system cells that also carry CD4 receptors.

The virus's replication cycle has several stages. (See figure. Note that the elements are not drawn to scale—the virus is really smaller in relation to the host cell than depicted in the figure.) (Also, see Web Activities 17.2 and 17.3.)

1. **Binding.** When a virus particle meets one of the host's CD4 cells, one of the molecules on the viral envelope, called **gp120**, binds to a CD4 receptor molecule on the cell's plasma membrane, as well as to a nearby **co-receptor** molecule. The co-receptor can be one of at least three different molecules, known as CCR5, CCR2, and CXCR4. Viral particles can bind effectively only to cells that carry both the CD4 receptor *and* a co-receptor.

2. **Fusion.** The virus's entry into the cell cytoplasm is accomplished by a second viral envelope glycoprotein, which promotes fusion of the viral envelope with the cell's plasma membrane.

3. **Entry.** As soon as fusion occurs, the viral capsid disintegrates and releases its contents—viral RNA and several enzymes—into the host cell's cytoplasm.

4. **Reverse transcription.** The viral RNA, now in the host cell's cytoplasm, is transcribed (copied) into double-stranded viral DNA, similar to the DNA of our own genes. This step is carried out by a viral enzyme called **reverse transcriptase**.

5. **Nuclear translocation.** The DNA is moved from the cytoplasm of the host cell into the nucleus. A specific viral protein called **Vpr** plays a key role in this step.

6. **Genomic integration.** The viral DNA is inserted into the DNA of one of the host cell's chromosomes. This step is accomplished by another viral enzyme called **integrase**.

7. **Transcription.** The viral genes are now treated like the cell's own genes and are transcribed into RNA many times over. The

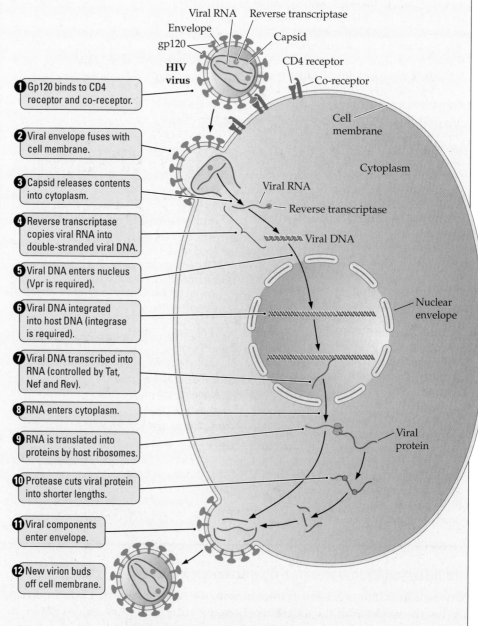

❶ Gp120 binds to CD4 receptor and co-receptor.

❷ Viral envelope fuses with cell membrane.

❸ Capsid releases contents into cytoplasm.

❹ Reverse transcriptase copies viral RNA into double-stranded viral DNA.

❺ Viral DNA enters nucleus (Vpr is required).

❻ Viral DNA integrated into host DNA (integrase is required).

❼ Viral DNA transcribed into RNA (controlled by Tat, Nef and Rev).

❽ RNA enters cytoplasm.

❾ RNA is translated into proteins by host ribosomes.

❿ Protease cuts viral protein into shorter lengths.

⓫ Viral components enter envelope.

⓬ New virion buds off cell membrane.

BOX 17.3 (continued)

host cell's own enzymes carry out the work of transcription. The process is controlled, however, by three viral proteins called **Tat**, **Nef**, and **Rev**. Tat is an "amplifier" that makes the cell produce more of the viral RNA than it otherwise would. Rev is a switch that tells the cell when to start producing viral RNA in a form suitable for export. Nef is necessary for the virus to be pathogenic, but its exact mode of operation is uncertain. (A few lucky Australian hemophiliacs were transfused with blood containing a mutant HIV lacking Nef—they were all infected, but none of them got sick.)

8. **Cytoplasmic translocation.** The new viral RNA behaves like the cell's own RNA. First, it moves from the nucleus into the cytoplasm.

9. **Translation.** Once in the cytoplasm, the viral RNA is translated into protein by the host cell's ribosomes. As with transcription, a single RNA molecule is translated many times over.

10. **Cutting.** The viral gene products are very long proteins that must be trimmed into shorter lengths to make enzymes and other functional viral proteins. This cutting is accomplished by another viral enzyme, a **protease**.

11. **Assembly.** The viral RNA and proteins move to the vicinity of the plasma membrane, and viral envelope proteins gp120 and gp41 insert themselves into the membrane. The membrane bulges outward, and a new viral capsid assembles within the bulge.

12. **Export.** The bulging section of the plasma membrane (now forming the viral envelope) buds off from the cell. How these last two steps are accomplished is still poorly understood. A cell, though infected with only a handful of viral particles, may export tens of thousands of new ones.

As described elsewhere in this chapter, several of these steps have been made the target of attack by specifically designed drugs.

CD4 receptor A receptor in the cell membrane of CD4 lymphocytes.

gp120 An HIV glycoprotein that binds to the host cell receptor, CD4.

co-receptor A receptor that plays a secondary role in binding.

reverse transcriptase An enzyme produced by a retrovirus that transcribes viral RNA into DNA.

Vpr An HIV protein involved in movement of viral DNA into the host cell nucleus.

integrase An enzyme that inserts viral DNA into the genome of the host cell.

Tat An HIV protein that promotes the production of viral RNA.

Nef An HIV protein whose function is uncertain but which is necessary for the virus to be pathogenic.

Rev An HIV protein that triggers production of viral RNA in a form suitable for export from the cell.

protease An enzyme that cuts proteins at specific locations.

---

of white blood cells that make up an important part of the body's immune system. Other cell types may also be infected. During this initial period there are no symptoms, and the infected person's immune system has not yet produced significant levels of antibodies to the virus. Thus the person is "HIV-negative," meaning that the usual HIV blood test, which detects the presence of antibodies to HIV, gives a negative response. Nevertheless, the virus itself is present at high levels and can be detected by a technique called the polymerase chain reaction (PCR). Thus the person is capable of infecting other people. This is the reason why members of high-risk groups are not allowed to donate blood, even if they test HIV-negative.

At some point, usually between 6 weeks and 6 months after infection, the infected person's immune system does mount a response to the virus—antibodies appear in the blood, and the person tests HIV-positive. This change is called **seroconversion**. Seroconversion may be preceded or accompanied by an acute flu-like illness that is marked by fever, nausea, muscle pain, and sometimes a rash; however, some people experience no symptoms at all during this phase. Even those who do may mistake the symptoms for some other illness.

The immune response to the HIV greatly reduces the level of virus in the infected person's blood. The symptoms of acute illness subside, and the person now enters a prolonged asymptomatic period that may last 7 to 10 years or even longer. This period is not a time of quiescence, however, but a long, drawn-out war between HIV and the infected person's immune system. The immune system is initially able to replace the CD4 cells killed by the virus, but this replacement process eventually falls behind. Thus the level of CD4 cells in the blood gradual-

seroconversion The change from negative to positive on an antibody test, such as occurs a few weeks or months after HIV infection.

HIV-symptomatic disease Health problems caused by HIV, especially those that occur before the criteria for an AIDS diagnosis have been met.

wasting Progressive and extreme loss of body weight.

AIDS dementia A broad cognitive impairment caused by HIV infection.

antiretroviral drugs Drugs effective against retroviruses.

ly declines from their normal level of about 1000 cells per microliter (cells/μL), and levels of the virus in the blood begin to rise again. The decline in CD4 cells typically takes place at a rate of about 80 to 100 cells/μL per year in untreated individuals, but genetic differences between individuals, as well as between different viral strains, affect the rate of decline. By the time CD4 counts have declined to 200 to 350 cells/μL, there is a risk that symptoms of overt disease—AIDS—will appear. At a level below 100 cells/μL, the risk is substantial.

Some signs and symptoms may begin to appear several years before the diagnosis of AIDS. These signs include thrush (a fungal infection of the mouth and throat), shingles (a painful rash caused by reactivation of a latent chicken pox infection), unexplained fever, diarrhea, night sweats, and a generalized swelling of lymph nodes. To distinguish these disorders from full-blown AIDS, they are referred to collectively as **HIV-symptomatic disease**.

HIV-positive people are considered to have AIDS when their CD4 levels drop below 200 cells/μL or when certain illnesses appear. These illnesses include infections, such as unusual forms of pneumonia or meningitis, that are able to take hold because of the infected person's poorly functioning immune system. Other AIDS-defining illnesses include certain cancers, including cervical cancer and lymphoma. Besides these and other illnesses, people with advanced AIDS often show generalized **wasting**. They may also suffer broad cognitive impairment (**AIDS dementia**). Without any treatment, people diagnosed with AIDS (not just HIV infection) typically survive for less than a year before succumbing to one or another of the complications of the disease.

Treatment of AIDS Is Directed at Both the Complications and the Viral Replication Cycle

Before the introduction of effective anti-HIV drug regimens (**Figure 17.18**), the mainstay of AIDS medicine was the use of drugs to prevent and treat the complications, especially the opportunistic infections. These drugs are still used extensively, especially for people whose CD4 counts are low in spite of anti-HIV drug treatment.

Antiretroviral drugs, which target the virus itself, were first introduced in 1987. The drugs available today fall into four classes that target four of the phases of the virus's replication cycle that are described in Box 17.3:

FAQ Thanks to the drugs I'm taking, my HIV viral load is now "undetectable." Can I have sex without a condom?
The risk that you will infect your partner is lower than before. However, the virus is still present in your body, and viral levels can rebound without warning. The only responsible behavior is to continue using condoms. By doing so, you'll also protect yourself from reinfection with a drug-resistant strain of HIV.

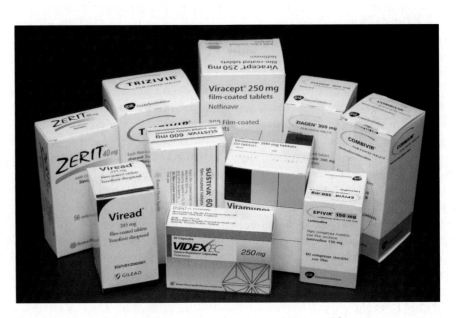

Figure 17.18 Anti-AIDS drugs reduce symptoms and improve life expectancy.

- *Entry inhibitors* prevent the attachment of the virus to the host cell's outer membrane and thus its passage into the cell. They do this by binding either to the virus itself or to one of the receptors or co-receptors on the surface of the target cell.

- *Reverse transcriptase inhibitors* block the copying of the viral RNA into DNA.

- *Integrase inhibitors* block the insertion of this DNA into the host cell's own genome.

- *Protease inhibitors* block the cutting of newly synthesized viral proteins into the shorter lengths that are required for function.

Typically these drugs are administered in combinations of about three different drugs, so as to attack the virus on several fronts and reduce its ability to develop resistance. These combined drug regimens are called **highly active antiretroviral therapy (HAART).**

HAART has greatly reduced the death rate from AIDS in the United States and other developed countries (**Figure 17.19**). Twenty-year-olds diagnosed with HIV today can now expect to live into their sixties (Antiretroviral Therapy Cohort Collaboration, 2008) (**Figure 17.20**). Still, current antiretroviral therapy has several shortcomings:

- It does not eradicate the virus from the body—viral levels rebound after therapy is stopped.

- Resistance to multiple drugs can eventually develop, making treatment difficult.

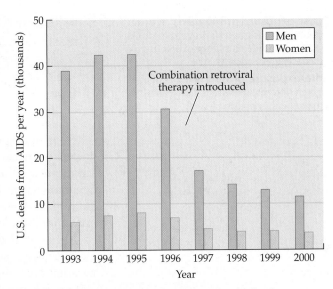

Figure 17.19 U.S. deaths from AIDS per year (in thousands), showing the decline related to the introduction of combination retroviral therapy. Since 2000, U.S. AIDS deaths have remained level at about 14,000 per year. (Data from Centers for Disease Control, 2002b.)

highly active antiretroviral therapy (HAART) Combinations of antiretroviral drugs that have proved effective in the treatment or prevention of AIDS.

(A)

(B)

(C)

Figure 17.20 Living with HIV (A) Olympic diver and author Greg Louganis was diagnosed with HIV in 1988. (B) Basketball star and businessman Magic Johnson announced he had HIV in 1991. (C) Former Playboy Playmate and safer-sex advocate Rebekka Armstrong has been HIV-positive since 1994.

post-exposure prophylaxis A drug treatment designed to prevent establishment of an infection after exposure to a disease agent such as HIV.

pre-exposure prophylaxis A drug taken before exposure to a disease agent to prevent infection.

- Many of the drugs have serious side effects that limit their usefulness.
- Antiretroviral therapy is burdensome. Failure to follow the prescribed regimen contributes to the emergence of drug-resistant forms of the virus, with a dramatic reduction in the effectiveness of treatment.
- Antiretroviral therapy is expensive: The projected lifetime drug costs for a person starting HAART are nearly $500,000 (Schackman et al., 2006).

There is some uncertainty about when to begin combination therapy. The desire to prevent irreversible damage to the immune system is balanced by the possible occurrence of harmful side effects and eventual drug resistance. Current recommendations are that treatment be started when CD4 counts fall below 350 cells/μL or an AIDS-defining illness sets in, whichever occurs first (Panel on Antiretroviral Guidelines for Adults and Adolescents, 2008).

Although antiretroviral therapy cannot eradicate an established HIV infection, it might prevent an infection from taking hold if administered immediately after exposure to the virus. This **post-exposure prophylaxis** has been used with some apparent success in cases of occupational exposure (needlesticks by medical personnel), sexual assaults by HIV-positive men, and sexual encounters between sero-opposite couples (i.e., couples where one partner is infected and the other is not) (Nwokolo & Hawkins, 2001), but there is a down side in terms of possible side effects and expense. People who believe they have been exposed to HIV should get medical advice immediately—preferably within a couple of hours and no later than 72 hours after exposure. A brief course of antiretroviral therapy can greatly reduce the likelihood of mother-to-child transmission during the perinatal period.

In spite of an enormous research effort, no AIDS vaccine has so far proved effective in clinical trials, and there are no promising candidates among those currently being tested (Fauci et al., 2008). Another so-far fruitless area of research has been the search for a vaginal microbicide that could inactivate HIV at the point of transmission (Grant et al., 2008). Research in these important areas continues.

Two novel drug strategies against AIDS are under development. One is a drug regimen that could be used by at-risk HIV-negative individuals to lower their chances of becoming infected (**pre-exposure prophylaxis**). This approach is currently being tested in Africa (Centers for Disease Control, 2008c). Another, less far-advanced strategy is to identify a class of drugs that could force HIV out of its hidden cellular reservoirs within the body, thus potentially ridding a person of HIV altogether. For decades, few have dared to speak of a "cure" for AIDS, but basic research in immunology could make this a reality (Stevenson, 2008).

There Are Several Ways to Reduce the Likelihood of STD Transmission

In spite of the many medical advances documented in this chapter, STDs remain a major public health problem. Well-meaning people disagree on the best strategies for combating them. Here we consider the main options.

Abstinence Prevents STDs

Although it may seem too obvious to be worth saying, people who have no sexual contacts with others cannot acquire or transmit any disease by the sexual route. (They can still acquire some "STDs" by nonsexual routes such as needle sharing, of course.)

Complete abstinence from sexual contacts has other potential benefits besides disease prevention. It offers complete protection against unwanted pregnancy without the expense and potential side effects of contraceptive techniques (see Chapter 12). It may allow people to concentrate their time and energies on non-physical relationships as well as on nonsexual goals, such as career advancement. The decision whether or not to be sexually abstinent is a highly personal one. It should also be borne in mind that "abstinence" is interpreted in different ways by different people. If it is interpreted to allow for sexual contacts other than coitus it may not offer much protection against STDs (see below).

Sexually Active People Can Reduce Their Risk of STDs by Their Choice of Partners

People who do not choose to be abstinent still have options for reducing their risk of acquiring STDs. One way they can do this is to reduce the total number of people with whom they have sexual contact and to select partners who are unlikely to have an STD. Two virgins who enter into a monogamous relationship have a low risk of passing an STD between them. Even in this situation, however, an STD can be transmitted if one partner has acquired a sexually transmissible infection through nonsexual means. Furthermore, it is difficult to know for certain whether one's prospective partner is really a virgin or whether they engage in sex with others after the supposedly monogamous relationship has begun. People have different understandings of terms such as "having sex" and "being a virgin," as we've seen in earlier chapters. The best one can do is to choose partners with whom one can discuss these matters freely and honestly, and not enter into a sexual relationship until one has done so (**Box 17.4**).

Different individuals may have different likelihoods of acquiring an STD even when their total number of sex partners is the same, on account of demographic variations in STD prevalence. For example, a white American male who has had only one sex partner in his lifetime has about a 2% chance of contracting herpes, but a black woman in the same situation has about a 33% chance (Leone & Corey, 2005). However, the seriousness of some STDs makes playing the numbers game a risky business: It may be a better strategy simply to assume that one's partners stand a good chance of carrying an STD and act accordingly.

Ideally, both partners would be tested for a variety of STDs, including HIV, before a sexual relationship begins. In real life that doesn't usually happen, but there are still useful steps that can be taken. The couple can discuss each other's sexual histories and whether either partner has an STD or is likely to have been exposed to one. Second, it is a good idea to visually inspect the other partner, especially his or her genitals. This strategy is particularly useful for women because STDs tend to be more visible in men than they are in women. A visible genital sore, wart, or discharge is a good reason to abstain from sexual contact. STD testing can of course be done at any time during a relationship. Unfortunately, genital inspection, if it happens at all, comes rather late in the proceedings. Too commonly, people judge their potential partners' STD status by irrelevant criteria, such as their youth, attractiveness, or generally healthful appearance.

Some Sexual Behaviors Are Riskier than Others for STD Transmission

In terms of STD prevention, the distinction between "abstinence" and "having sex" may be confusing and counterproductive because it suggests that any kind of sexual contact carries the same high risk of disease transmission. In reality, men and women who are sexually active can greatly influence their likelihood of acquiring or transmitting an STD by the choice of sexual behaviors they engage in (**Box 17.5**).

Coitus, anal sex, and anilingus (mouth-to-anus contact) are high-risk sexual behaviors, with anal sex being the riskiest with regard to HIV transmission. Anilingus has a low likelihood of transmitting HIV, but it is a risky practice

Society, Values, and the Law

BOX 17.4 Partner Notification

In late April, 2002, state health officials knocked at the dorm room of Nikko Briteramos, a 6-foot-7 basketball star at tiny Huron University in South Dakota. A few weeks previously, Briteramos had been told that he was HIV-positive—the discovery was made when he attempted to donate blood. Now the officials wanted to interview him about his sex partners in order to notify them of their possible exposure to the virus. But Briteramos didn't let the officials into his room. The reason soon became obvious: He was in bed with his girlfriend. That same day, Briteramos was arrested and charged with five counts of intentionally exposing his girlfriend to the AIDS virus through unprotected sex. He was convicted, received a suspended 5-year prison term, and was ordered to spend 120 days in jail. His girlfriend tested HIV-negative, but two other women who had sex with Briteramos have tested positive. Those two women told officials that they, in turn, had recently engaged in sex with 50 other persons (Simon, 2002).

Briteramos's alleged behavior is not uncommon. In a 1998 study led by Michael Stein of Brown University, 40% of people who received primary HIV care at two urban hospitals said that they had not disclosed their HIV status to all their recent sex partners. Among these admitted nondisclosers, 57% said that they did not use condoms during all sexual encounters (Stein et al., 1998).

Probably few of you would dispute that it is wrong for people who know they are HIV-positive to engage in unprotected sex without telling their partners of their HIV status. South Dakota is one of 21 states that make such behavior a crime regardless of whether the virus is actually transmitted or not. Even if a condom is used, you might question the morality of withholding this information.

What about the situation where a person hasn't been tested but might have reason to believe

In Minnesota and other states, this Web site makes anonymous partner notification easy. (Courtesy of Internet Sexuality Information Services.)

that they are infected with HIV or another STD? This issue came before the California Supreme Court in 2006. A woman sued her ex-husband for damages because (she alleges) he infected her with HIV. He had denied having engaged in any risky sex before or outside of their marriage, but she discovered emails that revealed his "rampant, high-risk secret homosexual lifestyle," according to her lawyers' statements. The court ruled that the case can proceed; it has not yet come to trial (KNBC.com, 2008).

An even trickier ethical question concerns the role of doctors and health officials in the partner notification process. Generally speaking, doctors' ethical responsibilities are directed toward their patients and include a responsibility to maintain confidentiality. What if doctors or other medical professionals know that HIV-positive patients have not notified their sex partners?

The Centers for Disease Control has taken the position that partner notification programs should be voluntary. In other words, officials should notify an HIV-positive person's partners only if that person gives consent. The CDC believes that mandatory notification programs could discourage potentially infected people from getting tested and are therefore likely to be counterproductive. The ACLU and AIDS activists have taken a similar position.

Nevertheless, the majority of states have enacted mandatory partner notification laws. Although the details vary from state to state, these programs often require medical personnel or officials to ask HIV-positive people about their sexual contacts and to inform those partners about their risk of exposure (usually without identifying the HIV-positive person). In most states, however, HIV-positive people are not legally required to provide the names of their sexual contacts. In that sense, even "mandatory" programs are voluntary.

because of the likelihood of transmission of hepatitis A or B (in the anus-to-mouth direction), as well as other STDs.

Oral sex (fellatio or cunnilingus) is a moderate-risk behavior. Transmission of HIV by oral sex is far less common than by coitus or anal sex, but some other STDs, such as gonorrhea and syphilis, are readily transmitted by this route.

Other sexual behaviors, such as kissing, fondling, hand–genital contact, and general body contact, are low-risk behaviors. They are certainly not free of risk—

Research Highlights

BOX 17.5 Reducing STD Prevalence: Strategies That Work

The U.S. government spends a great deal of money on abstinence-only sex education, even though research suggests that such programs have little or no effect on people's sexual behavior. What does work? A 1995 study from Jackson State University in Mississippi suggested part of the answer (St Lawrence et al., 1995). The researchers focused on 246 low-income black adolescents who visited a community health center. The youths were assigned at random to one of two programs. One program consisted of a single session in which the youths were given educational instruction concerning HIV and AIDS. The other was an 8-session program that presented the same education about HIV and AIDS but added training in skills such as correct condom use, risk recognition, assertiveness, how to refuse requests for sex, and self-management. The youths who participated in the skills-training program engaged in more protected intercourse and less unprotected intercourse than did the youths who received the education-only program. The skills-training program did not incite youths to begin sexual activity; in fact, of the youths who were sexually abstinent at the start of the skills-training pro-

gram, only 11.5% were sexually active a year later, compared with 31.1% of those who took the education-only program. In other words, appropriate skills training, even though it includes training in condom use, seems to help adolescents refrain from sexual activity.

Another effective strategy takes advantage of the fact that people's behavior is readily influenced by individuals regarded as leaders within their peer group or friendship network. In a study from the University of California, San Francisco, researchers identified opinion leaders within the young gay male communities of two West Coast cities (Kegeles et al., 1996). These opinion leaders were asked to deliver messages endorsing safe-sex practices to small gatherings of their friends and acquaintances. These personal contacts were backed up by risk reduction workshops and by distribution of printed materials in places where young gay men gathered. Over the course of the project, the fraction of young gay men in the target cities who engaged in unprotected anal sex with people other than their primary partners dropped by nearly half. No change occurred over the same period in a control community that was not tar-

geted. A comparable program directed at inner-city black women has also been successful in changing behavior (Lauby et al., 2000).

As advertisers well know, people's behavior can be modified by frequent and prolonged exposure to simple messages, such as TV commercials or public service announcements. In some countries, the mass media approach has been extraordinarily successful in combating STDs. In Thailand, for example, a mass media campaign to promote condom use, along with a condom distribution program and measures to ensure condom use by sex workers, led to a sixfold increase in condom use, an 85% decrease in STDs among men, and a decrease in HIV prevalence among pregnant women (Rojanapithayakorn & Hanenberg, 1996).

Another much-cited program is the "ABC campaign" in Uganda (U.S. Agency for International Development, 2003). This is an AIDS prevention program that emphasizes Abstinence (or delayed initiation of sexual behavior by teens), Be faithful (to one partner), and use Condoms. Begun in the early 1990s, the program has reduced HIV prevalence rates by as much as two-thirds, which makes it the biggest success story in Africa. A detailed longitudinal study in one region of Uganda found that condom use was the only behavior that changed in a positive direction, suggesting that it played the key role in reducing HIV prevalence (Altman, 2005).

Unfortunately, political considerations and standards established by the television networks have prevented any media campaigns in the United States equivalent to the programs in Thailand and Uganda. In fact, television programming is rife with depictions of sex or references to sex, but these episodes almost never include any mention of STDs or measures to prevent them. Only the pornographic movie industry has taken steps in this direction—many of these movies now show condoms in use.

In general, it seems that public health programs can have a substantial impact on STD prevalence, but they need to be based on methods that have been proven effective, and they need to be delivered broadly in time and space, not just for a few months in a few communities.

Safe-sex messages may have more effect when spread by peer networks.

This 2001 campaign to educate Thai youth about condom use was sponsored by condom manufacturer Durex.

herpes and syphilis, for example, can both be transmitted by these behaviors—but they are so much safer than the high- and moderate-risk behaviors described above that they offer a sensible alternative for sexually active people when STD transmission is a concern.

Condoms Are the Mainstay of STD Prevention

The condom is the key to STD prevention for sexually active people. The proper use of condoms has already been described in the context of contraception (see Chapter 12). Two points are worth reemphasizing in the context of STD protection:

1. Natural-tissue ("lambskin") condoms, although possibly effective as contraceptives, do not provide adequate protection against STDs because they have pores through which viruses can pass. No disease agents can pass through an unbroken latex or polyurethane condom.

2. Anal sex places greater demands on a condom than does vaginal sex. For anal sex, extra-strength condoms are recommended. This is particularly important when the insertive partner is known to be HIV-positive.

Female condoms are probably at least as effective as male condoms for STD prevention. Unfortunately, female condoms have not achieved widespread consumer acceptance.

No condom offers complete protection against STDs. With typical use, condoms occasionally break. Furthermore, some STDs, such as syphilis and herpes, can be transmitted to or from skin regions that are not covered by the condom. Still, using condoms is the single most effective step that sexually active men and women can take to reduce STD transmission.

Bear in mind that some "sexually transmitted" diseases may also be transmitted by other means, especially by the sharing of syringes or needles. It is not only risky to engage in such practices; it is also risky to have sex with someone who does.

Not Everything Is an STD

By this point, you quite likely have diagnosed several STDs in yourself, including a couple of fatal ones! If so, it's time for a reality check. HIV is uncommon in the college student population and very uncommon among heterosexual students. Hepatitis usually cures itself. Syphilis and gonorrhea can be easily cured with antibiotics. Herpes won't kill you.

Students often mistake other medical conditions, or even perfectly healthy traits, for STDs. **Figure 17.21** shows some examples of conditions that are not STDs but might be interpreted as such by people without medical training. Shaving the pubic area may cause a rash that is misinterpreted as herpes; if the rash gives rise to infected boils, these may be interpreted as gonorrhea or syphilis. Little bumps around the head of the penis, called "pearly penile papules," are natural and harmless growths, not genital warts caused by HPV. A round swelling on the labia is more likely to be caused by a blocked mucus gland than any kind of STD. Canker sores within the mouth have many causes, but they are not the result of infections, sexual or otherwise.

We encourage you to take all reasonable steps to protect your own health and that of your sex partners. By all means get yourself checked out if you are in doubt

FAQ Is there any way to reduce STD risk during cunnilingus?

For oral stimulation of the vulva or the anus you can buy flat sheets of latex called "dams"—some are flavored. Ask at your campus health center, go to a Web site that sells condoms, or make your own by cutting a condom lengthwise. Place it over the area that will be contacted. Water-based lubricant can be placed between the dam and the vulva or anus.

(A)

(B)

(C)

(D)

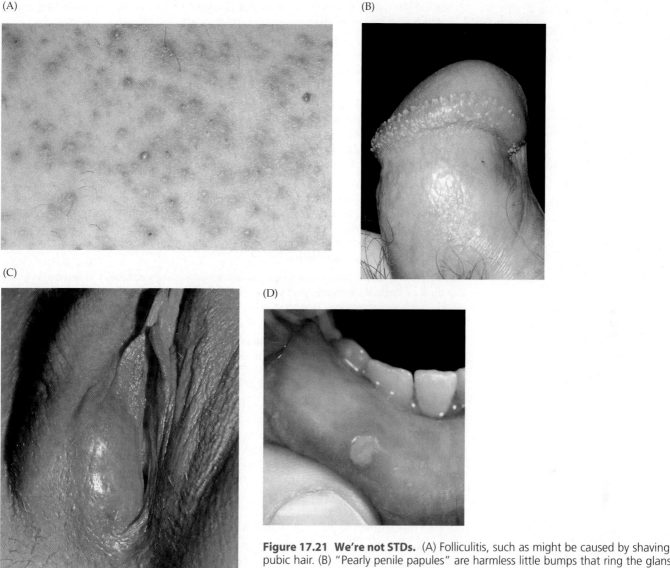

Figure 17.21 We're not STDs. (A) Folliculitis, such as might be caused by shaving pubic hair. (B) "Pearly penile papules" are harmless little bumps that ring the glans of the penis in some men. (C) This cyst on the labia was caused by blockage of the duct of a mucous gland. (D) A canker sore in the mouth may result from accidental biting or other causes.

about whether you have an STD or would like to be screened for HIV. But don't let fear of AIDS or other sexually transmitted diseases so preoccupy you as to leave no room for emotional or physical intimacy.

Summary

1. Nineteen million new cases of sexually transmitted diseases (STDs) occur annually in the United States. STDs are caused by insects, protozoans, bacteria, and viruses. In spite of medical advances, STDs remain a major public health problem. They also bolster a perception of sex as something dangerous or immoral.

2. Insect infestations that can be transmitted sexually include pubic lice and scabies. Pubic lice attach themselves to hair shafts, especially in the pubic region. Scabies mites burrow under the surface of the skin. Both infestations can cause severe itching but do not

REFER TO THE

Human Sexuality

WEBSITE AT

www.sinauer.com/levay3e

for activities, study questions, quizzes, and other study aids.

otherwise threaten health. Pubic lice and scabies mites can be eliminated by use of insecticidal lotions or shampoos.

3. Trichomoniasis is an infection of the vagina or urethra with a protozoan. In women it causes discomfort, a vaginal discharge, and the urge to urinate frequently. In men, the infection is usually asymptomatic. It is generally eliminated by a single oral dose of Flagyl.

4. Syphilis is caused by infection with the bacterium *Treponema pallidum*. The disease has several stages. Primary syphilis is marked by a sore (chancre) at the site of infection. Some weeks later, a rash and fever occur (secondary syphilis). The infection then becomes latent, but it may eventually attack a variety of organ systems (tertiary syphilis) and cause death. The disease is readily curable with penicillin in its early stages.

5. Gonorrhea is caused by infection with the bacterium *Neisseria gonorrhoeae*. In men it usually infects the urethra, causing painful urination. In women it can infect the cervix, causing a vaginal discharge. The infection in women is commonly asymptomatic, but it can spread to the internal reproductive tract, causing pelvic inflammatory disease (PID) and reduced fertility. Rectal and oral infections can occur in either sex. Gonorrhea can be treated with antibiotics.

6. Infection with the bacterium *Chlamydia trachomatis* is very common. It can cause a urethral or vaginal discharge and painful urination, but many infected men and women do not have symptoms. Anal and oral infections can occur. Chlamydia is readily treatable with antibiotics. In women, untreated chlamydia infections can lead to PID.

7. Molluscum contagiosum is a common skin condition caused by a pox virus. It consists of small skin growths that usually disappear permanently after a few months. Although any kind of interpersonal contact can allow for transmission, molluscum in the genital area is usually the result of sexual transmission.

8. Genital herpes is a very common condition caused by infection with the herpes simplex virus type 1 or 2 (HSV-1 or HSV-2). It causes an outbreak of sores at the site of infection, which is usually somewhere in the anogenital region but can also be in the mouth. The initial outbreak heals spontaneously, but it may be followed by further outbreaks at the same location that recur for the remainder of the person's life. Herpes infection is incurable, but outbreaks can be limited by antiviral drugs.

9. Cytomegalovirus (CMV) infection is usually asymptomatic in healthy people. The main concern with this virus is that a woman who is infected during pregnancy can pass the infection to her fetus, which may die or suffer serious disability.

10. Human papillomaviruses (HPV) cause genital warts and other lesions of the genital skin and urogenital tract. Genital warts can be removed by a variety of treatments. Some HPV types (not those that cause bulky, raised genital warts) infect the cervix and are the principal cause of cervical cancer and anal cancer. An HPV vaccine is available.

11. Hepatitis A and B are viral infections of the liver that can be acquired sexually as well as by other routes. Anal penetration and anilingus are the sexual behaviors most likely to transmit hepatitis A. Hepatitis B is transmitted by coitus or oral sex; in a minority of cases it leads to chronic liver disease and liver cancer. No cure exists for either form of hepatitis, but effective vaccines are available.

12. Acquired immune deficiency syndrome (AIDS) is caused by infection with the human immunodeficiency virus (HIV). The virus originated in central Africa, but a worldwide pandemic began with outbreaks in gay male communities in the United States in the late 1970s. Transmission now occurs by both male–female and male–male sexual contacts (principally by coitus and anal penetration), as well as by exposure to contaminated blood.

13. HIV infection can be marked by an acute illness followed by a several-year asymptomatic period. Eventually the infection impairs the person's immune system to the point that certain opportunistic infections and cancers may occur. Symptomatic AIDS is a life-threatening condition that cannot be cured, but it may be held in check with a combination of drugs that interfere with various stages of the virus's replication cycle.

14. Women and men can reduce their risk of acquiring STDs by a variety of means. Complete sexual abstinence offers complete protection. Sexually active people can reduce their risk by keeping their number of sexual partners low (ideally, by forming a mutually monogamous relationship), by discussing STDs and sexual history with prospective partners, by getting tested for STDs, and by engaging in relatively low-risk sexual behaviors as an alternative to coitus or anal sex. Careful and consistent use of condoms is key to lowering the risk of acquiring and transmitting STDs.

Discussion Questions

1. Do you think that there are any circumstances in which it would be acceptable for someone who has an STD not to inform their sex partner? If others in your class have a different opinion, discuss the reasons for your differing views and attempt to reach a consensus on the subject.

2. Do you think that legal action should ever be taken to punish someone who transmits a serious STD to a partner? Or do you think that such action is counterproductive? Should everybody simply be held responsible for protecting themselves from STDs?

3. Imagine you are embarking on a sexual relationship with your first partner or a new partner. How would you bring up the matter of STDs and what to do about them? Try to imagine the actual conversation you would have and what the difficulties might be.

4. Imagine you are returning to your high school to give a half-hour presentation about STDs. What age students would you choose to speak to? What would be the main goals you'd like to accomplish? Do you think any particular styles of communication would be particularly effective? Is there any way in which you think you could do a better job than an STD specialist from the local health department? Do you think you could communicate equally effectively with boys and girls, and with students of all races and ethnicities?

Web Resources

AIDS Information Global Education System www.aegis.org

Centers for Disease Control, Division of HIV/AIDS www.cdc.gov/hiv

Centers for Disease Control, Division of Sexually Transmitted Diseases
www.cdc.gov/std/

Center for Disease Control's 24-hour STD and AIDS hotline www.doe.state.in.us/
sservices/hivaids_cdchotline.html

Joint United Nations Program on HIV/AIDS www.unaids.org

National Minority AIDS Council www.nmac.org/

University of California, San Francisco HIV InSite http://hivinsite.ucsf.edu/InSite

Recommended Reading

Barnett, T., and Whiteside, A. (2006). *AIDS in the twenty-first century: Disease and globalization* (2nd ed.). Palgrave Macmillan.

Marr, L. (2007). *Sexually transmitted diseases: A physician tells you what you need to know* (2nd ed.). Johns Hopkins University Press.

Shilts, R. (1987). *And the band played on: Politics, people, and the AIDS epidemic.* St. Martin's Press.

CHAPTER 18

Unwanted sexual attention can lead to assault, harassment, or worse.

Sexual Assault, Harassment, and Partner Violence

This chapter deals with the dark side of sex. Sex is not limited to balanced, happy interactions between loving couples. It can be grossly one-sided, involving sexual desire on one person's part and disinterest, perhaps aversion, on the other's. It can involve physical assault. And intimate sexual relationships can be marred by cruelty and violence. We touched on these issues earlier: In Chapter 10 we discussed the difficult feelings resulting from unrequited love, as well as the breakup of relationships. In Chapter 15 we described paraphilias, such as exhibitionism and pedophilia, that can lead to the victimization of women and children. Here we take a broader look at sex as a context for physical and psychological injury.

What Is Rape?

The terms that describe acts of sexual victimization have been given many different definitions. Here we use these terms in ways that correspond approximately to legal usage. **Rape** or forcible rape is used to mean penetration of the vagina, anus, or mouth by the penis when performed by force or the threat of force. (Legal definitions vary: Sometimes oral or anal penetration is not considered rape, and sometimes vaginal or anal penetration by a finger or an object *is* considered rape.) **Sexual assault** is a broader term that includes any sexual act performed by force or the threat of force. **Statutory rape** means coitus, anal penetration, or oral penetration performed without force, but also without the partner's consent; it is usually applied to cases in which the partner cannot legally give consent on account of young age or mental incapacity. When we use the term "rape" without qualification, we are excluding statutory rape.

For a rape charge to stick, it must usually be shown that the victim made evident to the rapist her (or his) unwillingness to engage in sex. This unwillingness is often expressed by physical resistance, but not necessarily: A verbal refusal is sufficient. The courts are aware that physical resistance is sometimes impossible or unwise.

Rape law does not necessarily cover every sexual situation. A situation in which a man has sex with a woman who hasn't said either "yes" or "no" and who has not offered even token resistance is unlikely to be considered rape, legally speaking. If a woman says "yes" only because she's drunk, that's also unlikely to meet the legal definition of rape, (but it is statutory rape if she is too intoxicated to give meaningful consent). One state appellate court (in Maryland) has

rape Coitus (and sometimes other penetrative sex acts) accomplished by force or the threat of force.

sexual assault Coercive or nonconsensual sexual contact: a broader category of behaviors than rape.

statutory rape Penetrative sex when a partner is legally unable to give consent on account of young age, intellectual disability, or unconsciousness.

Figure 18.1 Age of rape and sexual assault victims
Young women are most at risk. (Data from U.S.
Department of Justice, 2000.)

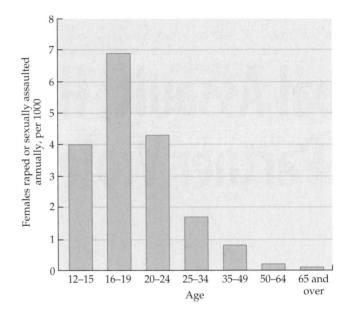

even ruled that it is not rape for a man to continue engaging in coitus after the woman says "stop," so long as she did consent to the initiation of coitus (Colb, 2006). In other words, there is a sphere of morally questionable or reprehensible behavior that extends beyond the limits of what the law may recognize as "rape."

It's also important to be aware that the details of laws governing rape and sexual assault vary considerably from state to state (American Prosecutors Research Institute, 2008). For example, the California Supreme Court has ruled in a fashion exactly opposite to the Maryland ruling just cited: In California, it *is* rape for a man to persist with intercourse after a woman says "stop" (Colb, 2003).

Young Women Are the Most Frequent Victims of Rape

Because many rapes are not reported to the police, the rape statistics we cite here are based on random-sample surveys of the U.S. population. In 2005, according to the National Crime Victimization Survey (NCVS), there were about 0.5 rapes per year for every 1000 people over 12 years old (Bureau of Justice Statistics, 2006). This may not seem like very many, but the rate is much higher in women than in men, and among women it is highest in the younger age groups (**Figure 18.1**). Thus about 7 in every 1000 women in the most victimized age range (16 to 19) are raped each year. It is possible that there are even more rapes that women do not disclose to interviewers, either because of shame or because of ignorance about what circumstances meet the definition of rape.

Thankfully, there has been a marked long-term decline in the incidence of rape: The rape rate in 2005 was only about 20% of what it was before 1980 (**Figure 18.2**). The rates for all violent crime have declined markedly during this period, but the rape rate has fallen the most. The reasons are not known for certain, but improving economic circumstances and greater awareness about rape and rape prevention among both women and men are likely to be factors. The decline in the rape rate appears to be continuing: Based on reports to law enforcement at least, there was a further 6% decline in the rape rate between 2005 and 2007 (Federal Bureau of Investigation, 2008).

Most Rapes Are Not Reported

Only about one-third of rapes and attempted rapes are reported to law enforcement (Rennison, 2002). This is much lower than the reporting rate for other vio-

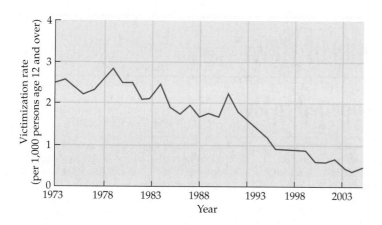

Figure 18.2 Declining U.S. rape rates This graph shows the number of rapes per 1000 persons over 12. (Data from Bureau of Justice Statistics, 2006.)

lent crimes. Reporting rates are highest when the perpetrator is a stranger and lowest when he is a current or former husband or boyfriend. When asked why they did not report a rape or attempted rape to the police, victims gave the following reasons (in order of frequency):

1. It was a personal matter.
2. They were afraid of reprisals.
3. They wanted to protect the perpetrator.
4. They believed the police were biased.

Most rape prevention organizations encourage a person who has been sexually assaulted to report the crime. They believe that doing so can help the victim regain a sense of control and can reduce the likelihood that the perpetrator will offend again. They also acknowledge, however, that this is a deeply personal decision that only victims can make for themselves.

Most Perpetrators Are Men Known to the Victim

Who are the people who commit rape or sexual assault? Contrary to what one might imagine, more than 2 out of 3 of them are known to the victim; of these, the majority are friends or acquaintances, and the remainder are spouses or other intimate partners, according to NCVS data (U.S. Department of Justice, 2006) (**Figure 18.3**).

Nearly all rapes and the great majority of sexual assaults are committed by men. Of people incarcerated for sexual assault—typically the more serious offenders—nearly 99% are male (Greenfeld, 1997). Still, aggressive sexual behavior by women, including sexual assault and even rape, does occur, and it deserves more study than it has received (Anderson & Struckman-Johnson, 1998).

Although the circumstances of rape vary greatly, what unifies all rapes is their severe effects on the raped woman or man. These effects are illustrated by first-person accounts of rape (**Box 18.1**).

College Rapes Are Common

Based on a large-scale survey of college women, researchers at the University of Cincinnati estimated that a female student has a 20% to 25% chance of experiencing a completed or attempted rape in the course of a 5-year college career (Fisher et al., 2000). They also estimated that a college campus with 10,000 female students would see at least 350 completed or attempted rapes per year. (In this survey, "rape" referred to penetration of the vagina or anus by the penis, a finger,

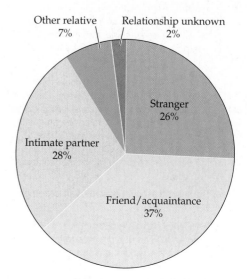

Figure 18.3 Most rapists are known to their victims. The graph shows the relationships of perpetrators of rape and sexual assault to their victims. (Data from U.S. Department of Justice, 2006.)

Personal Points of View

BOX 18.1 It Happened to Me

Rape is a horrific experience for the victim, regardless of the exact circumstances of the rape or the level of violence involved. In this box we present three first-person accounts from rape survivors, two by women and one by a man, that give some idea of the range of circumstances in which rape can occur.

The first account describes what is the most common form of rape: acquaintance rape that includes the involvement of alcohol or drugs:

> Steph: The girl invited me to a party that her friends were having. So I went there with her. I met the girls having the party, and they seemed very nice. I started talking to a guy who seemed to be a few years older then me. He was very nice and polite. Maybe I should have seen it coming.
>
> I had a boyfriend at the time, so I just talked to him with only intentions of friendship. To make this story shorter, I ended up in a room with him. I have no idea how. He ended up touching me and removing quite a bit of my clothing. I struggled and I cried the whole time. He took off his pants as well. Then he tried to go inside of me, which he succeeded at. But to be very blunt, it was only a few thrusts of going in and out. It was all so horrible and hurt so much. I ended up getting out from underneath of him. Not quite sure how. He apologized as I ran out of the room very quickly. I wanted to get home, into my house, and into my bed as fast as I could. I never wanted to see this guy again.
>
> Since I was a virgin at the time, I think I lost my virginity to him. However, it might sound silly, but I do not consider that to be very true. I consider it to be the time with my boyfriend now. In my head I have a definition of losing virginity that involves love. What he did to me did not contain any love."

The second account describes an extremely violent stranger rape.

> Maple: I had been out running for about an hour. I was getting close to home when I saw a van parked in a "no parking" zone; there were two men inside looking at a map. When I turned I saw two more men standing at the back of the van. I assumed they had gotten out to stretch their legs. I was wrong.
>
> As I walked past them I felt a hand on my shoulder. It was a strong grasp. I tried to pull away, but the grip got stronger, it was then that I knew that I was in trouble. I was pulled into the back of the van. There were two more men in there. I was gagged and handcuffed. I was terrified. I don't know how long we drove.
>
> When the van stopped they opened the door and got out. I heard them discussing whether or not they were sure that I wouldn't be heard if I screamed. They were not focused on me and I decided that I should try to get away. I eased myself out of the van and as soon as my feet hit the ground I started to run. I didn't get far when I was tackled from behind. Oh, how it hurt. I was told that it was a stupid thing to do and that I would have to be punished. That was when the knife came out. I remember the searing pain as it cut through the tender skin of my face.
>
> I was picked up and taken inside an old building. Once inside the handcuffs and gag were removed and I was told to scream as much as I wanted, I wouldn't be heard. I didn't scream, but I begged them not to hurt me anymore. The tears that ran down my cheeks stung when they reached the gash opened up by the knife.
>
> I was told to take off my clothes. I couldn't; the knife came out again. I finally did. I was humiliated already. I was told to lay down. That was the first time that I noticed the mattress on the floor. I couldn't lay down there, I felt that if I did it would mean that I was consenting to what I knew was about to happen. All I could do was say, "Please NO." The knife came out again, and then I was pushed onto the mattress.
>
> They all took off their clothes and stood around the mattress. I was told to open my legs, I couldn't, there came the knife, and my legs were pried open. The first was the worst one, it hurt so much. After that I started to go numb, and as each one took their turn I felt my body slipping away from me.

Male-on-male rape in prison is also common. The trauma of this kind of rape is compounded by the frequent lack of recourse or (as described here) the fear of retribution for "snitching," as well as by the possibility of HIV transmission.

> R. D.: While serving my sentence at a former institution, I was severely beaten and gang-raped, both orally and anally....It started by inmate [A] coming by my cell and waking me up at approximately 4:00 A.M. He said he wanted to come in and watch television with me. I didn't think nothing of it because we've had no prior problems before. I did think it was odd though. So he came in and sat on my bed. About 5 to 10 minutes after that, inmates [B], [C], and [D] came into my cell. Then inmate [D] said, 'We want some ass.' I said, 'I don't think so, I don't play that shit.' When he said this, I said to myself, 'Oh no! I'm in trouble!' I looked toward the door for an escape route. Finding it blocked, I went into myself to prepare for the worst.
>
> Inmate [B] then stood in front of me and pulled out his penis and forced it into my mouth. Inmate [C] then took his turn. Pulling me to my feet, he then took my boxers off, bent me over and forced his penis inside. Inmate [D] laid on the bed, took my head, and forced himself inside my mouth. All four of them, plus one more, took turns anally and orally raping me at the same time. Somewhere in the middle of this, inmate [F] entered. During the rape, I believe it was him that said 'Suck this dick, you ... bitch.' One said 'If you snitch on us, we'll kill you!!' The other said, 'And if you do and you get transferred, you'll still die.' At that time, I really believed them, and I still think this today.

Sources: Survive-UK, 2001; Human Rights Watch, 2001b.

or an object, as well as fellatio or cunnilingus, using force or the threat of force. This is a broader definition of rape than those used in some state laws.)

In the survey, most of the rapes occurred after 6:00 P.M. in residences—most commonly the victim's own residence. Most of the victims knew the perpetrator, who was usually a classmate, friend, ex-boyfriend, or acquaintance. (The phrase **date rape** or acquaintance rape is frequently used as shorthand to refer to these kinds of circumstances, although the two persons may not have been "dating" in the traditional sense.) About 20% of the rapes involved additional injuries, such as bruises and cuts.

About half of the victims who described incidents that the survey categorized as completed rapes did not themselves consider those incidents to be rapes. The reasons for this are unclear. These women may have believed that to be called rape, an encounter must involve coitus or must be accomplished by actual force, rather than by the threat of force. To some critics of this and similar studies, the fact that so many "rape" victims do not categorize the reported incidents as rape suggests that unrealistic criteria are being used to categorize the incidents. Still, whatever the acts are called, they are clearly serious crimes.

An acquaintance rape-prevention workshop at Hobart College, New York

Colleges have become very conscious of the problem of campus rape. Many have introduced policies that are more restrictive than state laws. Most have their own reporting, treatment, and counseling services. At the same time, colleges have to ensure fair treatment for students accused of sexual assaults. This issue came to national attention in 2006, when three members of the Duke University lacrosse team were accused of rape by an exotic dancer (and student at another Durham school) who had been hired to entertain at a team party. The university suspended two of the men (the third had already graduated), canceled the remainder of the lacrosse season, and fired the lacrosse coach, but all criminal charges against the three men were later dropped in the face of evidence that the woman had fabricated her accusations (Wilson, 2007). The university apologized for its failure to support the accused men and invited the two non-graduates to return to Duke, but they did not.

> **FAQ** Do women provoke rape by the way they dress or act?
> Women's actions may increase or decrease their risk of being raped, but nothing they do or fail to do changes the culpability of the rapist.

An important question is whether students accused of sexual assaults should be dealt with by college disciplinary procedures—in which case suspension or expulsion is the most severe punishment they are likely to experience—or whether they should be turned over to law enforcement officials and processed through the regular judicial system. The National Organization for Women takes the view that colleges are too protective of men accused of sexual assault and rarely fulfill their legal obligation to report criminal offenders to law enforcement agencies (National Organization for Women, 1999).

The Number One "Date Rape Drug" Is Alcohol

In recent years, a lot of attention has been paid to the use of drugs to facilitate date rape (National Women's Health Information Center, 2004). The drug that has received the most attention is **Rohypnol**, a Valium-type drug. Rohypnol is not legally available in the United States—it was banned in 1996 because of its reputation as a date rape drug—but it is smuggled in from overseas. There have been increasing reports of the use of Rohypnol to induce stupor in rape victims. The drug may also impair the victim's memory of the event. Another drug that has been used to facilitate rape is **gamma-hydroxybutyrate (GHB)** (Nicholson & Bal-

date rape Rape between dating or socially acquainted couples. Also called acquaintance rape.

Rohypnol A tranquilizer that has been used to facilitate rape.

gamma-hydroxybutyrate (GHB) A central nervous system depressant that has been used to facilitate rape.

(A)

(B)

Figure 18.4 Date rape drugs (A) Alcohol is commonly associated with rape—a fact recognized by this poster created by the Los Angeles District Attorney's Office as part of a public awareness campaign to prevent alcohol- and other drug-related rapes. (B) Rohypnol is called "the date rape drug," but alcohol has a better claim to this title. (A courtesy of the Los Angeles County District Attorney's Office; B courtesy of the Orange County Sheriff's Office.)

ster, 2001; Gahlinger, 2004). GHB is a central nervous system depressant that can be lethal when consumed in combination with alcohol or other depressants. A third drug sometimes used for the same purpose is **ketamine ("K")**, a veterinary anesthetic and recreational drug. Reports indicate that these drugs are given to women surreptitiously, often by placing them in a drink. Anyone who believes that they may have been given such a drug should go to an emergency room promptly for medical treatment and urine testing.

To assess the actual prevalence of the use of Rohypnol in rape, toxicologists analyzed over 1000 urine samples from rape victims who were suspected of being under the influence of illicit drugs (ElSohly & Salamone, 1999). Eight percent of these samples did contain Rohypnol or some kind of Valium-type drug. However, *38% of the samples contained alcohol.* Of course, merely identifying the presence of these substances in the victim's system says little about how they got there or the role they played in the rape. Alcohol may cloud a woman's judgment about prudent behavior or about how to extricate herself from a dangerous situation, and it may make her physically incapable of resisting rape just as effectively as any street drug (**Figure 18.4**). Alcohol also promotes rape when consumed by the rapist—by reducing his inhibitions. In one survey of college women, two-thirds of the women who had experienced a sexual assault said that the perpetrator was drinking at the time of the attack (Frintner & Rubinson, 1993). All in all, alcohol is probably the number one "date rape drug," whether consumed by the rapist or his victim.

Rape Can Have Severe Ill Effects on the Victim

There are many steps women can take to reduce the likelihood that they will be raped (**Box 18.2**). If a woman is raped, however, many options and services are available to help her, aid her recovery and reduce the long-lasting psychological harm that rape may cause.

Services Are Available for Rape Victims

The first and foremost step toward recovery is getting medical attention. The best place for this is an emergency room or a specialized forensic clinic, in which the staff are trained in the appropriate medical and reporting procedures (Patel & Minshall, 2001). A victim can also go to her own doctor, but that option may involve a delay, and the doctor might not have adequate expertise. Many colleges

ketamine ("K") An anesthetic and recreational drug that has been used to facilitate rape.

Sexual Health

BOX 18.2 Reducing the Risk of Rape

Rape and sexual assault are never the fault of the victim. Nevertheless, you can take precautions to reduce the risk of being raped. Rape crisis centers and rape prevention organizations offer the following advice:

General

- A man who has sexual contact with you against your will is committing a serious crime, no matter what his relationship to you and no matter what the circumstances. By reporting the crime you can help prevent someone else from becoming a victim.
- Prepare yourself for "fight or flight": Take self-defense and fitness classes.

Preventing acquaintance rape

- Until you know a man well, meet him in a group environment in which there are other women present, or in a public place.
- Pay for some of the expenses of the date, so that he can't self-justify an assault on the grounds that you "owe him something."
- Avoid drugs and excessive alcohol use, and take the man's use of either, or his attempts to persuade you to use them, as a warning sign. Don't leave your beverage unattended or accept a drink from an opened container that could have been spiked with a date rape drug.
- Be explicit if you don't want to have intercourse (or any kind of sex), especially if you are heading for his or your home. Be assertive, not coy. Don't let the man self-justify an assault on the grounds that you "led him on."
- If the man commences an assault, protest vehemently, threaten to call the police, escape from the situation if possible, use physical force if necessary, or create a loud disturbance, such as turning over tables and chairs.

Self-defense training helps women protect themselves against sexual assault.

Preventing stranger rape

- Make your home secure. Do not open the door to strangers. If you are a woman living alone, do not make that fact obvious.
- Keep your car doors locked whether you are inside or out of the car. Park where it will be safe for you to return—think about what the environment will be like after dark. Avoid deserted or ill-lit places. Jog with friends or at times and places where other people jog.
- Never hitchhike or pick up hitchhikers.
- If you find yourself in a threatening situation, run away. If that's not possible, resist forcefully. Fighting or creating a loud disturbance is more effective than pleading or offering no resistance.
- Carry an alarm device such as an air horn. If you carry any kind of weapon, be sure you know how to use it and what the law is. Generally, a person who is in imminent danger of rape may inflict whatever injury is necessary to prevent it, but no more than that, and only if other means of prevention (such as escape) are not available.

If you become a victim of a sexual assault

- Whether or not there was a completed rape, call the police or go to an emergency room immediately or call 1–800–656–HOPE.
- Do not shower, wash, douche, change your clothes, urinate, eat, drink, or clean up the location of the assault before you go—you may be destroying evidence. Take spare clothes with you.
- If the assailant was a stranger, try to remember his appearance and clothes and any details, such as a car license plate number or any part of it.
- If you do not report the assault right after it happens, do so later. The passage of time does not make the crime any less serious.
- Consider contacting a rape crisis center, where you can get expert advice and understanding in a confidential environment. Seeking help is the best way to head off long-lasting trauma.

and rape crisis centers will provide a rape advocate—a volunteer who will accompany the victim to the hospital and provide various kinds of practical and emotional support.

All healthcare providers are required to report rapes and other sexual assaults to the police, but this does not mean that the victim herself is obliged to coop-

Rape crisis centers provide support to victims, education, and advocacy.

erate or to press charges. In many communities, a woman can have a full, evidence-collecting examination and still not press charges. Thus she can keep her options open until she is sure whether or not she wants to pursue the matter legally. The desire not to report the crime should not prevent a woman from getting medical attention.

Providers who examine rape victims must assess and treat the physical and psychological injuries that the victims have sustained (Linden, 1999; McConkey et al., 2001). Careful assessment is important because there may be injuries of which the victim is unaware—particularly if, as is likely, she is in a state of emotional shock. In one study of women who had been sexually assaulted and were seen at an emergency room, 53% had general body injuries and 20% had genital or anal injuries (Sugar et al., 2004). The provider can assess the likelihood of pregnancy or disease transmission and suggest steps to prevent either eventuality. You may recall from Chapter 12 that hormonal pills can be used within 5 days after coitus to reduce the likelihood of pregnancy. Prophylaxis against STDs may include antibiotics. If there seems to be a substantial risk of HIV transmission, a short course of antiretroviral medications (post-exposure prophylaxis) might be advised.

Counseling, both in the acute aftermath of the rape and in the longer term, plays a vital role in helping "victims" of rape become "survivors." Such counseling, which may be conducted on an individual or group basis, is offered by many schools and colleges, rape crisis centers, and governmental agencies.

Rape Can Inflict Long-Lasting Psychological Injury

The effect of rape is likely to extend far beyond the immediate shock or any physical injury that the victim may sustain (Resnick et al., 1997). Rape is the denial of a person's autonomy in the most intimate aspect of their life. Different people react to the immediate experience of rape in different ways—some with an emotional outpouring, some with tightly controlled feelings—but all are at risk of developing a collection of long-term symptoms akin to the post-traumatic stress disorder experienced by survivors of other horrific events. In the context of rape or attempted rape, these symptoms have been called **rape trauma syndrome** (Burgess & Holmstrom, 1974). These symptoms may include feelings of numbness or disconnection, alternating with flashbacks and preoccupation with the rape; irrational self-blame; anxiety, depression, or anger; sleeplessness, inability to concentrate, and physical symptoms such as headaches and digestive disturbances. In the first 2 weeks after being raped, 94% of women have symptoms of rape trauma syndrome, and 46% still exhibit symptoms at 3 months after the event. Even several years later, women who have been raped are at increased risk of depression, anxiety, and substance dependency. The long-term ill effects are particularly severe for people who were raped at a young age and for those belonging to ethnic groups in which rape victims are highly stigmatized.

Not surprisingly, rape trauma syndrome can be marked by severe sexual problems. In one follow-up study of 81 female rape victims, 40% of the women said that they did not engage in any sexual contacts for several months after the rape, and almost 75% of the women, when they were interviewed 4 to 6 years after the rape, said their frequency of sexual activity was still reduced (Burgess & Holmstrom, 1979). The reasons given for the low sexual activity included a loss of interest in sex, difficulty with arousal, painful intercourse, vaginismus, and difficulty experiencing orgasm. Male rape victims have been less intensively studied. They appear to suffer psychological effects comparable to those reported by women, but they may be less able or willing to seek help, and they may be exposed to repeated rapes, especially if they are incarcerated (Mezey & King, 2000).

rape trauma syndrome A cluster of persistent physical and psychological symptoms seen in rape victims, comparable to post-traumatic stress disorder.

595 SEXUAL ASSAULT, HARASSMENT, AND PARTNER VIOLENCE

Many forms of help can facilitate a rape victim's psychological recovery. Partners, family, and friends can offer practical and emotional support by, for example, offering a place to stay, being willing to listen in a loving and nonjudgmental fashion, accepting the victim's account of what happened, emphasizing that the rape was not the victim's fault, and giving the rape survivor time and space to make their own decisions about how to deal with the situation. In a more general way, we all help people who have been raped when we do our part to create a culture that rejects rape, both as an actual deed and as the subject of humor, boasting, wishful thinking, and the like.

Counseling or group therapy may help head off lasting ill effects. Therapy focuses on countering the isolation, self-blame, and disrupted sense of control that rape victims commonly suffer (Regehr et al., 1999), as well as treating any sexual dysfunctions. For rape victims who do develop long-term psychological symptoms, **exposure therapy** may be more useful than regular counseling (Foa & Street, 2001). This is a form of cognitive–behavioral therapy in which the person recalls the traumatic event in a controlled, safe, supportive environment, usually in combination with relaxation techniques such as breathing exercises to counteract her negative emotions.

It's useful to bear two points in mind: First, recovery from rape, as from other traumatic events, does not occur overnight—whatever therapeutic measures are undertaken. Second, most people who have experienced rape or sexual assault are eventually able to recover, think of themselves as survivors rather than victims, and get on with their lives.

Male Victims Have Special Concerns

Males can be sexually victimized by females or by other males. Although female-on-male rape is uncommon—in fact, it may be impossible according to the definitions of rape used in some states—other kinds of sexual assaults on men by women are not at all rare.

There are many similarities between men and women's experiences of sexual victimization, but there are also some differences (Walker et al., 2005). Men (or male youths) who have been sexually assaulted by women may experience little support or understanding from their peers, who may treat the matter as a joke. Male victims may believe that rape crisis centers, medical staff, therapists, and the legal system are all geared toward the males-as-perpetrators concept and thus are not likely to be sympathetic or helpful to male victims. Oftentimes this belief is false, because professionals who deal with sexual assault are familiar with the fact that men can be victimized. Even if false, however, this belief tends to inhibit male victims from obtaining the help they need. In addition, men may feel guilty about being sexually assaulted, because they have violated an ethic of male self-reliance.

Males who are sexually assaulted, especially if they are assaulted by other males, may develop problems revolving around their sexual orientation. A heterosexual youth may feel "I must be gay." Conversely, a gay youth may feel that he is being punished for being gay and make efforts to become straight.

Rapes in prisons are something of a special case, not only because they are mostly male-on-male, but because they involve considerations of power as well as sex, and because they are very difficult for the victims to escape. Historically, prison authorities have not taken effective steps to prevent prison rape or to punish offenders. This has changed somewhat with the passage in 2003 of the Prison Rape Elimination Act and the issuance of a 2008 report on the subject by the Department of Justice. In some prisons, up to 16% of male prisoners report having been raped, according to the report (Shapleigh, 2008). Because HIV infection rates are consider-

FAQ I didn't fight back—will people blame me?
People understand that rape victims' main concern is to survive. Rapists can be successfully prosecuted without evidence that the victim fought back, even when no weapon is involved.

exposure therapy A form of psychotherapy for victims of rape or abuse in which they are encouraged to recall the traumatic event in a safe environment.

ably higher in prisons than elsewhere (Bureau of Justice Statistics, 2008), a man who is raped in prison has a relatively high risk of acquiring an HIV infection.

Prisoners who are small, young, nonviolent, mentally ill, gay or transgender, in prison for the first time, or lacking a gang affiliation are particularly vulnerable to being raped or sexually abused. The fact that a prisoner is known to have been raped makes him a likely target for further abuse. According to the organization Stop Prisoner Rape, prison authorities could greatly reduce the incidence of prison rape by housing these at-risk prisoners separately from known sexual predators (Stop Prisoner Rape, 2008).

Rape Laws Have Become More Protective of Victims

As recently as the eighteenth century, women were considered the property of men, and rape of women was considered an offense against men—against the woman's father if she was unmarried and against her husband if she was married (Geddes & Lueck, 2000). A woman who was raped lost value, was shamed, and brought shame on her family. Thus her kinsfolk might reject her, in addition to seeking vengeance on the rapist. These ideas still persist in some traditional patriarchal societies; for example, many of the countless Bengali women who were raped by Pakistani soldiers during the 1971 war for the independence of Bangladesh were cast out by their families. Moreover, in countries governed by traditional Islamic law, it may be near-impossible to bring a successful rape prosecution, because of unrealistic requirements such as the need to provide four male witnesses who saw the actual act of penetration. If a rape prosecution fails, the woman herself may be at risk of punishment for adultery, and she might be killed by a member of her own family.

U.S. law inherited from English law the concept of a "marital exemption" to rape, meaning that it was not rape for a man to force sex on his wife. The thinking was that the wife had given consent to sex by virtue of her marriage vows and could not retract it. Marital rape did not become a crime in all U.S. states until 1993.

Even today, many states allow a man to have sex with his wife in circumstances that would constitute *statutory* rape if it took place between unmarried persons, such as when the wife is unconscious, mentally impaired, or underage.

As an informal extension of the marital exemption, the legal system used to be quite forgiving of rapes that occurred between cohabiting or socially acquainted couples, rapes of dates or pick-ups, or rapes of prostitutes. The women in these circumstances were viewed as having voluntarily placed themselves at the man's disposal. Defendants could often escape severe penalties by arguing that the episode had been inflated as a consequence of domestic discord or that the victim had signaled her willingness to engage in sex. She might be judged to have done so by dressing or acting provocatively, by voluntarily going to the defendant's home, by entering his bedroom, or by engaging in noncoital sexual behavior.

In 2006, some Pakistani women demonstrated *against* the repeal of traditional laws that made rape prosecutions difficult. Nevertheless the laws were repealed.

Simply demonstrating that the victim was of "unchaste character" was often enough to secure an acquittal or to get the charges reduced. Evidence that the victim used contraceptives even though unmarried, that she frequented bars, or that she had a reputation as a promiscuous woman might be introduced for this purpose. In other words, rape laws were used primarily to protect "women of virtue"—women who either were virgins or were married to someone other than the perpetrator.

Reforms Began in the 1970s

The women's movement brought about many significant changes in the ways in which the legal system and the general public view rape. Beginning in the 1970s, **rape shield laws** were introduced. These laws protect rape victims in a number of ways, most notably by preventing the alleged perpetrator from introducing evidence about the victim's prior sexual history. In other words, the defendant can no longer get off by painting the victim as a "slut."

Laws have also been modified to introduce a range of sexual offenses in addition to rape, as traditionally defined. These offenses are called sexual battery, sexual assault, forcible or aggravated sodomy, and the like. The definitions of such offenses vary considerably from state to state. The key point is that it is no longer necessary to prove that coitus occurred, which makes it easier to obtain convictions in many cases—although the sentences are often much lighter than for a rape conviction. In addition, it is no longer necessary in many states to prove that the victim physically resisted the rape or assault, nor is it necessary to provide corroborating evidence from third parties.

Critics point to cases in which the alleged perpetrator's legitimate defense appears to have been undermined by the new laws (Young, 1998). One such case involved a Columbia University graduate student, Oliver Jovanovic, who was accused in 1996 of kidnapping, sexually assaulting, and torturing a female Barnard College student. Jovanovic argued that the encounter was a consensual BDSM encounter. Citing New York's rape shield law, the judge excluded from evidence a set of emails from the woman to Jovanovic in which she expressed an interest in sadomasochistic sex. Jovanovic was convicted and sentenced to 15 years in prison. After he had been in prison for 20 months, an appellate court ruled that the trial judge had applied the rape shield law improperly, and the case was eventually dismissed after the woman refused to testify in a retrial (Fritsch & Finkelstein, 2001).

What Happens to Men Who Rape?

Since the majority of rapes are not reported to law enforcement officials, we can assume that the majority of rapists go unpunished. Nevertheless, about 23,000 adults or juveniles are arrested for forcible rape in the United States each year (Federal Bureau of Investigation, 2008).

Some rape reports, of course, are judged by law enforcement officials to be unfounded or malicious. In one study, these constituted 8% of the total (Greenfeld, 1997). In another study, no fewer than 41% of all the reports of completed rape in a small Midwestern city were eventually retracted by the alleged victims (Kanin, 1994). The fact that the allegations were retracted does not necessarily mean that they were false, of course: Victims may be motivated to retract true allegations for the same reasons that most victims do not file reports in the first place. But people can also fabricate accusations; according to Kanin, they may be motivated to do so by a desire for revenge, by a wish for sympathy or attention, or to justify some action taken by the accuser.

rape shield laws Laws that protect rape victims, for example, by limiting the introduction of evidence about their prior sexual behavior.

FAQ I was raped 7 years ago—can I still file charges?
The statute of limitations varies from state to state, and it varies according to exactly which charge is brought against the perpetrator. In California, for example, the statute of limitations is 6 years for rape in most circumstances but could be longer if DNA evidence is involved. Prosecuting old cases can be difficult unless there is very strong evidence.

About half of all men arrested for rape are convicted (usually of felony rape)—most, after a guilty plea. Over two-thirds of convicted defendants received a prison sentence; the average term was 14 years. Another 19% of convicted defendants were sentenced to terms in local jails, and 13% were placed on probation. Convicted rapists typically serve about half of their prison terms before release. At any one time, about 90,000 Americans are in prison for rape or sexual assault.

Why Do Men Rape?

Understanding the reasons why men rape seems like an important first step toward developing effective strategies for preventing rape. This question has been approached from a variety of different perspectives, and there is no consensus on what are the most important causal factors. Here we review some of the main lines of thought on the topic, breaking them down into three basic questions:

1. Why does the human species possess the capacity for rape?
2. Why do some individuals have more propensity to rape than others?
3. How do social forces make rape more or less likely to occur?

Rape May Have Evolutionary Roots

As discussed in Chapter 2, forced copulation is quite common among nonhuman animals. It is seen in species ranging from insects all the way to primates, and in some of these species it is clearly an evolutionary adaptation: That is, the behavior has evolved because it increases the animals' reproductive success. Often, male animals copulate with females by force when regular courtship strategies are unsuccessful.

In their 2000 book, *A Natural History of Rape*, Randy Thornhill and Craig Palmer argued that human rape should be viewed through the lens of evolutionary psychology. They made the case that the human capacity for rape is either itself an adaptation or that it is *by-product* of adaptive traits, such as sexual desire and aggressiveness, which have evolved for reasons that have no direct connection with the benefits or costs of rape.

Some aspects of rape do suggest that it might be an evolutionary adaptation. For example, men most commonly rape women who are in their peak reproductive years (see Figure 18.1). Also, as in animals, human males who have failed to obtain sex partners by consensual means have an increased likelihood of doing so by coercion (Figueredo, 2000). From the perspective of evolutionary psychology, these and similar findings suggest that the capacity for rape has been shaped by rape's reproductive costs and benefits.

On the other hand, one attempt to model the reproductive costs and benefits of rape, using real-world data from a preliterate American Indian population in Paraguay, found that the reproductive *costs* of rape (such as the risk of death at the hands of the woman or her relatives) outweighed its reproductive *benefits* tenfold (Smith et al., 2001). The main reason for this outcome was that sex at a random time stands a low probability of falling within the woman's six-day "fertile window." These findings, if found to be generally true, would throw doubt on the idea that the capacity for rape could be an evolutionary adaptation. Also, the findings suggest a possible reason why ovulation in humans is concealed (not evident to others), in contrast to many other animals in which it is conspicuously advertised by physical changes and behavior ("heat"). Concealed ovulation may serve to reduce the frequency of rape by making it less profitable, in reproductive terms, to the men who rape.

Gang rape? Four male mallard ducks attempt to copulate with one (barely visible) female.

Some Characteristics Distinguish Rapists from Non-Rapists

A great deal of attention has been focused on men who commit rape. The hope is that through such study it might be possible to identify personality traits, early experiences, or other factors that predispose these men to commit their crimes.

Some extremely violent rapists have severe personality disorders or are driven by sadistic impulses (see Chapter 15). The majority of rapists, especially those who commit acquaintance or date rape, are fairly unremarkable people, but in a statistical sense at least they do differ from non-rapists. They tend to be of lower socioeconomic status, to have had less education and worse relationships with their parents, to have more self-centered personalities, and to have less capacity for empathy (Chantry & Craig, 1994; Gannon & Ward, 2008). These attributes are common in other criminal offenders, however, so they do not by themselves account for a proclivity to rape. In fact, the commonality between rapists and other criminal offenders is highlighted by studies of recidivism: When rapists reoffend, their crimes are somewhat more likely to be nonsexual offenses such as robbery than another sexual offense (Hanson & Bussière, 1998; Simon, 2000). (Child molesters, in contrast, are more likely to commit a second sexual offense.)

The inclination to rape seems to be quite common. In one survey of male college students by Neil Malamuth of UCLA, carried out at a time when rape was more common than it is today, 37% of the men said that there was some likelihood that they would commit rape if they knew that they wouldn't be caught (Malamuth, 1981). One in 12 men admitted to actually having committed acts that would meet the legal definition of rape, although most of these men denied that their acts constituted rape. In another study, 43% of college-aged men admitted to having used some kind of coercion, such as ignoring a woman's protests, to have sex (Rapaport & Posey, 1991).

Malamuth and his colleagues have done extensive studies of male college students to investigate factors associated with an inclination to rape. They reported that male college students who grew up in a violent home environment, were abused as children, became involved in juvenile delinquency, had large numbers of sex partners, were interested in impersonal sex, or had dominating or hostile attitudes toward women all expressed a greater willingness to engage in coercive sex than did other men. Over a 10-year follow-up period, such men were more likely than other men to actually engage in aggressive sexual or nonsexual behavior toward women (Malamuth et al., 1995). The researchers also found, however, that men who were capable of empathy were less likely to be aggressive toward women, even when all other factors predisposed them to be so (Dean & Malamuth, 1997).

Social Forces Influence the Likelihood of Rape

Social scientists and feminists have generally taken the view that rape is a learned behavior. Here is an expression of this point of view by Diana Russell, professor emeritus of sociology at Mills College in Oakland, California:

> Males are trained from childhood to separate sexual desire from caring, respecting, liking or loving. One of the consequences of this training is that many men regard women as sexual objects, rather than as full human beings. … [This view] predisposes men to rape. Even if women were physically stronger than men, it is doubtful that there would be many instances of female rapes of males: Female sexual socialization encourages females to integrate sex, affection, and love, and to be sensitive to what their partners want (Russell, 1984).

Anthropologist Peggy Sanday, of the University of Pennsylvania, has argued that U.S. society is an especially rape-prone culture, on account of a dominant patriarchal ideology. Rape was well-controlled in seventeenth-century New England, according to Sanday, because men were held accountable for their actions. Later, she argues, there developed a cultural tolerance of rape, based on the notion that men have an inherently uncontrollable sexual urge, so that men who rape were considered less culpable than those who committed other crimes (Sanday, 1996).

Here is a specific example that seems to illustrate a "culture of rape" in at least one sector of U.S. society. After the 2000 Puerto Rican Day parade in New York, a mob of men assaulted, stripped, groped, or sexually abused 50 women in Central Park. There was no intervention by police or bystanders. Some bystanders did provide videotapes to the police, but these videotapes were broadcast repeatedly on local TV stations, further traumatizing the victims. To some cultural critics, the media reaction to the event focused inappropriately on "mob psychology" and ignored the culture of sexism that permitted it to occur (Katz & Jhally, 2000).

In general, there does seem to be a connection between a "macho" masculine ideology and the acceptance and perpetration of sexual violence against women (Murnen et al., 2002). Men who feel a need to control women are especially prone to commit sexual violence (Christopher & Kisler, 2004). Thus, in the view of many feminists, changing the nature of relationships between men and women is a necessary step before rape can be eliminated (Buchwald et al., 2004).

In the United States, social forces work not only to encourage rape but also to restrain it. One social institution, the criminal justice system, presents a major deterrence to would-be rapists. In the 2000 Puerto Rican Day case just mentioned, for example, 30 men were charged and 18 were convicted for their roles in the incident and given sentences of up to 5 years of imprisonment (Finkelstein, 2001). In many parts of the world there would have been no prosecutions in connection with an incident of this kind.

The power of social controls is illustrated by what happens when they collapse, as may happen during a military invasion. In such situations the rape rate is likely to skyrocket. In fact, rape has sometimes been used as an apparent instrument of military policy, as occurred during World War II (**Box 18.3**) and more recently during fighting in the Democratic Republic of Congo, where hundreds of thousands of women and girls have been raped (McGreal, 2006).

The fact that the rape rate has fallen markedly in the United States over the last 35 years illustrates the power of social influences on the actions of individuals. It is likely that the feminist-led movement to end the victimization of women helped create a culture in which rape is less tolerated than it was a generation ago.

Theorists Have Debated Whether Rape Is Sexual

An idea first put forward by feminists in the 1970s is that rape is motivated not by sexual desire at all but rather by either hostility to women or the desire to exert power over them. Perhaps the most influential early expression of this view was the 1975 book *Against Our Will* by Susan Brownmiller. Here is a quote from the book:

> Man's discovery that his genitalia could serve as a weapon to generate fear must rank as one of the most important discoveries of prehistoric times, along with the use of fire and the first crude stone axe. From prehistoric times to the present, I believe, rape has played a critical function. It is nothing more or less than a conscious process of intimidation by which *all* men keep *all* women in a state of fear (Brownmiller, 1975).

Brownmiller's assertion that all men commit or consciously approve of rape as a tool to subjugate women may strike many people today as an extreme example of 1970s male-bashing. But the notion that rape is essentially *nonsexual* is still widespread. Many rape crisis and rape prevention centers carry statements such as the following on their Web sites:

Sex in History

BOX 18.3 The "Comfort Women"

Rape by conquering troops has been a part of most wars since time immemorial, but before and during World War II Japan institutionalized the practice. The Japanese took women from the countries they colonized (or conquered) to serve as sex slaves for their soldiers. An estimated total of 200,000 to 400,000 women were enslaved; most were Korean, but others were Taiwanese, Chinese, Filipino, Indonesian, or Dutch. The practice was begun in 1932 in Shanghai but eventually spread to all territories reached by Japanese soldiers. The enslaved women were euphemistically called *jugun ianfu* ("military comfort women").

Here are remarks by two former "comfort women":

Yun Doo Ree: When my cuts and bruises had healed slightly, they put me back into the same room. Another officer was waiting for me. They must have warned him about me. He did not wait and did not give me a moment to even think of protesting. He swiftly knocked me down and started pushing his thing inside of me. It happened all so fast. I found myself bleeding. I wasn't even sure where the blood was coming from. I only felt pain. Something in my body was torn apart. I

put my teeth into his cheek. Now we were both bleeding, he from his face and I, somewhere below.... I was 15.

Ok Seon Lee: I am filled with *han* [unresolved grief]. Nothing—not even the deaths of every Japanese soldier—can bring back my lost life.

Most of these sex slaves died during the Second World War, many at the hands of the Japanese. The Japanese government has declined to provide restitution out of public funds, despite protests by former comfort women (see figure) and others. It claims that the "comfort women" program was not official Japanese policy. In 2007 the government of Prime Minister Shinzo Abe created a furor across Asia when it denied that the military had coerced women into prostitution at all. According to historian Hirofumi Hayashi of Kanto-Gakuin University in Yokohama, however, the program "was not only carried out by the total involvement of every section of the military but also by administrative machinery at every level of the Japanese state. [The Emperor] certainly had power to stop it." *Sources*: Kim-Gibson, 1999; Kang, 2001; Onishi, 2007.

MYTH: Men rape women because they are sexually aroused or have been sexually deprived.

FACT: Men rape women to exert control and confirm their power.

(California Coalition Against Sexual Assault, 2005)

Let's take a look at some of the arguments and counterarguments used in debating the proposition that rape is not sexual or not primarily sexual:

Argument: Rapists choose their victims on the basis of their vulnerability, not their attractiveness (Groth, 1979).

Counterargument: Rape victims are predominantly in the age range that men find most physically attractive (see Figure 18.1). The most vulnerable females—female children and old women—are less commonly raped than are physically stronger young adult women.

Argument: Rapists do more physical harm to their victims than necessary to complete the act of coitus. Therefore, physical harm must be an end in itself (Harding, 1985).

Counterargument: Studies of victims' accounts of rape have found that, while some rapes are extremely violent, most are accomplished only by the threat of violence or by the minimal force required to complete coitus (pushing or holding) (McCahill et al., 1979).

Argument: Victorious soldiers often rape women among the defeated enemy; this shows that hostility is the motivation (Brownmiller, 1975).

Counterargument: This behavior could equally be the result of the low cost of rape in this situation. Also, victorious soldiers preferentially rape young women, a pattern that is not explained by the hostility theory (Gottschall, 2004).

Argument: Rapists often say that they raped for reasons of power, control, or vengeance, rather than sex (Scully, 1990).

Counterargument: Rapists' accounts of their crimes may describe either nonsexual or sexual motivations.

Here is one example illustrating sexual motivation:

She stood there in her nightgown, and you could see right through it—you could see her nipples and breasts, and, you know, they were just waiting for me (Groth, 1979).

Although this controversy remains unresolved, it seems likely that sexual desire plays a significant role in most rapes, especially date rapes. Although force or the threat of force is associated with all rapes by definition, this does not by itself mean that violence is part of the motivation. Thornhill and Palmer argue that drawing such a conclusion would be as illogical as concluding that men who pay prostitutes for sex are motivated by charity (Thornhill & Palmer, 2000).

Intervention Programs Are of Uncertain Value

Treatment programs aimed at reducing rapists' likelihood of reoffending typically employ cognitive-behavioral therapy in a group setting. These programs do seem to reduce recidivism, but the effect is small: In one meta-analysis, treatment reduced recidivism by only about 6% compared to nontreated controls (Lösel & Schmucker, 2005).

Partly because of the disappointing results with men who have already raped, there have been widespread efforts to prevent rape by changing attitudes and behaviors in young people. Because the peak age for the sexual victimization of females is 16 to 19, many females experience sexual assaults and rapes while they are still in high school. One survey of female students in the ninth through twelfth grades in Massachusetts found that about 10% of them had been sexually assaulted at least once by a dating partner (Silverman et al., 2001).

Given that sexual violence begins early, rape prevention programs have been developed that are aimed at adolescents who are beginning to date. A team led by Vangie Foshee of the University of North Carolina tested the effectiveness of one such program, which they called the Safe Dates Project (Foshee et al., 1996, 1998, 2000). Fourteen schools in a rural, mostly white North Carolina county were randomly assigned to offer the program, or not. In the schools that offered the program, eighth- and ninth-grade students were exposed to a ten-session curriculum, a play, and a poster contest. These activities focused on changing norms for dating violence and gender stereotyping, as well as improving conflict management skills and awareness of services. The program also had a community element, involving a crisis telephone line, training of counselors, and a support group.

When students were surveyed a month after completing the program, the results seemed quite promising: The students in the schools in which the program had been offered were less likely either to suffer or to inflict violence or psychological abuse in a dating context than were students in the control schools. In 12 months, however, these behavioral differences between the two groups of students had disappeared, although there was still an improved awareness of conflict resolution techniques and of the availability of community services among the students who took the program. Follow-up "booster programs" failed to help students maintain their improvements; students who participated in such a program 2 years after the initial program did not preserve or recover their initial behavioral benefits (Foshee, 2001, pers. comm.).

One reason for the limited success of such programs may be that they come too late. It has been forcefully argued that a key step in preventing violence by adults is promoting the development of empathy in young children (Swick, 2005). Empathy is a necessary precondition for loving relationships and interpersonal respect. Although all children have a natural capacity for empathy, this capacity needs to be fostered, or it will wither and die. This seems to be especially true for boys, who typically grow up in a highly competitive culture that rewards aggressive, goal-seeking behaviors. Whether programs to foster the early development of empathy could actually reduce sexual violence, however, is a question that remains to be studied.

Sexual Harassment Occurs in Many Environments

Sexual harassment is unwelcome sexual behavior in the workplace or in other structured environments. Most sexual harassment is perpetrated by men on women, but men are sometimes sexually harassed, either by women or by men (**Figure 18.5**). Presumably, women are occasionally harassed by other women.

The concept of sexual harassment did not really come to the attention of the American public until the mid-1970s, when the term began to be widely used by women's rights activists. Two activists, Lin Farley and Catherine MacKinnon, published influential books on the topic in the late 1970s (Farley, 1978; MacKinnon, 1979). Farley represented sexual harassment as a tool used by men to control women, just as Susan Brownmiller had done for rape a few years earlier. Farley's ideas are supported by recent experimental studies, which have found that women who violate gender expectations are harassed the most (Berdahl, 2007).

MacKinnon, a law professor, attempted to convince the legal community that sexual harassment constitutes illegal sex discrimination. She was successful in this aim: In 1980, the U.S. Equal Employment Opportunity Commission (EEOC) declared that sexual harassment in the workplace is a form of sex discrimination that violates the 1964 Civil Rights Act.

The EEOC defines sexual harassment as follows:

> Unwelcome sexual advances, requests for sexual favors, and other verbal or physical conduct of a sexual nature constitutes sexual harassment when submission to or rejection of this conduct explicitly or implicitly affects an individual's employment, unreasonably interferes with an individual's work performance or creates an intimidating, hostile or offensive work environment (Equal Employment Opportunity Commission, 2008).

It is ironic that the man who led the EEOC from 1982 to 1990, Clarence Thomas, was himself later accused of sexual harassment (**Box 18.4**).

Similar problems can arise in faculty–student relationships at colleges and between doctors, therapists, lawyers, ministers, and other professionals and their patients or clients. Unwelcome sexual behavior in these environments is not always illegal, but it is widely prohibited by college administrations, professional governing bodies, and the like.

There Are Two Kinds of Workplace Sexual Harassment

Sexual harassment in the workplace takes two different forms. The first involves an explicit or implicit "deal": "If you go out with me, I'll see that you get a merit

sexual harassment Unwanted sexual advances or other intimidating sexual behavior, usually in the workplace.

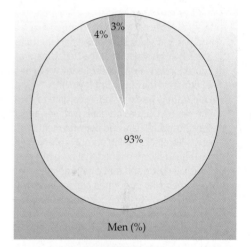

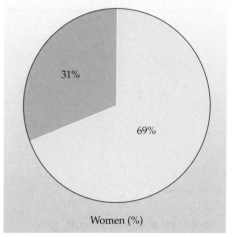

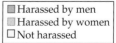

Figure 18.5 Who is harassed by whom? (Data from Louis Harris Poll, 1994.)

Sex in History

BOX 18.4   He Says, She Says: The Clarence Thomas Hearings

In 1991, U.S. Supreme Court Justice Thurgood Marshall announced his intention to retire, and President George Bush nominated Judge Clarence Thomas as Marshall's replacement. Thomas, like Marshall, was African American, but ideologically he was far to the right of Marshall. Thomas's appointment was opposed by many organizations, including the NAACP, who feared he would help roll back affirmative action and other liberal programs.

The U.S. Senate held its confirmation hearings later that year. The hearings became a media circus when Anita Hill, a law professor at the University of Oklahoma, charged that Thomas had sexually harassed her when she worked as his assistant at the Department of Education as well as subsequently when he was chairman of the Equal Employment Opportunity Commission. According to Hill, Thomas had requested dates with her, and after she refused, he harassed her with mentions of sexual topics, including pornographic movies. He repeatedly mentioned that his penis was unusually large and that it gave great pleasure to women who performed oral sex on him. "One of the oddest episodes I remember," said Hill, "was an occasion in which Thomas was drinking a Coke in his office. He got up from the table at which we were working, went over to his desk to get the Coke, and asked, 'Who has put pubic hair on my Coke?'" Hill said that the harassment caused her physical and emotional suffering and eventually caused her to leave her job. Thomas denied all of Hill's charges, which he considered politically motivated. "A high-tech lynching for uppity blacks" was his memorable description of the proceedings.

The Senate, which at the time included only two women, voted 52 to 48 to confirm Thomas's appointment. This result could be seen as a defeat for people concerned about sexual harassment. From a wider perspective, however, the Clarence Thomas hearings probably helped aid their cause by focusing public attention on the issue. Between 1991 and 1996, filings with the EEOC increased from about 6000 per year to about 14,000 per year, and total awards to victims increased from about $8 million to about $28 million. By 2007 the number of filings had fallen slightly, to 12,500 per year, but the total awards to victims had risen to about $50 million (Equal Employment Opportunity Commission, 2008).

Although the U.S. Senate was narrowly divided in its vote on Clarence Thomas, it took unanimous action 3 years later when it cen-

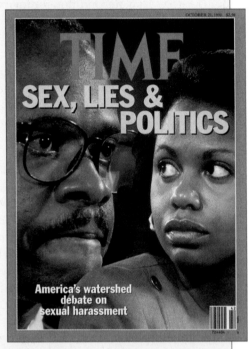

sured one of its own members, Senator Bob Packwood of Oregon, for sexually harassing female employees and campaign workers. Packwood resigned the day after the vote.

---

raise," or "If you don't have sex with me, you can kiss your job goodbye." This kind of sexual harassment is called **quid pro quo** ("what for what?") **harassment**. It is generally considered the more reprehensible kind—if the facts are not in dispute, there can be little doubt about its illegal and damaging nature.

The second kind of sexual harassment, called **hostile-environment harassment**, involves a pattern of unwelcome sexual attention that simply makes life difficult for the victim. This kind of harassment causes a great deal of suffering, but it is not so easy to characterize and document. For one thing, it depends on the victim's reactions to the perpetrator's actions. Men are less likely to be upset by sexual advances from women than women are by sexual advances from men. Even among women, some will feel more harmed than others. Also, in many cases, it's not obvious how effectively the victim communicated the unwelcomeness of the behavior to the harasser. Thus it's not always easy to draw the line between acceptable social behavior and sexual harassment. It is the hostile-environment cases that have aroused the most criticism from conservatives—including conservative women's groups.

Hostile-environment harassment cases often involve free speech issues. In one important case adjudicated in 1991, a female welder, Lois Robinson, brought an

quid pro quo harassment
Unwelcome sexual advances, usually made to a worker in a subordinate position, accompanied by promises or threats.

hostile-environment harassment
Sexual harassment involving a pattern of conduct that creates an intimidating work environment.

action against her employer, Jacksonville Shipyards, saying that male workers had harassed her by posting nude pinups around the workplace and making sexually suggestive remarks. The shipyard argued that firing the men would constitute an infringement of their First Amendment right to free speech. The court ruled that when an employee's exercise of free speech undermines workplace morale, an employer may fire them without infringing on their right to free speech.

The free speech defense has fared much better on college campuses, partly because they are not likely to count as workplaces if the alleged harassment occurs among students or between students and faculty. In a 1994 case, University of New Hampshire professor Donald Silva got himself into trouble during a technical writing class. In attempting to explain the meaning of the word "simile," Silva quoted the words of belly dancer Little Egypt: "Belly dancing is like Jell-O on a plate with a vibrator under the plate." Seven women in the class complained of sexual harassment, and Silva was ordered to apologize and undergo counseling. He refused and sued the school, whereupon the school suspended him without pay. Two years later, a federal court ordered Silva reinstated, saying that the school had violated his First Amendment rights by punishing him (Honan, 1994). The school had to pay Silva substantial damages. Thus, in establishing sexual harassment policies, colleges must tread a delicate path between preventing sexual abuses and infringing on free speech. In general, sexual harassment means a pattern of behavior, not a one-time incident like this one.

Sexual Harassment Begins Early

For many children, sexual harassment begins as soon as they enter puberty—if not before. In one national survey of students in grades 8 through 11 attending U.S. public schools, 63% of the girls and 56% of the boys said that they experienced sexual harassment "often" or "occasionally" (**Table 18.1**).

It is possible that many sexually colored incidents in schools are of no great significance. A school in Lexington, North Carolina, for example, earned national ridicule in 1996 when it suspended a 6-year-old boy for kissing a female classmate (Nossiter, 1996). But sexual harassment in school can be persistent and traumatic, as was made clear by the 4000 letters received by *Seventeen* magazine in response to an article and poll on the subject (Stein, 1999). Here is one typical letter, from a 12-year-old Mexican-American student in Michigan:

TABLE 18.1

Types of Sexual Harassment Experienced in School by Boys and Girls in Grades 8–11

	Boys (%)	Girls (%)
Sexual comments, jokes, gestures, or looks	34	48
Touched, grabbed, or pinched in a sexual way	20	29
Intentionally brushed up against in a sexual way	20	28
Flashed or mooned	18	22
Had sexual rumors spread about them	14	21
Had clothing pulled at in a sexual manner	14	16
Shown, given, or left sexual messages or pictures	15	10
Forced to kiss someone	7	7
Called gay or lesbian	19	13

Source: American Association of University Women, 2001.

A woman often experiences touching by a man to be unwelcome sexual contact, but the man may be unaware of this unless the woman tells him.

In my case there were 2 or 3 boys touching me, and trust me they were big boys. And I'd tell them to stop but they wouldn't. This went on for about 6 months until finally I was in one of my classes in the back of the room minding my own business when all of them came back and backed me into a corner and started touching me all over. So I went running out of the room and the teacher yelled at me and I had to stay in my seat for the rest of the class.

A common theme of the letters, as in this one, was the lack of concern shown by teachers and school officials; often the girls felt that they were treated as offenders rather than victims.

In one survey, sexual harassment in schools was found to cause more harm than bullying. Girls suffered more harm than boys: They experienced lower self-esteem, poorer mental and physical health, and more trauma symptoms (Gruber & Fineran, 2008). Gay and lesbian students were also traumatized by sexual harassment.

Schools are beginning to take sexual harassment more seriously, partly as a result of successful legal actions by students who have been harassed. A key case was that of LaShonda Davis, a fifth-grade student in Forsythe, Georgia. Davis was sexually taunted for months by a male classmate, but the school authorities failed to stop the abuse. LaShonda's mother sued the school board, and the case went all the way to the U.S. Supreme Court. In 1999 the court ruled in her favor, stating that federally funded schools that are willfully indifferent to student-on-student sexual harassment can be held liable.

Sexual Harassment Harms Its Victims

Although adults are better able to resist sexual harassment than are schoolchildren, the harmful effects of harassment in adulthood are still considerable (Willness et al., 2007). The effects on harassed workers include decreased job satisfaction, lower organizational commitment, withdrawing from work, physical and mental ill-health, and even symptoms of post-traumatic stress disorder. Employers also suffer in terms of lost productivity and the costs of insurance premiums or claim settlements. Nearly 1 in 4 female college students has avoided classes or dropped courses on account of sexual harassment (Paludi, 1996).

College policies on sexual relationships vary in their restrictiveness (Rimer, 2003). At Duke University, for example, faculty members are "strongly discouraged" from becoming sexually involved with students for whom they have academic responsibility; if they do so, they must report the fact to a dean and be removed from authority over the student. Yale University *bans* sexual relationships between faculty members and their own students. The University of California, Berkeley bans sexual *or romantic* relationships between faculty members and their own students. The College of William and Mary bans sexual or romantic relationships between faculty members and *any* undergraduate students, as have a few other schools. These policies have been challenged by some college faculty. Psychology professor Paul Abramson, for example, who teaches a human sexuality course at UCLA, argues that policies restricting consensual, nonexploitative relationships between faculty and students infringe on constitutionally guaranteed freedoms (Abramson, 2007).

Victims of Sexual Harassment Can Take Steps to End It

Many organizations, such as the AFL-CIO, the National Partnership for Women and Families, and the Feminist Majority, have formulated recommendations for dealing with sexual harassment:

- Know your rights. Consult your organization's written policies concerning sexual harassment.

- Tell your harasser that they are harassing you. Recount what they are doing, explain how it affects you, and demand that they stop. Make sure your tone of voice, facial expression, and body language match the seriousness of your message. Don't accept any excuses the harasser may offer or be sidetracked by diversionary topics. If the harassment is especially severe, so that you might anticipate a violent response to your complaint, do not confront the harasser directly.

- Keep a journal documenting every incident of harassment as it happens, how it affected you, and how you responded. Keep photographs or the originals of any offensive messages or images you receive.

- Tell other people, such as trusted coworkers, about the harassment as it occurs. Ask whether others have experienced sexual harassment from the same person, whether they have witnessed the harassment that you have experienced, and whether they will support you if you take action.

- If the harasser does not stop the offensive behavior or responds with any vindictive action, complain to your supervisor, your supervisor's boss, your union steward, your personnel department, your principal, or your student advisor or file an official complaint via the channels established by your organization. Keep records of these actions and their results.

- If you do not get satisfaction through these channels, consider obtaining a lawyer and filing a complaint with the EEOC, your state's Fair Employment Practice agency, or the U.S. Department of Education's Office of Civil Rights. Such complaints must be filed within a certain deadline (within 6 months of the last incident of harassment, in the case of the EEOC). These agencies may help you settle the case, or they may give you a "right-to-sue" letter that will facilitate a private lawsuit. If criminal behavior such as sexual assault is involved, you should go directly to the police.

A sexual harassment awareness poster

Most large companies provide training programs that cover sexual harassment issues. In fact, such programs may be required by state employment laws. The training is typically provided by contracting companies and it is probably quite effective in increasing awareness of sexual harassment and the harm that it causes.

There Are Three Kinds of Stalkers

If rape is the dark side of sex, then **stalking** is the dark side of love. A stalker is emotionally obsessed with a particular victim, and that obsession usually has, or once had, a romantic element. Stalkers put their victims in fear by repeatedly following them, harassing them, lying in wait for them, making phone calls or sending messages to them, vandalizing their property, and the like. Stalking via the Internet (**cyberstalking**) is an increasing problem (U.S. Department of Justice, 1999; Bocij, 2008).

According to data from the National Violence Against Women (NVAW) survey, which was conducted in the mid-1990s, 1% of women and 0.4% of men were stalked in the previous 12 months (Tjaden & Thoennes, 1998, 2006). About half of all victims are between 18 and 29 years old.

There are three distinct kinds of stalking. The most common is **intimate partner stalking**, in which the victim is stalked by a current or former spouse, cohab-

stalking Obsessive pursuit of someone in such a way as to put that person in a state of fear.

cyberstalking Stalking via the Internet.

intimate partner stalking Stalking of a current or former spouse or other intimate partner.

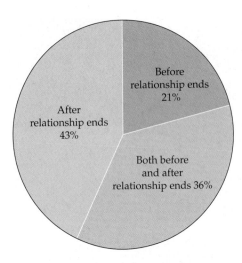

Figure 18.6 When does stalking occur?
The graph shows the timing of stalking of women by intimate partners. (Data from Tjaden & Thoennes, 1998.)

itational partner, boyfriend, girlfriend, or date. Fifty-nine percent of female stalking victims and 30% of male victims are stalked by intimate partners. It is often assumed that intimate partner stalkers do their stalking after the relationship has broken up, but in actuality, stalking can take place while a relationship is still intact (Tjaden & Thoennes, 1998) (**Figure 18.6**). Intimate partner stalkers often show a controlling or suspicious attitude toward the victim even before the stalking behavior begins. Anger is a major motivational factor in intimate partner stalking. These stalkers often have a prior psychiatric or criminal history (Meloy et al., 2000), and over half are alcohol or drug abusers (Macfarlane et al., 1999).

According to Brian Spitzberg of San Diego State University and William Cupach of Illinois State University, intimate partner stalking is an extreme example of a common behavior pattern that they call **obsessive relational intrusion** (Cupach & Spitzberg, 1998). A rejected lover will frequently make attempts to continue a relationship, perhaps in an attempt to see whether the rejection is wholehearted or not. Most women and men have experienced this kind of unwanted attention at some time or another, as described in Chapter 10. Certain personality traits in the pursuer, such as a tendency toward exploitation, coerciveness, or obsessive thinking, may help turn this behavior into persistent stalking.

In the second kind of stalking, **delusional stalking**, the stalker has the fixed belief that the victim is in love with him or could easily be made to fall in love with him, even though there has never been an intimate relationship between the two of them. This kind of delusional thinking is sometimes called **erotomania**. The victim may be an acquaintance—often a person in some kind of authority position or one who has given the stalker some attention, such as a teacher, doctor, or therapist. Alternatively, the victim may be a celebrity whom the stalker has never met. Being stalked is an occupational hazard in the entertainment industry. Delusional stalkers are generally socially inept people with few intimate relationships. The less the stalker and victim actually know each other, the more likely that the stalker has a serious mental illness.

The third type of stalking is **grudge stalking**, in which the stalker pursues the victim to seek revenge for some actual or imagined injury. This kind of stalking is not usually sexual; common targets are coworkers, employers, administrators, and the like.

Being stalked is an extremely traumatic and stressful experience and one that may go on for years. Besides having to deal with the constant harassment, the victim is often in fear that the stalking will escalate to violence—and with good reason. In the NVAW survey, 81% of women who were stalked by a current or former intimate partner were also physically assaulted by the stalker, and 31% were also sexually assaulted. Stalking can culminate in murder.

Doreen Orion, a psychiatrist at the University of Colorado who was stalked for 8 years by a female client, has suggested an extensive list of precautions that stalking victims should take (Orion, 1998):

- Tell the stalker "no" once and once only. Thereafter, avoid all contact.
- Keep your address and phone number private. Block your address at the Department of Motor Vehicles and Registrar of Voters. Use a post office box. Be cautious about revealing personal information online.
- Get a dog. Take self-defense classes. Carry a cell phone at all times. Drive to a police station if your car is being followed.
- Make a record of all stalking incidents, and keep all letters and messages received from the stalker.
- Join a stalking victims' support group.
- Consider moving if your case warrants it.

obsessive relational intrusion
Obsessive pursuit of a person by a rejected lover.

delusional stalking Stalking motivated by the delusional belief that the victim is in love with, or could be persuaded to fall in love with, the stalker.

erotomania The delusional belief that a sexually desired but unattainable person is actually in love with oneself.

grudge stalking Nonsexual revenge stalking.

- Consider obtaining a restraining order against your stalker, but bear in mind that most stalkers violate these orders (Tjaden & Thoennes, 1998) and that the police are not going to spend time guarding you.
- Shred all documents before disposal and limit the personal information that you post on the Internet.

Stalking is illegal in all 50 states, and stalking across state lines is a federal offense. In many states, however, first-offense stalking is only a misdemeanor, in which case the penalties may be minor. Furthermore, it may not be enough just to prove that you were put in fear by the stalker—in some jurisdictions, the stalker must make "credible threats" against you in order to be convicted of a crime.

(A)

(B)

Celebrities are common victims of delusional stalkers. (A) Actress Rebecca Schaeffer (right; seen here with her television costar Pam Dawber) was shot dead at her front door by a deranged admirer, Robert Bardo, who got her address from the Department of Motor Vehicles. (B) Talk show host David Letterman was stalked for a decade by a woman, Margaret Ray, who claimed to be his wife. Ray broke into his house and was once caught driving his Porsche. She eventually committed suicide.

Intimate Partner Violence Is a Crime with Many Names

The terms have changed over the years—from "wife beating" to "battering" to "spousal abuse" to "domestic violence" to **intimate partner violence**. The ugly reality remains the same: violent acts committed within what are supposed to be loving sexual relationships. The term is increasingly used to cover psychological trauma as well as physical violence.

The National Crime Victimization Survey (NCVS) found that about 655,000 violent crimes were committed against intimate partners in 2002 and that about 75% of these crimes were committed against women. Nearly 1% of women and 0.1% of men said they had experienced intimate partner violence during the previous 12 months (U.S. Department of Justice, 2004a). The National Violence Against Women (NVAW) survey came up with somewhat higher figures: 1.5% of women and 0.9% of men had experienced intimate partner violence during the previous 12 months. Lifetime rates were 25% for women and 8% for men (U.S. Department of Justice, 1998). The higher numbers in the NVAW survey probably reflect the inclusion of assaults that might not be considered crimes, such as pushing and grabbing. Of course, to the extent that victims may be unwilling to disclose domestic violence to interviewers, all these figures might be underestimates.

Of the criminal acts reported to the NCVS (**Figure 18.7**), the majority were simple assaults, meaning assaults that were carried out without a weapon and that caused no injury or caused minor injury. About 35% were aggravated assaults, sexual assaults, robberies, or murders. About 50% of the crimes were reported to the police.

Intimate partner violence represents a significant part of all the violence experienced by women. In 36% of cases in which women go to hospital emergency rooms with injuries resulting from violence, an intimate partner was the perpetrator (U.S. Department of Justice, 1997). One in three murders of women are committed by intimate partners, compared with only one in 25 murders of men.

intimate partner violence Violence between sex partners.

About one-third of all assaults on women are committed by their intimate partners.

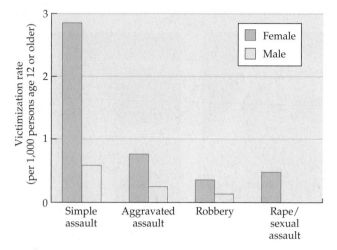

Figure 18.7 Violent crimes against intimate partners
This bar graph shows the average annual rate of nonfatal intimate partner violence, 2001–2005. Simple assault is assault without a weapon that results in no injuries or only minor injury. Aggravated assault is assault that causes serious injury or that involves a weapon. Information about rape victimization of males is not provided because the small number of cases is insufficient for reliable estimates. (Data from Bureau of Justice Statistics, 2007a.)

battered-woman syndrome A version of post-traumatic stress disorder affecting women who are victims of intimate partner violence, characterized especially by a cessation of attempts to escape from the abusive situation.

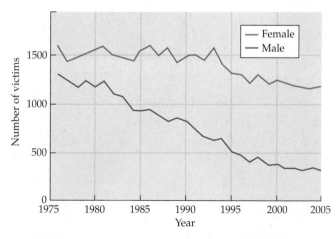

Figure 18.8 Decline in murders of intimate partners This graph shows the numbers of women and men murdered by their intimate partners from 1975–2005. (Data from Bureau of Justice Statistics, 2007b.)

Besides being female, risk factors for intimate partner violence include being African-American, young, divorced or separated, living in a city, and having a low income. The association with poverty is particularly marked: Women living in the lowest-income households experience intimate partner violence at 7 times the rate of women in affluent households. (It is possible that this difference is exaggerated if affluent people are less willing to report violence.)

Intimate partner violence is a particular problem on college campuses, where it is strongly associated with alcohol use. Among male and female students who are heavy drinkers, over half have committed some kind of aggression (including psychological aggression) against an intimate partner in the previous 12 months (Fossos et al., 2007). Although both men and women commit these acts, those perpetrated by men are more frequent, and they tend to cause more serious injuries.

More significant than the physical injuries in most cases are the psychological effects of domestic violence: depression, suicidal thoughts and suicide attempts, lowered self-esteem, substance abuse, and post-traumatic stress disorder (National Research Council, 1996). The specific variety of post-traumatic stress disorder that occurs in these circumstances is called **battered-woman syndrome**; it is characterized by a sense of inability to escape from the situation and therefore by a cessation of attempts to do so (Walker, 1999).

Children are present in 43% of households in which intimate partner violence occurs (NCVS data) and are at risk of being assaulted themselves. The violent atmosphere may profoundly affect the children's social development, increasing the likelihood that they, too, will commit intimate partner violence, abuse children, and exhibit other behavioral problems in adolescence and adulthood (Straus, 1992).

The one bright side to the story is that, as with rape, intimate partner violence has been on the decline, and this includes murders of intimate partners (**Figure 18.8**). The decline has been more marked for male victims than for female victims. Even so, between 1993 and 2002 the overall rate of intimate partner violence against women dropped by about half, and most of this decline was accounted for by a drop in violence among minorities, according to NCVS data (U.S. Department of Justice, 2004a).

Intimate Partner Violence Follows an Escalating Cycle

Domestic violence typically occurs as one phase of a three-phase cycle (Walker, 1979) (**Figure 18.9**):

1. *The tension-building phase* In this phase, the longest of the three, the abuser may be increasingly moody, nitpicky, or sullen. He may threaten the victim or commit minor assaults or property damage. The victim may attempt to stop the progression of the cycle by trying to calm him, by avoiding confrontation, or by satisfying his demands (e.g., keeping the children quiet, having food ready on time, etc.).

2. *The violent phase* The actual violent behavior constitutes the shortest phase, typically lasting no more than a day. As many as 9 out of 10 perpetrators are under the influence of alcohol or drugs during the assault, which is often carried out in the presence of children (Brookoff et al., 1997). The

victim tries to protect herself, fights back, kicks the abuser out, or flees. The victim, other family members, or neighbors may call the police, who have usually been to this address several times before.

3. *The reconciliation phase* In this phase, the perpetrator is apologetic and tries to make amends by declarations of love. He promises to cease the abusive behavior, to stop drinking, or to seek treatment. He showers the victim with gifts and attention. The victim is relieved and happy, forgives the abuser, and returns to him (or allows him back, if he has left). The victim may retract statements made to the police with the hope of stopping legal proceedings or may lie to doctors about the cause of her injuries.

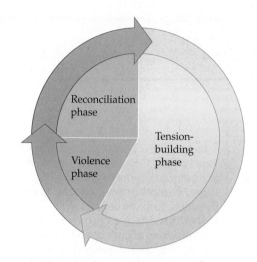

Figure 18.9 The cycle of intimate partner violence

Often, the severity of the violence escalates from cycle to cycle, so it may be more descriptive to refer to a "spiral of violence" rather than a cycle. Some relationships degenerate into a condition of nonstop violence; in a study of cases in which police were called to scenes of domestic violence, 35% of the victims said that they were assaulted every day (Brookoff et al., 1997).

Diverse Theories Attempt to Explain Intimate Partner Violence

Evolutionary psychology and feminist theory are in agreement that persistent domestic violence is a method used by men to dominate and control women. The phrase "patriarchal terrorism" has been used to characterize this interpretation (Johnson & Ferraro, 2000). In evolutionary psychology, the desire to assert control is seen as part of the man's evolutionary inheritance, and it serves (or once served) the function of protecting the man's paternity interests—in other words, it prevents his mate from having sex with other men (Wilson & Daly, 1992). Evolutionary psychologists see sexual jealousy (see Chapter 10) as the main motivator of intimate partner violence.

Most feminist and learning theorists think that men batter women because boys are socialized to be perpetrators of violence and girls are socialized to be victims. This socialization may not be simply a matter of individual training within the family, but also the result of an entire cultural and political structure that legitimizes this form of violence and, in essence, turns a marriage license into a "license to batter" (Yllö & Bograd, 1988). Men batter, according to this line of thought, because they have learned that it serves their interests to do so.

A somewhat different theory holds that men batter because they are psychologically wounded. The commonest version of this theory is the "cycle of violence," according to which men batter their wives because they themselves were abused during childhood or witnessed their fathers abusing their mothers. A number of studies have reported a statistical link between witnessing marital violence during childhood and later engaging in it (Gelles, 1976; Straus, 1992). It is possible, however, that this statistical link exists not because of any causal connection but because children and their parents tend to grow up in similar circumstances and therefore are exposed to many of the same risk factors.

Anger management programs, which use cognitive-behavioral methods, have a reasonable record of success with perpetrators of intimate partner violence (Howells & Day, 2003). These treatment programs tend to work better with persons who have voluntarily entered treatment than with those who do so under court order.

Breaking Up Is Hard to Do

Sympathetic outsiders who see a victim—usually a woman—sticking with her abusive mate through escalating cycles of violence often ask, "Why on earth does she stay with that awful man?!" Some of the answers to this question are appar-

Personal Points of View

BOX 18.5 What's Love Got to Do With It?

Rock diva and eight-time Grammy winner Tina Turner (born in 1939) was in a 16-year marriage with her musical partner and manager Ike Turner. The marriage deteriorated as the couple's artistic successes began to wane in the early 1970s and Ike developed a serious cocaine habit. According to Tina's autobiography (Turner & Loder, 1986) and the testimony of others, Ike beat her frequently and severely and also humiliated her, for example, by openly having sex with other women in their own home. Tina stayed with her abusive husband because he isolated her and controlled her physically, emotionally, and financially. Also, few social supports for battered women existed at that time.

After a particularly severe beating in a Dallas airport limousine in July 1976, she fled Ike and took refuge, bruised and blood-soaked, at a nearby hotel. Eventually she moved in with friends, where she did domestic work to earn her keep. Although written off by critics and saddled by debts, Turner gradually rebuilt her career, which culminated in 1984 with the number one bestselling album *What's Love Got to Do With It?* She has enjoyed many successes since then. In 1985 she met her boyfriend Erwin Bach, 16 years her junior, and the couple has remained together since then. Turner credits her conversion to Buddhism as giving her the inner strength to leave her abusive husband.

Diver Greg Louganis (born in 1960) won two gold medals in the 1984 Olympic Games and two more in 1988. In spite of his public celebrity during those years, Louganis was actually living in an abusive relationship with his manager, Jim Babbitt, who on one occasion raped him at knifepoint. As with Ike and Tina Turner, Babbitt controlled Louganis financially and emotionally, playing on Louganis's insecurity, especially concerning his homosexuality and his attractiveness.

Louganis attributed his failure to leave Babbitt to his own lack of self-esteem: "Looking back, it makes me sad that I thought so little of myself that I didn't just walk away from [Jim]. Like most battered spouses, I just wanted love and approval, and I thought [Jim] was the only one who could give it to me. I kept thinking, if I'm better, if I try harder, then maybe he'll love me. I should have thought, Run for your life!" (Louganis & Marcus, 1995). In 1988, after he had

Tina Turner (played by Angela Bassett) and Ike Turner (played by Laurence Fishburne) in the 1993 film *What's Love Got to Do With It?*

to spend some months away from Babbitt while training for the Olympics, Louganis gathered the strength to break off the abusive relationship. He took over his own financial affairs, came out as gay, wrote a best-selling autobiography, and is now in a loving relationship with another man.

Violence also happens within lesbian relationships. Here is one anonymous account, from a study of lesbian partner abuse by Janet Ristock: "It was my first long-term relationship. I was head over heels madly in love and I thought this is the relationship for life. And it started out really good. This woman was nine years older than myself. It was verbal abuse to start off with and then physical. Quite often I had black eyes

and she almost killed me once. Strangled me and then, this went on for three years. I was too young and insecure about the whole relationship, gay relationships, whatever. Anybody could have walked all over me." (Ristock, 2002)

When men are abused by female partners, which does happen, they may have a hard time making anyone believe their stories. Here is one account: "I was in a hellish marriage with a woman who had difficulty controlling her rage, which would frequently erupt with her hitting, verbal abuse, and screaming. If fighting with her did occur, it was self-defense; if she threw a punch or kicked, I defended myself. In one particular case, after she initiated a fight by kicking and throwing punches, she called the police to report me as the violent abuser! When they responded, I was seen as the bad guy, she was the victim! Attempts at counseling did not work, only separation and eventually divorce finally extracted me from this nightmare." (Menweb, 2001)

ent from narratives written by the victims themselves (Weiss, 2004). Information also comes from research studies (Walker, 1999).

Victims of intimate partner violence may stay with their partners because they are socially isolated, economically dependent, lack self-esteem, or believe that separation and divorce are wrong. Learned helplessness—a depressive, pessimistic response to a harmful situation—may leave victims without the will to remove themselves from the abusive situation. Victims often fear that breaking up will bring shame on them and that the perpetrator will pursue and punish them—a fear that is frequently well justified. Victims may also fear that their children will suffer in a breakup. Perpetrators may sense and reinforce all these traits; in particular, they often keep the victim socially isolated and punish her for reaching out to any potential sources of help. Nevertheless, many victims do eventually break free from their abusive relationship and are able to start new lives (Weiss, 2004) (**Box 18.5**).

Help Is Available

Services are available to help battered women, whether or not they remain in an abusive relationship:

- Emergency room staff are trained to treat domestic violence injuries and to recognize their cause. When a victim has multiple head and neck injuries at different stages of healing and there is no other predisposing factor, such as a neurological disorder, domestic violence is likely to be the cause.

- Law enforcement officers and lawyers can assist a domestic violence victim who decides to leave an abusive relationship by arresting the abuser or by helping the victim obtain a restraining order. In some states, such as California, prosecutors will continue domestic violence cases even when the victims retract their accusations ("no-drop policy"). Legal assistance is often available to low-income victims.

- Hotlines, battered women's shelters, women's crisis centers, and city social services can provide practical assistance for women who leave abusive relationships temporarily or permanently.

- Psychotherapists and support groups can help abused women understand the process of victimization and regain the strength and motivation to end it.

Services for male victims and for victims of same-sex abuse are less well developed than those for women who are abused by men. Still, most public services for abuse victims are gender-neutral, and the gay and lesbian organizations in many metropolitan areas have domestic violence services. The Los Angeles Gay and Lesbian Center, for example, provides survivors' groups, a batterers' treatment program, crisis counseling, shelter referrals, and educational programs (Los Angeles Gay and Lesbian Center, 2001).

Summary

1. Rape means coitus or other penetrative sex acts accomplished by force or the threat of force. Sexual assault covers a wider range of coercive sex acts. Although both men and women of all ages may experience rape, young women in the 16-to-19 age range are at the highest risk: About 7 in 1000 women in this group are raped each year in the United States. The great majority of perpetrators are male.

2. The rape rate has decreased markedly over the past 30 years. The majority of rapes and sexual assaults are committed by people known to the victim (acquaintances, relatives, or intimate partners).

3. According to one study, a college campus with 10,000 female students will experience 350 rapes or attempted rapes per year, although this figure includes many incidents that the victims do not consider to have been rape. Most campus rapes are perpetrated by acquaintances or current or former boyfriends. About 20% of campus rapes involve additional injuries.

REFER TO THE

Human Sexuality

WEBSITE AT

www.sinauer.com/levay3e

for activities, study questions, quizzes, and other study aids.

4. "Date rape drugs" such as Rohypnol may be used in the perpetration of rape, but alcohol (consumed by the perpetrator or the victim) is a factor more commonly associated with rape, including rapes on college campuses.

5. Besides physical injuries, victims of sexual assaults may suffer a variety of ill effects, including post-traumatic stress disorder. These effects may be countered by counseling and survivors' groups, which help victims regain a sense of control.

6. The law has become increasingly protective of rape victims, but many victims of rape and sexual assault do not report the crimes, perhaps because of shame, a sense of responsibility for the assaults, or a fear of retribution. Men who are convicted of rape are typically sentenced to lengthy prison terms.

7. Conflicting theories attempt to explain rape. Evolutionary psychologists have raised the possibility that it is a behavioral adaptation, meaning that it evolved because it increased the reproductive success of men who committed it. Individual men may be predisposed to rape on account of childhood abuse, personality disorders, or a lack of empathy. Social forces may encourage a "culture of rape" or, conversely, they may discourage rape, as for example through the criminal justice system.

8. Theorists have debated whether rape is primarily an act of hostility toward women or is sexually motivated. Most observations suggest that rapes are at least partly sexually motivated in most cases.

9. Rape prevention programs teach teenagers rape awareness and avoidance, attempt to overcome gender stereotypes, and promote conflict management skills. The effectiveness of these programs is uncertain. It is possible that efforts to help parents foster empathy development in their young children would be a more effective long-term strategy.

10. Unwelcome sexual attention in the workplace (sexual harassment) is a form of illegal sex discrimination. It can take the form of quid pro quo harassment, in which a demand for sex is accompanied by some inducement or threat, or hostile-environment harassment, in which the sexual attention makes life difficult for the victim. Harassment can also occur in other structured environments, such as schools and colleges.

11. Sexual harassment causes psychological and practical problems for its victims and reduces workplace productivity. Victims can take steps to end sexual harassment by confronting their harasser or by reporting the harassment.

12. Stalking is obsessive following, lying in wait, calling, sending mail or messages, and the like, all directed at a specific victim. In intimate partner stalking, the stalker is a current or former spouse or romantic partner, and the stalking is motivated by sexual jealousy and anger. In delusional stalking, the stalker is mentally disturbed and believes that the victim (often an acquaintance, teacher, therapist, or celebrity) is in love with him or could be made to fall in love with him. In grudge stalking, the stalker is not motivated by sexual interest. Whatever the type of stalking, it can progress to violence. Stalking is illegal, but legal remedies are of limited effectiveness.

13. Over 600,000 million violent crimes are committed against spouses or intimate partners annually. About 1 in 4 women and 1 in 12 men experiences intimate partner violence at least once in their lifetime.

14. Intimate partner violence causes both physical and psychological injuries. Battered women may come to see the violence as inevitable and therefore do little to escape it. Children often witness parental violence and may themselves be injured. The rate of intimate partner violence has dropped substantially over the past 30 years.

15. Intimate partner violence typically follows a three-phase cycle of tension-building, violence, and reconciliation. As the cycle repeats, the violent phase tends to intensify and may eventually occur without interruption.

16. Victims of intimate partner violence often stay with their partner. The reasons for this may include social isolation, economic dependence, low self-esteem, shame, and fear of retribution. Many services are now available to help victims of intimate partner abuse, whether or not they remain in their abusive relationship.

Discussion Questions

1. "On this campus, men still get away with a lot of sexist talk, sexual harassment, and even date rape." "On this campus, political correctness has got to the point that men are scared to show normal friendly behavior to women." Which of the former statements corresponds more closely to your opinion, and why? Do you think your sex influences your opinion?

2. If you had to establish your college's policy regarding faculty-student sex, what considerations would be most important to you in setting the policy? What would the policy be, and how would it compare with your college's actual policy? (If you don't know what your college's actual faculty-student sex policy is, find out about it.)

3. Having read some of the conflicting views about rape, what's your opinion—should rape be considered a sexual act or not? And do you think that the answer to this question is relevant to strategies for rape prevention?

4. How would you advise a female friend who tells you she is being stalked by a former boyfriend? Would your advice be different if it were a man being stalked by a former girlfriend?

5. Both men and women may sometimes give unclear signals about whether they are willing to engage in sexual contact when they are in a potentially sexual situation. How can a man or woman best make sure that their partner is really willing to engage in sex? What if you or your companion have had a few drinks?

6. Not uncommonly, victims recant accusations that their partners beat them. Would you support a "no-drop policy" in your community (i.e., a policy to continue a prosecution in these circumstances)? What kind of evidence could be used to get a conviction if the victim recants?

Web Resources

Men Can Stop Rape www.mencanstoprape.org

National Coalition Against Domestic Violence—hotline: 1-800-799-SAFE www.ncadv.org

National Sexual Violence Resource Center www.nsvrc.org

Rape, Abuse, and Incest National Network—hotline: 1–800–656-HOPE www.rainn.org

Stop Prisoner Rape www.spr.org

Recommended Reading

Brownmiller, S. (1975). *Against our will: Men, women and rape.* Simon and Schuster.

Buchwald, E., Fletcher, P. R., and Roth, M. (2004). *Transforming a rape culture* (2nd ed.). Milkweed Editions.

Hicks, G. L. (1995). *The comfort women: Japan's brutal regime of enforced prostitution in the Second World War.* W. W. Norton.

Lalumiere, M., et al. (Eds.). (2005). *The causes of rape: Understanding individual differences in male propensity for sexual aggression.* American Psychological Association.

Mullen, P. E., Pathé, M., and Purcell, R. (2000). *Stalkers and their victims.* Cambridge University Press.

Petrocelli, W., and Repa, B. K. (1999). *Sexual harassment on the job: What it is and how to stop it* (4th ed.). Nolo Press.

Schewe, P. A. (Ed.). (2002). *Preventing violence in relationships: Interventions across the lifespan.* American Psychological Association.

Thornhill, R., and Palmer, C. T. (2000). *A natural history of rape: Biological bases of sexual coercion.* MIT Press.

Walker, L. E. A. (2000). *The battered woman syndrome* (2nd ed.). Springer.

Weiss, E. (2004). Surviving domestic violence: Voices of women who broke free. Volcano Press.

CHAPTER 19

The marketing of sex has pervaded many human cultures throughout history.

Sex as a Commodity

Like anything that people want, sex has a cash value. Indeed, in one way or another, sex fuels a significant part of the U.S. economy. In this chapter, we focus primarily on the selling of sex itself (prostitution) and the commercial production of sexually arousing materials (pornography). The selling of sex raises a variety of ethical concerns, and few aspects of sex so sharply divide conservatives and liberals.

Can Money Buy You Love?

A great deal of wealth is transferred between sexual and romantic partners, the bulk of it flowing from men to women. From this perspective, prostitution is merely an unvarnished and extreme expression of something that goes on in many or most sexual relationships. What is morally offensive to many people about prostitution is not simply that money is involved, for many women receive their entire financial support from their husbands or boyfriends without bringing their moral status, or that of their partners, into question. Rather it is that the relationship between prostitute and client is brief and loveless and that the payment is for sex only, not as part of the complex web of commitments, attachments, and dependencies that characterize more durable relationships. Prostitution violates many people's belief that sexual behavior is morally justified only in the context of a loving, committed relationship, as discussed in Chapter 10.

There is some inconsistency in the use of terms that refer to prostitution and related activities. Here is how we use them. A **prostitute** is a person (of either sex) who engages in sex for money. Old slang or abusive terms for prostitutes, such as "hooker" and "whore," have to some extent been reclaimed by present-day prostitutes and the organizations that represent them (as for example in the name of San Francisco's Hookers' Ball). Male prostitutes are often called **hustlers**. The term **sex trader** is broader, referring to anyone who exchanges sex for money, drugs, or some other material incentive. Even broader is the term **sex worker**: This includes sex traders as well as people who work in related occupations, such as phone sex operators, exotic dancers, and the like.

Historically, Prostitution Was Viewed as a Necessary Evil

Prostitution is often called "the oldest profession," and with good reason. For millennia, prostitution was just about the only way in which unattached women could support themselves. Jewish and Christian scriptures include frequent references to prostitutes (or "harlots"), and Christian tradition holds that one of Jesus' followers, Mary Magdalene, was a reformed prostitute (**Figure 19.1**).

prostitution The practice of engaging in sex for pay.

hustler A male prostitute.

sex trader A person who exchanges sex for money, drugs, or other benefits; a broader term than prostitute.

sex worker A person who engages in prostitution, pornography, or another sex-related occupation.

Figure 19.1 St. Mary Magdalene was often portrayed with immodestly long red hair—a reference to her supposed earlier life as a prostitute. This painting is by the nineteenth century British artist Anthony Sandys.

Prostitution, like all sex between unmarried people, has been condemned as "fornication" throughout the Christian era. Still, moralists such as St. Augustine and St. Thomas Aquinas condoned the social structure of prostitution because they saw it as providing a necessary "safety valve" for the release of male sexual energy. In some non-Christian religions there has been a tradition of prostitution associated with religious institutions (**Box 19.1**).

Serious efforts to eradicate prostitution did not begin until the Protestant Reformation of the sixteenth century. They were driven not only by moral concerns, but also by the problem of sexually transmitted diseases. Prostitution continued to flourish, however. In fact, the heyday of prostitution was probably the late-eighteenth and nineteenth centuries, when large numbers of men migrated to cities and women were in short supply. In response to the terrible conditions experienced by prostitutes in London, William Booth founded the Salvation Army in 1865; its first shelter for prostitutes and vagrant girls opened 3 years later.

In the latter part of the nineteenth century, most U.S. cities saw the development of "red-light districts," in which prostitution was tolerated or, in a few locations, even legal. In the early-twentieth century, however, a coalition of reformers, early feminists, and health authorities forced most of these districts out of existence. Epidemics of gonorrhea and other diseases during the First World War triggered a major campaign against prostitution, and the profession went underground.

Prostitution Is on the Decline

Over the last century, prostitution has become much less prevalent. Kinsey estimated that men's usage of female prostitutes had dropped by nearly 50% over the few decades prior to the time of his survey, and he attributed this decline to a greater willingness of unmarried women to engage in sex with men. College-educated men in particular were no longer visiting prostitutes in great numbers. Still, Kinsey's survey showed that the average unmarried man in his thirties visited a prostitute once every 3 weeks (Kinsey et al., 1948).

A further major decline in prostitution accompanied the sexual revolution of the 1960s and its aftermath. Thanks to oral contraceptives and a sea change in sexual morality, unmarried women became much more willing to have sex with their boyfriends, so the main incentive for men to visit prostitutes disappeared. Whereas 7% of men born between 1933 and 1937 lost their virginity to a prostitute, only 1.5% of men born between 1968 and 1974 did so, according to National Health and Social Life Survey (NHSLS) data. During this same period, employment opportunities for many women expanded greatly, so the main incentive for women to work as prostitutes also lost much of its force. Ironically, prostitution declined during a period when opposition to prostitution also declined.

Statistics on the prevalence of prostitution today are hard to come by. One of the best studies of prostitution was conducted in Chicago by the Center for Impact Research (O'Leary & Howard, 2001). According to this study, an estimated minimum of 1800 to 4000 women and girls work as prostitutes in the Chicago metropolitan area at any one time. Because the Chicago metropolitan area has a female population of about 5 million, this estimate implies that the fraction of all females in that area that are engaged in prostitution could be less than 1 in 1000. The fraction in nonmetropolitan areas is likely to be even lower. These estimates are complicated by the fact that some women engage in prostitution part-time and that sex traders who exchange sex for drugs were not included in the Chicago data.

Although most prostitutes are female, the proportion of prostitutes who are male or transgendered is significant in some large cities. In San Francisco, for

Cultural Diversity

BOX 19.1 Temple Prostitution

Rani Bai is married to God, but she has sex with men—for cash. In her late thirties, and a remarkably beautiful woman, Rani Bai is a **devadasi**, a religious prostitute in southern India. When she was 6 years old she was "dedicated" to the goddess Yellamma: This means that her parents sold her into a life of temple prostitution. Soon after her first menstrual period a shepherd paid 500 rupees ($38 at the then-going rate), as well

Two devadasis with their children

as a silk sari and a bag of millet, for the right to take her virginity, which he did by force in the face of her physical resistance. Since then, she has had sex with as many as ten men every day. She is one of thousands of devadasis, mostly from the lowest and most destitute ranks of Indian society, who are loosely associated with

the temple of Yellamma. In practical terms, Rani Bai's life is little different from that of the many nonreligious prostitutes who work in the same area, but she perceives that Yellamma watches over her and gives her a special status in society. "We are not like the ordinary whores," she says (Dalrymple, 2008).

The present-day practice of devadasi, which the Indian government has tried in vain to stamp out, represents the degraded remnants of a once-noble tradition. Centuries ago, devadasis were highly educated and respected women, often of royal blood. Some were poets. Ironically, it was British missionaries who hastened the debasement of the tradition by attacking it as immoral.

The tradition of temple prostitution is not limited to India. Three millennia ago, the Babylonian temple of Mullitu (Mylitta) was the home of a custom whereby all women had to prostitute themselves once in their lives. At any one time, according the ancient Greek historian Herodotus, hundreds of women could be seen in the temple's courtyard, waiting for customers willing to pay for sex with them (Strassler, 2007). Some needed only to wait a few minutes, while

others—the less attractive ones—might have to wait for several years. Whatever the religious significance of temple prostitution—it may have been associated with fertility rites—the practice undoubtedly enriched the temples where it took place. Temple prostitution was widespread through the Middle East in Old Testament times, to judge from biblical references.

In Mexico at the time of the Spanish conquest, male adolescents served as prostitutes in the Aztec temples; this practice so disgusted the conquistadors that they used it as justification for acts of genocide against the Aztecs (Carrasco, 2008). There may even be echoes of temple prostitution in contemporary U.S. cults, some of which have incorporated sex into religious rituals or forced cult adherents into sexual relationships with cult leaders.

In India, some of the devadasis have organized themselves into collectives to improve their situation and to oppose the practice of "dedicating" young girls. They have received financial support in this campaign from the Canadian government (India Together, 2007). Rani Bai herself has made a good income from her work, and she now owns some land. She dreams of retiring from prostitution and running a dairy business. But that's not likely to happen. The AIDS virus has already killed both her daughters, her brother is dying of the disease, and she herself is HIV-positive. "The goddess dries our tears," she says. "Yellamma never wanted it to be like this" (Dalrymple, 2008).

devadasi An Indian temple prostitute.

example, an estimated 20% to 30% of prostitutes are male, and 25% are male-to-female transgenders (Prostitutes Education Network, 2008). Most of the transgenders have not undergone sex-reassignment surgery, but they may have breast implants and/or be taking estrogens.

All forms of prostitution are illegal everywhere in the United States except for 11 non-urban counties of Nevada, in which brothel prostitution is legal, and Rhode Island, where off-street prostitution is legal. Enforcement varies greatly, however. Prostitution that is publicly visible is much more likely to run afoul of the law than other types of prostitution. Some jurisdictions have instructed their police forces to make the enforcement of prostitution laws a low priority. A proposition to halt all enforcement of prostitution laws was on the November 2008 ballot in San Francisco, but lost by a wide margin. Other cities have set up "diversion programs" that spare prostitutes jail time and help them move on to other occupations without the stigma of a criminal record. In Canada and Britain, off-street, non-brothel prostitution is legal, but public solicitation for prostitution is not, nor is managing or living off the earnings of prostitutes (pimping).

There Is a Hierarchy of Prostitution

Prostitution is difficult to characterize because it takes many different forms. In general there is a hierarchy, ranging from forms that are street-based, cheap, and dangerous, to less visible forms involving larger sums of money and greater security for the prostitutes and the prostitutes' clients.

Street Prostitution Has Many Risks

In the Chicago study just described, 30% to 35% of the prostitutes worked on the streets. Street prostitution (or "streetwalking") is the most visible and familiar part of the industry. Streetwalkers are usually picked up by clients ("johns") driving automobiles, but they may also be picked up in bars located near a recognized streetwalking zone. After agreement between prostitute and client about the kind of sex to be engaged in and the fee, sex takes place in the automobile, in a pay-by-the-hour motel, or at some other location.

Street prostitutes (in the United States and worldwide) occupy the lowest rank of the prostitution hierarchy, and they charge the lowest prices. Some experience a lifetime of social degradation, beginning with a violence-ridden childhood and continuing into homelessness, alcoholism, and drug use (Raphael, 2004). The risk of being beaten or raped exists every time a streetwalker steps into a stranger's car. Street prostitutes may be less able or likely to insist on condom use than are other prostitutes, so they face a greater risk of acquiring sexually transmitted diseases and becoming pregnant. For example, one study of women who smoked crack cocaine and exchanged sex for money (or drugs) found that 30% had not used a condom in the previous month (Edlin et al., 1994), and in some cities, up to one-third of these women were HIV-positive. A British study of street-based prostitutes found that every one of them was drug- or alcohol-dependent; for most, their days were a nonstop cycle of selling sex, buying and using drugs, and then returning to work (Jeal & Salisbury, 2004; Jeal et al., 2008). In another study, which focused on young men who exchanged sex for money (or drugs) in Harlem, New York, 41% of the men tested HIV-positive (El-Bassel et al., 2000).

Because most street prostitutes come from poor and disadvantaged backgrounds, it is not surprising that minorities are greatly overrepresented in this population (O'Leary & Howard, 2001). Minority prostitutes are more likely to get into trouble with the law than are white prostitutes because they are more likely than white prostitutes to operate on the street, where arrests are most common.

The majority of female street prostitutes are mothers (Dalla, 2000). Although the fathers are not usually the women's customers, they are very often unavailable to support the children. The prostitute herself may give up or lose her parental rights. Street prostitutes who retain custody of their children experience considerable shame and anxiety about their own and their children's safety and may be reluctant to avail themselves of social services in case they should be deemed unfit mothers and lose custody of their children (Sloss & Harper, 2004).

Only a minority of prostitutes solicit customers on the streets, but they form the most visible part of the industry and are exposed to the greatest risks.

Female, Male, and Transgendered Streetwalkers Have Different Experiences

Although female, male, and transgendered streetwalkers all service male clients and all receive about the same payment per client, their experiences are otherwise quite different (Weinberg et al., 1999) (**Table 19.1**). Female and transgendered prostitutes tend to be in their late twenties, while male prostitutes are younger. Prostitution is more of a full-time occupation for women: They service more clients and earn a larger weekly income from prostitution than do either transgenders or men. Men spend about twice as much time with each client as do either women or transgenders. In other words, prostitution is a better economic prospect for women than for men, which is hardly surprising, given that the majority of potential clients are heterosexual men.

The nonfinancial aspects of prostitution work out better for men, however. Most significantly, men and transgenders are much less likely to be beaten or raped by a client than are women. They cannot become pregnant and for the most part do

Male-to-female transgendered prostitutes, such as these two in Paris, might deceive their clients about their anatomical sex, but some men specifically seek them out.

TABLE 19.1

Life Experiences of Female, Male-to-Female Transgendered, and Male Prostitutes in San Francisco's Tenderloin District

	Female	M-to-F	Male
Mean age	29.3	29.7	23.8
Used hard drugs (narcotics) at least weekly (%)	59	25	26
Income			
Prostitution was only source of income (%)	62	53	32
Mean weekly income in 1990	$1030	$688	$507
Workload			
Mean number of clients per week	26	15	10
Mean time with client (minutes)	24	29	45
Enjoyment			
Ever got sexual pleasure from giving oral sex to client (%)	28	72	64
Usually or always experienced orgasm during sex with client (%)	5	7	45
Negative effects (mean number of occasions in previous year)			
Raped by client	0.41	0.13	0.00
Beaten by client	0.46	0.23	0.09
Arrested for prostitution	0.63	0.48	0.83
Married or cohabiting (%)	52	19	11
Sexual orientation (%)			
Attracted to men only	65	71	37
Bisexual	35	29	50
Attracted to women only	0	0	13
Mean number of noncommercial sex partners in previous year			
Male partners	1.9	11.0	15.2
Female partners	0.2	0.3	6.9

Source: Weinberg et al., 1999.

Note: These data are not necessarily representative for all cities; arrest rates, for example, may be higher in cities that are less tolerant of prostitution than San Francisco.

pimp A man who manages prostitutes in exchange for part of their earnings.

not have children to worry about (see below). Also, men in general have more interest in casual sex and in having multiple sex partners than do women. Accordingly, male prostitutes get more sexual enjoyment and experience orgasm more often in the course of their work than do women. (Transgenders often get sexual enjoyment, but because they don't usually use their penis in commercial sex, they rarely experience orgasm.) Not surprisingly, most male prostitutes describe themselves as gay or bisexual, but some (13% in the Weinberg study mentioned earlier) describe themselves as heterosexual. Most male prostitutes are single and have multiple (mostly male) sex partners outside of their work.

Another difference that traditionally worked to the advantage of male prostitutes was that they tended to be independent agents working only for themselves, whereas women often worked for **pimps**. The women gave the pimps part or all of their earnings and also commonly had sex with them. In return, the pimps set up the women's living and working arrangements, protected their turf, provided drugs, and paid off mobsters and the police (or, if that didn't work, bailed the women out of jail).

In spite of the glorification of the pimp lifestyle in hip-hop culture (Sharpley-Whiting, 2007), pimps have become much less common in recent years. In Weinberg's San Francisco study, only 4% of the women prostitutes worked for pimps, and the Chicago study quoted law enforcement officials as saying there were few remaining pimps in that area. To some extent, the pimps' role has been taken over by gang members who control the street economy (Roane, 1999).

A good deal of deception occurs in street prostitution. Prostitutes often con their clients: At least half the prostitutes in the Weinberg study said they had failed to provide promised services or demanded more money than initially agreed to. Transgendered prostitutes frequently deceive their clients about their anatomical sex. They may tape back their penis and refuse to remove their panties, saying that they are having their period. Alternatively, they may use their anus or even their hands to fake coitus.

However, transgendered prostitutes do not always need to deceive because plenty of men are specifically attracted to transgenders, whom they call "she-males." According to the transgenders interviewed in the Weinberg study, it happened about 13 times a year that a client initially thought that the transgender was a woman but discovered the truth during the course of the encounter. About 15% of these clients responded violently; of the remainder, about half broke off the encounter, but the others simply carried on, suggesting that the discovery did not affect their enjoyment in a substantial way.

A rather distinct group of street prostitutes are *homeless* or *runaway youths* (of both sexes). Numerically, these prostitutes form a small portion of the total prostitute population—or of those who come to the attention of law enforcement, at least. Still, they arouse a great deal of concern because they are often fleeing an abusive home environment, and they are vulnerable to further abuse, exploitation, and disease.

Homeless youths enter prostitution, and the broader street economy, for several reasons (Gwadz et al., 2008). These include lack of access to regular employment (because of lack of education, incarceration, or mental illness), the financial rewards of prostitution, severe economic need, and active recruitment by others. Programs to address youth prostitution have either greatly reduced it or driven it underground in many cities (O'Leary & Howard, 2001). Some runaway youths are "adopted" by men who provide them with shelter and other resources in exchange for a sexual relationship; such arrangements are largely invisible to law enforcement or social services and might not be illegal, depending on the jurisdiction and the youth's age.

Massage Parlors and Strip Joints Are Often Fronts for Prostitution

The second kind of prostitute works at or out of a fixed commercial location such as a **massage parlor** or an exotic dance venue ("strip joint"). Massage parlors are often the most readily available locations for prostitution in suburban areas, but because they have become so associated with prostitution they have become a frequent target for police raids. For that reason some prostitution rings have moved to other locations. In the early 2000s, for example, prostitution rings started doing business in some chiropractors' clinics. Between 2001 and 2002 the police raided 23 clinics in Southern California, and the California chiropractic board stripped 11 practitioners of their licenses for involvement in prostitution (Morin, 2002).

Services at these kinds of locations vary, but hand–genital contact (often referred to as "massage" in escort-service ads) is the most common. At strip joints, exotic dancers may provide sex by rubbing their body against the customer's genitalia during a "lap dance." Alternatively, sex may take place in a "VIP room" or off-site after the show. In many communities, massage parlors and strip joints are periodically raided by the police. Not all masseurs and exotic dancers are prostitutes, of course, but ads or word of mouth usually make it clear what services are available at a particular establishment.

The one kind of locale for prostitution that is hard to find in the United States today is an old-fashioned **brothel** or **whorehouse**, whose traditional red lantern, placed in the doorway, gave "red-light districts" their name. Brothels are establishments entirely dedicated to prostitution and lack any cover activity such as massage, drinking, or entertainment. Thus they have little defense against police raids. Today, durable working brothels can be found chiefly in the rural counties of Nevada, where brothel prostitution is legal, and in remote mining and logging communities, where it may be tolerated. Only a handful of the countless brothels that once flourished in the United States have been preserved for their historical value (**Box 19.2**). Legal brothels do exist in quite a few other countries, including the Netherlands (**Box 19.3**) and in three Australian states.

In 2008, the Nevada brothels took a beating from the economic downturn and the run-up in gas prices: Business fell by almost half, according to the Nevada Brothel Owners Association (Ramirez, 2008). One brothel, the Moonlight BunnyRanch in Carson City, got creative: Men who spent their $600 economic stimulus check at the ranch were promised $1200 in services—three girls and a bottle of champagne.

Escort Services Are the Main Form of Prostitution in the United States

The third and most prevalent form of prostitution in the United States is **escort-service** prostitution. This is a form of off-street prostitution that is not tied to a specific service location. **Escorts** (or **call girls**) advertise their services by means of ads in weekly newspapers, adult entertainment magazines, or the Yellow Pages; by cards in telephone booths, bars, and other locations; by their own Web sites; or by word of mouth. There are also Internet sites and chat rooms that help guide men to prostitution services or to individual prostitutes who can meet their needs. However clients identify the

Strip joints and massage parlors are often fronts for prostitution.

massage parlor An establishment for massage that may also offer the services of prostitutes.

brothel A house of prostitution.

whorehouse Obsolete or slang term for a brothel.

escort service A service that provides prostitutes, generally contacted by telephone.

escort Euphemism for a prostitute who advertises by print, word of mouth, or the Internet.

call girl An escort-service prostitute, especially one who is relatively upscale in terms of clientele and price.

Even though prostitution is illegal, advertisements for "escorts" and similar services are ubiquitous.

Sex in History

BOX 19.2 The Best Little Whorehouse in Montana

The Dumas Hotel, on Mercury Street in Butte, Montana (Figure A), was built in 1890. In spite of its name, it was designed specifically as a brothel. It functioned as one until 1982, when its last madam, Ruby Garrett, was convicted of tax evasion.

(A) The Dumas Hotel. The tall windows allowed passers-by a good view of the prostitutes within.

The Dumas Hotel was originally built as a high-class "parlor house" brothel, and the upper floor still boasts the luxurious suites that would have been used by the wealthiest men in Butte (Figure B). Later, the basement and first floor were remodeled to serve humbler folk. The basement was subdivided into a warren of "cribs"—tiny cubicles just big enough to accommodate a bed. This is where Butte's miners spent their hard-earned wages on low-paid prostitutes, who worked in three shifts to accommodate the round-the-clock mining schedule. Some of the first-floor cribs opened directly onto the notorious "Venus Alley" behind the brothel, so that prostitutes in the cribs could solicit customers walking in the alley. Several other brothels, as well as gambling dens and saloons, stood on the same street.

In its earliest years, a customer could "get lucky" for as little as 50 cents, an amount a miner could earn in about 5 hours. The prostitutes either rented a crib for a few dollars a day or worked for the owner, who took 60% of their earnings. Even at the time of its closing, sex could be had for as little as $20.

The brothel owners bribed the police and the city council to leave them alone. In addition, the city authorities shared St. Thomas Aquinas's view—that prostitution was necessary if women of virtue were to be kept safe from lust-filled men. During the Second World War, however, the police sealed off the Dumas Hotel's basement cribs as part of a national campaign against venereal disease. The upper floors contin-

ued to operate, though more discreetly; women no longer paraded in the windows. The Dumas Hotel was designated a National Historic Landmark in 1973—while it was still operating. It is now a museum and has finally been renamed the "Dumas Brothel"—a quarter of a century after it ceased being one.

Another one-time brothel—though not purpose-built—was the Oasis Bordello in the old mining town of Wallace, Idaho. Because the Oasis was left intact when it stopped operating in 1988, present-day visitors can view the entire contents of the brothel, including a then-current price list still posted on the wall. Fifteen minutes of "half and half" (oral plus vaginal sex) cost $25.

(B) One of the upper rooms at the Dumas Hotel

outcall A form of escort-service prostitution in which the client and prostitute engage in sex at a location controlled by the client, such as his hotel room or residence.

incall A form of escort-service prostitution in which the client and the prostitute engage in sex at a location controlled by the prostitute or the service.

desired prostitute, they contact them or their manager via telephone or e-mail using certain accepted code words to describe what they want. ("Massage rates" means that the prostitute will stimulate the client by hand; "full companionship" means coitus, and so on.)

Escort-service prostitutes may go to the client's residence or hotel room or to a motel room rented for the encounter (**outcall**). Alternatively, the client may come to an apartment rented by the escort or the escort's service (**incall**). Escort-service prostitutes are generally expected to be better looking and more presentable than street prostitutes—an obvious drug user would not fare well at this level of the prostitution hierarchy. They also charge more than street prostitutes—$300 an hour would not be unusual. If the escort is working for a service, the fee has two parts: an "agency fee," which goes to the service, and a larger "tip," which goes to the escort.

Cultural Diversity

BOX 19.3 Prostitution: The Dutch Model

Prostitution has long been legal in Holland. Technically, brothels were illegal, but they have always flourished in the red-light districts of Amsterdam and other communities (especially in towns along the German and Belgian borders, in which they serve visitors from those countries). In 2000, brothels were officially legalized, and the law now concerns itself primarily with underage and involuntary prostitution.

In Amsterdam's Burgwallen district, the ground floors of many buildings have been converted into sets of small, narrow rooms, rather like the "cribs" in the Dumas Hotel (see Box 19.2). Each has a tall, doorlike window facing onto the street, and the prostitutes sit on high stools in these windows, advertising themselves to the passers-by (see figure). A man who is interested in a particular prostitute knocks on her window and is admitted, whereupon she draws the blinds. The prostitute may offer basic sex for as little as $20, but extra fees tend to get added on in the course of the encounter—for complete nudity, nonstandard positions, extra time, and the like.

The brothels are licensed, which allows the city some oversight over conditions in them. The prostitutes are not individually licensed, but

they are expected to declare their occupation and their earnings on their income tax, and medical services are provided for them. There is

also an active prostitutes' union, De Rode Draad (Red Thread).

While most or all of the window prostitutes are women, both male and female prostitutes can be found in sex clubs, which offer a more convivial atmosphere and a better opportunity to get to know the prostitutes before making a choice. They are more expensive—$80 and up, plus drinks or a substantial cover charge.

After the legalization of the Amsterdam brothels, their numbers increased greatly—there are now about 500 "display windows," and total annual earnings from prostitution are estimated at about $100 million per year. The brothel business has been taken over to a large extent by organized crime syndicates from Eastern Europe and Russia, and murders, drugs, and trafficking in women have become commonplace. In 2008, the Amsterdam city council said "enough." They voted to begin a process of purchasing and closing down the brothels (Simons, 2008). No one expects the Burgwallen district to be completely sanitized, but the anything-goes atmosphere that made it an international magnet may soon be a memory.

The actual encounter between escort and client is somewhat ritualized. On the escort's arrival at the client's hotel or other location, there is some discussion to settle what is wanted, the amount of time, and the payment. The client then pays the escort, usually by placing money (or a credit card) on a table rather than giving it to the escort directly. Assuming that the escort works for a service, the escort will then call the service to start the clock running. (The call also serves as a security measure.) After that there is conversation, foreplay, putting on of a condom, and whatever sex acts have been agreed upon. Some clients offer the prostitute an extra payment to engage in sex without a condom; how often such offers are accepted is uncertain.

In terms of sexual behavior, the encounter between a client and an escort may be much like a noncommercial sexual encounter. The fact that the client is paying, however, ensures that the focus is on the client's needs. After sex, there may be more conversation. When the encounter is over the escort will call the service again, or the service will call when the allotted time expires.

Many clients want a "girlfriend experience," which means a friendly conversational interaction in addition to sex, and more intimacy, such as cuddling and kissing, including open-mouth kissing. Sometimes the term is understood to mean

madam A woman who manages a brothel or an escort service.

gigolo A male prostitute who caters to women.

coitus without a condom. Escorts who have the skills to provide a girlfriend experience can charge more, and if extra time is involved the costs can quickly escalate.

In the Chicago study, escorts accounted for at least 50% of all prostitutes. This form of prostitution is somewhat safer for the prostitute—hygiene and contraception are easier to control, the clients tend to be more predictable (many are traveling businessmen), and arrests are fewer. Also, because there are relatively few public complaints about escorts, the police tend to leave them alone. These advantages are all relative to street prostitution, of course; compared with most "straight" jobs, even escort-service prostitution carries a high risk of injury, disease, and arrest.

Although much of this work is anonymous and loveless, some escorts see the same clients over and over again, and their relationships with these "regulars" can become quite intimate and pleasurable to both parties. "Regulars" are also desirable because they are predictable and therefore safer for the prostitute.

An unknown but growing number of teenagers are engaging in escort-style prostitution. Unlike the runaway youths mentioned above, most of these teens come from stable working-class or middle-class white families (Estes & Weiner, 2001). They engage in prostitution while still living at home but without their parents' knowledge, and they are motivated more by thrill-seeking and the desire for luxury goods than by any desperate economic need. This trend echoes a phenomenon in Japan—the so-called telephone clubs, which enable men to contact middle-class teenage girls for "compensated dates." The trend has been facilitated by text-messaging and other communication technologies.

At the top of the prostitution hierarchy are the real escorts—beautiful and well-bred young women or men that a client can take to dinner or a show without embarrassment. Such a prostitute might stay with a visiting businessperson for an entire weekend or even travel abroad to spend time with a well-heeled oil sheik. These top-end escort-service prostitutes often work for **madams** who have some access to affluent society; alternatively, they may work for prostitution rings (**Box 19.4**).

Real escorts are the only kind of prostitute that women use in any significant numbers. Male escorts who are paid by women are called **gigolos**. Gigolos are not common in the United States. In fact, one young man who spent months seeking gigolo work on behalf of *Hustler* magazine landed not a single assignation but was repeatedly victimized by scammers (Campbell, 2001). There is a well-accepted gigolo tradition in Europe, however, where affluent women have long enjoyed more sexual freedom than their American counterparts. One Switzerland-based agency offers a range of personable men for as little as $60 per hour, plus expenses, with a 3-hour minimum. Clients may specify every detail about the gigolo online before the encounter, including the cologne he should wear and the topics of conversation he should be versed in (Gigolos Begleitagentur, 2008).

Rather than hire expensive European gigolos, some older white women travel to Africa for sexual pleasure. In the coastal resort communities of Kenya, for example, female sex tourists from Britain and other countries can obtain sex and companionship from strapping 20-year-old Maasai tribesmen, sometimes for as little as a pair of sunglasses. Some of these women engage in sex without condoms, in spite of the high prevalence of HIV infection in the areas they visit (Clarke, 2007).

Good Pay Is the Main Motive for Prostitution

We have already mentioned two traditional motives for prostitution: economic necessity on the part of the prostitutes and lack of a sex partner on the part of unmarried clients. Today, strict economic necessity is probably the motive for only a minority of prostitutes in the United States—for runaway youths in particular. For other prostitutes, it's not so much that they can't survive by other means, but that they can do

A young Kenyan man with a white female tourist on the beach in Mombasa.

Society, Values, and the Law

BOX 19.4 The Governor and the Call Girl

The 2008 prostitution scandal that cost New York governor Eliot Spitzer his job cast some light on high-end prostitution, a world of beautiful young women and wealthy men that is unknown to most Americans. Spitzer, who is married with three daughters, spent $80,000 on prostitutes in New York, Washington D.C., and Florida over a period of several years, according to the *New York Post* (Dicker, 2008). His activities would have never come to public attention had not a bank reported to the IRS on some suspicious transactions in Spitzer's account. Federal investigators, thinking that the transactions were part of some politically corrupt dealing, put a wiretap on Spitzer's phone, and they got an earful.

Spitzer, it turned out, was making calls to the Emperors Club, a New York-based call-girl service whose clients are said to have included European aristocrats. The club's escorts were ranked on a 3- to 7-star scale. A 1-hour session with a 3-star girl could be had for as little as $500; a day with a 7-star would set a client back as much as $31,000, according to the club's now-defunct Web site. On one occasion, Spitzer hired a woman called "Kristen," who later turned out to be a 22-year-old New Yorker, Ashley Dupré. On February 13, 2008, Dupré traveled to Washington and had a 2-hour assignation with Spitzer at the Mayflower Hotel; Spitzer gave her $4000 in cash.

On March 6, four men were arrested and charged with running an illegal prostitution ring, and the Emperors Club was forced to close. On March 10, the *New York Times* broke the story of Spitzer's involvement (Hakim & Rashbaum, 2008). Two days later, Spitzer announced his resignation. On March 15, Dupré was granted immunity from prosecution in exchange for her testimony against the Emperors Club's executives. She became an instant celebrity: Her fees for a *New York Post* photo shoot, downloads of her songs, and other sources dwarfed the money she received from Spitzer, and reality TV show contracts are said to be in the offing.

The Spitzer–Dupré scandal evoked memories of Heidi Fleiss, the "Hollywood Madam" who was convicted in 1997 on tax evasion and attempted pandering charges. Fleiss's "little black book" was said to have contained the names of some of the richest and most famous men in Hollywood. One of them, actor Charlie Sheen, testified at Fleiss's trial that he had paid $50,000 for encounters with her call girls. After serving 21 months in prison, Fleiss was able to

Eliot Spitzer (with his wife) at a press conference apologizing for his involvement with a prostitution ring.

capitalize on her notoriety, earning millions from books, videos, a store, and the sale of movie rights. She moved to Pahrump, Nevada, where she planned to open the state's first legal brothel for women clients, but so far she has opened only a laundromat (Fleeman, 2007).

---

so much better by prostitution. Even at the streetwalking level, a single 20-minute "trick" is equivalent to about a day's work at minimum wage. In the Weinberg study, the great majority of the streetwalkers said that they would switch to a different job if they could get the same rate of pay. Given their limited education and blank résumés, however, they would not be likely to land such a job, so switching to "straight" work would lower their standard of living. At the escort level, the rewards are much higher, even after overheads such as the agency's cut or room rental, so the motivation to stay in prostitution is high. Still, some do leave the profession.

Two kinds of prostitutes have special financial needs that make a high income important. One kind, of course, is prostitutes who are addicted to drugs. The other kind is transgenders, about half of whom are trying to get the money together for sex-reassignment surgery. Based on Weinberg's income data, transgendered street prostitutes who saved half their income could pay for surgery in less than 2 years.

Men Use Prostitutes for Many Reasons

What about the motives of the men who use prostitutes? We mentioned that the traditional motive—the unavailability of sex partners for unmarried men—has largely disappeared in the United States. Some men do still have difficulty finding unpaid sex partners, however, for a wide variety of reasons. They may be shy, unlikable, physically unattractive, or severely disabled. They may be away from home or recently separated from a partner. Some men who could get unpaid sex partners prefer to pay in order to avoid the hassles and obligations they perceive to be associated with regular dating. In addition, men who do have regular partners may seek out prostitutes because their partner does not want to have sex as often as they do or does not want to participate in the particular sex practices that they enjoy. The men may also simply be looking for sexual variety, for someone more attractive than their regular partner, or for the excitement of "forbidden" sex.

Some feminists see men's use of prostitutes as misogynistic. "When men use women in prostitution, they are expressing a pure hatred for the female body," said anti-prostitution and anti-pornography crusader Andrea Dworkin (Dworkin, 1994). Prostitution, according to Dworkin, is "gang rape punctuated by money exchange." Yet some men who are open about their use of prostitutes express a great deal of interest in the women they pay and take great pains to please them. "I have found that escorts are some of the finest and most interesting women you'll ever meet and it's a real treat to get to know them," writes Marc Perkel, author of an online guide to escort-service prostitution. "I recommend that you prepare for your escort's arrival the same way you would for a date. After all, escorts offer more than just sex. Often you can get good conversation and personal companionship as well. And you get these other services by being as nice to them as to any other woman you date" (Perkel, 2008). In reality, it is likely that the dealings between prostitutes and their clients can range from amiable to abusive.

The Prostitutes' Rights Movement Works for Decriminalization

In 1973, Margo St. James founded COYOTE (for "Call Off Your Old Tired Ethics") to serve and represent prostitutes working in San Francisco (**Figure 19.2**). Within 2 years, COYOTE had several offshoots around the country and boasted over 10,000 members. COYOTE's mission was, and still is, to improve the image and working conditions of prostitutes. COYOTE and other prostitutes' organizations that have emerged subsequently see **decriminalization**—that is, the simple elimination of laws that outlaw prostitution—as the key to their goals. After decriminalization, the thinking goes, prostitution would become just another job, subject to normal labor practices, unionization, and the like.

Initially, the prostitutes' rights movement gained a lot of sympathy because it was seen as part of the sexual revolution of the time. The National Organization for Women endorsed decriminalization in the same year that COYOTE was founded, and St. James was portrayed positively in feminist magazines such as *Ms.* The movement took a major hit from the AIDS epidemic, however: Many people saw prostitutes as vectors of the disease, and attitudes toward them became much more conservative.

In the 1980s, some feminists (such as Andrea Dworkin, mentioned above) argued that prostitution was part of the exploitation of women by men. One effect of these feminist views was the redirection of some of the legal persecution of female prostitutes toward the men who were associated with them—that is to say, the pimps and the "johns," their customers. Pimps, as mentioned earlier in this chapter, have become a less important factor in prostitution. Johns

decriminalization Removal of laws that criminalize activities such as prostitution

Figure 19.2 Margo St. James (right), ex-San Francisco prostitute and founder of the prostitutes' rights group COYOTE, seen here talking with actress Jane Fonda. St. James also instituted the Hookers' Ball, a cultural phenomenon in San Francisco, and nearly won election to the Board of Supervisors in 1996.

are now arrested in numbers approaching those of prostitutes, and some cities, such as St. Paul, Minnesota, publish their names and photographs, along with those of arrested prostitutes, on the Internet as a form of deterrence (St. Paul Police, 2008). In addition, "schools for johns," have spread across America. These programs are organized like traffic schools: In exchange for having their arrests expunged from their records, the johns attend a one-day seminar during which they are lectured by feminists, ex-prostitutes, or law enforcement officials about the evils of prostitution.

Although the movement for decriminalization is making little headway today, there is some support for an alternative strategy, **legalization with regulation**. This corresponds roughly to the conditions under which Nevada's legal brothels operate. Prostitutes would be allowed to work in prescribed locations and under defined conditions. They might be required to be licensed, to take safe-sex classes, or to have periodic medical examinations for STDs. Proponents argue that this system would reduce the harmful side effects of prostitution, such as disease, unwanted pregnancy, violence, and organized crime. Opponents argue that it would increase the total amount of prostitution, thus increasing the harm (Raymond, 2004).

In the European experience, there has been a negative relationship between the strictness of regulations governing prostitution and the extent to which prostitutes follow them. In the Netherlands, for example, prostitutes are not individually licensed or compelled to have medical tests; thus, most Dutch prostitutes are happy to operate within the legal structure, although underage girls and nonresident aliens do still operate illegally. In Germany, where individual registration and occasional health examinations are required, only an estimated 25% of prostitutes operate within the law. In Greece, where prostitutes must register individually and receive mandatory health inspections twice a week, less than 10% of prostitutes operate legally; for the remaining 90%, health and social services are largely inaccessible (European Intervention Projects AIDS Prevention for Prostitutes, 2001). And in Nevada, the 300 or so prostitutes who work at the legal brothels are greatly outnumbered by those who work illegally as escorts in Las Vegas and elsewhere in the state. (Of course, the remoteness of the legal brothels from the large cities also makes it difficult for them to compete for clients.)

Anyone concerned with legal reform of prostitution in the United States needs to bear in mind the reality of this trade-off. It might not be an easy matter to reinvent America's freewheeling system of prostitution as a state-regulated industry. The prostitutes' rights organizations oppose this kind of reform altogether, demanding instead that prostitutes be free to conduct their business how and where they choose (Prostitutes Education Network, 2008).

A major roadblock to reform is the fact that most Americans, even young ones, still have moral reservations about prostitution. In a national poll, 4 out of 5 teens said they considered prostitution a "very serious matter," placing it somewhere between hate crimes and shoplifting on a scale of seriousness (Marcovitz & Snyder, 2001). In a random-sample survey of New York voters conducted in the wake of the 2008 Eliot Spitzer exposé (see Box 19.4), sizeable majorities of voters, especially women, disagreed with the idea that prostitution is a "victimless crime" and said that they did not want prostitution to be legalized (Jose, 2008) (**Figure 19.3**).

The stigmatization of prostitution by traditional feminists has been rejected by some more recent feminists such as Martha Nussbaum, a professor of law and ethics at the University of Chicago. "Spitzer's offense was an offense against his family," Nussbaum wrote. "It was not an offense against the public. If he broke any laws, these are laws that never should have existed and that have been repudiated by sensible nations. The hue and cry that has ruined one of the nation's

legalization with regulation
Conversion of an activity such as prostitution from a crime to a governmentally regulated occupation.

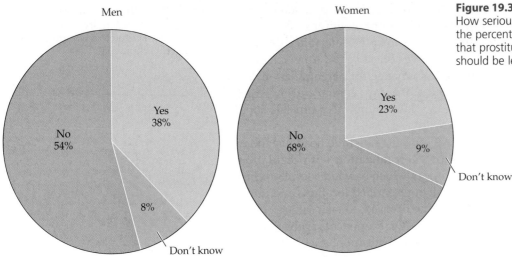

Figure 19.3 Should prostitution be legalized? How serious is prostitution? These graphs show the percentages of New Yorkers who believe that prostitution involving persons over 18 should be legal. (Data from Jose, 2008.)

most committed political careers shows our country to itself in a very ugly light" (Nussbaum, 2008).

The Debate on Prostitution Is Worldwide

Prostitution exists worldwide, of course, and conditions for prostitutes are worse in developing countries than they are in the United States or Europe. In some countries, for example, it is very difficult for prostitutes to demand that their clients use condoms. Still, for many, the economic benefits are real: Prostitutes in countries such as Thailand earn an average of about $800 a month, which is significantly higher than the general level of pay for unskilled labor in Southeast Asia. Prostitution and related activities such as exotic dancing account for 2% to 14% of Southeast Asian economies, and the International Labor Organization (ILO), an arm of the United Nations, has urged governments to recognize these industries and treat them like any other (Lim, 1998). In this way, the ILO believes, prostitutes would enjoy better working conditions and governments would receive more tax revenues. The World Health Organization has also called for the decriminalization of prostitution (Ahmad, 2001).

A different line is taken by feminists Janice Raymond and Dorchen Leidholdt, founders of the Coalition against Trafficking in Women (see Web Resources at the end of this chapter). Raymond, of the University of Massachusetts, echoed Andrea Dworkin when she asserted that prostitution is "rape that's paid for" (Raymond, 1995). The Coalition's goal is to achieve the worldwide criminalization of everyone connected with prostitution—johns, pimps, procurers, and traffickers—except the prostitutes themselves, whom they see only as victims (Coalition Against Trafficking in Women, 2008). The Coalition, as well as some other feminists, oppose the use of the phrase "sex workers," favored by many U.N. agencies and officials, because they feel it legitimizes prostitution, makes it morally equivalent to any other form of work, and masks the particular harms that prostitutes are liable to experience.

Underage and Coerced Prostitution Are Global Problems

Three aspects of prostitution that are of particular concern in a global context are prostitution by minors, involuntary prostitution, and transnational trafficking of prostitutes. The numbers of minors involved in prostitution are impossible to estimate, but young prostitutes are very evident in many countries. Although the term "child prostitution" is often used, it may be somewhat misleading, as most prostitution by minors involves adolescents in the 12 to 18 age range.

Most of the demand for underage prostitutes comes from local men, but visitors from overseas are also an important factor because of their disproportionate wealth. These visitors can be tourists, businessmen, or military personnel. Even the arrival of U.N. peacekeeping forces has spurred the development of underage prostitution in several countries, according to a study by the United Nations itself (ECPAT International, 2001). In 2007, 114 U.N. peacekeepers were expelled from Haiti for sexually exploiting women and girls as young as 13, paying them as little as $1 for sex (Williams, 2007).

Transnational trafficking of women is often connected with involuntary prostitution. Women and girls are moved from country to country—usually from poorer to richer countries—to supply the demand for prostitutes (**Figure 19.4**). For example, many women are transported from Bangladesh to Pakistan and India, from Myanmar (Burma) to Thailand, from Vietnam to China, and from the Philippines and Thailand to Japan. Women are trafficked to the United States from places all over the world, including Latin America, Southeast Asia, Eastern Europe, and Russia. Western Europe is also a major destination for trafficking of prostitutes.

A fairly typical U.S. case came to light in 2007. A Chinese national living in Minneapolis, Liqing Liu, earned $70,000 per month from the earnings of 100 Chinese and Korean women, according to police reports. The women operated out of apartment buildings, serving mostly upper-middle-class white businessmen and professionals who paid $80 a session. The women turned this money over to Liu in repayment for their transportation to the United States and upkeep (Capecchi,

Juvenile prostitutes are highly visible in some cities around the world, such as here in Bangkok, Thailand.

transnational trafficking of women
Transportation of women from one country to another, usually for purposes of prostitution.

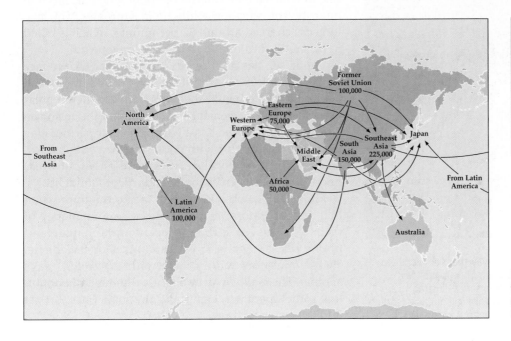

Figure 19.4 Traffic in women and girls for prostitution flows largely from poorer to richer countries. (Terrorism Research Center.)

FAQ Can I have sex with a minor in another country if it is legal there?
United States and Canadian laws make it a crime to travel to any foreign country to have sex with minors.

phone sex Erotic telephone conversations, usually carried out for pay.

2007). Liu and another man were convicted of trafficking women across state lines for purposes of prostitution (Associated Press, 2007c).

How voluntary is this trafficking? In one sense, none of it is: All the women are responding to economic forces that are greater than themselves. But there is clearly a lot of variation in how willingly they participate in the trafficking. Some women know what they are letting themselves in for and see it as a chance for economic betterment. At the other extreme, some women are deceived, enslaved, held prisoner in the host country, and forced to engage in prostitution against their will. Most cases fall into a gray area: The women travel voluntarily and know that they will be working in the sex industry, but they experience some degree of deception or coercion. For example, they may have to work longer as prostitutes in the host country to "pay back" their traffickers than they were initially led to believe.

Groups such as the Coalition against Trafficking in Women take an unreservedly negative view of this trade. "To say that these women are voluntarily allowing themselves to be trafficked is to ignore the powerful social conditions that push women and girls into that kind of life," says Dorchen Leidholt. "The valuation of women as commodities in the global marketplace is devastating to the rights of all women."

Laura Agustín of Connexions for Migrants, an organization that seeks to help migrants avoid exploitation, criticizes the Coalition's stance. "They call themselves radical feminists, and they say it's impossible to have any kind of voluntary prostitution. It's a theoretical line that says, even if you say you consent because you prefer it to cleaning floors or working in the fields, it can't be that way. It's a motherly stance. It turns women working as prostitutes into children: 'They don't know what they're doing, so we have to save them.' It's not realistic" (Gardiner, 2001).

Phone Sex Blends Prostitution and Pornography

Several kinds of sex work straddle the boundary between prostitution and pornography. One is exotic dancing or stripping, which may or may not involve actual sexual contact with customers. Another is **phone sex**, in which a man calls an operator who engages him in erotic conversation while he masturbates. The customer is charged around $2 per minute, which is billed to his credit card or added to his telephone bill.

Phone sex has a lot of advantages over face-to-face prostitution. It is easier and safer for the operators and allows them to organize their work around their regular lives. It is more convenient and cheaper for the customer. Also, a customer who has a wife or regular partner may feel more comfortable with phone sex than with face-to-face prostitution because (in his judgment, at least) phone sex doesn't cross the boundary into infidelity.

Phone sex companies like to create the impression that their operators are motivated by sex, not money, of course. "Missy is a diagnosed nymphomaniac and phone sex is her therapy," announces one Web site. "Most operators will orgasm with the caller," says another. The reality may be slightly different, but doubtless some operators, especially the male ones, do get into the swing of things.

Phone sex operator "Jade" earns a living in a way that allows her to stay home and take care of her young daughter. This "paperclay" sculpture by Norma Jean Almodovar is one of a series illustrating sex work in America. Almodovar, a retired Beverly Hills call girl, is a leading prostitutes' rights activist. (Courtesy of Norma Jean Almodovar.)

There are phone sex operators for every conceivable taste. Some position themselves as "sex therapists"—no doubt to the annoyance of therapists who have professional training in the subject—or "sex surrogates." Many phone sex outfits have Web sites, where it is possible for the client to view photographs of the operator—or supposedly of the operator—while talking with them.

In Europe there has been a move toward televised sex lines, such as the U.K.-based Babestation. In this format viewers can see the operators, but it is not usually possible for a phone caller to watch or interact with the specific operator with whom he is talking.

Pornography Has Always Been Part of Human Culture

The word **pornography** (often abbreviated as *porn* or *porno*) refers to depictions of people or behaviors that are intended to be sexually arousing. Pornography is estimated to be a $13 billion-a-year industry in the United States (Family Safe Media, 2008).

The depictions can be in any medium, but the most common ones are written text, drawing/painting, photography, and video/film. Sometimes the term pornography is restricted to the more down-market products or products of which the speaker disapproves. More expensive works, those that are considered to have literary or artistic merit or those that are less obviously commercial in purpose, may be called **erotica**. This distinction is very subjective, of course. One catchall, nonjudgmental term that is popular with academics and policymakers is **sexually explicit materials**. Even the medical text *Gray's Anatomy* is sexually explicit, however, and it hardly fits in the category we are talking about here because it is not intended to be sexually arousing. So we will stick with the term "pornography."

Pornographic works survive from many ancient cultures. Often, as with the sexually themed ceramics created by pre-Incan and Incan cultures, the intent of the artist remains mysterious—they may have intended the works to have a ceremonial significance, to be sexually arousing, or merely to be humorous. However, some ancient works, such as the sculptures and wall paintings that decorated the brothels of the ancient Roman city of Pompeii, are clearly intended to be sexually arousing.

pornography Material (such as art, writing, photographic images, and film) that is intended to be sexually arousing. Also called porn or porno.

erotica Sexually themed works, such as books or sculpture, deemed to have literary or artistic merit.

sexually explicit materials A nonjudgmental phrase denoting pornography.

obscene Related to sexually themed publications, art, films, performances, or behavior that is deemed offensive to public morals or that violates legal standards of acceptability.

Pornography Has Battled Censorship

Although early Christian tradition was largely anti-sex, pornography did reemerge in the Italian Renaissance. Early examples include the *Decameron* of Boccaccio (1313–1375), a series of stories that featured some naughty priests and nuns. The Roman Catholic Church banned the book but relented after the clerical characters were recast as laypeople (Bullough & Bullough, 1995). In the later Renaissance, erotic sculptures appeared.

Like Boccaccio, English-language pornographers have had to battle the censors. John Cleland's bawdy novel *Fanny Hill, The Memoirs of a Woman of Pleasure,* was a huge success when it was published in England in 1748 (and is still a delightful read), but Cleland was charged with "corrupting the King's subjects." He had to agree to publish no more works of that kind, but he violated the order with another erotic novel that he published anonymously.

The battle between pornography and censorship heated up in the nineteenth century, when almost anything that was potentially arousing was considered **obscene**—that is, sexually offensive or threatening to public morality. In the United States, the federal Comstock Act of 1873 and comparable state laws criminalized the sale or possession

Incan erotic pottery showing fellatio.

Michelangelo's *Dying Slave* (1513–1514) has been viewed as pornographic by some art historians.

of obscene materials. Some writings were banned as obscene even though they had no content that would be considered pornographic today. These included writings about contraception and homosexuality. The legal suppression of such materials continued well into the twentieth century.

During the second half of the twentieth century several important obscenity cases ended up at the U.S. Supreme Court, but the court had a great deal of difficulty defining pornography and establishing what may be banned under state laws. Some justices consistently argued that all pornography, or all pornography involving adults, was protected as free speech under the First Amendment of the U.S. constitution. Others argued that states should be allowed to restrict pornography as they saw fit.

At present, the law is governed by the Supreme Court's decision in the 1973 case *Miller v. California.* (Marvin Miller ran a mail-order pornography business.) According to *Miller*, there is no broad, first-amendment protection for pornography, but states may restrict a pornographic work only under certain conditions:

- The average person, applying contemporary community standards, must find that the work, taken as a whole, appeals to the prurient interest (i.e., is intended to be sexually arousing).
- The work depicts or describes, in a patently offensive way, sexual conduct or excretory functions.
- The work, taken as a whole, lacks serious literary, artistic, political, or scientific merit.

The *Miller* decision has allowed states to restrict pornography in significant ways, such as enacting zoning ordinances that banned pornographic bookstores and strip joints from certain areas. It has also limited government action, however, for example in the area of child pornography, as we will discuss below.

In recent years *Miller* has become difficult to interpret and apply. The reason is the increasing globalization of pornography, facilitated by the Internet, which has made it harder to establish which "community's" standards should be used to judge any particular work. In addition, the use of the term "contemporary" has ensured that legal standards must shift with changing public opinion, which has gradually become more tolerant of pornography. The practical result has been a general lessening or even abandonment of efforts to restrict print- and Internet-based pornography, except for pornography involving (or marketed to) minors.

New Technologies Mean New Kinds of Pornography

Developments in communication technologies have always affected pornography in important ways. The first book printed with movable type, for example, was Gutenberg's Bible of 1455, but it was quickly followed by an outpouring of less elevated material, such as the *Facetiae* of Poggio Bracciolini (published in 1474), a collection of sexual jokes and stories such as the following:

A messenger once asked a high-born lady of my acquaintance whether she desired him to take any letters from her to her husband, who was long away from home, as ambassador of the

Early photographic porn. This erotic image dates from around 1850.

Figure 19.5 Hugh Hefner with Playboy bunnies Shelia Levell (left) and Holly Madison at the Playboy Mansion.

republic. "How can I write him?" she said, "when he has taken his pen away with him and left my inkwell dry?" Which is a clever and honorable reply (cited in Bullough & Bullough, 1995).

While this may have been racy enough for fifteenth-century consumers, pornography became more explicit as technology advanced. By the eighteenth century, erotic books such as *Fanny Hill* were readily affordable by the wealthy and even the middle classes. Photography, invented in the early nineteenth century, was immediately used for pornographic purposes, and the same thing happened with film in the mid-twentieth century.

Glossy magazines became affordable to most levels of society in the 1950s. In 1953, Hugh Hefner founded the magazine *Playboy*; by 1971 it was selling 7 million copies a month. *Playboy* was **soft-core** pornography—it included no images of actual penetrative sex. Still, the magazine waged war on what Hefner considered America's puritanical aversion to sexual pleasure. Hefner's hedonistic empire expanded to include *Playboy* mansions, hotels, resorts, and casinos (**Figure 19.5**). Playboy was followed by more adventurous magazines that ventured into **hard-core** pornography, such as *Hustler*, founded by Larry Flynt in 1974.

By the 1970s, **adult bookstores** throughout the United States offered brief pornographic movies that could be watched in coin-operated viewing booths (peep-shows), and full-length movies were offered in dedicated porno movie theaters. Films that incorporated humor, such as hits *Deep Throat* (starring Linda Lovelace, 1972) and *The Devil in Miss Jones* (1974), helped to dissipate the furtiveness associated with the genre (**Figure 19.6**). These were movies that people could talk about socially and watch as couples, so they won a degree of middle-class acceptance.

Figure 19.6 *Deep Throat* (1972) is probably the most famous pornographic film of all time. It featured a woman (played by Linda Lovelace) whose sex life was unexciting until a doctor discovered that her clitoris was located in her throat—a finding that triggered a bonanza of oral sex. The humor in this film broadened its appeal.

The introduction of videocassettes in the late 1970s, followed by DVDs in the 1990s, had a major impact on pornography. These media made the production and distribution of porno movies much easier and cheaper, and a great diversity of movies catering to every taste appeared. By the 1990s, thousands of "adult" videos were being produced annually, and they accounted for a quarter of all video sales. Because videos could be rented and watched at home, they put most porno theaters out of business, though some theaters (especially those that catered to gay men) survived by serving as informal sex clubs. The quality of individual offerings was generally lower than in the time when films were released to theaters.

Computers and the Internet are just the latest of the many technological innovations that have changed pornography. Sexually explicit Web sites, bulletin boards, newsgroups, and chat rooms flourish. Thanks to instant messaging technology, typing speed has become the limiting factor in online sex. By facilitating sexual interactions across distance and time, the Internet has blurred the boundary between pornography, phone sex, and regular sex.

With the spread of broadband connections and Webcams, more and more users are able to interact in real time through video and audio links. Video porn chat is a growing business. Increasingly, corporations, studios, and advertising agencies are cut out of the equation as individual performers market themselves directly to consumers. Disturbingly, even children can and do become their own online porn entrepreneurs (Eichenwald, 2005).

A specialized Web-based technology that is now being used for sexual purposes is virtual reality (Biever, 2006). The online virtual reality game Second Life, for example, has its own red-light district called Amsterdam, where players take the roles of prostitutes and their customers, and the site has difficult-to-access sex rooms where avatars are anatomically correct and behavior is unrestricted. More recent virtual-reality sites, such as Redlight Center, are wholly devoted to sex. Another site, called Sociolotron, focuses on activities that would be illegal in the real world, such as rape. The site boasts a "plastic surgery system that allows the description of a character to be altered over time to correct natural alteration from giving birth, lactation or sexual torture."

There Is Some Pornography for Women

Although most pornography is marketed to men, a small sector of the industry does provide material for women. In the 1970s, *Playgirl* magazine appeared as a women's counterpart to *Playboy*; it sported centerfolds of ultramasculine men with semierect penises. It was not a huge success with women; in fact, it probably sold better among gay men. The print version of *Playgirl* ceased publication in 2008.

We mentioned in Chapter 8 that women's sexual fantasies typically include more elements of romance and affection than do those of men. Thus one might expect that women would prefer erotic materials that contain such elements, and this turns out to be generally the case. In studies in which women and men were shown a variety of erotic photographs and videos, women preferred the materials that contained indicators of affection and psychological intimacy and were turned off by too-graphic depictions of sex acts and by violence (Mosher & MacIan, 1994). Not surprisingly, then, some commercial pornography directed toward women is soft-core and has a romantic flavor.

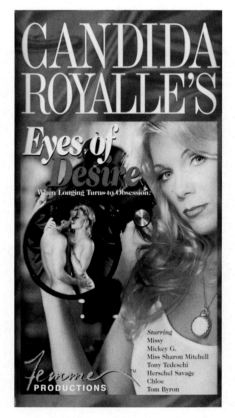

Figure 19.7 Woman-oriented pornography In Candida Royalle's film *Eyes of Desire*, a beautiful photographer experiences a sensual awakening, aided by a high-powered telescope. "Through this new lens of desire, she's drawn into a dangerous game of mystery and lust when she discovers that she, in turn, is being watched by a mysterious stranger from a nearby abandoned estate" (from the film's promotional material).

Still, hard-core, woman-oriented porno movies can be successful. Candida Royalle, a well-known porn star from the 1970s, turned to producing woman- and couple-oriented pornography in the 1980s. Her company, Femme Productions, turns out hard-core videos that present sex from the woman's perspective. Some of the sex scenes in her videos correspond to what one might expect—that is, passionate sex between a woman who is looking for love and a tall dark stranger who just might be Mr. Right (**Figure 19.7**). However, there are also "quickies" with men in elevators. Royalle describes her mission as "giving women permission to enjoy sex."

A woman-oriented genre that has no close male equivalent is the romance novel. Many of these novels would hardly be considered pornographic because they focus almost exclusively on relationships rather than on sex acts. The ubiquitous Harlequin Romance novels belong to this category. However, Harlequin now publishes more explicitly sexual stories under the Harlequin Temptation imprint, and other publishers have similar imprints. This phenomenon reflects a general trend toward acceptance of more explicit material by women than they were comfortable with in the past.

Lesbians have long been pacesetters in women's pornography. Of course, plenty of male-oriented pornography features "lesbian" sex—even *Fanny Hill* had a steamy woman-on-woman sex scene. Little of this material appeals to most lesbians, however, since the female actors, even when they have sex with each other, are usually presented as objects of heterosexual male desire. Thus lesbians who want pornography have had to generate their own. In 1984, lesbian feminists Nan Kinney and Debbie Sundahl founded *On Our Backs*, a magazine that was far more physical and explicit than anything seen before (**Figure 19.8**). Women plied each other with whips, used vulgar language, and gloried in their G-spots. The magazine also launched the career of "sexpert" Susie Bright (Bright, 1999). *On Our Backs* ceased publication in 2006, but lesbian-oriented videos are still a flourishing niche market.

Figure 19.8 The lesbian magazine *On Our Backs* pioneered lesbian pornography in the 1980s.

There Are Conflicting Perspectives on the Value or Harm of Pornography

Although the pornographers have basically won their battle with the censors—only pornography involving minors is still generally suppressed in the United States—there is still debate about the effects of pornography on society. On the one hand, it can be argued that pornography is victimless: The people who create it do so voluntarily and get paid, and the people who consume it also do so voluntarily and get sexual pleasure. On the other hand, it can be argued that the production and consumption of pornography has deleterious social consequences beyond its effects on the producers and consumers and should therefore be banned or regulated by society in some way.

What might these harmful social consequences be? According to *religious conservatives*, pornography promotes general moral decay and undermines traditional social institutions such as the family. Such allegations are very hard to prove or disprove, and we will therefore not consider them further here.

Anti-porn march through the Times Square area of New York in 1979. The march was led by feminists including Susan Brownmiller, Andrea Dworkin, Gloria Steinem, and Bella Abzug. Dworkin's speech at the closing rally is available online (Dworkin, 1979). The film showing at the theater (marquee in background), *The Possession of Nurse Sherri*, was a hugely successful drive-in slasher movie that, in its original uncut version, contained some lurid sex scenes.

More focused allegations come from the *radical feminist* perspective. The possibility that has provoked the most discussion is that pornography promotes physical or sexual violence or other forms of harm against women. In Chapter 18 we mentioned the feminist idea that men are taught by society to feel hostile toward women and that this teaching process is the cause of rape. We cited Diana Russell's arguments in support of this notion. Russell and some other radical feminists, such as Andrea Dworkin and Catherine MacKinnon, believe that pornography is an important part of this teaching process. In fact, Russell defined pornography in a way that incorporates this alleged effect. Heterosexual pornography, she says, is "material created for heterosexual males that combines sex and/or the exposure of genitals with the abuse or degradation of females in a manner that appears to endorse, condone, or encourage such behavior." All other sexually suggestive material, she said, constitutes erotica (Russell, 1994). In the 1970s and 1980s, radical feminists declared war on pornographic publishers.

Trends in *postfeminist* thought (which stresses diversity among women and a wide spectrum of ideas rather than the battle against male oppression) have led to some different viewpoints on pornography. "Pornography must continue to play a central role in our cultural life," wrote Camille Paglia. "Pornography is a pagan area of beauty, vitality, and brutality, of the archaic vigor of nature. It should break every rule, offend all morality" (Paglia, 1994).

The *liberal* perspective generally downplays any harmful effects of pornography and even sees beneficial effects in terms of encouraging sexual exploration or providing a harmless outlet for fantasies that could be dangerous in real life. Liberals also argue that pornography is protected by the First Amendment and that exceptions to First Amendment protection cover only forms of expression that put people in immediate danger.

Some writers have combined liberal and postfeminist threads in the defense of pornography. Nadine Strossen, a professor at New York Law School and president of the American Civil Liberties Union (ACLU), has argued that the sensual representation of women in pornography is a valid use of free expression and that free expression itself is central to women's equality (Strossen, 1995).

The question of pornography's harmful effects has long been a political football. A commission appointed by President Lyndon Johnson reported in 1970 that there was no evidence linking pornography to sexual crimes. A commission appointed by President Ronald Reagan (the "Meese Commission") came to the opposite conclusion, reporting in 1986 that "substantial exposure to sexually violent materials. . . . bears a causal relationship to antisocial acts of sexual violence" (Meese, 1986).

Research Has Not Resolved the Question of Pornography's Effects

A great deal of research has been done on the question of whether the consumption of pornography by men causes them to harm women. Some studies have been done on "regular" men with no special history of sexual violence. Male college students, for example, may be asked to provide information about their use of pornography and asked questions that assess their likelihood of committing violent acts against women. In more elaborate studies, men are exposed to various kinds of pornographic and non-pornographic materials in a laboratory setting. Then they may be given the opportunity to "harm" a woman by, say, giving her a (fictional) electric shock.

According to a meta-analysis of such studies, most men are not rendered more likely to harm women by exposure to any kind of pornography. Still, a minority of men—about 7% or so—do seem to become more likely to harm women after exposure to pornography (Malamuth et al., 2000; Vega & Malamuth, 2007). These

Society, Values, and the Law

BOX 19.5 Extreme Pornography

In 2002 Patrick Russo, a worship leader and music director at a church near Austin, Texas, was found guilty of the murder of Austin resident Diane Holik. Holik's body was found in her own home; she had been strangled, and her wrists were tied. Russo had gained access to her home by pretending to be interested in purchasing it. He was identified as a suspect because another woman, whom Russo had also approached as a would-be home buyer, became suspicious and took his car license plate number.

Police investigators searched Russo's home and examined his computer. They found that it contained about 1200 images from the Web site Necrobabes, to which Russo was a paid subscriber. Necrobabes, which described itself as offering "erotic horror for adults," presented numerous gruesome images of female murder victims, some of them strangled. These images were staged, but many were quite realistic. In addition, Russo had performed Web searches under the keyword "asphyx." This evidence for Russo's interest in sex murder and asphyxiation contributed to his conviction (CNET News, 2007).

A year after Russo's crime, a similar case occurred in England (Carter, 2007). A 35-year-old man, Graham Coutts, killed a woman and kept her body in a storage unit for a month—during which time he visited the unit several times and had sexual contact with the body—

before he finally incinerated it. Police investigations revealed that Coutts had visited the Necrobabes site and other similar sites before the murder. At his trial, Coutts admitted to an obsessive interest in sexual strangulation. Both Russo and Coutts were sentenced to life imprisonment.

It's quite possible that these two men would have committed their crimes even without having viewed the Necrobabes images. Still, as discussed in the text, there is evidence that some men with a predisposition to sexual violence are made more likely to offend by exposure to violent pornography. The Necrobabes site does not appear to have violated any laws in the United States. In fact, legally speaking, it may not have even qualified as pornography, since its images did not show genitals or portray sex acts.

The United Kingdom has taken a stronger line against this kind of material. In 2004 the British government tried without success to have the U.S. attorney general close down Necrobabes and similar sites. In 2008 a new British law banned the possession of what it termed "extreme pornography" (Office of Public Sector Information, 2008). This was defined as the portrayal for purposes of sexual arousal of

This staged image resembles those on the Necrobabes Web site.

behavior likely to cause severe injury or death, or intercourse with a human corpse or an animal. The law covers not only real acts but also those that are staged, so long as a reasonable person might believe that they are real.

The Necrobabes site is currently unavailable, except for its home page, which states that "the material we produce is fanciful, even cartoonish in many regards; there is nothing realistic about it. Our viewers know this. Far from normalizing violence, it relegates it squarely into the realm of fantasy."

---

are men with a preexisting hostility toward women or a violence-prone personality, perhaps as a result of childhood experiences. Not surprisingly, exposure to pornographic material that portrays violence (such as sadomasochistic behavior) has a greater effect on these men than do other forms of pornography (**Box 19.5**).

There is some question about the relevance of these findings to the problem of real-world violence against women. For that reason, studies have been done on men who have been convicted of actual violent crimes against women (along with control groups of men who have not committed such crimes). These studies have basically come up negative: Perpetrators of violent crimes against women do not report a greater exposure to pornography—or only a slightly greater exposure—compared with men in the control groups (Allen et al., 2000).

Cross-cultural studies also suggest that pornography consumption and violence against women do not necessarily go hand in hand. In Japan, for example, pornography—including violent pornography—is produced and consumed in very large quantities, yet sex crimes against women are relatively infrequent. During the period from 1972 to 1995, when the availability and consumption of pornography exploded, the annual number of reported rapes in Japan fell from 4677 per year to 1500 per year (Diamond & Uchiyama, 1999). In fact, a broad analysis of pornography availability and sex crime rates in numerous countries suggests that the Japanese experience is typical: Sex crimes become fewer when pornography consumption increases. This may be because pornography gives potential sex criminals an alternative outlet (Diamond, 1999), or it may be that some underlying social process, such as sexual liberation, causes both an increase in pornography and a decrease in sex crimes.

Such findings suggest that if pornography does promote sexual violence in the United States, there must be specific cultural factors at work here that facilitate the causal link. It might be more useful to study and address those cultural influences than to campaign for restrictions on pornography itself, because it seems unlikely at this point that any major restrictions on adult pornography are likely to be accepted or ruled constitutional.

Underage Pornography Is Widely Condemned, but Common in Some Countries

The situation is different with pornography involving minors. Although it is often called "child pornography" or "kiddie porn," the bulk of this material involves adolescents, so we'll call it **underage pornography**.

In the United States it is illegal to produce, distribute, purchase, download, or possess pornography featuring males or females under the age of 18. Simple nude pictures of minors are permissible in some circumstances, as are depictions of underage sexuality in a serious scientific or artistic context, such as a performance of Shakespeare's play *Romeo and Juliet*. (In the play, Juliet was 13.)

What about *simulated* underage pornography, such as may be produced by computer modification of adult images or videos? The distribution or acquisition of such pornography is illegal if the purveyor suggests, or the consumer believes, that it portrays real minors, according to a 2008 U.S. Supreme Court ruling (Greenhouse, 2008). In fact, the court ruled that even offering to buy or sell *nonexistent* works of underage pornography is a crime. The case arose out of the arrest of a man who offered to sell pornographic photographs of his 4-year-old daughter that he did not actually have.

Japan has long been the world leader in the production of underage pornography. According to a 1999 estimate by the international law enforcement organization Interpol, 80% of the world's commercial underage pornography is produced in that country, mostly using non-Japanese minors, and 40% of Japanese pornographic Web sites contain images of minors (Reitman, 2001). Many Japanese men have an unabashed sexual interest in girls between puberty and adulthood; this interest is so well known that it has a name, *rori kon*, which is derived from the English phrase "Lolita complex." (Lolita was the 12-year-old target of a middle-aged man's desire in Vladimir Nabokov's 1955 novel of that name.) In fact, some Japanese schoolgirls make money for expensive purchases by prostituting themselves to adult men; these transactions are arranged by so-called telephone clubs, as mentioned earlier. Traditionally, the age of consent in some Japanese cities, including Tokyo, was 12, but in 1999 it was raised to 18. At the same time, underage pornography was banned.

Canada, however, has slightly eased its restrictions on pornography involving minors. In 2001 Canada's Supreme Court ruled that videotapes of lawful sexual activity between minors aged over 14 could legitimately be made and used for personal, unshared consumption (Farley, 2001). Since then the legal age of consent has been raised to 16, so 16 would now be the youngest permissible age for sub-

underage pornography Pornography involving models or actors who are minors.

jects in this kind of material. For commercial pornography the youngest age is 18, but prosecutions involving youths over 16 are unusual.

A major concern about underage pornography is the potential for harm to the underage actors themselves. Even some adult porn actors, such as *Deep Throat* star Linda Lovelace, have portrayed their experience as abusive (Lovelace & McGrady, 1980); the risk that it will be so for minors is much greater. Thus there is broad agreement in the United States that the ban on the production of pornography that involves real minors should be actively enforced. Even the ACLU supports this ban, although it took a strong position against the ban on simulated underage pornography. The Association of Sites Advocating Child Protection (ASACP), an industry watchdog group, attempts to monitor and report Internet Web sites that feature underage actors.

Sex Is Part of the Mass Media

Sexually themed content on television and in advertising is rarely as explicit as it is in pornographic videos and the like. However, television and advertising reaches a much wider audience, including children and people who may not have chosen to see erotic material. Thus even mildly provocative sexual material can elicit a great deal of protest.

Images of the genitalia, anuses, and female nipples, hard-core sex, and sexual slang words such as "fuck" are all off-limits on network TV and many cable channels. Still, fleeting examples of these are starting to be seen or heard, even on "family-oriented" shows. For example, a contestant's penis was visible (in a nonsexual context) on CBS's reality show *Survivor: Gabon* in September 2008, and the word "fucking" was spoken on the same network's *Big Brother* in August of the same year (Parents Television Council, 2008b). Considering that these were edited shows, the airing of these incidents was probably not accidental.

Although explicit examples such as these are still uncommon, television programs in general are rife with sexual content—most of it verbal references to sex. A study by the Parents Television Council (PTC), a group that works to reduce the amount of sex, violence, and foul language on television, found that the number of sexual references or incidents on prime-time network television nearly tripled between 1989 and 1999. References to certain sexual topics, such as masturbation, oral sex, "kinky" sex, the genitalia, and homosexuality increased even faster; references to homosexuality led the field with a 265-fold increase over the decade. Since 1999, there has been a significant decline in the amount of sexual material aired during prime time (Parents Television Council, 2003). Still, the PTC claims that television glorifies adultery and promiscuity while portraying marital sex as dull or nonexistent (Parents Television Council, 2008a). Whether the PTC's campaign against sex on television is having any effect on viewership is open to question. Sometimes it seems as if a damning critique from the PTC actually helps *increase* a show's viewership (**Figure 19.9**).

Sexual references on TV are not necessarily harmful. Increased references to homosexuality, for example, could be seen as long overdue, given that the topic was virtually taboo until the 1980s. Some of the examples that the PTC study cites seem to have more of a consciousness-raising purpose than a salacious one. In one example, a closeted action-movie star tells a film executive that he wants to be open about his sexual orientation: "My life is a living hell. The shame, the hiding. I want to be able to walk down the street with my man and say to the world…'This is the man that I share my bed with'."

Increasing references to homosexuality on television might have the effect of familiarizing the public with homosexuality and thus decreasing anti-gay dis-

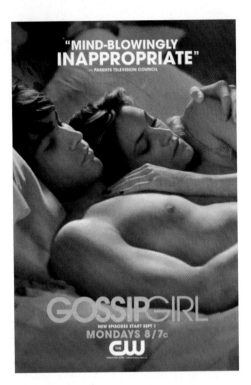

Figure 19.9 Backhanded compliment? The CW channel used a comment from the Parents Television Channel to promote the 2008 season of its teen sex drama, *Gossip Girl*.

crimination, or it might improve the self-esteem and mental health of gays and lesbians directly. Similarly, increasing references to masturbation might help reduce people's feelings of guilt about engaging in that behavior. Even general sexual references might be helpful, given that people's reluctance to discuss sexual matters has often been cited as a cause of relationship problems.

Still, it's hard not to conclude that an educational opportunity is being missed. Of the 14,000 sexual references the typical American teenager saw on television each year in the mid-1990s, only 150 dealt with sexual responsibility, abstinence, or contraception (American Academy of Pediatrics, 1995). It is doubtful that the situation has changed much since then. One longitudinal study from the RAND Institute found that teens who saw a great deal of sexual content on television were twice as likely to become pregnant (or cause a female to become pregnant) during the 3-year follow-up than teens who saw little of such content (Chandra et al., 2008). It is not known whether this association represents a causal relationship, but it is certainly a matter of concern.

In 1996, the U.S. television industry was ordered by Congress to introduce a "voluntary" ratings system that indicates the presence and intensity of sexual content (and violence and foul language) in individual programs. In combination with the V-chip—a device built into all new television sets and available as a set-top box for older sets—this system allows parents to filter out classes of programs they deem unsuitable for their children. The ACLU opposed the system, saying that it amounted to government censorship. One network—NBC—refused to go along with the full ratings system. In any case, it appears that the V-chip is little used, even by parents who have it on their TV and who have been personally shown how to use it (Hazlett, 2004).

Sex Sells, Sometimes

Sex has been used in advertising for as long as advertising has existed (**Figure 19.10A**), and roughly one-fifth of all advertising has overt sexual content (Reichert & Lambiase, 2003). People often pay attention to and recall sexy ads better than ads containing nonsexual imagery (Gallup and Robinson, 2008).

A problem with the use of sexual content in advertising is that it may distract the viewer from attending to or remembering the name of the product or the advertising message (Jones et al., 1998). Thus sexual content is most effective when the product itself is related to sex—as perfume is, for example. Sex doesn't sell car batteries so well.

Another problem is that people may be turned off by sexual material they don't find attractive, and women tend to react negatively to ads containing female nudity. For example, when market researchers interviewed women about an ad for Obsession perfume (**Figure 19.10B**), most responses were strongly negative. One woman described it as "obscene—nothing about love—purely physical pornography. Absolutely useless for selling perfume" (Gallup and Robinson, 2008). Still, Obsession was a blockbuster success.

One way advertisers may attempt to circumvent the kind of negative reaction just described is to present sexual material in forms that are not consciously perceived as such. These include "embeds" (small, imperceptible sexual images within a larger, nonsexual image) and symbols suggestive of genitals (such as rockets) or of sexual acts (insertion of a plug into a socket). Supposedly this kind of subliminal sexual content triggers arousal and attention without reaching the viewer's awareness (Key, 2003). Advertisers generally deny that they employ such strategies, however, and their efficacy has not been well documented (Reichert, 2002).

Advertisers are constantly trying to extend the limits of acceptability. In 1995, Calvin Klein was forced by public protest to terminate an ad campaign that featured apparently underage models in sexually suggestive poses (Lippert, 1995).

(A)

(C)

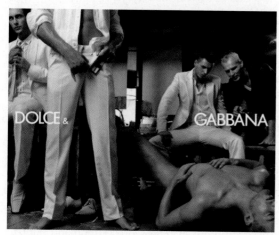

(B)

Figure 19.10 Sex in advertising (A) The first known illustrated advertising poster, a 1491 woodcut used to advertise the book *Histoire de la belle Mélusine*. Note the suggestion of autoerotic activity on the part of the mermaid. (B) Women reacted negatively to this ad for Calvin Klein's Obsession perfume but bought the perfume anyway. (C) This Dolce & Gabbana ad is perhaps suggestive of a gang rape, with a man as the victim.

For their spring 2007 campaign, Dolce and Gabbana used an ad in which a woman was pinned to the ground by a kneeling, barechested man while four other men looked on. It provoked a storm of criticism. The National Organization for Women, for example, accused Dolce and Gabbana of glorifying gang rape (National Organization of Women, 2007), and in Italy the ad was banned outright. Stefano Gabbana defended the ad by claiming that it was intended to represent an "erotic dream." (Women may indeed have rape fantasies, as we discussed in Chapter 8.) The company pulled the ad from publications worldwide but in the following year came out with a similar ad in which the "victim," now completely nude, was a man (**Figure 19.10C**).

Advertisers sometimes use their financial clout in an attempt to influence sex-related editorial content in the media. In 1997, for example, the golf ball manufacturer Titleist and shoe maker Foot-Joy pulled $1 million in ads from *Sports Illustrated* after the magazine reported that 20,000 lesbian fans attended the Dinah Shore LPGA tournament (Hiestand, 1997). In the same year Wendy's, Chrysler, and J.C. Penney all pulled their advertising from the episode of the comedy series *Ellen* in which Ellen DeGeneres' character announced that she was lesbian (Carey & Staimer, 1997). Yet *Ellen* helped normalize the representation of gay people on television. Six years later, when the gay-themed series *Will and Grace* aired the first romantic kiss between two men, Wendy's (along with Chevrolet and Old Navy) was happy to sponsor the episode.

Summary

1. Many relationships involve an exchange of resources for sex. Prostitution—paid sex— is the extreme version of this phenomenon. Prostitutes can be female, male, or transgendered, but nearly all users of prostitutes are male. Prostitution is illegal almost everywhere in the United States, but enforcement varies.

2. Historically, prostitution has been condemned as wrong but also tolerated as necessary. Concern about STD transmission has been a major factor in anti-prostitution campaigns. Prostitution declined greatly during the twentieth century in the United States, probably because unmarried women became more willing to engage in sexual relations with men.

3. Streetwalkers are the lowest-paid prostitutes. They face a relatively high risk of violence and STDs, and many use drugs. Street prostitutes who are minors may be runaways or homeless; these prostitutes face heightened risks. Among street prostitutes, women do better economically than men, but men enjoy their work more. Female street prostitutes traditionally worked for pimps, but increasing numbers are independent operators or are controlled by gangs.

4. Some prostitutes work at commercial locations such as massage parlors or exotic dance venues. Brothels—establishments that have the sole purpose of prostitution—are rare today and, in the United States, are legal only in some rural parts of Nevada.

5. Escorts are off-street prostitutes who obtain clients by advertising or by word of mouth. They may go to the client's location (outcall) or receive clients at a fixed location (incall). Many work for escort services, which arrange their appointments. Escorts are more numerous than street prostitutes; they charge more, and they work in somewhat safer conditions.

6. Women and men prostitute themselves principally because they can earn much more from prostitution than from other occupations, but sexual pleasure plays some role for high-end escorts and for some male prostitutes. Men use prostitutes for a wide variety of reasons, including difficulty in obtaining unpaid partners, sexual variety, or the excitement of illicit sex. According to some feminists, men use prostitutes to express their hatred of women, but some accounts by men suggest otherwise.

7. Prostitutes' rights organizations campaign for the total decriminalization of prostitution. Feminists have campaigned successfully for increased prosecution and punishment of men who use prostitutes. There is some support for regulated legalization of prostitution, as has happened in some European countries.

8. Conditions for prostitutes in developing countries are poor, but the occupation does offer them an above-average income. Some international agencies believe that prostitution should be recognized, governed by fair labor codes, and integrated into regional economies. Some international women's groups believe that activities associated with prostitution, but not prostitutes themselves, should be criminalized.

9. Underage prostitution is a particular concern in an international context. Overseas travelers are important users of underage prostitutes.

10. Many women are trafficked between countries for purposes of prostitution. Some women participate in this traffic voluntarily in search of economic betterment; others are enslaved and prostituted against their will.

11. Pornography consists of depictions of people or behaviors that are intended to be sexually arousing. Pornography has existed throughout history. Censorship of pornography increased greatly in Victorian times but eased after the Second World War. In 1973, the U.S. Supreme Court ruled that the legality of sexually explicit work must be judged by "contemporary community standards."

12. Developments in communication technologies—the printing press, photography, film, and the computer— have all affected pornography in important ways. Feature-length pornographic movies became popular in the 1970s. The introduction of the videocassette format made production and consumption easier and allowed for greater diversity of content. Thanks to the Internet, consumers can now create their own pornogra-

phy for sale or exchange. Virtual-reality sites allow for the enactment of sexual fantasies with like-minded others.

13. Pornography for women tends to be less sexually graphic than male-oriented pornography and to emphasize intimacy and romance. Still, there is a trend toward more sexually explicit material for women. Some lesbians have pioneered a more hard-core approach to pornography.

14. There is debate about the potential harmful effects of pornography. Religious conservatives see pornography as undermining traditional family values. Radical feminists argue that pornography promotes violence against women. Some postfeminist thinkers disagree, saying that pornography plays an important cultural role. Liberals see the restriction of pornography as a violation of free expression.

15. Research studies suggest that most normal men are not made more likely to harm women by viewing any kind of pornography, but pornography that includes violence may make a few men more likely to harm women. Studies of convicted sex offenders indicate that they have not had greater exposure to pornography than other men. Countries with high rates of pornography consumption do not necessarily have high rates of violence against women.

16. Pornography featuring real sexual activity by underage actors is illegal in the United States and many other countries. Simulated underage pornography may also be criminalized, according to a recent U.S. Supreme Court decision.

17. Sexual content on television increased greatly during the 1990s. Responding to public and Congressional concern, the television industry introduced a rating system that warns of sexual (and violent) content. In combination with the "V-chip," it allows parents to filter out material they don't want their children to see.

Discussion Questions

1. Do you think that prostitution should be legalized with regulation, decriminalized, or be illegal? Give your reasons.

2. If prostitution remains illegal, should the emphasis be on prosecuting prostitutes or on prosecuting their customers ("johns")? Should law enforcement devote equal resources to reducing street prostitution and escort-service prostitution?

3. Should all depictions of sex involving underage people (whether real or simulated) be illegal? Why or why not?

4. Female college students have sometimes been hired as high-priced call girls. What do you think would be the pros and cons of this occupation? If your best friend considered this as a way to pay a tuition bill that was overdue, what would you advise her?

5. Parents are often very upset to find their young sons reading pornographic material. How would you advise parents to respond in that situation?

6. Do you think children should be protected from seeing pornographic material on the Internet? If you do, how would you accomplish this?

Web Resources

Association of Sites Advocating Child Protection (porn industry association)
www.asacp.org/index.php

Coalition Against Trafficking in Women www.catwinternational.org/

End Child Prostitution in Asian Tourism (ECPAT) www.ecpat.net/eng/index.asp

Parents Television Council www.parentstv.org/

ProCon.org (*Should prostitution be legal?*) www.prostitution.procon.org

Prostitutes' Education Network www.bayswan.org/penet.html

Recommended Reading

Delacoste, F., and Alexander, P. (Eds.). (1998). *Sex work: Writings by women in the sex industry* (2nd ed.). Cleis Press.

Dworkin, A. (1981). *Pornography: Men possessing women.* Putnam.

Elias, J. E., Bullough, V. L., Elias, V., and Brewer, G. (Eds.). (1999). *Prostitution: On whores, hustlers, and johns.* Prometheus Books.

Lane, F. S. (2000). *Obscene profits: The entrepreneurs of pornography in the cyber age.* Routledge.

Nagel, J. (1997). *Whores and other feminists.* Routledge.

Raphael, J. (2004). *Listening to Olivia: Violence, poverty, and prostitution.* Northeastern University Press.

Reichert, T., and Lambiase, J. (Eds.). (2003). *Sex in advertising: Perspectives on the erotic appeal.* Lawrence Erlbaum Associates.

Strossen, N. (1995). *Defending pornography: Free speech, sex, and the fight for women's rights.* New York University Press.

Whisnant, J., and Stark, C. (2005). *Not for sale: Feminists resisting prostitution and pornography.* Spinifex Press.

Glossary

5α-dihydrotestosterone (or DHT) An androgen that plays an important role in the development of the male external genitalia.

5α-reductase deficiency The congenital absence of the enzyme 5α-reductase, which converts testosterone to dihydrotestosterone.

5α-reductase The enzyme that converts testosterone to 5α-dihydrotestosterone.

acne A skin disorder caused by blockage and inflammation of sebaceous glands.

acquired immune deficiency syndrome (AIDS) The disease caused by the human immunodeficiency virus (HIV); its onset is defined by the occurrence of any of a number of opportunistic infections, or on the basis of blood tests.

acrosome A structure at the front of a sperm that contains enzymes and receptors required for penetration of the zona pellucida of an ovum.

acrosome reaction The opening of a sperm's acrosome, releasing enzymes necessary for penetration of the zona pellucida of the ovum.

action potential An electrochemical signal that travels rapidly along an axon.

activational effect The influence of a sex hormone on the function of brain circuitry in adulthood.

acyclovir A drug used in the treatment of genital herpes.

adaptive Helping the propagation of an organism's genes.

adolescence The period of psychosexual and social maturation that accompanies and follows puberty.

adrenal gland A gland near the kidney that secretes a variety of steroids including sex steroids.

adult baby An adult who obtains sexual satisfaction from acting as a baby or toddler.

adult bookstore Euphemism for a store dealing in pornography.

afferent Carrying signals toward the CNS.

afterbirth The placenta, whose delivery constitutes the final stage of labor.

afterplay Sexual behavior engaged in after coitus or orgasm, or at the end of a sexual encounter.

AIDS dementia A broad cognitive impairment caused by HIV infection.

alpha-fetoprotein A protein whose presence at elevated levels in the blood of a pregnant woman is suggestive of neural tube defects in the fetus.

alveolus (pl. alveoli) Microscopic cavity, such as one of those in the breast where milk is produced.

Amazon A female Scythian warrior; more generally, any tall or powerful woman.

amenorrhea Absence of menstruation.

amniocentesis The sampling of the amniotic fluid for purposes of prenatal diagnosis.

amnion The membranous sac containing amniotic fluid and the fetus.

amniotic fluid The fluid within which the fetus develops.

anabolic Tending to increase tissue mass.

anal fold The posterior portion of the urethral fold, which gives rise to the anus.

anal sex Penetration of the anus by the penis, or any sexual behavior involving the anus.

anatomist Researcher who studies the structure of the body.

androgen Any of a class of steroids—the most important being testosterone—that promote male sexual development and have a variety of other functions in both sexes.

androgen insensitivity syndrome (AIS) An intersexed condition caused by absent or nonfunctional androgen receptors.

andropause In men, the gradual decline of fertility with age; a hypothetical male equivalent of menopause.

androphilic Sexually attracted to men.

anilingus Sexual contact between the mouth or tongue and the partner's anus.

anorgasmia Difficulty experiencing or inability to experience orgasm. In women, also called female orgasmic disorder.

anthropology The study of cultural or biological variations across the human race.

anti-Müllerian hormone (AMH) A peptide hormone secreted by Sertoli cells of the testis that prevents the development of the female internal reproductive tract.

antiretroviral drugs Drugs effective against retroviruses.

antrum The cavity that forms in an ovarian follicle as it matures.

anus The exit of the gastrointestinal tract.

aphrodisiac A substance believed to improve sexual performance, enhance sexual pleasure, or stimulate desire or love.

areola The circular patch of darker skin that surrounds the nipple.

aromatase An enzyme that converts testosterone to estradiol.

artificial insemination An assisted reproduction technique that involves the placement of semen in the vagina or uterus with the aid of a syringe or small tube.

artificial insemination by donor (AID) Artificial insemination using sperm from a man who is not the woman's partner.

asexual Describes a person who never experiences sexual attraction.

asexual reproduction Reproduction in which all the offspring's genes are inherited from a single parent.

assisted reproductive technology (ART) In vitro fertilization and related technologies.

asymptomatic carrier Someone who is infected with a disease organism but is not experiencing symptoms.

attachment theory The idea that relationship styles are influenced by the quality of the early parent–child bond.

autoerotic Providing sexual stimulation to oneself or being aroused sexually by oneself.

autoerotic asphyxia Self-strangulation for purposes of sexual arousal.

autogynephilia A form of male-to-female transexuality characterized by sexual arousal at the thought of becoming a woman.

autonomic ganglion A cluster of autonomic neurons outside the CNS.

autonomic nervous system The portion of the nervous system that controls smooth muscles and glands without our conscious involvement.

autosome Any chromosome other than a sex chromosome.

aversion therapy A form of behavior therapy that attempts to eliminate unwanted desires or behaviors by associating them with some unpleasant experience, such as a noxious smell.

axon The extension of a neuron that conveys impulses, usually in a direction away from the cell body. Also called nerve fiber.

bacterial vaginosis A condition in which the normal microorganisms of the vagina are replaced by anaerobic species, causing discomfort and a foul-smelling discharge.

balanitis Inflammation of the glans of the penis.

bar mitzvah Jewish coming-of-age ceremony for boys.

barrier method Any contraceptive technique in which a physical barrier, such as condom or diaphragm, prevents sperm from reaching the ovum.

Bartholin's glands Glands at the introitus that discharge a small amount of fluid during sexual arousal.

basal body temperature (BBT) Body temperature measured in the morning before getting out of bed.

basal ganglia Deep non-cortical structures of the forebrain.

bat mitzvah Jewish coming-of-age ceremony for girls.

bathhouse A facility, usually in the form of a private club, used for casual sex between men.

battered-woman syndrome A version of post-traumatic stress disorder affecting women who are victims of intimate partner violence, characterized especially by a cessation of attempts to escape from the abusive situation.

BDSM An all-inclusive term for forms of sexual expression that involve inflicting and receiving physical pain, restraint, or humiliation. Often construed as a compressed acronym for bondage and discipline, dominance and submission, and sadism and masochism.

bear In gay slang, a burly gay man with plenty of body hair; more generally, a member of a gay male subculture that rejects many of the prevailing standards of gay male attractiveness and behavior.

behavior therapy Treatment of paraphilias or other disorders based on conditioning or other theories of behavioral psychology. Also called behavior modification.

behavioral couples therapy (BCT) Therapy focused on improving styles of communication between partners in relationships.

benign prostatic hypertrophy An enlarged but noncancerous prostate gland.

bestiality Obsolete term for sexual contact between a person and an animal.

bigamy In law, the crime of marrying someone while already married to another spouse.

biopsy A tissue sample from a living person for diagnostic or (less commonly) for therapeutic purposes.

biphobia Prejudice against bisexuals.

birth canal The canal formed by the uterus, cervix, and vagina, through which the fetus passes during birth.

birthing center A facility specializing in childbirth care.

bisexuality Sexual attraction to persons of both sexes.

blastocyst A conceptus shortly before implantation, when it takes the form of a sphere of cells with a central cavity.

bondage The use of physical restraint for purposes of sexual arousal.

Boston marriage In nineteenth-century New England, the cohabitation of two women.

Bradley method A method of childbirth instruction that stresses the partner's role as birth coach and that seeks to avoid medical interventions.

brainstem The region of the brain between the forebrain and the spinal cord.

Braxton-Hicks contractions Irregular uterine contractions that occur during the third trimester of pregnancy. Also called false labor.

breast bud The first stage of breast development at puberty.

brothel A house of prostitution.

bulbospongiosus muscle A muscle that attaches to the base of the penis or clitoris and assists with erection and (in men) ejaculation.

bulbourethral glands Two small glands near the root of the penis whose secretions ("pre-cum") may appear at the urethral opening during sexual arousal prior to ejaculation. Also known as Cowper's glands.

butch Masculine-acting, often used to describe certain lesbians.

calendar rhythm method A fertility awareness method of contraception that takes account of variability in the length of a woman's menstrual cycles.

call girl An escort-service prostitute, especially one who is relatively upscale in terms of clientele and price.

candidiasis A fungal infection, for example, of the vagina. Also called thrush or a yeast infection.

capacitation A chemical change in the surface of a sperm within the female reproductive tract that allows it to swim more forcefully and respond to the presence of the ovum.

capsid An array of protein molecules surrounding the core of a virus.

casual sex Sexual encounters that do not take place within a durable sexual relationship.

CD4 lymphocytes A type of lymphocyte that carries the CD4 receptor; one of the major targets of HIV.

CD4 receptor A receptor in the cell membrane of CD4 lymphocytes.

celibate Living under a vow not to marry or (by implication) to engage in sexual relations.

cell body The part of a neuron where the nucleus is located.

central nervous system (CNS) The brain and spinal cord.

cerebral cortex Convoluted, layered gray matter that covers most of the brain.

cerebral hemispheres The uppermost and largest portion of the brain, divided into left and right halves.

cervical cap A small rubber of plastic cap that adheres by suction to the cervix, used as a contraceptive.

cervical mucus Mucus, the consistency of which varies around the menstrual cycle, secreted by glands in the cervix.

cervical mucus method A fertility awareness method of contraception that depends on observing changes in the cervical mucus.

cervix The lowermost, narrow portion of the uterus that connects with the vagina.

cesarean section (C-section) The delivery of a baby through an incision in the abdominal wall and the uterus.

chancre A primary sore on the skin or a mucous membrane in a person infected with syphilis. (Pronounced SHANK-er.)

child molester An adult who has had sexual contact with a pre-pubescent child.

chlamydia A sexually transmitted disease caused by infection with the bacterium *Chlamydia trachomatis.*

chorionic villus sampling The sampling of tissue from the placenta for purposes of prenatal diagnosis.

chromosome A rod-shaped nuclear organelle composed of DNA and associated proteins.

chronic pelvic pain syndrome An alternative, more-inclusive term for chronic prostatitis.

cilia Microscopic, hairlike extensions of cells, often capable of a coordinated beating motion.

classical (Pavlovian) conditioning A form of behavioral learning in which a novel stimulus is tied to a pre-existing reflex.

climacteric The transition to infertility at the end of a woman's reproductive life, lasting for several years and culminating in menopause.

clinical psychologist Clinician (usually not a medical doctor) who assesses or treats mental or behavioral problems.

clitoral hood A loose fold of skin that covers the clitoris.

clitoridectomy Removal of the entire external portion of the clitoris.

clitoris The erectile organ in females, whose external portion is located at the junction of the labia minora, just in front of the vestibule.

cloaca The common exit of the gastrointestinal and urogenital systems; in humans it is present only in embryonic life.

cognitive Related to the aspects of the mind that process knowledge or information.

cognitive therapy Therapy based on changing a person's beliefs and thought processes.

cohabitation A live-in sexual relationship between two persons who are not married to each other.

coital alignment technique A variation of the man-above position for coitus that increases clitoral stimulation.

coitus Penetration of the vagina by the penis.

colostrum The milk produced during the first few days after birth; it is relatively low in fat but rich in immunoglobulins.

colposcopy The examination of the cervix with the aid of an operating microscope.

come out of the closet (or "come out") Reveal a previously concealed identity, such as being gay.

commitment The cognitive component of love; the decision to maintain a relationship.

companionate marriage A form of marriage in which the husband and wife are expected to be emotionally intimate and to engage in social activities together.

compulsive sexual behavior Sexual behavior perceived subjectively as involuntary and diagnosed as a symptom of a compulsive disorder. Also called obsessive–compulsive sexual disorder.

conception Fertilization of the ovum.

conceptus The developing organism from the 2-cell stage onward, including both embryonic and extraembryonic tissues.

concubine A woman who cohabits with a man but is not his wife, usually in polygamous cultures.

conditioning The modification of behavior by learning through association and/or reinforcement.

congenital adrenal hyperplasia (CAH) A congenital defect of hormonal metabolism in the adrenal gland, causing the gland to secrete excessive levels of androgens.

conjugation Contact between two bacteria accompanied by the transfer of a short stretch of DNA from one to the other.

constant-dose combination pill An oral contraceptive regimen in which all pills (except any dummy pills) contain the same drug dosage.

contraception The prevention of fertilization and pregnancy.

contraceptive implants A device implanted in the body that slowly releases a hormonal contraceptive.

contraction In childbirth, a periodic coordinated tightening of the uterine musculature, felt as a cramp.

Coolidge effect The revival of sexual arousal caused by the presence of a novel partner.

copulation Sexual intercourse or coitus.

co-receptor A receptor that plays a secondary role in binding.

corona The rim of the glans of the penis.

corpus callosum A band of axons interconnecting the left and right cerebral hemispheres.

corpus cavernosum (pl. corpora cavernosa) Either of two elongated erectile structures within the penis or clitoris, which also extend backward into the pelvic floor.

corpus luteum A secretory structure in the ovary derived from an ovarian follicle after ovulation.

corpus spongiosum A single midline erectile structure. In both sexes it fills the glans; in males it extends backward along the underside of the penis, surrounding the urethra.

cortex The outer portion of an anatomical structure, as of the cerebral hemispheres or the adrenal gland.

courtship behavior Behavior that attracts a mate.

courtship disorder A paraphilia or cluster of paraphilias seen as a disorder of normal courtship behavior.

couvade Pregnancy-like symptoms in the male partner of a pregnant women.

covenant marriage A form of marriage that requires a stronger vow of commitment than a regular marriage and that makes divorce harder to obtain.

covert sensitization A variation of aversion therapy in which the unpleasant experience is provided by the subject's own imagination.

cremaster muscle A striated muscle that wraps around the spermatic cord and the testis.

cross-dress To wear the clothing of the other sex, for any of a variety of reasons.

crowning The appearance of the fetal scalp at the vaginal opening.

crus (pl. crura) Internal extension of a corpus cavernosum of the clitoris or penis.

cryptorchidism Failure of one or both testicles to descend into the scrotum by 3 months of postnatal age.

cultural psychologist Researcher who studies the interactions between culture and mental processes or behaviors.

cumulus cells A layer of cells, derived from the granulosa cells of an ovarian follicle, that surrounds the ovum after ovulation.

cunnilingus Sexual contact between the tongue or mouth of one person and the vulva of another.

cyberstalking Stalking via the Internet.

cycle of abuse The cycle in which some abused children grow up to repeat similar forms of abuse on others. Also called victim–perpetrator cycle.

cytomegalovirus (CMV) A virus that can be transmitted sexually or nonsexually. It can be hazardous to fetuses and persons with weakened immune systems.

dartos A sheet of smooth muscle underlying the skin of the scrotum, which when contracted causes the skin to become thick and wrinkled.

date rape Rape between dating or socially acquainted couples. Also called acquaintance rape.

dating relationship A nonmarital sexual relationship between two persons who do not live together but who see each other on a more-or-less regular basis.

DAX-1 A gene that promotes development of the ovaries.

decriminalization Removal of laws that criminalize activities such as prostitution.

deep kissing Kissing with entry of the tongue into the partner's mouth.

delayed ejaculation Difficulty achieving or inability to achieve orgasm or ejaculation. Also called male orgasmic disorder.

delayed labor Labor that occurs more than 3 weeks after a woman's due date.

delayed puberty Failure of onset of puberty by some criterion age, usually 13 or 14 in girls and 14 in boys.

delusional jealousy Persistent false belief that one's partner is involved with another person.

delusional stalking Stalking motivated by the delusional belief that the victim is in love with, or could be persuaded to fall in love with, the stalker.

dendrites The extensions of a neuron that receive incoming signals from other neurons.

Depo-Provera An injectable form of medroxyprogesterone acetate, used as a contraceptive in women or to decrease the sex drive in male sex offenders.

Depo-SubQ Provera A form of Depo-Provera designed for subcutaneous injection.

depressive psychosis Depression accompanied by seriously disordered thinking.

designer steroids Synthetic steroids intended to evade detection in drug tests.

devadasi An Indian temple prostitute.

***Diagnostic and Statistical Manual of Mental Disorders* (DSM)** A compilation of diagnostic criteria for mental disorders published by the American Psychiatric Association and updated periodically.

diaphragm A barrier placed over the cervix as a contraceptive.

diethylstilbestrol (DES) A synthetic estrogen receptor agonist that was once used to prevent miscarriage but that caused cancer and fertility problems in some of the daughters born of these pregnancies.

dilation In childbirth, the expansion of the cervical canal. Also called dilatation.

dilation and evacuation (D and E) A procedure involving the opening of the cervix and the scraping out of the contents of the uterus with a curette (spoonlike instrument). May be done as an abortion procedure or for other purposes. The term is sometimes used to refer to vacuum aspiration.

dildo A sex toy, often shaped like a penis, used to penetrate the vagina or anus.

diploid Possessing the full complement of chromosomes.

discrepant sexual desire The situation in which one partner in a relationship has much more interest in sex than the other.

disorders of sex development An alternative term for intersexed conditions.

dissociation The distancing of oneself from the emotions evoked by some traumatic experience or memory.

DNA (deoxyribonucleic acid) The linear molecul that forms the chemical basis of genes in all species except some viruses.

dominance The use of humiliation or subservience for purposes of sexual arousal.

dominatrix A woman who acts the role of the dominating partner in a BDSM setting.

dopamine A catecholamine that serves as a neurotransmitter and also as a hormone, inhibiting the release of prolactin from the anterior lobe of the pituitary gland.

dorsal horn The rear portion of the gray matter of the spinal cord. It has a sensory function.

dorsal root A bundle of sensory axons that enters a dorsal horn of the spinal cord.

double standard The application of different moral standards to males and females.

douche To rinse the vagina out with a liquid; the liquid so used.

Down syndrome A collection of birth defects caused by the presence of an extra copy of chromosome 21.

drag The wearing of exaggeratedly feminine clothing by a man, often for entertainment purposes.

dysmenorrhea Menstruation accompanied by pain.

dyspareunia Pain during coitus.

ectoderm The upper, outermost layer of embryonic cells, which will give rise to the skin and most of the nervous system.

ectopic pregnancy Implantation and resulting pregnancy at any site other than the uterus.

effacement Thinning of the cervix in preparation for childbirth.

efferent Carrying signals away from the CNS.

effleurage Light rhythmic stroking—a part of the Lamaze childbirth method.

ejaculatory duct Either of the two bilateral ducts formed by the junction of the vas deferens and the duct of the seminal vesicle. The ejaculatory ducts empty into the urethra within the prostate.

elective abortion An abortion performed in circumstances when the woman's health is not at risk.

embryo The portion of the conceptus that develops into the fetus. Used loosely to describe the entire conceptus from the 2-cell stage onward.

embryonic stem cell A cell found in the inner cell mass of the blastocyst, capable of developing into any type of cell.

emergency contraception Use of high-dose contraceptives after unprotected sex to prevent pregnancy.

emission The loading of the constituents of semen into the posterior urethra immediately before ejaculation.

emotional jealousy Fear that one's partner is becoming emotionally committed to another person.

emotionally focused couples therapy Therapy focused on uncovering emotional problems that harm relationships.

endocrine disruptors Environmental pollutants that have endocrine effects.

endocrinologist Researcher who studies hormones or chemical messengers.

endocrinology The study of glands and hormones.

endoderm The lower, innermost layer of embryonic cells, which will give rise to the digestive system and lungs.

endometrial cancer Cancer of the endometrium of the uterus.

endometriosis The growth of endometrial tissue at abnormal locations.

endometrium The internal lining of the uterus.

engagement The sinking of a fetus's head into a lower position in the pelvis in preparation for birth. Also called lightening.

envelope A lipid outer membrane possessed by some viruses.

ephebophile A person whose sexual feelings are directed mainly toward postpubertal teenagers.

epididymis (pl. epididymides) A structure attached to each testis through which sperm must pass before entering the vas deferens.

epididymitis Inflammation of the epididymis.

epidural anesthesia Anesthesia administered just outside the membrane that surrounds the spinal cord.

episiotomy A cut extending the opening of the vagina backward into the perineum, performed by an obstetrician with the intention of facilitating childbirth or reducing the risk of a perineal tear.

erectile dysfunction A persistent inability to achieve or maintain an erection sufficient to accomplish a desired sexual behavior such as coitus to orgasm.

erection The expansion and stiffening of the penis, clitoris, or nipples in response to sexual stimulation or fantasy.

erotica Sexually themed works, such as books or sculpture, deemed to have literary or artistic merit.

erotomania The delusional belief that a sexually desired but unattainable person is actually in love with oneself.

escort Euphemism for a prostitute who advertises by print, word of mouth, or the Internet.

escort service A service that provides prostitutes, generally contacted by telephone.

Essure A method of tubal sterilization that blocks the oviducts by use of implants.

estradiol The principal estrogen, secreted by granulosa cells in ovarian follicles.

estrogen Any of a class of steroids—the most important being estradiol—that promote the development of female secondary sexual characteristics at puberty and have many other functions in both sexes.

estrus The restricted period within the ovarian cycle when females of some species are sexually receptive; "heat."

ethnography The study of a cultural group, often by means of extended individual fieldwork.

eukaryote An organism whose cells contain nuclei.

eunuch A man who has been castrated.

evolution The change in the genetic makeup of living populations over time.

evolutionary psychologist Researcher who studies the influence of evolution on mental processes or behavior.

excitement phase The beginning phase of the sexual response cycle.

exhibitionism A paraphilia involving exposure of the genitalia to strangers, sometimes with masturbation. Also called "flashing."

exposure therapy A form of psychotherapy for victims of rape or abuse in which they are encouraged to recall the traumatic event in a safe environment.

extended-use regimen A regimen of contraceptive pills that allows for fewer or no menstrual periods.

external genitalia The sexual structures on the outside of the body.

extrafamilial child molester A person who has had sexual contact with children outside his immediate family.

extra-pair relationship A sexual relationship in which at least one of the partners is already married to or partnered with someone else.

fantasy An imagined experience, sexual or otherwise.

fascia A tough sheet or sheath of connective tissue.

fellatio Sexual contact between the mouth of one person and the penis of another.

female circumcision Any of several forms of ritual cutting or excision of parts of the female genitalia.

female condom A plastic pouch inserted into the vagina as a contraceptive and/or to prevent disease transmission.

female sexual arousal disorder Insufficient physiological arousal in women, such as to make sex unpleasurable or painful.

FemCap A type of cervical cap that has a raised brim.

feminism The movement to secure equality for women; the study of social and psychological issues from women's perspectives.

femiphobia Prejudice against femininity in males.

femme Feminine-acting, often used to describe certain lesbians or bisexual women.

fertility awareness methods Contraceptive techniques that rely on avoiding coitus during the woman's fertile window. Also called rhythm methods or periodic abstinence methods.

fertilization The entry of a sperm into an ovum, thus transforming the ovum into a genetically unique diploid organism capable of development (conceptus).

fetal alcohol syndrome A collection of physical and behavioral symptoms in a child who was exposed to high levels of alcohol as a fetus.

fetishism Sexual arousal by inanimate objects, materials, or parts of the body.

fetus The developing organism between the time when the main anatomical structures of the body have been established (in humans, 6 weeks after conception) and birth.

fibrin A protein responsible for the coagulation of body fluids.

fibrinogen The precursor to fibrin.

fibroid A noncancerous tumor arising from smooth muscle cells of the uterus.

fimbria A fringe-like set of extensions from the infundibulum of the oviduct, or a single extension.

first polar body A small body containing the discarded chromosomes from an oocyte's first meiotic division.

flagellum A whip-like fiber extending from a spermatozoon or other cell that confers motility.

fluctuating asymmetry A difference between the left and right sides of the body that results from random perturbations of development.

follicle An oocyte with its supporting cells within the ovary.

follicle-stimulating hormone (FSH) One of the two major gonadotropins secreted by the pituitary gland; it promotes maturation of gametes.

follicular phase The phase of the menstrual cycle when follicles are developing under the influence of gonadotropins.

fondling Any kind of sexual touching of the partner's body.

forebrain The cerebral hemispheres and basal ganglia.

foreplay Sexual behavior engaged in during the early part of a sexual encounter, with the aim of increasing sexual arousal.

foreskin The loose skin that partially or completely covers the glans in males who have not been circumcised.

fornication Obsolete term for sex between unmarried persons; viewed as a sin.

frenulum A strip of loose skin on the underside of the penis, running between the glans and the shaft.

frotteurism A paraphilia involving touching or rubbing the clothed genitals against a stranger without their consent or without their knowledge, as in a crowded public place.

fructose A simple sugar (monosaccharide) present in semen.

functional magnetic resonance imaging (fMRI) A form of magnetic resonance imaging that maps brain activity by detecting the associated changes in blood flow.

gamete A germ cell (ovum or sperm) that fuses with another to form a new organism.

gamete intrafallopian transfer (GIFT) An assisted reproduction technique in which ova and sperm are placed together in a woman's oviducts without prior in vitro fertilization.

gamma-hydroxybutyrate (GHB) A central nervous system depressant that has been used to facilitate rape.

ganglia Collections of neurons outside the central nervous system.

gay bashing Hate crimes against gay people. Sometimes includes verbal abuse as well as physical violence.

gaydar The ability to recognize gay people on the basis of unconscious behaviors, voice quality, gait, and so on.

gender The collection of psychological traits that differ between males and females.

gender constancy A child's understanding that sex is a fixed attribute.

gender dysphoria The unhappiness caused by discordance between a person's anatomical sex and gender identity.

gender identity A person's subjective sense of being male or female.

gender role The expression of gender identity in social behavior.

gender schema A collection of ideas about gender that influences perception and judgment.

gender-variant Atypical in gender characteristics.

gene A stretch of DNA that is transcribed as a functional unit; a unit of inheritance.

General Social Survey (GSS) A long-running periodic survey of the U.S. population run by the National Opinion Research Center.

geneticist Researcher who studies the mechanisms of inheritance.

genital end-bulbs Specialized nerve endings found in erogenous zones, which probably detect the mechanical stimulation associated with sexual activity.

genital herpes An infection of the genital area caused by HSV-2 or (less commonly) HSV-1.

genital ridge One of two bilateral clusters of cells in the embryo that give rise to the gonads.

genital swelling Regions of the genitalia in the embryo that give rise to the labia majora (in females) or the scrotum (in males).

genital tubercle A midline swelling in front of the cloaca, which gives rise to the glans of the clitoris (in females) or penis (in males).

genital warts Wartlike growths on or near the genitalia or anus, caused by infection with human papillomavirus.

genome An organism's entire complement of DNA, including all its genes. In some viruses, such as HIV, the genome is composed of RNA.

gestation Bearing young in the uterus; pregnancy.

gestational age A fetus's age timed from the onset of the mother's last menstrual period.

gigolo A male prostitute who caters to women.

glans The terminal knob of the clitoris or penis.

glycogen A polymer of glucose used for energy storage.

gonad An organ that produces gametes (a testis in males; an ovary in females).

gonadal intersexuality The existence of ovarian and testicular tissue in the same individual. Also called true hermaphroditism.

gonadotropin A hormone that regulates the function of the gonads.

gonadotropin-releasing hormone (GnRH) A hormone secreted by the hypothalamus that stimulates the release of gonadotropins from the anterior lobe of the pituitary gland.

gonorrhea A sexually transmitted disease caused by infection with the bacterium *Neisseria gonorrhoeae*.

gp120 An HIV glycoprotein that binds to the host cell receptor, CD4.

gp41 An HIV glycoprotein that promotes fusion of the virus with the host cell membrane.

Gräfenberg spot (G-spot) A controversial area of increased erotic sensitivity on or deep within the front wall of the vagina.

granulosa cells Cells within an ovarian follicle that support the oocyte and secrete sex steroids.

granulosa-lutein cells Cells of the corpus luteum, derived from follicular granulosa cells, that secrete progesterone.

gray matter A region of the central nervous system containing the cell bodies of neurons.

group marriage Three or more people living together in a marriage-like relationship.

growth hormone A protein hormone secreted by the pituitary gland that promotes growth.

grudge stalking Nonsexual revenge stalking.

gubernaculum Either of two bilateral fibrous bands that are involved in the descent of the gonads in the fetus.

gynecomastia Enlargement of one or both breasts in a male.

gynephilic Sexually attracted to women.

habituation The psychological or physiological process that reduces a person's response to a stimulus or drug after repeated exposure.

haploid Possessing half the usual complement of chromosomes.

hard-core Related to explicit pornography, such as images of penetrative sex and ejaculation.

harem 1. The quarters for wives and children in a polygamous Muslim household. 2. In some species, the group of females who live and mate with a single male.

health psychologist Person who assesses or treats mental or behavioral difficulties that arise out of physical disease.

heavy petting Sexually touching the partner's genitalia or breasts.

hepatitis A Liver disease caused by the hepatitis A virus. It is sometimes transmitted sexually.

hepatitis B Liver disease caused by the hepatitis B virus, a virus that is often transmitted sexually.

hepatitis viruses Viruses that cause liver disease.

heritable Capable of being passed down from parent to offspring.

hermaphrodite An organism that combines male and female reproductive functions.

heterosexual Sexually attracted to persons of the opposite sex.

heterosexuality Sexual attraction only (or predominantly) to persons of the other sex.

highly active antiretroviral therapy (HAART) Combinations of antiretroviral drugs that have proved effective in the treatment or prevention of AIDS.

hijra A member of a class of male-to-female transexuals in northern India and Pakistan.

HIV-symptomatic disease Health problems caused by HIV, especially those that occur before the criteria for an AIDS diagnosis have been met.

homogamy The tendency of sexually partnered couples, or married couples, to resemble each other in a variety of respects.

homophily The tendency to be attracted to people who resemble oneself.

homosexual Sexually attracted to persons of one's own sex.

homosexuality Sexual attraction only (or predominantly) to persons of one's own sex.

hooking up Uncommitted sex with an acquaintance.

hostile-environment harassment Sexual harassment involving a pattern of conduct that creates an intimidating work environment.

hot flashes (hot flushes) Episodes of reddening and warmth of the skin associated with menopause.

human chorionic gonadotropin (hCG) A gonadotropin secreted by the conceptus and by the placenta; its presence in a woman's blood is an indicator of pregnancy.

human immunodeficiency virus (HIV) The retrovirus that causes AIDS.

human papillomavirus (HPV) Any of a group of viruses that can be sexually transmitted and which cause genital warts or other lesions; some types predispose infected persons to cancer of the cervix or anus.

hustler A male prostitute.

hydrocele A collection of fluid around a testicle.

hymen A membrane, usually perforated or incomplete, that covers the opening of the vagina. It may be ruptured by first coitus or for other reasons.

hypersexuality Excessive sexual desire or behavior.

hypoactive sexual desire disorder Low or absent interest in sex, when this condition causes distress. Also called low sexual desire.

hypogonadal Suffering from low function of the testes or ovaries, usually taken to indicate a deficiency of sex steroids.

hypospadias An abnormal location of the urethral meatus on the underside of the glans, the shaft of the penis, or elsewhere.

hypothalamus A small region at the base of the brain on either side of the third ventricle; it contains cell groups involved in sexual responses and other basic functions.

hysterectomy Surgical removal of the uterus, sometimes along with the ovaries and oviducts.

hysterotomy An abortion performed via a surgical incision in the abdominal wall and the uterus.

identity The sense of self, self-labeling, or group affiliation.

idiopathic Lacking an identifiable cause.

Implanon An implanted hormonal contraceptive.

implicit association test A psychological test that is intended to reveal unconscious or unstated preferences.

in vitro fertilization (IVF) Any of a variety of assisted reproduction techniques in which fertilization takes place outside the body.

INAH3 (third interstitial nucleus of the anterior hypothalamus) A cell group in the hypothalamus that differs in size between men and women and between gay and straight men.

incall A form of escort-service prostitution in which the client and the prostitute engage in sex at a location controlled by the prostitute or the service.

inclusive fitness The likelihood that an individual's genes will be represented in future generations, both in direct descendants and in the descendants of close relatives.

indecent exposure The crime of exposing the genitals or female breasts in public—exact legal definitions vary.

induced abortion An abortion performed intentionally by medical or surgical means.

induced labor Labor induced artificially by drugs.

infant formula Manufactured breast milk substitute.

infertility Inability (of a man, woman, or couple) to achieve pregnancy.

infibulation The most invasive form of female circumcision, involving clitoridectomy plus the sewing together of the labia majora over the vestibule. Also known as pharaonic circumcision.

inguinal canal A short canal passing through the abdominal wall in the region of the groin in males.

inhibin A peptide hormone involved in the interaction between the pituitary gland and the gonads as well as in other functions.

integrase An enzyme that inserts viral DNA into the genome of the host cell.

internal fertilization Fertilization within the body.

interneuron A neuron whose connections are local.

interpersonal scripts Patterns of behavior that develop between couples.

intersexed Having a biological sex that is ambiguous or intermediate between male and female.

intimacy The sense of connectedness in an established relationship.

intimate partner stalking Stalking of a current or former spouse or other intimate partner.

intimate partner violence Violence between sex partners.

intracytoplasmic sperm injection (ICSI) An assisted reproduction technique in which a single sperm is injected into the cytoplasm of an ovum.

intrafamilial child molester A person who has had sexual contact with his own children or stepchildren. Also called incest offender.

intrauterine device (IUD) A device placed in the uterus as a contraceptive.

introitus The entrance to the vagina, usually covered early in life by the hymen.

investment The commitment or expenditure of resources for a goal, such as reproductive success.

ischiocavernosus muscle One of the muscles that attaches to the internal portions of the penis and clitoris. It assists with erection and (in men) ejaculation.

isoflavones Estrogen-like compounds of plant origin.

jaundice Yellowing of the skin and mucous membranes, caused by liver disease.

jealousy Fear that a partner may be sexually or emotionally unfaithful.

Kallmann syndrome A developmental syndrome characterized by delayed puberty, inability to smell, and other problems.

Kegel exercises Exercises to strengthen pelvic floor muscles, with the aim of improving sexual function or alleviating urinary leakage.

ketamine ("K") An anesthetic and recreational drug that has been used to facilitate rape.

kin selection The theory that it can be advantageous, in evolutionary terms, to support the reproductive success of close relatives.

kisspeptin A hormone produced in the hypothalamus that is involved in the initiation of puberty.

koro A social panic based on the fear that the penis will retract and disappear, causing death.

labia majora The outer lips: fleshy skin folds, partially covered in pubic hair, that extend from the mons.

labia minora The inner lips: hairless, loose folds of skin located between the labia majora and immediately flanking the vestibule.

labor The process of childbirth.

lactation The production of milk in the mammary glands.

lactiferous sinuses One of the storage areas for milk near the nipple.

Lamaze method A method of childbirth instruction that focuses on techniques of relaxation and other natural means of pain reduction.

laparoscopy Abdominal surgery, such as tubal sterilization, performed through a small incision with the aid of a laparoscope (a fiber-optic viewing instrument).

latent phase An asymptomatic phase of syphilis or other infectious disease.

Lea's shield A type of diaphragm with a one-way valve.

legalization with regulation Conversion of an activity such as prostitution from a crime to a governmentally regulated occupation.

leptin A hormone secreted by fat cells that may play a role in triggering puberty.

Leydig cells Cells located between the seminiferous tubules in the testis that secrete steroids. Also called interstitial cells.

lobe A subdivision of a gland or other region.

lobules A small subdivision of an organ, such as the breast.

lochia A bloody vaginal discharge that may continue for a few weeks after childbirth.

locus coeruleus A nerve center in the pons that helps regulate the state of consciousness.

lordosis In female rodents, an inverse arching of the back that exposes the vulva for intromission by a male.

luteal phase The phase of the menstrual cycle between ovulation and the beginning of menstruation.

luteinizing hormone (LH) One of the two major gonadotropins secreted by the pituitary gland; it promotes the secretion of androgens and, in females, participates in the regulation of the menstrual cycle.

Lybrel A contraceptive pill designed for complete elimination of menstrual periods.

machismo The traditional Latino culture of manliness, which delineates sharp gender roles and gives men certain obligations and privileges.

madam A woman who manages a brothel or an escort service.

mahu A man who took a female gender role in Polynesian society and performed ritual dances.

male condom A sheath placed over the penis as a contraceptive and/or to prevent disease transmission.

mammary glands The milk-producing glands within the breasts.

mammography Radiographic inspection of the breasts.

marriage and family counselor Therapist who assesses or treats interpersonal problems arising between spouses or other intimate partners.

masculinize Cause to become male or male-like.

masochism Sexual arousal from being subjected to pain, bondage, or humiliation.

massage parlor An establishment for massage that may also offer the services of prostitutes.

mastectomy Surgical removal of a breast.

mastitis Inflammation of the breast.

masturbation Sexual self-stimulation. Sometimes also used to refer to manual stimulation of another person's genitalia.

mate guarding A behavior in which a male animal prevents sexual contact between his mate and other males.

media fetishism Sexual attraction to materials such as rubber or silk. Also called material fetishism.

medial preoptic area A region of the hypothalamus involved in the regulation of sexual behaviors typically shown by males.

median eminence A region of the hypothalamus where GnRH is secreted, located immediately above the pituitary gland.

medical abortion An abortion induced with drugs.

medulla The portion of the brainstem closest to the spinal cord.

meiosis A pair of cell divisions that produces haploid gametes.

menarche The onset of menstruation at puberty.

menopausal hormone therapy (MHT) Use of hormones to treat symptoms occurring during or soon after menopause.

menopause The final cessation of menstruation at the end of a woman's reproductive years.

menorrhagia Excessively heavy menstrual bleeding.

menstrual cramps Sharp pelvic pains that may accompany or precede menstruation.

menstrual cup A cup placed within the vagina that collects the menstrual flow.

menstrual toxic shock syndrome A rare but life-threatening illness caused by a staphylococcal infection and associated with tampon use.

menstruation The breakdown of the endometrium at approximately monthly intervals, with consequent loss of tissue and blood from the vagina.

mesoderm The middle layer of embryonic cells, which will give rise to bone, muscle, connective tissue, and the cardiovascular system.

mesonephros A transitory embryonic kidney that provides tissue to the gonads.

methotrexate A drug used in some medical abortions.

microbiologist Researcher who studies microscopic organisms, especially those that cause disease.

micropenis A penis shorter than about 2 cm (0.8 inches) in stretched length at birth.

midbrain The region of the brainstem between the pons and the thalamus.

midpiece The portion of the tail of a sperm that is closest to the head, containing mitochondria.

mifepristone A progestin receptor antagonist used to induce abortion. Also known as RU-486.

milk let-down reflex The ejection of milk into the milk ducts in response to suckling. Also called milk-ejection reflex.

mini-laparotomy Abdominal surgery, such as tubal sterilization, performed through a short incision.

Mirena A hormone-releasing IUD.

misattribution of arousal The tendency of nonsexual arousal, such as fear, to facilitate sexual arousal.

misoprostol A prostaglandin used in medical abortions.

mitosis Cell division in which the chromosome number is preserved.

mittelschmerz Pain associated with ovulation.

molluscum contagiosum A skin condition marked by small raised growths; it is caused by a pox virus.

monoamines Compounds containing an amine group, including catecholamines and serotonin.

monogamy 1. Marriage limited to two persons. 2. A sexual relationship in which neither partner has sexual contact with third parties.

mons veneris (mons) The frontmost component of the vulva: a mound of fatty tissue covering the pubic symphysis.

morula The conceptus when it consists of about 16 to 32 cells arranged in a compact spherical mass.

motor neuron A neuron that triggers the contraction of muscle fibers.

mounting A male-typical sexual behavior: climbing onto the female to reach a position in which intromission is possible. (Used mostly for nonhuman animals.)

mucosa A surface layer of cells (epithelium) that is lubricated by the secretions of mucous glands.

mucus A thick or slippery secretion.

Müllerian duct One of two bilateral ducts in the embryo that give rise to the female reproductive tract.

mut'a A contract to marry for a fixed period of time.

mutation A change in an organism's genome.

mycoplasmas A group of very small cellular organisms that may cause urethritis.

myometrium The muscular layers of the wall of the uterus.

myotonia A general increase in muscle tension.

Naegele's rule A traditional rule for the calculation of a pregnant woman's due date: 9 calendar months plus 1 week after the onset of the last menstrual period.

National Health and Social Life Survey (NHSLS) A national survey of sexual behavior, relationships, and attitudes in the United States, conducted in the early 1990s.

National Survey of Sexual Attitudes and Lifestyles (NSSAL) A British survey of sexual behavior, relationships, and attitudes conducted in the early 1990s.

natural selection The survival and reproduction of those individuals that are best adapted to their environment.

necking Kissing or caressing of the head and neck.

necrophilia A paraphilia involving sexual arousal from viewing or having contact with dead bodies.

Nef An HIV protein whose function is uncertain but which is necessary for the virus to be pathogenic.

negative feedback A control system in which a compound directly or indirectly lowers its own rate of synthesis or secretion.

neuromuscular junction A synapse between an axon and a muscle fiber.

neuron A single nerve cell with all its extensions.

neuropharmacology The study of drugs that affect the brain.

neuroscientist Researcher who studies the nervous system.

neuroses Mental disorders such as depression that, in Freudian theory, are coping strategies against repressed sexual conflicts.

neurotransmitter A compound released at a synapse that increases or decreases the excitability of an adjacent neuron.

nitric oxide A dissolved gas that functions as a neurotransmitter in erectile tissue.

nocturnal emission Ejaculation during sleep.

nocturnal orgasm Orgasm during sleep.

nongonococcal urethritis (NGU) Urethritis not caused by gonorrhea.

nuchal translucency test The ultrasonographic measurement of the skin fold at the neck of a fetus, useful in the prenatal diagnosis of Down syndrome and other congenital anomalies. Also called nuchal fold test.

nucleus In neuroanatomy, a recognizable cluster of neurons in the central nervous system.

NuvaRing A contraceptive ring placed in the vagina.

object fetishism Sexual arousal by inanimate objects. Also called form fetishism.

obscene Related to sexually themed publications, art, films, performances, or behavior that is deemed offensive to public morals or that violates legal standards of acceptability.

obsessive–compulsive disorder (OCD) A mental disorder marked by anxiety, repetitive thoughts or urges, and behaviors that temporarily relieve those urges.

obsessive relational intrusion Obsessive pursuit of a person by a rejected lover.

oligomenorrhea Infrequent or irregular menstruation.

Onuf's nucleus A sexually dimorphic group of motor neurons in the sacral segments of the spinal cord that innervates striated muscles associated with the penis and clitoris.

oocyte A cell capable of developing into an ovum.

oral herpes Herpes infection of the mouth, caused by HSV-1 or (less commonly) HSV-2.

orchiectomy Surgical removal of one or both testicles.

orchitis Inflammation of a testicle.

organizational effect The influence of a sex hormone on the development of brain circuitry.

orgasm The intense, pleasurable sensations at sexual climax and the physiological processes that accompany them.

orgasmic platform The outer portion of the vagina and surrounding tissues, which thicken and tense during sexual arousal.

Ortho Evra A contraceptive patch.

os The opening in the cervix that connects the lumen of the vagina with the cervical canal.

osteoporosis Reduction in the mineral content of bone, predisposing to fractures.

outcall A form of escort-service prostitution in which the client and prostitute engage in sex at a location controlled by the client, such as his hotel room or residence.

outercourse Sexual activities other than coitus, promoted as a means to prevent unwanted pregnancy and avoid sexually transmitted diseases.

ovarian cysts Cysts within the ovary that can arise from a number of different causes.

ovary The female gonad; the organ that produces ova and secretes sex steroids.

oviduct Either of two bilateral tubes that lead from the uterus toward the ovaries; the usual site of fertilization. Also called fallopian tube.

ovulation Release of an ovum from the ovary.

ovum (pl. ova) A mature female gamete, prior to or immediately after fertilization.

oxytocin A hormone secreted by the pituitary gland that stimulates uterine contractions and the secretion of milk.

pair bond A durable sexual relationship between two individuals.

Pap test The microscopic examination of a sample of epithelial cells taken from the cervix or (less commonly) the anus.

Paragard A copper-containing IUD.

paraphilia An unusual form of sexual arousal or behavior that is considered to be a psychological problem.

paraphimosis Entrapment of the retracted foreskin behind the corona.

paraplegia Paralysis affecting the lower half of the body.

parasympathetic nervous system A division of the autonomic nervous system; among other functions, its activity promotes erection of the penis and clitoris.

paraurethral glands Glands situated next to the female urethra, thought to be equivalent to the larger prostate gland in males. Also called Skene's glands.

parthenogenesis Asexual reproduction from an unfertilized ovum; "virgin birth."

partialism Fetishistic attraction to specific parts of the body.

parturition Delivery of young; childbirth.

passion The overwhelming feeling of attraction typical of the early stage of a loving relationship.

paternity test A test to identify an individual's father by DNA analysis.

pathologist Doctor or researcher who studies the diseased body.

pedophile A person whose sexual feelings are directed mainly toward prepubescent children.

pelvic examination A visual and digital examination of the vulva and pelvic organs.

pelvic floor A muscular sling that underlies and supports the pelvic organs.

pelvic inflammatory disease (PID) An infection of the female reproductive tract, often caused by sexually transmitted organisms.

pelvic nerves Nerves that convey parasympathetic signals from the lower spinal cord to the genitalia and other organs.

penile bulb An expansion of the corpus spongiosum at the root of the penis.

penile implant An implanted device for treatment of erectile dysfunction.

penis The erectile, erotically sensitive genital organ in males.

penis captivus Inability of a male to withdraw his penis from the vagina for some time after ejaculation due to spasm of the vaginal musculature.

peptide A polymer of amino acids, usually shorter than a protein.

perfect-use failure rate The percentage of women using a contraceptive technique correctly who will become pregnant in a year.

perimenopause The phase prior to menopause that is marked by irregular menstrual cycles.

perimetrium The outer covering of the uterus.

perineum The region of skin between the anus and the scrotum or vulva.

peripheral nervous system The motor and sensory connections between the central nervous system and peripheral structures such as muscles and sense organs.

persistent genital arousal disorder Long-lasting physiological arousal in women, unaccompanied by subjective arousal or pleasure.

personality The collection of mental and behavioral traits, especially those related to emotions and attitudes, that characterize an individual.

perversion An obsolete term for atypical sexual desire or behavior, viewed as a mental disorder.

petting Sexually touching the partner's body (often taken to exclude the breasts or genitalia).

Peyronie's disease Pathological curvature of the penis.

pheromone A volatile compound that is released by one organism and that triggers a specific behavior in another member of the same species.

phimosis A tightening of the foreskin, preventing its retraction from the glans.

phone sex Erotic telephone conversations, usually carried out for pay.

pimp A man who manages prostitutes in exchange for part of their earnings.

pituitary gland A gland situated below and under the control of the hypothalamus; its posterior lobe secretes oxytocin and vasopressin, and its anterior lobe secretes gonadotropins and other hormones.

placenta A vascular organ, partly of fetal and partly of maternal origin, by which gases, nutrients, hormones, and waste products are exchanged between the fetus and its mother.

Plan B A progestin used for emergency contraception.

plateau phase The phase of the sexual response cycle during which arousal is maintained at a high level.

polyamory The formation of nontransient sexual relationships in groups of three or more.

polyandry The marriage or mating of one female with more than one male.

polycystic ovary syndrome (PCOS) A condition marked by excessive secretion of androgens by the ovaries.

polygamy Marriage to or (mostly in animals) mating with more than one partner.

polygyny The marriage or mating of one male with more than one female.

polymastia The condition of possessing more than two breasts; supernumerary breasts.

polymorphism A common genetic variation between individuals in a species.

polythelia The condition of possessing more than two nipples; supernumerary nipples.

pons A region of the brain above the medulla.

pornography Material (such as art, writing, photographic images, and film) that is intended to be sexually arousing. Also called porn or porno.

post-exposure prophylaxis A drug treatment designed to prevent establishment of an infection after exposure to a disease agent such as HIV.

postganglionic neuron A neuron with cell body in an autonomic ganglion and an axon that innervates glands or smooth muscles in a peripheral organ such as the genitalia.

postmenopausal hormone therapy Hormone treatment extending for a long time after menopause.

postnuptial agreement A financial agreement between spouses.

postovulatory phase An alternative term for luteal phase.

postpartum The period after birth.

postpartum depression Depression in a mother during the postpartum phase.

post-traumatic stress disorder A cluster of physical and psychological symptoms that can affect persons who have experienced severe trauma.

preadolescence The age range including the beginning of puberty, from approximately 8 to 12 or 8 to 13.

preantral follicle A follicle that has enlarged but does not yet have an antrum.

precocious puberty Puberty that begins early enough to be considered a medical problem.

pre-exposure prophylaxis A drug taken before exposure to a disease agent to prevent infection.

preganglionic neuron An autonomic motor neuron in the spinal cord.

pregnancy The state of carrying a living, implanted conceptus, embryo, or fetus.

preimplantation genetic screening Testing of in vitro fertilization embryos for genetic defects prior to implantation.

premature birth Birth that occurs before 37 weeks of gestational age. Also called pre-term birth.

premature ejaculation Ejaculation before the man wishes, often immediately on commencement of coitus. Also called rapid ejaculation.

premenstrual dysphoric disorder (PMDD) PMS-associated mood changes that are severe enough to interfere with relationships.

premenstrual syndrome (PMS) A collection of physical and/or psychological symptoms that may begin a few days before the menstrual period and continue into the period.

prenuptial agreement A contract signed before marriage, spelling out the disposition of wealth in the event of divorce.

preovulatory follicle The single, enlarged antral follicle that will ovulate in a particular cycle.

preovulatory phase An alternative term for follicular phase.

primary amenorrhea Failure to commence menstruation at puberty.

primary disorder A disorder that is not preceded by any period of healthy function.

primary oocyte An oocyte arrested in its first meiotic division.

primary syphilis The first phase of syphilis, marked by the occurrence of a chancre.

primordial follicle An undeveloped primary oocyte with its surrounding granulosa cells.

primordial germ cells The cells that give rise to oocytes and to the progenitors of sperm.

proceptive behavior Behavior by females that may elicit sexual advances by males.

pro-choice Believing that abortion should be legal under some or all circumstances.

procreation Production of offspring.

progesterone A steroid hormone secreted by the ovary and the placenta; it is necessary for the establishment and maintenance of pregnancy.

progestin (or progestagen) Any of a class of steroids, the most important being progesterone, that cause the endometrium to proliferate and help maintain pregnancy. (The term progestin is sometimes reserved for synthetic compounds.)

progestin-only pill An oral contraceptive that contains progestin but no estrogen. Also called the "mini-pill."

prolactin A peptide hormone secreted by the anterior lobe of the pituitary gland that promotes breast development, among other effects.

prolapse The slipping out of place of an organ, such as the uterus.

pro-life Opposed to abortion; believing that abortion should be illegal under most or all circumstances.

promiscuity Engaging in numerous casual or short-lived sexual relationships.

pronucleus A nucleus containing a haploid set of chromosomes derived from a sperm or ovum.

prostaglandin E₁ (alprostadil) A hormone that is injected into the penis to produce an erection.

prostaglandins A group of nonsteroidal signalling molecules that, among many other functions, help prepare the uterus for childbirth.

prostate cancer Cancer of the prostate gland.

prostate gland A single gland at the base of the bladder, surrounding the urethra; its secretions are a component of semen.

prostate-specific antigen (PSA) An antigen characteristic of cells of the prostate gland, whose presence at high levels in the blood is suggestive of, but not diagnostic of, prostate cancer.

prostatitis Inflammation of the prostate gland; may be acute or chronic.

prostitution The practice of engaging in sex for pay.

protease An enzyme that cuts proteins at specific locations.

protein A long polymer made up of amino acids.

pseudohermaphroditism Outdated term for intersexed conditions involving structures other than the gonads.

psychobiologist Psychologist who is interested in the biological bases of mental processes and behavior.

psychology The study of mental processes and behavior.

puberty The biological transition to sexual maturity.

pubic hair Hair that appears on portions of the external genitalia in both sexes at puberty.

pubic lice Insects (*Phthirus pubis*) that preferentially infest the pubic region.

pubic symphysis The junction of the left and right pubic bones, the frontmost elements of the pelvic skeleton.

pubococcygeus muscle Muscles in the pelvic floor that form a sling around the vagina.

pudendal nerves Peripheral nerves supplying the external genitalia.

quadriplegia Paralysis affecting almost the entire body below the neck.

quickening The onset of movements by the fetus that can be felt by the mother.

quid pro quo harassment Unwelcome sexual advances, usually made to a worker in a subordinate position, accompanied by promises or threats.

quinceañera Hispanic coming-of-age ceremony for girls.

radical prostatectomy Surgical removal of the entire prostate gland and local lymph nodes.

rape Coitus (and sometimes other penetrative sex acts) accomplished by force or the threat of force.

rape shield laws Laws that protect rape victims, for example, by limiting the introduction of evidence about their prior sexual behavior.

rape trauma syndrome A cluster of persistent physical and psychological symptoms seen in rape victims, comparable to post-traumatic stress disorder.

raphe The midline ridge of the perineum.

real-life experience A period of living in the role of the other sex as a prelude to sex reassignment.

receptor A molecular structure to which a hormone or neurotransmitter binds. Upon binding, the receptor triggers a specific cellular activity.

recessive trait An inherited trait that shows itself only when the responsible gene is present on both homologous chromosomes.

recidivism The tendency of convicted offenders to reoffend.

rectum The final, straight portion of the large bowel. It connects to the exterior via the anus.

Red Queen hypothesis The idea that sexual reproduction is advantageous because it helps defend organisms against parasites.

refractory period A period of reduced or absent sexual arousability after orgasm.

relapse prevention therapy Therapy aimed at training a person to avoid or cope with situations that trigger criminal behavior.

reproductive physiologist Researcher who studies fertility and pregnancy.

reproductive tract The internal anatomical structures in either sex that form the pathway taken by gametes or the conceptus.

resolution phase The phase of the sexual response cycle during which physiological arousal subsides.

rete testis A network of spaces between the testis and epididymis, through which sperm must pass.

retrovirus An RNA virus whose genome is translated into DNA within the host cell.

Rev An HIV protein that triggers production of viral RNA in a form suitable for export from the cell.

reverse transcriptase An enzyme produced by a retrovirus that transcribes viral RNA into DNA.

Rh factor An antigen on the surface of red blood cells that, when present in a fetus but not in its mother, may trigger an immune response by the mother, resulting in life-threatening anemia of the fetus or newborn.

Rohypnol A tranquilizer that has been used to facilitate rape.

rubella German measles, a viral infection that can cause developmental defects in fetuses whose mothers contract the disease during pregnancy.

sadism Sexual arousal by the infliction of pain, bondage, or humiliation on others, or by witnessing the recipient's suffering.

sadomasochism (S/M) The infliction and acceptance of pain or humiliation as a means of sexual arousal.

saline-induced abortion An abortion induced by use of a strong salt solution.

scabies Infestation with a mite (*Sarcoptes scabiei*) that burrows within the skin.

script theory The analysis of sexual and other behaviors as the enactment of socially instilled roles.

scrotum The sac behind the penis that contains the testicles.

Seasonale An extended-use contraceptive pill.

Seasonique An extended-use contraceptive pill.

sebaceous glands Oil-secreting glands associated with hair follicles.

second polar body A small body containing the chromosomes discarded during the second meiotic division of an ovum.

secondary amenorrhea Absence of menstruation in a woman who has previously menstruated normally.

secondary disorder A disorder that follows some period of healthy function.

secondary oocyte The oocyte in a preovulatory follicle after it has completed its first meiotic division.

secondary sexual characteristics Anatomical characteristics, such as breasts and facial hair, that generally differ between the sexes but are not used to define an individual's sex.

secondary syphilis The second phase of syphilis, marked by a rash and fever.

selective serotonin reuptake inhibitors (SSRIs) A class of drugs, including antidepressants such as Prozac, that depress sexual function.

semen The fluid, containing sperm and a variety of chemical compounds, that is ejaculated from the penis at male sexual climax.

seminal plasma The noncellular constituents of semen.

seminal vesicles Two glands situated on either side of the prostate; their secretions are a component of semen.

seminiferous tubules Convoluted microscopic tubes within the testis; the site of spermatogenesis.

sensate focus A form of sex therapy that involves graduated touching exercises.

sensitive period A period of development during which the survival or growth of a biological system depends on the presence of some factor, such as a hormone.

serial monogamy Involvement in a series of monogamous relationships.

seroconversion The change from negative to positive on an antibody test, such as occurs a few weeks or months after HIV infection.

serotonin A monoamine derived from the amino acid tryptophan that functions as a neurotransmitter.

Sertoli cell A type of cell within the seminiferous tubules that nurtures developing sperm and secretes hormones.

sex 1. The category of male or female. 2. Sexual feelings and behavior.

sex chromosome Either of a pair of chromosomes (X or Y in mammals) that differ between the sexes.

sex determination The biological mechanism that determines whether an organism will develop as a male or a female.

sex hormones Chemical messengers that influence sexual and reproductive processes.

sex play A variety of playful activities that add pleasure to sexual interactions.

sex-reassignment surgery Surgery to change a person's genitals or other sexual characteristics.

sex research The scientific study of sex.

sex steroid Any of the steroid hormones that are active in sexual and reproductive physiology.

sex therapist A person who treats sexual disorders, usually by means of psychotherapy and sexual exercises.

sex trader A person who exchanges sex for money, drugs, or other benefits; a broader term than prostitute.

sex worker A person who engages in prostitution, pornography, or another sex-related occupation.

sexology The scientific study of sex, especially of sexual dysfunctions.

sexual addiction The idea that a person may be addicted to certain forms of sexual behavior by a mechanism similar to that of substance addiction.

sexual assault Coercive or nonconsensual sexual contact: a broader category of behaviors than rape.

sexual dimorphism An anatomical difference between the sexes.

sexual harassment Unwanted sexual advances or other intimidating sexual behavior, usually in the workplace.

sexual intercourse Sexual contact, usually understood to involve coitus.

sexual jealousy Fear that one's partner is engaging in sexual contacts with another person.

sexual monogamy A sexually exclusive pair bond.

sexual orientation The direction of a person's sexual feelings toward persons of the same sex, the other sex, or both sexes.

sexual reproduction Reproduction in which the offspring inherit genes from two parents.

sexual response cycle The sequence of physiological processes that accompany sexual behavior.

sexual scripts Socially negotiated roles that govern sexual behavior.

sexual selection The evolution of traits under the pressure of competition for mates or of choice by mates.

sexuality The feelings, behaviors, and identities associated with sex.

sexually dimorphic nucleus of the preoptic area (SDN-POA) A cell group in the medial preoptic area of the hypothalamus of rodents that is larger in males than females.

sexually explicit materials A nonjudgmental phrase denoting pornography.

sinusoids A vascular space, such as within erectile tissue, capable of being expanded by filling with blood.

situational disorder A disorder that appears only in certain circumstances.

smegma A whitish, greasy secretion that builds up under the prepuce of the penis or clitoris.

smooth muscle Muscular tissue that has no microscopic striations. Its contraction is usually involuntary and under the control of the autonomic nervous system.

social monogamy A pair bond that is not sexually exclusive.

social psychology The study of our relationship to others.

socialization The effect of social influences such as family, education, peer groups, and the media on the development of psychological or behavioral traits.

sociology The scientific study of society.

sodomy Obsolete term for anal sex, or for any homosexual contact. As a legal term it may refer to a variety of prohibited sex acts.

soft-core Related to relatively nonexplicit pornography.

softening The elimination of connective tissue from the cervix, allowing it to thin out and dilate during labor. Also called ripening.

sperm A male gamete, produced in the testis.

sperm bank A facility that collects, stores, and provides semen for artificial insemination.

spermatic cord Either of two bilateral bundles of structures, including the vas deferens, blood vessels, and the cremaster muscle, that pass through the inguinal canal to the testis.

spermatogenesis The production of sperm.

spermicide A chemical that kills sperm, available as a contraceptive in a variety of forms, such as foams, creams, and suppositories.

sphincter A circular muscle around an orifice whose contraction closes the orifice.

spina bifida A congenital malformation caused by incomplete closure of the neural tube.

spinal cord The portion of the central nervous system within the vertebral column.

spinal reflex A reflex mediated by neurons in the spinal cord, requiring no participation by the brain.

spiral arteries The arteries that supply blood to the endometrium.

spirochete Any of a class of corkscrew-shaped bacteria, including the agent that causes syphilis.

SRY (Sex-determining Region of the Y chromosome) A gene located on the Y chromosome that causes the embryo to develop as a male.

stalking Obsessive pursuit of someone in such a way as to put that person in a state of fear.

standard days method A simplified calendar method of contraception usable by women with regular cycles.

status orgasmus An orgasm or uninterrupted sequence of orgasms that last from 20 seconds up to a minute or more.

statutory rape Penetrative sex when a partner is legally unable to give consent on account of young age, intellectual disability, or unconsciousness.

sterilization A surgical procedure to eliminate fertility in either sex.

stop-start method A sex therapy technique for the treatment of premature ejaculation that involves alternating between stimulating and not stimulating the penis.

striated muscle Muscular tissue that has microscopic striations. Its contraction is usually under voluntary control.

subfertility Difficulty in establishing a pregnancy; arbitrarily defined as the absence of pregnancy after a couple has had frequent unprotected sex for 12 months.

subincision A form of male circumcision in which a cut is made along the underside of the penis, exposing the urethra.

subzonal insemination An assisted reproduction technique in which sperm are injected into the space between the zona pellucida and the plasma membrane of an ovum to facilitate fertilization.

suitor A person who is seeking to establish a romantic relationship with another.

sunnah Female circumcision limited to incision or removal of the clitoral hood.

superincision An unusual form of male circumcision in which the upper part of the foreskin is incised but not removed.

surgical abortion An abortion induced by a surgical procedure.

surrogate A person who stands in for another; for example, as a sex partner or as the bearer of a child.

suspensory ligament A ligament that connects the root of the penis to the pubic symphysis.

swingers Couples who agree to engage in casual sexual contacts with others.

sympathetic nervous system A division of the autonomic nervous system; among other functions, its activity inhibits penile erection but helps trigger ejaculation.

sympto-thermal method A rhythm method of contraception that uses the measurement of basal body temperature and the testing of cervical mucus to determine the time of ovulation and the fertile window.

synapse A junction where signals are transmitted between neurons or from neurons to muscle fibers.

synaptic cleft The narrow space between two neurons at a synapse.

syphilis A sexually transmitted disease caused by a spirochete, *Treponema pallidum*.

Tat An HIV protein that promotes the production of viral RNA.

tertiary syphilis The third phase of syphilis, marked by multiple organ damage.

testicle or testis The male gonad: one of the two glands within the scrotum that produce sperm and secrete sex steroids.

testosterone The principal androgen, synthesized in the testes and, in lesser amounts, in the ovaries and adrenal glands.

thalamus The uppermost region of the brainstem.

thecal cells Cells located on the periphery of an ovarian follicle that synthesize sex steroids.

theca-lutein cells Cells of the corpus luteum, derived from follicular thecal cells, that synthesize testosterone.

therapeutic abortion An abortion performed to safeguard a woman's life or health.

third interstitial nucleus of the anterior hypothalamus (INAH3) A sexually dimorphic cell group in the medial preoptic area of the human hypothalamus.

trabeculae Connective tissue partitions separating the sinusoids of erectile tissue.

transcription factor A protein that regulates gene expression.

transexual A transgendered person who seeks to transition to the other sex.

transgender A person who identifies with the other sex.

transgendered Having a gender identity that is discordant with one's anatomical sex.

transition The final phase of dilation of the cervix during labor.

transman A female-to-male transexual.

transnational trafficking of women Transportation of women from one country to another, usually for purposes of prostitution.

transvestism Wearing clothes of the other sex for purposes of sexual arousal. Sometimes applied to cross-dressing for any reason.

transwoman A male-to-female transexual.

tribadism Sexual behavior between two women, who lie front-to-front and stimulate each other's vulvas with thrusting motions.

trichomoniasis (or "trich") Infection with the protozoan *Trichomonas vaginalis*.

trimester One of three 3-month divisions of pregnancy.

triphasic combination pill An oral contraceptive regimen that varies the doses of estrogens and progestins around the menstrual cycle.

true hermaphroditism Outdated term for gonadal intersexuality.

tubal ligation Female sterilization by tying off the oviducts.

tubal sterilization A female sterilization technique that involves cutting, cauterizing, or tying off the oviducts. Also called tubal ligation.

tunica albuginea A fibrous capsule surrounding the corpora cavernosa.

two-spirit person In Native American cultures, a person with the spirit of both a man and a woman; a transgendered person. Also called berdache.

typical-use failure rate The percentage of women using a contraceptive technique with a typical degree of care who will become pregnant in a year.

ultrasound scan An imaging procedure that depends on the reflection of ultrasonic waves from density boundaries within the body. Also called ultrasonographic scan.

umbilical cord The vascular cord that runs from the umbilicus (navel) of the fetus to the placenta.

underage pornography Pornography involving models or actors who are minors.

unrequited love Love that is not reciprocated.

urethra The canal that conveys urine from the bladder to the urethral opening. It also serves for the discharge of semen or female ejaculatory fluids.

urethral folds Folds of ectodermal tissue in the embryo that give rise to the labia minora (in females) or the shaft of the penis (in males).

urethral meatus The opening of the urethra at the tip of the penis (in males) or in front of the vagina (in females).

urethritis Inflammation of the urethra, usually caused by an infection.

urogenital sinus The common opening of the urinary and genital systems in the embryo.

uterus The womb; a pear-shaped region of the female reproductive tract through which sperm are transported and where the conceptus implants and develops.

vacuum aspiration An abortion procedure in which the conceptus is destroyed and removed by suction.

vacuum constriction system A device for treating erectile dysfunction that creates a partial vacuum around the penis, thus drawing blood into the erectile tissue.

vagina A muscular tube extending 8–10 cm from the vestibule to the uterine cervix.

vagina dentata The mythical concept that the vagina has teeth that can devour the penis.

vaginal dilator A plastic cylinder used to enlarge the vagina or to counteract vaginismus.

vaginismus Inability to experience coitus due to spasm of the muscles surrounding the outer vagina, pain, or fear of pain.

varicocele Enlargement of the veins that drain the testis.

vas deferens (pl. vasa deferentia) Either of the two bilateral ducts that convey sperm from the epididymis to the ejaculatory duct.

vasectomy A male sterilization technique that involves cutting or tying off the vasa deferentia.

vasomotor control The physiological regulation of peripheral blood flow.

vasovasostomy Surgery to reverse a vasectomy.

venereal disease Obsolete term for a sexually transmitted disease.

ventral horn The portion of the gray matter of the spinal cord nearer to the front of the body, where motor neurons are located.

ventral root A bundle of motor axons that leaves a ventral horn of the spinal cord.

vestibular bulbs Erectile structures deep to the labia minora, on either side of the vestibule.

vestibule The potential space between the left and right labia minora.

vibrator An electrically powered vibrating device used to provide sexual stimulation.

virus An extremely small infectious agent. When not inside a host cell, viruses are metabolically inert but infectious.

voyeurism A paraphilia involving spying on persons while they are undressing, naked, or engaged in sex.

Vpr An HIV protein involved in movement of viral DNA into the host cell nucleus.

vulva The female external genitalia.

vulvar vestibulitis syndrome A form of dyspareunia marked by inflammation of the vestibule and increased tension in pelvic floor muscles.

waist-to-hip ratio The ratio of the width of the body at the waist to the width at the hip.

wasting Progressive and extreme loss of body weight.

wet nurse A woman who breast-feeds someone else's infant.

white matter A region of the central nervous system that contains bundles of axons but no neuronal cell bodies.

whorehouse Obsolete or slang term for a brothel.

withdrawal method A method of contraception in which the man withdraws his penis from the vagina prior to ejaculation.

Wolffian duct One of two bilateral ducts in the embryo that give rise to the male reproductive tract.

X chromosome A sex chromosome that is present as two copies in females and one copy in males.

Y chromosome A sex chromosome that is present only in males.

yolk sac A transient, early extraembryonic structure; the source of primordial germ cells.

zona pellucida The capsule surrounding an ovum that must be penetrated by the fertilizing sperm.

zonal drilling An assisted reproduction technique in which a hole is drilled through the zona pellucida of an ovum to facilitate fertilization.

zoophilia A persistent preference for sexual contacts with animals, considered a paraphilia.

zygote A cell formed by the fusion of gametes: a fertilized ovum.

Photo Credits

References

ABC News. (2007). *Oldest mum "lied to IVF clinic."* (http://www.abc.net.au/news/newsitems/200701/s1835045.htm)

Abcarian, R. (2006). Which way, WeHo? *Los Angeles Times*, May 28.

Abel, G. G. & Osborn, C. A. (2000). The paraphilias. In M. G. Gelder et al. (Eds.), *New Oxford textbook of psychiatry*. Oxford University Press.

Abel, G. G. & Rouleau, J. L. (1990). The nature and extent of sexual assault. In W. L. Marshall et al. (Eds.), *Handbook of sexual assault: Issues, theories, and treatment of the offender*. Plenum.

Abell, A., Ernst, E. & Bonde, J. P. (2000). Semen quality and sexual hormones in greenhouse workers. *Scandinavian Journal of Work and Environmental Health, 26*, 492–500.

Ablow, K. (2005). A perilous journey from delivery room to bedroom. *New York Times*, August 23.

Abramov, L. A. (1976). Sexual life and sexual frigidity among women developing acute myocardial infarction. *Psychosomatic Medicine, 38*, 418–425.

Abramson, P. R. (2007). *Romance in the ivory tower: The rights and liberty of conscience*. MIT Press.

Abramson, P. R. & Pinkerton, S. D. (2002). *With pleasure: Thoughts on the nature of human sexuality* (revised edition). Oxford University Press.

ACLU of Utah. (2006). *Utah's bigamy statute and the right to privacy and religious freedom.* (http://www.acluutah.org/bigamystatute.htm)

Adams Hillard, P. J. (2003). *Imperforate hymen.* (http://www.emedicine.com/med/topic3329.htm)

Adams, H. E., Wright, L. W., Jr. & Lohr, B. A. (1996). Is homophobia associated with homosexual arousal? *Journal of Abnormal Psychology, 105*, 440–445.

Addiction and Family Research Group. (2004). *Behavioral couples therapy: A 3-day training and facilitators guide.* (http://www.addictionandfamily.org/SecuredManuals/M09BCT3FacilitatorUNSECURED.pdf)

Adham, M. N., Teimourian, B. & Mosca, P. (2000). Buried penis release in adults with suction lipectomy and abdominoplasty. *Plastic and Reconstructive Surgery, 106*, 840–844.

Adoptive Families. (2008). *Getting started in international adoption.* (http://www.adoptivefamilies.com/internationaladoption.php)

Affara, N. A. & Mitchell, M. J. (2000). The role of human and mouse Y chromosome genes in male infertility. *Journal of Endocrinological Investigation, 23*, 630–645.

Agency for Healthcare Policy and Research. (1998). *Health services research on hysterectomy and alternatives.* (http://www.ahcpr.gov/research/hysterec.htm)

Agency for Healthcare Research and Quality. (2005). *Management of menopause-related symptoms.* (http://www.ahrq.gov/clinic/epcsums/menosum.htm)

Agency for Healthcare Research and Quality. (2008). *Statistics on hospital-based care in the United States, 2005.* (http://www.hcupus.ahrq.gov/reports/annualreport/HAR_2005.pdf)

Ager, S. L. (2004). *The wandering womb.* (http://www.arts.uwaterloo.ca/CLASS/womb.htm)

Ahmad, K. (2001). Call for decriminalisation of prostitution in Asia. *Lancet, 358*, 643.

Aho, M., Koivisto, A. M., Tammela, T. L. & Auvinen, A. (2000). Is the incidence of hypospadias increasing? Analysis of Finnish hospital discharge data 1970–1994. *Environmental Health Perspectives, 108*, 463–465.

Ahokas, A., Aito, M. & Rimon, R. (2000). Positive treatment effect of estradiol in postpartum psychosis: a pilot study. *Journal of Clinical Psychiatry, 61*, 166–169.

Ainsworth, M. D., Blehar, S., Waters, E. & Wall, S. (1978). *Patterns of attachment: A psychological study of the strange situation*. Erlbaum.

Albert, A. E., Warner, D. L., Hatcher, R. A., Trussell, J. & Bennett, C. (1995). Condom use among female commercial sex workers in Nevada's legal brothels. *American Journal of Public Health, 85*, 1514–1520.

Alexander, C. J., Sipski, M. L. & Findley, T. W. (1993). Sexual activities, desire, and satisfaction in males pre- and post- spinal cord injury. *Archives of Sexual Behavior, 22*, 217–228.

Alexander, M. A. & Hines, M. (2002). Sex differences in response to children's toys in non-human primates (*Cercopithecus aethiops sabaeus*). *Evolution and Human Behavior, 23*, 467–479.

Alexander, M. G. & Fisher, T. D. (2003). Truth and consequences: using the bogus pipeline to examine sex differences in self-reported sexuality. *Journal of Sex Research, 40*, 27–35.

Ali, L. & Kelley, R. (2008). The curious lives of surrogates. *Newsweek*, April 7.

Allen, L. S. & Gorski, R. A. (1990). Sex difference in the bed nucleus of the stria terminalis of the human brain. *Journal of Comparative Neurology, 302*, 697–706.

Allen, L. S., Hines, M., Shryne, J. E. & Gorski, R. A. (1989). Two sexually dimorphic cell groups in the human brain. *Journal of Neuroscience, 9*, 497–506.

Allen, M., D'Alessio, D. & Emmers-Sommer, T. M. (2000). Reactions of criminal sexual offenders to pornography: A meta-analytic summary. In M. Roloff (Ed.), *Communication Yearbook 22*. Sage Publications.

Althof, S. E. & Schreiner-Engel, P. (2000). The sexual dysfunctions. In M. G. Gelder et al. (Eds.), *New Oxford textbook of psychiatry*. Oxford University Press.

Althof, S. E. (2007). Treatment of rapid ejaculation: Psychotherapy, pharmacotherapy, and combined therapy. In S. R. Leiblum (Ed.), *Principles and practice of sex therapy*. Guilford Press.

Althuis, M. D., Brogan, D. D., Coates, R. J., Daling, J. R., Gammon, M. D., Malone, K. E., Schoenberg, J. B. & Brinton, L. A. (2003). Breast cancers among very young premenopausal women (United States). *Cancer Causes and Control, 14*, 151–160.

Altman, L. K. (2005). Study challenges abstinence as crucial to AIDS strategy. *New York Times*, February 24.

Alvarez, W. A. & Freinhar, J. P. (1991). A prevalence study of bestiality (zoophilia) in psychiatric in-patients, medical in-patients, and psychiatric staff. *International Journal of Psychosomatics, 38*, 45–47.

Amato, P. R. (2000). The consequences of divorce for adults and children. *Journal of Marriage and the Family, 62*, 1269–1287.

Amberson, J. I. & Hoon, P. W. (1985). Hemodynamics of sequential orgasm. *Archives of Sexual Behavior, 14*, 351–360.

American Academy of Family Physicians. (2004). *Vaginal estrogen preparations for relief of atrophic vaginitis.* (http://www.aafp.org/afp/20040501/cochrane.html)

American Academy of Pediatrics. (1995). Sexuality, contraception, and the media. *Pediatrics, 95,* 298–300.

American Academy of Pediatrics. (2004). Age terminology during the perinatal period. *Pediatrics, 114,* 1362–1364.

American Academy of Pediatrics. (2005) *Breastfeeding and the use of human milk.* (http://aappolicy.aappublications.org/cgi/content/full/pediatrics;115/2/496)

American Academy of Pediatrics. (2006). Menstruation in girls and adolescents: Using the menstrual cycle as a vital sign. *Pediatrics, 118,* 2245–2250.

American Academy of Pediatrics. (2007a). Cord blood banking for potential future transplantation. *Pediatrics, 119,* 165–170.

American Academy of Pediatrics. (2007b). *Should we have our son circumcised?* (http://www.aap.org/publiced/BR_Circumcision.htm)

American Association of Retired Persons. (1999). *AARP/Modern maturity sexuality survey.* (http://research.aarp.org/health/mmsexsurvey_1.html)

American Association of University Women. (2001). *Hostile hallways: Bullying, teasing, and sexual harassment in school.* (http://www.aauw.org/member_center/publications/HostileHallways/hostilehallways.pdf)

American Cancer Society. (2007). *Breast reconstruction after mastectomy.* (http://www.cancer.org/docroot/CRI/content/CRI_2_6X_Breast_Reconstruction_After_Mastectomy_5.asp)

American College of Obstetricians and Gynecologists. (2002). *Medical experts still recommend mammography.* (www.acog.org/from_home/publications/press_releases/nr02-03-02.htm)

American College of Obstetricians and Gynecologists. (2007). *New recommendations for Down syndrome: Screening should be offered to all pregnant women.* (http://www.acog.org/from_home/publications/press_releases/nr01-02-07-1.cfm)

American Prosecutors Research Institute. (2008). *State rape statutes.* (http://www.ndaa.org/pdf/vaw_rape_statute.pdf)

American Psychiatric Association. (2000). *Diagnostic and statistical manual of mental disorders, 4th edition, text revision (DSM-IV-TR 2000).* American Psychiatric Association.

American Psychiatric Association. (2008). *Report of the APA Task Force on the sexualization of girls.* (http://www.apa.org/pi/wpo/sexualizationsum.html)

American Psychological Association. (2000). *Guidelines for psychotherapy with lesbian, gay, and bisexual clients.* (http://www.apa.org/pi/lgbc/publications/guidelines.html)

American Psychological Association. (2004). *Sexual orientation, parents, and children.* (http://www.apa.org/pi/lgbc/policy/parents.html)

American Social Health Association. (2006). *STD/STI statistics: Fast facts.* (http://www.ashastd.org/learn/learn_statistics.cfm)

American Society for Reproductive Medicine. (2004). *Guidelines of number of embryos transferred.* (http://www.asrm.org/Media/Practice/NoEmbryosTransferred.pdf)

American Society for Reproductive Medicine. (2007). Financial compensation of oocyte donors. *Fertility and Sterility, 88,* 305–309.

American Society for Reproductive Medicine. (2008). *Frequently asked questions about infertility.* (http://www.asrm.org/Patients/faqs.html)

American Society of Anesthesiologists. (2007). *Practice guidelines for obstetric anesthesia.* (http://www.guideline.gov/summary/summary.aspx?ss=15&doc_id=10807&nbr=5632)

Amstey, M. S. (1994). The political history of syphilis and its application to the AIDS epidemic. *Womens Health Issues, 4,* 16–19.

Andersen, A. G., Jensen, T. K., Carlsen, E., Jorgensen, N., Andersson, A. M., Krarup, T., Keiding, N. & Skakkebaek, N. E. (2000). High frequency of sub-optimal semen quality in an unselected population of young men. *Human Reproduction, 15,* 366–372.

Anderson, G. L. & 43 others. (2004). Effects of conjugated equine estrogen in postmenopausal women with hysterectomy: the Women's Health Initiative randomized controlled trial. *JAMA, 291,* 1701–1712.

Anderson, P. B. & Struckman-Johnson, C. (Eds.) (1998). *Sexually aggressive women: Current perspectives and controversies.* Guildford Press.

Anderson, R. H., Fleming, D. E., Rhees, R. W. & Kinghorn, E. (1986). Relationships between sexual activity, plasma testosterone, and the volume of the sexually dimorphic nucleus of the preoptic area in prenatally stressed and non-stressed rats. *Brain Research, 370,* 1–10.

Andersson, A. M., Toppari, J., Haavisto, A. M., Petersen, J. H., Simell, T., Simell, O. & Skakkebaek, N. E. (1998). Longitudinal reproductive hormone profiles in infants: peak of inhibin B levels in infant boys exceeds levels in adult men. *Journal of Clinical Endocrinology and Metabolism, 83,* 675–681.

Andrews, L. R. (2002). Letter to the Editor. *New York Times,* July 5.

Anonymous (1999). Confessions of a LUG. *Cincinnati CityBeat,* August 26.

Antiretroviral Therapy Cohort Collaboration. (2008). Life expectancy of individuals on combination antiretroviral therapy in high-income countries: A collaborative analysis of 14 cohort studies. *Lancet, 372,* 293–299.

Anzaldúa, G. & Moraga, C. (Eds.) (1981). *This bridge called my back: Writings by radical women of color.* Kitchen Table/Women of Color.

Apfelbaum, B. (2000). Retarded ejaculation: a much-misunderstood syndrome. In S. R. Leiblum and R. C. Rosen (Eds.), *Principles and practice of sex therapy.* (3rd ed.). Guilford Press.

Apicella, C. L., Feinberg, D. R. & Marlowe, F. W. (2007). Voice pitch predicts reproductive success in male hunter-gatherers. *Biology Letters, 3,* 682–684.

Archer, J. (2004). Sex differences in aggression in real-world settings: A meta-analytic review. *Review of General Psychology, 8,* 291–322.

Arden, M. A. & Dye, L. (1998). The assessment of menstrual synchrony: comment on Weller and Weller (1997). *Journal of Comparative Psychology, 112,* 323–324; discussion 325–326.

Arevalo, M., Jennings, V., Nikula, M. & Sinai, I. (2004). Efficacy of the new TwoDay Method of family planning. *Fertility and Sterility, 82,* 885–892.

Aries, P. (1965). *Centuries of childhood: A social history of family life.* Random House.

Arnold, A. P., Xu, J., Grisham, W., Chen, X., Kim, Y. H. & Itoh, Y. (2004). Minireview: Sex chromosomes and brain sexual differentiation. *Endocrinology, 145,* 1057–1062.

Ascherson, B. (1996). *Black Sea: The birthplace of civilization and barbarism.* Vintage.

Associated Press. (1996). *Husband seeks divorce over on-line affair.* (http://www.lectlaw.com/files/fam22.htm)

Associated Press. (1999). Sex abuse charges against former day-care operator dismissed. *News-Times (Danbury, CT),* September 23.

Associated Press. (2004a). *Gay couples exchange vows in Massachusetts.* (http://www.msnbc.msn.com/id/4991967/)

Associated Press. (2004b). *In abortion debate, Mississippi shows how far a state can go with array of restrictions.* (http://www.kansascity.com/mld/kansascity/news/local/10508851.htm)

Associated Press. (2004c). *Kelli White accepts two-year ban for steroid use.* (http://www.wkrn.com/Global/story.asp?S=1883322&nav=1ugQNHo3)

Associated Press. (2005). *School steroid use silent, rampant.* (http://wireservice.wired.com/wired/story.asp?section=Breaking&storyId=986565&tw=wn_wire_story)

Associated Press. (2007a). *College students face sticker shock for birth control pills as companies end discounts.* (http://www.tucsoncitizen.com/ss/byauthor/45951)

Associated Press. (2007b). *Georgia sex offender housing restriction overturned.* (http://www.msnbc.msn.com/id/21917363/)

Associated Press. (2007c) *Man sentenced for role in Asian prostitution ring.* (https://www.examiner.com/a-1585287~Man_sentenced_for_role_in_Asian_prostition_ring.html)

Associated Press. (2007d). Paper: 8 men claim encounters with Craig. *Washington Post,* December 2.

Associated Press. (2007e). *Track star admitted to doping, will return prize money.* (http://sportsillustrated.cnn.com/2007/more/11/23/jones.annulled.ap/index.html)

Associated Press. (2008a). Bar-Jonah dies in prison. *Billings Gazette,* April 14.

Associated Press. (2008b). Feds outline steroids case vs. cyclist. *New York Times,* March 6.

Associated Press. (2008c). *Ruling ending "virgin" marriage shocks France.* (http://www.thestar.com/News/World/article/437106)

Association for the Treatment of Sexual Offenders. (1997). *Anti-androgen therapy and surgical castration.* (http://www.atsa.com/ppantiandro.html)

Association of Gay and Lesbian Psychiatrists. (2008). *AGLP online referral system.* (http://web.memberclicks.com/mc/page.do?sitePageId=31371&orgId=aglp)

Atashili, J., Poole, C., Ndumbe, P. M., Adimora, A. A. & Smith, J. S. (2008). Bacterial vaginosis and HIV acquisition: a meta-analysis of published studies. *AIDS, 22,* 1493–1501.

Atkins, D. (Ed.) (1999). *Lesbian sex scandals: Sexual practices, identities, and politics.* Haworth.

Auger, J., Kunstmann, J. M., Czyglik, F. & Jouannet, P. (1995). Decline in semen quality among fertile men in Paris during the past 20 years. *New England Journal of Medicine, 332,* 281–285.

AVERT. (2008). *AIDS orphans.* (http://www.avert.org/aidsorphans.htm)

Avis, N. E. (2000). Sexual function and aging in men and women: community and population-based studies. *Journal of Gender-Specific Medicine, 3,* 37–41.

Avis, N. E., Stellato, R., Crawford, S., Bromberger, J., Ganz, P., Cain, V. & Kagawa-Singer, M. (2001). Is there a menopausal syndrome? Menopausal status and symptoms across racial/ethnic groups. *Social Science and Medicine, 52,* 345–356.

Avis, N. E., Zhao, X., Johannes, C. B., Ory, M., Brockwell, S. & Greendale, G. A. (2005). Correlates of sexual function among multiethnic middle-aged women: results from the Study of Women's Health Across the Nation (SWAN). *Menopause, 12,* 385–398.

Bagatell, C. J., Heiman, J. R., Rivier, J. E. & Bremner, W. J. (1994). Effects of endogenous testosterone and estradiol on sexual behavior in normal young men. *Journal of Clinical Endocrinology and Metabolism, 78,* 711–716.

Bagby, D. (2008). Proud "mama's boys." *Southern Voice,* May 9.

Bailey, A. A. & Hurd, P. L. (2005). Finger length ratio (2D:4D) correlates with physical aggression in men but not in women. *Biological Psychology, 68,* 215–222.

Bailey, J. M. & Oberschneider, M. (1997). Sexual orientation and professional dance. *Archives of Sexual Behavior, 26,* 433–444.

Bailey, J. M. & Zucker, K. J. (1995). Childhood sex-typed behavior and sexual orientation: A conceptual analysis and quantitative review. *Developmental Psychology, 31,* 43–55.

Bailey, J. M. (2003). *The man who would be queen: The science of gender-bending and transsexualism.* Joseph Henry Press.

Bailey, J. M., Gaulin, S., Agyei, Y. & Gladue, B. A. (1994). Effects of gender and sexual orientation on evolutionarily relevant aspects of human mating psychology. *Journal of Personality and Social Psychology, 66,* 1081–1093.

Bailey, J. M., Kim, P. Y., Hills, A. & Linsenmeier, J. A. (1997). Butch, femme, or straight acting? Partner preferences of gay men and lesbians. *Journal of Personality and Social Psychology, 73,* 960–973.

Bailey, R. C., Plummer, F. A. & Moses, S. (2001). Male circumcision and HIV prevention: current knowledge and future research directions. *The Lancet Infectious Diseases, 1,* 223–231.

Bakker, J., Brand, T., van Ophemert, J. & Slob, A. K. (1993). Hormonal regulation of adult partner preference behavior in neonatally ATD-treated male rats. *Behavioral Neuroscience, 107,* 480–487.

Baldwin, J. I. & Baldwin, J. D. (2000). Heterosexual anal intercourse: an understudied, high-risk sexual behavior. *Archives of Sexual Behavior, 29,* 357–373.

Balter, M. (1999). Scientific cross-claims fly in continuing beef war. *Science, 284,* 1453–1455.

Bancroft, J. (Ed.) (2003). *Sexual development in childhood.* Indiana University Press.

Bancroft, J., Herbenick, D. L. & Reynolds, M. A. (2003a). Masturbation as a marker of sexual development. In J. Bancroft (Ed.), *Sexual development in childhood.* Indiana University Press.

Bancroft, J., Loftus, J. & Long, J. S. (2003b). Distress about sex: a national survey of women in heterosexual relationships. *Archives of Sexual Behavior, 32,* 193–208.

Bandura, A. (1969). Social-learning theory of identificatory processes. In D.A. Goslin (Ed.), *Handbook of socialization theory and research.* Rand McNally.

Barash, D. P. & Lipton, J. E. (2001). *The myth of monogamy: Fidelity and infidelity in animals and people.* W.H. Freeman.

Barbaree, H. E. (2008). Sexual deviance over the lifespan. In D. R. Laws and W. T. O'Donohue (Eds.), *Sexual deviance: Theory, assessment, and treatment* (2nd ed.). Guilford Press.

Barker, R. (1987). *The green-eyed marriage: Surviving jealous relationships.* Free Press.

Barnes, S. L. (2001). Stressors and strengths: A theoretical and practical examination of nuclear, single-parent, and augmented African American families. *Families in Society, 82,* 449–460.

Barnhart, K., Furman, I. & Devoto, L. (1995). Attitudes and practice of couples regarding sexual relations during the menses and spotting. *Contraception, 51,* 93–98.

Barrie, D. (director) (1999). In excess: The death of Michael Hutchence (documentary film, Channel 4, U.K.)

Bartels, A. & Zeki, S. (2000). The neural basis of romantic love. *Neuroreport, 11,* 3829–3834.

Bartels, A. & Zeki, S. (2004). The neural correlates of maternal and romantic love. *Neuroimage, 21,* 1155–1166.

Baseman, J. G. & Koutsky, L. A. (2005). The epidemiology of human papillomavirus infections. *Journal of Clinical Virology, 32 Suppl 1,* S16–24.

Baskin, L. S. (2004). Hypospadias. *Advances in Experimental Medicine and Biology, 545,* 3–22.

Basson, R. (2000). The female sexual response: a different model. *Journal of Sex and Marital Therapy, 26,* 51–65.

Basson, R. (2001). Human sex-response cycles. *Journal of Sex and Marital Therapy, 27,* 33–43.

Basson, R. (2007). Sexual desire/arousal disorders in women. In S. R. Leiblum (Ed.), *Principles and practice of sex therapy.* (4th ed.). Guilford Press.

Basson, R., McInnes, R., Smith, M. D., Hodgson, G. & Koppiker, N. (2002). Efficacy and safety of sildenafil citrate in women with sexual dysfunction associated with female sexual arousal disorder. *Journal of Womens Health & Gender-Based Medicine, 11,* 367–377.

Baumeister, R. F. & Dhavale, D. (2001). The two sides of romantic rejection. In M. R. Leary (Ed.), *Interpersonal rejection.* Oxford University Press.

Baumeister, R. F. & Tice, D. M. (2000). *The social dimension of sex.* Allyn and Bacon.

Baumeister, R. F., Wotman, S. R. & Stillwell, A. M. (1993). Unrequited love: On heartbreak, anger, guilt, scriptlessness, and humiliation. *Journal of Personality and Social Psychology, 64,* 377–394.

Baumgardner, J. & Richards, A. (2000). *Manifesta: Young women, feminism, and the future.* Farrar, Straus and Giroux.

Bawer, B. (1993). *A place at the table: The gay individual in American society.* Poseidon.

Bayer, R. (1981). *Homosexuality and American psychiatry: The politics of diagnosis.* Princeton University Press.

Bazelon, E. (2007). Is there a post-abortion syndrome? *New York Times,* January 21.

BBC News. (2004). *Cheney rejects gay marriage ban.* (http://news.bbc.co.uk/2/hi/americas/3596732.stm)

BBC News. (2008). *Parted-at-birth twins "married."* (http://news.bbc.co.uk/2/hi/uk_news/7182817.stm)

Becker, A. E. (2004). Television, disordered eating, and young women in Fiji: Negotiating body image and identity during rapid social change. *Culture, Medicine and Psychiatry, 28,* 533–559.

Behre, H. M., Kuhlage, J., Gassner, C., Sonntag, B., Schem, C., Schneider, H. P. & Nieschlag, E. (2000). Prediction of ovulation by urinary hormone measurements with the home use ClearPlan Fertility Monitor: comparison with transvaginal ultrasound scans and serum hormone measurements. *Human Reproduction, 15,* 2478–2482.

Beil, L. (2007). Abstinence education faces uncertain future. *New York Times,* July 18.

Beit-Hallahmi, B. (1985). Dangers of the vagina. *British Journal of Medical Psychology, 58,* 351–356.

Belizan, J. M., Althabe, F. & Cafferata, M. L. (2007). Health consequences of the increasing caesarean section rates. *Epidemiology, 18,* 485–486.

Bell, A. P. & Weinberg, M. S. (1978). *Homosexualities: A study of diversity in men and women.* Simon and Schuster.

Belzer, E., Whipple, B. & Moger, W. (1984). A female ejaculation. *Journal of Sex Research, 20,* 403–406.

Bem, S. L. (1974). The measurement of psychological androgyny. *Journal of Consulting and Clinical Psychology, 42,* 151–162.

Bem, S. L. (1981). Gender schema theory: A cognitive account of sex typing. *Psychological Review, 103,* 320–335.

Bem, S. L. (1989). Genital knowledge and gender constancy in preschool children. *Child Development, 60,* 649–662.

Benedetti, J., Corey, L. & Ashley, R. (1994). Recurrence rates in genital herpes after symptomatic first-episode infection. *Annals of Internal Medicine, 121,* 847–854.

Bentlage, B. & Eich, T. (2007). *Hymen repair on the Arab Internet.* (http://www.isim.nl/files/Review_19/Review_19–20.pdf)

Bentovim, A. (1993). Children and young people as abusers. In A. Hollows and H. Armstrong (Eds.), *Children and young people as abusers: An agenda for action.* National Children's Bureau.

Berdahl, J. L. (2007). The sexual harassment of uppity women. *Journal of Applied Psychology, 92,* 425–437.

Berenbaum, S. A. & Bailey, J. M. (2003). Effects on gender identity of prenatal androgens and genital appearance: evidence from girls with congenital adrenal hyperplasia. *Journal of Clinical Endocrinology and Metabolism, 88,* 1102–1106.

Berenbaum, S. A. & Snyder, E. (1995). Early hormonal influences on childhood sex-typed activity and playmate preferences: Implications for the development of sexual orientation. *Developmental Psychology, 31,* 31–42.

Berger, B. J., Kolton, S., Zenilman, J. M., Cummings, M. C., Feldman, J. & McCormack, W. M. (1995). Bacterial vaginosis in lesbians: a sexually transmitted disease. *Clinical Infectious Diseases, 21,* 1402–1405.

Berglund, H., Lindstrom, P. & Savic, I. (2006). Brain response to putative pheromones in lesbian women. *Proceedings of the National Academy of Sciences of the United States of America, 103,* 8269–8274.

Berlin, F. S. & Malin, H. M. (1991). Media distortion of the public's perception of recidivism and psychiatric rehabilitation. *American Journal of Psychiatry, 148,* 1572–1576.

Bernstein, I. H., Lin, T. D. & McClellan, P. (1982). Cross- vs. within-racial judgments of attractiveness. *Perception and Psychophysics, 32,* 495–503.

Berscheid, E., Dion, K., Hatfield, E. & Walster, G. W. (1971). Physical attractiveness and dating choice: A test of the matching hypothesis. *Journal of Experimental Social Psychology, 7,* 173–189.

Bertone-Johnson, E. R., Hankinson, S. E., Bendich, A., Johnson, S. R., Willett, W. C. & Manson, J. E. (2005). Calcium and vitamin D intake and risk of incident premenstrual syndrome. *Archives of Internal Medicine, 165,* 1246–1252.

Best, K. (1999). *Disabled have many needs for contraception.* (http://www.fhi.org/en/fp/fppubs/network/v19-2/nt1924.html)

Betzig, L. (1989). Causes of conjugal dissolution: A cross-cultural study. *Current Anthropology, 30,* 654–676.

Bevc, I. I. & Silverman, I. I. (2000). Early separation and sibling incest. A test of the revised Westermarck theory. *Evolution and Human Behavior, 21,* 151–161.

Bevier, P. J., Chiasson, M. A., Heffernan, R. T. & Castro, K. G. (1995). Women at a sexually transmitted disease clinic who reported same-sex contact: their HIV seroprevalence and risk behaviors. *American Journal of Public Health, 85,* 1366–1371.

Biale, R. (1984). *Women and Jewish law: An exploration of women's issues in Halakhic sources.* Schocken Books.

Biever, C. (2006). The irresistible rise of cybersex. *New Scientist,* June 15.

Billy, J. O. G., Brewster, K. L. & Grady, W. R. (1994). Contextual effects on the sexual behavior of adolescent women. *Journal of Marriage and the Family, 56,* 387–404.

Binik, Y. M., Bergeron, S. & Khalife, S. (2007). Dyspareunia and vaginismus. In S. R. Leiblum (Ed.), *Principles and practice of sex therapy.* Guilford Press.

Birkhead, T. R. (1998). Sperm competition in birds: mechanisms and functions. In T. R. Birkhead and A. P. Moller (Eds.), *Sperm competition and sexual selection.* Academic Press.

Birkhead, T. R. (2000). *Promiscuity: An evolutionary history of sperm competition.* Harvard University Press.

Biro, F. M., Lucky, A. W., Huster, G. A. & Morrison, J. A. (1990). Hormonal studies and physical maturation in adolescent gynecomastia. *Journal of Pediatrics, 116,* 450–455.

Bisson, M. A. & Levine, T. R. (2007). Negotiating a friends with benefits relationship. *Archives of Sexual Behavior.*

Bittles, A. H. (2004). Genetic aspects of inbreeding and incest. In A. P. Wolf and W. H. Durham (Eds.), *Inbreeding, incest, and the incest taboo.* Stanford University Press.

Black, D. L. & Lichter, D. T. (2004). Homogamy among dating, cohabiting, and married couples. *Sociological Review, 45,* 719–737.

Blanchard, R. & Hucker, S. J. (1991). Age, transvestism, bondage, and concurrent paraphilic activities in 117 fatal cases of autoerotic asphyxia. *British Journal of Psychiatry, 159,* 371–377.

Blanchard, R. (1993). Varieties of autogynephilia and their relationship to gender dysphoria. *Archives of Sexual Behavior, 22,* 241–251.

Blanchard, R., Barbaree, H. E., Bogaert, A. F., Dickey, R., Klassen, P., Kuban, M. E. & Zucker, K. J. (2000). Fraternal birth order and sexual orientation in pedophiles. *Archives of Sexual Behavior, 29,* 463–478.

Blanchard, R., Kuban, M. E., Blak, T., Cantor, J. M., Klassen, P. & Dickey, R. (2006). Phallometric comparison of pedophilic interest in nonadmitting sexual offenders against stepdaughters, biological daughters, other biologically related girls, and unrelated girls. *Sexual Abuse, 18,* 1–14.

Blanchard, R., Watson, M. S., Choy, A., Dickey, R., Klassen, P., Kuban, M. & Ferren, D. J. (1999). Pedophiles: mental retardation, maternal age, and sexual orientation. *Archives of Sexual Behavior, 28,* 111–127.

Blumstein, P. & Schwartz, P. (1983). *American couples: Money, work, sex.* Morrow.

Bocij, P. (2008). *Cyberstalking: Harassment in the Internet age and how to protect your family.* Praeger.

Boden, J. M. & Horwood, L. J. (2006). Self-esteem, risky sexual behavior, and pregnancy in a New Zealand birth cohort. *Archives of Sexual Behavior, 35,* 549–560.

Bogaert, A. F. (2004). Asexuality: prevalence and associated factors in a national probability sample. *Journal of Sex Research, 41,* 279–287.

Bohlen, D., Hugonnet, C. L., Mills, R. D., Weise, E. S. & Schmid, H. P. (2000). Five meters of H(2)O: the pressure at the urinary bladder neck during human ejaculation. *Prostate, 44,* 339–341.

Bornstein, K. (1994). *Gender outlaw: On men, women, and the rest of us.* Routledge.

Bortz, W. M., 2nd, Wallace, D. H. & Wiley, D. (1999). Sexual function in 1,202 aging males: differentiating aspects. *Journals of Gerontology Series A, Biological Sciences and Medical Sciences, 54,* M237–241.

Boswell, J. (1980). *Christianity, Social Tolerance, and Homosexuality.* University of Chicago Press.

Bowlby, J. (1973). *Attachment and loss: Volume 3: Separation.* Basic Books.

Bowlby, J. (1988). *A secure base: Parent-child attachment and healthy human development.* Basic Books.

Bozon, M. (2001). Sexuality, gender, and the couple: A sociohistorical perspective. *Annual Review of Sex Research, 12,* 1–32.

Bradford, J. M. (2001). The neurobiology, neuropharmacology, and pharmacological treatment of the paraphilias and compulsive sexual behaviour. *Canadian Journal of Psychiatry Revue Canadienne de Psychiatrie, 46,* 26–34.

Bradford, J. M. & Pawlak, A. (1993). Double-blind placebo crossover study of cyproterone acetate in the treatment of the paraphilias. *Archives of Sexual Behavior, 22,* 383–402.

Brahmbhatt, H., Kigozi, G., Wabwire-Mangen, F., Serwadda, D., Sewankambo, N., Lutalo, T., Wawer, M. J., Abramowsky, C., Sullivan, D. & Gray, R. (2003). The effects of placental malaria on mother-to-child HIV transmission in Rakai, Uganda. *AIDS, 17,* 2539–2541.

Braun, C., Gründl, M., Marberger, C. & Scherber, C. (2001). *Beautycheck: babyfaceness.* (http://www.uni-regensburg.de/Fakultaeten/phil_Fak_II/Psychologie/Psy_II/beautycheck/english/kindchenschema/kindchenschema.htm)

Brawer, M. K. (2004). Testosterone replacement in men with andropause: an overview. *Reviews in Urology, 6 Suppl 6,* S9–S15.

Bray, J. H. (1999). From marriage to remarriage and beyond: Finding from the Developmental Issues in Stepfamilies research project. In E. M. Hetherington (Ed.), *Coping with divorce, single parenting, and remarriage.* Lawrence Erlbaum Associates.

Bressler, E. & Balshine, S. (2006). The influence of humor on desirability. *Evolution and Human Behavior, 27,* 29–39.

Bressler, E., Martin, R. & Balshine, S. (2006). Production and appreciation of humor as sexually selected traits. *Evolution and Human Behavior, 27,* 121–130.

Bretschneider, J. G. & McCoy, N. L. (1988). Sexual interest and behavior in healthy 80- to 102-year-olds. *Archives of Sexual Behavior, 17,* 109–129.

Briere, J. & Runtz, M. (1989). University males' sexual interest in children: predicting potential indices of "pedophilia" in a non-forensic sample. *Child Abuse and Neglect, 13,* 65–75.

Bright, S. (1999). *Susie Sexpert's lesbian sex world* (rev. ed.). Cleis Press.

Brink, P. J. (1989). The fattening room among the Annang of Nigeria. *Medical Anthropology, 12,* 131–143.

British Broadcasting Corporation. (2002). *Human instinct: Deepest desires.* (http://www.bbc.co.uk/science/humanbody/tv/humaninstinct/programme2.shtml)

Brookoff, D., O'Brien, K. K., Cook, C. S., Thompson, T. D. & Williams, C. (1997). Characteristics of participants in domestic violence. Assessment at the scene of domestic assault. *JAMA, 277,* 1369–1373.

Brooten, B. (2000). *The Bible and love between women.* (www.brandeis.edu/projects/fse/christianity/chris-essays/chris-ess-brooten.pdf)

Brooten, B. (2008). *The Feminist Sexual Ethics Project.* (www.brandeis.edu/projects/fse/index.html)

Brotman, R. M., Klebanoff, M. A., Nansel, T. R., Andrews, W. W., Schwebke, J. R., Zhang, J., Yu, K. F., Zenilman, J. M. & Scharfstein, D. O. (2008). A longitudinal study of vaginal douching and bacterial vaginosis—a marginal structural modeling analysis. *American Journal of Epidemiology, 168,* 188–196.

Brown, B. B. (1999). "You're going with who?!" Peer group influences on adolescent romantic relationships. In W. Furman et al. (Eds.), *The development of romantic relationships in adolescence.* Cambridge University Press.

Brown, P. L. (2007). Gay enclaves face prospect of being passé. *New York Times,* October 30.

Brownmiller, S. (1975). *Against our will: Men, women and rape.* Simon and Schuster.

Brückner, H. & Bearman, P. S. (2005). After the promise: The STD consequences of adolescent virginity pledges. *Journal of Adolescent Health, 36,* 271–278.

Buchwald, E., Fletcher, P. R. & Roth, M. (Eds.) (2004). *Transforming a rape culture.* (2nd ed.) Milkweed Editions.

Bukovsky, A., Caudle, M. R., Svetlikova, M., Wimalasena, J., Ayala, M. E. & Dominguez, R. (2005). Oogenesis in adult mammals, including humans: a review. *Endocrine, 26,* 301–316.

Bullough, V. L. (1981). Age at menarche: A misunderstanding. *Science, 213,* 365–366.

Bullough, V. L. (1994). *Science in the Bedroom: A History of Sex Research.* Basic Books.

Bullough, V. L. & Bullough, B. (1995). *Sexual attitudes: Myths and realities.* Prometheus Books.

Bumpass, L. & Sweet, J. (1989). National estimates of cohabitation. *Demography, 26,* 615–625.

Bureau of Justice Statistics. (2006). *National Crime Victimization Survey violent crime trends, 1973–2005.* (http://www.ojp.usdoj.gov/bjs/glance/tables/viortrdtab.htm)

Bureau of Justice Statistics. (2007a). *Intimate partner violence in the U.S.* (http://www.ojp.usdoj.gov/bjs/intimate/circumstances.htm)

Bureau of Justice Statistics. (2007b). *There has been a decline in homicides of intimates, especially male victims.* (http://www.ojp.usdoj.gov/bjs/homicide/intimates.htm)

Bureau of Justice Statistics. (2008). *HIV in prisons, 2006.* (http://www.ojp.usdoj.gov/bjs/pub/html/hivp/2006/hivp06.htm)

Burgess, A. W. & Holmstrom, L. L. (1974). Rape trauma syndrome. *American Journal of Psychiatry, 131,* 981–986.

Burgess, A. W. & Holmstrom, L. L. (1979). Rape: sexual disruption and recovery. *American Journal of Orthopsychiatry, 49,* 648–657.

Burgoyne, P. S., Thornhill, A. R., Boudrean, S. K., Darling, S. M., Bishop, C. E. & Evans, E. P. (1995). The genetic basis of XX-XY differences present before gonadal sex differenti-

ation in the mouse. *Philosophical Transactions of the Royal Society of London Series B: Biological Sciences, 350,* 253–260 discussion 260–251.

Burkman, R. T. (2004). The transdermal contraceptive system. *American Journal of Obstetrics and Gynecology, 190,* S49–S53.

Burmeister, S. S., Jarvis, E. D. & Fernald, R. D. (2005). Rapid behavioral and genomic responses to social opportunity. *PLoS Biology, 3,* e363.

Buss, D. M. & Schmitt, D. P. (1993). Sexual strategies theory: A contextual evolutionary analysis of human mating. *Psychological Review, 100,* 204–232.

Buss, D. M. (1989). Sex differences in human mate preference: Evolutionary hypothesis tested in 37 cultures. *Behavioral and Brain Sciences, 12,* 1–149.

Buss, D. M. (1995). *The evolution of desire: Strategies of human mating.* Basic Books.

Buss, D. M. (2000). *The dangerous passion: Why jealousy is as necessary as love and sex.* The Free Press.

Bussey, K. & Bandura, A. (1984). Influence of gender constancy and social power on sex-linked modeling. *Journal of Personality and Social Psychology, 47,* 1292–1302.

Buster, J. E., Kingsberg, S. A., Aguirre, O., Brown, C., Breaux, J. G., Buch, A., Rodenberg, C. A., Wekselman, K. & Casson, P. (2005). Testosterone patch for low sexual desire in surgically menopausal women: a randomized trial. *Obstetrics and Gynecology, 105,* 944–952.

Byne, W. (1998). The medial preoptic and anterior hypothalamic regions of the rhesus monkey: cytoarchitectonic comparison with the human and evidence for sexual dimorphism. *Brain Research, 793,* 346–350.

Byne, W. (2006). Book review: *Human Sexuality,* by Simon leVay and Sharon M. Valente. *JAMA, 295,* 2539.

Byne, W., Tobet, S., Mattiace, L. A., Lasco, M. S., Kemether, E., Edgar, M. A., Morgello, S., Buchsbaum, M. S. & Jones, L. B. (2001). The interstitial nuclei of the human anterior hypothalamus: an investigation of variation with sex, sexual orientation, and HIV status. *Hormones and Behavior, 40,* 86–92.

Byrd, J. E., Hyde, J. S., DeLamater, J. D. & Plant, E. A. (1998). Sexuality during pregnancy and the year postpartum. *Journal of Family Practice, 47,* 305–308.

Cado, S. & Leitenberg, H. (1990). Guilt reactions to sexual fantasies during intercourse. *Archives of Sexual Behavior, 19,* 49–63.

Cahill, L. (2005). His brain, her brain. *Scientific American, 292,* 49–63.

California Coalition Against Sexual Assault. (2005) *Rape myths.* (http://www.calcasa.org/34.0.html)

Calikoglu, A. S. (1999). Should boys with micropenis be reared as girls? *Journal of Pediatrics, 134,* 537–538.

Cameron, P. & Biber, H. (1973). Sexual thought throughout the lifespan. *Gerontologist, 13,* 144–147.

Camilleri, J. A. & Quinsey, V. L. (2008). Pedophilia: Assessment and treatment. In D. R. Laws and W. T. O'Donohue (Eds.), *Sexual deviance: Theory, assessment, and treatment* (2nd ed.). Guilford Press.

Campbell, W. (2001). The gigolo blues. *Hustler,* April.

Canada.com. (2007). *C-section rate in Canada continues upward trend.* (http://www.canada.com/topics/bodyandhealth/story.html?id=cd328013-086c-4ad7-a03d-6211b1cf1f2d)

Canadian Paediatric Society. (2004). *Circumcision: Information for parents.* (http://www.caringforkids.cps.ca/babies/Circumcision.htm)

Candib, L. M. (2001). A new view of women's sexual problems: A family physician's response. In E. Kaschak and L. Tiefer (Eds.), *A new view of women's sexual problems.* Haworth Press.

Canli, T., Desmond, J. E., Zhao, Z. & Gabrieli, J. D. (2002). Sex differences in the neural basis of emotional memories. *Proceedings of the National Academy of Sciences of the United States of America, 99,* 10789–10794.

Cann, A. (1993). Evaluative expectations and the gender schema: Is failed inconsistency better? *Sex Roles, 28,* 667–678.

Cantor, J. M., Blanchard, R., Christensen, B. K., Dickey, R., Klassen, P. E., Beckstead, A. L., Blak, T. & Kuban, M. E. (2004). Intelligence, memory, and handedness in pedophilia. *Neuropsychology, 18,* 3–14.

Cantor, J. M., Kabani, N., Christensen, B. K., Zipursky, R. B., Barbaree, H. E., Dickey, R., Klassen, P. E., Mikulis, D. J., Kuban, M. E., Blak, T., Richards, B. A., Hanratty, M. K. & Blanchard, R. (2008). Cerebral white matter deficiencies in pedophilic men. *Journal of Psychiatric Research, 42,* 167–183.

Capecchi, C. (2007). Man faces federal charges in a sex ring in Minnesota. *New York Times,* December 2007.

Carey, A. R. & Staimer, M. (1997). Effects of pulling "Ellen" ads. *USA Today,* April 29.

Carlsen, E., Giwercman, A., Keiding, N. & Skakkebaek, N. E. (1992). Evidence for decreasing quality of semen during past 50 years. *British Medical Journal. 305,* 609–613.

Carlson, A. D., Obeid, J. S., Kanellopoulou, N., Wilson, R. C. & New, M. I. (1999). Congenital adrenal hyperplasia: update on prenatal diagnosis and treatment. *Journal of Steroid Biochemistry and Molecular Biology, 69,* 19–29.

Carmichael, M. S., Warburton, V. L., Dixen, J. & Davidson, J. M. (1994). Relationships among cardiovascular, muscular, and oxytocin responses during human sexual activity. *Archives of Sexual Behavior, 23,* 59–79.

Carnes, P. (2001). *Out of the shadows: Understanding sexual addiction.* (3rd ed.). Hazelden.

Carpenter, C. L., Ross, R. K., Paganini-Hill, A. & Bernstein, L. (2003). Effect of family history, obesity and exercise on breast cancer risk among postmenopausal women. *International Journal of Cancer, 106,* 96–102.

Carpenter, L. M. (2005). *Virginity loss: An intimate portrait of first sexual experiences.* New York University Press.

Carpenter, L. M., Nathanson, C. A. & Kim, Y. J. (2008). Physical women, emotional men: gender and sexual satisfaction in midlife. *Archives of Sexual Behavior,* (online publication, DOI 10.1007/s10508-007-9215-y).

Carrasco, D. (Ed.) (2008). *The history of the conquest of New Spain by Bernal Diaz del Castillo.* University of New Mexico Press.

Carroll, J. S. & Doherty, W. J. (2003). Evaluating the effectiveness of premarital prevention programs: A meta-analytic review of outcome research. *Family Relations, 52,* 105–118.

Cart, J. (2001). Utah paying a high price for polygamy. *Los Angeles Times,* September 9.

Carter, C. S. (1998). Neuroendocrine perspectives on social attachment and love. *Psychoneuroendocrinology, 23,* 779–818.

Carter, C. S. & Getz, L. L. (1993). Monogamy and the prairie vole. *Scientific American, 268,* 100–106.

Carter, H. (2007). Teacher's killer found guilty of sex murder on retrial. *Guardian* (London), July 5.

Caspi, A. & Herbener, E. S. (1990). Continuity and change: assortative marriage and the consistency of personality in adulthood. *Journal of Personality and Social Psychology, 58,* 250–258.

Caspi, A., Herbener, E. S. & Ozer, D. J. (1992). Shared experiences and the similarity of personalities: a longitudinal study of married couples. *Journal of Personality and Social Psychology, 62,* 281–291.

Caspi, A., McClay, J., Moffitt, T. E., Mill, J., Martin, J., Craig, I. W., Taylor, A. & Poulton, R. (2002). Role of genotype in the cycle of violence in maltreated children. *Science, 297,* 851–854.

Castellsague, X., Bosch, F. X., Munoz, N., Meijer, C. J., Shah, K. V., de Sanjose, S., Eluf-Neto, J., Ngelangel, C. A., Chichareon, S., Smith, J. S., Herrero, R., Moreno, V. & Franceschi, S. (2002). Male circumcision, penile human papillomavirus infection, and cervical cancer in female partners. *New England Journal of Medicine, 346,* 1105–1112.

Catlin, D. H., Sekera, M. H., Ahrens, B. D., Starcevic, B., Chang, Y. C. & Hatton, C. K. (2004). Tetrahydrogestrinone: discovery, synthesis, and detection in urine. *Rapid Communications in Mass Spectrometry, 18,* 1245–1049.

Cebeci Save, D., Erbaydar, T., Kalaca, S., Hermanci, H., Cali, S. & Karavus, M. (2004). Resistance against contraception or medical contraceptive methods: A qualitative study on women and men in Istanbul. *European Journal of Contraception and Reproductive Health Care, 9,* 94–101.

Centers for Disease Control. (2000). *Preventing the sexual transmission of HIV, the virus that causes AIDS: What you should know about oral sex.* (http://www.cdc.gov/hiv/resources/factsheets/pdf/oralsex.pdf)

Centers for Disease Control. (2001). *First marriage dissolution, divorce, and remarriage.* (http://www.cdc.gov/nchs/data/ad/ad323.pdf)

Centers for Disease Control. (2002a). *Cohabitation, marriage, divorce, and remarriage in the United States.* (http://www.cdc.gov/nchs/data/series/sr_23/sr23_022.pdf)

Centers for Disease Control. (2002b). *HIV/AIDS surveillance report.* (http://www.cdc.gov/hiv/stats/hasr1301.htm)

Centers for Disease Control. (2002c). *Sexually transmitted diseases treatment guidelines.* (http://www.cdc.gov/mmwr/preview/mmwrhtml/rr5106a1.htm)

Centers for Disease Control. (2004a). *Assisted reproductive technology success rates.* (http://www.cdc.gov/reproductivehealth/ART02/index.htm)

Centers for Disease Control. (2004b). *Births: Final data for 2002.* (http://www.cdc.gov/nchs/data/nvsr/nvsr52/nvsr52_10.pdf)

Centers for Disease Control. (2004c). *Genital candidiasis.* (http://www.cdc.gov/ncidod/dbmd/diseaseinfo/candidiasis_gen_g.htm)

Centers for Disease Control. (2004d). *Youth risk behavior surveillance: United States, 2003.* (http://www.cdc.gov/mmwr/PDF/SS/SS5302.pdf)

Centers for Disease Control. (2006a). *Sexually transmitted diseases: Treatment guidelines 2006.* (http://www.cdc.gov/std/treatment/2006/toc.htm)

Centers for Disease Control. (2006b). *STD surveillance 2006: Racial and ethnic minorities.* (http://www.cdc.gov/std/stats/minorities.htm)

Centers for Disease Control. (2007a). *Births: Final data for 2005.* (http://www.cdc.gov/nchs/data/nvsr/nvsr56/nvsr56_06.pdf)

Centers for Disease Control. (2007b). *Chlamydia: CDC fact sheet.* (http://www.cdc.gov/std/Chlamydia/STDFact-Chlamydia.htm)

Centers for Disease Control. (2007c). *Drug use and sexual behaviors reported by adults: United States, 1999–2002.* (http://www.cdc.gov/nchs/data/ad/ad384.pdf)

Centers for Disease Control. (2007d). *Genital herpes: Initial visits to physicians' offices, United States, 1966–2006.* (http://www.cdc.gov/std/stats/figures/figure40.htm)

Centers for Disease Control. (2007e). *Maternal mortality and related concepts.* (http://www.cdc.gov/nchs/data/series/sr_03/sr03_033.pdf)

Centers for Disease Control. (2007f). *One test. Two lives.* (http://www.cdc.gov/hiv/topics/perinatal/1test2lives/qa.htm#)

Centers for Disease Control. (2007g). *STD surveillance 2006.* (http://www.cdc.gov/std/stats/toc2006.htm)

Centers for Disease Control. (2007h). *Syphilis surveillance report.* (http://www.cdc.gov/std/Syphilis2006/Syphilis2006Short.pdf)

Centers for Disease Control. (2008a). *Breastfeeding in the United States: Findings from the National Health and Nutrition Examination Surveys, 1999–2006.* (http://www.cdc.gov/nchs/data/databriefs/db05.pdf)

Centers for Disease Control. (2008b). *Cases of HIV infection and AIDS in the United States and dependent areas, 2006.* (http://www.cdc.gov/hiv/topics/surveillance/resources/reports/2006report/default.htm)

Centers for Disease Control. (2008c). *CDC trials of pre-exposure prophylaxis for HIV prevention.* (http://www.cdc.gov/hiv/resources/Factsheets/prep.htm)

Centers for Disease Control. (2008d). *Deaths: Final data for 2005.* (http://www.cdc.gov/nchs/data/nvsr/nvsr56/nvsr56_10.pdf)

Centers for Disease Control. (2008e). *Hepatitis B.* (http://www.cdc.gov/hepatitis/HepatitisB.htm)

Centers for Disease Control. (2008f). *HIV/AIDS among African Americans.* (http://www.cdc.gov/hiv/topics/aa/resources/factsheets/aa.htm)

Centers for Disease Control. (2008g). *HIV/AIDS statistics and surveillance: Basic statistics.* (http://www.cdc.gov/hiv/topics/surveillance/basic.htm)

Centers for Disease Control. (2008h). *HIV incidence.* (http://www.cdc.gov/hiv/topics/surveillance/incidence.htm)

Centers for Disease Control. (2008i.) *HIV infection in the United States household population age 18–49 years: Results from 1999 to 2006.* (www.cdc.gov/nchs/data/databriefs/db04.pdf)

Centers for Disease Control. (2008j). *Trends in the prevalence of sexual behaviors: National YRBS, 1991–2007.* (http://www.cdc.gov/HealthyYouth/yrbs/pdf/yrbs07_us_sexual_behaviors_trend.pdf)

Central Conference of American Rabbis. (2000). *Resolution on same-gender officiation.* (http://www.ccarnet.org/cgibin/resodisp.pl?file=gender&year=2000)

Chahnazarian, A. (1991). Determinants of the sex ratio at birth: Review of the recent literature. *Social Biology, 35,* 214–235.

Chalett, J. M. & Nerenberg, L. T. (2000). "Blue balls": A diagnostic consideration in testiculoscrotal pain in young adults: A case report and discussion. *Pediatrics, 106,* 843.

Chalmers, K. (2004). Sad end to boy/girl life. *Winnipeg Sun,* May 10.

Chandra, A., Martino, S. C., Collins, R. L., Elliott, M. N., Berry, S. H., Kanouse, D. E. & Miu, A. (2008). Does watching sex on television predict teen pregnancy? Findings from a national longitudinal survey of youth. *Pediatrics, 122,* 1047-1054.

Chantry, K. & Craig, R. J. (1994). Psychological screening of sexually violent offenders with the MCMI. *Journal of Clinical Psychology, 50,* 430–435.

Chaturvedi, A. K., Engels, E. A., Anderson, W. F. & Gillison, M. L. (2008). Incidence trends for human papillomavirus-related and -unrelated oral squamous cell carcinomas in the United States. *Journal of Clinical Oncology, 26,* 612–619.

Chaudhary, P. (2000). *Racism in queer cyberspace: My personal experience in the Gay.com chatrooms.* (http://www.main.org/trikonetejas/queerracism1.html)

Chauncey, G. (1994). *Gay New York: Gender, urban culture and the making of the gay male world.* Basic Books.

Chen, K. K., Chan, S. H., Chang, L. S. & Chan, J. Y. (1997). Participation of paraventricular nucleus of hypothalamus in central regulation of penile erection in the rat. *Journal of Urology, 158,* 238–244.

Cheng, S.-T. (1997). Epidemic genital retraction syndrome: Environmental and personal risk factors in southern China. *Journal of Psychology and Human Sexuality, 9,* 57–70.

Chivers, M. L., Rieger, G., Latty, E. & Michael Bailey, J. (2004). A sex difference in the specificity of sexual arousal. *Psychological Science, 15,* 736–744.

Choi, P. Y. & Pope, H. G., Jr. (1994). Violence toward women and illicit androgenic-anabolic steroid use. *Annals of Clinical Psychiatry, 6,* 21–25.

Christiansen, C. G. & Sandlow, J. I. (2003). Testicular pain following vasectomy: a review of postvasectomy pain syndrome. *Journal of Andrology, 24,* 293–298.

Christopher, F. S. & Kisler, T. S. (2004). Sexual aggression in romantic relationships. In J. H. Harvey et al. (Eds.), *The handbook of sexuality in close relationships.* Lawrence Erlbaum Associates.

Christopher, F. S. & Sprecher, S. (2000). Sexuality in marriage, dating, and other relationships: A decade review. *Journal of Marriage and the Family, 62,* 999–1017.

Chu, H. (2006). Wombs for rent, cheap. *Los Angeles Times.* April 16.

Chun, A. B., Rose, S., Mitrani, C., Silvestre, A. J. & Wald, A. (1997). Anal sphincter structure and function in homosexual males engaging in anoreceptive intercourse. *American Journal of Gastroenterology, 92,* 465–468.

Clark, R. D. & Hatfield, E. (1989). Gender differences in receptivity to sexual offers. *Journal of Psychology and Human Sexuality, 2,* 39–55.

Clark, R. D., III & Hatfield, E. (2003). Love in the afternoon. *Psychological Inquiry, 14,* 227–231.

Clarke, J. (2007). *Older white women join Kenya's sex tourists.* (http://www.reuters.com/article/newsOne/idUSL1434216920071126)

Cleary-Goldman, J. & Robinson, J. N. (2003). The role of episiotomy in current obstetric practice. *Seminars in Perinatology, 27,* 3–12.

Clement, K., Vaisse, C., Lahlou, N., Cabrol, S., Pelloux, V., Cassuto, D., Gourmelen, M., Dina, C., Chambaz, J., Lacorte, J. M., Basdevant, A., Bougneres, P., Lebouc, Y., Froguel, P. & Guy-Grand, B. (1998). A mutation in the human leptin receptor gene causes obesity and pituitary dysfunction. *Nature, 392,* 398–401.

Clutton-Brock, T. (2007). Sexual selection in males and females. *Science, 318,* 1882–1885.

Cnattingius, S., Bergstrom, R., Lipworth, L. & Kramer, M. S. (1998). Prepregnancy weight and the risk of adverse pregnancy outcomes. *New England Journal of Medicine, 338,* 147–152.

CNET News. (2007). *Necrobabes.com leads to murder conviction.* (http://news.cnet.com/Police-Blotter-Necrobabes.com-leads-to-murder-conviction/2100-1047_3-6192232.html)

Coalition Against Trafficking in Women. (2008). *An introduction to CATW.* (http://www.catwinternational.org/about/index.php)

Cohen, F., Kemeny, M. E., Kearney, K. A., Zegans, L. S., Neuhaus, J. M. & Conant, M. A. (1999). Persistent stress as a predictor of genital herpes recurrence. *Archives of Internal Medicine, 159,* 2430–2436.

Colapinto, J. (2000). *As nature made him: The boy who was raised as a girl.* HarperCollins.

Colb, S. F. (2003). *Withdrawing consent during intercourse.* (http://writ.news.findlaw.com/colb/20030115.html)

Colb, S. F. (2006). *A Maryland state court rules that women may not withdraw consent after penetration.* (http://writ.news.findlaw.com/colb/20061115.html)

Cole, L. A., Khanlian, S. A., Sutton, J. M., Davies, S. & Rayburn, W. F. (2004). Accuracy of home pregnancy tests at the time of missed menses. *American Journal of Obstetrics and Gynecology, 190,* 100–105.

Coleman, E. (1996). *What sexual scientists know about compulsive sexual behavior.* (http://www.ssc.wisc.edu/ssss/wssk_csb.htm)

Coleman, M., Ganong, L. & Fine, M. (2000). Reinvestigating marriage: Another decade of progress. *Journal of Marriage and the Family, 62,* 1288–1307.

Collaborative Group on Hormonal Factors in Breast Cancer. (1996). Breast cancer and hormonal contraceptives: collaborative reanalysis of individual data on 53,297 women with breast cancer and 100,239 women without breast cancer from 54 epidemiological studies. *Lancet, 347,* 1713–1727.

Colon, I., Caro, D., Bourdony, C. J. & Rosario, O. (2000). Identification of phthalate esters in the serum of young Puerto Rican girls with premature breast development. *Environmental Health Perspectives, 108,* 895–900.

ColorQ World. (2000). *Racism in queer America.* (http://www.colorq.org/Articles/2000/gayracism.htm)

Coltrane, S. & Adams, M. (2003). The social construction of the divorce "problem": Morality, child victims, and the politics of gender. *Family Relations, 52,* 21–30.

Conaglen, H. M., Suttie, J. M. & Conaglen, J. V. (2003). Effect of deer velvet on sexual function in men and their partners: a double-blind, placebo-controlled study. *Archives of Sexual Behavior, 32,* 271–278.

Congregation for the Doctrine of the Faith. (2003). *Considerations regarding proposals to give legal recognition to unions between homosexual persons.* (http://www.catholic.com/library/homo_union_cdf1.asp)

Connellan, J., Baron-Cohen, S., Wheelwright, S., Batki, A. & Ahluwalia, J. (2001). Sex differences in human neonatal social perception. *Infant Behavior and Development, 23,* 113–118.

Cooke, B. M., Chowanadisai, W. & Breedlove, S. M. (2000). Post-weaning social isolation of male rats reduces the volume of the medial amygdala and leads to deficits in adult sexual behavior. *Behavioural Brain Research, 117,* 107–113.

Coon, J. T., Pittler, M. H. & Ernst, E. (2007). Trifolium pratense isoflavones in the treatment of menopausal hot flushes: a systematic review and meta-analysis. *Phytomedicine, 14,* 153–159.

Cooper, A. (Ed.) (2002). *Sex and the Internet: A guidebook for clinicians.* Brunner-Routledge.

Cordier, S. (2008). Evidence for a role of paternal exposures in developmental toxicity. *Basic & Clinical Pharmacology & Toxicology, 102,* 176–181.

Costa, P. T., Jr., Terracciano, A. & McCrae, R. R. (2001). Gender differences in personality traits across cultures: robust and surprising findings. *Journal of Personality and Social Psychology, 81,* 322–331.

Cowan, G. & Hoffman, C. D. (1986). Gender stereotyping in young children: Evidence to support a concept-learning approach. *Sex Roles, 14,* 211–224.

Cowan, R. S. (1992). Genetic technology and reproductive choice: An ethics for autonomy. In D. J. Kevles and L. Hood (Eds.), *The code of codes: Scientific and social issues in the human genome project.* Harvard University Press.

Cox, D. J. & Maletzky, B. M. (1980). Victims of exhibitionism. In D. J. Cox and R. J. Daitzman (Eds.), *Exhibitionism: Description, assessment, and treatment.* Garland Press.

Cramer, D. W. & Xu, H. (1996). Predicting age at menopause. *Maturitas, 23,* 319–326.

Cramer, D. W., Xu, H. & Harlow, B. L. (1995). Family history as a predictor of early menopause. *Fertility and Sterility, 64,* 740–745.

Creinin, M. D. & Pymar, H. C. (2000). Medical abortion alternatives to mifepristone. *Journal of the American Medical Womens' Association, 55,* 127–132, 150.

Crepault, C. & Couture, M. (1980). Men's erotic fantasies. *Archives of Sexual Behavior, 9,* 565–581.

Crews, D., Grassman, M., & Lindzey, J. (1986). Behavioral facilitation of reproduction in sexual and unisexual whiptail lizards. *Proceedings of the National Academy of Sciences of the United States of America, 83,* 9547–9550.

Crohan, S. E. (1996). Marital quality and conflict across the transition to parenthood in African American and white couples. *Journal of Marriage and the Family, 58,* 933–944.

Crosby, R., Milhausen, R., Sanders, S. A., Graham, C. A. & Yarber, W. L. (2008). Two heads are better than one: the association between condom decision-making and condom use errors and problems. *Sexually Transmitted Infections, 84,* 198–201.

Cupach, W. R. & Spitzberg, B. H. (1998). Obsessive relational intrusion and stalking. In B. H. Spitzberg and W. R. Cupach (Eds.), *The dark side of close relationships.* Lawrence Erlbaum Associates.

Curtis, R. & Miller, K. (1997). Believing another likes or dislikes you: Behavior making the beliefs come true. *Journal of Personality and Social Psychology, 51,* 284–290.

Dabbs, J. M., Jr. & Mohammed, S. (1992). Male and female salivary testosterone concentrations before and after sexual activity. *Physiology and Behavior, 52,* 195–197.

Dahlburg, J.-T. (1994). Where killing baby girls is "no big sin." *Toronto Star,* February 28.

Daling, J. R., Madeleine, M. M., Johnson, L. G., Schwartz, S. M., Shera, K. A., Wurscher, M. A., Carter, J. J., Porter, P. L., Galloway, D. A. & McDougall, J. K. (2004). Human papillomavirus, smoking, and sexual practices in the etiology of anal cancer. *Cancer, 101,* 270–280.

Dalla, R. L. (2000). Exposing the "Pretty Woman" myth: A qualitative examination of the lives of female streetwalking prostitutes. *Journal of Sex Research, 37,* 344–353.

Dalrymple, W. (2008). Serving the goddess. *New Yorker,* August 4.

Darling, C. A., Davidson, J. K., Sr. & Conway-Welch, C. (1990). Female ejaculation: perceived origins, the Grafenberg spot/area, and sexual responsiveness. *Archives of Sexual Behavior, 19,* 29–47.

Darling, C. A., Davidson, J. K., Sr. & Jennings, D. A. (1991). The female sexual response revisited: Understanding the multiorgasmic experience in women. *Archives of Sexual Behavior, 20,* 527–540.

Davey Smith, G., Frankel, S. & Yarnell, J. (1997). Sex and death: are they related? Findings from the Caerphilly Cohort Study. *British Medical Journal, 315,* 1641–1644.

Davies, S. L., Glaser, D. & Kossoff, R. (2000). Children's sexual play and behavior in pre-school settings: staff's perceptions, reports, and responses. *Child Abuse and Neglect, 24,* 1329–1343.

Davies, W. & Wilkinson, L. S. (2006). It is not all hormones: alternative explanations for sexual differentiation of the brain. *Brain Research, 1126,* 36–45.

Davis, D. L. (1996). Cultural sensitivity and the sexual disorders of DSM-IV. In J. E. Mezzich, A. Kleinman, H. Fabrega, Jr., and D. L. Parron (Eds.), *Culture and psychiatric diagnosis.* American Psychiatric Association.

Davis, E. C., Shryne, J. E. & Gorski, R. A. (1995). A revised critical period for the sexual differentiation of the sexually dimorphic nucleus of the preoptic area in the rat. *Neuroendocrinology, 62,* 579–585.

Davis, P. K. (1999). *The power of touch: The basis for survival, health, intimacy, and emotional well-being.* (rev. ed.). Hay House.

Davis, S. R. (2000). Androgens and female sexuality. *Journal of Gender-Specific Medicine, 3,* 36–40.

de Andrade, E., de Mesquita, A. A., Claro Jde, A., de Andrade, P. M., Ortiz, V., Paranhos, M. & Srougi, M. (2007). Study of the efficacy of Korean Red Ginseng in the treatment of erectile dysfunction. *Asian Journal of Andrology, 9,* 241–244.

de Graaf, H. & Rademakers, J. (2006). Sexual behavior or prepubertal children. *Journal of Psychology and Human Sexuality, 18,* 1–21.

de Jonge, F. H., Muntjewerff, J. W., Louwerse, A. L. & van de Poll, N. E. (1988). Sexual behavior and sexual orientation of the female rat after hormonal treatment during various stages of development. *Hormones and Behavior, 22,* 100–115.

De Vaus, D., Qu, L. & Weston, R. (2003). Premarital cohabitation and subsequent marital stability. *Family Matters, Winter,* 34–39.

de Waal, F. B. M. (1995). Bonobo sex and society. *Scientific American, 272* (March), 82–88.

Dean, J., Hackett, G. I., Gentile, V., Pirozzi-Farina, F., Rosen, R. C., Zhao, Y., Warner, M. R. & Beardsworth, A. (2006). Psychosocial outcomes and drug attributes affecting treatment choice in men receiving sildenafil citrate and tadalafil for the treatment of erectile dysfunction: results of a multicenter, randomized, open-label, crossover study. *Journal of Sexual Medicine, 3,* 650–661.

Dean, K. E. & Malamuth, N. M. (1997). Characteristics of men who aggress sexually and of men who imagine aggressing: risk and moderating variables. *Journal of Personality and Social Psychology, 72,* 449–455.

Dear, M. & Sibley, D. (2000). The one-way strategy for sex offenders makes nobody safe. *Los Angeles Times,* October 1.

Deaver, J. B. & McFarland, J. (1917). *The breast: Its anomalies, its diseases, and their treatment.* P. Blakiston's Son and Co.

Declercq, E., Barger, M., Cabral, H. J., Evans, S. R., Kotelchuck, M., Simon, C., Weiss, J. & Heffner, L. J. (2007). Maternal outcomes associated with planned primary cesarean births compared with planned vaginal births. *Obstetrics and Gynecology, 109,* 669–677.

Del Carmen, R. (1990). Assessment of Asian-Americans for family therapy. In F. Serafica et al. (Eds.), *Mental health of ethnic minorities.* Praeger.

DeLamater, J. (1987). A sociological approach. In J. H. Geer and W. T. O'Donohue (Eds.), *Theories of human sexuality.* Plenum.

D'Emilio, J. (1990). Gay politics and community in San Francisco since World War II. In M. Duberman et al. (Eds.), *Hidden from history: Reclaiming the gay and lesbian past.* Meridian Books.

Denizet-Lewis, B. (2004). Friends, friends with benefits and the benefits of the local mall. *New York Times,* May 30.

Denney, N. W., Field, J. K. & Quadagno, D. (1984). Sex differences in sexual needs and desires. *Archives of Sexual Behavior, 13,* 233–245.

Denny, D. & Bolin, A. (1997). *And now for something completely different: An outcome study with surprising results and important implications.* (http://www.symposion.com/ ijt/hbigda/vancouver/denny2.htm)

Derby, C. A., Barbour, M. M., Hume, A. L. & McKinlay, J. B. (2001). Drug therapy and prevalence of erectile dysfunction in the Massachusetts Male Aging Study cohort. *Pharmacotherapy, 21,* 676–683.

Dettwyler, K. A. (1994). *Dancing skeletons: Life and death in West Africa.* Waveland Press.

Diamond, L. M. (2003). Was it a phase? Young women's relinquishment of lesbian/bisexual identities over a 5-year period. *Journal of Personality and Social Psychology, 84,* 352–364.

Diamond, L. M. (2008a). Female bisexuality from adolescence to adulthood: Results from a 10-year longitudinal study. *Developmental Psychology, 44,* 5–14.

Diamond, L. M. (2008b). *Sexual fluidity: Understanding women's love and desire.* Harvard University Press.

Diamond, M. (1999). The effects of pornography: An international perspective. In J. Elias et al. (Eds.), *Pornography 101: Eroticism, pornography, and the First Amendment.* Prometheus Press.

Diamond, M. & Sigmundson, H. K. (1997). Sex reassignment at birth. Long-term review and clinical implications. *Archives of Pediatrics and Adolescent Medicine, 151,* 298–304.

Diamond, M. & Uchiyama, A. (1999). Pornography, rape, and sex crimes in Japan. *International Journal of Law and Psychiatry, 22,* 1–22.

Dicker, F. U. (2008). 80G "Addicted to love" gov. *New York Post,* March 12.

Dirie, W. (1998). *Desert flower: The extraordinary journey of a desert nomad.* William Morrow.

Dittmann, R. W., Kappes, M. E. & Kappes, M. H. (1992). Sexual behavior in adolescent and adult females with congenital adrenal hyperplasia. *Psychoneuroendocrinology, 17,* 153–170.

Dobie, K. (2007). Going all the way. *Washington Post Book World,* February 11.

Docter, R. F. & Prince, V. (1997). Transvestism: a survey of 1032 cross-dressers. *Archives of Sexual Behavior, 26,* 589–605.

Domb, L. G. & Pagel, M. (2001). Sexual swellings advertise female quality in wild baboons. *Nature, 410,* 204–206.

Dominguez, R. C., Nelke, C. F. & Perry, B. D. (2002). Child sexual abuse. In D. Levinson (Ed.), *Encyclopedia of crime and punishment.* Sage Publications.

Donohoe, M. (2006). *Cosmetic surgery past, present and future: Scope, ethics, and policy.* (http://www.medscape.com/ viewarticle/542448_1)

Doulin, T. (2001). Man's journal ruled obscene. *Columbus Dispatch,* July 4.

Dreifus, C. (2005). Declaring with clarity, when gender is ambiguous. *New York Times,* May 31.

Drescher, J., D'Ercole, A. & Schoenberg, E. (Eds.) (2003). *Psychotherapy with gay men and lesbians: Contemporary dynamic approaches.* Harrington Park Press.

Drummond, K. D., Bradley, S. J., Peterson-Badali, M. & Zucker, K. J. (2008). A follow-up study of girls with gender identity disorder. *Developmental Psychology, 44,* 34–45.

Dryden, W. (1999). *Overcoming jealousy.* Sheldon Press.

D'Souza, G., Wiley, D. J., Li, X., Chmiel, J. S., Margolick, J. B., Cranston, R. D. & Jacobson, L. P. (2008). Incidence and epidemiology of anal cancer in the multicenter AIDS cohort study. *Journal of Acquired Immune Deficiency Syndromes, 48,* 491–499.

Duberman, M. (1991). *Cures: A gay man's odyssey.* Dutton.

Duberman, M. (1993). *Stonewall.* Dutton.

Dunn, M. E. & Trost, J. E. (1989). Male multiple orgasms: a descriptive study. *Archives of Sexual Behavior, 18,* 377–387.

Dutta, T. C. & Eid, J. F. (1999). Vacuum constriction devices for erectile dysfunction: a long-term, prospective study of patients with mild, moderate, and severe dysfunction. *Urology, 54,* 891–893.

Dutton, D. G. & Aron, A. P. (1974). Some evidence for heightened sexual attraction under conditions of high anxiety. *Journal of Personality and Social Psychology, 30,* 510–517.

Dworkin, A. (1994). *Prostitution and male supremacy.* (http://www.igc.org/Womensnet/ dworkin/MichLawJournalI.html)

Dworkin, S. H. (2001). Treating the bisexual client. *Journal of Clinical Psychology, 57,* 671–680.

Dwyer, M. (1988). Exhibitionism/voyeurism. *Journal of Social Work and Human Sexuality, 7,* 101–112.

Eaker, E. D., Sullivan, L. M., Kelly-Hayes, M., D'Agostino, R. B., Sr. & Benjamin, E. J. (2007). Marital status, marital strain, and risk of coronary heart disease or total mortality: the Framingham Offspring Study. *Psychosomatic Medicine, 69,* 509–513.

Earls, C. M. & Lalumiere, M. L. (2002). A case study of preferential bestiality (zoophilia). *Sexual Abuse, 14,* 83–88.

Eason, E. & Feldman, P. (2000). Much ado about a little cut: is episiotomy worthwhile? *Obstetrics and Gynecology, 95,* 616–618.

Easton, D. & Liszt, C. A. (1998). *The ethical slut: A guide to infinite sexual possibilities.* Greenery Press.

Eastwick, P. W. & Finkel, E. J. (2008). Sex differences in mate preferences revisited: do people know what they initially desire in a romantic partner? *Journal of Personality and Social Psychology, 94,* 245–264.

Eaton, W. O. & Enns, R. (1986). Sex differences in human motor activity level. *Psychological Bulletin, 100,* 19–28.

Eckholm, E. (2006). Plight deepens for black men, studies warn. *New York Times,* March 20.

ECPAT International. (2001). *Child prostitution.* (http://www.ecpat.net/eng/CSEC/faq/faq2.asp)

Eddleman, K. A., Malone, F. D., Sullivan, L., Dukes, K., Berkowitz, R. L., Kharbutli, Y., Porter, T. F., Luthy, D. A., Comstock, C. H., Saade, G. R., Klugman, S., Dugoff, L., Craigo, S. D., Timor-Tritsch, I. E., Carr, S. R., Wolfe, H. M. & D'Alton, M. E. (2006). Pregnancy loss rates after midtrimester amniocentesis. *Obstetrics and Gynecology, 108,* 1067–1072.

Edlin, B. R., Irwin, K. L., Faruque, S., McCoy, C. B., Word, C., Serrano, Y., Inciardi, J. A., Bowser, B. P., Schilling, R. F. & Holmberg, S. D. (1994). Intersecting epidemics—crack cocaine use and HIV infection among inner- city young adults. Multicenter Crack Cocaine and HIV Infection Study Team. *New England Journal of Medicine, 331,* 1422–1427.

Efron, S. (2001). Baby bust has Japan fearing for its future. *Los Angeles Times,* June 24.

Eggermont, S. (2006). Television viewing and adolescents' judgment of sexual request scripts: a latent growth curve analysis in early and middle adolescence. *Sex Roles, 55,* 457–468.

Eibl-Eibesfeldt, I. (2007). *Human Ethology.* Aldine.

Eichenwald, K. (2005). Through his webcam, a boy joins a sordid online world. *New York Times,* December 19.

Eisenberg, N., Wolchik, S. A., Hernandez, R. & Pasternak, J. (1985). Parental socialization of young children's play: A short-term longitudinal study. *Child Development, 56,* 1506–1513.

Ejegard, H., Ryding, E. L. & Sjogren, B. (2008). Sexuality after delivery with episiotomy: A long-term follow-up. *Gynecologic and Obstetric Investigation, 66,* 1–7.

El-Bassel, N., Schilling, R. F., Gilbert, L., Faruque, S., Irwin, K. L. & Edlin, B. R. (2000). Sex trading and psychological distress in a street-based sample of low-income urban men. *Journal of Psychoactive Drugs, 32,* 259–267.

Elders, M. J., (1997) *The dreaded "M" word.* (http://www.nerve.com/Dispatches/Elders/mword/)

Eldh, J., Berg, A. & Gustafsson, M. (1997). Long-term follow up after sex reassignment surgery. *Scandinavian Journal of Plastic and Reconstructive Surgery and Hand Surgery, 31,* 39–45.

Eliason, M. J. (1997). The prevalence and nature of biphobia in heterosexual undergraduate students. *Archives of Sexual Behavior, 26,* 317–326.

Elliott, A. J. & Niesta, D. (2008). Romantic red: Red enhances men's attraction to women. *Journal of Personality and Social Psychology, 95,* 1150–1164.

Ellis, B. J. & Symons, D. (1990). Sex differences in sexual fantasy: An evolutionary psychological approach. *Journal of Sex Research, 27,* 527–555.

ElSohly, M. A. & Salamone, S. J. (1999). Prevalence of drugs used in cases of alleged sexual assault. *Journal of Analytical Toxicology, 23,* 141–146.

Equal Employment Opportunity Commission. (2008). *Sexual harassment.* (http://www.eeoc.gov/types/sexual_harassment.html)

Erikson, E. H. (1968). *Identity: Youth and crisis.* Norton.

Esquire. (2007). *The state of sex.* (http://www.esquire.com/features/ESQ0207stateofsex)

Estes, R. J. & Weiner, N. A. (2001). *The commercial sexual exploitation of children in the U.S., Canada and Mexico.* (http://www.hri.ca/children/CSE/Estes_Weiner_19sept01.pdf)

EU Business. (2008). *WTO rejects EU beef hormone ban but also raps US, Canada.* (http://www.eubusiness.com/news-eu/1206976621.9)

European Intervention Projects AIDS Prevention for Prostitutes. (2001). *General conclusions and recommendations.* (http://allserv.rug.ac.be/~rmak/europap/summary.html)

Evenhouse, E. & Reilly, S. (2004). A sibling study of stepchild well-being. *Journal of Human Resources, 34,* 248–276.

Exodus International. (2008). *Home page.* (http://www.exodus-international.org)

Fabes, R. A., Martin, C. L. & Hanish, L. D. (2003). Young children's play qualities in same-, other-, and mixed-sex peer groups. *Child Development, 74,* 921–932.

Faderman, L. (1981). *Surpassing the love of men: Romantic friendship and love between women from the Renaissance to the present.* William Morrow.

Faderman, L. (1991). *Odd girls and twilight lovers: A history of lesbian life in twentieth-century America.* Columbia University Press.

Fagot, B. I. (1985). Changes in thinking about early sex role development. *Developmental Review, 5,* 83–98.

Fagot, B. I., Leinbach, M. D. & O'Boyle, C. (1992). Gender labeling, gender stereotyping, and parenting behaviors. *Developmental Psychology, 28,* 440–443.

Family Safe Media. (2008). *Pornography statistics.* (http://www.familysafemedia.com/pornography_statistics.html)

Farley, L. (1978). *Sexual shakedown: The sexual harassment of women on the job.* McGraw-Hill.

Farley, M. (2001). Canada's high court allows some possession of child pornography. *Los Angeles Times,* January 27.

Fauci, A. S., Johnston, M. I., Dieffenbach, C. W., Burton, D. R., Hammer, S. M., Hoxie, J. A., Martin, M., Overbaugh, J., Watkins, D. I., Mahmoud, A. & Greene, W. C. (2008). HIV vaccine research: the way forward. *Science, 321,* 530–532.

Fausto-Sterling, A. (1992). *Myths of gender: Biological theories about women and men.* Basic Books.

Federal Bureau of Investigation. (2003). *Hate crime statistics, 2002.* (http://www.fbi.gov/ucr/hatecrime2002.pdf)

Federal Bureau of Investigation. (2007). *Hate crime statistics, 2006.* (http://www.fbi.gov/ucr/hc2006/table1.html)

Federal Bureau of Investigation. (2008). *Crime in the United States, 2007.* (http://www.fbi.gov/ucr/cius2007/index.html)

Fehr, B. (1988). Prototype analysis of the concepts of love and commitment. *Journal of Personality and Social Psychology, 55,* 557–579.

Feinberg, D. R., DeBruine, L. M., Jones, B. C. & Perrett, D. I. (2008). The role of femininity and averageness of voice pitch in aesthetic judgments of women's voices. *Perception, 37,* 615–623.

Feingold, A. (1988). Matching for attractiveness in romantic partners and same-sex friends: A metanalysis and theoretical critique. *Journal of Personality and Social Psychology, 59,* 981–993.

Feng, M. I., Huang, S., Kaptein, J., Kaswick, J. & Aboseif, S. (2000). Effect of sildenafil citrate on post-radical prostatectomy erectile dysfunction. *Journal of Urology, 164,* 1935–1938.

Fichtner, J., Filipas, D., Mottrie, A. M., Voges, G. E. & Hohenfellner, R. (1995). Analysis of meatal location in 500 men: wide variation questions need for meatal advancement in all pediatric anterior hypospadias cases. *Journal of Urology, 154,* 833–834.

Figueredo, A. J. (2000). A Brunswikian evolutionary-developmental theory of adolescent sex offending. *Behavioral Sciences and the Law, 18,* 309–329.

Finer, L. B. (2007). Trends in premarital sex in the United States, 1954–2003. *Public Health Reports, 122,* 73–78.

Finer, L. B. & Henshaw, S. K. (2006). Disparities in rates of unintended pregnancy in the United States, 1994 and 2001. *Perspectives on Sexual and Reproductive Health, 38,* 90–96.

Finer, L. B., Frohwirth, L. F., Dauphinee, L. A., Singh, S. & Moore, A. M. (2005). Reasons U.S. women have abortions: quantitative and qualitative perspectives. *Perspectives on Sexual and Reproductive Health, 37,* 110–118.

Fink, B., Neave, N., Manning, J. T. & Grammer, K. (2006). Facial symmetry and judgements of attractiveness, health and personality. *Personality and Individual Differences, 41,* 491–499.

Finkelstein, J. W., Susman, E. J., Chinchilli, V. M., D'Arcangelo, M. R., Kunselman, S. J., Schwab, J., Demers, L. M., Liben, L. S. & Kulin, H. E. (1998). Effects of estrogen or testosterone on self-reported sexual responses and behaviors in hypogonadal adolescents. *Journal of Clinical Endocrinology and Metabolism, 83,* 2281–2285.

Finkelstein, K. E. (2001). Man is sentenced to 5 years in attacks in Central Park. *New York Times,* May 19.

Finley, C., Gregg, E. W., Solomon, L. J. & Gay, E. (2001). Disparities in hormone replacement therapy use by socioeconomic status in a primary care population. *Journal of Community Health, 26,* 39–50.

Finney, A., Fukuda, A., Breuel, K. F. & Thatcher, S. S. (1992). Coagulation and liquefaction of seminal plasma. *Assisted Reproduction Reviews, 2,* 164–169.

Firestone, P., Bradford, J. M., McCoy, M., Greenberg, D. M., Curry, S. & Larose, M. R. (2000). Prediction of recidivism in extrafamilial child molesters based on court-related assessments. *Sexual Abuse, 12,* 203–221.

Firestone, P., Kingston, D. A., Wexler, A. & Bradford, J. M. (2006). Long-term follow-up of exhibitionists: Psychological, phallometric, and offense characteristics. *Journal of the American Academy of Psychiatry and the Law, 34*, 349–359.

Firman, R. C., Simmons, L. W., Cummins, J. M. & Matson, P. L. (2003). Are body fluctuating asymmetry and the ratio of 2nd to 4th digit length reliable predictors of semen quality? *Human Reproduction, 18*, 808–812.

Fisch, H. (2008). Declining worldwide sperm counts: disproving a myth. *Urologic Clinics of North America, 35*, 137–146.

Fisher, B. S., Cullen, F. T. & Turner, M. G. (2000). *The sexual victimization of college women.* (http://www.ncjrs.org/pdffiles1/nij/182369.pdf)

Fisher, H. E. (1989). Evolution of human sexual pair-bonding. *American Journal of Physical Anthropology, 78*, 331–354.

Fisher, H. E., Aron, A. & Brown, L. L. (2006). Romantic love: a mammalian brain system for mate choice. *Philosophical Transactions of the Royal Society of London Series B: Biological Sciences, 361*, 2173–2186.

Fisher, W. A. & Black, A. (2007). Contraception in Canada: a review of method choices, characteristics, adherence and approaches to counselling. *Canadian Medical Association Journal, 176*, 953–961.

Fisher, W. A., Rosen, R. C., Eardley, I., Sand, M. & Goldstein, I. (2005). Sexual experience of female partners of men with erectile dysfunction: the female experience of men's attitudes to life events and sexuality (FEMALES) study. *Journal of Sexual Medicine, 2*, 675–684.

Flaccus, G. (2007). L.A. archdiocese agrees to $600 million abuse settlement. *Washington Post*, July 15.

Flanagan, J. (2001). *South African men rape babies as "cure" for AIDS.* (http://portal.telegraph.co.uk/news/main.jhtml?xml=/news/2001/11/11/wrape11.xml&sSheet=/news/2001/11/11/ixhome.html)

Flaxman, S. M. & Sherman, P. W. (2000). Morning sickness: a mechanism for protecting mother and embryo. *Quarterly Review of Biology, 75*, 113–148.

Fleeman, M. (2007). Heidi Fleiss opens her own "Dirty Laundry." *People*, July 2.

Fletcher, J. C. (1983). Is sex selection ethical? In K. Berg and K. E. Tranoy (Eds.), *Research ethics.* Alan R. Liss.

Floyd, F. J. & Bakeman, R. (2006). Coming-out across the life course: implications of age and historical context. *Archives of Sexual Behavior, 35*, 287–296.

Foa, E. B. & Street, G. P. (2001). Women and traumatic events. *Journal of Clinical Psychiatry, 62*, 29–34.

Focus on the Family. (2007). *Hate-crimes bill would give gays special rights.* (http://www.citizenlink.org/CLNews/A000004181.cfm)

Ford, C. S. & Beach, F. A. (1951). *Patterns of sexual behavior.* Harper.

Forger, N. G. & Breedlove, S. M. (1986). Sexual dimorphism in human and canine spinal cord: Role of early androgen. *Proceedings of the National Academy of Sciences of the United States of America, 83*, 7527–7531.

Foshee, V. A., Bauman, K. E., Arriaga, X. B., Helms, R. W., Koch, G. G. & Linder, G. F. (1998). An evaluation of Safe Dates, an adolescent dating violence prevention program. *American Journal of Public Health, 88*, 45–50.

Foshee, V. A., Bauman, K. E., Greene, W. F., Koch, G. G., Linder, G. F. & MacDougall, J. E. (2000). The Safe Dates program: 1-year follow-up results. *American Journal of Public Health, 90*, 1619–1622.

Foshee, V. A., Linder, G. F., Bauman, K. E., Langwick, S. A., Arriaga, X. B., Heath, J. L., McMahon, P. M. & Bangdiwala, S. (1996). The Safe Dates Project: theoretical basis, evaluation design, and selected baseline findings. *American Journal of Preventive Medicine, 12*, 39–47.

Fossos, N., Neighbors, C., Kaysen, D. & Hove, M. C. (2007). Intimate partner violence perpetration and problem drinking among college students: The roles of expectancies and subjective evaluations of alcohol aggression. *Journal of Studies on Alcohol and Drugs, 68*, 706–713.

Fouts, G. & Burggraf, K. (2000). Television situation comedies: Female weight, male negative comments, and audience reactions. *Sex Roles, 42*, 925–932.

Fox, A. (1991). Development of a bisexual identity. In L. Hutchins and L. Kaahumanu (Eds.), *Bi any other name: Bisexual people speak out.* Alyson.

Fox, R. C. (Ed.) (2004). *Current research on bisexuality.* Routledge.

Francoeur, R. T. (2001). *The international encyclopedia of sexuality.* (http://www2.hu-berlin.de/sexology/IES/index.html)

Franke, W. W. & Berendonk, B. (1997). Hormonal doping and androgenization of athletes: a secret program of the German Democratic Republic government. *Clinical Chemistry, 43*, 1262–1279.

Frayser, S. G. (1994). Defining normal childhood sexuality: An anthropological approach. *Annual Review of Sex Research, 4*, 173–217.

Frazer, J. G. (1922). *The golden bough: A study of magic and religion (abridged ed.).* Macmillan.

Frederick, D. A. & Haselton, M. G. (2007). Why is muscularity sexy? Tests of the fitness indicator hypothesis. *Personality and Social Psychology Bulletin, 33*, 1167–1183.

Frederick, D. A., Fessler, D. M. & Haselton, M. G. (2005). Do representations of male muscularity differ in men's and women's magazines? *Body Image, 2*, 81–86.

Freeman, D. (1983). *Margaret Mead and Samoa: The making and unmaking of an anthropological myth.* Harvard University Press.

Freud, S. (1905/1975). *Three essays on the theory of sexuality.* Basic Books.

Freud, K. & Blanchard, R. (1986). The concept of courtship disorder. *Journal of Sex and Marital Therapy, 12*, 79–92.

Freund, K. & Seto, M. C. (1998). Preferential rape in the theory of courtship disorder. *Archives of Sexual Behavior, 27*, 433–443.

Freund, K. W. (1974). Male homosexuality: An analysis of the pattern. In J. A. Lorraine (Ed.), *Understanding homosexuality: Its biological and psychological bases.* Elsevier.

Freund, K., Seto, M. C. & Kuban, M. (1997). Frotteurism: The theory of courtship disorders. In D. R. Laws and W. T. O'Donohue (Eds.), *Sexual deviance: Theory, assessment, and treatment* (2nd ed.). Guilford Press.

Freund, K., Steiner, B. W. & Chan, S. (1982). Two types of cross-gender identity. *Archives of Sexual Behavior, 11*, 49–63.

Freund, K., Watson, R. & Rienzo, D. (1987). A comparison of sex offenders against female and male minors. *Journal of Sex and Marital Therapy, 13*, 260–264.

Freund, K., Watson, R. & Rienzo, D. (1989). Heterosexuality, homosexuality, and erotic age preference. *Journal of Sex Research, 26*, 107–117.

Freund, K., Watson, R., Dickey, R. & Rienzo, D. (1991). Erotic gender differentiation in pedophilia. *Archives of Sexual Behavior, 20*, 555–566.

Friedrich, W. N., Fisher, J., Broughton, D., Houston, M. & Shafran, C. R. (1998). Normative sexual behavior in children: a contemporary sample. *Pediatrics, 101*, E9.

Friedrich, W. N., Sandfort, T. G. M., Oostveen, J. & Cohen-Kettenis, P. T. (2000). Cultural differences in sexual behavior: 2–6 year old Dutch and American children. *Journal of Psychology and Human Sexuality, 12*, 117–129.

Frintner, M. P. & Rubinson, L. (1993). Acquaintance rape: The influence of alcohol, fraternity membership, and sports team membership. *Journal of Sex Education and Therapy, 19*, 272–284.

Frith, T. F., Cheng, H. & Shaw, P. (2004). Race and beauty: A comparison of Asian and Western models in women's magazine advertisements. *Sex Roles, 50*, 53–61.

Fritsch, J. & Finkelstein, K. E. (2001). Charges dismissed in Columbia sexual torture case. *New York Times*, November 2.

Fromm, E. (1956). *The art of loving.* Harper and Row.

Gabelnick, H. L., Schwartz, J. & Darroch, J. E. (2007). Contraceptive research and development. In R. A. Hatcher et al. (Eds.), *Contraceptive technology* (19th ed.). Ardent Media.

Gaffney, G. R., Lurie, S. F. & Berlin, F. S. (1984). Is there familial transmission of pedophilia? *Journal of Nervous and Mental Disease, 172*, 546–548.

Gagneux, P., Woodruff, D. S. & Boesch, C. (1997). Furtive mating in female chimpanzees. *Nature, 387*, 358–359.

Gagnon, J. H. & Simon, W. (1987). The sexual scripting of oral genital contacts. *Archives of Sexual Behavior, 16*, 1–25.

Gahlinger, P. M. (2004). Club drugs: MDMA, gamma-hydroxybutyrate (GHB), Rohypnol, and ketamine. *American Family Physician, 69*, 2619–2626.

Galenson, E. (1990). Observation of early infantile sexual and erotic development. In M. E. Perry (Ed.), *Handbook of Sexology, vol. 7. Childhood and adolescent sexology.* Elsevier.

Gallup and Robinson. (2008). *Sex in advertising.* (http://www.gallup-robinson.com/tableofcontents.html)

Gallup News Service. (2004). *Gallup surveys U.S. views on abortion.* (http://www.globalethics.org/newsline/members/issue.tmpl?articleid=04260418121771)

Gallup Organization. (1997). *Family values differ sharply around the world.* (http://www.gallup.com/poll/releases/pr971107.asp)

Gallup Organization (2000). *Americans are overwhelmingly happy and optimistic about the future of the United States.*

(http://www.gallup.com/poll/releases/pr001013.asp)

Gallup Organization. (2001). *Over half of Americans believe in love at first sight.* (http://www.gallup.com/poll/releases/pr010214d.asp)

Gallup Organization. (2005). *Americans closely divided into pro-choice and pro-life camps.* (http://www.gallup.com/poll/content/login.aspx?ci=16297)

Gallup Organization. (2006a). *Abortion views reviewed as Alito vote nears.* (http://www.gallup.com/poll/20983/Abortion-Views-Reviewed-Alito-Vote-Nears.aspx)

Gallup Organization. (2006b). *Americans at odds over gay rights.* (http://www.gallup.com/poll/23140/Americans-Odds-Over-Gay-Rights.aspx)

Gallup Organization. (2008). *CA ruling on same-sex marriage bucks majority view.* (http://www.gallup.com/poll/107305/Ruling-SameSex-Marriage-Bucks-Majority-View.aspx)

Gangestad, S. W. & Thornhill, R. (1997). The evolutionary psychology of extrapair sex: The role of fluctuating asymmetry. *Evolution and Human Behavior, 18,* 69–88.

Gangestad, S. W. & Thornhill, R. (1998). Menstrual cycle variation in women's preferences for the scent of symmetrical men. *Proceedings of the Royal Society of London Series B: Biological Sciences, 265,* 927–933.

Gannon, T. A. & Ward, T. (2008). Rape: Psychopathology and theory. In D. R. Laws and W. T. O'Donohue (Eds.), *Sexual deviance: Theory, assessment, and treatment* (2nd ed.). Guilford Press.

Ganong, L. H. & Coleman, M. (2003). *Stepfamily relationships: Development, dynamics, and interventions.* Springer.

Gardiner, S. (2001). The grey area of prostitution: Can it be an opportunity or is it always exploitive? *New York Newsday,* March 15.

Garland, R. J. & Dougher, M. J. (1990). The abused/abuser hypothesis of child sexual abuse: A critical review of theory and research. In J. R. Feierman (Ed.), *Pedophilia: Biosocial dimensions.* Springer.

Gates, K. (2000). *Deviant desires: Incredibly strange sex.* Juno Books.

Gay Asian Pacific Support Network. (2001). *The truth about GAM.* (http://www.gapsn.org/project2/discussion/changj.asp)

Gay, N. (2004). Four Raiders avoid '03 punishment. *San Francisco Chronicle,* November 21.

Geddes, R. & Lueck, D. (2000). *The gains from self-ownership and the expansion of women's rights.* (http://lawschool.stanford.edu/olin/workingpapers/WP181GEDDES.pdf)

Gelfand, M. M. (2000). Sexuality among older women. *Journal of Women's Health and Gender Based Medicine, 9,* S15–20.

Gelles, R. J. (1976). Abused wives: Why do they stay? *Journal of Marriage and the Family, 38,* 659–668.

Georgiadis, J. R., Kortekaas, R., Kuipers, R., Nieuwenburg, A., Pruim, J., Reinders, A. A. & Holstege, G. (2006). Regional cerebral blood flow changes associated with clitorally induced orgasm in healthy women. *European Journal of Neuroscience, 24,* 3305–3316.

Georgiopoulos, A. M., Bryan, T. L., Wollan, P. & Yawn, B. P. (2001). Routine screening for postpartum depression. *Journal of Family Practice, 50,* 117–122.

Ghiselin, M. (1974). *The economy of nature and the evolution of sex.* University of California Press.

Gibson, L. E. & Leitenberg, H. (2000). Child sexual abuse prevention programs: do they decrease the occurrence of child sexual abuse? *Child Abuse and Neglect, 24,* 1115–1125.

Gigolos Begleitagentur. (2008). *Gigolos: What women want.* (http://www.gigolos.ch)

Gilbert, R. M. (2006). *The eight concepts of Bowen theory: A new way of thinking about the individual and the group.* Leading Systems Press.

Gilbert, S. F. (2003). *The Kallman syndrome: Sex, smell, and specific adhesion.* (http://www.devbio.com/article.php?ch=13&id=135)

Gilligan, C. (1982). *In a different voice: Psychological theory and women's development.* Harvard University Press.

Gladyshev, E. A., Meselson, M. & Arkhipova, I. R. (2008). Massive horizontal gene transfer in bdelloid rotifers. *Science, 320,* 1210–1213.

Goddard, M. R., Godfray, H. C. J. & Burt, A. (2005). Sex increases the efficacy of natural selection in experimental yeast populations. *Nature, 434,* 636–640.

Godfray, H. C. J. & Werren, J. H. (1996). Recent developments in sex ratio studies. *Trends in Ecology and Evolution, 11,* 59–63.

Goldacre, M. J., Wotton, C. J., Seagroatt, V. & Yeates, D. (2005). Cancer and cardiovascular disease after vasectomy: an epidemiological database study. *Fertility and Sterility, 84,* 1438–1443.

Goldberg, A. B. & Grimes, D. A. (2007). Injectable contraceptives. In R. A. Hatcher et al. (Eds.), *Contraceptive technology* (19th ed.). Ardent Media.

Goldberg, C. (2001). System stands accused in a Montana man's case. *New York Times,* January 23.

Goldberg, C. & Elder, J. (1998). Public still backs abortion, but wants limits, poll says. *New York Times,* January 16.

Goldberg, S. (1991). Feminism against science. *National Review, 43,* 30.

Goldie, S. J., Kuntz, K. M., Weinstein, M. C., Freedberg, K. A. & Palefsky, J. M. (2000). Cost-effectiveness of screening for anal squamous intraepithelial lesions and anal cancer in human immunodeficiency virus-negative homosexual and bisexual men. *American Journal of Medicine, 108,* 634–641.

Goldstein, I. (2000). The mutually reinforcing triad of depressive symptoms, cardiovascular disease, and erectile dysfunction. *American Journal of Cardiology, 86,* 41F–45F.

Goldstein, I. & Berman, J. R. (1998). Vasculogenic female sexual dysfunction: vaginal engorgement and clitoral erectile insufficiency syndromes. *International Journal of Impotence Research, 10 Suppl 2,* S84–90; discussion S98–101.

Goldstein, J. M., Seidman, L. J., Horton, N. J., Makris, N., Kennedy, D. N., Caviness, V. S., Jr., Faraone, S. V. & Tsuang, M. T. (2001). Normal sexual dimorphism of the adult human brain assessed by in vivo magnetic resonance imaging. *Cerebral Cortex, 11,* 490–497.

Gooden, A. M. & Gooden, M. A. (2001). Gender representation in notable children's picture books, 1995–1999. *Sex Roles, 45,* 89–101.

Gootman, E. (2004). The killer gown is essential, but the prom date? Not so much. *New York Times,* June 15.

Gordon, A. E. & Shaughnessy, A. F. (2003). Saw palmetto for prostate disorders. *American Family Physician, 67,* 1281–1283.

Gordon, S. (2008). Symptoms plus blood test boost ovarian cancer detection. *Washington Post,* June 23.

Gorey, K. M. & Leslie, D. R. (1997). The prevalence of child sexual abuse: integrative review adjustment for potential response and measurement biases. *Child Abuse and Neglect, 21,* 391–398.

Gottman, J. M. & Krokoff, L. J. (1989). Marital interaction and satisfaction: a longitudinal view. *Journal of Consulting and Clinical Psychology, 57,* 47–52.

Gottman, J. M. & Levenson, R. W. (1999). What predicts change in marital interaction over time? A study of alternative models. *Family Process, 38,* 143–158.

Gottman, J. M. & Notarius, C. I. (2000). Decade review: observing marital interaction. *Journal of Marriage and the Family, 62,* 927–947.

Gottman, J. M., Levenson, R. W., Gross, J., Frederickson, B. L., McCoy, K., Rosenthal, L., Ruef, A. & Yoshimoto, D. (2003). Correlates of gay and lesbian couples' relationship satisfaction and relationship dissolution. *Journal of Homosexuality, 45,* 23–43.

Gottschall, J. (2004). Explaining wartime rape. *Journal of Sex Research, 41,* 129–136.

Gotz, M. J., Johnstone, E. C. & Ratcliffe, S. G. (1999). Criminality and antisocial behaviour in unselected men with sex chromosome abnormalities. *Psychological Medicine, 29,* 953–962.

Gould, T. (1999). *The lifestyle: A look at the erotic rites of swingers.* Vintage Canada.

Goy, R. W., Bercovitch, F. B. & McBrair, M. C. (1988). Behavioral masculinization is independent of genital masculinization in prenatally androgenized female rhesus macaques. *Hormones and Behavior, 22,* 552–571.

Grafenberg, E. (1950). The role of the urethra in female orgasm. *International Journal of Sexology, 3,* 145–148.

Graham, C. A., Crosby, R., Yarber, W. L., Sanders, S. A., McBride, K., Milhausen, R. R. & Arno, J. N. (2006). Erection loss in association with condom use among young men attending a public STI clinic: potential correlates and implications for risk behaviour. *Sex Health, 3,* 255–260.

Grant, R. M., Hamer, D., Hope, T., Johnston, R., Lange, J., Lederman, M. M., Lieberman, J., Miller, C. J., Moore, J. P., Mosier, D. E., Richman, D. D., Schooley, R. T., Springer, M. S., Veazey, R. S. & Wainberg, M. A. (2008). Whither or wither microbicides? *Science, 321,* 532–534.

Gravina, G. L., Brandetti, F., Martini, P., Carosa, E., Di Stasi, S. M., Morano, S., Lenzi, A. & Jannini, E. A. (2008). Measurement of the thickness of the urethrovaginal space in women with or without vaginal orgasm. *Journal of Sexual Medicine, 5,* 610–618.

Green, A. H. & Kaplan, M. S. (1994). Psychiatric impairment and childhood victimization experiences in female child molesters. *Journal of the American Academy of Child and Adolescent Psychiatry, 33,* 954–961.

Green, R. (1987). *The "sissy-boy syndrome" and the development of homosexuality.* Yale University Press.

Green, R. (1992). *Sexual science and the law.* Harvard University Press.

Greene, D. A. (2004). *The women's movement and the politics of change at a women's college.* Routledge.

Greene, J. & Haidt, J. (2002). How (and where) does moral judgment work? *Trends in Cognitive Science, 6,* 517–523.

Greenfeld, L. A. (1997). *Sex offenses and offenders: An analysis of data on rape and sexual assault.* (http://www.vaw.umn.edu/FinalDocuments/sexoff.asp#)

Greenhouse, L. (2008). Supreme Court upholds child pornography law. *New York Times,* May 20.

Greer, G. (1971). *The female eunuch.* McGraw-Hill.

Griffin, R. M. (2008). *All about genital piercing.* (http://www.webmd.com/skin-beauty/guide/all-about-genital-piercing)

Grimes, D. A. (2007). Intrauterine devices (IUDs). In R. A. Hatcher et al. (Eds.), *Contraceptive technology* (19th ed.). Ardent Media.

Grossl, N. A. (2000). Supernumerary breast tissue: historical perspectives and clinical features. *Southern Medical Journal, 93,* 29–32.

Grossman, K. (2008). *Penis piercing.* (http://menshealth.about.com/cs/teenhealth/a/penis_piercing.htm)

Grossman, M. (2007). *Unprotected: A campus psychiatrist reveals how political correctness in her profession endangers every student.* Sentinel.

Groth, A. N. (1979). *Men who rape: The psychology of the offender.* Plenum.

Grove, L. (1994). Barry Goldwater's left turn. *Washington Post,* July 28.

Gruber, J. E. & Fineran, S. (2008). Comparing the impact of bullying and sexual harassment victimization on the mental and physical health of adolescents. *Sex Roles, 59,* 1–13.

Gruenbaum, E. (2000). *The female circumcision controversy: An anthropological perspective.* University of Pennsylvania Press.

Grunbaum, J. A., Lowry, R., Kann, L. & Pateman, B. (2000). Prevalence of health risk behaviors among Asian American/Pacific Islander high school students. *Journal of Adolescent Health, 27,* 322–330.

Guay, A. T. (2001). Decreased testosterone in regularly menstruating women with decreased libido: a clinical observation. *Journal of Sex and Marital Therapy, 27,* 513–519.

Guerrero Pavich, E. (1986). A Chicano perspective on Mexican culture and sexuality. In L. Lister (Ed.), *Human Sexuality, Ethnoculture, and Social Work.* Haworth Press.

Gupta, R. & Wald, A. (2006). Genital herpes: antiviral therapy for symptom relief and prevention of transmission. *Expert Opinion on Pharmacotherapy, 7,* 665–675.

Guttmacher Institute. (2002). *U.S. policy can reduce cost barriers to contraception.*

(http://www.guttmacher.org/pubs/ib_0799.html)

Guttmacher Institute. (2003). *An overview of abortion in the United States.* (http://www.guttmacher.org/presentations/ab_slides.html)

Guttmacher Institute. (2005). *Contraceptive use.* (http://www.agi-usa.org/pubs/fb_contr_use.html)

Guttmacher Institute. (2006). *Facts on American teens' sexual and reproductive health.* (www.guttmacher.org/pubs/fb_ATSRH.html)

Guttmacher Institute. (2008a). *Facts on induced abortion in the United States.* (http://www.guttmacher.org/pubs/fb_induced_abortion.html)

Guttmacher Institute. (2008b). *An overview of abortion in the United States.* (http://www.guttmacher.org/presentations/abort_slides.pdf)

Guzick, D. S., Overstreet, J. W., Factor-Litvak, P., Brazil, C. K., Nakajima, S. T., Coutifaris, C., Carson, S. A., Cisneros, P., Steinkampf, M. P., Hill, J. A., Xu, D. & Vogel, D. L. (2001). Sperm morphology, motility, and concentration in fertile and infertile men. *New England Journal of Medicine, 345,* 1388–1393.

Gwadz, M. V., Gostnell, K., Smolenski, C., Willis, B., Nish, D., Nolan, T. C., Tharaken, M. & S. Ritchie, A. (2008). The initiation of homeless youth into the street economy. *Journal of Adolescence.* Published online, doi:10.1016/j.adolescence.2008.01.004.

Hage, J. J. (1996). Metaidoioplasty: an alternative phalloplasty technique in transsexuals. *Plastic and Reconstructive Surgery, 97,* 161–167.

Haggard, T. (2006). *Ted Haggard's letter to New Life Church.* November 5.

Haig, D. (2004). The inexorable rise of gender and the decline of sex: social change in academic titles, 1945–2001. *Archives of Sexual Behavior, 33,* 87–96.

Haignere, C. S., Gold, R. & McDanel, H. J. (1999). Adolescent abstinence and condom use: are we sure we are really teaching what is safe? *Health Education and Behavior, 26,* 43–54.

Haile, R. W. & 25 others. (2006). BRCA1 and BRCA2 mutation carriers, oral contraceptive use, and breast cancer before age 50. *Cancer Epidemiology, Biomarkers and Prevention, 15,* 1863–1870.

Hakim, D. & Rashbaum, W. K. (2008). Spitzer is linked to prostitution ring. *New York Times,* March 10.

Halata, Z. & Munger, B. L. (1986). The neuroanatomical basis for the protopathic sensibility of the human glans penis. *Brain Research, 371,* 205–230.

Haldeman, D. C. (1994). The practice and ethics of sexual orientation conversion therapy. *Journal of Consulting and Clinical Psychology, 62,* 221–227.

Halpern, C. T., Udry, J. R., Suchindran, C. & Campbell, B. (2000a). Adolescent males' willingness to report masturbation. *Journal of Sex Research, 37,* 327–232.

Halpern, C. T., Joyner, K., Udry, J. R. & Suchindran, C. (2000b). Smart teens don't have sex (or kiss much either). *Journal of Adolescent Health, 26,* 213–225.

Halpern, C. T., Kaestle, C. E. & Hallfors, D. D. (2007). Perceived physical maturity, age of romantic partner, and adolescent risk behavior. *Prevention Science, 8,* 1–10.

Halpern, C. T., Udry, J. R. & Suchindran, C. (1997). Testosterone predicts initiation of coitus in adolescent females. *Psychosomatic Medicine, 59,* 161–171.

Halpern, C. T., Udry, J. R. & Suchindran, C. (1998). Monthly measures of salivary testosterone predict sexual activity in adolescent males. *Archives of Sexual Behavior, 27,* 445–465.

Halpern, C. T., Udry, J. R., Campbell, B., Suchindran, C. & Mason, G. A. (1994). Testosterone and religiosity as predictors of sexual attitudes and activity among adolescent males: a biosocial model. *Journal of Biosocial Science, 26,* 217–234.

Hamer, D. H., Hu, S., Magnuson, V. L., Hu, N. & Pattatucci, A. M. (1993). A linkage between DNA markers on the X chromosome and male sexual orientation. *Science, 261,* 321–327.

Hamilton, W. D. (1964). The genetical evolution of social behavior. *Journal of Theoretical Biology, 7,* 1–52.

Hamilton, W. D., Henderson, P. A. & Moran, N. A. (1981). Fluctuation of environment and coevolved antagonistic polymorphisms as factors in the maintenance of sex. In R. D. Alexander and D. W. Tinkle (Eds.), *Natural selection and social behavior.* Chiron Press.

Hammock, E. A. & Young, L. J. (2005). Microsatellite instability generates diversity in brain and sociobehavioral traits. *Science, 308,* 1630–1634.

Hand, D. (1998). *The Michael Hutchence tribute: The coroner's report.* (http://www.inxsweb.com/tribute/coroner.shtml)

Hanrahan, S. N. (1994). Historical review of menstrual toxic shock syndrome. *Women and Health, 21,* 141–165.

Hansen, G. L. (1985). Perceived threats and marital jealousy. *Social Psychology Quarterly, 48,* 262–268.

Hanson, R. K. & Bussière, M. T. (1998). Predicting relapse: a meta-analysis of sexual offender recidivism studies. *Journal of Consulting and Clinical Psychology, 66,* 348–362.

Harding, C. F. (1985). Sociobiological hypotheses about rape: A critical look at the data behind the hypotheses. In S. Sunday and E. Tobach (Eds.), *Violence against women: A critique of the sociobiology of rape.* Gordian Press.

Hare, E. H. (1962). Masturbatory insanity: The history of an idea. *Journal of Mental Science, 108,* 1–25.

Harris, C. R. (2003). A review of sex differences in sexual jealousy, including self-report data, psychophysiological responses, interpersonal violence, and morbid jealousy. *Personality and Social Psychology Review, 7,* 102–128.

Harris, G. & Berenson, A. (2008). Drug makers near old goal: A legal shield. *New York Times,* April 6.

Hartmann, K., Viswanathan, M., Palmieri, R., Thorp, J. & Lohr, K. N. (2005). Outcomes of routine episiotomy. *JAMA, 293,* 2141–2148.

Hartmann, U. & Waldinger, M. D. (2007). Treatment of delayed ejaculation. In S. R.

Leiblum (Ed.), *Principles and practice of sex therapy* (4th ed.). Guilford Press.

Hartocollis, A. (2006). Women have seen it all on subway, unwillingly. *New York Times,* June 24.

Hasan, Z. (1996). *Polygamy, slavery and Qur'anic sexual ethics.* (http://www.shobak.org/islam/polygamy.html)

Haselton, M. G., Mortezaie, M., Pillsworth, E. G., Bleske-Rechek, A. & Frederick, D. A. (2007). Ovulatory shifts in human female ornamentation: near ovulation, women dress to impress. *Hormones and Behavior, 51,* 40–45.

Hassett, J. M., Siebert, E. R. & Wallen, K. (2008). Sex differences in rhesus monkey toy preferences parallel those of children. *Hormones and Behavior, 54,* 359–364.

Hatfield, E. (1994). Passionate love and sexual desire: A cross-cultural perspective. *Proceedings of the Annual Meeting, Society for the Scientific Study of Sexuality, Miami.*

Hatfield, E. & Rapson, R. L. (1993). *Love, sex, and intimacy: Their psychology, biology, and history.* HarperCollins.

Hatfield, E., Traupmann, J. & Walster, G. W. (1979). Equity and extramarital sex. In M. Cook and G. Wilson (Eds.), *Love and attraction.* Pergamon.

Hatfield, E., Walster, G. W. & Berscheid, E. (1978). *Equity theory and research.* Allyn and Bacon.

Hawkes, K., O'Connell, J. F., Jones, N. G., Alvarez, H. & Charnov, E. L. (1998). Grandmothering, menopause, and the evolution of human life histories. *Proceedings of the National Academy of Sciences of the United States of America, 95,* 1336–1339.

Hawton, K., Catalan, J. & Fagg, J. (1992). Sex therapy for erectile dysfunction: characteristics of couples, treatment outcome, and prognostic factors. *Archives of Sexual Behavior, 21,* 161–175.

Hayes, R. D. & Dennerstein, L. (2005). The impact of aging on sexual function and sexual dysfunction in women: a review of population-based studies. *Journal of Sexual Medicine, 2,* 317–330.

Hayes, R. D., Dennerstein, L., Bennett, C. M., Sidat, M., Gurrin, L. C. & Fairley, C. K. (2008). Risk factors for female sexual dysfunction in the general population: exploring factors associated with low sexual function and sexual distress. *Journal of Sexual Medicine, 5,* 1681–1693.

Hazan, C. & Shaver, P. (1987). Romantic love conceptualized as an attachment process. *Journal of Personality and Social Psychology, 52,* 511–524.

Hazlett, T. (2004). *Requiem for the V-chip.* (http://slate.msn.com/id/2095396/)

Healy, M. (2001). Breast-feeding beyond babyhood. *Los Angeles Times,* February 5.

Hedlund, P., Ny, L., Alm, P. & Andersson, K. E. (2000). Cholinergic nerves in human corpus cavernosum and spongiosum contain nitric oxide synthase and heme oxygenase. *Journal of Urology, 164,* 868–875.

Heiman, J. R. (2007). Orgasmic disorders in women. In S. R. Leiblum (Ed.), *Principles and practice of sex therapy* (4th ed.). Guilford Press.

Hekma, G. (1994). "A female soul in a male body": Sexual inversion in nineteenth-century sexology. In G. Herdt (Ed.), *Third sex, third gender: Beyond sexual dimorphism in culture and history.* Zone Books.

Hendrick, S. (1981). Self-disclosure and marital satisfaction. *Journal of Personality and Social Psychology, 40,* 1150–1159.

Hendrick, S. & Hendrick, C. (1992). *Liking, loving, and relating.* Brooks/Cole.

Hendrick, S. S., Hendrick, C. & Adler, N. L. (1988). Romantic relationships: Love, satisfaction, and staying together. *Journal of Personality and Social Psychology, 54,* 980–988.

Henton, C. L. (1976). Nocturnal orgasm in college women: its relation to dreams and anxiety associated with sexual factors. *Journal of Genetic Psychology, 129,* 245–251.

Herbst, A. L. (1999). Diethylstilbestrol and adenocarcinoma of the vagina. *American Journal of Obstetrics and Gynecology, 181,* 1576–1578.

Herdt, G. (2005). *The Sambia: Ritual, sexuality, and change in Papua New Guinea.* Wadsworth.

Herek, G. M. (2002). Heterosexuals' attitudes toward bisexual men and women in the United States. *Journal of Sex Research, 39,* 264–274.

Herman-Giddens, M. E., Slora, E. J., Wasserman, R. C., Bourdony, C. J., Bhapkar, M. V., Koch, G. G. & Hasemeier, C. M. (1997). Secondary sexual characteristics and menses in young girls seen in office practice: a study from the Pediatric Research in Office Settings network. *Pediatrics, 99,* 505–512.

Herpetic Eye Disease Study Group. (2000). Psychological stress and other potential triggers for recurrences of herpes simplex virus eye infections. *Archives of Ophthalmology, 118,* 1617–1625.

Herzog, L. W. (1989). Urinary tract infections and circumcision. A case-control study. *American Journal of Diseases of Children, 143,* 348–350.

Hess, N. H. & Hagen, E. H. (2006). Sex differences in indirect aggression: Psychological evidence from young adults. *Evolution and Human Behavior, 27,* 231–245.

Hess, R. A., Bunick, D., Lee, K. H., Bahr, J., Taylor, J. A., Korach, K. S. & Lubahn, D. B. (1997). A role for oestrogens in the male reproductive system. *Nature, 390,* 509–512.

Hetherington, E. M. & Kelly, J. (2002). *For better or for worse: Divorce reconsidered.* W.W. Norton.

Hezareh, M. (2005). Prostratin as a new therapeutic agent targeting HIV viral reservoirs. *Drug News & Perspectives, 18,* 496–500.

Hiestand, M. (1997). Titleist pulls ads from "SI." *USA Today,* April 29.

Highleyman, L. A. (2000). *A brief history of the bisexual movement.* (http://www.biresource.org/history.html)

Hill, C., Rubin, Z. & Peplau, L. A. (1976). Break-ups before marriage: The end of 103 affairs. *Journal of Social Issue, 32,* 147–168.

Hines, M. (2006). Prenatal testosterone and gender-related behaviour. *European Journal of Endocrinology, 155,* S115–S121.

Hines, T. M. (2001). The G-spot: a modern gynecologic myth. *American Journal of Obstetrics and Gynecology, 185,* 359–362.

Hite, S. (2003). *The Hite report: A nationwide study of female sexuality.* Seven Stories Press.

Hobfoll, S. E., Ritter, C., Lavin, J., Hulsizer, M. R. & Cameron, R. P. (1995). Depression prevalence and incidence among inner-city pregnant and postpartum women. *Journal of Consulting and Clinical Psychology, 63,* 445–453.

Holden, C. (2004). State of ART. *Science, 306,* 808.

Holmes, J. (2001). *The search for the secure base: Attachment theory and psychotherapy.* Brunner-Routledge.

Holstege, G., Georgiadis, J. R., Paans, A. M., Meiners, L. C., van der Graaf, F. H. & Reinders, A. A. (2003). Brain activation during human male ejaculation. *Journal of Neuroscience, 23,* 9185–9193.

Holt, V. L., Cushing-Haugen, K. L. & Daling, J. R. (2002). Body weight and risk of oral contraceptive failure. *Obstetrics and Gynecology, 99,* 820–827.

Honan, W. H. (1994). Professor ousted for lecture gets job back. *New York Times,* September 17.

Horvath, T. (1981). Physical attractiveness: the influence of selected torso parameters. *Archives of Sexual Behavior, 10,* 21–24.

Howells, K. & Day, A. (2003). Readiness for anger management: Clinical and theoretical issues. *Clinical Psychology Review, 23,* 319–337.

Hrdy, S. B. (1977). *The langurs of Abu: Female and male strategies of reproduction.* Harvard University Press.

Hsu, B., Kling, A., Kessler, C., Knapke, K., Diefenbach, P. & Elias, J. E. (1994). Gender differences in sexual fantasy and behavior in a college population: a ten-year replication. *Journal of Sex and Marital Therapy, 20,* 103–118.

Hubacher, D. & Grimes, D. A. (2002). Noncontraceptive health benefits of intrauterine devices: a systematic review. *Obstetrical and Gynecological Survey, 57,* 120–128.

Hubacher, D., Lara-Ricalde, R., Taylor, D. J., Guerra-Infante, F. & Guzman-Rodriguez, R. (2001). Use of copper intrauterine devices and the risk of tubal infertility among nulligravid women. *New England Journal of Medicine, 345,* 561–567.

Huffstutter, P. J. & Frammolino, R. (2001). Lights! Camera! Viagra! When the show must go on, sometimes a little chemistry helps. *Los Angeles Times,* July 6.

Human Genome Project. (2005). *How many genes are in the human genome?* (http://www.ornl.gov/sci/techresources/Human_Genome/faq/genenumber.shtml)

Human Rights Campaign. (2008). *Working for gay, lesbian, bisexual and transgender equal rights.* (http://www.hrc.org/)

Human Rights Watch. (2001a). *Hatred in the hallways: Violence and discrimination against lesbian, gay, bisexual, and transgender students in U.S. schools.* (http://www.hrw.org/reports/2001/uslgbt/)

Human Rights Watch. (2001b). *No escape: Male rape in U.S. prisons.* (http://www.hrw.org/reports/2001/prison/voices.html)

Hurley, D. (2005). Divorce rate: It's not as high as you think. *New York Times,* April 19.

Hutchins, L. & Kaahumanu, L. (1991). *Bi any other name: Bisexual people speak out.* Alyson.

Hutchins, L. (2007). *Sexual prejudice: The erasure of bisexuals in academia and the media.* (http://nsrc.sfsu.edu/MagArticle.cfm?Article=475&PageID=171&SID=2F61BCD15F440019472CA01253795FEB&DSN=nsrc_dsn)

Hyde, J. S. (2005). The gender similarities hypothesis. *American Psychologist, 60,* 581–592.

Hyde, J. S., Fennema, E. & Lamon, S. J. (1990). Gender differences in mathematics performance: A meta-analysis. *Psychological Bulletin, 107,* 139–155.

Hyde, J. S., Lindberg, S. M., Linn, M. C., Ellis, A. B. & Williams, C. C. (2008). Gender similarities characterize math performance. *Science, 321,* 494–495.

Imperato-McGinley, J., Guerrero, L., Gautier, T. & Peterson, R. E. (1974). Steroid 5-alpha-reductase deficiency in man: an inherited form of male pseudohermaphroditism. *Science, 186,* 1213–1215.

Imperato-McGinley, J., Miller, M., Wilson, J. D., Peterson, R. E., Shackleton, C. & Gajdusek, D. C. (1991). A cluster of male pseudohermaphrodites with 5-alpha-reductase deficiency in Papua New Guinea. *Clinical Endocrinology, 34,* 293–298.

Imperato-McGinley, J., Peterson, R. E., Gautier, T. & Sturla, E. (1979). Androgens and the evolution of male-gender identity among male pseudohermaphrodites with 5-alpha-reductase deficiency. *New England Journal of Medicine, 300,* 1233–1237.

Inan, M., Aydiner, C. Y., Tokuc, B., Aksu, B., Ayhan, S., Ayvaz, S. & Ceylan, T. (2008). Prevalence of cryptorchidism, retractile testis and orchiopexy in school children. *Urologia Internationalis, 80,* 166–171.

India Together. (2007). *Devadasis uniting to end "dedications."* (http://www.indiatogether.org/2007/apr/soc-devadasi.htm)

Inhorn, M. C. (1996). *Infertility and patriarchy: The cultural politics of gender and family life in Egypt.* University of Pennsylvania Press.

Institute for Reproductive Health. (2008). *Research to practice: The TwoDay method.* (http://www.irh.org/RTP-TDM.htm)

International Gay and Lesbian Association. (1999). *World legal survey.* (http://www.ilga.org/Information/legal_survey/Summary%20information/age_of_consent.htm)

iPledge. (2005). *Committed to pregnancy prevention.* (https://www.ipledgeprogram.com/)

Isay, R. A. (1989). *Being homosexual: Gay men and their development.* Farrar, Straus and Giroux.

Ishak, W. W., Berman, D. S. & Peters, A. (2008). Male anorgasmia treated with oxytocin. *Journal of Sexual Medicine, 5,* 1022–1024.

Isiramen, C. O. (2003) *Women in Nigeria: Religion, culture, and the AIDS pandemic.* (http://www.iheu.org/modules/wfsection/article.php?articleid=380)

Izenman, A. J. & Zabell, S. L. (1981). Babies and the blackout: The genesis of a misconception. *Social Science Research, 10,* 282–299.

Jaffee, S. & Hyde, J. S. (2000). Gender differences in moral orientation: a meta-analysis. *Psychological Bulletin, 126,* 703–726.

James, A. (2004). *"Autogynephilia": A disputed diagnosis.* (http://www.tsroadmap.com/info/autogynephilia.html)

Jankowiak, W. R. & Fischer, E. F. (1992). A cross-cultural perspective on romantic love. *Ethnology, 31,* 149–155.

Janssen, E. & Bancroft, J. (2006). The dual control model: The role of sexual inhibition and excitation in sexual arousal and behavior. In E. Janssen (Ed.), *The psychophysiology of sex.* Indiana University Press.

Janssen, E., Carpenter, D. & Graham, C. A. (2003). Selecting films for sex research: gender differences in erotic film preference. *Archives of Sexual Behavior, 32,* 243–251.

Jayson, S. (2005). Cohabitation is replacing dating. *USA Today,* July 17.

Jayson, S. (2008). Report: Overall abortion rates continue to drop. *USA Today,* January 18.

Jeal, N. & Salisbury, C. (2004). A health needs assessment of street-based prostitutes: cross-sectional survey. *Journal of Public Health (Oxf.), 26,* 147–151.

Jeal, N., Salisbury, C. & Turner, K. (2008). The multiplicity and interdependency of factors influencing the health of street-based sex workers: a qualitative study. *Sexually Transmitted Infections, 84,* 381–385.

Jenkins, P. (1998). *Moral panic: Changing concepts of the child molester in modern America.* Yale University Press.

Jennings, V. H. & Arevalo, M. (2007). Fertility awareness-based methods. In R. A. Hatcher et al. (Eds.), *Contraceptive technology* (19th ed.). Ardent Media.

Jentzen, J., Palermo, G., Johnson, L. T., Ho, K. C., Stormo, K. A. & Teggatz, J. (1994). Destructive hostility: the Jeffrey Dahmer case. A psychiatric and forensic study of a serial killer. *American Journal of Forensic Medicine and Pathology, 15,* 283–294.

Jha, P., Kumar, R., Vasa, P., Dhingra, N., Thiruchelvam, D. & Moineddin, R. (2006). Low female-to-male sex ratio of children born in India: national survey of 1.1 million households. *Lancet, 367,* 211–218.

Johansson, P., Hall, L., Sikstrom, S. & Olsson, A. (2005). Failure to detect mismatches between intention and outcome in a simple decision task. *Science, 310,* 116–119.

Johnson, A. A., Hatcher, B. J., El-Khorazaty, M. N., Milligan, R. A., Bhaskar, B., Rodan, M. F., Richards, L., Wingrove, B. K. & Laryea, H. A. (2007a). Determinants of inadequate prenatal care utilization by African American women. *Journal of Health Care for the Poor and Underserved, 18,* 620–636.

Johnson, K. L., Gill, S., Reichman, V. & Tassinary, L. G. (2007b). Swagger, sway, and sexuality: Judging sexual orientation from body motion and morphology. *Journal of Personality and Social Psychology, 93,* 321–334.

Johnson, L. G., Madeleine, M. M., Newcomer, L. M., Schwartz, S. M. & Daling, J. R. (2004). Anal cancer incidence and survival: the surveillance, epidemiology, and end results experience, 1973–2000. *Cancer, 101,* 281–288.

Johnson, M. A. (2007). *Essential reproduction* (6th ed.). Blackwell.

Johnson, M. H. & Everitt, B. J. (2000). *Essential reproduction* (5th ed.). Blackwell.

Johnson, M. P. & Ferraro, K. J. (2000). Research on domestic violence in the 1990s: Making distinctions. *Journal of Marriage and the Family, 62,* 948–963.

Johnson, S. M. (2003). The revolution in couple therapy: a practitioner-scientist perspective. *Journal of Marital and Family Therapy, 29,* 365–384.

Johnson, S. M. (2004). *The practice of emotionally focused marital therapy: Creating connection* (2nd ed.). Bruner/Routledge.

Johnston, P., Hudson, S. M. & Marshall, W. L. (1992). The effects of masturbatory reconditioning with nonfamilial child molesters. *Behaviour Research and Therapy, 30,* 559–561.

Johnston, V. S., Hagel, R., Franklin, M., Fink, B. & Grammer, K. (2001). Male facial attractiveness: Evidence for hormone mediated adaptive design. *Evolution and Human Behavior, 22,* 251–267.

Jones, B. C., Debruine, L. M., Little, A. C., Conway, C. A. & Feinberg, D. R. (2006). Integrating gaze direction and expression in preferences for attractive faces. *Psychological Science, 17,* 588–591.

Jones, J. C. & Barlow, D. H. (1990). Self-reported frequency of sexual urges, fantasies, and masturbatory fantasies in heterosexual males and females. *Archives of Sexual Behavior, 19,* 269–279.

Jones, M. Y., Stanaland, A. J. S. & Gelb, B. D. (1998). Beefcake and cheesecake: Insights for advertisers. *Journal of Advertising, 27,* 33–52.

Jones, R. K., Darroch, J. E. & Henshaw, S. K. (2002). Patterns in the socioeconomic characteristics of women obtaining abortions in 2000–2001. *Perspectives on Sexual and Reproductive Health, 34,* 226–235.

Jose, K. (2008). *Poll: New Yorkers pinning high hopes on Paterson.* (http://www.observer.com/2008/poll-new-yorkers-pinning-high-hopes-paterson)

Jost, A. (1953). Problems of fetal endocrinology: The gonadal and hypophyseal hormones. *Recent Progress in Hormone Research, 8,* 379–418.

Juberg, D. R. (2000). An evaluation of endocrine modulators: implications for human health. *Ecotoxicology and Environmental Safety, 45,* 93–105.

Judson, O. (2002). *Dr. Tatiana's sex advice to all creation.* Metropolitan Books.

Kafka, M. P. (2003). Sex offending and sexual desire: The clinical and theoretical relevance of hypersexual desire. *International Journal of Offender Therapy and Comparative Criminology, 47,* 439–451.

Kafka, M. P. (2008). Neurobiological processes and comorbidity. In D. R. Laws and W. T. O'Donohue (Eds.), *Sexual deviance: Theory, assessment, and treatment* (2nd ed.). Guilford Press.

Kahn, R. H., Voigt, R. F., Swint, E. & Weinstock, H. (2004). Early syphilis in the United States identified in corrections facilities, 1999–2002. *Sexually Transmitted Diseases, 31,* 360–364.

Kaiser, J. (2000). Endocrine disruptors: Panel cautiously confirms low-dose effects. *Science, 290,* 695–697.

Kaiser, J. (2008). Price is the main barrier to wider use of papillomavirus vaccine. *Science, 320,* 860.

Kanazawa, S. & Still, M. C. (2000). Teaching may be hazardous to your marriage. *Evolution and Human Behavior, 21,* 185–190.

Kandel, E. R. & Schwartz, J. H. (Eds.) (1985). *Principles of neural science.* Elsevier.

Kang, K. C. (2001). Japanese government knew about sex slaves, researchers say. *Los Angeles Times,* November 30.

Kanin, E. J. (1994). False rape allegations. *Archives of Sexual Behavior, 23,* 81–92.

Kano, T. (1992). *The last ape: Pygmy chimpanzee behavior and ecology.* Stanford University Press.

Kaplan, H. S. (1974). *The new sex therapy.* Brunner/Mazel.

Kaplan, H. S. (1979). *Disorders of sexual desire.* Simon and Schuster.

Kaplan, H. S. (1992). A neglected issue: the sexual side effects of current treatments for breast cancer. *Journal of Sex and Marital Therapy, 18,* 3–19.

Kaplowitz, P. B. & Oberfield, S. E. (1999). Reexamination of the age limit for defining when puberty is precocious in girls in the United States: implications for evaluation and treatment. Drug and Therapeutics and Executive Committees of the Lawson Wilkins Pediatric Endocrine Society. *Pediatrics, 104,* 936–941.

Karellas, A., Lo, J. Y. & Orton, C. G. (2008). Point/Counterpoint. Cone beam x-ray CT will be superior to digital x-ray tomosynthesis in imaging the breast and delineating cancer. *Medical Physics, 35,* 409–411.

Katz, G. (2006). Letter to the Editor. *New York Times,* July 5.

Katz, J. & Jhally, S. (2000). Put the blame where it belongs: On men. *Los Angeles Times,* June 25.

Katz, J. N. (1993). Plymouth Colony sodomy statutes and cases. In W. B. Rubenstein (Ed.), *Lesbians, gay men and the law.* New Press.

Katz, P. A. & Boswell, S. (1986). Flexibility and traditionality in children's gender roles. *Genetic, Social, and General Psychology Monographs, 112,* 103–147.

Kaur, G., Gonsalves, L. & Thacker, H. L. (2004). Premenstrual dysphoric disorder: a review for the treating practitioner. *Cleveland Clinic Journal of Medicine, 71,* 303–305, 312–303, 317–308 passim.

Kaushal, V., Rattan, K. N., Kaushik, V., Magu, S. & Kaushik, S. (2007). Feminizing adrenal adenoma presenting as isosexual precocious puberty. *Internet Journal of Pediatrics and Neonatology, 7* (http://www.ispub.com/ostia/index.php?xmlFilePath=journals/ijpn/vol7n1/adrenal.xml)

Kawahara, M., Obata, Y., Sotomaru, Y., Shimozawa, N., Bao, S., Tsukadaira, T., Fukuda, A. & Kono, T. (2008). Protocol for the production of viable bimaternal mouse embryos. *Nature Protocol, 3,* 197–209.

Keele, B. F. & 18 others. (2006). Chimpanzee reservoirs of pandemic and nonpandemic HIV-1. *Science, 313,* 523–526.

Kegeles, S. M., Hays, R. B. & Coates, T. J. (1996). The Mpowerment Project: a community-level HIV prevention intervention for young gay men. *American Journal of Public Health, 86,* 1129–1136.

Keightley, P. D. & Eyre-Walker, A. (2000). Deleterious mutations and the evolution of sex. *Science, 290,* 331–333.

Kendall-Tackett, K. A., Williams, L. M. & Finkelhor, D. (1993). Impact of sexual abuse on children: a review and synthesis of recent empirical studies. *Psychological Bulletin, 113,* 164–180.

Kendler, K. S., Thornton, L. M., Gilman, S. E. & Kessler, R. C. (2000). Sexual orientation in a U.S. national sample of twin and nontwin sibling pairs. *American Journal of Psychiatry, 157,* 1843–1846.

Kennedy, E. L. & Davis, M. D. (1983). *Boots of leather, slippers of gold: The history of a lesbian community.* Routledge.

Kenrick, D. T. & Gutierres, S. E. (1980). Contrast effects and judgements of physical attractiveness: When beauty becomes a social problem. *Journal of Personality and Social Psychology, 38,* 131–140.

Kenrick, D. T., Gutierres, S. E. & Goldberg, S. E. (1989). Influence of erotica on ratings of strangers and mates. *Journal of Personality and Social Psychology, 25,* 159–167.

Kerns, K. A. & Berenbaum, S. A. (1991). Sex differences in spatial ability in children. *Behavior Genetics, 21,* 383–396.

Kessel, B. (2000). Premenstrual syndrome. Advances in diagnosis and treatment. *Obstetrical and Gynecological Clinics of North America, 27,* 625–639.

Key, W. B. (2003). Subliminal seduction: The fountainhead for America's obsession. In T. Reichert and J. Lambiase (Eds.), *Sex in advertising: Perspectives on the erotic appeal.* Erlbaum.

Kiebert, G. M., de Haes, J. C. & van de Velde, C. J. (1991). The impact of breast-conserving treatment and mastectomy on the quality of life of early-stage breast cancer patients: a review. *Journal of Clinical Oncology, 9,* 1059–1070.

Kiess, W., Muller, G., Galler, A., Reich, A., Deutscher, J., Klammt, J. & Kratzsch, J. (2000). Body fat mass, leptin and puberty. *Journal of Pediatric Endocrinology and Metabolism, 13 Suppl 1,* 717–722.

Kimball, M. M. (1986). Television and sex-role attitudes. In T. M. Williams (Ed.), *The impact of television: A natural experiment in three communities.* Academic Press.

Kim-Gibson, D. S. (1999). *Silence broken: Korean comfort women.* Mid-Prairie Books.

Kimura, D. (1999). *Sex and cognition.* MIT Press.

Kindon, H. A., Baum, M. J. & Paredes, R. J. (1996). Medial preoptic/anterior hypothalamic lesions induce a female-typical profile of sexual partner preference in male ferrets. *Hormones and Behavior, 30,* 514–527.

King, M. C., Marks, J. H. & Mandell, J. B. (2003). Breast and ovarian cancer risks due to inherited mutations in BRCA1 and BRCA2. *Science, 302,* 643–646.

King, M. C., Wieand, S., Hale, K., Lee, M., Walsh, T., Owens, K., Tait, J., Ford, L., Dunn, B. K., Costantino, J., Wickerham, L., Wolmark, N. & Fisher, B. (2001). Tamoxifen and breast cancer incidence among women with inherited mutations in BRCA1 and BRCA2: National Surgical Adjuvant Breast and Bowel Project (NSABP-P1) Breast Cancer Prevention Trial. *JAMA, 286,* 2251–2256.

Kingsberg, S., Shifren, J., Wekselman, K., Rodenberg, C., Koochaki, P. & Derogatis, L. (2007). Evaluation of the clinical relevance of benefits associated with transdermal testosterone treatment in postmenopausal women with hypoactive sexual desire disorder. *Journal of Sexual Medicine, 4,* 1001–1008.

Kinlay, J. R., O'Connell, D. L. & Kinlay, S. (2001). Risk factors for mastitis in breast-feeding women: results of a prospective cohort study. *Australian and New Zealand Journal of Public Health, 25,* 115–120.

Kinsey, A. C., Pomeroy, W. B. & Martin, C. E. (1948). *Sexual behavior in the human male.* Saunders.

Kinsey, A. C., Pomeroy, W. B., Martin, C. E. & Gebhard, P. H. (1953). *Sexual behavior in the human female.* Saunders.

Kinsman, S. B., Romer, D., Furstenberg, F. F. & Schwarz, D. F. (1998). Early sexual initiation: the role of peer norms. *Pediatrics, 102,* 1185–1192.

Kiyomura, C. (2005). *DSHS may want slice of Letourneau wedding payoff pie.* (http://www.king5.com/localnews/stories/NW_050205WABletourneauSW.2376b0238.html)

Klar, A. J. S. (2005). Excess of counterclockwise scalp hair-whorl rotation in homosexual men. *Journal of Genetics, 83,* 251–255.

Klassen, A. D., Williams, C. J. & Levitt, E. E. (1989). *Sex and morality in the U.S.: An empirical enquiry under the auspices of the Kinsey Institute.* Wesleyan University Press.

Klein, J. & Sauer, M. V. (2002). Oocyte donation. Best *Practice & Research: Clinical Obstetrics & Gynaecology, 16,* 277–291.

Klein, M. (2006). *America's war on sex: The attack on law, lust, and liberty.* Praeger Publishers.

Klein, R. (1999). *Penile augmentation surgery.* (http://www.ejhs.org/volume2/klein/penis10.htm)

Klusmann, D. (2002). Sexual motivation and the duration of partnership. *Archives of Sexual Behavior, 31,* 275–287.

Knafo, D. & Jaffe, Y. (1984). Sexual fantasizing in males and females. *Journal of Research in Personality, 18,* 451–467.

KNBC.com. (2008). *Suit approved for woman who alleges ex-husband gave her AIDS.* (http://www.knbc.com/health/16551746/detail.html)

Knickmeyer, R. & Baron-Cohen, S. (2006). Fetal testosterone and sex differences. *Early Human Development, 82,* 755–760.

Kobayashi, K., Masumori, N., Hisasue, S. I., Kato, R., Hashimoto, K., Itoh, N. & Tsukamoto, T. (2007). Inhibition of seminal emission is the main cause of an ejaculation induced by a new highly selective alpha1A-blocker in normal volunteers. *Journal of Sexual Medicine, 5,* 2185–2190.

Kohlberg, L. A. (1966). A cognitive-developmental analysis of children's sex role concepts and attitudes. In E. E. Maccoby (Ed.), *The development of sex differences.* Stanford University Press.

Kolata, G. (2007). Training through pregnancy to be marathon's fastest mom. *New York Times,* November 3.

Kolodny, R., Masters, W. H. & Johnson, V. (1979). *Textbook of sexual medicine.* Little, Brown.

Kondrashov, A. S. (1988). Deleterious mutations and the evolution of sexual reproduction. *Nature, 336,* 435–440.

Korach, K. S., Couse, J. F., Curtis, S. W., Washburn, T. F., Lindzey, J., Kimbro, K. S., Eddy, E. M., Migliaccio, S., Snedeker, S. M., Lubahn, D. B., Schomberg, D. W. & Smith, E. P. (1996). Estrogen receptor gene disruption: molecular characterization and experimental and clinical phenotypes. *Recent Progress in Hormone Research, 51,* 159–186.

Koskela, P., Anttila, T., Bjorge, T., Brunsvig, A., Dillner, J., Hakama, M., Hakulinen, T., Jellum, E., Lehtinen, M., Lenner, P., Luostarinen, T., Pukkala, E., Saikku, P., Thoresen, S., Youngman, L. & Paavonen, J. (2000). Chlamydia trachomatis infection as a risk factor for invasive cervical cancer. *International Journal of Cancer, 85,* 35–39.

Kosters, J. P. & Goetzsche, P. C. (2008). *Regular self-examination or clinical examination for early detection of breast cancer.* (http://www.cochrane.org/reviews/en/ab003373.html)

Kotz, D. (2008). A risky rise in C-sections. *U.S. News and World Report,* April 7.

Kramer, M. S., Aboud, F., Mironova, E., Vanilovich, I., Platt, R. W., Matush, L., Igumnov, S., Fombonne, E., Bogdanovich, N., Ducruet, T., Collet, J. P., Chalmers, B., Hodnett, E., Davidovsky, S., Skugarevsky, O., Trofimovich, O., Kozlova, L. & Shapiro, S. (2008). Breastfeeding and child cognitive development: new evidence from a large randomized trial. *Archives of General Psychiatry, 65,* 578–584.

Kraut-Becher, J., Eisenberg, M., Voytek, C., Brown, T., Metzger, D. S. & Aral, S. (2008). Examining racial disparities in HIV: lessons from sexually transmitted infections research. *Journal of Acquired Immune Deficiency Syndromes, 47 Suppl 1,* S20–27.

Kritsberg, W. (1993). *The invisible wound: A new approach to healing childhood sexual trauma.* Bantam.

Krob, G., Braun, A. & Kuhnle, U. (1994). True hermaphroditism: geographical distribution, clinical findings, chromosomes and gonadal histology. *European Journal of Pediatrics, 153,* 2–10.

Kuliev, A. & Verlinsky, Y. (2008). Preimplantation genetic diagnosis: technological advances to improve accuracy and range of applications. *Reproductive Biomedicine Online, 16,* 532–538.

Kynard, B. E. (1978). Breeding behavior of a lacustrine population of threespine sticklebacks (*Gasterosteus aculeatus* L.). *Behavior, 67,* 178–202.

Ladas, A. K., Whipple, B. & Perry, J. D. (2004). *The G spot and other recent discoveries about human sexuality.* Holt.

LaFraniere, S. (2005). Poor lands treating far more AIDS patients. *New York Times,* January 27.

Lahdenpera, M., Lummaa, V., Helle, S., Tremblay, M. & Russell, A. F. (2004). Fitness benefits of prolonged post-reproductive lifespan in women. *Nature, 428,* 178–181.

Lalumiere, M. L. & Quinsey, V. L. (1998). Pavlovian conditioning of sexual interests in human males. *Archives of Sexual Behavior, 27,* 241–252.

Lamaze International. (2002). *Myths about Lamaze.* (http://www.lamaze.org/2000/myth.html)

Lambda Legal Defense and Education Fund. (2000). *Lambda to sue Reno school officials for failing to protect gay student.* (http://www.lambdalegal.org/cgi-bin/pages/documents/record?record=560)

Landolt, M. A., Bartholomew, K., Saffrey, C., Oram, D. & Perlman, D. (2004). Gender nonconformity, childhood rejection, and adult attachment: a study of gay men. *Archives of Sexual Behavior, 33,* 117–128.

Landsberg, M. (2000). McMartin defendant who "lost everything" in abuse case dies at 74. *Los Angeles Times,* December 17.

Laner, M. R. & Ventrone, N. A. (2000). Dating scripts revisited. *Journal of Family Issues, 21,* 488–500.

Langevin, R. & Watson, R. J. (1996). Major factors in the assessment of paraphiliacs and sex offenders. *Journal of Offender Rehabilitation, 23,* 39–70.

Langevin, R., Paitich, D., Freeman, R., Mann, K. & Handy, L. (1978). Personality characteristics and sexual anomalies in males. *Canadian Journal of Behavioural Sciences, 10,* 222–226.

Langstrom, N. & Zucker, K. J. (2005). Transvestic festishism in the general population: Prevalence and correlates. *Journal of Sex and Marital Therapy, 31,* 87–95.

Larsson, I. & Svedin, C. G. (2002a). Sexual experiences in childhood: young adults' recollections. *Archives of Sexual Behavior, 31,* 263–273.

Larsson, I. & Svedin, C. G. (2002b). Teachers' and parents' reports on 3- to 6-year-old children's sexual behavior: A comparison. *Child Abuse and Neglect, 26,* 247–266.

Larsson, I., Svedin, C. G. & Friedrich, W. N. (2000). Differences and similarities in sexual behavior among pre-schoolers in Sweden and USA. *Nordic Journal of Psychiatry, 54,* 151–157.

Lauby, J. L., Smith, P. J., Stark, M., Person, B. & Adams, J. (2000). A community-level HIV prevention intervention for inner-city women: results of the women and infants demonstration projects. *American Journal of Public Health, 90,* 216–222.

Laumann, E. O. & Michael, R. T. (Eds.) (2000). *Sex, love, and health in America: Private choices and public policies.* University of Chicago Press.

Laumann, E. O., Ellingson, S., Mahay, J., Paik, A. & Youm, Y. (Eds.) (2004). *The sexual organization of the city.* University of Chicago Press.

Laumann, E. O., Gagnon, J. H., Michael, R. T. & Michaels, S. (1994). *The social organization of sexuality: Sexual practices in the United States.* University of Chicago Press.

Laumann, E. O., Masi, C. M. & Zuckerman, E. W. (1997). Circumcision in the United States. Prevalence, prophylactic effects, and sexual practice. *JAMA, 277,* 1052–1057.

Laumann, E. O., Paik, A. & Rosen, R. C. (2000). Sexual dysfunction in the United States: Prevalence and predictors. In E. O. Laumann and R. T. Michael (Eds.), *Sex, love, and health in America: Private choices and public policies.* University of Chicago Press.

Lawrence, A. A. (2003). Factors associated with satisfaction or regret following male-to-female sex reassignment surgery. *Archives of Sexual Behavior, 32,* 299–315.

Lawrence, A. A. (2004). Autogynephilia: A paraphilic model of gender identity disorder. *Journal of Gay and Lesbian Psychotherapy, 8,* 69–87.

Lawrence, A. A. (2008). *Practice information.* (http://www.annelawrence.com/practice/index.html)

Lawrence, K.-A. & Byers, E. S. (1995). Sexual satisfaction in long-term heterosexual relationships: The interpersonal exchange model of sexual satisfaction. *Personal Relationships, 2,* 267–285.

Laws, D. R. (1999). Harm reduction or harm facilitation? A reply to Maletzky. *Sexual Abuse, 11,* 233–241.

Laws, D. R. & O'Donohue, W. T. (2008). *Sexual deviance: Theory, assessment, and treatment* (2nd ed.). Guilford Press.

Le, H. H., Carlson, E. M., Chua, J. P. & Belcher, S. M. (2008). Bisphenol A is released from polycarbonate drinking bottles and mimics the neurotoxic actions of estrogen in developing cerebellar neurons. *Toxicology Letters, 176,* 149–156.

Leap, W. L. (Ed.) (1999). *Public sex/Gay space.* Columbia University Press.

LeDoux, J. (2002). *Synaptic self: How our brains become who we are.* Viking.

Lee, G. R. & Shehan, C. L. (1989). Retirement and marital satisfaction. *Journal of Gerontology, 44,* S226–230.

Lee, J. K. P., Jackson, H. J., Pattison, P. & Ward, T. (2002). Developmental risk factors for sexual offending. *Child Abuse and Neglect, 26,* 73–92.

Lee, P. A. & Houk, C. P. (2004). Outcome studies among men with micropenis. *Journal of Pediatric Endocrinology and Metabolism, 17,* 1043–1053.

Lee, P. A., Houk, C. P., Ahmed, S. F. & Hughes, I. A. (2006). Consensus statement on management of intersex disorders. *Pediatrics, 118,* e488–500.

Lehtinen, M., Koskela, P., Jellum, E., Bloigu, A., Anttila, T., Hallmans, G., Luukkaala, T., Thoresen, S., Youngman, L., Dillner, J. & Hakama, M. (2002). Herpes simplex virus and risk of cervical cancer: a longitudinal, nested case-control study in the nordic countries. *American Journal of Epidemiology, 156,* 687–692.

Leiblum, S. R. (2007a). Persistent genital arousal disorder. In S. R. Leiblum (Ed.), *Principles and practice of sex therapy* (4th ed.). Guilford Press.

Leiblum, S. R. (Ed.) (2007b). *Principles and practice of sex therapy.* Guilford Press.

Leiblum, S. R. (2007c). Sex therapy today: Current issues and future perspectives. In S. R. Leiblum (Ed.), *Principles and practice of sex therapy* (4th ed.). Guilford Press.

Leinbach, M. D. & Fagot, B. I. (1993). Categorical habituation to male and female faces: Gender schematic processing in infancy. *Infant Behavior and Development, 16,* 317–332.

Leitenberg, H. & Henning, K. (1995). Sexual fantasy. *Psychological Bulletin, 117,* 469–496.

Lemieux, R. & Hale, J. L. (1999). Intimacy, passion, and commitment in young romantic relationships: Successfully measuring the triangular theory of love. *Psychological Reports, 85,* 497–503.

Lemieux, R. & Hale, J. L. (2000). Intimacy, passion, and commitment among married individuals: Further testing of the triangular theory of love. *Psychological Reports, 87,* 941–948.

Leone, P. & Corey, L. (2005). *Genital herpes: Prevalence, transmission, and prevention.* (http://www.medscape.com/viewarticle/502718_1)

Levant, R. (1997). *Men and emotions: A psychoeducational approach.* Newbridge Communications.

LeVay, S. (1991). A difference in hypothalamic structure between heterosexual and homosexual men. *Science, 253,* 1034–1037.

LeVay, S. (1996). *Queer science: The use and abuse of research into homosexuality.* MIT Press.

LeVay, S. & Nonas, E. (1995). *City of friends: A portrait of the gay and lesbian community in America.* MIT Press.

Levenson, J. S. & Macgowan, M. J. (2004). Engagement, denial, and treatment progress among sex offenders in group therapy. *Sexual Abuse, 16,* 49–63.

Lever, J. (1994). Sexual revelations: The 1994 Advocate survey of sexuality and relationships: The men. In *The Advocate,* pp. 17–24.

Lever, J. (1995). Lesbian sex survey. In *The Advocate,* pp. 21–30.

Lever, J., Frederick, D. A. & Peplau, L. A. (2006). Does size matter? Men's and women's views on penis size across the lifespan. *Psychology of Men and Masculinity, 7,* 129–143.

Levine, D. (2000). Virtual attraction: What rocks your boat. *CyberPsychology and Behavior, 3,* 565–573.

Lewin, T. (1997). Teen-agers alter sexual practices, thinking risks will be avoided. *New York Times,* April 5.

Lewis, R. J. & Janda, L. H. (1988). The relationship between adult sexual adjustment and childhood experiences regarding exposure to nudity, sleeping in the parental bed, and parental attitudes toward sexuality. *Archives of Sexual Behavior, 17,* 349–362.

Lewontin, R. C. (1995). Sex, lies, and social science. In *New York Review of Books,* April 20.

Li, C. Y., Kayes, O., Kell, P. D., Christopher, N., Minhas, S. & Ralph, D. J. (2006). Penile suspensory ligament division for penile augmentation: indications and results. *European Urology, 49,* 729–733.

Lichter, D. T., Qian, Z. & Mellott, L. M. (2006). Marriage or dissolution? Union transitions among poor cohabiting women. *Demography, 43,* 223–240.

Lieberman, D., Tooby, J. & Cosmides, L. (2003). Does morality have a biological basis? An empirical test of the factors governing moral sentiments relating to incest. *Proceedings of the Royal Society of London Series B: Biological Sciences, 270,* 819–826.

Lim, K. T., Casey, R. G., Lennon, F., Gillen, P. & Stokes, M. (2003). Cryptorchidism: a general surgical perspective. *Irish Journal of Medical Science, 172,* 139–140.

Lim, L. L. (Ed.) (1998). *The sex sector: The economic and social bases of prostitution in Southeast Asia.* International Labour Office.

Lim, M. M., Liu, Y., Ryabinin, A. E., Bai, Y., Wang, Z. & Young, L. J. (2007). CRF receptors in the nucleus accumbens modulate partner preference in prairie voles. *Hormones and Behavior, 51,* 508–515.

Lim, M. M., Wang, Z., Olazabal, D. E., Ren, X., Terwilliger, E. F. & Young, L. J. (2004). Enhanced partner preference in a promiscuous species by manipulating the expression of a single gene. *Nature, 429,* 754–757.

Lin, B. J., Chen, K. K., Chen, M. T. & Chang, L. S. (1994). The time for serum testosterone to reach castrate level after bilateral orchiectomy or oral estrogen in the management of metastatic prostatic cancer. *Urology, 43,* 834–837.

Lin, Y.-H. (1961). *The lolo of Liang Shan.* HRAF Press.

Lindau, S. T., Schumm, L. P., Laumann, E. O., Levinson, W., O'Muircheartaigh, C. A. & Waite, L. J. (2007). A study of sexuality and health among older adults in the United States. *New England Journal of Medicine, 357,* 762–774.

Lindberg, L. D., Jones, R. & Santelli, J. S. (2008). Noncoital sexual activities among adolescents. *Journal of Adolescent Health, 43,* 231–238.

Lindberg, L. D., Santelli, J. S. & Singh, S. (2006). Changes in formal sex education: 1995–2002. *Perspectives on Sexual and Reproductive Health, 38,* 182–189.

Linden, J. A. (1999). Sexual assault. *Emergency Medicine Clinics of North America, 17,* 685–697.

Linz, D., Blumenthal, E., Donnerstein, E., Kunkel, D., Shafer, B. J. & Lichtenstein, A. (2000). Testing legal assumptions regarding the effects of dancer nudity and proximity to patron on erotic expression. *Law and Human Behavior, 24,* 507–533.

Linzer, D. (2008). Same-sex divorce challenges the legal system. *Washington Post,* January 2.

Lipitz, S., Frenkel, Y., Watts, C., Ben-Rafael, Z., Barkai, G. & Reichman, B. (1990). High-order multifetal gestation—management and outcome. *Obstetrics and Gynecology, 76,* 215–218.

Lippa, R. A. (2000). Gender-related traits in gay men, lesbian women, and heterosexual men and women: The virtual identity of homosexual-heterosexual diagnosticity and gender diagnosticity. *Journal of Personality, 68,* 899–925.

Lippa, R. A. (2002). Gender-related traits of heterosexual and homosexual men and women. *Archives of Sexual Behavior, 31,* 83–98.

Lippa, R. A. (2005). *Gender, nature, and nurture* (2nd ed.). Erlbaum.

Lippa, R. A. (2006). The gender reality hypothesis. *American Psychologist, 61,* 639–640; discussion 641–642.

Lippa, R. A. (2008). Sex differences and sexual orientation differences in personality: findings from the BBC Internet survey. *Archives of Sexual Behavior, 37,* 173–187.

Lippert, B. (1995). The naked untruth. *Adweek,* September 18.

Little, A. C., Apicella, C. L. & Marlowe, F. W. (2007). Preferences for symmetry in human faces in two cultures: data from the UK and the Hadza, an isolated group of hunter-gatherers. *Proceedings Biological Science, 274,* 3113–3117.

Litwin, M. S. (1999). Health related quality of life in older men without prostate cancer. *Journal of Urology, 161,* 1180–1184.

Liu, C. (2002). Ridding the MTA of pests. *Los Angeles Times,* October 7.

Lively, C. M. & Dybdahl, M. F. (2000). Parasite adaptation to locally common host genotypes. *Nature, 405,* 679–681.

Lobdell, W. & Stammer, L. B. (2004). 4 percent of U.S. priests since 1950 may have abused. *Los Angeles Times,* February 27.

Loftus, E. F. & Davis, D. (2006). Recovered memories. *Annual Review of Clinical Psychology, 2,* 469–498.

Lönnerdal, B. (2003). Nutritional and physiological signifance of human milk proteins. *American Society for Clinical Nutrition, 77,* 1537S–1543S.

Lopez Bernal, A. & TambyRaja, R. L. (2000). Preterm labour. *Baillieres Best Practice and Research in Clinical and Obstretrics and Gynecology, 14,* 133–153.

LoPiccolo, J. (1992). Postmodern sex therapy for erectile failure. In R. C. Rosen and S. R. Leiblum (Eds.), *Erectile disorders: Assessment and treatment.* Guilford Press.

Los Angeles Gay and Lesbian Center. (2001). *STOP Domestic Violence Program.* (http://www.laglc.org/section05/S0512.htm)

Lösel, F. & Schmucker, M. (2005). The effectiveness of treatment for sexual offenders: A comprehensive meta-analysis. *Journal of Experimental Criminology, 1,* 117–146.

Louganis, G. & Marcus, E. (1995). *Breaking the surface.* Random House.

Love in Action. (2008). *Finding freedom in Jesus Christ.* (http://loveinaction.org/)

Lovelace, L. & McGrady, M. (1980). *Ordeal.* Carol Publishing Group.

Lu, M. C., Prentice, J., Yu, S. M., Inkelas, M., Lange, L. O. & Halfon, N. (2003). Childbirth education classes: sociodemographic disparities in attendance and the association of attendance with breastfeeding initiation. *Maternal and Child Health Journal, 7,* 87–93.

Ludwig, A. K., Katalinic, A., Thyen, U., Sutcliffe, A. G., Diedrich, K. & Ludwig, M. (2008). Physical health at 5.5 years of age of term-born singletons after intracytoplasmic sperm injection: results of a prospective, controlled, single-blinded study. *Fertility and Sterility* (online publication, DOI: 10.1016/j.fertnstert. 2007. 11.037).

Lumley, V. A. & Scotti, J. R. (2001). Supporting the sexuality of adults with mental retardation. *Journal of Positive Behavior Interventions, 3,* 109–119.

Lundstrom, J. N. & Olsson, M. J. (2005). Subthreshold amounts of social odorant affect mood, but not behavior, in heterosexual women when tested by a male, but not a female, experimenter. *Biological Psychology, 70,* 197–204.

Lussier, P. & Piché, L. (2008). Frotteurism: Psychopathology and theory. In D. R. Laws and W. T. O'Donohue (Eds.), *Sexual deviance: Theory, assessment, and treatment* (2nd ed.). Guilford Press.

Luzzi, G. A. & Law, L. A. (2006). The male sexual pain syndromes. *International Journal of STD and AIDS, 17,* 720–726; quiz 726.

Lykins, A. D., Meana, M. & Strauss, G. P. (2008). Sex differences in visual attention to erotic and non-erotic stimuli. *Archives of Sexual Behavior, 37,* 219–228.

Lyman, R. (2005). Trying to strengthen an "I do" with a more binding legal tie. *New York Times,* February 15.

Lynch, M., Blanchard, J., Houle, D., Kibota, T., Schultz, S., Vassilieva, L. & Willis, J. (1999). Spontaneous deleterious mutation. *Evolution, 53,* 645–663.

Lyon, K. (1998). *Witch hunt: A true story of social hysteria and abused justice.* Avon Books.

Macaluso, M., Demand, M., Artz, L., Fleenor, M., Robey, L., Kelaghan, J., Cabral, R. & Hook, E. W., 3rd. (2000). Female condom use among women at high risk of sexually transmitted disease. *Family Planning Perspectives, 32,* 138–144.

MacCarthy, T. & Bergman, A. (2007). Coevolution of robustness, epistasis, and recombination favors asexual reproduction. *Proceedings of the National Academy of Sciences of the United States of America, 104,* 12801–12806.

Maccoby, E. E. (1998). *The two sexes: Growing up apart, coming together.* Harvard University Press.

Maccoby, E. E. & Jacklin, C. N. (1987). Gender segregation in childhood. In H. W. Reese (Ed.), *Advances in Child Development and Behavior,* vol. 20. Academic Press.

Macfarlane, J. M., Campbell, J. C., Wiot, S., Sachs, C., Ulrich, Y. & Xu, X. (1999). Stalking and intimate partner femicide. *Homicide Studies, 3/4,* 300–317.

MacKinnon, C. (1979). *Sexual harassment of working women: A case of discrimination.* Yale University Press.

Mahay, J., Laumann, E. O. & Michaels, S. (2000). Race, gender, and class in sexual scripts. In E. O. Laumann and R. T. Michael (Eds.), *Sex, love, and health in America: Private choices and public policies.* University of Chicago Press.

Maheu, M. M. & Subotnik, R. B. (2001). *Infidelity and the Internet: Virtual relationships and real betrayal.* Sourcebooks.

Maines, R. (1999). *The technology of orgasm: "Hysteria," the vibrator, and women's sexual satisfaction.* Johns Hopkins University Press.

Mains, G. (1984). *Urban aboriginals: A celebration of leathersexuality.* Gay Sunshine Press.

Major, B., Cozzarelli, C., Cooper, M. L., Zubek, J., Richards, C., Wilhite, M. & Gramzow, R. H. (2000). Psychological responses of women after first-trimester abortion. *Archives of General Psychiatry, 57,* 777–784.

Malamuth, N. M. (1981). Rape proclivity among males. *Journal of Social Issues, 37,* 138–157.

Malamuth, N. M., Addison, T. & Koss, M. (2000). Pornography and sexual aggression: are there reliable effects and can we understand them? *Annual Review of Sex Research, 11,* 26–91.

Malamuth, N. M., Linz, D., Heavey, C. L., Barnes, G. & Acker, M. (1995). Using the confluence model of sexual aggression to predict men's conflict with women: a 10-year follow-up study. *Journal of Personality and Social Psychology, 69,* 353–369.

Malo, A. F., Roldan, E. R., Garde, J., Soler, A. J. & Gomendio, M. (2005). Antlers honestly advertise sperm production and quality. *Proceedings of the Royal Society of London Series B: Biological Sciences, 272,* 149–157.

Mamo, L. (2007). *Queering reproduction: Achieving pregnancy in the age of technoscience.* Duke University Press.

Mann, P. E. & Bridges, R. S. (2001). Lactogenic hormone regulation of maternal behavior. *Progress in Brain Research, 133,* 251–262.

Mann, R. E., Ainsworth, F., Al-Attar, Z. & Davies, M. N. (2008). Voyeurism: Assessment and treatment. In D. R. Laws and W. T. O'Donohue (Eds.), *Sexual deviance: Theory, assessment, and treatment* (2nd ed.). Guilford Press.

Manning, J. T. & Chamberlain, A. T. (1994). Fluctuating asymmetry in gorilla canines: A sensitive indicator of environmental stress. *Proceedings of the Royal Society of London Series B: Biological Sciences, 255,* 189–193.

Manning, J. T., Churchill, A. J. & Peters, M. (2007). The effects of sex, ethnicity, and sexual orientation on self-measured digit ratio (2D:4D). *Archives of Sexual Behavior, 36,* 223–233.

Manning, W. D. & Smock, P. (2007). Measuring and modeling cohabitation: New perspectives from qualitative data. *Journal of Marriage and the Family, 67,* 989–1002.

Mannino, F. (1988). Neonatal complications of postterm gestation. *Journal of Reproductive Medicine, 33,* 271–276.

Mannix, L. K. (2008). Menstrual-related pain conditions: dysmenorrhea and migraine. *Journal of Womens' Health, 17,* 879–891.

Marazziti, D., Di Nasso, E., Masala, I., Baroni, S., Abelli, M., Mengali, F., Mungai, F. & Rucci, P. (2003). Normal and obsessional jealousy: a study of a population of young adults. *European Psychiatry, 18,* 106–111.

Marchbanks, P. A., McDonald, J. A., Wilson, H. G., Folger, S. G., Mandel, M. G., Daling, J. R., Bernstein, L., Malone, K. E., Ursin, G., Strom, B. L., Norman, S. A., Wingo, P. A., Burkman, R. T., Berlin, J. A., Simon, M. S., Spirtas, R. & Weiss, L. K. (2002). Oral contraceptives and the risk of breast cancer. *New England Journal of Medicine, 346,* 2025–2032.

Marcovitz, H. & Snyder, G. (2001). *Gallup youth survey: Major issues and trends.* Mason Crest Publishers.

Marcus, E. (1992). *Making history: the struggle for gay and lesbian equal rights.* HarperCollins.

Marcus, E. (2002). *Making gay history: The half-century fight for lesbian and gay equal rights.* HarperPerennial.

Marcus, R., Leary, D., Schneider, D. L., Shane, E., Favus, M. & Quigley, C. A. (2000). The contribution of testosterone to skeletal development and maintenance: lessons from the androgen insensitivity syndrome. *Journal of Clinical Endocrinology and Metabolism, 85,* 1032–1037.

Margaret Sanger Papers Project. (2000). *Margaret Sanger: Biographical sketch.* (http://www.nyu.edu/projects/sanger/ms-bio.htm)

Mark Welch, D. & Meselson, M. (2000). Evidence for the evolution of bdelloid rotifers without sexual reproduction or genetic exchange. *Science, 288,* 1211–1215.

Mark Welch, J. L., Mark Welch, D. B. & Meselson, M. (2004). Cytogenetic evidence for asexual evolution of bdelloid rotifers. *Proceedings of the National Academy of Sciences of the United States of America, 101,* 1618–1621.

Markman, H. J. (1981). Prediction of marital distress: A 5-year follow-up. *Journal of Consulting and Clinical Psychology, 49,* 760–762.

Markman, H. J., Renick, M. J., Floyd, F. J., Stanley, S. M. & Clements, M. (1993). Preventing marital distress through communication and conflict management training: a 4- and 5-year follow-up. *Journal of Consulting and Clinical Psychology, 61,* 70–77.

Marques, J. K., Wiederanders, M., Day, D. M., Nelson, C. & van Ommeren, A. (2005). Effects of a relapse prevention program on sexual recidivism: Final results from California's Sex Offender Treatment and Evaluation Project (SOTEP). *Sexual Abuse, 17,* 79–107.

Marrazzo, J. M., Koutsky, L. A., Eschenbach, D. A., Agnew, K., Stine, K. & Hillier, S. L. (2002). Characterization of vaginal flora and bacterial vaginosis in women who have sex with women. *Journal of Infectious Diseases, 185,* 1307–1313.

Marshall, D. S. (1971). Sexual behavior on Mangaia. In D. S. Marshall and D. N. Suggs (Eds.), *Human sexual behavior.* Basic Books.

Marshall, W. L. & Fernandez, Y. M. (2003). *Phallometric testing with sexual offenders.* Safer Society Press.

Martin, C. L. & Halverson, C. F. (1983). The effects of sex-typing schemas on young children's memories. *Child Development, 54,* 563–574.

Martin, D. (2006). Tyron Garner, plaintiff in pivotal sodomy case, dies. *New York Times,* September 14.

Martin, D. (2008). Mildred Loving, who fought marriage ban, dies. *New York Times,* May 6.

Martinson, F. M. (1976). Eroticism in infancy and childhood. *Journal of Sex Research, 2,* 251–262.

Masonjones, H. D. (2001). The effect of social context and reproductive status on the metabolic rates of dwarf seahorses (*Hippocampus zosterae*). *Comparative Biochemistry and Physiology Part A, Molecular and Integrative Physiology, 129,* 541–555.

Masters, W. H. & Johnson, V. (1970). *Human sexual inadequacy.* Little, Brown.

Masters, W. H. & Johnson, V. E. (1966). *Human sexual response.* Little, Brown.

Masters, W. H. & Johnson, V. E. (1979). *Homosexuality in perspective.* Little, Brown.

Masters, W. H., Johnson, V. E. & Kolodny, R. C. (1982). *Human sexuality.* Little, Brown.

Matek, O. (1988). Obscene phone callers. *Journal of Social Work and Human Sexuality, 7,* 113–130.

Mathes, E. W., Brennan, S. M., Haugen, P. M. & Rice, H. B. (1985). Ratings of physical attractiveness as a function of age. *Journal of Social Psychology, 125,* 157–168.

Matteson, D. (1991). Bisexual feminist man. In L. Hutchins and L. Kaahumanu (Eds.), *Bi any other name: Bisexual people speak out.* Alyson.

Matthews, M. (1994). *Horseman: Obsessions of a zoophile.* Prometheus Books.

Mauck, C. K., Weiner, D. H., Creinin, M. D., Archer, D. F., Schwartz, J. L., Pymar, H. C., Ballagh, S. A., Henry, D. M. & Callahan, M. M. (2006). FemCap with removal strap: ease of removal, safety and acceptability. *Contraception, 73,* 59–64.

Maurice, W. L. (2007). Sexual desire disorders in men. In S. R. Leiblum (Ed.), *Principles and practice of sex therapy* (4th ed.). Guilford Press.

Mayo Clinic. (2005). *Vaginal dryness.* (http://www.mayoclinic.com/health/vaginal-dryness/DS00550)

Mayo Clinic. (2008) *Episiotomy: Can you deliver a baby without one?* (http://www.mayoclinic.com/health/episiotomy/HO00064)

McCahill, T. W., Meyer, L. C. & Fischman, A. M. (1979). *The aftermath of rape.* Lexington Books.

McClellan, A. C. & Killeen, M. R. (2000). Attachment theory and violence toward women by male intimate partners. *Journal of Nursing Scholarship, 32*, 353–360.

McClintock, M. K. (1971). Menstrual synchrony and suppression. *Nature, 229*, 244–245.

McClintock, M. K. (1999). Reproductive biology: Pheromones and regulation of ovulation. *Nature, 401*, 232–233.

McConaghy, N. (1998). Paedophilia: a review of the evidence. *Australian and New Zealand Journal of Psychiatry, 32*, 252–265.

McConaghy, N. (2005). Sexual dysfunction and disorders. In J. E. Maddux and B. A. Winstead (Eds.), *Psychopathology: Foundations for a contemporary understanding.* Erlbaum.

McConkey, T. E., Sole, M. L. & Holcomb, L. (2001). Assessing the female sexual assault survivor. *Nurse Practitioner, 26*, 28–41.

McDowell, M. A., Brody, D. J. & Hughes, J. P. (2007). Has age at menarche changed? Results from the National Health and Nutrition Examination Survey (NHANES) 1999–2004. *Journal of Adolescent Health, 40*, 227–231.

McFadden, D. & Pasanen, E. G. (1999). Spontaneous otoacoustic emissions in heterosexuals, homosexuals, and bisexuals. *Journal of the Acoustical Society of America, 105*, 2403–2413.

McGreal, C. (2006). Hundreds of thousands raped in Congo wars. *Guardian (London),* November 14.

McKibben, A., Proulx, J. & Lusignan, R. (1994). Relationships between conflict, affect and deviant sexual behaviors in rapists and pedophiles. *Behaviour Research and Therapy, 32*, 571–575.

McNeil, D. G. (2007a). Circumcision's anti-AIDS effect found greater than first thought. *New York Times,* February 23.

McNeil, D. G. (2007b). Redesigning a condom so women will use it. *New York Times,* November 13.

McNeilly, A. S. (2001). Lactational control of reproduction. *Reproduction, Fertility, and Development, 13*, 583–590.

McPherson, M., Smith-Lovin, L. & Cook, J. (2001). Birds of a feather: Homophily in social networks. *Annual Review of Sociology, 27*, 415–444.

McWhirter, D. P. & Mattison, A. M. (1984). *The male couple.* Prentice-Hall.

Mead, M. (1928). *Coming of age in Samoa: A psychological study of primitive youth for Western civilization.* Morrow.

Mead, M. (1935). *Sex and temperament in three primitive societies.* Morrow.

Mealey, L., Bridgstock, R. & Townsend, G. C. (1999). Symmetry and perceived facial attractiveness: A monozygotic co-twin comparison. *Journal of Personality and Social Psychology, 76*, 151–158.

Meese, E. (1986). *Attorney general (Edwin Meese) commission report.* U.S. Government Printing Office.

Mehren, E. (2004). Acceptance of gays rises among new generation. *Los Angeles Times,* April 11.

Meisel, R. L. & Sachs, B. D. (1994). The physiology of male sexual behavior. In E. Knobil and J. D. Neill (Eds.), *The physiology of reproduction* (2nd ed., Vol. 1). Raven.

Meloy, J. R., Rivers, L., Siegel, L., Gothard, S., Naimark, D. & Nicolini, J. R. (2000). A replication study of obsessional followers and offenders with mental disorders. *Journal of Forensic Sciences, 45*, 147–152.

Mendez, M. F., Chow, T., Ringman, J., Twitchell, G. & Hinkin, C. H. (2000). Pedophilia and temporal lobe disturbances. *Journal of Neuropsychiatry and Clinical Neurosciences, 12*, 71–76.

Menweb. (2001). *Men's personal stories.* (http://www.batteredmen.com/gjdvsto1.htm)

Merrick, J., Merrick, E., Morad, M. & Kandel, I. (2006). Fetal alcohol syndrome and its long-term effects. *Minerva Pediatrica, 58*, 211–218.

Mertz, G. J., Benedetti, J., Ashley, R., Selke, S. A. & Corey, L. (1992). Risk factors for the sexual transmission of genital herpes. *Annals of Internal Medicine, 116*, 197–202.

Messe, M. R. & Geer, J. H. (1985). Voluntary vaginal musculature contractions as an enhancer of sexual arousal. *Archives of Sexual Behavior, 14*, 13–28.

Meston, C. M. (1997). Aging and sexuality. *Western Journal of Medicine, 167*, 285–290.

Meston, C. M. & Bradford, A. (2007). Sexual dysfunctions in women. *Annual Review of Clinical Psychology, 3*, 233–256.

Meston, C. M. & Frohlich, P. F. (2003). Love at first fright: partner salience moderates roller-coaster-induced excitation transfer. *Archives of Sexual Behavior, 32*, 537–544.

Metts, S. & Cupach, W. R. (1989). The role of communication in human sexuality. In K. McKinney and S. Sprecher (Eds.), *Human sexuality: The societal and interpersonal context.* Ablex.

Meyer, I. H., Dietrich, J. & Schwartz, S. (2008). Lifetime prevalence of mental disorders and suicide attempts in diverse lesbian, gay, and bisexual populations. *American Journal of Public Health, 98*, 1004–1006.

Meyer, J. P. & Pepper, S. (1977). Need compatibility and marital adjustment in young married couples. *Journal of Personality and Social Psychology, 35*, 331–342.

Meyer, W. J. & Cole, C. M. (1997). Physical and chemical castration of sex offenders: A review. *Journal of Offender Rehabilitation, 25*, 1–18.

Mezey, G. C. & King, M. B. (Eds.) (2000). *Male victims of sexual assault* (2nd ed.). Oxford University Press.

Michigan Womyn's Music Festival. (2008). *General festival information.* (http://www.michfest.com/festival/index.htm)

Miller, C. L., Younger, B. A. & Morse, P. A. (1982). The categorization of male and female voices in infancy. *Infant Behavior and Development, 5*, 143–159.

Miller, G., Tybur, J. M. & Jordan, B. D. (2007). Ovulatory cycle effects on tip earnings by lap dancers: economic evidence for human estrus? *Evolution and Human Behavior, 28*, 375–381.

Miller, S. A. & Byers, E. S. (2004). Actual and desired duration of foreplay and intercourse: Discordance and misperceptions within heterosexual couples. *Journal of Sex Research, 41*, 301–309.

Mills, J. (2007). World's oldest mother, 66, who lied about her age to get IVF, is "stricken by cancer." *Daily Mail (London),* December 13.

Mimiaga, M. J., Mayer, K. H., Reisner, S. L., Gonzalez, A., Dumas, B., Vanderwarker, R., Novak, D. S. & Bertrand, T. (2008). Asymptomatic gonorrhea and chlamydial infections detected by nucleic acid amplification tests among Boston area men who have sex with men. *Sexually Transmitted Diseases, 35*, 495–498.

Mischel, W. (1966). A social-learning view of sex differences in behavior. In E. E. Maccoby (Ed.), *The development of sex differences.* Stanford University Press.

Mita, T. H., Dermer, M. & Knight, J. (1977). Reversed facial images and the mere-exposure hypothesis. *Journal of Personality and Social Psychology, 35*, 597–601.

Mitchell, E. A. & Milerad, J. (2006). Smoking and the sudden infant death syndrome. *Reviews on Environmental Health, 21*, 81–103.

Mitelman, S. (2007). *Sexpressions: Sexuality education and resources for our youth.* (http://sexpressions.ca/)

Mittendorf, R., Williams, M. A., Berkey, C. S. & Cotter, P. F. (1990). The length of uncomplicated human gestation. *Obstetrics and Gynecology, 75*, 929–932.

Mittwoch, U. (1996). Sex-determining mechanisms in animals. *Trends in Ecology and Evolution, 11*, 63–67.

Moffat, S. D., Hampson, E. & Hatzipantelis, M. (1998). Navigation in a "virtual" maze: Sex differences and correlation with psychometric measures of spatial ability in humans. *Evolution and Human Behavior, 19*, 73–87.

Møller, A. P. (1992). Female swallow preference for symmetrical male sexual ornaments. *Nature, 357*, 238–240.

Molnar, B. E., Buka, S. L. & Kessler, R. C. (2001). Child sexual abuse and subsequent psychopathology: results from the National Comorbidity Survey. *American Journal of Public Health, 91*, 753–760.

Money, J. & Ehrhardt, A. E. (1971). *Man and woman, boy and girl: The differentiation and dimorphism of gender identity from conception to maturity.* Johns Hopkins University Press.

Mongeau, P. A. & Carey, C. M. (1996). Who's wooing whom? II: An experimental investigation of date initiation and expectancy violation. *Western Journal of Communication, 60*, 195–213.

Mongeau, P. A. & Johnson, K. L. (1995). Predicting cross-sex first-date sexual expectations and involvement: Contextual and individual difference factors. *Personal Relationships, 2*, 310–312.

Mongeau, P. A., Jacobsen, J. & Donnerstein, C. (2007). Defining dates and first date goals. *Communication Research, 34*, 526–547.

Mongeau, P. A., Morr Serewicz, M. C. & Therrien, L. F. (2004). Goals for cross-sex first dates: Identification, measurement, and the influence of contextual factors. *Communication Monographs, 71,* 121–147.

Montgomery, M. J. & Sorell, G. T. (1998). Love and dating experience in early and middle adolescence: grade and gender comparisons. *Journal of Adolescence, 21,* 677–689.

Monto, M. A. (1996). Lamaze and Bradley childbirth classes: contrasting perspectives toward the medical model of birth. *Birth, 23,* 193–201.

Mooradian, A. D. (1991). Geriatric sexuality and chronic diseases. *Clinics in Geriatric Medicine, 7,* 113–131.

Mooradian, A. D. & Korenman, S. G. (2006). Management of the cardinal features of andropause. *American Journal of Therapeutics, 13,* 145–160.

Moore, E., Wisniewski, A. & Dobs, A. (2003). Endocrine treatment of transsexual people: a review of treatment regimens, outcomes, and adverse effects. *Journal of Clinical Endocrinology and Metabolism, 88,* 3467–3473.

Moore, F. R., Cassidy, C., Law Smith, M. J. & Perrett, D. I. (2006). The effects of female control of resources on sex-differentiated mate preferences. *Evolution and Human Behavior, 27,* 193–205.

Moore, M. (1998). The science of sexual signalling: Context and consequences. In G. G. Brannigan et al. (Eds.), *The sex scientists.* Longman.

Morin, J. W. & Levenson, J. S. (2008). Exhibitionism: Assessment and treatment. In D. R. Laws and W. T. O'Donohue (Eds.), *Sexual deviance: Theory, assessment, and treatment* (2nd ed.). Guilford Press.

Morin, M. (2002). Kinky therapy for your back. *Los Angeles Times,* May 3.

Morlin, B. (2005). *West tied to sex abuse in 70s, using office to lure young men.* (http://www.spokesmanreview.com/jimwest/)

Morr, M. C. & Mongeau, P. A. (2004). First-date expectations. *Communications Research, 31,* 3–35.

Morris, N. M., Udry, J. R., Khan-Dawood, F. & Dawood, M. Y. (1987). Marital sex frequency and midcycle female testosterone. *Archives of Sexual Behavior, 16,* 27–37.

Morris, T., Greer, H. S. & White, P. (1977). Psychological and social adjustment to mastectomy: a two-year follow-up study. *Cancer, 40,* 2381–2387.

Moses, S., Bailey, R. C. & Ronald, A. R. (1998). Male circumcision: assessment of health benefits and risks. *Sexually Transmitted Infections, 74,* 368–373.

Mosher, D. L. & MacIan, P. (1994). College men and women respond to X-rated videos intended for male or female audiences: Gender and sexual scripts. *Journal of Sex Research, 31,* 99–118.

Mosher, W. D., Chandra, A. & Jones, J. M. (2005). *Sexual behavior and selected health measures: Men and women 15–44 years of age, United States, 2002.* (www.cdc.gov/nchs/data/ad/ad362.pdf)

Muir, A. (2006). Precocious puberty. *Pediatrics in Review, 27,* 373–381.

Mukul, L. V. & Teal, S. B. (2007). Current management of ectopic pregnancy. *Obstetrics and Gynecology Clinics of North America, 34,* 403–419.

Mulcahy, J. J. (1999). Penile prostheses in the sildenafil era. *Molecular Urology, 3,* 141–146.

Munarriz, R., Maitland, S., Garcia, S. P., Talakoub, L. & Goldstein, I. (2003). A prospective duplex Doppler ultrasonographic study in women with sexual arousal disorder to objectively assess genital engorgement induced by EROS therapy. *Journal of Sex and Marital Therapy, 29 Suppl 1,* 85–94.

Munk-Olsen, T., Laursen, T. M., Pedersen, C. B., Mors, O. & Mortensen, P. B. (2006). New parents and mental disorders: a population-based register study. *JAMA, 296,* 2582–2589.

Murnen, S. K. & Stockton, M. (1997). Gender and self-reported sexual arousal in response to sexual stimuli: A meta-analytic review. *Sex Roles, 37,* 135–153.

Murnen, S. K., Wright, C. & Kaluzny, G. (2002). If "boys will be boys" then girls will be victims? A meta-analytic review of the research that relates masculine ideology to sexual aggression. *Sex Roles, 46,* 359–375.

Murphy, L. L., Cadena, R. S., Chavez, D. & Ferraro, J. S. (1998). Effect of American ginseng (Panax quinquefolium) on male copulatory behavior in the rat. *Physiology and Behavior, 64,* 445–450.

Murphy, M. R., Checkley, S. A., Seckl, J. R. & Lightman, S. L. (1990). Naloxone inhibits oxytocin release at orgasm in man. *Journal of Clinical Endocrinology and Metabolism, 71,* 1056–1058.

Murphy, P. & Stout, D. (2007). Idaho senator says he regrets guilty plea in restroom incident. *New York Times,* August 29.

Murphy, W. D. & Page, I. J. (2008). Exhibitionism: Psychopathology and theory. In D. R. Laws and W. T. O'Donohue (Eds.), *Sexual deviance: Theory, assessment, and treatment* (2nd ed.). Guilford Press.

Murray, S. L. & Holmes, J. G. (1999). The (mental) ties that bind: Cognitive structures that predict relationship resilience. *Journal of Personality and Social Psychology, 77,* 1228–1244.

Musgrave, B. (1980). Penis captivus has occurred. *British Medical Journal, 280,* 51.

Musick, K. & Bumpass, L., (2006) *Cohabitation, marriage, and trajectories in well-being and relationships.* (http://repositories.cdlib.org/ccpr/olwp/CCPR-003-06/)

Mustanski, B. S., Dupree, M. G., Nievergelt, C. M., Bocklandt, S., Schork, N. J. & Hamer, D. H. (2005). A genomewide scan of male sexual orientation. *Human Genetics, 116,* 272–278.

Nagel, S. C., vom Saal, F. S., Thayer, K. A., Dhar, M. G., Boechler, M. & Welshons, W. V. (1997). Relative binding affinity-serum modified access (RBA-SMA) assay predicts the relative in vivo bioactivity of the xenoestrogens bisphenol A and octylphenol. *Environmental Health Perspectives, 105,* 70–76.

Nair, H. P. & Young, L. J. (2006). Vasopressin and pair-bond formation: Genes to brain to behavior. *Physiology (Bethesda), 21,* 146–152.

Najman, J. M., Nguyen, M. L. & Boyle, F. M. (2007). Sexual abuse in childhood and physical and mental health in adulthood: an Australian population study. *Archives of Sexual Behavior, 36,* 666–675.

Nanda, S. (1990). *Neither man nor woman: The hijras of India.* Wadsworth.

NARTH. (2008). *Home page.* (http://www.narth.com)

Nath, J. K. & Nayar, V. R. (1997). India. In R. T. Francoeur (Ed.), *The international encyclopedia of sexuality.* Continuum.

Nation, E. F. (1973). Willam Osler on penis captivus and other urologic topics. *Urology, 2,* 468–470.

National Asian Women's Health Organization. (1997). *Expanding options: A reproductive and sexual health survey of Asian American women.* (http://www.nawho.org/atf/cf/%7BBC9650E6-A7EB-483F-A210-CC3E0D7445A6%7D/NAWHOOptions.pdf)

National Campaign to Prevent Teen and Unplanned Pregnancy. (2008). *Why it matters.* (http://www.thenationalcampaign.org/why-it-matters/default.aspx)

National Campaign to Prevent Teen Pregnancy. (2006a). *Teen birth rates: How does the United States compare?* (http://www.teenpregnancy.org/resources/reading/pdf/inatl_comparisons2006.pdf)

National Campaign to Prevent Teen Pregnancy. (2006b). *Teen pregnancy rates in the U.S., 1972–2002.* (www.teenpregnancy.org/resources/data/pdf/pregrate_Oct2006.pdf)

National Cancer Institute. (2004). *The prostate-specific antigen (PSA) test: Questions and answers.*

National Cancer Institute. (2008a) *Cancer stat fact sheets: Cancer of the anus, anal canal, and anorectum.* (http://seer.cancer.gov/statfacts/html/anus.html)

National Cancer Institute. (2008b). *Prostate cancer screening.* (http://www.cancer.gov/cancertopics/pdq/screening/prostate/HealthProfessional/page1)

National Center for Transgender Equality. (2007). *Hate crime laws.* (http://www.nctequality.org/Hate_Crimes.asp)

National Gay and Lesbian Task Force. (2008a). *Hate crimes laws map.* (http://thetaskforce.org/reports_and_research/hate_crimes_laws)

National Gay and Lesbian Task Force. (2008b). *State nondiscrimination laws in the U.S.* (http://www.thetaskforce.org/downloads/reports/issue_maps/non_discrimination_01_08_color.pdf)

National Opinion Research Center. (1998). *American sexual behavior: Trends, socio-demographic differences, and risk behavior.* (http://cloud9.norc.uchicago.edu/dlib/t-25.htm)

National Organization for Women. (1999). *Campus rape ignored...even when there's a videotape.* (http://www.now.org/nnt/fall-99/campus.html)

National Organization for Women. (2007). *Sexy or sadistic? Sexist, actually.* (http://www.now.org/issues/media/070319advertising.html)

National Prevention Information Network. (2008). *STDs today.* (http://www.cdcpnin.org/scripts/std/std.asp)

National Research Council. (1996). *Understanding violence against women.* National Academy Press.

National Women's Health Information Center. (2004). *Date rape drugs.* (http://www.4woman.gov/faq/rohypnol.htm)

Navarro, V. M., Castellano, J. M., Garcia-Galiano, D. & Tena-Sempere, M. (2007). Neuroendocrine factors in the initiation of puberty: the emergent role of kisspeptin. *Reviews in Endocrine & Metabolic Disorders, 8,* 11–20.

Nduru, M. (2007). *Southern Africa: One million people need AIDS treatment.* (http://ipsnews.net/news.asp?idnews=37937)

Nelson, A. (2000). Contraceptive update Y2K: need for contraception and new contraceptive options. *Clinical Cornerstone, 3,* 48–62.

Nelson, A. L. (2007). Combined oral contraceptives. In R. A. Hatcher et al. (Eds.), *Contraceptive technology* (19th ed.). Ardent Media.

Nelson, L. D. & Morrison, E. L. (2005). The symptoms of resource scarcity: Judgments of food and finances influence preferences for potential partners. *Psychological Science, 16,* 167–173.

New, M. I. & Wilson, R. C. (1999). Steroid disorders in children: congenital adrenal hyperplasia and apparent mineralocorticoid excess. *Proceedings of the National Academy of Sciences of the United States of America, 96,* 12790–12797.

Nichols, M. & Shernoff, M. (2007). Therapy with sexual minorities. In S. R. Leiblum (Ed.), *Principles and practice of sex therapy* (4th ed.). Guilford Press.

Nicholson, K. L. & Balster, R. L. (2001). GHB: a new and novel drug of abuse. *Drug and Alcohol Dependence, 63,* 1–22.

Nicolosi, J. (1991). *Reparative therapy of male homosexuality: A new clinical approach.* Jason Aronson.

Nicolosi, J. & Nicolosi, L. A. (2002). *A parent's guide to preventing homosexuality.* InterVarsity Press.

Nielsen, J. & Pernice, K. (2008). *Eyetracking Web usability.* New Riders Press.

Nishizawa, S., Benkelfat, C., Young, S. N., Leyton, M., Mzengeza, S., de Montigny, C., Blier, P. & Diksic, M. (1997). Differences between males and females in rates of serotonin synthesis in human brain. *Proceedings of the National Academy of Sciences of the United States of America, 94,* 5308–5313.

Nosek, B., Banaji, M. & Greenwald, A. (2004). *Implicit association test.* (https://implicit.harvard.edu/implicit/demo/selectatest.html)

Nosek, M. A., Howland, C. A., Rintala, D. H., Young, M. E. & Chanpong, G. F. (1997). *National study of women with physical disabilities: Final report.* (http://www.bcm.tmc.edu/crowd/national_study/national_study.html)

Nossiter, A. (1996). 6-year-old's sex crime: Innocent peck on cheek. *New York Times,* September 27.

Now. (2004). *Love and sex guide survey results.* (http://www.nowtoronto.com/minisites/loveandsex/2004/s_survey_results.php)

Nurnberg, H. G., Hensley, P. L., Heiman, J. R., Croft, H. A., Debattista, C. & Paine, S. (2008). Sildenafil treatment of women with antidepressant-associated sexual dysfunc-

tion: a randomized controlled trial. *JAMA, 300,* 395–404.

Nussbaum, M. (2008). Trading on American's puritanical streak. *Atlanta Journal-Constitution,* March 14.

Nwokolo, N. C. & Hawkins, D. A. (2001). Postexposure prophylaxis for HIV infection. *The AIDS Reader, 11,* 402–412.

O'Brien, M. (1990). On seeing a sex surrogate. *The Sun.*

Ockene, J. K., Barad, D. H., Cochrane, B. B., Larson, J. C., Gass, M., Wassertheil-Smoller, S., Manson, J. E., Barnabei, V. M., Lane, D. S., Brzyski, R. G., Rosal, M. C., Wylie-Rosett, J. & Hays, J. (2005). Symptom experience after discontinuing use of estrogen plus progestin. *JAMA, 294,* 183–193.

O'Connell, H. E., Hutson, J. M., Anderson, C. R. & Plenter, R. J. (1998). Anatomical relationship between urethra and clitoris. *Journal of Urology, 159,* 1892–1897.

O'Crowley, P. (2004). Student orientation: More teenage girls are testing gender boundaries. *Star-Ledger,* May 26.

Office of Public Sector Information. (2008). *Criminal Justice and Immigration Act 2008.* (http://www.opsi.gov.uk/acts/acts2008/ukpga_20080004_en_1)

Okami, P., Olmstead, R. & Abramson, P. R. (1997). Sexual experiences in early childhood: 18-year longitudinal data from the UCLA Family Lifestyles Project. *Journal of Sex Research, 34,* 339–347.

Okami, P., Olmstead, R., Abramson, P. R. & Pendleton, L. (1998). Early childhood exposure to parental nudity and scenes of parental sexuality ("primal scenes"): an 18-year longitudinal study of outcome. *Archives of Sexual Behavior, 27,* 361–384.

O'Leary, C. & Howard, O. (2001). *The prostitution of women and girls in metropolitan Chicago: A preliminary prevalence report.* (http://www.impactresearch.org/documents/prostitutionreport.pdf)

Oliver, M. B. & Hyde, J. S. (1993). Gender differences in sexuality: A meta-analysis. *Psychological Bulletin, 114,* 29–51.

Onishi, N. (2007). Japan stands by declaration on "comfort women." *New York Times,* March 16.

Orion, D. (1998). *I know you really love me: A psychiatrist's account of stalking and obsessive love.* Dell.

Oropesa, R. S. & Gorman, B. K. (2000). Ethnicity, immigration, and beliefs about marriage as a "tie that binds." In I. J. Waite et al. (Eds.), *The tie that binds: Perspectives on marriage and cohabitation.* Aldine de Gruyter.

Owen, R. L. (1998). M cells as portals of entry for HIV. *Pathobiology, 66,* 141–144.

Paechter, C. & Clark, S. (2007). Learning gender in primary school playgrounds: Findings from the Tomboy Identities Study. *Pedagogy, Culture and Society, 15,* 317–331.

Paglia, C. (1990). *Sexual personae: Art and decadence from Nefertiti to Emily Dickinson.* Yale University Press.

Paglia, C. (1994). *Vamps and tramps: New essays.* 1994.

Palmer, J. R., Hatch, E. E., Rosenberg, C. L., Hartge, P., Kaufman, R. H., Titus-Ernstoff, L., Noller, K. L., Herbst, A. L., Rao, R. S.,

Troisi, R., Colton, T. & Hoover, R. N. (2002). Risk of breast cancer in women exposed to diethylstilbestrol in utero: preliminary results (United States). *Cancer Causes and Control, 13,* 753–758.

Palmore, E. B. (1982). Predictors of the longevity difference: a 25-year follow-up. *Gerontologist, 22,* 513–518.

Paludi, M. A. (1996). Sexual harassment on college campuses: Abusing the ivory power (rev. ed.). State University of New York Press.

Panel on Antiretroviral Guidelines for Adults and Adolescents. (2008). *Guidelines for the use of antiretroviral agents in HIV-1-infected adults and adolescents.* (http://aidsinfo.nih.gov/ContentFiles/AdultandAdolescentGL.pdf)

Paolucci, E. O., Genuis, M. L. & Violato, C. (2001). A meta-analysis of the published research on the effects of child sexual abuse. *Journal of Psychology, 135,* 17–36.

Paredes, R. G., Tzschentke, T. & Nakach, N. (1998). Lesions of the medial preoptic area/anterior hypothalamus (MPOA/AH) modify partner preference in male rats. *Brain Research, 813,* 1–8.

Parents Television Council. (2003). *Sex loses its appeal: A state of the industry report on sex on TV.* (http://www.parentstv.org/ptc/publications/reports/stateindustrysex/main.asp)

Parents Television Council. (2008a). *Happily never after: How Hollywood favors adultery and promiscuity over marital intimacy on prime time broadcast television.* (http://www.parentstv.org/PTC/publications/reports/SexonTV/MarriageStudy.pdf)

Parents Television Council. (2008b). *PTC blasts CBS for nudity on "Survivor" premiere.* (http://www.parentstv.org/PTC/news/release/2008/0930.asp)

Parish, A. R. & de Waal, F. B. (2000). The other "closest living relative." How bonobos (*Pan paniscus*) challenge traditional assumptions about females, dominance, intra- and inter-sexual interactions, and hominid evolution. *Annals of the New York Academy of Sciences, 907,* 97–113.

Parsonnet, J., Hansmann, M. A., Delaney, M. L., Modern, P. A., Dubois, A. M., Wieland-Alter, W., Wissemann, K. W., Wild, J. E., Jones, M. B., Seymour, J. L. & Onderdonk, A. B. (2005). Prevalence of toxic shock syndrome toxin 1-producing *Staphylococcus aureus* and the presence of antibodies to this superantigen in menstruating women. *Journal of Clinical Microbiology, 43,* 4628–4634.

Pate, J. E. & Gabbard, G. O. (2003). Adult baby syndrome. *American Journal of Psychiatry, 160,* 1932–1936.

Patel, M. & Minshall, L. (2001). Management of sexual assault. *Emergency Medicine Clinics of North America, 19,* 817–831.

Patterson, C. J. (2006). Children of lesbian and gay parents. *Current Directions in Psychological Science, 15,* 241–244.

Paul, M. & Stewart, F. H. (2007). Abortion. In R. A. Hatcher et al. (Eds.), *Contraceptive technology* (19th ed.). Ardent Media.

Paulson, M. (2002). Catholic newspaper calls for look at celibacy. *Boston Globe,* March 15.

Pawlowski, M., Atwal, R. & Dunbar, R. I. M. (2008). Sex differences in everyday risk-taking behavior in humans. *Evolutionary Psychology, 6,* 29–42.

Peabody Museum. (2004). *The Sunrise Dance.*

Peltason, R. (2008). *I am not my breast cancer: Women talk openly about love and sex, hair loss and weight gain, mothers and daughters, and being a woman with breast cancer.* William Morrow.

Penn, D. J. & Potts, W. K. (1998). MHC-disassortative mating preferences reversed by cross-fostering. *Proceedings of the Royal Society of London Series B: Biological Sciences, 265,* 1299–1306.

Penton-Voak, I. S. & Perrett, D. I. (2000a). Consistency and individual differences in facial attractiveness judgements: An evolutionary perspective. *Social Research, 67,* 219–245.

Penton-Voak, I. S. & Perrett, D. I. (2000b). Female preference for male faces change cyclically: Further evidence. *Evolution and Human Behavior, 21,* 39–48.

Peplau, L. A. & Garnets, L. D. (2000). A new paradigm for understanding women's sexuality and sexual orientation. *Journal of Social Issues, 56,* 329–350.

Peplau, L. A., Spalding, L. R., Conley, T. D. & Veniegas, R. C. (1999). The development of sexual orientation in women. *Annual Review of Sex Research, 10,* 70–99.

Peretti, P. O. & Rowan, M. (1983). Zoophilia: Factors related to its sustained practice. *Panminerva Medica, 25,* 127–131.

Perez, K. M., Titus-Ernstoff, L., Hatch, E. E., Troisi, R., Wactawski-Wende, J., Palmer, J. R., Noller, K. & Hoover, R. N. (2005). Reproductive outcomes in men with prenatal exposure to diethylstilbestrol. *Fertility and Sterility, 84,* 1649–1656.

Perkel, M. (2008). *How to use escort services: A men's guide.* (http://sex.perkel.com/escort/index.htm)

Perper, T. (1985). *Sex signals: The biology of love.* ISI Press.

Perrett, D. I., May, K. A. & Yoshikawa, S. (1994). Facial shape and judgements of female attractiveness. *Nature, 368,* 239–242.

Persson, G. (1981). Five-year mortality in a 70-year-old urban population in relation to psychiatric diagnosis, personality, sexuality and early parental death. *Acta Psychiatrica Scandinavica, 64,* 244–253.

Peskin, M. & Newell, F. N. (2004). Familiarity breeds attraction: effects of exposure on the attractiveness of typical and distinctive faces. *Perception, 33,* 147–157.

Peters, M., Manning, J. T. & Reimers, S. (2007). The effects of sex, sexual orientation, and digit ratio (2D:4D) on mental rotation performance. *Archives of Sexual Behavior, 36,* 251–260.

Pew Research Center. (2006). *Less opposition to gay marriage, adoption and military service.* (http://people-press.org/reports/display.php3?ReportID=273)

Pfizer. (2004). *Safety information for Depo-Provera contraceptive injection.* (http://www.fda.gov/medwatch/SAFETY/2004/Depo-Provera_deardoc.pdf)

Phoenix, C. H., Goy, R. W., Gerall, A. A. & Young, W. C. (1959). Organizing action of prenatally administered testosterone propi-

onate on the tissues mediating mating behavior in the female guinea pig. *Endocrinology, 65,* 369–382.

Pick, S. (2003). Healthy sexuality for all: The role of psychology. In R. H. Rozensky, N. G. Johnson, D. G. Goodheart, and R. W. Hammond (Eds.), *Psychology builds a healthy world: Opportunities for research and practice.* American Psychological Association.

Pierce, A. P. (2000). The coital alignment technique (CAT): An overview of studies. *Journal of Sex and Marital Therapy, 26,* 257–268.

Pierik, F. H., Burdorf, A., de Jong, F. H. & Weber, R. F. (2003). Inhibin B: a novel marker of spermatogenesis. *Annals of Medicine, 35,* 12–20.

Pierrehumbert, J. B., Bent, T., Munson, B., Bradlow, A. R. & Bailey, J. M. (2004). The influence of sexual orientation on vowel production. *Journal of the Acoustical Society of America, 116,* 1905–1908.

Pincus, J. H. (2001). *Base instincts: What makes killers kill?* W.W. Norton.

Planned Parenthood Federation. (2000). *Margaret Sanger.* (http://www.plannedparenthood.com/about/thisispp/sanger.html)

Planned Parenthood Federation. (2008). *Cervical mucus method.* (http://www.plannedparenthood.org/health-topics/birth-control/fam-cervical-mucus-method-22140.htm)

Plaud, J. J. & Martini, J. R. (1999). The respondent conditioning of male sexual arousal. *Behavior Modification. 23,* 254–268.

Plaud, J., Gaither, G. A., Amato Henderson, S. & Devitt, M. K. (1997). The long-term habituation of sexual arousal in human males: A crossover design. *Psychological Record, 47,* 385–398.

Plöderl, M. & Fartacek, R. (2008). Childhood gender nonconformity and harassment as predictors of suicidality among gay, lesbian, bisexual, and heterosexual Austrians. *Archives of Sexual Behavior.* Advance online publication. Retrieved September 23, 2008, doi:10.1007/s10508-007-9244-6.

Polak, M. & Trivers, R. (1994). The science of symmetry in biology. *Trends in Ecology and Evolution, 9,* 122–124.

Pollack, A. E., Thomas, L. J. & Barone, M. A. (2007). Female and male sterilization. In R. A. Hatcher et al. (Eds.), *Contraceptive technology* (19th ed.). Ardent Media.

Pomerantz, S. M., Goy, R. W. & Roy, M. M. (1986). Expression of male-typical behavior in adult female pseudohermaphroditic rhesus: comparisons with normal males and neonatally gonadectomized males and females. *Hormones and Behavior, 20,* 483–500.

Pomerleau, A., Bolduc, D., Malcuit, G. & Cossette, L. (1990). Pink or blue: Environmental gender stereotypes in the first two years of life. *Sex Roles, 22,* 359–367.

Pope John Paul II. (1981). *Apostolic exhortation "Familiaris consortio."* (http://www.vatican.va/holy_father/john_paul_ii/apost_exhortations/documents/hf_jp-ii_exh_19811122_familiaris-consortio_en.html)

Posner, R. A. (1992). *Sex and reason.* Harvard University Press.

Potter, L., Oakley, D., de Leon-Wong, E. & Canamar, R. (1996). Measuring compliance

among oral contraceptive users. *Family Planning Perspectives, 28,* 154–158.

Powdermaker, H. (1933). *Life in Lesu: The study of a Melanesian society in New Ireland.* Norton.

Powlishta, K. K. & Maccoby, E. E. (1990). Resource utilization in mixed-sex dyads: The influence of adult presence and task type. *Sex Roles, 23,* 223–240.

Prause, N. & Graham, C. A. (2007). Asexuality: classification and characterization. *Archives of Sexual Behavior, 36,* 341–356.

Prentice, R. L., Chlebowski, R. T., Stefanick, M. L., Manson, J. E., Pettinger, M., Hendrix, S. L., Hubbell, F. A., Kooperberg, C., Kuller, L. H., Lane, D. S., McTiernan, A., Jo O'Sullivan, M., Rossouw, J. E. & Anderson, G. L. (2008). Estrogen plus progestin therapy and breast cancer in recently postmenopausal women. *American Journal of Epidemiology, 167,* 1207–1216.

Prentky, R. A., Knight, R. A. & Lee, A. F. (1997). Risk factors associated with recidivism among extrafamilial child molesters. *Journal of Consulting and Clinical Psychology, 65,* 141–149.

Presbyterian Church (U.S.A.). (1998). *Older youth guide.* Presbyterian Distribution Service.

Price, J. H., Allensworth, D. D. & Hillman, K. S. (1985). Comparison of sexual fantasies of homosexuals and of heterosexuals. *Psychological Reports, 57,* 871–877.

Price, R. A. & Vandenberg, S. G. (1980). Spouse similarity in American and Swedish couples. *Behavior Genetics, 10,* 59–71.

Priest, R. J. (2001). Missionary positions: Christian, modernist, postmodernist. *Current Anthropology, 42,* 29–68.

Prostitutes Education Network. (2008). *Prostitution in the United States: The statistics.* (http://www.bayswan.org/stats.html)

Public Health Agency of Canada. (2003). *Principles of sexual health education.* (www.phac-aspc.gc.ca/publicat/cgshe-ldnemss/cgshe_7e.htm)

Public Health Agency of Canada. (2004). *Oral sex and the risk of HIV transmission.* (http://www.phac-aspc.gc.ca/publicat/epiu-aepi/epi_update_may_04/13_e.html)

Puts, D. A., McDaniel, M. A., Jordan, C. L. & Breedlove, S. M. (2008). Spatial ability and prenatal androgens: meta-analyses of congenital adrenal hyperplasia and digit ratio (2D:4D) studies. *Archives of Sexual Behavior, 37,* 100–111.

Quale, G. R. (1988). *A history of marriage systems.* Greenwood Press.

Quart, A. (2008). When girls will be boys. *New York Times,* March 16.

Queen, C. (1998). Bend over boyfriend: A couple's guide to male anal pleasure. *Fatale Video.*

Quigley, C. A., De Bellis, A., Marschke, K. B., el-Awady, M. K., Wilson, E. M. & French, F. S. (1995). Androgen receptor defects: historical, clinical, and molecular perspectives. *Endocrine Reviews, 16,* 271–321.

Quinsey, V. L. & Lalumière, M. L. (2001). *Assessment of sex offenders against children* (2nd ed.). Sage Publications.

Quittner, J. (2001). Death of a two spirit. *Advocate,* August 28.

Rahman, Q., Abrahams, S. & Wilson, G. D. (2003a). Sexual-orientation-related differences in verbal fluency. *Neuropsychology, 17,* 240–246.

Rahman, Q., Kumari, V. & Wilson, G. D. (2003b). Sexual orientation-related differences in prepulse inhibition of the human startle response. *Behavioral Neuroscience, 117,* 1096–1102.

Ralph, D., Eardley, I., Kell, P., Dean, J., Hackett, G., Collins, O. & Edwards, D. (2007). Improvement in erectile function on vardenafil treatment correlates with treatment satisfaction in both patients and their partners. *BJU International, 100,* 130–136.

Ramesh, R. (2008). India will pay families to have girls to end foeticide. *Guardian (London),* March 4.

Ramirez, J. (2008). Feeling the pinch: Nevada's brothels hit hard times. *Newsweek,* June 16.

Rand, K. H., Hoon, E. F., Massey, J. K. & Johnson, J. H. (1990). Daily stress and recurrence of genital herpes simplex. *Archives of Internal Medicine, 150,* 1889–1893.

Randall, T. (2006). Letter to the Editor. *New York Times,* July 5.

Rao, S., Joshi, S. & Kanade, A. (1998). Height velocity, body fat and menarcheal age of Indian girls. *Indian Pediatrics, 35,* 619–628.

Rapaport, K. R. & Posey, C. D. (1991). Sexually coercive college males. In A. Parrot (Ed.), *Acquaintance rape: The hidden crime.* Wiley.

Raphael, J. (2004). *Listening to Olivia: Violence, poverty, and prostitution.* Routledge.

Rashid, A. (2006). *A rush to cream the fairness fetish.* (http://www.dnaindia.com/report.asp?NewsID=1050554)

Ravdin, P. M., Cronin, K. A., Howlader, N., Berg, C. D., Chlebowski, R. T., Feuer, E. J., Edwards, B. K. & Berry, D. A. (2007). The decrease in breast-cancer incidence in 2003 in the United States. *New England Journal of Medicine, 356,* 1670–1674.

Raymond, E. G. (2007). Progestin-only pills. In R. A. Hatcher et al. (Eds.), *Contraceptive technology* (19th ed.). Ardent Media.

Raymond, J. G. (1995). Prostitution is rape that's paid for. *New York Times,* December 11.

Raymond, J. G. (2004). Prostitution on demand: Legalizing the buyers as sexual consumers. *Violence Against Women, 19,* 1156–1186.

Redmond, G., Godwin, A. J., Olson, W. & Lippman, J. S. (1999). Use of placebo controls in an oral contraceptive trial: methodological issues and adverse event incidence. *Contraception, 60,* 81–85.

Reed, D., Carroll, C. & Chang, A. (2005). Molester's trail leads to San Jose. *San Jose Mercury News,* June 17.

Regan, P. C. & Berscheid, E. (1997). Gender differences in characteristics desired in a potential sexual and marriage partner. *Journal of Psychology and Human Sexuality, 9,* 25–37.

Regan, P. C., Levin, L., Sprecher, S., Christopher, F. S. & Cate, R. (2000). Partner preferences: What characteristics do men and women desire in their short-term sexual and long-term romantic partners. *Journal of Psychology and Human Sexuality, 12,* 1–21.

Regehr, C., Cadell, S. & Jansen, K. (1999). Perceptions of control and long-term recovery from rape. *American Journal of Orthopsychiatry, 69,* 110–115.

Rehman, J. & Melman, A. (2001). Normal anatomy and physiology. In J. J. Mulcahy (Ed.), *Male sexual function: A guide to clinical management.* Humana Press.

Reich, K. (2002). Nevada school district settles gay harassment suit. *Los Angeles Times,* August 28.

Reichenberg, A., Gross, R., Weiser, M., Bresnahan, M., Silverman, J., Harlap, S., Rabinowitz, J., Shulman, C., Malaspina, D., Lubin, G., Knobler, H. Y., Davidson, M. & Susser, E. (2006). Advancing paternal age and autism. *Archives of General Psychiatry, 63,* 1026–1032.

Reichert, T. (2002). Sex in advertising research: a review of content, effects, and functions of sexual information in consumer advertising. *Annual Review of Sex Research, 13,* 241–273.

Reichert, T. & Lambiase, J. (Eds.) (2003). *Sex in advertising: Perspectives on the erotic appeal.* Lawrence Erlbaum Associates.

Reilly, J. M. & Woodhouse, C. R. (1989). Small penis and the male sexual role. *Journal of Urology, 142,* 569–571; discussion 572.

Reiner, W. G. (2004). Psychosexual development in genetic males assigned female: the cloacal exstrophy experience. *Child and Adolescent Psychiatric Clinics of North America, 13,* 657–674, ix.

Reiss, I. L. (1986). *Journey into sexuality: An exploratory voyage.* Prentice-Hall.

Reiss, I. L. & Miller, B. C. (1979). Heterosexual permissiveness: A theoretical analysis. *Journal of Marriage and the Family, 42,* 395–410.

Reissing, E. D., Binik, Y. M., Khalife, S., Cohen, D. & Amsel, R. (2003). Etiological correlates of vaginismus: sexual and physical abuse, sexual knowledge, sexual self-schema, and relationship adjustment. *Journal of Sex and Marital Therapy, 29,* 47–59.

Reissing, E. D., Binik, Y. M., Khalife, S., Cohen, D. & Amsel, R. (2004). Vaginal spasm, pain, and behavior: an empirical investigation of the diagnosis of vaginismus. *Archives of Sexual Behavior, 33,* 5–17.

Reitman, V. (2001). Officer held as Japan moves to stem child pornography. *Los Angeles Times,* January 25.

Religious Tolerance.org. (2005). *Public opinion polls on abortion: Overview.* (http://www.religioustolerance.org/abopollover.htm)

Religious Tolerance.org. (2006). *Abortion access: U.S. public opinion polls, year 2005.* (http://www.religioustolerance.org/abopoll05.htm)

Religious Tolerance.org. (2007). *Same sex marriages and civil unions.* (http://www.religioustolerance.org/hom_marp.htm)

Religious Tolerance.org. (2008). *Bisexuality: The least common sexual orientation.* (http://www.religioustolerance.org/bisexuality.htm)

Rennison, C. M. (2002). *Rape and sexual assault: Reporting to police and medical attention, 1992–2000.* (http://www.ojp.usdoj.gov/bjs/pub/pdf/rsarp00.pdf)

Resnick, H. S., Acierno, R. & Kilpatrick, D. G. (1997). Health impact of interpersonal violence. 2: Medical and mental health outcomes. *Behavioral Medicine, 23,* 65–78.

Reuters News Service. (2005). *Condom testing reveals best brands.* (http://www.cnn.com/2005/HEALTH/01/04/best.condoms.reut/index.html)

Reverby, S. M. (2000). *Tuskegee's truths: Rethinking the Tuskegee syphilis study.* University of North Carolina Press.

Reynolds, M. A., Herbenick, D. L. & Bancroft, J. (2003). The nature of childhood sexual experiences. In J. Bancroft (Ed.), *Sexual development in childhood.* Indiana University Press.

Reznikov, A. G., Nosenko, N. D. & Tarasenko, L. V. (1999). Prenatal stress and glucocorticoid effects on the developing gender- related brain. *Journal of Steroid Biochemistry and Molecular Biology, 69,* 109–115.

Rice, M. E. & Harris, G. T. (2002). Men who molest their sexually immature daughters: is a special explanation required? *Journal of Abnormal Psychology, 111,* 329–339.

Richardson, J. (1995). The science and politics of gay teen suicide. *Harvard Review of Psychiatry, 3,* 107–110.

Richter, J. & Song, A. (1999). Australian university students agree with Clinton's definition of sex. *British Medical Journal, 318,* 1011.

Ridley, M. (1994). *The red queen: Sex and the evolution of human nature.* Macmillan.

Rieger, G., Chivers, M. L. & Bailey, J. M. (2005). Sexual arousal patterns of bisexual men. *Psychological Science, 16,* 579–584.

Rieger, G., Linsenmeier, J. A., Gygax, L. & Bailey, J. M. (2008). Sexual orientation and childhood gender nonconformity: evidence from home videos. *Developmental Psychology, 44,* 46–58.

Rimer, S. (2003). Love on campus: Trying to set rules for the emotions. *New York Times,* October 1.

Rind, B. (2001). Gay and bisexual adolescent boys' sexual experiences with men: an empirical examination of psychological correlates in a nonclinical sample. *Archives of Sexual Behavior, 30,* 345–368.

Rind, B., Tromovitch, P. & Bauserman, R. (1998). A meta-analytic examination of assumed properties of child sexual abuse using college samples. *Psychological Bulletin, 124,* 22–53.

Riordan, S. (1999). Indecent exposure: The impact upon the victim's fear of sexual crime. *Journal of Forensic Psychiatry, 10,* 309–316.

Ristock, J. (2002). *No more secrets: Violence in lesbian relationships.* Routledge.

Roane, K. R. (1999). Gangs turn to new trade: Young prostitutes. *New York Times,* July 11.

Roberts, S. (2006). To be married means to be outnumbered. *New York Times,* October 15.

Roberts, S. C., Havlicek, J., Flegr, J., Hruskova, M., Little, A. C., Jones, B. C., Perrett, D. I. & Petrie, M. (2004). Female facial attractiveness increases during the fertile phase of the menstrual cycle. *Proceedings Biological Science, 271, Suppl 5,* S270–272.

Roberts, S. C., Little, A. C., Gosling, L. M., Jones, B. C., Perrett, D. I., Carter, V. & Petrie, M. (2005). MHC-assortative facial preferences in humans. *Biology Letters, 1,* 400–403.

Robson, K. M., Brant, H. A. & Kumar, R. (1981). Maternal sexuality during first pregnancy and after childbirth. *British Journal of Obstetrics and Gynaecology, 88,* 882–889.

Rogge, R. D. & Bradbury, T. N. (1999). Till violence does us part: the differing roles of communication and aggression in predicting adverse marital outcomes. *Journal of Consulting and Clinical Psychology, 67,* 340–351.

Rohrlich, T. (2000). McMartin case's legal, social legacies linger. *Los Angeles Times,* December 18.

Rojanapithayakorn, W. & Hanenberg, R. (1996). The 100% condom program in Thailand. *AIDS, 10,* 1–7.

Roovers, J. P., van der Bom, J. G., van der Vaart, C. H. & Heintz, A. P. (2003). Hysterectomy and sexual wellbeing: prospective observational study of vaginal hysterectomy, subtotal abdominal hysterectomy, and total abdominal hysterectomy. *British Medical Journal, 327,* 774–778.

Rose, S. & Frieze, I. H. (1993). Young singles' contemporary dating scripts. *Sex Roles, 28,* 499–509.

Roselli, C. E., Larkin, K., Resko, J. A., Stellflug, J. N. & Stormshak, F. (2004). The volume of a sexually dimorphic nucleus in the ovine medial preoptic area/anterior hypothalamus varies with sexual partner preference. *Endocrinology, 145,* 478–483.

Rosen, R. C. (2007). Erectile dysfunction: Integration of medical and psychological approaches. In S. R. Leiblum (Ed.), *Principles and practice of sex therapy* (4th ed.). Guilford Press.

Rosenbaum, J. E. (2006). Reborn a virgin: adolescents' retracting of virginity pledges and sexual histories. *American Journal of Public Health, 96,* 1098–1103.

Rosenbaum, T. Y. (2007). Physical therapy management and treatment of sexual pain disorders. In S. R. Leiblum (Ed.), *Principles and practice of sex therapy* (4th ed.). Guilford Press.

Rosenthal, E. (2008). Drug makers' push leads to cancer vaccines' rise. *New York Times,* August 19.

Rosing, M. T. (1999). 13C-Depleted carbon microparticles in >3700-Ma sea-floor sedimentary rocks from west Greenland. *Science, 283,* 674–676.

Rosman, J. P. & Resnick, P. J. (1989). Sexual attraction to corpses: a psychiatric review of necrophilia. *Bulletin of the American Academy of Psychiatry and the Law, 17,* 153–163.

Ross, J., Zinn, A. & McCauley, E. (2000). Neurodevelopmental and psychosocial aspects of Turner syndrome. *Mental Retardation and Developmental Disabilities Research Reviews, 6,* 135–141.

Rothschild, A. J. (2000). New directions in the treatment of antidepressant-induced sexual dysfunction. *Clinical Therapeutics, 22,* A42–57.

Rothschild, B. M., Calderon, F. L., Coppa, A. & Rothschild, C. (2000). First European exposure to syphilis: the Dominican Republic at the time of Columbian contact. *Clinical Infectious Diseases, 31,* 936–941.

Roughgarden, J. (2004). *Evolution's rainbow: Diversity, gender, and sexuality in nature and people.* University of California Press.

Rovet, J. & Netley, C. (1983). The triple X chromosome syndrome in childhood: recent empirical findings. *Child Development, 54,* 831–845.

Rovet, J., Netley, C., Keenan, M., Bailey, J. & Stewart, D. (1996). The psychoeducational profile of boys with Klinefelter syndrome. *Journal of Learning Disabilities, 29,* 180–196.

Rowland, J. H., Holland, J. C., Chaglassian, T. & Kinne, D. (1993). Psychological response to breast reconstruction. Expectations for and impact on postmastectomy functioning. *Psychosomatics, 34,* 241–250.

Ruberg, B. (2007). Do you like to watch? *Village Voice,* July 24.

Rubin, A. J. (2000). Public more accepting of gays, poll finds. *Los Angeles Times,* June 18.

Russell, D. E. H. (1984). *Sexual exploitation: Rape, child sexual abuse, and workplace harassment.* Sage.

Russell, D. E. H. (1994). *Against pornography: The evidence of harm.* Russell Publications.

Rust, J., Golombok, S., Hines, M., Johnston, K. & Golding, J. (2000). The role of brothers and sisters in the gender development of preschool children. *Journal of Experimental Child Psychology, 77,* 292–303.

Sacher-Masoch, L. v. (1870, 2000). *Venus in furs.* Viking Penguin.

Sadowsky, M., Antonovsky, H., Sobel, R. & Maoz, B. (1993). Sexual activity and sex hormone levels in aging men. *International Psychogeriatrics, 5,* 181–186.

Saidi, J. A., Chang, D. T., Goluboff, E. T., Bagiella, E., Olsen, G. & Fisch, H. (1999). Declining sperm counts in the United States? A critical review. *Journal of Urology, 161,* 460–462.

Sainz, B., Loutsch, J. M., Marquart, M. E. & Hill, J. M. (2001). Stress-associated immunomodulation and herpes simplex virus infections. *Medical Hypotheses, 56,* 348–356.

Salazar, L. F., DiClemente, R. J., Wingood, G. M., Crosby, R. A., Harrington, K., Davies, S., Hook, E. W., 3rd & Oh, M. K. (2004). Self-concept and adolescents' refusal of unprotected sex: A test of mediating mechanisms among African American girls. *Prevention Science, 5,* 137–149.

Salo, P., Kaariainen, H., Page, D. C. & de la Chapelle, A. (1995). Deletion mapping of stature determinants on the long arm of the Y chromosome. *Human Genetics, 95,* 283–286.

Samal, P. K., Farber, C., Farooque, N. A. & Rawat, D. S. (1997). Polyandry in a central Himalayan community: An eco-cultural analysis. *Man in India, 76,* 51–56.

Samois (Ed.) (1987). *Coming to power: Writings and graphics on lesbian S/M* (3rd ed.). Alyson.

Sampselle, C. M., Harris, V., Harlow, S. D. & Sowers, M. (2002). Midlife development and menopause in African American and Caucasian women. *Health Care for Women International, 23,* 351–363.

Sand, M. & Fisher, W. A. (2007). Women's endorsement of models of female sexual response: The Nurses' Sexuality Study. *Journal of Sexual Medicine, 4,* 708–719.

Sanday, P. R. (1996). *A woman scorned: Acquaintance rape on trial.* Doubleday.

Sanders, S. A. & Reinisch, J. M. (1999). Would you say you "had sex" if...? *Journal of the American Medical Association, 281,* 275–277.

Sanders, S. A., Graham, C. A. & Milhausen, R. R. (2008). Predicting sexual problems in women: The relevance of sexual excitation and sexual inhibition. *Archives of Sexual Behavior, 37,* 241–251.

Sanders, T. (2005). *Sex work: A risky business.* Willan Publishing.

Sanders, T. (2008). *Paying for pleasure: Men who buy sex.* Willan Publishing.

Santelli, J. S., Kaiser, J., Hirsch, L., Radosh, A., Simkin, L. & Middlestadt, S. (2004). Initiation of sexual intercourse among middle school adolescents: the influence of psychosocial factors. *Journal of Adolescent Health, 34,* 200–208.

Santelli, J. S., Lindberg, L. D., Finer, L. B. & Singh, S. (2007). Explaining recent declines in adolescent pregnancy in the United States: the contribution of abstinence and improved contraceptive use. *American Journal of Public Health, 97,* 150–156.

Santiago, R. (2006). 5-year-old "girl" starting school is really a boy. *Miami Herald,* July 10.

Santoro, N. (2005). The menopausal transition. *American Journal of Medicine, 118 Suppl 12B,* 8–13.

Sauvageau, A. & Racette, S. (2006). Autoerotic deaths in the literature from 1954 to 2004: a review. *Journal of Forensic Sciences, 51,* 140–146.

Savic, I. & Lindstrom, P. (2008). PET and MRI show differences in cerebral asymmetry and functional connectivity between homo- and heterosexual subjects. *Proceedings of the National Academy of Sciences, 105,* 9403–9408.

Savic, I., Berglund, H. & Lindstrom, P. (2005). Brain response to putative pheromones in homosexual men. *Proceedings of the National Academy of Sciences of the United States of America, 102,* 7356–7361.

Savin-Williams, R. C. (2001). Suicide attempts among sexual-minority youths: Population and measurement issues. *Journal of Consulting and Clinical Psychology, 69,* 983–991.

Savin-Williams, R. C. (2005). *The new gay teenager.* Harvard University Press.

Savin-Williams, R. C. & Diamond, L. M. (2004). Sex. In R. M. Lerner and L. Steinberg (Eds.), *Handbook of adolescent psychology* (2nd ed.) Wiley.

Sayle, A. E., Savitz, D. A., Thorp, J. M., Jr., Hertz-Picciotto, I. & Wilcox, A. J. (2001). Sexual activity during late pregnancy and risk of preterm delivery. *Obstetrics and Gynecology, 97,* 283–289.

Schackman, B. R., Gebo, K. A., Walensky, R. P., Losina, E., Muccio, T., Sax, P. E., Weinstein, M. C., Seage, G. R., 3rd, Moore, R. D. & Freedberg, K. A. (2006). The lifetime cost of current human immunodeficiency virus care in the United States. *Medical Care, 44,* 990–997.

Schaeffer, A. J. (2004). Etiology and management of chronic pelvic pain syndrome in men. *Urology, 63,* 75–84.

Schaffir, J. (2006). Sexual intercourse at term and onset of labor. *Obstetrics and Gynecology, 107,* 1310–1314.

Schiavi, R. C. (1999). *Aging and male sexuality.* Cambridge University Press.

Schieve, L. A., Rasmussen, S. A., Buck, G. M., Schendel, D. E., Reynolds, M. A. & Wright, V. C. (2004). Are children born after assisted reproductive technology at increased risk for adverse health outcomes? *Obstetrics and Gynecology, 103,* 1154–1163.

Schmid, D. M., Schurch, B. & Hauri, D. (2000). Sildenafil in the treatment of sexual dysfunction in spinal cord- injured male patients. *European Urology, 38,* 184–193.

Schmidt, G. (Ed.) (2000). *Kinder der sexuellen Revolution.* Psychosozial-Verlag.

Schmidt, H. (1998). Supernumerary nipples: prevalence, size, sex and side predilection—a prospective clinical study. *European Journal of Pediatrics, 157,* 821–823.

Schmidt, P. J., Nieman, L. K., Danaceau, M. A., Adams, L. F. & Rubinow, D. R. (1998). Differential behavioral effects of gonadal steroids in women with and in those without premenstrual syndrome. *New England Journal of Medicine, 338,* 209–216.

Schmitt, D. P. (2003). Universal sex differences in the desire for sexual variety: tests from 52 nations, 6 continents, and 13 islands. *Journal of Personality and Social Psychology, 85,* 85–104.

Schmitt, D. P. (2004). Patterns and universals of mate poaching across 53 nations: The effects of sex, culture, and personality on romantically attracting another person's partner. *Journal of Personality and Social Psychology, 86,* 560–584.

Schneider, A. & Barber, M. (1998). Lives ruined because lessons ignored. *Seattle Post-Intelligencer,* February 27.

Schneider, J. S., Burgess, C., Sleiter, N. C., DonCarlos, L. L., Lydon, J. P., O'Malley, B. & Levine, J. E. (2005). Enhanced sexual behaviors and androgen receptor immunoreactivity in the male progesterone receptor knockout mouse. *Endocrinology, 146,* 4340–4348.

Schneider, J. S., Stone, M. K., Wynne-Edwards, K. E., Horton, T. H., Lydon, J., O'Malley, B. & Levine, J. E. (2003). Progesterone receptors mediate male aggression toward infants. *Proceedings of the National Academy of Sciences, USA, 100,* 2951–2956.

Schnyder, U., Schnyder-Luthi, C., Ballinari, P. & Blaser, A. (1998). Therapy for vaginismus: in vivo versus in vitro desensitization. *Canadian Journal of Psychiatry Revue Canadienne de Psychiatrie, 43,* 941–944.

Scholly, K., Katz, A. R., Gascoigne, J. & Holck, P. S. (2005). Using social norms theory to explain perceptions and sexual health behaviors of undergraduate college students: an exploratory study. *Journal of American College Health, 53,* 159–166.

Schoofs, M. (1999). AIDS: The agony of Africa, part 5. *Village Voice,* December 1.

Schothorst, P. F. & van Engeland, H. (1996). Long-term behavioral sequelae of prematurity. *Journal of the American Academy of Child and Adolescent Psychiatry, 35,* 175–183.

Schubach, G. (1996). Urethral expulsions during sensual arousal and bladder catheterization in seven human females. Ed.D. thesis, *Institute for Advanced Study of Human Sexuality.*

Schultz, W. W., van Andel, P., Sabelis, I. & Mooyaart, E. (1999). Magnetic resonance imaging of male and female genitals during coitus and female sexual arousal. *British Medical Journal, 319,* 1596–1600.

Schumm, W. R., Webb, F. J. & Bollman, S. R. (1998). Gender and marital satisfaction: data from the National Survey of Families and Households. *Psychological Reports, 83,* 319–327.

Schuster, M. A., Bell, R. M., Nakajima, G. A. & Kanouse, D. E. (1998). The sexual practices of Asian and Pacific Islander high school students. *Journal of Adolescent Health, 23,* 221–231.

Schwebke, J. R. (2000). Bacterial vaginosis. *Current Infectious Disease Reports, 2,* 14–17.

Science Daily. (2007) *Alcohol amount, not type—wine, beer, liquor—triggers breast cancer.* (http://www.sciencedaily.com/releases/2007/09/070927083251.htm)

Scully, D. (1990). *Understanding sexual violence: A study of convicted rapists.* Unwin Hyman.

Sears, J. T. & Williams, W. L. (Eds.) (1997). *Overcoming heterosexism and homophobia: Strategies that work.* Columbia University Press.

Seattle Times. (2004). *Green River killings.* (http://seattletimes.nwsource.com/html/greenriverkillings/)

Serbin, L. A., Poulin-Dubois, D., Colburne, K. A., Sen, M. G. & Eichstedt, J. A. (2001). Gender stereotyping in infancy: Visual preferences for and knowledge of gender-stereotyped toys in the second year. *International Journal of Behavioral Development, 25,* 7–15.

Sermon, K., Van Steirteghem, A. & Liebaers, I. (2004). Preimplantation genetic diagnosis. *Lancet, 363,* 1633–1641.

Seto, M. C. (2008). Pedophilia: Psychopathology and theory. In D. R. Laws and W. T. O'Donohue (Eds.), *Sexual deviance: Theory, assessment, and treatment* (2nd ed.). Guilford Press.

Sexton, W. J., Benedict, J. F. & Jarow, J. P. (1998). Comparison of long-term outcomes of penile prostheses and intracavernosal injection therapy. *Journal of Urology, 159,* 811–815.

Shackelford, T. K. & Larsen, R. J. (1997). Facial asymmetry as an indicator of psychological, emotional, and physiological distress. *Journal of Personality and Social Psychology, 72,* 456–466.

Shanghai Star. (2002). *China's missing girls.* (http://www.china.com.cn/english/Life/47238.htm)

Shangold, M. M., Kelly, M., Berkeley, A. S., Freedman, K. S. & Groshen, S. (1989). Relationship between menarcheal age and adult height. *Southern Medical Journal, 82,* 443–445.

Shapleigh, E. (2008). *Report advises how to prevent rape in prison.* (http://www.shapleigh.org/news/2135-report-advises-how-to-prevent-rapes-in-prison)

Sharpe, R. M. (1997). Do males rely on female hormones? *Nature, 390,* 447–448.

Sharpley-Whiting, T. D. (2007). *Pimp's up, ho's down: Hip hop's hold on young black women.* New York University Press.

Shea, A. K. & Steiner, M. (2008). Cigarette smoking during pregnancy. *Nicotine and Tobacco Research, 10,* 267–278.

Shell-Duncan, B. & Hernlund, Y. (Eds.) (2000). *Female "circumcision" in Africa: Culture, controversy, and change.* Lynne Rienner.

Shepher, J. (1971). Mate selection among second generation kibbutz adolescents and adults: Incest avoidance and negative imprinting. *Archives of Sexual Behavior, 1,* 293–307.

Sherwin, B. B. & Gelfand, M. M. (1987). The role of androgen in the maintenance of sexual functioning in oophorectomized women. *Psychosomatic Medicine, 49,* 397–409.

Shilts, R. (1982). *The mayor of Castro Street: The life and times of Harvey Milk.* St. Martin's Press.

Shilts, R. (1987). *And the band played on: Politics, people, and the AIDS epidemic.* St. Martin's Press.

Shostak, M. (2000). *Nisa: The life and words of a !Kung woman.* Harvard University Press.

Showstack, J., Lin, F., Learman, L. A., Vittinghoff, E., Kuppermann, M., Varner, R. E., Summitt, R. L., Jr., McNeeley, S. G., Richter, H., Hulley, S. & Washington, A. E. (2006). Randomized trial of medical treatment versus hysterectomy for abnormal uterine bleeding: resource use in the Medicine or Surgery (Ms) trial. *American Journal of Obstetrics and Gynecology, 194,* 332–338.

Shumaker, S. A., Legault, C., Kuller, L., Rapp, S. R., Thal, L., Lane, D. S., Fillit, H., Stefanick, M. L., Hendrix, S. L., Lewis, C. E., Masaki, K. & Coker, L. H. (2004). Conjugated equine estrogens and incidence of probable dementia and mild cognitive impairment in postmenopausal women: Women's Health Initiative Memory Study. *JAMA, 291,* 2947–2958.

Shumaker, S. A., Legault, C., Rapp, S. R., Thal, L., Wallace, R. B., Ockene, J. K., Hendrix, S. L., Jones, B. N., 3rd, Assaf, A. R., Jackson, R. D., Kotchen, J. M., Wassertheil-Smoller, S. & Wactawski-Wende, J. (2003). Estrogen plus progestin and the incidence of dementia and mild cognitive impairment in postmenopausal women: the Women's Health Initiative Memory Study: a randomized controlled trial. *JAMA, 289,* 2651–2662.

SIECUS. (2004). *A portrait of sexuality education and abstinence-only-until-marriage programs in the States.* (www.siecus.org/policy/states/index.html)

Signorile, M. (1997). *Life outside: The Signorile report on gay men.* Harper Perennial.

Silvera, S. A., Miller, A. B. & Rohan, T. E. (2005). Oral contraceptive use and risk of breast cancer among women with a family history of breast cancer: a prospective cohort study. *Cancer Causes and Control, 16,* 1059–1063.

Silverberg, C., (2008) *How to achieve male multiple orgasms.* (http://sexuality.about.com/od/orgasms/ht/htmalemultiples.htm)

Silverman, I. & Eals, M. (1992). Sex differences in spatial abilities: Evolutionary theory and data. In J. H. Barko, L. Cosmides, and J. Tooby (Eds.), *The adapted mind.* Oxford University Press.

Silverman, J. G., Raj, A., Mucci, L. A. & Hathaway, J. E. (2001). Dating violence against adolescent girls and associated substance use, unhealthy weight control, sexual risk behavior, pregnancy, and suicidality. *JAMA, 286,* 572–579.

Simon, J. A. & Snabes, M. C. (2007). Menopausal hormone therapy for vasomotor symptoms: balancing the risks and benefits with ultra-low doses of estrogen. *Expert Opinion on Investigational Drugs, 16,* 2005–2020.

Simon, L. M. J. (2000). An examination of the assumptions of specialization, mental disorder, and dangerousness in sex offenders. *Behavioral Sciences and the Law, 18,* 275–308.

Simon, S. (2002). AIDS scare at tiny college shakes town. *Los Angeles Times,* April 30.

Simon, W. & Gagnon, J. H. (1986). Sexual scripts: permanence and change. *Archives of Sexual Behavior, 15,* 97–120.

Simon, W. & Gagnon, J. H. (1987). A sexual scripts approach. In J. H. Geer and W. T. O'Donohue (Eds.), *Theories of human sexuality.* Plenum Press.

Simons, J. S. & Carey, M. P. (2001). Prevalence of sexual dysfunctions: results from a decade of research. *Archives of Sexual Behavior, 30,* 177–219.

Simons, M. (2008). Amsterdam tries upscale fix for red-light district crime. *New York Times,* February 24.

Simpson, J. A., Collins, W. A., Tran, S. & Haydon, K. C. (2007). Attachment and the experience and expression of emotions in romantic relationships: a developmental perspective. *Journal of Personality and Social Psychology, 92,* 355–367.

Sinclair, A. H., Berta, P., Palmer, M. S., Hawkins, J. R., Griffiths, B. L., Smith, M. J., Foster, J. W., Frischauf, A. M., Lovell-Badge, R. & Goodfellow, P. N. (1990). A gene from the human sex-determining region encodes a protein with homology to a conserved DNA-binding motif. *Nature, 346,* 240–244.

Sinclair, H. C. & Frieze, I. H. (2001). Initial courtship behavior and stalking: How should we draw the line? In K. E. Davis et al. (Eds.), *Stalking: Perspectives on victims and perpetrators.* Springer.

Singer, J. & Singer, I. (1972). Types of female orgasm. *Journal of Sex Research, 8,* 255–267.

Singh, D. (1994a). Ideal female body shape: role of body weight and waist-to-hip ratio. *International Journal of Eating Disorders, 16,* 283–288.

Singh, D. (1994b). Waist-to-hip ratio and judgment of attractiveness and healthiness of female figures by male and female physicians. *International Journal of Obesity and Related Metabolic Disorders, 18,* 731–737.

Singh, D. (1995). Female judgment of male attractiveness and desirability for relationships: role of waist-to-hip ratio and financial status. *Journal of Personality and Social Psychology, 69,* 1089–1101.

Singh, S., Darroch, J. E. & Bankole, A. (2003). *A, B and C in Uganda: The role of abstinence, monogamy and condom use in HIV decline.* (www.guttmacher.org/pubs/or_abc03.pdf)

Sionean, C., DiClemente, R. J., Wingood, G. M., Crosby, R., Cobb, B. K., Harrington, K., Davies, S. L., Hook, E. W., 3rd & Oh, M. K. (2002). Psychosocial and behavioral correlates of refusing unwanted sex among African-American adolescent females. *Journal of Adolescent Health, 30,* 55–63.

Sipski, M. L., Alexander, C. J. & Rosen, R. (2001). Sexual arousal and orgasm in women: effects of spinal cord injury. *Annals of Neurology, 49,* 35–44.

Skidmore, W. C., Linsenmeier, J. A. & Bailey, J. M. (2006). Gender nonconformity and psychological distress in lesbians and gay men. *Archives of Sexual Behavior, 35,* 685–697.

Skornogoski, K. (2003). He's guilty: Bar-Jonah convicted on three counts. *Great Falls Tribune,* February 26.

Slater, A., Von der Schulenburg, C., Brown, E., Badenoch, M., Butterworth, G., Parsons, S. & Samuels, C. (1998). Newborn infants prefer attractive faces. *Infant Behavior and Development, 21,* 345–354.

Sloss, C. M. & Harper, G. W. (2004). When street sex workers are mothers. *Archives of Sexual Behavior, 33,* 329–341.

Smith, A. D. (2001). Where men love big women. *Marie Claire* (September).

Smith, E. A., Borgehoff Mulder, M. & Hill, K. (2001). Controversies in the evolutionary social sciences: A guide for the perplexed. *Trends in Ecology and Evolution, 16,* 128–135.

Smith, J. S., Herrero, R., Bosetti, C., Munoz, N., Bosch, F. X., Eluf-Neto, J., Castellsague, X., Meijer, C. J., Van den Brule, A. J., Franceschi, S. & Ashley, R. (2002). Herpes simplex virus-2 as a human papillomavirus cofactor in the etiology of invasive cervical cancer. *Journal of the National Cancer Institute, 94,* 1604–1613.

Smith, S. M. (1988). Extra-pair copulation in black-capped chickadees: the role of the female. *Behaviour, 107,* 15–23.

SmithBattle, L. (2007). "I wanna have a good future": Teen mothers' rise in educational aspirations, competing demands, and limited school support. *Youth and Society, 38,* 348–371.

Smock, P. J. (1993). The economic costs of marital disruption for young women over the past two decades. *Demography, 30,* 353–371.

Smock, P. J. (2000). Cohabitation in the United States: An appraisal of research themes, findings, and implications. *Annual Review of Sociology, 26,* 1–20.

Somboonporn, W., Davis, S., Seif, M. W. & Bell, R. (2005). Testosterone for peri- and postmenopausal women. *Cochrane Database of Systematic Reviews,* CD004509.

Sommer, B., Avis, N., Meyer, P., Ory, M., Madden, T., Kagawa-Singer, M., Mouton, C., Rasor, N. O. & Adler, S. (1999). Attitudes toward menopause and aging across ethnic/racial groups. *Psychosomatic Medicine, 61,* 868–875.

Southern Center for Human Rights. (2008). *Georgia sex offender law back in federal court moments after being signed by Governor Perdue.* (http://www.schr.org/aboutthecenter/pressreleases/HB1059_litigation/PressReleases/press_lawsuitHB1059_SB1signed.htm)

Spalding, L. R. & Peplau, L. A. (1997). The unfaithful lover: Heterosexuals' stereotypes of bisexuals and their relationships. *Psychology of Women Quarterly, 21,* 611–625.

Spehr, M., Gisselmann, G., Poplawski, A., Riffell, J. A., Wetzel, C. H., Zimmer, R. K. & Hatt, H. (2003). Identification of a testicular odorant receptor mediating human sperm chemotaxis. *Science, 299,* 2054–2058.

Spitzer, R. L. (2003). Can some gay men and lesbians change their sexual orientation? 200 participants reporting a change from homosexual to heterosexual orientation. *Archives of Sexual Behavior, 32,* 403–417; discussion 419–472.

Sprecher, S. & Regan, P. C. (2002). Liking some things (in some people) more than others: Partner preferences in romantic relationships and friendships. *Journal of Social and Personal Relationships, 19,* 463–481.

Sprecher, S. (2001). Equity and social exchange in dating couples: Association with satisfaction, commitment, and stability. *Journal of Marriage and Family, 63,* 599–613.

Sroufe, L. A. (1985). Attachment classification from the perspective of infant-caregiver relationships and infant temperament. *Child Development, 56,* 1–14.

St Lawrence, J. S., Brasfield, T. L., Jefferson, K. W., Alleyne, E., O'Bannon, R. E., 3rd & Shirley, A. (1995). Cognitive-behavioral intervention to reduce African American adolescents' risk for HIV infection. *Journal of Consulting and Clinical Psychology, 63,* 221–237.

St. Paul Police. (2008). *Prostitution photographs.* (http://mnstpaul.civicplus.com/index.asp?NID=2351)

Stacey, J. & Biblarz, T. J. (2001). (How) does the sexual orientation of parents matter? *American Sociological Review, 66,* 159–183.

Stack, S. & Gundlach, J. H. (1992). Divorce and sex. *Archives of Sexual Behavior, 21,* 359–367.

Statistics Canada. (2004). *Canadian Community Health Survey 2003.* (http://www.statcan.ca/Daily/English/040615/d040615b.htm)

Stavis, P. F. (1991). *Sexual activity and the law of consent.* (http://www.cqc.state.ny.us/cc50.htm)

Stavnezer, A. J., McDowell, C. S., Hyde, L. A., Bimonte, H. A., Balogh, S. A., Hoplight, B. J. & Denenberg, V. H. (2000). Spatial ability of XY sex-reversed female mice. *Behavioural Brain Research, 112,* 135–143.

Stein, M. D., Freedberg, K. A., Sullivan, L. M., Savetsky, J., Levenson, S. M., Hingson, R. & Samet, J. H. (1998). Sexual ethics. Disclosure of HIV-positive status to partners. *Archives of Internal Medicine, 158,* 253–257.

Stein, N. (1999). *Incidence and implications of sexual harassment in K–12 schools.* (http://www.hamfish.org/pub/nan.pdf)

Steinberg, L. (Ed.) (2004). *Adolescence* (7th ed.). McGraw-Hill.

Stepp, L. S. (1999). Parents are alarmed by an unsettling new fad in middle schools: oral sex. *Washington Post,* July 8.

Stepp, L. S. (2007). *Unhooked: How young women pursue sex, delay love, and lose at both.* Riverhead.

Sternberg, R. J. & Barnes, M. (1985). Real and ideal others in romantic relationships: Is four a crowd? *Journal of Personality and Social Psychology, 47,* 1586–1608.

Sternberg, R. J. (1986). A triangular theory of love. *Psychological Review, 93,* 119–135.

Sternberg, R. J. (1998). *Love is a story: A new theory of relationships.* Oxford University Press.

Stevenson, M. (2008). Can HIV be cured? *Scientific American, 299(5),* 78–91 .

Stewart, F., Trussell, J. & Van Look, P. F. A. (2007). Emergency contraception. In R. A. Hatcher et al. (Eds.), *Contraceptive technology* (19th ed.). Ardent Media.

Stimpson, D., Jensen, L. C. & Neff, W. (1991). Cross-cultural gender differences in preference for a caring morality. *Journal of Social Psychology, 132,* 317–322.

Stokes, D., Damon, W. & McKirnan, D. J. (1997). Predictors of movement toward homosexuality: A longitudinal study of bisexual men. *Journal of Sex Research.* 34, 304–312.

Stoller, R. J. (1975). *Perversion: The erotic form of hatred.* Pantheon.

Stone, L. (1988). Passionate attachments in the West in historical perspective. In W. Gaylin and E. Person (Eds.), *Passionate attachments: Thinking about love.* Free Press.

Stone, T. H., Winslade, W. J. & Klugman, C. M. (2000). Sex offenders, sentencing laws and pharmaceutical treatment: a prescription for failure. *Behavioral Sciences and the Law, 18,* 83–110.

Stop Prisoner Rape. (2008). *Government report confirms: Sexual abuse in detention is preventable.* (http://www.justdetention.org/en/pressreleases/2008/08-26-08.asp)

Strassberg, D. S. & Lockerd, L. K. (1998). Force in women's sexual fantasies. *Archives of Sexual Behavior, 27,* 403–414.

Strassler, B. (Ed.) (2007). *The Landmark Herodotus: The histories.* Pantheon.

Strassmann, B. I. (1992). The function of menstrual taboos among the Dogon: Defense against cuckoldry? *Human Nature, 3,* 89–131.

Strassmann, B. I. (1996). Menstrual hut visits by Dogon women: A hormonal test distinguishes deceit from honest signaling. *Behavioral Ecology, 7,* 304–315.

Strassmann, B. I. (1997). The biology of menstruation in *Homo sapiens:* Total lifetime menses, fecundity, and nonsynchrony in a natural fertility population. *Current Anthropology, 38,* 123–129.

Strassmann, B. I. (1999). Menstrual synchrony pheromones: cause for doubt. *Human Reproduction, 14,* 579–580.

Straus, M. (1992). Children as witnesses to marital violence: A risk factor for lifelong problems among a nationally representative sample of American men and women. In D. F. Schwartz (Ed.), *Children and violence.* Ross Laboratories.

Strossen, N. (1995). *Defending pornography: Free speech, sex, and the fight for women's rights.* Scribner.

Suarez, S. S. & Pacey, A. A. (2006). Sperm transport in the female reproductive tract. *Human Reproduction Update, 12,* 23–37.

Sugar, N. F., Fine, D. N. & Eckert, L. O. (2004). Physical injury after sexual assault: findings of a large case series. *American Journal of Obstetrics and Gynecology, 190,* 71–76.

Sullivan, A. (1995). *Virtually normal: An argument about homosexuality.* Knopf.

Summersgill, R. (2004). *Sodomy laws around the world.* (http://www.sodomylaws.org/)

Supreme Court of Arkansas. (2002). *Jegley v. Picado.* (http://courts.state.ar.us/opinions/2002a/20020705/01-815.html)

Supreme Court of the United States. (2003). *Lawrence et al. v. Texas.* (http://www.supremecourtus.gov/opinions/02pdf/02-102.pdf)

Supreme Court of Wisconsin. (2008).*Wisconsin v. Grunke.* (http://www.wicourts.gov/sc/opinion/DisplayDocument.pdf?content=pdf&seqNo=33332)

Survive-UK. (2001). *It happened to me.* (http://survive.org.uk/stories.html)

Suschinsky, K. D., Lalumiere, M. L. & Chivers, M. L. (2008). Sex differences in patterns of genital sexual arousal: Measurement artifacts or true phenomena? *Archives of Sexual Behavior* (online publication, 10.1007/s10508-008-9339-8).

Swami, V. & Tovee, M. J. (2006). Does hunger influence judgments of female physical attractiveness? *British Journal of Psychology, 97,* 353–363.

Swan, S. H. (2006). Semen quality in fertile US men in relation to geographical area and pesticide exposure. *International Journal of Andrology, 29,* 62–68; discussion 105–108.

Swan, S. H., Elkin, E. P. & Fenster, L. (2000). The question of declining sperm density revisited: An analysis of 101 studies published 1934–1996. *Environmental Health Perspectives, 108,* 961–966.

Swick, K. (2005). Preventing violence through empathy development in families. *Early Childhood Education Journal, 33,* 53–59.

Syed, R. (1999). Knowledge of the "Grafenberg zone" and female ejaculation in ancient Indian sexual science. A medical history contribution. *Sudhoffs Archiv; Zeitschrift fur Wissenschaftsgeschichte, 83,* 171–190.

Szarewski, A. (2002). High acceptability and satisfaction with NuvaRing use. *European Journal of Contraception and Reproductive Health Care, 7 Suppl 2,* 31–36; discussion 37–39.

Szasz, T. S. (2000). Remembering Krafft-Ebing. *Ideas on Liberty, 50,* 31–32.

Talimini, J. T. (1982). *Boys will be girls: The hidden world of the heterosexual male transvestite.* University Press of America.

Talley, A. E. & Bettencourt, B. A. (2008). Evaluations and aggression directed at a gay male target: The role of threat and anti-gay prejudice. *Journal of Applied Social Psychology, 38,* 647–683.

Tanfer, K. & Aral, S. O. (1996). Sexual intercourse during menstruation and self-reported sexually transmitted disease history among women. *Sexually Transmitted Diseases, 23,* 395–401.

Tarin, J. J. & Gomez-Piquer, V. (2002). Do women have a hidden heat period? *Human Reproduction, 17,* 2243–2248.

Tat, H. (2005). *Racism in gay culture.* (http://www.tatmultimedia.com/Websites/Journal/)

Templeman, T. L. & Stinnett, R. D. (1991). Patterns of sexual arousal and history in a "normal" sample of young men. *Archives of Sexual Behavior, 20,* 137–150.

Templer, D. I. (2002). *Is size important?* Ceshore Publishing.

Tennov, D. (1979). *Love and limerence.* Stein & Day.

Testa, R. J., Kinder, B. N. & Ironson, G. (1987). Heterosexual bias in the perception of loving relationships of gay males and lesbians. *Journal of Sex Research, 16,* 245–257.

The Arc. (2007). *Sexuality.* (http://www.thearc.org/NetCommunity/Page.aspx?&pid=1375&srcid=405)

Thienhaus, O. J. (1988). Practical overview of sexual function and advancing age. *Geriatrics, 43,* 63–67.

Thompson, J. K. & Tantleff, S. (1992). Female and male ratings of upper torso: Actual, ideal, and stereotypical conceptions. *Journal of Social Behavior and Personality, 7,* 345–354.

Thompson, M. (1995). *Gay soul: Finding the heart of gay spirit and nature.* Harper San Francisco.

Thorneycroft, I. H. & Cariati, S. L. (2001). *Ultra-low-dose oral contraceptives: Are they right for your patient?* (http://www.medscape.com/Medscape/WomensHealth/journal/2001/v06.n04/wh0703.thor/wh0703.thor-01.html)

Thornhill, R. (1980). Rape in *Panorpa* scorpionflies and a general rape hypothesis. *Animal Behavior, 28,* 52–59.

Thornhill, R. & Gangestad, S. W. (1999a). Facial attractiveness. *Trends in Cognitive Science, 3,* 452–460.

Thornhill, R. & Gangestad, S. W. (1999b). The scent of symmetry: A human sex pheromone that signals fitness? *Evolution and Human Behavior, 20,* 175–201.

Thornhill, R. & Palmer, C. T. (2000). *A natural history of rape: Biological bases of sexual coercion.* MIT Press.

Thys-Jacobs, S. (2000). Micronutrients and the premenstrual syndrome: the case for calcium. *Journal of the American College of Nutrition, 19,* 220–227.

Tiefer, L. (2002). Sexual behaviour and its medicalisation. Many (especially economic) forces promote medicalisation. *British Medical Journal, 325,* 45.

Tillmann-Healy, L. M. (2001). *Between gay and straight: Understanding friendship across sexual orientation.* AltaMira Press.

Tjaden, P. & Thoennes, N. (1998). *Stalking in America: Findings from the National Violence Against Women survey.* (http://www.ncjrs.org/pdffiles/169592.pdf)

Tjaden, P. & Thoennes, N. (2006). *Extent, nature, and consequences of rape victimization: Findings from the National Violence Against Women Survey.* (http://www.ncjrs.org/pdffiles1/nij/210346.pdf)

Tomlinson, P. S. (1987). Spousal differences in marital satisfaction during transition to parenthood. *Nursing Research, 36,* 239–243.

Toro-Morn, M. & Sprecher, S. (2003). A cross-cultural comparison of mate preferences among university students: The United States vs. the People's Republic of China (PRC). *Journal of Comparative Family Studies, 34,* 151–174.

Townsend, L. (2007). *Leatherman's handbook II.* Booksurge Publishing.

Trager, J. D. (2006). Pubic hair removal—pearls and pitfalls. *Journal of Pediatric and Adolescent Gynecology, 19,* 117–123.

Trebay, C. (2008, February 7). The vanishing point. *New York Times.*

Trenholm, C., Devaney, B., Fortson, K., Quay, L., Wheeler, J. & Clark, M. (2007). *Impacts of four Title V, Section 510 abstinence education programs.* (http://www.mathematica-mpr.com/publications/pdfs/impactabstinence.pdf)

Trevathan, W. R., Burleson, M. H. & Gregory, W. L. (1993). No evidence for menstrual synchrony in lesbian couples. *Psychoneuroendocrinology, 18,* 425–435.

Trivers, R. L. & Hare, H. (1976). Haplodiploidy and the evolution of the social insects. *Science, 191,* 249–263.

Trussell, J. (2007). Choosing a contraceptive: Efficacy, safety, and personal considerations. In R. A. Hatcher et al. (Eds.), *Contraceptive technology.* Ardent Media.

Tugwell, P., Wells, G., Peterson, J., Welch, V., Page, J., Davison, C., McGowan, J., Ramroth, D. & Shea, B. (2001). Do silicone breast implants cause rheumatologic disorders? A systematic review for a court-appointed national science panel. *Arthritis and Rheumatism, 44,* 2477–2484.

Tuller, D. (2004). Gentlemen, start your engines? *New York Times,* June 21.

Tulviste, T. & Koor, M. (2005). "Hands off the car, it's mine!" and "The teacher will be angry if we don't play nicely": Gender-related preferences in the use of moral rules and social conventions in preschoolers' dyadic play. *Sex Roles, 53,* 57–66.

Turner, T. & Loder, K. (1986). *I, Tina: My life story.* HarperCollins.

Tyring, S. K., Douglas, J. M., Jr., Corey, L., Spruance, S. L. & Esmann, J. (1998). A randomized, placebo-controlled comparison of oval valacyclovir and acyclovir in immunocompetent patients with recurrent genital herpes infections. The Valaciclovir International Study Group. *Archives of Dermatology, 134,* 185–191.

Tyson, A. S. (2007). Military discharged fewer gays, lesbians in '06. *Washington Post,* March 14.

U.S. Agency for International Development. (2003). *The ABCs of HIV prevention.* (http://www.aidsuganda.org/pdf/ABCs_of_prevention.pdf)

U.S. Census Bureau. (2001). *America's families and living arrangements—2000.* (http://www.census.gov/prod/2001pubs/p20-537.pdf)

U.S. Census Bureau. (2007). *Marital status in the 2004 American Community Survey.* (http://www.census.gov/population/www/documentation/twps0483/twps0483.pdf)

U.S. Census Bureau. (2008) *Ranking tables 2008.* (http://factfinder.census.gov/servlet/GRTSelectServlet?ds_name=ACS_2007_1YR_G00_)

U.S. Department of Health and Human Services. (2004). *National adoption and foster care statistics.* (http://www.acf.dhhs.gov/programs/cb/dis/afcars/publications/afcars.htm)

U.S. Department of Justice. (1997). *Violence-related injuries treated in hospital emergency departments.* (http://www.ojp.usdoj.gov/bjs/pub/pdf/vrithed.pdf)

U.S. Department of Justice. (1998). *Prevalence, incidence, and consequences of violence against women: Findings from the National Violence Against Women Survey.* (http://ncjrs.org/pdffiles/172837.pdf)

U.S. Department of Justice. (1999). *1999 report on cyberstalking: A new challenge for law enforcement and industry.* (http://www.usdoj.gov/criminal/cybercrime/cyberstalking.htm)

U.S. Department of Justice. (2000). *Full report of the prevalence, incidence, and consequences of violence against women.* (http://www.ncjrs.org/pdffiles1/nij/183781.pdf)

U.S. Department of Justice. (2004a). *Crime characteristics.* (http://www.ojp.usdoj.gov/bjs/cvict_c.htm#violent)

U.S. Department of Justice. (2004b). *Criminal offenders statistics.* (http://www.ojp.usdoj.gov/bjs/crimoff.htm)

U.S. Department of Justice. (2006). *National Crime Victimization Survey: Criminal victimization, 2005.* (http://www.ojp.usdoj.gov/bjs/pub/pdf/cv05.pdf)

U.S. Food and Drug Administration. (1999). *Toxic shock syndrome: Reducing the risk.* (http://www.fda.gov/bbs/topics/consumer/con00116.html)

U.S. Food and Drug Administration. (2004). *Questions and answers for estrogen and estrogen with progestin therapies for postmenopausal women.* (http://www.fda.gov/cder/drug/infopage/estrogens_progestins/Q&A.htm)

Udry, J. R. & Talbert, L. M. (1988). Sex hormone effects on personality at puberty. *Journal of Personality and Social Psychology, 54,* 291–295.

Udry, J. R., Billy, J. O., Morris, N. M., Groff, T. R. & Raj, M. H. (1985). Serum androgenic hormones motivate sexual behavior in adolescent boys. *Fertility and Sterility, 43,* 90–94.

Ullian, D. Z. (1981). Why boys will be boys: A structural perspective. *American Journal of Orthopsychiatry, 51,* 493–501.

UNAIDS. (2008). *2008 Report on the global AIDS epidemic.* (http://www.unaids.org/en/KnowledgeCentre/HIVData/GlobalReport/2008/2008_Global_report.asp)

United Methodist Church. (2000). *The book of discipline of the United Methodist Church.* United Methodist Publishing House.

United Nations Development Program. (1997) *HIV and development programme.* (http://www.undp.org/hiv/mayors/abiintroe.htm)

University of Arizona Campus Health Service. (2005). *Sextalk.* (http://www.health.arizona.edu/Health%20Education%20OnLine%20Library/Sexual%20Health/sextalk2-28-05.pdf)

Uronis, H. E. & Bendell, J. C. (2007). Anal cancer: an overview. *The Oncologist, 12,* 524–534.

van Anders, S. M., Vernon, P. A. & Wilbur, C. J. (2006). Finger-length ratios show evidence of prenatal hormone-transfer between opposite-sex twins. *Hormones and Behavior, 49,* 315–319.

Van Goozen, S. H., Wiegant, V. M., Endert, E., Helmond, F. A. & Van de Poll, N. E. (1997). Psychoendocrinological assessment of the menstrual cycle: the relationship between hormones, sexuality, and mood. *Archives of Sexual Behavior, 26,* 359–382.

van Wieringen, J. C., Wafelbakker, F., Verbrugge, H. P. & de Haas, J. H. (1971). *Growth diagrams 1965 Netherlands: Second National Survey on 0-24-year-olds.* Netherlands Institute for Preventative Medicine TNO. Leiden and Wolters Noordhoff.

Vance, E. B. & Wagner, N. N. (1976). Written descriptions of orgasms: A study of sex differences. *Archives of Sexual Behavior, 5,* 87–98.

VanOss Marin, B., Coyle, K. K., Gómez, C. A., Carvajal, S. C. & Kirby, D. B. (2000). Older boyfriends and girlfriends increase risk of sexual initiation in young adolescents. *Journal of Adolescent Health, 27,* 409–418.

Vara-Orta, F. (2007). Majority of freshmen view gay marriage as OK. *Los Angeles Times,* January 19.

Varghese, B., Maher, J. E., Peterman, T. A., Branson, B. M. & Steketee, R. W. (2002). Reducing the risk of sexual HIV transmission: quantifying the per-act risk for HIV on the basis of choice of partner, sex act, and condom use. *Sexually Transmitted Diseases, 29,* 38–43.

Vasey, P. L. (2006). The pursuit of pleasure: An evolutionary history of female homosexual behaviour in Japanese macaques. In V. Sommer and P. L. Vasey (Eds.), *Homosexual behaviour in animals.* Cambridge University Press.

Vasey, P. L. & Bartlett, N. H. (2007). What can the Samoan "Fa'afafine" teach us about the Western concept of gender identity disorder in childhood? *Perspectives in Biology and Medicine, 50,* 481–490.

Veale, J. F., Clarke, D. E. & Lomax, T. C. (2008). Sexuality of male-to-female transsexuals. *Archives of Sexual Behavior, 37,* 586–597.

Vedam, S. (2003). Home birth versus hospital birth: questioning the quality of the evidence on safety. *Birth, 30,* 57–63.

Vega, V. & Malamuth, N. M. (2007). Predicting sexual aggression: the role of pornography in the context of general and specific risk factors. *Aggressive Behavior, 33,* 104–117.

Vennemann, B. & Pollak, S. (2006). Death by hanging while watching violent pornographic videos on the Internet—suicide or accidental autoerotic death? *International Journal of Legal Medicine, 120,* 110–114.

Vicinus, M. (1989). Distance and desire: English boarding school friendships, 1870–1920. In L. Duberman et al. (Eds.), *Hidden from history: Reclaiming the gay and lesbian past.* NAL Books.

Virk, J., Zhang, J. & Olsen, J. (2007). Medical abortion and the risk of subsequent adverse pregnancy outcomes. *New England Journal of Medicine, 357,* 648–653.

Voracek, M., Hofhansl, A. & Fisher, M. L. (2005). Clark and Hatfield's evidence of women's low receptivity to male strangers' sexual offers revisited. *Psychological Reports, 97,* 11–20.

Wainright, J. L., Russell, S. T. & Patterson, C. J. (2004). Psychosocial adjustment, school outcomes, and romantic relationships of adolescents with same-sex parents. *Child Development, 75,* 1886–1898.

Waite, L. J. & Joyner, K. (2001). Emotional and physical satisfaction with sex in married, cohabiting, and dating sexual unions: Do men and women differ? In E. O. Laumann and R. T. Michael (Eds.), *Sex, love, and health in America: Private choices and public policies.* University of Chicago Press.

Wald, A., Zeh, J., Selke, S., Warren, T., Ryncarz, A. J., Ashley, R., Krieger, J. N. & Corey, L. (2000). Reactivation of genital herpes simplex virus type 2 infection in asymptomatic seropositive persons. *New England Journal of Medicine, 342,* 844–850.

Waldinger, M. D. (2004). Lifelong premature ejaculation: from authority-based to evidence-based medicine. *BJU International, 93,* 201–207.

Waldinger, M. D. & Olivier, B. (2004). Utility of selective serotonin reuptake inhibitors in premature ejaculation. *Current Opinion in Investigational Drugs, 5,* 743–747.

Waldinger, M. D., Zwinderman, A. H. & Olivier, B. (2001). Antidepressants and ejaculation: a double-blind, randomized, placebo- controlled, fixed-dose study with paroxetine, sertraline, and nefazodone. *Journal of Clinical Psychopharmacology, 21,* 293–297.

Walen, S. R. & Roth, D. (1987). A cognitive approach. In J. H. Geer and W. T. O'Donohue (Eds.), *Theories of human sexuality.* Plenum Press.

Walker, B. G. (1983). *Woman's encyclopedia of myths and secrets.* Harper San Francisco.

Walker, J., Archer, J. & Davies, M. (2005). Effects of rape on men: a descriptive analysis. *Archives of Sexual Behavior, 34,* 69–80.

Walker, L. E. A. (1979). *The battered woman.* Harper and Row.

Walker, L. E. A. (1999). *The battered woman syndrome* (2nd ed.). Springer.

Wallen, K. (1996). Nature needs nurture: the interaction of hormonal and social influences on the development of behavioral sex differences in rhesus monkeys. *Hormones and Behavior, 30,* 364–378.

Wallen, K. (2001). Sex and context: hormones and primate sexual motivation. *Hormones and Behavior, 40,* 339–357.

Wang, C., Swedloff, R. S., Iranmanesh, A., Dobs, A., Snyder, P. J., Cunningham, G., Matsumoto, A. M., Weber, T. & Berman, N. (2000). Transdermal testosterone gel improves sexual function, mood, muscle strength, and body composition parameters in hypogonadal men. Testosterone Gel Study Group. *Journal of Clinical Endocrinology and Metabolism, 85,* 2839–2853.

Ward, I. L., Ward, O. B., Winn, R. J. & Bielawski, D. (1994). Male and female sexual behavior potential of male rats prenatally exposed to the influence of alcohol, stress, or both factors. *Behavioral Neuroscience, 108,* 1188–1195.

Ward, T. & Beech, A. R. (2008). An integrated theory of sexual offending. In D. R. Laws and W. T. O'Donohue (Eds.), *Sexual deviance: Theory, assessment, and treatment* (2nd ed.). Guilford Press.

Warner, L. & Steiner, M. J. (2007). Male condoms. In R. A. Hatcher et al. (Eds.), *Contraceptive technology* (19th ed.). Ardent Media.

Warner, M. (2000). *The trouble with normal: Sex, politics, and the ethics of gay life.* Harvard University Press.

Warner, P. & Bancroft, J. (1987). A regional clinical service for sexual problems: A three-year survey. *Sexual and Marital Therapy, 2,* 115–126.

Washington, H. A. (2007). *Medical apartheid: The dark history of medical experimentation on black Americans from colonial times to the present.* Doubleday.

Watson, N. V. & Kimura, D. (1991). Nontrivial sex differences in throwing and intercept-

ing: Relation to psychometrically-defined spatial functions. *Personality and Individual Differences, 12,* 375–385.

Wawer, M. J. & 13 others. (2005). Rates of HIV-1 transmission per coital act, by stage of HIV-1 infection, in Rakai, Uganda. *Journal of Infectious Diseases, 191,* 1403–1409.

Wax, J. R., Cartin, A., Pinette, M. G. & Blackstone, J. (2004). Patient choice cesarean: an evidence-based review. *Obstetrical and Gynecological Survey, 59,* 601–616.

Wedekind, C. & Furi, S. (1997). Body odour preferences in men and women: do they aim for specific MHC combinations or simply heterozygosity? *Proceedings Biological Science, 264,* 1471–1479.

Weinberg, M. S., Shaver, F. M. & Williams, C. J. (1999). Gendered sex work in the San Francisco tenderloin. *Archives of Sexual Behavior, 28,* 503–521.

Weinberg, M. S., Williams, C. J. & Pryor, D. W. (1995). *Dual attraction: Understanding bisexuality.* Oxford University Press.

Weise, E. R. (1991). Bisexuality, *The Rocky Horror Picture Show,* and me. In L. Hutchins and L. Kaahumanu (Eds.), *Bi any other name: Bisexual people speak out.* Alyson.

Weise, E. R. (1992). *Closer to home: bisexuality and feminism.* Seal Press.

Weisfeld, G. (1999). *Evolutionary principles of human adolescence.* Basic Books.

Weisfeld, G. E., Czilli, T., Phillips, K. A., Gall, J. A. & Lichtman, C. M. (2003). Possible olfaction-based mechanisms in human kin recognition and inbreeding avoidance. *Journal of Experimental Child Psychology, 85,* 279–295.

Weiss, E. (2004). *Surviving domestic violence: Voices of women who broke free.* Volcano Press.

Weiss, K. R. (2001). Eggs buy a college education. *Los Angeles Times,* May 27.

Weller, A. & Weller, L. (1997). Menstrual synchrony under optimal conditions: Bedouin families. *Journal of Comparative Psychology, 111,* 143–151.

Weller, A. & Weller, L. (1998). Prolonged and very intensive contact may not be conducive to menstrual synchrony. *Psychoneuroendocrinology, 23,* 19–32.

Weller, L., Weller, A. & Avinir, O. (1995). Menstrual synchrony: only in roommates who are close friends? *Physiology and Behavior, 58,* 883–889.

Wellings, K., Field, J., Johnson, A. M. & Wadsworth, J. (1994). *Sexual behavior in Britain: The national survey of sexual attitudes and lifestyles.* Penguin Books.

Wendler, D., Emanuel, E. J. & Lie, R. K. (2004). The standard of care debate: can research in developing countries be both ethical and responsive to those countries' health needs? *American Journal of Public Health, 94,* 923–928.

Weng, X., Odouli, R. & Li, D. K. (2008). Maternal caffeine consumption during pregnancy and the risk of miscarriage: a prospective cohort study. *American Journal of Obstetrics and Gynecology, 198,* 279 e271–278.

Wessells, H., Lue, T. F. & McAninch, J. W. (1996a). Complications of penile lengthening and augmentation seen at 1 referral center. *Journal of Urology, 155,* 1617–1620.

Wessells, H., Lue, T. F. & McAninch, J. W. (1996b). Penile length in the flaccid and erect states: guidelines for penile augmentation. *Journal of Urology, 156,* 995–997.

Westneat, D. F. (1994). To guard or go forage: Conflicting demands affect the paternity of red-winged blackbirds. *American Naturalist, 144,* 343–354.

Westphal, S. P. (2004). Glad to be A: If you absolutely, positively, have no desire to have sex, you're not alone. *New Scientist,* October 16.

Whipple, B., Ogden, G. & Komisaruk, B. R. (1992). Physiological correlates of imagery-induced orgasm in women. *Archives of Sexual Behavior, 21,* 121–133.

Whisman, M. A. & Snyder, D. K. (2007). Sexual infidelity in a national sample of American women: Differences in prevalence and correlates as a function of method of assessment. *Journal of Family Psychology, 21,* 147–154.

Whisman, V. (1996). *Queer by choice: Lesbians, gay men, and the politics of identity.* Routledge.

Whitam, F. L. (1983). Culturally invariant properties of male homosexuality: Tentative conclusions from cross-cultural research. *Archives of Sexual Behavior, 12,* 207–226.

Whitam, F. L. & Dizon, M. J. (1979). Occupational choice and sexual orientation in cross-cultural perspective. *International Review of Modern Sociology, 9,* 137–149.

White, L. K. (1991). Determinants of divorce: A review of research in the eighties. In A. Booth (Ed.), *Contemporary families: Looking forward, looking back.* National Council on Family Relations.

Whitfield, J. (2004). Everything you always wanted to know about sexes. *PLoS Biology, 2,* E183.

Whitty, M. T. (2005). The realness of cybercheating. *Social Science Computer Review, 23,* 57–67.

Wilcox, A. J., Baird, D. D., Weinberg, C. R., Hornsby, P. P. & Herbst, A. L. (1995a). Fertility in men exposed prenatally to diethylstilbestrol. *New England Journal of Medicine, 332,* 1411–1416.

Wilcox, A. J., Day Baird, D., Dunson, D. B., McConnaughey, D. R., Kesner, J. S. & Weinberg, C. R. (2004). On the frequency of intercourse around ovulation: evidence for biological influences. *Human Reproduction, 19,* 1539–1543.

Wilcox, A. J., Weinberg, C. R. & Baird, D. D. (1995b). Timing of sexual intercourse in relation to ovulation. Effects on the probability of conception, survival of the pregnancy, and sex of the baby. *New England Journal of Medicine, 333,* 1517–1521.

Wiley, D. & Bortz, W. M., 2nd. (1996). Sexuality and aging—usual and successful. *Journals of Gerontology Series A, Biological Sciences and Medical Sciences, 51,* M142–146.

Williams, C. J. (2007). U.N. confronts another sex scandal. *Los Angeles Times,* December 15.

Williams, C. J. & Weinberg, M. S. (2003). Zoophilia in men: a study of sexual interest in animals. *Archives of Sexual Behavior, 32,* 523–535.

Williams, T. J., Pepitone, M. E., Christensen, S. E., Cooke, B. M., Huberman, A. D., Breedlove, N. J., Breedlove, T. J., Jordan, C.

L. & Breedlove, S. M. (2000). Finger-length ratios and sexual orientation. *Nature, 404,* 455–456.

Williams, W. L. (1986). *The spirit and the flesh: Sexual diversity in American Indian culture.* Beacon Press.

Willness, C. R., Steel, P. & Lee, K. (2007). A meta-analysis of the antecedents and consequences of workplace sexual harassment. *Personnel Psychology, 60,* 127–162.

Wilson, C. (2004). "Chemical condom" tantalisingly close. *New Scientist,* April 10.

Wilson, C. A. & Davies, D. C. (2007). The control of sexual differentiation of the reproductive system and brain. *Reproduction, 133,* 331–359.

Wilson, D. (2007). Former Duke players cleared of all charges. *New York Times,* April 11.

Wilson, G. & Rahman, Q. (2005). *Born gay: The psychobiology of sexual orientation.* Peter Owen.

Wilson, M. & Daly, M. (1992). The man who mistook his wife for a chattel. In J. H. Barkow et al. (Eds.), *The adapted mind: Evolutionary psychology and the evolution of culture.* Oxford University Press.

Wilson, S. K., Delk, J. R., 2nd & Billups, K. L. (2001). Treating symptoms of female sexual arousal disorder with the Eros-Clitoral Therapy Device. *Journal of Gender-Specific Medicine, 4,* 54–58.

Winters, S. J., Brufsky, A., Weissfeld, J., Trump, D. L., Dyky, M. A. & Hadeed, V. (2001). Testosterone, sex hormone-binding globulin, and body composition in young adult African American and Caucasian men. *Metabolism: Clinical and Experimental, 50,* 1242–1247.

Wisner, K. L., Perel, J. M., Peindl, K. S., Hanusa, B. H., Piontek, C. M. & Findling, R. L. (2004). Prevention of postpartum depression: a pilot randomized clinical trial. *American Journal of Psychiatry, 161,* 1290–1292.

Wisniewski, A. B. & Migeon, C. J. (2002). Gender identity/role differentiation in adolescents affected by syndromes of abnormal sex differentiation. *Adolescent Medicine, 13,* 119–128.

Wisniewski, A. B., Migeon, C. J., Gearhart, J. P., Rock, J. A., Berkovitz, G. D., Plotnick, L. P., Meyer-Bahlburg, H. F. & Money, J. (2001). Congenital micropenis: long-term medical, surgical and psychosexual follow-up of individuals raised male or female. *Hormone Research, 56,* 3–11.

Wiswell, T. E., Enzenauer, R. W., Holton, M. E., Cornish, J. D. & Hankins, C. T. (1987). Declining frequency of circumcision: implications for changes in the absolute incidence and male to female sex ratio of urinary tract infections in early infancy. *Pediatrics, 79,* 338–342.

Wolff, C. (1986). *Magnus Hirschfeld: A portrait of a pioneer in sexology.* Quartet Books.

Wolin, L. D. (2003). Gender issues in advertising: An oversight synthesis of research, 1970–2002. *Journal of Advertising Research, 43,* 112–129.

Women's Health Initiative. (2002). Risks and benefits of estrogen plus progestin in healthy postmenopausal women: Principal results from the Women's Health Initiative randomized controlled trial. *JAMA, 288,* 321–333.

Woods, N. F. (1987). Premenstrual symptoms: another look. *Public Health Reports. Suppl,* 106–112.

Working Group for a New View of Women's Sexual Problems. (2001). A new view of women's sexual problems. In E. Kaschak and L. Tiefer (Eds.), *A new view of women's sexual problems.* Haworth Press.

World Health Organization. (1993). *The ICD-10 classification of mental and behavioural disorders* (4th ed.) World Health Organization.

World Health Organization. (2001). *Estimated prevalence rates for FGM, updated May 2001.* (http://www.who.int/frh-whd/FGM/ FGM%20prev%20update.html)

World Professional Association for Transgender Health. (2008). *WPATH standards of care.* (http://www.wpath.org/ publications_standards.cfm)

Wrangham, R. & Peterson, D. (1996). *Demonic males: Apes and the origins of human violence.* Mariner Books.

Wright, L. (Ed.) (1996). *The bear book: Readings in the history and evolution of a gay male subculture.* Haworth Press.

Wu, Z. (2007). *Shacked up: A demographic profile of non-marital cohabitation.* (http://www.fedcan.ca/english/pdf/advocacy/BOHWuslides1007.pdf)

Wyatt, R. C. (2001). *An interview with John Gottman, Ph.D.* (http://www.psychotherapistresources.com/bios/totmframe.html)

Wylie, K. R. & Eardley, I. (2007). Penile size and the "small penis syndrome." *British Journal Urology, International, 99,* 1449–1455.

Xie, R. H., He, G., Liu, A., Bradwejn, J., Walker, M. & Wen, S. W. (2007). Fetal gender and postpartum depression in a cohort of Chinese women. *Social Science and Medicine, 65,* 680–684.

Xu, F., Sternberg, M. R., Kottiri, B. J., McQuillan, G. M., Lee, F. K., Nahmias, A. J., Berman, S. M. & Markowitz, L. E. (2006). Trends in herpes simplex virus type 1 and type 2 seroprevalence in the United States. *JAMA, 296,* 964–973.

Yang, Q., Wen, S. W., Leader, A., Chen, X. K., Lipson, J. & Walker, M. (2007). Paternal age and birth defects: how strong is the association? *Human Reproduction, 22,* 696–701.

Yang, Y. (2008). Social inequalities in happiness in the United States, 1972–2004: An age-period-cohort analysis. *American Sociological Review, 73,* 204–226.

Yang, Z. & Schank, J. C. (2006). Women do not synchronize their menstrual cycles. *Human Nature, 17,* 433–447.

Yarab, P. E., Sensibaugh, C. C. & Allgeier, E. R. (1998). More than just sex: Gender differences in the incidence of self-defined unfaithful behavior in heterosexual dating relationships. *Journal of Psychology and Human Sexuality, 10,* 45–57.

Yardley, J. (2005). Fearing future, China starts to give girls their due. *New York Times,* January 31.

Yllö, K. & Bograd, M. (Eds.) (1988). *Feminist perspectives on wife abuse.* Sage.

Yogani. (2004). *Advanced Yoga practices.* (http://www.geocities.com/advancedyogapractices/T30.html)

Yonkers, K. A., O'Brien, P. M. & Eriksson, E. (2008). Premenstrual syndrome. *Lancet, 371,* 1200–1210.

Yoo, J. (2008). *Beauty: The Korean way.* (http://web.mit.edu/cultureshock/fa2006/ www/essays/koreanbeauty.html)

Yoshizaki, A. (1991). I am who I am: A married bisexual teacher. In L. Hutchins and L. Kaahumanu (Eds.), *Bi any other name: Bisexual people speak out.* Alyson.

Young, C. (1998). Don't shield juries from the truth in sex cases. *Wall Street Journal,* April 20.

Young, L. J., Nilsen, R., Waymire, K. G., MacGregor, G. R. & Insel, T. R. (1999). Increased affiliative response to vasopressin in mice expressing the V1a receptor from a monogamous vole. *Nature, 400,* 766–768.

Young, L. Y., Paxman, C. G., Koehring, C. L. E. & Anderson, C. A. (2008). The application of a face work model of disengagement to unrequited love. *Communication Research Reports, 25,* 56–66.

Young-Bruehl, E. (1996). *The anatomy of prejudices.* Harvard University Press.

Yupanqui, T. (1999). *Becoming woman: Apache female puberty sunrise ceremony.* (http://www.webwinds.com/yupanqui/ apachesunrise.htm#Introduction)

Zahavi, A. & Zahavi, A. (1997). *The handicap principle: A missing piece of Darwin's puzzle.* Oxford University Press.

Zak, P. J. (2008). The neurobiology of trust. *Scientific American, 298,* 88–95.

Zaviacic, M. & Whipple, B. (1993). Update on the female prostate and the phenomenon of female ejaculation. *Journal of Sex Research, 30,* 148–151.

Zdravkovic, T., Genbacev, O., Prakobphol, A., Cvetkovic, M., Schanz, A., McMaster, M. & Fisher, S. J. (2006). Nicotine downregulates the l-selectin system that mediates cytotrophoblast emigration from cell columns and attachment to the uterine wall. *Reproductive Toxicology, 22,* 69–76.

Zebrowitz, L. A. (1997). *Reading faces: Window to the soul?* Westview Press.

Zhang, S. M., Cook, N. R., Manson, J. E., Lee, I. M. & Buring, J. E. (2008). Low-dose aspirin and breast cancer risk: results by tumour characteristics from a randomised trial. *British Journal of Cancer, 98,* 988–991.

Zourlas, P. A. & Jones, H. W. (1965). Clinical, histologic, and cytogenetic findings in male pseudohermaphroditism: Male hermaphrodites with feminine external genitalia (testicular feminization). *Obstetrics and Gynecology, 25,* 768–778.

Zucker, K. J. (2005). Gender identity disorder in children and adolescents. *Annual Review Clinical Psychology 1,* 467–492.

Zucker, K. J. & Blanchard, R. (1997). Transvestic fetishism: Psychopathology and theory. In D. R. Laws and W. T. O'Donohue (Eds.), *Sexual deviance: Theory, assessment, and treatment* (2nd ed.). Guilford Press.

Zverina, J., Hampl, R., Sulocava, J. & Starka, L. (1990). Hormonal status and sexual behaviour of 16 men after surgical castration. *Archivio Italiano di Urologia, Nefrologia, Andrologia, 62,* 55–58.

Author Index

Subject Index

ABOUT THE BOOK

Editor: Graig Donini

Project Editor: Kathaleen Emerson

Copy Editor: Jean Zimmer

Photo Editor: David McIntyre

Production Manager: Christopher Small

Book Design: Jefferson Johnson

Cover Design: Joanne Delphia

Book Layout: Joan Gemme

Illustration Program: Dragonfly Media Group, Joanne Delphia, and Joan Gemme

Manufacturer: Courier Corporation, Inc.